# Encyclopedia
## of the
## American Presidency

# Editorial Board

# Encyclopedia
# of the
# American Presidency

### Editors
**LEONARD W. LEVY**
**LOUIS FISHER**

**Volume 2**

SIMON & SCHUSTER

*A Paramount Communications Company*

New York   London   Toronto   Sydney   Tokyo   Singapore

Simon & Schuster
Academic Reference Division
15 Columbus Circle
New York, New York 10023

A Paramount Communications Company

Printed in the United States of America

printing number
2  3  4  5  6  7  8  9  10


**Library of Congress Cataloging-in-Publication Data**

Encyclopedia of the American presidency

Leonard W. Levy, Louis Fisher, editors.
v. cm.

Includes bibliographical references and index.

1. Presidents—United States—Encyclopedias.   2.
Presidents—United States—Biography.   I. Levy, Leonard
Williams, 1923–   .   II. Fisher, Louis.
JK511.E53 1994      353.03'13'03—dc20      93-13574 CIP

ISBN 0-13-275983-7 (Set)
0-13-276148-3 (Vol. 2)

The paper used in this publication meets the minimum
requirements of the American National Standard for
Information Sciences—Permanence of Paper for Printed Library
Materials ANSI Z39.48-1984.

# Abbreviations Used in This Work

**Ala.** Alabama
**Ariz.** Arizona
**Ark.** Arkansas
**Art.** Article
**b.** born
**c.** circa, about, approximately
**Calif.** California
**cf.** confer, compare
**chap.** chapter (pl., chaps.)
**CIO** Congress of Industrial Organizations
**Cong.** Congress
**Colo.** Colorado
**Conn.** Connecticut
**d.** died
**D** Democrat, Democratic
**D.C.** District of Columbia
**Del.** Delaware
**diss.** dissertation
**DR** Democratic-Republican
**ed.** editor (pl., eds); edition
**e.g.** exempli gratia, for example
**enl.** enlarged
**esp.** especially
**et al.** et alii, and others
**etc.** et cetera, and so forth

**exp.** expanded
**f.** and following (pl., ff.)
**F** Federalist
**Fla.** Florida
**Ga.** Georgia
**GOP** Grand Old Party (Republican Party)
**H.R.** House of Representatives
**I** Independent
**ibid.** ibidem, in the same place (as the one immediately preceding)
**Ida.** Idaho
**i.e.** id est, that is
**Ill.** Illinois
**Ind.** Indiana
**IRS** Internal Revenue Service
**Kan.** Kansas
**Ky.** Kentucky
**La.** Louisiana
**M.A.** Master of Arts
**Mass.** Massachusetts
**Me.** Maine
**Mich.** Michigan
**Minn.** Minnesota

**Miss.** Mississippi
**Mo.** Missouri
**Mont.** Montana
**n.** note
**N.C.** North Carolina
**n.d.** no date
**N.Dak.** North Dakota
**Neb.** Nebraska
**Nev.** Nevada
**N.H.** New Hampshire
**N.J.** New Jersey
**N.Mex.** New Mexico
**no.** number (pl., nos.)
**n.p.** no place
**n.s.** new series
**N.Y.** New York
**Okla.** Oklahoma
**Ore.** Oregon
**p.** page (pl., pp.)
**Pa.** Pennsylvania
**pt.** part (pl., pts.)
**R** Republican
**rev.** revised
**R.I.** Rhode Island
**S.** Senate
**S.C.** South Carolina

**S.Dak.** South Dakota
**sec.** section (pl., secs.)
**ser.** series
**ses.** session
**supp.** supplement
**Tenn.** Tennessee
**Tex.** Texas
**U.N.** United Nations
**U.S.** United States, United States Reports
**USA** United States Army
**USAF** United States Air Force
**USN** United States Navy
**U.S.S.R.** Union of Soviet Socialist Republics
**v.** versus
**Va.** Virginia
**vol.** volume (pl., vols.)
**Vt.** Vermont
**W** Whig
**Wash.** Washington
**Wis.** Wisconsin
**W.Va.** West Virginia
**Wyo.** Wyoming

# E

**EARLY, STEPHEN** (1889–1951), White House press secretary. Franklin D. Roosevelt appointed Early his WHITE HOUSE PRESS SECRETARY in 1933. He was the first modern holder of that post. Early, who had previously known the President for two decades, served until Roosevelt's death in 1945.

An experienced and respected newsman, Stephen Tyree Early was an efficient and businesslike press secretary. Press releases went out promptly; policy statements appeared in a coordinated and timely fashion. Early saw the President every morning and held daily press briefings where he provided "news" in a manner that reporters considered intelligent and objective. Early suggested that Roosevelt hold direct talks with reporters, and he participated in them, characterizing the President's statements and even answering questions himself. He established rules for newsgathering by the WHITE HOUSE PRESS CORPS, managed coverage of special events, and coordinated and often edited news releases of other government agencies.

Early often defended newsmen to President Roosevelt. He staffed the administration with experienced journalists, whom he instructed to work in a professional manner. He strongly opposed any "official" government publication of news.

Still, Early was a Roosevelt loyalist, a member of the White House inner circle of poker games, sports "pools," skits, and banter. He protected the President by discouraging comment on Roosevelt's paralysis. He staged newsreel coverages to convey positive personal images of the President. During the campaign of 1944, Early masked Roosevelt's declining health by arranging short press conferences and brief appearances that were carefully photographed to create the impression of a vigorous and robust President.

Nor could Early objectively distance himself from his cultural values. A Virginian, whose ancestors had included the Confederate general Jubal A. Early, he excluded African American journalists from press conferences until 1944, when the President personally invited them to the White House.

Stephen Early was an able and effective spokesman for the Roosevelt administration and developed techniques that both aided that President and substantially shaped the modern presidency.

### BIBLIOGRAPHY

Winfield, Betty H. *FDR and the News Media*. 1990.

GEORGE MCJIMSEY

**EAST FLORIDA.** Since the conquistadores first probed the coast of the Gulf of Mexico in the early sixteenth century, Florida played an integral geographic role in the strategy that gave Spain dominance over the region from CUBA to Mexico. As a New World pawn in the game of conquest, Florida fell victim to the international ambitions of many nations. The Spanish repelled a French challenge along the Atlantic Coast, only to lose the peninsula to Great Britain in the Peace of Paris at the conclusion of the Seven Years War (1763). During their twenty-year rule the English divided Florida into East and West. East Florida comprised much of the present-day state westward to the Apalachicola River. By crown proclamation of 1774 West Florida extended from that body to the Mississippi River south of 32° 28′ latitude (including Pensacola and Mobile).

East Florida agriculture took root under British rule and the population increased sharply, due in part to the influx of exiled British loyalists during the American Revolution. The Americans invaded Florida in 1778, hoping to add it to the new republic, but a smaller British force repulsed them. Geography and the results of the most recent European war obliged the English to return Florida to Spain in the Peace of Paris in 1783.

By the second Spanish period (1783–1821), Florida had become an international community, including Irish, Greek, Scots, Minorcan, Swiss, Italian, and African (free and slave) immigrants. St. Augustine, which has left an enduring architectural legacy, boasted a population that reached two thousand. The Spanish, racked by the Napoleonic Wars and a widespread colonial independence movement, however, could not control Florida's borderlands bandits, marauding Indians, and English merchants. Spain's weakness revealed itself in the west as land-hungry Americans declared their independence in 1810 and in the east when both the British and Americans occupied Pensacola during the WAR OF 1812.

Following the War, Secretaries of State James Monroe and John Quincy Adams attempted unsuccessfully to persuade the Spanish to cede the Floridas to the United States. An embarrassing incursion by General Andrew Jackson in 1818, following a series of Seminole INDIAN raids, prompted a reconsideration of policy. On 22 February 1819, the crown relinquished the Floridas to the United States in the Transcontinental (Adams-Onis) Treaty. In exchange for the territories, Spain received a boundary between her western possessions and the LOUISIANA PURCHASE and the American government agreed to pay $5 million in claims held against Spain by United States citizens. The transfer of East Florida occurred at St. Augustine on 10 July 1821 and Andrew Jackson served briefly as governor at Pensacola. An act of Congress signed by President Monroe united the two provinces in 1822 and provided a new western boundary for the Florida Territory at the Perdido River.

### BIBLIOGRAPHY

Fretwell, Jacqueline K., and Susan R. Parker, eds.. *Clash Between Cultures: Spanish East Florida, 1784–1821.* 1988.
Wright, J. Leitch. *Anglo-Spanish Rivalry in North America.* 1971.

JOHN M. BELOHLAVEK

## ECONOMIC STABILIZATION ACT (1970).

During the early years of his presidency, Richard M. Nixon faced a variety of economic problems, including rising unemployment, persistent inflation, growing trade deficits, and a weakened dollar. Strongly averse to wage and price controls as a result of his WORLD WAR II experience in the Office of Price Administration, Nixon opposed direct governmental controls over the private sector. Rather, he preferred to rely on monetarist solutions, hoping that Federal Reserve policy limiting growth of the money supply would restrain price increases.

By mid 1970, it appeared that Nixon's monetarist stance would not suffice to remedy the nation's economic ills. Congressional Democrats, sensing an election year advantage, passed the Economic Stabilization Act over the President's protest that it would grant him powers he neither wanted nor would use. Under the act, the President received discretionary administrative authority to control prices, rents, wages, and salaries. Nixon signed the act, notwithstanding his complaint that Congress, if it truly desired controls, should have enacted a mandatory program.

During 1971, Nixon's mounting economic problems seemed destined to threaten his coming reelection bid. On 15 August 1971, Nixon dramatically announced a new anti-inflation program consisting of a ninety-day wage and price freeze, to be followed by mandatory controls administered by a Cost of Living Council, a Price Commission, and a Pay Board. The inflation program was part of an astounding reversal of economic policy and incorporated suspension of dollar convertibility, imposition of an import tariff surcharge, and fiscal stimulus through tax reductions.

Nixon's experiment with controls, the most extensive peacetime effort of its type in American history, continued through four phases of varying stringency before ending in 1974. The administration's efforts were uneven and did little to moderate inflationary pressures that continued throughout the 1970s. In retrospect, Nixon characterized controls as "politically necessary" but "wrong."

### BIBLIOGRAPHY

Nixon, Richard. *RN: The Memoirs of Richard Nixon.* 1978.
Silk, Leonard. *Nixonomics.* 2d ed. 1973.
Stein, Herbert. *Presidential Economics: The Making of Economic Policy from Roosevelt to Reagan and Beyond.* 2d rev. ed. 1988.

RALPH MITZENMACHER

## EDUCATION, DEPARTMENT OF. The history

of the U.S. Department of Education mirrors the growth of federal involvement in setting public EDUCATION POLICY. From an agency that was created mainly to collect statistics on education, the department has grown to oversee an increasing number of federal programs representing a multibillion-dollar chunk of the federal budget. This involvement has developed despite the lack of a clear constitutional mandate for federal responsibility for education.

The idea of a federal agency to oversee education dates back to 1800. President Thomas Jefferson seconded a proposal for a national council on education and proposed it to Congress, but the concept received scant support. It was revived in 1838 by Henry Barnard, a secretary of schools in Connecticut. Barnard petitioned Washington for what he termed a "permanent statistical bureau . . . which would present an annual report on the educational statistics and progress of the country." Thirty years elapsed, however, before Barnard could secure its creation. Ohio Congressman and future President James A. Garfield introduced a bill in 1866 to create a federal educational agency. Garfield was especially education-minded, having been a college teacher and college president.

Garfield's bill passed both Houses and in 1867 President Andrew Johnson signed it into law. The act established a U.S. department of education, with a commissioner but without CABINET status. Its function was informational in nature. Two years later, the new department became an "office" of education and was relegated to the DEPARTMENT OF THE INTERIOR. In 1939 the agency was transferred to the Federal Security Agency, and in 1953 the office was placed under the jurisdiction of the newly created Department of Health, Education and Welfare. There it remained until 1979, when it became a department with Cabinet rank at the urging of President Jimmy Carter. By that time the agency had outgrown its original informational purpose to oversee innumerable government programs.

**Expanding Its Function.** By the 1880s the office was assigned the responsibility of administering the education portion of the MORRILL LAND GRANT ACT. Gradually the office was given more responsibility over federal education laws.

By the 1930s, the office oversaw some eighty federal education programs. After the Soviet Union's launch of the spacecraft *Sputnik* in 1957, President Dwight D. Eisenhower successfully lobbied for passage of the National Defense Education Act to improve science education. President Lyndon B. Johnson's GREAT SOCIETY programs sought to improve the education of the poor. Under Johnson, some sixty education bills were enacted, creating programs to help African Americans and other minorities, women, disabled people, and non–English speaking students.

In the 1860s the Department of Education consisted of four staff members and had a budget of $15,000. In

1965, the Office of Education was staffed by more than two thousand employees and had a budget of $1.5 billion. In fiscal 1992, the U.S. Department of Education had some forty-five hundred employees and a budget of $32.3 billion.

The department still collects data and supervises federal education research, but it also focuses on national education issues, oversees federal education programs, and enforces federal statutes prohibiting discrimination in federally funded programs.

Although the responsibilities of the U.S. Department of Education have been increasing, the monies allocated to states and localities through federal programs is relatively low. The federal portion of national education costs was approximately 6 percent in 1992, down from a high of 10 percent during the Johnson administration.

**Achieving Cabinet Status.** By the twentieth century, interest had grown in making the Office of Education into a Cabinet-rank department. Seventy bills to create such a department were introduced into Congress between 1918 and 1925. In 1929, President Herbert Hoover commissioned the National Advisory Committee on Education, which recommended, among other things, the establishment of a Cabinet-level education department. In 1943, President Franklin D. Roosevelt's policy arm, the National Resources Planning Board, recommended that the office of education take a larger role to "offer educational leadership to the nation." But it was not until the mid 1970s that interest was renewed in creating a department of education. The drive was led by the National Education Association (NEA), and the issue became that teachers' union's litmus test for supporting any presidential candidate. The NEA, with some two million members, had become the chief representative of the education lobby. In 1976, the organization decided to support a presidential candidate for the first time. It lent its considerable resources, both financial and human, to Democratic candidate Jimmy Carter when he agreed to create a department of education should he be elected.

The rationale of the NEA leaders was that a department of education would provide both a symbolic and substantive role for education. NEA leaders argued that the United States was the only major industrial nation without a national education department or ministry. Granting Cabinet status, they felt, would give education a national focus. Moreover, it would better coordinate the many education programs that were strewn over innumerable government agencies. Some sixty other educational organizations supported the move.

*Secretaries of Education*

| President | Secretary of Education |
| --- | --- |
| 39 Carter | Shirley M. Hufstedler, 1979–1981 |
| 40 Reagan | Terrel H. Bell, 1981–1985 |
| | William J. Bennett, 1985–1988 |
| | Lauro F. Cavazos, 1988–1989 |
| 41 Bush | Lauro F. Cavazos, 1989–1991 |
| | Lamar Alexander, 1991–1993 |
| 42 Clinton | Richard W. Riley, 1993– |

Opposition to a new department came from a number of sectors. Many feared further centralization of government. Others felt that another layer of needless bureaucracy would be created. Much of the opposition came from the old coalition of labor, education, and civil rights. Some believed the department was unnecessary and others contended that it should be created only when needed to execute a major policy. Even President Carter's Secretary of Health, Education and Welfare, Joseph Califano, Jr., was against the plan.

Carter wavered. But renewed pressure from NEA leaders compelled Carter to honor his campaign pledge. Passage of the bill establishing the department was not easy, however. It barely received the endorsement of the Government Operations Committee and passed the House with a mere four-vote margin. On 17 October 1979, President Carter signed the bill. He appointed a federal judge from California, Shirley Hufstedler, as the first secretary of the department.

**An Ideological Department.** No sooner did President Carter establish the new department than an attack aiming to dismantle it began. In the presidential campaign of 1980, Ronald Reagan pledged to eliminate what he considered an unnecessary bureaucratic agency. Moreover, Reagan wanted to diminish federal involvement in education. As President, Reagan had difficulty in choosing a Secretary of Education who would preside over the department's liquidation. He finally chose Terrel H. Bell, a former commissioner of the Office of Education under Presidents Richard M. Nixon and Gerald Ford. Bell, a moderate, had hoped to convince Reagan of the need to promote education.

Without the support of the conservatives in the Reagan administration, Bell authorized a study of the status of American education. Published in April 1983, the department's study, *A Nation at Risk: The Imperative for Educational Reform*, galvanized the nation for educational reform. The study decried the state of American education as lagging behind that of other developed nations. Alarmist and political in tone, *A Nation at Risk* ushered in "excellence" reform with these provocative words: "If an unfriendly foreign power had attempted to impose on America the mediocre performance that exists today we might have viewed it as an act of war."

The essence of excellence reform was the raising of academic standards. It was cost-neutral and appealed to President Reagan as a solution to America's economic decline in the face of strenuous foreign competition, especially from Japan. Reagan became a leading advocate of excellence reform and reversed his position on abolishing the new department.

President George Bush inherited the Reagan education agenda. He augmented excellence reform by advocating national standards, national testing, and a choice plan that would provide federal-government vouchers that, theoretically, would enable all students to select from among private, parochial, and public schools. The Department of Education thus promoted a conservative education program to the nation, and its influence on American education was strong.

### BIBLIOGRAPHY

Berube, Maurice R. *American Presidents and Education.* 1991.
Lapati, Americo D. *Education and the Federal Government: A Historical Record.* 1975.
Stickney, Benjamin D., and Lawrence R. Marcus. *The Great Education Debate: Washington and the Schools.* 1984.

MAURICE R. BERUBE

**EDUCATION POLICY.** American Presidents have taken varying roles regarding education. Limited by constitutional constraints, Presidents have, for the most part, been hesitant to involve themselves in national education policy. Two periods in American history have witnessed a consistent and concerted involvement of Presidents in setting education policy. The first of these was during the early years of the Republic; the second was after WORLD WAR II.

**The Early Republic.** The Founders saw an educated citizenry as one of the best methods to preserve the newly founded democracy. The vehicle for a national focus on education was a national university. The first six Presidents—George Washington, John Adams, Thomas Jefferson, James Madison, James Monroe, and John Quincy Adams—favored a national university. In 1790, President Washington sent a request to Congress for the establishment of a national university. His rationale was that such a university would substantially contribute "to the security of a free Constitution" in various ways, "not the least being" by teaching the people themselves "to know and to value their own rights." A number of presidential proposals to amend the Constitution to found a national university were ultimately submitted, but these proposals were not strongly enough backed by the Presidents who submitted them. After the end of Madison's term, no further proposals for a national university were offered, closing the first period of presidential interest in education.

The Framers' failure to mention education in the Constitution meant that power over education had been reserved by the states. In turn, states delegated much of that responsibility to localities. These constitutional constraints limited, and in many cases inhibited, Presidents in setting national education policy. Consequently, few American Presidents have exercised distinctive and wide-ranging educational leadership.

For the remainder of the nineteenth century, Presidents showed scant interest in education. The lone exception was Abraham Lincoln, who, although not an advocate of education either as a state legislator in Illinois or as President, signed the MORRILL LAND GRANT ACT (1862), which provided public land to support the state university system. These land-grant colleges were to be centers of training in science, agriculture, and engineering. The act, with its thrust for egalitarian admissions policy, had a signal effect on American higher education. Moreover, it was a major response to a national concern, shoring up a sagging agricultural economy as the Industrial Revolution intensified.

By the early twentieth century, presidential interest in education had become sporadic. Woodrow Wilson signed bills establishing vocational education, and Herbert Hoover appointed a commission to study the possibility of creating a U.S. department of education. But, for the most part, education was not yet seen as essential to America's economic growth.

**After World War II.** The second period of concerted presidential interest in education came after World War II. America emerged as a world economic and political power. Somewhat reluctantly, American Presidents were confronted with the educational demands of a technological age.

World War II proved an economic watershed. The question was no longer how much America could manufacture, but how sophisticated its products were. And advanced technology required a more educated workforce. These facts confronted Presidents.

Higher education was aided by federal government policies. For America's educators after World War II, the task was to convince political leaders that rising levels of education were needed. As the historian of education Diane Ravitch concludes, "Technological change created a need for an educated people, and educated people stimulated technological change."

Franklin D. Roosevelt made substantive contributions to education's becoming a national issue. First, Roosevelt was responsible for the GI Bill of Rights, which provided subsidized higher education for veterans and ushered in the era of mass higher education. Second, Roosevelt introduced a crucial philosophical concept that emerged from the GI Bill of Rights process: the right to education.

The idea of a right to education was first presented by Roosevelt in a 1942 report on the development of natural resources. Roosevelt called for the extension of the Constitution's Bill of Rights. Among the "new freedoms" Roosevelt enunciated was "the right to education."

The GI Bill of Rights transformed American higher education, enabling more than two million World War II and KOREAN WAR veterans to take advantage of higher education and creating mass higher education in the process.

President Harry S. Truman pursued the idea of a right to education. In 1947, he appointed the Commission of Higher Education, which concluded that education was an American "birthright" and recommended fourteen years of free schooling. The idea of a right to education later received a severe setback, however, when the U.S. Supreme Court in its 5-to-4 decision in *San Antonio School District v. Rodriguez* (1973) concluded that "education, of course, is not among the rights afforded explicit protection under our federal constitution."

Truman can be credited with beginning the effort to pass a federal aid-to-education bill. By 1965, when the Johnson administration saw the first such bill enacted, some two dozen had been introduced in Congress.

On 4 October 1957, during Dwight D. Eisenhower's second term, the Soviet Union launched the first spacecraft, *Sputnik*, setting off a wave of public hysteria. Americans feared that the Soviets, the arch COLD WAR enemy, had gained superiority in the space race and also perhaps in national defense. Eisenhower himself was swept up in the *Sputnik* hysteria. But federal interference created an ideological problem for him. Although opposed to a strong federal role in education, he saw the need for some federal action. Some historians believe that Eisenhower missed a grand opportunity to lead major education reform in America.

The National Defense Education Act of 1958 was Eisenhower's—and the Democratic Congress's—response to the threat posed by *Sputnik*. The heart of the act provided loans to students interested in pursuing studies in science. By 1964, almost three quarters of a million students had received NDEA monies.

John F. Kennedy failed to enact a federal aid-to-education bill. Nevertheless, his constant pressure on Congress laid the ground for Lyndon Johnson's later success. Indeed, as one analyst observed, "What was refused during [Kennedy's] lifetime was given freely after his death."

**The Great Society.** The civil rights movement of the 1960s defined the agenda of Johnson's GREAT SOCIETY. The discovery of substantial poverty in America, as documented in works such as Michael Harrington's *The Other America* (1962), led to federal education programs' emphasis on educating the poor.

For Johnson, education was the key element of the Great Society agenda. He promoted education both through the BULLY PULPIT and with substantive education programs. Johnson wanted to be remembered chiefly as the "education President." He could point to more than sixty education bills signed into the law during his tenure—including the historic first federal aid-to-education act, the Elementary and Secondary Education Act of 1965.

Johnson's major accomplishments in education fell into three categories. First, Johnson scored a breakthrough with the first federal aid-to-education bill, which forced school districts to abandon racial segregation to qualify for federal funds. Second, he followed suit with a higher education act. And, third, he incorporated preschool education for the children of the poor—the Head Start program—in his antipoverty measures. On balance, these programs were reasonably successful.

President Richard M. Nixon offered few innovative departures. For the most part, he continued Great Society educational programs, with their emphasis on the education of the poor. One new idea that Nixon did offer was to establish a federal agency for research on education. In his message on education reform in 1970, Nixon created the National Institute of Education to encourage and direct research on education. He also launched an experimental schools program that was not successful.

Jimmy Carter continued the federal presence in education. Most significantly, Carter created a separate DEPARTMENT OF EDUCATION, an accomplishment achieved at the urging of the largest teachers' union, the National Education Association.

**"Excellence" Reform.** Ironically, the second "education President" of the latter half of the twentieth century was Ronald Reagan. Reagan became an "education President" by accident: he intended neither to reform nor strongly influence American education. Indeed, he favored shoring up private schooling and decreasing federal funds and the federal role in public education. In 1980, he made a campaign pledge to dismantle the newly created Department of Education.

Competition from abroad (notably Japan), however, made the American public wary about economic decline. This, in turn, created a desire to make our public schools "excellent" to supply the brainpower that would restore America to its position of economic dominance. With the 1983 publication of the Department of Education's jeremiad *A Nation at Risk: The Imperative for Education Reform*, the excellence reform movement was officially launched. *A Nation at Risk* was deliberately alarmist in its critique of American public education: "If an unfriendly foreign power had attempted to impose on America the mediocre performance that exists today," the authors intoned, "we might have viewed it as an act of war."

The aim of the excellence reform movement was to raise educational standards to groom the best and the brightest students to make the United States economically competitive once again. Education reform became a national political issue. Reagan, who recognized a good idea when he saw it, used the bully pulpit to preach the virtues of excellence reform. For Reagan and his successor, George Bush (who inherited and carried on the Reagan agenda), excellence reform had the advantage of being "cost-neutral." They urged the states to assume greater financial obligation in restructuring schools. For the most part, Bush, like Reagan, practiced an educational politics of the bully pulpit. He declared that, for him, educational leadership would be mainly "hortatory." Like Reagan, he perceived education to be the responsibility of the states. Bush did call for national standards and national testing and laid emphasis on the teaching of basic subjects in his plan for educational reform.

The excellence reform movement initially provided some positive results. Scores on the Scholastic Aptitude Tests (SATs) stabilized. In nearly every state, education became the single largest budget item. Modest increases in scores in math, science, reading, and writing were made. The national focus on education continued as America grappled with its declining economic position.

## BIBLIOGRAPHY

Bell, Terrel H. *The Thirteenth Man: A Reagan Cabinet Memoir.* 1988.
Berube, Maurice R. *American Presidents and Education.* 1991.
Clowse, Barbara Barksdale. *Brainpower for the Cold War: The Sputnik Crisis and the National Defense Education Act of 1958.* 1981.
Cremin, Lawrence A. *American Education: The National Experience, 1783–1876.* 1980.
Finn, Chester E., Jr. *Education and the Presidency.* 1977.

Graham, Hugh Davis. *The Uncertain Triumph: Federal Education Policy in the Kennedy and Johnson Years.* 1984.

Jeffrey, Julie Roy. *Education for the Children of the Poor.* 1978.

Ravitch, Diane. *The Troubled Crusade: American Education, 1945–1980.* 1983.

MAURICE R. BERUBE

**EISENHOWER, DWIGHT D.** (1890–1969), thirty-fourth President of the United States (1953–1961). Dwight David Eisenhower was the last President born in the nineteenth century and, in a way, belonged to the nineteenth-century tradition of Presidents born in a log cabin—although in his case it was the Texas equivalent, a shack beside the railroad tracks in Denison. He is one of a handful of Presidents who had a secure worldwide reputation before he entered the White House. Critics at the time widely regarded his presidency as lackluster, marked by few reforms and few innovations. The 1950s as a whole, and the Eisenhower administration specifically, were characterized by comedians as "the bland leading the bland."

But this characterization is unfair. In fact, Eisenhower successfully led the nation and the world through eight years of high tension. Eisenhower adopted and continued Harry S. Truman's policy of the CONTAINMENT of communism. Eisenhower was convinced of two things: First, a nuclear war—which he was frequently urged to initiate during numerous war scares by politicians from both parties and nearly all his advisers—would be as disastrous for the "winner" as for the loser. Second, in time communism would collapse as a consequence of its internal contradictions. The 1950s were bland, in large part, because Eisenhower wanted them to be that way. The alternative, at the height of the COLD WAR, was too frightening to contemplate.

In contrast both to his immediate predecessors, Franklin D. Roosevelt and Truman, and to some of his successors, Eisenhower issued no stirring call to arms. Far from expanding the power of his office, he consciously strove to reduce it. He launched no great moral crusade, nor did he engage in an idealistic pursuit of some overriding national goal. His critics charged that Eisenhower was quite content to preside over a fat, happy, satisfied nation that devoted itself to enjoying life.

The charge possessed truth. Eisenhower's rebuttal also contained an elementary truth. He felt that, following the upheavals of the Great Depression, WORLD WAR II, and the KOREAN WAR, the nation needed a chance to catch its breath, to build and expand its material prosperity, to have a respite from tension and war. He often pointed out that the Declaration of Independence states that one of man's unalienable rights is the pursuit of happiness. In the 1950s Eisenhower tried, with much success, to create a climate in which American citizens could fully exercise that right.

He made peace in Korea, and he kept the peace thereafter. His proudest boast was, "The United States never lost a soldier or a foot of ground in my administration. We kept the peace. People asked how it happened—by God, it didn't just happen, I'll tell you that."

**Early Life.** Born in Dension, Texas, on 14 October 1890, Eisenhower was the third of five sons of David and Ida Eisenhower. In 1891 the family moved to Abileen, Kansas, where David worked as a mechanic. Dwight was a bright, competitive, ambitious, and athletic boy, a bit above average as a student. His popularity was reflected in his catchy nickname, Ike. In 1911 he went to the U.S. Military Academy at West Point, New York (where one other President, Ulysses S. Grant, received his education). On graduation in 1915 he was assigned to Fort Sam Houston, Texas, where he met and within a year married Mamie Dowd of Denver. They had two sons, one of whom died in infancy.

Eisenhower's early army career was humdrum, but it was excellent preparation for the high command in World War II and for the presidency, because he served most of the time as a staff officer in Washington, D.C. For fourteen years he was a major. His primary responsibilities were writing speeches for his superiors, including Chiefs of Staff John J. Pershing and Douglas MacArthur, and lobbying with Congress for the army. He was well known on Capitol Hill and learned to think about problems from the point of view of the high command. He became an expert on logistics, staff work, committee work, and global strategy.

**World War II.** On 7 December 1941—the day of the United States' entry into World War II—Army Chief of Staff GEORGE C. MARSHALL put Eisenhower on the Operations Division of the War Department, with the responsibility of planning a strategy for the war. He did so well that in March 1942, Marshall promoted him to major general. In May, he went to England to take command of American forces in Britain. In July he was promoted to lieutenant general and put in command of the Allied forces (British and American) for the invasion of North Africa.

As commander of an alliance force, Eisenhower's role was as much political as military. He worked on a daily basis with British Prime Minister Winston Churchill and, later, with Free French leader Charles de Gaulle; he had British, American, and Canadian air, sea, and land forces under his command. He became an expert in balancing the conflicting goals and aspirations of different nations and in persuading officers of different nationalities, services, and traditions to work together in a common cause.

He was a great success. In February 1943, he became a four-star general. In May, the last Axis troops in North Africa surrendered to Eisenhower in Tunisia. In July, he commanded the Allied armies, navies, and air forces that invaded Sicily. In September, British and American forces under his command invaded the Italian mainland. In December, he was selected by President Roosevelt to be the Supreme Commander of the Allied Expeditionary Force (AEF) for Operation Overlord, the invasion of France. It was the most coveted command in the war.

Operation Overlord was the largest amphibious operation in the history of warfare and one of the most complicated undertakings in history. It involved detailed planning by thousands, and the work of millions, of men and women. Eisenhower planned the invasion with the help of a large staff, always keeping the power of final decisions to himself. He chose the site, the time of attack, the assault divisions, and their commanders. He decided to use Allied bombers to disrupt the French railway system. He directed the deception plan and the overall training and preparation of troops. All this involved close coordination with Churchill, de Gaulle, and Roosevelt. Working with world leaders, making choices, and finding necessary compromises became second nature to him.

It was Eisenhower who made the decision to invade, despite chancy weather, on 6 June 1944 (known thereafter as D Day). His place in history was fixed by the time night fell. The invasion had succeeded; the Allies had established themselves in Normandy. As for George Washington after Yorktown or Grant after Appomattox, everything that happened to Eisenhower after Overlord, even the presidency, could only be an anticlimax.

In the campaign in northwestern Europe, June 1944 to May 1945, Eisenhower commanded American, British, Canadian, Norwegian, Polish, and French forces, as well as forces from smaller Allied nations. In December 1944, he was promoted to the new rank of five-star general. That month his troops stopped the German counteroffensive in the Ardennes and then, in the Battle of the Bulge, the biggest battle of the Western Front and the largest ever fought by the U.S. Army, won a smashing victory.

During the course of the European campaign, Eisenhower made many controversial decisions. Some angered the British, some the French, some his American colleagues. He managed to make his decisions

stick while simultaneously holding the Allied Expeditionary Force together as a team.

His most controversial decision, and one that would directly affect his presidency, was not to challenge the Red Army to a race to capture Berlin. Churchill and most of the British and General George S. Patton and many of the Americans wanted Berlin badly, and they urged Eisenhower to try to seize the city before the Soviet forces reached it. He refused. He feared the heavy casualties that would inevitably result from street-to-street fighting in Berlin (the Red Army went on to lose 100,000 men in the battle for the city), and in any event, he doubted that the AEF could get there before the Soviets did. But his reasons were as much political as military: he believed that peace in the postwar world depended on American-Soviet cooperation and goodwill, and he felt that a competition between the Red Army and the AEF over who got Berlin would be the worst way to end the war. Too, he saw no point in making an effort to take the city when the division of Germany into east and west (along the line of the Elbe River) and of Berlin into separate sectors occupied by the different Allied armies had already been agreed to by the U.S., Soviet, and British governments.

In the view of Eisenhower's critics, the Western Allies could have held Berlin had they taken it, thus avoiding some of the worst problems of the cold war. In Eisenhower's view, nothing short of hostilities could have kept the Red Army out of Berlin.

**Postwar Public Service.** By the spring of 1945, Eisenhower was exceedingly tired of war. He deplored wild talk about using the AEF not only to destroy Nazi Germany but to continue advancing eastward to destroy Soviet communism. Eisenhower had seen enough of war's depredations to last him a lifetime. He was bitterly angry with the Germans for not surrendering when the Allied armies crossed the Rhine River and it became obvious that the war was lost, thereby forcing him to destroy the country. He had personally signed thousands of letters of condolence to parents of young men killed in battle. When World War II ended, he wanted no more of war. Unlike Patton, he was a general who hated war. That attitude dominated his presidency.

On 8 May 1945, the Germans surrendered unconditionally. General Marshall's tribute to Eisenhower, sent by cable that day, summed up his accomplishments:

> You have completed your mission with the greatest victory in the history of warfare. You have commanded with outstanding success the most powerful military force that has ever been assembled. . . . You have made history, great history for the good

of mankind, and you have stood for all we hope for and admire in an officer of the United States Army.

Eisenhower emerged from the war as the most famous and popular of American leaders. He was a natural choice for the presidency; indeed, in 1944 there had been a small movement to draft him as the Republican candidate, a move that he had dismissed out of hand. At the POTSDAM CONFERENCE in July 1945, President Truman offered to support him for the Democratic nomination in 1948; Eisenhower said he wanted nothing to do with politics.

Instead, he stayed in the Army. From May until November 1945, he served as head of the occupation in the American zone, where he came to know and work with some leading German politicians, including Konrad Adenauer. He went to Moscow, where he met with Premier Joseph Stalin. He dealt on a regular basis with the Soviet generals in charge of the Soviet zone in eastern Germany and the Soviet sector in Berlin. It was as if he were being groomed for the presidency.

In late November 1945, he replaced Marshall as U.S. Army Chief of Staff, a post he held for two years—and a most disagreeable one, as he was presiding over the dissolution of an army. In February 1948, after serving his country for thirty-seven years, he retired. He had no savings, no investments, no property. But he had his memories. His memoir of the war, *Crusade in Europe* (1948), made him a rich man. It became one of the most widely translated and best-selling books of all time and is often compared to Grant's *Personal Memoirs* as a classic of military writing.

From 1948 through 1950, Eisenhower served as president of Columbia University in New York City. He was under intense pressure from both political parties to run for the presidency in 1948. Eisenhower took the position that a lifetime soldier ought not become a politician, and he refused.

In January 1951, Truman appointed Eisenhower the first Supreme Allied Commander Europe. From his Paris headquarters, Eisenhower put together the beginnings of the North Atlantic Treaty Organization (NATO) armed force. He came to know all the leaders of Western Europe on a personal basis. He urged the creation of a United States of Europe, with one army, one currency, and one federal government.

In 1952, Republican leaders, primarily from the East Coast and former supporters of New York governor THOMAS E. DEWEY, who had been the Republican presidential candidate in 1944 and 1948, persuaded Eisenhower that he had a duty to serve as President because the alternatives were socialism under the left-wing Democrats or isolationism under the right-wing

Republicans. He won the nomination only after a bitter struggle with Ohio Senator Robert Taft, who had voted against NATO.

Eisenhower chose Senator Richard M. Nixon of California as his running mate. Nixon's youth he was (thirty-nine) balanced Eisenhower's age (at sixty-two he was the oldest man, to that date, ever to have been nominated for the presidency). Nixon's standing with the right wing of the REPUBLICAN PARTY, thanks to his exposure of Alger Hiss as a Soviet spy, balanced Eisenhower's standing with the moderate-to-liberal East Coast Republicans. And Nixon had an aggressive campaign style that would allow Eisenhower to stay on the high road.

The Republicans in 1952 had a formula: $K_1C_2$, referring to the unpopular Korean War, the loss of China, and allegations that there were communists in the U.S. government. They condemned Truman's policy of containment for abandoning millions of people to communism, and Nixon went so far as to attack Democratic candidate ADLAI E. STEVENSON as a "graduate of the Cowardly College of Communist Containment." Eisenhower proposed a policy of liberation for the nations of Eastern Europe. But what won the election for him—beyond his popularity—was his pledge that, if elected, he would "go to Korea." Eisenhower won easily, 55 percent to 44 percent.

**Presidency.** On 20 January 1953, Eisenhower became the thirty-fourth President of the United States. His immediate goal was to shut down the costly, stalemated war in Korea. Most Republicans, especially Nixon and the new Secretary of State, JOHN FOSTER DULLES, wanted to end the war by winning it; they urged Eisenhower to go on the offensive, drive the Chinese Communists out of North Korea, unify the country, and perhaps even attack China itself with atomic weapons. Eisenhower, fearing a third world war and dreading the American casualties that would be suffered in an offensive, refused. In July, after much difficulty, he managed to achieve an armistice that left Korea divided along the thirty-eighth parallel (approximately the dividing line before the war began in 1950) but at peace.

*Domestic Policy.* Eisenhower's principal domestic goal was to balance the budget, which meant cutting defense spending even beyond the savings realized because of the end of the Korean War. This goal led Eisenhower to increase the pace of building nuclear bombs and the means of delivery while sharply reducing the size of the regular armed forces, especially the army. He called it the "new look" in defense policy. "More bang for a buck" was the popular slogan.

The right-wing Republicans had as their principal

domestic goal the repeal of the NEW DEAL and cutting taxes. Eisenhower would do neither. He kept most of the reforms of the 1930s in place and expanded the SOCIAL SECURITY system. He would not cut taxes until and unless the budget was balanced. His administration meanwhile launched the greatest public works project of all time, the Interstate Highway System (1956), and in cooperation with the Canadians built the SAINT LAWRENCE SEAWAY, opening the Great Lakes to oceangoing vessels.

Eisenhower was in agreement with the right wing of his party on the need to rid the government of subversives. They believed that the Truman administration had been lax, at best, in finding and dismissing communists in government. The Eisenhower administration moved quickly to fire supposedly disloyal federal employees, although not quickly enough to satisfy Republican Senator Joseph R. McCarthy of Wisconsin, who launched his own witch-hunt. Eisenhower refused to speak out against McCarthy's methods, but when the Senator began charging that the U.S. Army was harboring subversives and held the Army-McCarthy hearings (1954), the President did work behind the scenes to undercut McCarthy by encouraging Republic Senators to support a resolution censuring him.

*Cold War.* Eisenhower's most difficult and long-lasting problem was not alleged communists in the U.S. government but the Communists in Moscow. Since 1945 Eisenhower had hardened in his attitude toward the Soviet Union because of the imposition of Communist dictatorships in Eastern Europe and Communist aggression in Korea. As in domestic affairs, however, he was a moderate man. The Republicans wanted him to repudiate the accords reached at the 1945 YALTA CONFERENCE and take the offensive against communism in Eastern Europe, a goal that was consistent with his campaign promise to liberate the Soviet satellites, but he would not. While holding firmly to Truman's policy of containment, he tried to reach out to the Soviets in search of a modus vivendi. Stalin's death in March 1953 provided the opportunity for him to deliver (on 16 April 1953) the finest speech of his presidency, "The Chance for Peace."

In this address, Eisenhower proposed calling off the arms race. In ringing words, he spoke of its cost: "Every gun that is made, every warship launched, every rocket fired, signifies, in the final sense, a theft from those who hunger and are not fed, those who are cold and are not clothed." He warned that if the arms race continued, "The worse to be feared and the best to be expected can be simply stated. The worst is atomic war. The best would be this: a life of perpetual fear and tension; a burden of arms draining the wealth

and the labor of all peoples." He offered to devote the savings achieved by ending the arms race "to a fund for world aid and reconstruction. . . . The monuments to this new kind of war would be these: roads and schools, hospitals and homes, food and health." The Soviets failed to respond, then or later, when, at the Geneva Summit of 1955, he proposed an "Open Skies" policy in which each side would open its airspace to the other so as to reduce the fear of surprise attack and thus diminish the need for a hair-trigger retaliatory force. So the cold war went on.

Eisenhower's search for peace with the Soviets was offset by his policy of actively resisting communist revolutions or the establishment of left-wing governments in the developing world. In 1953 he directed the CENTRAL INTELLIGENCE AGENCY (CIA) to overthrow an elected but apparently procommunist government in Iran headed by Mohammad Mosaddeq. The CIA sponsored a coup that restored the shah to his throne. In 1954, at Eisenhower's urging, the CIA carried out a covert action in Guatemala that overthrew the elected government of Jacobo Arbenz Guzmán. Through the remainder of the Eisenhower administration, the CIA, under the direction of the Secretary of State's younger brother, Allen Dulles, continued to carry out COVERT OPERATIONS against third-world governments thought to be unfriendly to the United States. Although Truman had created the CIA, it was Eisenhower who made it into a principal weapon in the cold war.

He fought communism not only with the CIA but also with economic and military aid to Asian, African, and Latin American nations. But he refused to get into a real war. In early 1954, when the French garrison at Dien Bien Phu in Vietnam was about to fall to the communist Viet Minh, Eisenhower's advisers, to a man, urged him to intervene. Secretary of State Dulles, Vice President Nixon, and the Chairman of the JOINT CHIEFS OF STAFF, Admiral Arthur Radford, wanted to use atomic bombs to save the French garrison.

Eisenhower refused. He feared the divisive effect of another Asian war less than a year after the armistice in Korea; he doubted that the United States could send sufficient forces to maintain French rule in Indochina; and he wanted no part of supporting COLONIALISM. He also refused to fight without allies, and the British would not participate. So he said no. After the garrison fell in May 1954, Eisenhower and Dulles responded to the French defeat by accepting the 1954 Geneva Conference's division of Vietnam into north and south. The President and Secretary of State then backed the SEATO TREATY, which gave birth to a new collective security arrangement, the Southeast Asia Treaty Organization, and they brought the pro-Western government of South Vietnam into SEATO. Over the next six years the Eisenhower administration gave economic and military support to the government of Ngo Dinh Diem in Saigon. By the end of 1960, the United States was fully committed to the defense of South Vietnam against North Vietnam and the communist Vietcong rebels. Some six hundred American officers were serving as advisers to the South Vietnamese army.

Eisenhower also came to the support of the Nationalist Chinese. In 1949, the communist Chinese had driven Chiang Kai-shek's forces off the mainland. Chiang set up his government on Formosa (Taiwan). The communist government in Beijing made preparations to invade the island. In December 1954, Eisenhower signed a mutual-defense treaty with the Nationalists that declared that an armed attack on either party would be regarded as an act of war against the other. To back it up he continued Truman's policy of maintaining the U.S. Seventh Fleet in the Formosa Strait. Although the communists continued to harass Chiang's forces, no invasion was ever attempted.

***The 1956 election.*** Throughout his life Eisenhower had enjoyed robust health, but on 23 September 1955, he suffered a moderate heart attack. He was incapacitated for a week or so, which frightened the American people and led to intense speculation about whether he would run for a second term and, if so, whom he would choose as his running mate. His recovery, though slow, was complete, and in early 1956 he announced that he would be a candidate for a second term. There was a move by moderates in the Republican Party to dump Nixon, something Eisenhower seemed to encourage. But when Nixon showed great strength among party regulars, Eisenhower decided to keep him on the ticket. Adlai Stevenson was once again the Democratic candidate.

The Democrats hardly had an issue. The economy was booming. The budget was balanced. The nation was at peace, Stevenson advocated a nuclear test ban, something Eisenhower was working for behind the scenes but refused to make into a public issue.

There were two simultaneous crises during the last weeks of the 1956 campaign. One came in Hungary, where there was a popular uprising to overthrow the communist dictatorship. Soviet leader Nikita Khrushchev sent tanks to Budapest to crush the revolt. The Hungarian rebels called out to the United States for help. The CIA was eager to move, and American anticommunists urged Eisenhower to intervene. He refused. Hungary was surrounded by Soviet satellites, and Eisenhower could see no hope in challenging the communists in the heart of their empire. He was also constrained by what was happening in the Middle East, where Egyptian leader Gamal Abdel Nasser had seized the Suez Canal to provide revenue to build dams on the Nile River. Great Britain and France, which had jointly owned the canal, entered into a cabal with Israel (which was subject to endemic hit-and-run attacks from Arab nationalists) to attack Suez with British and French paratroopers and Sinai with Israeli tanks and infantry. The conspirators kept their plans secret from Eisenhower.

When they launched the attack, Eisenhower moved immediately to stop what he considered nineteenth-century-style colonialism. He persuaded the UNITED NATIONS to adopt resolutions requiring the British, French, and Israelis to abandon their gains or face economic sanctions, specifically an oil embargo by the United States (in the 1950s, the U.S. was a major oil exporter). This action was the first direct American intervention into the politics of the Middle East. The result was humiliation for the conspirators, some criticism of Eisenhower from conservatives who argued he should have supported Israel and America's NATO allies, and much praise for Eisenhower from third-world countries, who could hardly believe that the United States would side with an Arab country against Israel and its European partners.

The coincidence of the Hungarian and Suez crises with the election led people to "trust Ike" more than ever. He won a smashing reelection victory on 6 November, 35 million to 25 million votes. But the Republicans, who had lost control of both houses of Congress in the 1954 elections, failed to regain either house. For the first time in American history, a President was reelected without his party controlling either house of Congress. The Democrats had won the House and Senate in the 1954 congressional election, so Eisenhower's last six years in office set a pattern that persisted through much of the second half of the twentieth century—a Republican President and a Democratic Congress.

In March 1957, in the wake of the Suez crisis, Eisenhower persuaded Congress to pass a resolution giving the President authorization to employ American troops and to provide economic and military aid in support of any Middle Eastern nation that requested such aid. The resolution, known as the EISENHOWER DOCTRINE, gave him a blank check to intervene in the Middle East whenever he saw fit.

***Brown and Little Rock.*** In the fall of 1957 Eisenhower had two crises to manage, one domestic, the other foreign. The domestic crises concerned civil rights. When Eisenhower took office in 1953, the United States maintained a system of rigid racial segregation in nearly every aspect of life. The single important exception was in the armed services, which Truman had integrated during the Korean War. Eisenhower's first and by far his most important appointment to the Supreme Court had come early, in 1953, when he had nominated Governor Earl Warren of California as Chief Justice. In 1954, Attorney General HERBERT BROWNELL had argued before the Court that the 1896 decision in *Plessy v. Ferguson*, which had sanctioned segregation on the basis of "separate but equal" promises, was unconstitutional. Warren had agreed and written the unanimous opinion in *Brown v. Board of Education* (1954), which outlawed segregation by race in the schools and ordered public school systems throughout the country to desegregate "with all deliberate speed." The burden of implementing the court decision fell on the administration.

Eisenhower was unhappy. Although not a racist, he was a segregationist. But he was also a President determined to do his duty, and his duty was clear—to enforce desegregation. He did so, but reluctantly. When white southerners defied the law, he was at pains to see the problem from their point of view. He refused ever to speak out in favor of *Brown*, a silence that encouraged white southerners to believe they need not obey the law.

The LITTLE ROCK CRISIS came in September 1957, when Governor Orvil Faubus of Arkansas called out the state national guard to block court-ordered desegregation of Central High School in his state's capital city. Whatever Eisenhower's feelings on segregation, he would never allow direct defiance of the federal government. He called out airborne troops from the U.S. Army and sent them to Little Rock to enforce the court decree. Southern politicians protested vigorously, but Eisenhower persisted. He thus made an important contribution to civil rights by making it clear that the South could not use force to uphold segregation.

That same year, the Eisenhower administration guided the first civil rights bill since RECONSTRUCTION through the Democratic Congress. It was primarily concerned with VOTING RIGHTS and was so weakened by amendments in the Senate that many African American political and religious leaders urged Eisenhower to veto it. Nevertheless, he signed. [*See* CIVIL RIGHTS ACT OF 1957.]

*Foreign Affairs.* The foreign crisis of 1957 was created by a Soviet technological advance that was a great blow to American pride. On 4 October 1957, the Soviets fired into orbit the world's first artificial satellite, named *Sputnik*. The public had a near-hysterical reaction to which the Democrats played by charging that Eisenhower had allowed a missile gap to develop because of his insistence on a balanced budget. This, they claimed, had made America number two in space and thus vulnerable to a surprise Soviet missile attack.

The President tried to reassure the people. He said that *Sputnik* was more a stunt than a serious scientific breakthrough, which was true. He said that the United States' defenses were more than adequate and that America's ability to produce and deliver weapons of mass destruction was far greater than that of the Soviets, which was also true. But for the first time since 1942 the people refused to "trust Ike." Foundations created committees to find out what was wrong with American education, to call for more military research and development, greatly to expand the defense budget, and vastly to increase the production of armaments.

Eisenhower said no. He insisted there was no reason for panic. He did create the President's Science Advisory Committee (PSAC) and centralized space research under civilian control with the National Aeronautics and Space Administration (NASA). Soon the United States caught up with—and then quickly surpassed—the Soviets in space [*see* SPACE POLICY]. Nevertheless the missile gap remained the Democrats' best issue.

A major reason for Eisenhower's relative calm about America's defense posture was intelligence about the Soviet position. As a general and as President, Eisenhower had insisted on obtaining all the intelligence he could about his enemies. This effort had led him greatly to increase the CIA's intelligence-gathering capacities. In 1956 the agency had come up with the U-2 spy-in-the-sky plane. It penetrated Soviet air space at altitudes too high to be shot down and, using the latest photographic techniques, took pictures of Soviet military installations. These photographs convinced Eisenhower that America was well ahead in the arms race. The problem was that he could not reveal his source, as the U-2 flights violated international law and were kept secret (that is, from the American people; the Soviets knew about them).

In 1958 Eisenhower again intervened in the Middle East under the terms of the Eisenhower Doctrine. The government in Lebanon, fearful that Nasser's bid to unite all Arabs under Egyptian leadership would lead to its overthrow, asked for help. Eisenhower responded by sending a division of U.S. Marines to Beirut on 15 July. He limited the scope of the intervention by insisting that the Marines secure the airfield and the capital only. No pan-Arabist coup was attempted. In October, Eisenhower withdrew the Marines. This, the first use of U.S. troops in the Middle East in the twentieth century, set a precedent for later administrations.

In the fall of 1958, with off-year elections for Congress coming up, Eisenhower had a personnel problem. His White House Chief of Staff, Sherman Adams, was accused of accepting gifts from a businessman who had tax difficulties. Angered by the charges, which seemed to him to be partisan, Eisenhower tried to keep Adams but eventually was forced to let him go by Republicans up for reelection. The Democrats retained control of both houses of Congress anyway, winning a dramatic victory.

On 1 January 1959, another foreign crisis developed, as Fidel Castro marched into Havana and took control of the government of Cuba. Eisenhower's initial response to Castro was cautious, but he soon became convinced that Castro was a communist and decided to put the CIA to work to drive him from power. The CIA created a paramilitary force consisting of Cuban exiles living in Florida and began planning for an invasion of Cuba. The plan called for landing the exiles at the Bay of Pigs on Cuba's southern coast, with the hope that it would set off an anti-Castro uprising throughout the island. Eisenhower refused to implement it while he was in office, not because he disapproved but because he insisted that the exiles had to create a government-in-exile first and they were unable to get together behind one leader.

***The Peacemaker.*** Castro was an irritant rather than a threat. Eisenhower wanted peace and prosperity, which could not be attained without coming to some accommodation with the Soviet Union. Eisenhower's efforts to achieve that goal had included his Open Skies proposal, an offer (called Atoms for Peace) to share atomic stockpiles with the U.N., and constraints imposed on the American defense budget. But Khrushchev failed to respond. Instead, he threatened to blockade Berlin in order to force the Western governments to abandon their occupation rights in the city and pull their troops out, leaving all of Berlin in the control of the communist East German government.

Eisenhower called Khrushchev's bluff. Although he admitted that the situation in divided Berlin was "abnormal," he would not consider pulling out. If necessary, America would fight. Khrushchev backed down, withdrawing his ultimatum. Khrushchev's retreat showed that the United States had military superiority, which Eisenhower had all along insisted was the case. But the President wanted peace, a balanced budget, and prosperity more than armed strength. For his last year in office, he set as his goal nothing short of achieving a genuine worldwide peace. He traveled around the world on Air Force One, on a mission of peace and was greeted by tumultuous crowds wherever he went.

But the ability to make peace rested with Khrushchev, not with the people of the world. Eisenhower reached out to him. He offered to meet in a summit in Paris in May 1960 to seek an agreement on a nuclear test ban treaty and a resolution of the status of Berlin. Both sides had made propaganda use of the issues, especially the test ban, playing on peoples' fears about radioactive fallout. Meanwhile, both sides continued to test new weapons at the limit of their capacity. If achieved, a test ban would have been the first limitation on armaments since the prohibition of gas warfare after World War I, the first in the atomic age, and the first step toward world peace. Eisenhower made it his last major goal, and Khrushchev seemed agreeable. Eisenhower had reached the high-water mark of his remarkable career.

But on 1 May 1960, on the eve of the Paris summit, the Soviets shot down a U-2 flying over their country. Khrushchev used the U-2 incident as an excuse to break up the meeting. Eisenhower was deeply depressed. He canceled visits to the Soviet Union and Japan. The cold war went on. Eisenhower called the failure of the summit the biggest disappointment of his life.

He had another in the 1960 presidential election. He had been exceedingly slow to endorse his Vice President for the Republication nomination, but once Nixon became the candidate and Senator John F. Kennedy became the Democratic nominee, he strongly supported Nixon. But his ambivalent feelings toward Nixon led him to make a gaffe during a news conference that may have cost Nixon the election. Nixon had been stressing his experience in government, in contrast to Kennedy; he insisted that he had been involved in decision making throughout the Eisenhower administration. The Democrats had been charging that Eisenhower had delegated his authority, that he was content to reign, not rule. Eisenhower hated that charge. So when he was asked by a reporter to name one decision Nixon had participated in making, Eisenhower insisted that he made all the decisions himself. When reporters persisted, he snapped, "Give me a week and I might think of one." In one of the closest presidential elections in history, Kennedy was declared the winner. Eisenhower was bitterly disappointed, as he regarded Kennedy unfit for office.

In his farewell address, delivered on 17 January 1961, Eisenhower spoke to the most basic theme of his administration. He had overseen the buildup of America's nuclear strike capacity from a few hundred to many thousands of bombs, but he had hated doing so and was terribly worried about the effect of the arms race and the military-industrial complex on American life. He pointed out that the cold war had forced the nation to create a "permanent armaments industry of vast proportions" and a large standing peacetime army. "This conjunction of an immense military establishment and a large arms industry is new in the American experience," he noted, and he warned, "In the councils of government, we must guard against the acquisition of unwarranted influence, whether sought or unsought, by the military-industrial complex." These became the most quoted—and ignored—words of his presidency. He concluded, "Disarmament . . . is a continuing imperative."

**Later Life.** In retirement, Eisenhower spent his summers and falls at a farm outside Gettysburg, Pennsylvania, and his winters and springs in Palm Desert, California. He wrote extensively, and successfully. His two volumes of political memoirs, *Mandate for Change* (1963) and *Waging Peace* (1965), were up to the standards he had set with *Crusade in Europe*. A volume of informal memoirs, *At Ease: Stories I Tell My Friends* (1967), delighted a large readership. He painted, in oils and watercolors. He played golf. He commented on current events, although he took care not to be too critical of his successors; even though he disapproved of Kennedy's handling of the BAY OF PIGS INVASION (1961) and the BERLIN CRISIS (1961), he expressed his feelings only privately. He strongly and publicly supported President Lyndon B. Johnson on the VIETNAM WAR; he strongly but privately criticized Johnson's GREAT SOCIETY.

He and Mamie loved living on their Gettysburg farm (the first home they had ever owned). They had the pleasure of seeing their grandson David marry Nixon's daughter Julie and of seeing Nixon win the 1968 election. On 28 March 1969, shortly after Nixon's inauguration, Eisenhower died.

**Assessment of Eisenhower's Presidency.** Eisenhower was the general who hated war, the President who sought peace. He was a man quick to anger, quicker to forgive, usually sunny in his disposition. He took pride in his triumphs, but his instant instinct after victory was to reach out his hand to the defeated opponent. He was intelligent, well educated, widely read, a man of the broadest experience, but the characteristic that mattered most was that he was a man full of love, for life and for people. He made it a consistent motto never to question another man's motives. His wisdom, yes, but not his motives. And Eisenhower always assumed the best about others, until shown otherwise.

He was a man of his word (although there were exceptions after be became a politician), a feature emphasized by his open, honest manner and marvelously expressive face, highlighted by a wonderful grin and infectious laugh. "He has but to smile at you," said the British Field Marshal Bernard Montgomery, "and you trust him at once."

Eisenhower had a genuine modesty and a justified self-confidence. He had great respect for men with talent and an ability to bring them all together as a team. He got them to *want* to pull together, if only to please him. To quote Montgomery again: "He has the power of drawing the hearts of men as the magnet draws the piece of metal."

What he accomplished can be simply stated. He headed the great Allied force that crushed the Nazis, and he managed the crises of the 1950s—from Korea and Vietnam to Berlin and the Middle East—without blowing up the world or sacrificing any national interest.

When he left office, his rank with intellectuals was about as low as his popularity with the people was high. It was charged that he was a do-nothing President who let Dulles run foreign policy and Adams take care of the domestic side while he played golf. In fact, he was always in charge. The man who commanded Operation Overlord was never one to shrink from responsibility or decision making. He made no great innovations as President; most of his decisions were negative (e.g., not to go over to the offensive in Korea in the spring of 1953, not to intervene in Vietnam in 1954, not to launch an atomic attack against China, not to intervene in Hungary or support the British-French-Israeli invasion of Egypt in 1956).

Eisenhower was not a reformer, but one of the great changes in American life came about because of his appointment of Earl Warren as Chief Justice and because of his use of force to support *Brown v. Board of Education* in Little Rock in 1957. He was a great builder. It has been said that no government program of the twentieth century had so great an impact on American life as his Interstate Highway System. He brought peace and prosperity, and many regard the 1950s as the best decade of the twentieth century. There were no wars during his administration. There was some progress in civil rights. Americans enjoyed the sharpest rise in real wages of any decade in the century, and, consequently, home buying, auto purchases, road building, and other capital investment all went up at a record pace. Surely Eisenhower's fiscal policies—his refusal to cut taxes or increase defense spending, his insistence on a balanced budget—played some role in creating this happy situation.

After the excesses of the 1960s, and the failed

presidencies of Johnson, Nixon, Gerald Ford, and Jimmy Carter, Eisenhower's reputation even among intellectuals began to climb, helped immeasurably by the documentary evidence that became available to scholars at the Eisenhower Library in Abilene, Kansas. That reputation continued to climb through the 1980s, when a consensus was reached that he was a strong, forceful, successful President, very much in charge. In the 1990s a new generation of historians began to take issue with this revised assessment. They pointed, rightly, to serious shortcomings and failures, as in civil rights policy and dealings with underdeveloped countries. But that he will continue to rank among the few truly great Presidents of the twentieth century is clear.

### BIBLIOGRAPHY

Ambrose, Stephen. *Eisenhower the President.* 1984.
Ewald, William Bragg, Jr. *Eisenhower the President.* 1981.
Greenstein, Fred. *The Hidden-Hand Presidency.* 1982.
Hughes, John Emmet. *The Ordeal of Power: A Political Memoir of the Eisenhower Years.* 1963.
Larson, Arthur. *Eisenhower: The President Nobody Knew.* 1968.
Lyon, Peter. *Eisenhower: Portrait of the Hero.* 1974.
Neustadt, Richard. *Presidential Power: The Politics of Leadership.* 1960.
Pach, Chester, and Elmo Richardson. *The Presidency of Dwight D. Eisenhower.* 1990.
Parmet, Herbert. *Eisenhower and the American Crusades.* 1972.

STEPHEN E. AMBROSE

**EISENHOWER, MAMIE** (1896–1979), First Lady, wife of Dwight D. Eisenhower. Although entering the political world late in life, Mamie Doud Eisenhower had several decades of experience as the spouse of a man in the public eye. Eisenhower's earlier experience as military leader and university president allowed her to perfect the hostess skills that she later brought to the WHITE HOUSE. She took no leadership role in any important project or cause but became popular for the way she wore her hair, selected clothing, retained a youthful appearance, and insisted on an atmosphere of homey familiarity in the Executive Mansion. In fact, this popular public image constituted her greatest asset to her husband's presidency. Mamie Eisenhower saw the job of FIRST LADY as managerial and social: she was noted for her attention to detail in running the executive mansion and for personally greeting thousands of visitors every year.

### BIBLIOGRAPHY

Eisenhower, John S. D. *Strictly Personal.* 1974.
Teasley, Martin M. "Ike Was Her Career: The Papers of Mamie Doud Eisenhower." In *Modern First Ladies: Their Documentary Legacy.* Edited by Nancy Kegan Smith and Mary C. Ryan. 1989.

BETTY BOYD CAROLI

**EISENHOWER DOCTRINE.** A law passed in 1957 authorizing the President to give military and economic aid to any Middle Eastern nation that requested it embodies the Eisenhower Doctrine. In the wake of the Suez crisis of October and November 1956, President Dwight D. Eisenhower decided that the President needed advance authorization to intervene in the Middle East with military force if the Soviet Union attacked the area or if pan-Arab nationalists attempted to overthrow a Middle Eastern government that was friendly to the United States. He also wanted to provide economic and military aid to friendly governments in the region. On 5 January 1957, he went to Capitol Hill to deliver a special message to Congress on the Middle East. In this message, he asked for authorization to provide arms and money to "any nation or group of nations which desires such aid" as well as authorization to employ U.S. troops "to secure and protect the territorial integrity and political independence of such nations . . . against overt armed aggression from any nation controlled by International Communism." He assured Congress that he would not use the authority to intervene "except at the desire of the nation attacked."

Congressional opposition came from friends of Israel and from conservatives who opposed all foreign aid, but Eisenhower used his persuasive powers and his political skills to overcome it. He was helped by Israeli intransigence over Gaza (Egyptian territory occupied by Israel in 1956) and by the pro-Soviet, anti-American propaganda of Egyptian leader Gamal Abdel Nasser. In March 1957, Congress passed the Eisenhower Doctrine and the President signed it into law. The resolution gave the President a blank check to intervene in the Middle East whenever he saw fit.

On 15 July 1958, Eisenhower implemented the doctrine when he sent a division of U.S. Marines to Lebanon. The government in Beirut had requested assistance to ward off a coup by pro-Nasser pan-Arab nationalists. There was great fear in the West that the Soviets were behind Nasser's attempt to create a single Arab nation, one that would be unfriendly to the United States and that would deny Middle Eastern oil to America's European allies.

Eisenhower limited the scope of the intervention by insisting that the Marines secure the airfield and the capital only. The coup was never attempted. The last of the U.S. troops were withdrawn in October. This, the first use of U.S. troops in the Middle East, set a precedent: President Ronald Reagan sent Marines to Lebanon, and President George Bush sent nearly half a million fighting men and women to Saudi Arabia, Kuwait, and Iraq, though neither cited the Eisenhower Doctrine.

BIBLIOGRAPHY

Eisenhower, Dwight D. *Waging Peace.* 1965.
Stookey, Robert W. *America and the Arab States: An Uneasy Encounter.* 1975.

STEPHEN E. AMBROSE

**ELECTION, PRESIDENTIAL.** For discussion of the process by which Presidents are elected, see CAMPAIGN STRATEGY; CAUCUSES, PRESIDENTIAL; DEBATES, PRESIDENTIAL; ELECTORAL COLLEGE; ELECTORAL REFORM; NOMINATING PRESIDENTIAL CANDIDATES; PRIMARIES, PRESIDENTIAL. See also CAMPAIGN SLOGANS; DARK HORSES; PACS; PLATFORMS, PARTY; THIRD PARTIES; THIRD-PARTY CANDIDATES. For discussion of specific elections, see the following fifty-two articles on each presidential election from 1788 to 1992.

**ELECTION, PRESIDENTIAL, 1788.** The election of 1788, the first under the newly ratified Constitution, was in many ways the most unusual in American history. Political factions and even political parties were well established in a number of the states. On top of that, the people had divided sharply over the adoption of the new federal charter. Two states— Rhode Island and North Carolina—had refused to ratify the Constitution, and several others had suggested numerous, immediate amendments. Yet there was never any question as to who would fill the highest office were the Constitution approved. Indeed, the Constitutional Convention might never have proposed an executive office as powerful as the presidency if its own presiding officer had not been present as a living proof that great executive authority could be entrusted to men of great virtue. For Federalists and Anti-Federalists alike, approval of the Constitution left two questions. Would General Washington accept the nation's undisputed will? And who would fill the second-highest office?

**Washington's Stature.** By 1788 Washington already occupied a place and served a purpose for the nation that would never be repeated. As commander of the Continental Army, he had been indispensable to national success. Washington was not a brilliant field commander. In the Revolution, he was beaten time and time again; yet every time he rose and fought again until the opportunity for final victory appeared at Yorktown. Through it all, he understood that the United States could not be subjugated if, despite its woeful inability to feed and fill the ranks, it could maintain a Continental Army and exhaust Great Britain's willingness to fight. His sound strategic sense, his irrepressibility, and his ability to win incredible devotion from his officers and troops were equalled only by his brilliance as a revolutionary politician.

Washington was faultless in his deference to civil leaders, even when they starved the army or conceded him a dictatorial authority that he declined to use because he was ever-mindful of the republican ideals for which the war was being fought. By 1783, when he insisted that the grievances of the disbanding army be redressed by legal means and then surrendered his commission with a promise of a permanent return to private life, he had become a living legend. Contemporaries thought of him as an embodiment of the republican ideal of public service. They compared him to the Roman general, Cincinnatus, who had left his farm to save his country's liberties and then had sheathed his sword when liberty became secure. Washington, in turn, deliberately attempted to conform his personality and conduct to the same ideal.

Of course, retirement to MOUNT VERNON did not mean that Washington withdrew entirely from public life. The great commander took an active role in Virginia's effort to open the navigation of the Potomac, kept a careful watch on national events, and wrote repeatedly to influential men throughout the country, siding with and even spurring the reformers who were coming to believe that radical revision of the Articles of Confederation might be necessary to preserve the Union and the Revolution. When these reformers finally succeeded in securing a CONSTITUTIONAL CONVENTION and insisted that his presence was essential, he realized that his commitment and his reputation would compel him to relinquish his determination never to resume a public role. Washington's attendance at the convention was critical to its success. For many voters, Washington's endorsement of the Constitution was sufficient. For many who opposed the Constitution and insisted on amendments, only a Cincinnatus could be trusted with the awesome powers that a President would hold. The great commander's personal prestige was needed once again to put the government into effect.

**The Vice Presidency.** On 2 July 1788, the twelfth anniversary of the congressional resolution for American independence, the President of the Confederation Congress announced that nine states had ratified the Constitution, the minimum required to put it into operation among the ratifying states. As Article II required, Congress moved immediately to set the dates for the selection of presidential electors and for their meeting in their several states to cast two ballots, one of which would have to be for a person from another state. Congress approved the first Wednesday in January 1789 and the first Wednesday in February 1789, with the First Federal Congress to assemble on the first Wednesday in March.

New York, the seat of the Confederation Congress, had served since the adjournment of the Constitutional Convention as a clearinghouse for national information and for efforts to coordinate the national campaign for the approval of the Constitution. Now, it served again as a planning center for the national election. Taking Washington's election as a given (and bombarding him with letters fervently insisting that the public good required him to forgo his personal desires), ALEXANDER HAMILTON, James Madison, and other leading Founders turned their thoughts to who should fill the second office. Nearly everyone, it seems, assumed that sectional considerations virtually demanded that a southern president be balanced with a man from Massachusetts, the second-largest state and northern pillar of the Revolution.

Neither Hamilton nor Madison was thrilled about this prospect. It pointed automatically to Governor John Hancock or to John Adams, the Confederation's current minister to Britain, whose service in the early revolutionary congresses, as draftsman of the Massachusetts constitution, as peace commissioner, and in a wide variety of diplomatic posts identified him as another hero of the Revolution. But Hancock, Madison lamented, was "weak, ambitious, a courtier of popularity, given to low intrigue, and lately reunited by a factious friendship with Samuel Adams," who had initially opposed the Constitution. Hancock's own enthusiasm for the Constitution was in doubt; he was a known proponent of amendments; and he was widely thought to owe his current office to the participants in Shays' rebellion, to whom his government had offered numerous concessions. John Adams was at least a firm supporter of the Constitution, though Madison insisted that the minister to Britain had "made himself obnoxious to many, particularly in the southern states, by the political principles avowed in his [recent] book," a treatise in which Adams had attacked the unicameralists in France on lines that seemed to mark him as an admirer of the British system. "Others," Madison reflected, "knowing his extravagant self-importance," and aware of his abiding love of dignified positions, "conclude that he would not be a very cordial second to

the General, and that an impatient ambition might even intrigue for a premature advancement" to the presidency itself.

Still, Madison and Hamilton saw little choice except to push for Adams, though Hamilton decided to employ his influence in Connecticut to advocate a scattering of second ballots, which might be necessary to avoid the sort of accident that could produce a tie in the Electoral College. New England sentiment was moving in the same direction, partly because of widespread doubts about Hancock's health and rumors that the popular governor might disdain the powerless office.

**The Result.** Washington did nothing that might even hint of personal ambition. Indeed, he may have been entirely candid when he answered numerous entreaties by insisting that his "great and sole desire [was] to live and die, in peace and retirement, on my own farm." He would, he wrote, "unfeignedly rejoice" if the electors passed the choice to someone else and saved him from "the dreaded Dilemma of being forced to accept or refuse." Washington was genuinely doubtful that his qualities were suited to the office and concerned that it could only tarnish his assured historical repute. He called on Heaven to witness that "nothing in this world" could draw him from retirement "unless it be a *conviction* that the partiality of my Countrymen had made my services absolutely necessary, joined to a *fear* that my refusal might induce a belief that I preferred the conservation of my own reputation and private ease, to the good of my Country." Even then, he solemnly observed, "this act would be the greatest sacrifice . . . that ever I have been called upon to make. It would be to forego repose and domestic enjoyment, for trouble, perhaps for public obloquy: for I should consider myself as entering upon an unexplored field, enveloped on every side with clouds and darkness."

Of course, this sacrifice was just what Washington's contemporaries called on him to make. The Constitution provided for the selection of presidential electors in whatever manner the state legislatures should direct. In several of the smaller states, the legislatures made the choice themselves. In Delaware, Massachusetts, Pennsylvania, Maryland, and Virginia, the voters chose tickets of electors proposed by meetings of leading state supporters of the Constitution. On 4 February 1789, electors gathered in ten states as each of their local legislatures had directed. (North Carolina and Rhode Island had not yet ratified the Constitution, and a deadlock between the two houses of the legislature in New York had rendered it unable to act.) Seventy-two electors had been chosen; sixty-nine voted. As was quickly known throughout the country, all sixty-nine electors cast one of their two ballots for George Washington. The second ballots were scattered broadly among several local favorites or distinguished national figures, partly as a way of throwing some of them away. John Adams led the list with thirty-four of the possible sixty-nine, only five of which (all from Virginians) were from states south of Delaware. JOHN JAY of New York, another revolutionary diplomat and soon to be the first Chief Justice, garnered nine electoral votes, mostly from Delaware and New Jersey. Hancock got three, as did Governor GEORGE CLINTON of New York. Robert H. Harrison of Maryland and John Rutledge of South Carolina each received six votes as favorite sons. Six other candidates divided the remaining eight electoral ballots.

Punctilious to the end, the President-elect stayed quietly at home until the last formalities had been completed. In New York, the first House of Representatives found a quorum on 1 April, the Senate on 6 April. The House then joined the Senate in its chamber, where the Senate's president pro tem, John Langdon of New Hampshire, opened and counted the electoral ballots. Charles Thomson of Pennsylvania, the longtime secretary of the old Confederation Congress, was appointed to carry the official news to the new President. Sylvanus Bourn was given the honor of notifying Vice President Adams.

Thomson reached Mount Vernon on 14 April, and Washington wrote immediately to Langdon to notify the Congress of his acceptance. Two days later, his diary entry read: "About ten o'clock I bade adieu to Mount Vernon, to private life, and to domestic felicity; and with a mind oppressed with more anxious and painful sensations than I have words to express, set out for New York in company with Mr. Thompson and Colonel Humphries, with the best dispositions to render service to my country in obedience to its call, but with less hope of answering its expectations." Acclaimed at every stop, he reached the city on 23 April and was inaugurated as the first chief magistrate on 30 April 1789.

### BIBLIOGRAPHY

DenBoer, Gordon, ed. *The Documentary History of the First Federal Elections, 1788–1790.* Vol. X. 1989.
Fitzpatrick, John C. *The Writings of George Washington.* 39 vols. 1931–1944.
Flexner, James Thomas. *George Washington.* 4 vols. 1965–1972.
Howe, John R., Jr. *The Changing Political Thought of John Adams.* 1966.
Miller, John C. *The Federalist Era, 1789–1801.* 1960.
Morris, Richard B. *The Forging of the Union, 1781–1789.* 1987.
Wills, Garry. *Cincinnatus: George Washington and the Enlightenment.* 1964.

LANCE BANNING

**ELECTION, PRESIDENTIAL, 1792.** In 1789 George Washington accepted unanimous election to the nation's highest office in the fervent hope that he would not be called upon to serve a second term. Four years, he reasoned, would be long enough to organize the government, establish its authority among the people, and get the nation past its sharp division over the adoption of the Constitution. At that point, he would be able to enjoy an honorable retirement; and by giving up his post, he could set a precedent for a rotation in the presidential office that would be his final contribution to the vigor and success of democratic institutions. In the spring of 1792, with most of his original ambitions solidly fulfilled, he asked James Madison to draft a farewell address.

**The Emergence of Parties.** In 1789, however, neither Washington nor any of his colleagues had anticipated the ferocious conflict that developed after the adoption of the Constitution. Three years later, that conflict was working to divide the government and people into two emerging parties. The argument had started in the second session of the infant Federal Congress, when Madison disputed the morality and policy of ALEXANDER HAMILTON's proposals for the funding of the debt. With help from Thomas Jefferson, the Secretary of State, this first collision had been settled by the Compromise of 1790, which traded the enactment of the funding plan for an agreement that the federal government would move in 1800 to a permanent location on the Potomac River. In 1791, however, Hamilton proposed creation of a national bank and federal encouragement of native manufactures. Jefferson as well as Madison insisted that incorporation of a national bank was not within the powers granted by the Constitution. Both men increasingly suspected that the Secretary of the Treasury was following a course that could result in concentrated central power; domination of the South and West by the commercial and financial East; subversion of the federal government's responsiveness to popular control; oppression of the agricultural majority of people; and, in time, a threat to the survival of republicanism itself. Hamilton, in turn, suspected that the two Virginians were determined to destroy a Union that they had not been able to control.

In the summer of 1791, after the adjournment of the First Congress, Jefferson and Madison embarked upon a pleasure tour of New England and upstate

New York. Hamilton's supporters were convinced that the Virginians meant to link the Philadelphia opponents of his program with the followers of Governor GEORGE CLINTON, who had opposed the Constitution and were longtime foes of Hamilton's supporters in New York. Before he left, moreover, Jefferson had accidentally initiated a tremendous furor in the press. Angered by the antidemocratic tone of high society in Philadelphia and by a growing disapproval of developments in France, he had attached a private note condemning "the political heresies which have sprung up among us" to a copy of Thomas Paine's defense of the French Revolution. This note found its way into the press and prompted a widely printed rejoinder, the "Letters of Publicola," which everyone mistakenly identified with Vice President John Adams rather than his son, John Quincy. By the opening of 1792, the Cabinet as well as Congress was bitterly divided. And by that time, the two Virginians had succeeded in negotiations that persuaded the revolutionary poet, Philip Freneau, to come to Philadelphia to launch a national newspaper opposing Hamilton's measures. Hamilton responded with anonymous (but hardly secret) essays attacking Jefferson's connection with the *National Gazette*.

With the election rapidly approaching, the two emerging parties hurled themselves into a full-blown newspaper war. In August, Washington appealed to both of his secretaries for an end to public quarrels; but Hamilton continued his campaign against the opposition, and Jefferson insisted that his rival's program would "demolish the republic" and subvert the Constitution, "which he has so often declared to be a thing of nothing which must be changed." In the *National Gazette*, which acted now as unofficial organ for an embryonic party, Madison, Freneau, and other opposition spokesmen pushed ahead with an intense campaign to influence the congressional elections.

**Washington and Adams.** Washington stood high above this dawning party war, which would develop in the years ahead into the sharpest in American history. Indeed, both sides insisted that the rising clamor was the strongest argument against the President's retirement. The North and South were held together, Jefferson declared, by Washington alone. Hamilton and Madison and countless others argued that a premature departure would endanger everything that Washington had struggled for throughout his long career. Attorney General EDMUND RANDOLPH warned the President that it could lead to fragmentation of the Union, even civil war.

Washington resisted. He was sixty now and feared his faculties were failing. Surely, he had earned a quiet

repose. But in the circumstances, he could hardly bring himself to issue an announcement that he simply would not serve. The Republicans—as Jefferson's and Madison's supporters usually identified themselves—focused their attention on securing a majority in Congress and on an effort to replace John Adams.

Always vain and often prickly, Adams was instinctively disliked by many national politicians, though few could boast a more distinguished record or a better grasp of western governmental theory. In addition, Adams had decided in the past few years to carry on a personal crusade against the intellectuals in France, fearing that their admiration for a single-chamber government was winning converts even in America and Britain. His three-volume *Defense of the Constitutions of Government of the United States,* published in 1787 and 1788, defended the bicameral legislatures and strong executives of both America and Britain against the democratic constitutionalism of the French Revolution. His *Discourses on Davila,* which appeared as a newspaper series in the Federalist *Gazette of the United States* in 1790, were even more insistent on the evils of radical democracy. Like the "Letters of Publicola," which answered Jefferson and Paine, these writings seemed to many to *prefer* the hated British constitution—monarchy and all—to more enlightened French ideas. For years, they made John Adams an appealing target for the rising fear that Federalists were plotting a revival of hereditary privilege and gradual replacement of the federal Constitution with a system of the British sort. The effort to replace him as Vice President became the centerpiece of the Democratic-Republican campaign.

**Party Conflict.** Party conflict, to be sure, was just beginning to assume a definite configuration at this point. In the first session of the Second Congress, which met from October 1791 until May 1792, Madison could ordinarily depend on all the members from Virginia and Georgia, all of those from North Carolina except John Steele, half of those from Maryland, Thomas Sumter of South Carolina, Thomas Tredwell of New York, and William Findley of Pennsylvania. Another group of roughly fifteen members, mostly from New England, voted against the opposition leader two-thirds of the time, while fully half of the House of Representatives aligned themselves consistently with neither of these groups. The embryonic parties plainly had their bases in New England and the South (except for South Carolina). This regional division was a natural consequence of Hamilton's financial program, which had benefited the commercial and financial interests at the South's expense. Both parties, nevertheless, were starting to attract a following in every section of the country. As supporters of a strong new government and advocates of economic growth, the Federalists appealed to merchants, artisans, and market farmers—indeed to all who feared that ordered liberty was threatened by the radical contagion started by the democratic revolutions. As opponents of a grasping central government, which seemed to shower favors on elitist special interests, the Democratic-Republicans appealed to former ANTI-FEDERALISTS and to the rising democratic sentiments of countless ordinary voters, former Anti-Federalists and Federalists alike. Divided sentiments and early efforts to construct true parties were especially apparent in New York and Pennsylvania, where persistent local parties had competed since the first years of the Revolution.

Jefferson and Madison had not, in fact, completed an alliance with New York's Clintonians during their travels of 1791. As supporters of the Constitution, the Virginians were reluctant to cooperate with Clinton—all the more so when his supporters reelected him as governor in 1792 by challenging returns for his opponent. By summer, nonetheless, it seemed apparent that the governor alone could manage to unite the opposition in this crucial state, and Jefferson and Madison acknowledged his appeal to former Anti-Federalists in Pennsylvania and Virginia. In September, as Republicans in Pennsylvania worked toward an agreement on a party ticket for the fall congressional elections, John Beckley, the Virginia clerk of the House of Representatives and an important link between the national leadership and local operatives in Pennsylvania, traveled to New York with a letter from the Philadelphia physician Benjamin Rush introducing him to AARON BURR as someone who enjoyed the confidence of both the Pennsylvanians and Virginians. In October, Burr responded with a letter introducing Melancton Smith as spokesman for the rising "Republican interest" in New York. Smith met with Beckley and a group of Pennsylvanians on 16 October, and it was generally agreed that the Republicans would back George Clinton.

**The Result.** Voters played a modest role in the election of 1792. In nine of the fifteen states, the legislatures kept the choice of presidential electors in their own hands. In many of the others, citizens were still indifferent to a central government that barely touched their lives; political disputes had not yet generated active parties; or parties were so poorly organized that they could hardly reach agreement on a ticket, much less march supporters to the polls. Even in Pennsylvania, several different slates were offered by a wide variety of individuals and groups, and several candidates were listed on the tickets of both parties. Popular participation must have been discouraged, too, by lack of any challenge to the President himself.

Certainly, the outcome held no great surprises. Voting in their several states on 13 February 1793, the electors cast 132 of a possible 136 ballots for George Washington. In the election for Vice President, with Maryland and Pennsylvania splitting their electoral votes, unanimous support for Clinton by the coalition of New York, Virginia, Georgia, and North Carolina could not defeat New England and New Jersey. The electors cast 77 ballots for John Adams, 50 for George Clinton, 4 for Thomas Jefferson, and 1 for Aaron Burr. Four years later, when the "father of his country" finally retired and Jefferson himself could be supported, the Democratic-Republicans would have another, better shot at "his rotundity," John Adams.

### BIBLIOGRAPHY

Adams, Charles Francis, ed. *The Works of John Adams.* 10 vols. 1850–1856.

Banning, Lance. *The Jeffersonian Persuasion: Evolution of a Party Ideology.* 1978.

Cunningham, Noble E., Jr. *The Jeffersonian Republicans: The Formation of Party Organization, 1789–1801.* 1957.

Flexner, James Thomas. *Washington: The Indispensable Man.* 1969.

Howe, John R., Jr. *The Changing Political Thought of John Adams.* 1966.

Miller, John C. *The Federalist Era, 1789–1801.* 1960.

LANCE BANNING

**ELECTION, PRESIDENTIAL, 1796.** The election of 1796 was momentous in the history of the presidency because it was the first contested election for that high office fought by two closely matched political parties. As long as George Washington stood ready to serve as CHIEF EXECUTIVE (1789–1797), none would challenge at the polls this symbol of national unity and revolutionary triumph. By 1796, however, sharp divisions over domestic and foreign policy had generated the formation of political parties throughout much of the country. The struggles between Federalists and Democratic-Republicans, which had first emerged at the nation's capital, spread to congressional and state elections and were bound to trigger party competition for the presidency once Washington retired from office.

**Parties and Issues.** By the spring of 1796 leaders in both parties believed that Washington would probably not seek a third term, but the President delayed making public his decision until September when he released to the press his FAREWELL ADDRESS. The stage was now set for a sharp partisan battle. The election of

1796, therefore, marked a new stage in the evolution of American politics. For the next half century presidential contests played a vital role in the development of a keenly partisan political culture.

In his Farewell Address President Washington warned the country against "the baneful effects of the spirit of party generally," and though he did not regard himself as a partisan, Washington was so perceived by the opposition, which had subjected him to withering press attack in his last years in office. The timing of the address, moreover, bore the marks of partisanship, for by delaying announcement of retirement, the President gave the opposition less time to organize a campaign against his preferred successor, Vice President John Adams. Washington's self-perception as a man above party was sincere, but he could no more avoid acting as a partisan in influencing the succession than other leaders who also contributed to party development while disclaiming partisan intent. The parties, however, became the instrument for settling the succession in an age when hereditary monarchy was still the norm, and they did so in accord with the republican principles of popular sovereignty, though the mode of election was not a direct popular vote. In this sense the election of 1796 was also a triumph for republican constitutionalism since it managed a disputed succession for control of the executive branch legally and peacefully.

Political divisions had first surfaced in the early 1790s over Secretary of the Treasury ALEXANDER HAMILTON's proposals for funding the national debt, establishing a national bank, promoting the growth of manufactures, and building a strong central state. Cumulative conflicts over these issues generated the formation of two parties, the FEDERALIST PARTY, led by the President and Hamilton, and the Democratic-Republicans, led by two Virginians, Thomas Jefferson and James Madison. When war broke out in Europe between the French republic and Great Britain, which was allied with other monarchies threatened by the spread of French revolutionary principles, the neutral United States, enjoying a booming trade with the belligerents, found it nearly impossible to preserve NEUTRALITY as first the British, and then the French, launched attacks on American vessels trading with their enemies. Disputes over foreign policy sharply intensified partisan division as Federalists tilted toward a pro-British neutrality, culminating in a bitter struggle over ratification of JAY'S TREATY during Washington's last year in office. The treaty enabled the United States to avoid war with Great Britain, but the Democratic-Republicans condemned it as a betrayal of national interests by a party sympathetic to British

monarchy. In the eyes of Jefferson and his supporters the Federalists had betrayed the French alliance that had secured American independence a generation earlier and they had also betrayed the spread of republicanism, which the French Revolution, for all its faults, had ignited all over Europe. In Federalist eyes, however, the pro-French bias of the opposition risked engulfing the country in war with Britain and the importation of blood-soaked, radical French revolutionary principles to American shores. Heated battles between Anglophiles and Gallophiles, each suspecting the other's loyalty to the Constitution of 1789, intensified partisan warfare because people suspected that the very stability of the republic seemed at risk. This furnished an enflamed backdrop to the election of 1796.

**The Nominees.** Despite the spread of partisan feeling on the eve of the 1796 election, party organization still remained rudimentary. The parties had no formal, regularized procedures for selecting candidates, including nominees for President and Vice President. Before Congress adjourned, Democratic-Republican notables caucused, and though Jefferson was the obvious choice for President, they could not agree on Vice President. Federalist notables conferred more informally, and they agreed to support Vice President Adams, but they also reached no consensus on the second spot. Despite the secretive, informal, and elitist nature of the nominating process, both Adams and Jefferson were the popular choices of their parties. Both had served the republic at home and abroad since the heroic days of the American Revolution; each possessed a strong regional base, Adams in New England, Jefferson in the South, and each enjoyed broad support within their party in all regions. Adams promised continuity, as Washington's anointed successor; Jefferson promised a change in direction for those alienated by eight years of Federalist rule. Neither man actively sought the nomination; neither could refuse the honor and obligation of service.

Though neither party reached a consensus on a candidate for vice president, many Democratic-Republicans supported New York's AARON BURR and Federalists supported South Carolina's Thomas Pinckney. The parties entered the campaign, however, highly vulnerable to factious intrigue by those who took advantage of the Constitution's provision that the person with the second highest number of electoral votes became Vice President. The Framers had not anticipated the formation of political parties and consequently, until the adoption of the TWELFTH AMENDMENT (1804), the two offices were not chosen separately, opening the possibility, as events turned out, for John Adams to win the presidency and Thomas Jefferson the vice presidency. This outcome thwarted the designs of those Federalist leaders, following Alexander Hamilton, who secretly plotted to elect Pinckney, whom they regarded as more pliable than the fiercely independent Adams, by arranging for the South Carolinian to outpoll the Vice President. ABIGAIL ADAMS warned her husband of Hamilton's treachery: "Beware of that Spair Cassius . . . O I have read his Heart in his Wicked Eyes many a time. The very devil is in them." Hamilton's scheme failed because Adams loyalists, fearing betrayal, refused to vote a straight party ticket, scattering enough votes for their second choice to allow Jefferson to come in just behind Adams. Likewise, many of Jefferson's supporters deserted Burr, who had personally campaigned among elites in New England, to make sure that he polled fewer votes than the Virginian.

**The Election.** The indirect mode of election depressed popular interest, as did the unfamiliarity with contested presidential elections and the absence of strong two-party competition in many states.

Pennsylvania was a notable exception, anticipating in some respects the style of partisan campaigns that later became the national norm. Here voters could chose electors on a statewide ticket. Democratic-Republican leaders constructed a carefully balanced list of popular notables representing different parts of the state and ethnic groups. Thousands of handbills flooded the commonwealth while the leading Democratic-Republican newspaper, Benjamin Franklin Bache's *Aurora*, aroused the faithful. The outcome was extremely close as most voters cast a straight ticket for all fifteen of the Federalist or Democratic-Republican electors, though the law required ballots to be handwritten. Jefferson polled well in Philadelphia where the party capitalized on the support it had gained among artisans and mechanics whose interests it championed in local matters. Some Quakers deserted the Federalists, opting for the pacific foreign policy Jeffersonians promised toward France. With an eye on the Pennsylvania vote, the French minister to the United States, Pierre Adet, sought to influence the election by informing the United States that France regarded Jay's Treaty as a pro-British measure that justified seizure of American vessels trading with the enemy. Whether Adet's war scare helped or hurt the Democratic-Republicans, the party entered the election weakened by its failure to block Jay's Treaty, which, for all its concessions to Britain, had preserved the peace and aroused strong popular support that had overwhelmed the congressional opposition.

Since in nearly half the states, legislatures chosen

months before the campaign picked the electors, electioneering had limited impact, further dampening popular interest. Neither Adams nor Jefferson themselves were active; in many parts of the country their friends could count on carrying the state without popular mobilization. The parties were still new and rudimentary. Neither offered a PARTY PLATFORM—that lay well into the future—but each candidate was identified with a set of policies and convictions that programatically differentiated the parties. Jefferson's friends boosted him as a friend of popular government, Adams as a closet monarchist, quoting out of context from Adams's voluminous writings on politics, excerpts that made him appear hostile to republicanism. Federalists lambasted Jefferson as unfit for Chief Executive, citing his failure as governor of Virginia during the American Revolution and his alleged partiality for France and Jacobinism. Scoffing at Jefferson's impractical idealism and penchant for airy philosophizing, Robert G. Harper, a Federalist, declared him more fit to "be a professor in a College" than President of the United States.

The election was extremely close. Adams garnered seventy-one to Jefferson's sixty-eight electoral votes in a highly sectionalized pattern. Adams swept New England and won nearly two-thirds of the electoral votes of the middle states but ran poorly in the south. Jefferson took most of the votes in the south and west but except for Pennsylvania, showed little strength elsewhere. Turnout is impossible to estimate because in seven states the legislatures chose the electors; in another seven there were popular elections either by districts, as in four states, or on a general ticket, in three states. Two states used a mixed system of both legislative and popular election.

Though by later standards party warfare only partially aroused the electorate, the intensity of the campaign was something new in presidential politics and alarming to contemporaries. "I fear America will never go through another Election without Blood Shed," Abigail Adams warned. "We have had a paper War for six weeks past, and if the Candidates had not themselves been entirely passive, Rage and Violence would have thrown the whole Country in a flame."

**The Aftermath.** Despite the heat of the campaign, President Adams enjoyed a brief honeymoon as partisanship subsided and the two rivals moved toward reconciliation. Jefferson sincerely wished the President well after his election. Adams, in turn, reached out to the opposition in his inaugural. The new President reaffirmed his devotion to republican government, reassuring those who suspected him of an affinity for a British-style aristocratic or monarchical system, and he reaffirmed, too, his desire to maintain friendly relations with France. Hamilton's treachery had not succeeded, but it left the new President leader of a divided party, with members of his own administration more loyal to the New Yorker than to their chief. "We are broken to pieces," the Massachusetts Federalist Congressman Fisher Ames lamented. "If the Federalists go to playing pranks," Adams confided half-jokingly to his wife, "I will resign the office, and let Jefferson lead them to peace, wealth, and Power if he will."

The wounds never entirely healed, and for a while reconciliation with the Democratic-Republicans seemed a possibility, but as continuing French attacks on American shipping brought the two nations closer to war, Jeffersonian Republican resistance to Federalist defense and tax policy revived the saliency of the foreign policy differences that had become defining issues between the parties earlier and now sowed the seeds for Federalist defeat in 1800.

In the longer perspective of partisan competition for the presidency, John Adams's election in 1796 stands as a victory for a centrist leader who moderated extremists in his own party who had first attempted to thwart the popular choice of most Federalists and then push the country toward war with France, which Adams ultimately resisted. Before his election, Adams presciently predicted the dilemma he later faced as President: "I am not enough of an Englishman, nor little enough of a Frenchman, for some people." Finally the election of 1796 contributed to party development by solidifying divisions in the electorate while at the same time demonstrating the successes with which the Constitution provided a diverse electorate with an orderly means of expressing intense differences of opinion on vital questions of public policy. In his INAUGURAL ADDRESS, President Adams affirmed his republican pride in presiding over a government that derived its legitimacy "fresh from the hearts and judgments of an honest and enlightened people."

### BIBLIOGRAPHY

Chambers, William N. *Political Parties in a New Nation.* 1963.

Cunningham, Noble E., Jr. *The Jeffersonian Republicans: The Formation of Party Organization.* 1957.

Dauer, Manning J. *The Adams Federalists.* 1953.

Kurtz, Stephen G. *The Presidency of John Adams, 1795–1800.* 1957.

Schlesinger, Arthur M., Jr., ed. *History of American Presidential Elections, 1789–1968.* 3 vols. 1971.

PAUL GOODMAN

**ELECTION, PRESIDENTIAL, 1800.** The election of 1800 tested the new Constitution, the nature of government in America, and the nation's new political party system. In the end, after much stress, the country weathered its first great political crisis under the Constitution, as Thomas Jefferson and AARON BURR, the candidates of the Republican Party (or the Democratic-Republican Party as it was also called), became the nation's third President and Vice President. Aside from the individuals involved, the election is notable for six reasons: the adoption of a blatantly political law—the Sedition Act of 1798—to help the incumbent John Adams defeat his likely opponent, Thomas Jefferson; the only tie in the voting history of the ELECTORAL COLLEGE; the first election thrown into the House of Representatives because no candidate had a majority of the Electoral College votes; the first election of an opposition candidate in the nation's history; the first election of someone who quite possibly was not supported by a majority of the nation's voters; and the adoption of a constitutional amendment (the TWELFTH AMENDMENT) to avoid repetition of the problems caused by a tie in the Electoral College vote.

The structure of the Electoral College under the Constitution of 1787 and the emergence of political parties in the 1790s shaped the 1800 election. In the Electoral College system, each elector voted for two candidates. The candidate with the most votes became President, the runner-up became Vice President. This system worked perfectly well for the first two elections as the electors unanimously chose George Washington for President with John Adams clearly second. The system worked less effectively in 1796. That year John Adams won the most votes, but his rival Thomas Jefferson won the second highest number of electoral votes. This set the stage for four years in which the President and the Vice President were at odds over almost all aspects of politics, and in which it was clear they would oppose each other in the coming election. Indeed, within a few months after the election of 1796, President Adams and Vice President Jefferson were barely on speaking terms.

**Adams versus Jefferson.** In July 1798 Federalists in the Congress adopted legislation to aid President Adams's reelection. The Sedition Act of 1798 punished anyone who falsely criticized the President, the Congress, or the government of the United States. Because the Act omitted the Vice President from those protected, the law was clearly designed to shield Adams while allowing criticism of Jefferson. This blatantly political act expired on 4 March 1801, the day the President elected in 1800 would take office. If Adams won reelection, he would not need the law; and if Jefferson won, he could not turn the law on Adams's supporters.

Federalists arrested twenty-five people under the sedition act, indicted fourteen, and tried and convicted ten. All of them were supporters of Jefferson. While small in numbers, these arrests and trials led many Americans to believe that Adams was a tyrant, intent on destroying American liberty. Adams and his supporters clearly misunderstood popular views of liberty on this issue, and hostility to the sedition act prosecutions hurt Adams far more than any newspaper articles could have. Indeed, had the Federalists not adopted the repressive ALIEN AND SEDITION ACTS it is quite possible they would have won the election of 1800.

The Federalists also lost popular support for their military and tax policies. In 1798 Congress authorized more than tripling the size of the national army in order to suppress dissent, enforce the Sedition Act, and possibly go to war with France. Jeffersonians argued that the larger standing army was a threat to liberty. Jeffersonians also complained about higher taxes—on salt, paper, carriages, and imports—that were in part collected to pay for the larger standing army.

Aside from the Sedition Act, the army, and taxes there were other real differences between Adams and Jefferson. In foreign policy Adams favored stronger ties with England, while Jefferson wanted the United States to support France or remain neutral when dealing with European issues. This foreign policy difference dovetailed with the economic interests of the Federalists and the Jeffersonians.

The Federalists wanted to stimulate foreign trade and build a stable economy based on government support for commercial and industrial development and the BANK OF THE UNITED STATES. The Federalists encouraged a lively import-export trade, with tariffs from imports and excise taxes supporting an expansive national government. Thus, the Federalists tilted toward Britain in foreign affairs because another war with the former mother country would have destroyed commerce. Support for the Federalists came from New England and the Middle States, where commerce was important, and from the wealthy planters of the South.

Jefferson and his followers were less concerned with international commerce, opposed the existence of the Bank of the United States, had an undying distaste for England and an affection for France. Where the Federalists saw the Constitution as a flexible document that would allow for an expansive national government, the Jeffersonians read the Constitution narrowly and strictly, with an eye toward limiting the size and power of the national government as well as its influence on the economy.

Social and cultural factors also affected the 1800 campaign. Federalists were likely to be Congregationalists (in New England), Episcopalians, or members of traditional, mainstream churches. Many Federalists still favored established churches in the states. Himself a deist, Jefferson was the nation's foremost proponent of the separation of church and state. Many of his followers were Baptists, Methodists, or members of other dissenting faiths. Immigrants, especially Catholics, tended to be Jeffersonians, since the Federalists had tried to limit immigration through the Alien Acts of 1798. Finally, opponents of SLAVERY in the North were more likely to be Federalists, as were free blacks who voted in most of the North as well as in North Carolina. The South, which by this time was fully committed to slavery as a permanent institution, voted overwhelmingly for Jefferson, a man who owned about 150 slaves when he took the oath of office as President.

The campaign was particularly nasty. Jeffersonians accused Adams of wanting to create a monarchy. They circulated rumors that Adams had arranged a marriage between one of his sons to a daughter of King George III of England in order to establish ties to the British monarchy, and that Adams backed down only when George Washington drew his sword and personally threatened him. Jeffersonians further claimed that Adams had sent General CHARLES COTESWORTH PINCKNEY to England to procure "pretty girls as mistresses" for Adams and Pinckney. The Jeffersonians also predicted the Federalists would cheat Jefferson out of a victory by improperly counting the electoral votes. Meanwhile, Federalists branded Jefferson an atheist who would set up a guillotine in the nation's new capital and bring the excesses of the French Revolution as well as libertine anarchy to America.

**The Electoral Vote.** In 1800 there was no popular vote, direct or indirect, for President or the presidential electors. Rather, the state legislatures chose the electors. Thus, the election was decided gradually, as each state chose a new legislature. In the end the Republicans won seventy-three electoral votes—fifty-three from the South and twenty from New York and Pennsylvania. The Federalists won all the electoral votes of New England, New Jersey, and Delaware, half of Maryland's, seven of Pennsylvania's fifteen, and a third of North Carolina's, for a total of sixty-five electoral votes. Jefferson's electoral victory was a narrow eight votes. It is quite possible that had there been a popular election Jefferson would have lost. Jefferson won all New York State's votes because of Aaron Burr's shrewd political maneuvering. A shift of a few hundred votes in New York City would have given

Adams the state and the election. In fact, with the exception of New York, Adams did better in 1800 than in 1796. Moreover, most of Jefferson's support came from slave states, whose electoral votes were augmented under the three-fifths clause. Without the electoral votes derived from slaves, Adams, not Jefferson, would have been the victor in 1800. Had a popular vote been counted, Adams might very well have had more votes than Jefferson, since his support came from the states with the most voters, while Jefferson's support came from southern states with fewer voters.

Under the then-existing electoral system, each elector voted for two candidates. The electors supporting Jefferson also agreed to vote for Burr, thus guaranteeing him the vice presidency. This marked the first time that electors pledged to a particular candidate also agreed on a vice presidential candidate. This plan undermined one of the goals of the Framers of the Constitution—which was to ensure that the best candidates were elected for both jobs, without regard to faction or party. But, it also appeared to eliminate the repetition of what happened in 1796, when rivals were elected to the nation's two highest offices.

However, when all the Republican electors voted for both Jefferson and Burr, this plan backfired and there was a tie for the presidency. Jefferson apparently expected one of his electors to vote for someone other than Burr, so that there would not be a tie for the presidency. One Adams elector from New Hampshire did just this by voting for JOHN JAY rather than Adams's vice presidential choice, Charles Cotesworth Pinckney. But Jefferson's supporters failed to take such a precaution. The result was that neither Jefferson nor Burr was elected. Jefferson's supporters expected Burr to step aside for Jefferson, but Burr refused. Seeing the chance to become President, he argued that he had as much right to the office because he had received just as many electoral votes as Jefferson.

**The House Decides.** The tie in the Electoral College threw the election into the House of Representatives, where each state had a single vote. To win the election, Jefferson or Burr had to carry nine states, a majority of the sixteen in the Union. Burr attempted to get Federalists to support him, although neither candidate made any important political bargains. The House began voting on Wednesday, 11 February 1801. On the first ballot eight states supported Jefferson, six states (with Federalist majorities in their House delegations) supported Burr, and two states were divided. The House cast twenty-seven ballots throughout the night, with no change in the votes. The House voted again on Thursday, twice on Friday, and three times

on Saturday, but after thirty-three ballots, not a single vote had changed. On Tuesday, 17 February, Federalists in the Vermont and Maryland delegations abstained, thereby giving those two deadlocked states to Jefferson; Delaware and South Carolina cast blank ballots. Thus, on the thirty-sixth vote Jefferson carried ten states, four went to Burr, and two abstained. The nation finally had a President. Three years after Jefferson took office the nation adopted the Twelfth Amendment, which required that electors designate their choice for President and Vice President, thus preventing a tie of two running mates in the future.

Despite the turbulence of the preceding months, Jefferson peacefully took office on 4 March and became the first President inaugurated in the nation's new capital on the Potomac. More importantly, his inauguration showed that an opposition candidate could peacefully take over the reigns of government under the new Constitution. Jefferson's inaugural address was a masterpiece of political conciliation. He characterized the bitter campaign as a "contest of opinion," suggesting that the real issues had been about ideas, despite the personal slurs both candidates had endured. Although he would later urge "a few wholesome prosecutions" of some of his political opponents, Jefferson began his administration on a high note, asserting the "sacred principle" that "the will of the majority . . . to be rightful, must be reasonable; that the minority possess their equal rights, which equal laws must protect, and to violate would be oppression." He urged his countrymen to reject political intolerance, declaring "we are all republicans—we are all federalists."

BIBLIOGRAPHY

Banning, Lance. *The Jeffersonian Persuasion: Evolution of a Party Ideology.* 1978.
Brown, Ralph Adams. *The Presidency of John Adams.* 1975.
Chambers, William Nisbet. *Political Parties in a New Nation: The American Experience, 1776–1809.* 1963.
Levy, Leonard W. *Jefferson and Civil Liberties: The Darker Side.* 1963.
McDonald, Forrest. *The Presidency of Thomas Jefferson.* 1976.
Peterson, Merrill. *Thomas Jefferson and the New Nation.* 1970.

PAUL FINKELMAN

**ELECTION, PRESIDENTIAL, 1804.** President Thomas Jefferson overwhelmingly won reelection to a second term in 1804, carrying all but two of seventeen states, and winning 92 percent of the electoral vote. Four years earlier Jefferson, the Democratic-Republican, running against President John Adams, the Federalist, narrowly won by only 52 percent of the vote.

The 1804 election revealed the virtual collapse of the FEDERALIST PARTY opposition, the result of that party's failings, but even more of Jefferson's successes in his first term.

**Jefferson's Strength.** "The power of the administration," explained the moderate Massachusetts Federalist John Quincy Adams, son of Jefferson's rival in 1800, "rests upon the support of a much stronger majority of the people throughout the union than the former administration ever possessed since the first establishment of the Constitution." The voters, Adams added, had "completely and irrevocably abandoned and rejected" the Federalist "system of measures."

During Jefferson's first term, the country enjoyed peace and prosperity. His predecessor had avoided war with France but Jefferson reaped the blessings. With the danger of war passed, Democratic-Republicans lowered taxes and reduced the army and navy as well as government spending. Jefferson made no wholesale removals of Federalist officeholders, but methodically rewarded his friends and thereby altered the political composition of the federal officialdom. The FEDERAL JUDICIARY remained a bastion of Federalist influence, but even here the President pursued a cautious policy. The impeachment and removal of Judge John Pickering was readily justified on grounds of mental instability and intemperance. Nor did the Jeffersonians overturn that pillar of Federalist financial policy, the BANK OF THE UNITED STATES, which remained a useful institution. The President scored his greatest coup with the LOUISIANA PURCHASE (1803), which vastly increased the size of the United States at modest cost and secured the free navigation of the Mississippi, thereby assuring unfettered development of the trans-Appalachian West. Where other nations expanded by military means, Jefferson boasted, he had relied upon "truth and reason," which proved to be "more powerful than the sword." Finally, the President sought, through subtle gestures, to fashion a republican style of governance by abandoning some of the high-toned practices of his Federalist predecessors that had served to underscore the distance between the rulers and the ruled. The Democratic-Republican President abolished the stuffy weekly levees at the White House; he dressed casually and refused to ride in a coach mounted by liveried outriders; nor would he agree to public celebrations of his birthday and suggestions from his northern supporters for a grand tour, such as Washington had made. Democratic-Republican modesty and simplicity set the tone and sought to underline a new relationship between the President and the people. In a republic a President's authority derived not from the office, the title, or aristocratic trappings, but from the votes and confidence of the people.

By 1804 the President had gone far to weaken the sharp partisan cleavages that had bitterly divided the country in the late 1790s. In his first inaugural he reached out to the opposition by affirming that "we are all republicans: we are all federalists," a play on the generic meaning of words that emphasized the common ground on which most Americans stood, devotion to popular sovereignty and the Constitution of 1789 that left power divided between the states and the nation. Jefferson's moderate policies enabled the Democratic-Republicans to make substantial inroads among many Federalists. The dire warnings of national disaster should the Democratic-Republicans win power, failed to materialize. Not even Massachusetts, once the keystone of Federalist power in New England, resisted the Jeffersonian tide in 1804. After the election, the President boasted to a French friend: "The two parties which prevailed with so much violence when you were here are almost wholly melted into one." The "mass of the people," he claimed, "have joined us," leaving Federalist leaders isolated and brooding "over their angry passions."

**Federalist Pessimism.** Dealt a weak hand by Jefferson's shrewd course in his first term that deprived them of issues, Federalist leaders were pessimistic about recouping their party's fortunes and fell to quarreling among themselves. Moderates like John Quincy Adams drifted towards the Democratic-Republican Party. Extreme Federalists, however, centered in New England, the party's stronghold, remained convinced that the Jeffersonians were dangerous democratic levellers out to destroy "every influential Federalist and every man of considerable property who is not of the reigning sect." Because there seemed little hope of recapturing national power, some toyed with a scheme to dismember the Union and establish a northern confederacy that extended from New York to Maine, a region that would fall under Federalist control. "The people of the East cannot reconcile their habits, views, and interests with those of the South and West," explained Timothy Pickering, a Massachusetts Federalist leader who had served in the Adams Cabinet. Yet other Federalists who shared Pickering's forebodings of Jeffersonian rule resisted his conclusions. Separation, they argued, would solve nothing because the sources of the political evils in the country were in "the political theories of our country and in ourselves." The country was hopelessly democratic, though "democracy in its natural operation" led to "government of the worst." Not until the excesses of democratic politics ended in crisis and chaos would conservative statesmen have the chance to reform the system by limiting the suffrage, some Federalist leaders concluded.

The plan of disunionists like Pickering rested on enlisting support from Vice President AARON BURR who, they hoped, could deliver New York for the northern confederacy. Burr was a powerful New York politician who had played a key role in carrying his state for Jefferson in 1800, although he fell out with Jefferson and the Democratic-Republicans after the election because he opportunistically sought to thwart the popular will by taking advantage of the unexpected tie between himself and Jefferson in the ELECTORAL COLLEGE. The tie vote forced the election into the House of Representatives where Burr's maneuvers stamped him in the eyes of Democratic-Republicans as a traitor and in the eyes of historians as the "Machiavelli of American politics." Jefferson was elected President and Burr became Vice President. Burr hoped to recoup his fortunes by running for governor of New York in 1804 in alliance with the Federalists. His defeat for governor, however, doomed the plot to establish a northern confederacy.

When in July 1804 Burr killed ALEXANDER HAMILTON in a duel, triggered by Hamilton's opposition to Burr's election as governor and to disunionism, the Federalist Party lost its greatest leader.

**The Election.** Facing a divided and demoralized opposition, leading a united Democratic-Republican party, and enjoying widespread popularity, Jefferson entered the election of 1804 supremely confident. In November 1804, pointing to the Federalist extremists, Jefferson proclaimed: "To me will have fallen the drudgery of putting them out of condition to do mischief." Earlier in that year a large public caucus of Democratic-Republican Congressmen, breaking with the earlier practice of the secret caucus, chose Jefferson as the party's standard bearer and replaced Burr with Governor GEORGE CLINTON of New York as his running mate. The Federalists held no caucus but private and newspaper discussion led to half-hearted support on behalf of South Carolina's General CHARLES COTESWORTH PINCKNEY and New York's Senator RUFUS KING. Federalists hoped that Pinckney, a southerner who had served as John Adams's running mate in 1800, might make inroads in the slave states. His refusal to pay a bribe to the French when sent to Paris to avoid war in 1797 ("No! No! Not a sixpence.") had won him popularity as a tough defender of national honor and interests.

Neither Jefferson nor Pinckney campaigned directly. Jefferson's insistence that "respect for myself as well as for the public requires that I should be the silent and passive subject of their consideration" belied his efforts and those of his supporters behind the scenes. One Democratic-Republican Congressman from each state headed a state campaign committee. Democratic-

Republican organization was most active where party competition remained intense and electioneering might pay off. Newspaper agitation, parades, and dinners all worked to rally Democratic-Republican voters. By contrast, the Federalists, who had never matched the Democratic-Republicans at popular mobilization, made only token efforts. In many parts of the country it was difficult to know that a contested election was under way. Even before 1804, Federalists had suffered substantial losses in Congress; some Federalists withdrew from public life in discouragement; while the spread of population into the new states of the West, all monolithically Jeffersonian, only made a desperate situation worse.

Six states still gave the choice of electors to the state legislatures, limiting popular campaigns to eleven states. The Federalists carried only Connecticut and Delaware and two of Maryland's eleven Electoral College votes. Pinckney demonstrated little appeal in the South, not even in his native South Carolina. The Federalists won Connecticut because of the strength of elite families of wealth, education, and social status buttressed by an established Congregationalist church in a state that grew slowly, undergoing only modest economic and demographic diversity, conditions that favored Jeffersonian party-building elsewhere. In other states Democratic-Republicans demonstrated remarkable success in fashioning a broad-based coalition appealing to those who felt excluded by long-entrenched Federalist elites. As author of the Virginia Statute of Religious Freedom, Jefferson had immense appeal to Baptists and Methodists and others who still suffered persecution or disadvantage, especially in New England with its remaining religious establishments. The Democratic-Republican Party became the champion of voluntarism in religious matters.

Likewise the party won support from mechanics and artisans in cities such as New York, Philadelphia, and Baltimore by advancing their particularistic interests as well as the broader principles of popular participation. In addition to the nearly unchallenged support among southern planters and small farmers, the party captured control of many large maritime and commercial centers along the eastern seaboard. In Salem, Massachusetts, for example, the Crowninshields, a powerful family engaged in overseas trade, especially with the French Empire, ousted a Federalist merchant elite that had long dominated the port. Jeffersonian support among entrepreneurial interests, demanding state bank charters to break the Federalist monopoly, and artisans, demanding charters of incorporations for their societies, underlines the heterogeneous character of the party. The historian Henry Adams identified the strikingly disparate character of the Jeffersonian coalition: "While the mobile, many-sided, restless democracy of New England, New York and Pennsylvania, exhibited its faults, and succeeded, with much personal abuse, in thrusting out the elements foreign to its character which retarded its movement, the society of the Southern States was classically calm. Not a breath disturbed the quiet which brooded over the tobacco and cotton fields between the Potomac and Florida." Yet belying the political calm of a virtually one-party South lay another source of disquiet, the institution of SLAVERY, which generated one of the periodic violent struggles for freedom. In Jefferson's native state, Gabriel's Revolt (1801) seized white southerners with terror, but Jefferson had long abandoned any efforts to act on his antislavery principles, though they stood deeply rooted in his belief in human rights and Christian virtue. Instead he and others trapped by the peculiar institution sought refuge in the illusion of colonizing the blacks abroad or diffusing them by spreading them across the southwest.

Over a party so mixed in character and a country so divided between free and slave, Jefferson presided in 1804 as undisputed master in a period of national calm and prosperity. The day of reckoning lay in the future. Victory by such a majority as Jefferson received in 1804, however, proved dangerous. "Rarely has a Presidential election better calculated to turn the head of a President," Henry Adams reflected. In his second term, Jefferson faced new, unexpected challenges that strained the limits of his political leadership. "In a government like ours," he said, the Chief Magistrate's duty is *to do all the good* which his station requires" and "*to unite in himself* the confidence of the *whole people*." Yet four years after his triumphant reelection in 1804 Jefferson left public life tired and sorely frustrated, uncertain whether he still commanded that popular confidence on which a President's power to govern must rest.

### BIBLIOGRAPHY

Adams, Henry. *History of the United States of America during the Administrations of Thomas Jefferson and James Madison*. 7 vols. 1891–1896.

Cunningham, Noble E., Jr. *The Jeffersonian Republicans in Power*. 1963.

Johnstone, Robert M., Jr. *Jefferson and the Presidency*. 1978.

Malone, Dumas. *Jefferson the President, First Term, 1801–1805*. 1970.

Schlesinger, Arthur M., Jr. *History of American Presidential Elections, 1789–1968*. 3 vols. 1971.

PAUL GOODMAN

**ELECTION, PRESIDENTIAL, 1808.** Americans tend to view the presidency as a permanent fixture that has not evolved radically over the two centuries of national existence, yet the election of James Madison to the presidency in 1808 was unrelated to modern experience.

**Jefferson's Successor.** Thomas Jefferson's election in 1800, after a near disaster showed deficiencies in the ELECTORAL COLLEGE, brought on a constitutional amendment (the TWELFTH AMENDMENT) to remedy the problem (a tie between AARON BURR and Jefferson lasted until the thirty-sixth ballot in the House). The system of the party caucus, which permitted the leading Representatives and Senators in a political party to choose their presidential candidate, however, was not affected. Jefferson had been chosen that way in 1796, 1800, and again in 1804, and in this short period the so-called caucus system worked. Clearly Jefferson was favored by most of his party, and until the waning days of his second term, Jefferson was in complete control of his party and of the Congress.

When the choice of Jefferson's successor was discussed by Republican (that is, Democratic-Republican) Congressmen and Senators, party chieftains knew the President's wishes. Jefferson wanted his Secretary of State, James Madison, to succeed him and carry on his policies. Accordingly, Senator Stephen Bradley of Vermont posted a notice for all members of Congress to attend a meeting in mid January 1808 to select a presidential candidate. Only Republicans loyal to Jefferson attended, and they chose Madison as the party's candidate, eighty-three votes in Madison's favor, six against. In practical terms, this meant that in each state either the legislators or specially chosen electors would align behind the Madison candidacy. In the state contests, candidates committed to Madison would make their loyalty known, and if elected their duty was clear. Since the Republicans controlled most of the state legislatures outside of New England in the spring of 1808 and seemed headed for victories in the fall, the election of Madison would have appeared to be a certainty once the caucus decision was announced.

Several obstacles to an easy victory for Madison soon surfaced. Representative John Randolph of Virginia, bitterly opposed to the Jefferson administration, had already fired a blast at Madison and tried to derail his candidacy by recommending James Monroe to fellow Republicans as an alternative to the President's hand-picked candidate. Randolph's following was thin and his venomous attacks on both Jefferson and Madison made his efforts suspicious. Monroe, his feelings hurt by a diplomatic rebuff by the administration, allowed his name to be entered in the contest. His candidacy was doomed from the start.

The other roadblock to Madison's easy victory was

the conduct of New York Republicans, who supported GEORGE CLINTON nominally but may have really worked for DEWITT CLINTON's subrosa campaign. As the sitting Vice President George Clinton was placing his party in an anomalous position, for could he run for both Vice President and President at the same time? He preferred to keep his silence and confuse the issue, while his ambitious nephew DeWitt Clinton courted votes that could have kept the state of New York out of Madison's electoral column.

Still another circumstance in 1808 made a comparison with modern campaigning unrealistic. George Washington had not campaigned for the presidency, and in ignoring the election process he set a precedent followed by all his successors. Indeed, a presidential candidate who appeared to have desired the office and made speeches or written newspaper editors soliciting support would have alienated the voters. John Adams and Jefferson had ached to be elected, but in public they appeared indifferent to the contest. Now Madison was expected to follow this same route, by keeping busy at his tasks in the State Department and pretending not to be a candidate for the presidency. Meanwhile, Monroe wrote close friends and sought their help, while George Clinton warded off all queries and only added to the confusion of Federalists, who had no real candidate but did not want Madison to win by default.

**Candidates and Issues.** After some preliminary inquiries apparently took place, Federalist leaders gathered in New York and gave up on an attempted coalition with the Clintonians. CHARLES COTESWORTH PINCKNEY, the South Carolina diplomat-soldier, was named to head the Federalist ticket, with New York Senator RUFUS KING as his running mate. Their candidacy sprang out of despair rather than optimism, for the South and West were already disposed to support Madison. Only defections there, plus a turnaround in the key states of New York and Pennsylvania, made a Federalist victory possible. Early fall elections would tell whether New England was pulling away from its Republican allegiances or not.

A new force in American politics soon tipped the odds in Madison's favor. Newspapers had played an important role in bringing on the Revolution in 1775 and in the ratification struggle over the Constitution in 1787–1788. Now nearly three hundred newspapers, most of them weeklies, supplied readers with information about the candidates in a most partisan fashion. Except in a few Federalist strongholds in New England, most newspapers were fiercely Republican in their bias and quickly endorsed Madison as their presidential choice. A few defectors, such as William

Cheetham, a Clinton supporter who edited the New York *American Citizen*, soon attacked Madison as a slaveholder who was part of the so-called Virginia dynasty and unworthy of the presidency. (That Washington and Jefferson had been Virginians was not held against them.) The pro-Federalist Boston *Columbian Centinel* blasted Madison as the handpicked choice of a sordid caucus system, as did the pro-Monroe Richmond *Virginia Argus*. But the Philadelphia *Aurora*, the Republican mouthpiece of party regular William Duane, threw such charges back as scurrilous attacks on a qualified, loyal public servant. And in the nation's capital, the *National Intelligencer* (the leading pro-administration newspaper) insisted that Madison was committed to the "Principles of '98," which meant simply that Madison would be a President in the Jeffersonian tradition and would be vigilant to preserve CIVIL LIBERTIES, keep the national debt on its course toward extinction, and not spend taxes wastefully to keep a large navy and army at the ready.

Nothing harmed Madison's chances more than the discredited EMBARGO ACTS, which he had helped formulate while in Jefferson's Cabinet. The embargo closed down the American shipping industry, idled thousands of sailors and shipwrights, and damaged American commerce and agriculture by prohibiting an export trade with European belligerents. New England reacted violently to the program by underhanded smuggling operations, and in the fall elections of 1808, Federalists made heavy inroads in New England. Repeal of the embargo was not a campaign issue elsewhere, however, and Republicans loyally proclaimed their support of the policy despite its depressing effect on southern farm prices. In effect, the hottest issue of the campaign was never discussed publicly by any of the presidential candidates.

Desperate for an issue, the New York dissidents tried to paint Madison as a French sycophant who would truckle to Napoleon once in office. The flimsy excuse for the charge was that Madison had accepted an offer of French citizenship in 1793. Madison ignored the charges while his friends pointed out that Washington and ALEXANDER HAMILTON had been similarly granted French citizenship along with Madison. No more promising for the opposition were feeble efforts from James Monroe's allies to discredit Madison. Except for a small coterie in Richmond Monroe had no support for his candidacy. Even so, he refused to withdraw from the race. "For the public good and your future prospects," an old friend pleaded, "put a stop to the contest." Monroe still refused and clung to the hope that some miracle would occur in the mid-Atlantic and New England regions to make his candidacy viable. A friendly letter from Jefferson, probably meant to nudge Monroe out of the way, was instead flaunted by Monroe as proof of his fitness for the high office.

**The Result.** Notwithstanding the infighting of the New York Republicans, little changed in the way the campaign was conducted. Nor was the outcome ever in real doubt. Although early returns from Vermont indicated Federalist strength in a former Republican bastion, the real test came in New York where Clinton supporters mustered only six of nineteen electoral votes. From early September onward the flow of returns from Ohio and the western country, along with solid victories in the South, made the Richmond *Enquirer* safely predict that the Monroe boomlet was dead and that Madison would be a sure victor when the Electoral College met. In his home state, Madison had a landslide victory with a 11,000-vote plurality over Monroe.

The final returns showed Madison's victory was devastating for the Federalists and for Monroe personally. Madison won 122 electoral votes, Pinckney 47, and Clinton a token 6 from his New York friends. Monroe received no votes for President and 3 for Vice President, while Clinton was reelected Vice President with 112 votes to scattered opposition. Madison's move to the presidency, which Jefferson desired and had predicted fifteen years earlier, meant that the Republican hold on the White House was firm. With a few exceptions, the Democratic-Republican hold on the presidency would remain in place until 1861.

### BIBLIOGRAPHY

Brant, Irving. "The Election of 1808." In *History of American Presidential Elections, 1789–1968.* Edited by Arthur M. Schlesinger, Jr., and Fred L. Israel. 4 vols. 1971.

Cunningham, Nobel E., Jr. "The Jeffersonian Republican Party." In *History of U.S. Political Parties.* Edited by Arthur M. Schlesinger, Jr. 4 vols. 1973.

Rutland, Robert A. *The Presidency of James Madison.* 1990.

ROBERT A. RUTLAND

**ELECTION, PRESIDENTIAL, 1812.** With rare exceptions the American electorate has given incumbent Presidents the benefit of the doubt at election time, unless a grave depression struck during the first term. In 1812, James Madison was under pressure from his party because of a depression in shipping and agriculture that threatened the national prosperity; moreover, some rabble-rousers in his own party accused him of avoiding a war with Great Britain that they believed would bring Canada into the Union as a new state. Farmers saw commodity prices drop but had a patriotic sense that Madison's administration was doing the right thing by constricting the British market.

In fact, Madison had tried to negotiate a peace with the British and had winked at French insolence to avoid a fight with Napoleon, but in the end, he called for a war and thus probably assured his reelection in 1812.

**Challenges to Madison.** Madison's nomination by the dominant Republican Party was accomplished by the congressional caucus, which had become a fixture in presidential politics. In May 1812 the majority of Republican Senators and Representatives attended a special meeting in the Capitol chambers, voted overwhelmingly to recommend Madison to the nation as the party choice, and picked John Langdon as the vice presidential candidate to replace the late GEORGE CLINTON; there was no obstreperous John Randolph to condemn the process and bring forward another candidate, as he had done in 1808. But the nation was nervous about the threat of war, and DEWITT CLINTON was scurrying about in New York lining up disaffected Democratic-Republicans who thought Madison was beatable.

Madison waited impatiently to hear from a last-ditch effort to bring peace with the British. A Federalist Congressman who thought the chances for war were disappearing gleefully predicted that a settlement of the differences with Great Britain would soon occur. Then, the New Englander predicted, "Madison's Presidential career will close with the 3d of March 1813." Madison upset the timetable by sending a war message to Congress, and by June 1812 the war hawks prevailed (79 to 49 in the House, 19 to 13 in the Senate). The United States was at war with Great Britain, and Madison became the country's first wartime President.

To say the young Republic was unprepared for the WAR OF 1812 is a grave understatement. The army was a small frontier force, the navy was a token force, and the Treasury Department operated on a pay-as-you-go basis. Yet an angry Federalist accurately predicted that no war taxes would be enacted "because it might endanger Madison's reelection."

Other forces were at work to make Madison a one-term Chief Executive. Clinton's supporters in New York called for a convention to challenge the caucus nomination of Madison as "hostile to the spirit of the federal constitution, dangerous to the rights of the people, and to the freedom of election." During the summer doldrums, Clinton supporters tried to forge an alliance with dispirited Federalists and to appeal to voters by challenging Madison's competence. Clinton, voters were told, would relieve the nation of "an inefficient administration" that was bumbling the war effort and ignoring the fact that the treasury was nearly empty.

Clinton was not everybody's favorite. Hardcore New England Federalists, distrusting Clinton as overly ambitious and untrustworthy, thought Chief Justice John Marshall would be a better match for Madison. Marshall, flattered by the prospect, condemned the war but refused to throw the door open for his nomination. In quiet desperation, Clinton's friends called a convention in New York in mid September and after hearing speeches calling for Marshall or John Jay as an alternative, endorsed Clinton's candidacy. Federalist wire-puller RUFUS KING of New York denounced the whole affair and advised New England friends to nominate a true Federalist as a sacrificial lamb, then "acquiesce in Mr. Madison's re-election," and capitalize on the debacle that would surely follow four more years under a Democratic-Republican President.

**The Campaign.** Events in the summer of 1812 gave credence to such a possibility. The so-called war hawk faction in Congress welcomed the outbreak of war and expected Canada to be easily conquered, but the surrender of Fort Detroit by General William Hull on 16 August shocked the nation. Madison delayed a shakeup of his military commanders but tried to take the initiative in the campaign by sending messages to the New Jersey Democratic-Republican convention promising a relentless war on the British to be followed by an honorable peace. Democratic-Republican newspapers printed Madison's war cry as proof of the President's commitment to victory and used a similar message to South Carolina Democratic-Republicans who had told Madison "the glory of the issue will be commensurate with the righteousness of our cause." Otherwise, Madison did no campaigning and depended on state and local leaders to keep party regulars loyal to the ticket.

As in 1808, newspapers carried the brunt of the campaign into the enemy's camp, but fraternal orders also contributed to the election in 1812. Democratic-Republicans embraced the Tammany societies that originated in New York as a vehicle for party discipline, and "Sons of Tammany" groups with rituals and dues spread to New England and westward to Ohio. Federalists countered with their Washington Benevolent Society, where the first President's name and likeness were used as propaganda tools for electioneering against Madison's return to the White House. Although voting was still limited in most states to white males who owned some property, there was overall excitement generated by the expanding weekly press,

and rival societies appealed to voters up to the very moment they cast their ballots.

Clinton's friends in the South, knowing the war was popular there, painted him as a warrior who had long favored war preparations and a vigorous Canadian campaign. Where the war was not popular, as in New England, Clinton's banners proclaimed "Peace and Commerce." As the pro-administration *Washington National Intelligencer* noted, the Federalists "have been compelled to form a monstrous alliance with the apostate Republicans. . . . Like the camelion [sic] in the fable, Dewitt is one thing to one man, a different thing to another." Bribery scandals involving bank charters in New York left their taint on Clinton's campaign, too, and historian Henry Adams's judgment was: "Clinton strove to make up a majority which had no element of union but himself and money."

Federalists disgusted with the Clinton alliance held a rump convention of their own in western Virginia and nominated Rufus King as their candidate. King ignored the proceedings but Virginia Federalists did not, and a last-minute suggestion by discouraged Clintonians that their man might withdraw and throw his support to King proved futile. Meanwhile, Madison squelched a peace feeler from British sources that fell short of ending the obnoxious impressment of American seamen. He never seems to have doubted the eventual outcome of the war, despite Hull's disgrace that summer, and his confidence may have been a vital link with the electorate that historians so critical of Madison's conduct have overlooked.

Diehard Federalists could not accept King's negative strategy and hoped Madison's failure would revive their moribund party. In Boston, the influential *Columbian Centinel* rejected King's advice and declared that defeat by England would be no "more complete and degrading than that which must befall us under [four more years of] MADISON. . . . *no condition can be worse* . . . under the administration of DEWITT CLINTON." New Englanders appeared to agree and her political leaders hoped Pennsylvania might defect from the Democratic-Republican columns, too. Without Pennsylvania, strategists figured, Madison probably would fall short in the Electoral College.

**The Result.** Pennsylvania proved to be safely in the Democratic-Republican camp, however, owing in part to the popularity of the war there. Late in October, after a Federalist party committee published its endorsement of Clinton, Madison men who had wavered suddenly came back to the Democratic-Republicans. In the balloting on 30 October, Madison won in forty counties and lost only five to the Clinton ticket by garnering 63 percent of the votes. In adjacent Ohio, the vote on 11 November gave the President 72 percent.

Madison was never in danger of losing. Clinton could have won, if he had carried Pennsylvania and still lost Ohio, but their total of 32 electoral votes tipped the balance in Madison's favor. When the presidential electors convened, Madison received the votes of all the southern and western states, lost only New England, Delaware, New York, and part of Maryland, and had a total of 128 votes to 89 for Clinton.

Could a presidential candidate hope to win without a major foothold in the West and South? In retrospect, it would seem that Clinton was never taken too seriously beyond the borders of New York, that New England support was half-hearted at best, and Madison's incumbency worked in his favor against Clinton's ambivalence and ambition. Moreover, Madison's precedent would stand, for never have voters rejected an incumbent President during a war.

### BIBLIOGRAPHY

Brant, Irving. *James Madison: Commander in Chief.* 1961.
Risjord, Norman. "The Election of 1812." In *History of American Presidential Elections. 1789–1968.* Edited by Arthur M. Schlesinger, Jr., and Fred L. Israel. 4 vols. 1971.
Rutland, Robert A. *The Presidency of James Madison.* 1990.

ROBERT A. RUTLAND

**ELECTION, PRESIDENTIAL, 1816.** The most distinctive feature of the presidential election of 1816 was the behind-the-scenes maneuvering within the Democratic-Republican Party prior to the meeting of the congressional nominating caucus, which was still the party nominating agency. FEDERALIST PARTY leaders, oppressed by anticipation of defeat, made no significant effort to mount a presidential campaign. The Federalists had been fatally damaged by their opposition to the war and the secessionist movement behind the Hartford Convention. By 1816 the Federalists had no real identity except as the party of the elite. The Democratic-Republicans had long taken over Federalist measures, culminating in the rechartering of the BANK OF THE UNITED STATES in 1817. Moderate Federalists had already made their way into the Democratic-Republican Party, and the issues over which the parties had once disagreed were emerging as divisive factors within the Democratic-Republican Party itself—a development that took final form in the new party alignments of the 1830s.

**Monroe's Prospects.** There was never any doubt that the Democratic-Republicans, as the "party of true patriots," would again be victorious in 1816. After the

appointment of James Monroe as Secretary of State in 1811, most Democratic-Republicans assumed that he would be the party's candidate in 1816. It was considered his due as one of the founders of the party, a proper reward for his long public career, and a recognition of his close association with Thomas Jefferson and James Madison. By 1813, however, Monroe's nomination was far from assured. Not only was there a widespread sense of weariness over the prolonged reign of the so-called Virginia Dynasty, but strains within the party had been evident since Jefferson's second term. Southern conservatives were displeased by the moderate nationalism adopted by the party. Many northern leaders, while approving of nationalist programs, were unhappy over foreign policy measures that they saw as damaging to commercial interests. The New York Democratic-Republicans in particular felt that it was time their state was assigned first place on the national ticket.

The dissidents within the party were not in agreement on either a party program or a candidate—other than not wanting another Virginian. Indeed, this was the only real objection to Monroe's candidacy: if he had been from any other state, he would not have encountered any serious opposition. Southern conservatives favored the former Georgia Senator, Secretary of War WILLIAM H. CRAWFORD, who was enormously popular with the members of Congress. Crawford did not enjoy the same national fame as Monroe, whose long public career had made him well known to the people and to state leaders. Monroe was seen as the last of the revolutionary generation (and a hero to boot) who would be eligible for the presidency. During the winter of 1815–1816 he received many endorsements from state legislatures and conventions. President Madison, following Jefferson's example, remained outwardly neutral, but it was generally accepted that Monroe was his choice. The columns of the semiofficial Washington *National Intelligencer*, whose contents were widely copied, were filled with accounts of Monroe's career, praising his patriotic devotion. In the fall of 1815 Madison bolstered Monroe's position in New York by appointing Solomon Southwick, editor of the influential Albany *Register*, postmaster of Albany. Southwick and Smith Thompson (later Monroe's Secretary of the Navy), who were allies of Martin Van Buren, exerted their influence on Monroe's behalf.

Although the forty-four-year-old Crawford was reportedly reluctant to challenge his senior colleague, he failed to clarify his position in a convincing manner. On 1 February 1816, his successor in the Senate, William W. Bibb, published a letter stating that Crawford did not wish to be considered as a competitor for the nomination. This belated statement and similar indirect statements were considered something less than a formal withdrawal. Many doubted Crawford's sincerity and continued to regard him as willing to run if nominated. Crawford later maintained that his supporters had disregarded his instructions to inform the caucus that his name was being introduced without his consent. Crawford's failure to make an explicit withdrawal subsequently became a factor exacerbating the distrust Monroe felt toward Crawford after 1820.

Monroe, aware of the divisions within the party, sought to strengthen his candidacy. In 1812 he had wanted to leave the State Department for a military command, which would have enhanced his public reputation. This plan was frustrated by the personal animosity of the Secretary of War, John Armstrong, who blamed Monroe for robbing Robert R. Livingston (Armstrong's brother-in-law) of credit for the LOUISIANA PURCHASE. After Armstrong's forced resignation in 1814, Monroe had the satisfaction of winning public approval for his efficient administration of the War Department. In 1815, Monroe acted to silence unfounded rumors current in Virginia that he did not have Jefferson's approval to become Madison's successor. Although Monroe needed his native state's support, he wanted to avoid being identified as the Virginia candidate. Some of the most powerful state leaders (the so-called Richmond Junto) were not well disposed toward him because he had allowed dissident Democratic-Republicans (the so-called Old Republicans) to enter his name against Madison in the presidential election of 1808 in order to voice their disapproval of administration foreign policy.

Late in 1815, Monroe sent his son-in-law, George Hay, to win over the state leaders, especially Judge Spencer Roane and Thomas Ritchie, the editor of the influential Richmond *Enquirer*. Hay succeeded in this mission and also in persuading the Richmond Junto not to permit the state legislature to nominate Monroe prior to the meeting of the Congressional caucus. The legislative caucus simply chose electors known to be favorable to Monroe. Monroe had already reconciled the Old Republicans, many of whom had not approved of his decision to enter Madison's Cabinet in 1811. Only John Randolph of Roanoke, who had little influence, remained implacable.

During the winter of 1815–1816 many Republican papers carried articles condemning the perpetuation of Virginia influence in the national government, but they did not mount direct attacks on Monroe: his long service to the party and the nation shielded him. Regional and local papers devoted space to praising DANIEL D. TOMPKINS and JOHN C. CALHOUN. The caucus

was also frequently condemned as an undemocratic method of nominating presidential candidates. The only overt attack on Monroe was made by Armstrong in an anonymous pamphlet, *Exposition of the Motives for Opposing the Nomination of James Monroe . . .* (Washington, 1816), which criticized Monroe's career. Armstrong's attack, obviously a highly personal affair, had no effect on the nomination or the election.

**Maneuvers in New York.** The decision of the Democratic-Republican Party in New York was regarded as of prime importance in the selection of the party candidate. The New Yorkers' dissatisfaction over the long Virginia domination had been expressed in 1812 when dissident Republicans and Federalists supported DeWITT CLINTON against Madison in the presidential election. In 1816 the New York Democratic-Republicans were engaged in a bitter contest between Ambrose Spencer (a Clintonian) and Van Buren for control of the state party machinery. National political considerations were secondary in this contest for power in the state organization. Spencer and Van Buren both wanted to prevent the selection of another presidential candidate from Virginia, but the moment that Spencer announced his support for Crawford Van Buren totally committed his followers to Tompkins, the popular wartime governor. The fact that Tompkins, who was little known outside New York state, had no chance of winning the presidential nomination did not deter Van Buren. To defeat Spencer, Van Buren was prepared to accept a Virginian as the presidential nominee, since the New Yorker could secure for Tompkins the second place on the ticket. When the state legislative caucus met on 14 February 1816, Van Buren was able to secure the endorsement of Tompkins, accompanied by a resolution recommending that the state congressional delegation oppose any Virginia-sponsored candidate. Van Buren, who had visited Washington in January, knew that fifteen of the twenty-one members of the New York congressional delegation (elected in 1815) supported Crawford. The action of the state legislative caucus and Van Buren's personal influence were sufficient to hold the delegation pledged to Tompkins until the meeting of the congressional caucus. The distribution of the New York vote remained secret until the balloting in the caucus.

**The Congressional Caucus.** The conflict over the nomination was centered in Congress during the winter of 1815–1816, where the exact strength of the forces supporting Monroe and Crawford remained uncertain. Although Monroe seemed to have the advantage, a close vote in the caucus would be an embarrassment. Capitalizing on the widespread criticism of the caucus, Monroe and Senator James Barbour of Virginia, who functioned as Monroe's manager in Congress, decided to prevent a caucus nomination. They considered the nominations made by state legislatures to be sufficient. Crawford's friends, confident of victory, circumvented Barbour's plan by issuing an anonymous call for a caucus to meet on 12 March 1816, considerably later in the session than had been customary in the past. Earlier caucuses had been arranged by senior party members. Since fewer than half the Democratic-Republicans attended, a second meeting was set for 16 March. With HENRY CLAY's cooperation, Monroe's friends intended to prevent the caucus from making a nomination.

At the second meeting, attended by 118 Republicans (twenty-four were absent), Clay's resolution that it was inexpedient to make a nomination was voted down, as was a resolution condemning the caucus system introduced by John W. Taylor, a Monroe backer from New York. Monroe was then nominated by the narrow margin of sixty-five votes to fifty-four for Crawford. Fifteen New Yorkers voted for Crawford, four for Monroe, and two abstained. Among those voting for Monroe were three former War Hawks (Peter B. Porter, John W. Taylor, and Enos Throop) who had worked closely with Monroe supporting defense measures prior to the declaration of war in 1812 [see WAR OF 1812]. If the distribution of the New York vote had been known in advance, the outcome in the caucus might have been different. Several known Crawford backers, including Senator Bibb, failed to attend. Either they had accepted Crawford's statement as a sincere withdrawal or felt reluctant to deny the nomination to Monroe, whose long service merited the party accolade. (Crawford would have his turn in 1824.)

Undoubtedly the influence of state party leaders was an important factor in Monroe's victory. Those Congressmen who had been elected early in 1815 could not ignore the pressure from state parties. Not unexpectedly, the vice presidential nomination went to Tompkins with eighty-five votes to thirty for Simon Snyder of Pennsylvania—an arrangement satisfactory to Van Buren, since he had routed Spencer's forces. Although Tompkins was running for Vice President on the national ticket, Van Buren engineered his reelection as governor of New York. The state party, however, refused to agree that Tompkins could hold state office while running for the vice presidency. Clinton was chosen as Tompkins's replacement as gubernatorial candidate—a temporary setback for Van Buren. For reasons that can only be explained as a protest against Van Buren's tyranny, the fifteen New Yorkers who voted for Crawford also voted for Snyder as the vice presidential candidate.

The Federalists, who had never utilized the caucus method of nomination, selected RUFUS KING of New York as their presidential candidate after their customary habit of private (written) consultation among prominent northern leaders. No attempt was made to establish contact with southern Federalists. The vice presidential nominee was John Eager Howard of Maryland. The Federalists made no effort to publicize their selection. With the exception of New York, Federalist electoral slates were chosen only in New England—where Federalists controlled the state legislatures—and in Maryland and Delaware, where the district system of choosing electors prevailed.

**The Result.** Accepting the inevitability of defeat, the Federalist press mounted feeble attacks on Monroe, usually confining its criticism to his conduct as minister to France during the George Washington administration. The Democratic-Republican press dutifully lauded Monroe as a revolutionary hero and a dedicated patriot. Monroe and Tompkins swept the field, receiving 183 electoral votes (including those of Vermont and New Hampshire). Thirty-four votes (those of Massachusetts, Connecticut, and Delaware) were cast for King. The lack of coordination among the Federalists, as well as their prevailing sense of defeat, can be seen in the vice presidential vote: Howard received twenty-two votes; twelve votes were scattered for favorite sons; and three Federalist electors from Maryland and one from Delaware never bothered to vote at all. Although the Federalists continued as a force in New England and in New York, where they often held the balance of power between rival Democratic-Republican factions, the presidential election of 1816 was the Federalist Party's last appearance on the national scene, marking the end of the first two-party system. Many Democratic-Republicans, however, remained apprehensive of a Federalist revival. The fact that many former Federalists were prominent advocates of a ban on SLAVERY in Missouri as a condition for its statehood in 1819 led to entirely unjustified suspicions that the restrictionists were attempting to revive the old party system on an antislavery basis.

## BIBLIOGRAPHY

Ammon, Harry. *James Monroe: The Quest for National Identity.* Rev. ed. 1990.

Cole, David R. *Martin Van Buren and the American Political System.* 1984.

Livermore, Shaw, Jr. *The Twilight of Federalism: The Disintegration of the Federalist Party, 1815–1830.* 1984.

Mooney, Chase Curran. *William H. Crawford, 1772–1834.* 1974.

Raybeck, Joseph G. "A Myth Re-examined: Martin Van Buren's Role in the Presidential Election of 1816." *American Philosophical Society Proceedings* 124 (1980): 106–118.

Remini, Robert V. "New York and the Presidential Election of 1816." *New York History* 31 (1950): 208–223.

HARRY AMMON

## ELECTION, PRESIDENTIAL, 1820.

The election of 1820 proved one thing beyond doubt: the first American two-party system was dead. In his FAREWELL ADDRESS, President George Washington had warned his countrymen against political parties because they would be divisive and a threat to the very existence of the Republic. Jefferson's Democratic-Republican Party had arisen in opposition to the Hamiltonian FEDERALIST PARTY. John Adams, Washington's successor, proved to be the only Federalist to win the presidency. The next three, Presidents Thomas Jefferson, James Madison, and James Monroe, were Democratic-Republicans from Virginia. The Federalists had managed to nominate candidates in every election before 1820 except for 1812 when they went along with DeWITT CLINTON, a disaffected Democratic-Republican. But in 1816 the Federalists, weaker than they knew, tried again with the nomination of RUFUS KING. When he lost to James Monroe, the message was clear. Any Federalists who lingered would do so at the local, state, and congressional level. In presidential politics the Federalists had breathed their last. For more than a decade all presidential contenders would be members of the Jefferson party.

**Monroe's Dominance.** After his first inauguration in 1817, President Monroe toured New England, haven of Federalists still smarting from "Mr. Madison's War" and the defeat of the effort to amend the Constitution in ways proposed by the Hartford Convention. When Monroe reached Boston, he was greeted warmly by the town's Federalists, and a Boston newspaper headlined the visit as an ERA OF GOOD FEELINGS. During his first term Monroe assembled a brilliant Cabinet. Foreign relations flourished under Secretary of State John Quincy Adams, who achieved diplomatic triumphs with England and Spain especially. JOHN C. CALHOUN in the War Department built on Jefferson's Treasury Secretary ALBERT GALLATIN's important transportation report when he advocated a system of roads and canals financed and built by the national government. WILLIAM CRAWFORD ran an efficient Treasury Department, and Benjamin Crowninshield (1817–1818) and, later, Smith Thompson ran the Navy Department. Return Meigs served as Postmaster General and Richard Rush (1817) and WILLIAM WIRT were Attorneys General. Two major problems during the first term were the panic of 1819 and the question of SLAVERY (and the admission of Missouri as a state).

There was no formal nomination for President in 1820. The time-honored congressional caucus attempted to do so, but only about fifty members of Congress attended the meeting of that body, and they adjourned without making a nomination. Nineteen states had cast votes in their electoral colleges in 1816; since then four new states had entered the Union: Mississippi, Illinois, Alabama, and Maine. Monroe signed the bill in March 1820 enabling Missouri to enter the Union and Missouri adopted a constitution in July 1820, but Congress did not admit that state until August 1821 after Missouri pledged not to interfere with the privileges and immunities of citizens of other states wishing to move to that place. Though there was debate about the matter, Missouri's electoral vote of three was counted in the election of 1820.

**The Result.** The twenty-four states of the Union chose electors in a variety of ways in that election. Nine continued to use the somewhat old-fashioned and less democratic method of having state legislators name electors. Four of these were southern states (Delaware, South Carolina, Georgia, and Alabama); Vermont and New York in the Northeast; Indiana in the Old Northwest; and Louisiana and Missouri in the New West (beyond the Mississippi) used the same method. Nine states had statewide direct election of electors: five were in the Northeast (New Hampshire, Connecticut, Rhode Island, New Jersey, and Pennsylvania); three in the South (Virginia, North Carolina, and Mississippi); and Ohio in the Old Northwest also used that method. Four states chose all electors by district: Illinois in the Old Northwest and Maryland, Kentucky, and Tennessee in the South. And two states in New England (Massachusetts and Maine) used a combination of district and at-large statewide elections.

The sizes of state delegations in Senate and House dictated that there be 235 electoral votes in 1820. Only 232 were cast, for three electors (one each from Pennsylvania, Tennessee, and Mississippi) died before their colleagues met. Of the 232 votes cast, President Monroe received all but one. William Plumer of New Hampshire disliked Monroe and voted for John Quincy Adams. Over the years the legend arose that Plumer wanted no one but Washington to have the honor of unanimous choice.

There was a minor contest for Vice President. The incumbent, DANIEL TOMPKINS of New York, received 218 votes, while four others received fourteen in all. Of these, Richard Stockton of New Jersey got eight;

Daniel Rodney of Delaware obtained all of that state's votes; Robert G. Harper of Maryland received the vote of one of his state's electors; and Richard Rush of Pennsylvania got the vote of a New Hampshire elector.

**Monroe Reviews the Issues.** Monroe's program was set forth in two documents: his fourth STATE OF THE UNION MESSAGE of 14 November 1820 and his second INAUGURAL ADDRESS of 5 March 1821 (delivered on that day because 4 March was a Sunday). In the state of the union message Monroe saw "much cause to rejoice in the felicity of our situation." Every individual enjoyed fully his rights, said Monroe, in a nation where the national government operated "with complete effect" in every part of the country "without being felt . . . except by the ample protection which it affords" and where state governments performed "their equal share." Monroe thanked the "Supreme Author of All Good" for such a glorious and gratifying spectacle.

At the same time he felt obliged to examine some unhappy conditions, most of which, he declared, were the result of the "peculiar character of the epoch in which we live," resulting from "convulsions" and "long and destructive wars" abroad. Even five years after peace came, the "state of Europe is unsettled," wrote the President. Monroe hoped for Spanish ratification of the Florida treaty, for British relaxation of trade privileges in the West Indies, and for Spanish accommodation to the revolutions of independence in her Latin American colonies. Monroe outlined a number of steps in progress to repair and improve the coastal fortifications of the country "in the event of another war." Such improvements would save the lives of citizens and their property. More important, such fortifications would go far to prevent war, he declared.

President Monroe alluded to an act of 1820 that made participation in "that disgraceful traffic,'" the slave trade, punishable by death. American naval vessels had been sent to Africa's coast to enforce the law. He also discussed INDIAN relations, pointing out that "game is their sustenance and war their occupation" in "their original state." "Left to themselves their extirpation is inevitable," he added. Through trade with Indian tribes, "we supply their wants, administer to their comforts, and gradually, as the game retires, draw them to us." By the maintenance of posts "we acquire a more thorough and direct control over them," and bring about "a complete change in their manners." Finally, President Monroe made one reference only to the effects of the panic and depression. He urged Congress to pass legislation to relieve purchasers of public land who were attempting to pay their installments.

The second inaugural, delivered nearly four months later, revealed Monroe's insights at that time. Referring to his landslide victory, Monroe indicated that the strength and stability of the Union had drawn the people together. The President saw himself as the instrument rather than "the cause of the union which has prevailed in the late election." He believed that "like accord" would be permanent in the nation. Monroe detailed further progress in the erection of coastal fortifications designed to prevent war and to "mitigate its calamities" if it came. He applauded Spanish ratification of the Florida treaty, and he underscored the fact that NEUTRALITY would continue to be American policy toward Spain and her former colonies. He hoped for better commercial treaties with France and Britain, and he declared that American interests continued to require naval presence in the Mediterranean and in the Pacific. Noting that he had urged the repeal of internal taxes and that Congress had concurred, he now added that deficits required reinstitution of certain internal duties, believing as he did that "the demands of the current year, especially in time of peace, should be provided for by the revenue of that year." Returning to the topic of Indian relations, he revealed that dealing with Indians as nations had "flattered their pride" and "retarded their improvement." He hoped for elimination of tribal title to land and for division of property among individuals. Indians, he claimed, had a right to expect magnanimity and justice from the government. Finally, he praised American principles that vested authority in the people who, in turn, transferred their power "to bodies of their own creation" which possessed "all the energies of any government ever known to the Old World," but had "utter incapacity to oppress the people."

## BIBLIOGRAPHY

Ammon, Harry. *James Monroe: The Quest for National Identity.* 1971.

Cresson, W. P. *James Monroe.* 1946.

Dangerfield, George. *The Awakening of American Nationalism, 1815–1828.* 1965.

Dangerfield, George. *The Era of Good Feelings.* 1952.

Roseboom, Eugene H. *A History of Presidential Elections.* 2d ed. 1964.

Schlesinger, Arthur M., Jr., ed. *History of U.S. Political Parties.* Vol. I. 1973.

Stanwood, Edward. *A History of the Presidency from 1788 to 1897.* 1898.

Turner, Lynn W. "Elections of 1816 and 1820." *History of American Presidential Elections,* 1789–1968. Edited by Arthur M. Schlesinger, Jr., and Fred L. Israel. 4 vols. 1971.

RAYMOND H. ROBINSON

**ELECTION, PRESIDENTIAL, 1824.** The election of 1824 is one of the most complicated and controversial in American history. In the election of 1820 only one electoral vote was cast against the successful incumbent, James Monroe, whose victory represented the high point of the Jeffersonian ascendancy, with its emphasis on political consensus and the determining role of the congressional caucus in selecting the next President. At the same time, a number of important developments began to undercut the Jeffersonian belief that the running of the country should be left in the hands of a small group of wise and virtuous politicians. The economic changes that followed the end of the WAR OF 1812 created a variety of new and competing interests, leading to tensions that were exacerbated by the difficulties unleashed by the Panic of 1819. Congress had engaged in an extended debate between 1819 and 1821 over the admission of Missouri as a slave state. And there was a widespread revival of STATES' RIGHTS thought that came in reaction to a series of ultranationalist decisions handed down by the United States Supreme Court. The class, sectional, and constitutional antagonisms uncovered by these developments broadened popular interest in politics and broke apart the Democratic-Republican Party, which had dominated the presidency since Jefferson's election in 1800. Moreover, by the early 1820s an overwhelming majority of the states chose presidential electors by popular vote instead of by the state legislature, further diminishing the influence of entrenched politicians.

**The Candidates.** WILLIAM H. CRAWFORD of Georgia, Monroe's Secretary of the Treasury, was the early front-runner in the election of 1824. In 1816 he had received considerable support for the presidency, and had only barely been defeated in the caucus by a vote of 64 to 54. Many considered him to be Monroe's heir apparent. In addition to his home state, Crawford's chief backing came from politicians in the states of New York, Delaware, Virginia, and North Carolina. Most of them were Old Republicans, critics of the aggressive nationalism and preoccupation with economic development that followed the end of the War of 1812. But Crawford was virtually eliminated when he suffered a paralytic stroke in late 1823. Despite this he did receive the caucus nomination, although it did not mean very much since only 66 out of a possible 216 congressmen attended the meeting. This was the last caucus ever to nominate a presidential candidate.

Crawford had several rivals. This group included JOHN C. CALHOUN, the brilliant, young, energetic Secretary of War under Monroe. Extremely nationalistic, Calhoun was a proponent of a protective tariff, a national bank, and a federal program of INTERNAL IMPROVEMENTS, which, taken together, were known as

the AMERICAN SYSTEM. Calhoun's positions put him at odds with Crawford throughout most of Monroe's two administrations. Although he did not effectively rival Crawford in the South, Calhoun did have a firm hold on his home state of South Carolina as well as strong political connections with the dominant politicians in Pennsylvania and with many Federalists in Maryland, New Jersey, and the New England states. Another rival was HENRY CLAY, the popular Speaker of the House of Representatives, a particularly effective legislative leader. He, too, championed the nationalist policies of the American System. Clay viewed himself as the choice of the West, the fastest-developing section of the country. He anticipated carrying the states of Ohio, Tennessee, Indiana, Illinois, Missouri, and his home base of Kentucky, and to pick up some votes in other parts of the country. Even more formidable was John Quincy Adams of Massachusetts. He had an extensive career in government service, and had proved to be a brilliant Secretary of State under Monroe, successfully managing the acquisition of Florida and formulating the principles behind the MONROE DOCTRINE. His main political base was New England. He also vigorously supported the American System. Beyond this, he was widely respected for his abilities and integrity, and local considerations and personal resentments aside, most established politicians throughout the country viewed him as perhaps the best man for the presidency.

The great surprise of the election of 1824 was the emergence of Andrew Jackson. Widely known as the military hero who had beaten the British at New Orleans and as an Indian fighter who had won a number of important victories in the old southwest and who had crushed the Seminoles in Florida in 1818, Jackson was not considered a political figure when the Tennessee legislature nominated him for the presidency in July 1822. At first, most of his more established rivals did not take Jackson's candidacy very seriously, but his popularity with the voters soon became clear, and his supporters overwhelmed the Calhoun forces in Pennsylvania, Maryland, and New Jersey. Realizing what had happened, Calhoun withdrew from the presidential race and instead ran, virtually unopposed, for the vice presidency on the Jackson and Adams tickets. Jackson also significantly cut into Crawford's and Clay's support in the South and West. Only in New England did he not catch on. For the most part, no one really knew where Jackson stood on the key political issues of the day.

In 1824 the different candidates did not "run" for office. Instead they "stood" for election, which meant that they allowed other people to make their case to the public and to engage in whatever other political machinations were necessary. Jackson's supporters were particularly aggressive in this regard. They made a considerable effort to counter charges that he was an impulsive and violent man unfit by temperament, as well as lacking the political experience to govern the country. In response they pointed out that Jackson had never been part of the established Jeffersonian leadership with which the public had become so disenchanted, and that as a decisive and successful military leader he could bring the country back to the original principles of the American Revolution, from which would flow prosperity and happiness.

**Bargaining for the Presidency.** In the ensuing election, Jackson came in first, receiving 152,901 popular votes and 99 electoral votes. Adams placed second, with 114,023 popular votes and 84 electoral votes. Crawford came in third, with 46,979 popular votes and 41 electoral votes. Fourth place went to Henry Clay, with 42,217 popular votes and 37 electoral votes. Since Jackson received only a plurality of the electoral votes and not a majority, the United States Constitution, as revised by the TWELFTH AMENDMENT, required that the election be decided by the House of Representatives, with the entire congressional delegation from each state casting one vote from among the three leading candidates. This eliminated Clay, but as Speaker of the House he played an important role in the politics that followed. Calhoun easily captured the Vice Presidency.

Crawford's illness effectively removed him from serious consideration; the real choice was between Jackson and Adams. Jackson believed that he had a moral claim to the presidency since he had obtained both the largest popular and electoral vote, but, as far as scholars have been able to determine, he did not get involved in the politicking that preceded the decision by the House of Representatives, though a few of his supporters did have some contact with Clay. Adams, on the other hand, was willing to bargain. He had several meetings with Congressmen who wanted political favors and whose votes were going to be especially important. He also had an extended confidential interview with Clay. It is not known exactly what transpired between the two men except that some kind of understanding was reached. Throughout his life Adams kept a full and careful account of his days' activities in his diary, but he never wrote up his meeting with Clay. He did leave a blank space, and perhaps expected to write it up later. Why did Adams, who clearly was uncomfortable with political haggling, but who desperately wanted to be President, refuse to detail what his distinguished biographer, Samuel Flagg Be-

mis, called "one of the most important conversations that he ever had in his life!"? Bemis believed that Adams's conscience would not let him do it. To support his case, he cites a letter Adams wrote to one of his sons a few years later admonishing him to maintain his diary:

> A man who commits to paper from day to day the employment of his time, the places he frequents, the persons with whom he converses, the actions with which he is occupied, will have a perpetual guard over himself. His record is a second conscience. He will fly from worthless associates and from dishonest deeds, to avoid the alternative of becoming a self-accuser or of falsifying by the suppressio veri his own testimony to his own actions. I will appeal to yourself whether your interruptions in your diary, according as you have kept or neglected it have not been most frequently owing to a sense of shame, an unwillingness to put upon the record time worse than wasted, and actions of which you were ashamed.

**The Result.** When the House voted on 9 February 1825, Adams was elected President on the first ballot, receiving the votes of thirteen states to seven for Jackson and four for Crawford. Clay's support of Adams was decisive. He played a key role in convincing a number of Congressmen from Illinois, Louisiana, Missouri, Ohio, and Kentucky to vote for Adams despite the fact that Jackson had either carried their states or come in second to Clay in the popular vote. In fact, the Kentucky legislature actually instructed its Representatives to vote for Jackson, but they ignored it. In part Clay opposed Jackson because he viewed him as a very formidable rival for western support. He also did not believe that Jackson had either the experience or the temperament to be a good President, and he correctly suspected that Jackson was no friend to the American System.

On the other hand, although Clay and Adams did not personally like each other, they shared similar views on public-policy issues. Further, a few days after his election as President, Adams appointed Clay Secretary of State. Clay had desired this position in 1817 when Adams got it, and many considered it an important stepping-stone to the presidency. Following the announcement of Clay's appointment, the disappointed Jacksonians raised the cry of "Bargain and Corruption" throughout the country and claimed that the people's will had been thwarted by cynical and self-serving politicians. Although an act of corruption had not taken place, the people's will had been denied, and this fact did not lend itself to an easy explanation. Indeed, Clay and Adams spent the rest of their political careers dealing with these charges. As for Jackson, he had launched the campaign that was to capture the presidency for him in 1828.

The election of 1824 effectively brought an end to Jeffersonian hegemony and rule by the Virginia dynasty of Thomas Jefferson, James Madison, and James Monroe. It destroyed the one-party system of presidential politics that dominated the elections of 1816 and 1820, and in addition to renewing popular interest in the presidency it was an important phase in the emergence of a permanent two-party system of presidential politics that dominated all elections beginning in 1828.

### BIBLIOGRAPHY

Bemis, Samuel Flagg. *John Qunicy Adams and the Union.* 1956.

Dangerfield, George. *The Awakening of American Nationalism.* 1965.

Heale, M. J. *The Presidential Quest: Candidates and Images in American Political Culture, 1781–1852* (1982).

Hopkins, James F. "The Election of 1824." In *History of American Presidential Elections, 1789–1968.* Edited by Arthur M. Schlesinger, Jr., and Fred L. Israel. 4 vols. 1971. Vol. 1, pp. 349–410.

McCormich, Richard P. *The Presidential Game: The Origins of American Presidential Politics.* 1982.

Remini, Robert V. *Andrew Jackson and the Course of American Freedom, 1822–1832.* 1981.

Sellers, Charles G. "Jackson Men with Feet of Clay." *American Historical Review* 42 (1957): 537–551.

Sellers, Charles. *The Market Revolution: Jacksonian America, 1815–1846.* 1991.

RICHARD E. ELLIS

**ELECTION, PRESIDENTIAL, 1828.** The election of 1828, one of the most significant in American history, unquestionably initiated in national politics a popular and enthusiastic style of campaigning quite distinct from earlier practice. It also sent Andrew Jackson to the White House for the first of two tumultuous terms, during which he strengthened and transformed the office of the President. And the campaign marked a major step in the emergence of a new political party system.

**Opposition to Adams.** The campaign of 1828 began as soon as the election of 1824 concluded with the selection by the House of Representatives of John Quincy Adams as President and Adams's appointment of HENRY CLAY as his Secretary of State. Jackson had mustered a plurality of both the popular and electoral votes in 1824, and although he reluctantly accepted the House's decision as constitutionally legitimate, he believed the appointment of Clay reeked of bargaining and corruption. It appeared that Adams had awarded the State Department, which was the stepping stone to the presidency, to Clay in exchange for Clay's support in the House election. Jackson forces cried "Corrupt Bargain," and resolved to replace Adams in 1828. The "Corrupt Bargain" charge helped associate Jackson with the democratic ideals of majority rule and egalitarianism. Adams's election by the House, in contrast, identified him with old-style politics, in which a small coterie of political leaders determined the course of events.

Adams's nationalistic program of economic development, redolent of Clay's AMERICAN SYSTEM, had considerable public support, especially in New England and in Mid-Atlantic states like Pennsylvania. It also had the formidable backing of numerous established political leaders, led by Clay and DANIEL WEBSTER. But Adams's extravagant recommendations for INTERNAL IMPROVEMENTS, education, and other measures to advance the public welfare disturbed many and provided a focal point of opposition. Large portions of the country remained attached to the Jeffersonian legacy of limited government and STATES' RIGHTS. Even Clay thought Adams was going too far.

**Alignments and Organization.** Because of Adams's policies, a number of political groups soon moved into the Jackson camp, bringing Old Hickory the additional numbers that elevated his plurality in 1824 to a clear-cut majority in 1828. First to join was the newly elected Vice President, JOHN C. CALHOUN of South Carolina. The politically ambitious Calhoun now confronted the possibility that the Adams-Clay alliance would monopolize the White House for sixteen years. Furthermore, the bold assertion of federal powers that underlay the Adams presidency clashed with South Carolina's escalating antitariff and NULLIFICATION movements. Calhoun's commitment to his state and section, therefore, drew him to Jackson as much as did his political aspirations. Adams's Vice President thus became Jackson's running mate.

Even more important numerically to Jackson was the support of the so-called Radical or Old Republican faction. Directed by New York's Martin Van Buren, the Radicals were devoted to reviving the essential elements of the original Jeffersonian Republican party. To Van Buren, this meant a tight political organization, adherence to limited government principles, and the reestablishment of an alliance between "the planters of the South and the plain Republicans of the North." A party built along these lines, Van Buren was convinced, would prevent excessive concentration of power in the national government. Of course, Van Buren's own political prospects would flourish as well. By the spring of 1827, Van Buren maneuvered the Radicals behind Jackson, giving him a bloc of support in New York, Virginia, Georgia, North Carolina, and elsewhere. In Clay's own state of Kentucky, a group known as the Relief, or New Court, Party also sided with Jackson. Some New Court leaders, such as Amos KENDALL and FRANCIS P. BLAIR, would become close advisers of Jackson after he took office.

As these groups coalesced, an unprecedented degree of political organization and popular campaigning took place. To be sure, neither the Jackson nor the Adams followers constituted a full-fledged political party. Both considered themselves "Republicans." It would be two or three more years before the Jackson men were generally known as "Democrats" and the Adams followers as "National Republicans." Nevertheless, in structure and technique, the Jackson and Adams organizations progressed far beyond the personal factions and limited campaigning associated with the ERA OF GOOD FEELINGS. This was partly due to structural changes in the political environment. By 1828, only two states, Delaware and South Carolina, left the selection of presidential electors to the state legislatures. Everywhere else, the voters decided, and with the exception of a few states, that meant the adult, white male population. In part, too, the political culture now validated a more active and participatory role for this expanded electorate. The Jackson and Adams organizations, therefore, advanced a major step toward becoming the national, popular, participatory parties that would emerge in the 1830s.

The Jackson men led the way, constructing an elaborate, extensive, grassroots organization to mobilize the electorate. Of crucial importance was a network of pro-Jackson newspapers, including the *United States' Telegraph*, established in early 1826 in Washington, D.C., by Duff Green who pioneered in making the *Telegraph* the central agency of a national newspaper network.

Meanwhile, Jackson leaders in Washington established a central committee to distribute election material, and Congressmen raised money and used their free mailing privileges to circulate information. In the states, the story was much the same. The Jacksonians formed a jumble of local, county, and state committees to direct campaign activities. They also held state conventions, and the election of 1828 became the first presidential election in which a majority of the states held conventions to endorse a national candidate. Throughout the country, the Jackson committees organized rallies, barbecues, parades, militia musters, and other entertainment to attract voters. Hickory poles, emblematic of Old Hickory, were a featured part of these Jackson celebrations.

While custom still constrained candidates from actively campaigning on their own behalf, Jackson cautiously circumvented this tradition. He kept abreast of campaign developments, and collected and prepared material for distribution to committees and newspapers. He even embarked on a trip to New Orleans in January 1828, taking advantage of the anniversary of his victory over the British in 1815 to engage in vote gathering. Jackson's appreciation of the benefits of organization and the need to rally public support, characteristic of his presidency, were already evident during this election.

The Adams forces, though also making strides in adopting modern campaign techniques, nevertheless lagged behind the Jacksonians. There were rallies, meetings, and parades, but there were too few skilled politicians like Clay and Webster, too few newspapers, and too little coordination of the committee network. Nor did Adams help his own cause. Adhering to the old-fashioned ideal of a high-minded statesman, Adams considered himself above parties and partisanship. He refused to remove officeholders who opposed his reelection, or to assist those who, like Clay, were trying to build a party. He made only occasional, and futile, attempts to woo the electorate.

**The Campaign.** The election of 1828 was one of the coarsest in American history. Adams's newspapers accused Jackson of the cold-blooded murder of six militiamen for desertion during the Creek War. They embellished and broadcast stories of his duels and gambling, and a labeled Jackson's wife, Rachel, an adulterer, his mother a prostitute. The Jackson camp gave as good as they got.

Mudslinging aside, in a campaign that emphasized personal considerations, Jackson had the advantage. While Adams acknowledged his "reserved, cold, austere, and forbidding manners," Jackson conveyed an impression of decisive action. Moreover, the self-made quality of his rise to prominence and his seemingly providentially inspired victory at New Orleans presented a more appealing image than did Adams's prominent birth, extensive education, and vast experience as a diplomat.

The contest also hinted that a Jackson presidency would bring changes in policy. Jackson viewed his candidacy as a means of saving the Republic from the corruption of power evident in the principles and program of the Adams administration. Showing greater solicitude for traditional Jeffersonian states' rights and limited government principles, he recommended a "judicious" tariff, payment of the public debt, which he labeled a "national curse," and limitations on government expenditures for internal improvements.

**The Result.** Jackson's traditional appeal to Jeffersonian precepts, combined with his popularity and innovative organization resulted in a resounding victory.

Voting in the country took place from September to November, and Jackson received about 56 percent of the better than 1,150,000 votes cast. He won approximately 647,200 votes to Adams's 507,700. The total popular vote increased substantially compared to previous presidential elections, partly due to laws that now permitted the people, rather than legislatures, to select presidential electors, but also because of higher voter interest and competition between the rival organizations. Adams received a substantial tally, but Jackson won virtually every electoral vote south of the Potomac River and west of New Jersey. He even polled substantial minorities in parts of New England.

The election of 1828 sent Andrew Jackson to the White House. It also advanced the formation of political parties and popular campaign techniques. Much remained to be done. Political organization, even for the Jackson forces, was uneven, and while voter turnout rose, it registered only about 56 percent of the eligible electorate. In the years following this election, political parties would fully emerge, and the United States would experience a mass, participatory party system whose outlines were first disclosed during the election of 1828.

### BIBLIOGRAPHY

Bemis, Samuel Flagg. *John Quincy Adams and the Union.* 1956.

Dangerfield, George. *The Awakening of American Nationalism: 1815–1828.* 1965.

Heale, M. J. *The Presidential Quest: Candidates and Images in American Political Culture, 1787–1852.* 1982.

McCormick, Richard P. *The Presidential Game: The Origins of American Presidential Politics.* 1982.

Remini, Robert V. *The Election of Andrew Jackson.* 1963.

Remini, Robert V. "Election of 1828." In vol. 1 of *History of American Presidential Elections: 1789–1968.* Edited by Arthur M. Schlesinger, Jr., Fred L. Israel, and William P. Hansen. 4 vols. 1971.

Ward, John William. *Andrew Jackson: Symbol for an Age.* 1955.

Weston, Florence. *The Presidential Election of 1828.* 1938. Repr. 1974.

RICHARD B. LATNER

**ELECTION, PRESIDENTIAL, 1832.** The principal protagonists in the presidential election of 1832 were President Andrew Jackson, who successfully ran for reelection on the Democratic ticket, and HENRY CLAY, longtime advocate of the AMERICAN SYSTEM and leader of the congressional opposition, who ran as a National Republican. When he captured the presidency in 1828, Jackson had expected to serve only one term, but an unfinished political agenda combined with the failure of a consensus to emerge within the DEMOCRATIC PARTY about who should be his successor forced him to reconsider. In retrospect, Jackson's reelection seems inevitable. He was immensely popular with the great mass of the people and the country was prospering. Yet in the summer and fall of 1832, the President and his closest advisers were quite nervous about the likelihood of his success since his first administration had been rocked by a major social scandal, a variety of personality conflicts, and a number of clear-cut stands on controversial political issues that had given the opposition several strong rallying points.

**Jackson's Problems.** Jackson's first year in office was marred by a notorious feud that preoccupied the meetings of his official Cabinet and that divided the followers of his two most important political allies; JOHN C. CALHOUN (Vice President of the United States) and Martin Van Buren (Secretary of State), both of whom wanted to succeed Jackson to the presidency. It began when Mrs. Calhoun and a number of other socially prominent women in Washington, D.C., including the wives of several of Jackson's Cabinet members, socially ostracized Peggy Eaton, who had just married Jackson's close friend and Secretary of War, John Eaton. Mrs. Eaton was the daughter of a Washington tavern keeper who had a reputation for being promiscuous, and her first husband, a naval officer, had killed himself at sea, reportedly out of despair over an affair she was having with Eaton. At Jackson's urging, the couple quickly married. Their marriage became a political issue when Jackson and Van Buren, a widower, sided with the Eatons and tried to force their social acceptance upon the Cabinet and Washington society. But they failed when even Jackson's own niece refused to entertain Mrs. Eaton. Infuriated, Jackson stopped meeting with his Cabinet. These developments soon became known to the public. They embarrassed the President in large part because they seemed to support the claims of his opponents that he was unfit by temperament, experience, and ability to govern the country effectively.

The open split that took place between Jackson and Calhoun during his first administration further enhanced the view of those who argued that the President was petty and vindictive and had allowed himself to become preoccupied with irrelevant considerations. The split started shortly after the Eaton affair ended, when the Vice President's enemies let it be known that at secret Cabinet meetings in 1818, when Calhoun was Secretary of War, he had vehemently criticized General Jackson's invasion of Florida and had pushed for his censure and removal from office. This development enraged Jackson, who believed that Calhoun had supported him in 1818. He demanded an explanation from the Vice President. Various letters were exchanged between the two, but nothing was settled, and the President broke off relations with his Vice President. The publication of the correspondence in early 1831, at Calhoun's direction, did not make Jackson look very good. In addition, the administration had lost the support of an important southern leader.

During his first administration, Jackson took strong stands on a number of controversial issues that alienated important groups and interests. In his inaugural address he espoused the doctrine of rotation of office. He indicated his intention to remove the numerous federal officeholders under his jurisdiction because long tenure had made them corrupt, indifferent to the public interest, and inclined to consider their positions "as a species of property." Forcing people out of office every few years, the President believed, would have a cleansing effect and would make the federal government more sensitive to the needs of the people. This philosophy did not sit well with the numerous savvy and active political appointees who had acquired their offices during the long period of the Jeffersonian ascendancy (1801–1828) and who, until Jackson became President, had believed their positions were secure.

The concept of rotation of office in the United States dated back to the Articles of Confederation and a number of the more democratic state Constitutions of the revolutionary era. It had not, however, been included in the United States Constitution, a development that had been a major concern of the ANTI-FEDERALISTS in 1787–1788. Jackson's advocacy of it in 1829 was considered by his opponents to be, in effect, a direct assault on the Constitution itself. There was some truth to this charge since throughout his administration Jackson also urged that the Constitution be altered to eliminate the ELECTORAL COLLEGE, to limit the tenure of the President and Vice President to a single term of four or six years, to provide for the popular election of Senators and members of the federal judiciary, and to give self-government to the District of Columbia. Jackson and many of his closest advisers were also critical of the broad powers of interpretation that the Supreme Court had arrogated to itself over the past twenty-five years. In particular, they favored a repeal of section 25 of the Judiciary Act of 1789 and denied that the Supreme Court was either the exclusive or final arbiter of constitutional disputes.

During his first administration, Jackson also found it difficult to keep the disparate and conflicting groups that had elected him united. A firm advocate of STATES' RIGHTS and of a strict interpretation of the federal Constitution, Jackson disappointed many of his western followers by opposing, on both constitutional and policy grounds, a federal program of INTERNAL IMPROVEMENTS. Jackson's policy on the tariff during his first administration also caused political problems. He did not push very hard to lower it, despite considerable pressure from the South, because he did not want to cause political difficulties for Van Buren whose state, New York, favored protection.

By far, Jackson's most controversial action was to veto the rechartering of the Second BANK OF THE UNITED STATES. This occurred on 10 July 1832, after Nicholas Biddle, president of the bank, following Clay's advice, asked for an early rechartering, thus linking the issue to the coming election. This angered Jackson, who believed the bank was trying to intimidate him. In a powerful veto message, written with the aid of AMOS KENDALL and ROGER B. TANEY, the President declared the bank to be unconstitutional and warned that it was too powerful an institution not to be amenable to popular control. Playing upon popular fears, he pointed out that much of the stock was held by foreigners, and that it was essentially an aristocratic institution. The federal government, he argued, must "take a stand against all new grants of monopolies and exclusive privileges, against any prostitution of our government to the advancement of the few at the expense of the many."

Jackson's opponents denounced the veto. The President's assault on the bank, they claimed, would destabilize the currency and ruin the economy. To this end Clay and the National Republicans, with the underwriting of the bank, distributed copies of the veto message expecting that it would reveal the President's numerous prejudices and inadequacies in dealing with economic issues. But they were mistaken and soon had to change tactics, for the great majority of the people loved it. Jackson, much more so than his opponents, understood what the electorate wanted to hear.

**The Campaign.** The election of 1832 also spawned two new political developments: the first national THIRD PARTY, the ANTI-MASONIC PARTY, and the first presidential nominating conventions. The Anti-Masonic Party had its origins in the mysterious disappearance of William Morgan, a former Freemason who had threatened to publish the secrets of the Masonic Order, from Batavia, New York, in 1826. The party stressed its opposition to all secret societies with evangelical fervor. Its strength was concentrated in the rural area of western New York and New England, but it also spread into Pennsylvania and parts of the Midwest. The Anti-Masons opposed Jackson's reelection because he was a Freemason, and they refused to support Clay, a former member of the order, who was unwilling to renounce it. They, therefore, decided to hold a convention to select their own candidate. Meeting in Baltimore in September 1831, the Anti-Masons nominated WILLIAM WIRT of Maryland for President and Amos Ellmaker of Pennsylvania for Vice President.

The two major national parties immediately emulated this procedure for selecting candidates. The National Republicans assembled at Baltimore in December 1831 and proceeded to nominate Henry Clay for President and John Sergeant of Pennsylvania for Vice President. The Democrats also met in Baltimore in May 1832 and unanimously endorsed Jackson for the presidency. They then selected Van Buren for the vice presidency, replacing Calhoun. The Democratic convention also adopted the two-thirds rule (which lasted until 1936), which required two-thirds of the delegates to support a candidate before an actual choice was made. There was no platform.

In the ensuing election, Clay supported a continuation of the American System, especially a federal program of internal improvements, a high protective tariff, and the rechartering of the Second Bank of the United States. He also was very critical of Jackson's disregard of various United States Supreme Court decisions, especially *McCulloch v. Maryland* (1819) and *Worcester v. Georgia* (1832). He attracted the support of business interests and others who believed the federal government should play a key role in the country's economic development, the partisans of a nationalist interpretation of the Constitution, various members of the old Jeffersonian political establishment, and political conservatives fearful of Jacksonian reforms. The National Republicans also criticized Jackson's policy of INDIAN removal from areas east of the Mississippi River. Their critique was particularly popular with Quakers and other humanitarian groups in New England, New Jersey, Pennsylvania, and Ohio.

The Democrats vigorously defended Jackson and his policies. They praised his integrity, his willingness to make hard decisions, his leadership qualities, the fact that he spoke for the people and not politicians and other special interests, and his democratic philosophy of government. They defended the record of his first administration and pointed with pride to his success in dismantling the American System. Their rhetoric appealed in particular to small farmers, mechanics, laborers, agrarians, frontiersmen, intellectuals, and states' rights and old Republican types opposed to any kind of concentration of economic and political power in a distant and centralized government.

**The Result.** Jackson won the election of 1832 decisively. He carried sixteen of the twenty-four states,

mainly in the South, the West and the Middle-Atlantic region with 219 electoral votes and 685,502 popular votes. Clay garnered 49 electoral votes, carried six states (Massachusetts, Rhode Island, Connecticut, Delaware, Maryland, and his home state of Kentucky), and received 530,189 popular votes. William Wirt carried only Vermont, for which he received seven electoral votes; while in South Carolina, the legislature, now under the control of antitariff and anti-Jackson nullifiers, cast its 11 electoral votes for John Floyd of Virginia.

It is hard to say with precision what motivated the electorate, but Jackson's popularity and the bank question seemed to have been the decisive factors. Certainly Jackson viewed the election as a vindication of both himself and his policies and as a popular mandate to continue to move the country toward states' rights and democracy and to sever all ties, as quickly as possible, between the federal government and the Bank of the United States.

### BIBLIOGRAPHY

Chase, James S. *Emergence of the Presidential Nominating Convention, 1789–1832.* 1973.

Ellis, Richard E. *The Union at Risk: Jacksonian Democracy, States Rights, and the Nullification Crisis.* 1987.

Gammon, Samuel Rhea, Jr. *The Presidential Campaign of 1832.* 1922.

McCormick, Richard P. *The Presidential Game: The Origins of American Presidential Politics.* 1982.

Remini, Robert V. "Election of 1832." In vol. I. of *History of American Presidential Elections, 1789–1968.* Edited by Arthur M. Schlesinger, Jr., and Fred L. Israel. 4 vols. 1971.

Sellers, Charles. *The Market Revolution: Jacksonian America, 1815–1846.* 1991.

Vaughn, William P. *The Anti-Masonic Party in the United States, 1826–1843.* 1983.

RICHARD E. ELLIS

**ELECTION, PRESIDENTIAL, 1836.** The presidential election of 1836 marked a decisive step in the establishment of the second American party system. The WHIG PARTY emerged as the major opposition to the Democrats, with impressive support in all parts of the country. The election also demonstrated the popular appeal of William Henry Harrison, who would become the first successful Whig presidential candidate four years later. As for the Democrats, the election of 1836 showed that the party could win without Andrew Jackson on the ticket. But their victory was considerably narrower than in 1828 and 1832, forecasting the close contests that typified the rest of the nineteenth century.

The campaign originated in the NULLIFICATION and banking controversies that arose during Jackson's second term. Old Hickory's spirited defense of the Union and its laws, embodied in the FORCE BILL of 1833, unsettled many southerners, who thought him insufficiently attentive to their complaints about high tariffs and who accused him of adopting principles that dangerously broadened federal and executive powers. Although the crisis was resolved peaceably in March 1833, the nullification controversy sparked an exodus of southern radicals from the Democratic Party and strained the loyalty of others in the South.

Then, in the fall of 1833, Jackson announced that the federal government would no longer deposit its money in the BANK OF THE UNITED STATES. Considering the institution dangerous to the country, Jackson placed the government's revenues in state banks, dubbed "pet banks" by the opposition. The removal of the government's deposits from the Bank created a political furor. Most Democrats stood by the President, but many voiced reservations, and a number of Democrats abandoned the party for the opposition.

**The Democratic Ticket.** In the midst of this political upheaval, the Democrats looked to the coming presidential election. The leading contender to succeed Jackson was his Vice President, Martin Van Buren. A New York politician of extraordinary skill, Van Buren was Jackson's personal choice to lead the party, but Van Buren's popular appeal was uncertain. The New York elections in the fall of 1834 became a test of Van Buren's ability to rally the public behind Jackson's removal policy. When the Democrats won a sweeping victory, Van Buren's nomination was assured.

In May 1835, more than six hundred delegates met at the Democratic convention in Baltimore and unanimously chose Van Buren as their candidate. Even though there was no question about Van Buren's selection, his designation by the convention had a special significance. Democrats were well aware of the differences between Jackson and his heir. Jackson was a national hero, a leader with charismatic qualities. Van Buren, on the other hand, was the "Little Magician," the "Sly Fox," a professional politician whose achievements depended upon the skillful manipulation of men and institutions, rather than force of character. A nomination by delegates "fresh from the people" compensated for these deficiencies by investing Van Buren with the authority of the party's name and principles.

While harmony reigned at the top of the ticket, serious disagreement erupted among the delegates over the selection of Van Buren's running mate. Jackson and other party leaders favored RICHARD M. JOHNSON of Kentucky. A military hero—he was thought to have killed Tecumseh during the WAR OF 1812—

Johnson was also popular in the West and among eastern labor groups for his stands against imprisonment for debt and for the delivery of mail on Sundays. Johnson's nomination promised to strengthen the party's appeal in the West and in the border region, especially if HENRY CLAY entered the race.

But Johnson provoked considerable opposition, particularly among southern Democrats. He had two daughters from a longstanding and open relationship with a mulatto mistress, which made him "not only unpopular . . . but affirmatively odious" among slaveholders. Many southern Democrats, therefore, favored Jackson's former minister to France, the Virginian William C. Rives. Johnson managed to secure the necessary two-thirds vote for the nomination, but Virginia refused to accept the convention's choice and eventually gave its vice presidential vote to Judge William Smith of Alabama.

**The Rise of the Whigs.** The Democratic ticket faced a new and potent challenge in 1836. During the removal controversy, groups of Anti-Masons, nullifiers, STATES' RIGHTS advocates, and disaffected Democrats joined with National Republicans to form the Whig Party. The party's name was employed during the New York City municipal elections in the spring of 1834 and given prominence in a Senate speech by Henry Clay, and it was in general use by the summer of 1834. Condemning "executive usurpation," the corruptions of party and patronage, and the disruption of established financial arrangements, the Whigs proclaimed themselves the protectors of liberty against Democratic abuses of power.

In this early stage of the party's development, it proved easier for the Whigs to unite against Jackson than to concentrate support behind one candidate. The party's three major leaders, Henry Clay, JOHN C. CALHOUN, and DANIEL WEBSTER—the Great Triumvirate—were political rivals. Since each was determined to test the political waters, a national political convention was out of the question. None of these candidates captured the public's favor, however, and, by the fall of 1835, both Calhoun and Clay had withdrawn from the field. Only Webster remained, and he attracted little support beyond New England.

In this inchoate situation, two new and unexpected political figures emerged—William Henry Harrison and Hugh Lawson White. Harrison, the son of a signer of the Declaration of Independence, had been governor of the Indian Territory and had also achieved a degree of military fame at the Battle of Tippecanoe. While tending his Ohio farm and serving as clerk of the Cincinnati Court of Common Pleas, he assumed the position of Van Buren's major opponent in the

North and the West when, in December 1835, he was nominated by both the Anti-Masons and the Whigs of Pennsylvania.

Meanwhile, in the South, White provided the rallying point for the Whig Party. A Tennessean and a U.S. Senator, White was a longtime personal and political friend of Jackson's. He had provided constant support for Jackson's controversial policies, including removal. But the vain and ambitious White was dismayed by Van Buren's rise to power, and, in December 1834, he consented to stand as a presidential candidate. White did not claim the Whig label. Instead, his supporters directed their attacks at Van Buren and asserted that White stood firmly behind the republican principles of Jefferson and Jackson. White, therefore, captured a large and disparate following of states' rights advocates, business-oriented Democrats, and southerners who considered a slaveholding candidate safer than Van Buren.

**The Campaign.** Democrats alleged that the Whigs deliberately ran three regional candidates in order to defeat Van Buren by throwing the election into the House of Representatives. But the multiple candidacies were not a planned strategy. Like the failure to call a national convention, they were actually evidence that the Whig Party was a new and not yet fully developed organization. Yet even with such structural weaknesses, the Whigs were able to mount an effective and innovative campaign. They harped on Van Buren's reputation as a trimmer, a fop, and a mere politician—a "third-rate man," according to one Whig. They also seized the banner of democracy by denouncing the Democratic national convention as a caucus of officeholders, while claiming that their candidates had been brought forth by the people.

The election also highlighted programmatic differences between the parties. In contrast to the Democrats, the Whigs generally sanctioned government initiatives to promote economic growth. Harrison strongly endorsed the distribution of revenue to the states for INTERNAL IMPROVEMENTS, and both he and White indicated that they would be willing, under certain conditions, to approve a new national bank. Webster's close ties to banking and manufacturing interests were well known. When Jackson turned in a hard-money direction and issued his SPECIE CIRCULAR in July 1836, ordering that only gold and silver be accepted as payment for public lands, the Whigs blasted this assault on bank paper and credit.

In the South, the Whigs framed a distinctive appeal based on the emergence of the abolitionist movement (*see* ABOLITIONISM). The abolitionists had recently attempted to distribute their "incendiary" publications in the South and to petition Congress to use its powers on behalf of freedom. White's supporters exploited regional anxieties by alleging that the northerner Van Buren was a "radical abolitionist." Noting as well Johnson's personal practice of "amalgamation," they drove home the obvious point: the South required a "Slave holding President."

As the contest intensified, the Whig Party noticeably discarded the elitism of the National Republican Party from which it had emerged. Although Webster largely shunned popular campaigning, both Harrison and White became active in their own behalf. White delivered campaign speeches at dinners and rallies, but it was Harrison who especially reached out to the electorate. By means of campaign tours, speeches, and letters, the "farmer of North Bend," as he was dubbed, demonstrated the same kind of rapport with the people that Jackson did. Whig politicians also adopted the organization and campaign techniques necessary to compete successfully with the Democrats. Party leaders entertained and mobilized voters, issued addresses and pamphlets, established newspapers, and raised money.

The Democrats responded vigorously to the Whig assault by invoking party loyalty and capitalizing on their proficiency in party organization. Identifying Van Buren as the "executor" of the Democratic Party's principles, they argued that a vote for any Whig was, in effect, a vote for "bankism, nullification . . . anti-Jacksonism, and everything that is anti-republican." They warned that the Whigs were attempting to subvert the will of the majority by throwing the election into the House of Representatives.

Although avoiding personal campaigning, Van Buren made extensive use of public letters to explain his position. He endorsed the measures of the Jackson administration, including the Specie Circular, and took special care to assure southerners that, as President, he would resist "the slightest interference" with SLAVERY in the southern states. In May 1836, Democrats in Congress underscored Van Buren's remarks by passing the so-called gag rule, automatically tabling abolitionist petitions without reference or printing.

Jackson was also active on Van Buren's behalf. He not only denounced White as a "red hot federalist," but also quieted potentially divisive and damaging issues. In 1835, a protracted disagreement with France over spoliation claims resulted in the virtual severance of diplomatic relations. The French refused to pay the claims unless Jackson made satisfactory explanations—an apology—for statements the French considered unacceptable. Jackson initially refused to stand down at the "arrogance" of France, but, in December

1835, with the Whigs accusing him of rash and warlike behavior and with the election approaching, he disclaimed any intention of menacing or insulting France. The French accepted this explanation, and the controversy was resolved by February 1836. A few months later, Jackson reluctantly signed the Deposit Act of 1836, which distributed the government's surplus revenue to the states, despite his objections to such a policy. Returning money to the states was enormously popular, of course, even among Democrats.

**The Results.** The election of 1836 took place on various days between 4 November and 23 November. The returns registered a victory for Van Buren, who captured 170 electoral votes and just under 51 percent of the popular vote. Harrison followed with 73 electoral votes, and his evident popularity made him a leading contender for the presidency in 1840. White won 26 electoral votes, Webster claimed only Massachusetts's 14, and South Carolina gave its 11 votes to Willie P. Mangum. The average voting turnout was only slightly larger than that of 1832, but the distribution of votes produced a close contest in many more states than previously. The average national percentage difference between the two parties was only 11 percent, compared to 36 percent in 1832, showing the emergence of an organized Whig Party in the South and West and increased Democratic strength in New England.

The election of 1836 revealed the general outlines of politics for the next twenty years. Party competition became national. In most states, the parties were well organized, the electorate was engaged, and the vote was close. At the same time, the election provided a reminder of the imperfections of American political parties. When Virginia Democrats refused to vote for Johnson as vice president, he failed to gain the necessary majority in the ELECTORAL COLLEGE. The election became the responsibility of the Senate, where, in February 1837, Johnson was chosen by a vote of 33 to 16. The Democratic ticket had triumphed, but the jubilation did not last long. Shortly after Van Buren's inauguration, an economic panic and depression struck the country and loosened the Democratic Party's lock on the White House.

### BIBLIOGRAPHY

Brown, Thomas. *Politics and Statesmanship: Essays on the American Whig Party.* 1985.

Brown, Thomas. "From Old Hickory to Sly Fox: The Routinization of Charisma in the Early Democratic Party." *Journal of the Early Republic* 11 (1991): 339–369.

Cole, Donald B. *Martin Van Buren and the American Political System.* 1984.

Cooper, William J., Jr. *The South and the Politics of Slavery: 1828–1856.* 1978.

Heale, M. J. *The Presidential Quest: Candidates and Images in American Political Culture, 1787–1852.* 1982.

Latner, Richard B. *The Presidency of Andrew Jackson: White House Politics, 1829–1837.* 1979.

McCormick, Richard P. *The Second American Party System: Party Formation in the Jacksonian Era.* 1966.

Silbey, Joel H. "Election of 1836." In vol. 1 of *History of American Presidential Elections: 1789–1968.* Edited by Arthur M. Schlesinger, Jr., Fred L. Israel, and William P. Hansen. 4 vols. 1971.

RICHARD B. LATNER

**ELECTION, PRESIDENTIAL, 1840.** The WHIG PARTY elected its first President in the "Hurrah" campaign in 1840, when William Henry Harrison defeated the Democratic incumbent, Martin Van Buren. The election pivoted on two separate, if intertwined, axes, both determined by the presidential office and its occupants. Harrison's victory was partly due to the immediate impact on many Americans of an economic panic and the Van Buren administration's ineffectual response to it. But, the election was also shaped by the evolution, in the decade and a half before 1840, of a competitive, national two-party system out of the policy controversies ignited by former Presidents John Quincy Adams and Andrew Jackson. The election was a concluding moment in a process of national political clarification and institutionalization that had been underway for some time.

The Democrats had clearly manifested a commitment to limited federal government power in directing economic affairs; they were hostile to a central bank and a protective tariff. They believed that Whig policies benefited only part of the American population at the expense of the greater number of simple farmers and artisans who, in their daily labors and lives, needed no artificial support for their endeavors. In their turn, the Whigs had established themselves as the party of commitment to vigorous federal authority to promote commercial development. They argued that protection of home markets and infant industries through tariffs, federal support for the expansion of credit, and a variety of similar matters were proper responsibilities of the federal government. At the same time, the sharp ethnic and religious antagonisms of earlier years had led different, hostile groups to align with one or the other party. Many of these antagonisms reached back into their European past but had often been stimulated by new tensions in the United States. Thus, for one example, many religious groups found Puritan moralizing and determination to legislate proper behavior in society hard to accept and the occasion for political mobilization. The Whig party was identified as the home of such Puritan busybodies, while the Democrats were seen as having a more pluralist approach. In short, by 1840, political parties expressed current hopes and fears while also embodying future expectations and past resentments.

**Issues and Candidates.** During the depression that began in 1837, President Van Buren, true to his Democratic principles, resisted any direct federal involvement in promoting commercial activity—the establishing of banks or protective tariffs, the easing of credit, or the subsidization of INTERNAL IMPROVEMENTS such as roads and canals. His administration pursued a policy of tight money, balanced budgets, and denial of federal subsidies to economic enterprises. The Whigs fought the Van Burenites fiercely on behalf of their policies of federally aided commercial expansion. The Whigs believed that the argument over presidential policy gave them an unprecedented opportunity to wrest the office from the Democrats. Their determination to make the most of their opportunity directly affected their choice of standard-bearer in 1840.

The first Whig national convention met in Harrisburg, Pennsylvania, on 4 December 1839. There had already been a great deal of preliminary, behind-the-scenes maneuvering among party leaders. Hard-nosed party strategists such as Thurlow Weed of New York had doubts about the electability of the party leader, HENRY CLAY. Clay had been in politics too long, was too closely identified with many controversial battles of the past, and had too many enemies; he would not mobilize the votes that the Whigs needed in order to win, particularly from those voters who though not normally attracted to the Whigs were potentially winnable because of the depression. In Clay's place, the Whig convention settled on William Henry Harrison of Indiana. Harrison's fame was not political. A resolute general in the WAR OF 1812 and the victor over the hostile INDIANS of the Ohio Valley, Old Tippecanoe, as he was nicknamed, offered the electorate a set of accomplishments untainted by involvement in the domestic policy disasters of the previous few years. Harrison could be seen as a nonpartisan candidate who would draw to himself the now-indifferent supporters of an earlier frontier general, Andrew Jackson. The Whig vice presidential nomination went to John Tyler of Virginia, who was an ally of Clay's, a native of one of the largest states in the Union, and a representative of the large states' rights bloc that remained in the Whig party despite its centralizing tendencies. Thus the slogan "Tippecanoe and Tyler Too!" was coined.

The Whigs did not issue a national platform in 1840, because PARTY PLATFORMS were still deemed unconventional and unusual. But the party's stance on current issues and its policy preferences were clear from the record, its candidates' speeches, and the mounds of printed material party spokesmen had produced over the previous decade.

The Democrats met in Baltimore, Maryland, in early May 1840. They began their third national convention by agreeing to a platform emphasizing their well-known commitment to strict construction of the Constitution, defending their policies over the previous few years, and celebrating Democratic achievements in freeing Americans from past restrictions. No one could doubt that, were the Democrats reelected, their policy course regarding banks, tariffs, and government power generally would remain steady. They readily renominated their standard-bearer Van Buren, whatever qualms some of them may have had about his electability. His controversial Vice President, RICHARD M. JOHNSON, was not formally renominated at the convention, with the decision on whom to support being left to state Democratic parties. But Johnson became the de facto candidate as the campaign progressed, and most Democrats accepted him.

**The Campaign.** The 1840 campaign is remembered for the great increase in each party's organized activities and its extraordinary carnival-like atmosphere. All the electioneering techniques that had developed to mobilize voters were more extensively and systematically applied than ever before. Careful organization and strategy underlay every campaign move. The Whigs proved masters of hoopla, overwhelming their opponents with their energy. Party managers carefully built up a pyramid of committees—from the local through the county, district, and state levels—to run their campaign. Tippecanoe clubs appeared everywhere, as did committees of vigilance, Old Hickory clubs, and similar mobilizing institutions. These committees and clubs identified voters, made sure they received campaign material, got them out to rallies and constantly and repetitively reminded them of their duty to vote.

The centerpiece of each party's efforts was the mass rally, which drew hundreds, sometimes thousands, of people—men, women, and children—from the surrounding countryside. Rally participants were entertained by rousing speeches denouncing their party's enemies as well as parades, dances around hickory or "liberty" poles, representations of the Battle of Tippecanoe or models of Harrison's birthplace in Ohio. Prominent speakers appeared at major events, including Harrison himself, who made more public speeches than the Democrats considered seemly.

Campaigns of this kind needed to marshal information on which to build rhetorical assaults and to frame answers to negative portrayals throughout the large, spread-out country. The parties' national and state central committees made sure that broadsides and pamphlets were plentiful and that reprints of speeches and editorials were mailed throughout the nation. Their contents were echoed repeatedly. Party newspapers came into their own in 1840: both parties had flagship journals in Washington, D.C.—the Whig *National Intelligencer* and the Democratic *Globe*—as well as major organs in every state. Special campaign newspapers also appeared, including the *Extra Globe* and HORACE GREELEY's Whig *Log Cabin*. These set the tone for the faithful, were widely distributed (often by Democratic postmasters to the Whigs' chagrin), their editorials providing the raw materials for speeches on the hustings and debates between the faithful.

Beyond the hoopla, both parties played on substantive themes. Every American politician was an egalitarian by 1840—at least in public; commitment to the common man had become a standard of American political culture. But the parties continued to contest, as they had done since John Quincy Adams and Jackson, how best to promote and protect American freedom. There were no surprises. As noted in their platform, the Democrats continued to favor a restricted role for the government in both economic and social life, refusing to promote certain industries over others and, equally, refusing to interfere in how people chose to live, worship, or behave. The Whig position was no less clear-cut: they continued their commitment to energetic, helpful, directive government power.

The country's economic condition was also a staple of the Whig campaign. It was no accident that in a depression year the Whigs concentrated on emphasizing the plainness of Harrison's life, the simple log cabin in which he had been born, and the contrast this made with Van Buren's luxurious life in the Executive Mansion, with its servants and gold plate. Nor was it accidental that the Democrats reminded voters of ancient fears and threats to American liberty and their suspicions about the elitist Whigs' late conversion to popular democracy. Behind their enemies, Democrats claimed, lurked the excesses of federalism and high toryism.

**The Result.** There was no single election day in 1840; in different locales, ballots were cast for President on different days, from early fall through November. Polls were open during daylight hours, and party workers brought the faithful to the polling places in wagons, supplied voters with ballots, and guarded the poll against last-minute efforts by the other side. Party leaders carefully checked off who had turned out and who had not, making a final push to contact the no-shows.

Their energetic efforts paid off. More than 80 percent of those eligible to vote did so, as compared to just over 56 percent four years before. It was the highest turnout in a presidential contest yet recorded. Throughout the United States there were clear signs of the power of issues and party organization. The contest for the presidency was more critically important to the American people than it had ever been before.

The results were also clear. Harrison won overwhelmingly in the ELECTORAL COLLEGE, taking nineteen states (234 electoral votes) against Van Buren's seven (60 votes). The Whigs also won control of both houses of Congress for the first time. The popular result was actually much closer than the electoral count suggests. Nationally, Harrison won 52.9 percent of the more than 2.4 million votes cast; Van Buren, 46.8 percent (a small third party, the antislavery Liberty party, garnered 0.3 percent). Clearly, the Whigs and Democrats had retained the support of many of their traditional partisans, but the Whigs had converted some voters, had gotten more of their supporters to the polls, and had won over many of the uncommitted. Overall, however, there was little change in the socioeconomic sources of each party's vote. In five states (with a total of 93 electoral votes) Harrison won very narrowly—reflective of the close competition between the parties throughout the country. Switches of allegiance or failure to turn out by a few voters could easily have changed the result.

The presidential election of 1840 was a defining contest in the history of American politics. The modern political tendency toward organization reached fruition. The control exercised by party leadership and the dedicated commitment of the party faithful assumed a significant mix. Moreover, the 1840 election was not a singular episode but rather marked the beginning of a long era in American political life dominated by popular hoopla, party organization, and voter commitment.

## BIBLIOGRAPHY

Carwardine, Richard. "Evangelicals, Whigs, and The Election of William Henry Harrison." *Journal of American Studies* 17 (1983): 47–75.

Chambers, William N. "Election of 1840." In *History of American Presidential Elections*. Edited by Arthur M. Schlesinger, Jr., and Fred L. Israel. 4 vols. 1971.

Curtis, James. *The Fox at Bay: Martin Van Buren and the Presidency, 1837–1841.* 1971.

Gunderson, Robert. *The Log Cabin Campaign.* 1957.

Holt, Michael F. "The Election of 1840, Voter Mobilization, and the Emergence of Jacksonian Voting Behavior." In *A Master's Due:*

*Essays in Honor of David Herbert Donald.* Edited by William Cooper et al. 1985.

McCormick, Richard P. *The Second American Party System: Party Formation in the Jacksonian Era.* 1966.

JOEL H. SILBEY

**ELECTION, PRESIDENTIAL, 1844.** On Wednesday, 29 May 1844 Democratic delegates gathered in convention in Baltimore nominated James K. Polk for the presidency. They accomplished this on the ninth ballot during the third day of a convention that had seen deadlock, intense behind-the-scenes maneuvering, and even the threat of physical violence. At adjournment, the delegates had unanimously agreed upon the first DARK HORSE candidate in the history of the presidency.

**Preelection Issues.** The fierce excitement and violent disagreements that plagued the convention resulted from significant tensions and divisions that had been building within the Democratic Party for more than a decade. By 1840, bitter animosity between those supporting a moralistic, hard-money position and those favoring a more pragmatic, entrepreneurial posture had seriously fragmented the party. Supporters of Martin Van Buren, champion of the radical hard-money men, meant to purge the party of its business component and to vindicate their leader by electing him to the presidency in 1844. For their part, entrepreneurial groups within the party—convinced that Van Buren and his radical supporters represented a distinct threat to a progressive business climate within the nation—intended to rid themselves of these troublemakers. They could not, however, coalesce around a single candidate; instead they remained divided behind such men as LEWIS CASS, James Buchanan, or RICHARD M. JOHNSON. In addition, JOHN C. CALHOUN loomed in the background. Thus, Democrats approached the election year of 1844 ripe for an intraparty fight. At the same time, though, the majority hoped for some issue and some man that could unite and reinvigorate their fractious party.

The issue proved to be expansionism. Ironically, a Whig President, John Tyler, injected this issue into the campaign of 1844. Upon his ascendancy to the presidency following the death of William Henry Harrison, Tyler, who had been a STATES' RIGHTS Democrat, found himself repudiated by the Whig Party. Desperate to retain his hold on the presidency, Tyler anxiously sought an issue around which he could build a third party. He hit upon the idea of forcing the question of the ANNEXATION OF TEXAS.

Consequently, his Secretary of State, Abel P. Upshur, a Virginia supporter of Calhoun, negotiated an annexation treaty. Upon Upshur's accidental death on board a naval vessel, Tyler gave in to political pressure and appointed Calhoun to head the State Department. By April 1844, Calhoun had a treaty. However, anxious to separate Van Buren from the Texas issue, Calhoun wrote a letter to the British minister, Richard Pakenham, that clearly linked the annexation of Texas with the protection of SLAVERY. He then submitted the treaty, called by some the Texas bombshell, to the Senate. Both Van Buren and HENRY CLAY—the two obvious choices to be their parties' standard-bearers in 1844—publicly declared their opposition to the immediate annexation of Texas. Time would tell whether each man had acted wisely or was to be politically destroyed by the Texas issue.

**The Conventions.** Certainly Clay could not have been more pleased with the Whig convention that met in Baltimore on 1 May amidst jubilant harmony. The city itself was a veritable Whig camp: boxes of live raccoons—symbolic of the "old coon" himself, Henry Clay—appeared everywhere along with Clay portraits, Clay hats, Clay cigars, and other bits of Clay memorabilia. Mirroring this exuberance, the convention delegates nominated Clay unanimously by acclamation. They then selected Theodore Frelinghuysen, former Senator from New Jersey and prominent moral reformer and nativist, to be Clay's running mate. After that the delegates adopted a platform espousing traditional Whig attitudes but maintaining a cautious silence on the Texas issue.

Martin Van Buren did not fare nearly so well as his friend Henry Clay. Indeed, when the Democrats gathered in Baltimore at the end of May, Van Buren's supporters encountered a hotbed of opposition that threatened to deadlock and possibly destroy the party. Quite simply, a significant number of delegates intended to rid their party of both its hard-money, antibusiness bias and of Martin Van Buren, the major proponent of those positions. For their part, Van Buren supporters meant to purge "the rotten portion of the party" from the ranks of the Democrats. Neither side would compromise; thus, once the delegates adopted a rule making it mandatory for a candidate to receive a two-thirds majority to gain the nomination, each side aimed at preventing the other from achieving the nomination even if it meant that the convention might break up in confusion.

Van Buren entered the convention with a clear majority of delegates but short of the necessary two thirds. His intransigence on money matters as well as on the annexation of Texas, however, worked against him. After seven ballots it became clear that he could not be nominated: with each ballot Cass gained delegates while Van Buren's support slipped. If something was not done quickly, Van Buren men feared that "the damned rotten corrupt venal Cass cliques" would gain the victory. In order to prevent this, Van Buren men from Ohio took matters into their own hands and provoked a melee that forced an adjournment for the night.

Throughout the evening of 28 May and the early morning of 29 May three men—Gideon Pillow, George Bancroft, and Benjamin Butler—worked feverishly to find a way to derail the bandwagon rolling in support of Cass. They were successful. On the ninth ballot James K. Polk of Tennessee (a man of impeccable Jeffersonian principles and a close friend of Andrew Jackson) received the unanimous support of the convention. On the following day the convention nominated GEORGE M. DALLAS of Pennsylvania for the vice presidency and endorsed a party platform articulating traditional Democratic principles. There was, however, a new plank: unequivocal support for the "reoccupation of Oregon and the reannexation of Texas." After committing the Democratic Party to expansion, the delegates headed home relieved at their party's seemingly providential escape from self-destruction.

**The Campaign.** This sense of well-being did not last long; Democrats soon found themselves embroiled in a raucous campaign. A Whig handbill declared Polk "destitute of the commanding talent—the stern political integrity—the high moral fitness—the Union should possess at this crisis." In addition, "having been twice rejected for the Office of Governor in his own State—and having no hold upon the confidence or affections of his countrymen at home, and no talent to command respect for us abroad he is not the man for the times or for the Union." Democrats brought out the old "corrupt bargain" charge of 1824 and accused Clay of being a "notorious *Sabbath-breaker, Profane Swearer, Gambler, Common Drunkard, Perjurer, Duellist, Thief, Robber, Adulterer, Man-stealer, Slave-holder, and Murderer.*" In addition, they described Polk as a man of the people and Clay as the candidate of the aristocracy.

The candidates themselves worked to advance their own cause. In order to placate ambitious party leaders and thus to draw together the various factions within the Democratic Party, Polk publicly pledged himself to a single term. Further, in order to stave off a rebellion within his own party on the tariff issue, Polk sent a carefully worded letter to John K. Kane, a Philadelphia supporter of Van Buren, that sanctioned "such moderate discriminating duties, as would produce the amount of revenue needed, and at the same time afford reasonable incidental protection to our home industry." After this point Polk shrewdly maintained a discreet silence on troublesome issues.

The same could not be said of Henry Clay. Under antislavery pressure from the LIBERTY PARTY candidate, James G. Birney, and anxious to appease his southern supporters, Clay wrote several public letters equivocating on his opposition to the annexation of Texas. This correspondence led to a gleeful Democratic gibe: "He wires in and wires out, And leaves the people still in doubt, Whether the snake that made the track, Was going South, or coming back." At the same time Democrats found themselves vulnerable in certain parts of the country on the issue of the extension of slavery. A pamphlet written by Robert J. Walker, in attempting to convince Georgia Whigs to vote for Polk, warned that the South and its peculiar institution would be endangered by the election of Clay. Whigs quickly circulated the pamphlet in Ohio in order to take advantage of that state's growing antislavery sentiment.

**The Result.** The presidency went to Polk in an extremely narrow victory. He carried fifteen states with a combined electoral vote of 170 while Clay won eleven states with 105 electoral votes. The popular vote, though, was much closer. Polk's percentage of the vote stood at barely 1.4 over Clay's; a scant 38,181 votes separated the two men out of more than 2.5 million cast. Birney and the Liberty Party, while gaining no electoral votes, garnered more than 60,000 popular votes. It is quite clear that the party system had achieved equilibrium by 1844. The persistence rate of voters was astounding. For example, the Democrats carried Westmoreland County, Pennsylvania, in 1840 and 1844 by identical votes of 4,704 to 2,778. In Davidson County, Tennessee, the Whig candidates for governor in 1843 and 1845 carried the county each time by exactly 583 votes; Clay achieved that same majority in the presidential election of 1844. Although such results are certainly atypical, partisan constancy measured for the years 1836 to 1860 is striking indeed. For many scholars, then, the fact that voters maintained their party identifications from one campaign to another is more important in understanding political activity in the late antebellum period than are particular candidates or specific issues.

This perspective contradicts the standard explanation for Polk's victory in 1844: that the Liberty Party drained enough antislavery votes away from Clay in New York to swing that state, and thus the election, to Polk. Adherents of partisan constancy maintain that Polk's victory resulted primarily from party lines holding firm in 1844. The party system incorporated the issue of the extension of slavery rather than being disrupted by it. Thus, individuals voted for or against expansion according to party loyalty; they did not arrive at a choice of party on the basis of the issue itself.

It does not appear that the issue of the extension of slavery swung the election one way or the other. Polk gained New York and very likely Georgia as a result of expansion, but he lost Ohio. Clearly, the issue cut both ways; remove it and Polk would still have been the victor. Given this fact, a state such as Pennsylvania assumes even greater importance. There Polk's letter to Kane certainly helped his cause. But there and in New York as well other issues intruded. Both Philadelphia and New York City had been racked by ethnic and religious tensions. A strong nativist backlash, closely associated with the Whigs, appeared. The vast numbers of Irish in both cities could not support a party ticket that included Frelinghuysen. It seems clear, then, that in an era of party equilibrium the shifting allegiance, indifference, or unusual turnout of certain relatively small groups within the electorate had a disproportionate effect upon election results. The observation by Charles Sellers that "Texas, abolition, Nativism, and the tariff had little to do with most of the votes cast, but everything to do with the result of the election" neatly expresses this viewpoint.

From a slightly different perspective, though, issues and candidates retain a great deal of significance. Why Polk gained the nomination and why he won the election are two quite different questions. If the answer to the latter does not require reference to the issue of the extension of slavery, the former cannot be understood without it. Had it not been for this issue, Polk would not have been nominated. He would not have become the vigorous President who embroiled the country in the MEXICAN WAR—that "dose of arsenic" that brought the nation to civil war. Here, the observation of a Vermont Congressman following Polk's election is truly prophetic. Upon viewing a Democratic victory banner flying over a slave market, this Whig partisan exclaimed: "That flag means *Texas*, and *Texas* means *civil war*, before we have done with it."

### BIBLIOGRAPHY

Alexander, Thomas. "The Dimensions of Voter Partisan Constancy in Presidential Elections from 1840 to 1860." In *Essays on American Antebellum Politics, 1840–1860*. Edited by Stephen E. Maizlish and John J. Kushma. 1982.

Holt, Michael F. *The Political Crisis of the 1850s.* 1978.

Niven, John. *Martin Van Buren: The Romantic Age of American Politics.* 1983.

Remini, Robert. *Henry Clay.* 1991.

Sellers, Charles. "Election of 1844." In *History of American Presidential Elections, 1789–1968.* Edited by Arthur M. Schlesinger, Jr., and Fred L. Israel. 4 vols. 1971.

Sellers, Charles. *James K. Polk: Continentalist, 1843–1846.* 1966.

ROBERT E. SHALHOPE

**ELECTION, PRESIDENTIAL, 1848.** If ever a political year cried out for political parties to take a stand, it was 1848. The issue was SLAVERY in the Mexican Cession, the vast area that ultimately became the states of California, Utah, Nevada, New Mexico, Arizona, and portions of other states as well acquired by the TREATY OF GUADALUPE HIDALGO.

**The Slavery Issue.** In 1846 the WILMOT PROVISO, forbidding slavery in any land acquired from Mexico, passed the House but was defeated in the Senate. Public opinion divided into four positions. Two were seen as extreme views; two others took the form of compromise or moderate solutions.

Many Northerners believed that Congress had constitutional authority to forbid slavery in all territories. For Southerners, the words of the Fifth Amendment denying Congress power to deprive any person of property without due process of law meant that slaveholders could not be denied the right to take their slaves with them to territories. Some Southerners believed also that Congress should enact a territorial slave code to protect slaves in all territories.

One of the compromise solutions called for the extension of the MISSOURI COMPROMISE line of 36° 30′, which had applied to the LOUISIANA PURCHASE, through the Mexican Cession. In that event area north of the line would be closed to slavery, and, presumably, lands south of the line would be open. The other compromise solution was advocated primarily by LEWIS CASS, Democratic Senator from Michigan. Cass believed in popular, or squatter, sovereignty, that is, letting the people of territories decide during the territorial phase the matter of slavery or freedom.

**Parties and Candidates.** Of the four proposed solutions to the dilemma in 1848 the WHIG PARTY accepted none and the Democratic candidate embraced popular sovereignty. It remained for the FREE-SOIL PARTY, newly created in the summer of 1848, to advocate the extreme Northern position.

The DEMOCRATIC PARTY met in Baltimore from May 22 to 26. The convention reaffirmed the two-thirds rule of earlier Democratic conventions. The nominee would need two-thirds of the votes to win his place on the ticket. Four ballots were required to nominate a presidential candidate. On the first ballot, Cass had 125 votes of a necessary 168. James Buchanan of Pennsylvania and Levi Woodbury of New Hampshire had 55 and 53 votes respectively. Three others had less than 10 votes each. On the fourth ballot Cass emerged as victor with 179 votes. For Vice President, after two ballots, the convention decided on General William O. Butler of Kentucky.

The PARTY PLATFORM was adopted on the last day. The

document that emerged was essentially the same as the Democratic platforms of 1840 and 1844. Delegate William L. Yancey of Alabama sought unsuccessfully to convince the convention to embrace the words of the Fifth Amendment as they were seen to apply to the slavery-in-the-territories controversy. The delegates thought the Yancey proposal unnecessary since one of the resolutions lifted from the 1844 platform condemned abolitionist activity "to induce Congress to interfere with questions of slavery" as potentially threatening to the very existence of the Union.

Popular sovereignty ideas did not appear in the Democratic platform, but Cass had adopted his personal plank on the matter. Cass believed that it would be "revolting to the common sense and practice of mankind" for the United States to forego acquisition of Mexican territory. As for the Wilmot Proviso, Cass stated that he did not believe that Congress had that kind of authority and that it was better to leave to the states-to-be, the territories, the matter of slavery during the territorial time.

The Whigs gathered in Philadelphia on 7 June and balloting for a presidential nominee began the next day. Four ballots were necessary for the party to make its choice. On the first ballot General Zachary Taylor, cotton grower and slaveholder from Louisiana and one of the victorious generals of the Mexican War, led by three votes but lacked a majority. At sixty-four, "Old Rough and Ready" had never voted in an election. He had devoted his life to military service, and his political views were rather vague. He believed that Congress's will regarding tariffs and internal improvements ought to be "respected by the Executive," and he noted that presidential vetoes had been too much used in the recent past. As for the Mexican War, he rejoiced at the "prospect of peace" and declared that the United States could afford to be "forbearing" and "even magnanimous to our fallen foe."

Five other Whigs received votes on the first ballot: HENRY CLAY and DANIEL WEBSTER had 119 votes between them; John McLean of Ohio and John M. Clayton of Delaware had a total of six. The other hero of the late war, Old Fuss and Feathers, WINFIELD SCOTT, had 43. In the next three ballots Scott gained votes as the others, save for Taylor, lost them. But in the end Taylor captured the nomination with 171 of 280 possible votes. Twelve persons received votes for Vice President, but Millard Fillmore of New York and Abbott Lawrence of Massachusetts were strongest. On the second ballot Fillmore was named.

No platform was adopted by the Whigs at the convention. But within days after adjournment Whigs adopted resolutions that noted that Taylor would have voted for Clay if he had voted. The resolutions praised Taylor as the man who could bring peace, prosperity, and union to the American people. Taylor was a man who had lived and worked "under the broad banner of the Nation," the Whigs wrote, and his interests and loyalties were not to state or section. Furthermore, if elected, Taylor would use as a model for his administration that of President George Washington. General Taylor himself said nothing about slavery but noted that, if elected, he would do all that he could "to cement the bonds of our Union."

The failure of the Whigs and Taylor to speak forthrightly on the slavery-territory issue and irritation with popular sovereignty led to the formation of an outspoken and committed THIRD PARTY, the Free-Soil, in August. Attracted to the national convention that created the party in Buffalo, New York, were disaffected Northern Whigs and Northern Democrats (like the Barnburners) who joined with the LIBERTY PARTY members (who had already nominated Senator John P. Hale of New Hampshire). Represented at Buffalo were about 300 men from seventeen of the thirty states; on their first ballot they named Martin Van Buren, favorite of the New York Barnburners, over John P. Hale, the Liberty Party man. For Vice President the Free Soilers chose former Whig Charles Francis Adams, grandson and son of earlier American Presidents.

The platform categorically opposed the extension of slavery to the territories and called on Congress to legislate as much. Free Soilers cried "No more Slave States and no more Slave Territory." "Let the soil of our extensive domains be kept free," they wrote, "for the hardy pioneers of our own land, and the oppressed and banished of other lands seeking homes of comfort and fields of enterprise in the New World." Other planks called for cheap postage, INTERNAL IMPROVEMENTS, a tariff sufficiently high to defray expenses and to pay the debt, and, most important, the granting of free land to actual settlers. In a ringing conclusion the Free-Soil men adopted the slogan "Free Soil, Free Speech, Free Labor, and Free Men" and promised to "fight on" and "fight ever, until a triumphant victory shall reward our exertions."

**The Result.** Only in South Carolina did the legislature continue to choose electors. In the others states, voters went to the polls and chose electors on general statewide tickets, and the political party with the most votes got all the electoral votes of that state. Van Buren and Adams received popular votes for their electors in eighteen states but won no electoral votes. They received no popular votes in twelve southern states and only 125 in Maryland, 80 in Delaware, and 9 in

Virginia. The Free Soilers were clearly a Northern party.

In New England, Maine and New Hampshire went for Cass while Vermont, Massachusetts, Connecticut, and Rhode Island decided for Taylor. The three Mid-Atlantic states (New York, New Jersey, and Pennsylvania) cast votes for Taylor too. All of the five states of the Old Northwest (Ohio, Indiana, Illinois, Michigan, and Wisconsin) voted for Cass. Of the eleven Southern states east of the Mississippi River, seven (Delaware, Maryland, Kentucky, Tennessee, North Carolina, Georgia, and Florida) went for Taylor and four (Virginia, South Carolina, Alabama, and Mississippi) for Cass. Of the five states west of the river, Iowa, Missouri, Arkansas, and Texas were for Cass; only Louisiana, Taylor's home state, decided for him.

A total of 2,871,906 popular votes for electors was cast in the 1848 election. As a measure of public opinion, about 47 percent of the voters preferred Taylor, about 42 percent favored Cass, and slightly more than 10 percent were for Van Buren. No one had an overall majority of the popular vote, but Taylor's electors cast 163 electoral votes in the colleges in fifteen states, while Cass obtained only 127 in the other fifteen states. The percentages were 56 and nearly 44. Taylor would be President. Neither he nor his party had come to grips with the pressing issue of the year—slavery in the Mexican Cession. Perhaps that explains his victory as much as anything.

### BIBLIOGRAPHY

Bauer, K. Jack. *Zachary Taylor.* 1985.
Hamilton, Holman. "Election of 1848." *History of American Presidential Elections, 1789–1968.* Edited by Arthur M. Schlesinger, Jr., and Fred L. Israel. 4 vols. 1971.
Hamilton, Holman. *Zachary Taylor: Soldier of the Republic.* 1941.
Hamilton, Holman. *Zachary Taylor: Soldier in the White House.* 1951.
Rayback, Joseph G. *Free Soil: The Election of 1848.* 1970.
Roseboom, Eugene H. *A History of Presidential Elections.* 2d ed. 1964.
Schlesinger, Arthur M., Jr., ed. *History of U. S. Political Parties.* Vol. 1, 1789–1860.
Smith, Elbert B. *The Presidencies of Zachary Taylor & Millard Fillmore.* 1988.
Stanwood, Edward. *A History of the Presidency from 1788 to 1897.* 1898.

RAYMOND H. ROBINSON

**ELECTION, PRESIDENTIAL, 1852.** The presidential election of 1852 was the last contest between the DEMOCRATIC PARTY and the WHIG PARTY. Originally formed around issues of economic policy, these parties had gradually muted their differences and come to concentrate more and more on winning elections by organization and turning out their voters. This strategy was based on the realities of party loyalty and party balance. Party votes varied little from election to election. Party loyalty was considered a duty, party switching an apostasy. Party strength was evenly balanced nationally so that neither party drew its votes disproportionately from one part of the country. Even the vast majority of counties were closely contested.

**Threats to the Party System.** But this strategy was weakening voter loyalties. By 1852, many believed that parties cared more for winning office than for addressing the voters' concerns. Concentrating on the mechanics of politics, the parties experienced factionalism, as one group contended against another for control of the party machinery and the spoils of office. Such competition spurred further acts and charges of corruption, blurring even more the distinctions between the parties and weakening their claims on voter loyalties.

At the same time, new issues confused the political scene. A wave of economic prosperity sent Americans scrambling for railroad charters and other favors from government, worrying many voters that both parties were catering to selfish special interests. In response, religious leaders, moral reformers, and young men of political ambition advocated a new civic morality of high purpose and principle. In many northern states some advocated temperance legislation and in 1851 achieved a major victory when Maine adopted a PROHIBITION law. This issue, which the parties were not prepared to confront on a partisan basis, occurred near the crest of a wave of Roman Catholic immigration from Ireland and Germany. Both parties coveted so rich a treasure of votes but were checked by the suspicions and fears of native-born Protestant voters, who disapprovingly noted how Irish and German Catholics celebrated their Sundays with song and beer. By 1852, many nativists and temperance advocates had organized reform groups demanding that the parties adopt their principles or lose their votes.

Also threatening the party system was the SLAVERY issue. Since its founding, the Republic had been held together by a consensus that the national government should balance the interests and opportunities of slavery and freedom. Whigs and Democrats both followed this line, taking advantage of the federal nature of the United States' electoral system to picture their candidates as antislavery in the North or proslavery in the South. This consensus had thwarted the efforts of JOHN C. CALHOUN of South Carolina to assume southern leadership on an openly proslavery platform and those of the antislavery LIBERTY PARTY and FREE-SOIL PARTY to mount a national attack on slavery.

The COMPROMISE OF 1850 left the party system generally intact. Voting on the compromise revealed splits between procompromise northern Democrats and proslavery Deep South Democrats and between antislavery northern Whigs and procompromise southern Whigs. Although these divisions had been contained by the party consensus, a growing number of Deep South politicians, often younger men, advocated SECESSION from the Union and denounced the proslavery provisions of the compromise as inadequate. To counter their appeals, Democratic and Whig unionists formed coalitions that temporarily succeeded in defeating the secessionists but soon fractured as voters returned to their traditional party loyalties.

**The Conventions.** The Democratic Party opened its national convention in Baltimore on 1 June. Prominent candidates for the presidential nomination were Senator LEWIS CASS of Michigan, the party's standard-bearer in 1848; James Buchanan of Pennsylvania, who had served as Secretary of State in the James Polk administration; William L. Marcy of New York, who had been Secretary of War under Polk; and Senator STEPHEN A. DOUGLAS of Illinois, who had maneuvered the Compromise of 1850 to passage. In one form or another, all supported the Compromise of 1850 and all were acceptable to the South, which offered no candidate of its own. The trouble for the party, then, was over neither principles nor party unity; it was the fact that the convention rules required a two-thirds vote of the delegates to nominate a candidate, and the number of aspirants, each with a loyal constituency, guaranteed a stalemate. This circumstance provided the opportunity for supporters of Franklin Pierce of New Hampshire. Although he came from a distinguished political family in his native New Hampshire and had himself won political honors that had extended from the statehouse to the United States Senate, Pierce had no desire for the presidency but was willing to serve as a compromise candidate. This strategy, which corresponded to the realities of the convention, his supporters readily adopted.

The Democrats took three days and forty-nine ballots to choose their nominee. Each of the major candidates surged in the voting from time to time, but none came within sixty votes of the two-thirds standard. Pierce entered on the thirty-fifth ballot but for several rounds mustered only a puny thirty votes. Then a combination of fortuitous events—decisions by the leaders to "experiment" with other candidates, the exhaustion and desperation of delegates to nominate someone to avoid a party collapse, and, above all, the tireless efforts of Pierce's supporters—won him the nomination. At the critical moment, North Carolina unexpectedly announced for Pierce and the stampede was on. In the movement to Pierce southern states were as active as northern, giving no one reason to doubt that the party had found a formula for unity. For Vice President the convention chose Senator WILLIAM R. KING of Alabama, a unionist and party regular. The party platform bowed deeply to party traditions of limited government, economic individualism, and suspicion of banking; denounced abolitionists; and endorsed the Compromise of 1850 by promising to "abide by and adhere to a faithful execution" of its provisions.

Ten days after the Democrats had left the city, the Whigs arrived for their convention. Southerners who had supported the compromise were determined to nominate President Millard Fillmore, whose support of the compromise, many believed, had made its passage possible, in part because Fillmore was a bitter factional rival of New York Senator WILLIAM H. SEWARD, who had opposed the compromise. Actually, Seward and many other northern Whigs were torn between the obvious popularity of the compromise and evidence that Free Soilers held the balance of power in many crucial northern states and thus needed to be courted. Seward's candidate was Gen. WINFIELD SCOTT, who had led United States armed forces to victory in the MEXICAN WAR. Following the standard practice of Whig military candidates, Scott had uttered no statements about the compromise or any other issue. A third candidate, DANIEL WEBSTER of Massachusetts, had supported the compromise and then resigned to become Fillmore's Secretary of State. Once one of the nation's most formidable political orators and a founding father of the Whig Party, Webster had suffered badly from his support of the proslavery features of the compromise. Now deteriorated in health so that he would not live out the year, he commanded just enough support to deny Fillmore and Scott the majority required by the convention rules.

The convention first took up the platform, which bowed to the South by endorsing the compromise and pledging to carry out its terms. (Some northern Whigs voted for the platform, believing that if Scott were nominated he would repudiate it.) The balloting then settled into a maddening repetition of Webster's thirty votes, denying Fillmore and Scott a majority. Southerners supported Fillmore almost unanimously, but Fillmore, who had no desire for the nomination, could not get enough northern votes to give Webster a majority and the southerners would not support Webster. The result was a gradual drift toward Scott, who picked up enough northern votes to win on the fifty-third ballot. When formally told of his nomination, the general, by impulse or design, declared that he supported the entire Whig platform, thus apparently distancing himself from Seward and the Free Soilers. Southern Whigs left the convention convinced, like the Democrats, that they had found a formula for party unity.

With the return of the Free-Soil Democrats to their former party, the Free Soilers had hoped the Whigs would endorse antislavery principles. Now, however, it seemed to many of them that another third-party nomination was the only means to keep their cause before the voters. Encouraged by northern Whigs who hoped a Free-Soil candidate would attract votes from the Democrats, the Free Soilers held a convention in Pittsburgh, where they nominated Senator John P. Hale of Hew Hampshire, adopted a platform containing many Democratic Party principles, and changed their name to the Free Democrats.

For the most part, the campaign followed traditional midcentury lines. Committees flooded the nation with pamphlets and handbills. Campaign biographies rolled off the presses. "Clubs" rallied support, provided space for meetings, and distributed literature. Rallies, speeches, and parades entertained and inspired the electorate. Much of the campaigning attacked the opposing candidate personally. Pierce was charged with anti-Catholicism, alcoholism, and abolitionism, Scott with anti-Catholicism, incompetence, and abolitionism. As such attacks suggested, both sides hoped to attract the immigrant, Catholic vote, which they believed held the balance of power in key states such as Ohio and Indiana. Hoping to overcome the popular association of their party with nativism, the Whigs sent Scott on a speaking tour of the Ohio Valley, where he conspicuously praised immigrants and even attended a Catholic mass.

**The Result.** Such tactics did the Whigs no good. Scott carried only four states (Vermont, Massachusetts, Kentucky, and Tennessee) and 42 electoral votes to Pierce's twenty-seven states and 254 electoral votes, the most lopsided victory since Andrew Jackson's reelection in 1832.

Issues of nativism and slavery hurt the Whigs more than the Democrats. Scott's flirtation with ethnic Catholics offended many northern Whig Protestants. Perceptions that Scott was influenced by the antislavery Seward alienated slave-state voters, particularly in the Deep South. Whig hopes that Hale's Free-Soil candidacy would take votes from the Democrats backfired as Free-Soil Democrats voted for Pierce and Whig Free Soilers in the crucial state of Ohio voted for Hale.

One notable feature of the voting was the overall decline in popular participation. The rate of voter turnout was the lowest of any election between 1840 and 1860. The Whig vote especially declined in the slave states, where Scott's association with Seward failed to overcome his support of the Compromise of 1850.

In general the returns sustained voting patterns of previous Democratic-Whig contests. The greatest variations were surges toward the Whigs in Massachusetts and toward the Democrats in Alabama, Georgia, Mississippi, Maryland, and Virginia. Elsewhere the shifts were modest and the parties remained strongly competitive. Pierce carried thirteen states with 156 electoral votes by less than five percentage points each, a margin the Whigs might well expect to overcome in four years.

As is usually the case in history, the significance of the election was the meaning people attached to it. Most Whig leaders discounted the positive signs, interpreted the outcome as a disaster, and concluded that the party should try to rebuild itself by concentrating on state issues. Pierce, who had benefited from the unanimous support of his party, now found himself besieged by its factional leaders, each demanding rewards that overlapped and conflicted. He tried to please them all but only left them discontented and aggressive.

The election of 1852 was neither a transitional election nor an indicator of future trends. It was a stage-setting election that stocked the political arena with disillusioned voters and a dispirited Whig Party whose search for new directions in the North would lead it toward nativism, temperance, and antislavery. In the center it placed a Democratic Party presided over by a compromise President who owed his nomination to too many factional leaders. It was a setting that did not guarantee a political conflict over slavery; but it was one that could not easily contain such a conflict if it arose.

### BIBLIOGRAPHY

Alexander, Thomas B. "The Dimensions of Voter Constancy in Presidential Elections from 1840 to 1860." In *Essays on American Antebellum Politics, 1840–1860*. Edited by Stephen E. Maizlish and John J. Kushuma. 1982.

Cooper, William J., Jr. *The South and the Politics of Slavery, 1828–1856*. 1978.

Freehling, William H. *The Road to Disunion*. 1990.

Gienapp, William E. *The Origins of the Republican Party*. 1987.

Holt, Michael F. *The Political Crisis of the 1850s*. 1978.

Nichols, Roy F. *Franklin Pierce*. 1931.

Sewell, Richard H. *Ballots for Freedom*. 1976.

GEORGE MCJIMSEY

**ELECTION, PRESIDENTIAL, 1856.** The election of 1856 marked the collapse of the second party system, in which Democrats and Whigs competed primarily over government economic policies, and the rise of a new system, in which Democrats and Republicans would battle primarily over issues involving slavery. The Democratic presidential and vice presidential candidates, James Buchanan and JOHN CABELL BRECKINRIDGE, defeated the Republican candidates, JOHN C. FREMONT and W. L. Dayton, by 1,838,169 votes to 1,341,264 votes. The candidates of the KNOW-NOTHING (AMERICAN) PARTY, Millard Fillmore and Andrew J. Donelson, received 874,534 votes. The three tickets received 174, 114, and 8 electoral votes respectively.

**Slavery and Immigration.** The election revolved around the issue of SLAVERY. Both the DEMOCRATIC PARTY and the WHIG PARTY had worked to keep that issue out of national elections, because it threatened to divide each party along sectional lines. However, this policy could work only as long as the parties divided along issues that most American voters considered more important than slavery, or as long as most voters believed the issue so dangerous to the maintenance of the Union that they recoiled from it. In fact, the COMPROMISE OF 1850, supported by the leadership of both parties, was supposed to have settled the slavery issue forever.

Even by the early 1850s, however, the old concerns had lost much of their salience. As the parties seemed ever more alike, Americans began to complain that they served no purpose other than to further the ambitions and interests of the politicians. Charges of corruption multiplied. People complained that the parties were unable to deal with new and pressing problems. Interest in politics and voter turnout declined.

In this environment, a powerful current of anti-immigrant and anti-Catholic feeling had developed. Many Americans believed that the great German and Irish immigration of the late 1840s and 1850s threatened the character of American society. They believed that the Catholicism of many of the immigrants was inconsistent with democratic institutions and that the immigrants did not share the same moral standards as American Protestants. The result was the apparently spontaneous organization of secret, anti-Catholic, nativist societies around the nation, whose members agreed to vote only for political candidates who shared their anti-immigrant, anti-Catholic beliefs; who would support measures to curb immigrants' political power; and who favored passing laws to enforce Protestant morality by law—for example, by prohibiting the production and sale of alcoholic beverages.

This Know-Nothing movement, so called because its members claimed to "know nothing" about it, disrupted old political alliances. Most Democratic leaders, who traditionally received the votes of Catholic immigrants, denounced the movement, while many Whigs thought they could harness it. But many Democratic voters were attracted and many Whigs repelled by Know-Nothingism, wrecking party lines.

At the same time, Democrats in Congress passed legislation framed by Illinois Senator STEPHEN A. DOUGLAS to provide local government for the Nebraska territory, part of the LOUISIANA PURCHASE. The new territory was mostly north of the Missouri Compromise line, where slavery was not permitted according to the MISSOURI COMPROMISE OF 1820. To satisfy southerners, however, the party leaders arranged to split the territory into two parts, Nebraska and Kansas. They would allow the settlers to vote on whether to permit slavery, as the Compromise of 1850 had provided in territories conquered from Mexico—a policy that came to be called popular sovereignty. Since Kansas lay adjacent to slaveholding Missouri, it seemed likely that its first settlers would vote to permit slavery in the territory. Strongly backed by the administration of President Franklin Pierce, the new law announced that the Compromise of 1850 had repealed the Missouri Compromise.

Reaction in the North was furious. But although northern Whigs opposed the Kansas-Nebraska Act, most northern voters' anger was channeled through new political organizations, created by the leaders of old antislavery splinter parties, dissident Whigs and Democrats, and Know-Nothings disgusted with both parties. The new organizations, called Republican parties, People's parties, and by other names, often endorsed both antislavery and nativism. In other places, rival third parties organized, stressing one theme or the other. In the local and congressional elections of 1854, the Democrats lost votes throughout the North, while the new parties gained them. In the Deep South the Whig party collapsed, although it remained viable in the upper tier of slave states.

**Party Realignment.** It had been unclear at first whether the new opposition to the Democrats would be based primarily on antislavery or on anti-immigrant sentiments. After 1854 the coalition that had defeated the Democrats broke apart. Voters and leaders who considered slavery the most important issue formed the Republican Party, while those who stressed the danger of Catholic immigration formed the American Party. However, after some jockeying for two years, it was the antislavery movement that attracted more solid support. As the elections of 1856 approached, the American Party broke apart over slavery, with most northern members going over to the Republicans. Old Whigs came to dominate the American organization, which remained strong in the border states and upper South, and stressed its Unionism as much as its nativism. Its convention met in Philadelphia in February 1856—early because the party was disintegrating and it hoped to influence the later Democratic and Republican conventions. It nominated former Whig President Millard Fillmore for the presidency and a protégé of Andrew Jackson, Andrew J. Donelson of Tennessee, for Vice President.

The Democratic convention met on June 2 in Cincinnati. Fearing to nominate anyone closely identified with the Kansas-Nebraska Act, including President Pierce and Senator Douglas, the convention instead turned to Philadelphia Democratic leader James Buchanan, who had been serving as ambassador to Russia during the controversy. As his running mate the Democrats chose a Douglas ally, Representative John C. Breckinridge of Kentucky. The platform reiterated old Democratic positions on economic issues, blasted religious and ethnic bigotry, denounced antislavery agitation as a danger to the Union, and confirmed the party's commitment to popular sovereignty in the territories.

The new Republican Party held its first national convention in Philadelphia on June 17, with its leaders divided over whether to appeal to nativism or repudiate it. On one side, many northern nativists were antislavery and could be attracted by a campaign stressing both issues. But on the other, Republicans had learned in local elections that appeals to nativism repelled voters who opposed all bigotry and also repelled immigrants who were antislavery. In the end the Republicans neither endorsed nor repudiated nativism. Their platform stressed slavery almost entirely. A plank opposing legislation that would impair "equality of rights among citizens" sounded like a condemnation of nativism, but it did not repudiate nativist demands to deny citizenship to immigrants for a long probationary period.

Republicans promoted the same ambiguity by their nominations. They refused to nominate Ohio Governor SALMON P. CHASE, who was too radical on the slavery issue and had dallied with the American Party, or the conservative Supreme Court Justice William McLean, who was known to be the candidate most acceptable to them. They might have nominated William H. Seward, who had always sharply criticized nativism, but he refused to allow his name into nomination because he knew he could not win the election without nativist support. Instead, the Republicans enthusiasti-

cally nominated a young military hero and explorer, John C. Frémont, a self-described former Democrat who had said little on slavery or nativism. Rejecting propositions to name someone acceptable to Americans for Vice President, the convention balanced the ticket with ex-Senator William L. Dayton of New Jersey, a former Whig.

**The Campaign and the Result.** In the campaign, the American Party eschewed nativism and ran as the party that would suppress controversy over slavery in order to preserve the Union. On that platform it secured a good deal of support in New York, New Jersey, Pennsylvania, Illinois, and California, as well as the South, where it received the votes of most old Whigs. Republicans responded that it was slavery that put the Union at risk. A slaveholding aristocracy had taken control of the southern states, suppressing freedom of speech and press and driving nonslaveholders to the margins of society, Republicans argued. Through their control of the Democratic Party these slaveholders were promoting policies that would do the same in the West and ultimately even in the North. The only remedy was to pass laws barring slavery in all the territories, thus assuring the supremacy of free institutions in the Union.

Many of the Republican campaigners believed they were engaged in a crusade to save liberty from slavery, and many northern voters came to agree. Republican enthusiasm made up for the disorganization in their new party. The Republicans organized huge rallies, with Wide-Awake clubs marching through the streets in torchlight parades.

Democrats were assured of the southern states, despite the substantial support for the American Party there, but they were hard pressed in the North. They insisted that the settlers of territories north of the old Missouri Compromise line were sure to vote down slavery under the system of popular sovereignty. They warned that antislavery legislation in Congress would break up the Union. They appealed to racism, accusing Republicans of favoring complete civil and political equality for blacks. They charged Republicans with nativism and religious intolerance.

In the end the Democrats were able to carry enough northern states to win the presidential election—California, Illinois, New Jersey, and Pennsylvania. But the Republican performance was remarkable. With a barely organized party, the Republicans had carried almost every northern state. Although future Republican success was by no means inevitable, to retain power Democrats would have to devise a way to reassure Northerners about the future of free institutions. If they proved unable to do so, they could expect disaster.

BIBLIOGRAPHY

Foner, Eric. *Free Soil, Free Labor, Free Men: The Ideology of the Republican Party before the Civil War.* 1970.

Gienapp, William E. *The Origins of the Republican Party, 1852–1856.* 1987.

Holt, Michael F. *The Political Crisis of the 1850s.* 1978.

Nichols, Roy Franklin. *The Disruption of American Democracy.* 1948. Chapter 1, "Conservatives to the Rescue."

MICHAEL LES BENEDICT

**ELECTION, PRESIDENTIAL, 1860.** No American presidential election had greater consequences for the history of the country than this one. Whatever the social forces underlying SECESSION, the result of the election of 1860 provided its proximate political cause. The political parties ran skillful and spectacular campaigns of the sort only the United States afforded in the middle of the nineteenth century. As a result, voter turnout was astonishingly high. And yet, an able analyst could have predicted the outcome of the election four years in advance.

**Parties and Candidates.** The results of the 1856 election revealed the burgeoning strength of the newly formed REPUBLICAN PARTY. Ominously, the Republicans represented precisely what George Washington had warned against in his famous FAREWELL ADDRESS: a sectional political party. Their appeal lay in the most populous section of the country, however, and in order to win in 1860, they needed only to retain the states they won in 1856 (essentially the upper tier of northern states) and gain Pennsylvania along with either Indiana or Illinois. Already in 1856 the Republican Party embraced leaders shrewd enough to adopt the proper strategies: broaden the economic appeal of the party, especially with Pennsylvania's manufacturing interests in mind; avoid offense to anti-Catholic voters moving over from the KNOW-NOTHING (AMERICAN) PARTY into the Republican, and perhaps choose a candidate with special appeal in Indiana or Illinois.

Of course, the strategy was not as obvious to contemporaries; otherwise, New York's WILLIAM H. SEWARD would not have been regarded as the front-runner for the nomination to be decided at the Republican convention in 1860. Moreover, many critical political events intervened to confuse politicians. The United States Supreme Court in 1857 issued its *Dred Scott* decision declaring that Congress could not ban SLAVERY from the territories—essentially outlawing the principal plank in the Republican platform (*see* DRED SCOTT V. SANDFORD). A continuing struggle for control of Kansas Territory caused a bitter split between the Democratic President, James Buchanan, and the leading northern Democrat in Congress, STEPHEN A. DOUGLAS, of Illinois, as well as deep alienation of southern political leaders from the rest of the DEMOCRATIC PARTY. And in 1859 the abolitionist John Brown attempted to raise a slave rebellion in a raid on Harpers Ferry, Virginia. The continuing sectional agitation ultimately aided the Republicans, who were an anti-Southern party.

The antisectional party, called the Constitutional Union Party, united remnants of the old WHIG PARTY and Know-Nothing Party. On 9 May 1860, they nominated JOHN BELL, of Tennessee, for President, with Edward Everett, of Massachusetts, as running mate. They appealed to love of the Union and made the Constitution, the Union, and enforcement of the laws their platform.

The troubled Democratic Party had met in Charleston, South Carolina, in April. Southern delegates demanded a platform plank for protection of slave property in the territories, the common property of all the states, as they saw it. Democratic supporters of Douglas, the front-runner, would not yield on this point. He stood on a platform advocating popular sovereignty, that is, local territorial control of the slave question. His supporters also expressed willingness to obey a Supreme Court decision on what power Congress and territorial legislatures held over slaves brought into unsettled territories. When Douglas's plank was adopted, many Southern delegates walked out, led by the Alabama "fire-eater" William L. Yancey.

Before the Democrats reconvened, the Republicans met on 16 May in Chicago in a building called the Wigwam. They were determined to broaden their platform and to nominate a moderate candidate. Seward's reputation as an antislavery radical and his record of cooperation with Catholics in New York when he was governor hurt him. Indiana and Illinois delegates insisted he could not carry their states; in Pennsylvania the vote of anti-Catholic former Know-Nothings seemed crucial. Other prominent candidates offered even fewer assets. Missouri's Edward Bates had only recently declared himself opposed to slavery's expansion into the territories. SALMON P. CHASE, by contrast, seemed too radical on the slavery question and could not unite the delegates of his own state, Ohio. Simon Cameron, of Pennsylvania, had a reputation for corruption. Illinois's Abraham Lincoln, about whom little was known, stood as the inoffensive second choice of many delegates.

"I suppose I am not the *first* choice of a very great many," Lincoln had told an Ohio politician on 24 March 1860. "Our policy, then, is to give no offence to others—leave them in a mood to come to us, if they shall be compelled to give up their first love." Lincoln had a sound record on the slavery expansion issue, as evidenced especially in his 1858 campaign against Douglas for the U.S. Senate. But because he had not been active in antislavery political movements before 1854 especially, as Chase and Seward had been, Lincoln bore no scent of radicalism. As "an old HENRY CLAY tariff whig"—that was Lincoln's self-description in a private letter of 11 October 1859—he carried a consistent record on an issue of great importance in tariff-mad Pennsylvania. He had lived, moreover, for long periods in both Indiana and Illinois.

Lincoln had been introduced to eastern Republicans on 27 February 1860, when he delivered a speech at the Cooper Institute in New York City. The Young Men's Republican Union, dominated by anti-Seward New York Republicans like William Cullen Bryant and HORACE GREELEY, had invited him. The speech, usually called the Cooper Institute Address, was widely republished. Lincoln researched the opinions of the Founders of the country, as revealed in voting on early restrictions on slave expansion, to argue that the Republican Party adhered to the original ideas of the Founders; opposition to slavery's expansion was thus truly conservative policy. He ridiculed John Brown's raid and emphasized the defensive nature of Republican policies:

> You say we have made the slavery question more prominent than it formerly was. We deny it. We admit that it is more prominent, but we deny that we made it so. It was not we, but you, who discarded the old policy of the fathers. We resisted, and still resist, your innovation; and thence comes the greater prominence of the question.

Lincoln's strategy worked and he won the nomination on the third ballot. HANNIBAL HAMLIN, a former Democrat from Maine, was the running mate for the former Whig, Lincoln. The platform now included appeals not only to keep slavery out of the territories but also for a transcontinental railroad, protective tariffs, and homestead legislation.

The Democrats reconvened in Baltimore on 18 June, refused to let bolting Southerners back in, and nominated Douglas. Herschel V. Johnson, of Georgia, was their vice presidential nominee. Other Southerners withdrew and, the next day, nominated JOHN C. BRECKINRIDGE, of Kentucky, for President. Joseph Lane, of Oregon, was his running mate. In addition to demanding a federal slave code for the territories, their platform urged the acquisition of CUBA and condemned state laws frustrating the capture of FUGITIVE SLAVES.

**The Contests.** Though many assumed that the Democratic split would assure Lincoln's election, the parties left nothing to chance and ran spirited campaigns. The Republicans set the tone of the canvass at first, adopting the old Whig style of "hurrah" campaign used for William Henry Harrison twenty years earlier. They ignored issues and stressed parades, fireworks, music, and rallies. Democrats followed suit, even copying their rivals' young men's marching clubs, called "wide awakes" by the Republicans. The methods proved enviably successful. Voter turnout in the North exceeded 80 percent and, though quantified estimates for the South are not readily available, turnout certainly increased there and was high.

Two two-way contests developed, one between Lincoln and Douglas in the North and the other between Breckinridge and Bell in the South. Neither section learned much about the other; instead, voters heard sectional enemies vilified and caricatured. Following the accepted custom for presidential candidates, Lincoln gave no speeches. Breckinridge gave one. Both Bell and Breckinridge forces laid claim to holding the best plan to save slavery, and Breckinridge men stressed the need for Southern unity more than they avowed secessionism.

Douglas shattered tradition, campaigning throughout the North and in the upper South in summer. When key states that held gubernatorial elections in October went Republican, Douglas headed into the Deep South and, denouncing secession, pleaded heroically for the Union in numerous speeches.

This image of devotion to the Union would cling to Douglas's reputation ever after, but it made little headway in the South, where Democrats despised him as a betrayer of Southern interests in the political conflict over Kansas back in 1857. Lincoln's campaign image endured as well. At the Chicago nominating convention an old settler had produced parts of a rail fence Lincoln had hewn in his youth, and the candidate was christened "the railsplitter." The emphasis thus placed on his birth in a log cabin and his subsequent rise to success fit the economic message of the Republican Party, which depicted the South as economically retarded because of slavery and therefore unable or unwilling to offer economic opportunity to the common man. The Republicans championed free labor and free soil. Lincoln, also known popularly as "Honest Abe," stood apart from the aura of corruption that tarnished the waning administration of President Buchanan.

Lincoln was so little known even after his nomination for the presidency that the first paperback campaign biography of him produced after the adjournment of the Republican convention misspelled his name as "Abram." If the "hurrah" campaign and observation of the custom of not giving electioneering speeches as the presidential candidate limited understanding of Lincoln's positions on the issues, they were nevertheless readily available in the book version of his famed debates with Douglas, published in the spring of 1860. The book went through many printings. To Lincoln this and the Chicago platform seemed enough. When asked for explanations of his beliefs he replied, typically, as in this letter of 23 October:

> I appreciate your motive when you suggest the propriety of my writing for the public something disclaiming all intention to interfere with . . . slavery in the States; but in my judgment, it would do no good. I have already done this many—many, times; and it is in print, and open to all who will read. Those who will not read, or heed, what I have already publicly said, would not read, or heed, a repetition of it.

Lincoln may have been correct, but all that is known for sure is that without such assurances he was generally depicted as an abolitionist in the South. Conversely, Republicans questioned southern unanimity in denouncing the North; they dismissed predictions of secession as bluff and bluster and blackmail that did not really threaten the security of the Union.

**The Result.** The voting on 6 November gave Lincoln 39 percent of the popular vote. These voters, concentrated in populous states, gave the Republican 180 electoral votes to 72 for Breckinridge, 39 for Bell, and 12 for Douglas (even though Douglas came in second in popular votes). Lincoln took all the Northern states except New Jersey, which split its electoral vote. He would have won the Electoral College vote even if the popular votes of his opponents had been concentrated on one candidate. There was no real contest in New England. Lincoln took Vermont, for example, by a vote greater than triple that of his opponents combined, and all the other states in the region by thumping majorities. Lincoln carried New York by 362,646 to 312,510 and Pennsylvania 268,030 to 208,612 for his opponents combined and the rest of the upper tier of states by substantial majorities. The states of the Old Northwest were closer. In Indiana, Lincoln gained 139,033 to 138,110 for his combined opposition, for example.

Lincoln did not get a single vote in any future Confederate state except Virginia, where he polled under 2,000. In the border slave states he did best in Delaware and Missouri. Bell won Kentucky, Tennessee, and Virginia and ran very close in Maryland. Douglas won Missouri, split New Jersey's electoral vote with Lincoln, and ran close in California. The future states of the Confederacy, save for Virginia and Tennessee, belonged to Breckinridge.

With that display of Southern unity, the slave states of the lower South began to secede in December.

### BIBLIOGRAPHY

Crenshaw, Ollinger. *The Slave States in the Presidential Election of 1860.* 1945.
Luthin, Reinhard H. *The First Lincoln Campaign.* 1944.
Potter, David M. *The Impending Crisis, 1848–1861.* 1976.

MARK E. NEELY, JR.

**ELECTION, PRESIDENTIAL, 1864.** The historian James A. Rawley referred to the election of 1864 as a "perilous experiment." Only once before—in 1812—had the United States held an election during wartime. James Madison's situation, however, battling a Britain already embroiled in the Napoleonic Wars, bore scant resemblance to the plight of Abraham Lincoln a half-century later.

**Lincoln's Predicament.** In the spring of 1864, the President's fate seemed to hinge more on success on the battlefield than on the campaign trail. In an effort to hasten victory on both the political and military fronts, Lincoln brought the controversial General Ulysses S. Grant to Washington to command and coordinate all Union forces. Grant would move against the legendary Robert E. Lee in Virginia, while William Tecumseh Sherman attacked Joseph E. Johnston in Georgia. Immediate Yankee triumphs would serve the dual purpose of ending the war and insuring Lincoln's reelection. The strategy foundered quickly. In May, Grant engaged Lee at the battles of the Wilderness and Spotsylvania Court House resulting in Union defeats with heavy casualties. Sherman met with little more success against Johnston, who stalled the Union forces outside Atlanta.

Frustration produced by military failure, intersecting with the President's philosophical and political concerns, placed a dark cloud over his reelection bid. He had to face not only angry opposition Democrats, but hostile elements within the REPUBLICAN PARTY. Although the risks of violence at the polls, demoralization of the armies, and fragmentation of the Northern populace loomed large, Lincoln apparently gave no serious thought to postponing the election. The President took the opposite tack, viewing the contest as an opportunity to clarify the issues, obtain a mandate, and unify the nation preparatory to the final push for military victory.

During his first administration Lincoln had made numerous enemies. Many Democrats resisted Republican economic efforts to involve the federal government in the economy. The EMANCIPATION PROCLAMATION infuriated many northern Democrats. Some were willing to fight a war to preserve the Union, but few were willing to advance the cause of African Americans. Lincoln also alienated the opposition with his suspension of many CIVIL LIBERTIES, particularly the writ of habeas corpus in the spring of 1861 [see HABEAS CORPUS, SUSPENSION OF]. Arbitrary arrests abounded, thousands were imprisoned, and freedom of the press was curtailed. Antiwar peace Democrats were prosecuted, and their outspoken leader, Ohio congressman Clement Vallandigham was exiled in 1863. Vallandigham had intrigued with Confederate agents, supporters of a Northwest Confederacy, and with the Sons of Liberty, a secret antiwar society. His return to Ohio in 1864 bode ill for the President.

Within his own party, Lincoln's cautious approach to the war—emphasizing preservation of the Union— agitated many of his compatriots. These RADICAL REPUBLICANS envisioned the conflict as an agent for rapid and dramatic social change in the South. Lincoln often shared their vision, but he disagreed with them about timing and about what locus of power should effect change. The Radicals resented Lincoln's moderation and insistence on executive control of RECONSTRUCTION. Some Congressmen disapproved of his maintenance or appointment of conservatives, even Democrats, to vital positions in the army and Cabinet. While the Radicals could work with Lincoln, they hoped for a more amenable candidate in 1864.

The Radicals found promise in the boomlets launched for Secretary of the Treasury SALMON P. CHASE and General JOHN C. FREMONT. Their campaigns garnered only minimal support, however, since most party loyalists remained reluctant to replace a strong incumbent President. In February 1864, Chase and his managers unwisely began a pamphlet campaign to promote the secretary's candidacy among party regulars. Quickly outmaneuvered by the President, an embarrassed Chase offered to resign. The President declined, but Chase's candidacy ended in early March. Four months later, after the Republican convention, Chase resubmitted his resignation and Lincoln accepted. Although Chase continued to agitate the President, Lincoln nominated him as Chief Justice of the United States in December to placate the Radicals.

Frémont's challenge, while more enduring, was likewise unthreatening. The General had a checkered military career that reached back to the MEXICAN WAR. He had won a reputation in Missouri in 1861 when he prematurely emancipated the slaves in a Union state. While unconstitutional, this bold act made him the favorite of abolitionists and German Americans. The strong antislavery elements in the party had welcomed the Emancipation Proclamation but became increasingly troubled at the slow pace at which slaves were gaining their freedom. Their concern increased in late spring when the House of Representatives failed to pass a constitutional amendment to end all slavery in the United States. Eager for a President who would press this issue with more alacrity, 350 delegates formed a rump convention in Cleveland, Ohio, on 31 May 1864, and nominated Frémont. The platform of the Radical Democratic Party not only embraced equality before the law but also advocated redistribution of confiscated Confederate lands and condemned Lincoln's suspension of civil liberties. Charges were leveled that the movement had become a tool of the Democrats to divide the Republicans, prompting most abolitionists to remain loyal to the President.

When the Republicans, calling themselves the National Union Party met in Baltimore on 7 June, Lincoln easily won renomination. In a show of national unity, the leadership dumped Vice President HANNIBAL HAMLIN of Maine, replacing him with Democrat Andrew Johnson of Tennessee. This seemingly unimportant decision was to have far-reaching effects on Reconstruction. Unable to stop Lincoln, the disenchanted Radicals contented themselves with strong platform statements in support of the war, emancipation, and the use of African American troops. The party approved Lincoln's war measures and rejected any peace negotiations with the Confederacy unless they included unconditional surrender.

**The Radical Challenge.** The unanimous renomination of the President belied the ongoing tension between him and the Radicals in Congress. Although Lincoln pledged himself to freedom, his position on black rights in the newly reconstructed states of Louisiana and Arkansas suggested the need for a stronger stance. His proposals empowered neither blacks nor Radicals in either state and allowed locals far too much discretion for congressional palates. In voting to deny the admission of Congressmen from these two states, Congress both challenged Lincoln's power of executive Reconstruction and declared its unhappiness with his scheme of social reform.

On 2 July, Congress passed the Wade-Davis bill, an affirmation of legislative authority and sharp challenge to the state readmission procedure proposed by Lincoln. The measure insisted that 50 percent (not Lincoln's slim 10 percent) of those who had voted in 1860 take an "iron-clad oath" that they had not supported the Confederate government. It also contained provisions to protect the rights of new freedmen. Lincoln threw down the gauntlet by pocket-vetoing the measure.

The President recognized that the combination of peace activism, military stagnation, and Radical opposition might yet doom his reelection bid. The spring campaigns had produced sixty thousand casualties in Virginia as Grant moved on Richmond, but without capturing the ultimate prize. By June, the struggle bogged down, with Union troops reduced to trench warfare at Petersburg. Grant boldly attempted to break the stalemate on 30 July with an innovative attack by means of explosives planted under Lee's lines (the Crater). When this creative, but poorly executed, assault turned into a fiasco, the Union troops settled in for a prolonged seige that lasted until April 1865. Sherman provided a flicker of hope as he continued his slow advance against the Rebels outside Atlanta. Attempting to deliver a telling blow, he launched a frontal attack at Kenesaw Mountain (27 June) but was repulsed. Sherman resumed a more patient flanking strategy that would eventually succeed but, again, the inability to produce a dramatic victory in the field hurt Lincoln.

Battlefield doldrums manifested themselves economically and politically. The Yankee greenback dollar declined in value to 39 cents in gold, while the peace movement renewed its efforts at ending hostilities. HORACE GREELEY, Republican Radical and the eccentric editor of the *New York Tribune,* learned that two Confederate agents had arrived in Niagara Falls, Canada, and were prepared to negotiate. The President, stung by criticism that he was not supportive of peace, dispatched his private secretary, JOHN HAY, to accompany Greeley to Canada. Although skeptical of the Confederates' intent, Lincoln instructed Greeley and Hay to certify their credentials and assure them that he welcomed peace based on reunion and emancipation. Although the Southerners had no credentials, both the Confederates and the President used his demands for their respective propaganda purposes. In an effort to defuse the peace forces, Lincoln empowered a second mission in mid July to visit Richmond and meet with Confederate president JEFFERSON DAVIS and secretary of state Judah P. Benjamin. The message of "reunion and emancipation," however, elicited only a defiant statement from Davis, who stood fast for "independence . . . or extermination."

Unable to satisfy his opponents in such a volatile climate, the President endured ongoing criticism from both inside and outside his party. On 5 August, Congress issued the Wade-Davis Manifesto. This Radical response to the President's veto reflected congressional frustration with the executive, attacked the unconstitutional nature of Lincoln's actions, his usurpation of legislative powers, and the establishment of "oligarchies" in the reconstructed states. General Benjamin Butler, a Democrat, surfaced as the dissidents sought a fresh face to displace the incumbent. A group of political leaders met in New York City on 14 August and called for a new Union Party convention. The conservative New York political boss Thurlow Weed and the Radical editor Horace Greeley both informed correspondents that Lincoln's future was dim. The pessimistic President agreed. On 23 August he informed his Cabinet that it was "exceedingly probable" that he would not be reelected.

**The Democratic Candidate.** A week later a divided DEMOCRATIC PARTY met in Chicago at the Wigwam—the scene of Lincoln's nomination in 1860. Sensing victory, the Democrats moved to achieve harmony. Peace Democrats, who desired an armistice with the South, championed New York Governor HORATIO SEYMOUR. War Democrats, who supported a continuation of the war but opposed emancipation, presented General GEORGE B. MCCLELLAN. A compromise resulted. The peace faction wrote the platform, emphasizing states' rights (which apparently included slavery), civil liberties, and a call for an armistice. The Democrats would play the racial card and paint the Republicans with a pro-black brush. Seymour withdrew, but the peace element received Ohio Congressman George Pendleton as the vice presidential nominee. Although war Democrats got McClellan as the presidential choice, the general would not accept the armistice plank in the platform. In his acceptance letter he rejected the measure, demanding union first, thus antagonizing many in the peace faction.

In spite of the confusion over the compatibility of the nominee and the platform, the Democrats presented a viable threat to Lincoln. Fortunately for the President, fate intervened in the most welcome form—military victory. Sherman's defeat of new Confederate commander John Bell Hood and the subsequent capture of Atlanta on 2 September formed a turning point in the war. The victory at Atlanta, combined with the recent victory of Admiral David Farragut at Mobile Bay, gave Lincoln the strength to press on toward November. Even the Radical Republicans understood that Lincoln's seemingly hesitant posture on African American rights (he had also begun to backpedal on the linkage of reunion and abolition in late August) was far better than what might be expected from McClellan. Butler's candidacy evaporated and Frémont withdrew his thirty-party bid on 22 September. Lincoln promptly replaced conservative Postmaster General Montgomery Blair, who was anathema to the Radicals. Although the hated WILLIAM H. SEWARD remained in the State Department, concessions were made. The dual moves united the party a month before the election.

**The Result.** The 8 November election presented voters with a clear choice. The Democrats remained divided, with McClellan at odds with the peace faction over the issue of the preeminence of union or peace. Both opposed emancipation and spoke of restoration, not reconstruction. The Republicans wanted to prosecute the war to a victorious conclusion and promoted emancipation. The results gave the President an overwhelming victory in the ELECTORAL COLLEGE (212–21). The voter turnout was 74 percent, and Lincoln swept the popular vote 2.2. million to 1.8 million (55 percent to 45 percent). McClellan won only Delaware, Kentucky (both slave states), and New Jersey, although the crossover of a few thousand voters in key states such as New York and Pennsylvania would have placed those states in the Democratic column.

The Republicans scored equally well in state legislative and congressional races. In the next Congress, Republicans mustered 145 of 185 members in the House and 42 of 52 in the Senate. The soldiers who voted in huge numbers no doubt contributed significantly to the Republican gains, but the overall balloting suggests the widespread appeal of Lincoln and the war party in 1864. The President now had the power to pursue the conflict to its conclusion (only six months away) and to seek greater accommodation with the Radicals over Reconstruction. The election doomed the peace elements and painted the Democratic Party with the brush of disloyalty for a generation. Lincoln's triumph ensured military victory, political union, and freedom for African Americans.

### BIBLIOGRAPHY

Kirkland, Edward. *The Peacemakers of 1864.* 1927.

Nelson, Larry. *Bullets, Ballots and Rhetoric: Confederate Policy for the United States Presidential Contest of 1864.* 1980.

Rawley, James A. *Turning Points of the Civil War.* 1966.

Sears, Stephen. *George B. McClellan.* 1988.

Trefousse, Hans. *The Radical Republicans.* 1969.

Williams, T. Harry. *Lincoln and the Radicals.* 1941.

Zornow, William. *Lincoln and the Party Divided.* 1954.

JOHN M. BELOHLAVEK

**ELECTION, PRESIDENTIAL, 1868.** In the election of 1868, the Republican presidential and vice presidential candidates, Ulysses S. Grant and SCHUYLER COLFAX, defeated Democrats HORATIO SEYMOUR and FRANCIS P. BLAIR by 214 electoral votes to 80. (The electoral vote of Georgia was challenged. The Senate counted it, the House did not. Therefore, the electoral vote was formally reported to Congress in the alternative, Seymour receiving 80 electoral votes according to the Senate and 71 according to the House.) Grant won the popular vote by a much narrower margin— 3,012,833 votes to 2,703,249. The central issue of the campaign was the Republican program of RECONSTRUCTION after the CIVIL WAR. Economic and financial issues were secondary.

**The Issues.** The Reconstruction program involved several elements. Through the Fourteenth Amendment to the Constitution and the CIVIL RIGHTS ACT OF 1866 Republicans had defined citizenship in a way that included black Americans, secured basic civil rights against deprivation by the state, and disqualified many ex-Confederates from holding state or federal office. When Southerners refused to accept these provisions as the settlement of Civil War issues, Republicans had placed the former Confederate states under military occupation until they agreed to frame new constitutions to eliminate racial discrimination in civil and political rights, thus enfranchising black Southerners. By the time of the election, Republicans had restored all but three of the Southern states to normal relations in the Union on this basis. All of them had Republican governments, relying mostly on black voters for support.

Not only Democrats but also Andrew Johnson, who had become President upon Abraham Lincoln's assassination, sharply criticized the Republican program. They argued that it violated the rights of the states to control local affairs and their own political structures. They bitterly assailed Republicans for placing the Southern states under military control, even temporarily, after peace had been reestablished. They called for white supremacy, insisting that black Americans remain second-class citizens in both North and South, without political rights and subject to whatever laws states deemed appropriate.

In response, Republicans claimed credit for saving the Union and charged the Democrats with defeatism and pro-Southernism. They appealed to Americans' belief that all people were entitled to basic civil rights. They pointed out that black Southerners had remained loyal to the Union when Southern whites endorsed treason and that hundreds of thousands of black Americans had served in the Union army. They warned that most white Southerners had not yet accepted the results of the war and that renewed conflict was inevitable if the old Southern leaders returned to power without some political force in the Southern states to counteract them. They acted cautiously, imposing new constitutions on the South only after Southern intransigence forced them to do so. The

Republican arguments and approach had proven successful politically, leading to big victories in the congressional elections of 1866.

However, Americans were also concerned with other issues in the 1868 elections. Many were critical of postwar conservative economic and financial policies. During the war, the government had issued large numbers of legal-tender notes—paper money without gold to back it. After the war, the government began to withdraw this circulation in an effort slowly to put the currency back on a specie (gold and silver) basis. The resulting contraction of the currency led to an economic recession that was particularly painful in the South and the states west of Ohio, where money was needed to finance recovery and economic development. The situation was exacerbated by changes the government had made in the banking system and by a policy of repaying the money borrowed to finance the war in specie, even though it had often been lent in paper. The result of these policies was to increase taxes, raise prices on domestic and imported goods, and to drain money from the South and West to the North and East, because most of the banks in the new system were located there.

**The Parties.** These policies divided both the Republican and Democratic parties along regional lines. Influential Democrats and Republicans in the northeast, the Atlantic states, and in urban financial centers tended to favor them; Southern and western Republicans and Democrats vigorously opposed them. By 1867, many Democrats, especially in the West, wanted to make financial issues as important as the Reconstruction issue in the upcoming presidential election. They began to rally behind ex-Representative George H. Pendleton of Ohio, the Democratic vice presidential candidate in 1864, who advocated paying the national debt in paper money. Others favored Indiana Senator THOMAS A. HENDRICKS, who took a somewhat less radical position. Although they applauded President Johnson's denunciation of Republican Reconstruction policy, they blamed him for continuing conservative financial policies. Therefore, while Johnson wanted the Democratic nomination as a vindication of his course, hoping to combine Democratic backing with that of other conservatives, he could not secure western Democratic support.

These western Democrats were also among the most trenchant critics of Reconstruction and equal rights for African Americans. After Lincoln issued the EMANCIPATION PROCLAMATION, Pendleton had become a leader of the peace wing of the Democratic party. Republicans had denounced Democrats like him as unpatriotic COPPERHEADS. Many eastern Democrats, disliking Pend-

leton's position on financial issues, warned that no Peace Democrat could win the presidency in 1868.

But the conservative Democrats had no strong candidate to oppose Pendleton and Hendricks. Originally supportive of Johnson, they abandoned him as he alienated more and more Northern voters and refused to cooperate fully with the Democratic Party. Their strongest possibility, ex-Governor Horatio Seymour of New York, was vulnerable to the same charge of Copperheadism as Pendleton.

Although they disagreed about finances, Republicans were united in their desire to protect the results of their Reconstruction policy. But as of 1867 many Republicans wanted a more radical reconstruction of the South, the enfranchisement of black Americans in the North, and the impeachment of President Johnson. These RADICAL REPUBLICANS tended to favor SALMON P. CHASE of Ohio, the Chief Justice of the United States, or Ohio Senator Benjamin F. Wade, for the Republican presidential nomination. But more conservative Republicans feared that such radical policies would alienate too many voters and that such well-known radicals would prove unelectable. They favored the immensely popular Gen. Ulysses S. Grant, who was credited with winning the war and who appeared cautious and safe on Reconstruction issues. The state elections of 1867, in which Republicans lost ground to Democrats, confirmed their fears. The Grant candidacy boomed in the following months. By February 1868 his nomination was certain.

**The Nominees.** As Chase's chances for the Republican nomination faded, he became attractive to some of the conservative Democrats, especially in New York, who had earlier supported Johnson. Chase had been known for his Radical Republicanism, but he had become more critical of Republican Reconstruction. He was especially hostile to the use of the military to superintend Reconstruction; he worried that Republican policies were undermining state rights. He opposed the Republican effort to impeach Johnson in spring 1868, using his position as the presiding officer over the trial in the Senate to undermine the Republican position. He favored a general amnesty for all Southerners. He had long supported black suffrage, but because it clearly remained anathema to most Democrats, he told them that he was willing to let the individual states decide.

The nomination of Chase on the Democratic ticket promised a new departure for the party. It would neutralize the Copperhead charge and the taint of extreme racism, thereby allowing Democrats to appeal to floating voters and conservative Republicans unhappy with the more radical aspects of Republican

Reconstruction policy. Moreover, Chase was safe on financial questions. As Secretary of the Treasury under Lincoln, he himself had authored the financial policies eastern Democrats wanted to preserve.

The Republicans nominated Grant, as expected, at their national convention held in Chicago, 20 and 21 May 1868. The hard-fought vice presidential nomination went to Speaker of the House Schuyler Colfax of Indiana. The Republicans stressed their moderation, pronouncing Reconstruction complete for all practical purposes. The platform left the enfranchisement of black Americans outside the South up to the individual states. It remained largely silent on economic issues, promising tax reductions as soon as possible but hinting that the national debt should be repaid in specie. In his brief letter of acceptance, Grant appealed to Americans' desire to put the Civil War issues behind them. "Let us have peace," he urged.

The Democratic national convention met on 4 July in New York, where Democratic leaders maneuvered behind the scenes for Chase's nomination. The platform arraigned Republican Reconstruction policy but was ambiguous about the remedy. Instead it promised primarily to change national financial and economic policy. New York's Democratic leaders planned to prevent Pendleton from securing the two-thirds vote needed to win the nomination. At the right moment, they intended to bring Chase's name forward and stampede the convention in his favor. But when Pendleton's supporters saw that Pendleton could not succeed, they swung their support to New York's Seymour. New York delegates rushed to Seymour's support instead of bringing out Chase as planned, and Seymour swept to the nomination. To balance the ticket, the Democrats nominated ex-Missouri Congressman Francis Preston Blair, a strong Unionist who was known to take an extremely hard line against Republican Reconstruction policy.

**The Result.** The Democrats found themselves in a difficult position in the election. By nominating Seymour, they had abandoned the economic issues on which they might have appealed to western voters and the new departure that might have won over conservative Republicans. Many of Johnson's supporters formally announced for Grant, while the President remained silent. Matters worsened when a belligerent letter that Blair had written before his nomination appeared in the press. He opined that a Democratic President should declare Reconstruction null and void, order the army to disperse the Republican governments in the South, and let white Southerners reorganize new ones. Republicans effectively cited the so-called Brodhead Letter to prove that Grant was the candidate of peace while Seymour and Blair promised continued strife and instability. Democrats were unable to undo the damage.

Nonetheless, the election proved surprisingly close. Although Grant carried the North by almost the same margin as Lincoln had in 1864, Southern whites overwhelmingly backed the Democrats. The votes of black Southerners provided Grant's margin of victory in the popular vote. The Democrats won the electoral votes only of five Southern and border states, as well as New York, New Jersey, and Oregon.

The presidential election of 1868 amounted to a referendum on whether to accept the Republican Reconstruction program as a final settlement of the Civil War issues. The Republican victory in effect ratified the program and emboldened Congress to frame the Fifteenth Amendment, securing racially nondiscriminatory suffrage throughout the country, as a final measure. Although Democrats would soon regain power in the South, reducing and finally eliminating African American political power there, they would be forced to accept the principles of equal civil and political rights embodied in the Fourteenth and Fifteenth amendments before they could make a credible effort to regain the American presidency.

### BIBLIOGRAPHY

Benedict, Michael Les. *A Compromise of Principle: Congressional Republicans and Reconstruction, 1863–1869.* 1974.

Coleman, Charles H. *The Election of 1868: The Democratic Effort to Regain Control.* 1933.

Silbey, Joel H. *A Respectable Minority: The Democratic Party in the Civil War Era, 1860–1868.* 1977.

MICHAEL LES BENEDICT

**ELECTION, PRESIDENTIAL, 1872.** In the presidential election of 1872, the Republican candidates for President and Vice President, incumbent President Ulysses S. Grant and Massachusetts Senator HENRY WILSON, defeated HORACE GREELEY and B. Gratz Brown, the candidates of the Democratic and Liberal Republican parties, by 3,597,132 votes to 2,834,125. Grant received 286 electoral votes. Greeley died before the ELECTORAL COLLEGE cast its ballot. His electors divided 66 electoral votes among five candidates.

By electing Grant in 1868 the American people had clearly indicated a desire to treat CIVIL WAR issues as settled. This wish had created problems for both Democratic and Republicans political leaders, since the appeals of both parties had been based on their positions on issues that were now passé while they were divided on newly arising concerns.

**Republicans and Democrats.** Rival factions of the Republicans Party had begun maneuvering for influence with Grant and for control of the party immediately. On one side were leaders who had acquired power during the Civil War and RECONSTRUCTION—especially United States Senators who transformed their control over federal appointments into control over the parties of their states. They had achieved their positions by stressing sectional issues and were reluctant to give them up. Against these leaders stood other Republican politicians who had lost power as the Senators gained it—among them Congressmen, state governors, newspaper editors, and sometimes rival Senators. Allied with these dissidents were members of an intellectual elite who also felt frozen out of positions of influence.

Calling themselves reformers, these challengers charged that the established leaders concentrated on outmoded slavery and war-related issues and ignored important new questions. The reformers called for currency reform, by which they meant steadily reducing the amount of paper money in circulation until the United States was back on a specie (gold and silver) standard. They opposed government intervention in the economy—for example, regulation of railroad freight rates, the establishment of a ten-hour work day, and especially protective tariffs and other subsidies for industries. They urged reform of the CIVIL SERVICE by substituting merit for political considerations in making appointments and removals, in part because they wanted to undermine their opponents' control of the patronage but also because they believed that a modern, progressive society required expert civil servants.

The reformers recognized that as long as Civil War issues remained paramount, the established Republican leaders would retain their support among Republican voters. Therefore, they urged a policy of amnesty and forgiveness toward former Confederates and minimized reports of violence against former slaves and Republicans in the South. When this policy led most Southern Republicans, especially black Republicans, to ally with the established leadership, Republican reformers joined Democrats in a campaign to vilify Southern Republicans as corrupt "carpetbaggers" and "scalawags."

President Grant had at first sympathized with much of the reform program and had tried to avoid getting entangled in Republican factional politics. But by the summer of 1870 it had become clear that the Republican Party was drifting. Moreover, reformer-allied Liberal Republicans in the South were disrupting their fragile Republican parties so badly that Democrats were returning to power. As a result Grant came down firmly on the side of the regular party leadership, returning control of the patronage to them and endorsing legislation to stop anti-Republican violence in the South. By spring 1871 reform Republicans were in open revolt, charging Republican regulars with stirring up wartime hatreds and with fostering corruption in the civil service. Many of the leading Republican newspapers in the country openly opposed Grant's renomination. More and more dissident Republican politicians joined them, advocating currency, tariff, and especially CIVIL-SERVICE REFORM. They hoped for support not only from rank-and-file Republicans who agreed with them on reform issues but also from large numbers of German immigrant voters, who were alienated by Republicans' tendency to support the temperance movement and Democrats' sympathy for France in the recent Franco-Prussian War.

Democrats faced similar problems after 1868. They had rejected the opportunity to cut free of wartime issues in the election of that year. Many Democrats still bitterly opposed the enfranchisement of black voters in the South and tried strenuously to prevent the ratification of the Fifteenth Amendment, which barred racial discrimination in voting qualifications anywhere in the nation. But this stance enabled Republicans to continue to tie them to their pro-peace, racist wartime policies, and it prevented them from appealing to the dissatisfied Republicans.

Just as among Republicans, personal and factional ambitions played an important role. Longtime Democratic leaders with aspirations to the party's presidential nomination, such as Indiana Senator THOMAS A. HENDRICKS, Ohio Congressman George H. Pendleton, and New York Governor John T. Hoffman, were identified with the old issues and probably would have to give way to a reform Republican presidential candidate if the two groups coalesced. But as Republican divisions deepened, the temptation to modify old Democratic positions and ally with the reform Republicans increased. Finally, in May 1871 one of the best-known advocates of the hard-line Democratic position, Ohio's Clement L. Vallandigham, the leading Peace Democrat during the war, electrified Democrats by publicly advocating a "New Departure." Democrats bitterly debated the issue, but by spring 1872 the New Departure Democrats were clearly in the ascendant. Democrats grudgingly announced that they accepted the results of the war as embodied in the Thirteenth, Fourteenth, and Fifteenth amendments and would no longer contest the legitimacy of the Southern state governments reorganized under the Reconstruction Acts of Congress.

**The Reform Republicans.** This decision paved the way for an alliance between Democrats and dissident Republicans in the election of 1872. In January Missouri reform Republicans issued a call for a national convention of Liberal Republicans in Cincinnati, Ohio, to be held 1–3 May, well before either the Democratic or Republican conventions. The idea was to pressure one party or the other to accept the Liberal Republican candidate, although the chances of stopping Grant's renomination were already slim.

Many of the leading reformers hoped to nominate Charles Francis Adams, the scion of the great, conservative Massachusetts family. However, Adams had himself played almost no role in organizing opposition to Grant and remained aloof from politics. He might excite enthusiasm among the movement's intellectuals, but his cool demeanor rendered any wider appeal doubtful. Other reformers gravitated toward Illinois Senator Lyman Trumbull, whose commitment to state rights, dislike for regular Republican bosses in the Senate, and deteriorating political position in Illinois had led him into the reform camp. Others had smaller bases of support but could emerge as compromise candidates.

However, as May approached, two less acceptable candidates emerged. One was Supreme Court Justice David Davis, whose always active political cronies touted him as a friend of the working man. Shortly before the Cincinnati convention the judge's friends secured him the nomination of a small workingman's party. Since the Liberal Republican convention was to be open to any dissident Republican who chose to participate, many reformers feared that Davis's henchmen might flood the meeting.

Equally controversial was a growing movement to nominate Horace Greeley, fueled by his newspaper, the *New York Tribune*, the most important Republican journal in the country. Grant had alienated Greeley and his supporters in the New York Republican Party by giving control of federal patronage to Greeley's rival, Senator Roscoe Conkling. Greeley had been a longstanding supporter of amnesty for Confederate leaders and rapprochement with the South, but he had never been known as a friend of civil-service reform; among his political allies were some of the worst wire-pullers in New York. Worse, he was one of the most forceful advocates of a protective tariff in the country—a position that was anathema to many Democrats and nearly all the reform Republicans. Worst of all, he was one of the best-known advocates of temperance in the nation, sure to alienate the German-born voters the Liberal Republicans were courting.

On the other hand, the support of Greeley's *Tribune* and his still-powerful political organization in New York was tempting to the reform leaders. And Davis's drive for the nomination seemed more threatening. Therefore, despite anguished pleas from many reformers, key convention organizers admitted his representative into a conspiracy to attack Davis in the major reform newspapers and derail his candidacy. The price was to omit tariff reform from the Liberal Republican platform, which as a result stressed primarily civil-service reform and conciliation of the South.

The conspirators' plan succeeded in blocking Davis, but Greeley's henchmen then made a deal with the backers of Missouri's Governor B. Gratz Brown, who threw their support to Greeley. Greeley also picked up support from Southern delegates, who were far more attracted by Greeley's conciliatory Southern policy than they were by civil-service or other reforms. The balloting finally wound down to a contest between Adams and Greeley. In the end Greeley won, to the dismay of the convention leaders. The old editor had been a vigorous antislavery man and a somewhat utopian reformer all his life. Large numbers of Republicans regarded him with a bemused affection, while Adams seemed cold and aloof. Completing the deal, the convention nominated Brown for the vice presidency.

The Greeley nomination threw reform Republicans into serious disarray. Many refused to endorse him and reluctantly returned to the Republican fold. The German-American vote at best was split. Many Democrats found the nomination equally distasteful, and for a brief time resistance to coalition with the Liberal Republicans flared anew. Most Democratic leaders, however, concluded that to nominate their own candidate would merely split the anti-Grant vote. On July 9 and 10 the Democratic convention, meeting in Baltimore, nominated Greeley and Brown, and adopted the Liberal Republican platform word for word.

Meanwhile, Republicans had renominated Grant at their convention, held in Philadelphia 5 and 6 June, although they nominated Massachusetts Senator Henry Wilson for Vice President in place of the incumbent Schuyler Colfax. The platform praised the accomplishments of the Republican Party in general and the Grant administration in particular. It tried to offset the Liberal Republican-Democratic appeal by endorsing civil-service reform, amnesty for ex-Confederates, and STATES' RIGHTS.

**The Campaign.** Ironically, by nominating Greeley the Liberal Republicans had deprived themselves of nearly all the issues upon which they had attacked Grant and the Republicans. Greeley was even more clearly associated with the protective tariff than the Republicans were. His New York political organization was as corruption-riddled as any Republican machine and just as hungry for patronage. Although Greeley may have been somewhat more firmly committed to hard money (that is, specie-backed currency) than the Republicans, the Liberals and Democrats could not stress that issue because so many western Democrats favored paper money.

Ultimately, the main difference between Grant and Greeley turned out to be over how to treat the South, precisely where the Democrats were weakest and the Republicans strongest. Any criticism of Republican Southern policy by a Democratic-backed candidate reawakened Northern suspicions of Southern and Democratic intentions. This suspicion was exacerbated by congressional testimony about Southern Ku Klux Klan violence in 1871 that Republicans published through the summer of 1872.

As the campaign continued, the Democratic character of the Democratic-Liberal Republican coalition become more pronounced. The more the appeal of the Liberals to Republicans eroded, the more the Democrats insisted that they ought to control the nominations for local office. But this insistence led to further erosion, as more Republicans perceived the coalition as a mere cover for a Democratic resurgence.

In the summer of 1872, Republicans won local elections that foretold the result of the presidential election to follow. The enthusiasm of Democratic voters waned quickly, while most Republicans returned to the party fold. Many Democrats ultimately did not vote at all; a few voted for an ill-organized straight-out Democratic ticket. As a result Grant won the election easily.

The election of 1872 confirmed the power of the regular Republican leaders and the ability of war-related issues to mobilize the loyalty of Republican voters. It demonstrated to Democrats the necessity of jettisoning the old issues and turning to new ones, but at the same time it led them to conclude that this change had to be accomplished by the party itself; they abandoned the idea of formal coalitions with dissident Republicans.

## BIBLIOGRAPHY

Gerber, Richard Allen. "The Liberal Republicans in Historiographical Perspective." *Journal of American History* 62 (1975): 40–73.
Gillett, William. *Retreat from Reconstruction, 1869–1879.* 1979. Chapter 2, "Double Liability: The Presidential Campaign of 1872."
McGerr, Michael. "The Meaning of Liberal Republicanism. The Case of Ohio." *Civil War History* 28 (1982): 307–323.
Ross, Earle Dudley. *The Liberal Republican Movement.* 1919.

Sproat, John G. *"The Best Men": Liberal Reformers in the Gilded Age.* 1968.

MICHAEL LES BENEDICT

## ELECTION, PRESIDENTIAL, 1876.

**ELECTION, PRESIDENTIAL, 1876.** The election of 1876 and its resulting Compromise of 1877 mark the end of the Reconstruction era of United States history. They also ended the national government's first major effort to grant equal citizenship to African Americans.

**The Situation of the Parties.** The election occurred in the wake of a dramatic upsurge of Democratic voting that reduced previously overwhelming Republican majorities to an equal balance between the parties. The most important cause of this shift was the prolonged economic depression that began in the fall of 1873. Following an opportunistic strategy, the Democrats promised hard-pressed taxpayers honest and frugal government, temporarily allied with midwestern farmer parties seeking railroad regulation, and mobilized German voters against Republican-sponsored temperance legislation. In 1874 the Democrats captured several governorships and won control of the House of Representatives for the first time since the elections of 1856.

The most significant result of the Democratic landslide of 1874 was the election of Samuel J. Tilden to the governorship in New York. Long a party workhorse, Tilden had become one of America's wealthiest men, largely by refinancing bankrupt railroads and marketing corporate securities. Cold and aloof but fiercely ambitious and egotistical, Tilden entered office determined to rejuvenate the Democratic Party by cutting the taxes of depression-pressed voters. Tilden immediately attacked and destroyed his state's Canal Ring, a combination of contractors and state legislators who rigged bids to repair the state's canal system. Tilden's strategy was to divert attention from the issues of Reconstruction and to make the Democratic Party the party of inexpensive government.

The depression, however, bedeviled Tilden and his party over the currency issue. Long a supporter of "hard money" and an opponent of the greenback paper currency, Tilden was horrified when several midwestern Democrats, led by Governor William Allen of Ohio, advocated expanding the paper issues to combat hard times. When Allen ran for reelection that fall, many Ohio Democrats accused Tilden and other New Yorkers of secretly aiding his opponent, Rutherford B. Hayes. Allen's narrow defeat did not quiet the issue but shifted inflationist leadership to Indiana's governor Thomas A. Hendricks. When the

Democratic-controlled House convened in December 1875, Tilden's supporters were able to counter Hendricks and the inflationists by electing to the speakership Michael Kerr, an Indiana Congressman who opposed the greenbacks.

Further weakening the Republicans was the decline of the party's southern wing. By 1873, in states where the African American vote was too small to make a Republican majority, the Democratic Party had won control. In the remaining states Democrats adopted a "white line" strategy to "draw the color line in politics" and to use violence and threats of violence against all Republicans. In 1874 these tactics brought Democratic victories in Arkansas and Alabama, leaving only Mississippi, Louisiana, Florida, and South Carolina in Republican hands.

In previous years the national Republicans had countered Democratic terrorism with federal intervention. Now, however, they acquiesced in such tactics. In December of 1874, Congress convened for the last time that decade with the Republicans in control of both Houses and the presidency. Frustrated by years of political disorder in the southern states and morally weakened by racist suspicions that African Americans were incapable of honest and efficient government, Republicans believed the time had come to make concessions to southern whites, especially those of "property and education." When, on request of the Louisiana Republican Party, federal troops entered the lower house of the state legislature and removed several Democratic members who themselves had been seated by force, a hostile northern outcry forced the national Republicans to arrange a compromise that returned the house to the Democrats. Subsequently, the Republicans refused to intervene in Arkansas, where the Democrats took complete control. Congress did pass the broad CIVIL RIGHTS ACT OF 1875 that forbade discrimination in public facilities but left it to individuals to enforce their rights by suing in the federal courts.

In 1874, the Republicans had been seriously split on the currency issue when Congress had voted to increase the greenback circulation and President Ulysses S. Grant had vetoed the bill. Hoping to reconcile their divergent interests, the Republican majority passed the Resumption Act, which promised to redeem the greenbacks in gold on 1 January 1879, while permitting an indefinite expansion of national bank notes.

Taken together, the Republican decisions to accommodate southern whites rather than to employ national power to protect southern blacks, to enact symbolic and ineffectual civil rights legislation, and to mollify business interests with the hard-money Re-

sumption Act constituted a compromise of 1875 that pointed in the direction of the more dramatic compromise two years later. Events later that year further shaped the presidential election. In the Ohio gubernatorial contest, Rutherford B. Hayes, a Republican Party regular, won, campaigning against state support for Roman Catholic schools and paper money. Warned that further intervention in the South would doom Hayes's gubernatorial candidacy, the Grant administration permitted the Republican government in Mississippi to fall to Democratic terrorism. Hayes's victory seemed to justify the strategy of nonintervention and also made the governor presidential timber.

**The Conventions.** Public discontent with Republican scandal and corruption further boosted Hayes's prospects. By early 1876 several members of Grant's Cabinet had resigned under charges of corruption, as had the President's private secretary. To counter this image and the popularity of Democratic reformers like Tilden, many Republicans wanted to nominate a candidate with a reputation for honesty. Two likely candidates were Grant's Secretary of the Treasury Benjamin H. Bristow and Governor Hayes, whose life and administration reflected only the smooth, bland surfaces of middle-class respectability. The reformers especially hoped to defeat the candidacy of Speaker of the House JAMES G. BLAINE, who was discovered to have helped certain railroads obtain land grants in return for various financial benefits. The revelations, however, did not cause Blaine to withdraw, and he entered the convention leading in delegate support.

But Blaine was only one of several hopefuls as the Republican convention opened in Cincinnati on 14 June. For the first time since 1860 the Republicans had neither an incumbent nor a popular military hero to preempt their nomination. Other challengers included Senator Roscoe Conkling, whose strength rested on the patronage he controlled in New York, and Senator Oliver P. Morton of Indiana, who was strong in the southern states. Secretary Bristow, who came from Kentucky, was popular in his area and among Republican reformers.

Blaine led the early balloting but could get no closer than seventy votes of the nomination. Ultimately, however, Blaine was defeated not by the softness of his support but by the animosities of his rivals. When the Speaker's vote gained early on the seventh ballot, Morton, Bristow, and Conkling all withdrew in favor of Hayes, who quickly picked up the extra votes needed for victory. The convention balanced the ticket regionally by nominating Senator WILLIAM WHEELER of New York for Vice President. The platform and Hayes's acceptance letter stressed honest government, hard money, and an end to conflict in the South: the compromise formula of 1875. The anti-Catholic theme of Hayes's gubernatorial race appeared in a plank supporting a constitutional amendment to deny public funds to any school "under sectarian control."

On 27 June, the Democratic national convention assembled in St. Louis. From his base in New York, Tilden had assiduously courted delegates at county and state conventions, especially in the South, and by convention time his organization had created an impression of his invincibility. On the first ballot Tilden received 400½ of the 491 required with his closest challenger, Hendricks, at 140. The second ballot put Tilden within 12 votes of the nomination and occasioned switches that put him over the top.

Like the Republicans the previous year, the Democrats strove to resolve their differences over the currency issue. After all-night wrangling, the resolutions committee proposed a plank that bowed to the inflationists by proposing to postpone the date upon which the Resumption Act would take effect. The Tilden men accepted this deviation from financial orthodoxy and offered another concession to the inflationists by nominating Hendricks for Vice President. In July, Tilden and Hendricks met at Saratoga Springs, New York, and issued statements that papered over their differences.

The move of the major parties toward hard money highlighted the appeal of the National GREENBACK PARTY, which in May had nominated the eighty-five-year-old New York philanthropist Peter Cooper on a platform that called for repeal of the Resumption Act and the issue of paper currency backed by United States bonds. Although they would receive less than 1 percent of the popular vote, the Greenbackers held the balance in the crucial state of Indiana.

**A Disputed Election.** The November balloting produced one of the closest and certainly most controversial results in United States history. Tilden received a majority of the popular vote (considerably enlarged by Democratic intimidation of African American voters in the southern states). But the United States' system of electing a President had always held out the possibility that the winner of the popular vote might not win the ELECTORAL COLLEGE vote, which awarded all of a state's electoral votes to the largest vote-getter in that state only. Careful checking by Republicans in New York City showed that Hayes might yet win if he could carry South Carolina, Florida, and Louisiana (the three southern states still under Republican control). Instructions went out to the southern Republican regimes, which controlled the vote count, to "hold your state."

In the three weeks between the popular voting and the casting of the Electoral College vote, the parties fought furiously over the contested states. Students of the election, attempting to balance Republican manipulation of the vote counting against Democratic violence and intimidation against Republican voters have concluded that a fair count would probably have elected Tilden; a free vote would have elected Hayes. In the end Republican and Democratic electors cast separate ballots in their states and dispatched competing sets of electoral votes to Washington. At issue were twenty electoral votes, all of which Hayes needed in order to have a one-vote majority, 185 to 184, over Tilden.

In South Carolina and Louisiana the parties set up rival governors and legislatures. When Congress convened in December, separate returns had also arrived from Oregon, where Hayes had won a majority but the Democratic governor had appointed a Democratic elector on the death of a Republican elector. The Constitution did not specify how to deal with such a situation and Congress, divided between a Democratic House and a Republican Senate, was temporarily stalemated. Certain spokesmen for both parties advocated force or threats of force, and the fierce partisanship of the average voter might well have enlisted behind such a call. But neither Hayes, Tilden, nor Grant was inclined to risk civil conflict and their views were supported by the nation's major commercial interests.

From these leadership groups emerged three approaches to settle the election peacefully. Tilden compiled legal precedents to show that the House should count the electoral ballots for President, which would either elect him outright or disqualify the contested votes and elect him by a vote of the House itself. He undermined his cause, however, by advising the House Democrats simply to debate until the Republicans gave in, worrying many party leaders that so passive a strategy would give the Republicans a chance to steal the election. Friends of Hayes hoped to crack the House Democratic majority by promising southern Democrats patronage and economic subsidies (most notably a federal grant to a Texas & Pacific Railroad that would run from Marshall, Texas, to San Diego, California). Before the plans of either could mature, however, moderates of both parties produced a bill to establish an ELECTORAL COMMISSION to count the vote. The commission was to contain five Senators, five Representatives, and five Supreme Court Justices. The bill's sponsors assumed that seven would be Republicans, seven Democrats, and one independent, presumably Justice David B. Davis. But just before Davis was offered the position, the Illinois legislature elected him to the United States Senate. The position then went to Justice Joseph P. Bradley. When the commission considered the disputed returns, Bradley voted in every case with the Republicans and for the election of Hayes.

This result was a major embarrassment to the Democrats, who had supported the commission believing it would surely elect Tilden. In their frustration, rage, and confusion some House Democrats threatened to filibuster against completing the electoral count. Nervousness about this possibility caused certain Ohio Republicans to renew their promises of patronage and economic favors to the South and to promise that Hayes would recognize the Democratic regimes in South Carolina and Louisiana. Eager to profit from a hopeless situation, the Democrats accepted the assurances, thus completing the Compromise of 1877. The commission's report was received and Hayes was peacefully inaugurated.

The election of 1876 and the Compromise of 1877 that completed the count accomplished the transition from the politics of Reconstruction. Hayes recognized the Democratic governments in South Carolina and Louisiana, appointed former Democrats and Republican reformers to his Cabinet, and was soon embroiled in PATRONAGE battles with disappointed Republican factions. The voting patterns of the election persisted into the 1880s and created a stalemate between the major parties. From time to time Republicans paid lip service to supporting equal rights for African Americans but in practice respected white home rule in the South. The nation's next crusade on behalf of its disadvantaged citizens would advocate regulating big business and would take place in an era of racial segregation.

### BIBLIOGRAPHY

Hoogenboom, Ari. *The Presidency of Rutherford B. Hayes.* 1988.
Polakoff, Keith Ian. *The Politics of Inertia.* 1973.
Woodward, C. Vann. *Reunion and Reaction.* 1951.

GEORGE MCJIMSEY

**ELECTION, PRESIDENTIAL, 1880.** Residual issues and personalities from the CIVIL WAR and RECONSTRUCTION dominated political rhetoric as the election of 1880 approached. But the United States was in a major transition from a society based on agricultural and extractive economics and small-town culture to one resting on industrialism and urban life. Every year more Americans lived in cities or large towns and worked in shops and factories. Whatever their ideals and collective memories, voters faced a new kind of politics based on issues arising from that industrialization.

Party politics naturally faced both backward and forward. It had been a mere twenty years since SECESSION, fifteen since the end of the war, and four since the disputed election of 1876, which had signaled that Reconstruction was over. Both parties had sectional bases, the Democrats in the South, the Republicans in New England and the old Northwest. The electoral battleground was in the states stretching from New Jersey to Illinois. The Republicans, as a new party, feared losing the presidency and its national power and symbolism. The Democrats needed to win the office to regain their respectability and national appeal.

**The Republican Nominee.** A large minority of Republicans favored former President Ulysses S. Grant as their convention approached in 1880. Major party leaders such as Senators Roscoe Conkling of New York, Don Cameron of Pennsylvania, and John A. Logan of Illinois supported him. Whatever the failings of his administration, Grant represented authority and remained a powerful emotional force to Republican voters. His world travels after leaving the presidency had supposedly fitted him to be President again. If his managers could adopt a unit rule at the convention, by which a majority of a state's delegates determined the state's entire vote, Grant might easily win the 379 votes needed for the nomination. Critics saw the Grant movement as a return to the past at a moment when the party needed to chart new territory and doubted that he could ever be a successful President. They also attacked the idea of a third term for anyone. Liberal Republicans, who had bolted to form a separate ticket in 1872 because they disliked Grant's apparent opposition to reforming the federal CIVIL SERVICE, might bolt again. A divided party could not win.

Senator JAMES G. BLAINE of Maine, who had sought the nomination in 1876, attracted Republicans who wanted a new party program. While he was popular with many younger Republicans, Blaine never shook off an aura of unethical conduct in Congress. The party's safest candidate was Secretary of the Treasury JOHN SHERMAN of Ohio, famous for his mastery of complex financial policies. But his inability to please both hard- and soft-money elements and his forbidding personality prevented Sherman from developing wide appeal.

The convention, held in Chicago in June, rejected the unit rule, leaving Grant a few votes short of victory, and deadlocked. After many verbal pyrotechnics, the meeting turned to the former Congressman and newly elected Senator from Ohio, James A. Garfield. To soothe the Grant element, the Garfield managers chose Chester A. Arthur of New York for the vice presidential slot. The platform was circumspect and moderate on most issues, including CIVIL-SERVICE REFORM and MONETARY POLICY, and favored tariff protection, a long-standing party policy.

**The Democratic Nominee.** The Democrats faced a similar situation. A few diehards wished to renominate SAMUEL J. TILDEN of New York, the defeated candidate in 1876. Tilden played something of a guessing game with the party, but his age and health worked against a nomination. So did his role in apparently trying to bargain for the presidency in 1876, as a series of congressional investigations had revealed after 1877. Few Democrats wanted to risk another bitter personal campaign and disputed election.

The next most prominent contender for the Democratic nomination was Senator Thomas F. Bayard of Delaware, noted for his stand in favor of hard money and for general probity in politics. This spotless record appealed to those who wished to move beyond war issues to a campaign emphasizing a new departure. But, somewhat like the Republican Sherman, Bayard seemed aloof and detached, a statesman rather than a politician with whom voters might identify. Senator Allen G. Thurman of Ohio was a remote possibility, though he lacked a significant base beyond his own state.

The chief outsider, or DARK HORSE, was Gen. WINFIELD HANCOCK, nominally from Pennsylvania but stationed in New York in 1880. He was attractive to southerners because he had been a lenient military governor in Texas and Louisiana during Reconstruction. Northern Democrats saw him as someone who might harmonize intraparty factions in New York and the Midwest. Above all, he had taken no debatable stands on any issues. The Democratic national convention, held in Cincinnati in late June, chose Hancock on the second ballot and named William H. English of the crucial state of the Indiana as the vice presidential candidate.

THIRD PARTIES did not play an important role in 1880, but their rhetoric and platforms foreshadowed campaigns to come. The most prominent of these was the GREENBACK PARTY, which stood for an expanded currency and moderate inflation to help indebted farmers and for government regulation of the railroads and the workplace. It named Congressman JAMES WEAVER of Iowa for President and B. J. Chambers of Texas for Vice President. The PROHIBITION PARTY, dedicated to banning liquor as a means of transforming society, named Neal Dow of Maine for President and A. M. Thompson of Ohio for Vice President.

**The Campaign.** In the late nineteenth century, presidential campaigns were run from state organizations, with national committees acting as coordinators and fund-raisers. This accommodated local issues and made state leaders important in any elected administration. A national campaign promoted a set of large ideals and programs in the party's name and covered the dangers in local issues with an appealing candidate. Such an effort required a great deal of money, which was not readily available. Assessments against federal officeholders, along with gifts from candidates' friends and supporters, were the traditional source of campaign funds. Business contributions were not yet large in 1880. The amounts raised and spent were minuscule by later standards, and, contrary to popular belief, the money was not generally used to buy votes, though this did happen in both parties. Most campaign funds disappeared very quickly to pay for speakers, for organized events such as mass meetings and parades, and especially to meet the voracious demand for printed matter and newspaper coverage. The electorate was interested, read and listened to party messages, and wanted to participate where possible, all of which cost campaign organizations money.

The campaign of 1880 was thus as intense and partisan as any previous campaign. Garfield hoped to remain at his farm in Mentor, Ohio, aloof from intraparty battles while the organizations made their bids. He stood for something new in Republican politics—a general emphasis on youth, recent experience that was relevant to national problems, and some concern for industrial issues. Hancock clearly proposed to say little (and certainly nothing inflammatory), to appear unifying, and to hope for the best.

Two incidents altered these plans and revealed the power of the unexpected in politics. The Republicans gradually began to emphasize tariff protection as their major issue in order to capture votes from varied business and labor interests that feared foreign competition. Hancock and the Democrats hoped to avoid this divisive issue. Democrats generally, though not always, opposed protection, and their 1880 platform called for "a tariff for revenue only," an opaque phrase that upset some normally Democratic business elements. To calm such fears, Hancock said in an October newspaper interview that he favored reasonable protection and saw the tariff as a legitimate way to raise federal revenue, and he declared that "the tariff question is a local question." There was some truth in the observation, since a multitude of local interests combined to create a national party stand. But the remark made Hancock seem ignorant about this major issue. The Republicans quickly used this slip to denigrate him as a potential national leader. The second incident was a classic instance of the DIRTY TRICKS so common in American politics, especially in a negative campaign. In late October, the *New York Truth*, a noted scandal sheet despite its name, printed a letter supposedly from Garfield to one H. L. Morey, a Massachusetts businessman, dated 23 January 1880 and written on House of Representatives stationery. The letter stated that Garfield accepted the immigration of cheap Chinese labor and assumed that employers would hire as cheaply as they could. If true, these views would cost Garfield votes, perhaps the election, especially in California, which had a long-standing antipathy to Chinese immigration. Garfield delayed denouncing the letter until 23 October, chiefly to check his office files to make sure that a clerk had not sent such a missive. There was no H. L. Morey; the letter was a forgery.

**The Result.** All parties recognized the close balance in American politics, and the outcome of the voting on 2 November seemed uncertain to the end. Some 78.4 percent of eligible voters (that is, white males over twenty-one years of age) cast ballots and gave Garfield the victory. But the popular returns were indeed close, with a mere seven thousand out of 10 million votes separating the two major party candidates nationally. The votes were distributed for a sound ELECTORAL COLLEGE win, however: 214 votes for Garfield to 155 for Hancock, who carried the now-solid South. Garfield carried every northern state except New Jersey, and Nevada and California. New York made the difference and could have given the victory to either candidate. The 300,000 Greenback votes were not critical, but if the Greenback votes cast in Indiana had all gone to Hancock, he would have won that state. If Garfield had polled them in New Jersey and California, he would have carried those states. The Prohibitionists received a mere ten thousand votes.

Hancock awoke the morning after the election to hear his wife say, "It has been a complete Waterloo for you." The exhausted candidate replied, "That is all right. I can stand it," and went back to sleep. And for Garfield victory hardly brought unmixed joy. A note of resignation if not of sadness entered his private musings: "I close the year with a sad conviction that I am bidding goodbye to private life and to a long series of happy years which I fear terminate in 1880." He was correct, for he faced bitter personal wrangling in forming an administration. CHARLES GUITEAU shot the new President in July 1881, and Garfield died that September. Chester A. Arthur filled out almost an entire term.

The contest of 1880 was dramatic and anxiety laden for its protagonists as well as for the voters. It began with residual war issues and personalities but ended with an emphasis on the tariff question. The Republican failure to win any southern electoral votes also compelled the party to abandon efforts at Reconstruction and to develop a constituency based in industrial strongholds.

### BIBLIOGRAPHY

Clancey, Herbert J. *The Presidential Election of 1880.* 1958.
Morgan, H. Wayne. *From Hayes to McKinley: National Party Politics 1877–1896.* 1969.
Peskin, Allan. *Garfield.* 1978.
Reeves, Thomas C. *Gentleman Boss: The Life of Chester A. Arthur.* 1975.

H. WAYNE MORGAN

**ELECTION, PRESIDENTIAL, 1884.** The election of America's twenty-second President was one of the most bitter, scandal-ridden contests in the history of the presidency. During the campaign, the leading political issues of the Gilded Age—tariff, currency, and CIVIL SERVICE REFORM, labor unrest, Chinese exclusion, and control of the public utilities—were overshadowed by sensational disclosures about the candidates' loose morals and crooked financial dealings. When the orgy of mudslinging was over, the governor of New York had clinched a narrow victory for the DEMOCRATIC PARTY, exiling the Republicans from the White House for the first time since the CIVIL WAR.

**The Candidates.** No fewer than seven candidates, representing the REPUBLICAN PARTY, Democratic Party, Temperance Party, GREENBACK PARTY, PROHIBITION Party, Equal Rights Party, American Party, and American Prohibition National Party, vied for the presidency in 1884. The campaign, however, boiled down to a bitter contest between Stephen Grover Cleveland, a forty-eight-year-old lawyer from Buffalo, New York, and his Republican opponent, JAMES G. BLAINE of Augusta, Maine.

Blaine was one of the best-known politicians of his time. Blessed with a magnetic personality, a gift for speechifying, a powerful pen, and a razor-sharp wit, Blaine was a veteran of political experience and a fixture on Capitol Hill. Elected to Congress in 1862, he served in Washington, D.C., as a Representative, Speaker of the House, Secretary of State, and Senator—a career recounted in his massive two-volume history *Twenty Years of Congress*. Though his party nominated him only once for the presidency, Blaine—who was dubbed the "Plumed Knight" by Robert G. Ingersoll at the 1876 Republican national convention—was a formidable presence in national politics and a viable nominee at all Republican conventions from 1876 through 1892. Cleveland, by contrast, had never visited Washington and was virtually unknown outside of his home state of New York. Born in 1837, he was a stern, bull-necked bachelor whose 240-pounds would make him the nation's heftiest President until the election in 1908 of the 340-pound William Howard Taft.

Cleveland began his political career as a ward supervisor in Buffalo, New York. During the Civil War, he accepted a patronage appointment as assistant district attorney and in 1870 was elected sheriff of Erie County, New York. In 1881, he was elected mayor of Buffalo, and in 1882 became governor of the Empire State. Though bereft of Blaine's political expertise, Cleveland had something the Plumed Knight lacked: a reputation for honesty and political integrity. These qualities were coveted in post-Civil War America, a nation wracked by corruption, fraud, bribery, favoritism, and PATRONAGE at all levels of government. As governor, Cleveland won acclaim from CIVIL SERVICE reformers—middle-class and mainly Protestant Americans who aspired to clean government of corruption—by making appointments based on merit, vetoing bills that would have misappropriated public funds, and blocking the nomination of Tammany Hall candidates for state office.

Blaine, for his part, was seen as a quintessential spoilsman. His reputation had been tarnished in 1876, when the Democratic Party revealed the so-called Mulligan Letters, documents that linked Blaine, who was then Speaker of the House, with the granting of congressional favors to the Little Rock and Fort Smith Railroad. Although Blaine proclaimed his innocence in a histrionic appeal from the floor of the House, the affair cost him the presidential nomination in 1876 and 1880. By 1884, however, many in the Republican Party had come to believe that the Plumed Knight's time had come. He was finally nominated in June at the Republican national convention in Chicago, along with running mate, Sen. John A. Logan.

Blaine's nomination split the Republican Party. "Mugwumps"—gentlemen reformers who viewed Blaine as a font of corruption—repudiated the party's nominee and threw their support to Cleveland. Their decision divided friends and families. Henry Ward Beecher, the famous minister of Brooklyn's Plymouth Congregational Church, backed Cleveland, but his sister, Harriet Beecher Stowe, the author of *Uncle Tom's Cabin*, stood firm for Blaine. Mark Twain tried to convince the novelist William Dean Howells to abandon Blaine, but the author declined, as did many Republicans who, like Sen. George F. Hoar of Massachusetts, considered the renegades "the vilest set of political assassins that ever disgraced this or any other country."

Blaine's popularity among Irish Americans further ruptured the Republicans. Seen as a friend of Catholics for his anti-British stance as Secretary of State, Blaine was shunned by many nativist Yankees who saw in his nomination what the *Springfield Republican* called the "Pope's toe moving toward the presidential mahogany."

The Democratic Party also faced challenges from within. At the party's national convention, also held in Chicago, the Cleveland forces locked horns with representatives of Tammany Hall, Irish Americans who viewed Cleveland's penchant for civil service reform as a plot to deprive Irish Catholics of patronage jobs. The party's rural, middle class, and largely Protestant delegates, however, distrusted Irish Catholic immigrants, despised their urban political machine, and viewed Cleveland as the party's ticket to the White House. Accordingly, the party nominated Cleveland for President on 11 July, and chose THOMAS A. HENDRICKS of Indiana as his running mate.

**The Campaigns.** The two candidates mounted very different campaigns. Cleveland made only two public appearances during the campaign, in Newark, New Jersey, and Hartford, Connecticut, where he stressed civil service reform, tax reduction, and labor issues. Blaine, meanwhile, undertook an unprecedented whirlwind tour of the country, delivering more than four hundred speeches about protectionism, a sound currency, the reconstructed South, and the virtues of agriculture.

Issues, however, would be buried by sensational newspaper reports about sexual impropriety and political misconduct. The campaign's first bombshell exploded on 21 July, when the Buffalo *Evening Telegraph* reported that Cleveland had had an affair with a Buffalo widow, Maria Halpin, and that a son, who was alleged to be his, had been born on 14 September 1874. Republicans quickly seized on the story in an effort to transform Cleveland's image as a man of virtue into that of a scoundrel who had violated the mores of Victorian America. The *New York Sun* branded him as a "coarse debauchee who might bring harlots to the White House," while Republican cartoons showed a confounded Cleveland covering his ears as a distraught baby screamed "I WANT MY PA!" More damaging were the lyrics of a Republican campaign song:

Ma! Ma! Where's my pa?
    Gone to the White House,
    Ha! Ha! Ha!

Cleveland responded with candor. He admitted paternity, declared that he had supported the child, and had helped Halpin set up a business. "Whatever you say," Cleveland wired his anxious campaign managers, "tell the truth." His policy of full disclosure accorded with Cleveland's reputation for honesty and may have left him a stronger, if chastened, candidate.

Blaine's fall from grace began on 15 September, when the *Boston Journal* published a new series of "Mulligan Letters," missives that Blaine had written in 1876 to the Boston firm that handled his questionable railroad stock transactions. On the back of one of the letters, Blaine had scrawled "Burn This Letter"—an unheeded order that found a comfortable home in Democratic songsters:

Blaine, Blaine, James G. Blaine
     The Continental Liar from the State of Maine,
     Burn this Letter!

The news wreaked havoc on Blaine's campaign. Cartoonists, such as Thomas Nast, had a field day, portraying Blaine as a crook who could not be trusted with the nation's highest office. Newspapers, such as the *New York Times*, joined the fray, calling Blaine "a prostitutor of public trusts, a scheming jobber and a reckless falsifier." No charge, it seemed, was too outrageous. One Democratic paper charged that Blaine was anti-Catholic, even though his mother adhered to the faith and his sister was a nun. Even physicians were quoted as saying that Blaine suffered from palsy, leprosy, insanity, and a host of other ailments.

Both campaigns continued in spectacular fashion despite bad press. Hundreds of men showed up at a Blaine rally in New York, wearing papier-mâché suits of armor and waving tall plumes and swords. When Cleveland returned to Buffalo at the end of the campaign, *Harper's Weekly* observed that he was greeted with an enormous parade in which "all the principal streets of the city were decorated with flags, transparencies, and pictures of the Governor. Chinese lanterns were burning all over the front of many buildings and upon ropes stretched from one building to another across the streets. The scene was such as had never been witnessed before in Buffalo."

During the final week of the campaign, Blaine committed a number of tactical blunders which may have cost him the election. At a meeting of Protestant clergymen in New York's Fifth Avenue Hotel, the Reverend Samuel D. Burchard of the Murray Hill Presbyterian Church described the Democratic Party, in Blaine's presence, as the party of "Rum, Romanism, and Rebellion." Exhausted after his tour of the country, Blaine failed to distance himself from this expression of anti-Catholic prejudice, an error that may have sent thousands of Irish voters back to the Democratic Party.

Blaine's image was further tarnished when, six days before the election, he joined Jay Gould, Russell Sage, John Jacob Astor, Andrew Carnegie, and other millionaires for a banquet at Delmonico's, an opulent New York restaurant. The next day, the *New York World* insinuated that Blaine was indifferent to poverty and unemployment when it ran a front page cartoon headlined "The Royal Feast of Belshazzar Blaine and the Money Kings." The accompanying story described the soiree as "a merry banquet," where "champagne frothed and brandy sparkled in glasses that glittered like jewels."

**The Result.** Over 10 million Americans went to the polls on 4 November 1884 in one of the closest elections in American history. Cleveland won by a margin of only 23,005 popular votes, garnering 4,874,986 votes to Blaine's 4,851,981. The Democrat carried nineteen states, capturing the South, the border states of Delaware, Kentucky, Maryland, Missouri, West Virginia, and New Jersey, as well as Indiana and Connecticut. Blaine carried eighteen states.

The outcome was determined in New York State, where Cleveland edged Blaine by only 1,149 popular votes—enough for Cleveland to capture the state's 36 electoral votes, and enough for him to squeeze out a 219 to 182 victory in the ELECTORAL COLLEGE. If Blaine had gained just 600 more votes in New York, he would have won the White House. Pondering his defeat, the Plumed Knight would later write: "I should have carried New York by 10,000 if the weather had been clear on election day and Dr. Burchard had been doing missionary work in Asia Minor or Cochin China."

The presidential election of 1884 was a political slugfest of unprecedented bitterness, in which mudslinging preempted serious and sustained discussion of political issues. It thus prefigured the negative campaigns of the late twentieth century, in which candidates' personalities and peccadilloes were subjected to more scrutiny than their political beliefs. The contest also marked a departure from a time-honored tradition in which presidential candidates refrained from speaking or actively soliciting public support for themselves during campaigns. With the exception of William Henry Harrison, who took to the stump during the log-cabin and hard-cider election of 1840, and Stephen A. Douglas, Abraham Lincoln's chief rival in 1860, most presidential candidates preferred to remain silent during campaigns. Blaine, however, broke this pattern in 1884, setting out on a massive tour of the country in an effort to clear his name. His mission was ultimately unsuccessful, but his strategy of taking the election to the people would set a precedent for personal campaigning that would be repeated several years later by the "Great Commoner," WILLIAM JENNINGS BRYAN and that perpetual campaigner, Theodore Roosevelt.

Finally, 1884 marked a subtle turning point in the organization of presidential campaigns. Although the campaign of 1884 boasted brass bands, torchlight parades, and other popular rituals, party leaders were beginning to pay less attention to pomp and parades and more attention to strengthening their organizations, appealing to voters, and educating the electorate. This new emphasis, which was just beginning to crystallize in 1884, would later transform the American presidential campaign into a highly managed and professional operation—one that bore little resemblance to the rip-roaring festivals of popular democracy that characterized the Gilded Age.

### BIBLIOGRAPHY

Brown, Thomas N. *Irish-American Nationalism, 1870–1890*. 1966.

Hirsch, Mark G. "Election of 1884." In vol. 2 of *History of American Presidential Elections, 1789–1968*. Edited by Arthur M. Schlesinger, Jr., and Fred C. Israel. 4 vols. 1971.

Keller, Morton. *Affairs of State: Public Life in Late Nineteenth Century America*. 1977.

McFarland, Gerald W. *Mugwumps, Morals and Politics, 1884–1920*. 1975.

McGerr, Michael E. *The Decline of Popular Politics: The American North, 1865–1928*. 1986.

Melder, Keith. *Hail to the Candidate: Presidential Campaigns From Banners to Broadcasts*. 1992.

Morgan, H. Wayne. *From Hayes to McKinley: National Party Politics, 1877-1896*. 1969.

Nevins, Allan, ed., *Letters of Grover Cleveland, 1850–1908*. 1933.

MARK G. HIRSCH

**ELECTION, PRESIDENTIAL, 1888.** Although the presidential election of 1888 occurred amid the partisan fervor that characterized the post-RECONSTRUCTION United States, it was perhaps the least frenzied of the quadrennial contests. The Republic faced no major threats, internal or external, CIVIL WAR passions had become muted, and both parties' candidates were stolid, conservative, and basically unexciting. The gap between the two major parties was so narrow throughout this period that the outcome of the voting in a couple of key states, such as New York and Indiana, could throw the national victory to one party or the other. Campaigning and attention focused on these swing states, so it was hardly surprising that the major parties' presidential candidates hailed from New York and Indiana.

**The Democratic Incumbent.** The New Yorker was the Democratic incumbent, President Grover Cleveland. Few had doubted that Cleveland would run for reelection in 1888. He had gained a national reputation as a reform governor of the Empire State and had been the candidate of a united party in 1884. In that year, he had won in an extremely close race over the Republican candidate, JAMES G. BLAINE, in a contest remarkable, even in an era of unrestrained partisanship, for its mudslinging and personal attacks. Cleveland was the first Democrat to capture the White House after the Civil War, and his election helped complete the reintegration of the southern states into the Union. As President, Cleveland demonstrated forthrightness and lived up to his campaign promise to hold public office as a public trust.

He did break with precedent in 1887 when he devoted his entire STATE OF THE UNION MESSAGE to the tariff. The U.S. Treasury annually amassed tens of millions of dollars more than it was authorized to spend, and the President favored lowering the high customs duties on many imports to eliminate the surplus. His call for prudent reductions in the tariff schedules failed to move Congress that summer. The Republicans could not have been happier with Cleveland's stance and with his party's failure to enact legislation. They portrayed Cleveland and Democrats in general as advocates of free trade—an extreme position that very few Democrats considered wise and one that Cleveland certainly did not favor.

The incumbent did almost nothing to enhance his position during the presidential campaign, confining his personal electioneering to writing a formal letter accepting his party's nomination by acclamation and a few private letters that were later publicized. A seasoned but aging and very weary warhorse—the vice presidential candidate, Allen G. Thurman of Ohio—was left to do the ticket's active campaigning. The management of the DEMOCRATIC PARTY under William H. Barnum and Calvin S. Brice was equally uninspired. Cleveland apparently believed that the leadership of these two businessmen would reassure those who feared he would undermine the protective tariff edifice that had existed largely unchanged since the passage of high import taxes during the Civil War. The Democratic candidate, the PARTY PLATFORM, and the campaign thus provided the opposition with an ideal issue for the 1888 contest, one that any prominent Republican could be comfortable debating.

**The Republican Challenger.** Because James G. Blaine had come so close to defeating Cleveland in

1884, many expected the Plumed Knight from Maine to insist upon a rematch. But he had no intention of entering the lists again, preferring to act as the senior statesman of the REPUBLICAN PARTY and ultimately accepting a second tour as Secretary of State in the new administration. The possibility of a last-minute boom for Blaine cast a cloud over the ambitions of other potential Republican contenders. The most prominent of these was JOHN SHERMAN, an Ohio statesman who had demonstrated intelligence and competence both in Congress and in Cabinet posts for several decades. At the party's convention in June, Sherman led the pack in early balloting but failed to gain strength on succeeding ballots. Two other leading candidates were Walter Q. Gresham of Illinois and Chauncy Depew of New York, both of whom started out with more delegate support than did Indiana's Benjamin Harrison.

Inconclusive roll calls gave dealmakers an opportunity to exercise their art. A key player was Thomas C. Platt, the wily Republican boss of New York, who convinced Depew to drop out in favor of Harrison. While the convention was adjourned over a weekend, Stephen B. Elkins, a Senator from West Virginia, received a coded communication from Blaine in Europe, designating Harrison as his choice as well. When balloting resumed on Monday, 25 June, Harrison pulled ahead. The eighth roll call gave him a majority, and the delegates then approved a motion to make the nomination unanimous.

Harrison possessed ideal credentials for a political candidate in the Gilded Age. He was the grandson of William Henry Harrison, the popular military hero who had won the presidency in 1840, only to die shortly after his inauguration. Young Benjamin Harrison established a law practice in Indianapolis, where he was a prominent member of the Presbyterian church. He also had the most important requisite for high political office in that era: an outstanding military record. He had joined the Union Army in 1862 and distinguished himself during Gen. William T. Sherman's Georgia campaign. Harrison ended the war with the rank of brevet brigadier general.

Although he was mentioned frequently as a potential political candidate after the war, Harrison's only government service had been a six-year term in the United States Senate that had ended in 1887. Nonetheless, as early as 1884, his friends had begun laying the foundations for his 1888 presidential candidacy. Blaine's late endorsement helped Harrison's chances at the convention, but far less than the elder statesman's decision not to become a candidate himself.

The convention delegates selected LEVI P. MORTON, a New York banker, to be Harrison's running mate. The party's platform featured undeviating loyalty to the protective tariff dogma. It was a tried and true political philosophy that sounded as good to Republicans in 1888 as it had at the party's founding in the 1850s.

**The Campaign.** Whereas Cleveland's campaign suffered from lackluster management, the Republican effort was run by two clever political pros: the New Yorker Platt and Matthew Quay of Pennsylvania. Quay recruited John Wanamaker, a Philadelphia department store magnate, and he in turn organized a nationwide advisory board of businessmen. The board solicited contributions of as much as $10,000 each from eastern businessmen, eventually collecting an unprecedented campaign chest of $3 million, far more than the Democrats could muster.

The money went for many purposes, but it was not spent directly by Harrison. Blaine had broken with tradition in 1884 when he conducted an exhausting cross-country campaign, delivering speeches at dozens of locations. Harrison, however, revived a technique that James A. Garfield had pioneered in 1880 and that William McKinley would hone to perfection in 1896. He remained in Indianapolis and spoke from the front porch of his own home to partisan delegations brought for that purpose from across the country. While high tariffs figured prominently in the ninety-four addresses Harrison delivered, he carefully tailored each one to match the interests of the delegation of the day, a technique that generated frequent and favorable press coverage for the candidate.

In an age when voter turnout frequently exceeded 90 percent and when party loyalty was a fundamental article of faith with the electorate, even an effective speaking schedule had little impact on the fundamental political equation. The boisterous Mugwumps—Liberal Republicans who had opposed Blaine and who claimed to have won the election for Cleveland in 1884—did not wield any substantial influence. Although some Mugwumps continued to thump for the incumbent, their actions were a pale shadow of the outspoken and widely publicized reform effort that had been mounted four years earlier.

Occasionally, the level playing field did allow a minor event to seem more important than it was. Two such events created momentary flashes of excitement in 1888, causing embarrassment in one party and glee in the other. The Republicans suffered chagrin in their candidate's home state when the so-called Dudley Letter was published. It was widely believed that many people in Indiana routinely sold their votes to the highest bidder. Shortly after a late poll showed Cleveland leading in the state, the Democratic press published a letter purportedly distributed by W. W. Dudley, treasurer of the Republican National Committee. A Hoosier himself, Dudley was alleged to have written the letter as a circular to the members of the Indiana state committee, urging them to take strong steps to manipulate the vote. "Divide the floaters into blocks of five," he was quoted as saying in reference to those willing to sell their votes, "and put a trusted man with the necessary funds in charge of these five, and make him responsible that none get away and that all vote our ticket." Although Dudley denied having sent the letter, Harrison was incensed and refused to have anything to do with Dudley afterward.

Another letter proved as embarrassing to the Democrats. In this instance, the author admitted to having written the letter, but only as an unsuspecting pawn in a campaign trick. A California Republican named Charles Osgoodby, masquerading as an English citizen named Charles F. Murchison, wrote to the British legation in Washington, asking which American party the United Kingdom preferred. Sir Lionel Edward Sackville-West, the British minister, foolishly drafted a reply endorsing the reelection of Cleveland. His letter was published in late October and stirred the cauldron of anti-British sentiment that was always near the boiling point in nineteenth-century America. Republicans cited this letter as incontrovertible evidence that the Democratic President was in league with the hated British—and, worse yet, as a confirmation of his alleged free trade attitudes, because Great Britain was the world's leading advocate of free trade. Cleveland was furious and sent the British minister home in disgrace.

**The Result.** It is doubtful that either of these late-breaking sensations had much impact on Election Day. The key battleground was New York, which Cleveland had won by an eyelash in 1884. David B. Hill, the Democratic governor, had failed to measure up to the reform standards that the President and his Mugwump friends advocated, but he had won nomination for a second term at the state convention in September 1888. Although Hill campaigned for the presidential ticket, Cleveland was uncomfortable being associated with him. The political situation in New York City was even worse. There, Mayor Abram S. Hewitt, a reform Democrat, became mired in a three-way contest with a Republican and a fellow Democrat supported by Tammany Hall. The bitter exchanges between the Democratic mayoral candidates did nothing to ennoble the party, and they demonstrated its deep divisions in the President's home state. Meanwhile, the united Republicans ran an effective campaign for their man. Harrison reversed the 1,139-vote plurality Cleveland had won in 1884 in the Empire State and ran up a comfortable 13,002 margin in 1888.

New York's thirty-six electoral votes, combined with fifteen from Indiana, constituted the nationwide margin of victory for Harrison. Cleveland had carried both those states in 1884; their loss was fatal to his hopes for victory in 1888. The rest of the tally followed predictable patterns: the Democratic Party handily won all the electoral votes in the South; the Republican candidate carried all the northern states except for New Jersey and Connecticut. Harrison had 233 electoral votes, and Cleveland ran a distant second with only 168. But, in a most peculiar aspect of this otherwise unremarkable election, Cleveland's popular vote total exceeded that of the victorious Harrison by 100,000 votes. Much of Cleveland's surplus could be attributed to extra and therefore extraneous ballots cast in the southern states, where the Republican Party candidate was a hopeless ALSO-RAN.

Harrison's elevation to the White House coincided with the establishment of a slim Republican majority in the House of Representatives and of a more solid Republican hold in the Senate. For the first time in many years, the Republican Party enjoyed complete control of the federal government. President Harrison's party capitalized on this control to produce several landmark pieces of legislation in the 1890 congressional session, including the SHERMAN ANTI-TRUST ACT and the MCKINLEY TARIFF. But the Republicans had little time to savor their triumph. First their party lost control of the House in the fall of 1890. Then Grover Cleveland ran against Harrison again in 1892 and won back his place in the White House, the only President in American history to serve two nonconsecutive terms.

### BIBLIOGRAPHY

Baumgardner, James L. "The 1888 Presidential Election: How Corrupt?" *Presidential Studies Quarterly* 14 (1984): 416–427.

Campbell, Charles S., Jr. "The Dismissal of Lord Sackville." *Mississippi Valley Historical Review* 44 (1958): 635–648.

Lichtman, Allan J. "Political Realignment and Ethnocultural Voting in the Nineteenth-Century American." *Journal of Social History* 16 (1983): 55–82.

Socolofsky, Homer E., and Alan B. Spetter. *The Presidency of Benjamin Harrison.* 1987.

Welch, Richard E., Jr. *The Presidencies of Grover Cleveland.* 1988.

Wesser, Robert R. "Election of 1888." In vol. 2 of *History of American Presidential Elections.* Edited by Arthur M. Schlesinger, Jr., Fred L. Israel, and William P. Hansen. 3 vols. 1971.

JOHN M. DOBSON

**ELECTION, PRESIDENTIAL, 1892.** The presidential election campaign of 1892 exceeded all others in the Gilded Age for boredom and irrelevance. The incumbent Republican, Benjamin Harrison, ran against his predecessor, Democrat Grover Cleveland, and both men were determined to conduct dignified and quiet campaigns as befitted men who had held the highest office in the land. In retrospect, it made no difference to the country which of the two won; and both men campaigned in a manner that indicated that they did not think it mattered much either. Cleveland was conservative; Harrison, more so. Unlike the six previous quadrennial battles to select a new President there were no folk heroes running, such as Ulysses S. Grant in 1868 and 1872, no disputed state totals as occurred in 1876, no October surprises such as the Morey letter of 1880, no charges of fathering illegitimate children as opponents brought up against Cleveland in 1884, and no disparities between the popular and electoral vote totals as the nation witnessed in 1876 and 1888. And, unlike the three presidential elections of the 1880s, where the outcome in New York determined the victor, in 1892 the votes of no single state affected the final result.

Both Harrison and Cleveland lacked charm and neither aroused passionate or ferocious loyalty. Harrison, in particular, made any room seem colder just by entering it. Nonetheless, Republican and Democratic politicos had little choice but to back their party candidates if they hoped to obtain any of the spoils that the victorious candidates would distribute to party followers who worked hard to elect the ticket. There is little indication, however, that they were happy about it. The party platforms reflected the dullness of their leaders. The vice presidential candidates were Whitelaw Reid (Republican) and ADLAI E. STEVENSON (1835–1914) (Democratic).

**Issues of the Campaign.** Harrison ran on his record, which included presiding over the executive branch until the Fifty-first, or "Billion Dollar," Congress (1889–1891) squandered the federal surplus on a vast array of public works and huge pension benefits for veterans of the Union Army. The Fifty-First Congress also enacted the MCKINLEY TARIFF ACT in 1890, which Democrats attacked in their platform as "the culminating atrocity of class legislation." This tariff infuriated voters by raising duties to a level that increased the costs of consumer goods without providing working people with any apparent benefits in return. Conservatives of both parties also opposed passage of the Silver Purchase Act of 1890, which authorized the federal government to buy and mint monthly 4.5 million ounces of silver, thereby inflating the currency. Yet six prosilver western states—North and South Dakota, Montana, Washington, Idaho, and Wyoming—which had entered the Union in 1889 and 1890, prevented passage of the McKinley Tariff until Congress approved the Silver Purchase Act. President

Harrison also supported passage of the "force bill," which had already been passed by the House of Representatives. If the Senate concurred as well, the federal government would have been able to monitor state elections thereby protecting the voting rights of African Americans in the South.

Cleveland, on the other hand, opposed the "force bill" because he needed the votes of the white South and also because he generally believed in allowing state and local governments to take care of their own affairs. He had sought the Democratic nomination, in part, because he favored a lower tariff and opposed the free coinage of silver. The former President and other Democratic conservatives feared that unless he captured the nomination, it might go to an agrarian candidate who favored inflation. As President from March 1885 through March 1889, Cleveland had not been particularly popular but his low-tariff stance had won public approval. Thus, in 1892, the positions that he had taken and his prestige as the DEMOCRATIC PARTY's only living former President helped propel his candidacy.

The platform that the Democrats adopted condemned the McKinley Tariff, attacked reciprocity as a sham, and, concerning currency, pledged to use "both gold and silver without discriminating against either metal." Fortunately, the Silver Purchase Act was not a major issue in the campaign because Cleveland, as a "sound money" man, had no intention of compromising on the gold standard.

Cleveland also benefited in 1892 from the brutal assaults that summer upon striking laborers at the Homestead steel plant in Pittsburgh and the silver mines at Coeur d'Alene, Idaho. Many Americans viewed the Homestead strike as proof that the Harrison administration's high-tariff policy not only revealed a callousness toward labor but a Republican identification with the nation's plutocrats as well. Although former President Cleveland also associated with Wall Street investors and bankers, and did not openly support labor interests, he did condemn those, like the beneficiaries of the high tariff, who had "received open subsidies" from the federal government, and he pledged to work for import duties which would help to improve the laborers' lot. Some workers interpreted this as a nod in their favor, and the Democratic nominee received their backing as well as votes from others who were incensed either by the largesse of the Fifty-first Congress or the barriers erected by the McKinley Tariff.

**The Campaign.** During the campaign both Harrison and Cleveland attempted to gain support from important party members. Since the state of New York proved crucial during the previous three elections, each presidential nominee made some efforts with politicians in the Empire State. Republican Tom Platt, who controlled the party in New York, met with Harrison at the White House on 5 September and agreed to work for the President's reelection. Cleveland met with "Boss" Richard Croker of New York City's Tammany Hall and other prominent Democrats in the state on 8 September and listened to their desires. "No promises" is how he allegedly committed himself but the Democrats knew that electing him meant greater potential for PATRONAGE than staying with Harrison.

Neither Cleveland nor Harrison went out on the campaign trail. The President vacationed with his ill wife at Loon Lake in the Adirondak Mountains and returned to Washington at the end of the summer where he remained with her until she died on 25 October.

While he watched his wife deteriorate, the campaign held little interest for him. After she died, Harrison seemed even less concerned with the political outcome. In a similarly detached vein from the political arena, Cleveland spent most of the summer nursing his own case of gout and enjoying the cool breezes at his vacation home in Buzzards Bay, Massachusetts. He ventured out only a few times to make speeches in important swing states like New Jersey and New York.

The only spark to the 1892 campaign came from the People's Party, or the Populists, as they were known. Composed mostly of agrarians and silverites from the South and West who had been hurt by the depression of the 1880s, the Populists nominated JAMES B. WEAVER of Iowa, along with an ex-Confederate, James Field of Virginia, as his running mate, to bring reform to the country. Their party platform called for the most radical changes the nation had ever seen. Populists wanted, among other proposals, to nationalize the railroads and the telegraph, institute a graduated income tax, increase the money supply and inflate the currency, institute an eight-hour working day on government projects, elect Senators directly, and give the people the power both to initiate legislation and to repeal bills that had already won legislative approval.

The Populists frightened conservatives with a platform stating that the "wealth belongs to him who creates it, and every dollar taken from industry without an equivalent is robbery," but they won over many farmers, mostly those in the West who favored free silver. Although the party ultimately garnered 1,027,329 supporters, which equalled 8.5 percent of the popular vote, Populists won only twenty electoral votes from Colorado, Idaho, Kansas, and Nevada, and two others: one each in Oregon and North Dakota.

The zeal of the most dedicated reformers did not affect the outcome of the election.

In three states, Illinois, Indiana, and New York, the combined votes garnered by the Populist Party and PROHIBITION PARTY, however, probably took enough voters away from the Republicans to propel those states into the Democratic column. The totals in Illinois were: 426,281 Democratic; 399,288 Republican; 22,207 Populist; 25,870 Prohibition. In Indiana the results were: 262,740 Democratic; 255,615 Republican; 22,208 Populist; 13,050 Prohibition. In New York the totals were: 654,868 Democratic; 609,350 Republican; 16,429 Populist; 38,190 Prohibition.

**Cleveland's Victory.** Because of the influence of the minor parties, the Democrats won a broader mandate than had been anticipated. In victory, Cleveland prevailed with 277 electoral votes and 5,554,414 (or 46 percent) popular votes; Harrison received 145 electoral votes and 5,190,802 (43 percent) popular votes. The Democrats carried the South, the border states, and the Middle Atlantic region with the exception of Pennsylvania. The swing states of the 1880s—Connecticut, Indiana, New Jersey, and New York—went into the Democratic column as did those of Illinois and Wisconsin, two states that had not given a majority to a Democratic presidential candidate since before the Civil War. Cleveland also picked up 1 electoral vote in Ohio, 1 in North Dakota, 5 in Michigan, and 8 in California. His coattails were long and he brought along 218 Democrats, compared with the 127 the Republicans elected, to the House of Representatives; the Democrats won a slight majority in the Senate as well. For the first time since before the Civil War, the Democrats would preside over the White House while controlling majorities in both the Senate and House of Representatives.

Factors contributing to Cleveland's victory included the skill of his campaign manager, William C. Whitney of New York, popular opposition to the high duties levied by the McKinley Tariff, and the support of just about every major labor union official. Also helpful was the switch, two weeks before the election, of Walter Q. Gresham, a mainstream and highly regarded Republican from Harrison's home state of Indiana. Gresham had a reputation for wanting tariff reform, and his repudiation of Harrison and his backing of Cleveland was believed to have finished even the slim chance that the President still had for reelection.

In retrospect, it seems that Cleveland's election was inevitable. Several states had already rejected the Republicans in the 1890 congressional and state elections, primarily in response to the McKinley tariff, which, in combination with local issues, resulted in the ousting of several Republican governors and other officials. Harrison's lack of popularity also handicapped his cause. His legislative "accomplishments" were seen as failures, labor abhorred him, and a barely noticed anti-Harrison undercurrent ran through much of the nation. Although many southern farmers saw Cleveland as a tool of the Eastern banks that kept them in poverty, their alternative was either the radical Populists or the nominee of the party that had freed the slaves and now wanted to protect black voting rights in the region. To much of the nation, moreover, Cleveland seemed less conservative than Harrison.

After reading the election totals, one of President Harrison's supporters declared it "humiliating to think that the slums of Chicago, Brooklyn and New York should settle the destinies of this country for four years." Without actually saying so, he meant the votes of the immigrants who lived in those communities. It was a prescient remark whose implications the speaker may not have been quite aware of at the time. For in subsequent elections those city dwellers, their descendants, and other newcomers, mostly from southern and eastern Europe, would have a great deal to say about who would live in the White House.

After the election, a downturn in the national economy dashed the hopes of the 1892 voting majority, and Cleveland had to think of solutions even before he reentered the White House in March 1893. The new President then frustrated millions of Americans by demanding the repeal of the Sherman Silver Purchase Act. During the ensuing depression he alienated labor even more than Harrison had when he sent troops to Pullman, Illinois, to derail the 1894 PULLMAN STRIKE, and before his term ended, Cleveland's policies resulted in the loss of most of his Democratic supporters and the ascendancy of the agrarian influence to a commanding role in the party. Never again would the national Democratic Party be as conservative as it was in the year that it reelected Grover Cleveland to a second term in the White House.

### BIBLIOGRAPHY

Dozer, Donald Marquand. "Benjamin Harrison and the Presidential Campaign of 1892." *American Historical Review* 54 (1949): 49–77.

Fratkin, Robert A. "The Election of 1892." In *Running for President.* Edited by Arthur M. Schlesinger, Jr. 1992.

Lorant, Stephan. "1892: The Twenty-Seventh Election." In Stephan Lorant, *The Glorious Burden.* 1968. Pp. 411–426.

Morgan, Wayne. "The Election of 1892." In *History of American Presidential Elections, 1789–1968.* Edited by Arthur M. Schlesinger, Jr., and Fred L. Israel. 4 vols. 1971.

LEONARD DINNERSTEIN

## ELECTION, PRESIDENTIAL, 1896.

The presidential election of 1896 marked a turning point in the political history of the United States and in the institution of the presidency. The victory of the Republican candidate, William McKinley of Ohio, over the Democratic-Populist nominee, WILLIAM JENNINGS BRYAN of Nebraska, ended the quarter-century of electoral stalemate that had marked national politics since the victory of Ulysses S. Grant over HORACE GREELEY in 1872. In office, McKinley strengthened the presidency and set it on a course that it has followed during the twentieth century.

The dominant fact of national politics as the election year of 1896 approached was the economic depression that had begun in 1893. Three years of hard times had made the administration of Grover Cleveland virtually a caretaker presidency while the nation waited for a change of leadership. Cleveland's actions had split the Democrats over the issue of MONETARY POLICY. Cleveland favored the gold standard, but Democrats in the South and West endorsed the concept of free silver, a form of currency inflation, as the answer to the depression. The People's Party (Populists), representing unhappy farmers in the same regions, also favored free silver as a way to raise farm prices and relieve the burden of debt that farmers faced. Most Republicans favored the gold standard and wanted to see an increase in the protective tariff. The few Republicans who favored free silver were concentrated in the Rocky Mountain states.

The protective tariff was the other major issue of the day. The WILSON-GORMAN TARIFF ACT that the Democrats had passed in 1894 satisfied no one. Cleveland had let it become law without his signature. The Democrats and Populists disavowed it. Republicans charged that it was not protective enough to restore business confidence.

**The Republicans.** In the elections of 1894, the Republicans had scored impressive gains in one of the most decisive off-year contests in the nation's history. They gained 117 seats in the House of Representatives, won a number of Senate seats, and laid claim to being the nation's majority party. To complete their dominance, they needed to win the White House in 1896.

The leading Republican candidate was William McKinley. A former Ohio congressman and governor, McKinley enjoyed national popularity within his party for his longtime support of the tariff, his ability to carry his home state, and his moderate views on gold and silver. Finishing his gubernatorial term in 1896, McKinley and his close friend Marcus (Mark) Alonzo Hanna, a Cleveland industrialist, were already embarked on a strategy to secure a first-ballot nomination at the Republican national convention. The campaign's slogan called McKinley the Advance Agent of

Prosperity. None of McKinley's potential Republican rivals, including the Speaker of the House, Thomas B. Reed, could match his standing with most Republicans. During the first half of 1896, McKinley piled up delegates as the time for the convention in St. Louis approached.

The money issue provided the only threat to McKinley's selection. Eastern Republicans wanted a strong affirmation of the gold standard. McKinley sought a more balanced position. In the end, the party decided on a platform plank that came out "unreservedly for sound money" and the gold standard but that also called for efforts to secure an international agreement for the wider use of silver in world trade. Once the platform had been settled, some silver Republicans bolted the party. McKinley easily won the nomination. GARRET A. HOBART of New Jersey was chosen as the vice presidential nominee to offset McKinley's "Western" allegiance. The nominee and his party expected to build their campaign around the theme that the Republicans would raise the tariff and restore prosperity.

**Democrats and Populists.** The Populists decided to hold their national convention after the Republicans and Democrats had met. The leaders of the People's Party calculated that if both their rivals nominated advocates of the gold standard then the Populists would have the only candidate for free silver. The Democrats, however, did not cooperate with this strategy. During 1895 and early 1896, pro-silver forces had been taking control of the party away from Cleveland's supporters. Their task was to find a candidate to give expression to the free-silver sentiment sweeping the Democrats. The more prominent figures were not inspiring: Richard Parks Bland of Missouri—whose nickname was "Silver Dick"—stirred little enthusiasm, and Horace Boies of Iowa was only a lukewarm silver supporter. The situation was ripe for a newcomer to champion the free-silver cause.

William Jennings Bryan, a former Nebraska Congressman, saw himself as "the logic of the situation" for the Democrats. Bryan, thirty-six years old, had served in the House between 1891 and 1895, where he had become famous for his compelling oratory. Defeated in a Senate race in 1894, he frequently spoke at party functions during 1895, reminding his fellow Democrats of the need to pick a candidate dedicated to silver. He urged them to think of him as a compromise choice should the front-runners falter. It seemed improbable, but Bryan had calculated his chances shrewdly.

His opportunity came when the Democratic national convention, held in Chicago, debated the monetary issue for its platform. Bryan was the last speaker for the pro-silver forces. He had rehearsed his speech until he had mastered the oration. With a clear, musical voice that reached all the corners of the hall, he gave the Cross of Gold speech, one of the most famous addresses in the nation's political history. "You shall not press down upon the brow of labor this crown of thorns," he said. "You shall not crucify mankind upon a cross of gold." Enraptured Democrats went wild in a prolonged demonstration.

The next day Bryan was chosen as the nominee on the fifth ballot. As his running mate, the delegates selected Arthur Sewall, a pro-silver shipping executive from Maine. The country's enthusiasm for Bryan grew after his dramatic nomination. "The Chicago convention has changed everything," said Mark Hanna.

Bryan's selection upset the Populist strategy and placed the third party in a precarious predicament. If they, too, nominated Bryan and fused their campaign with that of the Democrats, then why should they remain a third party at all? If they selected their own candidate, they would split the silver coalition and deliver the election to the Republicans and the gold standard. At the People's Party convention in St. Louis in late July, the delegates faced this dilemma. "If we fuse, we are sunk," said one leader, but "if we don't fuse, all the silver men will leave us for the more powerful Democrats." After a rancorous meeting, the Populists nominated Bryan but tried to save their separate role by selecting Thomas E. Watson of Georgia as their vice presidential candidate.

As it turned out, a fourth party entered the race: the Cleveland wing of the Democratic Party split off, becoming the Gold Democratic Party and putting forward John M. Palmer of Illinois as its presidential choice and Simon Bolivar Buckner as his running mate. The Gold Democrats took votes away from Bryan in states such as West Virginia, Kentucky, and Delaware.

**The Campaign.** The main contest, however, was between McKinley and Bryan. The Democratic candidate decided to campaign across the nation personally to compensate for his party's lack of campaign funds. Making the first true whistle-stop tour, Bryan crossed the country speaking to receptive audiences. He journeyed eighteen thousand miles and made almost six hundred formal appearances. His free-silver message reached all who wished to hear it during the autumn of 1896.

His party's division and the limits of his program hampered Bryan's efforts. When he spoke in New York at Madison Square Garden, he swayed few minds. Coordinating the efforts of the Populists and the Democrats proved difficult. The Republican press hammered away at Bryan's alleged "radicalism" and his relative youth. The enthusiasm of the summer proved difficult to sustain during the fall.

McKinley and the Republicans confronted Bryan with a well-organized strategy. Rather than trying to match Bryan's touring, McKinley conducted a front-porch campaign that brought visiting delegations to his home in Canton every day. His speeches to the visitors stressed the danger of inflation that free silver would bring and emphasized the prosperity that the protective tariff would provide. McKinley was very effective in this role, and, using these controlled circumstances, he put his message out with as much force as Bryan achieved through his whistle-stop method. By the time the campaign ended, McKinley had spoken to 750,000 people from thirty states.

Hanna raised money from corporate contributors to finance the Republican campaign. Estimates were that the Republican war chest exceeded $4 million. The money was spent to pay for campaign pamphlets; some 250 million were distributed, with five million families receiving literature from the McKinley headquarters each week. Cadres of party speakers toured the country on McKinley's behalf. The Republicans conducted what Hanna called a "campaign of education," and by late September the results of their effort became evident. The Bryan tide ebbed. An English journalist captured the nation's mood as the balloting neared, writing, "McKinley offers change, but not too big a change, and so McKinley it is."

**The Result.** That was indeed how things turned out on election day. McKinley received 271 electoral votes to Bryan's 176. The popular-vote totals stood at 7,035,638 ballots for McKinley compared with 6,467,945 for Bryan and the Democratic-Populist ticket. McKinley's popular-vote majority was the largest since Grant's in 1872. His victory confirmed his party's off-year success in 1894 and made the Republicans the majority party of the United States for the next generation.

Bryan had run a better race than any other Democratic contender could have. Burdened with the legacy of the Cleveland administration and confronted with a divided party, he had made the race closer than it would have been with a more conventional candidate. It proved difficult to sustain a campaign on the single issue of silver, but the campaign established Bryan as a major figure in national politics.

Popular interest in the contest was intense. In the North more than 78 percent of the eligible white male voters went to the polls. The Republicans ran strongly among factory workers, prosperous farmers, businessmen, and professionals. Democrats charged that big business had coerced labor to vote for McKinley, but the potential impact of Bryan's inflationary policies on wages had more to do with inducing skilled workers to vote Republican than did threats from employers. Bryan carried the South and ran strongly in the Plains and Rocky Mountain states. He did poorly in the cities and in the more settled areas of the Midwest.

The Republican electoral coalition of northern city dwellers, commercial farmers, industrial workers, and ethnic groups (other than Irish Americans), proved to be a lasting force in national politics. The 1896 election gave the Democrats a minority-party status that, with the exception of Woodrow Wilson's two terms, they did not escape until the NEW DEAL. The McKinley victory also ended the career of the People's Party as a serious element in national political affairs.

In office, McKinley strengthened the power of the presidency, won the war with Spain, and saw prosperity return by 1900. He easily prevailed in a rematch with Bryan in 1900. A shrewd, effective candidate, McKinley helped to make the presidential election of 1896 one of the most important shifts in political allegiance in U.S. history.

### BIBLIOGRAPHY

Coletta, Paolo. *William Jennings Bryan.* Vol. 1. 1964.
Glad, Paul. *McKinley, Bryan and the People.* 1964.
Jensen, Richard. *The Winning of the Midwest.* 1971.
Jones, Stanley L. *The Presidential Election of 1896.* 1964.
Morgan, H. Wayne. *William McKinley and His America.* 1963.
Williams, R. Hal. *Years of Decision: American Politics in the 1890s.* 1978.

LEWIS L. GOULD

**ELECTION, PRESIDENTIAL, 1900.** The election of 1900 matched the two candidates of the 1896 presidential election, Republican William McKinley and Democrat WILLIAM JENNINGS BRYAN, against each other for a second time. The victory of McKinley by an even larger margin solidified the electoral supremacy that the Republicans had established during the 1890s and represented a popular endorsement of the overseas expansion that accompanied the SPANISH-AMERICAN WAR of 1898.

Foreign policy provided the political setting within which the 1900 election was waged. In April 1898, after negotiations over the island of CUBA collapsed, the United States and Spain went to war. Three months of fighting brought overwhelming victories for the Americans: Spain left Cuba, the United States acquired PUERTO RICO, Guam, and the PHILIPPINES, and the nation became a world power. The war itself was short and relatively cheap. In the Philippines, however, the United States faced a popular insurrection that went on for three years amid casualties for American troops, much greater losses for Filipino rebels and civilians, and charges of atrocities on both sides. As 1900 opened, the ugly war in the Philippines continued.

**The Candidates.** While the guerilla fighting posed problems for the presidential administration of William McKinley, other political signs favored the REPUBLICAN PARTY. Spurred by the war and discovery of gold in the Yukon and South Africa, the American economy had recovered from the Depression of 1893–1897. The return of prosperity helped the Republicans, for few other domestic issues troubled the nation. The free silver craze of the depression years had faded. Apprehensions about the growth of monopolies and large corporations were spreading but had not yet reached an intense stage. McKinley was a popular President who could say in late 1899, "The hum of industry has drowned the voice of calamity, and the voice of despair is no longer heard in the United States."

During the first half of 1900, McKinley faced some troublesome problems over trade relations between the United States and Puerto Rico as well as the negotiations with Great Britain about a canal across Central America. The Republicans worked out a compromise on the Puerto Rican tariff issue, and the treaty to settle the dispute with Great Britain was postponed until after the election. The President escaped from these episodes with little damage to his political prospects. He also persuaded his old friend, Senator Marcus A. Hanna of Ohio, to be his campaign chairman once again.

The major issue that the President faced was the selection of his running mate. Vice President GARRET A. HOBART died in November 1899 and a clamor arose at once for the nomination of Governor Theodore Roosevelt of New York. Roosevelt had won fame in Cuba during the war, and he was very popular among younger Republicans, especially in the West. McKinley and the men around him regarded Roosevelt as immature and impetuous. They looked for an alternative candidate. None of the men they discussed, including Secretary of the Navy John D. Long, Cornelius N. Bliss of New York, or Jonathan P. Dolliver of Iowa, aroused the enthusiasm that Roosevelt evoked.

Roosevelt did not think that the vice presidency was the best stepping-stone to the White House, and he resisted blandishments to run from his friends such as Senator Henry Cabot Lodge of Massachusetts. The governor issued statements disavowing any interest in the nomination but the public and his supporters refused to take these remarks as a final renunciation. Roosevelt himself was careful not to foreclose his

options as the Republican national convention neared. Meanwhile, the Republican leader in New York, Sen. Thomas Collier Platt, had concluded that it would be best for Roosevelt to be kicked upstairs to the vice presidency before his criticisms of corporate power caused more trouble for the party among its wealthy campaign contributors.

The Republican national convention in mid June 1900 at Philadelphia produced Roosevelt's nomination to the vice presidency. He decided that he had to appear at the convention and he came onto the floor with his Rough Rider hat from Cuba. Republican insiders concluded that he was wearing "an acceptance hat." Senator Hanna dreaded the prospect of Roosevelt on the ticket, but could not persuade McKinley to veto his selection. On 19 June, McKinley announced that the administration "has no candidate" of its own, which cleared the way for Roosevelt.

With Senator Platt pushing his candidacy, Roosevelt was nominated 21 June 1900. McKinley had allowed the party to make the wisest choice available in that Roosevelt added energy and enthusiasm to the Republican campaign. Flushed with their own success, the Republicans boasted of the nation's prosperity and how their policies had promoted its reappearance. A Republican magazine editor, however, was troubled. The Republican Party, he told a friend, "is a little too fat and sleek and prosperous, and its moral tone is not quite what it ought to be. It looks back with pride, rather than forward with aspiration."

Soon after his defeat in November 1896, Bryan was being talked of as the Democratic candidate four years later. He never stopped running for the nomination and found that no serious rival emerged within the party to challenge him. Bryan served as a volunteer officer during the war with Spain, but the White House prevented him from seeing action in Cuba. He opposed IMPERIALISM, but blundered when he recommended that Democratic Senators support the peace treaty ending the war in 1899. Even the waning of his major issue of free silver did not provide any serious obstacle to his renomination. By the end of 1899, it was clear that Bryan was the front-runner.

There was a brief flurry of enthusiasm for Admiral George Dewey, the hero of the battle of Manila Bay, but Dewey's lack of political experience produced mistakes that made his candidacy a public joke. Democratic state conventions endorsed Bryan in spring 1900 and his nomination was assured. At the national convention in Kansas City, the party platform placed its greatest emphasis on the question of imperialism, which it identified as "the paramount issue of this campaign." The document also called for Philippine independence under an American protectorate. Bryan succeeded in winning a reaffirmation of the doctrine of the free coinage of silver at a ratio of 16 to 1 with gold. Bryan's vice presidential nominee was ADLAI E. STEVENSON of Illinois, who had been Grover Cleveland's Vice President from 1893 to 1897.

There were no serious THIRD PARTY CANDIDATES in 1900. The Populists nominated Bryan and selected Charles A. Towne as his running mate. The Silver Republicans also selected Bryan and left their vice presidential slot open. EUGENE V. DEBS was the nominee of the Socialist Party.

**The Campaign.** As an incumbent President, McKinley observed the tradition that it would be undignified for him to campaign actively. He delivered an acceptance speech on 12 July in which he asserted that "American authority must be supreme" in the Philippines. He rejected a "scuttle policy" (withdrawal from the islands), and made the same point in his letter of acceptance issued 8 September. The President spent the summer in Washington dealing with the problem of the Boxer Rebellion in China and other foreign policy issues. Then he went to his home in Canton, Ohio, for the rest of the presidential campaign.

Roosevelt carried the brunt of the Republican canvas. He toured the nation in a series of hard-hitting campaign stops and told audiences "that the incoming of Mr. Bryan would mean terrible and widespread disaster." Roosevelt was popular with his crowds, and a friend concluded: "Theodore has had a very successful trip, has addressed great crowds, has spoken extremely well, and has helped the party enormously."

The Republicans had ample funds, more than $2.5 million, to carry on a well-organized campaign. They sent out 125 million documents and more than 21 million postcards. Six hundred speakers took to the campaign trail, and the campaign headquarters took crude polls to gauge popular opinion. There was no doubt about the outcome: the republicans radiated confidence in McKinley's success.

Bryan was never able to settle on a winning issue. In his acceptance speech in August, he promised that if elected he would call a special session of Congress to provide the Philippines with a stable government. Independence would follow with American guarantees that would protect the islands. It was not clear how this policy differed from McKinley's assurance that the islands needed a stable government under American authority. Bryan soon discovered that anti-imperialism was not gaining votes.

In mid September he switched his emphasis to the issue of the trusts. The Republican Party, he charged, "stands sponsor at the cradle of more trusts than ever sprang into existence before." It was an issue with potential appeal, as there had been a spread of business consolidations since 1895. The Republicans counterattacked by citing the weak antitrust record of the Cleveland administration and the involvement of some prominent Democrats with antitrust violations in New York. The trust issue would work for the Democrats in future elections, but the persistence of prosperity in 1900 undercut attacks on corporate power. Bryan also revived the silver issue where it had sectional support. The Republicans used monetary policy against him as they had in 1896.

As with any campaign, there were some moments of concern for the victors. A strike among coal miners in September required the intervention of Senator Hanna to produce a settlement. The Senator also went out on the campaign trail himself despite the worries of party managers. He proved to be a popular speaker who did well in the Middle West. By October McKinley was told that the prospects for the Republicans were "very favorable, and we continue to receive encouraging reports from all parts of the country."

**The Result.** The election occurred 6 November 1900. McKinley won a decisive victory, receiving 7,218,491 ballots to 6,356,734 for Bryan. The result in the ELECTORAL COLLEGE was 292 for McKinley to 155 for Bryan. The Republicans polled 114,000 more votes than they did in 1896, while Bryan garnered 146,000 fewer ballots. The winner got 51.7 percent of the popular vote; the loser received 45.5 percent. Bryan carried the states of the South, Idaho, Montana, Nevada, and Colorado. McKinley won all the other states.

Voter turnout slipped from the peak level of 1896: 71.6 percent of voters in the northern states came to the polls as compared with 78.3 percent four years before. The trend of lower voter turnout would be a significant feature in future presidential contests. The Republicans also did well in the congressional races. They controlled the Senate with 55 seats to 31 for the Democrats and 4 for the minor parties. The Republican total in the House was 197 seats to 151 for the Democrats. It was clear that the Republicans had become the majority party of the nation.

The important elements in the outcome of the election were voter happiness with the economy and the Republicans. The issue of anti-imperialism did not change many votes. Americans did not want to overturn the consequences of the war with Spain, but neither did they wish the McKinley administration to be more expansive in the future. The President saw himself as endorsed by the American people. "I can no longer be called the President of a party," he said. "I am now the President of the whole people." For

McKinley his second administration lasted only about six months until his assassination in September 1901. The accession of Theodore Roosevelt to the presidency opened a new era in American history and relegated the election of 1900 to a historical obscurity from which it has not escaped. In the process the political skill of William McKinley and his success as an electoral leader have also faded from view.

### BIBLIOGRAPHY

Coletta, Paolo. *William Jennings Bryan*. Vol. 1. 1964.
Gould, Lewis L. *The Presidency of William McKinley*. 1980.
Gould, Lewis L. *Reform and Regulation: American Politics from Roosevelt to Wilson*. 1986.
Koenig, Louis. *Bryan*. 1971.
Morgan, H. Wayne. *William McKinley and His America*. 1963.
Williams, R. Hal. *Years of Decision: American Politics in the 1890s*. 1978.

LEWIS L. GOULD

**ELECTION, PRESIDENTIAL, 1904.** The election of 1904 was the first landslide election of the twentieth century and the most significant political victory of Theodore Roosevelt's career. As the incumbent Republican President, Roosevelt easily won a decisive triumph over the Democratic nominee, ALTON B. PARKER. His success at the polls enabled Roosevelt to launch the economic reforms of his second term that made him a Progressive. For the Democrats the election demonstrated that they could not regain the presidency as long as the Republicans remained united. Their effort to run Parker as the conservative alternative to the popular Roosevelt had ended in electoral disaster.

**Roosevelt and Hanna.** The election of 1904 took shape during the summer of 1901, when President William McKinley announced that he would not be a candidate for a third term. Theodore Roosevelt, McKinley's Vice President, immediately began tentative preparations for a campaign to secure the Republican nomination in 1904. Other hopefuls within the party, including CHARLES W. FAIRBANKS of Indiana, Leslie M. Shaw of Iowa, and McKinley's longtime friend, Senator Marcus A. Hanna of Ohio, also looked to 1904.

The assassination of McKinley on 6 September 1901 changed the dynamics of the fight for the Republican nomination. Roosevelt was now the President, and his performance in office would determine the outcome of that interparty struggle. The youthful and energetic Roosevelt soon proved to be a formidable political operator. He revitalized the SHERMAN ANTITRUST ACT through the prosecution of the Northern Securities Company in 1902. His intervention in the anthra-

cite-coal strike later that year ended the walkout and showed him to be an evenhanded mediator between capital and labor. In foreign policy, he settled the Alaska boundary controversy, built up the navy, and secured the PANAMA CANAL Zone in 1904. Republicans soon recognized that they had a leader of almost unlimited popular appeal.

One apparent obstacle to nomination worried the President. He wanted the support of Senator Hanna, fearing that Hanna, McKinley's closest political ally, might oppose him to run as the candidate of big business. Hanna had little interest in the White House and recognized that his age and health probably ruled out a presidential race. Nonetheless, he resented the way that Roosevelt pressed him for an endorsement. As chairman of the Republican national committee, Hanna took the position that he should not make a public pledge that would rule out other candidates. Roosevelt listened to party members who said that Hanna planned to block Roosevelt's nomination.

After a year of uneasy maneuvering, in spring 1903 Roosevelt seized an opportunity to make Hanna declare himself. As Ohio Republicans prepared to hold a party convention, Senator Joseph B. Foraker, an enemy of Hanna's, proposed a resolution to endorse Roosevelt. When Hanna wavered, Roosevelt insisted on a public endorsement from the convention. Hanna agreed but did not himself come out directly for Roosevelt. During the remainder of 1903, Roosevelt sought Hanna's support amid further talk that the Senator might be a candidate. A showdown seemed imminent until Hanna fell ill and died in February 1904. The path to Roosevelt's nomination was now open.

**The Conventions.** As he prepared for the election, Roosevelt took a conservative posture on most controversial issues. He made sure that the Republican platform emphasized the party's record and was vague on the protective tariff. He did not interfere when the convention named Fairbanks, a colorless conservative, as his running mate. Roosevelt designated George B. Cortelyou, his former secretary and a current CABINET member, to run the campaign. Interparty feuds in the key states of Wisconsin and Illinois were solved and repressed. At a harmonious but dull convention, Theodore Roosevelt was unanimously nominated on the first ballot.

The Democrats encountered much more difficulty selecting their standard-bearer in 1904. After WILLIAM JENNINGS BRYAN's second defeat in 1900, the conservative wing of the party decided that it would dominate the candidate-selection process four years later. The Democrats, said one party newspaper, should "return from following after strange gods." During the period 1901 to 1903, the conservatives generally defeated the Bryan supporters in party conventions. Their problem, though, was that they had neither a strong issue nor an attractive candidate to run against the popular and exciting Roosevelt. The President's attacks on large corporations and his handling of the coal strike had deprived the Democrats of two potential lines of criticism. They would need more than denunciations of Roosevelt as a "pigmy autocrat" to regain the White House.

The range of potential candidates was small. Some talked of a fourth race for Grover Cleveland, but he aroused little enthusiasm. Bryan mentioned some of his supporters, but no one took them very seriously. There seemed to be two real aspirants. On the left of the party, William Randolph Hearst, the newspaper publisher, hoped to win voters by attacking trusts and supporting organized labor. Unfortunately, his personal life was vulnerable: one critic termed him a "low voluptuary."

The conservative Democrats preferred Alton B. Parker of New York, who, his friends claimed, could carry his home state against Roosevelt. As a state appeals court judge, he had been silent on the issues and thus had offended few. Soon, wealthy Democrats got behind his candidacy. Critics in New York charged that Parker showed to "the inquiring vision all the salient qualities of a sphere," but his safety and conservatism brought him enough delegates to produce his nomination at the national convention.

During the convention, Bryan insisted that the party platform be as progressive as possible. He wanted the party to avoid repudiating free silver for which he had campaigned in 1896 and 1900. The delegates decided to leave the issue of silver out of the platform completely. Such a strategy did not suit Judge Parker. He sent the convention a telegram insisting that the delegates endorse the gold standard. A tumultuous debate followed until the convention allowed Parker to interpret the monetary issue as he wished. For Parker's running mate, the convention chose Henry Gassaway Davis of West Virginia, who was eighty-two years old and whose wealth, so the Democrats hoped, would make him a generous campaign contributor.

**The Campaign.** The Democrats began confidently. Their strategy was to build on the 150 electoral votes that they could count on from the Solid South, which always turned out for the Democratic nominee. If Parker could carry New York, New Jersey, and Connecticut and the Democrats could win the border states of Delaware, West Virginia, and Maryland, then capturing a midwestern state such as Indiana would put the nominee into the White House. The Democrats hoped to argue that Parker provided a safe alternative to Roosevelt's radicalism and impetuosity. The choice, said one, was "between the hair trigger man and the judicial mind."

The campaign started badly for Parker. He delivered his acceptance speech at his home in Esopus, New York, but his remarks failed to attract the attention that his "gold" telegram to the national convention had received. He tried to run a "front porch" campaign, as McKinley had done in 1896, but few people came to see him at his remote home. The Democratic national committee had ample funds but spent them inefficiently. Many Bryan Democrats simply did not support Parker openly, and neither Bryan nor Hearst gave the candidate anything more than lukewarm backing. The prosperity of the nation in 1904 also contrasted vividly with the depression of the early 1890s, when the Democrats had been in power.

The Republicans waged a campaign than supported a popular candidate with techniques of advertising and merchandising. In observance of the tradition that an incumbent President did not campaign, Roosevelt delivered his formal speech accepting the nomination, issued his letter of acceptance to set the themes of the race, and then stayed in the White House. "I wish I were where I could fight more effectively," he said. Under Cortelyou's skillful management, the Republicans put an array of speakers in the field to stress Roosevelt's virtues. The Republicans made strong inroads into normally Democratic ethnic voters. Irish Catholic voters particularly responded to Roosevelt's religious tolerance in his appointments and policies.

From the outset the Republicans could not believe the strength of their campaign. Parker appeared "to be a blank cartridge," said Senator Jonathan P. Dolliver of Iowa. The electorate seemed unusually quiet, and one editor called it "the most apathetic campaign ever heard of since James Monroe's second election." The militarized campaigns of the late nineteenth century, featuring large parades of voters organized into campaign clubs, were a fading memory as the parties stressed the merits of their individual candidates.

With his campaign faltering as the election neared, Parker endeavored to stimulate popular interest. Using information from a business friend, he attacked the Republican campaign fund and Cortelyou. As the former Secretary of Commerce and Labor, the Republican chairman had once had access to corporate records. Parker charged that the Republicans were using that knowledge to extract campaign contributions. The trusts, said Parker, were being asked "to buy protection" from the Republicans. Democratic newspapers attacked "Cortelyou and Corruption."

Roosevelt was infuriated. He thought that Parker was attacking his honesty, and he insisted that a $100,000 contribution from Standard Oil be returned and sent out letters rebutting the allegations. In fact, the Republicans had indeed raised money from business, but Roosevelt did not go deeply into that issue.

Parker returned to the attack on 3 November, five days before the voting. Roosevelt immediately issued a personal statement that labeled Parker's charges "unqualifiedly and atrociously false." Unfortunately for Parker, his informant about the campaign funds had made him promise to maintain secrecy about his identity. Parker failed to substantiate the charges, and, in the public's mind, Roosevelt won the battle.

**The Result.** The election was a decisive triumph for Roosevelt. He received 7,628,875 votes, or 56.4 percent, to Parker's 5,084,442, or 37.6 percent. In the ELECTORAL COLLEGE, the President received 336 votes, the most that any candidate had gained to that time; Parker had 140 electoral votes. In the popular totals, Parker ran about 1.3 million ballots behind what Bryan had polled in 1900. Some Democrats supported the Socialist ticket of EUGENE V. DEBS, who received about 400,000 votes. Other Democrats cast their ballots for Roosevelt or just stayed at home. For the electorate at large, the 1904 result showed a decline in popular interest. Turnout in the northern states fell from 71.7 percent in 1900 to 64.7 percent in 1904. Roosevelt had achieved a true landslide without bringing more voters to the polls.

On election night, Roosevelt announced that he would not be a candidate in 1908. Now President, as he put it, "in my own right," he began the campaign for government regulation that would mark his full term. That program would, by 1908, divide the REPUBLICAN PARTY and open the way for the Democrats' victory in 1912. In the immediate aftermath of 1904, however, Roosevelt had nothing but pleasure in the personal triumph he had achieved. The election of 1904 was the high-water mark of his remarkable popularity with the American people.

### BIBLIOGRAPHY

Blum, John M. *The Republican Roosevelt*. 1954.
Broesamle, John M. "The Democrats from Bryan to Wilson." In *The Progressive Era*. Edited by Lewis L. Gould. 1974.
Gould, Lewis L. *Reform and Regulation: American Politics from Roosevelt to Wilson*. 1986.
Harbaugh, William H. "Election of 1904." In *History of American Presidential Elections, 1789–1968*. Edited by Arthur M. Schlesinger, Jr., and Fred L. Israel. 4 vols. 1971.

LEWIS L. GOULD

**ELECTION, PRESIDENTIAL, 1908.** The election was the last of WILLIAM JENNINGS BRYAN's three presidential races; it shifted power within the REPUBLICAN PARTY from Theodore Roosevelt to William Howard Taft, and foreshadowed the divisive split that the GOP suffered in 1912. In the contest itself, Taft defeated Bryan because of his own success as a candidate and the strong support of President Roosevelt. By ending Bryan's presidential hopes, the election allowed the Democrats to look to other, more electable candidates in the future.

**The Republican Candidate.** The opening event in the 1908 election occurred on the evening of Election Day in 1904. Having won a landslide victory over ALTON B. PARKER, Roosevelt told the American public that he would not be a candidate for renomination in 1908. "The wise custom which limits the President to two terms regards the substance and not the form," he said in making the announcement. Roosevelt adhered to his pledge faithfully over the four years that followed. As a result, a succession crisis occurred among the Republicans to see who would replace the popular and exciting Roosevelt.

Although he would not be a candidate himself, Roosevelt did want to play a large role in selecting the Republican standard-bearer in 1908. He expected that the party's nominee would be someone identified with the domestic policies that Roosevelt supported during his second term. These programs included railroad regulation embodied in the Hepburn Act of 1906, control of large corporations, and such laws as the Pure Food and Drug Act of 1906 and the Meat Inspection amendment adopted that same year. Any Republican who did not endorse the "Roosevelt policies" was unlikely to receive a presidential blessing.

If Roosevelt could have picked the candidate himself, he would probably have selected his Secretary of State, ELIHU ROOT. Unfortunately, Root was in his late sixties, in uncertain health, and had a background in corporate law. As the President surveyed the other Republican hopefuls, few of them met his political standard. Vice President CHARLES W. FAIRBANKS was colorless and conservative, Speaker of the House Joseph G. Cannon was vulgar and reactionary, and Senator PHILANDER C. KNOX of Pennsylvania had also moved to the right since his days as Roosevelt's Attorney General. Senator Joseph B. Foraker of Ohio was an ardent opponent of Roosevelt's regulatory program.

On the left, Senator ROBERT M. LA FOLLETTE of Wisconsin was deemed to be erratic and radical, and he had little support outside his native state. There was enthusiasm in the East for CHARLES EVANS HUGHES, elected governor of New York in 1906, and identified with attacking corruption in the insurance industry. Hughes and Roosevelt soon clashed over PATRONAGE policies, and Roosevelt regarded the New Yorker as a false progressive who could not be trusted.

The logical candidate in Roosevelt's mind was his Secretary of War, William Howard Taft. The two men were good friends, with Taft often proclaiming his loyalty to the President's policies. "He and I view public questions exactly alike," Roosevelt said in 1908. In fact Roosevelt and Taft had differing ideas about how the President should govern, but there was little reason to explore these issues before Taft was elected. One source of immediate tension within their relationship was Mrs. Taft's determination to see her husband become President. She was suspicious of Roosevelt's fidelity to his 1904 pledge, and she pressed the President for a declaration of support for her husband.

Roosevelt came out strongly for Taft early in 1907 in part to thwart Foraker's presidential candidacy. The Senator and the President had clashed over Foraker's criticism of Roosevelt's handling of the Brownsville episode, which involved African American soldiers and a shooting incident in south Texas. By March Roosevelt was telling his Cabinet that he had a "peculiar regard" for Taft's political views. He directed that Taft should have an important role in allocating patronage in Ohio and the South.

From that point on, Taft's road to the nomination was clear. Roosevelt denied any interest in a third term to block efforts at a renomination. He carefully upstaged Hughes when the New York governor made an important speech on national issues. The result was that Taft had the nomination in hand when the Republicans met in mid June 1908. He was selected on the first ballot, and agreed to have Congressman JAMES S. ("Sunny Jim") SHERMAN of New York as his running mate. The Republican platform was conservative, but it did pledge revision of the protective tariff as soon as the new President was inaugurated.

**The Democratic Strategy.** The Democrats entered the election with much optimism about their prospects. Since the overwhelming defeat of the conservative Alton B. Parker in 1904, William Jennings Bryan had once again emerged as the party's leader. The Democrats had made gains in the 1906 elections in the House. Without the popular Roosevelt as the Republican candidate the opposition party might have a strong chance to capture the White House. Bryan's themes were primarily procedural in 1908. He called for the direct election of Senators, the initiative, and the referendum. He asked the voters: "Shall the People Rule?"

With what amounted to a personal machine within the Democratic Party, Bryan controlled the delegate-selection process during the early months of 1908. The conservative challengers who ran against him such as George Gray of Delaware and John A. Johnson of Minnesota were no match for Bryan's popularity. Bryan placated the South with statements in favor of segregation, and he came out against Japanese immigration on the West Coast. He was easily nominated when the Democrats held their convention in Denver. John Worth Kern of Indiana was the vice-presidential candidate.

The Democratic platform called for lower tariffs, railroad regulation, and federal licenses for businesses that controlled the manufacture of more than 25 percent of a single product. More sensitive issues such as government ownership of railroads, the initiative, and the referendum were left out. The main goal was to achieve a united party to run against Taft and the Republicans.

Bryan thought that circumstances finally favored his candidacy as they had not done in 1896 or 1900. The economic downturn of late 1907 (the Panic of 1907) blocked the GOP from boasting about prosperity. Moreover, the Democrats could now count on the backing of the American Federation of Labor. The AFL disliked Republican support for the use of the labor injunction in case of strikes. In the North, some black voters were angry at Roosevelt. The Republicans were also divided in some midwestern states over the issue of prohibition.

The Democratic strategy was based on the South, where there were 125 solid electoral votes for Bryan. Adding Kentucky and the new state of Oklahoma would give him another fifteen electoral votes. The rest would come from New York, Illinois, Indiana, Missouri, and Bryan's own state of Nebraska. During the early weeks of the contest, prospects seemed favorable for the Democrats. "Things are looking well," Bryan observed during early October, "and I see no reason why they should not steadily improve."

**The Campaign.** The election of 1908 reflected the newer advertising style of campaigning that had emerged after 1900. Both parties still used the usual assortment of party speakers to address the faithful, but a greater emphasis was placed on "bureaus, subcommittees, and auxiliary committees" that tried "to reach the American people . . . in their lives and daily occupations." Most vestiges of campaign clubs and large rallies had now disappeared.

The campaign started slowly for the Republicans. Taft named Frank H. Hitchcock as his campaign manager. He spent the summer months in careful organizational work. Worries about Taft's candidacy mounted. Organized labor disliked him because of decisions he made against strikes as a federal judge during the 1890s. As a Unitarian, Taft evoked fears among more traditional Protestant denominations. Blacks were restive about Brownsville. Republican fund-raising also went slowly because Taft supported some public disclosure about campaign contributions. One newspaper reporter concluded: "This election is not going to be an open-and-shut affair."

By the middle of August, Taft decided that he would have to campaign personally to turn the election in his direction. He toured the Midwest, made a foray into parts of the South, and covered New York during the last six weeks of the canvass. He promised that he would fulfill the platform pledge for tariff revision, and he contended that "the Republican party is a more trustworthy instrument of government than the Democratic."

Roosevelt also made his presence felt in the campaign. He issued a number of public statements on behalf of the Republican nominee. He effectively attacked Bryan on the issue of campaign contributions. The weight of the presidency was put behind Taft, an asset that Bryan and the Democrats could not equal.

After its initial strong start, Bryan's campaign stalled during October. He did not follow a single theme in his speeches, but shifted back and forth among the trust issue, the tariff, and procedural change. His capacity to use the popular concern about campaign contributions was also reduced because of the charges made on that point about his own campaign treasurer.

In the end, the Republicans proved to have the stronger organization. Hitchcock's emphasis on the last four weeks of the election enabled the GOP to put its best speakers into the field at the key moment. Although campaign contributions were reduced, the Republicans still had enough to outspend their opposition. The labor vote did not defect to the Democrats, and African Americans remained loyal to the party of Taft and Roosevelt. Although there were internal strains among the Republicans, the coalition that William McKinley and Theodore Roosevelt had built held together for Taft and Sherman.

**The Result.** On 3 November 1908, Taft won a solid victory. He had 7,675,320 popular votes to 6,412,294 for Bryan. The winner amassed 321 electoral votes; Bryan received 162. Eugene V. Debs, the Socialist candidate, recorded almost 421,000 votes. The number of Americans voting rose as 1,367,000 more votes were recorded than in 1904. The election was a return to the pattern of 1896 and 1900. Of the sixteen states that Bryan won, he had carried thirteen of them twice before, including eleven in the South, Colorado, and Nevada. Voter turnout in the northern states was 67 percent, up slightly from the result in 1904. Taft ran particularly well in the cities where Republicans had been strong for more than a decade.

Beneath the surface, however, there were signs of Republican weakness. In five states that Taft carried, the Democrats elected governors, a sign that ticket-splitting was becoming more common. Most important, the election did not resolve the factional tensions among the Republicans. Both the progressive and conservative wings of the party expected Taft to support them in future disputes.

The election results in 1908 also laid the basis for future trouble between Roosevelt and Taft. A few days after the balloting, Taft wrote Roosevelt to say that "you and my brother Charlie made that possible which in all probability would not have occurred otherwise." Roosevelt bitterly resented having his contributions to Taft's victory bracketed with the President-elect's wealthy half-brother who had underwritten his candidacy. Resolving the differences in philosophy and temperament that separated Taft and Roosevelt would prove difficult during the four years that followed.

In that sense, the presidential election of 1908 represented a critical turning point in the political history of the early twentieth century. The electoral coalition that had brought the Republicans to dominance during the 1890s was showing signs of age after twelve years in office. Bryan had not been able to sweep it from power in his third run for the White House, but he had kept the Democrats together and provided a base from which others could triumph. As the Republicans battled during Taft's presidency, the fissures that opened between Roosevelt and his successor made possible the triumph of Woodrow Wilson and eight years of Democratic rule.

### BIBLIOGRAPHY

Coletta, Paolo E. "Election of 1908." In *History of American Presidential Elections, 1789–1968.* Edited by Arthur M. Schlesinger, Jr., and Fred L. Israel. 4 vols. 1971.

Gould, Lewis L. *Reform and Regulation: American Politics from Roosevelt to Wilson.* 1986.

Koenig, Louis. *Bryan: A Political Biography of William Jennings Bryan.* 1971.

McGerr, Michael. *The Decline of Popular Politics: The American North, 1865–1928.* 1986.

Pringle, Henry F. *The Life and Times of William Howard Taft.* 2 vols. 1939.

LEWIS L. GOULD

**ELECTION, PRESIDENTIAL, 1912.** The election of 1912 witnessed the high tide of the progressive movement. This movement, nationwide in scope, inevitably had a powerful impact on national politics, and by 1910 the traditional two-party system seemed incapable of assimilating and controlling it. The DEMOCRATIC PARTY, although strengthened by the support of organized labor, was on the national level a loose alliance of big-city bosses, southern politicians usually of probusiness and prorailroad stripe, and western mining interests. It was still largely a southern party, still tainted with charges of rebellion and of violence against African Americans, most of whom lived in the region. Progressivism's impact was strongest on the dominant REPUBLICAN PARTY, the one organization that seemed capable of governing the country. As late as 1910, control of the Republican Party on the national level still rested with conservative state bosses and a group in the Senate known as the Old Guard.

Theodore Roosevelt, Republican President from 1901 to 1909, had kept his party together by not alienating conservatives and, at the same time, by mollifying the rank and file by a vigorous antitrust campaign, conservation of the dwindling public domain, effective federal regulation of the railroads, and a mounting rhetorical campaign against "malefactors of great wealth." Roosevelt's chosen successor, William Howard Taft, split the Republican Party apart by signing and then praising the PAYNE-ALDRICH TARIFF ACT of 1909, whose high rates were achieved brazenly by special interests, and by permitting himself to appear as an anticonservationist. The inevitable explosion came during the primary and general elections of 1910, when anti-Taft Republicans, known as insurgents, were everywhere successful in the Midwest and West. Taft seemed repudiated by his own party, while the Democrats won control of the House of Representatives for the first time since 1892.

The next two years witnessed strenuous campaigns in both parties for the presidential nominations in 1912, because nothing less than control of the federal government was at stake. Republican insurgents, determined to prevent Taft's renomination, organized the National Progressive Republican League in January 1911 to fight for the nomination of ROBERT M. LA FOLLETTE, former governor of and now Senator from Wisconsin. But the majority of progressive Republicans, although they admired La Follette, thought that he could not win because he was too closely identified with the radicals. They turned instead to Roosevelt, who had become increasingly alienated from Taft. Convinced that only he could save his party from disaster, Roosevelt at last gave in to the pleas of his friends and announced his candidacy on 24 February 1912. Since 1910, Roosevelt had been developing an advanced progressive program, and his entry into the race galvanized the Republican Party's right wing. The one thing that most set conservatives' teeth on edge was Roosevelt's advocacy of the popular recall of judicial decisions, for the courts had been the chief defenders of property rights.

**The Nominees.** Thirty states instituted presidential primaries in 1912 (the first in American history), and Roosevelt and Taft slugged it out with increasing bitterness, even descending to name-calling. By the end of the primary campaign, there was no doubt about which man the rank and file wanted: Roosevelt had won 1,157,397 votes; Taft, 761,716; and La Follette, 351,043. Roosevelt had even carried Taft's home state, Ohio, by a two-to-one margin. But Taft had the support of 326 delegates from the South and other boss-controlled delegations, compared to Roosevelt's 432 and La Follette's 41. There were also 254 contested delegates, and, when the Republican national convention met in Chicago in mid June, the Taft-controlled national committee awarded 235 of the contested delegates to the President, enabling Taft to win renomination on the first ballot on 21 June.

Roosevelt came to Chicago to take personal command of his forces at the national convention. When it was obvious that the conservatives were going to steal the nomination, most of the Roosevelt delegates withdrew from the convention and agreed with their hero to return to Chicago and to organize the new PROGRESSIVE (BULL MOOSE) PARTY. Return they did on 5 August, gathering for what was more a revival meeting than a political convention. So excited were they by Roosevelt's acceptance speech, "A Confession of Faith," that they burst into "The Battle Hymn of the Republic" and "Onward Christian Soldiers."

Behind this drama and wild exuberance lay the substance of the Progressive platform, which embodied the program that Roosevelt called the NEW NATIONALISM. In historical perspective, the platform was the most important political document since the Populist platform of 1892 because it erected milestones for the development of public policy for at least the next fifty years. It approved all the objectives of the social reformers—child labor legislation, minimum wages and the eight-hour day for women workers, social and health insurance, workmen's compensation, and so on. On the political side it endorsed the initiative, referendum, and recall; the recall of judicial decisions; the direct election of Senators; the nomination of presidential candidates by preferential primaries; and, most important, woman suffrage by federal amendment. In the economic realm, it demanded the creation of powerful new federal agencies to regulate business and industry and the creation of a new currency issued by the government and not by private banks (as was the system in 1912).

Meanwhile, a struggle for control of the Democratic Party, equally critical if not as bitter as the Republican intraparty warfare, had been occurring. Soon after the congressional election of 1910, WILLIAM JENNINGS BRYAN announced that he would not be a presidential candidate for a fourth time (he had run in 1896, 1900, and 1908), and a host of new leaders vied to assume Bryan's mantle. Four front-runners soon led the pack: Woodrow Wilson, governor of New Jersey; James Beauchamp ("Champ") Clark of Missouri, Speaker of the House of Representatives; Representative Oscar W. Underwood of Alabama, Democratic majority leader in the House of Representatives; and Judson Harmon, governor of Ohio.

Wilson got off to the fastest start. Elected New Jersey governor in 1910, he pushed a comprehensive progressive program through the state legislature in the spring of 1911 and won Bryan's praise and the adulation of progressive Democrats across the country. He set out on the campaign trail with such vigor and effectiveness that by early 1912 it seemed he would easily win the Democratic presidential nomination. The Wilson campaign came near derailment, however, once the state primaries and conventions were held. Wilson's constituency turned out to be composed of urbanites, "highbrows," and well-educated Democrats. Wilson carried those states, such as Pennsylvania, North Carolina, Ohio, Texas, and Wisconsin, where these Democrats controlled the state organizations. But they were a minority within the party, and Wilson won not quite one-fourth (248) of the delegates to the Democratic national convention. Underwood, whose reputation derived solely from his advocacy of tariff reform, was never a national candidate, but he won more than a hundred delegates from Virginia and the Deep South. The great surprise of the Democratic preconvention campaign was the near tidal wave of support for Champ Clark. A longtime member of Congress who had always supported Bryan, he inherited most of Bryan's followers in the Midwest and Plains states. Elsewhere, with the exception of the South, he had the support of every big-city machine and conservative state organization. He also had the support of William Randolph Hearst, whose national network of newspapers and magazines flayed Wilson daily for his alleged conservatism and disdain of southern and eastern European immigrants. Clark emerged from the preconvention campaign the front-runner, with some 436 delegates.

Clark seemed unstoppable when the Democrats met in Baltimore on 25 June 1912; he seemed unbeatable when the ninety Tammany-controlled New York state delegates, nominally for Harmon, went to Clark on the tenth ballot and gave him a majority, but not the two-thirds majority then necessary for nomination. Then occurred one of the miracles of American political history: Wilson's nomination on the forty-sixth ballot. It was the result of the fanatical loyalty of the Wilson delegates and of the superb strategy of Wilson's managers. At the beginning of the balloting, they made a solemn compact with Underwood's managers that each other's delegates would never vote for Clark, but only for Wilson or Underwood, as the circumstances might determine. This agreement effectively blocked a Clark victory and gave the Wilson managers time to whittle away at Clark's strength. A stampede to Wilson began when Illinois swung its fifty-eight votes from Clark to Wilson on the forty-third ballot; then the Underwood delegates swung over to Wilson on the final, forty-sixth ballot. As his running mate, Wilson chose THOMAS R. MARSHALL, governor of Indiana.

**Campaign and Result.** The Democratic platform, crafted under Bryan's guidance, represented the final maturation of the Bryan-progressive tradition. It denounced the Payne-Aldrich tariff and promised honest downward revision; demanded legislation to destroy the so-called trusts and to establish a banking and currency system free from Wall Street control; approved the income tax and the direct election of Senators; and held out certain promises to organized labor. But it was silent on matters such as woman suffrage and advanced social and economic legislation.

Since Taft confined his participation in the campaign to his acceptance speech and a few public letters, the presidential campaign of 1912 turned into a verbal duel among Roosevelt, Wilson, and the Socialist Party candidate, EUGENE V. DEBS. Wilson highlighted the tariff issue at first but then, under the tutelage of Louis D. Brandeis, the "people's lawyer of Boston," found his issue in the emancipation of business and labor from monopolistic control. Lashing out at Roosevelt's New Nationalism, Wilson said that it would end in control of the federal government by big-business leaders and their enslavement of workers. In contrast, Wilson proposed to destroy monopolies and unleash the potential energies of businessmen by restoring conditions under which competition could flourish—by freeing the banking and currency systems from Wall Street control and strengthening the SHERMAN ANTITRUST ACT. Wilson called this program the NEW FREEDOM. In brief, it envisaged the destruction of special privileges, the restoration of the reign of competition, and reliance for future economic growth on individual enterprise.

Aware of the odds against him because he did not

have a nationwide party organization behind him, Roosevelt campaigned more strenuously than Wilson. Denouncing the New Freedom as "rural toryism" and a throwback to outmoded STATES' RIGHTS and laissez-faire doctrines, Roosevelt pressed the argument that Americans had to abandon individualism for democratic collectivism and use of the federal and state government as the regulators and protectors of business, industry, and workers. He said that Americans had to surrender their hostility to strong government and espouse a New Nationalism that would achieve Jeffersonian ends through Hamiltonian means.

There was much excitement when a madman shot Roosevelt, wounding him seriously, but not fatally, in Milwaukee on 14 October. This incident evoked much sympathy for the Bull Moose, as Roosevelt called himself, but brought him few additional votes on Election Day, 5 November 1912. The most striking fact of the campaign was Roosevelt's failure to draw enough Democrats to his side to create a majority progressive coalition. Wilson polled 6,293,120 popular and 435 electoral votes; Roosevelt, 4,119,582 popular and 88 electoral votes; Taft, 3,485,082 popular and 8 electoral votes; and Debs, 900,672 popular votes. On account of the split in the Republican vote, the Democrats gained a commanding majority in the House of Representatives and a narrow but workable majority in the Senate.

Looking to the future, Wilson could take small comfort from these returns, for he had received fewer votes than Bryan had polled in 1908 and failed to establish the Democratic Party as the majority party of the country. In defeat, Roosevelt was the real winner in 1912. He did better than any THIRD-PARTY CANDIDATE in American history. More important, his New Nationalism would live to challenge all administrations until its final enactment—as the NEW DEAL—during the presidency of Franklin D. Roosevelt.

### BIBLIOGRAPHY

Filler, Louis. *Appointment of Armageddon.* 1976.

Kelly, Frank L. *The Fight for the White House.* 1961.

Link, Arthur S. *Wilson: The Road to the White House.* 1947.

Link, Arthur S., et al., eds. *The Papers of Woodrow Wilson.* 69 vols. 1966–1993. Vols. 20–25.

Mowry, George E. "Election of 1912." In vol. 3 of *History of American Presidential Elections, 1789-1968.* Edited by Arthur M. Schlesinger, Jr., and Fred L. Israel. 4 vols. 1971. Pp. 2134–2241.

Mowry, George E. *Theodore Roosevelt and the Progressive Movement.* 1946.

ARTHUR S. LINK

**ELECTION, PRESIDENTIAL, 1916.** The election of 1916 was the first U.S. presidential contest since 1808 to have worldwide repercussions. It came, of course, during WORLD WAR I, and, as events turned out, its outcome determined who would lead the American people during their participation in that war and be their spokesman at the peace conference that would follow. It was also a referendum on the domestic achievements of the administration of Woodrow Wilson.

Wilson and the Democratic Congress's achievements were extensive and impressive enough to give the President a good chance of reelection. Before the presidential campaigns began in the spring of 1916, Wilson had pushed through Congress the most comprehensive reform program in American history to that date. Wilson had overcome lobbyists and special-interest groups to win passage of the UNDERWOOD TARIFF ACT (1913), which drastically reduced the rates of the PAYNE-ALDRICH TARIFF ACT of 1909. The President then went from one legislative triumph to another: the Federal Reserve Act (1913), which created a new decentralized, federally controlled banking system and currency; the CLAYTON ACT (1914), which strengthened the SHERMAN ANTITRUST ACT of 1890; the Federal Trade Commission Act (1914), to monitor business and prevent restraint of trade before it occurred; the Seamen's Act (1915), which freed sailors from bondage to their labor contracts; and other measures of lesser note, such as the Jones Act (1916), which gave near autonomy to the PHILIPPINES.

In foreign affairs, some of them very perilous, Wilson had achieved a record probably excelling that of any other President since Thomas Jefferson. He had supported the Mexican revolution against its American and European foes; he had staunchly, if only rhetorically, defended American neutral rights against the encroachments of the British navy; and, most importantly, he had forced the haughty imperial German government to observe the rules of civilized warfare in its submarine attacks on merchant shipping.

On the other hand, the United States was still a predominantly Republican country in 1916 (as it had been since 1896), and Wilson in his first term was a minority President who held office and had a Democratic Congress only because the REPUBLICAN PARTY had split asunder in 1912. The result of the coming presidential election was very much in doubt in the early months of 1916. Everything would depend on what would happen between then and November, most importantly what the Republican and Progressive parties would do.

**The Candidates.** The first augury—the result of the congressional elections of 1914—was not promising for Wilson and his party. The PROGRESSIVE (BULL MOOSE)

PARTY had been a one-man party in 1912 (that man being Theodore Roosevelt), without a viable nationwide organization. It went to pieces in the election of 1914, and, since most Progressives reverted to traditional voting habits, the Republicans reduced the Democratic majority in the House of Representatives to twenty-five and carried state elections in many large and key states. Republican leaders in 1916 were determined not to do anything openly to woo back remaining apostates to the fold. This was evidenced when Roosevelt entered the Republican presidential primaries and carried not a single state.

The main task of the Republicans was to find a candidate who was acceptable to both conservatives and progressives and who had offended no one on issues such as military preparedness and policies vis-à-vis the European belligerents. The Republican preconvention campaign turned up only favorite-son candidates, none of whom could successfully challenge Wilson. When the Republican national convention opened in Chicago on 7 June, 1916, all Republican eyes turned toward a noncandidate, CHARLES EVANS HUGHES, an Associate Justice of the Supreme Court. Hughes had impressive credentials as a reform governor of New York from 1907 to 1910. More importantly, he had not said a word on public issues since donning his judicial robes in 1910. He yielded to a draft when the convention nominated him on the third ballot on a moderately progressive platform, one that carefully avoided any hint of favoritism toward either side in the European conflict.

There was never any doubt that the Democrats would renominate Wilson, but there were many questions at the beginning of 1916 about Wilson's thoughts and future policies concerning important items still on the national reform agenda. In answer to those who wondered whether Wilsonian reform had run its course, the President showed that he was bent on a new course of advanced progressivism that went far beyond the NEW FREEDOM program. On 28 January 1916, he taunted conservatives by appointing Louis D. Brandeis, the country's most ardent foe of big business, to the Supreme Court. (Brandeis was confirmed on 1 June 1916 after a long struggle in which Wilson played the decisive role.) On 24 January, Wilson endorsed the establishment of a federal tariff commission to take the tariff out of politics, a proposal that Roosevelt had advocated and Wilson had ridiculed in 1912. On the same day that he sent Brandeis's nomination to the Senate, Wilson met with congressional leaders and approved a bill to establish a federally funded system of long-term rural credits. In 1914, he had blocked a similar bill by threatening to veto it. Congress enacted

all the above-mentioned measures into law in a relatively short time. Wilson had also struck out on another new course in late 1915 and early 1916 by championing a program of moderate military preparedness in land forces and a significant increase in American naval strength. He sincerely believed in the necessity of such a program, but he also was responding to a movement whose staunchest champion was Theodore Roosevelt.

Wilson personally oversaw the drafting of the platform that was presented to the Democratic national convention, which opened in St. Louis on 14 June 1916. It made an open bid for Progressive support by promising adoption of federal social legislation, including a CHILD LABOR law and a model program for all employees of the federal government. This program included payment of a living wage, the eight-hour day, workmen's compensation, protection of women, and pensions for retired federal employees. The platform also endorsed a neutral foreign policy, supported Wilson's program of "reasonable" preparedness, and commended American membership in a postwar league of nations "to assist the world in securing peace and justice." The platform, which also lauded the progressive legislation working its way through Congress, was as radical as the Progressive platform of 1912, except on the issue of woman suffrage. (This it approved, but only on the basis of enfranchisement by the states.)

The convention approved the platform and renominated Wilson, but otherwise Wilson's plans for the conclave went awry. Before the convention met, the President directed that it should make "Americanism," patriotism, and, presumably, willingness to go to war to defend American rights, the keynotes. The keynote speaker, former governor Martin H. Glynn of New York, sounded these themes, but the delegates responded with a notable lack of enthusiasm. Then Glynn, discussing Wilson's NEUTRALITY policies, made what he thought would be a brief recital of past instances when the country had chosen peace over war. It was as if a bolt of lightning had struck the hall; delegates began to shout, "Hit him again!" Departing from his text, Glynn went off into a paean of praise of neutrality. "What did we do?" he asked after reciting each instance. "We didn't go to war!" the delegates roared in answer. The permanent chairman of the convention, Senator Ollie M. James of Kentucky, was even more eloquent in extolling the President's neutrality in his speech the next day. He was followed by WILLIAM JENNINGS BRYAN, who had resigned as Secretary of State in June 1915 because he thought Wilson was standing too rigidly in the crisis with Germany occasioned by the German torpedoing of the British liner Lusitania. Bryan came down from the reporters' box to add his blessing to Wilson the peace-lover. And at the last moment someone inserted the slogan "He kept us out of war" in the platform.

**The Campaign.** Hughes began his campaign vigorously with a cross-country tour, denouncing Democratic inefficiency and iniquities and Wilson's alleged meddling in Mexico and calling for a high tariff and "unflinching maintenance of all American rights on land and sea." But, everywhere he spoke, this "bearded iceberg," as Roosevelt called him, evoked little enthusiasm. Hughes also blundered in California by consorting only with right-wing Republicans there and ignoring the Progressive senatorial candidate, Governor Hiram W. Johnson. Hughes did finally find an issue in early September, when Wilson averted a nationwide railroad strike by pushing the Adamson Act through Congress. The law satisfied railroad workers by imposing the eight-hour day on all interstate railroads. Wilson had cravenly surrendered to the railroad unions, Hughes said, declaring that "no power on earth" had the right to dictate to the President and Congress. It seemed like a turning point: money flowed into the Republican campaign coffers, while contributions to the Democrats' campaign fell to a trickle.

Wilson was too busy to enter the fray before September. Aside from preventing the railroad strike, he also pushed through the federal child labor and workmen's compensation bills, which had been stalled in the Senate, and was overseeing passage of a "soak the rich" tax bill. But all these distractions were behind him when he opened his campaign with his acceptance speech on 2 September 1916. It was a frank appeal for the support of progressives in general and of former Rooseveltian Progressives in particular. "We have in four years come very near to carrying out the platform of the Progressive party, as well as our own," he said, "for we also are progressives."

In the contest that followed, Hughes continued on his inept course, while Wilson was at his magnificent best as a campaigner. When Hughes continued to pound away at the Adamson Act, Wilson replied that he favored the eight-hour day for all workers, not just railroad workers. Hughes flirted with pro-German citizens; in contrast, Wilson publicly rebuked a German American who had sent him an insulting telegram. Then, in a speech on 30 September, Wilson went for Hughes's jugular. The "certain prospect" of a Republican victory, he said, "is that we shall be drawn, in one form or other, into the embroilments of the European war, and that, to the south of us, the force of

the United States will be used to produce in Mexico the kind of law and order which some American investors in Mexico consider most to their advantage." Democratic campaign managers and speakers all over the country now rushed to exploit the peace theme. Bryan was in the forefront of this army, sounding the call of peace up and down the prairie and plains states.

Wilson's conjoining the themes of peace and advanced progressivism caused a division in American politics the likes of which the country had not seen since 1896. The left-wing of progressivism, including many socialists, social workers, suffrage leaders, and intellectuals and their journals (for example, *The New Republic* and *The Nation*) moved en masse into the Wilson ranks. Most of the leaders of the near-defunct Progressive Party repudiated Roosevelt and supported Wilson. Also enthusiastic were the railroad brotherhoods, the American Federation of Labor, and farm organizations. Finally, practically all independent newspapers and magazines came to Wilson's side.

**The Result.** Still, the outcome was in doubt to the very end of the campaign. The first sign was a bad augury for the Democrats: in mid September Republicans made a clean sweep in Maine, the only state to hold state and congressional elections before November. "I don't see how we can lose now," Hughes said. His prediction seemed on the mark when the returns began coming in on election day, 7 November. They indicated a tidal wave for Hughes: by 10 P.M. that evening he had carried all non-southern states east of the Mississippi except for New Hampshire and Ohio. Wilson was philosophical in his seeming defeat. In fact, he had already made plans to arrange for Hughes' immediate succession in the event that Hughes won. (Wilson would have appointed Hughes as Secretary of State; then Wilson and Vice President THOMAS R. MARSHALL would have resigned, and Hughes would have succeeded to the presidency.)

Returns from the west began to come in early in the morning of 8 November; they indicated a strong trend toward the Democrats. By midnight Wilson had 251 electoral votes to Hughes's 247. Final returns from California, Minnesota, North Dakota, and New Mexico would determine the election. The outcome was known late on 9 November: Wilson had carried California, New Mexico, and North Dakota, with a total of 9,129,606 popular and 277 electoral votes. Hughes had 8,538,221 popular and 254 electoral votes. Wilson's victory was a narrow one: for example, he carried California by 3,806 votes and North Dakota by 1,735, and he lost Minnesota by only 392 votes.

Wilson's victory must be reckoned one of the notable achievements in American political history. Overall, he increased his popular vote in 1916 by nearly 50 percent over the three-way race of 1912. In some states he doubled his popular vote. Wilson won because he consummated the union of the south and west, which Bryan had failed to do in 1896. In addition, he overwhelmingly carried the vote of organized labor and a disproportionate number of the votes of former Progressives. He also won about 300,000 votes from Socialists who deserted their candidate, Allan Benson. But no observer could say that Wilson had established the DEMOCRATIC PARTY as the dominant party or that the coalition he put together in 1916 could endure the strains that future events would put on it.

### BIBLIOGRAPHY

Link, Arthur S. *Wilson: Campaigns for Progressivism and Peace.* 1965.

Link, Arthur S., et al., eds. *The Papers of Woodrow Wilson.* 69 vols. 1966–1993. vols. 36–38.

Link, Arthur S., and William M. Leary, Jr. "Election of 1916." In *History of American Presidential Elections, 1789–1968.* Edited by Arthur M. Schlesinger, Jr., and Fred L. Israel. 4 vols. 1971.

Lovell, S. D. *The Presidential Election of 1916.* 1980.

Mowry, George E. *Theodore Roosevelt and the Progressive Movement.* 1946.

ARTHUR S. LINK

**ELECTION, PRESIDENTIAL, 1920.** The 1920 presidential election, coming only two years after the end of WORLD WAR I, decided the direction the United States would take in the postwar world. The new President could either continue President Woodrow Wilson's active foreign policy or turn the country inward toward the isolationist policies that had preceded entry into the war. In domestic affairs the election would decide whether the federal government was to continue the progressive initiatives begun by President Theodore Roosevelt, strengthened by President William Howard Taft, and consolidated by President Wilson in his first term.

The election was fought over one overriding issue: whether the United States would join the LEAGUE OF NATIONS. All other issues from PROHIBITION to unemployment were politically secondary.

**The Issues.** Woodrow Wilson after serving two terms was expected to follow precedent and not seek a third term. Instead, he chose to remain in the White House and await a third nomination. At the same time there was considerable concern about the President's health after his stroke in September 1919. This left the DEMOCRATIC PARTY, along with possible presidential contenders, in a quandary. The party could not unseat a sitting President, and the contenders could not

actively pursue the nomination without risk of being seen as usurpers.

Woodrow Wilson had been elected by forming a coalition made up in part by labor, which found that it could look to Wilson to protect its interests. The administration passed a labor program that included the controversial Adamson Act of 1916, making the eight-hour day mandatory on interstate carriers, a measure for which Wilson's support was essential; the Keating-Owen Child Labor Act, which epitomized the best impulses of the progressive era; the Kern-McGillicuddy law, which provided workmen's compensation for federal employees; and the La Follette Seamans Act, which Wilson supported after coming to know the terrible labor conditions in the merchant marine. Farmers occupied a vital place in the Wilson coalition. They warmed to the antimonopoly measures and agricultural education programs that Wilson enacted, the regulation of railroad rates and promotion of good roads, the generous loans to agriculture coupled with the advancement of credit against warehouse stocks. Progressives also made up an important part of the coalition. The President captured not only the loyal Democratic followers of WILLIAM JENNINGS BRYAN, but also some of Theodore Roosevelt's Progressive adherents who saw Wilson enact, one by one, the important elements in the PROGRESSIVE (BULL MOOSE) PARTY platform of 1912.

By 1919 the coalition lay in ruin. When labor, having made consistent gains during the war, called a series of strikes organized to retain and extend wartime gains, the Justice Department had sided with management. Wilson denounced the 1919 Boston police strike as a "crime against civilization." When the bituminous coal miners went on strike Attorney General A. Mitchell Palmer, mentioned as a possible successor to Wilson, obtained two federal injunctions against the strikers. Palmer, along with antagonizing labor, damaged Wilson among progressives with the Red Scare in 1919, which involved mass deportations of aliens accused of subversive activities [*see* PALMER RAIDS]. The deportation delirium itself ended early in the election year of 1920.

Woodrow Wilson, the hero of Versailles, had made a drastic error; by keeping the Republicans out of the peace process, he had made the League of Nations and the TREATY OF VERSAILLES a partisan issue in the election of 1920. The Republicans had the choice of forcing the Democrats to accept their amendments or discrediting and defeating the treaty on the Senate floor, and thus injuring Wilson or his successor in the process.

The main point in the treaty that the Republicans, led by Senator Henry Cabot Lodge, wanted altered was Article X. This provision they interpreted as violating United States sovereignty by allowing the League and not Congress to decide when and where United States troops would be used overseas. The Republican Senators wanted to amend the treaty to empower Congress, and not the League, to decide when and where the United States would use troops to protect vital interests. Wilson had submitted three drafts of the treaty to the Senate. Republican leaders found all three unsatisfactory. After his final draft was rejected, Wilson would brook no further interference or changes in "his" League, and went so far as to ask the voters to make the issue their reason for electing Democrats to Congress in 1918, to no avail, however. Wilson's partisanship toward the League in two Senate votes made it an issue in the 1920 presidential election. The Republicans called for the League's defeat, and the Democrats were forced to back a treaty that many Americans believed to be flawed without the amendments proposed by the Senate.

**The Nominees.** There were six Republican possibilities for the presidential nomination of 1920. General Leonard Wood, commander of the Rough Riders in the SPANISH-AMERICAN WAR, and military governor of CUBA, had advocated preparedness prior to the nation's entry into World War I. Wood, who appealed to eastern conservatives and had support from former President Taft, was opposed by organized labor. Senator Hiram Johnson, former progressive Governor of California and vice presidential nominee in 1912, was Wood's main opponent in the primaries. He was a vocal opponent of the League. With the death of Theodore Roosevelt in 1919, Johnson believed he was the natural heir to the Roosevelt Progressives. Senator Henry Cabot Lodge, the senior Senator from Massachusetts and the leader of the opposition to the League in the Senate, was a credible contender. Frank O. Lowden, governor of Illinois and a member of the Republican national committee, appealed to both liberals and conservatives and was considered a possible compromise candidate. Herbert Hoover, the best known possible contestant, had been Food Administrator in the United States during the war and in 1919 was director general of European Relief to a war-torn Europe. He was viewed as a progressive but opposed the closed shop and therefore had the opposition of labor. Senator Warren G. Harding of Ohio, the DARK HORSE candidate, was a party regular who had first entered the race to maintain control of the Ohio delegation, but retained the backing of many of the party bosses who were impressed with Harding's ability to follow their advice.

The presidential campaign would be an ordeal for any Democratic candidate who would attempt to face up to the burdens of the League and of intraparty disorder; yet nevertheless, three leading Democrats actively sought their party's nomination. JAMES M. COX, three-term governor of Ohio, was an avowed wet who openly ridiculed the Volstead Act. Liberals and labor leaders perceived A. Mitchell Palmer, Wilson's Attorney General, as an embodiment of the reaction and betrayal that appeared to characterize the Wilson administration during its second term. William Gibbs McAdoo was the most distinctly Wilsonian candidate. Many of his supporters had held administration posts; and as Secretary of the Treasury through the war McAdoo had worked closely with such loyal Wilsonians as Carter Glass and Josephus Daniels. McAdoo, Wilson's son-in-law, was seen as the heir apparent. But because the President would not step aside or support him he did not persist in his efforts and was denied the nomination that many party elders had thought to be his for the asking.

The Republican convention met in June 1920 at the Chicago Coliseum. The Republican platform did not call for a repudiation of the League as many had feared, but instead left room for compromise. Throughout the primaries no candidate had been able to capture enough delegates to capture the nomination. Wood had won in New Hampshire, South Dakota, New Jersey, and Massachusetts; Johnson in North Dakota, Michigan, Illinois, and Nebraska; Harding in the delegate-rich states of California and Ohio. After only the fourth ballot the convention was adjourned without a roll call in an effort to prevent a deadlock. It was from this meeting that the popular image of the smoke-filled room would emerge in many of the accounts concerning the nomination.

In an all-night meeting, party leaders chose Harding as their nominee. Harding was pushed along by his political manager, HARRY M. DAUGHERTY, a former state legislator who many Republicans regarded as the consummate fixer. When the convention resumed it took six more ballots for Harding to gain the nomination of his party. Calvin Coolidge, the conservative governor of Massachusetts, best known for his stand against the Boston police strike of 1919, gained the nomination on the first ballot as vice presidential candidate.

At the Democratic convention, which began later in June in San Francisco, the delegates voted for a platform that called for ratification of the League of Nations along with an evasive statement about a willingness to accept "interpretive" amendments. After forty ballots Cox finally won the nomination and chose as his running mate former Assistant Secretary of the Navy Franklin Delano Roosevelt. Roosevelt brought to the ticket not only name recognition but political and geographical balance.

**The Campaign.** Bound to the disastrous issue of the League, and pitted against a popular political mood that forecast almost certain defeat, Cox and Roosevelt crisscrossed the country preaching progressivism and calling for the ratification of the peace treaty and the League. Added to their problems was the near dormancy of the party organization since the congressional elections of 1918.

The Republican strategy was to run a "front porch" campaign. Harding ensconced himself on the porch of his home in Marion, Ohio, and awaited party leaders and other political supplicants. Rather than calling for a progressive future for the United States, the Republican nominee yearned for a return to the past, "America's present need," he said, " is not heroics, but healing; not nostrums, but normalcy; not revolution, but restoration; not agitation, but adjustment; not surgery, but serenity, not the dramatic, but the dispassionate; not experiment, but equipoise; not submergence in internationality, but sustainment in triumphant nationality."

The real Republican quarry was the incumbent President, not the Ohio governor. On the general issue of the League the people may have been undecided or indifferent, but toward the Wilson League considerable numbers were by 1920 unquestionably hostile, having become estranged from the austere and unbending President.

Just six weeks before the election, Harding was forced off his porch by attacks by Cox, who asserted that the Republicans had established a slush fund from illegal contributions. After Harding publicly challenged those charges, Cox was forced to retract them.

As the campaign wound down Samuel Gompers, the president of the American Federation of Labor, endorsed Cox and Roosevelt. But it was too late to help the Democrats. Cox had become more virulent in his attacks on Harding, who in one pronouncement had said he would back the League, and in another that he would fight against it. In his last public speech before election day, Cox told an audience that anyone who voted for Harding was a traitor. Roosevelt on the other hand took the higher road, and for the most part stayed with praising the Democratic record, and stressing the need for an international association to keep world peace. He appealed more to the intellect of the voters than to their emotions. Neither line of attacks could help the Democratic Party in 1920. The Republicans predicted a landslide, and were not disappointed.

**The Result.** In the popular vote, Harding received 16,181,289 votes, Cox 8,141,750. In the ELECTORAL COLLEGE Harding carried thirty-seven states with 404 votes against Cox's 127 votes and eleven states. The Republicans won the House of Representatives with 303 seats to 131 seats for the Democrats, the largest majority in the party's history. In the Senate the Republicans gained 10 seats, which gave them a 22-seat majority. Harding and the REPUBLICAN PARTY viewed the election as a complete repudiation of Wilsonian progressivism and a call by the American people for a conservative isolationist federal government.

BIBLIOGRAPHY

Bagby, Wesley M. *The Road to Normalcy: The Presidential Campaign and Election of 1920*. 1962.
McCoy, Donald R. "Election of 1920." In *History of American Presidential Elections, 1789-1968*. Edited by Arthur M. Schlesinger, Jr., and Fred L. Israel. Vol. 3. 1971.

MICHAEL P. KELLY and DAVID BURNER

**ELECTION, PRESIDENTIAL, 1924.** The death of Warren G. Harding on 2 August 1923 had brought Vice President Calvin Coolidge to the White House as the thirtieth President of the United States. As soon as Coolidge took his oath of office talk began among Republicans in Washington, D.C., about who would be the Republican nominee the next year.

Coolidge soon managed to create a conservative administration, although as governor of Massachusetts he had been considered a mild liberal. Coolidge quickly gained public confidence by settling a serious Pennsylvania coal strike, and ridding himself of those who were associated with the corruption in the Harding administration. He appointed competent, qualified people to office as well as a special counsel to investigate the scandals that had arisen during Harding's tenure. [See TEAPOT DOME SCANDAL.]

**The Republican Contest.** In the fall of 1923, Senator Hiram Johnson of California announced his intention to seek the Republican presidential nomination. He represented the isolationists within the party. He spoke against the World Court as he had the League of Nations and vehemently opposed the sale of arms to liberal forces in Mexico. He called for an end to all oriental immigration and joined the American League in supporting the immediate payment of the veterans' bonus.

By using PATRONAGE to consolidate his hold over Republican officeholders and officeseekers in the South, Coolidge was able to dominate the southern delegations. Johnson's strength in some of the farm states was offset by the President's increase in wheat tariffs and in the availability of farm loans. His candidacy forced the President to adopt a more progressive stance and especially to rid his house of corruption. Johnson was probably instrumental in the movement that led Coolidge to fire Attorney General HARRY M. DAUGHERTY and to accept the resignation of the Secretary of the Navy who had leased naval oil reserves. When Coolidge defeated Johnson even in the progressive Republican's home state of California, Johnson decided to drop out of the race.

In mid May when the official Coolidge headquarters opened, it had become clear that the only interesting event of the Republican campaign would be the choosing of the vice presidential candidate. Senator William Borah declined the honor; other candidates included General CHARLES G. DAWES, Secretary of Commerce Herbert Hoover, and Governor Frank Lowden of Illinois.

The Republican convention opened on 10 June. Little debate arose over the choice of the presidential nominee since a combination of preferential primaries and state conventions supplied Coolidge with a commanding lead in pledged delegates. On the first ballot he received all but thirty-four delegate votes.

The delegates nominated Governor Lowden for Vice President, and the President wrote him a letter of congratulations on being selected. But he refused to accept. Charles G. Dawes, a brigadier general of WORLD WAR I was unpopular with organized labor but had wide support among convention delegates and especially conservatives, who liked his denunciation of the closed shop. Hoover was disliked by wheat farmers for his role in price fixing during the war. Dawes defeated Hoover by 682 votes to 234.

Dawes was a useful choice. He would aggressively carry the partisan campaign for Coolidge. For his efforts to ease the harsh payment terms for the reparations imposed on Germany, moreover, he might secure a large number of the German-American votes. These might otherwise go to the Progressive Party candidate ROBERT M. LA FOLLETTE who as a Wisconsin Republican had attracted the support of many midwesterners of German descent.

The PARTY PLATFORM contained few changes from the 1920 platform. No mention was made of the KU KLUX KLAN and the document only briefly mentioned plans for joining the World Court and helping farmers. The platform focused on the administration's impressive record in creating a strong economy and pledged tax reduction and a continuation of things as they were. The "Honest Government" plank spoke of maintaining high standards of government. Prosecution of the participants in the Teapot Dome scandal had already started. When asked to comment on how those involved in the scandal would be dealt with, Coolidge simply declared "those guilty will be punished."

Because of the death of his son, the President gave few speeches and rarely traveled outside of Washington, D.C. The Coolidge campaign focused on prosperity, economy, stability and harmony, and respectability and promised tax cuts, which would allow a rise in purchasing power.

**The Democratic Contest.** Democrats looked optimistically toward the 1924 election. In 1922 they had captured seventy-eight congressional seats that had been held by Republicans and every incumbent Democrat won. As a result the Republican Party majorities were reduced to eight in the Senate and eighteen in the House. Democrats believed that if they could galvanize anger at the Harding scandals and produce a qualified candidate, they might win the presidency.

Hostility to immigrants, to Catholics, to alcohol, to cities and political machines motivated Democrats in small towns and the countryside. Urban Democrats returned the hostility.

The rural camp presented former Secretary of the Treasury William Gibbs McAdoo as its candidate. The sixty-year-old McAdoo entered the convention with about 300 delegates pledged to him, 194 of them through presidential primaries. During his wartime administration of the railroads, he had become popular with labor; and as a progressive and as Woodrow Wilson's son-in-law, he was a favorite of the Wilsonians. The primary results showed that McAdoo had wide appeal throughout the country. He appeared to be strongest in the South and West, where much of his support came from the drys and—perhaps to his dismay—from the Ku Klux Klan. McAdoo remained neutral on the Klan issue, neither actively seeking its support nor denouncing Klansmen outright.

Opposition to McAdoo came from big business in the East and from factions north and east of the Ohio River reacting to the nativist, anti-Catholic, and prohibitionist Democrats with whom McAdoo was associated. The Teapot Dome scandal had also touched him. And despite McAdoo's reputation for progressivism, some Democrats suspected him of opportunistic plays to public opinion.

Urban Democrats supported the liberal Catholic governor from New York, ALFRED E. SMITH. His original reason for seeking the nomination had been to block McAdoo on behalf of the eastern bosses. In the 1922 congressional elections the Democratic Party made gains in the cities and regions of rapid industrialization. Smith's followers came from states with big electoral votes, New York, Massachusetts, and Illinois, the kind of states that could swing an election.

The Democratic platform deplored CHILD LABOR, pitied the farmer, and included some radical demands such as federal aid to education, an excess profits tax in wartime, vigorous prosecution of monopolies, and "strict public control and conservation of all the nation's natural resources, such as coal, iron, oil and timber." The controversial issue of whether to censure the Ku Klux Klan by name caused immense problems for the platform committee. The Smith faction demanded denunciation of the Klan. Bryan and McAdoo, while not friends of the Klan, believed that denouncing it by name would betray their supporters. In the ensuing vote, the Klan barely escaped censure.

With the party split in two, the rule requiring a two-thirds majority for nomination crippled the chances of both candidates by giving each a veto. McAdoo wanted to drop the two-thirds rule, but his Protestant supporters preferred to keep their veto power over a Catholic candidate, and the South regarded the rule as a protection of sectional interests. A deadlock developed. Smith never won more then 368 of the 729 votes needed for nomination, and McAdoo reached his highest point of 528 on the seventieth ballot. On ballot after ballot some votes also went to Oscar Underwood of Alabama, an opponent of PROHIBITION and the Klan. Tammany Hall Democrats tried to prolong the convention until the hotel bills became too expensive for most delegates; they also packed the galleries with noisy rooters. Smith suggested that all delegates be released from their pledges, to which McAdoo agreed on condition that the two-thirds rule be eliminated. No accord was reached. At one point, Smith offered to withdraw if McAdoo would do likewise, but McAdoo refused.

Lesser candidates also refused to withdraw from the race. One of them, JOHN W. DAVIS began to gain strength. On the 103d ballot, after fourteen days of bickering and after the withdrawal of Smith and McAdoo, Davis was nominated as the Democratic candidate. Charles W. Bryan, governor of Nebraska since 1922 and brother of WILLIAM JENNINGS BRYAN, became the vice-presidential nominee on the first ballot. The stiff, retiring Davis could not ignite a challenge to the Republican Party with its promise of expanded prosperity in already prosperous times.

Powerful railroad unions and progressives lacking faith in either major party, enthusiastically sought a THIRD-PARTY option.

**The Progressive Party.** In July twelve hundred delegates to the Progressive Party convention nominated Senator La Follette. At the foundation of his program was an attack on monopolies, as violators of social justice and traditional American liberties. He called for government ownership of water power and a gradual nationalization of the railroads. He opposed prohibition and spoke for the antiwar strain of progressivism. La Follette immediately and clearly disavowed the Ku Klux Klan and repeatedly dissociated himself from the communists. La Follette's running mate was Senator Burton K. Wheeler, Democrat of Montana.

The Progressive Party and its candidate had serious weaknesses. La Follette had a history of serious illness and was unable to handle an extensive speaking itinerary. The party lacked press coverage, substantial funds, and local candidates who could promote the ticket, and the party was seriously hurt by the rise in wheat prices over the summer, which afforded Coolidge a substantial number of farm votes. La Follette's radicalism attempted to unite labor and farmers, but organized labor was not strong enough to carry La Follette's campaign. The Progressive Party was further plagued by a host of election technicalities.

The 1924 campaign introduced major historical additions to politics: the use of the bonus system and radio broadcasting of the conventions and political party advertisements. The bonus system awarded extra convention votes to any states that had supported the party's presidential candidate in the previous election. In 1924 the Republican Party used this system for the first time, but the Democrats did not until 1944. The innovative and widely used art of photojournalism offered a quick record of the convention and publicity shots of its candidates. And the use of radio for convention coverage and political campaigning foreshadowed the use of media techniques for exposure of political candidates.

**The Result.** The resilient economy and a divided Democratic Party, along with the effective "Keep Cool with Coolidge" campaign slogan, helped Coolidge and Dawes easily defeat their opponents. The Republican ticket received more popular votes, 15,719,921 (54 percent), and electoral votes, 382, than the other two parties combined. Davis garnered 136 electoral votes in twelve states, and 8,386,704 (28.8 percent) of the popular vote. La Follette won only Wisconsin's thirteen electoral votes and 4,988,398 (17.2 percent) of the popular vote. Coolidge's simple policies of tax reduction, government economy, and aid to private business without accompanying restraints, helped to keep the focus of the campaign on prosperity and the economy. His rectitude gained the confidence and support of the people.

## BIBLIOGRAPHY

Burner, David. *The Politics of Provincialism: The Democratic Party in Transition, 1918–1932*. 1986.

Murray, Robert K. *The 103rd Ballot*. 1976.

Rice, Arnold S. *The Ku Klux Klan in American Politics.* 1962.

Roseboom, Eugene H. *The History of Presidential Elections: From George Washington to Richard M. Nixon.* 1970.

Schlesinger, Arthur M., Jr., and Fred L. Israel, eds. *History of American Presidential Elections.* 4 vols. 1971.

Schlesinger, Arthur M., Jr., ed. *History of the United States Political Parties, Vol. III, 1910-1945: From Square Deal to New Deal.* 1973.

SHARI LEE OSBORN and DAVID BURNER

**ELECTION, PRESIDENTIAL, 1928.** The 1928 presidential contest between Democrat ALFRED E. SMITH, governor of New York, and Republican Herbert Hoover, Secretary of Commerce, brought out the intellectual best in the two men and the worst in their supporters. Their most publicized differences centered on the emotionally charged issues of religion (Smith was a Catholic) and PROHIBITION. Neither candidate directly attacked the other, largely because Hoover refused to conduct his campaign through debate or even to mention Smith's name in pubic. He also denounced support for the REPUBLICAN PARTY based on bigotry, but at the state and local levels vicious battles were waged between Protestant "drys" and Catholic "wets" because of the controversial Eighteenth (Prohibition) Amendment.

**The Campaign.** Racism also entered the campaign scene in the South, with the Democrats circulating a picture purportedly showing Hoover dancing (a social grace he never mastered) with Mary Booze, a black Republican committeewoman, along with rumors about his relationships with black women during his Mississippi flood-relief work. They also exploited the fact that Hoover had abolished segregation in the Department of Commerce. Southern Republicans in turn tried to connect Smith with the rising expectations of African Americans in New York, distributing a picture of a Harlem politician dictating to a white stenographer. This racism was nothing, however, compared to the anti-Catholic aspect of the campaign or to the passions that flared over prohibition.

The campaign's dirty, bigoted tactics obscured the fact that there were few substantive differences between the two candidates. Though Hoover and Smith were portrayed as exact opposites, they, and the PARTY PLATFORMS of both parties, exhibited more similarities than differences as each tried to capitalize on the pervasive underlying theme of the campaign: prosperity. Smith, however, took greater exception to certain planks in the Democratic platform than did Hoover to the Republican, with Smith specifically objecting to his party's support for the Eighteenth Amendment. Also Smith was never able to convince westerners that he both understood and sincerely supported the Farm Bureau's "equalization fee," which would have allowed the government to purchase surplus commodities.

In fact, neither Hoover nor Smith had been enthusiastically chosen by the professional politicians of their respective parties even though both were chosen on the first ballot. Each was ultimately assigned a packaged image by both supporters and opponents. Smith proved more difficult to sell to the public at large because he deliberately flaunted such New York Catholic characteristics as his Lower East Side brogue, his brown derby, and a taste for alcohol. The selling of political contenders through advertising techniques having little to do with political principles, now so common, was effective for the first time in 1928 because of two new means of national communication—radio and newsreels. Although Smith had a reputation in New York as an effective public speaker and although he made more speeches, he was no better at using radio than was the inarticulate Hoover. Outside New York State, Smith's accent irritated more Americans than it persuaded, and he stubbornly refused to try to alter it. Hoover looked and acted pained by the political process, but his discernible midwestern accent and his monotonous delivery proved less grating on the ears of the listening public in the last prosperous year of the New Era. Neither vice presidential candidate—Republican CHARLES CURTIS of Kansas and Democratic Senator Joseph T. Robinson of Arkansas—contributed anything distinctive to the campaign.

Their speech-pattern difficulties notwithstanding, both Hoover and Smith made conscious use of the radio as a campaign device. In May 1928, Hoover's New York campaign manager, Alan Fox, made the startling announcement that if Hoover were nominated his campaign would consist almost exclusively of radio broadcasts and films. Hoover made only seven major speeches, and all were based on the Republican platform. Hoover's technical knowledge and association with the radio industry as Secretary of Commerce had made him very aware of its potential political value. Smith had begun using radio broadcasts as early as 1924 to force New York Republican leaders to lower state income taxes. Although he later said he found radio "a cold affair," he actually delivered more radio addresses than did Hoover during the course of the 1928 campaign. Unfortunately, the radio campaigns of their supporters intensified emotionalism on the religious and prohibition questions instead of clarifying where their respective candidates stood on public power, AGRICULTURAL POLICY, and FOREIGN AFFAIRS.

**The Candidates.** Despite their contrasting appearances, religions, and attitudes toward alcohol, the two candidates were both self-made men—Smith's career was the urban counterpart to Hoover's rural rag-to-riches story. Both had reputations as efficient, progressive administrators (Hoover achieved governmental reorganization at the national level, Smith at the state level). Both received labor support: Hoover because he had consistently opposed "excessive use of injunctions in labor disputes" and Smith for having worked hard to improve the conditions of city workers in New York State and because of his good personal relationships with labor leaders (Hoover gained additional support from unions, however, because they did not want to support the loser, as they had in 1924). Both made a conscious effort to appeal to women voters in 1928, although Hoover captured the endorsement of the militant National Women's Party because Smith opposed the Equal Rights Amendment. Both surrounded themselves with experts for advice on economic and social reform matters. Both refused to succumb to red scare hysteria and other reactionary and nativist trends in the 1920s, such as the revival of KU KLUX KLAN. And, finally, both defended capitalism, big business, and the prosperity of the period and could count numerous millionaires among their supporters.

In one area, however, there was a distinct difference. Hoover was considered apolitical, never having run for public office, while Smith had an undisputed reputation as a professional politician and a "miracle worker in electioneering," having lost only one political contest in twenty-five years. Smith's progressive record as governor of New York, despite his Tammany Hall connections, was based on his administrative reforms and on his support not simply for state regulation of public power but for government ownership of power facilities in direct competition with private enterprise. Other evidence of his progressive stance included his strong CIVIL LIBERTIES record, especially with respect to protecting the rights of socialists, and his support of social welfare legislation aimed at improving working conditions, housing, and recreational facilities. But Smith was no WILLIAM JENNINGS BRYAN or ROBERT M. LA FOLLETTE—nor even a neo-Populist, much to the disappointment of the most progressive elements in the DEMOCRATIC PARTY.

Ostensibly committed to McNary-Haugenism (federal legislation that embodied a two-price system based on high domestic and low export prices), the New York governor had serious reservations about executing it and no convincing alternative program to offer farmers. Even this lack did not stop George N. Peek, a successful midwestern farm-implement executive and president of the American Council of Agriculture who had clashed with Hoover in the 1920s, from trying to

deliver the traditionally Republican farm vote into Smith's camp. Smith naturally frightened many Democratic conservatives and is usually described as the liberal candidate because he represented the urban masses—especially second-generation immigrants who neither abided by the laws against drinking nor conformed to traditional American social and religious values. His domestic socioeconomic and political views, however, were more traditionally conservative than Hoover's, if only because they were more provincial. The same is true of Smith's foreign policy—a subject he ignored almost entirely during the postwar decade. During the campaign, both Smith and Hoover agreed on high tariffs and nonintervention in Latin America.

Voters in 1928 assumed that "rum and Romanism" played an important role in Smith's defeat; certainly these issues accounted for the unusually high voter turnout. But, in fact, neither prohibition nor Smith's Catholicism appears in retrospect to have been a significant factor in the final results. Despite his wet Catholic liabilities, Smith ran better than had the two previous Democratic candidates of the decade. His greatest strength lay in his attractiveness to city voters of foreign white stock; his greatest weaknesses rested in his stubborn refusal to mitigate his own urban provinciality with a broadly based progressive campaign and in his insistence on contradicting his own party's plank on prohibition. Even given New Era prosperity, Smith was his own worst enemy in 1928, once replying to a reporter's question about how he would meet the needs of western states with the query, "What are the states west of the Mississippi?"

Just as Smith was not as liberal as his partisans wanted the electorate to believe, neither was Hoover as narrowly WASPish as they claimed. Hoover's support did not depend exclusively on Anglo-Saxon, small-town, middle-class citizens who were clinging to Protestantism and prohibition. Although Hoover did call prohibition "noble in motive," his views and public image represented a highly successful blend of the modern with the traditional. He was the businessman as well as the farm boy; the engineer as well as the humanitarian, a Progressive without the taint of socialism, a champion of America and yet an internationalist and man of the world, a "square dealer" with labor as well as with management, a successful administrator and yet not a politician, and an orphan and millionaire rolled into one. Finally, he stood for individualism as well as cooperation. He was thus "ten candidates in one," offering something to everyone, and what he offered appeared to be the best of the 1920s. To the majority of Americans in 1928, however, Hoover was simply an immensely successful "superexpert," a practical man of action who could be counted on to solve any problem with his facts and figures. During the campaign his publicity staff did little to modify this image, although they did try to humanize it somewhat.

**The Result.** Voter turnout was the largest in history up to that time, with 8 million more people voting than in 1924. Hoover's smashing victory further enhanced his reputation and heightened public expectations. Hoover carried all but eight states, and won 444 electoral votes to Smith's 87, accumulating 58 percent of the popular vote: 21,392,190 compared to Smith's 15,016,443. At the time this was the second biggest landslide in a presidential race. (By the 1990s, it ranked fifth behind the landslide elections of 1936, 1964, 1972, and 1984).

Probably no Democrat could have beaten Hoover, let alone an Irish Catholic "wet" from the slums of New York. Even so, Hoover took no chances. Once he obtained Calvin Coolidge's lukewarm endorsement after the nominating convention, Hoover ran an almost flawless (albeit boring) campaign, making a conscious effort to minimize factionalism within the party since he could not automatically rely on either Republican Progressives or the old guard for support. For its time, his was the best-financed campaign in history, and by refusing to debate with Smith directly over the most controversial and emotional issues Hoover united behind him such disparate Republicans as CHARLES EVANS HUGHES and Idaho Senator William E. Borah. In the long run, however, Hoover's landslide victory proved less impressive than Smith's defeat. Democratic victories in the nation's twelve largest cities and in fifty of the largest urban counties indicated that a new partisan realignment, which had been gradually building over the decade among the northern urbanites, was becoming a reality. In short, Smith cracked the traditionally solid support for the Republican Party in the Northeast. Publicly, Smith graciously accepted his overwhelming defeat. Privately, his supporters raged against the victory as an example of religious bigotry when, in fact, neither religion nor prohibition, however symbolically important in the election, determined voting patterns in 1928.

### BIBLIOGRAPHY

Bornet, Vaughan Davis. *Radio, Television, and American Politics.* 1969.

Burner, David. *The Politics of Provisionalism: The Democratic Party in Transition.* 1968.

Shover, John L. "The Emergence of the Two-Party System in Republican Philadelphia, 1924–1936." *Journal of American History* 60 (Mach 1974): 985–1002.

Silva, Ruth. *Rum, Religion, and Votes.* 1962.

JOAN HOFF

**ELECTION, PRESIDENTIAL, 1932.** Republican Herbert Hoover won the 1928 presidential election as the optimistic spokesman of a new era of prosperity. The election of 1932 was held with the United States mired in what had become the worst economic depression in its history. The decline in business activity that followed the stock market crash of October 1929 had resulted in more than thirteen million unemployed by 1932. Hoover balked at a massive public works program or federal relief for the unemployed because of the threats such measures represented to the balanced budget and thus to the business confidence required for recovery.

**The Candidates.** Hoover's political difficulties were heightened by a chilly personality that made him appear remote from, even callous to, the widespread suffering. Nevertheless, he retained so iron-clad a grip on the REPUBLICAN PARTY machinery as to foreclose any challenge to his renomination. A group of former Theodore Roosevelt Republicans looked to Senator Hiram Johnson of California or Governor Gifford Pinchot of Pennsylvania as possible alternatives. Johnson, however, was not tempted, and though Pinchot did test the political waters, he abandoned the idea of running because of lack of support. Former President Calvin Coolidge squelched a "draft Coolidge" movement that appeared in fall 1931. Other dissidents hoped New Jersey Senator Dwight Morrow, Charles Lindbergh's father-in-law, might run, but Morrow died in late 1931. Hoover's sole public rival for the Republican nomination was Dr. Joseph I. France, a former Senator from Maryland who mustered only four votes at the Republican national convention in mid-June 1932. The gloomy delegates also proceeded to renominate Hoover's 1928 running mate, the lackluster Vice President CHARLES CURTIS. The platform coupled defense of the Hoover administration's record with the promise to continue upholding the gold standard, the balanced budget, and the protective tariff. The convention's only excitement was over PROHIBITION. The plank adopted was a straddle that defended prohibition while simultanously affirming that "the people should have an opportunity to pass upon a proposed amendment . . . which . . . shall allow the States to deal with the problem as their citizens may determine."

The Democrats had profited from the hard times to make impressive gains in the 1930 congressional elections. Hoover's continuing decline in popularity promised a Democratic victory in the presidential contest if the party could avoid tearing itself apart. At the beginning of 1932, the front runner for the Democratic nomination was New York governor Franklin D. Roosevelt. Although a 1921 attack of poliomyelitis had left him unable to walk more than short distances, and then only with the aid of leg braces and canes, Roosevelt had remained active in politics. After ALFRED E. SMITH—then New York governor—had won the 1928 Democratic presidential nomination, Smith had asked Roosevelt to run for New York governor to offset the negative effect of Smith's Roman Catholicism on the presidential race in that state. Roosevelt won the election narrowly, then won reelection in 1930 by an unprecedented three-quarter-million-vote margin. As governor, Roosevelt supported labor and welfare legislation, tax relief for farmers, public power development, and stricter regulation of utility and telephone rates. As the depression continued to worsen, he began to call for stronger state action to aid the victims of the economic downturn. His major achievement was the 1931 establishment of the Temporary Emergency Relief Administration, headed by social worker HARRY L. HOPKINS, which assisted almost 10 percent of New York state's families.

In early 1932, Roosevelt assembled a group of campaign advisers and speechwriters for his bid for the presidency, including three Columbia University professors—the economist REXFORD G. TUGWELL, lawyer Adolf A. Berle, Jr., and the political scientist RAYMOND MOLEY—whom the newspapers labeled the BRAIN TRUST. Roosevelt's longtime adviser and confidant, the former newspaperman LOUIS M. HOWE, worked closely with JAMES A. FARLEY, the New York Democratic committee chairman, to line up the support of local and state party organizations. The backbone of Roosevelt's support lay in the South, because party leaders there saw him as the likeliest man to avoid a repeat of the battles over religion and prohibition that had divided the DEMOCRATIC PARTY during the 1920s. By contrast, many liberals distrusted Roosevelt, thinking him a political trimmer because of his failure to act against Tammany Hall corruption.

**The Race for the Democratic Nomination.** One stumbling block to Roosevelt's nomination was the effort by the party's "wets" (i.e., opponents of prohibition) and eastern conservatives, led by the chairman of the Democratic national committee, John J. Raskob, a wealthy DuPont executive, to make repeal of national probition the number one campaign issue. Even more threatening was the resentment felt by Al Smith toward Roosevelt and Smith's own ambition to have another try at the White House. When Roosevelt pictured himself as the champion of "the forgotten man at the bottom of the economic pyramid," Smith replied with an attack against "any demagogic appeal . . . setting class against class." Although Smith had no realistic chance of winning the nomination, the danger

existed that, given the party's two-thirds rule for nomination, he could tie up a sufficient number of delegates to block Roosevelt and thus open the door for a favorite son candidate. The most formidable favorite son was Speaker of the House of Representatives JOHN NANCE GARNER of Texas, who had the backing of the influential newspaper publisher William Randolph Hearst.

After a strong opening, the Roosevelt campaign ran into difficulties in spring 1932. Smith beat Roosevelt by a three-to-one margin in the Massachusetts primary and ran more strongly than expected in Pennsylvania; Garner defeated Roosevelt in the California primary. When the Democratic national convention met in Chicago in late June, Roosevelt was more than a hundred votes short of the required two-thirds majority on the first ballot. The next two roll calls saw no significant gains for Roosevelt; only Louisiana's Huey Long prevented the Mississippi delegation's breakaway from Roosevelt, which could have started a stampede. The most probable beneficiary of Roosevelt's defeat would have been NEWTON BAKER, a successful corporation lawyer who had been Secretary of War under Woodrow Wilson.

While the convention recessed, the Roosevelt managers worked frantically to save the day. Early in 1932, Roosevelt had appeased Hearst, Garner's most important backer, by coming out against U.S. membership in the LEAGUE OF NATIONS. But Garner himself was the key. Convinced that a deadlocked convention could ruin the party's chances, he threw his support to Roosevelt. When the fourth ballot reached California, delegation leader William G. McAdoo announced its switch to Roosevelt. The rest of the delegates, except for the diehard Smith people, followed. Although Garner personally did not want the vice presidential nomination, his Texas followers insisted on his being selected.

To quiet questions about his health, Roosevelt broke with precedent by flying to Chicago to deliver the first-ever acceptance speech to a nominating convention. When a cartoonist picked up on his closing pledge of "a new deal for the American people," the term NEW DEAL became identified with Roosevelt and his program.

Nineteen other parties were represented on the ballots of the different states. These included the Socialist Labor Party, the Farmer-Labor Party, and the Liberty Party. The Socialist Party put forward NORMAN THOMAS on a platform that demanded "social ownership" of principal industries along with immediate reforms such as unemployment relief, maximum-hour and minimum-wage legislation, abolition of child labor, and higher income taxes. Making his strongest appeal to intellectuals doubtful about Roosevelt's reform credentials, Thomas optimistically hoped to poll at least two million votes. The Communist Party, whose nominee was William Z. Foster, called for "the revolutionary way out of the crisis, for the overthrow of capitalism . . . [and] establishment of the workers' and farmers' government." The Prohibition Party—protesting against repeal or weakening of the Eighteenth Amendment—also ran a presidential candidate.

**The Campaign.** In late July 1932, Hoover signed the Relief and Construction Act, authorizing loans to states and localities for self-liquidating public works and relief. But he proceeded to dole out the funds grudgingly. The final nail in his political coffin was the BONUS ARMY incident. An estimated twenty thousand WORLD WAR I veterans came to Washington, D.C., in May and June to petition Congress for immediate payment of a bonus promised for 1945; they built a shantytown at Anacostia Flats on the outskirts of the city and took over vacant land and unused government buildings on Pennsylvania Avenue near the Capitol. While many went home after the Senate voted against the bonus on 17 June, others stayed on. Alarmed by exaggerated stories about Communist infiltration, Hoover panicked and ordered the army to clear the veterans from downtown Washington. On 28 July, army units that included tanks, cavalry with sabers, and infantry with bayonets and tear gas and that were personally commanded by the Chief of Staff, General Douglas MacArthur, went further than Hoover had ordered, driving the veterans from their Anacostia Flats camp and burning their shacks. Even though MacArthur had exceeded his authority, the use of military force against the veterans solidified popular hostility against the President. When Roosevelt heard what had happened, he reportedly exclaimed, "This will elect me."

Although the Republicans were more richly funded than their rivals, the party machinery directed by Republican national committee chairman Everett Sanders, a former Congressman who had been President Coolidge's secretary, was in disarray. The major burden of running the Republican campaign fell on Hoover's own shoulders as most Republican Congressmen and state and local party organizations tried to disassociate themselves from him. By election day, many midwestern and western progressive Republican Senators had jumped on the Roosevelt bandwagon. In long, turgid speeches crammed with statistics, Hoover defended his record while warning that Roosevelt and his advisers represented an alien philosophy ("the fumes of the witch's cauldron which boiled in Russia") that threatened the American way. Audiences were turned off, a British journalist observed, by Hoover's "sour, puckered face of a bilious baby, his dreary, nasal monotone reading interminably, and for the most part inaudibly, from a typescript without a single inflection of a voice or gesture to relieve the tedium."

By contrast, the Democratic campaign organization—managed by Farley, whom Roosevelt had arranged to have elected national committee chairman—operated with efficiency and resourcefulness. Campaign publicity director Charles Michaelson did a brilliant job of tarring Hoover as cold and heartless. The Democratic platform was a bland affair that restated familiar party themes. Its most radical plank was a call for the repeal of the Eighteenth Amendment.

To remove any doubts about his physical vigor, Roosevelt undertook whistle-stop tours through the West and South. Although Roosevelt was a far more dynamic personality than Hoover, his speeches were vague, even contradictory. He promised to aid farmers, for example, without spending any government money. He denounced Hoover as a reckless spender, attacked his overcentralizing power in Washington, and pledged to cut federal spending by 25 percent. Sympathetic historians have strained to find in his speeches foreshadowings of later New Deal programs. Some did make an appearance: support for public power, advocacy of stricter regulation of Wall Street, even an allusion to a planned economy. Hoover later blamed Roosevelt for dashing the recovery by frightening business, but during the campaign Roosevelt avoided controversial issues that could cost him votes—even if he had a future agenda spelled out in his mind.

**The Result.** Roosevelt won by a landslide, with 57.4 percent of the popular vote (22.8 million) to Hoover's 39.7 percent (15.74 million). His margin in the ELECTORAL COLLEGE was 472 (forty-two states) to Hoover's 59 (Maine, Vermont, New Hampshire, Connecticut, Pennsylvania, and Delaware). Socialist Norman Thomas attracted a disappointing 881,000 votes. The Communist Party vote of 102,000 only marginally exceeded the Prohibition Party's tally of almost 82,000. All the minor parties combined received only 1.16 million votes (2.9 percent of the total).

Roosevelt saw the results as a mandate for more vigorous action by the national government to combat the depression. And his political success appeared to confirm that reading of the popular mood. Most important, 1932 constituted a turning point in American political history at which the Democrats replaced the Republicans as the nation's majority party.

BIBLIOGRAPHY

Burner, David. *Herbert Hoover: A Public Life.* 1979.

Daniels, Roger. *The Bonus March: An Episode of the Great Depression.* 1971.

Fausold, Martin. *The Presidency of Herbert Hoover.* 1985.

Freidel, Frank. "The Election of 1932." In *The Coming to Power: Critical Presidential Elections in American History.* Edited by Arthur M. Schlesinger, Jr. 1972.

Freidel, Frank. *Franklin D. Roosevelt: The Triumph.* 1956.

Lisio, Donald. *The President and Protest: Hoover, Conspiracy, and the Bonus March.* 1974.

Rosen, Elliot A. *Hoover, Roosevelt, and the Brain Trust: From Depression to New Deal.* 1977.

Schlesinger, Arthur M., Jr. *The Age of Roosevelt: The Crisis of the Old Order.* 1956.

JOHN BRAEMAN

**ELECTION, PRESIDENTIAL, 1936.** President Franklin D. Roosevelt sought reelection in 1936 amidst bitter conflict and political division. The NEW DEAL had stirred a heated debate about the role of government and presidential power, and the 1936 election promised to be an important turning point in that debate. Roosevelt faced a difficult battle against not only his Republican opponent, but also potential THIRD-PARTY CANDIDATES, leaders of mass movements of all political stripes. Would the popular mandate given Roosevelt in 1932 be continued four years later, endorsing New Deal reform and the growth of intervening activist government? Would an emerging coalition of voters, forming since ALFRED E. SMITH's campaign of 1928, confirm the Democrats as the majority party? The results of this election shaped American politics for decades to come.

**The Opposition.** The REPUBLICAN PARTY entered the 1936 campaign in disarray. As demographic changes altered the American electorate, the Republican Party had failed to address the needs of the urban immigrant, or of the African Americans migrating north and west. Furthermore, during the 1920s the Republicans had split into two factions of progressives and conservatives. Mostly, however, it was the Great Depression that saddled the party with a crushing burden. Herbert Hoover and the Republicans became synonymous with unemployment lines and soup kitchens. Roosevelt's victory in 1932 humiliated the Republicans, an insult repeated with another Democratic victory in the 1934 midterm elections.

By 1936 the Republicans lacked leadership and direction, resulting in a dearth of possible presidential candidates. Eventually, seeking a compromise between the conservative and progressive elements, and hoping to pull in the midwestern vote, the Republi-

cans looked to Governor ALFRED M. LANDON of Kansas, a moderate progressive, and the only Republican governor reelected in 1934. Alf Landon's progressive credentials dated back to Theodore Roosevelt's PROGRESSIVE (BULL MOOSE) PARTY of 1912. Although he supported several New Deal programs, he balked at the spending levels of the New Deal, called for a balanced budget, and opposed Roosevelt's prolabor measures, a stance that won the allegiance of conservatives. Eighty percent of the nation's newspapers, following the lead of William Randolph Hearst and William Allen White, enthusiastically endorsed the Republican candidate. The party's platform was vague and confusing, even including some New Deal ideas, but it was strongly anti-Roosevelt in rhetoric. When Arthur Vandenberg of Michigan seconded Landon's nomination at the Republican convention in June, he summed up the Republican agenda for 1936: "Stop Roosevelt."

The Republican's best chance of regaining the presidency came through the possibility that the radical discontents emerging since 1933 would rob Roosevelt of votes. Mass movements on the left and the right produced a myriad of colorful and controversial figures, including Louisiana's Huey Pierce Long. An early Roosevelt supporter, by the end of 1933 the "Kingfish" had blasted the New Deal for its failure to redistribute America's wealth. Despite frequent charges of corruption, Long's Share Our Wealth Society gained much public support. By mid 1935 many predicted that the Louisiana politician could seriously jeopardize Roosevelt's chances, but in September 1935, an assassin ended Long's career.

Into the void created by Long's death stepped a Roman Catholic priest, Father Charles E. Coughlin, the "Radio Priest." Like Long, Coughlin had supported Roosevelt in 1932, but soon grew frustrated with the New Deal's conservatism, accusing "Franklin Double-Crossing Roosevelt" of being a friend only to big business. Born in Canada, Coughlin could not run for President, but with a radio audience of 40 million, he could be a valuable asset to his chosen candidate. He joined forces with Dr. Francis E. Townsend of Long Beach, California, whose Old Age Revolving Pension Plan spurred the creation of more than forty-five hundred Townsend Clubs. As leader of the National Union for Social Justice, Coughlin convinced Congressman William Lemke of North Dakota to lead the Union Party, predicting that he could pull 6 percent of the electoral vote away from Roosevelt, jeopardizing his reelection.

There were challengers on the far right as well. The American Liberty League, founded in 1934, included a combination of business tycoons like John Jacob Raskob and disgruntled Democrats like Al Smith, who, with his fellow league members, complained that the New Deal was only socialism in disguise. (This caused problems for socialist NORMAN THOMAS who waged his third bid for the presidency in 1936.) The league claimed nonpartisan status, but existed solely to oppose the New Deal. It sought to give back to business the independence it once enjoyed, free from unwanted government regulation.

**Roosevelt's Renomination.** For Roosevelt the 1936 election meant vindication or repudiation of four years of liberal reform. Unemployment was down by more than a third, industrial output had increased, farm income had grown, and national income had risen more than 60 percent. Organized labor made great strides with presidential support. Millions, including African Americans, qualified for federal relief and found jobs in public works agencies. America's elderly, among the most vulnerable to economic crises, would soon enjoy the benefits of SOCIAL SECURITY. Despite such successes, Roosevelt also had to concede some measure of failure, since full economic recovery remained elusive, and important programs such as the National Recovery Administration and the Agricultural Adjustment Administration were terminated or severely curtailed by the conservative Supreme Court. Roosevelt responded to these setbacks by becoming increasingly militant throughout 1936. The campaign became more than just a bid for reelection; it was a crusade to continue the New Deal.

Roosevelt set the tone of the campaign at the Democratic national convention in Philadelphia in June. Having quietly pushed through a repeal of the old two-thirds rule in order to weaken the power of southern conservatives, he easily took the nomination with a simple majority. His acceptance speech was a strong affirmation of the New Deal. Clearly, he was prepared to do battle with the "economic royalists," the representatives of wealth and big business that controlled the nation's purse strings. He attacked those who built "new dynasties" out of wealth and power, denying free opportunity to all Americans and placed the federal government firmly on the side of the working man and woman, for "against economic tyranny such as this, the American citizen could appeal only to the organized power of Government." His rousing speech in Philadelphia left few doubts about Roosevelt's commitment to reform and the expanding role of the government. "Better the occasional faults of a Government that lives in a spirit of charity," he told the crowd, "than the consistent omissions of a Government frozen in the ice of its own indifference."

Roosevelt understood the years ahead would be difficult, but he also predicted their importance. "There is a mysterious cycle in human events," he continued. "To some generations much is given. Of other generations much is expected. This generation of Americans has a rendezvous with destiny."

**The Campaign.** Landon launched his campaign early, promoting his progressive record, speaking out against racism and bigotry, and especially courting the farm vote in his native Midwest. But these tactics alienated the conservative Republican old guard that was his strongest financial base and dominated his circle of advisers, subjecting Landon to frequent charges of inconsistency. "You cannot be an old-guard Republican in the east," Roosevelt taunted, "and a New Deal Republican in the west." Roosevelt, on the other hand, did not officially open his campaign until late September, but he completed a "nonpolitical" tour of the flood-damaged Midwest in August. Everywhere he went, by train or by car, cheering crowds greeted him. He heard frequent cries of "He saved my home," or "He gave me a job." The campaign climaxed at Madison Square Garden on 31 October 1936, where Roosevelt delivered a fiery speech. "I would like to have it said of my first Administration," he shouted to be heard over the roaring crowd, "that in it the forces of selfishness and lust for power met their match. I should like to have it said of my second Administration that in it these forces met their master!"

Surrounded by family and friends at HYDE PARK on Election Day, Roosevelt awaited results. Many of his closest advisers, including his wife, ELEANOR ROOSEVELT, worried about reelection, but the President remained optimistic. Perhaps he understood better than anyone else the dominant mood of the people, and possibly he could discern in those approving crowds the many elements of a developing Democratic coalition. The same demographic changes that worked against the Republican Party helped the Democrats. Al Smith's unsuccessful bid for the presidency in 1928 brought to the polls many first-time voters, especially the urban immigrant, who joined the Democratic Party's traditional stronghold, the South and northern Catholics, to expand the party's voting base. The New Deal completed that trend, further mobilizing the beneficiaries of New Deal programs: the millions on relief, organized labor, some farmers, and particularly African Americans, who turned their backs on the party of Lincoln to give nearly total support to the Democrats. By 1936 Roosevelt could rely upon a diverse, national vote.

Even on Election Day the forecasts were ambiguous. The public's response and important endorsements from such organizations as the Nonpartisan League and the National Progressive Conference failed to convince many political experts that a Roosevelt landslide was in the making. Some anticipated a narrow Landon victory; others forecast a Republican landslide. The Republicans certainly had outspent the Democrats—$14 million to $9 million. The straw poll of the *Literary Digest*, which had accurately called every presidential election since 1920, predicted an electoral victory of 370 to 161 for Landon, but others, including George Gallup's new poll, declared that Roosevelt would easily win. JAMES A. FARLEY, an aide to Roosevelt, reassured the President that he would take every state but Maine and Vermont.

**The Result.** When the first results reached Hyde Park, showing that the new coalition was indeed working, the President's reaction was "Wow!" The results should not have been a surprise. Without Long's leadership, and plagued by internal dissension caused mostly by Coughlin's vicious attacks on Roosevelt, the Union Party peaked in the summer and fizzled out by fall. Landon was no match for the popular and charismatic President. The Liberty League's blatant probusiness platform only alienated a population still locked in the depression. And when Norman Thomas was asked later to explain the demise of socialism in America, he answered: "Roosevelt, in a word."

Roosevelt won by 27.7 to 16.6 million votes, carrying, as Farley predicted, all but Maine and Vermont, leaving only eight electoral votes for Landon. He took 60.8 percent of the popular vote. (Lemke received 2 percent of the popular vote and no electoral votes; Thomas received 0.4 percent of the popular vote.) Roosevelt's popularity spilled over into Congress, and the Democratic majority in the House of Representatives climbed to 331, with only 89 seats left in Republican control. In the Senate the Democrats enjoyed a whopping 76 to 16 majority. The election results also showed Roosevelt's support to be nationwide. Not surprisingly, he received 76 percent of the vote in the South (98 percent in South Carolina), but he also took 68 percent in the West, 61 percent in the middle states, and 59 percent in the East. Never before had sectional differences been so minimal, as class emerged as a deciding factor with 42 percent of the upper income, 60 percent of the middle income, and 76 percent of the lower income casting votes for Roosevelt.

The 1936 election gave Roosevelt the popular mandate to continue New Deal reform. The voters resoundingly endorsed the new role of government, approving the growth of a welfare and activist regulatory state. The election also completed a trend of voter realignment and mobilization that established the Democrats as the majority party, a position, supported by the "Roosevelt coalition," that they would maintain for thirty years.

### BIBLIOGRAPHY

Allswang, John M. *The New Deal and American Politics: A Study in Political Change.* 1978.

Andersen, Kristi. *The Creation of a Democratic Majority, 1928–1936.* 1979.

Leuchtenburg, William E. "Election of 1936." In *History of American Presidential Elections, 1789–1968.* Edited by Arthur M. Schlesinger, Jr., and Fred L. Israel. 4 vols. 1971.

Lubell, Samuel. *The Future of American Politics.* 3d. ed. 1965.

Patterson, James T. *Congressional Conservatism and the New Deal: The Growth of the Conservative Coalition in Congress, 1933–1939.* 1967.

Sternsher, Bernard. "The New Deal Party System: A Reappraisal." *Journal of Interdisciplinary History* 15 (Summer 1984): 53–81.

Sundquist, James L. *Dynamics of the Party System: Alignment and Realignment of Political Parties in the United States.* 1973.

OTIS L. GRAHAM, JR., and ELIZABETH KOED

**ELECTION, PRESIDENTIAL, 1940.** The dangerous international situation dominated the 1940 presidential election. The German *Blitzkrieg* that swept over Europe from April to June 1940 reinforced the commitment of President Franklin D. Roosevelt to all-out aid to Great Britain and was a crucial factor in his decision to run for a third term. Although Roosevelt appears to have decided to run by late May 1940, his continued secrecy about his intentions allowed him to keep his options open while handcuffing potential rivals.

**The Race for the Republican Nomination.** Early in 1940, there were three leading candidates for the Republican nomination. Profiting from his reputation as a racket-buster, THOMAS E. DEWEY, the thirty-seven-year-old district attorney of New York County (Manhattan), ran strongly in the primaries and was regarded as the front-runner. But he was handicapped by his youth, his lack of political experience, and his straddling on foreign policy. Robert A. Taft of Ohio, the son of President William Howard Taft, had made his mark as a strong opponent of the NEW DEAL after his election to the Senate in 1938. Along with his alignment with the Republican old guard on domestic issues, Taft had an isolationist voting record on foreign policy matters. Although a first-rate intellect, he had a chilly and aloof personality. More personable—and more long-winded—Senator Arthur H. Vandenberg of Michigan was a bit more liberal than Taft domestically but was a hard-line isolationist. As the German armies swept over Western Europe, Republican internationalists rallied behind a forty-eight-year-old dark horse, WENDELL L. WILLKIE. A lawyer who had become a utility company executive, Willkie had gained national attention when, as president of the giant holding company Commonwealth and Southern, he had led the opposition to the Tennessee Valley Authority (TVA). Although his fight to block the TVA failed, he won what many businessmen thought was a moral victory by selling his firm's subsidiary in the Tennessee Valley region to the TVA and local municipalities for a handsome price. Willkie also had the advantage of an informal, folksy manner—including a Hoosier twang from his Indiana upbringing—that appealed to many Americans. A youthful admirer of Woodrow Wilson, Willkie had been a delegate to the Democratic national conventions in 1924 and 1934. He had switched his party affiliation from Democratic to Republican only in 1939. Old guard Republican Senator James Watson reportedly told him, "Well, Wendell, you know that back home in Indiana it's all right if the town whore joins the church, but they don't let her lead the choir the first night."

Although talk about Willkie's running for the presidency had surfaced as early as August 1939, when *New York Times* columnist Arthur Krock named him as the "darkest horse," he appears not to have thought seriously about running until early 1940 and not to have fully committed himself to doing so until spring, after most of the primaries had been held. Crucial to his decision was his conviction that aid to Britain was essential to U.S. security. A small group of Willkie admirers lined up business, magazine, and newspaper support, launched a whirlwind publicity campaign that boosted Willkie's standing in the polls, and recruited a nucleus of professional politicians looking for a winner. When the Republican convention met in Philadelphia in late June, the Willkie forces flooded the delegates with letters, telegrams, and phone calls and packed the galleries. Despite secret negotiations the night before the voting, neither Dewey nor Taft would give way to the other. Dewey led on the first ballot, with 360 votes to Taft's 189, Willkie's 105, and Vandenberg's 76. When the bandwagon that Dewey's managers hoped for failed to materialize, his support ebbed away to Willkie, who won on the sixth ballot. The vice presidential nomination went to Charles L. McNary of Oregon, the Senate minority leader, who was an isolationist but a supporter of public power development.

**The Democratic Convention.** Roosevelt wished to give the appearance of yielding to a spontaneous draft of the delegates when the Democratic national convention met in Chicago in mid July. But he personally managed the proceedings through HARRY L. HOPKINS, who had a direct telephone line from his Chicago hotel suite to the White House. Alarmed by Willkie's rise, party leaders saw Roosevelt as the Democrats' only hope. He won the nomination on the first ballot, with 946 votes to JAMES A. FARLEY's 72 and JOHN NANCE GARNER's 61. To the unhappiness of many southern Democrats and big-city bosses, Roosevelt insisted on selecting Secretary of Agriculture HENRY A. WALLACE as his running mate. Why he picked Wallace is not known. Perhaps he hoped that Wallace would strengthen the ticket in the midwestern farm states. Roosevelt ruled out the other candidate whom he seriously considered, Senator JAMES F. BYRNES of South Carolina, partly because Byrnes was a southerner and partly because of possible Roman Catholic hostility over the fact that Byrnes had been born a Roman Catholic but had become an Episcopalian. With Roosevelt threatening to turn down the nomination if Wallace were not nominated, the delegates grudgingly gave Wallace the nod on the first ballot with 626 votes to 329 for Speaker of the House William Bankhead of Alabama. Farley was so embittered by what he regarded as Roosevelt's betrayal that he resigned as Democratic national chairman and Postmaster General. Roosevelt replaced him as Democratic national chairman with the skillful political manager Edward J. Flynn, boss of the Bronx in New York City.

**The Campaign.** Domestic issues played a secondary role in the 1940 campaign. The Democratic platform duly recalled how bad things had been in 1933 and extolled the New Deal's accomplishments. But the Republican platform accepted many of the New Deal programs, and Willkie personally went even farther in that direction. He publicly endorsed the WAGNER ACT (National Labor Relations Act), pledged to continue aid to farmers, and promised to extend SOCIAL SECURITY. In a position paper that appeared in the April 1940 issue of *Fortune*, Willkie affirmed that "government, either state or federal, must be responsible not only for the destitute and the unemployed, but for the elementary guarantees of public health, the rehabilitation of farmers, rebuilding of the soil, preservation of the national forests, clearance and elimination of city slums." He even picked up the support of union leaders John L. Lewis, of the United Mine Workers, and Harry Bridges, head of the West Coast longshoremen. The third-term issue remained troublesome for Roosevelt. Many conservatives, and not a few old-line progressives, had come to see despotic ambitions in Roosevelt. The COURT-PACKING PLAN had done much to fuel that suspicion, and opponents of the executive reorganization plan proposed by the BROWNLOW COMMITTEE in 1938 attacked that proposal as yet another Roosevelt power grab. His breach of what had been a rule of American politics since George Washington, the TWO-TERM TRADITION, reinforced distrust of Roosevelt as a would-be dictator.

Even the third-term issue, however, was overshadowed by the international crisis. In his radio address accepting the Democratic nomination, Roosevelt underlined what he would make the dominant theme of his campaign: the danger that "untried hands . . . will . . . substitute appeasement and compromise with those who seek to destroy all democracies everywhere." Speaking before the graduating class of the University of Virginia in June, he had pledged that the United States would "extend to the opponents of force the material resources of this nation." Then, just before the Republican convention, he nominated two leading Republican supporters of aid to Britain to key posts—HENRY L. STIMSON, who had been Secretary of War under Taft and Secretary of State under Herbert Hoover, to head the War Department and Chicago publisher Frank Knox, the 1936 Republican vice presidential nominee, to head the Navy Department. But Roosevelt took pains to avoid getting too far ahead of the voters. He shied away from endorsing the Burke-Wadsworth selective service bill to institute peacetime conscription until private preparedness groups had swung public opinion to its support. The most delicate issue was the British request for overage American destroyers to counter the German submarine threat in the Atlantic. After hesitating at first, Roosevelt hit on the gambit of trading, via an EXECUTIVE AGREEMENT that bypassed Congress, the U.S. destroyers for leases on bases in Newfoundland and the Caribbean. In his press conference early in September, Roosevelt hailed the DESTROYERS FOR BASES deal as "the most important action in the reinforcement of our national defense that has been taken since the Louisiana Purchase." And he sharply attacked the isolationist voting record of the Republican leaders in Congress.

Representative Joseph W. Martin, Jr., of Massachusetts, the House minority leader—whom Willkie had brought in as Republican national chairman to appease party regulars despite Martin's "old guard" and isolationist record—proved a poor choice as Republican campaign manager. Willkie could not match Roosevelt as a speaker. Worse, he had difficulty in finding a focus for his campaign. His complaints that the New Deal had failed to bring recovery were undercut by the economic revival under way because of defense spending. His attacks on the administration's neglect of national defense were similarly neutralized by Roosevelt's "inspection" tours of defense plants and military bases. In his 17 August acceptance speech, Willkie expressed himself in favor of the fullest possible aid to Britain. He even publicly endorsed the

destroyers for bases deal. But then he backtracked under pressure from Republican isolationists and denounced the move. With his campaign lagging, Willkie in late September began to attack the Democrats as the war party and warned that Roosevelt's election would mean war within six months. Stung by these attacks and alarmed by Willkie's gains in the polls, Roosevelt flatly assured his listeners that "your boys are not going to be sent into any foreign wars"—omitting the qualifying phrase "except in the case of attack" that he had placed in the Democratic platform. Willkie, listening to the radio, exclaimed, "That hypocritical son of a bitch! This is going to beat me."

**The Result.** Minor parties had no significant impact in 1940. The Prohibition Party candidate Roger Babson polled approximately 57,000 votes. The Socialist Labor Party's John W. Aiken tallied under 15,000. The Socialist Party again went with NORMAN THOMAS, who warned that U.S. involvement in the war would destroy CIVIL LIBERTIES and likely result in fascism in the United States. Thomas attracted only about 100,000 votes. In 1935, the Communist Party had adopted the "popular front" line for a broad alliance against fascism. After the Hitler-Stalin pact in August 1939, the Communists had attacked the European conflict as an "imperialist war," demanded that the United States stay out, and denounced Roosevelt as a warmonger. This turnabout disillusioned many fellow travelers, and Communist standard-bearer Earl Browder drew slightly more than 48,000 votes. Roosevelt defeated Willkie, 27.24 million to 22.30 million votes. His margin in the ELECTORAL COLLEGE was 449 (thirty-eight states) to 82 (ten states). Willkie made a substantial showing in the midwestern farm states (carrying the Dakotas, Nebraska, Kansas, Colorado, Iowa, Michigan, and Indiana) and cut into Roosevelt's support among German, Irish, and Italian American voters. Roosevelt kept the Solid South while simultaneously gaining the black vote in the North. But the key to Roosevelt's victory lay in the large majorities he won in working-class and lower-middle-income districts in the cities as voting closely followed class lines.

The immediate consequence of the election of 1940 was popular ratification of Roosevelt's policy of all-out aid to Britain. While anxieties over the dangerous international situation contributed to his success in overcoming the third-term issue, the results showed the continuing impact of the political realignment brought by the New Deal.

## BIBLIOGRAPHY

Burke, Robert E. "Election of 1940." In *The Coming to Power: Critical Presidential Elections in American History.* Edited by Arthur M. Schlesinger, Jr. 1972.

Donohoe, Bernard F. *Private Plans and Public Dangers: FDR's Third Term Nomination.* 1965.

Freidel, Frank. *Franklin D. Roosevelt: A Rendezvous with Destiny.* 1990.

Johnson, Donald D. *The Republican Party and Wendell Willkie.* 1960.

Leuchtenburg, William E. *Franklin D. Roosevelt and the New Deal, 1932–1940.* 1963.

Madison, James H., ed. *Wendell Willkie: Hoosier Internationalist.* 1992.

Neal, Steve. *Dark Horse: A Biography of Wendell Willkie.* 1984.

Parmet, Herbert S., and Marie B. Hecht. *Never Again: A President Runs for a Third Term.* 1968.

JOHN BRAEMAN

**ELECTION, PRESIDENTIAL, 1944.** The election of 1944 was the first presidential election since that of 1864 to take place during wartime. The Democratic incumbent, Franklin D. Roosevelt, garbed his campaign in the patriotic mantle of Commander in Chief, as had Abraham Lincoln eighty years earlier.

New York governor THOMAS E. DEWEY easily secured the Republican Party nomination, defeating the nominal head of the Republican Party, WENDELL WILLKIE, who had been its candidate in 1940. Willkie had lost his party's support through his championing of unorthodox one-world liberalism, and he was virtually eliminated from the nomination contest after an overwhelming defeat in the Wisconsin primary. Meeting in Chicago in June, the Republican national convention chose Ohio governor John Bricker as Dewey's running mate. Otherwise undistinguished, Bricker did offer midwestern Republicans the solace that power in the Republican Party had not seen completely seized by Dewey's faction—the eastern financial establishment.

Rumors had circulated for months that President Roosevelt might be too ill to seek a fourth term, but on 11 July he allayed doubts by announcing that he would run. The only surprise at the Democratic convention concerned Roosevelt's running mate. Hashing out a bargain in the convention's smoke-filled rooms, Democratic powerbrokers arranged for Vice President HENRY A. WALLACE to be dropped from the ticket and replaced by Senator Harry S. Truman of the border state of Missouri. Unlike Wallace, who represented the party's liberal-labor coalition, Truman was a political moderate, and the "Missouri Compromise of 1944" proved acceptable to all the party's factions.

**The War.** Despite the fact that some of the bloodiest battles of WORLD WAR II lay ahead, the issues that animated the campaign had a great deal more to do with domestic than with international affairs. But of course the war and its far-reaching ramifications could hardly be excluded from the arena of partisan conflict. Dewey had to tread carefully so as not to appear less than patriotic in criticizing administration initiatives abroad. Roosevelt unequivocably embraced America's leadership role in the world order that would follow the war, and he called for expanded executive powers to fulfill that responsibility. Although the Republicans had spent the better part of a decade lambasting Roosevelt's imperial pretensions, Dewey was afraid to seem out of step with the national mood, and he quickly endorsed American participation in a postwar "United Nations." To make matters worse for the Republicans, the progress of the war and the drift of war-related events favored the President. D-Day and the victories in France that followed provided a great lift for the Democrats, as did the enormously popular GI bill, which Roosevelt signed in the summer of 1944.

The administration's policies did come under Republican criticism. Senator Robert A. Taft of Ohio warned, "the New Dealers are determined to make the country over under the cover of war if they can." And Dewey used his acceptance speech to rail against an epidemic of government ineptitude, regimentation, and bureaucracy fostered by the war. But the Democrats were equally adept at playing the patriotism tactic in reverse. The President, smarting from a series of legislative setbacks at the hands of a growing conservative coalition in Congress, ominously declared, "The Republicans are in the midst of a campaign to sow discord among us."

**Dewey's Personality.** Such accusations scared Dewey's people. In the early weeks of the campaign, therefore, Dewey tried his best to seem composed, judicious, even aloof—a mien that his advisers considered "presidential" but that a great many others, including the press, found bland and boring. Dewey's speeches were practically soporific as he studiously avoided attacking Roosevelt's conduct of the war or even the President's social objectives. He ended up endorsing the essentials of most landmark NEW DEAL legislation (SOCIAL SECURITY, unemployment insurance, relief, collective bargaining), thereby earning himself the sobriquet "Little Sir Echo."

His exaggerated "presidential" prudence earned Dewey a reputation for being prim, stuffy, slick, icy, fastidious, humorless, and rigid. He was smothered by the excessive sense of his own dignity, in the public's mind becoming the "Boy Orator of the Platitude"—someone suffering from "intellectual halitosis" and so self-important he could "strut while sitting down." The contrast with Roosevelt's wit, self-confidence, and mastery of spontaneous "conversational oratory" could hardly have been starker or more damning.

**Roosevelt's Health.** The Republican tactic of choice was to harp on Roosevelt's evident frailty and exhaustion and to depict the administration as a group of "tired old men." Republican Party publicists encouraged gloomy speculations about Roosevelt's health, circulating photographs of him taken during his acceptance speech in Chicago in which he appeared haggard and glassy-eyed, his body ravaged. It was a shrewd ploy, as the President's diminishing vigor was painfully obvious. For example, when Roosevelt returned from a tour of the Pacific to make a nationwide broadcast from the Bremerton Navy Yard outside Seattle, he was visibly experiencing excruciating pain; he had to hold on to the lectern for support and consequently had trouble turning the pages of his text, which lent the speech a faltering, tepid quality. This was a great shock for the millions used to his customary composure and cheerfulness, and polls taken immediately afterward registered a dramatic slump in support for the President. Rumors that he was seriously ill and hence unable to campaign, much less endure the rigors of a fourth term, were rife.

At Washington's Statler Hotel on the evening of 25 September, everything changed. Addressing a supportive group of officials of the Teamsters Union, Roosevelt delivered what was, in the opinion of SAMUEL ROSENMAN, the greatest campaign speech of his long career. The speech was carried to the nation over the radio, and in it the President recaptured all the charm, wit, and strength of past campaigns—and managed, besides, to transform a humble Scottish terrier into the most famous PRESIDENTIAL PET in history. This was in response to an insinuation made by Harold Knutson, an obscure Republican congressman from Michigan, that Roosevelt had extravagantly abused the public treasury while on a trip to Alaska, when he allegedly sent a naval destroyer all the way back to the Aleutian Islands to pick up the family dog, Fala, which had been left behind inadvertently. Feigning a righteous anger, hilariously indignant, Roosevelt rushed to his dog's defense:

> The Republican leaders have not been content to make personal attacks on me—or my wife—or my sons—they now include my little dog, Fala. Unlike the members of my family, Fala resents this. When he learned that the Republican fiction writers had concocted a story that I left him behind on the Aleutian Island and had sent a destroyer to find him—at a cost to the taxpayer of two or three or twenty million dollars—his Scotch soul was furious. He has not been the same dog since. I am accustomed to hearing falsehoods about myself, but I think I have a right to object to libelous statements about my dog.

When the applause and laughter died down, Roosevelt went on to counter the political damage caused by his age and, subtly, to raise fears of a return to the depression should the Republicans regain power: "Well, here we are again, after four years—and what years they have been! I am actually four years older—which seems to annoy some people. In fact, millions of

us are more than eleven years older than when we started in to clean up the mess that was dumped in our laps in 1933."

The speech had an electric effect, giving new life to the President and greatly irking the previously passive Dewey. The Republican candidate lashed back in a speech to a packed Municipal Auditorium in Oklahoma City, castigating Roosevelt for "mudslinging, ridicule, and wisecracks," of "plumbing the depths of demogoguery," and of making "reckless charges of fraud and falsehood" that Dewey felt compelled, however reluctantly, to respond to. Dewey argued that Roosevelt had never managed to solve the depression and that the President had demonstrated a woeful ineptitude in readying the United States for war—making mistakes that had led to countless unnecessary American deaths.

**Campaign Nastiness.** The second stage of the campaign had begun—and it was a far cry from the careful politeness of the first stage. In keeping with the new, combative tone of their candidate's Oklahoma City diatribe, Dewey's advisers instructed him that the campaign's final rounds demanded "body punches and head-rocking"; they proved themselves up to the fight. Republican spokesmen added a "red bogeyman" to the symbolic vernacular of presidential electioneering when they repeatedly alleged a connection between Roosevelt and the Communist Party of the United States.

The ammunition for this Republican red-baiting was provided by the Political Action Committee of the CIO (Congress of Industrial Organizations, the large labor group). The CIO's PAC, which played an important role in the Democratic campaign, had been established to help solve one of the greatest threats to the Democratic Party—the gradually increasing apathy among poor and working-class voters, which had shown itself in the midterm elections of 1942. PAC, which was described by *Time* magazine as disseminating "far and away the slickest piece of political propaganda in a generation," energetically attacked the problem of voter apathy. Through fourteen regional centers, it mounted registration drives in factories in critical cities such as Detroit, Chicago, San Francisco, St. Louis, and Los Angeles.

The chairman of PAC was Sidney Hillman, a Jewish refugee and onetime socialist who was one of the CIO's founders. As a Jew, an immigrant, and an ex-radical, Hillman was a perfect target for the Republican strategists. They seized on a rumor reported by *New York Times* Washington correspondent Arthur Krock—whose conservative leanings were well known—that during the Democratic convention Roosevelt had told his party's leaders that they had to "clear it with Sidney" before choosing his running mate.

"Clear it with Sidney" became the favorite catcall of the Republicans, who mercilessly exploited a poisonous political logic. If Hillman was so powerful, then the CIO must also possess enormous control over the presidency. And because it was known that there was an active Communist Party faction within the CIO, then it was evident that the communists exerted power over the presidency as well. Dewey's supporters suggested that, whether consciously or not, Roosevelt and his party had fallen victim to a communist conspiracy.

Republican Party broadsides asked, "Sidney Hillman and Earl Browder's Communists have registered. Have you?" (Browder was general secretary of the Communist Party, U.S.A.) Dewey's language, in a speech in Boston late in the campaign, was shrill: "This is that same Earl Browder who was convicted as a draft dodger . . . convicted again as a perjurer and pardoned by Franklin Roosevelt in time to organize the campaign for his fourth term." Addressing voters in Connecticut, vice presidential candidate Bricker warned, "First the New Deal took over the Democratic Party and destroyed its very foundation. Now the Communistic forces have taken over the New Deal and will destroy the very foundations of the republic."

This unprecedented effort to paint a sitting President as a subversive naturally brought a response. PAC began bending over backwards to emphasize its "Americanism," and Hillman condemned the Republicans for "red-baiting and Jew-baiting." Roosevelt chastised Dewey and Bricker: "When any political candidate stands up and says, solemnly, that there is a danger that the Government of the United States—your Government—could be sold out to Communists—then I say that candidate reveals a shocking lack of trust in America."

Despite all the smoke and fire, however, the electorate's concerns centered on two unknowns: the well-being of the postwar economy and health of the President. Roosevelt forthrightly addressed both anxieties. He reiterated his commitment to an economic bill of rights and in a speech at Soldiers Field in Chicago cheered his legions of poor and working-class supporters by forecasting an economy that would add sixty million jobs after the war was over—an economy of abundant new homes, highways, and hospitals that would forever inter the grim memory of Herbert Hoover and the Great Depression.

Meanwhile, Roosevelt allayed fears about his own health by perpetuating the image of renewed strength he had displayed at the Teamsters dinner. In New York City on 21 October, thousands of onlookers witnessed Roosevelt's remarkable seeming vitality: in a bitterly cold wind and driving rain, Roosevelt rode in an open car during a four-hour-long procession through the city.

**The Result.** By the end of October, Roosevelt's reelection was a certainty. Governor Dewey conceded defeat at 3:00 A.M. on election night at the Roosevelt Hotel in New York. Although it was Roosevelt's slenderest presidential victory, he still managed to carry thirty-six states for a total of 432 electoral votes. His winning margin of 53.4 percent of the popular vote was slightly less than the 54.7 percent he had taken in 1940. PAC received much of the credit for the unexpectedly high voter turnout of forty-eight million. The campaign was considered by many, including Roosevelt, as particularly nasty, and so the victory was especially gratifying to the President.

### BIBLIOGRAPHY

Blum, John Morton. *V Was for Victory: Politics and American Culture during World War II*. 1976.

Burns, James MacGregor. *Roosevelt: The Soldier of Freedom, 1940–45*. 1970.

Garson, Robert A. *The Democratic Party and the Politics of Sectionalism, 1941–48*. 1974.

Markowitz, Norman. *The Rise and Fall of the People's Century: Henry A. Wallace and American Liberalism, 1941–48*. 1973.

Polenberg, Richard. *War and Society: The United States, 1941–45*. 1972.

Smith, Richard Norton. *Thomas E. Dewey and His Times*. 1982.

STEVE FRASER

**ELECTION, PRESIDENTIAL, 1948.** In the 1948 election there were four rather than two prominent candidates, and one of them surprised the nation by winning the contest. That upset is the election's best-known feature, but others also deserve emphasis, including the place of the election in the histories of the NEW DEAL, civil rights, the CONTAINMENT policy, and the second red scare.

**Truman's Situation.** Going into the election, the Democratic Party controlled the presidency but appeared to be a mix of weaknesses as well as strengths. It had become the majority party during the 1930s and still appeared to occupy that position, but a Republican revival seemed to be under way for the Republicans had gained control of both houses of Congress in the 1946 elections.

Furthermore, Roosevelt's coalition seemed to be falling apart. By 1948, the component that controlled the White House faced challenges from both left and right. HENRY A. WALLACE, Roosevelt's first Secretary of Agriculture and second Vice President and Harry S.

Truman's first Secretary of Commerce, challenged from the left. Supported by communists as well as noncommunist liberals, he decided to run as a THIRD-PARTY CANDIDATE, denounced Truman's policy of Soviet containment as imperialistic and certain to lead to war, and seemed capable of depriving Truman of votes he needed.

On the right, Truman encountered discontent among southern Democrats. Worried about their loss of strength in their party, they feared the rising challenge to segregation. Truman in a speech in February 1948 had proposed broad civil rights legislation. Feeling betrayed, southerners protested.

To the pollsters in early 1948, Truman looked like a loser. Truman and his aides, however, prepared for victory. Determined to run, he had help from the White House staff, led by CLARK CLIFFORD, and from the Democratic national committee. They saw Truman's personality and the party's stand on domestic issues as the means to rally Democratic voters. They advised the President to move boldly against both Wallace and the Republicans, and he did so in a series of speeches in early 1948 but became more cautious on civil rights as southern discontent grew.

At least one sign encouraged Truman: most labor leaders lined up behind him. Pleased by his veto of the TAFT-HARTLEY ACT in 1947 and fearing a weakening of the Democratic Party, they refused to support Wallace. Instead, they endorsed Truman's anti-Soviet foreign policy.

The Americans for Democratic Action (ADA), a new liberal anticommunist organization, also helped. Wanting a strong Democratic Party and charging that the Wallace movement was a communist effort to destroy Truman's foreign policy, the ADA helped Truman by hurting Wallace.

Furthermore, the Soviet Union helped Truman by backing a communist coup in Czechoslovakia in February 1948 and imposing a blockade against land and water traffic to and from Berlin in June. Because of the importance of liberals in the toppled government, the coup suggested to many that Wallace was wrong in assuming liberals and communists could work together. And the blockade gave Truman an opportunity for dramatic action. He responded by airlifting supplies to the pressured city and sending bombers to Europe.

Truman helped himself in several additional ways. He gained support from Jewish-Americans and others by granting de facto recognition to ISRAEL in May, and he made a cross-country speaking tour in June.

**The Conventions.** Meanwhile, a flock of Republicans, encouraged by the difficulties of the Democrats, competed for Truman's job. Governor THOMAS E. DEWEY of New York, a moderate on both domestic and foreign issues, was in the lead. His challengers included HAROLD STASSEN, a former governor of Minnesota and a militant internationalist; Senator Robert A. Taft of Ohio, a conservative critic of the administration; Earl Warren, the liberal governor of California; General Douglas MacArthur, a war hero now in charge of the American occupation of Japan and an advocate of greater attention to Asia, and Senator Arthur Vandenberg of Michigan, a participant in the development of Truman's foreign policy. According to the polls, several of the Republicans—Dewey, Vandenberg, Stassen, and MacArthur—could defeat Truman.

Republicans assembled in June to ratify their platform and make their decision on candidates. They had chosen Philadelphia for their convention because of its access to television. After endorsing the UNITED NATIONS and containment and several liberal domestic programs, they nominated Dewey on the third ballot. He seemed certain to win in the fall.

Soon after the Republicans left, a gloomy group of Democrats moved into Philadelphia for their first televised convention. The platform called for continuation of New Deal programs and containment and included a stronger civil rights plank than the White House favored; the delegates nominated Truman, although not unanimously. His confident acceptance speech called for a special session of Congress to test Republican sincerity.

During the convention fight over civil rights, some southerners walked out and immediately joined others to form the States' Rights Democrat Party. Denouncing the centralization of power in Washington, the Dixiecrats, as these southerners were called, emphasized the preservation of segregation and nominated Governor STROM THURMOND of South Carolina as their presidential candidate, hoping to throw the election into the House of Representatives where they could bargain with the presidential candidates.

Later in July, Wallace and his followers covened their new PROGRESSIVE PARTY, also in Philadelphia. In addition to nominating Wallace for the presidency, the Progressives called for Soviet-American cooperation, criticized Truman's foreign and military policies, and advocated wide-ranging reform of American life. They also gave their critics new opportunities to charge that communists controlled the party.

**The Campaigns.** Truman did not wait for Labor Day to begin his campaign. In late July, he issued two EXECUTIVE ORDERS on federal employment, both military and civilian, that strengthened his standing with black voters. Then, he pressured the special session to pass domestic measures promised in the Republican as well as the Democratic platforms, and when the lawmakers refused to act, he had the support he wanted for a charge that the Republican-controlled Congress of 1947–1948 was a "do-nothing" body.

Then, from Labor Day to Election Day, the President stumped the country by train, traveling over twenty thousand miles and making more than 250 speeches. Greeted by impressive crowds that bolstered his confidence, he presented himself as a "common man" and a champion of the "people" against the "special interests." Truman often spoke of the benefits of the New Deal and portrayed the Republicans as a threat to it. Concentrating on the East, the Midwest, and the Far West, he made only two stops in the South outside of Texas and said little about civil rights before visiting Harlem late in the campaign. He continued to charge that communists controlled Wallace, added that support for him would hurt the party of effective liberalism, and denied that containment would lead to war.

Dewey made a less strenuous effort. Several factors restrained him: his confidence that he would win, his belief that he had been too militant against Roosevelt in 1944, and his fear of advertising the conflicts within the Republican Party on both international and domestic issues. Furthermore, he hoped to move easily from the campaign to the presidency. Thus, rather than take a strong stand on issues, he appealed for national unity, did not praise the Republican-controlled Congress, and only mildly criticized Truman. While he did use the communist-in-government issue, he relied upon others to point out that Republicans had supported Truman's foreign policy.

The other candidates made quite different races. Thurmond waged only a small campaign, limiting it to the South and focusing on government centralization and civil rights. His task, as he saw it, was to defend the "southern way of life" against the on-rushing federal government. Wallace, on the other hand, campaigned strenuously. He traveled even more miles than Truman and made large efforts in all parts of the country. He spoke often of civil rights, doing so in the South as well as the North, but emphasized foreign policy, regarding all else as dependent upon it. He encountered much opposition, some of it violent, was often barred from speaking, and lost more ground.

**Truman Defeats Dewey.** By Election Day only Truman had risen in the polls. Nevertheless, the prediction stayed the same. The pollsters and the press remained convinced that Dewey would win.

Yet, on 2 November, Truman won. Picking up more than 24 million votes or 49.5 percent of the total, he received 303 electoral votes to 22 million (45.1 percent) and 189 electoral votes for Dewey. Thurmond and Wallace trailed far behind with only slightly more than one million votes each. Thurmond did pick up 39 electoral votes, but Wallace failed to win any.

Although Truman failed to carry New York, New Jersey, Pennsylvania, and Michigan, he achieved much of his success in the cities, especially among the working classes, Catholics, Jews, and blacks. While the President's identification with the New Deal explained much of his success, he also benefited from his anti-communist foreign policy, his support for Israel, and his efforts for civil rights.

Thurmond succeeded only in the Deep South: South Carolina, Alabama, Mississippi, and Louisiana. Elsewhere in the South, attachment to the Democratic Party remained firm after campaigners emphasized, not the threat to the racial order, but the benefits of Democratic economic policies.

Carrying the West and the Middle West, Truman gained more support from farmers than Roosevelt had in 1940 and 1944. Truman had reminded those people of New Deal benefits and portrayed the Republicans as likely to do away with them. Farmers rewarded the President with especially significant support in Ohio, Wisconsin, and Iowa.

Surprising as Truman's victory was, the outcome reflected weaknesses as well as strengths. It was victory by a narrow margin, only 4.4 percent, the smallest since Woodrow Wilson defeated CHARLES EVANS HUGHES by 3 percent in 1916. Roosevelt's margins had averaged nearly 15 percent, for Roosevelt was more successful than Truman in the East and the South. Furthermore, the latter achieved his victory in a low-turnout election. A million more voters had come to the polls in 1940; 12 million more people would vote in 1952. This suggests that even on Election Day in 1948, Truman was not a popular President; it also indicates that his opponents were not popular either.

Truman's victory was more a party victory than a personal one. The Democrats gained control of Congress and most state governments, and he ran behind congressional Democrats and some Democratic gubernatorial candidates. In maintaining control of the presidency, the Democrats demonstrated that the New Deal, the programs of the 1930s that made the federal government and the unions more important in the economic system, had substantial political strength. The election also revealed that civil rights and fear of communists inside the U.S. had become important parts of the political agenda. Still further, the election strengthened containment. Three of the four presidential candidates—Dewey and Thurmond as well as Truman—supported it, while the candidate who opposed it—Wallace—suffered a humiliating defeat.

## BIBLIOGRAPHY

Donovan, Robert J. *The Presidency of Harry S. Truman.* 2 vols. 1977, 1982.

Hamby, Alonzo L. *Beyond the New Deal: Harry S. Truman and American Liberalism.* 1973.

Kirkendall, Richard S. "Election of 1948." In *History of American Presidential Elections, 1789–1968.* Edited by Arthur M. Schlesinger, Jr., and Fred L. Israel. 4 vols. 1971.

Kirkendall, Richard S., ed. *The Harry S. Truman Encyclopedia.* 1989.

McCullough, David. *Truman.* 1992.

Markowitz, Norman D. *The Rise and Fall of the People's Century: Henry A. Wallace and American Liberalism, 1941–1948.* 1973.

Ross, Irwin. *The Loneliest Campaign: The Truman Victory of 1948.* 1968.

Smith, Richard Norton. *Thomas E. Dewey and His Times.* 1982.

RICHARD S. KIRKENDALL

**ELECTION, PRESIDENTIAL, 1952.** By defeating ADLAI E. STEVENSON (1900–1965) on 4 November 1952, Dwight D. Eisenhower became the first Republican since Herbert Hoover in 1928 to win the presidency. Eisenhower's election, however, was less a partisan than a personal triumph. Although the Republicans also won control of Congress, their narrow majorities—eight seats in the House, one in the Senate—were hardly as impressive as Eisenhower's 55.1 to 44.4 percent advantage in the popular vote and 442 to 89 margin in the ELECTORAL COLLEGE. Eisenhower achieved such a smashing victory because the voters "liked Ike." They considered him a hero whose geniality, integrity, and military experience were just what the nation needed to deal with a stalemated KOREAN WAR, sensational accusations of communist subversion, and political scandal in Washington.

**Courting Eisenhower.** Pressure mounted on Eisenhower during late 1951 to run for the presidency, but he hesitated because of his fidelity to duty. Eisenhower could not abide the mixing of military responsibility and political ambition. Nor did he want to resign as Supreme Commander of North Atlantic Treaty Organization armed forces, a position he had assumed only at the beginning of 1951. Yet Eisenhower privately criticized President Harry S. Truman for what he considered inept handling of communist challenges at home and abroad and demagogic promotion of FAIR DEAL policies that smacked of socialism.

Aware of Eisenhower's scruples, a host of Republican politicians and business leaders organized grassroots support for Eisenhower, then traveled to NATO headquarters near Paris to convince the general of his duty to accept the summons of the nation. They reinforced their appeals by warning that Eisenhower's inaction would give the Republican nomination to Sen. Robert A. Taft of Ohio, who declared his candidacy on 16 October. While Eisenhower generally shared Taft's conservative positions on domestic matters, he could not accept the Senator's ultranationalist views on international affairs, which included reducing foreign aid and avoiding commitments, such as NATO, to defend other nations.

Gradually, Eisenhower found a way to reconcile duty and ambition. First, he announced in January 1952 that he would accept the Republican nomination but would not campaign for it. Then, after winning the New Hampshire primary and seeing film of a frenetic Eisenhower rally in Madison Square Garden, he declared that he would return to the United States in early June to campaign for the nomination that so many people were calling on him to accept.

When the Republican convention met in Chicago on 7 July, Taft had a small lead in delegates over Eisenhower. The decisive battle for the nomination occurred over the seating of the Georgia and Texas delegations. With Taft supporters in control, the credentials committee voted to accredit pro-Taft delegations from those two states. The Eisenhower forces retaliated with their own power play, loftily entitled the Fair Play resolution, which empowered the full convention to determine which delegations to seat. With help from two favorite-son candidates, Earl Warren, governor of California, and HAROLD E. STASSEN, a former governor of Minnesota, Fair Play passed, and Eisenhower then won a narrow first-ballot victory. For the vice presidential nomination, Eisenhower selected Sen. Richard M. Nixon of California because of his youth and his reputation for hunting communist subversives.

**The Democratic Candidate.** The contest for the Democratic nomination was more dramatic and even longer in doubt. By late 1951, Truman had decided not to seek reelection but refrained from making a public announcement in order to retain maximum influence over the choice of the Democratic nominee. At first he had little effect. He tried unsuccessfully to interest Chief Justice Fred Vinson in the presidency. ALBEN BARKLEY was willing to run, but Truman could not overcome his fears that the vice president, who was seventy-four, was too old. Unacceptable to Truman were all the declared candidates, some of whom began their campaigns for the nomination even before Truman revealed his intentions. Sen. Richard B. Russell of Georgia, Sen. Robert S. Kerr of Oklahoma, and Gov. W. Averell Harriman of New York all had, in the President's estimate, some major personal or political liability. The worst was Sen. Estes Kefauver of Tennessee, whom Truman loathed because his highly publicized investigations of organized crime had embarrassed several local and state Democratic organizations. Following a shocking and painful loss to Kefauver in the New Hampshire primary, Truman announced on 29 March that he would not run again.

Before his withdrawal, Truman tried to throw his support to Stevenson. The President lauded Stevenson as "the best all-around candidate" because of his administrative experience in the Navy and State departments and as a delegate to the United Nations, his progressive record as governor of Illinois since 1949, and his ability to wage a "forthright and energetic campaign." Stevenson, however, demurred and declared in mid April that he would seek only a second term as governor. Despite his statement, Stevenson remained interested in the nomination. He simply recognized the advantages of remaining independent of Truman while positioning himself to accept the call of the convention.

When the Democratic convention met in Chicago on 21 July, no candidate controlled nearly enough delegates to be nominated. Stevenson lifted his prospects with a stirring welcome address, while Kefauver and Harriman weakened theirs with unsuccessful maneuvering to block the seating of several southern delegations that opposed civil rights and that refused to pledge their support for the party's platform and nominees. Stevenson emerged as the one candidate acceptable to all major factions, including organized labor, liberals, and southerners. After trailing Kefauver on the first ballot, he triumphed on the third roll call, with the help of Truman's timely intervention with party leaders. Stevenson chose Sen. John Sparkman of Alabama as his running mate, after Truman effectively vetoed his first choice—Kefauver. In accepting the nomination, Stevenson proclaimed the major theme of his campaign, "Let's talk sense to the American people."

**The Campaign.** After the convention, Stevenson clumsily tried to distance himself from Truman. He thought that if he ran as Truman's designated successor, he was certain to lose. Without consulting the White House, he selected Stephen A. Mitchell to succeed Frank McKinney, Truman's appointee, as Democratic national chairman. A more damaging blunder was a careless reply to a reporter's inquiry in which Stevenson proclaimed that he indeed knew how to "clean up the mess in Washington." Republicans boasted that even Stevenson agreed with their favorite description of Truman's policies, while the President

boiled and resolved to sit out the campaign. But Truman changed his mind and vented his frustrations by traveling across the country and lambasting the Republicans. Yet he remained bitter toward Stevenson and hoped for a Democratic victory mainly to provide personal vindication.

Eisenhower was far more adept at unifying his party behind his candidacy. On 12 September, he met with Taft for the first time since the convention. At Eisenhower's Morningside Heights office in New York City, the two men agreed on a statement that dismissed their basic differences over foreign policy as matters of degree and described the campaign's most important issue as "liberty against the creeping socialism in every domestic field." Stevenson denounced the meeting as the "Munich of Morningside Heights," and some independents and liberal Republicans deserted Eisenhower because they feared that he had tilted too far to the right.But Eisenhower gained far more than he lost. Taft immediately endorsed the Republican ticket, an action that mobilized conservatives who had been waiting for the Senator's direction. Such support was critical, since in early September, the Gallup Poll indicated a close race, with Eisenhower leading Stevenson by 51 to 43 percent, with 6 percent undecided.

Only a few days after his meeting with Taft, Eisenhower faced the greatest crisis of his campaign when newspapers published allegations that Nixon had profited from a political slush fund established by California business leaders. The accusation was especially embarrassing because Republicans had hammered away at Democratic corruption after revelations in 1951 of bribery and influence peddling in the Reconstruction Finance Corporation and the Bureau of Internal Revenue. Nixon replied on 23 September in a televised address in which he recounted his financial history and insisted he was not guilty of any improprieties. The speech was trite and sappy, especially when Nixon vowed that he would not break his daughters' hearts by returning a gift cocker spaniel puppy named Checkers. Yet Nixon seemed genuine and sincere to most viewers, and the telegrams and letters that poured into Republican National Committee headquarters favored him by a margin of 350 to 1. The crisis quickly dissipated, but Republican speakers tempered their attacks on Truman administration scandals for the remainder of the campaign.

The Checkers speech was only the most dramatic example of the Republicans' more effective use of television, which, for the first time, played a major role in a presidential campaign. Hoping to capitalize on Eisenhower's friendly manner, Republican strategists commissioned a series of thirty-second commercials in which Eisenhower offered folksy but informed answers to questions about issues on the minds of voters, such as inflation and taxes. Stevenson deprecated these advertisements as an "indignity to the democratic process." He relied instead on telecasts of speeches so that voters could hear his eloquent analyses of the issues. But problems occurred, as when Stevenson's election eve address over live television exceeded the time limit and the network cut him off.

That mistake was only one of many difficulties that beset the Stevenson campaign. Stevenson's basic strategy was to concentrate first on explaining his positions on the issues before taking the offensive against Eisenhower. The strategy produced a series of brilliant speeches but small crowds and little popular enthusiasm, especially because of Stevenson's reluctance to deviate from his prepared text. The columnist Stewart Alsop coined the campaign's most memorable term when he wrote that Stevenson appealed mainly to a small group of "eggheads." If voters found Stevenson distant and formal, many southern Democratic leaders considered him unacceptably rigid. His views on civil rights, although more moderate than Truman's, still persuaded such powerful Senators as Russell of Georgia and Harry F. Byrd of Virginia to refrain from campaigning. His forthright declaration that the federal government, not the states, owned the oil pumped from offshore wells helped convince James F. Byrnes of South Carolina and Allan Shivers of Texas, both Democratic governors, to stump for Eisenhower.

Eisenhower was far more opportunistic, even to the point of raising doubts about the strength of his convictions. While campaigning in Milwaukee, he deleted from his speech a passage praising Gen. GEORGE C. MARSHALL, who had selected him to command Allied troops in WORLD WAR II. Eisenhower did so to avoid a partisan wrangle with Sen. Joseph R. McCarthy (R-Wis.), who was on the platform as he spoke and who had alleged that Marshall was part of a conspiracy of communist subversives and sympathizers that controlled Truman's foreign policy [see McCARTHYISM]. For his silence, Eisenhower endured a flurry of criticism from editorial writers and from Stevenson, who wondered about his opponent's "backbone." But once more, the benefits of the incident for Eisenhower exceeded the losses. McCarthy and other anticommunist zealots viciously retaliated by attacking Stevenson's patriotism and attributing the problems of the Korean War to Democratic bungling and disloyalty. Then, in Detroit on 24 October, Eisenhower dramatically turned popular frustration over the war to his advantage by promising to go to Korea if elected to find a way to bring peace.

**The Result.** Korea, communism, and corruption—$K_1C_2$, according to the popular shorthand of 1952—contributed to Eisenhower's overwhelming victory on Election Day. So too did Democratic difficulties in holding the Solid South while courting the black vote. Stevenson won heavy majorities among African American voters, but he lost the traditionally Democratic states of Texas, Virginia, and Florida. While Stevenson impressed many voters with his eloquence and wit, Eisenhower inspired trust, confidence, and hope in many more. Stevenson gave better speeches, but Eisenhower was a more effective campaigner. Stevenson may have remained truer to his principles in dealing with controversial issues, but Eisenhower maneuvered around them more adroitly. In the end, the career army officer running his first campaign for public office was the superior politician.

### BIBLIOGRAPHY

Ambrose, Stephen E. *Eisenhower.* Vol. 1: *Soldier, General of the Army, President-Elect, 1890–1952.* 1983.

Donovan, Robert J. *Tumultuous Years: The Presidency of Harry S. Truman, 1949–1953.* 1982.

Greene, John Robert. *The Crusade: The Presidential Election of 1952.* 1985.

Martin, John Bartlow. *Adlai Stevenson of Illinois.* 1976.

McCoy, Donald R. *The Presidency of Harry S. Truman.* 1984.

McKeever, Porter. *Adlai Stevenson: His Life and Legacy.* 1989.

Pach, Chester J., Jr., and Elmo Richardson. *The Presidency of Dwight D. Eisenhower.* Rev. ed. 1991.

Patterson, James T. *Mr. Republican: A Biography of Robert A. Taft.* 1972.

CHESTER J. PACH, JR.

# ELECTION, PRESIDENTIAL, 1956.

On 6 November 1956, Dwight D. Eisenhower won a second term as President by once again defeating ADLAI E. STEVENSON (1900–1965), the former governor of Illinois. By an even wider margin than in 1952, voters preferred Eisenhower over Stevenson. The President carried forty-one states, two more than in the previous election, and garnered 57.6 percent of the popular vote, an increase of 2.5 percent. Yet Eisenhower's reelection was by no means a Republican triumph. Indeed, Eisenhower became the first candidate to win the presidency since Zachary Taylor in 1848 without his party gaining control of either house of Congress. The election of 1956 was an individual victory for Eisenhower, a resounding vote of confidence in one of the most popular Presidents in American history.

**Eisenhower's Renomination.** The only major obstacle to Eisenhower's reelection was his health. In September 1955, Eisenhower suffered a heart attack, and his convalescence kept him from resuming a full schedule of duties until the beginning of 1956. Eisenhower's recovery was very much a public event. His physicians released detailed information about his condition, and his chief cardiologist, Dr. Paul Dudley White, finally declared in mid-February that there was no medical reason why Eisenhower could not serve another term. These reports reassured the public, but new concern arose in June when Eisenhower had to undergo emergency abdominal surgery because of an ileitis attack. Although the President recovered fully and quickly, many voters wondered whether Eisenhower could withstand the rigors of a second term.

The heart attack encouraged Eisenhower to think deeply about his political future. During his first two years in office, Eisenhower had told close friends that he hoped to retire after a single term. He offered a variety of reasons for not seeking reelection: his age (he would turn sixty-six before the election), his desire for the emergence of new leadership in the REPUBLICAN PARTY, and his conviction that he had performed his duty to his country. Yet after his heart attack Eisenhower could not think of a single Republican in whom he had confidence who could win the presidency. Eisenhower admired Attorney General HERBERT BROWNELL, Deputy Secretary of Defense Robert B. Anderson, and White House Chief of Staff SHERMAN ADAMS, yet he knew that none of them had much political appeal. Vice President Richard M. Nixon would have been able to secure the nomination, but Eisenhower had doubts about whether Nixon was mature enough for the presidency. Such ruminations persuaded Eisenhower by the beginning of 1956 that there really was no alternative to his running again. The heart attack only reinforced his tendency to see his reelection as essential to Republican success and the nation's well-being.

Since he faced no opposition to his renomination, Eisenhower's main political concern after announcing his candidacy on 29 February was his choice of a running mate. Eisenhower knew that his heart attack had focused attention on the vice presidency, and he feared that Nixon would be a political liability. Republican regulars loved Nixon's strident, partisan rhetoric, but Democrats were sure to question Nixon's fitness to serve, if necessary, as Chief Executive. Eisenhower tried to nudge the Vice President off the ticket by suggesting that Nixon take a Cabinet position. Nixon, however, refused to follow this advice unless Eisenhower would bluntly tell him to step aside, and that the President would not do. Yet Eisenhower clearly wanted to rid himself of Nixon, since he offered the vice presidential nomination to Robert Anderson. But Anderson declined, and after months

of uncertainty, Nixon finally told Eisenhower in April that he wanted to remain on the ticket.

Eisenhower's ileitis operation provoked one last attempt to replace Nixon. This time HAROLD STASSEN, Eisenhower's disarmament adviser, took the initiative. But Stassen's candidate, Governor Christian A. Herter of Massachusetts, failed to attract much support and withdrew just as the Republican national convention began in San Francisco on 20 August. Two days later, after nominating Eisenhower by acclamation, the delegates chose Nixon with only one dissenting vote.

The awkward handling of the vice presidential nomination distressed Nixon, but it did nothing to diminish Eisenhower's enormous popularity. At the beginning of the campaign, two-thirds of the American people approved of Eisenhower's performance in office. The President's standing was so high because he had secured an armistice in the KOREAN WAR, met with Soviet leaders at Geneva in 1955 in the first East-West summit conference since the end of WORLD WAR II, and presided over a robust economy. Eisenhower was eager to run on this record, and his CAMPAIGN SLOGAN was "Peace, Prosperity, and Progress."

**Stevenson's Renomination.** The Democrats had little chance of defeating such a popular President, but the contest for both spots on their ticket was nonetheless exciting. Stevenson was the front runner, a position he enjoyed by virtue of heading the ticket in 1952 and of working vigorously for Democratic causes and candidates during the following three years. Stevenson also cultivated a reputation as a statesman with a world tour in 1953 that produced a popular series of articles in *Look* magazine, lectures at Harvard University in 1954 on America's world role (later published as a best-selling book, *Call to Greatness*), and a radio address criticizing the Eisenhower administration for risking nuclear war during the Quemoy-Matsu crisis of 1954-55. While Stevenson had reservations about Eisenhower's foreign policy, he worried even more about drift and complacency at home. Stevenson clearly wanted the nomination, and, unlike 1952, he decided to declare his candidacy openly and early: he entered the race on 15 November 1955.

Stevenson had at first anticipated little difficulty securing the nomination, but Eisenhower's coronary changed his outlook. New York Governor W. Averell Harriman indicated in late September that he was now interested in the nomination, while Lyndon B. Johnson of Texas, the Senate majority leader, also recovering from a heart attack, started to maneuver himself into the position of compromise choice should the convention deadlock. But Stevenson's most formidable opponent was Senator Estes Kefauver of Tennessee, whose progressive views on civil rights and crusading investigations of organized crime had made him popular with liberals, reformers, and those weary of politics as usual. The prospect of a fight for the nomination forced Stevenson to enter several primaries, contests he had previously hoped to avoid. Still, with endorsements from many party leaders, he remained confident that he would win the nomination without great difficulty.

Such optimism vanished with the first primaries. Kefauver won an uncontested victory in New Hampshire on 13 March and a week later pulled off a stunning upset in Minnesota. The latter defeat forced major changes in Stevenson's campaign tactics. He relied less on lofty, eloquent rhetoric and more on direct, simple discussion of the issues that could mobilize voters. He also stepped up the pace of an already grueling schedule. On 21 May, he faced Kefauver in Miami in the first nationally televised PRESIDENTIAL DEBATE between two presidential candidates. Eight days later, Stevenson squeaked out a victory in the Florida primary and then won a landslide victory in California the following week.

The nomination was now his. Kefauver withdrew in late July and threw his support to Stevenson. Harriman got a last-minute boost from an endorsement by former President Harry S. Truman just before the national convention began on 13 August in Chicago. But Stevenson's lead was too great, and he won an easy first-ballot victory. In a dramatic gesture, Stevenson turned the choice of the vice-presidential nominee over to the convention, and Kefauver prevailed on the second ballot.

**The Campaign.** From the beginning of the campaign, Stevenson found it difficult to dent the President's enormous popularity. He criticized Eisenhower for forging peace maintained by nuclear terror, settling for prosperity that excluded many farmers and small businessmen, and exulting in "progress" that forced children to endure a shortage of schools and teachers. He also chastised Eisenhower for leadership so narrow, weak, and even indolent that the President devoted more energy to his golf game than to driving important legislation through Congress. Stevenson offered proposals for a "New America," a series of programs to raise the quality of life by providing federal aid for educational programs, medical research, economic development of depressed areas, and health care for the elderly. Yet these campaign initiatives did little more than frustrate Stevenson, since so many voters liked Eisenhower and exempted him from responsibility for the failings of his own administration.

Adding to Stevenson's difficulties was his inability to project an image of vitality that would remind voters of Eisenhower's age and fragile health. While Stevenson maintained an exhausting schedule of speeches and meetings, Eisenhower limited his campaigning. The result, especially on television, was that Eisenhower often looked more energetic and younger, even though he was ten years older than Stevenson. Eisenhower's television appearances also were smoother and more skillfully produced, thanks to the coaching of actor Robert Montgomery.

An even greater advantage for Eisenhower was Stevenson's decision to concentrate on two defense issues, suspension of nuclear testing and termination of the draft. Stevenson argued that neither reform would weaken national defense. The American nuclear arsenal could already obliterate the Soviet Union many times over and so there was no need to poison the atmosphere with nuclear fallout; a switch from conscription to an all-volunteer force would result in longer terms of service and improved readiness in armed forces dependent on ever more sophisticated military technology. Stevenson advocated both proposals because he thought they were right rather than politically popular, but he never imagined how badly they would backfire. Eisenhower firmly replied that the United States could not maintain adequate military forces without a draft. Then, in mid October, Soviet Premier Nicolai A. Bulganin endorsed the test ban and noted approvingly its popularity "with certain prominent public figures in the United States." Bulganin's embrace of Stevenson's issue was a kiss of death. Nixon condemned Stevenson as an appeaser, while Eisenhower scorned his challenger for injecting a delicate international issue into the campaign. On both the test ban and the draft, most people trusted Eisenhower's judgment, since he remained the nation's most respected soldier.

That trust also helped Eisenhower when crises erupted in the Suez and Hungary in the final days of the campaign. Distressed over Egyptian nationalization of the Suez Canal, Great Britain, France, and Israel launched a coordinated, surprise attack against Egypt on 29 October. Eisenhower loathed Egyptian President Gamal Abdel Nasser, but he knew that military action would only rally Arab support behind Nasser. Even though Britain and France were U.S. allies he refused to support them and used American leverage to secure a cease-fire. While the British and French fought for the vestiges of colonialism, the Soviets used force to maintain their empire by sending 200,000 troops into Hungary. Eisenhower condemned the Soviet invasion, but there was nothing he could do to stop it. Stevenson went on national television and insisted that the fighting in the Suez reflected "the bankruptcy of our policy." Privately, he conceded, though, that the political effect of these crises was to rally support behind the President.

**The Result.** On Election Day, Eisenhower won a landslide victory. The President ran up a plurality of almost ten million popular votes and an advantage of 457 to 73 in the ELECTORAL COLLEGE. Stevenson carried only the core of the Solid South—six states in the heart of Dixie—plus Missouri. He even lost Louisiana, the first time that state had voted Republican since the end of RECONSTRUCTION. While the Suez and Hungarian crises may have widened Eisenhower's margin of victory, there seems little doubt that the President would have won handily even if international tensions had not intruded on the last week of the campaign. Eisenhower's record was just too strong and his personality too appealing. The voters simply liked Ike—overwhelmingly.

### BIBLIOGRAPHY

Ambrose, Stephen E. *Eisenhower.* Vol. 2: *The President.* 1984.

Ambrose, Stephen E. *Nixon.* Vol. 1: *The Education of a Politician, 1913–1962.* 1987.

Martin, John Bartlow. *Adlai Stevenson and the World.* 1977.

McKeever, Porter. *Adlai Stevenson: His Life and Legacy.* 1989.

Pach, Chester J., Jr., and Elmo Richardson. *The Presidency of Dwight D. Eisenhower.* Rev. ed. 1991.

Parmet, Herbert S. *Eisenhower and the American Crusades.* 1972.

CHESTER J. PACH, JR.

**ELECTION, PRESIDENTIAL, 1960.** Thanks to the flair of "idealized advocacy" journalism, the 1960 election remains in lore as a modern confrontation between good and evil, a David and Goliath contest in which John F. Kennedy's sling felled the contentiously partisan Vice President, Richard M. Nixon. "Camelot" was born, the politics of a new American enlightenment repelling the ominous champion of a new dark age. A sort of fog settled over that year's realities, only to be further obscured by such later events as the assassination in Dallas and Richard Nixon's forced resignation from the presidency in 1974. In fact, as each man became his party's nominee in 1960, a number of skeptics wondered about how different the two men really were.

**The Candidates and the Parties.** The incumbent Vice President was only forty-seven and at his peak, experienced and articulate, a credible formulator of positions as well as a loyal Republican "soldier." He was so close to his party's central establishment that his nomination as Dwight D. Eisenhower's successor was

virtually preordained, even among Grand Old Party ultraconservatives already enamored with an ideologue from Arizona, Senator BARRY M. GOLDWATER.

When, just before his nomination, Nixon negotiated what became known as the Compact of Fifth Avenue with his more liberal rival, Governor NELSON A. ROCKEFELLER of New York, he neutralized just about all remaining pockets of resistance. Not that all fellow Republicans were pleased. Senator Goldwater called the agreement, in which Nixon acceded to Rockefeller positions about the party's platform, "the Munich of the Republican Party." Nixon, however, by adding to his ticket Henry Cabot Lodge, Jr., the U.S. Ambassador to the United Nations and former Senator from Massachusetts, chose a man congenial with the party's moderates and acceptable to most conservatives. Most of all, Nixon was the man of experience. He was "Ike's boy" and better known than just about anyone else.

Kennedy's mission was far more difficult. Doubts about his fitness for the top office were so serious that, on 2 January 1960, even as he announced his candidacy for his party's nomination, he stressed that he would not settle for the vice presidency. He had, by the age of 43, come a long way to establish his credibility, especially his fitness to command a party still largely enthralled by the legacy of the NEW DEAL and the FAIR DEAL. The presidential wing, mainly party leaders whose power was not centered on Capitol Hill, according to an analysis made by an eminent political scientist, still clung to progressive liberalism. Favorites of that wing ranged from such potential heirs to the Roosevelt-Truman period as Senator HUBERT H. HUMPHREY of Minnesota and ADLAI E. STEVENSON (1900–1965), the former governor of Illinois who had distinguished himself even while losing twice to Eisenhower, to Capitol Hill moderates like Senator Stuart Symington of Missouri and Lyndon B. Johnson, the Senate's majority leader. In that field, the boyish-looking young man from Massachusetts seemed out of place.

He was even more at a disadvantage because of his own background. His congressional career, following his victory from the Bay State's Eleventh District in 1946, placed in the House of Representatives the sallow-faced, sickly son of a very rich and widely disliked man, Joseph P. Kennedy.

**Kennedy's Background.** Kennedy's early congressional career had gone from notoriety as an indifferent playboy Representative to a Senator who did his best to avoid voting on the condemnation of Joseph McCarthy. On that other great moral issue of the day, civil rights, Kennedy played an equally innocuous role, voting on the 1957 bill in a way that left an impression of straddling the issue. On foreign policy matters, he did deliver several significant and even bold statements from the Senate floor, notably on Southeast Asia in 1954 and the Algerian revolution three years later, but except for some valuable work during the deliberations that led to the Landrum-Griffin Labor Relations Act of 1959, he was never regarded as among the leaders of the Senate, or as a member of their inner circle. To liberals, he was neither a Humphrey nor a Stevenson; to those focused on Capitol Hill, he was no Johnson. ELEANOR ROOSEVELT, the greatest living symbol of the New Deal era, mocking the title of Kennedy's Pulitzer Prize-winning book, said he should show more courage and less profile.

*Profiles in Courage*, published in 1956 and awarded a Pulitzer Prize for history and biography, played a key role in advancing the young man's career. Appearing as it did just before that year's Democratic convention, it drew prominent notices. The Massachusetts Senator, already a WORLD WAR II hero after rescuing the survivors of his destroyed PT boat, had earlier written a book, *Why England Slept*, based on his Harvard college senior thesis. His second work, one that celebrated figures who had taken courageous stands in defiance of political caution, was an inspiring contribution to the sense of national idealism. Some of that valor might, he hoped, brush off on him, perhaps making people forget about his timidity toward Joseph McCarthy. It was, nevertheless, as the author of *Profiles in Courage* that his name was placed alongside that of Senator Estes Kefauver of Tennessee during the 1956 convention as a potential running mate for presidential nominee, Adlai Stevenson. Kennedy, during the highlight of an otherwise lackluster affair, came within a few delegate votes of defeating Kefauver. At the moment, his loss hurt, but his spontaneity and graciousness in defeat captivated viewers. The Pulitzer Prize for *Profiles* followed soon afterward. Kennedy, with his aides having already taken the pains to convince the party that a Roman Catholic could win the presidency, was squarely on the road toward the White House.

Led in large part by the talents of a superb organizer, speechwriter, and key aide, THEODORE SORENSEN, the Kennedy drive almost immediately began the effort of selling the young man. Sorensen had circulated an analysis that showed his candidate's Roman Catholicism would, on balance, actually result in a net gain of electoral votes even if he were to decline in the popular count. Doubts, however, were not easy to overcome, with some Catholic politicians among the most reluctant to reopen the wounds that they still felt lingered from the campaign of ALFRED E. SMITH in 1928. With the sharpest criticism of the Eisenhower administration, and especially of Nixon, coming from the liberal Democratic wing, Kennedy pitched his prenomination campaign to overcome that resistance. Stevenson had already been defeated twice and those on the left considered Johnson too much of a Southern conservative and hostile toward labor. HUBERT H. HUMPHREY's liberal background, especially his identification with the early civil rights movement, loomed as Kennedy's chief obstacle for winning over the New Deal traditionalists. An assemblage of academics went to work turning out position papers and books. Sorensen skillfully placed articles under Kennedy's byline in a wide variety of publications. Kennedy undertook speaking tours to all parts of the country.

In 1960, candidates were still chosen by party nominating conventions; there were, that year, only thirteen PRESIDENTIAL PRIMARIES, a number that would nearly triple within the next two decades. In an era before party reforms changed the rules, delegates were chosen by Democratic Party professionals attending controlled conventions. Still, Kennedy, to overcome doubts about the winning potential of a Catholic, took on Humphrey in key primaries held in Wisconsin and West Virginia. He won both, but his 61 percent in heavily fundamentalist Protestant West Virginia gave him a commanding advantage for the Democratic convention in Los Angeles, one that easily withstood the late entry campaign of Lyndon Johnson and a last minute floor rally for Adlai Stevenson. His first-ballot victory was no surprise. But Kennedy's choice of Lyndon B. Johnson as his vice presidential running mate, largely because of the majority leader's potential ability to deliver the South, was a master stroke that stunned both professionals and amateurs alike. Johnson's acceptance seemed almost as astonishing.

**Campaign Strategy.** Having gone that far, the advantages then became Kennedy's. Nixon was hampered in ways Kennedy was not. He was bound by his need to defend the administration's record, which, apart from the Eisenhower personality, was open to sharp criticism. Since 1958, with only a brief respite, the economy had been sluggish, burdened by both stagnation and inflation, giving rise to a new word popularized by the media, stagflation. Several industrial centers were especially hard hit by high unemployment. Moreover, in the wake of the Soviet launching of the first outer space satellite, *Sputnik*, on 4 October 1957, and the collapse of the projected summit conference after the Soviets shot down an American U-2 spy plane in Soviet airspace, the Eisenhower defense posture was under increasing political fire. Kennedy, sensing campaign issue, latched on to the perception (later proved erroneous) that a "missile gap" would soon tilt the military balance in favor of the Soviets and that the administration was shortsighted in not equipping the military with the flexible-force capability to counter the most likely forms of battlefield engagement. Nixon's private closeness to Kennedy's views on this matter had, of necessity, to be muted. He even had to attack Kennedy's suggestion, made during their nationally televised PRESIDENTIAL DEBATES, favoring military intervention that could, if not overthrow Fidel Castro, at least destabilize his Communist hold over CUBA. Then, when the Reverend Dr. Martin Luther King, Jr., was jailed on a technicality and sent to a remote Georgia prison, Nixon could only stand by, fearful of jeopardizing the Republican Party's new-found standing in the South, while Robert and Jack Kennedy wooed the black vote by getting King released after contacting De Kalb County Judge Oscar Mitchell.

The debates themselves, four in all and novel for a presidential campaign, vitiated Nixon's claim to unique preparation for the presidency. They debated the wisdom of an activist federal government, U.S. policies toward the off-shore islands near Communist China, and Cuba. Kennedy, anticipating an Eisen-hower-administration preelection attempt to topple Castro, strongly advocated military intervention. Fearing adverse reactions if he failed to agree to meet the challenge in that manner, and still confident of how well he could handle the media after his 1952 "Checkers" speech, Nixon nevertheless inadvertently made his rival a more credible opponent. He never recovered from the negative effects of the first debate, in which Kennedy's articulate certitude enhanced his stature. The debates succeeded in elevating Senator Kennedy to the Vice President's level merely by presenting the candidates as equals.

Nixon's campaign strategy similarly placed him at a disadvantage. His vow to touch down in all fifty states, made more difficult by a brief but costly hospitalization from a knee injury early in the campaign, placed him in Alaska on the final weekend, wooing that state's three electors while Kennedy canvassed the rich New York metropolitan area.

Through it all, conservative Republicans were displeased that Nixon, reminiscent of THOMAS E. DEWEY in 1948, was waging an updated "me-too" campaign. There was more agreement than confrontation, the essential difference centering on the extent of federal intervention in the economy. Nixon was not with the Goldwater Republicans, which also made him vulnerable to their subsequent attacks.

He also suffered from President Eisenhower's belated campaigning. Eisenhower's health kept him from participating until the final days. In the interim, Eisenhower's ostensible put-down, during a news conference, of Nixon's claim to experience was a clear embarrassment to the Vice President. When he did take up the cause, most notably in speeches in Philadelphia and New York, Eisenhower did so with enthusiasm and polls showed Nixon catching up to Kennedy's lead. Election Day came with the two men in a dead heat.

**The Result.** Nixon did not concede until the next morning. Kennedy's early advantage in the East, where he took astonishingly large majorities in recession-wracked industrial cities, faded as Nixon strength became apparent from the rest of the country. In the end, Kennedy took 303 electoral votes to Nixon's 219, a success made possible by Johnson's efforts in the South. The popular count was more imprecise, the exact numbers dependent upon the method used to calculate ballots from southerners who found both men unacceptable and voted for uncommitted electors. Most counts placed Kennedy's plurality at below 120,000 out of 69 million cast. Though without verifiable evidence, suspicion lingered long afterward that Mayor Richard J. Daley of Chicago, a Democrat, had tampered with the vote returns in Cook County; combined with irregularities in Texas and Missouri it was enough to deny Nixon victory. Nixon, to his credit, rejected the advice of some that he challenge the votes by asking for a recount (Illinois by itself would not have been enough to overturn the result and Texas had no provision for a recount). Nevertheless, Kennedy's narrow victory, in addition to the composition of the new Congress, especially conservative control over key committees, made for a surprisingly cautious new administration, one that was in striking contrast to the bold vows of his inaugural address.

### BIBLIOGRAPHY

Ambrose, Stephen E. *Nixon: The Education of a Politician 1913–1962.* 1987.

Parmet, Herbert S. *JFK: The Presidency of John F. Kennedy.* 1983.

Schlesinger, Arthur M., Jr. *A Thousand Days: John F. Kennedy in the White House.* 1965.

Sorensen, Theodore C. *Kennedy.* 1965.

White, Theodore H. *The Making of the President 1960.* 1961.

HERBERT S. PARMET

**ELECTION, PRESIDENTIAL, 1964.** The presidential election of 1964 between Democrat Lyndon B. Johnson and Republican BARRY GOLDWATER stands out for the personalities heading the tickets, the issues evaded, extreme positions taken, the amateurish campaign waged by the Republican Party, and the decidedly one-sided nature of the outcome. Many voters would later say that they had been fooled into voting for the wrong candidate because what they had feared in Goldwater—militancy that might get the nation involved in a Southeast Asian war—turned out to be true of the Democratic victor instead.

**The Contest Records.** Johnson won with the highest-ever percentage of the vote in a presidential contest—61.1 as compared with Warren G. Harding's 60.3 in 1920 and Franklin D. Roosevelt's 60.7 in 1936, the previous record-holders. Moreover, the victory was Democratic at every level of the federal system.

This decidedly unbalanced result stands between two very close elections: the narrow defeat administered by John F. Kennedy to Richard M. Nixon in 1960, and the latter's narrow defeat of HUBERT H. HUMPHREY in 1968. The overwhelming victory scored by the Democrats in 1964 therefore warrants explanation. How could so crushing a defeat have possibly taken place in the middle of an eight-year interval that had such extremely close election results on either end?

The explanation may lie in the tide of events from 1960 to 1964, in change in Democratic leadership, and, especially, in the turmoil in the Republican Party. Much depends on whether one focuses on the dramatic personality, skills, and accomplishments of President Johnson, Kennedy's successor after the assassination of November 1963, or on the intellectual ferment, personalities, and chosen course of the Republican Party.

**The Candidates.** Johnson was a skilled politician who used wisely the team he had inherited from his dynamic predecessor. The country desired strong executive leadership at the time, and Johnson consciously emulated Franklin Roosevelt. In foreign affairs, he pursued the successful segments of the Kennedy path while avoiding repetition of early Kennedy errors. His interaction with Congress, born in his experience as majority leader was very effective.

On the other hand, the Republicans made suicidal mistakes in policies and procedures. The uncompromisingly conservative ideas of Barry Goldwater and his inexperienced team were pridefully advanced, while moderate Republican ideas and courses were scornfully ignored. Leaders who espoused any routes other than those of the stubborn candidate and his extremist faction were simply pushed aside.

In early 1964, the possible Republican candidates seemed to include three moderates: New York's governor NELSON A. ROCKEFELLER, Pennsylvania's William

Scranton, and Governor George Romney of Michigan. Conservative Arizona Senator Barry Goldwater's crushing victory over his rivals is not easy to explain. Dwight D. Eisenhower had not left a firm and identifiable political legacy. The Kennedy years had seen the nation's humiliation in the BAY OF PIGS INVASION fiasco, a reversal in world power relationships highlighted by the Soviet supremacy in space, and the upheaval of school desegregation mandated by the Supreme Court, so there was a widespread desire for decisive leadership. The civil rights movement had brought racial unrest manifested in protest marches, prompting retaliatory actions by some southern political and law-enforcement figures. The Supreme Court seemed to be in the hands of "liberals" even though Chief Justice Earl Warren was an Eisenhower appointee. Liberalism was ascendent in the 1964 Congress.

The Republican right wing came to consist of fundamentalist Christians, some John Birch Society types who cradled deep suspicions reminiscent of McCarthyism. Some white workers displayed concern about black employees entering the skilled workforce. Some people far from the Atlantic seaboard distrusted so-called eastern establishment leftists and UNITED NATIONS partisans. A sturdy conservative movement was also being born in some intellectual circles.

Goldwater was no intellectual; indeed, like Harry S. Truman before him, he was not even a college graduate, though he had spent a year at the University of Arizona. He came from a business background (he had been a department store owner) and was a high-ranking Air Force reservist who qualified as a multi-engine-airplane pilot. He was also a talented photographer. Although his vote against the CIVIL RIGHTS ACT OF 1964 alienated black voters, it did guarantee that GEORGE WALLACE would not form a THIRD PARTY. Goldwater was a practical man, in politics and everything else, yet he liked to say that principles were what politics ought to be rooted in. He was an attractive individual: friendly, open, candid, honest—by no means a cynical politician.

Some who found Goldwater's candidacy promising believed that there existed a vast, uncounted vote that could be tapped by a candidate who offered, as Goldwater certainly did, a clear-cut "choice, not an echo," as the title of Phyllis Schlafly's 1964 book promoting the Goldwater candidacy put it. Goldwater and his team thought the country had seen enough liberal, moderate, or progressive Republican candidates. His supporters believed that a hidden conservative majority could be mobilized for victory in 1964.

Johnson, the incumbent, was well positioned to perform well at the polls. His demeanor after

Kennedy's death had been flawless, as everyone admitted, and his succession to office had been a triumph of good administration. He handled the budget crisis in the winter of 1963–1964 quite well and soon thereafter aroused national interest in a War on Poverty program that enlarged and codified the plans and hopes of Kennedy subordinates. What would later become the VIETNAM WAR seemed for some time to be unimportant; it was being handled "much as Kennedy would have done." This was no accident, for Kennedy's Vietnam advisers stayed on.

Johnson met the need to display a politically appealing program in a Michigan speech on 22 May by reiterating the slogan GREAT SOCIETY as encapsulating his hopes. He intended to place future reforms in civil rights, welfare, education, conservation, medical care, and other areas under this umbrella. The Civil Rights Act of 1964 and Johnson's attitude strongly attracted the support of African American voters.

Republicans knew that their House leader, Charles Halleck, and Senate leader, Everett Dirksen, shared credit for the civil rights bill, so it would be hard to use it to recruit white votes in a partisan sense, even with Goldwater as the candidate. He privately agreed with Johnson not to make civil rights for minorities an issue in the election. The two men secretly met in the White House on 24 July and agreed to shun debate over civil rights and Vietnam. If civil rights became an issue, Goldwater said, "it could polarize the country." He promised he would not attack the President's position and expected quid pro quo.

Both candidates knew that the public was divided over the legitimacy of America's role in Vietnam and was uninformed about increasing American commitment there. "I asked to see you," Goldwater told Johnson, "because I do not believe it is in the best interest of the United States to make the Vietnam War or its conduct a political issue in this campaign. I have come to promise that I will not do so." The public knew nothing of this secret agreement. From the meeting stemmed a failure to air public unease concerning two major areas of nationwide discussion in 1964. This deprived citizens of the kind of analysis and position-taking that might have clarified these two divisive areas.

**The Campaign.** Goldwater did miserably in the early New Hampshire primary but performed better in later primaries. He used dual organizations, one from the conventional party and the other made up of his ideological partisans. The tactic worked best in those states that did not hold primaries. He was always surrounded by newcomers, many of whom thought adherence to principles more important than mere winning. Rockefeller suffered a political blow when he

divorced and remarried shortly thereafter. Romney's campaign never caught on.

Though Goldwater did well in the Republican primaries overall, he did not try to unite his party as the convention approached. His opponents, who called themselves "moderate" Republicans, found the ascendant conservative wing of their party dogmatic and uncompromising.

The Goldwater forces won a solid victory at the Republican national convention in San Francisco, but they lost party unity. There were few compromises in the platform committee, no concessions to the Rockefeller-Romney-Scranton moderate wing, and no gestures to unity when accepting the nomination. "Extremism in the defense of liberty is no vice. Moderation in the pursuit of justice is no virtue," Goldwater proclaimed. He kept the vice presidential nomination within his own faction, later saying flippantly that little-known Congressman William Miller was chosen "because he drives LBJ nuts."

The Democrats met in Atlantic City to endorse Johnson's candidacy and to rubber stamp his vice presidential choice. A divisive struggle over which Mississippi delegation should be seated was settled by an agreement on achieving racial equity in future conventions. The platform, entitled "One Nation, One People," built on the Great Society theme and offended few. LBJ maneuvered successfully to facilitate his choice of Hubert Humphrey as a running mate.

After the convention, Republican leaders met briefly to try to restore party unity. Differences between the conservative and moderate factions proved difficult to reconcile, however, especially over AGRICULTURAL POLICY. The extremism of the Goldwater ranks remained in force, but a new Citizens' Committee did try to bridge gaps between party factions.

Democrats worked hard to smear Goldwater. Vicious television commercials targeted his alleged positions on the use of nuclear weapons and on SOCIAL SECURITY. A slogan used by loyalist Republicans—"In your heart you know he's right"—was joyfully converted by the opposition to, "In your guts you know he's nuts." To his credit, Goldwater killed an offensive Republican film, *Choice*, bluntly saying that it was racist. The Johnson campaign built on the Kennedy mystique. Goldwater's tried to bury ill-advised remarks he had made early in the primary period. Except for their tone, his speeches somewhat resembled those of his predecessors on both foreign and domestic policy. Early on, his strategists wrote off New England while hoping, unrealistically, for some success in the South. Little effort was made to appeal to special interests or to specific groups of voters.

**Result and Significance.** Election day brought the Democrats all they wished, and more. The tally, 43,129,484 to 27,178,188, translated to a phenomenal 486 to 52 electoral votes. The Democrats won more than five hundred new seats in state legislatures and twelve new governorships. The Democrat-to-Republican ratios were now 295 to 140 in the House of Representatives and 68 to 32 in the Senate. Still, there was the possibility that many of the House seats gained in close races might not be permanent, for thirty-seven of the congressional winners enjoyed a less than 52.5 percent margin, and sixty-one had won with less than 55 percent of the total.

One measure of the completeness of the Johnson victory was his margin in every category of voter. He won practically all the black vote, three-quarters of the poor, well over half of the rich, and 83 percent of union members. He won among men and women, educated and uneducated, and various religious groups. Not surprisingly, Johnson's popularity stood at 69 percent a month after the election.

There was a great deal of post-election introspection within the Republican Party. What happened to Goldwater? many asked. For awed Democratic partisans who watched, the GOP's utter collapse was mind-boggling. The overall campaign, wrote Kennedy partisan John Barlow Martin, was "one of the silliest, most empty, and most boring campaigns in the nation's history."

A far deeper significance of the 1964 election emerged with the passage of time. The winner got an apparently unlimited mandate to govern as he saw fit, together with a lopsidedly partisan Congress obligated to help him. The losing party was split into hostile moderate and conservative factions, a polarization that would long continue. Johnson, a Vice President inheriting the presidency, became a powerful President in his own right, though from his earliest days in office he had helped build the Kennedy mythology, which pleased the latter's partisans and helped his own progress.

The significance of the election seems threefold. First, the Republican Party's new leadership violated first principles of presidential politics, especially the idea that the vast center of the body politic must be wooed at all costs. They relied in vain on an invisible, hypothetical conservative electorate, presuming without research that there was a hidden majority.

Americans had watched the winner promise vast changes for the better. His speechwriters did this so plausibly that a great many citizens probably believed that major improvement would surely result. The remarkable thing was that the reelected President actually did carry through with landmark legislation in 1965 and later, both in areas mentioned in campaign speeches and in some that were not. Hell bent for a massive victory, he had promised that he would not send American boys to fight in an Asian war, but this promise was by no means to be honored.

The winner was certain that he had a mandate to move in whatever direction he wished. From this belief flowed the Great Society programs, unguarded moves toward a catastrophic undeclared war overseas, and excesses in erecting an outsized Johnson image.

Conservative Republicans observed that they had lost only the initial battle in what they promised would be a long "crusade." Some visionaries reflected hopefully that they might recoup their fortunes later on in the person of Ronald Reagan. For the new Democratic majority led by President Lyndon Johnson, however, 1965 would prove to be the greatest single year for liberal legislation since the crisis months of 1933. The election of 1964 was an election that had indeed made a difference.

### BIBLIOGRAPHY

Bornet, Vaughn Davis. *The Presidency of Lyndon B. Johnson.* 1983.
Cummings, Milton C., Jr., ed. *The Presidential Election of 1964.* 1966.
Lamb, Karl A., and Paul A. Smith. *Campaign Decision-Making: The Presidential Election of 1964.* 1968.
Lokos, Lionel. *Hysteria 1964: The Fear Campaign against Barry Goldwater.* 1967.
White, Theodore H. *The Making of the President, 1964.* 1965.

VAUGHN DAVIS BORNET

**ELECTION, PRESIDENTIAL, 1968.** In 1968 the REPUBLICAN PARTY under Richard M. Nixon took back the executive branch of the national government from the DEMOCRATIC PARTY after a hiatus of eight years. They did so in a year marked by a controversial war overseas, a deteriorating peace at home, the assassinations of two prominent leaders, and race rioting in the streets of major cities. A determined third-party effort was mounted from the South. The year also witnessed the decision of an incumbent President not to run again, as well as the return from political limbo of a politician many journalists had written off as no longer electable to any office.

**Candidates and Issues.** Positioning by candidates for the 1968 election was noticeable throughout the preceeding year. President Lyndon B. Johnson's VIETNAM WAR policy was publicly endorsed by the Western States Democratic Conference in late August 1967. When race riots erupted in more than fifty cities during the summer of 1967 the response was partisan.

The election of 1966 had increased Republican seats in Congress, so that the House no longer voted semiautomatically for whatever President Johnson wanted. Vice President Hubert H. Humphrey called for a "Marshall Plan" to help ghetto dwellers, and Senator Robert F. Kennedy called for a low-cost housing program, but little changed. The President sent troops to Detroit on 24 July to control rioters, thus embarrassing Michigan's Republican governor, George Romney (a possible presidential candidate), even though he agreed with the drastic action. The report of a federal Advisory Commission on Civil Disorders was a legacy of 1967 to the future.

Many public figures were guarded in their utterances. Governor Ronald Reagan of California favored "honorable disengagement" from Vietnam—but first he wanted to win the war. He did not know how, exactly, but thought that perhaps better targeting of U.S. bombing raids would help. Nixon favored "massive pressure" as opposed to Johnson's policy of "gradual escalation."

Protest, both in and outside the electoral process, became prominent. A National Conference for a New Politics met in Chicago from 31 August to 4 September 1967, with two thousand delegates representing some two hundred disaffected, chiefly radical, groups. A new, right-wing Patriotic Party of 250 delegates duly nominated Governor George Wallace of Alabama at a 1967 Kansas City meeting. Another emerging national figure was Democratic Senator Eugene McCarthy of Minnesota, who courted college students and others who agreed that the Asian war was immoral. He rejected "party unity" as a goal. Senator Kennedy, too, soon began to criticize the war (which he had earlier supported) as one that targeted women and the innocent. Kennedy thought that the South Vietnamese weren't exerting enough effort. Vice President Humphrey praised their courage, however, and attacked any "new isolationism." Republican governor Nelson A. Rockefeller of New York called for a "just society" at home and the deemphasizing of the burgeoning national government vis-à-vis the states.

By autumn 1967, Romney was an official candidate, Rockefeller was refusing to declare himself a candidate (he later did), and Nixon (who like Romney had visited Vietnam in 1967) was saying that division at home was a factor prolonging the war. Governor Reagan remained a favorite son, a campaigning "noncandidate." The public thought that President Johnson was certain to run for reelection.

As the election year approached, therefore, political divisions among the parties were rooted in the Vietnam War (never actually a declared war), in the need for racial stability at home, and the supremacy of Washington in the federal system. Whether Johnson's Great Society of social-welfare programs was really working received less attention than it had earlier.

The nation in early 1968 was obsessed with Vietnam—where, by January 1968, 492,900 American military personnel were deployed and where nearly 17,000 had already died. Late January—the time of the Vietnamese new year (Tet)—brought the fierce Tet offensive attack by North Vietnam and the Vietcong. The American public and media were shocked, and Johnson's credibility suffered additional decline. Now came changes in the public perception of "progress" in Southeast Asia, even though Tet was a military defeat for North Vietnam. Such awesome events impinged on presidential politics. As the President failed to lead the public mind, television news and commentary led the public to see the war as unwinnable without an unacceptable level of effort.

In the White House, February brought indecision, and with March came serious discussions by influential insiders on how to get peace negotiations going. It was determined that the President would give a major TV speech on Sunday, 31 March, to announce that the United States would halt the bombing if serious talks on "peace" began promptly. Johnson closed his somber speech with a dramatic, surprise announcement that he would not run in 1968 for a new four-year term.

Johnson's opponents joyfully proclaimed, then and later, that they had forced a hated President from office. Recent primary results from New Hampshire, where Johnson was a write-in candidate but McCarthy got 42 percent of the vote, had indeed been disappointing to Johnson. Still, there is more than ample evidence that his retirement had long been planned in view of his marginal health (Johnson had suffered a heart attack in 1956 and had many physical problems). Soon after New Hampshire, McCarthy's candidacy was joined by that of Robert Kennedy. Charges of party disloyalty could no longer be mounted.

It quickly became evident that the administration would be uniting behind the liberal and dependable Vice President. The three figures now battled it out in the remaining primaries, seeking delegates to bring success at the Democratic national convention in Chicago in August.

**Primaries and Conventions.** The outcome of the Democratic primaries was hard to predict. Kennedy won California after he unexpectedly lost to McCarthy in Oregon, then was assassinated.

Meanwhile, Richard Nixon, long a favorite of organization Republicans, headed toward an easy victory in the Republican convention in Miami Beach. The biggest surprise there was his choice of Governor SPIRO T. AGNEW of Maryland as his running mate. Since Nixon's acceptance speech was an unexpected success, it seemed that he had a decent chance in November against the sharply divided Democrats. Johnson's withdrawal, aimed at peace, had been quickly overshadowed by the assassination of African American leader Martin Luther King, Jr., in Memphis on 4 April and the riots that followed. The electorate was now emotionally disturbed over both foreign and domestic issues, and the national psyche was apprehensive.

Late August brought a dramatic event in American electoral history: the violent Chicago Democratic convention, witnessed on television by millions. Threats by a variety of political and cultural radicals to disrupt the proceedings seemed credible to Chicago police authorities. As youths interdicted convention-goers in an orgy of protest, the Chicago police reacted to the baiting by beating demonstrators—a response that to many observers seemed as repulsive as the extralegal display that had caused it. The inability of Humphrey, the eventual convention victor, to win back many of the disaffected McCarthy and Kennedy elements quickly made the Democrats glum.

Labor's support did not loom as large as usual, for both Nixon and Wallace had some support among blue-collar workers. Humphrey and his running mate, Maine Senator Edmund Muskie, got little help from an underfunded Democratic National Committee. White House help was conjectural, for Johnson was now obsessed with forcing the ticket's endorsement of every aspect of his Vietnam policy. In any case, the presence in the primaries of three Democrats of contrasting views on the war divided the party seriously. Another disturbing factor was the noisy third-party candidacy of George Wallace, which threatened to be effective nationally. Wallace, who had just retired as governor of Alabama, chose Air Force General Curtis LeMay as his running mate for the racist, STATES' RIGHTS, jingoistic campaign on behalf of the newly formed American Independent Party. His hard line on civil rights and Vietnam alike brought hecklers in the North and due appreciation from racists, militants, and devoted southerners. While an unedifying spectacle, his campaign nevertheless drew some southern support away from the Democrats.

**The Vietnam Issue.** Vietnam had long been expected to dominate the campaign issues, but Kennedy's death and the subsequent Humphrey nomination intervened. Unknown to the public, Nixon had used evangelist Billy Graham to convey to Johnson his private pledge not to make the American presence in Vietnam an election issue. Never would it be "Johnson's War." This basic position, however, did not keep Nixon from making charges of mismanagement and serious mistakes in setting the level of military action. Humphrey, who as Vice President was an integral part of the administration, was in an awkward position to absorb the former Kennedy and McCarthy supporters in the party into his campaign, for he could hardly challenge the major policies of the President.

In a speech in Salt Lake City on 30 September, Humphrey tried to woo dovish elements in the party without actually repudiating his boss. He would be "willing to stop the bombing," he said, as "an acceptable risk for peace." To do that, he would need "direct or indirect evidence that the enemy would restore the Demilitarized Zone" between North and South Vietnam. The press helped make this evasive promise into considerably more than it was, and privately Johnson seethed.

Johnson played both helper and spoiler roles in the election. His mishandling of two abortive Supreme Court appointments in late summer strengthened opposition forces, and he kept candidate Humphrey nervous and irritable with private threats mixed with hints of ultimate White House help—when the time should be ripe.

The capture of an American intelligence ship, the USS *Pueblo,* off North Korea early in the year had weakened Johnson's posture as an international leader, for there seemed little that could be done to remedy that situation, short of still more use of force in Asia. A last-minute presidential effort to defuse the Vietnam quagmire only days before the election nearly did prove decisive. Johnson claimed that a breakthrough in peace negotiations in Paris warranted the announcement of a total bombing halt. The bombing had long been a major campaign issue because of North Vietnamese claims that women, children, and hospitals were deliberately targeted—charges that, in modified form, were being repeated at home. The dramatic and timely move alarmed Republicans. It was, wrote Nixon later, "a pretty good bomb in the middle of my campaign," one that he could not attack. Instead, he said that, as Dwight D. Eisenhower had promised vis-à-vis Korea in 1952, he would go to Saigon after the election to help bring peace. He said, too, that he had a plan to win the war. Although Johnson said privately that Nixon was a better war supporter than Humphrey, he nevertheless finally forced himself to stump in Texas for his Vice President. Even so, Humphrey was angry at Johnson after the end of his close but unsuccessful election campaign.

**The Result.** When the votes were counted a gap of only 449,704 votes separated winner and loser. Nixon's total of 31,770,237 and Humphrey's nearly identical 31,270,533 added up to vastly more than Wallace's 9,906,141. The vote percentages were 43.4, 42.7, and 13.5, respectively, contrasting sharply with the triumphant Democratic victory of 1964. Some 60.2 percent of eligible voters had come to the polls. In the increasingly black-populated District of Columbia, Nixon got only 18.2 percent of the vote, showing, especially in light of three Johnson-sponsored civil rights bills, that the party of Abraham Lincoln had become predominantly white. Wallace's reactionary effort did take between 37 and 66 percent of the vote in some southern states, but he did much less well elsewhere (10 percent in Michigan, for example). A motley list of third parties made an unimpressive showing, with a total of under 250,000 votes.

The Democrats lost the presidency for many reasons. Johnson's conduct as President (the "credibility gap") lost some supporters, especially in the media. The Republican campaign organization was far superior to that of the Democrats. Unrest in the country over lawlessness, a backlash to vigorous pressure by African-American for long-denied civil rights, and the failure of the electorate to appreciate some Great Society programs were all factors.

The election of 1968 could have had an entirely different outcome, for Nixon still had his enemies of old, still lacked a glowing television presence, and inherited what was, in the wake of the 1964 defeat, a still-unnerved party machine. The assassination of Robert Kennedy eliminated the possibility of a John F. Kennedy replacement, and ensuing dispair diminished the willingness of young Democrats to work for an "old fashioned liberal candidate" like Humphrey. Humphrey proved to be a weaker candidate than hoped, despite his many admirable qualities—especially his visionary idealism. Some partisans of the Kennedy brothers sat on their hands, considering the Minnesota Senator no match for their fallen heroes. All in all, so Humphrey judged later, "We defeated ourselves." Nevertheless, he could hardly have worked more vigorously for his cause.

Although the election returned moderate Republicans to power in the executive branch, the party did not win Congress. Nixon's 302 electoral votes (versus 191 for Humphrey and 45 for Wallace) did not bring control of Congress, where the postelection seat totals were 57 Democrats and 43 Republicans in the Senate, 243 Democrats and 192 Republicans in the House. The Republicans had gained five seats in the Senate but a mere four in the House. As usual, the third-party effort was only at the presidential level. Nine African Americans won election to the House. The Republicans won five additional governorships.

The change in administration went unusually smoothly, as Johnson and his team showed signs of relief that their ordeal was over. The country hoped that the new administration would somehow bring relief to its traumas at home and abroad. At home, Johnson's exit from power (and from the headlines) did bring some feeling of relief, for there was a new chief of state and there would be some consolidation of the far-reaching legislation of the Johnson era. Abroad, the new President seemed determined to bring a gradual end to the war, and to "de-Americanize it," as the Republican PARTY PLATFORM had promised. Overall, the election produced no mandate for the victor, but there were to be some meaningful changes in Nixon's years.

### BIBLIOGRAPHY

Bornet, Vaughn Davis. *The Presidency of Lyndon B. Johnson.* 1983.
Knappman, Edward W. *Presidential Election 1968.* 1970.
Lamb, Karl A., and Paul A. Smith. *Campaign Decision-Making: The Presidential Election of 1968.* 1968.

VAUGHN DAVIS BORNET

**ELECTION, PRESIDENTIAL, 1972.** The VIETNAM WAR dominated the 1972 election campaign as it had the campaign in 1968. In 1968 Republican candidate Richard M. Nixon had claimed he had a plan to end the war. When President Lyndon Baines Johnson had announced, a week before election day, that he was instituting a bombing halt throughout most of North Vietnam and that peace talks would begin the day after the election, Nixon had undercut him by persuading President Nguyen Van Thieu of South Vietnam to announce that his government would not participate. Nixon had then won a narrow victory over Democratic candidate HUBERT H. HUMPHREY.

Nixon's plan to end the war turned out to be what he called Vietnamization—that is, a plan to end American participation in the war. He gradually withdrew American ground troops from Vietnam while increasing American air support for the Army of South Vietnam (ARVN). In 1972 the North Vietnamese Army (NVA) launched a massive offensive into South Vietnam. Nixon responded by bombing Hanoi and mining Haiphong harbor. The offensive was stopped, but the war went on.

**The Democrats' Situation.** Antiwar Americans were dismayed and desperate. Their numbers had grown during the Nixon administration to the point that they numbered more than 40 percent of the population—and a majority within the DEMOCRATIC PARTY. The Democrats had meanwhile instituted structural changes in their party convention rules, changes that required a certain percentage of the delegates to be minority members, young people, and women. This worked to the advantage of the author of the changes, South Dakota Senator GEORGE MCGOVERN, the most liberal of the Democratic candidates. McGovern was also helped in that Nixon thought he would be the weakest candidate the Democrats could nominate. Consequently, during the primary season, Nixon's people carried out a series of DIRTY TRICKS against the man Nixon most feared would be nominated, Senator Edmund Muskie of Maine.

McGovern's delegates dominated the July convention in Miami. They gave an appearance of being anti-religion and pro-drugs, anti-profit and pro-welfare, anti-family and pro-abortion, anti-farmer and pro–migrant worker, anti-Saigon and pro-Hanoi, anti–armed forces and pro–draft dodgers. Delegates booed Humphrey and former President Johnson; some were heard to cheer the name of Ho Chi Minh, the North Vietnamese leader.

The convention was the high-water mark of the New Left's participation in national politics. For both the New Left and the Democratic Party, the campaign was a disaster. McGovern won the nomination, then selected Senator Thomas Eagleton of Missouri as his running mate. Two weeks later, Eagleton admitted that a story just revealed by the newspaper columnist Jack Anderson was true: he had undergone electroshock therapy for depression. McGovern at first said he was behind Eagleton "1,000 percent," but as the controversy over Eagleton's mental health swelled, McGovern realized that unless he did something that issue would dominate the campaign. He therefore asked Eagleton to step down and then suffered the embarrassment of having a number of prominent Democrats rebuff his invitation to join the ticket. Eventually former PEACE CORPS director Sargent Shriver agreed to run.

McGovern's problems were overwhelming. Many Democratic party professionals (especially in the South) and leaders of organized labor refused to support him. His pledge to end the war the day he took office lost some of its appeal as Nixon continued to withdraw American troops from Vietnam and the casualty figures went down. Nixon had earlier reached out to ease COLD WAR tensions by visiting China in February 1972 and signing the Strategic Arms Limitation Treaty (SALT) at a summit in Moscow in May 1972.

Nixon's greatest fear was that Governor GEORGE WALLACE of Alabama would run on a third-party ticket, as he had in 1968; Wallace could be expected to win the votes of white southerners who regarded McGovern as unacceptably radical but who had no great love for Nixon. On 15 May, however, while campaigning in Laurel, Maryland, for the Democratic nomination, Wallace was shot and badly wounded. He dropped out of contention.

**Nixon's Strategy.** At the Republican convention held in August in Miami, Nixon and his Vice President, SPIRO T. AGNEW, were renominated by acclamation. In his platform and in the ensuing campaign, Nixon emphasized patriotism, family values, opposition to forced busing as a means of achieving school desegregation, a get-tough policy on crime and drug use, his foreign policy triumphs, and progress toward "peace with honor" in Vietnam. He never used the words *Republican, Democrat,* or *Nixon.* Instead, he attacked McGovern by name. Emphasizing his office, Nixon's campaign organization was called the Committee to Re-Elect the President (or CREEP, as the Democrats preferred to say). Nixon's campaign chairman was his former Attorney General, JOHN MITCHELL.

Nixon's strategy of appealing to disgruntled Democrats who were unhappy with McGovern was a brilliant success. In Texas, former governor John Connally organized "Democrats for Nixon," a group composed of rich Texans who had been supporters of Lyndon Johnson. Johnson himself stayed out of the fray, refusing to campaign for McGovern because of his antiwar stance.

McGovern had terrible difficulty in raising money for his campaign; Nixon, meanwhile, had the most successful fund-raising effort ever seen in American politics. Much of the money was gathered illegally, in cash. Big corporations were all but ordered to contribute. Nixon's chief fund-raiser, Maurice Stans, gathered in $60 million (the previous high had been in 1968, when Nixon's campaign had spent $36.5 million). Nixon used the money for television advertisements and made few public appearances and almost no campaign speeches. Since the polls indicated that he had a lead over McGovern of 64 to 39 percent, this was a wise strategy.

Nixon had two areas of potential vulnerability. One was his failure to end the war. The other was the WATERGATE AFFAIR. On 17 June, a team of burglars working for CREEP had broken into the offices of the Democratic National Committee in the Watergate apartment and office complex in Washington, D.C. They were attempting to place a bug in the telephone of Larry O'Brien, the chairman of the Democratic

Party. The purpose was to find out what O'Brien knew about Nixon's relations with billionaire Howard Hughes, a heavy contributor to Nixon's campaigns through the years but also a man with a close association with O'Brien, who was on his payroll. Money carried by the burglars, who were caught and arrested, was quickly traced to CREEP.

Nixon moved immediately to cover up any White House involvement and to minimize the importance of what had happened. He ordered his Chief of Staff, H. R. (Bob) Haldeman, to tell the CENTRAL INTELLIGENCE AGENCY (CIA) to instruct the FEDERAL BUREAU OF INVESTIGATION (FBI) to back off the case on the grounds that NATIONAL SECURITY was involved (one of the burglars had once worked for the CIA, and a number had been involved in the BAY OF PIGS INVASION). The CIA refused to cooperate, however, and the FBI did investigate. Two federal judges were more helpful to Nixon. Judge Charles Richey, to whose court the Democrats' civil suit against CREEP was assigned, delayed the trial until after the election, and Judge John Sirica, who would preside over the trial of the burglars, did the same. Congressman Gerald Ford (R-Mich.) worked successfully to undercut hearings by the House Banking Committee into the money trail.

On the public relations side, Nixon managed to trivialize the case. At a news conference on 22 June, he said, "This kind of activity . . . has no place whatever in our electoral process or in our governmental process. . . . The White House has had no involvement whatever in this particular incident." McGovern called the break-in "shocking" and charged that it was the "legacy of years of snooping" by the Nixon administration, but he was unable to make an issue of Watergate. In a late-August news conference, Nixon laid it to rest—at least for the duration of the campaign—when he said that under his direction,

> Counsel to the President, Mr. [John] Dean, has conducted a complete investigation of all leads which might involve any present members of the White House Staff. . . . I can say categorically that his investigation indicates that no one in the White House Staff, no one in the Administration, presently employed, was involved in this very bizarre incident.

Only later did the public learn that Dean had made no investigation; Nixon just made it up.

Nixon's strategy was to ignore McGovern. On 3 October, McGovern charged that Nixon was the most deceitful President and the head of the "most corrupt administration" in history. He also charged that Nixon's Vietnam policy was the worst crime since the Holocaust and that Nixon was the number one warmaker in the world. Nixon's response, in a news conference, was, "I am not going to dignify such comments."

**The Campaign.** Nixon's surrogate speakers, mainly members of the CABINET and Republican Senators, went after McGovern. Their basic theme was the "triple A": acid (i.e., LSD, referring to liberal attitudes toward drug use), abortion, and amnesty. McGovern hardly advocated the use of heavy drugs, but he did call for removing criminal penalties from marijuana use, for women's right to choose abortion, and for amnesty for draft dodgers. Nixon was clearly in much closer touch with American attitudes than was McGovern. On issues such as busing, amnesty, drugs, defense spending, and taxes, Nixon spoke for a large majority of the people, while McGovern was talking to a shrinking minority.

Nixon even made Vietnam work for him. In October, HENRY KISSINGER, Nixon's NATIONAL SECURITY ADVISER, entered into serious negotiations with the North Vietnamese in Paris. An agreement was reached. The United States would withdraw all its armed forces in return for the prisoners of war held by Hanoi. The government in Saigon would stay in charge. Nixon called the agreement "complete" and characterized it as a victory. At a news conference on 26 October, Kissinger declared, "We believe that peace is at hand." An enormous wave of relief swept over the country.

McGovern made a plea to the American people: "Don't let this man fool you again." But the euphoria continued. Nixon's already huge lead in the polls increased. When President Nguyen Van Thieu said that South Vietnam would not accept the agreement because it left 160,000 NVA troops in his country, Nixon made his first televised political broadcast of the campaign (2 November), in which he said, "We are going to sign the agreement when the agreement is right, not one day before—and when the agreement is right, we are going to sign without one day's delay." The following day he defended the settlement and said, "We have made a breakthrough in the negotiations which will lead to peace." On election eve he repeated that claim.

**The Result.** On Election Day, 7 November, Nixon got 47 million votes (60.7 percent) to McGovern's 29 million (37.5 percent), winning every state except Massachusetts. (McGovern also won the District of Columbia.) It was the third-largest victory margin in a contested presidential election, behind Lyndon Johnson's 61.1 percent in 1964 and Franklin D. Roosevelt's 60.8 percent in 1936.

The aftermath, however, was not so happy for Nixon. The Vietnam agreement broke down; on 18 December Nixon began a massive bombing campaign against Hanoi. The Democrats, and some Republicans, were furious. They felt that "Tricky Dick" Nixon had tricked them again. Meanwhile, investigations into the Watergate break-in by the courts, the FBI, and newspaper reporters revealed that it was much more serious than Nixon had admitted, and that White House personnel, up to and including Haldeman, were involved. The investigations also began to reveal Nixon's dirty tricks, the extent of CREEP's illegal fund-raising, and other peccadillos of his campaign.

Even worse for Nixon, his insistence on centering the campaign exclusively on reelecting "the President" and his refusal to use the word *Republican* or to campaign for Republican candidates contributed to a Democratic sweep in the Congressional elections. When the Ninety-third Congress opened its session in January 1973, the Democrats used their control of Congress to create a Senate committee to investigate illegal acts in the campaign. What those and other investigations revealed forced Nixon to resign less than two years after his greatest triumph.

### BIBLIOGRAPHY

Ambrose, Stephen E. *Nixon: The Triumph of a Politician, 1962–1972.* 1989.
Ehrlichman, John. *Witness to Power: The Nixon Years.* 1982.
Haldeman, H. R., with Joseph DiMona. *The Ends of Power.* 1978.
Nixon, Richard. *The Memoirs of Richard Nixon.* 1978.
Stans, Maurice. *The Terrors of Justice.* 1978.

STEPHEN E. AMBROSE

**ELECTION, PRESIDENTIAL, 1976.** The 1976 bicentennial of the independence of the United States coincided with a presidential election year in a nation shaken by economic woes and the bitter memories of the Vietnam War and the Watergate affair. Two years earlier, in the congressional elections of 1974, only 38 percent of the eligible electorate had bothered to go to the polls, the lowest turnout for an off-year election since World War II. Frustrated by energy shortages and a souring economy and disgusted by Watergate—and especially by President Gerald Ford's full and unconditional pardon of the disgraced ex-President Richard M. Nixon—voters in 1974 had increased the Democratic majorities in both the House of Representatives and the Senate.

**The Nominees.** Further undermining his standing with the public, Ford proved to be the most conservative President since Herbert Hoover. As a congressman he had opposed virtually every Great Society measure, and, in his first year in the White House, Ford vetoed thirty-nine pieces of legislation, including

federal aid to education and health-care bills. He opposed busing to achieve racial balance in schools, and he urged federal agencies to do nothing to disturb "maximum freedom for private enterprise." The nation was enduring its worst recession since 1958, but rather than stimulating the economy, Ford drove interest rates to all-time highs and vetoed a tax cut designed to give consumers more money to spend. With nearly 60 percent of voters having gone Democratic in 1974 (the second-largest Democratic congressional victory ever), 1976 appeared to be a promising year in which to challenge the vulnerable Republican incumbent—who was the first Chief Executive who had not been elected to the presidency or the vice presidency. (Ford had been appointed Vice President by Nixon after the resignation of Spiro T. Agnew.) As one ebullient Democrat crowed, "We could run an aardvark this year and win." Unsurprisingly, there were many Democrats vying for their party's nomination; former California governor Ronald Reagan announced he would run against Ford in the Republican presidential primaries.

As the recognized leader of the most conservative faction of the Republican Party, Reagan lambasted Ford for selecting the liberal Republican Nelson A. Rockefeller as his Vice President and for his adherence to detente as a dangerous and unwarranted surrender to Soviet interests. Reagan called for a massive buildup of American arms, supported taking a hard line against the Soviet Union, and called for a reassertion of national pride and self-assurance. Reagan won his greatest support in denouncing Ford's efforts to end U.S. rule of the Canal Zone and to give away the Panama Canal. Reagan charged that the President was becoming too used to the cozy deal-making of Washington and was losing touch with the concerns of ordinary Republicans, and he stressed his own opposition to student radicalism, promiscuity, abortion, and the Equal Rights Amendment. Running as an outsider untainted by Watergate corruption and scorning Ford for compromising conservative values with practical politics, Reagan defeated the President in a series of western and southern primaries and won enough delegates to keep the nomination in doubt even as the Republicans assembled for their convention. But when Reagan stunned and angered conservative Republicans by announcing that his running mate would be the very liberal Richard Schweiker of Pennsylvania, Ford secured the Republican nomination. He then unified his party for the campaign by jettisoning Rockefeller and selecting sharp-tongued Senator Robert Dole of Kansas, a favorite of party regulars, for the second spot on the ticket, accepting a conservative platform that adopted most of Reagan's positions, and blocking completion of an arms-control agreement with the Soviet Union and suspending negotiations on the Panama Canal treaty.

An obscure former one-term governor of Georgia, James Earl (Jimmy) Carter emerged from a wide field of Democratic contenders that had initially included Senator Birch Bayh of Indiana, Kennedy in-law Sargent Shriver, and Arizona Representative Morris Udall. Carter surprised political pundits by overcoming a name-recognition factor of only 2 percent to win the Iowa precinct caucuses in January and then the New Hampshire primary in February. More quickly than most Democrats, Carter understood the extent to which the new rules by which the Democrats selected delegates to the national nominating convention had significantly reduced the power of party leaders, labor union officials, and state organization stalwarts to hand pick the nominee. The new rules gave the edge to well-financed candidates who could devote full time to the quest for delegates in many parts of the country. Holding no political office in 1973, Carter had begun his lengthy and ultimately successful direct appeals to the affluent and middle-class Democratic activists who would vote during the half-year-long gauntlet of state primaries and caucuses in 1976.

Against the background of Watergate secrecy and corruption, Carter had crisscrossed the country promising honesty and openness, pledging again and again that "I will never lie to you" and emphasizing his lifelong distance from the scandals and failures of the federal government. "I'm not a lawyer," he said. "I'm not a member of Congress, and I've never served in Washington." He then stressed his southern roots and "born again" Protestant credentials to defeat GEORGE WALLACE in the southern primaries, proving his ability to capture the votes of white southerners who had deserted the Democrats in the previous two presidential elections. Portraying himself as someone who could give the nation fresh and untainted leadership and promising a government as good, as competent, as moral, and "as filled with love as are the American people," Carter continued to accumulate delegates, foiling the efforts to halt his bandwagon that were mounted by late entries Governor Jerry Brown of California and Senator Frank Church of Idaho. By June he had enough delegates pledged to him to win nomination on the first ballot of the Democratic national convention, which was held in New York City. To mollify Democratic liberals bothered by Carter's longtime support for the Vietnam War, his disavowal of many Great Society programs, his embrace of budget balancing, and his disdain for Washington insid-

ers, Carter chose Minnesota Senator WALTER F. MONDALE, an outspoken liberal closely identified with HUBERT H. HUMPHREY, as his running mate.

**The Campaign.** The smoothly run and harmonious Democratic convention combined with the continued lack of enthusiasm for Ford to give Carter a 33-percent lead in public opinion polls at the start of the campaign. Victory in November seemed assured, although most Americans still claimed not to know much about the Georgian who had seemingly come out of nowhere to garner the Democratic nomination.

In the main, the contest between Ford and Carter lacked excitement. Both nominees avoided specific commitments. Ford chose to stay in the White House most of the time, trying to look presidential. The press soon labeled his effort the "Rose Garden campaign." Although his affability was a welcome contrast to Nixon's moody self-isolation, Ford remained haunted by Republican involvement in Watergate and his pardon of Nixon, as well as by his having presided over the frenzied, humiliating departure of the last American troops from Vietnam.

Consequently, Ford tried to do all he could to maintain the support of the "middle American" former Democrats who had voted for Wallace in 1968 and Nixon in 1972. He publicly shared their outrage at the excesses of the 1960s; blamed Democratic liberals for assaulting the church, the family, patriotism, and morality; and emphasized his opposition to school busing, feminism, the abolition of school prayer, and to permissiveness toward pornography and sexual license. He both affirmed middle Americans' values and assuaged their sense of having been neglected and slighted. In addition, Ford sought to counter Carter's main appeal by portraying himself as a trustworthy leader who would bring even greater economy and efficiency to Washington.

But Carter, who had never held federal office, retained the distinct advantage in the aftermath of Watergate. Repeating his convention themes, Carter played the innocent novice, castigating the administration for not disciplining the "confused and overlapping and wasteful federal bureaucracy" and for not reducing government expenditures sufficiently. He presented himself as both a fiscal conservative and a social liberal, as one who would restrain government spending and fight for tax reform, a national health program, and a comprehensive energy policy. In foreign affairs, Carter stressed that the United States would work for human rights, arms control, and nonintervention. Most of all, he emphasized that, as "an engineer, a planner, and a nuclear physicist," he would make government competent once again and that, as a good Christian, down-home farmer (he was frequently photographed wearing blue jeans), and family man, he would restore homespun honesty, decency, and compassion to the American political process.

In one of the few exciting moments in the campaign, *Playboy* magazine published an interview with Carter in which he admitted that he had "looked on a lot of women with lust [and] committed adultery in my heart many times" but said he was sure that God had forgiven him. The article appalled conservative evangelicals, and many urban sophisticates found Carter's priggish piety troubling and were uncomfortable with the notion of a devoutly religious President, with his evangelist sister, Ruth Carter Stapleton, and his outrageous brother Billy.

Then Ford blundered. Following Carter's repeated jibes that the President was "hiding in the Rose Garden," Ford reluctantly agreed to hold three televised PRESIDENTIAL DEBATES with his challenger, the first such debates since 1960. Carter stood to gain more, benefiting from the national exposure and the opportunity to appear on an equal footing with the President. Ford's assertion, during the second debate, that there was "no Soviet domination of Eastern Europe, and there never will be under a Ford administration" revived images of Ford as a well-meaning but bumbling President. Further embarrassing the President, a newspaper decided to publish a privately told obscene joke about African Americans that a reporter had overheard Secretary of Agriculture Earl Butz make.

Ford hammered away at Carter's inept attempts to be all things to all voters and to hedge on the issues, and, indeed, increasing numbers of Americans seemed uneasy with Carter's refusal to take a straightforward stand on difficult issues.

**The Result.** By Election Day, neither Carter nor Ford was inspiring great public enthusiasm, and neither candidate was widely perceived as "presidential." Polls revealed that 80 percent of likely voters gave a negative assessment of Carter's leadership abilities, and Ford did not do much better, with 76 percent assessing his leadership ability negatively. Other polls showed widespread disaffection and resignation on the part of the American people, especially those in the lower and working classes, toward the entire governmental system. Many Americans chose not to vote, having little faith in the leaders of either party or in politics itself as a vehicle for securing change. Just 54 percent of those eligible to vote cast ballots, the lowest percentage in any presidential election since World War II. Those who did not vote in 1976 were younger, poorer, less well educated, and more likely to be nonwhite than those who went to the polls. The greatest declines in voter participation came in the districts with the highest rates of unemployment and poverty.

Carter's failure to emphasize the traditional economic issues of greatest concern to needy Americans enabled Ford to make a close race out of what had initially seemed would be a Democratic cakewalk. Carter squeaked to victory with 40.8 million votes to Ford's 39.1 million, a gap of a scant two percentage points. His narrow 291-to-241 triumph in the ELECTORAL COLLEGE was the closest margin of victory since Woodrow Wilson's reelection in 1916. Carter did, however, manage to reassemble most of the NEW DEAL coalition among those who voted, uniting the South and the industrial Northeast and capturing the votes of organized labor, minorities, and urban liberals to win twenty-three states and the District of Columbia. Ford carried the entire West (except Hawaii) plus a scattering of states in New England and the upper Midwest to garner twenty-seven states. Carter won Texas on the strength of his appeal to African American and Mexican American voters and, spurred by regional pride and an affinity with Carter's evangelical Protestantism, the ballots of both black and white southerners enabled Carter to sweep every border and southern state, save Virginia. Carter received more than 90 percent of the African American vote, and blacks' votes provided the margin of victory in Ohio and Pennsylvania as well as in the South.

The election was also a referendum on Ford's handling of the economy, and the outcome was a victory for lower- and middle-class voters over the wealthy and the upper middle class. Some 70 percent of voters had identified economic issues as their basic concern. Carter won 75 percent of the votes of those who were primarily worried about unemployment as well as the lion's share of votes from those who feared further recession. The future political fortunes of the new President would depend on how well he addressed these economic matters. Carter had skillfully exploited popular disenchantment with political corruption, Washington insiders, and economic disarray to gain the White House; now he would have to rectify the nation's woes or else become the victim, rather than the beneficiary, of American cynicism about government.

### BIBLIOGRAPHY

Carroll, Peter. *It Seemed Like Nothing Happened*. 1983.

Carter, Jimmy. *Keeping Faith*. 1982.

Ford, Gerald R. *A Time to Heal*. 1979.

Glad, Betty. *Jimmy Carter*. 1980.

Hartmann, Robert T. *Palace Politics: An Inside Account of the Ford Years*. 1980.

Reichley, A. James. *Conservatives in an Age of Change: The Nixon and Ford Administrations.* 1981.

White, Theodore H. *America in Search of Itself: The Making of the President, 1956–1980.* 1982.

Witcover, Jules. *Marathon.* 1977.

HARVARD SITKOFF

**ELECTION, PRESIDENTIAL, 1980.** The 1980 presidential election year coincided with the federal government's decennial census. The census figures bolstered the belief of many politicians that the nation's dominant political mood had turned conservative: the number of senior citizens had increased by 24 percent during the previous decade; the number of retired persons had jumped by more than 50 percent; and Americans continued to migrate from the "Frostbelt" states of the Northeast and Midwest to the Sunbelt states of the South and West—a region that had historically been both politically conservative and intensely suspicious of Washington. Too, a larger number and percentage of Americans than ever before lived in suburbs, paid middle-class taxes, and identified with fundamentalist and/or evangelical Christianity.

Many Americans who claimed they had been "born again" and personally experienced salvation believed that they had an obligation to become politically involved on the side of traditional, "pro-life" moral values. They supported candidates who would ban ABORTION, oppose the EQUAL RIGHTS AMENDMENT, condemn homosexuality, halt school busing for racial balance, outlaw pornography, restore prayer to public schools, impose ceilings on property taxes, and put stringent limits on spending for social programs. They also opposed liberals, militant feminists, and affirmative action and reverse discrimination. Religious conservatives made up part of an important political force known as the New Right and joined a powerful coalition supporting the right-wing war horse Ronald Reagan, who had narrowly lost the 1976 Republican nominating contest to Gerald Ford. By 1978, however, Reagan was actively campaigning for the 1980 nomination.

**The Candidates.** In the Republican presidential race of 1980, after an initial stumble in the Iowa caucuses, Reagan triumphed easily over his more moderate opponents, Representative John Anderson of Illinois and former CIA director George Bush of Texas. Following his defeat of Anderson in the congressman's home state in mid March, Reagan was widely conceded to be the certain nominee despite the fact that twenty-five primaries remained. By the time

of the Republican convention, he had handily won twenty-nine primaries (losing just six to Bush) by appealing to New Right concerns.

Reagan controlled the nominating convention. After failing to convince former President Ford to accept the vice presidential slot, he chose Bush as his running mate and pushed through a conservative platform that mirrored the themes of his campaign.

Four years earlier, Jimmy Carter had likewise presented himself to frustrated, angry voters as a savior who would recover all the best that had been lost in American life. But his popularity had flagged early in his administration, and by the time of the Democratic convention in August 1980 only 21 percent of the Gallup Poll's sample approved of his overall performance as President (with only 18 percent approving of his handling of foreign affairs). Carter's rating was even lower than Harry S. Truman's had been during the nadir of the KOREAN WAR or Richard M. Nixon's at the height of the WATERGATE AFFAIR.

The humiliating, infuriating spectacle that had begun when militant Iranians seized the American embassy in Tehran and took fifty-three Americans hostage in October 1979, however, overshadowed all else throughout the election year. The media gave the IRANIAN HOSTAGE CRISIS extensive coverage, and the ordeal of the hostages became a national cause. None of Carter's diplomatic moves, however, had brought the hostages' release. Confidence in Carter's leadership dropped precipitously. Although Carter's inability to gain the release of the hostages was most likely what ultimately sealed his fate with the electorate, the nightly television pictures of mobs in Tehran mocking the United States had initially caused Americans to rally around the President. But as the crisis dragged on, many Americans blamed the President for the stalemate, and an embarrassing failed rescue attempt, DESERT ONE, reinforced images of Carter as an irresolute bumbler and of the United States as a declining power unable to protect its citizens abroad.

Many Democrats stuck with their leader despite the fact that they found themselves in greater agreement with the views of his major rival, Senator Edward Kennedy of Massachusetts, who announced his bid for the nomination in November 1979. But lingering doubts about Kennedy's character led many Democrats to distrust Kennedy more than they disliked Carter. However inept he might be, Carter was still viewed as a decent and honest man. Also, no matter how much Kennedy's policies appealed to party activists, many conceded that his old-fashioned liberalism was out of tune with the 1980 electorate. Banking on Kennedy's liabilities, Carter refused to campaign against him in the primaries, claiming that his presence was required in the White House. This "Rose Garden" strategy worked, and Carter won two-thirds of the delegates without ever leaving Washington. And so the delegates to the 1980 Democratic national convention enthusiastically cheered Kennedy, whom they had rejected, and tepidly renominated the Jimmy Carter–WALTER F. MONDALE team they thought would not win.

**The Campaign.** Carter concentrated first on the Anderson factor. Having lost the Republican nomination to Reagan, the Illinois congressman had bolted the REPUBLICAN PARTY to run for President as an independent. Although Anderson had no organization and his primary appeal to voters was his self-proclaimed integrity and competence, early polls showed him receiving about 15 percent of the vote, with Carter and Reagan running even. Carter believed he could win by portraying Reagan as a dangerous reactionary and siphoning off most of the middle-of-the-road Democratic voters who were attracted to Anderson because of their disapproval of the President's performance. By ignoring Anderson in his campaign speeches, and by refusing to participate in a three-way debate that included him, Carter effectively demolished Anderson as a viable alternative. By October the overwhelming preponderance of voters were resigned to a choice between Carter and Reagan.

Defeating Reagan in the general election, however, proved a more difficult matter for Carter than dealing with Kennedy or Anderson had been. In sharp contrast to Carter's pessimism and gloom, Reagan exuded optimism and hope. Reagan projected common sense and competence; offered simple, reassuring answers to complex questions; and spoke grandly of renewal, strength, and national pride. Most importantly, the darling of the New Right toned down his conservative rhetoric, avoiding mentioning his more extreme beliefs (such as his dislike of the SOCIAL SECURITY system) and concentrating on Carter's inability to free the hostages, which for Reagan epitomized Carter's ineffectual and indecisive presidency. Moreover, Reagan showed real wit: when Carter quibbled with him over economic definitions, Reagan retorted, "I'm talking in human terms and he is hiding behind a dictionary. If he wants a definition, I'll give him one. A recession is when your neighbor loses his job. A depression is when you lose yours. A recovery is when Jimmy Carter loses his."

Nevertheless, many Americans harbored doubts about the former actor. Reagan would soon turn seventy, and some found him too old as well as too uninformed and too conservative. And they particularly feared him as a dangerous militarist who would likely get the United States into war. Those doubts shrank significantly after the Carter-Reagan debate held in Cleveland, Ohio, on 28 October. Confident that his greater intelligence and command of the facts would make Reagan appear "unpresidential," Carter badly miscalculated: after all, his challenger had been trained as an actor. Standing toe to toe with the President, Reagan appeared poised, self-assured, genial, and not at all the mad, untrustworthy scrooge the Democrats had depicted him as. Reagan carried the day when, in his closing remarks, he stared directly at the television camera and advised Americans, "Ask yourself, are you better off today than you were four years ago? Is America as respected throughout the world as it was four years ago?"

**The Result.** A week later, the American people went to the polls and resoundingly answered no. They voted their lack of confidence in a President whom they considered too ineffective to fix the economy or retrieve the hostages and their conviction that it was time for a change. Carter became the second consecutive presidential incumbent to suffer defeat. Reagan garnered 43.9 million votes (50.8 percent of the total) to Carter's 36.4 million (41 percent) and Anderson's 5.7 million (6.6 percent). Carter won only four small states plus his home state of Georgia, Mondale's Minnesota, and the District of Columbia, for a total of 49 electoral votes. Reagan won 489 electoral votes, managing to collect the support of blue-collar, middle-class, Catholic, ethnic, and southern voters, about half the labor union and Jewish voters, and nearly a third of Hispanic voters. Of the NEW DEAL coalition forged by Franklin D. Roosevelt in the 1930s, only African American voters remained staunchly Democratic. Although most congressional Democrats ran well ahead of Carter, the Republicans nevertheless picked up an additional fifty-three seats in the House of Representatives and twelve in the Senate, gaining a majority in the upper house for the first time since 1954 and defeating some of the most prominent liberal Democrats in the country, including Birch Bayh in Indiana, Frank Church in Idaho, George McGovern in South Dakota, and Gaylord Nelson in Wisconsin, who had been specifically targeted by conservative PACS (POLITICAL ACTION COMMITTEES).

The 1980 election, however, also showed that Americans' loss of faith in voting and politics was continuing. Just 53 percent of the eligible electorate voted, making the "party" of nonvoters the largest group in the American political spectrum. Although he won by a lopsided margin, the President-elect had been chosen by only 28 percent of the potential electorate. Many who did not vote were former Democrats who no longer saw any political party as representing their economic interests; many were poor and working-class people who were convinced that the entire system of government was rigged by, and for the benefit of, a small elite. While two-thirds of those employed in manual-labor jobs had voted in 1964, only 48 percent did so in 1980. Significantly, Carter's biggest decline in support from 1976 to 1980 was among white working men, especially Catholics, blue-collar workers, and labor union members. Believing the Democrats too liberal on social issues such as abortion, school busing, and the Equal Rights Amendment, they had either opted out of the political process or become "Reagan Democrats." They were not to return to the Democratic fold anytime soon.

### BIBLIOGRAPHY

Blumenthal, Sidney. *The Rise of the Counter-Establishment*. 1986.
Carter, Jimmy. *Keeping Faith*. 1982.
Dallek, Robert. *Ronald Reagan*. 1984.
Drew, Elizabeth. *Portrait of an Election*. 1981.
Hargrove, Erwin. *Jimmy Carter as President*. 1988.
Steinfels, Peter. *The Neo-Conservatives*. 1979.
White, John Kenneth. *The New Politics of Old Values*. 1988.
Wills, Garry. *Reagan's America: Innocents at Home*. 1985.

HARVARD SITKOFF

**ELECTION, PRESIDENTIAL, 1984.** In a landslide victory in forty-nine states, with 59 percent of the popular vote, Ronald Reagan was reelected President in 1984. Accumulating 525 electoral votes, the Republican incumbent lost only the District of Columbia and Minnesota, the home state of Democratic opponent WALTER MONDALE.

**Significance of the Election.** Reagan's performance was matched in American electoral history only by Franklin D. Roosevelt's reelection nearly half a century earlier, in 1936. Reagan won a smaller percentage of the popular vote than Roosevelt, but he carried more states and gained more electoral votes than the New Deal Democrat. (In 1984, there were two more states, Alaska and Hawaii, and three more electoral votes, cast by the District of Columbia.) In contemporary times, his triumph was further notable because it was the first victory by an elected incumbent President in some thirty years, since Dwight D. Eisenhower's second victory in 1956.

The 1984 election results carried implications for public policy, the character of American campaigns and voting coalitions, and the institution of the presidency. First, the Reagan victory had important conse-

quences for presidential policy. In his first term, Reagan had changed the course of American government. His program of lower taxes, reduced domestic programs, and increased military spending marked a sharp turn in an ideologically conservative direction. Those policies were challenged by Mondale, a prominent liberal, who explicitly stated that he would propose tax increases if elected.

Reagan's overwhelming reelection was widely interpreted as a popular endorsement of his first term's actions. Yet, there was no popular mandate, since there was little focus in the Republican campaign on the likely future programs of a second Reagan administration. Indeed, polls showed that most voters held positions contrary to Reagan's own views on such important issues as abortion, increased governmental aid to the poor, and a freeze on the deployment of nuclear weapons. On election night, indirectly acknowledging the lack of a mandate, Reagan only promised the voters that, "You ain't seen nothing yet!"

The election results did carry one specific policy implication for the future. After Mondale's massive defeat, conventional wisdom held that taxes could not be raised. Accepting this interpretation, neither the President nor Congress would propose significant new programs, however desirable. Furthermore, with significant spending reductions also unacceptable, the President and Congress could do little to control the soaring national budget deficit and its detrimental impact on the nation's economy and international position.

Beyond its economic effects, the 1984 election had other impacts on the presidency. With a strong popular endorsement, the administration felt more confident in Reagan's control of foreign policy. This confidence led both to historic disarmament agreements with the Soviet Union and to the IRAN-CONTRA AFFAIR, which tarnished Reagan's second term. The reelected President also moved to consolidate conservative control of the Supreme Court and to use the executive power to achieve such party goals as restrictions on legalized ABORTION.

**Impact on Party Politics.** The Reagan triumph also had major impacts on national party politics. Reagan won a national victory in more than simple arithmetic terms, for the incumbent President's support showed similar degrees of strength across the nation, rather than large variations in his vote from one region to another. Within this uniformity, however, some areas of particular appeal were evident. Most prominent on the electoral map was the Republicans' strength west of the Mississippi. In all but two of the fourteen states from the Great Plains to the western slopes of the

Rockies, from the wheat fields of North Dakota to the desert of Arizona, Reagan won at least five votes out of eight. Reagan's other geographical base was in the more advanced economies of the South, particularly the growing population centers of Virginia, Florida, and Texas. His large pluralities in these states were, in part, simply expansions of the Republicans' recent bases in Dixie. They also showed the party's particular appeal to areas that had high-technology, recent industrial growth, and a relatively low proportion of black voters.

Democratic party strength in the election was obviously more narrowly confined. Mondale had no notable support in any state in the Rocky Mountain region and performed adequately in the South only in states with a large black electorate. The Democrats did better in the Northeast, where they had a traditional base of support among city residents, factory workers, and members of minority and ethnic groups. They also ran decent races in states of established liberal Republican support, the upper Midwest and the northern Pacific Coast.

The geographical patterns of the 1984 election indicated the emergence of a stable Republican majority, at least in presidential elections. Its vigor was demonstrated again in the next election, when Reagan's Vice President, George Bush, would win the White House with a similar, although diminished, coalition, again centered on the Rocky Mountains and the South.

The Reagan presidential majority claimed support from specific social groups. Traditionally, Republican support came from white Protestants, residents of small communities and farms, college graduates, persons of higher income, and those in white-collar and managerial positions. Reagan's percentage among these groups—in keeping with his party's historical support—was larger than that of his national vote overall.

More notably, Reagan made inroads among traditional Democratic groups. Regionally, the most striking change was the conversion of the white South from solidly Democratic to solidly Republican—a result in part due to the industrialization and urbanization of the region and the aftermath of the CIVIL RIGHTS movement. Republican gains were also evident among social groups in the rest of the nation that once were core members of the New Deal Democratic coalition. Although Catholics still supported the Democratic Party more than Protestants, some had slowly drifted away, as a result of their better economic status and their endorsement of the Republican position on such issues as abortion and crime control.

This trend was part of a larger drift toward the Republicans of "middle America"—skilled workers, high school graduates, and persons of moderate income. The result in 1984 was that Reagan had gained sufficient support among the broad middle strata to blur traditional class differences in the vote. Indeed, Reagan still would have won even if the electorate had been restricted to persons with annual incomes less than the national median, $24,000.

The 1984 election witnessed two new cleavages among the voters, on the basis of sex and age. In most years, women's votes had been no different from those of men. By 1984, however, a "gender gap" had appeared, so that Mondale's vote was about 6 percent higher among women than men (or, in mirror image, that Reagan's vote was about 6 percent higher among men). The reason for this difference probably goes beyond the Democrats' historic selection of a woman, GERALDINE FERRARO, for their vice presidential candidate. It was probably related to women's new social roles and to emerging differences between the sexes on issues of domestic and foreign policy.

Particularly significant for the future were age differences in the vote. Although there was little difference in the actual 1984 vote between younger and older voters, there were encouraging portents for the Republicans. In the past, new and younger voters had tended to vote Democratic, reflecting that party's basic majority among their parents' generation. By 1984, a plurality of the younger voters expressed an identification with the Republicans and gave that party at least as much support as their elders at the polls.

The campaign for the White House, just as the vote itself, evidenced change in the nature of presidential politics. However, the campaign did not change the vote. For the most part, Reagan led by the same substantial margin in polls taken throughout the calendar year. The preelection contest, however, did clarify the causes of Reagan's triumph. The skilled Republican Party effort emphasized Reagan's positive claims. Despite the deep recession in the early years of his first term, there had been astonishing economic growth—over 10 percent early in 1984—along with low inflation. In foreign policy, Reagan boasted that "America is back, standing tall," citing the successful and popular American intervention in Grenada [see GRENADA INVASION], and increased military spending.

Republican campaigners developed artful television spots proclaiming, "It's morning again in America," showing a wedding, a family moving into a new home, fertile fields, and rugged construction workers. Depicting Reagan wrapped in the American flag, the longest advertisement concluded with a virile policeman raising the star-spangled banner before a group of attractive female athletes.

**Changed Role of the Presidency.** The 1984 campaign altered the character of the presidency as an institution. Focusing on the candidates' personal characteristics, it augmented the long-term transformation of the presidency from a formal role to a personal office. In the televised PRESIDENTIAL DEBATES, seen by more than one hundred million voters, the emphasis was on personality. Although the debates ostensibly were about the candidates' positions on the issues, the latent message was more important and dramatic. Most viewers would find it difficult to sort out the claims, statistics, and refutations of the debaters. They could more easily make a judgment of their competence, trustworthiness, and abilities. This meant more than the candidates' "images," or personalities; it meant their character, their leadership and vision, their basic fitness for the highest office.

The personal stress of the debates altered the campaign. In the first debate, Mondale made a strong impression by combining courtesy toward the President with a pointed attack on his policies and, even more, his competence. Reagan added to his problems, by admitting that he was "confused," and by giving a rambling closing statement, cluttered with statistics, as if he were a college student who had crammed too much for a final exam.

The first debate raised the question of the President's age. Was his mediocre performance an indication that the nation's oldest Chief Executive was unable to continue? The second presidential debate ostensibly centered on foreign policy. Mondale again stressed Reagan's lack of competence. On this occasion, however, Reagan was more equal to the challenge. On the critical issue of his age, he ended all discussion with the best quip of the campaign: "I will not make age an issue in this campaign. I am not going to exploit for political purposes my opponent's youth and inexperience."

This personal emphasis was also evident in the voters' decisions. Reagan's victory, while more than a triumph of personality, was an endorsement of his individual record. While there was no clear electoral mandate on policy directions, there was considerable coherence in evaluations of the ability of the two candidates and the two parties to deal with these issues. Voters might not know what to do about a particular policy problem, but they showed far more agreement on who they believed was more trustworthy and competent in handling the problem.

**The Result.** In mid October, by a four to three margin, the electorate was more inclined "to trust the future of this country" to the Republicans. The voters considered Reagan better able to handle the economy, control inflation and the federal budget deficit, maintain strong military defenses and keep the nation out of war, and stand up to the Soviet Union. Democrats were preferred in regard to providing fairness, aid to the poor, and social security, but these were not the dominant concerns of voters as they judged the record of the previous four years.

The voters themselves acknowledged the personal character of their judgment. Three out of five cited "strong leadership" and "experience" as major reasons for their decisions. In assessing Reagan's qualifications, the voters were far more favorable in 1984 than in 1980, as actual performance in office led them to give him higher ratings for intelligence, a command of the issues, ability to maintain peace, and even, despite his advancing years, physical capability.

In summary, the lasting effects of the 1984 election were the retrospective endorsement of a conservative turn in public policy, a step in the gradual development of a Republican voting majority for the White House, and an intensification of long-term trends toward the personalization of the presidency.

### BIBLIOGRAPHY

Abramson, Paul, John Aldrich, and David Rhode. *Change and Continuity in the 1984 Elections.* 1986.

Fiorina, Morris. *Retrospective Voting in American National Elections.* 1981.

King, Anthony, ed. *The New American Political System.* 2d. ed. 1990.

Mayer, Jane, and Doyle McManus. *Landslide.* 1988.

Nelson, Michael, ed. *The Elections of 1984.* 1985.

Pomper, Gerald, ed. *The Election of 1984.* 1985.

Wattenberg, Martin. *The Rise of Candidate-Centered Politics.* 1991.

GERALD M. POMPER

**ELECTION, PRESIDENTIAL, 1988.** In the first presidential campaign in two decades that did not involve an incumbent President, Vice President George Bush defeated Governor MICHAEL S. DUKAKIS of Massachusetts to extend Republican control of the White House four years beyond the Reagan presidency. Character issues, raised in slashing personal attacks and in unprecedented intrusions into the candidates' private lives, largely eclipsed any public dialogue on the economy and on America's role in a changing world. Although Dukakis declared that the contest should be decided on the basis of competence rather than ideology, the Republicans succeeded in branding him as both liberal and incompetent.

**The Candidates.** George Bush began his quest for the Republican nomination with two advantages: his experience as a candidate in two previous national campaigns and the fact that he was the sitting Vice President. Launching his candidacy soon after the 1984 Republican landslide, Bush embarked on a nationwide "party-building" odyssey, while assembling a powerful fund-raising apparatus. The REPUBLICAN PARTY's hierarchical tradition of promoting its leaders in succession worked to his advantage. Legions of experienced professional operatives and key Republican governors joined Bush's campaign, as did most of the party's state activists and large contributors.

Beyond the nomination, however, the vice presidency has not offered historically the surest springboard for promotion. Not since Martin Van Buren's 1836 election had one of Bush's predecessors reached the presidency through the ballot. With his fate tied to the fortunes of President Ronald Reagan, Bush had to play the role of loyal supporter rather than leader. If his subservience to Reagan initially made Bush appear weak, it later threatened to exact a higher price after a series of scandals rocked the administration. The most serious of these was a clandestine operation to arm Nicaraguan rebels with weapons bought with profits from secret arms sales to Iran. For months questions about the so-called IRAN-CONTRA AFFAIR dogged Bush on the campaign trail. While evasively denying that he had been privy to the deliberations surrounding the illegal operation, Bush resisted his advisers' urging to distance himself from Reagan. Bush's loyalty enabled him to inherit the Reagan mantle despite the Republican right's lingering skepticism toward him.

Bush's Republican rivals also sought recognition as Reagan's heir by contrasting their conservatism with Bush's more moderate record. Representative Jack Kemp of New York advocated supply-side economic prescriptions that resonated with economic conservatives. Minor candidates Sen. Pete DuPont and Gen. Alexander Haig also tried to compete for the conservative vote, but they were consequential only as props for the other candidates. The television evangelist Pat Robertson mobilized the religious right with his fundamentalist, anti-Washington rhetoric. After Robertson briefly seized control of the party machinery in Michigan and shocked Bush in the Iowa caucuses, his political inexperience and limited support became more apparent. Bush's most formidable rival for the support of the party establishment was the Senate Republican leader, Robert Dole. Although Dole had the allegiance of his Senate colleagues, they usually did not command extensive grass-roots organizations comparable to those that Republican governors were able to mobilize for Bush.

The prospects for a Democratic victory attracted a large field of contestants in that party's primary race. Sen. Gary Hart of Colorado reignited his 1984 campaign to begin the 1988 cycle as the Democratic favorite. When his candidacy collapsed in the wake of revelations of marital infidelity, the race became a free-for-all in which the remaining candidates were subjected to intense personal scrutiny. The next to fall was Sen. Joseph Biden of Delaware, who faced charges of rhetorical plagiarism as he prepared to preside over the confirmation hearing of Robert Bork, who had been nominated by Reagan to the Supreme Court. Dukakis himself was almost forced out of the race by the revelation that, despite his previous denials, his campaign had distributed the videotape that had precipitated Biden's downfall.

The field of contenders remained crowded, despite the attrition. Hart reentered the race but never regained his earlier momentum. Liberal and minority voters responded to the stirring oratory of the Rev. Jesse Jackson, another veteran of 1984, while southern whites gravitated to the regional candidacy of Sen. Albert Gore, Jr., of Tennessee [see GORE, AL]. The presence of two midwesterners in the race—Rep. Richard Gephardt of Missouri and Sen. Paul Simon of Illinois—divided that section's support, thus aiding Dukakis. Gephardt, the most formidable rival, articulated a powerful message of economic populism, but his overstated rhetoric contradicted his own record, while inadequate funds caused his campaign to stall. Dukakis capitalized on a superior fund-raising operation, an advantageous primary calendar, and a careful allocation of resources on Super Tuesday, a cluster of sixteen primaries and five caucuses on 8 March.

Super Tuesday was the brainchild of conservative Democrats, who had devised a primary schedule that they hoped would produce a nominee compatible with their views. By scheduling multiple southern state primaries early in the process, they hoped to diminish the influence of the more liberal Democratic voters in Iowa and New Hampshire, while forcing candidates to spend more time addressing southern audiences and issues. Super Tuesday proved to have unintended consequences, however. The liberal Jesse Jackson carried five southern states by taking an overwhelming share of the black vote. Dukakis also emerged with a respectable showing by engineering a "four corners" plan that concentrated resources on Texas, Florida, Maryland, and the Washington state caucuses. His careful targeting and his superior financial resources enabled him to outlast his rivals and to capture the nomination.

It was the Republican candidate, George Bush, who really capitalized on Super Tuesday. To offset Bush's anticipated loss in Iowa, Bush's campaign manager, Lee Atwater, had constructed a "southern firewall" with aggressive field organizations in key states. After inducing Dole and Robertson to compete in Bush strongholds, Atwater shifted media budgets forward, targeting the closely contested states and effecting a clean sweep of the southern primaries. By the time the battle moved to the Midwest, Bush had virtually clinched the nomination.

The two national conventions transformed huge halls into television studios, but neither went according to the script. In Atlanta, negotiations with Jesse Jackson distracted the Dukakis campaign until last-minute concessions on the party platform and rules broke the impasse. The Republicans' well-orchestrated convention scenario was disrupted after Bush announced his vice presidential selection. Revelations and rumors surrounding his choice, Sen. Dan Quayle of Indiana, touched off a media frenzy that dominated the news and threw the campaign off balance. Dukakis's earlier selection of Sen. Lloyd Bentsen of Texas as his running mate sought to rekindle the Kennedy-Johnson spirit of 1960, but the hope of defeating Bush in his home state proved unrealistic.

**The Campaign.** Despite the provisions for federal financing of presidential campaigns, both parties mounted massive fund-raising drives under the guise of party building. The Democratic National Committee raised a record $56 million for the 1988 cycle, while the Republican total was almost $97 million. These war chests of "soft money" accentuated the influence of large contributors and political action committees, further undermining public confidence in the political process.

While the Democrats wasted valuable time, the Republicans engaged in elaborate planning for the fall campaign. Bush's collective campaign leadership structure yielded command to the veteran organizer JAMES A. BAKER III, who resigned as Secretary of the Treasury to run Bush's campaign. The Vice President's operatives assumed control of the state party machinery to ensure that the coordinated campaigns served his interest, while staff changes at the White House also advanced Bush's efforts.

Republican strategists used focus groups of Reagan Democrats to develop a series of negative attacks on Dukakis. One television ad, which depicted Boston Harbor's pollution, sought to neutralize criticism of the Republicans' poor environmental record. Other attacks ridiculed the Massachusetts governor's lack of experience in foreign policy and his weakness on defense issues. Even his patriotism and the state of his mental health became targets. But the most effective

assaults charged that Dukakis was soft on crime, citing as evidence his support of gun control, his opposition to the death penalty, and his defense of a controversial prison furlough program. The Republicans personalized the furlough issue by reciting the case of a convicted murderer, William Horton, who, while on furlough, had terrorized a Maryland couple. Dukakis's failure to respond to these attacks and his campaign's inability to define the candidate or even to present a clear message allowed the Republicans' image of Dukakis to prevail in the public mind.

**The Result.** As Dukakis's support in the South evaporated, the contest increasingly focused on the industrial Midwest, as well as New Jersey and Pennsylvania. In the election, Bush swept the Sunbelt and defeated the Democrat in the hotly contested states of Illinois, Michigan, and Ohio. Bush's decisive 56 percent of the popular vote translated into an even larger victory in the electoral vote: 426 to 111, with one elector casting his vote for Lloyd Bentsen.

Bush employed a "no new taxes" promise, first against Dole in the pivotal New Hampshire primary, then against Dukakis in the fall campaign. Although this declaration aided the Vice President's victory, it would later haunt his presidency and his reelection efforts. Without flexibility in fiscal policy, he could neither stimulate the sagging economy nor reduce the soaring budget deficit. When he was ultimately forced to renege on his pledge in 1990 by approving a tax increase, he destroyed his credibility and incurred conservative wrath.

Although the nation's sense of economic prosperity was perhaps the greatest factor in Bush's election, many observers believed that he was also aided by Dukakis. The flawed, inexperienced candidate embarked on the fall campaign with no strategy or message and with little real understanding of how to win. Even more than the Republican attacks, Dukakis's own performance as a candidate raised valid questions about his fitness for the presidency.

Press coverage of the campaign also came under criticism. The media's event-driven emphasis on the horse-race elements of the campaign led to an excess of photo opportunities and shrinking sound bites. The press also became an unwitting pawn of negative campaigning by reporting attack ads as straight news stories, thus magnifying their impact. The experience of 1988 led the press to reform its coverage of subsequent campaigns. Political advertising and candidates' claims became subject to greater scrutiny for accuracy and appropriateness.

Above all, the race sharply increased the public's resistance to negative campaigning. When Bush ran for reelection four years later, his personal attacks on the Democratic nominee, Bill Clinton, proved to be a costly miscalculation.

BIBLIOGRAPHY

Blumenthal, Sidney. *Pledging Allegiance: The Last Campaign of the Cold War.* 1990.

Cramer, Richard Ben. *What It Takes.* 1992.

Drew, Elizabeth. *Election Journal: Political Events of 1987–1988.* 1989.

Germond, Jack W., and Jules Witcover. *Whose Broad Stripes and Bright Stars?: The Trivial Pursuit of the Presidency, 1988.* 1989.

Gillette, Michael L., interviewer. *Snapshots of the 1988 Presidential Campaign.* 3 vols. 1992.

Runkel, David R., ed. *Campaign for President: The Managers Look at '88.* 1989.

MICHAEL L. GILLETTE

**ELECTION, PRESIDENTIAL, 1992.** In early 1991, standing at the foot of Pennsylvania Avenue, George Bush appeared invincible as he saluted thousands of troops marching by him in review. The Commander in Chief was the victor in the one-hundred-hour GULF WAR, freeing Kuwait from its occupation by Iraqi dictator Saddam Hussein. After organizing an unprecedented international coalition and winning congressional approval of the use of force (despite opposition by the Democratic leadership), his skill as diplomat and politician seemed beyond reproach. Bush's reelection was generally conceded to be a foregone conclusion.

**A Vulnerable President.** The President hailed from an atrophied wing of the REPUBLICAN PARTY—the Eastern Establishment. Bush grew up mainly in the cloistered town of Greenwich, Connecticut; his father, Prescott, a Wall Street banker and political friend of Governor THOMAS E. DEWEY of New York, was elected a U.S. Senator from Connecticut. After serving as a Navy pilot in WORLD WAR II and graduating from Yale, young Bush moved to Texas to prove his mettle. Relying on his father's business connections, he established himself as an oilman and entered Texas politics just as the GOP was emerging as a conservative force in that state. Bush was elected as a congressman from a safe, wealthy Republican district in Houston, but also lost two Senate races. From the start, he tried to accommodate himself to the ascendant right-wing in an effort to shed the offensive taint of his old-money background.

He rose to prominence as a protégé. President Nixon appointed him ambassador to the UNITED NATIONS and chairman of the Republican National Committee. President Ford named him U.S. diplomatic representative to China. In 1980, Bush ran in the Republican presidential primaries, expressing his main theme as having "the Big Mo" (the big momentum). He was decisively defeated by Ronald Reagan. After being chosen as his running mate, Bush was determined never to be caught outside the shadow of Reagan's conservatism. Bush's election as President in 1988 was believed to have proved conclusively the case for the GOP's electoral superiority.

President Bush saw himself principally as a foreign policy President. Consistent with laissez-faire economic doctrine, he believed he should do little but adhere to his campaign promise not to raise taxes— "Read my lips, no new taxes!"—the emblem of his consistency with Reagan (In 1980, Bush had labeled Reagan's economic prescriptions as "voodoo economics."). By maintaining the domestic status quo, Bush hoped to pacify the Republican right wing, which remained suspicious of him, and free himself for important international issues. The President saw the role of Chief Executive basically as one of senior diplomat, directing tactical maneuvers in the COLD WAR. On this score he intended to break with Reagan. Bush believed that Mikhail Gorbachev's internal reforms in the Soviet Union and overtures to the West were a new, more dangerous, form of the cold war. So, for six months, in early 1989, Bush refused to act on Reagan's ultimate policy, which was founded on the notion that the cold war was ending and which was criticized by the right wing. Bush dismissed his predecessor's view as naive and utopian. By the time Bush began to deal with Gorbachev in earnest, Eastern Europe was swept by revolutions that overthrew the old totalitarian regimes and united Germany. Bush moved closer to Gorbachev, identifying the U.S. interest almost completely with his fate, but failing to provide him with significant aid beyond gracious diplomatic gestures.

By the opening of the election year, the main pillars of Republican support were crumbling. Getting tough with the Soviets no longer had any meaning for either foreign policy or national defense. In August 1991, when communism was overthrown in the Soviet Union after an unsuccessful hardliners' coup, being the cold warrior became anachronistic. Without an external threat, Bush's foreign-policy credential lost its power in domestic politics. On social issues, a majority of women, including suburban women who had voted Republican in the past, were angry at the GOP for its opposition to ABORTION and for Bush's 1991 appointment to the Supreme Court of Clarence Thomas, who was accused by a former colleague, Anita Hill, of sexual harassment. On economic issues, Bush bore the burden of a recession. He had broken his campaign promise of no new taxes in late 1990, an act which had not fostered prosperity. Conservatives painted him as a betrayer of Reagan's legacy, and white-collar employees, who tended to vote Republican, were especially hurt in the economic downturn.

On the eve of the election year, in December 1991, the President traveled to Japan. Public opinion polls showed that most Americans regarded Japan as an economic threat. At a state dinner, Bush became ill, vomiting in the lap of the prime minister and rolling under the table. This unfortunate incident was widely felt to be symbolic of U.S. economic decline.

Suddenly vulnerable, Bush faced a challenge for the nomination from the Republican right in the person of Patrick Buchanan, a syndicated columnist and media commentator from Washington, D.C. "America First" was his slogan, self-consciously adopted from the pre-World War II, isolationist old right. With the end of the cold war, the ancient fissures of the GOP were opened again. Though Buchanan did not win a single primary, he inflicted severe damage on Bush as his first opponent to crystalize his negative image as indifferent about the country. "Message—I care!" Bush pleaded in New Hampshire.

**A Persistent Challenger.** During the months after the Gulf War, when Bush appeared as the conqueror, many of the seemingly obvious Democratic candidates decided not to run. One figure swiftly took the lead: Governor Bill Clinton of Arkansas. Clinton had had a modest, small-town upbringing ("the man from Hope," voters learned, had struggled with an abusive, alcoholic stepfather); was a striver who became a Rhodes Scholar; met his equally driven and accomplished wife, his closest political adviser, HILLARY RODHAM CLINTON, at Yale Law School; had run the Texas organization for the McGovern campaign in 1972; in 1978, at the age of thirty-two, was elected the youngest governor in the country; lost two years later in the Reagan landslide, partly for pushing too hard and fast on progressive causes; and returned from the political dead as a cannier, more careful politician. Clinton diligently made friends across the political spectrum of the DEMOCRATIC PARTY and was involved in many of the free-floating policy debates of the experts. Above all, he called for a national economic strategy and investment in public infrastructure and education, a rejection of the economic conservatism of the 1980s.

Just as Clinton became the frontrunner, a former nightclub singer, Gennifer Flowers, claimed she had had a twelve-year affair with him. She was paid more than $100,000 for her charges by the tabloid *National Inquirer*. Bill and Hillary Clinton attempted to defuse the scandal by explaining the solidity of their marriage on CBS's "60 Minutes." Then a 1969 letter Clinton had written to a member of his draft board mysteriously surfaced. In it he discussed his opposition to the VIETNAM WAR. Critics flayed Clinton as a draft-dodger.

By an extraordinary display of persistence and stamina, however, he came in second in New Hampshire. Clinton's main opponents for the nomination were former Senator Paul Tsongas of Massachusetts, who focused on the deficit, and former Governor Jerry Brown of California, a chameleon-like figure who appeared as a left-wing crusader. Both men decried Clinton's presumed lack of integrity. But, in state after state, Clinton's perseverance allowed him to triumph over the obstacle of the so-called character issue. Yet his negative ratings spiraled upward. And most of the Democratic Party leadership was convinced he was unelectable as President.

In May, after police officers were acquitted of charges arising from beating an unarmed black motorist, a riot engulfed large sections of Los Angeles. A week later President Bush visited the still-smoldering ruins, but seemed helpless. The principal response of the administration was a speech by Vice President DAN QUAYLE condemning a lack of self-discipline in the underclass and permissiveness promoted by the "cultural elite." The particular object of his criticism was "Murphy Brown," a television situation comedy that featured an unwed mother.

**The Conventions and the Campaign.** Disorder in the country, it became commonly believed, reflected "gridlock" in Washington. With Bush passive and Clinton discredited, a new candidate emerged—a Texas billionaire, H. ROSS PEROT, whose business success was widely taken as a sign of what he could do for America. Perot's campaign was launched with an appearance on a television talk show, "Larry King Live." He expressed a thorough contempt for the two parties and politics itself. Decline, he argued, could be reversed simply, by putting the man of action in the White House. In June, Perot ran ahead of both Bush and Clinton on the polls. But stories appeared in the press describing his extensive history of suspicion, conspiracy-mongering, mythomania, authoritarianism, and vendettas. Perot insisted that the stories were all part of a Republican plot against him.

In July, Clinton selected Senator AL GORE of Tennessee as his running mate. Gore, whose father had been a liberal senator, was a Southern progressive, much like Clinton. Gore specialized in futuristic issues, such as the environment and new technologies. Clinton and Gore were only a year apart in age, both in their mid-forties, and their appearance itself presented an image of generational succession. Theirs was the first complete ticket of leaders from the post-

World War II generation. The choice of Gore gave many voters an opportunity to reevaluate Clinton, who leaped ahead of Bush and Perot—a lead he never lost. The Democratic convention in New York City was marked by unity; unlike recent Democratic conventions, devisiveness was almost completely absent. On the day of Clinton's nomination, Perot, whose poll numbers were plummeting toward single digits, withdrew, claiming that he wanted to spare the country a deadlocked election that would be decided by the House of Representatives. Most of Perot's supporters were disillusioned by their putative leader, and they turned to Clinton as the candidate who stood for change. Immediately after the convention, Clinton and Gore embarked on a tumultuously received bus trip through the Midwest, seeking to dramatize concern for ordinary citizens. Bus trips through other regions became a regular feature of Clinton's campaign.

A month later, in August, the tone of the Republican convention in Houston was set with the first speech, delivered by Patrick Buchanan. In it, he called for a "cultural war," a "religious war," as well as suggesting a race war—drawing enthusiastic cheering from the delegates. An effort was made to undo the damage on "Family Values Night" with a soothing appearance by BARBARA BUSH, whose popularity exceeded her husband's. But a speech by Marilyn Quayle denigrating working women and exalting "women's essential nature" compounded Buchanan's emphasis. The Houston event was the most self-destructive convention since the Democratic convention of 1968.

Perot now decided to reenter the race. His announcement was made at a rump gathering in Dallas of what he called his "volunteers" (almost all handpicked, with many in his pay). Both the Bush and Clinton campaigns sent delegations of senior officials, who obsequiously praised Perot at press conferences.

Bush followed a series of disjointed campaign strategies, overseen by his friend, JAMES A. BAKER III, who quit as Secretary of State to serve as White House chief of staff for the duration. The president unveiled an economic plan to much fanfare, but forgot about it a week later when it failed to stimulate his poll numbers. Strategists from the British Conservative Party, who had succeeded in winning an election earlier in the year against the odds, were imported. They suggested that bush attack Clinton on trust and taxes. Bush took the advice, making his campaign almost wholly negative. His attacks included charges that Clinton was a draft-dodger and that he had made a trip to Moscow as a student in 1969 that was somehow suspicious. Baker, for his part, developed a strategy dependent on Perot

splitting the anti-Bush vote in such a way that Bush might win reelection. Bush's senior aides did not believe the President could win a majority of votes.

The President on the stump hit shrill notes, even calling Clinton and Gore "two bozos." But Clinton, with MICHAEL DUKAKIS's previous passivity always in mind, deftly parried Bush's assaults and focused on "the economy, stupid," as a slogan posted in his headquarters put it. Three PRESIDENTIAL DEBATES showcased Perot's gift for simple aphorism, Clinton's ability to connect with ordinary citizens, and Bush's apparent disengagement. At one point, he checked his watch several times. The vice presidential debate was notable only for the confusion of Perot's running mate, retired Admiral James Stockdale, a former Vietnam prisoner of war, who remarked: "Who am I? Why am I here?" Perot spent more than $60 million of his own money on his campaign, more than either Bush or Clinton. Nine days before the election, Perot announced that he had quit in July because the Republicans were going to disrupt his daughter's wedding and distribute fabricated pictures of her involved in lesbian sex. He produced no evidence.

**The Result.** Ross Perot finished with 19 percent of the vote, a protest vote expressing deep disenchantment with the political and economic system, more than any independent candidate had gained since Theodore Roosevelt ran in 1912, though Perot did not win a single state. President Bush received only 38 percent, a lower vote than that for Herbert Hoover in 1932 and BARRY GOLDWATER in 1964. Bill Clinton won 43 percent, the same percentage won by Richard Nixon in 1968, at the start of the Republican-dominated era. In the ELECTORAL COLLEGE, Clinton beat Bush by 370 electoral votes to 168. Bill Clinton's victory was a general mandate for change to counter economic decline.

BIBLIOGRAPHY

Duffy, Michael, and Dan Goodgame. *Marching in Place: The Status Quo Presidency of George Bush.* 1992.
Levin, Robert E. *Bill Clinton: The Inside Story.* 1992.
Phillips, Kevin. *Boiling Point: Republicans, Democrats, and the Decline of Middle Class Prosperity.* 1993.
Pomper, Gerald, et. al. *The Election of 1992: Reports and Interpretations.* 1993.

SIDNEY BLUMENTHAL

**ELECTORAL COLLEGE.** The body of electors empowered under the Constitution to select a President is popularly known as the Electoral College. Article II, Section 1 provides: "Each State shall appoint in such manner as the Legislature thereof may direct, a Number of Electors, equal to the whole Number of Senators and Representatives to which the State may be entitled in the Congress," with the proviso that no Senator or Representative or officer of the U.S. government may be an elector. The census, performed every ten years, determines the size of a state's membership in the House of Representatives and therefore the number of its electors in the Electoral College.

**The Institution.** Although in the early years of the Republic state legislatures frequently chose the electors themselves, every state now provides for popular election. To succeed, a presidential candidate must receive a majority in the Electoral College, which in 1992 was 270 out of 538 votes. Formally, voters choose a slate of state electors who are pledged to support a particular candidate's election in the Electoral College. Rarely do the names of the electors appear on the ballot. The total electoral vote of a state accrues to the winner of the popular vote.

By law, the electors meet in their respective state capitals on the first Monday after the second Wednesday in December and cast their votes for President and Vice President. A certified copy of the state results is dispatched to the president of the U.S. Senate. On 6 January, in a joint session of Congress, he opens the certificates and announces the result.

Despite the formally indirect method of election, the result basically reflects the popular will. But the popular will is expressed in a distinctive pattern—state by state rather than by a national referendum. This "federalized" mode of choosing a President is the heart of the Electoral College election process.

If no candidate gains a majority in the Electoral College, the Constitution prescribes a contingency procedure: the House of Representatives, voting by state delegations rather than by individual Representatives selects the President from the three candidates (originally five) who earned the highest number of electoral votes. Only twice, in 1800 and in 1824, has the House been called upon to decide. If no vice presidential candidate receives a majority in the Electoral College the Senate chooses from the top two candidates in the college. Only once, in 1837, has the Senate made that choice.

**Origins.** What prompted the Framers to adopt such a complex system of election? The progressive historians J. Allen Smith and Charles Beard claim that the complicated, indirect method reflected the Framers' deep distrust of democracy. This thesis was rejected by the political scientist John P. Roche, who argued that the Electoral College was simply a last-minute compromise designed to allow the CONSTITUTIONAL CONVENTION to wind up its business. It was, according to Roche, merely a "jerry-rigged improvisation."

More recent scholarship, based on a close reading of the Constitutional Convention records, suggests a third explanation. The Electoral College system did have a clear design and purpose, but antimajoritarianism did not inspire its adoption. According to this thesis, the Electoral College emerged at Philadelphia as a second chapter of the Connecticut Compromise to resolve the fundamental dispute between large and small states at the convention.

Both the Virginia and New Jersey plans, the documents on which the Constitution was based, advocated election of the executive by the legislature, the practice most common in the states. But this method, it was felt, would violate the principle of the SEPARATION OF POWERS and compromise the executive's independence. To avoid these undesirable consequences it was at first decided to limit the President to one rather lengthy term of office (seven years). Some delegates, however, objected to the bar on reeligibility. They advocated moving the choice from the legislature to the people since popular election would avoid undue influence on the executive by the legislature and remove any barrier to reeligibility. Many delegates, including James Madison, GOUVERNEUR MORRIS, and JAMES WILSON, strongly supported the idea of popular elections. But two groups objected to removing the choice from the legislature. The smaller states had gained a distinct advantage in the upper house (ultimately the Senate) after the Connecticut Compromise secured equality for them in that body. The slave states had gained an increment in voting power in the lower house (ultimately the House of Representatives) by virtue of the rule that made a state's representation in the House proportional to its white population plus three-fifths of its black population, although only the white population would vote. Transferring the choice from the legislature to the public at large would eliminate the built-in advantages that these two groups of states had secured in the legislature. Those favoring election by Congress and those favoring popular election remained locked in battle until practically the end of the Convention.

At the last minute, the Brearley Committee on Unfinished Parts proposed the Electoral College scheme, which successfully preserved the advantages of the small and slave states without compromising the executive's independence. Since each state would be entitled in the Electoral College to the same number of votes that it would enjoy in a joint session of Congress, both small and slave states were amenable to transferring the task of selecting a president from the real Congress to this ad hoc single-purpose congress. Since the electors would never assemble together at one national site but would meet to vote "in their respective States" and immediately thereafter disband, there was no danger of corruption, plotting, or cabal. To help prevent the larger states from dominating the selection process, each elector was to vote for two persons, one of whom, at least, would not be a citizen of his own state. At the same time, since a majority was required for selection of the President, no elector would be prone to throw away his second vote. Thus a national figure would likely be chosen at the first round. If no candidate received an absolute majority in the Electoral College, the House of Representatives would choose the President from the five candidates receiving the highest totals in the Electoral College.

The delegates saw the Electoral College scheme as an equitable system for electing a President and one that reserved considerable influence for the states. This influence was reflected not only in the composition of the Electoral College but also in the state's power to determine the manner of appointment of the electors and in the contingency arrangements granting the House of Representatives, voting by states, the ultimate choice. An incidental by-product of the new scheme was the emergence of the office of Vice President, designed to take care of the electors' second vote.

The Electoral College, a one-purpose congress, was a well-wrought compromise, blending national and federal elements in the selection of a President. Thus ALEXANDER HAMILTON, in FEDERALIST 68, could declare with pride that if "the mode of appointment of the Chief Magistrate is . . . not perfect it is at least excellent."

**Operation.** Not surprisingly, the Electoral College worked smoothly in the first two presidential elections, those of 1788 and 1792. Since George Washington was the unanimous choice of the electors both times, the only issue dividing them was how to cast their second vote in choosing a Vice President. On both occasions John Adams was chosen.

By 1796, however, the advent of political parties radically transformed the Electoral College from a conclave of independent-minded men of "information and discernment" (as Hamilton had envisaged) engaged in a search for the most qualified executive, into a body of committed politicans pledged to cast their votes in accordance with prearranged instructions. The double ballot for President, designed to give the smaller states a chance to land a President and to preclude a straight-out vote for favorite sons, could lead to highly undesirable results, as events proved.

Two parties were now vying for control of the

government—the FEDERALIST PARTY, which advocated federal supremacy, and the Democratic-Republicans, who espoused greater state autonomy. The 1796 race was closely fought, and a split result ensued: Federalist John Adams captured the presidency (71 votes), and Democratic-Republican Thomas Jefferson gained the vice presidency (68 votes). In 1800, when every Democratic-Republican elector faithfully cast his two votes for the party's nominees—Jefferson for President and AARON BURR for Vice President—the result was that both received exactly the same number of votes (73) in the Electoral College, thereby propelling the final choice into the House of Representatives. Federalists predominated in the House, and many were intent on punishing Jefferson by awarding the presidency to Burr. Only the strong intervention of Hamilton swung the election to Jefferson after six days of debate and thirty-six ballots.

This situation revealed yet a further danger. Had Burr conspired with the Federalists, he would assuredly have become President. The double vote to which each elector was entitled in the College opened the way for the minority party to connive with the majority party's vice presidential candidate to make him President. The only solution was to separate the Electoral College vote for President from the vote for Vice President. This was effected by adoption of the TWELFTH AMENDMENT to the Constitution in 1804. (Additionally, the amendment prescribed that the election of a Vice President in the College required a majority vote, not just a plurality, and that in the contingency procedure the House would choose the President from the top three candidates, not from the top five, as previously.) The large state–small state dichotomy that, in large measure, had prompted the adoption of the Electoral College, had now been attenuated by the emergence of political parties.

The politicization of the election process also affected the pattern of state voting in the Electoral College. By 1836, all states except South Carolina had instituted popular election of electors. Likewise, all the states had adopted the general ticket system, with the winner taking all. The dominant political party in each state preferred this system since it magnified the party vote in the college. James Madison himself gave the greatest spur to the general ticket system. In 1800, realizing that Democratic-Republican candidate Jefferson faced a close contest to win the presidency from Federalist Adams, Madison induced the Virginia state legislature to abandon the district system, which previously operated in that state, and to switch to the general ticket system. This effectively shut out the Federalists from any share in Virginia's electoral vote.

This general ticket system, which has prevailed with

only rare exceptions, has had profound consequences for the course of American political history. On the one hand, it has been responsible, in no small measure, for the existence of a two-party system in the United States. Since a political party must be capable of capturing a plurality in an entire state in order to score in the Electoral College, third parties have invariably fallen by the wayside in their endeavor to make inroads in the presidential sweepstakes. Even where a regional third party has arisen, as has happened on occasion in the South, it has never gained sufficient strength to modify the outcome of an election. Ideological parties have never made headway in the United States since they have never succeeded even in capturing a state's electoral vote much less secure a majority in the college. The end result is that the United States is dominated by two large political parties, each of which is a conglomerate of different interests and ideologies.

The general ticket system has also influenced the nature of the political campaign in presidential elections. Since the winner takes all, candidates have tended to concentrate their efforts on the states with the highest number of electoral votes. In recent times this has sometimes led political parties to exhibit particular sensitivity in their PLATFORMS to the needs of the ethnic minorities concentrated in the large, populous urban centers.

Moreover, the system has operated to magnify the winner's margin of victory in the Electoral College. Even a razor-thin popular victory, such as that won by John F. Kennedy over Richard M. Nixon in 1960 (49.5 percent to 49.3 percent) produced an unequivocal Electoral College vote of 303 to 219. In short, the general ticket system helps convert even a modest victory into a decisive and categorical verdict.

By the same token, a winning candidate in the Electoral College may well be a minority President and may even receive a smaller popular vote than his chief rival. In sixteen elections (1824, 1844, 1848, 1856, 1860, 1876, 1880, 1884, 1888, 1892, 1912, 1916, 1948, 1960, 1968, 1992) a candidate gained a majority in the Electoral College without commanding a majority of the popular vote. The most notable instance of a minority President is Abraham Lincoln in 1860, who garnered just under 40 percent in the popular vote. Twice, the loser in the popular-vote contest has prevailed in the Electoral College. In 1876 Democrat SAMUEL J. TILDEN polled 4,287,670 votes against 4,035,924 for Republican Rutherford B. Hayes. In the Electoral College Tilden scored 184 votes to Hayes's 165, with a further 20 electoral votes, mainly from Southern states still under RECONSTRUCTION, in dispute. A majority in the College consisted of 185; thus Tilden

was one vote short of outright victory. An electoral commission set up by Congress ultimately ruled that all 20 disputed votes accrued to Hayes, who thereby prevailed by 185 votes to 184. Hayes's promise to the Democrats to end Reconstruction and remove federal troops from the South induced them to accept the results. In 1888 Democrat Grover Cleveland, the incumbent, received 5,540,309 votes, about 95,000 votes more than Republican Benjamin Harrison (5,444,337). Nonetheless, Cleveland lost the election because Harrison scored 233 electoral votes to Cleveland's 168.

The politicization of the Electoral College process has also given rise to the unexpected problem of the maverick, or wayward, elector who refuses to vote as pledged. In contrast to the independence electors were initially expected to possess, electors were now bidden to adhere faithfully to the choice of those who appointed them. To act otherwise constituted a betrayal of trust. Fortunately, the number of electors who have presumed to act independently over the years has been miniscule and their impact nil. Between 1820 and 1988 more than eighteen thousand electoral votes were cast for President, but only seven of these can categorically be said to constitute misvotes. Nonetheless, complaints about potentially unfaithful electors has fueled criticism of the Electoral College system as presently constituted. A number of states have adopted legislation (of doubtful constitutionality) requiring electors to abide by their party commitment.

Adoption in 1961 of the TWENTY-THIRD AMENDMENT to the Constitution, allotting Washington, D.C., the same number of electors to which the least populous state is entitled, confirmed the attenuation of state influence in the Electoral College process.

**Proposals for Reform.** No provision of the Constitution has drawn so much criticism over the years nor provoked so many constitutional amendments as has the Electoral College clause. Whatever the considerations of the Framers in creating the College, many believe that its retention under a democratic form of government is an anachronism. In truth, the real target of the criticism of the Electoral College is less the college itself than an incidental aspect of the scheme— the general ticket system. Critics maintain that, by awarding the winner in a state the entire electoral vote of that state, the system distorts the popular vote nationally and robs nearly half of the electorate of its say in the selection of a President. Four reform schemes have been proposed.

*The Automatic Plan.* This is the least-innovative scheme since it retains the College and keeps the general ticket system intact while eliminating the role of elector. The state's electoral vote would automatically go to the victor in the popular vote, and no unfaithful electors could disturb the result. For most reformers the automatic plan constitutes no reform at all since it would furnish constitutional fiat to the general ticket system, which at present is based on custom.

**The District Plan.** The Electoral College would be retained in this scheme, but each state would be divided into electoral districts in accordance with its electoral vote. The people in each district would choose one elector and the national totals would faithfully reflect the measure of national support accorded each candidate. While the district plan would not promote ideological splinter parties it would be open to gerrymandering by state legislatures. Moreover, it would not preclude a minority President or even recourse to the House of Representatives under the Constitution's contingency procedures.

**The Proportional Plan.** In this plan, the Electoral College as an institution would be eliminated, but electoral votes would continue to be distributed among the states as at present. The assignment of a state's votes to the candidates, however, would not be on the basis of winner-take-all but would be proportionate to the percentage of the popular vote each candidate has scored. Gerrymandering would become pointless, and every voter's ballot would count. Tallying up the national vote of each candidate would be a simple matter of aggregating the electoral vote scored in each state. To be elected, a candidate would have to receive at least 40 percent of the electoral vote. If no candidate received that percentage of the national vote there would be a contingency procedure, with members of Congress, in joint session, voting as individuals to select the President from the top two candidates or alternatively a runoff election.

This plan was proposed several times in Congress, most notably in the late 1940s and early 1950s, when it was strongly promoted by Senator Henry Cabot Lodge of Massachusetts and Congressman Ed Gossett of Texas. The major criticism of the so-called LODGE-GOSSETT PLAN was that it would encourage the emergence of splinter parties and, given the narrowness of most victories, would fail to provide a President with a categorical mandate.

**The Direct Vote Plan.** This plan would eliminate the Electoral College entirely and provide for direct election of the President by the national electorate. Under some variations of the plan, winning a plurality would be sufficient to be elected, eliminating the need for any contingency arrangement. Under another variation the victor would have to receive at least 40 percent of the popular vote to be pronounced winner; if no candidate received 40 percent, there would either be a runoff election between the two top contenders or the Congress, in joint session, would choose between them. The great advantage of direct popular election of the President is that it serves as a true national referendum; the primary criticism is that it would encourage splinter parties and would not produce a categorical result.

Denying the need for reform, numerous commentators have extolled the virtues of the Electoral College as at present constituted, claiming that the College continues to fulfill a vital federal function. The United States remains a nation of states, as reflected in the continuing requirement of equality in state representation in the Senate—a requirement that cannot be modified under the Constitution. Furthermore, although the Supreme Court has endorsed the rule of "one person, one vote" in the formulation of electoral districts for state and national elections, the Court in 1966 refused to entertain an action by Delaware and other states against New York that alleged that these states were disadvantaged by the winner-take-all arrangement of the Electoral College system (*Delaware v. New York*). The argument that the Electoral College system is not consistent with a democratic system of government is simply a non sequitur since the very existence of a constitution represents a bar on absolute majority rule. Proponents say that the Electoral College operates to ensure that a President will be elected only on the basis of a special kind of majority—a federative one—and that the result will reflect a wide consensus in the national choice.

Supporters maintain that the Electoral College has stood the test of time, successfully providing the nation with Chief Executives for more than two centuries without any major upheavals. The last time the contingency procedure was invoked was in 1824. To attempt to radically modify a system that has operated so flawlessly is to take a leap in the dark, not knowing what lies at the other end. If the presidential sweepstakes tends to advantage larger states and to give a premium to urban centers and their ethnic minorities, this serves to balance the rural influence dominant in Congress. Whatever adverse consequences arise under the Electoral College scheme should be balanced against the great benefits accruing from this set-up, including the two-party system, the forestalling of splinter parties, the stability that derives from the nonideological character of American political parties, and a categorical rendering of the outcome of the election so that no matter how narrow the margin of victory the decision is clear-cut, giving the winner an unchallengeable mandate to govern. The broad national consensus that a victor must command in the Electoral College is said by some to constitute the foremost prescription for sound government.

While in recent years, the demand for reform has been quiescent, if a runner-up in the popular vote is elected, or if the contingency procedure involving the House of Representatives is brought into operation because of the candidacy of a third party, the nation may once again reverberate with the call to reform the Electoral College system.

### BIBLIOGRAPHY

Best, Judith. *The Case against Direct Election of the President.* 1975.
Bickel, Alexander. *Reform and Continuity: The Electoral College, the Convention and the Party System.* 1968.
Diamond, Martin. *The Electoral College and the American Idea of Democracy.* 1977.
Pierce, Neal R., and Lawrence D. Longley. *The People's President: The Electoral College in American History and the Direct Vote Alternative.* Rev. ed. 1981.
Sayre, Wallace S., and Judith H. Parris. *Voting for President: The Electoral College and the American Political System.* 1970.
Slonim, Shlomo. "The Electoral College at Philadelphia: The Evolution of an Ad Hoc Congress for the Selection of a President." *Journal of American History* 73 (1986): 35–58.
Wilmerding, Lucius, Jr. *The Electoral College.* 1958.
Zeidenstein, Harvey. *Direct Election of the President.* 1973.

SHLOMO SLONIM

**ELECTORAL COMMISSION.** The Electoral Commission was established 29 January 1877 as a mechanism to settle a dispute between the Republican Senate and the Democratic House of Representatives regarding the counting of electoral votes from several states in the presidential election of 1876. Rival sets of electoral votes came from Florida, Louisiana, and South Carolina, where both Democrats and Republicans claimed to have won the election. In Oregon, the governor attempted to replace a Republican elector with a Democrat, because the Republican was ineligible to serve.

The Constitution provides that should no candidate receive a majority of the electoral vote, the House of Representatives must then vote for President from among the three leading candidates. In this case the House would choose between the Democratic candidate, SAMUEL J. TILDEN, who was one vote short of a majority even without the disputed electoral votes, and the Republican Rutherford B. Hayes, who needed all the disputed votes to win. However, the Republican Senate denied that the provision applied to a case of disputed returns. It insisted that the Republican president pro tem of the Senate, whom the Constitution

designates to count the electoral vote, must simply count the votes certified by the proper state authorities—thus electing Hayes. House Democrats insisted Congress could go behind the official returns and instead count the alternative votes. If the two chambers disagreed about which votes to count, preventing either candidate from securing a majority, the House would select a President according to the constitutional provision—thus electing Tilden.

The Electoral Commission was created as a compromise in the dangerous conflict. Both sides agreed to submit the disputed electoral votes to the commission. The commission was made up of fifteen members: five each from the House, the Senate, and the Supreme Court. The commission's decision as to which votes to count could be reversed only by the vote of both chambers of Congress. The commission began deliberations on 31 January 1877 and adjourned *sine die* on 2 March 1877. The eight Republicans on the commission decided to count the votes cast for the Republican candidates, thus electing Hayes and his running mate, WILLIAM WHEELER, while the seven Democrats dissented. Democrats protested, but efforts in the Democratic House to disrupt the formal vote count failed and Hayes took office on 4 March 1877.

[*See also* ELECTION, PRESIDENTIAL, 1876.]

### BIBLIOGRAPHY

Benedict, Michael Les. "Southern Democrats in the Crisis of 1876–1877: A Reconsideration of *Reunion and Reaction.*" *Journal of Southern History* 44 (1980): 489–524.
Fairman, Charles. *Five Justices and the Electoral Commission of 1877.* Supplement to vol. 7 of *Oliver Wendell Holmes Devise History of the Supreme Court of the United States.* Edited by Paul A. Freund and Stanley N. Katz. 1988.
Polakoff, Keith Ian. *The Politics of Inertia: The Election of 1876 and the End of Reconstruction.* 1973.
Woodward, C. Vann. *Reunion and Reaction: The Compromise of 1877 and the End of Reconstruction.* 1951.

MICHAEL LES BENEDICT

**ELECTORAL REFORM.** The system for electing the President is a mixture of constitutional provisions, federal and state laws, rules of the House of Representatives, and tradition. The Constitution, in Article II, Section 1 and in the TWELFTH AMENDMENT, outlines the basic features of what is known as the ELECTORAL COLLEGE, as well as the essentials of a contingency (or run-off) election in the House of Representatives. Federal law fixes the date of the national election. State laws determine how the electors are chosen inside the states and, in some cases, try to mandate how the electors vote. House rules govern the conduct of the contingency election. Finally, tradition now holds that the electors should be selected by the people and bound by the popular vote.

**Supposed Flaws.** Calls for reform rest on claims that the system is flawed, but there are major disagreements about what constitutes a flaw. Four problems have been identified.

First is the possibility that a candidate who loses the popular vote may win the electoral vote and become President. Referred to as the problem of the "minority" President, this possibility results mostly from the current winner-take-all laws in place today in all but two of the states. Under these laws, all of a state's electoral votes are awarded to the candidate who receives a plurality of the popular vote. A minority President has occurred in one clear-cut instance, when Benjamin Harrison was elected over Grover Cleveland in 1888 after losing the popular vote. The objection to a minority President is that the popular will is ignored.

A second problem, which derives from the same winner-take-all provisions, is the claim that the system is already highly undemocratic because it encourages candidates to base their strategies on winning an electoral majority, not a popular majority. Candidates thus pay more attention to voters in some states than in others. Generally speaking, voters in the largest (and perhaps the smallest) states are favored. Furthermore, the absence of genuine competition in all of the states is said to discourage voter participation.

A third problem is the possibility that electors will use their discretion under the Constitution to vote for a candidate different from the one to whom they were pledged. This so-called "faithless elector" problem has occurred some seven times in the twentieth century, although none of these indiscretions has affected the outcome of an election. But there is a more serious problem, which has figured vaguely in the electoral strategies of certain THIRD-PARTY CANDIDATES. This scenario comes into play in the event of an election in which no candidate wins an electoral majority outright. In this instance, a candidate might well try to decide the election in a bargaining process using his electoral votes, or the electors themselves might attempt to bargain their votes. The problem is that the electors are no longer regarded as the legitimate officers to exercise this kind of discretion, which would put the entire election result in question.

A fourth problem (or set of problems) is connected with the existing contingency election that comes into play when no candidate receives a majority of the electoral votes. Under this plan, the House of Representatives chooses the President from among the top three electoral-vote recipients by a vote in which each state casts one vote and in which a majority of the states are needed to elect. This provision has not been used since 1824, in large part because of the existing electoral system and the dominance of two parties. Still, the plan remains in effect, and there are both substantive and technical objections to it. Some contend that the Congress is an inappropriate body to select the President, and many more argue that, whatever one may think of an election by Congress, the specific arrangement is deeply flawed. A vote by states undervalues dramatically the wishes of voters in the large states and thus of the people in general. Moreover, there is no assurance that a President can even be chosen, as the votes of a majority of states is required to elect.

**Proposed Reforms.** The various reforms that have been proposed address one or more of these problems. A judgment of their merits depends, first, on an analysis of the seriousness of the problem in question and, second, on whether the proposed reform resolves the problem without also creating other and more serious problems.

First, there is a proposal to eliminate the existing electoral system and replace it with a direct popular election. To ensure that the victor has a sufficient base of popular support, most variants of this plan stipulate that if no candidate receives more than 40 percent of the vote, a run-off popular election will be held between the top two vote recipients. This plan has been offered chiefly to deal with the minority President possibility, but it is also favored because it makes elections more democratic and eliminates all difficulties connected with the contingency election plan.

The direct election plan is the most radical of all the reform proposals. It breaks with the principle of federalism, which presently accords considerable weight to state concerns, and substitutes for it the simple idea of a national electorate. A direct election plan would also produce pressure to nationalize electoral administration. If a vote in Chicago is worth the same as a vote in Jackson, then citizens should presumably be registered and vote under the same rules. The plan would also change, for better or worse, the calculus of presidential campaigns, as candidates would fashion strategies that are less attentive to (certain) state interests and more attentive to certain demographic categories. Finally, the direct election plan with a run-off provision could very well have the effect of encouraging serious third-party candidates. Under this system, a vote for a third party in the first round might not appear—as it now does—to be wasted, because it could force a second election and enable a third party to negotiate with one of the major candidates.

Second, there is a proposal to eliminate state winner-take-all laws by an amendment that would require two of the electors in each state be selected statewide (like Senators) and the others be chosen individually by congressional district. Interestingly, this district system is achievable in theory without a constitutional change. States have the authority to set their own laws for the selection of the electors, and two states—Maine and Nebraska—have adopted a district system. A few other states have recently been examining this possibility. Without an amendment, however, the adoption of a district system is likely to be only partial.

The district plan, like the direct-election plan, is designed to address the problem of the minority President. Yet, while it reduces somewhat this possibility, it does not eliminate it entirely. Moreover, this plan would probably require a change in the method of drawing congressional districts, as these districts would now hold the key to presidential politics. Civil rights provisions that call for districts that favor election of blacks and Hispanics to Congress would also have to be reviewed.

Third, there is a plan to abolish the office of the elector, while leaving the rest of the system essentially unchanged. Under this plan, states would assign the electoral votes according to a formula determined by state law. This plan is designed to solve the problem of the faithless elector, including the circumstance in which candidates or electors in a three-way race might try to bargain votes to decide the election.

Fourth, there are two plans to change the existing contingency-election system. The first is to eliminate Congress from the process altogether and hold a run-off election between the top two electoral vote recipients. The run-off would be decided by electoral votes. A second plan is to maintain the choice of the President by Congress, but to select in a joint session of the House and Senate, with each member having a single vote. Decision on a certain date by a plurality vote could also guarantee that a new President would be chosen.

None of these proposed amendments has made much headway. The direct-election plan has had the most fervent supporters, but also the most opponents. The supporters argue for its simplicity and fairness. Opponents contend that the likelihood of a minority President is slight. Given the damage to the federal principle, as well the possible ill-effects on the two party system, it is better to leave things alone. Purely as a practical matter, moreover, passage of this plan—at least before the occurrence of the election of another minority President—seems doubtful, because of the states' heavy involvement in the ratification process.

BIBLIOGRAPHY

Berns, Walter, ed. *After the People Vote: Steps in Choosing the President.* 1983.

Best, Judith. *The Case against the Direct Election of the President.* 1975.

Longley, Lawrence. *The Politics of Electoral College Reform.* 1972.

JAMES CEASER

**ELECTRONIC SURVEILLANCE.** Government wiretapping for law-enforcement purposes began to become controversial in the early twentieth century. Not until 1928, however, did the Supreme Court decide whether government interception of telephone communications with no authorization from the courts or Congress violated the Fourth Amendment's limitations on searches and seizures. The Court in OLMSTEAD V. UNITED STATES (1928) held that communications over telephone lines were not tangible and did not constitute property protected by the Constitution. It maintained this position for almost forty years. Further developments narrowed the permissible scope and utility of electronic surveillance techniques, but *Olmstead* essentially left the development of electronic surveillance law to executive practice and congressional deliberation.

Congress inquired into executive practices periodically, and the Federal Communications Act of 1934 made it unlawful to intercept any interstate or foreign wire or radio communication and "divulge or publish" its contents. The Supreme Court ruled in *Nardone v. United States* (1937) that this statute barred using evidence at a criminal trial if it had been obtained from wiretaps. A later ruling, *Nardone v. United States* (1939), also barred any evidence that resulted from using information obtained by wiretaps.

The executive branch interpreted these decisions as barring the interception *and* disclosure of communications, not prohibiting the interception of communications. Thus, executive-branch policy continued to allow electronic surveillance so long as information obtained was not used in evidence.

The Supreme Court first indicated concern regarding its electronic-surveillance decisions in *Goldman v. United States* (1942). Then, in *Silverman v. United States* (1961), the Court recognized that conversations could be "seized" and that their acquisition from a private area could require a warrant even where officials did not enter.

Finally, in *Berger v. United States* (1967), regarding state practices, and KATZ V. UNITED STATES (1967), regarding federal activities, the Supreme Court held that the Fourth Amendment applies to electronic surveillance of telephone communications for law-enforcement purposes and that prior judicial approval is required in most circumstances. The *Katz* test for determining whether the Fourth Amendment applies is whether there exists a "reasonable expectation of privacy," that is, whether the communicant expects the communication to be private and whether society will respect that expectation in the circumstances.

Congress reacted by enacting Title III of the Omnibus Crime Control and Safe Streets Act of 1968, which established a detailed procedure for obtaining a court order before using microphones, wiretapping, and other forms of electronic surveillance to obtain evidence. A judge must determine that there is probable cause to believe certain crimes have been or are about to be committed. The target is notified not more than ninety days after the denial of a request or termination of the surveillance, although delays can be approved.

This statute was broadened by the Electronic Communications Privacy Act of 1986 because of technological developments. The 1986 act's provisions cover electronic mail, computer records, cellular and portable telephones, video teleconferencing, telephone records, paging devices, and beepers. The general rule remains that a prior court order is required to monitor communications with a reasonable expectation of privacy.

Electronic surveillance related to NATIONAL SECURITY has always received exceptional treatment. In 1940 President Franklin D. Roosevelt specifically authorized the Attorney General to use electronic surveillane in "defense of the nation." The federal courts and Congress also have recognized that the Fourth Amendment's warrant clause may not apply to national security–related electronic surveillance.

The *Katz* decision, which required a warrant for law-enforcement surveillance, left open the question whether safeguards other than a prior court order would satisfy the Fourth Amendment in a situation involving national security. Justice Byron White emphasized this reservation and expressed his view that no warrant should be required where the President or Attorney General authorized electronic surveillance in the interests of national security.

In enacting the 1968 wiretap law, Congress had explained it was not altering the President's constitutional power to protect national security. Also, information acquired under that authority could be used as evidence if the interception was "reasonable." This presidential power was narrowed when the Supreme Court determined in UNITED STATES v. UNITED STATES DISTRICT COURT (1972) that warrantless electronic surveillance is unconstitutional when the target is a domestic organization and the purpose is maintaining internal security, not gathering foreign intelligence about foreign powers or their agents. The 1968 wiretap law did not authorize warrantless national-security surveillance or admit that the President could do so but only recognized that the President claimed such power. The Court did not decide whether prior judicial review is required when surveillance of foreign powers or their agents is undertaken.

The lower federal courts have explained the practical difficulties of requiring a prior court order for such cases. For example, the Third Circuit Court of Appeals recognized in *United States v. Butenko* (1974) that requiring officials conducting electronic surveillance of foreign powers for foreign intelligence purposes to interrupt their operations and "rush to the nearest magistrate" to protect the privacy of a United States citizen would be disruptive.

Thus, the Fourth Amendment allows the President, exercising constitutional power to conduct foreign affairs and direct the armed forces, or, under *United States v. Ehrlichman* (1976) the Attorney General when the President delegates that power, to authorize electronic surveillance directed against a foreign power or its agents for foreign intelligence purposes.

From 1940 until 1978, the Attorney General acted for the President to authorize such activities. The basis for this action was not always clear. Since 1976, the President's authority has been delegated to the Attorney General in public EXECUTIVE ORDERS, and under Executive Order 12333, the Attorney General may approve surveillance for foreign-intelligence purposes against a "United States person" abroad where a warrant would be required if the same activity were conducted for law-enforcement purposes. In such cases, the Attorney General is acting in the place of a judge and applies legal principles developed in the law-enforcement area as a guide.

In 1978 Congress enacted the FOREIGN INTELLIGENCE SURVEILLANCE ACT (FISA) requiring that all electronic surveillance of targets within the United States for foreign-intelligence purposes be approved by the Attorney General and, in most cases, authorized by specially designated federal district court judges. Even in designing a judicial role in foreign-intelligence surveillance, Congress included unique national-security features. For example, the Attorney General may approve such surveillance without judicial review when the targeted communications are between foreign powers and are unlikely to involve United States persons. Further, Congress made clear that FISA does not apply to electronic surveillance against foreign-intelligence targets outside the United States. Standards and procedures for overseas surveillance may be different from those that apply within the United States.

Abroad, therefore, electronic surveillance for foreign-intelligence purposes remains subject to approval by the Attorney General where the Fourth Amendment would require a warrant if the activity were undertaken for law-enforcement purposes. Executive-branch policy requires Attorney General approval for such surveillance abroad only when directed against United States citizens, permanent resident aliens, groups largely composed of such persons, and United States corporations. This standard has been found to be lawful in *United States v. Hawamda* (1988).

Under United States law, no approval is necessary for such activities when directed against foreign nationals abroad since, as recognized in *Berlin Democratic Club v. Rumsfeld* (1976), the Fourth Amendment has never been read to require a warrant for law-enforcement surveillance in such circumstances. The Supreme Court has held in *United States v. Verdugo-Urquidez* (1990), that the Fourth Amendment does not limit United States government law-enforcement searches directed at aliens and their property abroad even if the foreign national is in the custody of the United States at the time.

### BIBLIOGRAPHY

Brown, William F., and Americo Cinquegrana. "Warrantless Physical Searches for Foreign Intelligence Purposes: Executive Order 12333 and the Fourth Amendment." *Catholic University Law Review* 35 (1985): 97.

Cinquegrana, Americo. "The Walls (and Wires) Have Ears: The Background and First Ten Years of the Foreign Intelligence Surveillance Act of 1978." *University of Pennsylvania Law Review* 137 (1989): 793.

"Developments in the Law—The National Security Interest and Civil Liberties." *Harvard Law Review* 85 (1972): 1130.

"The Foreign Intelligence Surveillance Act: Legislating a Judicial Role in National Security Surveillance." Note. *Michigan Law Review* 78 (1980): 1116.

"Foreign Security Surveillance and the Fourth Amendment." Note. *Harvard Law Review* 87 (1974): 976.

Gasque, Aubrey. "Wiretapping: A History of Federal Legislation and Supreme Court Decisions." *South Carolina Law Review* 15 (1963): 593.

AMERICO R. CINQUEGRANA

**EMANCIPATION PROCLAMATION.** The proclamation was a presidential order freeing the slaves in areas in rebellion against the United States. Although Abraham Lincoln considered himself "naturally antislavery" and could not remember when he "did not so think, and feel," he entered office believing that the Constitution bound him not to interfere with SLAVERY where it already existed. When General JOHN C. FRÉMONT issued a proclamation on 30 August 1861, freeing the slaves of rebels in Missouri, Lincoln revoked it. "Can it be pretended," Lincoln asked on 22 September, "that it is any longer the government of the U.S.—any government of Constitution and laws,—wherein a General, or a President, may make permanent rules of property by proclamation?"

One year after denouncing Frémont's proclamation as "dictatorship," Lincoln announced his own proclamation. He had changed his mind about both principle and policy in that year, but Lincoln had, at the time of Frémont's proclamation, already come some distance on the constitutional question. "I do not say," Lincoln then wrote, "Congress might not with propriety pass a law . . . just such as General Frémont proclaimed. I do not say I might not, as a member of Congress, vote for it. What I object to, is, that I as President, shall expressly or impliedly seize and exercise the permanent legislative functions of the government."

Lincoln's mind had to travel farther in regard to policy. Early in the war he feared that antislavery measures might drive the loyal slave states, especially Kentucky, into the Confederacy, but when Union military campaigns in the East failed in the spring of 1862, Lincoln determined that to win the war he must "change . . . tactics" and lay "a strong hand on the colored element." He made the decision alone, wrote the first draft of the proclamation in secret, and presented it to his Cabinet on 22 July as a decided policy. Lincoln ignored Montgomery Blair's objection that it would hurt Republicans in the fall elections but heeded WILLIAM H. SEWARD's plea to await a military victory so it would not look like a desperation measure.

While Lincoln waited, he provided the public occasional misleading signals, including his reply on 22 August to a *New York Tribune* editorial written by HORACE GREELEY. "My paramount object . . . *is* to save the Union," Lincoln said, "and is *not* either to save or to destroy slavery. If I could save the Union without freeing *any* slave I would do it, and if I could save it by freeing *all* the slaves I would do it; and if I could save it by freeing some and leaving others alone I would also do that." Lincoln's words disappointed antislavery advocates and insulted black people, but a close reader might have noticed that he expressed no doubts about his constitutional power to abolish slavery.

On 22 September 1862, five days after the Battle of Antietam, Lincoln issued a preliminary Emancipation Proclamation, threatening to free the slaves of persons in states or parts of states still in rebellion one hundred days hence. He based the document on his powers as COMMANDER IN CHIEF.

By chance, the hundredth day afterward was 1 January 1863, and Lincoln signed the final proclamation after the traditional White House New Year's Day reception. Revisions of the preliminary text had eliminated a foreign-policy gaffe in the document, which, in discontinuing enforcement of the Fugitive Slave Act, had sounded like an invitation to servile insurrection. The final document also explicitly endorsed the acceptance of freedmen in the Union armed forces.

Lincoln may have doubted the document's legality but not its wisdom—hence his work in 1864 for the Thirteenth Amendment to the Constitution, which would guarantee slavery's end no matter what the Supreme Court might say about the proclamation.

### BIBLIOGRAPHY

Franklin, John Hope. *The Emancipation Proclamation.* 1963.

MARK E. NEELY, JR.

**EMBARGO ACTS** (1807–1809). At the end of the first decade of the nineteenth century, the world's two mightiest powers, England and France, committed acts against American shipping warranting a DECLARATION OF WAR by the United States. President Thomas Jefferson adopted an alternative to war: economic coercion in the form of an embargo on American trade. The embargo, which lasted fifteen months, from December 1807 until the last day of Jefferson's administration, failed to persuade the European powers to respect American maritime rights in return for a restoration of American trade.

Congress adopted five embargo acts. The second and third covered loopholes in the first and increased penalties for violation. The third also applied to exports by land as well as by sea. The fourth was a drastic force act that carried the administration to the precipice of unlimited and arbitrary powers, concentrating powers in the President in an unprecedented way, employing the navy for enforcement purposes, and disregarding the Fourth Amendment's protections against unreasonable searches and seizures. The President personally administered some provisions of the acts on a daily basis, although his Secretary of the Treasury, ALBERT GALLATIN, supervised enforcement.

Organized resistance spread because of the economic injury inflicted on Americans by the embargo caused. Jefferson proclaimed the existence of an insurrection in Vermont near Lake Champlain and called out state militias. By mid 1808 Gallatin advised that "arbitrary powers" that were "dangerous and

odious" must be employed to make the embargo work, and Jefferson insisted that Congress "must legalize all *means* which may be necessary to obtain its *end.*" One means used by the administration was prosecution for treason, but a stinging opinion by U.S. Supreme Court Justice Brockholst Livingston, a Jefferson appointee, censured the administration's dangerous misuse of that charge. Another Jefferson appointee, Justice William Johnson, ruled that the President's detaining of shipments exceeded his statutory authority.

Undaunted, Jefferson obtained a fifth embargo act, authorizing the use of the armed forces to enforce the embargo, the only time in American history that the President was empowered to use the army in time of peace—and against beleaguered American citizens—for day-to-day execution of the laws. The act also authorized seizures on mere suspicion that goods might be intended for export. Collectors ransacked homes, businesses, ships, and wagons seeking incriminating evidence and seizing suspect property without due process of law. The fifth embargo act remains as repressive and unconstitutional as any legislation ever enacted by Congress in time of peace. And no other peacetime President has ever sought or received so vast a concentration of powers at the expense of provisions of the Bill of Rights. Civil disorders continued, however, and the embargo policy was a complete failure, both as a domestic measure and as a means of coercing England and France. Leaving the presidency, Jefferson contemplated retirement as if he were a "prisoner, released from his chains." The country felt the same.

### BIBLIOGRAPHY

Levy, Leonard W. *Jefferson and Civil Liberties: The Darker Side.* 1963.
Spivak, Burton. *Jefferson's English Crisis: Commerce, Embargo, and the Republican Revolution.* 1979.

LEONARD W. LEVY

**EMERGENCIES, NATIONAL.** See EMERGENCY POWERS; NATIONAL EMERGENCIES ACT.

**EMERGENCY BANKING ACT** (1933). The events leading up to the Emergency Banking Act of 1933 began when Michigan's governor, William A. Comstock, declared an eight-day banking holiday, or closure, on 14 February 1933. By 4 March, the day of Franklin Delano Roosevelt's inauguration, almost every state had declared a holiday or severely restricted banking practices.

On 5 March, President Roosevelt issued two proclamations. The first summoned Congress into special session beginning on 9 March. The second declared a national bank holiday "in order to prevent export, hoarding or earmarking of gold or silver coin or bullion or currency."

Congress convened at noon on 9 March and immediately received a message from Roosevelt and a draft bill that had been prepared by Herbert Hoover's Secretary of the Treasury, Ogden L. Mills, and Roosevelt's Secretary of the Treasury, William Woodin. The bill went through Congress at record speed. By 8:36 that evening, President Roosevelt signed the Emergency Banking Act of 1933. Two hours later he issued a proclamation extending the bank holiday indefinitely.

The act had five basic provisions. Title I validated the banking holiday. Congress confirmed that the authorization to close the banks was included in the 1917 Trading-with-the-Enemy Act. Additionally, it expanded the power of the President to regulate member banks of the Federal Reserve. Title II entitled "Bank Conservation Act" established guidelines for opening banks with impaired assets. Title III authorized the sale of preferred stock to the public or the RECONSTRUCTION FINANCE CORPORATION in order to increase capital. Title IV broadened the Federal Reserve Act. Title V appropriated $2 million dollars for the execution of the act.

The act proved to be successful as recovery from the crisis was rapid and efficient. Of the banks that reopened under the Emergency Banking Act only nine national and six state members suspended operations by the end of 1933. Further modifications in banking would be made throughout 1933 including the Robinson-Steagall Act and the Banking Act of 1933.

### BIBLIOGRAPHY

Burns, Helen M. *The American Banking Community and New Deal Banking Reforms, 1933–1935.* 1974.
Colt, C. C., and N. S. Keith. *28 Days: A History of the Banking Crisis.* 1933.
Kennedy, Susan Estabrook. *The Banking Crisis of 1933.* 1973.

JEFFREY D. SCHULTZ

**EMERGENCY POWERS.** In the context of the U.S. governmental system, emergency powers are those authorities and controls—deriving in varying degrees from the Constitution, the statutes, or a concept of EXECUTIVE PREROGATIVE—used to address an emergency. While there can be varying understandings of what constitutes an emergency, its characteristics generally are sudden and unforseen occurrence, endangerment of life and well-being, and require-

ment of an immediate response, which rule and law may not always provide. In the midst of the crisis of the Great Depression, the majority opinion of the Supreme Court in *Home Building and Loan Association v. Blaisdell* (1934), for example, described an emergency in terms of urgency and relative infrequency of incidence as well as equivalence to a public calamity resulting from fire, flood, or like disaster not reasonably subject to anticipation.

**The Political Theory of Emergency Powers.** The necessity of having some special arrangements to preserve a state in the face of an emergency has long been recognized in political theory. Almost five centuries ago, the Italian political realist Niccolo Machiavelli warned in his *Discourses on Titus Livy* of the necessity for republics, when in imminent danger, to have recourse to dictatorship or some form of authority analogous to it to avoid ruin. Similarly, the seventeenth-century English philosopher, John Locke—a preeminent exponent of government by law and not by men—argued in his *Second Treatise of Civil Government* that occasions may arise when the executive must exert a broad discretion in meeting special exigencies or "emergencies" for which the legislative power has provided no relief and existing law grants no necessary remedy.

*The Founders.* During the course of the CONSTITUTIONAL CONVENTION of 1787, emergency powers, as such, failed to attract much attention. In its aftermath, ALEXANDER HAMILTON addressed one obvious emergency issue in FEDERALIST 23. There he argued against "constitutional shackles" on "authorities essential to the care of the common defense" because, in his view, "it is impossible to foresee or to define the extent and variety of national exigencies, and the correspondent extent and variety of the means which may be necessary to satisfy them." It appears, however, that little else was offered on the matter of emergencies by Hamilton or his *Federalist* coauthors. Nonetheless, the Constitution does contain some obvious emergency powers, such as congressional authority to declare war or call forth the militia to execute the laws, suppress insurrections, and repel invasions; congressional power to suspend habeas corpus when public safety is endangered by rebellion or invasion; presidential authority to call special sessions of Congress; and the guarantee to the states of protection against invasion or domestic violence. These are explicit or enumerated constitutional powers that have pertinence for a condition of emergency.

Through the tradition of interpretive derivation of implied constitutional authority have come other emergency powers. From time to time, for example,

Presidents have relied generally upon the COMMANDER IN CHIEF clause or the FAITHFUL EXECUTION CLAUSE to exercise police powers relative to an emergency.

**Statutory grants of power.** Apart from the Constitution but resulting from its prescribed procedures and provisions of legislative authority, there are statutory grants of power—both explicit and implied—for emergency conditions. Sometimes these laws are only temporary, such as the ECONOMIC STABILIZATION ACT (1970), which mandated presidential imposition of wage and price controls for about three years before it eventually expired in 1974.

Many of these laws, however, are permanent and readily available for presidential use in responding to an emergency. The Defense Production Act (1950), for example, gives the executive authority for prioritizing and regulating the manufacture of military goods and material. Others have been enacted on a stand-by basis and delegate to the President certain powers that become available with a formal declaration of the existence of a national emergency.

**Prerogative.** Finally, Presidents have occasionally exercised powers in response to an emergency by relying on a concept of EXECUTIVE PREROGATIVE. Locke had counseled that the executive, faced with an emergency for which neither the legislature nor available law afforded counteraction, must exert a broad discretion in responding. Assertion of independent prerogative in this regard was sufficient if the exercise might advance the "public good." Theodore Roosevelt's STEWARDSHIP THEORY of the presidency was consistent with Locke's concept of executive prerogative. In his *Autobiography* (1913) the former Chief Executive contended that it was not only the President's right "but his duty to do anything that the needs of the Nation demanded unless such action was forbidden by the Constitution or by the laws."

A rather different understanding of executive prerogative in time of emergency guided the actions of President Abraham Lincoln. By the time of his inauguration, seven states of the lower South had announced their secession; the Confederate provisional government had been established; JEFFERSON DAVIS had been elected and installed as president of the Confederacy; and an army was being mobilized by the secessionists. When Lincoln assumed office, Congress was not in session. He delayed calling a special meeting of the legislature and ventured into its constitutional domain. Without making a DECLARATION OF WAR or asking for one, he took the legally suspect step of blockading the ports of the secessionist states, ordered the addition of nineteen vessels to the navy, extended the blockade, and ordered increases in armed forces

personnel. In his July message to the newly assembled Congress, Lincoln suggested that his recent emergency actions, "whether strictly legal or not, were ventured upon under what appeared to be a popular and a public necessity, trusting then, as now, that Congress would readily ratify them. It is believed," he wrote, "that nothing has been done beyond the constitutional competency of Congress." Congress did, indeed, give its approval, and did so again concerning some other questionable emergency actions. Clearly, the President had made a quick unilateral response to the emergency at hand—the rebellion and SECESSION of the Southern states. Congress, for reasons of partisan politics and popular approval, gave post factum sanction to these assertions of executive prerogative, as Lincoln had anticipated.

Partisan political controversy arose concerning emergency actions taken by Presidents Woodrow Wilson and Franklin D. Roosevelt. Both men exercised extensive emergency powers with regard to world hostilities; Roosevelt also used emergency authority to deal with the Great Depression. Their emergency actions, however, were largely supported by statutory delegations and a high degree of public approval.

**Proclamations.** Furthermore, it was during the Wilson and Roosevelt presidencies that a major procedural change came about in the exercise of emergency powers—the use of a PROCLAMATION to declare a national emergency, which activated all stand-by statutory provisions that delegated authority to the President during such an emergency. The first such proclamation was issued by President Wilson in February 1917 (39 Stat. 1814), pursuant to a statute establishing the United States Shipping Board (39 Stat. 728). It was statutorily terminated along with a variety of other wartime measures in March 1921 (41 Stat. 1359).

The next such proclamations were promulgated by Roosevelt with regard to the Great Depression and the oncoming war. A March 1933 proclamation declared the famous "bank holiday" (48 Stat. 1689), which closed banks until they were certified that they were able to comply with the new emergency banking law (48 Stat. 1).

Later, in September 1939, Roosevelt declared a "limited" national emergency, though the qualifying term really was legally insignificant (54 Stat. 2643). Almost two years later, in May 1941, he issued a proclamation of "unlimited" national emergency (55 Stat. 1647). While it did not make any significant new powers available, it served to apprise the American people symbolically of the worsening conflict in Europe and growing tensions in Asia.

Both the war-related proclamations remained operative until 1947, when certain of the provisions of law they had activated were statutorily rescinded (61 Stat. 449). After Congress terminated the declaration of war against Germany in 1951 (65 Stat. 451) and a treaty of peace with Japan was ratified the following year, legislation was required to keep certain emergency provisions in effect (66 Stat. 54, 96, 137, 296, and 330; 67 Stat. 18 and 131). President Harry S. Truman terminated the 1939 and 1941 proclamations in April 1952 (66 Stat. c 31), supposedly leaving operative those emergency authorities continued by statutory specification.

Truman's 1952 termination, however, specifically exempted a December 1950 proclamation of national emergency, which he had issued in response to hostilities in the KOREAN WAR (64 Stat. A454). Furthermore, two other national-emergency proclamations resulted before Congress once again returned to these matters. Faced with a postal strike, President Richard M. Nixon declared a national emergency in March 1970, which permitted him to use ready reserve military units to move the mail (84 Stat. 2222). He issued another proclamation in August 1971 to control balance-of-payments difficulties by temporarily suspending certain trade agreement provisos and imposing supplemental duties on some imported goods (85 Stat. 926).

**Controlling Emergency Powers.** In the years following the conclusion of U.S. armed forces' involvement in active conflict in Korea, expressions of concern regarding the continued existence of Truman's 1950 national-emergency proclamation, long after actual conditions prompting its issuance had disappeared, were occasionally heard in Congress. There was some annoyance that the President retained extraordinary delegated powers intended only for times of genuine emergency, and there was a feeling that the continued failure of the Chief Executive to terminate the declared national emergency was thwarting the legislative intent of Congress. However, no immediate corrective action was taken.

*Congressional interest.* Several years later, growing public and congressional displeasure with presidential exercise of war powers and deepening U.S. involvement in hostilities in the VIETNAM WAR prompted interest in a variety of related matters. One of these was the exercise of statutory emergency powers that remained available to the President as a consequence of the unrescinded 1950 national-emergency proclamation. In response, the Senate created a special committee to study and investigate the termination of this proclamation and "to consider problems which might arise as the result of the termination and to consider what administrative or legislative actions might be necessary." Initially chartered in June 1972 as the Special Committee on the Termination of the National Emergency, the panel did not begin operations before the end of the year.

Reconstituted by the 93d Congress in 1973, the panel soon found its mission to be more complex and more burdensome than its creators had originally thought it would be. Staff research revealed that there was not just one proclamation of national emergency in effect but four—those issued in 1933, 1950, 1970, and 1971. The country was in a condition of national emergency four times over, and with each proclamation, the whole collection of statutorily delegated emergency powers was activated. Consequently, in 1974, the study panel was rechartered as the Special Committee on National Emergencies and Delegated Emergency Powers.

The panel produced several studies, including one identifying 470 provisions of federal law delegating extraordinary authority to the executive in time of national emergency. Not all of them required a declaration of national emergency to become operative, but they were, nevertheless, extraordinary grants. Furthermore, there was no ready procedure for terminating the four outstanding national-emergency proclamations. Consequently, the panel began developing corrective legislation for the situation. The resulting reform bill was unanimously recommended in a July 1974 committee report and was introduced in the Senate by the panel's chairman late in the following month. Scheduling complications in the House, however, delayed consideration of the measure; it was reintroduced in the next Congress in early 1975. Eventually, the legislation received final congressional approval during this summer of 1976 and was signed into law in September by President Gerald Ford.

*Legislation.* As enacted, the NATIONAL EMERGENCIES ACT (90 Stat. 1255) generally returned all stand-by statutory delegations of emergency power activated by an outstanding declaration of national emergency to a dormant state two years after the date of the law's approval. The statute did not actually cancel the 1933, 1950, 1970, and 1971 emergency proclamations because of their issuance by the President pursuant to Article II of the Constitution. Nevertheless, it rendered them ineffective by returning to dormancy the stand-by statutory authorities they had made operational, thereby necessitating a new declaration for any reactivation. Also, some provisions of emergency law were amended and others were repealed.

According to the procedural provisions of the act, the President, when declaring a national emergency, must specify the stand-by authorities he is activating. Congress may negate this action with a resolution disapproving the emergency declaration or the activation of a particular statutory power. The statute was amended in 1985 (99 Stat. 448) to require the use of a joint resolution in this regard, which must be approved through the constitutionally provided legislative process. Originally, a so-called LEGISLATIVE VETO could be effected with a concurrent resolution approved by both chambers of Congress. Any national-emergency declaration that is not previously terminated by the President or Congress expires automatically on the anniversary date of the declaration, unless the President, within the ninety-day period prior to each anniversary date, gives notice to Congress and in the *Federal Register* that the emergency is to continue in effect. The act also sets certain reporting and accounting requirements for each national emergency declaration.

**Aftermath.** In the years immediately following the enactment of the National Emergencies Act, a few emergency-powers statutes were modified, but no sweeping changes were made. One of the most ambitious of these was the division of the President's international economic regulatory authority between the Trading with the Enemy Act of 1917 and the new International Emergency Economic Powers Act of 1977 (91 Stat. 1626).

In subsequent years, several matters identified in the Senate special committee's final report received slight congressional attention. These included investigation of emergency-preparedness efforts conducted by the executive branch, attention to congressional preparations for an emergency and continual review of emergency law, halting open-ended grants of authority to the executive, investigation and institution of stricter controls over delegated powers, and improving the accountability of executive decision making.

The procedures of the National Emergencies Act were first used for a presidential declaration of national emergency in 1979. In November, President Jimmy Carter issued Executive Order 12170 blocking the Iranian government's access to its property within U.S. jurisdiction in response to the seizure of American citizens as hostages in Teheran during the IRANIAN HOSTAGE CRISIS. Five months later, Carter issued Executive Order 12211, which declared another national emergency and set further prohibitions on economic and commercial transactions with Iran. Similar emergency declarations were made in 1985 regarding Nic-

aragua (E.O. 12513) and South Africa (E.O. 12532), in 1986 regarding Libya (E.O. 12543), in 1988 regarding PANAMA (E.O. 12635), in 1990 regarding Iraq (E.O. 12722), and in 1991 regarding HAITI (E.O. 12775). National emergencies also were declared in 1980 (E.O. 12211), 1983 (E.O. 12444), and 1990 (E.O. 12735) to continue export-control regulations when the Export Administration Act, failing to be congressionally reauthorized, automatically expired. Finally, in November 1990, President George Bush declared a national emergency (E.O. 12735) with regard to the international proliferation of chemical and biological weapons. Generally, Congress concurred in these actions. Thus, while the presidential exercise of emergency powers is somewhat more regulated as a consequence of the National Emergencies Act, a variety of functional and geographic crises continue to be addressed.

## BIBLIOGRAPHY

Rankin, Robert S., and Winfried R. Dallmayr. *Freedom and Emergency Powers in the Cold War.* 1964.

Rossiter, Clinton L. *Constitutional Dictatorship.* 1963.

Smith, J. Malcolm, and Cornelius P. Cotter. *Powers of the President During Crisis.* 1960.

U.S. Senate. Special Committee on National Emergencies and Delegated Emergency Powers. *A Brief History of Emergency Powers in the United States.* 93d Cong., 2d sess., 1974. Committee Print.

U.S. Senate. *National Emergencies and Delegated Emergency Powers.* 94th Cong., 2d sess., 1976. S. Rept. 94–922.

U.S. Senate. Special Committee on the Termination of the National Emergency. *Emergency Powers Statutes.* 93d Cong., 1st sess., 1973. S. Rept. 93–549.

HAROLD C. RELYEA

**EMPLOYMENT ACT** (1946). A few months after the end of World War II, Congress enacted the Employment Act of 1946, which ushered in a new era in the making of economic policy for presidential administrations and for Congress. In the later stages of the war, many government officials, economists, and labor and business leaders directed their attention to the nation's ability to make the transition from a wartime to a peacetime economy. There was widespread concern that the economy might well revert to its poor performance of the 1930s as a result of sharp cutbacks in war production, layoffs of millions of war workers, and the discharge of about 10 million men and women from military service, which would greatly swell the army of workers seeking jobs in the civilian sector.

Given this outlook, President Roosevelt set the stage for a new formulation of national economic policy when he said in January 1944 that every American has "the right to a useful and remunerative job." In essence, he pledged, full employment of manpower and resources would become a major focal point of economic policy in a peacetime economy.

Because of wartime restrictions on the production and consumption of consumer goods and on the construction of housing and a corresponding reduction in plant capacity for the production of civilian goods, there existed considerable pent-up demand for a wide variety of consumer goods and services. For a while this demand would undoubtedly spur the economy, but many economists still had serious reservations about the nation's ability to avoid a recession after its immediate needs were met.

Though a strong free market economy remained the central policy goal, many believed the government would have to play an important role in promoting economic growth and full employment. In a campaign speech given on 21 September 1944, the Republican presidential candidate, Thomas E. Dewey, stated: "If at any time there are not sufficient jobs in private employment to go around, the government can and must create job opportunities, because there must be jobs for all in this country."

On 22 January 1945, Sen. James Murray (D-Mont.) introduced the Full Employment Act of 1945. It declared that "all Americans able to work and seeking work are entitled to an opportunity for useful, remunerative, regular, and full-time employment" in any field of work. Moreover, the bill stated that "the federal government has the responsibility, with the assistance and concerted efforts of industry, agriculture, and labor and state and local government . . . to assure continuing full employment." If continuing full employment could not be maintained solely by the efforts of the private sector of the economy, the federal government would provide "such volume of federal investment and expenditures as may be needed to assure full employment."

Following House and Senate consideration, major changes were made in the wording of the legislation, and its title was changed from the Full Employment Act to the Employment Act of 1946 (P.L. 79-304). The act, as finally passed on 20 February 1946, did not contain a declaration of the right to employment opportunity or of the federal responsibility for maintaining full employment. Instead, the act declared that it is the continuing policy and responsibility of the federal government "to pursue all practicable means . . . to promote maximum employment, production, and purchasing power."

To carry out this new mandate, the act requires the President to submit to Congress an annual Economic Report outlining the policies and programs the President wishes to follow in meeting the declared policy objectives of the act. To assist and advise the President in his conduct of economic policy, the act created a three-member Council of Economic Advisers.

The act also established a new joint congressional committee, the Joint Economic Committee on the Economic Report (better known as the Joint Economic Committee). This committee, composed of ten members of the House and ten members of the Senate, holds hearings on the Economic Report of the President and (1) makes "a continuing study of matters related to the Economic Report," (2) studies "means of coordinating [federal] programs in order to further the policy of this act," and (3) files a report with the Senate and House of Representatives "containing its findings and recommendations with respect to each of the main recommendations by the President in the Economic Report." Over the years, the committee has also held hearings and sponsored economic studies on a wide variety of policy issues and economic matters of concern to a broad spectrum of interests.

Though many proponents of the original Full Employment Act concept were disappointed with the final statutory language, it was generally agreed that the act's passage by Congress marked an important milestone in the nation's economic history. For the first time, Congress explicitly recognized that the government could no longer play a passive role in the economic life of the nation.

No major changes were made in the act until 1978. During the second half of the 1970s the nation faced several difficult economic problems: sluggish economic growth, exceedingly high unemployment, persistent inflation, and a worsening trade balance. In seeking to address these problems, Congress (following several years of debate) enacted the Full Employment and Balanced Growth Act of 1978 (P.L. 95-523), which amended and substantially changed the scope and goals of the Employment Act of 1946.

This new legislation, popularly known as the Humphrey-Hawkins Act, declared that it is the responsibility of the federal government, in cooperation with private enterprise, to pursue policies and programs that would most effectively promote full employment, ensure balanced economic growth, achieve adequate growth in productivity, increase real income, give proper attention to national priorities, achieve a balanced budget, improve the nation's trade balance, and achieve reasonable price stability. The law requires the President to establish five-year numerical goals for employment, unemployment, production, real income, productivity, and prices. These projections are to be contained in each annual Economic Report submitted to Congress. Humphrey-Hawkins also required the President's budget to include the economic goals set forth in the Economic Report.

The act specified a goal of reducing the unemployment rate to 4 percent by 1983 (compared to 6.1 percent in 1978). After this goal was achieved, each succeeding Economic Report of the President was to "have the goal of achieving as soon as practicable and maintaining thereafter full employment and a balanced budget." The act specified that the inflation rate should be reduced to a level of not more than 3 percent by 1983 (compared to 9 percent in 1978). Thereafter, it was to be reduced to 0 percent, provided that the policies and programs followed for reducing the rate did not impede the goal of promoting full employment. The act, however, allows the President to recommend modifications in the timetables for achieving these goals for unemployment and inflation.

Among other provisions, the act for the first time required the Federal Reserve Board to report to Congress twice a year on its monetary policies and how they relate to the goals of the act. At the time, monetary policy was considered the most potent tool available to the government in combating economic problems, especially high inflation. Humphrey-Hawkins also mandates that the semiannual report set forth the Fed's objectives and plans with regard to the target ranges it sets for the growth in the supply of money and credit and that it consider how these objectives and plans relate to the short-term goals set forth in the most recent Economic Report of the President and any short-terms goals approved by the Congress.

The results of Humphrey-Hawkins have been mixed. The unemployment rate rose sharply from about 6 percent in 1978 to more than 10 percent in 1982. Afterward it declined steadily to a level of 5.3 percent in 1989 but increased again to more than 7.4 percent in 1992. Inflation, following a steep acceleration to double-digit levels from 1978 through 1981, improved significantly in the first half of the 1980s. After reaching a low of about 2 percent in 1986, the rate rose again to much higher levels in the remainder of the decade and ranged between 3 and 5 percent annually during the early 1990s. Finally, the Carter, Reagan, and Bush administrations were not successful in balancing the budget during the 1980s and early 1990s, as envisioned by the Humphrey-Hawkins Act. Though the deficit was the subject of intense political debate, it remained exceedingly large throughout this period.

BIBLIOGRAPHY

Bailey, Stephen Kemp. *Congress Makes a Law: The Story behind the Employment Act of 1946.* 1980.
Knight, Edward. "Economic Policy and Inflation in the United States: A Survey of Developments from the Enactment of the Employment Act of 1946 through 1974." In *Studies in Price Stability and Economic Growth.* Prepared for the use of the Joint Economic Committee, Congress of the United States. 1975.
Norton, Hugh S. *The Employment Act and the Council of Economic Advisers, 1946–76.* 1977.
United States Congress. Joint Economic Committee. *A Symposium on the 40th Anniversary of the Joint Economic Committee.* Hearings, 99th Cong., 1st sess., 1986.
United States Congress. Joint Economic Committee. *Thirtieth Anniversary of the Employment Act of 1946—A National Conference on Full Employment.* Hearings, 94th Cong., 2d sess., 1976.

EDWARD KNIGHT

**ENERGY, DEPARTMENT OF.** On 1 October 1977 the Department of Energy (DOE) became the twelfth Cabinet-level agency, fulfilling President Carter's campaign promise to bring together the patchwork of existing federal energy programs and to implement a more concerted national energy policy. America's fragmented energy policy was a legacy of the government's traditional focus on, and limited intervention in, markets for specific energy resources. However, a broader concept of energy policy began to emerge in the early 1970s as the nation recognized that its energy resources were limited. The Arab oil embargo in 1973–1974 and the natural gas shortages of 1976–1977 shocked energy markets, disrupted daily life, and riveted the nation's attention on the "energy crisis."

**Creation.** The creation of DOE was a major step in a succession of federal responses to the crisis. As an outgrowth of President Nixon's efforts to coordinate federal energy policy and to respond to the embargo, Congress created the Federal Energy Administration (FEA) to address what many thought was a temporary crisis. After the oil embargo was lifted in March 1974, President Ford approved the creation of the Energy Research and Development Administration (ERDA), brining together parts of the ATOMIC ENERGY COMMISSION (AEC), the DEPARTMENT OF THE INTERIOR, and other scattered programs to pursue technological avenues to energy independence. ERDA also inherited the nuclear weapons research and production complex.

In the summer of 1977, Carter's energy reorganization plan eased through the Democratic Congress after the natural gas shortages revived public anxiety over energy. Meanwhile, James Schlesinger, Director of the White House Energy Policy and Planning Of-

*Secretaries of Energy*

| President | Secretary of Energy |
| --- | --- |
| 39 Carter | James R. Schlesinger, 1977–1979 |
| | Charles W. Duncan, 1979–1981 |
| 40 Reagan | James B. Edwards, 1981–1983 |
| | Donald P. Hodel, 1983–1985 |
| | John S. Herrington, 1985–1989 |
| 41 Bush | James Watkins, 1989–1993 |
| 42 Clinton | Hazel R. O'Leary, 1993– |

fice, sought passage of Carter's national energy plan, which was to be implemented by DOE. The plan was a blueprint for increased federal management of energy resources, with an emphasis on conservation. Carter signed the Department of Energy Organization Act on 4 August 1977, creating a new department that would merge ERDA and FEA with energy programs from nine other departments or commissions. Schlesinger, who as AEC chairperson under Nixon had expanded research into broader energy fields, became the first Secretary of Energy. Rather than follow patterns set by the organizations inherited by DOE, Schlesinger structured the core DOE offices in accordance with Carter's plan to manage energy resources through various developmental stages, from basic research to commercialization. The Energy Information Administration collected and disseminated energy-related data. The nearly autonomous Federal Energy Regulatory Commission inherited the regulatory functions of the Federal Power Commission and shared responsibility for regulating petroleum with the department's Economic Regulatory Administration. The Office of Defense Programs oversaw the nuclear weapons complex and controlled one-third of the department's budget.

Congress was more deliberate and less accommodating in its consideration of Carter's energy policy than it was in establishing DOE. Schlesinger concentrated on working toward passage of Carter's policy and on the difficulties of reshaping existing bureaucracies into a new organization. The National Energy Act of 1978, signed in November, consisted of about half of the program originally proposed by Carter. Two months later Iranian oil exports were cut off, and Americans experienced another disruption of petroleum markets. While Carter renewed his call for stricter conservation measures, gradual decontrol of oil prices, and a windfall profits tax, DOE officials from the Economic Regulatory Administration stepped up efforts to enforce price and allocation controls. As the crisis eased in the summer of 1979, Schlesinger resigned, and Carter named Charles Duncan as the new Secretary of Energy. Duncan abandoned Schlesinger's organizational structure in favor of a more traditional arrangement of DOE offices by fuel or technology. At the close of Carter's term, DOE's emphasis on conservation and energy security was evident in reduced oil consumption and imports.

**The Reagan Administration.** President Reagan promised to abolish DOE, reduce government intervention in energy markets, and strengthen the nation's security. The efforts of his first Energy Secretary, James Edwards, to dismantle the department met with congressional resistance. Reagan succeeded in shrinking DOE's involvement in energy markets by implementing further deregulation, eliminating many conservation programs, and cutting back the department's efforts to commercialize new energy technologies. Reagan's focus on NATIONAL SECURITY led to a continued commitment to DOE's research and development of energy technologies and increased funding for the NUCLEAR WEAPONS complex.

Reagan's second Secretary of Energy, Donald Hodel, began a massive research effort in support of the President's SDI (STRATEGIC DEFENSE INITIATIVE). Soon after his confirmation in February 1985, John Herrington, Reagan's third Energy Secretary, focused his attention on the nuclear weapons complex, where he found facilities and environmental problems dating back to the MANHATTAN PROJECT. By late 1988, the nuclear weapons complex had come under intense public criticism. Herrington proposed costly long-term programs to clean up and modernize the complex.

President Bush, Reagan's successor, assured employees that he would not dismantle DOE and appointed James Watkins as the sixth Secretary of Energy. Watkins moved quickly to cultivate "a new culture of accountability" at DOE by stressing its environmental, safety, and health responsibilities. He also established an Office of Environmental Restoration and Waste Management to coordinate clean-up efforts and opened the department to increased oversight by other agencies. Watkins backed off from Herrington's weapons complex modernization plans as the COLD WAR came to end. These efforts to transform the culture and composition of the weapons complex did not entirely overcome bureaucratic inertia and congressional skepticism.

Continued concern for energy security and a growing interest in the environmental impact of energy development led Watkins to draft a national energy strategy based on broad DOE, interagency, and public input. The Persian Gulf crisis brought on by Iraq's invasion of Kuwait in 1990 interrupted this process.

DOE helped stabilize petroleum prices and supplies by providing accurate information about the status of oil supplies and drawing down the Strategic Petroleum Reserve in cooperation with other nations to mitigate the loss of embargoed Iraqi and Kuwaiti oil. When America's leaders considered DOE's national energy strategy after the GULF WAR, they had a renewed concern for the nation's energy security. The strategy sought to encourage cleaner, more efficient energy production and consumption without resorting to renewed federal energy management. Just before the 1992 election, Congress incorporated key elements of Bush's energy strategy in the first comprehensive energy legislation passed in over a decade.

### BIBLIOGRAPHY

Department of Energy. *National Energy Strategy: Powerful Ideas for America.* 1st ed. 1991.
General Accounting Office. *Nuclear Weapons Complex: Major Safety, Environmental, and Reconfiguration Issues Facing DOE.* 1992.
Goodwin, Craufurd D., ed. *Energy Policy in Perspective: Today's Problems, Yesterday's Solutions.* 1980.

BRIAN WELLS MARTIN

**ENTITLEMENTS.** A federal entitlement is a provision of law providing a legal right to payments from the U.S. Treasury. Most entitlements are paid to individuals; some are provided to other (i.e., state or local) governments. Entitlements are a form of "spending authority" for which the funds are not provided in advance by appropriations acts. Most are classified in the federal budget as direct benefit payments to individuals and by the BUDGET ENFORCEMENT ACT of 1990 as direct spending.

The right to payment is typically established in substantive legislation rather than in appropriations acts. Some entitlements (such as SOCIAL SECURITY) are financed by trust funds whose monies become available without current action by Congress. Most, however, require annual appropriations, but Congress must provide sufficient funds to pay the mandated amounts.

Entitlement legislation has two main components: eligibility criteria and payment formulas. The legislation is usually open-ended; it does not specify or limit the total amount to be paid. The total is determined by the number of persons eligible and the payment to which each is entitled. The total is influenced by demographic trends (such as the age structure of the population) and economic conditions (such as the unemployment rate). Many payments are indexed to the inflation rate or other price changes.

Special rules govern the consideration of entitlement legislation in Congress. The principal control is a pay-as-you-go (PAYGO) rule imposed by the 1990 Budget Enforcement Act. PAYGO requires that any increase in entitlement spending due to new legislation be offset by legislation to decrease other entitlements, legislation to increase revenues, or SEQUESTRATION, that is, the automatic cancellation of certain entitlement authority.

Entitlements account for a rising share of federal budget outlays. They amounted to about one-third of total spending in 1970, almost one-half in 1990, and were projected to comprise about 60 percent by the end of the century. Because this trend has been largely determined by economic and demographic conditions, efforts to control the rise in entitlement spending have generally been unsuccessful. During the 1980s, for example, Congress took actions that, by official estimates, pared more than $50 billion from Medicare spending. During that decade, however, Medicare outlays rose from $31 billion to $96 billion.

The federal budget has become principally a means of supporting the income of American households rather than a means of financing federal agencies. Entitlements are the main financial "safety net" for the elderly, low-income persons, and workers who have lost their jobs. The number of recipients is so large that legislation affecting major entitlements can have extraordinary political impact. In the early 1990s, more than 40 million Americans received social security checks, more than 30 million participated in Medicare, and more than 20 million received food stamps.

The rise of entitlements has weakened the budgetary role of the President. During the postwar era, the budget was the means by which the President recommended financial and legislative changes to Congress. While Presidents typically recommended the continuation of most existing programs, they concentrated on spending initiatives financed by the rise in federal revenues. Budgetary debate in Congress generally focused on proposed increases, giving the President a substantial voice in budget policy.

Entitlements, however, gradually robbed the President of incremental budget choice. These expenditures have risen regardless of the fiscal preferences of the President or other demands on the budget. In some years, they have consumed virtually all incremental resources, reducing the President's role to little more than an accounting of the cost of past decisions. Even when a President has sought to counter incremental trends by proposing substantial cutbacks, as Ronald Reagan did in the 1980s, he has had difficulty getting Congress to consider his proposals seriously.

Entitlements also diminish the President's control of budget totals and make it difficult to balance revenues and expenditures. Because of the sensitivity of major entitlements to economic conditions, total spending and the deficit often vary significantly from planned levels.

During the 1980s, the President frequently sought to overcome budgetary weakness by negotiating BUDGET SUMMIT agreements with congressional leaders. But these were rarely successful, because neither the President nor Congress was willing to take forceful action to bring entitlements under control.

### BIBLIOGRAPHY

U.S. Congressional Budget Office. *Mandatory Spending: Trends and Sources of Growth.* 1992.

Weaver, R. Kent. *Automatic Government: The Politics of Indexation.* 1988.

ALLEN SCHICK

**ENVIRONMENTAL POLICY.** Prior to the 1960s, few Americans paid much attention to ecology or to the relationship between humans and nature. Since the beginning of the twentieth century, conservationists had warned the nation about the neglect, abuse, depletion, and monopolization of natural resources, but conservation never become a coherent, broadly based movement. Only a few Presidents—notably the two Roosevelts—incorporated resource issues into their legislative agendas. The environmental movement that swept over the country in the mid sixties generated much greater public concern, but, as with conservation, only a few Presidents exhibited much devotion to environmental issues.

**Conditions after World War II.** The environmental movement grew out of profound changes in American society that occurred in the years following WORLD WAR II. The disposable income of Americans doubled from 1945 to 1970, and the population grew from 131 million in 1940 to 180 million in 1960. The production of houses, autos, and a wide range of appliances dramatically increased, and these products used vast quantities of natural resources and contributed to air, water, and soil pollution. In addition, more and more Americans lived in large cities. For example, from 1950 to 1960, U.S. cities of more than fifty thousand people grew by an average of 65 percent. Cheap gasoline and massive federal subsidies to build interstate highways and finance housing allowed most cities to grow out rather than up; the consequent traffic congestion, smog, urban blight, and other features of modern life made Americans more sensitive to their surroundings. So did technology. One petrochemical company coined the slogan, "Better things for better living through chemistry," and more and more chemicals found their way into the biosphere. But now they could be measured by new devices such as the gas chromatograph, which detected amazingly small traces of toxic or carcinogenic substances. Scientists and politicians had a much harder time deciding how much, if any, of these substances could or should be tolerated as the price of economic prosperity. Moreover, changes in the life-style of middle-class Americans resulted in a redefinition of human health as optimum fitness and longevity, not just the absence of disease.

If any one event characterized the birth of the modern environmental movement, it was the publication of Rachel Carson's *Silent Spring* in 1962—a book that focused the concerns of the early 1960s as well as helped to change them. Carson limited her discussion to the abuse of chemical pesticides and herbicides, particularly DDT. Pesticides, however, were symbolic of a wide range of potential environmental dangers ranging from radioactivity, to lead in gasoline and paint, to smog, to food preservatives. In simple but elegant language, Carson demonstrated that many agricultural chemicals killed birds, cats, and other creatures besides the "target species," and that some poisons persisted in the soil and water for years—insects became resistant long before the chemicals degraded into harmless elements.

Earlier critics had warned about the dangers of pollution and the American penchant for unlimited economic growth. But none had carried such a frightening message. In Carson's book for the first time, a popular writer had fitted human beings into nature in a way that attracted the attention of the American public. Man, Carson warned, was ultimately the most vulnerable of all mammals because DDT became more concentrated in foods at the top of the food chain. She had many other ominous messages: that Americans could not trust the experts they had relied on for so long; that science had been corrupted by the alliance of universities and chemical corporations; that what you could not see *could* hurt you. She warned that while American farmers were addicted to the cultivation of a single crop and maximum productivity, which required heavy reliance on chemicals, diversity was the key to biological health; man's fatal conceit was that he could control nature. Within two years of the book's appearance, forty states restricted the use of DDT, and ultimately it resulted in complete bans or severe limitations on the use of that chemical and a dozen other pesticides and herbicides Carson had described. Her long-range contribution was much more profound; she changed the focus of the policy debate from the use of natural resources to the preservation of human health.

**The Policies of Kennedy and Johnson.** The book had little immediate influence in Washington. Soon after John F. Kennedy assumed the presidency in 1961, he sent a series of messages to Congress recommending specific legislation; one focused on resource policies. Nevertheless, on his agenda, conservation competed unsuccessfully with HEALTH POLICY, EDUCATION POLICY, CIVIL RIGHTS POLICY, economic policy, consumer protection, WELFARE POLICY, and other issues that had more appeal to the voters. Kennedy cared deeply about the preservation of natural beauty, and he supported successful legislation to use the fees paid by those who used federal lands as an additional source of revenue to buy land for three national seashores and other federal reserves. His very effective Secretary of the Interior, STEWART UDALL, noted that Kennedy "knows the issues and recognizes their importance," but he lamented that the President refused to raise those issues himself. Kennedy exercised little leadership beyond selecting dedicated people to run the natural resource agencies and calling the first White House Conference on Conservation in fifty-four years.

Although his presidency was preoccupied with the VIETNAM WAR along with the War on Poverty and civil rights, Lyndon Baines Johnson conceded in his 1971 memoirs that "conservation could no longer be approached in the manner it had been in the time of Theodore Roosevelt." Something had to be done to control "careless technology," as he called it, particularly as that technology choked the environment with the by-products of affluence. In 1959 President Dwight D. Eisenhower had vetoed a water-pollution-control bill on the grounds that the problem was "a uniquely local blight." Kennedy had increased federal aid for the construction of sewage-treatment plants, but both he and Congress had refused to deal directly with the issue of setting water-quality standards. In 1965, however, Johnson recommended a measure to Congress that doubled federal grants for sewage systems but required the states to set minimum standards and permitted the federal government to do so when the states failed to comply. This measure, the Water Quality Act, not only expanded federal authority over water, it was the first statute to set up a federal agency specifically concerned with pollution. (Although the water-quality agency was established in the Department of Health, Education, and Welfare [HEW], many of its functions were subsequently moved to the DEPARTMENT OF THE INTERIOR).

Johnson showed far more interest in the environment than previous Presidents, but the pressure for change came mainly from such environmental groups as the Sierra Club, the Audubon Society, and the Wilderness Society and from the Senate. For example, Senator Edmund Muskie of Maine soon expressed dissatisfaction with the 1965 law and pushed a much more ambitious six-year cleanup program that carried a price tag of $6 billion and that imposed tough national water-quality standards. That effort failed, and while the Clean Water Act of 1966 authorized the President to spend up to $3.5 billion over five years cleaning up the nation's lakes and streams, Johnson and President Richard M. Nixon spent less than one-third of these funds. Similarly, Muskie pushed for stronger air-pollution-control legislation. Opposition to federal air standards was even stronger than opposition to water standards. In January 1967, Johnson proposed legislation mandating national standards and monitoring of air quality, including federal auto-emission-control inspections. But he quickly backed off when sulfur standards prompted strenuous protests from eastern coal-producing states. Although compromise legislation gave the HEW Secretary power to review and modify state-imposed standards, the states were slow to comply. By the end of 1970, only twenty-one states had submitted air-pollution standards, and none had been approved in Washington.

**Nixon's Environmental Policy.** Nixon came to office at the peak of public concern for the environment (1969–1970). By 1969, public opinion polls revealed that environmental protection had become a critical national issue, surpassed in public interest only by the Vietnam War and jobs. During his first year in office, the new President promised the nation an environmental program he described as "the most comprehensive and costly program in this field ever in the nation's history." He enthusiastically supported the 1970 Clean Air Act, which allowed the federal government to set minimum air-quality standards and promised a reduction in auto emissions of 90 percent by 1975. Even though much of Nixon's environmental program was designed to reduce Muskie's public appeal—Muskie was considered his likely opponent in 1972—his conversion to the new cause was suspect. In 1971 Muskie proposed legislation to eliminate the discharge of all pollutants into navigable waters by 1985 in yet another attempt to move away from the inadequate state water-quality standards mandated by the 1965 water law. The proposal also ordered the government to draft federal standards for toxic chemicals and made it permissible to sue violators. Nixon vetoed the legislation, but Congress overrode the veto.

In September 1970, Nixon established the Environmental Protection Agency (EPA) as an independent agency to coordinate antipollution efforts, but he did so in part as an alternative to creating a more powerful Department of Natural Resources and the Environment, which was the course favored by many environmentalists. Moreover, other presidential actions and policies demonstrated scant regard for the environment. Nixon supported construction of the supersonic transport (SST), an airplane that flew much higher than conventional aircraft, even though many scientists warned that it was far too noisy and would damage the ozone layer. The Senate finally killed the project in May 1971. And when Secretary of the Interior Walter Hickel stopped oil drilling on the continental shelf following the great Santa Barbara oil spill of January 1969, and seemed to have second thoughts about construction of the eight hundred-mile-long Alaska pipeline, Nixon fired Hickel late in 1970. The President supported a 1970 law making oil companies liable for cleaning up spills, but that legislation limited corporate liability to $14 million. He also vetoed a 1972 bill that provided more than $24 billion for sewage treatment plants on the grounds that it was inflationary and recommended that the expenditure be cut by 75 percent. By that time, Nixon openly attacked "environmental extremists." "We are not going to allow the environmental issue to be used," he declared, "sometimes falsely and sometimes in a demagogic way, basically to destroy the system."

**The Policies of Ford, Carter, and Reagan.** By 1973, environmental issues no longer seemed as urgent as they had a few years earlier. With suspension of the draft and the withdrawal of troops from Vietnam, new issues, including inflation, "crime in the streets," and an Arab oil embargo, took center stage. When Nixon resigned in 1974 after the WATERGATE AFFAIR, he was replaced by his Vice President, Gerald Ford. Ford, and later Ronald Reagan, believed that, in Ford's words, new regulatory agencies such as the EPA were "stifling American productivity, promoting inefficiency, eliminating competition and even invading personal privacy. Red tape surrounded and almost smothered us." Reagan went even further in his desire to cut taxes and reduce spending on social programs. He had no environmental agenda and no sympathy for environmental issues. His appointee as EPA chief, Anne Gorsuch, proposed an EPA budget only one-fourth the size of that agency's budget during the Carter administration and proved so sympathetic to polluters that Congress launched an investigation that led to her resignation in March 1983. Reagan's Secretary of the Interior, JAMES WATT, a symbol of the "sagebrush rebellion," wanted

to "privatize" the public domain by turning large parts over to the states and selling off timber and minerals at low prices. He also wanted to slash the cost of administering the national parks and open offshore oil lands to drilling. He, too, resigned under fire, and Reagan's attempt to undermine the clean-air-and-water legislation of the sixties and seventies largely failed.

Of all the Presidents since the sixties, Jimmy Carter showed the greatest sensitivity to environmental issues. Carter made the same commitment to deregulation and to curbing government spending as Reagan, but he also supported strengthening antipollution laws, which was done in 1977. In addition, he pushed through Congress a comprehensive (though ultimately largely ineffective) national ENERGY POLICY (1978); he strongly supported a "superfund," which was created in 1980 to provide for the disposal of toxic wastes; and, above all, he reserved more than 150 million acres of Alaska lands. These included 97 million acres set aside for new parks and wildlife refuges, which doubled the amount of public land reserved for these purposes within the United States, and 56 million acres designated as wilderness, which tripled the amount of public land reserved for that purpose. Ironically, his ability to work with Congress and to lead the nation was seriously impaired by his attempt to scrap wasteful and inefficient western water projects. His October 1978 veto of the annual public works bill alienated almost every Democratic leader in Congress and haunted him for the rest of his presidency.

Most Presidents have come to the White House with years of experience in practical politics. They well understand the art of compromise, and they quickly learn that many environmental issues do not easily lend themselves to compromise or to quick, easy explanations on television. And even those Presidents with the training or temperament to formulate coherent environmental policies know that too close identification with environmentalists can be used to label them "extremists." In the decades following World War II, environmentalists were often characterized as arrogant elitists and visionaries who lacked an understanding of the "real world." They were also criticized for having more interest in the lives of birds and trees than in the welfare of working Americans. So while the environmental legislation enacted by Congress after the mid sixties was amazingly diverse, even Presidents with a strongly defined environmental consciousness shied away from such controversial issues as population control and the protection of endangered species and fish and wildlife habitats. They preferred lower-risk issues that promised direct benefits to voters, particularly pollution abatement and beautification.

Environmental issues score high in the polls but do not prompt the same visceral reaction among the mass of voters as their concerns about unemployment, inflation, taxes, or crime. Occasionally, fears that depletion of the ozone layer or cutting away the Amazon rain forest might imperil the future of mankind create a flurry of excitement in Washington, but no President has been able to place the relationship between man and nature at the center of his legislative agenda.

### BIBLIOGRAPHY

Carson, Rachel. *Silent Spring.* 1962.

Carter, Jimmy. *Keeping Faith: Memoirs of a President.* 1982.

Davies, J. Clarence, III. *The Politics of Pollution.* 1977.

Fox, Stephen. *John Muir and His Legacy: The American Conservation Movement.* 1981.

Hays, Samuel P. *Beauty, Health, Permanence: Environmental Politics in the United States, 1955–1985.* 1987.

Lash, Jonathan. *A Season of Spoils: The Story of the Reagan Administration's Attack on the Environment.* 1984.

Nash, Roderick F. *American Environmentalism.* 1990.

Petulla, Joseph M. *American Environmental History.* 1988.

DONALD J. PISANI

**EQUAL RIGHTS AMENDMENT.** In 1923 an equal rights amendment (ERA) to the Constitution was introduced in Congress by supporters of the radical National Women's Party. It was immediately opposed by organized labor and most WOMEN'S RIGHTS groups who feared that an ERA would invalidate progressive-supported legislation that gave special protection to women. Although the amendment was introduced in every subsequent session of Congress, it was not until the 1950s that support began to pick up. ELEANOR ROOSEVELT dropped her opposition and President Dwight D. Eisenhower stressed his support and that of both political parties for an ERA. In 1963, however, President John F. Kennedy's Commission on the Status of Women concluded that there was no need for an ERA "now."

By 1967, support for an ERA had grown. The new National Organization for Women (NOW) made amendment passage its number one priority. In May 1970 the Senate began hearings on the amendment. One month later, after only an hour's debate the House of Representatives passed the ERA by a vote of 350 to 15. It read: "Neither the United States nor any state shall, on account of sex, deny to any person within its jurisdiction the equal protection of the laws." Senate passage was more time-consuming as a series of substitute languages dealing with the draft and "functional differences" between men and women were offered and debated. On 22 March 1972, the Senate adopted the House version on a vote of 84 to 8 and the amendment was sent to the states for their ratification. Although supported by Presidents Richard M. Nixon, Gerald Ford, and Jimmy Carter the amendment, after a fast start, faltered quickly. The political climate was changing and an effective opposition was able to associate the amendment with much that was wrong with society. Although amendment supporters were able to convince Congress to extend the original seven-year time period for ratification to 10 years, in 1980, as the time for ratification was running out, the REPUBLICAN PARTY abandoned its support of the ERA for the first time and its standard-bearer, Ronald Reagan adamantly opposed the amendment. The ERA died in June 1982 when it fell three states short of the thirty-eight necessary for ratification.

### BIBLIOGRAPHY

Boles, Janet. *The Politics of the Equal Rights Amendment.* 1979.

Mansbridge, Jane. *Why We Lost the ERA.* 1986.

KAREN O'CONNOR

**ERA OF GOOD FEELINGS.** This phrase, coined by the Federalist Boston *Columbian Centinel* at the time of President James Monroe's visit in 1817, was intended to epitomize the advent of a new era in American politics—an age without political parties. This ideal, shared by Federalists and Democratic-Republicans alike, had been articulated in George Washington's FAREWELL ADDRESS in which he denounced parties as hostile to republican institutions. The *Centinel*'s phrase was ironic—within a decade American politics was infused by a rancor unequalled since the 1790's.

The Federalists, bankrupted by their opposition to the WAR OF 1812 and the Hartford Convention, welcomed reconciliation with the Democratic-Republicans, who had adopted so much of the Federalist program. The newly elected President accepted this ideal. He intended, as he often repeated, to be the chief magistrate of the nation and not the head of a party. To signal his commitment he undertook a tour of the nation—the first President to do so since Washington. Starting late in the summer of 1817 he first visited New England. Everywhere he was greeted with public demonstrations, banquets, and formal addresses as Federalists vied with Democratic-Republicans to honor the Chief Executive. His old foe, the aged John Adams, welcomed him at his home in Braintree. Monroe met with an equally enthusiastic reception two years later in the South and West. Although Federalists continued as a political force in New England, they vanished from the national scene.

Ex-Federalists still in Congress, such as RUFUS KING, supported administration policies. Pressures from within the Democratic-Republican Party prevented Monroe from cementing the reconciliation by appointing Federalists to high office.

With the disappearance of parties Monroe could not utilize party loyalty to ensure congressional approval of his measures. He had to rely on personal contacts with members of Congress and most importantly on the congressional followings of his Cabinet members who were seen as likely candidates for the succession. John Quincy Adams (State), WILLIAM H. CRAWFORD (Treasury), and JOHN C. CALHOUN (War) all had substantial blocks of supporters in Congress. This system worked well during Monroe's first term, but eroded after 1820, when administration measures were increasingly subjected to factional attacks. These divisions resulted from the rivalries over the presidential succession and the resurgence of sectional animosities. By 1820 the number of presidential aspirants had increased to five: Crawford (a close contender for the nomination in 1816), Adams, Calhoun, HENRY CLAY, and Andrew Jackson, fresh from the invasion of Florida. Each candidate, except for Adams and Calhoun, sought to establish distinct identities by attacking administration measures. After the war the nationalist spirit, which had infused the Democratic-Republicans, was supplanted by sectional differences over the tariff, internal improvements, and the BANK OF THE UNITED STATES. The furious debates over the Missouri question in 1819–1820 [see MISSOURI COMPROMISE] created a seemingly unbridgeable North-South animosity. However, these differences were not fully evident until after the election of 1820. Monroe was reelected overwhelmingly with 231 electoral votes—one New Hampshire elector for personal reasons voted for John Quincy Adams.

The one-party system had a direct impact on the practical business of winning elections. The two parties had provided a ready means of candidate identification. How could voters choose between candidates belonging to the same party? The task of restoring order to the political chaos was assumed by Senator Martin Van Buren of New York, who denounced Monroe for betraying the true principles of the party, the so-called Monroe heresy. After 1820, Van Buren made frequent trips in the South, touting Crawford as the candidate for 1824 and promising to restore the party to its STATES' RIGHTS principles. Northern economic developments had reduced the earlier commitment to nationalism. He also offered a tacit understanding that the southern position on slavery would not be challenged.

Although Van Buren was working to restore the old New York–Virginia alliance, he had not eliminated support for the other candidates. Until Calhoun's withdrawal early in 1824, partisan battles raged in Congress and the press creating an unrestrained "era of bad feelings." In 1824 Crawford was nominated by the caucus (then widely condemned as undemocratic), although he was literally physically prostrated by illness throughout the year. No candidate received a majority of the electoral vote. Jackson had a plurality, but Clay's influence in the House of Representatives was sufficient to win the presidency for Adams. During the next four years Van Buren, now supporting Jackson, completed the groundwork for the formation of the DEMOCRATIC PARTY on the ruins of the Democratic-Republican Party. The new party was committed to states' rights and proslavery principles—an arrangement that endured for three decades.

### BIBLIOGRAPHY

Ammon, Harry. *James Monroe: The Quest for National Identity.* 1990.

Dangerfield, George. *Era of Good Feelings.* 1952.

Livermore, Shaw, Jr. *The Twilight of Federalism: The Disintegration of the Federalist Party 1815–1830.* 1984.

Remini, Robert V. *Martin Van Buren and the Making of the Democratic Party.* 1970.

Sydnor, Charles S. "The One Party Period in American History." *American Historical Review* 51 (1950): 201–223.

HARRY AMMON

## ESCH-CUMMINS TRANSPORTATION ACT

(1920). Addressing problems of postwar adjustment in his annual message of December 1918, Woodrow Wilson called railroad policy his greatest concern. Nevertheless, Wilson offered no specific legislative proposals concerning the critical issues affecting railroads. Consolidations of redundant competing lines, rate structures that would support weak lines without permitting excessive profits to strong lines, maintenance backlogs, chronic railway labor disputes, and the future role of the Interstate Commerce Commission all required attention.

Wilson's wartime railroad administrators, William McAdoo and Walker Hines, urged that governmental operation of railroads be extended by five years. Glenn Plumb of the Organized Railway Employees proposed outright nationalization. Congress, little disposed to extreme proposals, focused instead on prompt resumption of private control and operation.

Senator Albert Cummins, Chairman of the Committee on Interstate Commerce, shaped a bill creating a strong new Transportation Board having broad powers to compel consolidations, set rates and guarantee minimum profits, and settle labor disputes. Representative John Esch, Chairman of the House Committee on Interstate and Foreign Commerce, fashioned a less ambitious bill. The conference bill, passed in February 1920 to meet the President's timetable for resumption of private railroad operation on 1 March 1920, encouraged railroad consolidations—authorizing the I.C.C. to recommend but not compel implementation of consolidations plans—and established a new Railroad Labor Board empowered to arbitrate labor disputes. Additionally, the act provided for short-term federal financing of railroad improvements and empowered the I.C.C. to recover a portion of profits earned by strong lines and to subsidize weak lines.

Wilson signed the Esch-Cummins Act over the opposition of organized labor. The measure was mildly successful in encouraging consolidations and moderating wasteful competition within the railroad industry.

### BIBLIOGRAPHY

Clements, Kendrick A. *The Presidency of Woodrow Wilson.* 1992.

Dixon, Frank Haigh. *Railroads and Government: Their Relations in the United States, 1910–1921.* 1922.

Leonard, William Norris. *Railroad Consolidation under the Transportation Act of 1920.* 1946.

Martin, Albro. *Railroads Triumphant: The Growth, Rejection, and Rebirth of a Vital American Force.* 1992.

RALPH MITZENMACHER

**EXECUTIVE AGREEMENTS.** An executive agreement is a U.S. international agreement other than a treaty, but is similarly binding on the U.S. government as a matter of international law. Executive agreements are concluded without Senate ADVICE AND CONSENT. Although State Department parlance seeks to limit the term to mean those presidential agreements that rest entirely on INHERENT POWERS conferred on the President by the Constitution, the term is also commonly used to cover nontreaty international agreements that are authorized by legislation or by prior treaties.

The Constitution does not mention executive agreements, explicitly authorizing only treaties, which are negotiated by the President and approved by the Senate, for the formalization of U.S. international commitments. Nonetheless, historians have variously identified the first such agreement as being either a 1792 postal agreement with the British colonies in Canada or the 1817 United States–Great Britain agreement to limit their naval forces on the Great Lakes.

Executive agreements represent the predominant form of international agreement for the United States, with more than six thousand in force as compared to roughly one thousand treaties. Most cover routine military or diplomatic matters. Congress in 1972 implicitly ratified the general constitutionality of the executive-agreement process by enacting the CASE ACT, which requires the Secretary of State to transmit the text of agreements other than treaties to each house of Congress for informational purposes within sixty days of their taking effect. Moreover, the trend toward increasing their use is manifest. Between 1945 and 1980, roughly 95 percent of U.S. international agreements were in the form of executive agreements, as compared to about 50 percent a century earlier.

Treaties may authorize subsequent executive agreements relative to their implementation. An example is the NATO TREATY, which has been regarded as authorizing hundreds of agreements on the status of military forces and other matters.

**Congressional Authorization.** Congress may also authorize executive agreements through statutes. Areas in which Congress has authorized the President to negotiate executive agreements include postal relations, trade matters, and foreign assistance. Congress has also authorized the President to conclude certain agreements that have already been negotiated, as in the case of the Headquarters Agreement with the UNITED NATIONS and various multilateral agreements establishing international organizations, for example, the United Nations Relief and Rehabilitation Administration, the International Bank for Reconstruction and Development, the International Monetary Fund, and the International Refugee Organization.

Except for the subject of foreign trade, explicitly assigned by the Constitution to Congress as part of its regulatory authority, the source of power for Congress to legislate on international matters is unclear. Theoretical uncertainties, however, have not at all impeded the use of legislatively authorized executive agreements (sometimes called congressional-executive agreements). In large part, this is because virtually all these agreements represent commitments that international law recognizes as within the sovereign power of the United States. So long as Congress and the President concur in these commitments, the often difficult question of domestic law—that is, the question as to which branch is the actual repository of that power—need not be faced. Like a treaty, such an agreement becomes the law of the land, superseding inconsistent state laws as well as inconsistent provisions in earlier treaties, other international agreements, or acts of Congress.

Legislatively authorized executive agreements afford the President two advantages over treaties in international relations. Because such agreements may be approved by a simple majority of both houses, the Senate cannot veto an executive agreement by the one-third-plus-one vote sufficient to defeat a treaty. Thus, for example, after anti-expansionist Democrats and others from sugar-growing southern states blocked a treaty for the ANNEXATION OF HAWAII, President William McKinley successfully sought statutory authorization for annexation by executive agreement, which was accomplished in 1898. (President John Tyler had made the identical move in order to bring about the ANNEXATION OF TEXAS.) Also, including the House of Representatives in the process helps assure that the House will not resist any later presidential effort to secure whatever legislative implementation, including appropriations, may be required to put an international agreement into effect.

**Unilateral Agreements.** Agreements that rest entirely on presidential authority (so-called unilateral agreements) are less numerous—perhaps only 2 to 3 percent of the total—but more controversial, though they are often of great diplomatic significance. The State Department's traditional position has been that the President's FOREIGN AFFAIRS powers, role as COMMANDER IN CHIEF, LAW ENFORCEMENT powers, and generalized EXECUTIVE POWER may all legitimate an executive agreement lacking congressional authorization. The Commander-in-Chief power, for example, supports armistice agreements and, arguably, wartime commitments on territorial and political issues for a post-war era, such as at the YALTA CONFERENCE and POTSDAM CONFERENCE. The President also has sole exercise of the RECOGNITION POWER, and the Supreme Court held in UNITED STATES V. BELMONT (1937) that this power is sufficient to authorize unilateral executive agreements to settle issues that are necessary to establish diplomatic relations.

The danger of according the President unlimited discretion to make unilateral executive agreements on any foreign relations matter is that such a doctrine would not only obliterate Article II's express check of Senate consent to treaties but would substantially weaken any legislative check on U.S. international commitments. Any such commitments that did not require subsequent legislative implementation, for example, would never be reviewed by either the House or Senate. It is historically clear that the motivation behind certain congressional-executive agreements was precisely to circumvent the Senate two-thirds-majority requirement for treaties, but it is less certain to what degree, if any, circumventing Congress altogether has been an impetus to unilateral agreements. A possible example is Franklin D. Roosevelt's 1940 agreement to lend Great Britain fifty overage destroyers, arguably breaching the obligations of the United States as a neutral in the conflict with Germany at a time when the American public still substantially favored NEUTRALITY as national policy.

To recognize this danger, however, is not to suggest any solution. Neither courts nor commentators have been able to articulate any clear, principled line dividing those initiatives for which the President may properly rely on exclusive and inherent powers and those that, if taken unilaterally, would trespass on the Senate's role. The Supreme Court has not yet held any executive agreement ultra vires (beyond the scope of presidential authority) for lack of Senate consent, nor has it given other guidelines that might define the President's power to act alone. The State Department's foreign affairs manual specifies criteria to be considered in deciding whether to proceed by treaty or nontreaty agreement but offers no rule other than an instruction to the department's Legal Adviser to seek appropriate consultations with Congress on difficult cases. The criteria to be considered include the degree to which an anticipated agreement would affect the nation as a whole, whether the agreement would be intended to affect state laws, whether subsequent legislative action would be needed for implementation, past practice on similar agreements, Congress's preferences with regard to a particular category of agreement, the desired level of formality, the proposed duration and need for prompt conclusion of an agreement, and general international practice with respect to the sort of agreement in question.

In 1981 the Supreme Court in DAMES & MOORE V. REGAN evaded this difficult set of issues with respect to a very common use of executive orders, namely, their use to settle international claims disputes. The agreement at issue—facilitating the end of the IRANIAN HOSTAGE CRISIS—had not been congressionally authorized and did not fall within any category of unilateral agreement already approved by the Court. The Court's majority, however, upheld the agreement based on Congress's implicit authorization, evidenced largely by a consistent history of ratifying prior claims-settlement agreements through implementing legislation.

It is possible to identify at least two likely limitations on the unilateral executive-agreement power that would not apply to treaties or congressional-executive agreements. First, courts are unlikely to treat unilateral executive agreements as overriding prior statutes. In UNITED STATES V. GUY W. CAPPS (1953), a federal circuit court refused to give effect to an executive agreement regulating the export of potatoes from Canada to the United States. The court regarded the agreement, effecting a regulation of interstate and foreign commerce, as lying not only within presidential authority, but also within Congress's power to regulate such trade. Because the agreement conflicted with provisions of the Agricultural Act of 1948, the Court held that the agreement was invalid; the President's inherent foreign affairs powers were insufficient to permit him to override Congress's determinations as to trade.

The requirement that Presidents respect prior statutes does not necessarily prohibit a President from making an executive agreement regarding a matter on which Congress could legislate but has not. Unilateral executive agreements would seem to be unlawful, however, in any area for which the courts have determined that affirmative legislative authority is a prerequisite to government initiative. An important example is extradition. The Supreme Court held in *Valentine v. United States* (1936) that extradition, "albeit a national power, is not confined to the executive in the absence of treaty or legislative provision." It would seem to follow that an extradition pursuant to a unilateral executive agreement would be unlawful.

Federal courts have struck down executive agreements that violate constitutional rights. In SEERY V. UNITED STATES (1955) the Court of Claims invalidated an executive agreement insofar as it denied a woman compensation that she was entitled to receive under the Fifth Amendment. Two years later, in REID V. COVERT (1957), the Supreme Court declared an executive agreement invalid because it permitted American military courts in Great Britain to use trial by court-martial for offenses committed by dependents of American military personnel, depriving them of the constitutional right to trial by jury.

If an executive agreement is within the President's power, there are no formal requirements as to how it must be made. It may be signed by the President or on his behalf; it can be made by the Secretary of State, an ambassador, or a lesser authorized official; in fact, there is no reason why it must be formal or even written.

It is not clear to what degree, if any, Congress may legislatively proscribe unilateral executive agreements. The BRICKER AMENDMENT of 1953, a proposed comprehensive limit on such agreements, failed to be enacted. To the extent, however, that the WAR POWERS RESOLUTION of 1973 purports to limit the President's authority to deploy U.S. military forces, it prohibits his use of executive agreements to promise such deploy-

ment as well. The Arms Control and Disarmament Act of 1962 prohibits arms limitation or reduction agreements except through treaties or as legislatively authorized. The Fishery Conservation and Management Act of 1972 provides that no international fishery agreement may take effect until sixty days after its transmission to Congress, during which time Congress reserves authority to prohibit the agreement by statute.

### BIBLIOGRAPHY

American Law Institute. *Restatement of the Law: Foreign Relations Law of the United States.* 1965. Rev. Tentative Draft No. 1. 1980.

Bloom, Evan. "The Executive Claims Settlement Power: Constitutional Authority and Foreign Affairs Applications." *Columbia Law Review* 85 (1985): 155–189.

Byrd, Elbert. *Treaties and Executive Agreements of the United States.* 1960.

Fisher, Louis. *Constitutional Conflicts between Congress and the President.* 3d ed. 1991.

Gilbert, Amy M. *Executive Agreements and Treaties, 1946–1973: Framework of the Foreign Policy of the Period.* 1973.

Glennon, Michael J. *Constitutional Diplomacy.* 1990.

Henkin, Louis. *Foreign Affairs and the Constitution.* 1972.

McClure, Wallace. *International Executive Agreements: Democratic Procedure under the Constitution of the United States.* 1967.

PETER M. SHANE

**EXECUTIVE BRANCH.** See CHIEF EXECUTIVE; EXECUTIVE DEPARTMENTS.

**EXECUTIVE DEPARTMENTS.** In designing the organization for the government they were creating, the Framers of the Constitution did not rely on classical political philosophy nor on the example of Great Britain or France, the two great nation-states of the period. Instead, the Framers relied largely upon their own experience in trying to wage the Revolutionary War against a global power and in attempting to manage the national confederation of states after the close of hostilities in 1781. Their personal experiences became the crucible for political thought.

**Organization of the Executive Branch.** While questions regarding how best to organize the executive branch were raised at the CONSTITUTIONAL CONVENTION, the Constitution itself is nearly silent on organizational matters. There are only two indirect references to the question of administrative organization in the Constitution, namely, that the President "may require the Opinion, in writing, of the principal Officer in each of the executive Departments, upon any Subject relating to the Duties of their respective Offices" and that "the Congress may by Law vest the Appointment of such inferior Officers, as they think proper, in the President alone, in the Courts of Law, or in the Heads of Departments" (Article II, Section 2, clauses 1 and 2).

The paucity of language in the Constitution respecting organizational matters should not be interpreted, however, as showing lack of interest or concern on the part of the Framers. Quite to the contrary, there was lively concern for organizational matters. The Framers were influenced by eighteenth-century Enlightenment philosophy rather than nineteenth-century social-revolutionary philosophy. Enlightenment philosophy stressed reason, and reason embraced scientific methodology. ALEXANDER HAMILTON was articulate in his arguments that public administration was a "science" and that the United States could organize a government that was at once efficient and representative. Writing in FEDERALIST 9, Hamilton states,

> The science of politics, however, like most other sciences, has received great improvement. The efficacy of various principles is now well understood, which was either not known at all or imperfectly known to the ancients. The regular distribution of power into distinct departments; the introduction of legislative balances and checks; the institution of courts composed of judges holding their offices during good behavior; the representation of the people in the legislature by deputies of their election; these are wholly new discoveries, or have made their principal progress toward perfection during modern times.

The important point is that the Framers believed that it was possible to create a rational and democratically accountable administrative structure. They believed that there were principles of organization that ought to be followed and that deviation from these principles should require the promoters to meet a higher standard of proof. The role of historical and legal precedent in the evolution of the federal executive establishment came into play during the First Congress. Much that takes place today in the field of organizational management can be traced back in origin to the very first years of the Republic.

One of the first orders of business for the new Congress in 1789 was the establishment of executive departments. Three "organic" statutes were passed creating three great departments: Treasury, State, and War. A problem arose with respect to the numerous domestic activities of government that did not fit neatly into these three departments. The First Congress made an attempt to establish a "Home Department," such as existed in England, to which these domestic functions might be assigned. Opposition to this proposal arose from several sources. There was concern that such a department would lead to a diminution of the states and their responsibilities for providing basic services to the citizenry. Also, Congress

was wary of creating another department under the President's authority. The rejection of the Home Department proposal led to the parceling out of many domestic activities among the three departments and the creation of some long-standing anomalies.

Just a few of these anomalies are worth noting. The STATE DEPARTMENT was given responsibility for conducting the census and for supervising the Mint. The TREASURY DEPARTMENT was assigned the Coast Survey, General Land Office, and the Revenue Cutter Service, later to be the U.S. Coast Guard. And the WAR DEPARTMENT was assigned responsibility for supervising INDIAN affairs and for national construction projects (Army Corps of Engineers).

The underlying concepts behind the executive branch structure were that it should be a unitary organizational structure and that departments should be headed by a single individual, not a committee. Both George Washington and Hamilton were opposed to a plural executive in any form. Some dispute arose as to the supervision of these departments. While Congress accepted the premise that FOREIGN AFFAIRS and national defense were essentially executive functions and therefore properly the responsibility of the President, they did not accept the view that national finances were an executive function. Congress, since the earliest days of the Continental Congress, had kept the supervision of the Treasury and the appointment of its officers within its orbit. Under the Constitution, Congress agreed to share the supervision of the new Treasury, but only up to a point.

Unlike the departments of State and War, Treasury was not styled an executive department, and many in Congress anticipated that the Secretary of the Treasury and lesser statutorily designated officials (e.g., the Comptroller) would be "agents" of Congress. Hamilton, as the first Secretary of the Treasury, relished his special relationship with Congress, but he disappointed those in Congress who hoped he would be satisfied with an agent's role. Hamilton held himself accountable first and foremost to the President.

**Expansion of the Departments.** President Washington assembled his department secretaries for advice and counsel, and in 1793 this informal group became popularly known as the CABINET. In addition to the three secretaries (after 1798 there was a fourth secretary representing the new Department of the Navy), the ATTORNEY GENERAL was considered a member of the Cabinet. The Attorney General was initially a private lawyer on retainer ($1,500 annually) to the federal government. Only later did the Attorney General become a full-time officer of the United States, finally becoming the head of the newly created DEPARTMENT OF

| EXECUTIVE BRANCH |
| --- |

| Executive Departments |
| --- |
| Department of Agriculture |
| Department of Commerce |
| Department of Defense |
|   Joint Chiefs of Staff |
| Department of Education |
| Department of Energy |
| Department of Health and Human Services |
|   Social Security Administration |
| Department of Housing and Urban Development |
| Department of the Interior |
| Department of Justice |
|   Attorney General |
|   Solicitor General |
|   Office of Legal Counsel |
|   Federal Bureau of Investigation |
|   Office of the Pardon Attorney |
| Department of Labor |
| Department of State |
| Department of Transportation |
|   Saint Lawrence Seaway Development Corporation |
| Department of the Treasury |
|   United States Secret Service |
| Department of Veterans Affairs |

| Independent Commissions |
| --- |
| Commodity Futures Trading Commission (CFTC) |
| Consumer Product Safety Commission (CPSC) |
| Federal Communications Commission (FCC) |
| Federal Election Commission (FEC) |
| Federal Energy Regulatory Commission (FERC) |
| Federal Maritime Commission (FMC) |
| Federal Mine Safety and Health Review Commission |
| Federal Reserve System, Board of Governors of the Federal Trade Commission (FTC) |
| Interstate Commerce Commission (ICC) |
| National Labor Relations Board (NLRB) |
| Nuclear Regulatory Commission (NRC) |
| Occupational Safety and Health Review Commission |
| Postal Rate Commission |
| Securities and Exchange Commission (SEC) |
| U.S. International Trade Commission (ITC) |

JUSTICE in 1870. The POSTMASTER GENERAL, though head of the POST OFFICE, was not a member of the Cabinet until 1829. The Post Office became an executive department in 1872, a status it held until 1971, when it was redesignated by Congress as "an independent establishment of the executive branch."

The first major new addition to the list of executive departments was the DEPARTMENT OF THE INTERIOR, created in 1849. Transferred to this department were the already existing General Land Office, Office of Indian Affairs, Pension Office, Patent Office, and census activities. Over succeeding decades the role of the department evolved, with Interior eventually becoming the custodian of the nation's natural resources and parks.

As functions were assumed by the federal government, they were assigned to new or existing departments. Before 1860, only four permanent "detached agencies" were created: the Library of Congress, the Smithsonian Institution, the Botanical Gardens, and the Government Printing Office. For the first hundred years or so of the Republic, the executive branch, with few exceptions, consisted of departments headed by single administrators under the authority of the President.

**Supervision: Competing Claims.** The Constitution and political customs of the United States provide the basis for a continuing struggle between the President and Congress over who should be the primary supervisor of the administrative agencies. Many of the complex issues involving statutory authority, lines of accountability, tenure, and organizational management were first aired in the dispute over the President's right to remove officers of the executive branch. This dispute and its resolution have come down to us in history as the DECISION OF 1789.

Soon after Washington's inauguration, a major crisis loomed. In proposing legislation to establish the departments of Foreign Affairs (later State), War, and Treasury, James Madison included language providing that the secretaries of these departments would be "removable by the President." Many members of Congress objected to this provision, arguing that the Constitution's silence concerning where the REMOVAL POWER would reside indicated that removals were to be guided by the same authority as that specified in the appointment clause, which required Senate approval of all appointments. According to this reasoning, removals, other than by the IMPEACHMENT process, would require Senate confirmation as well.

| Government Corporations |
| --- |
| African Development Foundation |
| Export-Import Bank of the United States |
| Farm Credit Administration |
| Federal Deposit Insurance Corporation (FDIC) |
| Federal Housing Finance Board |
| Inter-American Foundation |
| Legal Services Corporation |
| National Railroad Passenger Corporation (Amtrak) |
| Pennsylvania Avenue Development Corporation |
| Pension Benefit Guaranty Corporation |
| Resolution Trust Corporation |
| Tennessee Valley Authority (TVA) |

| Other Agencies and Boards |
| --- |
| ACTION |
| Administrative Conference of the U.S. |
| Central Intelligence Agency (CIA) |
| Commission on the Bicentennial of the U.S. Constitution |
| Commission on Civil Rights |
| Defense Nuclear Facilities Safety Board |
| Environmental Protection Agency (EPA) |
| Equal Employment Opportunity Commission (EEOC) |
| Federal Emergency Management Agency (FEMA) |
| Federal Labor Relations Authority |
| Federal Mediation and Conciliation Service |
| Federal Retirement Thrift Investment Board |
| General Services Administration |
| Merit Systems Protection Board (MSPB) |
| National Aeronautics and Space Administration (NASA) |
| National Archives and Records Administration |
| National Capitol Planning Commission |
| National Credit Union Administration |
| National Foundation on the Arts and the Humanities |
| National Mediation Board |
| National Science Foundation |
| National Transportation Safety Board |
| Office of Government Ethics |
| Office of Personnel Management |
| Oversight Board for the Resolution Trust Corporation |
| Peace Corps |
| Railroad Retirement Board |
| Selective Service System |
| U.S. Arms Control and Disarmament Agency (ACDA) |
| U.S. Information Agency (USIA) |
| U.S. International Development Cooperation Agency |
| Agency for International Development (AID) |
| U.S. Office of Special Counsel |
| U.S. Postal Service |

Washington and Madison strongly disagreed with this argument and the interpretation of the Constitution it reflected. They contended that the power of removal belonged exclusively with the President and is incident to the President's general EXECUTIVE POWER under the Constitution. The debate in both houses of Congress was sophisticated in its theoretical nuances and in its evaluation of the likely practical consequences that would follow if a particular choice were made. At one point Madison concluded, "Vest [the removal power] in the Senate jointly with the President, and you abolish at once that great principle of unity and responsibility in the Executive department which was intended for the security of liberty and the public good."

The final vote on the removal issue favored Washington's and Madison's position that the President should have the exclusive right to remove department heads and, with a few exceptions, all officers of the executive branch. Although the issue appeared resolved, it was not. Congress has sought on several occasions to limit the President's power to remove executive-branch officials [see TENURE OF OFFICE ACT]. Additionally, the Supreme Court in several cases has approved limitations on the authority of the President to remove officers (e.g., HUMPHREY'S EXECUTOR V. UNITED STATES [1935]).

The Federalist period (1789–1801) was a period of extraordinary achievement in many fields, not the least being organizational design and management. The decision to establish a unitary administrative structure, an innovation much admired at the time, was designed by the Federalists to complement their more comprehensive theory of government. Although the main lines of Federalist philosophy of organizational management would remain in place throughout the Jeffersonian period (1801–1829), the institutional presidency gradually declined in power vis-à-vis Congress. Congress began to assert its authority over executive agencies more energetically with each passing year, forcing nineteenth-century Presidents, with several notable exceptions, to rely heavily on the APPOINTMENT POWER, the removal power, the veto, and personal persuasion to exert whatever influence they might have over the course of administrative affairs.

The period between 1829 and 1900 was a period of congressional dominance over the presidency, a period characterized by a devolution of authority and of responsibility for the administration of the United States government. The once-small departments were required by rapidly escalating demands for services to devolve their authorities and capacities to subunits. The creation within departments of bureaus marked by specialization of personnel and tasks was a dominant feature of the nineteenth century. Often these bureaus developed their own cultures and sets of loyalties that were at odds with the objectives of departmental secretaries.

The movement toward bureaus within departments and the development of field structures to bring services directly to the people highlighted the issue as to whom these bureaus were accountable. Initially, Congress resisted the creation of bureaus because they associated them with increased expenditures. Later, however, Congress tended to encourage their creation since bureaus could serve the interests of their constituents more directly and were also more amenable to congressional intervention.

The idea that the President ought to be an active manager of the executive branch was not one of the burning issues of the nineteenth century. Presidents tended to be jealous of their institutional and legal prerogatives and on occasion would fight tenaciously for some particular administrative or managerial concept. By and large, however, Presidents tended to be deferential to Congress on organizational management questions. Congress had control over the purse-strings, and thus Congress was the initiator of most reorganizations and changes in administrative practices.

The dominance of Congress in matters of administrative oversight notwithstanding, the earlier appeal of the unitary executive branch retained its persuasiveness throughout the nineteenth century. The first substantial break with departmentalism, and with the idea of a single administrative head for each bureau, did not occur until the 1880s, with the creation of the Civil Service Commission (1883) and the Interstate Commerce Commission (1887). This break was associated in many respects with the newly triumphant movement for CIVIL-SERVICE REFORM and with a growing recognition by Congress that it was institutionally unable to oversee the growing body of regulatory activities. Thus, Congress was increasingly sympathetic

to the idea of delegating some of its managerial and regulatory authority to the President and executive agencies, but not necessarily to department secretaries.

The problem, however, was that the institutionalized presidency was unable to substantially enhance either its political or managerial leverage over the executive departments. The President had virtually no staff, no budgetary authority over departments, and few general management laws through which the departments and agencies could be supervised collectively. The situation was ripe for change.

**The President as Chief Manager.** The new century ushered in new opportunities for American Presidents to exert their leadership skills. Government institutions were growing rapidly not only in size but in their resource requirements. The executive branch needed new organizational forms and a skilled manager, and the President was looked upon to furnish this leadership.

Under the banner of Progressivism, the doctrines of "scientific management" were promoted for application in the executive branch. With respect to organizational management, Progressives, by and large, favored four reforms: reorganization of the executive branch into functional departments and agencies, promotion of the President's authority to manage a unified executive branch, introduction of an executive budget, and development of a neutrally competent management class for departmental leadership. Progressives believed that progress was not only possible but inevitable if certain sound principles of organizational management were followed.

Under the Progressives' scheme, the President was to be the chief manager of the executive branch, which was to be reorganized as an integrated structure with strict lines of responsibility and accountability leading to the President. Reorganization of the executive departments and agencies was viewed as a critical precondition for effective governance.

Throughout the twentieth century a large number of commissions have been established by Congress, the President and, on occasion, jointly to study the organization and management of the executive branch and to make recommendations for change. Several of these commissions have achieved landmark status—most notably the BROWNLOW COMMITTEE (1937), the first of the HOOVER COMMISSIONS (1949), and the ASH COUNCIL (1970). For the most part, at least through the Ash Council, the commissions' reports recommended a stronger institutionalized presidency and greater reliance on departments rather than independent agencies. Collectively, the three commissions noted above promoted a group of organizational management concepts that came to be known as the orthodox theory of federal organization. A brief review of the recommendations of these commissions is useful for understanding the present status of executive departments.

***Brownlow Committee.*** As his second term approached, President Franklin D. Roosevelt sought to develop a comprehensive organizational strategy that would enhance his capacity to manage the executive branch. He named a three-member committee headed by Louis Brownlow to provide him with organizational recommendations. The Brownlow Committee recommended the creation of two additional departments (of public works and of social welfare) and the reintegration into the departmental structure of most existing independent agencies, regulatory commissions, and government corporations. The committee's report was particularly critical of the independent regulatory commissions, referring to them as the "headless fourth branch of government."

The Brownlow report has been characterized as the "high noon of orthodoxy" because of its advocacy of clear lines of accountability, departmentalism, and the doctrine that responsibility for making policy and setting standards ought to reside in the President and departmental secretaries rather than being devolved to the agency level. Congress did not accept the 1937 legislation that would have implemented much of the report's recommendations in part because its timing coincided with Roosevelt's ill-fated COURT-PACKING PLAN. Roosevelt had to be satisfied with the achievement, in 1939, of a law establishing the EXECUTIVE OFFICE OF THE PRESIDENT and the assignment of some REORGANIZATION POWER to the President.

***First Hoover Commission.*** In the immediate aftermath of WORLD WAR II, there was a fairly broad consensus favoring governmental "retrenchment." Congress enacted and President Harry S. Truman signed a bill creating a commission headed by former President Herbert Hoover to comprehensively review the entire organizational management of the federal government. The premise underlying the Hoover Commission recommendations was similar to the orthodox approach of the earlier Brownlow Committee. The commission made proposals to strengthen the President as manager and secretaries as administrative chiefs of their departments. The commission criticized the tendency toward dispersing functions to independent agencies and called for a renewed, hierarchical administrative structure. "The unity of administration of the executive branch as planned by the Constitution must be restored," said the commission report, which called for grouping agencies "as nearly as possible by major purposes." Concerning departmental secretaries, the Commission stated, "Under the President, the heads of departments must hold full responsibility for the conduct of their departments. There must be a clear line of authority reaching down through every step of the organization and no subordinate should have authority independent from that of his superior."

The consensus that the President should be the chief manager of the executive branch and that he should have the necessary legal and organizational resources to perform these responsibilities permitted the passage of a number of far-reaching laws providing generic management direction for the departments and agencies. Two large, functionally based departments were created (DEPARTMENT OF DEFENSE, 1949; Department of Health, Education, and Welfare, 1953) in part as a consequence of Hoover Commission recommendations.

***Ash Council.*** A third commission worth highlighting was the Ash Council, which submitted its report to President Richard M. Nixon in 1970. The council's objective was to provide the President with a comprehensive reorganization proposal that would improve the President's capacity to manage—even control—the executive branch while rationalizing the structure of the executive branch to reflect new service demands being placed on government.

The council recommended more centralized and politically responsible lines of authority within the executive branch. It advocated a package approach to reorganization that combined various elements of the New Federalism (e.g., revenue sharing) with executive-branch reorganization. In proposing its restructuring of the executive branch, the council recommended a move away from the narrow, constituency-oriented traditional departments toward broader functional departments. In March 1971, Nixon sent four bills to Congress that had as their intent the reorganization of seven existing departments and various independent agencies into four large super departments of Human Resources, Community Development, Natural Resources, and Economic Affairs.

It was a dramatic proposal, the logical conclusion of the orthodox public administration values embodied in the earlier Brownlow Committee and Hoover Commission reports. Policy directions and lines of accountability to the department secretaries would be strengthened while administrative functions (e.g., awarding of grants) would be decentralized, often to standardized regional offices. In short, the four pieces of legislation embodied a comprehensive conceptual approach, yet Congress was not persuaded. No action was forthcoming.

With the failure of Nixon's comprehensive strategy to reorganize the executive branch according to orthodox principles, the commission and report approach to organizational management fell into disrepute. President Jimmy Carter initiated a large reorganization effort—but one without a commission, without a report, and without, according to its executive director, a distinctive theoretical basis, orthodox or otherwise. Two new departments were created during Carter's tenure, ENERGY and EDUCATION, but these two constituency-based departments represented a further fragmentation of the executive branch, not a return to administrative unity.

President Ronald Reagen, noting the relative failure of his predecessor in structuring a comprehensive organizational strategy, rejected the commission approach to reorganizing government and relied instead on the budget and regulatory review processes as tools for management. The one substantial commission during the Reagan years, the Grace Commission (1984), was principally concerned with program management and control and did not recommend the creation or abolition of any departments.

The appeal of the commission approach, despite the negative opinions of late-twentieth-century Presidents, remains high in Congress, and it is a rare session in which there is not some legislation considered for a new commission of some sort. In 1988, for instance, legislation to establish a National Commission on Executive Organization based on the Hoover Commission model was passed. The key provision was that the new President in 1989 would have the discretion to convene such a commission. The newly elected President, George Bush, decided for various reasons that such a commission was not needed.

**The Executive Branch in the 1990s.** By 1992 there were fourteen departments in the executive branch, the most recent department to be established being the DEPARTMENT OF VETERANS AFFAIRS (1988). The others (and the dates of their creation or reorganization) are as follows: DEPARTMENT OF AGRICULTURE (1889), DEPARTMENT OF COMMERCE (1903; 1913), Department of Defense (1789; 1949), Department of Education (1979), Department of Energy (1977), DEPARTMENT OF HEALTH AND HUMAN SERVICES (1953; 1980), DEPARTMENT OF HOUSING AND URBAN DEVELOPMENT (1965), Department of the Interior (1849), Department of Justice (1870), DEPARTMENT OF LABOR (1903; 1913), Department of State (1789), DEPARTMENT OF TRANSPORTATION (1966), and Department of the Treasury (1789). In addition to these departments, the executive branch includes more than fifty independent agencies, regulatory commissions, government corporations, and quasi-governmental units.

With the exception of portions of several commission reports discussed above, there is very little in the literature of government on the subject of institutional types. The absence of principles to guide the choice of institutions for performance of functions results in decisions that are based more on intuition than on experience. There are no general laws defining the structure, powers, and immunities of the several categories of institutions. A department, for instance, has only those powers assigned in its enabling act. Other attributes of a department singularly or of departments as a class are determined by custom, precedent, judicial interpretation, congressional agreement, and subsequent laws amending the original legislation.

The strength of departments as a class of organization lies largely in their potential to bring leadership initiatives into play to address complex policy issues. A department does provide the organizational context and limits within which budgetary and personnel decisions can be made. Department secretaries are able to deal with one another on reasonable parity, thus providing a channel of communications and policy accommodation between constituent agencies, but agencies that are not in departments may find themselves without a high-level defender in the inevitable bureaucratic wars of government. When the President meets with the Cabinet, most of the executive branch is represented, and some (often quite modest) degree of administrative coherence, moving the administration in a single direction, is achieved in these meetings.

The case for departmentalism, while retaining much of its persuasiveness, is no longer the dominant political thrust of organizational management in the executive branch. Following congressional rejection of Nixon's 1971 proposals for four super departments, a fundamental shift in organizational philosophy occurred. Presidents, by and large, retreated from the view that having a comprehensive organizational strategy is a necessary basis for political leadership. The integrated, unitary executive branch was no longer an ideal worth expending political capital to achieve.

Disaggregation, not integration, became the primary motivating force behind most reorganizations. Although Congress might give lip service to the principles of departmentalism enunciated by the first Hoover Commission, in practice Congress sought to increase political and administrative leverage at the expense of department leadership. Increasingly, agencies in departments (e.g., the Federal Aviation Administration in the Department of Transportation, the Office of Thrift Supervision in the Department of the Treasury) were assigned their authority directly by statute, bypassing the secretaries in the process. Additionally, more functions, including functions of a governmental character, were being assigned to third-party contractors because of budgetary and personnel limitations placed on departments.

Congress, in the absence of the interest or leadership of the President or the OFFICE OF MANAGEMENT AND BUDGET (OMB), has increasingly intervened in organizational management issues traditionally viewed as the province of the executive branch. Agencies and programs that might once have been assigned to departments are now given almost routinely to bodies of deliberately ambiguous legal status that function in a "twilight zone" between the governmental and private sectors. Bodies such as the Resolution Trust Corporation, National Endowment for Democracy, and the Federal National Mortgage Association ("Fannie Mae") are products of this retreat from departmentalism.

There is little doubt that if the Federalists and the Progressives were permitted a return visit, they would be disappointed with the state of organizational management in the executive branch. They would be displeased with the loss of presidential will and capacity to enunciate and promote a comprehensive organizational management strategy. The erosion of a unified departmental structure would, in all likelihood, be a cause for their special concern as more and more activities have been assigned to nondepartmental bodies. Reorganizations of executive agencies and programs continued apace in the early 1990s (e.g., the proposal to establish a Department of Environmental Affairs) but without any discernible theoretical basis. Executive reorganizations tend to be influenced most by immediate political considerations, with structural options simply becoming chips in the political game.

The future of departments as a class of organization in the executive branch is not in danger. They will not disappear; indeed, there are likely to be more rather than fewer departments. But the mission of departments as centers for political and administrative leadership has become less clear. In the 1980s and 1990s, laws creating departments and agencies were distinguished by their length, detail, regulatory emphasis, and conflicting lines of accountability. The exciting action in government has tended to move away from departments and toward other categories of organization. The big challenge, therefore, to those who seek to reorient and reinvigorate the federal government to confront both domestic and international problems more effectively is to rethink the role and structure of departments. The organizational structure and management of departments is a critical factor to any successful comprehensive political strategy in the third century of the Republic.

BIBLIOGRAPHY

Arnold, Peri E. *Making the Managerial Presidency: Comprehensive Managerial Reorganization Planning, 1905–1980.* 1986.

Fairlie, John A. *The National Administration of the United States.* 1905.

Fisher, Louis. *Constitutional Conflicts between Congress and the President.* 3d rev. ed. 1991.

Moe, Ronald C. "Traditional Organizational Principles and the Managerial Presidency: From Phoenix to Ashes." *Public Administration Review* 50 (1990): 129–140.

Seidman, Harold, and Robert S. Gilmour. *Politics, Position, and Power: From the Positive to the Regulatory State.* 4th rev. ed. 1986.

Short, Lloyd M. *The Development of National Administrative Organization in the United States.* 1923.

U.S. Commission on the Organization of the Executive Branch of Government (First Hoover Commission). *The Hoover Commission Report.* 1949.

U.S. Office of Management and Budget (Ash Council). *Papers Relating to the President's Departmental Reorganization Program.* 1971.

U.S. President's Committee on Administrative Management (Brownlow Committee). *Report With Special Studies.* 1937.

Wallace, Schuyler C. *Federal Departmentalization: A Critique of Theories of Organization.* 1941.

RONALD C. MOE

## EXECUTIVE OFFICE OF THE PRESIDENT (EOP).

The Executive Office of the President, created in 1939, houses the President's staff. It was formally established by President Franklin D. Roosevelt through Reorganization Plan No.1 and Executive Order 8248 in 1939, under the authority granted to the President by the Reorganization Act of 1939.

**Establishment.** The proposal to establish an Executive Office of the President originated in the report of the President's Committee on Administrative Management (the Brownlow Report) of January 1937. In its attempt to strengthen presidential leadership of the executive branch, the BROWNLOW COMMITTEE proposed to bring the principal managerial units of government firmly under presidential control by housing those agencies concerned with budgeting, efficiency research, personnel, and planning in the proposed EOP along with the White House office, home of the President's immediate and intimate personal staff. "The canons of efficiency," said the committee, "require the establishment of a responsible and effective chief executive as the center of energy, direction, and administrative management."

Initially, the EOP functioned primarily as a managerial institution, consistent with the Brownlow blueprint. In addition to the White House office, Executive Order 8248 placed four presidential agencies within the EOP: the Bureau of the Budget, the National

Resources Planning Board, the Liaison Office for Personnel Management, and the Office of Government Reports. All of these agencies were new except the Bureau of the Budget, which had hitherto been located in the Department of the Treasury. The executive order also provided for the establishment of an emergency management office in the EOP in the event of a national emergency and, within a year, President Roosevelt had utilized this authority to create the first of several but vitally important management agencies to coordinate the war effort. Long before Franklin Roosevelt came to the presidency, managing the activities of a rapidly expanding executive branch had grown beyond the capabilities of one person. The establishment of the Executive Office was a significant attempt to match the President's managerial responsibilities with managerial capacity.

**Divisions.** The agencies established within the EOP are not necessarily permanent. They can be disbanded when they have outlived their usefulness and new presidential staff units, serving different purposes, can be added when needed. A variety of agencies, more than forty in all, have been housed in the Executive Office of the President since 1939 and only a small proportion have survived the administration that created them.

Divisions of the EOP can be created and disbanded by statute, by a reorganization plan (when presidential reorganization authority has been granted by Congress), or by EXECUTIVE ORDER. The President, therefore, is not the sole determinant of the structure of the EOP and, on more than one occasion, Congress has demonstrated its capacity to shape the presidential staff system by adding or removing staff units from the executive office irrespective of whether or not the

President at the time approves of its decisions. For example, two of the most important divisions currently in the EOP, the NATIONAL SECURITY COUNCIL and the COUNCIL OF ECONOMIC ADVISERS, were devised in the corridors of Congress rather than the White House, and it was Congress, not the President, that decided to terminate the existence of one of the major original agencies, the National Resources Planning Board, after just four years.

Currently, the Executive Office of the President consists of twelve divisions (with the date of inclusion in the EOP in parentheses): WHITE HOUSE OFFICE (1939); Bureau of the Budget/OFFICE OF MANAGEMENT AND BUDGET (1939/1970); Council of Economic Advisers (1946); National Security Council (1949); Council on Environmental Quality (1969); Office of Special Representative for Trade Negotiations/OFFICE OF THE UNITED STATES TRADE REPRESENTATIVE (1974); OFFICE OF SCIENCE AND TECHNOLOGY POLICY (1976); Domestic Policy Staff/OFFICE OF POLICY DEVELOPMENT (1977); OFFICE OF ADMINISTRATION (1977); National Critical Materials Council (1984); Office of National Drug Control Policy (1988); and National Economic Council (1993).

The EOP has an annual budget in excess of $200 million and a full-time staff conservatively estimated at sixteen hundred. Because of the large staff, a number of EOP staff have offices some distance from the OVAL OFFICE.

**Politicization.** Over the course of its development since 1939 the EOP has also gradually outgrown the Brownlow blueprint. Presidential staff in the EOP operates in a much broader range of government activity than the Brownlow Report originally planned. Whereas Brownlow's EOP was intended to be an agency for centralized administrative management and coordination, today's executive office is very much involved in policy advice, policy-making, policy implementation, and political strategy, in addition to the management and coordination of executive branch activities. Furthermore, some of the major functions that Brownlow did intend the EOP to perform, particularly long-term resource planning and personnel management, have never figured prominently in the work of the executive office.

Because the reach of the EOP now extends across the whole range of public policy, it often overlaps, second-guesses, and conflicts with the work done in the executive-branch departments and agencies. This, together with the budgetary control exercised by the Office of Management and Budget, is the principal source of the generally adversarial relationship between the EOP and the executive branch, a relationship that Brownlow had never intended to encourage but that has become a recurring pattern in post-WORLD WAR II presidencies. By the mid 1980s, political scientist Nelson W. Polsby felt compelled to suggest that perhaps the most interesting political development of the postwar period "is the emergence of a presidential branch of government separate and apart from the executive branch."

The most significant deviation from the spirit and ethos of the Brownlow Report is the preeminence of the White House Office, which has become the directing force and the most powerful division within the EOP. To a great extent, the major EOP agencies operate as satellites of the White House Office with key political appointees directing the work of the various staffs. As a consequence, the distinction made in the Brownlow Report between an institutional staff for the presidency and the President's personal staff has been substantially eroded over the years. The EOP is no longer a permanent, professional, nonpartisan, expert staff serving the presidency irrespective of who holds the office at any one time. The senior echelons of the executive office are now filled by noncareer, highly partisan presidential loyalists, many of whom lack professional expertise in government or even prior experience in the executive branch. In that sense, the EOP has become politicized or, as some political scientists would say, "deinstitutionalized."

The deinstitutionalization of the executive office has been criticized by many experts on the presidency, particularly in the post-Watergate era. Politicization, together with the growing power and expanding size of the EOP, were seen as major defects in the system of government and a significant contributor to the events of the WATERGATE AFFAIR. There was a widely shared feeling that the presidential staff system was out of control, that the growth of the EOP should be curtailed, that staff be made more accountable, that the CABINET ought not to be neglected, and the flow of power from the departments to the EOP be reversed. The post-Watergate literature was especially critical of the practice of placing loyal presidential appointees in those key EOP posts originally intended to be occupied by career professionals. It cost the presidency the benefits of expertise, professionalism, objectivity, continuity and institutional memory. Advocates of reform have urged future Presidents to think institutionally, to consider the long-term organizational interests of the presidency and to restore the values of neutral-competence to the executive office. Almost all of the post-Watergate critics of the EOP have urged a return to the fundamentals of the Brownlow Report.

Notwithstanding the events of Watergate and the IRAN-CONTRA AFFAIR, both of which were generated from within the EOP, post-Watergate Presidents have been unresponsive to the post-Watergate reform agenda. The size of the executive office has not been reduced significantly, nor has its power, nor has there been any meaningful attempt to restore policy-making responsibility and authority to the Cabinet and, through it, to the departments and agencies. Neither has there been any effort to depoliticize the EOP. The classical textbook virtues of neutral-competence, institutional continuity, and objective, nonpartisan, professional advice have had little appeal for post-Watergate Presidents.

Some literature has suggested that these classic textbook virtues are found only in textbooks and have little relevance to the real world of the presidency and the highly political framework within which any contemporary President has to work. The evidence since the 1970s does seem to indicate that what Presidents really want, and think they need, is a staff unit that is primarily politically sensitive and politically responsive and that they are better served by expanding the responsibilities of their staff, by centralizing decision making in the EOP, and by politicizing what was meant to be an institutional arm of the presidency. Indeed, Presidents might wonder why they are being criticized for not thinking institutionally with regard to the role and function of the EOP when, from their point of view, it is the advocates of reform who ought to be criticized for not thinking politically.

**An Assessment.** The Executive Office of the President is a very significant innovation in American government. As Clinton Rossiter once argued, it was a vital creation that had helped to save the presidency from paralysis and the Constitution from oblivion, and it enabled future Presidents to cope with the exigencies of the modern state. But, like many other reforms in post-World War II American politics, the creation of the EOP has had unintended consequences, and, in the aftermath of Watergate, it appeared to many commentators that the EOP was yet another reform gone wrong.

Any assessment of the performance of the EOP would have to recognize that the EOP's mission to help the President coordinate and manage the activities of the executive branch of government has been interpreted as a mandate to control the executive branch and, in establishing control, the EOP has set itself up as a counterbureaucracy and a separate presidential branch of government. It has interposed itself between the President and the executive branch and has upset what was the traditional relationship between the CHIEF EXECUTIVE and his top political executives in the departments and agencies. As a consequence, the nature of decision making in American government has changed since 1939 with a marked decline in the status and authority of the members of the Cabinet.

The EOP has not only challenged the power of the executive branch, but it has also challenged the constitutional prerogatives of the legislative branch by frustrating its attempts to intervene in and oversee the policy-making process. A large, powerful, and highly developed presidential staff system reduces the President's dependency on the executive branch for advice, information, and policy initiatives and so renders the legislature's ties with the departments and agencies less potent than they once were.

The EOP was originally designed as an administrative-management entity but has evolved into a political body competing for power at the very center of government in a highly fragmented and pluralistic political system. The consequences of this evolution have been mixed. The EOP has undoubtedly enhanced the capacity of the President to do the things that the President wants to do, but its record in helping Presidents do what Presidents ought to do is much less obvious. Enhanced management of the executive branch has been achieved at the cost of a seemingly permanent adversarial relationship between the President and the bureaucracy, and, while it is difficult to generalize about the quality of public policy that has emerged from the EOP over the years, it is far from proved that centralization of decision making in the EOP has been, even on balance, a beneficial development (see Walter Williams for a critique of the policy performance of the EOP). Good public policy can never be guaranteed by any institutional innovation in government. The rise of the EOP to center stage of political decision making has been largely unchecked and unconstrained, even after the Watergate and Iran-contra affairs, thus there can be no certainty that presidential staff in a future EOP will not produce their own version of Watergate or Iran-contra in the name of the President whom they have been appointed to serve.

### BIBLIOGRAPHY

Burke, John P. *The Institutional Presidency.* 1992.
Graham, George A. "The Presidency and the Executive Office of the President." *Journal of Politics* 12 (1950): 599–621.
Hart, John. *The Presidential Branch.* 1987.
Moe, Terry. "The Politicized Presidency." In *The New Direction in American Politics.* Edited by John E. Chubb and Paul E. Peterson. 1985.
Rossiter, Clinton. "The Constitutional Significance of the Executive Office of the President." *American Political Science Review* 43 (1949): 1206–1217.
Williams, Walter. *Mismanaging America: The Rise of the Anti-Analytic Presidency.* 1990.

JOHN HART

**EXECUTIVE ORDER 9835** (1947). This order, (12 Fed. Reg. 1935) also known as the Loyalty Order, was issued by President Harry S. Truman on the premise that "maximum protection must be afforded the United States against infiltration of disloyal persons into the ranks of its employees, and equal protection from unfounded accusations of disloyalty must be afforded to the loyal employees of the Government." The order was part of the early days of the COLD WAR and part of the anticommunist excesses subsequently referred to as MCCARTHYISM after Senator Joseph McCarthy (R-Wis.).

The Loyalty Order required a loyalty investigation of *every* person entering the federal executive branch. The investigations were highly problematic from the point of view of civil rights because the order never specifically defined "loyalty" or "disloyalty." It did list the following as grounds for an adverse finding: sabotage, espionage, or attempts thereof; treason, sedition, or advocacy thereof; advocacy of revolution or the use of force or violence to alter the constitutional regime; intentional unauthorized disclosure of certain documents or information; serving the interests of another government, on the job, in preference to those of the United States; membership, affiliation, or sympathetic association with subversive organizations, as identified by the U.S. Attorney General.

These grounds were not meant to be exhaustive, and loyalty investigations ranged widely over subjects such as the individual's views regarding racial equality and integration, marriage and premarital sex, appropriate reading material, peace, civil liberties, and even religious practices. Government employees were entitled to hearings before departmental loyalty boards. Adverse findings could be appealed to a national Loyalty Review Board within the U.S. Civil Service Commission. Fourteen regional loyalty boards were used to screen applicants. Initially the standard for dismissal or refusal of employment was "on all the evidence, reasonable grounds exist for belief that the person involved is disloyal to the government of the United States." However, in 1951 more of the burden of persuasion was transferred to the individual by allowing adverse actions whenever there was "a reasonable doubt as to the loyalty of the person involved."

The hearings fell far short of constitutional due process from the perspective of the 1990s. The charges against an individual were stated only as specifically as security considerations permitted in the eyes of those making them. Confrontation and cross-examination were not required, and statements against individuals might not be sworn. A total of 560 persons were removed under the Loyalty Order; another 1,192 left federal service after receiving interrogatories or charges under the order.

The constitutionality of Executive Order 9835 was upheld by an equally divided Supreme Court in *Bailey v. Richardson* (1951). The order was replaced by Executive Order 10450 (the Security Order; 18 Fed. Reg. 2489 [1953]).

### BIBLIOGRAPHY

Bontecou, Eleanor. *The Federal Loyalty-Security Program.* 1953.
Brown, Ralph. *Loyalty and Security.* 1958.
Emerson, Thomas, and David Helfeld. "Loyalty among Government Employees." *Yale Law Journal* 58 (1948): 1–143.
Rosenbloom, David H. *Federal Service and the Constitution.* 1971.

DAVID H. ROSENBLOOM

**EXECUTIVE ORDER 9981** (1948). This order (13 Fed. Reg. 4313), by President Harry S. Truman, established a policy of "equality of treatment and opportunity for all persons in the armed forces without regard to race, color, religion, or national origin" and created a presidential committee to oversee its implementation. The emphasis in the implementation effort was on desegregation, since proponents of non-discrimination believed that "separate but equal" was per se discriminatory. As a desegregation policy, the presidential order was effectively implemented by its scheduled deadline, and on 1 January 1955, the Defense Department announced that there were no longer any all-black units in the armed forces.

Truman issued Executive Order 9981 eight years after the Selective Service Act of 1940 had stipulated that in the selection and training of men under the act there should be no discrimination against any person on account of race or color. In actual practice, however, throughout WORLD WAR II the army (and the air force as a part of the army) followed a racial policy that restricted enlisted strength to 10 percent black, segregated units, and greatly limited job opportunities. The navy did not accept blacks in any capacity other than as mess attendants until it began receiving its manpower through Selective Service in February 1943, and at that time the War Manpower Commission insisted that the navy accept blacks in the same proportion as the other branches.

At least as late as May 1948, Truman did not intend to issue an executive order regarding discrimination in the armed forces. Rather, his policy was to pursue gradual change administratively, and he neither sought nor supported legislative action on the matter. Events that occurred after May caused a change in strategy. Armed forces desegregation became an important point of conflict in the congressional controversy over a new draft law; the Republican convention in late June adopted a platform that opposed racial segregation in the armed services; and after the civil rights platform fight on the floor at the Democratic convention in mid July, Mississippi and Alabama delegates walked out. President Truman convened the "do-nothing" Republican Eightieth Congress to prove that the Republicans would not act on their civil rights platform, and on 26 July, the eve of his appearance before the special session of Congress, he announced his Executive Order 9981.

While Truman issued his order in 1948 for campaign reasons, he fully intended that the policy be effected. Under the leadership of Charles Fahy, former Solicitor General, the Committee on Equality of Treatment and Opportunity in the Armed Services quietly worked behind the scenes with the services to implement the President's policy and hence did not arouse opposition. Since the presidential order offered loopholes for those who might seek them and lacked a time limit for implementation, much depended upon the committee members and their decisions and the attitude of the military command, as well as upon presidential support.

James Forrestal, who succeeded Frank Knox as Secretary of the Navy in 1944, did not resist efforts to change the status of blacks as Knox had and was fully committed to integrating the navy; and W. Stuart Symington, who became the first secretary of an independent air force in September 1947, was also determined to achieve racial integration in that service. The situation in the army was markedly different. Some of the highest-ranking army officials maintained that the President's order did not require an end to segregation. Gordon Gray, Secretary of the Army, was slow in reconciling differences with the Fahy Committee, especially on the issues of racial quotas and policies and procedures on assignments. In fact, the army would not have moved as speedily toward desegregation had not the KOREAN WAR begun in June 1950. Even then, Gen. Douglas MacArthur refused to use the available black troops to their fullest capacity or to integrate them. This situation changed only when Gen. Matthew Ridgway replaced MacArthur.

### BIBLIOGRAPHY

Dafiume, Richard M. *Desegregation of the U.S. Armed Forces.* 1969.

McCoy, Donald R., and Richard S. Ruetten. *Quest and Response*. 1973.

MacGregor, Morris J., and Bernard C. Nalty. *Blacks in the United States Armed Forces: Basic Documents*. 13 vols. 1977.

President's Committee on Equality of Treatment and Opportunity in the Armed Forces. *Freedom to Serve*. 1950.

RUTH P. MORGAN

**EXECUTIVE ORDER 10340** (1952). Signed by President Harry S. Truman late in the evening of 8 April 1952, less than three hours before the United Steel Workers of America, CIO, were to begin a nationwide steel strike, Executive Order 10340 (17 Fed. Reg. 3139) directed the Secretary of Commerce to take possession of the steel mills and keep them operating. Among other things, Secretary of Commerce Charles Sawyer was specifically ordered to "determine and prescribe terms and conditions of employment under which the plants . . . and other properties . . . shall be operated." This aspect of the President's order was particularly irksome because executives of the steel companies feared that when the businesses were returned to private hands after the seizure was terminated, they would be stuck with the terms of a labor contract negotiated between the steel workers and the government, which they saw as partial to the union.

Throughout the winter of 1951–1952 a dispute had simmered over the size of the wage increase demanded by the union and how such a wage increase would be paid for. The companies argued that any wage hike required an increase in the price of steel; the government contended that industry earnings were more than ample to afford both a wage increase and substantial profits and that any boost in steel prices would only add fuel to already-spiraling inflation. Rejecting the imposition of an eighty-day cooling-off period under the TAFT-HARTLEY ACT (1947) as both inequitable (because the union had already twice voluntarily postponed its strike) and ineffective (because after eighty days the union would still be legally entitled to strike), President Truman ordered seizure of the mills as the only alternative to doing nothing.

The government disclaimed reliance on either the Defense Production Act (64 Stat. 798 [1950]) or the Universal Military Training and Service Act (63 Stat. 1067 [1949]) in justifying the seizure. In order to justify the seizure or taking of private property (with the corollary requirement that just compensation be paid), the former act required that the government institute regular condemnation proceedings while the latter required that the government place orders for specific articles or materials. Not only had Congress failed to authorize the steel seizure, but it had in fact specifically rejected seizure as a method of resolving labor-management disputes in legislative debate over the Taft-Hartley Act and on other occasions.

In the absence of reliance on any statutory basis for governmental seizure of private industry in peacetime, the executive order cited the President's 16 December 1950 declaration of a national emergency, which authorized U. S. military support for the United Nation's effort to repel North Korean aggression against South Korea during the KOREAN WAR. Although Congress was never asked to declare war and the military response came to be labeled "a police action," the executive order justified seizure of the mills on the grounds that maintenance of steel production was crucial to military success and the safety of American troops. The Supreme Court subsequently held the seizure to be unconstitutional in YOUNGSTOWN SHEET & TUBE CO. v. SAWYER (1952).

BIBLIOGRAPHY

Marcus, Maeva. *Truman and the Steel Seizure Case: The Limits of Presidential Power*. 1977.

Westin, Alan F. *The Anatomy of a Constitutional Law Case*. 1958.

CRAIG R. DUCAT

**EXECUTIVE ORDER 11063** (1962). This order (27 Fed. Reg. 11527), by President John F. Kennedy, declared an official national public policy of nondiscrimination in federally assisted housing and established the Committee on Equal Opportunity in Housing. The President charged the committee to coordinate federal activities under the order, to examine all agency rules, to make recommendations, to report to the President, and to encourage educational programs by private groups. The housing order fulfilled Kennedy's campaign promise and was the culmination of more than two decades of effort by various groups.

When Kennedy assumed the presidency, the government had been a participant in housing programs for three decades. During this time only minor gains toward nondiscrimination in housing had been made through a few administrative rules and regulations. Federal housing programs included publicly owned and operated housing and financial assistance for private housing, both operated through private industry or local public authorities. The major racial issue in the federal housing program was the extent to which the national government should control the discriminatory practices of private business and local public agencies. As a practical matter, policies with regard to the housing of racial minorities depended on the agencies involved.

Pressure began during the administration of Harry

S. Truman for a fair housing EXECUTIVE ORDER and continued through the administration of Dwight D. Eisenhower. Civil rights groups insisted that the housing agencies had ample authority to issue regulations to prevent segregation in housing financed in whole or in part by federal funds. By 1961, however, the Federal Housing Administration (FHA), the Public Housing Administration, and the Urban Renewal Administration had made it clear that further steps to assure equal opportunity to all Americans would await presidential or legislative direction.

In addition to the recommendations of interested groups and both private and governmental study committees, the two major parties pledged for the first time in 1960 to take action to prohibit discrimination in federally assisted housing. To offset the pressures from civil rights advocates, others (such as representatives of the real estate interests, southern politicians, and some administrators in the housing agencies) opposed an executive order on fair housing. They argued that it would slow down the construction program and that the South would simply refuse federal aid, thus hurting the minorities the order was designed to aid.

Executive Order 11063 included federally owned housing, public housing, urban renewal, and housing financed with the aid of FHA-insured or Veterans Administration-guaranteed loans, but it did not include conventional loans and mortgages by financial institutions regulated by federal agencies. The order placed primary responsibility for obtaining compliance with the nondiscrimination policy on the various executive agencies that administered housing programs—first through conciliation, and then through sanctions. The sanctions included canceling the contract for federal aid, barring the violator from further aid, and refusing to approve a lending institution as a beneficiary under any program. Agencies were also authorized to refer violations to the Attorney General for civil or criminal action under existing laws.

In 1964 Congress passed legislation that in effect validated Executive Order 11063. However, Title VI of the CIVIL RIGHTS ACT OF 1964 only covered federally assisted public housing, and therefore Executive Order 11063 continued to apply to the FHA mortgage insurance programs and VA-guaranteed loans. President Lyndon B. Johnson shifted the emphasis from executive action to legislation and requested a federal open-housing law in his STATE OF THE UNION MESSAGE on 12 January 1966. His proposals were accepted in a measure that he signed on 11 April 1968, which banned discrimination in housing by progressive stages, the first stage to cover housing already included in the 1962 executive order.

BIBLIOGRAPHY

McKay, David H. *Housing and Race in Industrial Society.* 1977.
Morgan, Ruth P. *The President and Civil Rights: Policy Making by Executive Order.* 1970.
U.S. Commission on Civil Rights. *Hearings on Housing.* 2 vols. 1959.

RUTH P. MORGAN

**EXECUTIVE ORDER 11246** (1965). This order (30 Fed. Reg. 12319, 12935), by President Lyndon B. Johnson, abolished the President's Committee on Equal Employment Opportunity and transferred its functions to the Civil Service Commission and the Department of Labor. Made possible by the passage of the CIVIL RIGHTS ACT OF 1964, the order signaled the culmination of efforts of five Presidents from Franklin D. Roosevelt to Johnson to implement policies of fair employment practices. Title VII of the Civil Rights Act of 1964 banned discriminatory employment practices and created the first statutory committee, a five-member Equal Employment Opportunity Commission, with enforcement responsibilities.

Presidents pledged to support legislation on fair employment practices beginning with the 1944 Republican platform and the 1948 Democratic platform. In spite of wide support for fair employment legislation, no fair employment practices bill ever came to a vote in the Senate, and on only one occasion did such a bill pass in the House until Congress passed the Civil Rights Act of 1964. The bills proposed were of two general types: those with enforcement or penalty provisions (compulsory) and those with persuasive or educational provisions (voluntary).

Congressional and administrative declarations of nondiscrimination policies had existed with little effect before President Roosevelt issued Executive Order 8802 in 1941, the first in a series of orders on fair employment practices. The subsequent pattern of presidential activity for two decades was one of incremental change—a reemphasis upon a mandate against discrimination and the search for adequate machinery to enforce the mandate. With increasing experience, succeeding EXECUTIVE ORDERS contained stronger mandates.

Presidents Roosevelt, Harry S. Truman, Dwight D. Eisenhower, and John F. Kennedy issued ten executive orders during their presidencies that set policies and created seven different committees to implement them: the first and second Committee on Fair Employment Practice (Roosevelt, Executive Order 8802, 6 Fed. Reg. 3109 [1941] and Executive Order 9346, 8 Fed. Reg. 7183 [1943]); Fair Employment Board in the Civil Service Commission (Truman, Executive Order 9980, 13 Fed. Reg. 4311 [1948]); Committee on Government Contract Compliance (Truman, Executive Order 10308, 16 Fed. Reg. 12303 [1951]); Government Contract Committee (Eisenhower, Executive Order 10479, 18 Fed. Reg. 4899 [1953]); Committee on Government Employment Policy (Eisenhower, Executive Order 10590, 19 Fed. Reg. 409 [1955]); and Committee on Equal Employment Opportunity (Kennedy, Executive Order 10925, 26 Fed. Reg. 1977 [1961]). The three other fair employment practices executive orders strengthened the authority of these committees (Truman, Executive Order 9664, 10 Fed. Reg. 15301 [1945]; Eisenhower, Executive Order 10557, 19 Fed. Reg. 5655 [1954]; and Kennedy, Executive Order 11114, 28 Fed. Reg. 6485 [1963]).

Prohibiting discrimination in employment within the executive branch by executive order without statutory authority posed no legal problem. In order to reach private employment, President Dwight D. Eisenhower introduced provisions in government contracts that eliminated discrimination in work done for the government as the means to prevent federal money from supporting discriminatory practices. But without statutory authority, presidential staffs found no way to reach labor unions or to reach thousands of firms not parties to government contracts.

Aside from the important positive achievements the presidential committees may have made in opening jobs and opportunities for members of minority groups, these Presidents laid the groundwork for subsequent legislation and for statutory committees. When the Equal Employment Opportunity Commission was created by Congress in 1964, and when the Department of Labor and the Civil Service Commission assumed the responsibilities of the President's Committee on Equal Employment Opportunity in 1965, all benefited from the many studies that had been made in previous years.

With the added responsibilities for the federal government under the Civil Rights Act of 1964, President Johnson asked Vice President HUBERT H. HUMPHREY to assume the task of coordinating the government's many programs on civil rights, including those on fair employment. The President formalized this arrangement by creating the President's Council on Equal Opportunity, established by Executive Order 11197 (30 Fed. Reg. 1721) in 1965 under independent constitutional authority and funded as an interdepartmental committee, with the Vice President as chairperson. After he had studied the activities of the various federal agencies involved in the field of civil rights, Humphrey wrote the President on 24 September 1965 to advise him that the time had passed when it was necessary to have special administrative machinery in

order to ensure compliance with a national policy of nondiscrimination. President Johnson thus abolished the Committee on Equal Employment Opportunity by Executive Order 11246; he also abolished the Council on Equal Opportunity by Executive Order 11247 (30 Fed. Reg. 12327 [1965]).

### BIBLIOGRAPHY

Norgren, Paul H., and Samuel E. Hill. *Toward Fair Employment*. 1964.
Ruchames, Louis. *Race, Jobs, and Politics: The Story of FEPC*. 1953.
Sovern, Michael I. *Legal Restraints on Racial Discrimination in Employment*. 1966.

RUTH P. MORGAN

**EXECUTIVE ORDER 12291** (1981). Soon after his inauguration, President Ronald Reagan promulgated Executive Order 12291, titled "Federal Regulation." The order requires executive agencies, to the extent permitted by statute, to observe cost-benefit principles when promulgating regulations. (The order does not apply to the independent regulatory agencies.) Affected agencies must prepare documents that evaluate proposed major rules according to a prescribed "regulatory impact analysis" (RIA). The overall purpose is to maximize net benefits to society from regulation. Accordingly, each RIA must estimate costs and benefits associated with a rule (in monetary terms where possible), and must identify the incidence of these effects. Proposed rules and accompanying RIAs must be sent to the OFFICE OF MANAGEMENT AND BUDGET (OMB), which reviews them and discusses them with the agencies. This function has since been placed in the OFFICE OF INFORMATION AND REGULATORY AFFAIRS (OIRA) within OMB. Agencies may not promulgate rules until review is complete, unless statutory or judicial deadlines for rulemaking intervene.

Congress has neither directly authorized nor forbidden this review program, which continued under the Bush administration. Accordingly, the legal basis for the program is the President's constitutional power to supervise the executive branch pursuant to his obligation to ensure the faithful execution of the laws, buttressed by his explicit authority to require subordinate officers to furnish him opinions in writing concerning their performance of their duties. The program builds on predecessor forms of executive review of regulation under the Nixon, Ford, and Carter administrations. All the earlier programs employed some form of cost-benefit analysis. The unique feature of Executive Order 12291 is that it empowers OMB not merely to review proposed rules, but to prevent their issuance while it does so. This feature of the order has given

OMB greatly enhanced leverage over agencies, and has made this the most effective of the review programs from the point of view of the President. Not surprisingly, substantial controversy, much of it political in nature, has dogged the program from its inception.

Controversy has centered on three aspects of the program. First, some important rules have encountered substantial delays, although most rules do not. Occasionally, delay caused by the review process has exceeded a statutory deadline for rulemaking. Whether the delay that necessarily attends adding a new layer of rule-making process is justified by producing better rules is a matter of political controversy [*see* RULE-MAKING POWER].

Second, to assuage congressional concerns that decisions placed in agencies by statute could be transferred to OMB, the order provides that it is not to displace the agencies' legal responsibilities. Nevertheless, charges that the review process became one of command not consultation have arisen and have been denied by OIRA. Overall, the process has been one of negotiation between OIRA and agencies. Tensions created by differences in institutional viewpoint are inherent in the system. Agencies consider themselves the experts in resolving fact and policy issues under their statutes; OMB and its components consider the agencies to be overly parochial in their priorities. These tensions parallel those that are familiar in the executive budgetary process.

Third, there has also been controversy about the appropriate degree of openness that the review program should embody. Because the process entails discussions at high levels in the executive branch, concepts of EXECUTIVE PRIVILEGE are relevant. OIRA asserts the value that underlies executive privilege—the need for policy debate in the executive to be confidential, so that it will be candid. Also, disclosure requirements have costs to executive efficiency. On the other hand, it is necessary to accommodate these considerations to administrative-law requirements that rules be based on known administrative records that fully support them. It is possible for special interests to channel policy arguments through sympathetic executive officers, thereby avoiding otherwise applicable requirements that rule-making submissions be public. After some years of experience under the program, a compromise was worked out between the administration and congressional committees. It provided that most written communications between OMB and the agencies be made public after the rule to which they pertain is promulgated, but that informal oral communications within the executive may remain confiden-

tial. Thus, the EXECUTIVE ORDER program has shown a characteristic of many experimental programs—early periods of trial and error eventually lead to more regularized and open processes.

### BIBLIOGRAPHY

Bruff, Harold H. "Presidential Management of Agency Rulemaking." *George Washington Law Review* 57 (1989): 533–595.

"Cost-Benefit Analysis and Agency Decision-Making: An Analysis of Executive Order No. 12,291." Symposium. *Arizona Law Review* 23 (1981): 1195–1298.

National Academy of Public Administration. *Presidential Management of Rulemaking in Regulatory Agencies.* 1987.

HAROLD H. BRUFF

**EXECUTIVE ORDER 12498** (1985). Executive Order 12498, promulgated by President Ronald Reagan in 1985, established a "regulatory planning process" to be implemented through formulation of an annual regulatory program for the executive agencies of the federal government. (Independent regulatory agencies are not included.) The head of each executive agency must send the OFFICE OF MANAGEMENT AND BUDGET (OMB) a draft regulatory program containing a description of all significant regulatory actions to be undertaken in the next year. After OMB reviews the plans for consistency with administration policy and discusses them with the agencies, final regulatory plans are drafted and combined into a comprehensive plan for the executive agencies, which is published as the Regulatory Program of the United States Government for the coming year.

This program is a companion to the cost-benefit process initiated by EXECUTIVE ORDER 12291 (1981). The purpose and effects of both orders are to give agency heads and OMB officials more control of regulatory initiatives that have begun in staff components of the agencies. If, instead, agency heads simply reacted to staff proposals once they were fully developed, the proposals could attain enough momentum to elude control by higher echelons. Thus, Executive Order 12498 reflects a perception that the political appointees who head agencies are subject to capture by their staffs of civil servants. The staffs have value preferences of their own, substantial expertise in the issues confronted by the agency, and enough longevity of tenure to press indefinitely for favored policies.

By ensuring that agency heads take time to set overall regulatory priorities each year and then conform them to administration policy, the order mimics the budgeting process. Without the discipline that the order imposes, it would be easy for busy agency heads to defer larger questions of overall priorities in favor of resolving the crisis of the moment. The order also responds to inherent differences in outlook between agencies and the OMB. Agencies tend to pursue their own statutory duties without attention to how they fit into broader national priorities. The OMB, situated at the apex of the executive branch, can weigh competing claims on scarce national resources and decide which ones are deserving of regulatory emphasis. Of course, these decisions must be made consistently with statutory directives concerning regulation. To ensure that Congress and the public can monitor executive priority-setting and its consistency with law, the OMB releases copies of agency drafts of their regulatory programs to the public after formulation of the final administration program for the year.

### BIBLIOGRAPHY

"Presidential Policy Management of Agency Rules Under Reagan Order 12498." Note. *Administrative Law Review* 38 (1986): 63.

Strauss, Peter L., and Cass R. Sunstein. "The Role of the President and OMB in Informal Rulemaking." *Administrative Law Review* 38 (1986): 181–207.

HAROLD H. BRUFF

**EXECUTIVE ORDERS.** Presidents have long made legally binding policy without the participation of Congress by issuing executive orders that command government officials to take or refrain from taking some kind of action. These orders have been used to craft foreign policy actions, like the order in 1992 directing the Coast Guard to return Haitian refugees found at sea to Haiti without a refugee claims assessment in a neutral location. Executive orders have also been used to make domestic policy, as in the case of the much debated Executive Order 12291 (1981) authorizing the Office of Management and Budget (OMB) to use wide-ranging powers of review over agency issuance of regulations.

**The Numbering System.** By the time Ronald Reagan left office in 1989, there had been approximately 12,667 executive orders promulgated. The number is approximate because the exact number of orders is unknown. The present numbering system was based upon an effort to backtrack in history to find the earliest executive order clearly delineated as such, which is taken to have been one issued by Abraham Lincoln, and numbering forward. However, because Presidents have historically issued the equivalent of executive orders that may have been called by other names and because there was no uniform process for publishing such orders until the passage of the Federal Register Act in 1935, the current numbering system is little

more than a useful approximation that is accepted as a matter of convention.

Although the Federal Register Act mandated publication of orders in the *Federal Register* and attempted to impose some degree of uniformity on the format in which they are promulgated, its provisions are very general. The more specific guideline for the issuance of executive orders is itself an executive order, E.O. 11030 (1962). However, even that order does little more than describe the general format and routing for the development of drafts and final publication. Security-classified orders are not published at all [*see* National-security directives].

Because of the problems of access to documentation and the late adoption of rules for uniform publication, a codification of all executive orders that would present all currently valid orders has been difficult to develop. After considerable effort, the Office of the Federal Register has published a codification of orders and Proclamations promulgated since the end of World War II.

**Types and Legal Force.** Executive orders issued on a valid assertion of constitutional or statutory authority are legally binding. Courts have held that the legislature may ratify an executive order after its issuance. The failure of the Congress to take any kind of action with respect to an order that is consequently permitted to stand for an extended period is taken as evidence of approval. This is the so-called acquiescence doctrine.

However, the President may not promulgate an executive order that violates a valid statute or usurps the constitutional authority of a coordinate branch of government. On that ground, Congress may nullify an executive order unless the President can demonstrate an independent basis of constitutional authority in Article II to support it.

The legal force of presidential action does not depend upon labeling it an executive order. The Supreme Court has held that there is no meaningful legal distinction between, for example, a presidential proclamation and an executive order. As a matter of form, a proclamation is generally directed to persons outside of government while an executive order governs actions by government officials and agencies. Proclamations are most often used for hortatory purposes like the declaration of a national day of celebration for a group or historical figure. However, they have been used for very important actions, like President George Washington's Proclamation of Neutrality.

In truth, the effort to distinguish between internal and external effect is not helpful, since orders directed to executive-branch officials or agencies are often aimed at commanding them to carry out policy governing all citizens in a certain way. Thus, orders directed at officers involved in immigration and refugee administration plainly affect asylum seekers. Similarly, orders like E.O. 12291 and EXECUTIVE ORDER 12498—mandating regulatory review by the Office of Management and Budget and President Bush's moratorium on agency rulemaking, while specifically directed to administrative agencies, affect the implementation of a wide variety of major policies and therefore clearly have an impact upon state and local governments as well as individual citizens.

Beyond the use of proclamations, Presidents have employed a variety of other formats to issue what are, in effect, executive orders. Thus President Bush's order in 1992 for executive agencies to impose a ninety-day moratorium on the issuance of new regulations and to review existing regulations to determine which ones could be eliminated or modified to be less burdensome, was issued in the form of a presidential memorandum (Memorandum for Certain Department and Agency Heads on the Subject of "Reducing the Burden of Government Regulations" 1992). Indeed, although E.O. 12291 was the basis for the Reagan administration's creation of the Vice President's Task Force on Regulatory Relief as part of the regulatory review process when George Bush was Vice President, later President Bush did not see the need for a new or amended executive order when he created the Vice President's Council on Competitiveness under Vice President DAN QUAYLE, which effectively replaced the Task Force on Regulatory Relief and gave the new body much greater power than that exercised by its predecessor.

Some Presidents have avoided reference to executive orders in part because there is no specific requirement for publication of other kinds of documents. For example, there has been considerable tension between the White House and Congress over the use of national security directives (NSDs). In a number of cases, the contents of these directives, issued by the President to various executive agencies, have not even been disclosed to Congress.

**Tensions with Congress.** Where there is no clear order or proclamation, as in the case of the Quayle commission, or where there are devices such as NSDs in use that are not disclosed, the possibilities for tensions between the President and Congress may be particularly high.

Similarly, where an order is issued unilaterally by the White House without much open public discussion or informal exchange with key figures in the Congress and if it concerns particularly important questions, the potential for conflict may be great. Thus, the issuance of E.O. 12356 (1982) governing security classifications

during the Reagan administration caused noticeable frustration on Capitol Hill. Although there is legislation prohibiting disclosure of classified information, the definition of security classification and government policy in the handling of classified material have historically been addressed by executive orders. The Carter administration revised the entire system in its executive order on security classification, E.O. 12065 (1978), through a relatively open and participative process, to reduce the amount of classified material and move toward as much declassification of existing material as possible. The Reagan replacement took a much more restrictive approach and did not involve conversations with the participants involved in the earlier version. The result was substantial strain in PRESIDENTIAL-CONGRESSIONAL RELATIONS.

History suggests that the significant use of executive orders by Presidents since Lyndon B. Johnson, and in particular Jimmy Carter and his successors, has been both a cause and effect of presidential-congressional tensions. Johnson promulgated EXECUTIVE ORDER 11246 (1965), which laid the basis for what came to be known, during the Nixon administration, as the PHILADELPHIA PLAN, requiring affirmative action in government contracting in part because he could not move the same policy through the Congress. Others have taken action that they thought was implied in more or less expansive terms by prior statutes. Presidents Richard M. Nixon and Carter both took significant action based in part on the assertion that existing legislation authorized their decisions. In August 1971, President Nixon issued a set of executive orders and proclamations, most importantly E.O. 11615 and Proclamation 4074, which imposed, among other things, a freeze on wages, prices, rents, and salaries and a 10 percent added fee on imports, claiming implied authority from the ECONOMIC STABILIZATION ACT of 1970 and the TRADE EXPANSION ACT of 1962. Similarly, President Carter's imposition of an oil import fee, later struck down by federal courts, was also based upon a broad reading of the trade act.

**Legal Challenges.** Despite the fact that the judiciary has struck down a variety of orders over time, it is very difficult to mount a legal challenge to such a presidential action. Some of the most celebrated cases, like the YOUNGSTOWN SHEET & TUBE CO. v. SAWYER (1952) ruling striking down President Harry S. Truman's EXECUTIVE ORDER 10340 directing the Secretary of Commerce to take over steel mills in order to keep them in operation during a labor dispute and the challenges to Nixon's wage-price freeze and Carter's oil import fee, involved cases where there was an immediate and direct effect upon specific property claims. There the parties were clear and the basis for a legal challenge was obvious.

However, in many cases, the situation is considerably more complex. Thus, when the Office of Management and Budget began to delay issuance of regulations by agencies obligated by statute to produce them, it became very difficult for frustrated critics to get the issue of the validity of the executive order into court. It was only when regulators like the Environmental Protection Agency, caught between congressional mandates and the OMB, provided information to such critics that a suit charging violations of statutory obligations in the name of regulatory review was made.

Even assuming that presidential critics can develop a case that will survive procedural roadblocks, the larger problems remain. Where there has been a lack of formal congressional opposition, courts tend to defer to the President. That is particularly, though not universally, true with respect to executive orders affecting foreign policy questions. The Supreme Court, for example, upheld the executive order issued by President Carter, E.O. 12283 (1981), and reaffirmed by President Reagan, suspending claims pending in United States courts involving Iranian assets affected by the agreement reached between the two countries for release of American hostages ending the IRANIAN HOSTAGE CRISIS [see DAMES & MOORE V. REGAN]. Even though there were obvious parties with clear property interests at stake, and despite the fact that Congress had taken no action on the presidential move, the Court concluded that there was legislative acquiescence in the Iran settlement that should be understood as congressional support. Coupled with the general judicial deference to presidential foreign policy decisions, that acquiescence was enough to sustain a dramatic presidential action.

More often, the nature of limits on executive orders is less obvious and direct. For example, the Reagan regulatory review orders asserted that the OMB was to proceed "to the extent permitted by law" but the mechanics and politics of the situation made it virtually impossible for the rulemaking process to meet both the substantive and procedural requirements of all of the applicable legislation. In some cases, the orders themselves do not contain language that suggests a problem of authority but other accompanying documents may. Thus, the full implications of E.O. 12498, the second Reagan regulatory review order, did not become clear to those outside government until they saw the White House memoranda to executive-branch agencies that were issued along with the executive order. These implementation guidelines defined terms and processes discussed in E.O. 12498 in such a way as to give the Office of Management and Budget a great deal more power than would be understood from a simple reading of the order itself.

If challenges to orders are difficult with respect to presidential actions purportedly based upon statutes, they are all the more problematic where the President grounds an executive order on a broad claim of constitutional authority. Historically, periods of war and national emergency have prompted some Presidents to issue large numbers of orders relying upon assumed powers which the Congress later ratified. Franklin Delano Roosevelt, for example, issued 3,727 executive orders during his years in the White House. However, in most instances modern Presidents have relied upon some kind of claim to statutory authority for their actions. During the Carter administration, however, the White House regularly made both particular assertions of statutory authority, either direct or implied, and more general claims that the President was acting under the authority "vested in me as President of the United States." Since then the President has more often asserted broad constitutional claims alone or with limited claims of statutory authority as the basis for action. Thus, the regulatory review process established by E.O. 12291 is grounded only on President Reagan's assertion of "the authority vested in me as President by the Constitution and Laws of the United States of America." The same was true of the executive order on the family (E.O. 12606 [1987]) and federalism (E.O. 12612 [1987]).

Where the President's order is considered to be directed at internal management functions and supervision of executive-branch employees, as in President Bush's E.O. 12674 (1989) setting forth "Principles of Ethical Conduct for Government Officers and Employees," there is often acceptance of a broad constitutional claim on grounds that the President is responsible for the operation of the executive branch under Article II. However, when the President ranges beyond that kind of action, the complexities grow. It is often uncertain just what provision of the "Constitution and laws" the President is asserting.

Hence, executive orders are flexible tools that offer the President a variety of options. At the same time, they are complex and sometimes dangerous in both legal and political terms. They have occasionally tempted Presidents to abuse powers conferred by statute or to claim constitutional powers they do not rightly possess.

## BIBLIOGRAPHY

Cash, Robert. "Presidential Power: Use and Enforcement of Executive Orders." *Notre Dame Lawyer* 39 (1963): 44–55.

Hart, James. *The Ordinance Making Powers of the President of the United States*. 1925.

Keenan, Hugh S. "Executive Orders: A Brief History of Their Use and the President's Power to Issue Them." In U.S. Senate. Report of the Special Committee on National Emergencies and Delegated Emergency Powers. *Executive Orders in Times of War and National Emergency*. 93d Cong., 2d sess. 1974. Committee Print.

Morgan, Ruth P. *The President and Civil Rights: Policy-Making by Executive Order*. 1970.

Office of the Federal Register. *Codification of Presidential Proclamations and Executive Orders, April 13, 1945–January 20, 1989*. 1990.

Rosenberg, Morton. "Beyond the Limits of Executive Power: Presidential Control of Agency Rulemaking under Executive Order 12,291." *Michigan Law Review* 20 (1981): 193–247.

U.S. House of Representatives. Committee on Government Operations. *Executive Orders and Proclamations: A Study of a Use of Presidential Power*. 85th Cong., 1st sess. 1957. Committee Print.

PHILLIP J. COOPER

**EXECUTIVE POWER.** Article II of the Constitution stipulates that all executive power resides in the hands of the President. Article II defines formal executive power, but like many constitutional provisions it is a framework, not a blueprint. While the President may initially define his own executive powers under the Constitution, his interpretations may be challenged before the Supreme Court and by Congress. For example, President Harry S. Truman, citing his constitutional authority as CHIEF EXECUTIVE and COMMANDER IN CHIEF, seized the steel mills in 1952 to prevent a crippling strike during the KOREAN WAR [*see* EXECUTIVE ORDER 10340]. However, in the *Steel Seizure Cases* (1952), the Supreme Court held that the President had exceeded his constitutional powers [*see* YOUNGSTOWN SHEET & TUBE CO. v. SAWYER].

**Overview.** The Framers of the Constitution, while recognizing the importance of the presidency, did not foresee the vast expansion of presidential power that eventually occurred. Article II states that "the executive Power shall be vested in a President" and that "the President shall be Commander in Chief of the Army and Navy of the United States, and of the Militia." Aside from providing that the President "shall take Care that the Laws be faithfully executed" and that "he may require the Opinion, in writing, of the principal Officer in each of the executive Departments," the Constitution does not specify how "executive" power is to be exercised.

Under the CHECKS AND BALANCES system, the Constitution specifies that certain executive powers are subject to senatorial ADVICE AND CONSENT: the TREATY-MAKING POWER and the power to "appoint Ambassadors, other public Ministers and Consuls, Judges of the supreme Court, and all other Officers of the United States whose Appointments are not herein otherwise provided for." But, "Congress may by Law vest the Appointment of such inferior Officers, as they think proper, in the President alone, in the Courts of Law, or in the Heads of Departments."

Article II gives the President direct and indirect legislative powers and responsibilities. He may veto congressional legislation, and his action can be overridden only by a two-thirds vote in the House and the Senate. Article II also provides that the President is from time to time, to recommend legislation to Congress and give Congress a STATE OF THE UNION MESSAGE. The President can also convene either or both houses of Congress on "extraordinary occasions."

Article II makes the President the ceremonial head of state, by providing, for example, that he must "receive Ambassadors and other public Ministers." The President represents that nation at home and abroad, and his ceremonial role enhances his informal powers by making him in a sense both a king and a prime minister.

**Chief Executive.** The Constitution provides that the President shall "take Care that the Laws be faithfully executed." This simple provision makes the President the nation's Chief Executive, and he alone exercises primary executive power. The executive branch is an extension of the presidency, and the President may "require the Opinion, in writing, of the principal Officer in each of the executive Departments, upon any subject relating to the Duties of their respective offices."

The Framers envisioned a small and easily controllable executive branch performing the essential executive functions of defense, foreign relations, revenue raising, LAW ENFORCEMENT, the post office, control over patents, regulation of navigation, territorial administration, and a few other miscellaneous responsibilities. Aside from 6,479 military personnel, 1,223 collectors of revenue, and 947 deputy postmasters, the entire executive branch in 1802 consisted of 588 persons. That figure contrasts with the over 2.5 million federal employees in the 1990s. Clearly the President's ability to control the modern executive branch is severely limited by its size, complexity, and vast responsibilities.

Regardless of changes in the scope and character of the executive branch over the years, the President's role as Chief Executive is firmly embedded in the Constitution. ALEXANDER HAMILTON in *Federalist* 72, recognized that one of the most important presidential duties was to be leader of the executive branch. He argued that since the President would appoint, albeit with the advice and consent of the Senate, members of the executive branch they should be considered as his assistants and "subject to his superintendence." Article II, coupled with Hamilton's arguments in THE FEDERALIST, support presidential control over the executive branch.

*Growth of the federal bureaucracy.* The President had little difficulty in supervising executive activities until the growth of the federal bureaucracy in the twentieth century, most notably during President Franklin D. Roosevelt's administration in the 1930s. The Hamiltonian theory that backed presidential domination of the executive branch surfaced during Roosevelt's presidency to support measures that would shore up the President's role as Chief Executive. Most importantly, the Report of the President's Committee on Administrative Management (BROWN-LOW COMMITTEE) in 1937 recommended that the President's staff be increased to give him the upper hand over the burgeoning NEW DEAL bureaucracy that threatened to run out of control completely. The committee, which Roosevelt had selected, supported his view that it was not only the constitutional responsibility of the President to be "Chief Administrator," but also that democracy and efficiency required the President to pay strict attention to his responsibilities as Chief Executive. In 1939, Roosevelt created the EXECUTIVE OFFICE OF THE PRESIDENT as a direct result of the committee's report, into which he placed the WHITE HOUSE STAFF and the then Bureau of the Budget (the OFFICE OF MANAGEMENT AND BUDGET) as central components.

Roosevelt's attempts to solidify the President's power as Chief Executive faced formidable opposition in departments and agencies that often were beholden to clientele groups and congressional committees for political support and appropriations. Presidents after Roosevelt continued attempts to buttress their powers as Chief Executive, only to find that White House control of the federal bureaucracy remained an elusive goal.

***Growth of the presidential bureaucracy.*** After Roosevelt, Democratic and Republican Presidents alike turned to their own bureaucracy, the Executive Office of the President, to help them deal with the regular bureaucracy, which had its own political constituencies separate from the President and much of which civil service rules protected from presidential removal. Both Lyndon B. Johnson and Richard M. Nixon, although from opposite sides of the political spectrum, agreed that presidential control of the bureaucracy was essential. To achieve this end both men expanded the Executive Office of the President and set the precedent of a powerful White House staff at the center of an increasingly institutionalized presidency. Later Presidents, Jimmy Carter, Ronald Reagan, and George Bush, agreed that the size and power of the federal bureaucracy was a major problem, and they kept the President's bureaucracy intact and expanded its power.

Future Presidents will undoubtedly continue to face obstacles as they strive to be effective Chief Executives. While the Constitution delegates the executive power to the President, it also creates a checks and balances system that often limits presidential power. Congress cannot directly exercise executive power, but it possesses major constitutional authority over the executive branch. Congress alone creates executive departments and agencies, unless through legislation it permits the President to do so. Congress also determines agency powers, and whether or not the courts will have the authority to review administrative decisions. Congress may create "independent" agencies that are mostly outside of presidential control. From the vantage point of Capitol Hill, the executive branch is an extension of Congress as much as of the President.

***Political limits.*** Formal constitutional prescriptions are only one component of presidential power. As the President seeks to carry out his role as Chief Executive his success depends as much upon his political skills as upon his constitutional powers. In the end, as Richard Neustadt pointed out in his famous work, *Presidential Power*, executive power depends more upon the President's responsibility to persuade others that their interests coincide with his than upon his formal powers. Departments and agencies are linked to powerful political constituencies and congressional committees that may combine to override presidential initiatives. In Neustadt's view, the Constitution makes the President a clerk, not a king. But a politically astute President can turn his clerkship into a powerful Chief Executive.

**Chief Legislator.** The role of the President as chief legislator, initially based on Article II, has vastly expanded in the twentieth century beginning with Roosevelt's administration. The President's constitutional responsibilities to recommend legislation to Congress and to inform the legislature about the state of the union from time to time, and most particularly his power to veto legislation, give him an important legislative role. But, with the exception of the veto authority, these constitutional provisions pale in comparison to important political changes that have occurred which support the President's power of LEGISLATIVE LEADERSHIP.

Outside of the Constitution, the President derives his legislative role from his position as political PARTY LEADER. Although presidential parties are loosely knit confederations of diverse interests that often cannot agree with each other, they do have PARTY PLATFORMS and represent interests that back public policies in many areas. Presidents have little influence on the platforms, and rarely even read them or know their contents. But they are sensitive to party interests. In the broadest sense the two major parties represent different national economic and social goals. Presidents stand at the head of their parties and derive a legislative role from the position.

The political mantle Presidents wear as head of their parties is further enhanced from the broad electoral base of the presidency that makes it the focus of democratic aspirations and the popularly chosen instrument for political change. This aspect of presidential power is in sharp contrast to the intentions of the Framers of the Constitution who envisioned the President as an indirectly elected statesman, not a down-to-earth politician.

*Power limits.* The President's power as chief legislator is even more limited than as Chief Executive. The Constitution makes the President Chief Executive, while it only indirectly gives him a legislative role, albeit an important one. The presidency of Franklin Roosevelt, which centralized power in the White House, marked the beginning of an ascendant presidency with a comprehensive legislative agenda. But presidential domination of the legislative sphere requires, both under the Constitution and politically, congressional assent that Presidents more often than not find elusive. The failure of parties to bridge the constitutional gap between the President and Congress is a major restraint on presidential power in the legislative arena.

*Delegation of legislative authority.* While Congress exercises the primary legislative authority under the Constitution, it may and often does delegate important legislative power to the President and executive departments and agencies [*see* DELEGATION OF LEGISLATIVE POWER]. The executive branch's role in policy implementation gives it an important voice in defining legislation. The executive fills in the details of often vaguely worded and ambiguous legislation. This is particularly true in the regulatory sphere where Congress usually cannot go very far beyond directing the executive to heed the public interest, convenience, and necessity in implementing REGULATORY POLICY and programs. By filling in legislative details under such circumstances the executive more than Congress gives legislation its true meaning.

**Commander in Chief.** Article II provides that the President "shall be Commander in Chief of the Army and Navy of the United States, and of the Militia of the several states, when called into the actual Service of the United States." The President is, in Hamilton's words, the first general and admiral of the confederacy. The President's role as Commander in Chief has assumed great proportions in times of crisis, such as during the CIVIL WAR and the wars of the twentieth century. As the power has evolved, the President makes war, even though the Constitution delegates to Congress the authority to declare war [*see* WAR, DECLARATION OF].

The Framers of the Constitution made the President Commander in Chief for two reasons. First, they wanted unequivocally to establish civilian control over the military, a principle that is essential to the preservation of constitutional democracy. Second, they found it only logical to make the President Commander in Chief as the presidency was the only office that was unified and could act with dispatch. Moreover, the Commander in Chief power is clearly executive in nature.

As Commander in Chief the President exercises EXECUTIVE PREROGATIVE power. Congress, however, checks the President. Congress alone has the power to declare war, to raise and support armies, and to determine the organization of the military and its appropriations. Presidents may claim prerogative power, but Congress may decide otherwise.

In the aftermath of the VIETNAM WAR, which its opponents saw as an abuse of presidential discretion, Congress enacted a wide range of checks upon executive power in foreign and military affairs, requiring the President to inform Congress before taking action in many areas, such as the sale of arms abroad. Congress also passed the WAR POWERS RESOLUTION of 1973, which technically required the President to gain congressional approval before committing American troops abroad for a time period longer than sixty days. Congress intended the resolution to limit the President's Commander in Chief powers that had grown so enormously in the twentieth century, although many saw the law ironically as a recognition for the first time of the constitutional authority of the President to make war. The resolution has had virtually no impact upon the President's extensive powers as Commander in Chief.

**Leader in Foreign Affairs.** So extensive is presidential power in making foreign policy that one political scientist, Aaron Wildavsky, has written that there are TWO PRESIDENCIES, one in foreign and the other in domestic affairs. When Harry Truman said categorically, "I make foreign policy," few disagreed. The two presidencies emerged after WORLD WAR II and Roosevelt's administration, which marked the beginning of an IMPERIAL PRESIDENCY in FOREIGN AFFAIRS.

During Roosevelt's administration Congress willingly delegated broad authority to the President as DIPLOMAT IN CHIEF to make foreign policy. In a historic decision, UNITED STATES V. CURTISS-WRIGHT (1936), the Supreme Court held that Congress could delegate far broader legislative authority to the President to make foreign policy than it could to make domestic policy. The *Curtiss-Wright* opinion contrasted with a prior case, SCHECHTER POULTRY CORP. V. UNITED STATES (1935), in which the Court announced the Schechter Rule, which held that in the domestic sphere the Constitution required Congress, not the President, to exercise legislative power. Congress could not delegate its exclusive authority to legislate to the President or to the executive branch. However, in the *Curtiss-Wright* case, the Court found that the Constitution gave to the President primary foreign–policy-making power that supported broad congressional delegations of authority to the executive in the foreign-policy sphere.

Presidential authority to conduct foreign policy is derived from his constitutional powers in Article II: to make treaties; nominate ambassadors and consuls; receive foreign ambassadors; and command the military forces.

The extent to which the President becomes personally involved in the conduct of foreign policy depends upon his style and the times. Foreign crises require personal presidential attention. The growth of the White House staff in the modern presidency, which includes the important post of NATIONAL SECURITY ADVISER, has enabled the White House to dominate the Secretary of State and his bureaucracy in foreign affairs.

Presidential power even over the area of foreign affairs, however, can never be absolute. Congress through legislation has restricted presidential authority in many areas and has delegated not only to the STATE DEPARTMENT but to more than forty administrative agencies the authority to make foreign-policy decisions. No President, even with a foreign-policy staff, can hope to control the bureaucratic maze that exists in foreign policy.

Moreover, the Constitution provides for the sharing of important foreign–policy-making between the President and the Senate. The Founding Fathers envisioned a major role for the Senate and as a minimum a sharing of foreign–policy-making responsibilities between the President and the Senate in the then important treaty-making area.

During much of the nineteenth century Congress and the President were equal partners in making foreign policy, with the Congress often dominant. But World War II marked at least a temporary end of important congressional power over foreign affairs. President Franklin D. Roosevelt had firmly established presidential supremacy with a cooperative Congress. Even in the area of treaty making, Presidents, starting with Franklin D. Roosevelt with an acquiescent Congress, have essentially turned to the use of executive agreements over which the President has virtually complete discretion in dealing with foreign nations.

Throughout United States history the President's power over foreign affairs has ebbed and flowed, but mostly flowed. As Justice George Sutherland wrote in his opinion in *Curtiss-Wright*:

> In the vast external realm [of foreign affairs] with its important, complicated, delegate and manifold problems, the President alone has the power [under the Constitution] to speak or listen as a representative of the nation. He *makes* treaties with the advice and consent of the Senate; but he alone negotiates. Into the field of negotiation the Senate cannot intrude; and Congress itself is powerless to invade it.

**Chief of State.** The President is the nation's chief of state by default. He exercises the ceremonial functions of the head of government, making him a king and prime minister. In Great Britain the monarch performs the ceremonial head-of-state role, but the President must carry out this demanding and time-consuming task in the United States. Being ceremonial head of state is not a "power" in the sense that being Chief Executive and Commander in Chief is, but it greatly adds to the strength of the presidency as he assumes a nonpolitical and symbolic mantle that places him above the crowd, and, particularly in times of foreign crises, helps to immunize him from political criticism. An attack upon the President under such circumstances can be viewed as unpatriotic.

As ceremonial chief of state the President represents the nation abroad as he travels, for example, to summit meetings and trade conferences. At home the President receives foreign ambassadors in elaborate ceremonies on the South Lawn of the White House, and presides over state dinners for foreign leaders. The President's ceremonial responsibilities extend far beyond activities relating to foreign affairs, and include such activities as receiving the Boy Scouts of America, Olympic athletes and other sports champions, lighting the national Christmas tree on the Washington Mall, proclaiming national holidays, and delivering messages supporting charities of all kinds. The President also must sign all bills, treaties, and certification of many appointments.

As ceremonial chief the President is also the voice of the American people. For example, President Franklin Roosevelt in 1941 expressed before a joint session of Congress the outrage of the American people at the Japanese attack on PEARL HARBOR. President George Bush similarly expressed popular outrage at the Iraq invasion of Kuwait that led to the GULF WAR in 1991.

Ceremonial functions are an important ingredient of presidential power. Presidents adopt different styles as they carry out their ceremonial role, stressing more or less White House glamour and glitz. All Presidents have recognized that being ceremonial "kings" adds to their power.

**The Reality of Presidential Power.** Popular expectations that the President is the person in charge and capable of changing the nation's course mark the modern presidency. Presidents are not expected simply to exercise narrow executive power, but to overcome the constitutional limits set by the separation of powers and checks and balances system. After Roosevelt, Presidents, regardless of affiliation, accepted the Roosevelt model of the presidency as the dominant political force.

*Contrasting views of executive power.* The ambiguity of Article II about many aspects of executive power left problems of definition to the future. The Framers of the Constitution themselves saw executive power differently and their contrasting views are best summarized by Alexander Hamilton on the one hand and James Madison on the other.

*The Hamiltonian model.* Hamilton wrote in *Federalist* 70 that "energy in the executive is a leading character in the definition of good government." Hamilton told the Constitutional Convention that what he preferred was an "elected monarch for life," something no other delegate would accept. Hamilton happily settled for the unified and independent presidency the Framers created. He viewed the separation of powers not as a limit on the executive but, because it created a presidency separate from Congress, a support for a strong even an "imperial" executive. The Constitution supported Hamilton's view by giving the President prerogative powers in Article II and a separate political constituency from that of the legislature. Ironically, from a Hamiltonian perspective, the very separation-of-powers system designed ostensibly to limit the President actually strengthened the office vis-à-vis Congress.

*The Madisonian model.* James Madison's view of executive power was the exact opposite of that of Hamilton. Madison saw the separation-of-power and checks-and-balances system as a strong limit upon the President who would be forced to carry out his responsibilities under a watchful and powerful Congress.

The history of executive power is cyclical, reflecting at different times the Hamiltonian and Madisonian models. The Hamiltonian executive prevails mostly in foreign affairs, while the weaker Madisonian executive characterizes domestic politics. Presidential ascendancy is never guaranteed.

*Presidential strengths.* The Constitution, when viewed from a Hamiltonian perspective, supports a strong executive. Political and economic changes, particularly in the twentieth century, have made the presidency the focus of national leadership, and both constitutional and political factors strengthen the executive.

*Unified office.* Unlike the plural executives of parliamentary countries, the American presidency is a single executive. Alexander Hamilton wrote in *Federalist* 70: "That unity is conducive to energy will not be disputed, decision, activity, secrecy, and dispatch, will generally characterize the proceedings of one man, in a much more eminent degree than the proceedings of any greater number; and in proportion as the number is increased, these qualities will be diminished." Inevitable internal dissention in a plural executive would "tincture the exercise of the executive authority with the spirit of habitual feebleness and dilatoriness." Moreover a plural executive would tend "to conceal faults, and destroy responsibility. . . . It often becomes impossible, amidst mutual accusations, to determine on whom the blame or the punishment of a pernicious measure . . . ought really to fall." The unified presidency has been particularly important to effective executive power in the American political system, which is characterized by political pluralism and the lack of disciplined parties. The centripetal force of the presidency has helped to aggregate diverse political interests by giving them an incentive to form national political parties to capture the presidency.

*Fixed four-year term.* Unlike prime ministers, who can lose their office upon a parliamentary vote of no confidence, Presidents have a constitutionally guaranteed four-year term subject only to the highly unlikely possibility of IMPEACHMENT. The TWENTY-SECOND AMENDMENT prevents the President from serving more than two terms, but while they are in office Presidents have some decision-making leeway. Alexander Hamilton wrote in *Federalist* 71: "Duration in office has been mentioned as the second requisite to energy of the executive authority."

*Independent constituency.* Another source of executive strength is the President's independent electoral constituency—the ELECTORAL COLLEGE. The Framers of the Constitution considered but rejected a plan to have Congress choose the President. Alexander Hamilton recognized that a strong and independent executive required an electoral constituency separate from that of Congress, which would both enable the President and give him an incentive to check Congress. Different electoral constituencies for the executive and legislature were central to the theory and practice of the separation-of-powers and checks-and-balances system. The President and Congress do not depend upon each other because they do not draw from the same base of electoral support. The President's constituency is far more national than that of the House or the Senate.

*Independent powers.* The President's prerogative powers as Chief Executive and Commander in Chief and his authority to veto legislation make the executive a powerful independent force. Executive initiatives do not depend upon legislative majorities as they do in parliamentary systems. Extreme presidential actions have occasionally been challenged in the courts, but with only a few important exceptions the judiciary has exercised self-restraint and refused to overturn presidential initiatives.

*Growth of executive responsibilities.* Franklin D. Roosevelt made the presidency the focus of leadership. The Roosevelt presidency assumed wide-ranging responsibilities to deal with the Great Depression. For the first time the President became the "Manager of Prosperity," to use Clinton Rossiter's apt phrase in his classic work *The American Presidency* (1956). Congress strengthened the executive's capacity to make economic policy by creating the COUNCIL OF ECONOMIC ADVISERS in 1946 and putting it directly under presidential control in the Executive Office of the President. Simultaneously Congress formed a Joint Economic Committee that was to work closely with the executive in economic policy.

World War II helped to solidify the President's powers as Commander in Chief and leader in foreign affairs. Responsibilities help to create power but do not guarantee it. Nevertheless, by the time of the Nixon administration, which began in 1968 and ended in disgrace with the President's resignation in 1974, critics of the executive described it as the "imperial presidency." Presidential power ebbed somewhat in the 1970s as Congress attempted to curb executive discretion to make war and foreign policy, but the constitutional and political forces that have supported executive dominance, particularly in foreign affairs, remain intact.

**Executive limits.** Both the Constitution and politics limit executive power. Ironically, the President's chosen instruments, the CABINET and the executive branch, restrain the President because they have both legal powers and political constituencies independent of the White House.

*Constitutional restraints.* Under the checks-and-balances system of shared powers the executive must gain congressional approval for executive appointments and treaties. However, these are not the most important constitutional powers the legislature has over the executive. Far more significant is the authority of Congress to control many aspects of the executive branch through authorization and appropriations legislation. Congress authorizes executive programs and determines the departments and agencies that will administer them and how they will be implemented.

The legislature sets policies for the executive branch. After authorizations the House and Senate appropriations committees determine how much money will be spent on executive programs. By separating the legislature from the executive the Constitution requires the President to deal with Congress as one of his political constituencies, seeking and sometimes even pleading for congressional support. The President has no automatic power over Congress, and in relation to Congress the executive is indeed more a clerk than a king.

Although not part of the original Constitution, the Supreme Court's power to review executive decisions when they are challenged in appropriate cases and controversies also constitutes a restraint, albeit a remote one [*see* SUPREME COURT DECISIONS ON THE PRESIDENCY].

*Political limits.* While the Constitution explicitly makes Congress a check upon the executive, Presidents also must heed a variety of other political constituencies to be effective leaders. Political pluralism complicates the President's task.

First, Presidents must deal not only with Congress as a whole, but separately with the House and the Senate and within those bodies with the numerous committees that control public policy and appropriations. Washington insider and former *New York Times* bureau chief Hedrick Smith, in his book *The Power Game* (1988), characterizes congressional committee chairmen as "Prime Ministers." A century before, Woodrow Wilson, then a young scholar, used the metaphor "feudal barons" to describe the chairmen of Congress's standing committees who had emerged as one of the most powerful forces in national politics. Congressional "prime ministers" have their own political constituencies independent not only of the President but of their own party chiefs, which requires the President to deal separately with committee chairmen as he tries to persuade them to follow him.

Presidential attempts to wield executive power require him to confront a pluralistic and often independent executive branch. EXECUTIVE DEPARTMENTS and agencies are beholden to their own independent political constituencies as they strive to maintain a balance of political support over opposition. Departments, such as Labor, Commerce, and Agriculture, may put client interests above those of the President. In other areas political IRON TRIANGLES, which define collusion among congressional committees, administrative agencies, and special interests, impede presidential control. Finally, congressionally imposed civil-service rules protect most of the federal bureaucracy from presidential removal.

Other political limits upon the President come from his own party as he strives to compromise diverse interests in order to maintain party support. Although more difficult to pinpoint, the media and public opinion may also put limits on presidential initiatives for no Chief Executive wants to be perceived as being outside of mainstream America.

The American presidency is a uniquely powerful and democratic institution that has become the focus of national leadership. Popular expectations require the President to set the domestic as well as the foreign agenda. The growth of presidential responsibilities has not always been accompanied by a commensurate increase in executive power, which in the future will require particularly skillful politicians in the White House to fulfill the demands of the modern presidency.

### BIBLIOGRAPHY

Barber, James D. *The Presidential Character: Predicting Performance in the White House*. 3d ed. 1985.
Corwin, Edward S. *The President: Office and Powers*. 4th ed. 1957.
Cronin, Thomas E. *The State of the Presidency*. 2d ed. 1980.
Greenstein, Fred, ed., *Leadership in the Modern Presidency*. 1988.
Milkis, Sidney M., and Michael Nelson. *The American Presidency: Origins and Development, 1776–1990*. 1990.
Nelson, Michael, ed. *The Presidency and the Political System*. 3d ed. 1990.
Neustadt, Richard. *Presidential Power*. 1980.
Rossiter, Clinton. *The American Presidency*. 2d ed. 1960.
Schlesinger, Arthur M., Jr. *The Imperial Presidency*. 1973.
Sorenson, Theodore C. *Decision-Making in the White House*. 1963.
Wildavsky, Aaron. "The Two Presidencies." In *American Government: Readings and Cases*. Edited by Peter Woll. 1993.

PETER WOLL

**EXECUTIVE PREROGATIVE.** The power of a monarch or chief executive officer of government to act, in certain areas, outside the bounds authorized by constitutions and laws is called the executive prerogative. The description of it that was familiar to most of the Framers of the U.S. Constitution was probably that contained in John Locke's *Second Treatise of Civil Government* (1690). The prerogative, Locke wrote, was "Power to act according to discretion, for the publick good, without the prescription of the Law, and sometimes even against it." Such a power was necessary because legislative bodies though "supream" were too slow to act, because the law could not foresee and provide for every contingency that might affect the public, because it was impossible to frame laws that would do no harm if executed "with inflexible vigor," and because a legislature that sat all the time would be "burthensome to the People" whereas the need for the executive was continuous.

**The English Background.** The concept of the prerogative that Americans inherited from England grew out of the late medieval distinction, formulated by Henry Bracton, Sir John Fortescue, and other commentators, between two channels through which royal authority was exerted. Bracton called them *jurisdictio* ("jurisdiction") and *gubernaculum* ("governance"); Fortescue wrote of a *dominium politicum et regale* ("political and regal domain"). What they meant was that in those areas of governance that concerned the preservation of domestic order and the defense of the realm from foreign enemies, the power of the crown was absolute and unrestrained; in matters that concerned the life, liberty, and property of free subjects, however, the king was bound by the law of the land. In other countries, the English believed, there was no such distinction, for in them whatever pleased the king had the force of law.

Over time, constitutional evolution changed the form but not the substance of the distinction. Earlier, the king had administered justice directly through courts over which he personally presided. By Bracton's time (late thirteenth century) the king's courts, though still acting in his name and though the judges were still appointed and removed at his pleasure, had become substantially independent. By Fortescue's time (mid to late fifteenth century), Parliament had emerged as a law-making body, under the king and subject to his dismissal. These two developments gave the law a more definite and predictable quality, and in time the term prerogative came into general usage to describe the specified royal powers that were exercised outside the law as defined by the common-law courts and Parliament.

The royal prerogative grew enormously in the sixteenth century under the Tudor monarchs, especially Henry VIII and Elizabeth I. It was extended to a broad range of subjects, from minute regulation of domestic commerce to the granting of charters giving a monopoly of trade. Most of this growth was in violation of the law, but it was justified under the dispensation power, the prerogative to dispense with the execution of particular laws in particular cases. There were two important new exercises of the royal prerogative. One was the issuance of proclamations that had the force of law. In 1539 Parliament enacted the Statute of Proclamations, giving such declarations the force of law except in regard to life or limb and the forfeiture of property, but when the statute was repealed a few years later, the effect was to do away with the exceptions, not to prevent proclamation law. The other major change was the creation of prerogative courts in which the king and his council participated directly and in which accused parties were denied the procedural protections afforded in the common-law courts. As a result of all this, by the time of Elizabeth's death

England had moved a long way from being a *dominium politicum et regale* toward being purely a *dominium regale*.

The aggrandizement of the prerogative by the Tudors ensured troubles for their seventeenth-century successors, the Stuarts, for it made enemies—or at least rivals—of two potent groups, parliamentarians and common-law lawyers. The unhappy reigns of James I, Charles I, Charles II, and James II, marked by repeated constitutional crises, can be fairly characterized as struggles between champions of the prerogative and champions of power in the hands of Parliament and the common-law courts. Except for the interregnum between the execution of Charles I in 1649 and the restoration of Charles II in 1660, the prerogative party had the better part of the battle the better part of the time.

It was the short reign of James II that brought an end to the struggle and, for practical purposes, to the prerogative itself. James, although a professed Roman Catholic, had sworn in his coronation oath to "defend the faith," meaning the established Anglican Church, but he was nonetheless determined to see England return to the papacy. To that end, he issued a Declaration of Indulgence in 1687 and another the next year, in effect suspending the Test Act, which prohibited Catholics from holding civil or military offices. He then began to appoint Catholics to various high posts. The English, though alarmed, might have been disposed to wait for James to die, for he was fifty-five, he had no male heirs, and his eldest daughter, Mary, was Protestant; but then his wife had a son, opening the prospect of a Catholic line of succession. A group of highly placed Englishmen invited Mary and her husband, William of Orange, to invade England and assume the throne as joint sovereigns. They accepted, and James fled the country.

As part of the Revolution Settlement (1688–1689) William agreed to severe limitations on the prerogative, including the abolition of the dispensing power, and during William's reign most of the remaining prerogative powers were, as Sir William Blackstone put it, "lopped off." During the eighteenth century Britain developed the system of government by cabinet ministers who also served as members of Parliament. In effect the Parliament and the ministers had arrogated the old prerogative unto themselves.

**The American Adaptation.** American political leaders were thoroughly versed in English constitutional history, and their knowledge as well as their experience with colonial governors (who were nominally vested with the prerogatives that kings had had before 1689) conditioned them to distrust executive power. They did venerate the person and regal office of the

king, and as the imperial crisis of 1763–1776 unfolded they not only absolved him of blame, protesting that the oppressive measures were the work of wicked ministers, they also repeatedly petitioned the king to reexert the prerogative to rein in Parliament. When the king instead declared them in rebellion and hired German mercenaries to put them down, their sense of betrayal was profound. The body of the Declaration of Independence, itemizing a long list of "injuries and usurpations," attributes those evils personally to George III. Moreover, in the Articles of Confederation and in the revolutionary state constitutions, Americans almost completely rejected executive authority.

By the time of the CONSTITUTIONAL CONVENTION of 1787, a good many political leaders had come to realize that government without a tolerably strong executive was no government at all, but uneasiness persisted. A third or more of the delegates preferred a plural executive, and until nearly the end of the convention the proposed plan made the President elected by and subordinate to Congress. In the final arrangements, instead of either dividing the presidency or making it dependent, the delegates sought to make the executive safe, though energetic, by fragmenting the prerogative itself.

Part of the traditional prerogative is vested exclusively in the President. Most important, the President is COMMANDER IN CHIEF of the armed forces; in addition, he has the power to grant reprieves and pardons, to receive foreign ministers, to call Congress into special session, and to adjourn Congress when the two houses disagree over adjournment.

Other parts of the prerogative are shared with one or both houses of Congress or conferred exclusively on Congress. Traditionally the crown was the fountain of all positions of honor or authority; in America the President's power to appoint judges, ambassadors, and other high officers is subject to the approval of the Senate (and the power to grant titles of nobility is absolutely prohibited). Traditionally the crown had the power to conclude treaties with foreign governments or sovereigns; in America that power is subject to senatorial approval. Historically, the crown had power to coin money, grant patents, regulate commerce, create courts, and construct forts and other military facilities; in America these powers belong to Congress, subject only to the presidential veto. And though the crown had the power to declare war, under the Constitution that power rests exclusively with Congress.

Finally, the Constitution departs from tradition in that the President is subject to IMPEACHMENT and removal upon conviction, whereas the king was beyond the reach of the law personally, though his ministers were not.

**Practical Adaptations.** In making these arrangements the Framers provided an effective set of barriers against executive tyranny. In trying to bring the prerogative under the rule of law, however, they were attempting the impossible. Virtually every presidential administration has found it necessary or expedient to transgress the boundaries of the Constitution and laws by resorting to the prerogative in the interest of what is deemed to be the public good.

A few examples will illustrate the point. Nowhere in the Constitution is the President authorized to issue PROCLAMATIONS, but in 1793 George Washington issued a neutrality proclamation—over the strong protests of Secretary of State Thomas Jefferson, who insisted that, inasmuch as only Congress could declare war, only Congress could declare NEUTRALITY. In 1794, Congress enacted the Neutrality Act and prosecutions were brought for violations under that statute. Jefferson himself, when President, repeatedly went outside the Constitution and laws, justifying his actions by saying that "the laws of necessity . . . are of higher obligation" than "scrupulous adherence to written law." Lincoln stretched the Constitution in the interest of the "higher obligation" of preserving the Union.

Twentieth-century administrations have exercised a discretionary, extraconstitutional prerogative in myriad ways. Every President since Theodore Roosevelt has employed EXECUTIVE AGREEMENTS to deal with matters not covered by senatorially ratified treaties (the Supreme Court has ruled that such agreements have the force of treaties, unless they conflict with a treaty or with a statute passed pursuant to congressional authority). Jimmy Carter granted a blanket amnesty to those who dodged the draft during the VIETNAM WAR. What is most telling of all, Presidents have despatched American troops into combat situations more than two hundred times without a DECLARATION OF WAR. Often these have been trivial affairs, but sometimes they have been enormous, as when President William McKinley sent seventy thousand troops to suppress a rebellion in the PHILIPPINES (they fought there for three years), or as in the Korean and Vietnamese wars.

In sum, prerogative power inheres in the presidential office, a situation that is dangerous but necessary. The restraints upon it are not constitutional but political: the Congress, the bureaucracy, the news media, and PUBLIC OPINION.

### BIBLIOGRAPHY

Arnhart, Larry. " 'The God-Like Prince': John Locke, Executive Prerogative, and the American Presidency." *Presidential Studies Quarterly* 9 (1979): 121–130.

Holdsworth, W. S. *A History of English Law.* 2d ed. Vol. 6. 1937.
McDonald, Forrest. *The American Presidency: Roots, Establishment, Evolution.* 1993.
Schlesinger, Arthur M., Jr. *The Imperial Presidency.* 1974.
Scigliano, Robert. "The President's 'Prerogative Power.' " In *Inventing The American Presidency.* Edited by Thomas E. Cronin. 1989.

FORREST MCDONALD

**EXECUTIVE PRIVILEGE.** The concept of executive privilege is not mentioned in the Constitution. As the Supreme Court observed in 1974, however, it does have "constitutional underpinnings." The principle emerged out of the more fundamental constitutional concept of SEPARATION OF POWERS. As Archibald Cox has written, "The controversy over executive privilege arises from our constitutional separation of government into coordinate legislative, executive, and judicial branches." In 1787, the Framers, fearful of creating a political system that would encourage tyranny, conceived a federal political system that emphasized separate institutions that would share power. Separation of powers, along with other concepts such as CHECKS AND BALANCES, FEDERALISM itself, and the concept of judicial review, were ideas incorporated explicitly or implicitly into the Constitution to reduce the risk of tyranny in the new republic.

**The Constitutional Framework.** Separation of powers, while also not mentioned explicitly in the Constitution, is implicit in the form of the distribution of powers among the three coordinate branches of the national government and between the central and state governments. Congress, the President, and the federal courts have sets of powers, enumerated in Articles I through III, that define the powers of each branch of government. The concept of separation of powers seems to suggest that none of the coordinate branches will intrude into areas of power reserved to the other coordinate branches. The legislature legislates; the executive implements legislation; and the federal courts judge the constitutionality of the legislation itself or of the way in which the legislation has been implemented by the executive.

In reality, however, the coordinate branches share power to some extent. Since the early days of the Republic an interactive relationship has developed between the coordinate branches of the national government. Because of this interaction and overlap of powers, there is no possibility that any of the branches will be absolutely insulated "within its own sphere," divorced from the actions of the other two branches. As the Supreme Court said in UNITED STATES v. NIXON (1974), the "separated powers were not intended to operate with absolute independence."

Given the fact that no formalistic separation of powers is possible or even desired, the reality of separate institutions sharing power leads to occasional conflict. Occasionally, the conflict between the Congress and the President over refusal to release executive information leads to a threat by the chair of an investigating congressional committee to hold the executive officer in contempt of Congress. If either house of Congress holds an executive official in contempt, the U.S. attorney convenes a grand jury to seek an indictment. In *United States v. House of Representatives* (1983), the Supreme Court was faced with the request to resolve a confrontation between the Republican President, Ronald Reagan, and the Democrat-controlled House. The Justices urged the two coordinate branches to seek compromise rather than confrontation. Judicial intervention in such confrontations, the Court said, "should be delayed until all possibilities for settlement have been exhausted."

The concept of executive privilege must be viewed in this context. In his battles with Congress and with federal judges over the release of information and audiotapes in his possession, for example, President Richard M. Nixon maintained that the only recourse to his use of presidential privilege to deny documents to congressional investigators and the courts would be "by IMPEACHMENT and through the electoral process." Viewing PRESIDENTIAL-CONGRESSIONAL RELATIONS since 1789, however, one sees grudging accommodation and compromise more often than the type of confrontation suggested by Nixon.

A President and his staff must be free to examine alternative strategies in the process of formulating policy for the nation. The conversations that take place among executive policy makers must be robust, free-wheeling, and confidential for the President to solicit frank views on controversial public policy matters. Furthermore, it may be necessary to keep certain NATIONAL SECURITY secrets from the courts. Congress, of course, has its own constitutional responsibilities in military and national security affairs. It is recognized that the national security rationale for refusing to release information may conceal a less honorable motivation, such as protecting the administration from embarrassment.

Executive privilege, then, is a derivative concept that emerges from the separation of powers idea and the need for the executive to encourage frank conversations and to protect the national security. As the Justices said in *Nixon*, the privilege "is fundamental to the operation of government and inextricably rooted in the separation of powers under the Constitution."

What happens, however, if these conversations (tape-recorded or transcribed) or papers and other materials are requested by the courts or Congress? Can an investigating committee of Congress looking into claims of fraud and malfeasance in a federal agency request papers and other materials from the executive in order to carry out the legislature's investigative function? Can a subpoena be issued, in line with rule 17(c) of the Federal Rules of Criminal Procedure, that requires a member of the executive branch, even the President, to turn over needed information so that the prosecution can adequately prepare its case for presentation to a federal grand jury investigating a criminal activity or to a petit jury in a criminal trial in a federal district court?

**Conflict among the Branches.** A presidential claim of executive privilege, that is, a claim made by the executive that information held by the executive will not be given to Congress or to a court, encourages a clash between coordinate branches. The President's power to withhold information conflicts with the power of a federal court to issue a subpoena and with the congressional power to call witnesses in the course of a legislative investigation.

While the term *executive privilege*, or *presidential privilege*, is of recent vintage, President George Washington had to wrestle with the concept as early as 1792. He met with his CABINET to discuss a request for information from the executive branch from a congressional committee investigating General Arthur St. Clair's ill-fated expedition against the INDIANS. According to Thomas Jefferson's notes of the meeting, Washington said that "the Executive ought to communicate such papers as the public good would permit, and ought to refuse those, the disclosure of which would injure the public." On that occasion, the Cabinet concluded that there would be no injury to the public if Washington turned over material to the legislative investigating committee.

That working definition of executive privilege has become a primary foundation block for Presidents and presidential advisers. Since 1792, Presidents have asserted executive privilege to deny Congress sensitive information dealing with foreign policy and national security matters. While the privilege is not an unqualified one, both the federal courts and Congress acknowledge that, under certain conditions, the executive should not have to turn over papers and other materials to the federal courts, nor should key members of the executive branch be compelled to testify before Congress. The question that plagues members of the coordinate branches is this: Under what circumstances can and should the claim of executive privilege be used by the President to avoid exposure of executive-branch discussions and decision making?

***Executive privilege in the courts.*** During the WATER-GATE AFFAIR, President Nixon acknowledged in a brief presented to the Supreme Court that executive privilege "cannot be claimed to shield executive officers from prosecution for crime." As the Court's *Nixon* decision clearly indicates, when a prosecutor preparing a criminal case for argument before a federal grand jury or before a trial jury in federal district court needs information held by the executive, then a subpoena can be issued to the President or any other and any member of the executive branch.

In *Nixon*, a unanimous Court ordered the President to turn over sixty-four tapes to the federal judge. An absolute, categorical executive privilege, which is what Nixon's attorneys argued for, would mean that criminal proceedings in federal courts would in some cases have to be based on incomplete evidence. Given the adversarial nature of the U.S. justice system, relevant information is necessary to determine guilt or innocence. Prosecuting and defense attorneys' need for compulsory means to obtain information—including the use of the subpoena to force persons to present vital information—overrides the presidential use of privilege. Federal prosecutors, however, must convince trial judges that the specific information sought is relevant, cannot be found elsewhere, and will be admissible as evidence. If persuaded, the judge makes an in camera inspection of the information to determine whether it is indeed relevant to the criminal proceedings. In *Nixon*, the general executive privilege to retain the tapes fell before the argument presented by the Watergate special prosecutor, Leon Jaworski.

***Executive privilege in the Congress.*** Although clashes have frequently occurred between Congress and the President over executive privilege, the federal courts, including the Supreme Court, have never created constitutional limits on the use of executive privilege to deny Congress information. Viewing these conflicts over history, one can see a pattern whereby this type of political dispute is resolved by the political process itself.

In certain political conflicts—as, for example, impeachments—Congress has had good access to materials and personnel in the executive branch. The Constitution gives the House of Representatives the "sole power of Impeachment," so it must have complete access to the materials it needs to conduct impeachment investigations. As President James K. Polk noted in 1846, the House has "the right to investigate the conduct of all public officers under the Government. . . . It could command the attendance of any and every agent of the Government, and compel them to produce all papers, public or private, official or unofficial, and to testify on oath to all facts within their knowledge."

Presidential privilege is also deemed inappropriate when employed in an effort to cover up official misconduct. The Supreme Court, in *Watkins v. United States* (1957), noted that the power of Congress to conduct investigations "comprehends probes into departments of the Federal Government to expose corruption, inefficiency, or waste." President Reagan's Attorney General, William French Smith said publicly in 1982, that he would never "shield documents which contain evidence of criminal or unethical conduct by agency officials from proper review." And Reagan himself, after the IRAN-CONTRA AFFAIR broke in 1986, allowed two top former NATIONAL SECURITY ADVISERS to testify before Congress.

Further, Congress has been successful in obtaining information regarding nominees put forward by the President. The Supreme Court, however, has tried to place some modest restrictions on the scope of the congressional investigatory power. A committee must demonstrate the relevance to its investigation of the information it seeks. However, the Court, as stated in *Barenblatt v. United States* (1959), as long as an legislative investigating committee "acts in pursuance of its constitutional power, the judiciary lacks authority to intervene on the basis of the motives which spurred the exercise of that power."

Generally, Congress recognizes the critical value of confidentiality of discussions in the executive branch. The President and his key staff must be able to discuss policy alternatives frankly, and the documents and preliminary drafts of policy statements prepared for such conversations are entitled to presidential privilege protection. Committee members acknowledge that presidential advisers and intimates have the shield of presidential confidentiality and should not be asked to reveal to Congress the substance of confidential discussions with the President.

**Executive Privilege and National Security.** The most sensitive area, which has occasionally been the basis for serious confrontation between the executive and the other two branches of national government, is that of national security and FOREIGN AFFAIRS. In the 1974 *Nixon* decision, a unanimous Supreme Court deferred to executive privilege in controversies involving "a claim of need to protect military, diplomatic, or sensitive national security secrets." For the Justices, even in camera inspection by a federal district judge of papers and documents involving military, diplomatic, or national security matters amounted to too great an interference by the judiciary into political matters.

Even when secret military or diplomatic information is needed for a trial, the Justices have deferred to the President when he employs executive privilege to justify nondelivery of presidential information. In *United States v. Reynolds* (1952), the Justices concluded that the federal courts "should not jeopardize the security which the [executive] privilege is meant to protect by insisting upon an examination of the evidence, even by the judge alone, in chambers." Since that time, however, Congress has explicitly authorized judges to inspect sensitive materials in camera.

While the Court has largely relinquished its review of national security materials, Congress, because of its constitutional responsibilities, cannot. Article I gives Congress the enumerated powers to declare war, to raise and support armies and navies, to provide for the common defense, and, through the necessary and proper clause, to create instrumentalities such as the Selective Service System to effectively implement their enumerated powers. Further, Congress has general oversight responsibility over the executive agencies responsible for implementing military and foreign policy. In the critically important areas of military, diplomatic, and national security policy, as the Court noted in *Japan Whaling Association v. American Cetacean Society* (1986), Congress and the President jointly play a premier role in the formulation and execution of foreign policy. Courts have continually urged Congress and the executive to resolve their disputes regarding the availability of executive information about military and foreign policy.

As Louis Fisher writes, the scope of executive privilege is shaped by vying claims by the three coequal branches of the national government. Fisher claims, "The integrity of the judicial process requires evidence; the executive branch needs a measure of confidentiality in its deliberations; and Congress depends on information to carry out its responsibilities." Accommodation among the three institutions sharing power is essential. The Supreme Court, very cautious when controversies come close to being nonjusticiable, is reluctant to referee such clashes and instead has consistently encouraged compromise between Congress and President.

## BIBLIOGRAPHY

Ball, Howard. *"We Have a Duty": The Supreme Court and the Watergate Tapes Litigation.* 1992.
Berger, Raoul. *Executive Privilege.* 1973.
Casper, Gerhard. "An Essay on Separation of Powers: Some Early Versions and Practices." *William and Mary Law Review* 30 (1989): 30–78.
Cox, Archibald. "Executive Privilege." *University of Pennsylvania Law Review* 122 (1974): 1383–1424.
Fisher, Louis. *Constitutional Conflicts between Congress and the President.* 3d rev. ed. 1991.
Freund, Paul A. "Foreword: On Presidential Privilege." *Harvard Law Review* 88 (1974): 30–107.
Kurland, Philip. *Watergate and the Constitution.* 1978.
Winter, Ralph K., Jr. "The Seedlings for the Forest." *Yale Law Journal* 83 (1974): 1730–1795.

HOWARD BALL

**EXECUTIVE RESIDENCE STAFF.** The staff of the Executive Residence of the President is responsible for the operation and general housekeeping of the Residence, which is the central part of the WHITE HOUSE and does not include the East and West Wings. The staff helps to maintain the Residence, not only as a home for the President and his family, but also as a site for official state and other ceremonial functions and as a national monument visited by over a million Americans each year.

Staff duties may be compared to those of the staff at a well-run small hotel but carry far greater responsibilities and resources. Before 1910, apart from a steward, usher, and nine doorkeepers, servants and other domestics working in the Residence were paid privately by the President. By 1992, a staff of approximately one hundred included administrators, domestics, tradesmen, and other professional and specialized employees.

A chief usher, aided by several assistants, is responsible for supervising and directing the staff. The chief usher's many duties include budgeting for food and other household supplies, receiving and attending to the needs of all personal and official guests, preparing for receptions, dinners, and official entertainment, and overseeing the daily maintenance of the Residence. A digital display board in the chief usher's office indicates the location in the White House or on the grounds of the President and members of his family.

Nearly half the staff is involved with domestic duties around the Residence and in the main kitchen. The basic housekeeping staff consists of nine maids, six housemen, and three doormen. The kitchen staff consists primarily of a maître d'hôtel (responsible for food service operations, including recommending menus), five chefs, five butlers, and four stewards.

For security reasons, all food served in the White House is prepared in the White House kitchen. Meals for the President and his family are prepared in a small kitchen on the second floor next to the President's dining room. The same chef usually prepares the meals for the First Family (i.e., duty is not rotated among the chefs).

State dinners may require food for as many as 140 guests, with hors d'oeuvres for 1,000 guests. During such events, a few extra chefs and as many as twenty additional butlers and pantry stewards may be hired to help prepare and serve meals.

State and ceremonial functions are made more elegant by the work of the five florists, five calligraphers, and five curators on the staff. The florists arrange and place live floral arrangements throughout the Residence, the calligraphers script invitations and other announcements, and the curators acquire, care for, and catalog furnishings and artworks in the Residence. Additional florists may be hired for large ceremonial functions.

Also on the staff are approximately thirty-four trades and maintenance workers who look after the mechanical systems providing heating, air conditioning, and ventilation for the White House. They include carpenters, painters, plumbers, electricians, and operating engineers.

The staff consists of well-trained, carefully screened professionals, who generally continue to serve from one administration to the next. They receive benefits and privileges similar to those received by other government employees, except that they are subject to dismissal at any time.

### BIBLIOGRAPHY

U.S. House of Representatives. Committee on Appropriations. *Treasury, Postal Service, and General Government Appropriations for Fiscal Year 1993.* Part 3. 102d Cong., 2d. sess., 1992.

ROGELIO GARCIA

**EX PARTE.** See Merryman, Ex Parte; Milligan, Ex Parte.

# F

**FAIRBANKS, CHARLES W.** (1852–1918), twenty-sixth Vice President of the United States (1905–1909). Charles Warren Fairbanks's tenure illustrated how an otherwise influential figure could be rendered relatively insignificant.

Fairbanks was born on 11 May 1852. Following admission to the bar, he became a successful bankruptcy lawyer. He was active in politics and in 1897 was elected to the Senate from Indiana on his second try. He became a strong supporter and ally of President William McKinley. Fairbanks was one of those mentioned as a possible running mate for President McKinley in 1900 but was passed over in favor of Governor Theodore Roosevelt of New York.

Four years later, he attracted wide support for the vice presidential nomination. The conservative wing of the REPUBLICAN PARTY, which had misgivings about Roosevelt, insisted upon Fairbanks's selection for the second spot. Roosevelt, then the incumbent President, preferred Representative Robert R. Hitt of Illinois. In the interest of party unity however, he deferred to the preference of the McKinley wing of the party and accepted Fairbanks who was selected without opposition. Fairbanks's selection illustrated the viability of several of the classic criteria of vice presidential selection. As a conservative, he balanced the ticket ideologically. As a member of the McKinley wing, he achieved party unity. As a Senator, his selection was popular with Republican legislators. And, as a son of Indiana, he enhanced the ticket's appeal in a competitive state.

Roosevelt, as incumbent President, chose not to campaign too widely and accordingly Fairbanks assumed the burden of the Republican campaigning in 1904. He traveled across the country by train, gener-ally carrying himself in a dignified manner, avoiding controversial issues, and defending Roosevelt's actions and policies. His presence on the ticket may have helped produce the unprecedented Republican majority in Indiana; nationally, the ticket won a sweeping victory.

In an 1896 article Roosevelt had advocated enhancing the office of the VICE PRESIDENT in part by including its incumbent in the CABINET, consulting him on all important issues, and giving him a vote in the Senate. In practice, however, Roosevelt never put any of these suggestions into effect. He and Fairbanks did not agree on the issues. Roosevelt had little respect for Fairbanks, made frequent derisive comments about him, and ignored him. Consequently Fairbanks, like most of his predecessors, played no significant role in the administration.

Fairbanks sought the presidential nomination in 1908, one of several candidates working to deny William Howard Taft the nomination. Fairbanks spent much of his time as Vice President traveling to enlist support for a presidential campaign. Although initially perceived as a front-runner, Fairbanks's campaign faltered in part due to the active support Roosevelt gave Taft. Ultimately, Taft won on the first ballot; Fairbanks finished a distant fifth. He declined an opportunity to run again for the vice presidency.

Fairbanks sought his party's presidential nomination again in 1916 but was unsuccessful. He was, however, the overwhelming choice for the second spot on the ticket with Justice CHARLES EVANS HUGHES, in part because of Indiana's importance as a swing state. With THOMAS MARSHALL, the incumbent Democratic Vice President, running for reelection, this election marked the first time both parties nominated vice presidential candidates from the same state. The Republicans carried Indiana but lost the election.

Fairbanks actively supported America's involvement in WORLD WAR I, an effort that brought a reconciliation with Roosevelt. Fairbanks wrote Roosevelt during early 1918 pledging to support his former rival for President in 1920. Fairbanks died, however, on 4 June 1918.

### BIBLIOGRAPHY

Gould, Lewis L. "Charles Warren Fairbanks and the Republican National Convention of 1900: A Memoir." *Indiana Magazine of History* 77 (1981): 358–371.

Rissler, Herbert J. *Charles Warren Fairbanks: Conservative Hoosier.* 1962.

Smith, William Henry. *The Life and Speeches of Hon. Charles Warren Fairbanks.* 1904.

JOEL K. GOLDSTEIN

**FAIR DEAL.** In his STATE OF THE UNION MESSAGE on 6 January 1949, President Harry S. Truman set as the principle of his domestic program that "every segment of our population and every individual has a right to expect from our government a fair deal." Two days later he sent to Congress his economic report, detailing the proposals. Truman meant every word of what he recommended. He had been an ardent New Dealer and wanted to continue NEW DEAL economic and social measures. As chief executive of Jackson County, Missouri (the county that contains Kansas City), and as junior Senator from Missouri beginning in 1935, Truman had ardently supported federal intervention in the economy together with measures for social reform. Indeed, in the Senate his record of voting for New Deal measures had been so regular that President Franklin D. Roosevelt often took his vote for granted and gave far more attention, and often PATRONAGE, to his anti–New Deal colleague, Senator Bennett C. Clark.

But the results of Truman's Fair Deal proposals were mixed. The President enjoyed a few triumphs. The minimum wage advanced from forty to seventy-five cents an hour. Congress included ten million more people under the SOCIAL SECURITY program, doubled old age and survivors' benefits, and improved provisions for children and the disabled. The Celler-Kefauver Act of 1950 forbade companies to buy assets of competitors, plugging a loophole in the CLAYTON ACT of 1914. Several of the economy and efficiency measures urged by the first of the HOOVER COMMISSIONS were passed. The President's losses nonetheless over-

weighed the gains. Proposals for reform of the agricultural assistance program advanced by Secretary of Agriculture Charles Brannan, which sought to exclude big farmers from benefits, gave way to a patchwork favoring producers of cotton, tobacco, and wheat. Civil rights advanced slowly. Truman had said after his 1948 electoral victory that "we shall win that civil rights battle just as we won the election." The principal gain was three Supreme Court decisions against railroad dining-car segregation, against separation of an African American student from other students at the University of Oklahoma, and against establishment of a separate law school for African Americans in Texas rather than allowing them to attend the University of Texas Law School. The African American activist lawyer Thurgood Marshall said after these cases, "The complete destruction of all enforced segregation is now in sight." Federal aid to primary and secondary education languished because of congressional arguments over equal allotment of money to black and white schools and money to parochial schools. Presidential proposals for a federal health care program collapsed after a campaign by the American Medical Association against "socialized medicine," although Congress did increase support for hospital construction. In May 1949, the House voted down the attempt to repeal the TAFT-HARTLEY ACT, which was hated by labor. Low-cost housing came to nought, for even though the President signed the Housing and Rent Control Act of 1949, only 156,000 units—an insignificant number—had been started under it by 1952. Increasing taxes for corporations and higher-income Americans proved difficult because of a recession in 1949, with unemployment up to 7.6 percent and a deficit of $1.8 billion in fiscal year 1949.

What brought this untoward result after the President's great electoral victory in November 1948, which included Democratic majorities in both the House and the Senate? The "Fair Deal majority" was an election-year conglomerate, not a unified coalition with a solid intellectual base. Members spoke for their own interests, regardless of party. Truman sarcastically described the powerful southerner, Richard Russell, as "the great Georgia Senator, representative of the National Chamber of Commerce, the Coca-Cola Company, et cetera." The only consistent congressional lineup was the right-wing coalition of conservative Democrats and Republicans.

Truman himself contributed to the almost intractable problems produced by conservatives of both parties in Congress. He should have disciplined the Dixiecrats of 1948 by working to deny them their committee seniorities. Moreover, he chose to hold grudges against Senators who, however wayward on small issues, could have aided him on the more important aspects of the Fair Deal. He disliked Senator J. William Fulbright of Arkansas, who in 1946 had suggested that the President resign because of the adverse congressional elections. Truman described Fulbright as "Senator Half-Bright" and sometimes as "an overeducated Oxford SOB." In addition, he disliked Clinton P. Anderson of New Mexico, who in 1948 had resigned as Secretary of Agriculture to run for the Senate (in effect abandoning Truman when he was fighting for his political life). Estes Kefauver of Tennessee annoyed him by pretending to be a mountaineer and wearing a coonskin cap. Kefauver also had the ill judgment to take his Senate crime committee (the Special Committee to Investigate Organized Crime in Interstate Commerce) to Missouri for open sessions.

The President perhaps gave up too quickly on the Fair Deal proposals. In a speech in 1949 he criticized the Eighty-first Congress worse than the Eightieth. That year he considered a speaking tour around the country but instead opted to keep Congress in session and to use private pressure to promote the Fair Deal. By April 1950, Truman was tiring and tried to cut down on appointments in the Oval Office, telling an assistant that "I just can't take it any more."

Voter indifference to a program that was attractive in general but not in detail may have lain behind the Fair Deal's failure. Moreover, public attention soon turned elsewhere: in June 1950, the KOREAN WAR began.

### BIBLIOGRAPHY

Donovan, Robert J. *Tumultuous Years: The Presidency of Harry S. Truman, 1949–1953.* 1982.

Hamby, Alonzo L. *Beyond the New Deal: Harry S. Truman and American Liberalism.* 1973.

McCoy, Donald R. *The Presidency of Harry S. Truman.* 1984.

McCoy, Donald R., and Richard T. Ruetten. *Quest and Response: Minority Rights and the Truman Administration.* 1973.

ROBERT H. FERRELL

**FAIR EMPLOYMENT PRACTICE COMMITTEE.** President Franklin Roosevelt established a Committee on Fair Employment Practice, known as the FEPC, by EXECUTIVE ORDER on 25 June 1941 to combat racial discrimination in the defense industry and the federal government. Roosevelt created the FEPC in response to a large demonstration to protest racial discrimination, scheduled for the nation's capital in July 1941 and organized by A. Philip Randolph's March on Washington Movement. Seeking to avoid the political embarrassment of the demonstration, Roosevelt negotiated its cancellation in exchange for the issuance of an executive order establishing the FEPC.

Roosevelt's Executive Order 8802, issued pursuant to the President's WAR POWER, mandated a policy of nondiscrimination on the basis of race, color, and national origin for both federal defense contractors and the federal government. The order established the FEPC to receive and investigate complaints of discrimination and to make recommendations to the President and other federal agencies concerning enforcement.

The FEPC itself had no real enforcement power. Although it could conduct hearings following the receipt of a complaint of discrimination and could make recommendations, it could not compel an employer to take any action. Moreover, even though contracting agencies of the federal government did have the authority to cancel contracts based on the FEPC's recommendations, such agencies were reluctant to do so because of the pressing need for wartime production. Nevertheless, by the end of the war the FEPC had conducted approximately thirty hearings and had successfully resolved by negotiation a number of discrimination complaints.

Political pressure forced the cancellation of some of the FEPC's scheduled hearings. Postponement in January 1943 of hearings involving the railroad industry prompted several of the FEPC's members to resign, which effectively terminated its activities. Roosevelt eventually reestablished the FEPC on 27 May 1943 by Executive Order 9346. This second order strengthened the committee by providing additional funding and imposing a nondiscrimination obligation on labor unions as well as defense contractors and government agencies.

Attacks on the FEPC by southern congressmen ultimately led to its demise. In 1944, Congress, concerned with both the expansion of EXECUTIVE POWER through the use of the executive order and in particular the activities of the FEPC, enacted legislation that prohibited operation of an executive agency for more than one year without Congressional authorization. Under the leadership of Georgia Senator Richard Russell, Congress eventually declined to continue to fund the FEPC, which led to its dissolution in June 1946. Yearly efforts to establish a permanent FEPC by congressional legislation failed until Congress established the Equal Employment Opportunity Commission as part of the CIVIL RIGHTS ACT OF 1964.

BIBLIOGRAPHY

Morgan, Ruth P. *The President and Civil Rights: Policymaking by Executive Order.* 1970.

Reed, Merl E. *Seedtime for the Modern Civil Rights Movement: The President's Committee on Fair Employment Practice, 1941–1946.* 1991.

Ruchames, Louis. *Race, Jobs, and Politics: The Story of FEPC.* 1953.

DAVISON M. DOUGLAS

**FAIR LABOR STANDARDS ACT** (1938). The Fair Labor Standards Act (FLSA) was conceived when New Deal reform sentiment was running at high tide. But its birth, repeatedly delayed, was nearly aborted by the gathering hosts of anti-New Deal reaction. From the moment the Supreme Court ruled the National Industrial Recovery Act (NIRA) unconstitutional in May 1935, President Franklin D. Roosevelt and some of his closest advisers, including Felix Frankfurter, Benjamin V. Cohen, Thomas Corcoran, and Labor Secretary Frances Perkins, urged on by their allies in the labor movement, began to devise ways of restoring the NIRA's minimum-wage–maximum-hour provisions. For Roosevelt and those around him influenced by Keynesian thinking, this was more than a matter of long-deferred social justice; it was just as much a hard-headed economic recovery strategy premised on the notion that restoring and increasing mass purchasing power was the key to reviving American industry and agriculture. Then as the newly established Committee for Industrial Organization (CIO) flexed its muscles in a wave of sit-down and mass strikes that swept across the country early in 1937, the pressure on the administration grew. The CIO, through its Labor's Non-Partisan League, had materially contributed to the President's landslide victory the previous November and understandably expected help in pursuing its own legislative priorities that naturally included a nationally mandated standard of hours and wages. By early that spring, Roosevelt was assuring the CIO leader, Sidney Hillman, that the administration was indeed committed to such a bill during the current congressional session.

In May, Senator Hugo Black introduced the bill in the Senate and Congressman Lawrence J. Connery did likewise in the House. Roosevelt publicly proclaimed his enthusiasm for a reform designed not only to establish livable standards of hours (forty per week) and wages (forty cents per hour) for millions of American workers, but one that would outlaw CHILD LABOR once and for all. But immediately the business community mobilized in opposition (including the National Association of Manufacturers and the United States Chamber of Commerce) as did the growing phalanx of conservative Democrats in the South and rural West, along with their ideological cousins across the aisle in the Republican Party. Economic self-interest, racial fears, and more dispassionate objections to government interference in the marketplace threatened to derail what the President had once imagined a popular and unifying piece of legislation. A process of crippling amendments began at once. By July, revisions in the Senate allowed for child labor under sixteen if such work did not endanger the health or education of the minor. Special interests from the retail, forestry, farming, dairying, fishing, and other industries lobbied successfully for exemptions.

When Congressman Connery died, Roosevelt called on Mary Norton of New Jersey to become the administration's spear carrier in the House, a job she performed with skill but without sufficient ammunition to prevent the conservative coalition, led by southern Democrats like Howard W. Smith of Virginia, from bottling up the bill in committee. Although the President pressed the issue again during the November special session called to deal with that fall's precipitous recession, only a new round of horse trading between the farm and labor lobbies produced enough votes to dislodge the bill from the Rules Committee. Next fratricidal quarrels within the house of labor between the American Federation of Labor (AFL) and the rival CIO led the AFL into opposition to the administration's "Norton bill." By the end of the special session it was a dead letter. Roosevelt grew desperate. He was even prepared to grant his southern opponents a regional minimum wage differential if necessary to get things moving again. By April 1938 the House Labor Committee had drafted a new bill. Then Claude Pepper's victory in the Florida primary, where he openly championed an hours-and-wages law, reinvigorated the administration's allies. Finally, on 14 June, more than a year after its original introduction, the FLSA was passed and on 25 June signed by an exhausted President.

Immediately at least, the FLSA accomplished more in principle that it did in practice. Its passage established the categorical right and responsibility of the state to guarantee basic labor standards, that is to maintain a universal egalitarianism of rights and not merely to protect specially defined subsectors of the labor market, like women and children. But as the act made its tortuous way through Congress, amendment after amendment narrowed its coverage, weakened its administrative authority, limited its investigative powers, and lowered its standards. An impressive armada of industries escaped coverage entirely—retailing, agriculture, dairying, food processing, fishing, seafaring, personal services, and nearly all transportation workers. In the end only 11 million workers or one-fifth of the labor force was protected and of those a mere 300,000 stood to benefit from the act's initial twenty-five-cent minimum wage. Women and black workers, because they labored disproportionately within the borders of the exempt industries, were left largely defenseless, belying the bill's universalist pretentions. Some did indeed benefit—those 1.4 million laboring more than the act's mandated forty-four-hour week, and those 200,000 or so children whom the bill excluded from the labor market. The act trebled the number previously protected by state laws and its time-and-a-half-for-overtime provision helped everybody, especially better-paid workers. The FLSA turned out to be a monument both to the President's good intentions as well as to the diminishing political fortunes of the New Deal he had authored.

The FLSA has been frequently amended, often at presidential instigation. The amendments have increased the minimum wage, $4.25 per hour in 1993, and have considerably extended the coverage of the statute to employees not previously protected. Most benefit from the act; executive, professional, and administrative employees and some engaged in agriculture are excluded.

### BIBLIOGRAPHY

Douglas, Paul, and Joseph Hackman. "The Fair Labor Standards Act of 1938: The Background and Legal History of the Act." *Political Science Quarterly* 53 (1938): 491–515.

Grossman, Jonathan. "Fair Labor Standards Act of 1938: Maximum Struggle for a Minimum Wage." *Monthly Labor Review* (June 1978): 22–30.

Patterson, James T. *Congressional Conservatism and the New Deal: The Growth of the Conservative Coalition in Congress, 1933–1939.* 1967.

Steinberg, Ronnie. *Wages and Hours: Labor and Reform in 20th Century America.* 1982.

STEVE FRASER

**FAITHFUL EXECUTION CLAUSE.** The provision of Article II, Section 3, of the Constitution of the United States that directs the President to "take Care that the Laws be faithfully executed" is best understood in broader terms of the rule of law. Government under law is the sustaining principle of constitutional empowerment. In short, authoritative power is derived from and enhanced by acceptance of legal constraints consistent with standards of reasonableness expected of government in a constitutional democracy.

Related fundamentals are also crucial: most specifically that, while separate institutions are created by the Constitution, the three branches share the authority and responsibilities of one national government. The faithful execution of the laws clause has sometimes been viewed, however, in terms of a system of competing branches, increasingly characterized by presidential aggrandizement.

The traditional perspective on faithful execution of the laws is more constrained, and the limits are urgently relevant to basic conditions of American government. Public confidence in political institutions and leaders has often been shaken by corruption, partisan spoils, and failures to collaborate as one government to achieve reasonable public purposes. Government has often been weakened by diminished popular trust. That is a crucial context in which faithful execution of the laws needs to be understood. It is a practical perspective, and in that sense it is much like the situation that prevailed when the clause was written into the Constitution, although contemporary problems of nonobservance of law are significantly different.

**Constitutional Origins.** Prior to implementation of the new Constitution in 1789, acts of the United States government could only be executed by the Continental Congress—and that could only be accomplished with great difficulty. The states under the Articles of Confederation retained their separate sovereignty and jealous independence. The United States, as a "congress assembled," as provided for by the Articles of Confederation, was relatively impotent to enforce compliance by the states with financial requisitions and other national actions. Delegates to the Philadelphia Convention sought to remedy that condition.

A national executive was conceived by many of the Framers as a necessary extension of the United States government. The purpose was to provide practical means for the national government to implement its decisions, giving rise to the faithful execution of the laws clause and related provisions. The initial language of the Virginia Plan demonstrated this practical orientation. It proposed creation of a "National Executive" to be chosen by Congress, with general authority to execute national laws. Proposed responsibilities of the executive were phrased at the CONSTITUTIONAL CONVENTION on 1 June 1787 by James Madison in these words: "with power to carry into execution the national laws, . . . and to execute such powers, not legislative or judiciary in their nature, as may from time to time be delegated by the national legislature." Roger Sherman said he considered the Executive "as nothing more than an institution for carrying the will of the Legislature into effect." The New Jersey Plan, phrased in terms of a plural executive system, proposed that "the Executives" should have general authority to execute federal acts. The Hamilton Plan, favoring the greatest authority of the executive, simply provided authority to execute all laws passed. Following deliberations and stylistic drafting, the provision emerged in its final version: "take Care that the Laws be faithfully executed."

In short, enhanced authority of the national government was a great concern in the processes of writing and ratification of the proposed, new constitution. Structuring of the United States government into three branches by the new charter was justified in THE FEDERALIST as a means to limit chances of tyranny that might more easily result from concentrated power. Clearly, the institutional arrangement was not aimed at creating an executive with authority to act independently as the government. Creation of an executive branch was quite simply a practical decision to facilitate action, within limits, by the one national government of the United States. Means were previously lacking to enforce laws; the new arrangement was designed to remedy that.

**Interpretations in Conflict.** Constitutional authority of the President under the faithful execution of the laws clause has been interpreted throughout American history as constrained, particularly by authority assigned by Congress to other governmental officers. But while limited, the authority has been understood as providing for crucial oversight by the President to assure faithful execution of laws, specifically with respect to executive-branch matters. Conflicts over presidential authority under the provision have arisen in recent decades, however, including some over assertions that executive acts can only be done under direction and control of the President. Associated with this activist theory of presidential power are interpretations that stress SEPARATION OF POWERS and ignore shared authority and responsibilities. This activist theory at its extreme nearly defines an executive branch that is subordinate to the President as the United States government.

Historical origins of the constitutional language, as summarized above, and practices throughout American history support a more constrained interpretation. Madison in the First Congress stated that the President's responsibility is to ensure "good behavior" and to "superintend" executive officers for that purpose (*Annals of Congress*, 1789, vol. 1, pp. 379 and 387). In 1823, during James Monroe's presidency, Attorney General William Wirt responded as follows to a request for his opinion on the President's authority to alter decisions of Treasury Department auditors and comptrollers: "The Constitution assigns to Congress the power of designating the duties of particular officers: the President is only required to take care that they execute them faithfully" (1 Op. Att'y Gen. 625). With respect to ministerial functions and quasi-judicial functions, presidential control is limited.

Chief Justice William Howard Taft, following his service as President, espoused active presidential authority. Specifically, in MYERS V. UNITED STATES (1926), he found authority for the President to remove a postmaster, without cause, before expiration of his term of office, and the Court held contrary provisions of the TENURE OF OFFICE ACT of 1867 unconstitutional. Nine years later, in the equally well-known case, HUMPHREY'S EXECUTOR V. UNITED STATES (1935), the President was held to lack authority to remove a member of the Federal Trade Commission, who was found to exercise no part of executive power but to function under quasi-legislative and quasi-judicial powers.

Taft's support in *Myers* of a "strong" presidency represented a mild brand of activism by contrast with a few later interpretations. In UNITED STATES V. NIXON (1974) for example, it was argued on behalf of the President, caught up in the WATERGATE AFFAIR, that the judiciary lacked jurisdiction because the matter was an in-house dispute within the executive branch. The Supreme Court rejected that view, however, and allowed the special prosecutor, an employee of the executive branch, to sue his hierarchical superior, the President. Later, the Reagan administration sometimes argued the view that the President has separate authority and responsibility to interpret the Constitution, Supreme Court decisions to the contrary notwithstanding. While such positions have rarely garnered much support, actions consistent with doctrines of separate and overriding presidential power have concerned careful observers of the national government. For example, persistent Reagan administration interventions into agency rulemaking and adjudications, under the guise of coordination, were seen by experts as troubling violations of traditional, constitutionally based limits.

Contrary to constitutional law, extensive literature of American public administration from the 1930s forward has supported aggrandizement of presidential power in a system characterized by a relatively strict separation of powers rather than by shared authority and responsibility. Many early public-administration leaders deliberately divorced themselves from the field of law. In his influential textbook first published in 1926, for example, Leonard White enjoined the field of public administration to leave aside concerns of law and to embrace, instead, those of the American Management Association. In 1936, the seminal report of the President's Committee on Administrative Management (the Brownlow Committee) established the doctrine of American public administration for the next forty years under the banner of executive leadership and hierarchical conformation and control. The two Hoover Commissions (1947–1949, 1953–1955) forcefully persisted in a similar vein.

Despite such sustained support of aggrandizement of presidential power, constitutional interpretation strongly supports the view that the three branches of United States government share authority and responsibilities. Congress can and does distribute ministerial and adjudicative duties among executive-branch officials without observing the hierarchical principles of public administration orthodoxy. Executive-branch officers, in turn, do implement the laws themselves, except that, in broad areas in which discretion is allowed, the President may exert direction and control.

**Failures of a Rule of Law.** Questions about the faithful execution of the laws clause most commonly have concerned means of enforcement of national laws and institutional conflicts among the three branches of the national government. Since the late 1960s, however, concerns have focused increasingly on whether governmental officials may properly place self-interests and partisan loyalties, especially to the President, above responsibility to a rule of law. Chronic failures to observe reasonable standards of law have so come to characterize the national government that traditional concerns of constitutional interpretation no longer suffice in analysis of the faithful execution of the laws clause.

Historically, despite such earlier scandals as territorial land-development schemes, shoddy Civil War procurements, crimes in dealing with Indian affairs, corruption of elections, and the Teapot Dome Scandal, it was generally assumed in public affairs that standards of a rule of law as well as reasonable compliance with specific laws would characterize conduct of national government officials. Although successes in maintaining government under law have continued to outnumber failures by far, since the 1960s increasingly destructive violations of reasonable standards have shaken public confidence. Spoils and corruption have ranged among public officials from Vice President Spiro T. Agnew to numerous presidential appointees of the Reagan administration and from former Speaker of the House of Representatives Jim Wright to a multitude of members of Congress in the House bank and post office scandals in the early 1990s. Official national government failures have included the Bay of Pigs invasion, Vietnam War, the Watergate affair, the Iranian hostage crisis, the Iran-contra affair, and numerous violations in defense and foreign-assistance contracting. Such failures demonstrate a deficiency of shared understanding and acceptance of the discipline of the rule of law.

Constitutional government under the rule of law requires the following conditions:

First, a culture of respect for law. Examples at the top and at all levels of government who do in fact take care that the laws are faithfully executed are essential to facilitate both the substance and image of integrity.

Second, responsible exercise of latitude in interpretation and applications of laws. Both professional expertise and political sensitivity are required to deal effectively with the complexities of public affairs, making shared responsibility among career civil servants and political officials in all branches of government essential.

Third, practices that reach well beyond obedience to specific laws. Most fundamentally, such practices involve a "search for reasonableness," building on experience that reaches back to such teachings as Plato's allegory of the cave. In administrative processes, for example, minimum guidelines that are accepted as basic to a rule of law include actions consonant with disciplined processes, experience, and knowledge; actions accessible to open inquiry; opportunities for fair hearings; authoritative purposes, the "ends of the law," always weighed positively in the balance.

### BIBLIOGRAPHY

Fisher, Louis. *The Politics of Shared Power: Congress and the Executive.* 1993.

Ledewitz, Bruce. "The Uncertain Power of the President to Execute the Laws." *Tennessee Law Review* 46 (1979): 757–806.

Miller, Arthur S. "The President and Faithful Execution of the Laws." *Vanderbilt Law Review* 40 (1987): 389–406.

Miller, Arthur S., and Jeffrey H. Bowman. "Presidential Attacks on the Constitutionality of Federal Statutes: A New Separation of Powers Problem." *Ohio State Law Journal* 40 (1979): 51–80.

Newland, Chester A. "Faithful Execution of the Law and Empowering Public Confidence." *Presidential Studies Quarterly* 21 (1991): 673–686.

CHESTER A. NEWLAND

**FAREWELL ADDRESS.** Like a father who desires to impart some final words of wisdom to his son before he makes his way into the world, George Washington, the Father of His Country, wished to deliver one final exhortation to his nation after declining to run for a third term as President in 1796. The result was the masterful Farewell Address, one of the crown jewels of the American political tradition. The address was held in such high regard during the nineteenth century that it was repeatedly reprinted in pamphlet form along with both the Declaration of Independence and the Constitution.

The address was written with the able assistance of ALEXANDER HAMILTON, James Madison, and JOHN JAY, all of whom, not inappropriately, had contributed to THE FEDERALIST during the battle for the Constitution's ratification. Nevertheless, the ideas and rhetorical style of the address are Washington's own. Forsaking the crass partisanship of the moment, Washington wrote for posterity, avoiding attacks on specific personalities and exhibiting in his comments the same solemn modesty that had been extraordinarily evident throughout his public career.

The underlying theme of the address is the necessity of morality to politics. According to Washington, republicanism cannot survive without moral virtue on the part of both the citizenry and its government. Structural devices such as CHECKS AND BALANCES and the SEPARATION OF POWERS will not stave off destruction if the people do not have enough temperance, wisdom, and justice to rule themselves.

Nearly two centuries have passed since the Farewell Address was first published, yet its specific applications of morality to politics remain disconcertingly relevant. Washington warned, for example, of the dangers of accumulating a large national debt during peacetime. He argued that citizens and their government had a sacred obligation to discharge the public debt as quickly as possible, rather than "ungenerously throwing upon posterity the burthen which we ourselves ought to bear." Washington also attacked the excessive influence of partisanship and special interests on the deliberative process. In his view, elections were the proper forum for making choices about the principles and policies of the national government; once elected, the nation's representatives had their mandate and were obliged to do their duty without being sidetracked by the agendas of an "enterprising minority." In the area of foreign affairs, Washington urged the observance of "good faith and justice towards all Nations" rather than permanent alliances with a few and he warned against manipulation of American foreign policy by foreign governments. More generally, Washington pleaded for all Americans to be united with one another as fellow citizens. Here he was trying to discourage the regional rivalries that would ultimately tear apart antebellum America; but his admonitions remain pertinent in light of the efforts of some to derive their primary identity from race or ethnicity rather than from their American citizenship. Finally, Washington pointed to religion

and education as the primary means for inculcating proper habits and cultivating the "enlightened public opinion" on which republicanism depends.

Though Washington expressed some fears for the future of his country in the Farewell Address, he held out even brighter hopes, viewing the rising American republic as the fulfillment of the promises of the Declaration of Independence. The declaration had proclaimed "the pursuit of happiness" as one of the fundamental ends for which governments are ordained. In the Farewell Address, Washington announced his hope that those who had pursued happiness in 1776 would now obtain it, allowing the world to profit from America's example by following her lead and adopting political liberty as the correct standard of human government. The rest of American history has been in large part a struggle to live up to Washington's demanding vision.

### BIBLIOGRAPHY

Bemis, Samuel Flagg. "Washington's Farewell Address: A Foreign Policy of Independence." *American Historical Review* 39 (1934): 250–268.

*George Washington: A Collection.* Edited by W. B. Allen. 1988.

McDonald, Forrest. *The Presidency of George Washington.* 1974.

Paltsits, Victor H. *Washington's Farewell Address.* 1935.

JOHN G. WEST, JR.

**FARLEY, JAMES A.** (1888–1976), Democratic Party national committee chairman, Postmaster General. Long active in New York State politics, James Aloysius Farley managed Franklin D. Roosevelt's successful gubernatorial campaign in 1928 and was named chairman of the state Democratic committee. Farley played a key role in securing the Democratic presidential nomination for Roosevelt in 1932 and became his campaign manager. His extraordinary talent for organization, winning personality, and knack for remembering names and faces served Roosevelt well. In 1933 Roosevelt named him POSTMASTER GENERAL, from which position he operated as the administration's PATRONAGE supervisor and political field general.

Farley found neither role easy to fill in the rapidly changing and fractious political environment of the NEW DEAL. An old-style politician used to dealing with party organizations and political bosses, he never adapted to the new style of interest-group politics that underlay the Roosevelt coalition. Farley's patronage job was complicated by the many new agencies' demands for professional talent; the heads of several New Deal agencies simply hired whomever they wanted, leaving Farley with the difficult task of coping with disgruntled local party bosses.

Even worse, Farley's relationship with Roosevelt, once close, grew strained. Though he ascribed his failure to crack the New Deal's inmost circle to social snobbery, others attributed the problem to Farley's inability to find common ground with Roosevelt on any level except the political. Farley resented not being consulted about the COURT-PACKING PLAN issue in 1937, and he opposed the President's attempted purge of the Democratic Party in 1938, in which Roosevelt tried to rid the Congress of conservative Democrats who opposed the New Deal. The final break came when Roosevelt dashed Farley's hopes of running for President by taking on the third-term campaign of 1940. Farley never actively opposed Roosevelt, but he withdrew to the sidelines in the 1940s.

## BIBLIOGRAPHY

Schlesinger, Arthur M., Jr. *The Age of Roosevelt.* 3 vols. 1957–1960.

WILLIAM LASSER

## FAST-TRACK AUTHORITY.

**FAST-TRACK AUTHORITY.** The Trade Act of 1974, which authorized the President specifically to enter into trade agreements to reduce nontariff barriers (NTBs), required that such trade agreements be approved and implemented by an act of Congress. Special procedures were devised for such enactment in order to protect the needs and concerns of both the executive and Congress. The need of the executive to preserve the integrity of an agreement already entered into, and thereby the credibility of the United States as a negotiating party, is protected by "fast track procedures" (sec. 151 of the act), providing for mandatory introduction and requiring expeditious consideration of an "implementing bill" submitted by the President. These procedures included deadlines for committee and floor consideration, limited debate, no amendments, and a mandatory vote. The same procedures were applied to newly authorized agreements establishing free-trade areas (FTAs). Fast-track procedures would apply only to those NTB and FTA agreements that would be concluded before 1 June 1993. They continue to apply, without a cut-off date or other requirements, to joint resolutions to approve agreements with nonmarket-economy countries providing for reciprocal most-favored-nation (MFN) treatment.

In return for these expedited procedures, the President must notify and consult with the Congress at various stages of the negotiations. The President must consult with all committees having jurisdiction over matters in the agreement; notify both Houses of Congress of his intention to enter into the agreement at least ninety calendar days before doing so; and submit to Congress an implementing bill (in practice, fashioned in cooperation with the Congress), a statement of proposed administrative action and required supporting information.

Fast-track procedures are denied to an NTB or FTA agreement-implementing bill if both Houses at any time adopt, within sixty days of each other, separate resolutions disapproving the procedures because of the President's failure or refusal to consult. Nor do they apply to a bill implementing an FTA agreement— nor can such agreement be entered into by the President—unless certain additional conditions have been fulfilled, among them a written notice of negotiations to the Senate Finance and the House Ways and Means committees at least sixty session days before the ninety-day advance notice of entry into the agreement, and consultation with them on the FTA agreement. Fast track also does not apply if either committee, within sixty session days after receiving the notice, disapproves the negotiation of such agreement.

Fast-track procedures have been enacted as an exercise of the rulemaking power of either House, and can be changed or eliminated in the same manner as any other rule.

## BIBLIOGRAPHY

Holmer, Alan F., and Judith H. Bello. "The Fast Track Debate: A Prescription for Pragmatism." *International Lawyer* 26 (Spring 1992): 183–199.

U.S. House of Representatives. Committee on Ways and Means. *President's Request for Extension of Fast Track Trade Agreement Implementing Authority.* Hearings. 102d Cong., 2d sess. 12 March and 11 April 1991. Serial 102-16.

VLADIMIR N. PREGELJ

## FEDERAL BUREAU OF INVESTIGATION

**FEDERAL BUREAU OF INVESTIGATION (FBI).** Since its founding in 1908, the FBI has been one of the most controversial institutions in American life. Its history can be divided into three parts: the years before J. EDGAR HOOVER, Hoover's years as director (1924–1972), and the post-Hoover period.

Before 1908, investigations of violations of federal crimes were handled by SECRET SERVICE agents from the TREASURY DEPARTMENT lent to the JUSTICE DEPARTMENT (or to other agencies with problems needing investigation). When Theodore Roosevelt investigated land frauds in Idaho involving members of the Idaho REPUBLICAN PARTY, Congress tried to stop the investigation by prohibiting the loan of Secret Service personnel to other departments, so Roosevelt set up the

Bureau of Investigation within the Justice Department. Initially, the Bureau was staffed by nine former Secret Service agents and twenty-five other investigators.

A pattern emerged during these early years: when the public became aroused over a real or perceived danger, Congress or the President would respond with new federal laws or EXECUTIVE ORDERS, and the Bureau would be thrown into action, characteristically emerging with a few high-profile arrests to demonstrate federal concern. During public hysteria over the so-called white slave menace in 1910, the Bureau arrested the controversial black heavyweight boxing champion, Jack Johnson, for a violation of the Mann Act. During WORLD WAR I, the Bureau brought the weight of the government down on draft resisters and antiwar activists, particularly members of the Industrial Workers of the World and the Socialist Party. After the war, the Bureau organized the PALMER RAIDS to round up and deport alien communists.

During the TEAPOT DOME SCANDAL of 1923 and 1924, the Bureau's efforts to intimidate critics of the Warren G. Harding administration instead discredited the Bureau. As a result, Calvin Coolidge's Attorney General, Harlan F. Stone, put the Bureau under guidelines that restricted it to investigations of federal crimes, a policy adhered to by its new director, J. Edgar Hoover, with few exceptions, until the Franklin D. Roosevelt administration. From 1924 to 1933, Hoover turned the Bureau into a model progressive law enforcement agency, making the Bureau indispensable to local forces by developing fingerprint files, establishing crime laboratories, collecting crime statistics, and providing advanced training facilities in police science.

But under Herbert Hoover the Bureau also began to perform rather innocuous political services for the President at his request—providing information on individuals and groups wishing to meet with the President, for example—that evolved into a regular routine of acting as the President's personal political intelligence agency, furnishing information to Roosevelt on rivals like Huey Long, the Liberty League, and the isolationist movement, to Harry S. Truman on Tommy Corcoran, and to the Kennedys on Martin Luther King, Jr., and on the implications of their romances. During the 1964 Democratic Convention, the Bureau kept Lyndon B. Johnson informed on anything that might disrupt his control of the event. The Bureau's need to be ready to service presidential inquiries undoubtedly was one of the motives—or excuses—for its tireless acquisition of information on public figures, a practice that unnerved political Wash-

ington during Hoover's lifetime and has fascinated the media ever since.

In 1933 the Bureau received a new mandate from Franklin Roosevelt's Attorney General, HOMER CUMMINGS. The news media and Hollywood had made celebrity gangsters a symbol of national demoralization during the early depression. Cummings put Hoover and the Bureau on the trail of outlaws such as Machinegun Kelly, Pretty Boy Floyd, Baby Face Nelson, and John Dillinger, and the impact of these cases was enormous: they propelled through Congress a package of federal laws vastly increasing the jurisdiction of the Bureau (renamed the Federal Bureau of Investigation in 1935) and touched off a "G-man" boom of FBI entertainment in the movies, radio, the comics, and pulp magazines. In addition, Roosevelt secretly put Hoover and the Bureau back in the business of investigating extremist organizations and individuals, especially communists and fascists. With the outbreak of WORLD WAR II in Europe, Roosevelt proclaimed a state of emergency and made the FBI publicly responsible for collecting information on espionage, sabotage, and subversive activities. After PEARL HARBOR, the FBI publicized its activities on the home front to prevent vigilante loyalty investigations of the World War I variety.

With the outbreak of the COLD WAR, Hoover's FBI embarked on the highly controversial task of investigating Soviet espionage activities and prosecuting the Communist Party U.S.A. under the Smith Act. The Bureau also provided assistance to congressional internal security investigative committees, notably the House Un-American Activities Committee, the Internal Security Subcommittee of the Senate Judiciary Committee and, eventually, Sen. Joseph McCarthy's investigative subcommittee. The FBI also worked with anticommunist journalists, politicians, and organizations and cooperated with the entertainment industry to create a climate of popular anticommunism and ensure support for the Bureau's plans to detain communists and other persons who represented security risks should hostilities break out between the United States and the Soviet Union.

Throughout the 1950s and 1960s and into the 1970s the FBI continued to raise the alarm about domestic communism, long after most observers felt the danger had passed. During the 1960s the Bureau was criticized for failing to enforce civil rights laws aggressively and for not protecting the safety of civil rights activists. Hoover was also faulted for maintaining a force of agents who were exclusively white and male and for permitting the Bureau to be a stronghold of institutional racism despite changes in the nation's standards of race relations. The FBI's hostility toward the civil rights movement and radical political protest culminated in the notorious COINTELPRO (Counter-Intelligence Program) of the 1960s, which was directed against the black power and student antiwar movements, and in the Bureau's outrageous harassment of Martin Luther King, Jr. (motivated by Hoover's personal hatred of the civil rights leader).

When Hoover died in 1972 the Bureau had become a focus for national fury over the VIETNAM WAR and the WATERGATE AFFAIR, and revelations of illegal FBI activities by Senate and House investigations in 1975 destroyed the Bureau's hard-won reputation as the country's bulwark against crime and communism, replacing it with the image of having itself been a criminal conspiracy against civil liberties and the constitutional political process. After 1978 two former federal judges, William H. Webster and then William S. Sessions, served as directors and moved the FBI into investigations of political corruption and white-collar crime. Recognizing the public and media distrust of the Bureau, they tried to keep away from the kind of publicity-generating activities favored by Hoover. In 1993 the Bureau had about eighty-seven hundred special agents across the country and was continuing to evolve, not without growing pains, into an organization reflecting the pluralistic character of American society.

### BIBLIOGRAPHY

Garrow, David J. *The FBI and Martin Luther King, Jr.* 1983.
Lowenthal, Max. *The Federal Bureau of Investigation.* 1950.
Powers, Richard Gid. *G-Men: Hoover's FBI in American Popular Culture.* 1983.
Powers, Richard Gid. *Secrecy and Power: The Life of J. Edgar Hoover.* 1987.
Theoharis, Athan G., and John S. Cox. *The Boss: J. Edgar Hoover and the Great American Inquisition.* 1988.
Ungar, Sanford J. *FBI.* 1976.

RICHARD GID POWERS

## FEDERAL ELECTION COMMISSION (FEC).

The Federal Election Commission was established by the 1974 amendments to the Federal Election Campaign Act (FECA) to administer the FECA, disburse public financing to presidential (and vice presidential) candidates and political party conventions, enforce the contribution and expenditure limitations and the PAC (POLITICAL ACTION COMMITTEE) and political party committee provisions, provide the means for comprehensive disclosure of political receipts and expenditures relating to federal candidacy, and preside over other aspects of federal election law.

The FEC is composed of six voting members appointed by the President and confirmed by the Senate. The terms of the appointments are staggered and are for six years each. No more than three of the appointees may be affiliated with the same political party. The commission elects from among its members a chair and a vice-chair—each of a different political party—and the officers serve a term of only one year, in order to prevent a particular party or interest from dominating agency decisions and actions.

The FEC is empowered to promulgate necessary rules and regulations, conduct audits and investigations, subpoena witnesses, and make reports to the Congress and the President.

The FEC has jurisdiction over civil enforcement of federal laws; it does not have authority to act as a court of law nor to deal with criminal enforcement, though it may refer such cases to the ATTORNEY GENERAL. The FECA specifically mandates the commission to encourage voluntary compliance with the law, and the commission has committed itself to correct or prevent violations by seeking conciliation before resorting to civil enforcement actions. Candidates and committees may agree to conciliation for a variety of reasons, such as the pressures of time, cost, and adverse publicity. Although the FEC does not formally adjudicate, the commission does interpret matters of law, determine matters of fact, and publicly declare violations of law. It may sue or be sued in civil actions and constitutional cases.

The FEC has within its jurisdiction a Clearinghouse on Election Administration. Unlike the FEC's main focus, which is on the flow of money in federal elections, the clearinghouse provides information services and studies to state and local governments in the administrative conduct of elections.

The FEC's mission as overseer of the election process requires it to strike a reasonable balance between enforcing the law and the goals of not chilling free speech nor inhibiting citizen participation in the electoral process.

### BIBLIOGRAPHY

Alexander, Herbert E. *Financing Politics: Money, Elections and Political Reform.* 4th ed. 1992.
Jackson, Brooks. *Broken Promise: Why the Federal Election Commission Failed.* 1990.

HERBERT E. ALEXANDER

## FEDERALISM.

The Framers of the Constitution in 1787 placed the President within a framework of government that provided for divided power between the new national government and the states. The question of how much the Constitution provided for a federal or a national government was not settled when the nation began. As James Madison put it in FEDERAL-IST 39, the Constitution was "in strictness, neither a national nor a federal Constitution, but a composition of both." The key idea that Madison advanced in *Federalist* 10 contended that a republican government needed a large area if it was to survive. In such an expanded government, the President, as the leader of the nation, played an important part in deciding where the balance should fall in the rivalry between the states and the national government. As a result, Presidents regularly addressed the issue of federal-state relations, especially as the power of the federal government increased during the twentieth century.

The issue of federalism presented itself in a direct way initially with the Kentucky and Virginia Resolutions of 1798 and 1799. A reaction to the ALIEN AND SEDITION ACTS, the resolutions, drafted by Thomas Jefferson and James Madison, asserted that if the federal government exceeded its powers, states had "the right and are in duty bound to interpose for arresting the progress of the evil, and for maintaining within their respective limits the authorities, rights, and liberties appertaining to them." Presidents in the years before the CIVIL WAR had to deal with the doctrine of NULLIFICATION that later evolved from these resolutions. SLAVERY and the sectional crisis often underlay the claims of state power that Presidents affirmed up until the 1860s.

**Dual Federalism.** In general, Chief Executives accepted the doctrine of what came to be called dual federalism down to 1861. Under this philosophy, the states and the nation were both sovereign within their spheres, but the emphasis was placed on the sovereignty of the states. Accordingly, the existence of state powers acted as a check on even the powers that the Constitution had delegated to the national government. Dual federalism was a concept that set the states and the national government into a competition for power and authority.

In practice, dual federalism fit well with both the philosophical assumptions and the policy beliefs of the nation's early Presidents. Consistency yielded, however, when some important goal was being pursued. So while Presidents appealed to principle in stating their position on federalism, they could be quite flexible in their practices.

Thomas Jefferson in his second INAUGURAL ADDRESS in March 1805 believed that a constitutional amendment was necessary before federal revenues could be used to promote "rivers, canals, roads, arts, manufactures,

education and other great objects within each state." A dozen years later, on 3 March 1817, President James Madison vetoed a bill to promote INTERNAL IMPROVE-MENTS in the states. He proclaimed "that the permanent success of the Constitution depends on a definite partition of powers between the General and State Governments." Because "no adequate landmarks would be left by the constructive extension of the powers of Congress" that the bill proposed, Madison refused to approve the measure.

Five years later in May 1822, James Monroe vetoed a bill to repair the Cumberland road. In a lengthy paper that accompanied the message, he argued that "The Government of the United States is a limited Government, instituted for great national purposes, and for those only." Accordingly, a constitutional amendment would be necessary for the federal government to construct internal improvements. "The States individually can not transfer the power to the United States, nor can the United States receive it," Monroe said.

John Quincy Adams went against this line of reasoning in his first Annual Message of 6 December 1825 in which he advocated the use of national power to promote internal improvements which he described as "important to the whole and to which neither the authority nor the resources of any State can be adequate." The political reaction to federal activism that Adams advanced was hostile, and his rhetorical challenge to dual federalism had little immediate impact.

Andrew Jackson at first maintained the view of federalism that most of his predecessors had adopted but then shifted it when his own prerogatives were challenged. In his veto of the Maysville road bill in 1830, he called the legislation one "of purely local character." Disregarding the distinction between appropriations for national and local purposes, Jackson said, "would, of necessity, lead to the subversion of the federal system." Jackson's veto of the second BANK OF THE UNITED STATES also represented a move against centralized control from the national government.

When the issue became, however, whether the state of South Carolina had the power to nullify the TARIFF ACT OF 1832, Jackson defended national prerogatives. For a state to assert a right to overturn a federal law of which it disapproved, would be "*incompatible with the existence of the Union*" [Jackson's emphasis]. The President concluded that "The Constitution of the United States, then, forms a government, not a league" and that the right of nullification or SECESSION could not be justified. The immediate controversy was resolved through a compromise, but Jackson's expansion of federal power would have important consequences later in the nineteenth century.

During the twenty-five years after Jackson left the White House, the Democratic Presidents remained faithful to dual federalism and the principle of STATES' RIGHTS that lay at the heart of their party. James K. Polk believed that both the federal government and the states were sovereign "within the sphere of its reserved powers." In 1854, Franklin Pierce vetoed a bill to grant public lands to the states for the benefit of the insane, as the reformer Dorothea Dix had advocated. Pierce could not "find any authority in the Constitution for making the Federal Government the great almoner of public charity throughout the United States." Doing so, he concluded would "be contrary to the letter and spirit of the Constitution and subversive of the whole theory upon which the Union of these States is founded."

James Buchanan took a similar position in 1859 when he vetoed a bill to grant public lands to states and territories for educational purposes. "Should the time ever come when the State Governments shall look to the Federal Treasury for the means of supporting themselves and maintaining their systems of education and internal policy, the character of both governments will be greatly deteriorated." Deference to states' rights, however, was less evident when these Presidents dealt with the issue of state laws to protect fugitive slaves.

**Lincoln's Federalism.** Faced with the problem of secession and rebellion, Abraham Lincoln advanced a view of federalism that built upon the position of Jackson in the nullification crisis. In a message to Congress on 4 July 1861, Lincoln attacked the idea of secession as based on the mistaken assumption "that there is some omnipotent and sacred supremacy pertaining to a *State*—to each State of our Federal Union" [Lincoln's emphasis]. He contended that "the States have their status in the Union and they have no other legal status." In the GETTYSBURG ADDRESS, by placing the nation first and stressing the Declaration of Independence with its promise of equality, Lincoln delivered a powerful blow to the older tradition of federalism. The outcome of the Civil War eliminated the doctrines of nullification and secession and shifted power toward the national government. The forces behind dual federalism, particularly among the Democrats, remained strong.

During the RECONSTRUCTION period, President Andrew Johnson, a former Democrat, reasserted the position on federalism that had been so long associated with that party. In vetoing the CIVIL RIGHTS ACT OF 1866 (which Congress then passed over his veto), Johnson claimed that the measure represented a movement "toward centralization and the concentration of all legislative power in the National Government." Johnson used federalism as a support for his racial position on Reconstruction. His opposition to the civil rights law helped to push Republican opinion behind the Fourteenth Amendment as a way of curbing state power to interfere with the rights of the newly freed slaves.

Thereafter, Republican Presidents reaffirmed the Lincoln position on federalism. The "decree" of war, said James A. Garfield in 1881, had established the supremacy of the Constitution and the laws made under it: "This decree does not disturb the autonomy of the States nor interfere with any of their necessary rights of local self-government, but it does fix and establish the permanent supremacy of the Union." In December 1883, Chester A. Arthur urged Congress to consider legislation regulating railroads "to protect the people at large in their interstate traffic against acts of injustice which the State governments are powerless to prevent." That step was taken with the creation of the Interstate Commerce Commission in 1887.

During his two terms as President, Grover Cleveland resisted the movement of power toward the central government. He urged Americans "to persistently check the increasing tendency to extend the scope of Federal legislation into the domain of State and local jurisdiction upon the plea of subserving the general welfare." For Cleveland this meant vetoing a bill to provide money for seeds in drought-affected Texas counties in 1887. "I do not believe," wrote the President "that the power and duty of the General Government ought to be extended to the relief of individual suffering which is in no manner properly related to the public service or benefit." On the other hand, Cleveland put aside his qualms about federal interference with the states in the PULLMAN STRIKE of 1894 when he sent troops to Chicago despite the objections of the Illinois governor, John P. Altgeld.

Benjamin Harrison returned to the Republican tradition when he endorsed the concept of federal legislation to reform state elections in the South, a measure that the Democrats labeled a force bill. In his annual message of 1890, the President said that the measure "has been denounced as if it were a new exercise of Federal power and an invasion of the rights of the States. Nothing could be further from the truth," he argued, citing other aspects of elections that Congress regulated. Nonetheless, the federal elections bill was defeated. The Presidents who followed Harrison took the position that the Constitution did not give the President the power to interfere in the racial affairs of states and localities. Federalism became an apparent barrier to presidential action to alleviate racial injustice.

Similar concerns restrained William McKinley from pursuing federal antitrust legislation at the end of the nineteenth century. Theodore Roosevelt had no such reservations. A strong advocate of national power, he regarded state rights as a way of avoiding the effective control of corporate power. "The States have shown that they have not the ability to curb the power of syndicated wealth," Roosevelt said in 1907, "and therefore, in the interest of the people, it must be done by national action." Accordingly, Roosevelt believed, "irresponsible outside business power. . .can only be controlled in one way—by giving adequate power of control to the one sovereignty capable of exercising such power—the National Government." A railroad president decided that Roosevelt was "trying to concentrate all power in Washington, to practically wipe out state lines, and to govern the people by commissions and bureaus."

**Growing Federal Dominance.** After Roosevelt left office in 1909, William Howard Taft and Woodrow Wilson oversaw important changes in the nature of federal-state relations. Congress enacted a number of measures such as the Weeks Act (1911), the Smith-Lever Act (1914), and the National Highway Act (1916) that tied cash grants from Washington to the states having met minimum standards and having submitted specific plans for spending the allotted funds. Before he became President, Wilson said that he "put the emphasis on the duties of the States rather than their 'rights' " and stressed "a fortunate liberty and variety in our methods of cooperation" between the national government and the states. Indeed, the programs of monetary grants and federal mandates have been described as "cooperative federalism" that characterized the period from the early part of the twentieth century through the mid 1960s. In place of the competing governments of dual federalism, cooperative federalism envisioned a kind of intergovernmental partnership between Washington and the states.

The Republican Presidents during the 1920s generally endorsed cooperative federalism in their public statements. The prohibition amendment posed issues of joint federal-state law enforcement that President Warren G. Harding discussed in a speech he made during a national tour in 1923. "The very basis of our political establishment is the idea of dual sovereignty of the States and the Nation," he said in Denver, and he spoke of "the necessity for real cooperation between National and State authority, if we will only develop effective means for the exercise therein of concurrent jurisdiction.

Two years later in a Memorial Day speech, Calvin Coolidge set forth a more restricted version of cooperative federalism when he argued that what the nation needed was not "more Federal Government but better local government." The reason for the "increasing demands" on the Federal government was "that the States have not discharged their full duties." Accordingly, he deplored the use of federal money to help the states build highways. "If there is to be a continuation of individual and local self-government and of State sovereignty, the individual and locality must govern themselves and the State must assert its sovereignty."

During the Great Depression, Herbert Hoover reminded his audiences that in his judgment the federal system placed limits on what the national government could do to alleviate hard times. In a speech in October 1930, he said that "tendencies of communities and states to shirk their own responsibilities or to unload them upon the Federal Government, or of the Federal Government to encroach upon the responsibilities of states, are destructive of our whole pattern of self-government." Because of these views, the President resisted pleas from the states for relief funds to fight the depression until the summer of 1932 when the administration allocated $300 million from future highway grants to states. Cooperative federalism under Hoover had limited impact on the nation's economic distress.

**The New Deal.** The presidency of Franklin D. Roosevelt permanently transformed the pattern of federal-state interaction. The amount of federal money allocated to the states rose from $220 million in 1932 to $2 billion three years later. Roosevelt believed "that forty-eight sovereignties cannot agree quickly enough or practically enough on any solution for a national economic problem or a national social problem." The varied programs of the NEW DEAL affected federalism in numerous ways. The federal government made direct grants to the states to promote such policies as relief for the unemployed and housing. It also developed aid programs in numerous areas such as aid to children, assistance for health services, and old-age care. By the end of the Roosevelt presidency, there were twenty-nine permanent grant programs. In addition, national legislation limited state power in labor relations and exercised supervisory control over public works. Although the Supreme Court initially resisted Roosevelt's concept of federalism, by 1937 it had capitulated.

Harry Truman faced the issue of federalism in an area that other twentieth-century Presidents had avoided: civil rights. Confronted with the rising expectations of African Americans after WORLD WAR II and their voting power in the North, the President came out strongly for civil rights legislation in his 1948 state of the union message. His call for "effective federal action" on the subject spurred the creation of the States' Rights Party in the South and the presidential candidacy of STROM THURMOND of South Carolina. In a less controversial area, Truman sponsored the first HOOVER COMMISSION (1947–1949) to examine the workings of the federal government.

The election of Dwight D. Eisenhower in 1952 brought a President with a more conservative attitude toward federalism issues than had been the case under Roosevelt and Truman. He set up the Kestnbaum Commission on intergovernmental relations in 1953 to look over the whole issue. Four years later, in 1957, he told the state governors that "Year by year, responding to transient popular demands, the Congress has increased Federal functions. So, slowly at first, but in recent times more and more rapidly, the pendulum of power has swung from our States towards the central government." The President then proposed the Joint Federal-State Action Committee, which produced only modest legislative results. Interestingly, Eisenhower supported an extensive system of interstate highways, in part by relating it to the needs of NATIONAL SECURITY.

**Advance and Retreat.** Since the 1960s, one President after another has addressed the issue of federalism with broad and innovative programs. The first to do so was Lyndon B. Johnson. He announced his approach in his GREAT SOCIETY speech of 22 May 1964. To meet the nation's social problems, he said, required "new concepts of cooperation, a creative federalism, between the National Capital and the leaders of local communities." During the five sessions of Congress of the Johnson presidency, 120 separate legislative acts related to issues of intergovernmental relations. Among the more prominent were the Economic Opportunity Act of 1964, the Medicare-Medicaid Act of 1965, the model Cities Act of 1966, the Public Broadcasting Act of 1967, and the Intergovernmental Cooperation Act of 1968. Despite Johnson's efforts, however, his programs involved no significant changes in the federal system.

Richard Nixon proposed his version of a New Federalism in August 1969. He called for a "new and dramatically different approach" in the manner in which "responsibilities are shared between the States and the Federal Government." His initiatives included a Family Assistance Program, which Congress did not adopt, revenue sharing with the states, block grants for community development, and comprehensive training for employment, which did become law. If Nixon's goal was to lessen the role of the national government, his policies actually shifted power toward Washington.

During the administrations of Gerald Ford and Jimmy Carter, the patterns established under Johnson and Nixon persisted.

Ronald Reagan, however, brought forward his own version of a New Federalism in his 1981 inaugural address. He sought "to curb the size and influence of the Federal establishment and to demand recognition of the distinction between the powers granted to the Federal government and those reserved to the states or to the people." The Reagan administration sought to cut back on the money that the states received from the federal government through grants-in-aid, an effort that achieved some success by 1985. The President also achieved the elimination of one hundred federal programs by the end of his first term. Block grants were consolidated, and a campaign was launched to return a number of welfare and aid programs back to the states. The New Federalism lost some of its momentum after the first two years of the Reagan presidency, and some analysts suggested that regulatory power had begun to flow back toward Washington on such issues as trucking standards, teen-age drinking, and state affirmative-action plans. George Bush continued the basic Reagan philosophy toward federalism, but without strong passion or commitment.

While Presidents have regularly asserted their commitment to the principles of federalism throughout American history, the trend of power has been toward the national government during the twentieth century. The large budget deficits of the 1980s and 1990s produced substantial reductions in federal aid to the states, and the clamor for a balanced-budget amendment made greater cuts more likely in the future. It is logical to expect further presidential pledges of a fidelity to the federal system and a corresponding strengthening of the authority and influence of the nation's Chief Executive.

## BIBLIOGRAPHY

Conlan, Timothy. *New Federalism: Intergovernmental Reform from Nixon to Reagan.* 1988.

Fausold, Martin, and Alan Shank, eds. *The Constitution and the American Presidency.* 1991.

Grodzins, Morton. *The American System: A New View of Government in the United States.* 1966.

Kammen, Michael. *A Machine That Would Go of Itself.* 1986.

Richardson, James D., comp. *A Compilation of the Messages and Papers of the Presidents, 1789–1897.* 1899.

Walker, David B. *Toward a Functioning Federalism.* 1981.

Wellborn, David M., and Jesse Burkhead. *Intergovernmental Relations in the American Administrative State: The Johnson Presidency.* 1989.

LEWIS L. GOULD

**FEDERALIST, THE.** In October 1787, ALEXANDER HAMILTON asked JOHN JAY and James Madison to join him in writing a series of essays designed to promote ratification of the Constitution. Taking Publius as their pseudonym and *The Federalist* as their title, the three authors eventually drafted eighty-five essays defending both the general necessity of the Constitution and its particular provisions. Originally published in newspapers in New York City, the essays were reprinted in other states and then in a two-volume edition in the spring of 1788. Although its impact on ratification may have been slight, *The Federalist* was soon recognized as the most comprehensive and authoritative commentary on the Constitution to emerge from the heated debates of 1787–1788. Its influence on modern interpretations of the Constitution has been enormous.

The principal essays dealing with the presidency (numbers 67–77) were written by Hamilton. But Madison offered revealing insights into his ideas of EXECUTIVE POWER while discussing the SEPARATION OF POWERS in *Federalist* 47–51, while Jay's analysis of treaty-making in *Federalist* 64 has important implications for executive responsibility in foreign affairs. All three men had closely considered the role of executive power in republican governments long before the Convention met: Hamilton from his attachment to the British constitution, Madison from his concern with the dangers of legislative domination in the state constitutions, and Jay from his experience as Secretary for Foreign Affairs under the Confederation.

By the time Hamilton's essays on the executive began to appear in March 1788, the major objections to which he had to respond were familiar. Hamilton opened *Federalist* 67 by complaining that ANTI-FEDERALISTS had reached new levels of rhetorical excess in denouncing the President as a potential tyrant more dangerous than the British crown. Hamilton devoted much of his ensuing analysis of Article II to explaining why this analogy was farfetched. The strongest refutation of this charge appeared in *Federalist* 69, in which Hamilton contrasted the limited term of office of the proposed executive, its shared powers over treaties and appointments with the Senate, and its limited veto over legislation, with the rule of a hereditary monarch possessing an absolute veto and unilateral authority over war and peace and appointments to office. But the comparison was also implicit in the defense of these provisions and others that Hamilton offered elsewhere in this series of essays. Throughout he was intent upon demonstrating that provisions for the election, reeligibility, and IMPEACHMENT of the President all erected adequate safeguards against the abuse of executive power.

Yet beyond recounting these safeguards, Hamilton also provided a compelling justification of the advantages of a vigorous and unitary executive in a republic. This was the central theme of *Federalist* 70, his longest and theoretically most powerful contribution to the series. Here Hamilton closely followed the dominant concerns that had prevailed at the CONSTITUTIONAL CONVENTION by arguing that unity was essential both to promote the efficient execution of the laws and to satisfy republican standards of accountability in government. By contrast, establishing a plural executive or even a single executive linked to a ministerial council would be a formula for indecision, cabal, and divided (and therefore uncertain) responsibility.

The virtues of unity were also reflected in Hamilton's discussion of the powers of the presidency. In *Federalist* 73, he defended the executive veto over legislation as a power designed to enable the executive both to protect itself against improper congressional meddling with its own duties and to serve more generally as a check against impetuous lawmaking by Congress. Here Hamilton's thinking was entirely consistent with the positions that his coauthor James Madison had taken both in the Convention and in his treatment of the separation of powers in *Federalist* 47–51. Because the veto was a necessary but potentially dangerous power, the arguments for efficiency and responsibility again justified its being vested in a unitary executive.

The same considerations were invoked when Hamilton examined presidential authority in foreign relations in *Federalist* 75. Here he echoed arguments that John Jay had previously made in *Federalist* 64. In contrast to modern claims that view the President as the principal maker of foreign policy as well as the exclusive agent for its conduct, Hamilton and Jay described an executive who should follow the advice of the Senate in framing the objects of negotiation, but who should enjoy significant latitude in the business of diplomacy.

In combining a candid treatment of the innovative elements of the Constitution with a defense of its prudential safeguards, the treatment of executive power in *The Federalist* is of a piece with the overall tone of the work as a whole.

## BIBLIOGRAPHY

Cook, Jacob E., ed. *The Federalist.* 1961.

Epstein, David F. *The Political Theory of The Federalist.* 1984.

Kesler, Charles R., ed. *Saving the Revolution: The Federalist Papers and the American Founding.* 1987.

JACK N. RAKOVE

**FEDERALIST PARTY.** The Federalist Party was one of the two main parties in the first American party system. Established in the mid 1790s, the party survived until its disintegration after the WAR OF 1812. Members of this party should not be confused with the group of the same name who supported ratification of the Constitution in 1787–1788. The Federalists of the 1780s never formed a true party (with a platform and organization) but were simply a loose alliance of people who shared a common position on the new Constitution.

The Founding Fathers established political parties only reluctantly. When the new government under the Constitution was launched in 1789, most Americans hoped that everyone would support its policies. Any organized opposition, they feared, would disrupt national harmony and undermine the fragile republican experiment. But ALEXANDER HAMILTON's financial program in the early 1790s divided Americans, and the breach widened over the administration's response to the French Revolution and the ensuing Anglo-French wars (1793–1815). When the administration lined up with Britain in JAY's TREATY of 1794, the breach became irreparable.

After James Madison and Thomas Jefferson organized the Democratic-Republican Party [see DEMOCRATIC PARTY] in the early 1790s, friends of the administration responded by establishing the Federalist Party. The party was strongest in the Northeast and was dominated by George Washington, who served two terms as President (1789–1797), John Adams, who served one term (1797–1801), and Alexander Hamilton, who served as Secretary of the Treasury from 1789 to 1795. The presidential elections of the 1790s mirrored the growth of the party system: while Washington received the unanimous vote of the ELECTORAL COLLEGE in 1788 and 1792, Adams prevailed over Jefferson in 1796 by a margin of only three votes, 71 to 68.

The Federalists had little sympathy for the growing egalitarian and democratic spirit of their age. They had an elitist bias, believing that society should be organized into distinct classes and that the lower classes should defer to the upper classes, especially on matters of state. They favored a broad interpretation of the Constitution (based on Hamilton's doctrine of IMPLIED POWERS) and were willing to use the machinery of government to foster and protect commerce. They also believed in a strong central government with a vigorous executive branch, a large peacetime defense establishment (both to deter and to prosecute war), and a stable system of public finance that included excise as well as import taxes, a funded debt, and a national bank.

The Federalists were hostile to the French Revolution and to the Napoleonic regime that came to power in France in the late 1790s. They saw Britain as the last bastion of civilization in Europe, the only thing that prevented the spread of France's destructive revolutionary ideals. They had little interest in the American West (where they had few constituents) and were against territorial expansion (which they feared would undermine their control of the government and disrupt sectional harmony). They were also hostile to immigrants (most of whom supported the Democratic-Republican Party) but were sympathetic to Native Americans (INDIANS) and slaves.

The Federalists dominated the national government in the 1790s largely because of the enormous prestige of Washington and the extraordinary genius of Hamilton. But their elitism and pro-British bias ran counter to prevailing sympathies, and the taxes and ALIEN AND SEDITION ACTS they adopted during the QUASI-WAR WITH FRANCE (1798–1801) further undermined their popularity. A quarrel between Adams and Hamilton split the party in 1800, and in the election that year Jefferson and AARON BURR each won 73 electoral votes to Adams's 65. With no clear winner, the election was thrown into the House of Representatives, where Federalists supported Burr and thus blocked Jefferson's selection until the thirty-sixth ballot.

After assuming the presidency in 1801, Jefferson pursued moderate policies in the hope of detaching the Federalist rank and file from their leaders. He was largely successful during his first term because the nation enjoyed peace and prosperity, but after 1805 intractable international problems shattered the political calm. Jefferson's attempt to force Britain and France to show greater respect for America's rights as a neutral during the Napoleonic Wars (1803–1815) by employing commercial sanctions—particularly the embargo (1807–1809)—boomeranged on the United States, undermining national prosperity and reducing government revenue. These problems gave new life to the Federalist Party, which only a few years before had seemed headed for extinction.

When Madison became President in 1809, he continued the policy of economic coercion until 1812, when the United States declared war on Britain. Federalists opposed the War of 1812 (1812–1815), and in the election of 1812 their candidate for the presidency, dissident Republican DEWITT CLINTON, won 89 electoral votes to Madison's 128. The outcome was much closer than the vote indicated, and the Federalists had done far better than in any presidential election since 1800.

Throughout the War of 1812 Federalists in Congress presented a united front, voting against all war legislation except measures related to the navy and coastal defense. In New England, where they controlled the state governments, Federalists feuded with Democratic-Republican officials in Washington over the deployment and command of the militia and ultimately convened the Hartford Convention, a regional conference summoned to air their grievances against the administration and its policies.

Although the Federalists made gains at all levels in elections held during the War of 1812, they emerged from the conflict tainted by their opposition, and the party quickly disintegrated as a national organization. The last Federalist candidate for the presidency, RUFUS KING, won only 34 of 221 votes in the election of 1816. Remnants of the party survived in parts of New England until the 1830s but had no significant impact on national politics.

Though in some ways out of touch with their times, the Federalists successfully launched the government in 1789, and most of their policies served the nation well. Their legacy of strong central government, loose construction of the Constitution, military preparedness, and sound public finance continues to inform public policy even today.

### BIBLIOGRAPHY

Broussard, James H. *The Southern Federalists, 1800–1816.* 1978.
Chambers, William N. *Political Parties in a New Nation: The American Experience, 1776–1809.* 1963.
Fisher, David H. *The Revolution of American Conservatism: The Federalist Party in the Era of Jeffersonian Democracy.* 1965.
Hofstadter, Richard. *The Idea of a Party System, 1780–1840.* 1969.
Kerber, Linda K. *Federalists in Dissent: Imagery and Ideology in Jeffersonian America.* 1970.

DONALD R. HICKEY

**FEDERAL REGISTER ACT** (1935). The Federal Register Act of 1935 responded to the great outpouring of legal documents from the executive branch of the federal government during the NEW DEAL. Before the act, there was no systematic method of gathering and publishing new rules and orders, including those emanating from the President. Many were simply held at the agency that generated them, or at the White House. Affected citizens, and even officials charged with enforcing government orders, could be wholly unaware of their provisions. Accordingly, the act created the *Federal Register* and the Code of Federal Regulations (CFR).

The *Federal Register* is an official government newspaper that is issued every working day and contains new PROCLAMATIONS, EXECUTIVE ORDERS, and regulatory actions issued by the executive branch. The volume of these materials is much greater than that of the statutes that they implement. Every agency document of "general applicability and legal effect" must be published in the *Federal Register*; otherwise, persons not having actual knowledge of such directives are not bound by them. If, however, materials are published in the *Federal Register*, everyone is bound by them regardless of actual knowledge of them. In recent years, effective efforts have been made to improve the comprehensibility of materials published in the *Federal Register*.

The CFR organizes these materials and retains them in more permanent form. Revised annually, it collects presidential materials in a separate part set aside for that purpose. The complete regulations of the agencies then appear, organized according to the titles of the United States Code that they implement. Thus, the act makes the large body of law generated in the executive branch both accessible to and binding upon the general public.

### BIBLIOGRAPHY

Schwartz, Bernard. *Administrative Law.* 3d ed. (1991).

HAROLD H. BRUFF

**FEDERAL RESERVE SYSTEM.** The Federal Reserve System consists of two major decision-making bodies, the Federal Reserve Board (or the Board of Governors of the Federal Reserve System) and the Federal Open Market Committee, which includes representatives from twelve Federal Reserve district banks. The Federal Reserve was established in 1913 to perform classic tasks of economic stabilization: serving as lender of last resort to the banking system, correcting periodic regional imbalances in the money supply, and guaranteeing a stable money supply to accommodate the needs of commerce, agriculture, and industry.

The Federal Reserve took its current institutional form in 1935. Reforms that year removed the Secretary of the Treasury from the board, made the Board of Governors the voting majority of the Federal Open Market Committee for the first time, and lengthened the term of board members to fourteen years. This structure has often been interpreted as ensuring political independence, but the view at the time was more mixed. Franklin D. Roosevelt's appointee as chairman, Marriner Eccles, intended the reforms to make the Federal Reserve an unambiguously public agency so that private financial interests could not block key portions of the New Deal program. Subsequently,

Eccles led the Federal Reserve in cooperating closely with White House policy.

This cooperation was reinforced by the demands of financing WORLD WAR II. Following the war, a conflict arose with the Truman administration when the Federal Reserve, then chaired by Thomas B. McCabe, proposed to fight inflation by permitting more variation in interest rates. This conflict was resolved in 1951 in an "accord" between the DEPARTMENT OF THE TREASURY and the Federal Reserve to the effect that interest rates would vary more widely and that the Federal Reserve would enjoy a wider range of independence.

The Federal Reserve Board has seven members, each appointed for fourteen years by the President with the ADVICE AND CONSENT of the Senate. The long terms, together with budgetary independence, are believed to be essential to the system's political independence. The chairman is appointed from among board members to a four-year term. The board has authority for a number of important decisions affecting MONETARY POLICY and the regulation of financial institutions. Because these decisions are central to the financial health of the nation, Presidents have a keen interest in Federal Reserve policy.

One important set of decisions involves the discount rate, the rate of interest at which banks, savings and loan institutions, and credit unions can borrow, short-term, directly from the Federal Reserve district banks. Typically this borrowing has little impact on the money supply, but it can be vital in addressing financial crises. For example, the Federal Reserve signaled unusual willingness to lend through the discount window following the Penn Central Railroad failure in 1970, the collapse of the Continental Illinois Bank in 1984, and the stock market crash of October 1987.

A second important set of decisions involves reserve requirements for virtually all depository institutions. Reserve requirements specify how much cash financial institutions must have immediately available in their own vaults or on deposit with the Federal Reserve. Other financial regulatory decisions made by the Federal Reserve involve consumer protection, the behavior of bank holding companies, and the behavior of state-chartered banks that are Federal Reserve System members.

The Federal Open Market Committee has twelve voting members: the members of the Federal Reserve Board plus five of the twelve district bank presidents. One of the five is always the president of the New York Federal Reserve Bank, which is responsible for implementing open market policy—that is, the buying and selling of government bonds in financial markets. The other four voting seats are rotated among the other district banks (all district bank presidents participate in all meetings even when not voting). The district bank presidents are appointed by the district bank boards of directors subject to approval by the Board of Governors.

It has been argued that high-level policymakers such as the district bank presidents should be presidential appointees, subject to Senate confirmation. The importance of these appointments is underscored by the observation that district bank presidents have generally favored more restrictive monetary policy than have members of the Board of Governors, who are direct presidential appointees. By implication, if the President appointed all the members of the FOMC, monetary policy might be marginally more stimulative. However, court challenges to the method of appointment have not succeeded.

The decisions that the Federal Open Market Committee makes about monetary-growth and interest-rate targets are now regarded as the most important decisions made by the Federal Reserve. The White House watches these decisions closely, and when the President or members of his administration call on the Federal Reserve to change interest rates, their comments are directed to the Federal Open Market Committee.

BIBLIOGRAPHY

Clifford, A. Jerome. *The Independence of the Federal Reserve System.* 1965.
Kettl, Donald. *Leadership at the Fed.* 1986.
Maisel, Sherman. *Managing the Dollar.* 1973.
Woolley, John T. *Monetary Politics: The Federal Reserve and the Politics of Monetary Policy.* 1984.

JOHN T. WOOLLEY

**FEDERAL TRADE COMMISSION ACT**(1914). The act, passed in tandem with the CLAYTON ANTITRUST ACT, constituted the first significant legislative modification of national antitrust law following adoption of the SHERMAN ANTITRUST ACT of 1890. It established the Federal Trade Commission as an independent administrative agency possessing both enforcement and rulemaking authority over "unfair methods of competition."

Its enactment followed long-standing controversy over the redirection of ANTITRUST POLICY. Theodore Roosevelt had sought to redefine national policy toward monopolies in a manner consistent with emerging concepts of progressivism. Roosevelt opposed overbroad application of the Sherman Act that indiscriminately invalidated all monopolies and trade restraints, wishing instead to distinguish between good trusts and bad trusts so as not to impair the benefits of large-scale industrial organization. Concurrently, he hoped to increase the scope of federal regulation so that the activities of big business would better serve the public interest. Not incidentally, he sought to shift the focus of antitrust interpretation away from the judiciary and also empowered a new executive agency, the Bureau of Corporations, to play a leading role in antitrust policymaking.

Roosevelt's emphasis on executive policymaking contrasted with that of his Republican successor, William Howard Taft. By the end of his presidency, Taft was more satisfied with existing law and with the prospect that judges, rather than administrators, would continue to occupy center stage in antitrust law interpretation.

By 1912, antitrust law was in crisis. The previous year, the Supreme Court had adopted the "rule of reason," applying Sherman Act restrictions selectively to those forms of conduct that judges found harmful. Proponents of strong antimonopoly controls feared that the rule of reason would emasculate future antitrust enforcement. At the same time, business leaders bemoaned the lack of clear guidance afforded by existing law and feared the prospect of selective enforcement of antitrust sanctions. Three different approaches to antitrust reform were obvious in the presidential contest of 1912. Taft Republicans called for legislative modifications defining specific business behaviors punishable in the federal courts. Roosevelt Progressives proposed a shift of antitrust policymaking from the courts to a strong, new federal regulatory agency. Wilsonian Democrats, stressing the restoration of "true" competition as a component of the NEW FREEDOM, were disinclined to establish a new federal bureaucracy that might suffer usurpation at the hands of powerful business interests. In January 1914 President Wilson urged a multipronged approach to antitrust reform. Among other recommendations, Wilson proposed that Congress supplement the Sherman Act to invalidate specific corporate practices such as price discrimination, exclusive dealing and tying arrangements, and the maintenance of interlocking directorates. Wilson also proposed that Congress create a weak form of interstate trade commission possessing advisory, not regulatory, powers.

In June 1914, Wilson came to recognize that his prior recommendation had underestimated the difficulty of specifying legislatively corporate behaviors that ought to be proscribed. The House of Representatives had already passed not only a strong antitrust

measure (the Clayton Act) authored by House Judiciary Committee Chairman Henry Clayton prohibiting specific corporate behaviors, but also a weak version of the Federal Trade Commission bill that Wilson had previously championed. But Wilson grew concerned that the Clayton bill would be evaded too easily and abandoned his prior opposition to a strong Federal Trade Commission. Wilson then threw his support behind a Senate amendment to the Federal Trade Commission bill that included commission authority to issue cease and desist orders as the centerpiece of its regulatory authority; the bill secured Senate approval with the bipartisan support of progressive Democrats and Republicans. The Senate bill, somewhat modified in conference committee to expand the power of courts to review commission orders, secured prompt approval by the full Congress.

In December 1914, Wilson reported to Congress that his program for regulation of business was "virtually complete." However, Wilson's initial appointments to the Federal Trade Commission were not distinguished, and progressives were generally disappointed by the commission's early efforts.

### BIBLIOGRAPHY

Clements, Kendrick A. *The Presidency of Woodrow Wilson.* 1992.
Link, Arthur S. *Woodrow Wilson and the Progressive Era, 1910–1917.* 1954.
Mason, Alpheus Thomas. *Brandeis: A Free Man's Life.* 1946.
Sklar, Martin J. *The Corporate Reconstruction of American Capitalism, 1890–1916.* 1988.

RALPH MITZENMACHER

**FERRARO, GERALDINE** (b. 1935), member of the House of Representatives, Democratic vice presidential nominee in 1984. Geraldine Ferraro was the first woman ever to be nominated for the vice presidency by a major political party. She was raised and educated in New York City and attended Fordham University Law School, from which she graduated in 1960. Ferraro married John Zaccaro shortly thereafter. While she raised three children, she practiced civil law and was active in local DEMOCRATIC PARTY politics. When her children reached school age, she went into private practice. In 1974 she became a district attorney in Queens County. She left that office in 1978 to run for Congress. During her three terms in the House of Representatives, Ferraro became a favorite of party leaders and was rewarded with several key appointments in the House as well as chair of the 1984 Democratic platform committee. But, Ferraro's moment in history came when WALTER MONDALE selected her to be his running mate in 1984.

As a candidate for the vice presidency, Ferraro faced far greater public scrutiny than any candidate for that position before or since. Questions about her husband's business dealings plagued her candidacy and she was routinely asked "women's questions" including whether she could bake blueberry muffins. During the vice presidential debate, Ferraro was asked if she could actually bring herself to "push the button" in case of a nuclear attack. After that debate, her opponent, then Vice President George Bush boasted he had "kicked a little ass."

Personal attacks on Ferraro did not stop after the debate. The normally gracious Barbara Bush, for example, coyly referred to Ferraro as a "four million dollar—I can't say it, but it rhymes with rich." Opposition from the Roman Catholic Church was also intense, due to Ferraro's support for legalized abortion.

In 1984, Ronald Reagan won reelection by a landslide. The Mondale-Ferraro Democratic ticket carried only one state, Minnesota. Nevertheless, given the lopsidedness of the election, most pollsters concluded that the "Ferraro factor" had little to do with the outcome of the race. She continues to be active in politics. In 1992 Ferraro was an unsuccessful candidate for the Democratic Party nomination for U.S. Senator in New York.

### BIBLIOGRAPHY

Ferraro, Geraldine. *Ferraro: My Story.* 1985.

KAREN O'CONNOR

**FIELD v. CLARK** 143 U.S. 649 (1891). This leading case concerning DELEGATION OF LEGISLATIVE POWERS arose out of efforts by the Benjamin Harrison administration to open foreign markets to American agricultural products. Secretary of State JAMES G. BLAINE feared that early versions of the MCKINLEY TARIFF ACT of 1890, by placing sugar and other agricultural imports on the free list, would hinder his ability to negotiate RECIPROCAL TRADE AGREEMENTS. President Harrison also believed that meaningful power to negotiate reciprocal trade agreements would be hampered if the effectiveness of such arrangements depended on congressional legislation or Senate treaty concurrence.

Reflecting administration concerns, section 3 of the McKinley Tariff permitted the President to suspend free entry of sugar, molasses, coffee, tea, and hides produced by any nation imposing duties on American exports that the President determined to be "recipro-

cally unequal and unreasonable." The President's power to suspend free entry would result in the imposition of duties on the offending nation's products at predetermined rates for so long as the President should "deem just." Armed with the power to suspend free entry, Harrison was able to conclude a number of reciprocal trade agreements during his presidency. Presidential discretionary authority became a common element of tariff measures adopted subsequent to the 1890 act.

In *Field v. Clark*, the Marshall Field & Company department store attempted to avoid McKinley Tariff Act duties by claiming, among other things, that section 3 unconstitutionally delegated legislative and TREATY-MAKING POWERS to the President. Justice John Marshall Harlan, on behalf of a seven-member majority, upheld section 3. Harlan's opinion reviewed a long history of congressional enactments that had granted presidential discretions concerning foreign trade. It also cited *Brig Aurora v. United States* (1813), in which the Supreme Court upheld, against a claim of unconstitutional delegation of congressional power, President James Madison's reimposition of Non-Intercourse Act sanctions against British imports. In reaching his conclusion, Harlan conceded that Congress cannot delegate legislative power to the President. He held, however, that Congress may direct the President, in his execution of laws, to engage in specified fact-finding activities and that the consequence of congressional enactments may depend on such presidential fact-finding.

Justices Joseph R. Lamar and Melville W. Fuller, appointees of Democrat Grover Cleveland, dissented. They argued that section 3 granted the President far more than fact-finding powers and that the extent of presidential discretion infringed on congressional legislative powers.

The rationale of *Field v. Clark*, permitting the delegation of mere fact-finding powers, was a preliminary step in the evolution of Supreme Court doctrine supporting the development of the administrative state. An earlier case, *Wayman v. Southard* (1825), permitted the delegation of discretion to "fill up the details" of congressional enactments. Later cases supported congressional delegations of rule-making authority to the executive or independent agencies where the exercise of administrative discretion was subject to "adequate legislative standards." Since the 1930s, when the Court occasionally did invoke the delegation of power doctrine to invalidate early NEW DEAL legislation, the Court has consistently approved delegations of administrative authority even under the vaguest of legislative standards.

BIBLIOGRAPHY

Barber, Sotirios A. *The Constitution and the Delegation of Congressional Power.* 1975.

Davis, Kenneth Culp. *Administrative Law Text.* 3d ed. 1972.

Jaffe, Louis L. *Judicial Control of Administrative Action.* 1965.

Terrill, Tom E. *The Tariff, Politics, and American Foreign Policy, 1874–1901.* 1973.

RALPH MITZENMACHER

**FILLMORE, MILLARD** (1800–1874), thirteenth President of the United States (1850–1853). Fillmore was born in dire poverty on a Cayuga County, New York, farm and grew up semiliterate, physically powerful, and accustomed to hard labor. His father did not even permit him to hunt or fish. At age fourteen he was apprenticed first to a clothmaker and then to a textile mill. With only a few months of formal schooling, he studied constantly and read extensively, and during a period of unemployment he enrolled at a local academy, where he was further inspired by Abigail Powers, a minister's daughter. Ultimately, he studied law, taught school for the money needed to buy off his apprenticeship, opened a law office, and married Powers.

**Early Career.** In Buffalo he soon became a successful attorney and model citizen. He and his wife were charter members of the first Unitarian Church Society and he helped found a high school association; was vice president of the lyceum; gave the YMCA time, money, and books; and served for many years as honorary chancellor of the University of Buffalo. In 1828 he was elected to the New York state assembly, where he promoted turnpike companies, ferries, banks, school charters, and dams, and led efforts to abolish imprisonment for debt and the religious oath for courtroom witnesses.

In 1832 he was elected to the U.S. House of Representatives, and DANIEL WEBSTER arranged for him to practice law before the Supreme Court. In the House he served creditably, but he refused to run for reelection in 1834. In 1836, however, he returned to the House and remained for three terms. During his third term, he was runner-up in the balloting for Speaker and chaired the powerful Ways and Means Committee. He won high praise for steering the 1842 tariff through the House, but in 1842 he again refused to seek reelection. He and his wife simply did not like Washington.

Meanwhile, strong jealousies had developed between the Seward-Weed Whigs in Albany and the western New York Whigs led by Fillmore. The powerful Albany editor, Thurlow Weed, dreamed of making his friend WILLIAM H. SEWARD President and viewed Fillmore as a potential rival. In 1844, Fillmore was defeated for governor by a small margin, although he ran well-ahead of HENRY CLAY, the Whig candidate. During the campaign he strongly opposed the annexation of Texas, and during the next four years he attacked President James K. Polk's domestic policies and denounced the MEXICAN WAR as a wicked scheme of conquest designed to add another vast slave territory to the Union. He also supported fully the WILMOT PROVISO, which prohibited SLAVERY in any of the new territories taken from Mexico.

In 1847, Fillmore was elected state comptroller by the largest margin ever won by a Whig in New York. In this position he got the Erie Canal basin enlarged and framed a new banking code. He designed a state currency system that would later be copied by the National Banking Act of 1861. Paper money in New York would henceforth be backed by state and federal bonds rather than commercial paper. With an impeccable reputation, many friends, and no enemies except jealous Whig rivals, he was an excellent choice for the 1848 vice presidential nomination, although he was surprised and somewhat dismayed by the honor.

Fillmore's support for the Wilmot Proviso and his status among Northern Whigs were vital to the election of Zachary Taylor. He assured Northern voters truthfully that Taylor, who owned 140 slaves, would not try to extend the institution. Also, after Taylor accepted an additional nomination from a group of South Carolina Democrats, Weed called for New York Whigs to abandon Taylor and nominate another candidate, but Fillmore denounced the idea and forced Weed to reconsider. Taylor carried seven Northern states, including New York, Pennsylvania, and Massachusetts.

**The Compromise of 1850.** President Taylor was certain that slavery could not expand into the territories taken from Mexico and considered the Wilmot Proviso to be both dangerous and unnecessary. He also believed that slavery's opponents had as much right to be heard as its defenders, and perhaps partly as a symbolic gesture he formed a close personal friendship with William H. Seward, the highly vocal antislavery New York Senator. This meant that the New York federal patronage went to the Seward faction and Fillmore's supporters were ignored. Fillmore had agreed to cooperate with Weed and Seward, but they had deceived him and left him less powerful politically than he had been as state comptroller. The ensuing twenty-seven months were very unhappy for Fillmore as he presided over the Senate during its angry sectional debates, receiving a steady stream of complaints and accusations from his disappointed New York friends and pining for his wife during her long visits back to Buffalo. During the same period he served as a regent of the newly created Smithsonian Institution and did much to promote its success.

In the Senate, Henry Clay proposed a compromise consisting of statehood for California, adjustment of the Texas–New Mexico boundary with monetary compensation for Texas, a New Mexican territorial government with no congressional action on slavery, a stronger federal fugitive slave bill, and abolition of the slave trade in the District of Columbia. Southerners combined these proposals into a single Omnibus bill, which President Taylor opposed because he was certain it could not pass without amendments that would give the slave state of Texas most of the free territory of New Mexico, which he was sworn to defend. Since states could make their own decisions on slavery, Taylor wanted California and New Mexico to become states as soon as possible, and the Omnibus Bill debates were preventing this. Fillmore agreed with Taylor, but with so many amendments being debated, no one knew for certain what the Omnibus Bill would be if it ever came to a final vote. Fearing that he might have to cast a tiebreaking vote, Fillmore was determined to "see what shape it assumes before I . . . say yea or nay." He informed Taylor that if he should feel it his duty to vote for the Omnibus Bill, it would not be from any personal hostility.

On 9 July 1850 Taylor died and Fillmore became President. Seward and Weed feared his revenge, but he made only a few significant changes and left most of their appointees undisturbed. He selected a distinguished Cabinet of three Southerners and four Northerners headed by Daniel Webster as Secretary of State. All had supported compromise, but some had opposed the Omnibus Bill. Most historians have emphasized the break between the Taylor and Fillmore administrations, but there was more continuity than change. Some have suggested that Taylor's death may have prevented a civil war over the Texas–New Mexico boundary, but Fillmore continued Taylor's policy and sent fifteen hundred additional troops to New Mexico.

On 31 July, Fillmore's close friend, Senator Alfred Pearce of Maryland, introduced amendments to the Omnibus Bill that resulted in its complete demolition, just as Taylor had wished. Senator STEPHEN A. DOUGLAS then introduced most of its parts as separate bills, and within a few weeks all had passed; together they are known as the COMPROMISE OF 1850. The Texas settlement came after Fillmore warned the Congress that he would meet force with force if Texas should attack

New Mexico. With considerable skill, Fillmore also used presidential influence to get the bills passed in a form acceptable to both North and South. He quickly signed all of them except the Fugitive Slave Act, which violated his conscience, but was a necessary part of the compromise, since the South got nothing else. Attorney General John J. Crittenden and Webster assured him that it was constitutional and persuaded him to sign it.

During the following months, the former political division between Whigs and Democrats in the South gave way to a new realignment of moderates and Unionists against radical secessionists. It was clear that a strict adherence to the compromises, including the fugitive slave law, would be necessary to prevent the secessionists from winning the Southern elections in 1850 and 1851. Fillmore, therefore, gave lip service to the Fugitive Slave Act and on a few occasions sent police or military force to the scene where the law had been violated, but his actions always came after the slave or slaves had escaped. His nominal support, however, helped enable the Unionists to win most of the Southern elections in 1850 and 1851. He also showed that he would not tolerate any moves toward secession. He included General WINFIELD SCOTT in Cabinet discussions of contingency policies to be followed in case of a SECESSION and strengthened the Charleston forts. He also stationed additional troops in South and North Carolina. When the South Carolina governor demanded an explanation, Fillmore replied that he would station troops wherever he saw a possible need and that he owed the governor no explanation.

**Foreign Policy.** In foreign policy, with first Webster and then Edward Everett as Secretary of State, Fillmore was reasonable and firm. Webster enjoyed great prestige, but his health gradually declined and Fillmore assumed more and more direct responsibility. He continued Taylor's earlier efforts to promote a canal connecting the Atlantic and Pacific oceans. Taylor, on his deathbed, had signed the CLAYTON-BULWER TREATY, in which Great Britain and the United States pledged not to seek any more territory in Central America, but the British still had their puppet Mosquito Indian kingdom in San Juan (Nicaragua) at the end of the proposed canal route. When a British warship forced an American ship to pay harbor dues claimed in San Juan, Fillmore ordered a U.S. warship to the scene, and the British disavowed the action. The American minister negotiated a treaty with Mexico whereby an American company could build a canal across the Tehuantepec Peninsula, but the Mexican Congress nullified the treaty because it validated an earlier land grant to Americans by a previous Mexican administration. Senator Judah P. Benjamin demanded action and threatened to send a private army of five hundred men to Mexico to start a war. Fillmore announced firmly that the United States would arrest anyone involved in such activity and the matter ended.

In 1843 the United States had recognized the independence of the Hawaiian Islands, but they were being threatened by both the British and French. The Hawaiian king suggested a secret treaty of annexation to the United States, but Fillmore would do nothing in secret. When Emperor Napoleon III of France tried to make Hawaii agree to a protectorate by the French, however, Fillmore informed Napoleon bluntly that the United States would tolerate no such action.

Japan had cut itself off from the world for almost 250 years, but the islands were potentially an excellent stopover for ships going to China and seemed to offer opportunities for valuable trade. The British had forced China to open its doors to the West, and Fillmore decided that the United States should do the same for Japan. He, Webster, and Everett planned and launched the expedition of Commodore Matthew Perry to Japan. The mission was completed during the administration of Franklin Pierce, but for better or worse the exhibition of military strength combined with peaceful assurances that brought Japan into the modern world was conceived, organized, and staffed by Millard Fillmore.

Respect for the rights of other nations was a basic principle with Fillmore. Daniel Webster ordered naval protection against Peru for an American expedition en route to remove guano from the Lobos Islands. Fillmore, however, reversed his secretaries of State and the Navy and announced that Americans removing guano without the consent of Peru would do so at their own risk.

Meanwhile, the filibustering efforts against CUBA that Taylor had opposed were being renewed. Narciso Lopez armed some four hundred young adventurers, most of them American Southerners, and prepared to sail. Southern leaders favored any action that might acquire Cuba for the United States, but Fillmore ordered naval officials in New Orleans to stop the expedition and announced that any volunteers would be violating U.S. laws and would receive no American protection. The New Orleans authorities allowed Lopez to sail, but the invasion was a fiasco. Lopez and 50 Americans, including the nephew of Attorney General Crittenden, were executed, and another 160 were taken to Spain for penal servitude in the mines. Americans were shocked, and a New Orleans mob sacked the Spanish consulate and a Spanish newspaper office.

Many Americans cheered, but Fillmore had Webster apologize to the Spanish government and promised a salute for the Spanish flag and proper treatment for the consul. This conciliatory attitude enabled Fillmore to negotiate the release of the 160 Americans imprisoned in Spain. While Fillmore flatly rejected any suggestion that the United States should forcibly annex Cuba, he refused to sign a treaty with the British and French stipulating that none of the three would ever annex Cuba. He warned that because of the island's strategic location, annexation might become necessary at some future date, and meanwhile the United States would not allow it to be taken by anyone else.

**Postpresidential Career.** When the country was wildly celebrating the passage of the 1850 compromise measures, Fillmore's popularity was at a zenith. If he had immediately announced his candidacy for 1852, his nomination would have been a certainty, and as the only Whig with a strong following in both North and South he might have been elected. Fillmore, however, was genuinely reluctant to seek another term. He had rejected Washington in favor of his happy life in Buffalo twice before, and he was eager to do so again. He had no taste for the unpleasant responsibilities and difficulties that pitted his personal feelings against political exigencies. He made no effort to use PATRONAGE for lining up delegates to support his nomination, and, indeed, left most of the officeholders recommended to Taylor by his enemies Weed and Seward in their places. In March 1851 he directed an editor friend to begin spreading the word that he would not run, and in December he repeated this intention to a close friend. He did not make a formal announcement, however, because it would weaken him significantly during the final year of his presidency.

Fillmore's weak efforts to enforce the Fugitive Slave Act had been designed to keep the Southern fire-eaters from winning the elections of 1850 and 1851, but they had also won him a status in the South enjoyed by no other Whig. Daniel Webster, however, had ached for the presidency for thirty years, and Fillmore genuinely wished to help the old man achieve his lifelong ambition. Webster's health was precarious, however, and William H. Seward had his own candidate, General Winfield Scott, ready to run. The possibility of Scott's nomination as the candidate of the one Whig most hated by the South was a death threat to the WHIG PARTY, but this was not as obvious to Fillmore in 1852 as it is to historians with the wisdom of hindsight. Driven in part by wishful thinking and longing to quit Washington, Fillmore continued to hope until it was too late that the ailing Webster could take the reins.

Letters urging Fillmore to run and messages and editorials offering support deluged the White House from every direction, and the dying Henry Clay rallied long enough to issue a ringing plea for the party to nominate Fillmore. Simultaneously, however, the Seward Whigs and their newspapers were denouncing their own President as a traitor who by supporting the compromise had sacrificed friends and principles for the sole purpose of getting elected. Much evidence indicates that in 1852 the Seward supporters wanted the election of a Southern Democrat who would oppose Northern economic interests and antislavery feelings and thereby ensure the election of a sectional Northern candidate, presumably Seward, in 1856. Fearing that this would happen, Fillmore reluctantly became a candidate after Seward already had most of the Northern delegates lined up for Scott.

For seven convention ballots, Fillmore led both Scott and Webster, and would have been easily nominated if Webster had thrown his meager support to Fillmore. After forty-six ballots, the weary delegates adjourned for a weekend recess. Fillmore's supporters offered to give Fillmore's 107 votes to Webster if Webster could get his total up to 40 votes. In turn, Webster should quit in favor of Fillmore if Webster could not reach 40 votes. Webster refused, however, until his delegates began to switch to Scott. He then gave the order, but it was too late. Seward persuaded Webster's leaderless New England delegates to support Scott, who was thereby nominated.

Scott was an impossible candidate. A Southern Whig convention in Washington resolved that no Southerner should vote for him, and the Southern Whigs voted almost en masse for Democrat Franklin Pierce, who was all things to all men. The Whig party that had been a bastion of nationalism had ceased to be a viable national party and it never rose again.

Fillmore and his wife had eagerly anticipated his retirement, but she stood in snow and slush at the Pierce inaugural and was dead from pneumonia a few weeks later. He grieved and brooded for more than a year, and then received another crushing blow when his favorite daughter, only twenty-two, also died. Desperate for a diversion, he reentered the political scene by joining the KNOW-NOTHING (AMERICAN) PARTY. The party had expanded primarily because of competition for jobs between the older ethnic stocks and the ever-increasing flood of immigrants, but its leading organizers were Whigs who had long complained that the Democrats were voting thousands of immigrants before they became citizens. Their basic goals were the restriction of immigration and a longer period before an immigrant could become a citizen and vote. To attract popular support, the party resorted to shameful appeals to anti-Catholicism and other cultural prejudices. It included also, however, a number of former Whigs who did not necessarily share its more extreme principles, but saw it as their only alternative to the radical free-soil Republicans and the Southern-dominated Democrats. More than a few also hoped that it might become a unifying force for the North and South. In the elections of 1854 the Know-Nothings elected seventeen Congressmen and won every state office in Massachusetts but two. It also carried Delaware and shared a victory with old-line Whigs in Pennsylvania. In 1855, while he was touring Europe, the Know-Nothings nominated Fillmore for President.

During the campaign Fillmore ignored the anti-Catholic and antiforeign sentiments of his new party, but in twenty-seven public speeches he dwelt upon the terrible civil war he believed would result from the election of JOHN C. FREMONT, the Republican candidate, who was the Northern candidate. He told at least one audience, "I have no hostility to foreigners . . . having witnessed their deplorable condition in the old country, God forbid I should add to their sufferings by refusing them an asylum in this." Fillmore received a respectable 28.6 percent of the vote and probably contributed significantly to the defeat of Frémont.

It was Fillmore's last political foray. He married a wealthy widow, resumed his role as Buffalo's most distinguished senior citizen, and gave generously of time and money to countless charities and civil activities. Four days after the Battle of Fort Sumter, he organized a giant Union demonstration and pledged $500 for the support of volunteers' families. He organized and led the Union Continentals, a corps of men who were too old to fight but were ready to act in any local emergency and did much to encourage enlistments among younger men. He and his wife helped organize a fair that raised $25,000 for the war effort. After the war he continued to be honored as the local patriarch until his death on 8 March 1874.

Fillmore's reputation has suffered much from his failure to win renomination and from his Know-Nothing candidacy. These events, however, should not obscure the fact that he overcame the disadvantages of desperate childhood poverty to become an outstanding state official and U.S. Representative and a responsible and highly effective President during a period of great national crisis.

### BIBLIOGRAPHY

Grayson, Benson L. *The Unknown President: The Administration of Millard Fillmore.* 1981.

Hamilton, Holman. *Prologue to Conflict: The Crisis and Compromise of 1850.* 1964.

*Millard Fillmore Papers.* Microfilm Collection. Buffalo Historical Society.

Rayback, Robert. *Millard Fillmore: Biography of a President.* 1959.

Richardson, James D., ed. *A Compilation of the Messages and Papers of the Presidents.* Vol. 5. 1900.

Severance, Frank., ed. *Millard Fillmore Papers.* Vols. 10–11. 1907.

Smith, Elbert B. *The Presidencies of Zachary Taylor and Millard Fillmore.* 1988.

Snyder, Charles M., ed. *The Lady and the President: The Letters of Dorothea Dix and Millard Fillmore.* 1975.

ELBERT B. SMITH

**FILMS, PRESIDENTS IN.** Presidents of the United States have been familiar figures on film ever since the first motion pictures were produced in the mid 1890s. Indeed, several of the earliest films, such as *President McKinley Taking the Oath* (1901) and *President Roosevelt's Fourth of July Oration* (1903) were simply documentary records of public events photographed by movie cameras. But with the rise of the Hollywood studios in the 1910s and the ascendancy of feature-length motion pictures that were scripted and directed for commercial mass entertainment, documentary representations of Presidents on film were relegated to newsreels in the wake of two new film categories. One was the historical drama, in which the life (or, more commonly, a portion of the life) of an actual President was depicted by professional actors. The other was entirely in the realm of fiction, in which imaginary Presidents were created for the purposes of comedy, mystery, adventure, melodrama, and romance. The evolution of these cinematic categories reveals some interesting attitudes about politics in general and Presidents in particular.

During the 1910s and 1920s, Presidents were conveyed on film primarily through the film genres of historical drama and biography, which usually provided reverent portraits of exalted leaders such as George Washington or Abraham Lincoln. Although Washington may have been "first in the hearts of his countrymen," he played a decided second to Lincoln in the total number of film representations. Perhaps because Lincoln's physical appearance (tall and thin, bearded, and with deep-set eyes) was so distinctive, or perhaps because the dramatic contours of his life (humble pioneer origins, plain but honest virtues, and martyred end) were so well suited for the screen, he has been the President by far the most frequently depicted in film. In the years through 1930, for example, Lincoln not only was the leading protagonist in *Lincoln's Gettysburg Address* (1912), *Lincoln the Lover*

(1913), *Lincoln's Thanksgiving Story* (1914), *The Life of Abraham Lincoln* (1915), *The Lincoln Cycle* (1917), *The Highest Law* (1921), *The Heart of Lincoln* (1922), *The Dramatic Life of Abraham Lincoln* (1924), and *Abraham Lincoln* (1930) but also appeared as a historical character in *Abraham Lincoln's Clemency* (1910), *The Battle of Gettysburg* (1913), *The Birth of a Nation* (1915), *The Crisis* (1916), *The Test of Loyalty* (1918), *Barbara Frietchie* (1924), *The Iron Horse* (1924), *The Man without a Country* (1925), *Hands Up!* (1926), *The Heart of Maryland* (1927), and *Court-Martial* (1928). In these films, Lincoln was almost invariably portrayed as kind-hearted Honest Abe and the Savior of the Union. Cinematic treatments of Washington, although always respectful—as in *The Life of Washington* (1910), *Washington at Valley Forge* (1914), *America* (1924), and *Winners of the Wilderness* (1927)—were both less frequent and less adulatory than those of Lincoln.

The subjects Hollywood chooses to treat often run in cycles. In the early 1930s, a string of films about imaginary Presidents appeared, calling attention to the apparent need for action and change in the midst of the Great Depression. First came a musical comedy, *The Phantom President* (1932), which opened with a shot of paintings of Washington, Lincoln, Thomas Jefferson, and Theodore Roosevelt coming to life and singing "The Country Needs a Man" to lead it out of hard times. A much more serious treatment was *Gabriel over the White House* (1933), in which a cynical and ineffectual President is transformed into a powerful, albeit dictatorial, leader when saved from death by the archangel Gabriel. The new President astonishes and delights the nation by suspending Congress and declaring martial law to solve the pressing problems of unemployment, hunger, crime, and world war in his own forceful way. Similar concerns were expressed in *The President Vanishes* (1934), in which a liberal President must fake his own kidnapping to counter the threat of right-wing business tycoons conspiring to drive the nation into war for their own profit. The undertext of all three films was that the U.S. was greatly in need of a strong, resourceful leader.

By the end of the decade, after the crisis of the early 1930s had abated somewhat, Hollywood's treatment of the presidency returned to the more usual fare of quasi-historical dramas involving Presidents and biographical pictures celebrating their virtues. Examples of the former included *The Gorgeous Hussy* (1936), which focuses on Cabinet-wife Peggy O'Neale Eaton's role in Andrew Jackson's administration; *This is My Affair* (1937), in which both William McKinley and Theodore Roosevelt are behind the busting of a bank-robbing syndicate; and *The Buccaneer* (1938), which briefly involves Andrew Jackson in the affairs of the pirate Jean Laffite. Prime examples of biographical pictures included a trio of Lincoln tributes: *Young Mr. Lincoln* (1939), which portrayed the President-to-be as a folksy but shrewd country lawyer; *Lincoln in the White House* (1939), which stressed his principles of democracy and humanitarianism; and *Abe Lincoln in Illinois* (1940), based on the Pulitzer Prize–winning play (1939) that covered the thirty years in Lincoln's life prior to his inauguration. The trend continued into the early 1940s with *Tennessee Johnson* (1942), which cast an unusually positive light on Lincoln's successor (the film's alternate title was *The Man on America's Conscience*), and *Wilson* (1944), perhaps the most elaborate presidential biography ever produced by Hollywood. Based on extensive research and a painstaking re-creation of the period, *Wilson* was an unabashed attempt to prove that the twenty-eighth President had been prescient in seeking greater international involvement (in, e.g., the LEAGUE OF NATIONS) for the U.S. after WORLD WAR I, and that the same mistake should not be repeated after WORLD WAR II.

Although *Wilson* was moderately successful at the box office, its failure to win an Academy Award for best picture, actor, or director was a great disappointment to its influential Hollywood producer, Darryl F. Zanuck, who had ballyhooed the film as "The Most Important Event in Fifty Years of Motion Picture Entertainment" and had spent an unprecedented $5.2 million (almost a million dollars more than *Gone with the Wind*) to make *Wilson* the most expensive picture in history up to that time. Perhaps as a result, Hollywood began to shy away from similarly grand ventures. The 1940s and 1950s saw only a few Presidents in film: *The Great Moment* (1944), which celebrated the first successful medical use of ether but is also notable for containing the only screen representation of Franklin Pierce; *Magnificent Doll* (1946), in which James Madison plays second fiddle to First Lady DOLLEY MADISON; *Unconquered* (1947), which has George Washington fighting the French and Indian War; *My Girl Tisa* (1948), which has Theodore Roosevelt as a minor character; *The Story of Will Rogers* (1952) in which Wilson appears, though only briefly; *The President's Lady* (1953), more the story of Andrew Jackson's wife, Rachel, than of Jackson himself; and a remake of *The Buccaneer* (1958), in which Jackson battles the British in the WAR OF 1812.

In the early 1960s, two biographical pictures reverently extolled the formative years of two Presidents-to-be: *Sunrise at Campobello* (1960), the story of Franklin Roosevelt's first struggle with polio; and *PT 109* (1963), a re-creation of John F. Kennedy's heroics during World War II. These were followed by two dramas about fictional but clear-thinking Presidents whose courage and wisdom save the country from imminent danger: the threat of a right-wing coup in *Seven Days in May* (1964) and nuclear annihilation in *Fail Safe* (1964). But another film on those topics released the same year, *Dr. Strangelove or: How I Learned to Stop Worrying and Love the Bomb* turned the President, given the rather unauthoritative name of Merkin Muffley, into an ineffectual bumbler who is powerless to stop the chain of events leading to the world's destruction. Extremely influential, *Dr. Strangelove* set a satirical and antiestablishmentarian tone for films about fictional Presidents that followed in the politically tumultuous 1960s and 1970s.

For example, the President in *In Like Flint* (1967) is abducted while playing golf and held hostage by a secret society of women planning to conquer the world. Similarly powerless is the President in *Colossus—The Forbin Project* (1970), whose actions are overridden by the world's most powerful computer. At the opposite extreme is the megalomaniacal President in *Hail to the Chief* (1972), who orders his secret police to massacre harmless hippies and dispatches other young dissenters to concentration camps. Similarly unorthodox leaders are those depicted in *The Virgin President* (1968), in which a President named Fillard Millmore is a thirty-five-year-old incompetent, unaware that his Cabinet is plotting to bomb China; *Putney Swope* (1969), whose President Mimeo is a marijuana-smoking midget seen frolicking in bed with the First Lady; and *Brand X* (1970), where the President holds a press conference with his mentally impaired wife on display. Perhaps the most bizarre Chief Executive, however, is Max Frost, who is overwhelmingly elected in *Wild in the Streets* (1968) after fourteen-year-olds have been given the vote and age requirements abolished for officeholders. One of President Frost's first acts is to dispatch everyone over thirty-five to retirement camps where hallucinogenic drugs are the regimen. When compared with such wildly improbable leaders, the portrayals of Presidents in two other films from the same period appear relatively mild. *Kisses for My President* (1964) portrays the first female President, though a large part of the film deals with the problems her spouse faces as "first husband." Reflecting the racial concerns of the time was *The Man* (1972), in which an unusual chain of events begets the nation's first African American President.

Whether there is a pattern to the portrayals of Presidents in films produced since the mid 1970s is still not entirely clear. On the one hand, there has been a return to relatively respectful historical dramas and biographical pictures, particularly in the docudramas and miniseries for television. These include *Give 'Em Hell, Harry!* (1975), *Truman at Potsdam* (1976), *Eleanor & Franklin* (1976), *Eleanor & Franklin: The White House Years* (1977), *Johnny, We Hardly Knew Ye* (1977), *Ike* (1979), *FDR: The Last Year* (1980), *George Washington* (1984), *Lyndon Johnson* (1987), *LBJ: The Early Years* (1987), and *Gore Vidal's Lincoln* (1988). It should be noted, however, that the same treatment was not extended to Richard Nixon, whose representations in *Washington: Behind Closed Doors* (1977), *Secret Honor* (1984), and *The Final Days* (1989) are less than flattering.

On the other hand, theatrical movies have more often opted for fictional representations of Presidents, especially ones who have frighteningly little control over world events. Examples include *Being There* (1979), in which the President is an extension of big business; *First Family* (1980), in which the family consists of a dim-witted Chief Executive, inebriated First Lady, and sex-starved daughter; *The Kidnapping of the President* (1980), in which the Chief Executive is seized for ransom by third-world terrorists; *Superman II* (1981), whose President is captured by a team of super-villains; *Escape from New York* (1981), in which he is held hostage by the inmates of a maximum-security prison; *Wrong Is Right* (1982), in which the President ineptly orders the assassination of an Arabian sheik, thereby setting in motion a new world war; and *Dreamscape* (1984), where the President is overwhelmed by nightmares of nuclear annihilation. Interestingly, these darker dramas are set in unspecified (but not-too-distant) years to come. Thus, while most of the presidential biographies of the post-1970s era gaze back nostalgically on the past, the fictional representations during this period seem to look ahead somewhat fearfully to the future.

### BIBLIOGRAPHY

Bidaud, Anne-Marie. "Les présidents américains au cinéma." *Cinéma* 263 (1980): 60–62.

Bidaud, Anne-Marie. "Réflexions sur l'iconographie présidentielle américaine." *Cinéma* 263 (1980): 50–59.

Christensen, Terry. *Reel Politics: American Political Movies from* Birth of a Nation *to* Platoon. 1987.

Custen, George F. *Bio/Pics: How Hollywood Constructed Public History.* 1992.

Gutman, Richard J. S. "A Roster of Early Lincoln Impersonations in the Cinema, 1909–1930." *Lincoln Herald* 78 (1976): 139–146.

Gutman, Richard J. S. "Three Outstanding 'Abes': Lincoln's Image in the Cinema, Part II, 1931–1977." *Lincoln Herald* 80 (1978): 122–132.

Knock, Thomas J. "History with Lightning: The Forgotten Film *Wilson*." *American Quarterly* 28 (1976): 523–542.

Ross, Nathaniel Lester. "Portraying Presidents." *Films in Review* 23 (1977): 482–488.

JAMES I. DEUTSCH

## FINANCING PRESIDENTIAL CAMPAIGNS.
See CAMPAIGN FINANCES.

## FINDING, PRESIDENTIAL.
A formal approval by the President authorizing a covert action abroad by the CENTRAL INTELLIGENCE AGENCY (CIA) or some other entity is called a presidential finding. From the administration of Harry S. Truman through that of Gerald Ford, the approval process for covert actions—that is, the secret use of propaganda, political activity, economic disruption, or paramilitary operations against foreign countries—was relatively informal and excluded Congress. The CIA, the agency usually employed for covert actions, did not wish to inform legislators about these sensitive activities, and, conveniently, neither did legislators wish to know about them. The political risks might have been too high for members of Congress if an operation went awry and became public; it was safer to remain outside this decision loop.

Nor did the NATIONAL SECURITY COUNCIL (NSC) within the White House approve, or even know of, every significant COVERT OPERATION carried out by the CIA. The tendency during these years was for the CIA to ask the NSC for broad grants of authority ostensibly covering large numbers of subsidiary operations—a good many arguably warranting separate and specific approval by the NSC.

In December 1974 Congress—in the wake of the WATERGATE AFFAIR and troubled by media revelations alleging domestic spying and unsavory covert actions in Chile—formally confronted this lack of accountability and took the first step toward reining in secret intelligence operations. In a flurry of last-minute legislative activity, Congress approved the HUGHES-RYAN ACT (1974), sponsored by Senator Harold E. Hughes (D-Iowa) and Representative Leo J. Ryan (D-Calif.). This legislation required the President to approve all important covert actions (approval was assumed to be in writing) and established a procedure for informing Congress of each approval. The law's key provision required that "no funds appropriated under the authority of this or any other act may be expended by or on behalf of the [CIA] for operations in foreign countries, unless and until the President *finds* that each such operation is important to the national security of the United States and reports, in a timely fashion, a description and scope of such operation to the appropriate committees of the Congress" [emphasis added].

The Hughes-Ryan legislation was a bold attempt by Congress to replace the so-called doctrine of plausible denial (by which a President could deny knowing about a covert action and thereby save face) with a clear trail of accountability for covert action that would lead straight to the OVAL OFFICE. The law formally forbade all covert actions—from placing false stories in foreign newspapers to overthrowing governments abroad—unless directly approved by the President.

From the verb *finds* in the statute comes the term *finding*, that is, the anticipated written document bearing the President's signature of approval. The "appropriate committees" to which the finding was to be delivered "in a timely fashion" (understood to be within twenty-four hours) were initially three in the House of Representatives and three in the Senate: the committees on appropriations, armed services, and foreign affairs. In 1976, legislators added the Senate Select Committee on Intelligence and, in 1977, the House Permanent Select Committee on Intelligence. Then, in 1980, with the passage of the Intelligence Accountability Act (known less formally as the INTELLIGENCE OVERSIGHT ACT), Congress trimmed the list back to include only the two intelligence oversight committees.

This 1980 law, the most important formal measure taken by legislators to tighten their control over intelligence operations, also required that the executive branch report a finding to the two oversight committees prior to the implementation of a covert action, replacing the ex post facto "timely fashion" standard. In emergency situations, the statute allowed the President to limit prior notice to eight leaders in Congress: the chairmen and ranking minority members of the intelligence committees, the Speaker and minority leader of the House of Representatives, and the majority and minority leaders of the Senate—the so-called Gang of Eight.

In 1991 Congress passed another Intelligence Oversight Act, allowing the President to delay "for a few days" the report on a finding to Congress in emergency situations, thereby relaxing the prior-notice standard by not even requiring a report to the Gang of Eight. President George Bush said at the time, though, that he would honor the concept of prior notice in all but the most pressing circumstances. The 1991 Intelligence Oversight Act also made explicit the understanding (violated by President Ronald Reagan during the IRAN-CONTRA AFFAIR of 1986–1987) that each finding

had to be in written, not oral, form. This law also prohibited the use of retroactive findings, that is, covert action approvals made by the President after an operation was already underway or perhaps even completed. (This had also occurred during the Iran-contra affair; indeed, the belatedly signed and retroactive finding for the covert sale of arms to Iran during the scandal explicitly forbade the CIA from honoring the reporting requirement of the 1980 act.)

From 1947 to 1974, the CIA decided on and conducted covert actions with only limited accountability. With the Hughes-Ryan Act, Congress insisted on a much more formal decision process. For better or worse, covert action had been democratized, with the President and members of Congress now more intimately involved in its supervision.

### BIBLIOGRAPHY

Jeffreys-Jones, Rhodri. *The CIA and American Democracy.* 1989.
Johnson, Loch K. *America's Secret Power: The CIA in a Democratic Society.* 1989.
Ransom, Harry Howe. "The Politicization of Intelligence." In *Intelligence and Intelligence Policy in a Democratic Society.* Edited by Stephen J. Cimbala. 1987.
Treverton, Gregory F. "Covert Action and Open Society." *Foreign Affairs* 65 (1987): 995–1014.
Turner, Stansfield. *Secrecy and Democracy: The CIA in Transition.* 1985.

LOCH K. JOHNSON

**FIRESIDE CHATS.** Thirty-one times during his presidency, Franklin D. Roosevelt made informal radio speeches to the American people. These "fireside chats" marked a new departure in American political rhetoric. Rather than addressing the people from on high, Roosevelt projected a reassuring, avuncular image, entering America's living rooms for seemingly impromptu conversations. The effect was dramatic, and Roosevelt used these opportunities to great political advantage.

Roosevelt delivered the first fireside chat on 12 March 1933, just eight days after assuming the presidency (the term *fireside chat* was not used until 7 May 1933, when it was coined in a press release by Harry Butcher of CBS News, but the tone and setting of the earlier address clearly establishes it as the first of the genre). In the midst of the national banking emergency, Roosevelt used the occasion to reassure the people that the nation's financial system was essentially sound and in good hands.

The fireside chats were perfectly adapted for radio. Roosevelt spoke in intimate terms, addressing his audience as "my friends" and speaking as if in personal conversation with every citizen. "We have provided the machinery to restore our financial system," he declared in the first chat, "and it is up to you to make it work." His language was typically inclusive rather than exclusive: "we must work and sacrifice"; "you and I have the utmost contempt for Americans who . . . have served the enemy propagandists"; "you and I will do our part." He used colloquial language and homey analogies (on the capture of Rome during WORLD WAR II, the first of the three Axis capitals: "One up and two to go!"; on appeasement with the Nazis: "No man can tame a tiger by stroking it.") To illustrate his points and make them more concrete, he spoke in particular terms of specific individuals rather than of anonymous groups: "I should like to tell you one or two stories about the men we have in our armed forces"; "let me cite to you the example of the salesman in a store in a large eastern city"; "I wish that all Americans could read all the citations for various medals recommended for our soldiers and sailors and marines. I am picking out one of those citations." And he used other innovative techniques as well: asking every American to "take out and spread before you a map of the whole earth, and to follow me in the references which I shall make," for example, or apologizing for not delivering his annual message to Congress in person because "like a great many other people, I have had the flu."

Roosevelt made thirty-one speeches that can be classified as fireside chats (SAMUEL ROSENMAN, the compiler of Roosevelt's official papers, put the number at only twenty-seven). As for FDR's other speeches, many distinguished speech writers contributed to the various addresses, though Roosevelt's influence is always apparent. Always Roosevelt spoke in what Rosenman called a "clear and resonant" voice that came across beautifully on the radio.

Of the thirty-one speeches, eight were delivered in Roosevelt's first term, eight in the second, and fifteen in the third (Roosevelt made no fireside chats in his month-long final term). Those of the first two terms dealt largely with domestic policy; not surprisingly, the wartime speeches were overwhelmingly devoted to foreign policy matters. Typically the fireside chats were not so much forums for new policy announcements as they were opportunities for the President to defend decisions already made, summarize the state of the union or of the war effort, and rally the nation's support. The tone of the speeches tended more toward reassurance and reflection than confrontation, though there were exceptions—most notably the 1937 speech defending the President's COURT-PACKING PLAN and the 1938 speech announcing the "purge" of conservatives from the Democratic Party.

A few of the speeches have become true classics. Among these are the "Arsenal of Democracy" speech (29 December 1940), which announced the Lend-Lease Program [see LEND LEASE ACT]; the Washington's Birthday address of 1942 calling on the American people to emulate the sacrifices and patriotism of General George Washington and his troops at Valley Forge; and the aforementioned Court-packing speech. Many more, though well crafted, dwell on matters of little interest to history.

In several ways, Roosevelt's chats provided a model for later Presidents. Jimmy Carter explicitly appropriated the concept and adapted it for television, appearing literally before a fireplace and clad in a cardigan sweater. Ronald Reagan used to great effect the technique of singling out particular individuals. Other Presidents learned to use television to speak directly and intimately to the American people, confiding in them and urging their support in times of war, economic emergency, or partisan conflict.

BIBLIOGRAPHY

Buhite, Russell D., and David W. Levy, eds., *FDR's Fireside Chats.* 1992.

WILLIAM LASSER

**FIRST LADIES.** From the ceremonial role played by Presidents' wives in the early days of the republic, the job of First Lady has grown to one of considerable clout, involving campaigning, speaking out on issues, heading a project or cause that complements the President's program, serving as one of the nation's emissaries abroad, and overseeing the WHITE HOUSE's management and its use as a national cultural center. The emphasis placed on any particular part of the job remains for each First Lady to define for herself in line with her own interests and personality, her relationship with the President, and her perception of what public attitudes will endorse.

Explanations for the growth in the distaff side of the presidency are numerous and complex, some of them tied up with the willingness of the women to play a public role and some with the wide latitude left to the chief executive to choose his advisers as he wishes—without the constraints of his party, as in a parliamentary system. As the public relations aspect of the presidency increased, incumbents turned to members of their families to augment their effectiveness, and spouses began to play a more prominent part.

**The Early Republic.** George Washington helped pave the way for spouses to participate in the presidency when he arranged for MARTHA WASHINGTON to arrive with some fanfare in New York City a month

*First Ladies*

| President | First Lady |
|---|---|
| 1 Washington | Martha Dandridge Custis Washington |
| 2 J. Adams | Abigail Adams |
| 3 Jefferson | Widower |
| 4 Madison | Dolley Madison |
| 5 Monroe | Elizabeth Kortright Monroe |
| 6 J. Q. Adams | Louisa Johnson Adams |
| 7 Jackson | Widower |
| 8 Van Buren | Widower |
| 9 W. H. Harrison | Anna Symmes Harrison |
| 10 Tyler | Letitia Christian Tyler; Julia Tyler |
| 11 Polk | Sarah Childress Polk |
| 12 Taylor | Margaret Mackall Smith Taylor |
| 13 Fillmore | Abigail Powers Fillmore |
| 14 Pierce | Jane Means Appleton Pierce |
| 15 Buchanan | Never married |
| 16 Lincoln | Mary Todd Lincoln |
| 17 A. Johnson | Eliza McCardle Johnson |
| 18 Grant | Julia Dent Grant |
| 19 Hayes | Lucy Webb Hayes |
| 20 Garfield | Lucretia Rudolph Garfield |
| 21 Arthur | Widower |
| 22 Cleveland | Frances Folsom Cleveland |
| 23 B. Harrison | Caroline Scott Harrison |
| 24 Cleveland | France Folsom Cleveland |
| 25 McKinley | Ida Saxton McKinley |
| 26 T. Roosevelt | Edith Kermit Carow Roosevelt |
| 27 Taft | Helen Herron Taft |
| 28 Wilson | Ellen Louise Axson Wilson / Edith Bolling Galt Wilson |
| 29 Harding | Florence Kling De Wolfe Harding |
| 30 Coolidge | Grace Goodhue Coolidge |
| 31 Hoover | Lou Henry Hoover |
| 32 F. D. Roosevelt | Anna Eleanor Roosevelt Roosevelt |
| 33 Truman | Elizabeth Wallace ("Bess") Truman |
| 34 Eisenhower | Mamie Doud Eisenhower |
| 35 Kennedy | Jacqueline Bouvier Kennedy |
| 36 L. B. Johnson | Claudia Alta Taylor ("Lady Bird") Johnson |
| 37 Nixon | Thelma Catherine ("Pat") Ryan Nixon |
| 38 Ford | Betty Bloomer Warren Ford |
| 39 Carter | Rosalynn Smith Carter |
| 40 Reagan | Nancy Davis Reagan |
| 41 Bush | Barbara Pierce Bush |
| 42 Clinton | Hillary Rodham Clinton |

after his inauguration. She had remained in Virginia while he took the oath of office partly because her responsibilities had not yet been defined. By the time she joined her husband in late May 1789, he had made additional decisions that tended to magnify her role: his official residence would also serve as his workplace, thus drawing his entire household into the government process. Within days of her arrival in the temporary capital, Martha Washington had assumed the role of a public personage, hosting a dinner and a party that mixed politicians with friends. Newspaper columns debated what her title should be and how much attention she merited.

While Martha Washington and most of her immediate successors refused to acknowledge any role in making presidential decisions, ABIGAIL ADAMS became known for her sharp wit and partisan views. Dubbed Mrs. President by some of her critics (who had tacitly approved the nonpartisanship of her predecessor by calling her Lady Washington), Abigail Adams wrote many letters attacking her husband's political enemies and lamenting the pro-French bent of the opposition. She complained that criticism of her husband and son was excessive and suggested limiting such criticism by law. Abigail Adams's strong partisan stance, following the relatively mild-mannered Martha Washington,

met a mixed reaction. Her husband's enemies found such intervention unwarranted and wrong while proponents of opinionated women lauded her as an excellent model.

For much of the nineteenth century, First Ladies followed the pattern set by Martha Washington rather than that of Abigail Adams. Most accepted that their husbands' elections propelled them into a public role, one that included entertaining at receptions and dinners, calling on other women in Washington, and overseeing the White House domestic staff—but all this without involving themselves in partisan disputes or taking sides in debates on public policy.

DOLLEY MADISON perfected the role of First Lady as social leader, showing in the process how a popular hostess could help win votes for her husband. Known for her charm and tirelessness, she attempted to call on everyone in the capital who expected a visit and she opened the White House for weekly public receptions. She is sometimes credited with helping her husband win reelection in 1812. Although Elizabeth Monroe and Louisa Adams were less popular than Dolley Madison (and both refused to make the number of social calls that she had made), they persevered in the nonpartisan, hostess role. Louisa Adams pointed to the contradiction in the job: on the one hand she was deemed ignorant of politics simply because she was a woman, and at the same time, she reported that she was scrutinized at each public appearance for some hint as to her husband's opinions.

**The Jacksonian Style.** After 1829, the arrival in the nation's capital of women from the new western states helped set the stage for a different kind of White House woman. Rachel Jackson did not live to see her husband inaugurated, but she had suffered many verbal attacks from the capital's social arbiters and announced that she had no desire to live in the White House. Her death in December 1829 left her husband bitter, convinced that her critics had hastened her demise. Historians have concluded that Rachel Jackson exercised from the grave more influence over the White House than did some other women who actually resided there. Andrew Jackson's loyalty to his wife's memory is offered as the most plausible explanation for his support of Peggy O'Neal, the woman whose marriage to Jackson's ally and friend, John Eaton, split Washington into opposing camps.

The Jackson presidency coincided with a new emphasis in America on youth, and for much of the next half century, Presidents' wives were often absent or willing to abdicate their public roles, turning to young substitutes (daughters, daughters-in-law, and nieces less than thirty years of age) whose youth protected them from the criticism of the capital's social leaders. Widowers and bachelors relied on young relatives rather than mature sisters or colleagues' spouses to oversee social events at the Executive Mansion.

An obvious exception to this pattern is Sarah Polk who, at a time when campaigning for one's husband had not yet become acceptable behavior, wished that it had. Educated at one of the better women's academies in the South, she chafed at being constrained to home while her husband was out trying to win votes; and in a letter to him, she confided that she had attempted (unsuccessfully) to influence local Democrats. In the White House she made a point of subjugating domestic responsibilities to political discussions, and she refused to hide her interest in questions of public policy. Although she escaped the strong criticism that Abigail Adams encountered, she was widely rumored to have influence in her husband's decisions.

Sarah Polk was not unique among nineteenth-century women in experimenting with the job of First Lady and testing the borders of its potential power. Julia Gardiner Tyler, the young, publicity-conscious second wife of John Tyler, paid an assistant to improve her public image; and Julia Grant cooperated with the press by supplying information about the Grant children's weddings, the youngest son's pets, and other family matters. MARY TODD LINCOLN's letters indicate that she used her position in the White House to gain special favors from merchants and jobs for friends and acquaintances.

**Development of a Public Role.** With Lucy Hayes, the job of First Lady took a slightly different turn. Although the term *first lady* had occasionally been used in the 1860s, it began to appear in print in the 1870s, and the President's wife was referred to as "the first lady of the land." Lucy Hayes, whose plain style contrasted with her predecessor's extravagance, became a popular national figure as a result of many newspaper and magazine articles about her. The Hayeses' trip across the continent—the first by a President and his wife—revealed the extent of her popularity, and temperance advocates continued to pressure her to speak up on their behalf. Although her biographer later concluded that Lucy Hayes (who abstained from alcoholic beverages herself) did not hold strong feelings about others' drinking, her ban on alcohol in the White House found wide public support. Rutherford Hayes acknowledged in his diary that his wife's advocacy had helped bring temperance votes into the Republican column.

As national magazines increased their attention to White House occupants in the late nineteenth century, Presidents' wives were singled out as favorite topics, and their relationships with their husbands were scrutinized for some indication as to the President's character. Frances (Frankie) Folsom Cleveland, the only bride of a President to be married in the White House, became enormously popular, and her face was used in commercial advertisements (a move lamented by one Congressman, who introduced legislation to make such use illegal). When unfounded charges were made public about Grover Cleveland's physical abuse of his wife, she replied in a public statement testifying to his good behavior.

This national attention focused on the First Lady helped increase the number of requests she received for help—from writers who explained that they would have communicated directly with the President had not they believed his wife to be kinder, more accessible, or more likely to respond. Lucy Hayes received letters from advocates of polygamy; Frances Cleveland heard from people who wanted her to promote various products; and Caroline Harrison responded to requests for all sorts of souvenirs: quilt patches cut from her discarded dresses and even locks of her hair.

**The White House.** Part of the public role for First Ladies developed out of their association with the Executive Mansion. Since the first occupancy of the White House in 1800, Presidents' wives had worked at furnishing and maintaining it. Their selections were taken as an indication of their taste, and their expenditures were carefully watched for hints of extravagance or frugality. Dolley Madison solidified the association of Presidents' wives with the mansion when she prevailed on Congress for an $11,000 appropriation and turned to the Surveyor of Public Buildings for assistance in outfitting the President's House. Elizabeth Monroe contributed to the shopping list compiled by her husband for the rebuilt White House when it reopened after being burned in 1814.

By the end of the nineteenth century, First Ladies were taking a larger public role in maintaining the mansion as a public monument. Lucretia Garfield set out to research the mansion's history at the Library of Congress because, as her husband wrote, "so little is known," and Caroline Harrison worked closely with an architect to develop plans for enlarging the White House into a horseshoe-shaped palace with separate wings for museum and office functions. When Congress refused to appropriate the necessary funds, she had to make do with a general cleanup.

This concern with the White House, as something more than a residence and office, would continue to preoccupy Presidents' wives in the twentieth century when the mansion's management would become one of their primary responsibilities. Edith Roosevelt conferred with architects and decorators about the 1902 renovation and helped engineer a change from the Victorian rococo-revival interior with its dark colors, heavy fabrics, and many fringes to rooms with a light, sparsely furnished look. She also originated the idea of displaying portraits of Presidents' wives ("myself included," she said) in the ground-floor corridor. EDITH WILSON arranged for china from previous Presidents' purchases to be displayed in a specially designated room on the lower level. Grace Coolidge appointed the first advisory committee ever formed to oversee the mansion's furnishings and decoration, and she prevailed on Congress to pass legislation permitting her and the committee to seek donations of furnishings and artwork much as boards of museums operate. When a public debate erupted about what styles were appropriate for the nation's most famous home, Calvin Coolidge called a halt to the whole project and thus only a few pieces of furniture were donated.

In 1961 JACQUELINE KENNEDY showed how valuable a popular First Lady can be to an administration when she embarked on a project to turn the White House into a showcase for the nation's finest art and furniture. That same year Congress passed legislation making the mansion's contents public property so that future residents could not discard items according to their personal whims. Jacqueline Kennedy brought a curator on loan from the Smithsonian and appointed an advisory committee to help in the refurbishing. Guidebooks about the house and its occupants went on sale to help finance the project.

Jacqueline Kennedy's enormous personal appeal helped draw attention to the White House and imprint on the public's mind a strong connection between it and the First Lady. After PAT NIXON turned to a new White House curator, Clement Conger, to help encourage donations of art and furniture, many gifts arrived. The emphasis during the Nixon years was on acquisitions that had once been in the White House (such as the chairs ordered by the Monroes for the Blue Room in 1817) rather than on reproductions or period pieces. Pat Nixon also endorsed the idea of making the White House a showcase for American workmanship rather than for the French styles that Jacqueline Kennedy had favored. NANCY REAGAN became embroiled in controversy when she announced a project to upgrade the family quarters with more than one million dollars that came from private donations.

Their association with the Executive Mansion's furnishings exposed First Ladies to criticism (and praise) that reflected on their husbands. Opinion is almost unanimous that Jacqueline Kennedy enhanced her husband's record with her refurbishing, which was highlighted in a nationally televised tour that she conducted of the White House public rooms. But Nancy Reagan's project to upgrade the family quarters brought unfavorable attention to the President, partly because it coincided with the administration's announced cuts in social programs.

As the White House took on more and more importance as a cultural showcase for the nation, First Ladies took responsibility for scheduling entertainment. Musicales, held first at the mansion during the Hayes administration, became common in the twentieth century, and concerts that had begun as gatherings of a few dozen people in the East Room were eventually carried on television to the entire nation because, ROSALYNN CARTER explained, "Jimmy and I knew there were so many people who had never been to the White House and would be so thrilled to be able to come."

In their choice of performers, a selection process in which they have the help of advisers, First Ladies have often gone beyond their own personal preferences to please popular tastes and thus add to the President's following or color his image. ELEANOR ROOSEVELT brought in many different ethnic groups and gave unknown performers, such as the conductor Antonia Brico, a chance to be seen and heard. Mrs. Roosevelt's defense of Marian Anderson's right to sing at the

Lincoln Memorial (when the Daughters of the American Revolution refused her the right to perform in Constitution Hall) also earned her support in many areas. MAMIE EISENHOWER's choice of groups led by Lawrence Welk and Fred Waring was credited by her husband with making Americans feel good about the White House and convincing them that it reflected popular tastes. Jacqueline Kennedy preferred more classically oriented programs, and Nancy Reagan often turned to Hollywood friends.

**Causes and Campaigns.** In addition to responsibility for overseeing the White House; choosing its china, glassware, and other furnishings; and arranging entertainment; the job of First Lady gradually came to include direction of a project or cause complementary to the President's agenda but separate from it. Hints of this development were already evident in the nineteenth century when Americans appealed to Harriet Lane, James Buchanan's niece, for help on matters relevant to artists or to American Indians. As mentioned, Lucy Hayes's valuable association with the temperance movement revealed the potential value of a President's wife taking on a cause, but not until the twentieth century did First Ladies select their own projects rather than simply respond to public pressure to champion a cause.

This particular way of contributing to the presidency, by spearheading a reform, got a firm start with Ellen Wilson in 1913. Before her death the following August, she had lent her name to slum-clearance projects and invited reformers to meet legislators at White House socials. Using official vehicles to transport observers around Washington, she showed how decrepit and inadequate some housing, within blocks of the President's home, had become. Her association with this cause became so popular that on the day she died, the Senate passed a housing bill in her honor. Her immediate successors linked their names with causes that found wide support, such as the Girl Scouts or the Red Cross.

Eleanor Roosevelt enlarged on these precedents by speaking out on many matters on which a national consensus had not yet formed. Citing her husband's partial paralysis as the reason for her traveling as his "eyes and ears," she eschewed a social leadership role for herself and turned to investigating problems that affected how people lived. She descended into mines, toured poverty-stricken areas, inspected troops in the Pacific, and then reported back to the White House and testified before a congressional committee. Although she insisted that she merely conveyed information and did not attempt to influence her husband on solutions, her own accounts belie this claim. She was widely believed to attract a more liberal following than did her husband (and thus increase his popularity with a particular segment of the population) on issues involving civil rights, WOMEN'S RIGHTS, federally subsidized housing, youth programs and artists' projects. Her regular meetings with the press and her own newspaper columns increased access to her and her views.

Not all her successors followed Eleanor Roosevelt's lead. Neither BESS TRUMAN nor Mamie Eisenhower adopted a project as her own, preferring to follow older models that featured the First Lady as social leader. But each President's wife after 1961 selected a cause as her own; its value to the President depended on how the project was perceived and whether or not the First Lady's concern seemed genuine. LADY BIRD JOHNSON was sometimes ridiculed for her enthusiasm about "beautifying" the nation by tearing down billboards and planting trees, but her actions coincided with a new interest in protecting the environment. Indeed, on balance, her contribution was considered an asset to the administration. Pat Nixon championed volunteerism, traveling thousands of miles and speaking to dozens of audiences about how they could donate time and effort to helping others and their nation. Because the President's staff chose not to publicize her efforts, her work did little for her husband's popular standing. BETTY FORD won some votes for her husband and endangered others because of her efforts to support the Equal Rights Amendment and her candor concerning her views on a woman's right to abortion. Rosalynn Carter, who also favored passage of the Equal Rights Amendment, concentrated the energies of her staff on mental health projects and on resettling Cambodian refugees. Nancy Reagan staked out a Foster Grandparents program early in her husband's presidency. When her ratings fell, however, thus causing some concern about a negative effect on the President's popularity, she turned to a program to discourage drug abuse. Billed as "Just Say No," her campaign included many public appearances and a White House conference attended by spouses of other nations' leaders. Barbara Bush sought to bolster her husband's initiative to be the "education president" by setting her own aims on raising literacy.

This increasingly prominent role as the leader of a project or cause coincided with the public acceptance of an important part for wives in the presidential campaign. Well into the twentieth century, women eschewed openly partisan speeches in their husbands' behalf, preferring to keep in the background in a subtle, supporting role. In 1928 Lou Hoover objected to wearing a campaign button for her husband, and later Eleanor Roosevelt expressed some doubts about the propriety of a woman's speaking out in her husband's favor. Bess Truman accompanied her husband on train campaigns but limited her appearances to smiling acknowledgment of her husband's introduction of her as "The Boss." Mamie Eisenhower put her name on an article in a major woman's magazine urging voters to "Vote for my husband or for Governor Stevenson but *please vote.*"

After 1960 spouses undertook increasingly partisan campaigning, and eventually their participation became an expected part of each election. Jacqueline Kennedy traveled and spoke for her husband until she announced her pregnancy and retired to Massachusetts to await the election results. Lady Bird Johnson, who set new records in 1964 when she toured the South in a train dubbed the Lady Bird Special, gave forty-seven speeches to crowds gathered along the way and she invited Democratic Party leaders to come on board for portions of the trip. Rosalynn Carter expanded the idea of spouse as campaigner when she went out on the campaign trail more than a year before the 1976 Democratic Party convention and talked to hundreds of groups, both large and small, in behalf of Jimmy Carter's nomination. She continued this very prominent and separate role in the general election and in the unsuccessful bid for reelection in 1980, explaining that by traveling separately she and her husband could cover more territory. By the 1980s, candidates' wives were accepting invitations for television interviews and for debates with the wives of other candidates.

**The Public Role.** Since the First Lady's duties have never been fully defined and funding for her efforts is made on an ad hoc basis, each woman experiments with the job's potential. In the twelve years that Eleanor Roosevelt served as First Lady, she enlarged the scope of the position considerably. Yet it is important to realize that she built on the foundations laid by her twentieth-century predecessors, who had attempted in different ways to bolster their husbands' standings and effectiveness.

Edith Wilson, who came to the White House as Woodrow Wilson's bride in December 1915, took on special importance after his paralyzing stroke in the fall of 1919. The Wilsons spent considerable time together after their wedding, and he admitted that he enjoyed working more when he was in her presence. He went less willingly to the West Wing office, and she often sat alongside and assisted him as he read confidential communications relevant to the war. She accompanied him to the peace conference at Versailles

and made a triumphant tour of Italy—the first such international tour by a First Lady. After their return to the United States and his illness, she monitored all his visitors and all communications addressed to him, resulting in cries that she had become the "Assistant President" or "petticoat government."

Historians have disagreed on the extent of Edith Wilson's influence during the six months or so that her husband was severely incapacitated. That she limited access to him is undisputed but that she actually made other decisions is questionable. For much of the winter of 1919–1920, few decisions came out of the White House. A miners' strike, a steel workers' strike, and controversy over the deportation of aliens evidently received little presidential attention. Edith Wilson is generally credited, however, with influencing her husband to dismiss appointees who did not meet with her approval, an intervention that is difficult to document because of the privacy that surrounds it. Her lack of interest in politics after leaving the White House lends credence to her claim that she was merely acting as a supportive wife in the White House—attempting to protect her husband's health and well-being—and that she took little interest in government.

Edith Wilson's successor, Florence Harding, had been an ardent promoter of her husband all through their marriage, and she continued to work hard in the White House to bolster his popularity. Staff members noted that she made frequent trips to the public rooms of the mansion to greet tourists and to have her photograph taken with delegations of sorority sisters, Masons, and whatever groups wanted to pose. She met informally with women reporters, although these meetings were not the publicized and well-attended meetings that Eleanor Roosevelt had with the press.

Grace Coolidge took no stands on public issues, but her enormous personal popularity helped soften her husband's image as cool and distant. The White House released photographs showing her with her dog, Rob Roy, and her pet raccoon, Rebecca, thus revealing her as an animal lover and endearing her to the public. Visitors to the White House would remark that she, rather than the President, remained their strongest memory.

Although she shrank from publicity and refused to be interviewed as First Lady, Lou Hoover worked hard for her husband's program and spoke on national radio urging Americans to fight the Great Depression with volunteerism. Her attempt to refurbish the Executive Mansion with authentic American antiques had little success in those economically bad times, but she did initiate a project to compile a record of the furniture and art in the White House collection.

The stage was thus set in 1933 for Eleanor Roosevelt to reconsider the role of First Lady and to enlarge the public role in its substantive (rather than merely social or decorative) aspects. Taking advice from friends who were more feminist than she, Eleanor Roosevelt expanded the job of First Lady in several ways. She agreed to meet regularly with members of the press, scheduling her first news conference within days of moving into the White House and well before her husband got around to his first encounter with the Fourth Estate. For the rest of her tenure, Eleanor Roosevelt met weekly with women reporters. She lifted her ban on men during World War II and permitted them to attend as well. Reporters could question her on any subject, including those that were political, although she had initially put a ban on such topics. News services that had not employed women felt obliged to hire them so as to have a representative present. These press conferences and her other public statements and writings that revealed her as more liberal than her husband on matters of civil rights and women's rights helped enlarge the President's following in some quarters.

Bess Truman chose not to continue regular meetings with the press, and she refused to take stands on matters of public policy. Except for her statement that she thought the White House should be repaired rather than torn down and replaced when it was found to have structural weaknesses, she issued few public announcements. Harry Truman insisted that he consulted her before making important decisions, including that of whether to use the atomic bomb in Japan in 1945, but supporting evidence (including the recollections of their daughter Margaret) is inconclusive on this matter. Bess Truman refused to answer questions, except some of those directed to her secretaries in writing, and she destroyed many of her papers before she died.

Mamie Eisenhower followed the Truman rather than the Roosevelt model in most respects, and none of Bess Truman's successors agreed to regular press conferences. When Presidents' wives met with reporters, the subject was generally limited to social matters: menus for state dinners, clothing to be worn for special events, guest lists, and new furniture or art acquisitions for the White House.

Betty Ford's press conference, held within weeks of moving into the White House in 1974, broke new ground. She announced that she did not always agree with her husband on important matters, including the recent Supreme Court decision concerning a woman's right to terminate a pregnancy. In staking out her own separate turf and attracting a following that was not necessarily in her husband's camp, she won some followers and antagonized others. Her candor following surgery for breast cancer was even more remarkable. First Ladies had generally kept their medical conditions private, but the Ford White House released details of her surgery, encouraging American women to go for checkups. In the process, Betty Ford came to realize the enormous potential in the job of First Lady.

Although Presidents had usually refused to acknowledge that their wives played any part in important decisions, Gerald Ford admitted that he talked over with his wife major questions and that she had been influential in his controversial decision to pardon Richard Nixon. The Carters continued this trend by emphasizing Rosalynn's role in the presidency. She attended Cabinet meetings, publicized her weekly "working lunches" with the President in the Oval Office, and acted as her husband's emissary abroad. Taking the first trip ever made by a presidential spouse on an international tour of a substantive (rather than ceremonial or investigative) nature, she spoke with leaders of seven nations in the Caribbean and Latin America on matters of defense and trade policy. Yet the criticism leveled at her on her return, since she traveled as an unelected and unappointed representative of the United States, is generally cited as the reason that she made no more such trips and that her successors limited themselves to goodwill missions when they traveled abroad in behalf of their husbands.

The Reagan presidency focused new attention on the President's wife as adviser. By the time Nancy Reagan left the White House in 1989, one major newspaper credited her with raising the job of First Lady to that of "Associate Presidency." Although she downplayed her part in any official decisions, observers were nearly unanimous in insisting that she participated actively, especially in her husband's selection of personnel and in his scheduling. Her prominence was no doubt affected by her husband's being temporarily disabled, first by an assassination attempt in March 1981 and then by subsequent surgeries. But a long list of evidence compiled by the press and by White House insiders suggests her involvement: her visible prompting of the President when he replied to reporters' questions; Chief of Staff DONALD REGAN's version of how she vetoed certain dates for the President's travels or meetings; various accounts of how she worked to ease out Cabinet members, campaign managers, and others on the Reagan team.

BARBARA BUSH did not continue this trend toward a more-opinionated, involved First Lady. Her literacy project was more in line with a traditionalist role for wives, and she kept most of her views to herself.

Observers ventured that her opinion on important questions differed from those held by the President—particularly on gun control and on a woman's right to terminate a pregnancy—but she refused to reveal her views to the public.

The Bush presidency rounded out two centuries in which the job of First Lady evolved from its ceremonial base to become deeply involved in the presidency. In the process a large office in the East Wing became the center of the First Lady's activities. Each woman's account of her years in the White House was read for information about how decisions had been made, and the autobiographies of Lady Bird Johnson, Betty Ford, Rosalynn Carter, and Nancy Reagan were especially revealing. In January 1993, Hillary Rodham Clinton became the first presidential spouse to bring an extensive professional career of her own to the job of First Lady. Graduate of Yale Law School and partner in an Arkansas law firm, she was repeatedly singled out as one of her husband's most trusted advisers, thus illustrating once again that the job of First Lady is one that each administration defines for itself.

### BIBLIOGRAPHY

Anthony, Carl Sferrazza. *First Ladies*. 2 vols. 1990–1991.

Boller, Paul. *Presidential Wives*. 1988.

Caroli, Betty Boyd. *First Ladies*. 1987.

Furman, Bess. *White House Profile*. 1957.

Gould, Lewis. "First Ladies and the Presidency." *Presidential Studies Quarterly* 20 (1990): 677–684.

Gutin, Myra. *The President's Partner: The First Lady in the Twentieth Century*. 1989.

Means, Marianne. *The Woman in the White House*. 1963.

Smith, Nancy Kegan, and Mary C. Ryan, eds. *Modern First Ladies: Their Documentary Legacy*. 1989.

BETTY BOYD CAROLI

**FIRST LADY'S OFFICE.** Although the origins of the FIRST LADY's office can be found in the nineteenth century in the ceremonial appearances of Presidents' spouses and in their management of the WHITE HOUSE, its development as a distinct segment of the executive branch occurred in the twentieth century. Edith Roosevelt paved the way when, in 1901, she brought on loan from the War Department a clerk, Isabella Hagner, to work as her social secretary and assist in answering correspondence, dealing with the press, and handling other tasks that came to the President's wife. Hagner remained throughout the Theodore Roosevelt presidency, working first out of Edith Roosevelt's bedroom on the second floor and then,

after the 1902 White House renovation, setting up a desk in the West Hall.

Provisions for Staff and space for the First Lady's office were made on an ad hoc basis until the 1940s. Presidents' wives paid out of their own funds for one or more social secretaries and relied on friends to assist them in answering letters, greeting well-wishers, arranging parties, promoting causes, improving the White House's appearance, and keeping a record of its furnishings and of the guests invited to each official event. Social secretaries compiled the materials that became "White House Social Files" for each administration. Because of the unstructured nature of the operation—involving high turnover, many volunteers, and a paid staff that came on loan from some other part of the executive branch and then left when a particular job was done—it is difficult to document the exact size and personnel of the First Lady's office.

After its construction in 1942, the East Wing of the White House became headquarters for the First Lady's office and whatever staff she chose to name. The East Wing also housed a correspondence division that handled the large volume of mail in and out of the Executive Mansion, including invitations to official events, greeting cards at holiday time, and unsolicited mail to any member of the President's family. The correspondence office grew considerably as more and more Americans reached out to their chief executive for help—in 1988 6 million communications were received. Presidents also sought to bolster their popularity by sending out individual cards to acknowledge birthdays, anniversaries, and the Christmas season. In 1990 the Bush White House reported it had sent 750,000 of these messages. Some actual addressing of cards was done by volunteers, but the entire correspondence office is under the First Lady's direction.

In 1953 the *Congressional Directory* made its first public acknowledgment of the First Lady when it listed Mary McCaffree as "Acting Secretary to the President's wife." In the following decade, the office of First Lady would take on an entirely new look. LADY BIRD JOHNSON shaped the operation into its modern version: a professionally trained, paid staff of about thirty people working out of the East Wing. In many ways the First Lady's staff mirrors the organization of the President's West Wing operation, with its own chief of staff (sometimes called staff director), press secretary, speech writers, project directors, and various other assistants for particular assignments.

Although ELEANOR ROOSEVELT served as her own press secretary, meeting with women reporters every week, her two immediate successors relied on their husbands' press secretaries to deal with the media. In

1961 JACQUELINE KENNEDY named her own press secretary—Pamela Turnure. Pierre Salinger, John Kennedy's Press Secretary, estimated that he controlled 90 percent of the access reporters had to Mrs. Kennedy and her children, but the job of a separate press person for the First Lady became accepted. Lady Bird Johnson turned to a seasoned Washington reporter, Elizabeth Carpenter, who doubled as staff director and worked hard to show her employer, in the most favorable light, teaching her how to get the most advantageous news coverage and thus enhance her husband's record. Carpenter's success showed the potential value of an activist First Lady and inspired attempts to imitate her. As demands increased for information about the President's family, the First Lady's press secretary became an important part of the White House operation and the sole source for photographs of the presidential family. (Photos of the President and official visitors came from his press office.)

Since 1963 a specially designated project director coordinates the activities intended to promote the First Lady's association with whatever project she has announced as her own: beautification (Lady Bird Johnson); volunteerism (PAT NIXON); support for the arts and passage of the Equal Rights Amendment (BETTY FORD); mental health reforms (ROSALYNN CARTER); Foster Grandparents and fighting drug abuse (NANCY REAGAN); literacy (BARBARA BUSH). The project director and other staff members schedule speaking trips and other public appearances, arrange conferences, and generally work to highlight the First Lady's project as a positive contribution to the President's record.

Each First Lady arranges her own office as she chooses. Rosalynn Carter maintained headquarters in the East Wing and made a point of announcing that she went there regularly to work. Betty Ford kept an office in the residence on the second floor, installing her own telephone for lobbying and partisan pursuits. Nancy Reagan and Barbara Bush also worked out of the residence, but both of them downplayed the "office" aspect of being First Lady.

In her role as manager of the White House, the First Lady has the help of several experts, although they do not technically fall under the rubric of her "office." The Chief Usher, presiding out of a room just inside the north entrance, oversees a staff of slightly more than one hundred and works closely with the First Lady to monitor upkeep of the Executive Mansion and all traffic through it. Since 1961, a White House curator has advised the First Lady regarding exhibition of furniture and artworks in the State Rooms. Barbara Bush described herself as the unpaid guide to the second floor, but she had a sizable, knowledgeable staff to assist her.

Coordination between the First Lady's office and that of the President is not always smooth, and lines of authority frequently overlap. Rules for operation are developed by each administration, and personnel designations shift with each incumbent. Typically, however, the President's spouse heads a large office that figures prominently in each administration's plans for success.

## BIBLIOGRAPHY

Anthony, Carl Sferrazza. *First Ladies*. 2 vols. 1990–1991.
Caroli, Betty Boyd. *First Ladies*. 1987.
Gould, Lewis. "Modern First Ladies: An Institutional Perspective." in *Modern First Ladies: Their Documentary Legacy*. Edited by Nancy Kegan Smith and Mary C. Ryan. 1989.
Gould, Lewis. "Modern First Ladies and the Presidency." *Presidential Studies Quarterly* 20 (1990):677–683.
Gutin, Myra. *The President's Partner: The First Lady in the Twentieth Century*. 1989.

BETTY BOYD CAROLI

**FIRST USE OF NUCLEAR WEAPONS.** First use refers to the use of NUCLEAR WEAPONS by one nation against an enemy nation prior to the use of such weapons by the enemy. A first use could be an all-out attack upon the enemy nation, sometimes referred to as a first strike, or it could involve the introduction of tactical nuclear weapons in a battlefield situation. First use differs from second strike, which is a retaliation for a nuclear attack.

Over the years, the United States strategic nuclear policy has evolved from containment, to massive retaliation, to mutual assured destruction (MAD), to flexible response. Despite these shifts in policy and despite the overall theme of deterrence, sitting Presidents of both parties have uniformly declined to endorse a no-first-use position. A simple but perplexing question arises: Under the Constitution, does the President have the authority to order a first use or any use of nuclear weapons?

Article II, Section 2, of the Constitution provides that the President shall be the COMMANDER IN CHIEF of the armed forces of the United States. The Constitution does not further define this conferral of power, yet the broad outlines are reasonably certain: at all times, the President, as Commander in Chief, has the duty to defend the nation from foreign aggressors and, during times of war, the President operates as the supreme commander of the armed forces. Since the nuclear weapons arsenal is an integral part of the United States' armed forces, it follows that the President, as Commander in Chief, has authority over the use of nuclear weapons, both in times of peace and in times of war. Yet this constitutional authority is not unlimited; it is checked by the Article I legislative powers of Congress, including the powers to appropriate funds, to regulate the armed forces, and to declare war (*see* WAR, DECLARATION OF). The precise demarcation between presidential and congressional primacy in this realm cannot, however, be reduced to a simple formula, and is more likely to be defined by the practical realities of politics and war. Adding to the ambiguity, Congress has not directly regulated or limited the President's authority to use nuclear weapons.

If the United States is attacked by the nuclear forces of an enemy, accepted constitutional wisdom provides that the President may respond with nuclear weapons. A more complicated constitutional question is presented by the unilateral presidential order of a first use of nuclear weapons, either as a preemptive strike against a potential enemy or as an escalation of a preexisting conflict in which nuclear weapons have not yet been introduced. A preemptive strike ordered by the President might range beyond the legitimate scope of presidential authority, potentially running afoul of the congressional power to declare war. However, evidence of an imminent nuclear attack by an enemy could provide the President the authority to order a preemptive attack upon that enemy's nuclear forces as a defensive measure, the theory being that an imminent nuclear attack is tantamount to a sudden attack upon the nation. The resolution of the constitutional tensions in this latter scenario will be defined by the surrounding political circumstances and not by the fine tunings of constitutional theory. One would hope that the presidential decision would be informed by the republican principles that animate the Constitution.

First use in a preexisting conflict presents a slightly less ambiguous context. In the absence of congressional direction to the contrary, a presidential order to use nuclear weapons during an ongoing conflict would seem to fall within the President's prerogative as Commander in Chief. Some constitutional theoreticians have argued, however, that the introduction of nuclear weapons to an ongoing conflict would necessarily constitute a new war and, therefore, a presidential order of such use would be beyond the scope of presidential authority. The likelihood of such a theory having any practical measure is, however, slim. Although the President should and presumably would take the consequences of nuclear escalation into account, the ultimate decision to use those weapons in any particular conflict is, absent authoritative legislation to the contrary, a presidential decision. The USE OF ATOMIC BOMBS in WORLD WAR II is an example of precisely such a first use. President Harry S. Truman, aware of the devastating explosive force of the available atomic bombs, ordered their use without any guidance from Congress. That historical fact and its seeming validation by a positive public and congressional response lays a strong foundation for the President's prerogative in this realm.

### BIBLIOGRAPHY

Cimbala, Stephen J. *First Strike Stability: Deterrence after Containment.* 1990.

Lindsay, James M. *Congress and Nuclear Weapons.* 1991.

Martel, William C., and Paul L. Savage. *Strategic Nuclear War: What the Superpowers Target and Why.* 1986.

Raven-Hansen, Peter, ed. *First Use of Nuclear Weapons: Under the Constitution, Who Decides.* 1987.

ALLAN IDES

**FISCAL CORPORATION BILL** (1841). The Fiscal Corporation bill represented an effort to deal with the vacuum created in 1836 when the charter of the BANK OF THE UNITED STATES expired. As an interim measure, Congress established an INDEPENDENT TREASURY in 1840 to keep federal funds free from any connection with banks. The Independent Treasury was scheduled to take effect on 4 July 1840, but when the election of 1840 put the Whigs in power, Congress repealed the Independent Treasury. Interpreting the election as a referendum in favor of a national bank, Sen. HENRY CLAY introduced the bill for repeal.

The bank issue produced a major confrontation between Clay and President John Tyler, who cautioned Clay against trying to push for a national bank bill in the special session of Congress in 1841. Tyler warned that he might have to exercise his veto if such a bill reached him. A central part of the dispute concerned the power of Congress to establish branch banks. Was it necessary to obtain the consent of the state governments, or did the Constitution give Congress full power to create branches without state approval? Clay reluctantly modified the bill to provide for state permission for branch banks. State approval, however, would be assumed if a state legislature did not act during its first session after passage of the bank bill.

The bank bill was presented to Tyler on 6 August. After waiting the full ten days to consider the bill, Tyler vetoed it on the ground that it usurped state prerogatives. He found particularly offensive a provision that once a state assented to a branch, only Congress could withdraw it. The Senate sustained his veto.

Tyler then met with members of Congress to devise a substitute bill that might meet with his approval. These discussions led to the Fiscal Corporation bill, which used the term "agency" instead of "branch bank" and reduced the operating capital of the central bank. Tyler showed some enthusiasm for the measure at first but later backed away, concluding that it was a plot to discredit him. A "coffeehouse letter," written by Congressman John Minor Botts, suggested that the bank bill was drafted as a trap for Tyler: the Whigs would abhor him for vetoing it and the Democrats would condemn him if he signed it. Tyler vetoed the second bill, prompting his entire Cabinet, except for Secretary of State DANIEL WEBSTER, to resign. The House sustained the second veto.

### BIBLIOGRAPHY

Chitwood, Oliver Perry. *John Tyler.* 1964.
Peterson, Norma Lois. *The Presidencies of William Henry Harrison and John Tyler.* 1989.

LOUIS FISHER

**FISCAL POLICY.** The strategic use of spending and tax policies to achieve macroeconomic objectives constitutes fiscal policy. Since the NEW DEAL, Presidents have borne the primary political responsibility for promoting economic prosperity. Through budgetary programs and related stabilization policies, Presidents have attempted to control unemployment and inflation levels while fostering economic growth. Presidential advisory staffs, such as the COUNCIL OF ECONOMIC ADVISERS (CEA), provide institutional support for presidential economic leadership.

Presidential fiscal policy management is conditioned by policy and political constraints. Since the 1960s, the consensus on using budget deficits and surpluses to stimulate or restrain the economy has evaporated, leaving the President with few fiscal policy options. The President must also contend with an independent FEDERAL RESERVE BOARD setting monetary policy and, since 1974, with a Congress setting its own budget and fiscal policies, making it more difficult to forge a policy consensus. Most important, as deficit problems have grown more severe and spending control more intractable, the budget's utility as a fiscal policy tool has been diminished.

**New Deal Precedents.** The presidency of Franklin D. Roosevelt is considered a watershed in the evolution of fiscal policy management, although presidential economic responsibilities can be traced back to the beginning of the Republic. The conservative economic orthodoxy that governed public finance before Roosevelt, however, meant that presidential economic leadership was highly circumscribed. The Great Depression led to more activist and interventionist government and, ultimately, to a new fiscal policy orthodoxy.

According to most experts, Roosevelt did not pursue a deliberate fiscal policy strategy in 1933, nor did he completely abandon the balanced-budget principles he espoused before taking office. New Deal emergency spending programs, however, made deficits unavoidable, and Roosevelt placed a higher priority on funding employment and public assistance programs than on balancing the budget. Roosevelt's spending experiment anticipated much of the argument presented in John Maynard Keynes's *The General Theory of Employment, Interest, and Money* (1936), which provided the theoretical rationale for demand-based stimulus through spending increases or tax cuts.

Keynesian theory soon emerged as the dominant paradigm in economics, and the spectacular success of demand-based stimulus during WORLD WAR II accelerated this intellectual transformation. The New Deal era thus established aggressive presidential economic leadership and enhanced the appeal of Keynesian theory. It also put into place a national unemployment insurance program and other income transfer programs that serve as automatic stabilizers during economic downturns and are a primary component of modern fiscal policy management.

**Toward Aggressive Keynesianism.** From the end of World War II until the early 1960s, political leaders struggled to define a clear fiscal policy approach. President Harry S. Truman was forced by circumstances during the late 1940s to devote much of his attention to combating inflation. In practice, this meant balancing the budget rather than pursuing economic stimulus through tax cuts or spending increases.

Dwight D. Eisenhower placed an even higher priority on inflation control. In order to balance the budget and control inflation, Eisenhower repeatedly opposed tax cuts and other economic stimulus measures. The economic record of the period reflects Eisenhower's emphases and consistency. The budget was balanced three times during his tenure, and peacetime inflation rates were kept below 4 percent. At the same time, the economy went through three recessions, unemployment levels were comparatively high, and economic growth was sporadic.

With the administration of John F. Kennedy, Keynesian stimulus policy was finally and fully embraced, not just by economic advisers but also by a President. When the economy's brief recovery from the 1960 recession began to slow early in 1962, Kennedy first proposed countercyclical, targeted spending increases but then switched to politically more palatable tax cuts and to an aggressive defense of deliberate deficits. The rationale for Kennedy's tax program was presented in the fiscal year 1964 budget, which declared, "Our present choice is not between a tax cut and a balanced budget . . . [but] between chronic deficits arising out of a slow rate of economic growth, and temporary deficits stemming from a tax program designed to promote . . . more rapid economic growth."

The Revenue Act of 1964, passed after Kennedy's death, received much of the credit for the strong economic expansion that occurred during the mid-1960s. Since actual deficits were less than had been estimated, its underlying full-employment budget rationale gained credibility. The full-employment budget provided an alternative deficit measurement based on the economy growing at full capacity, replacing the goal of a balanced budget with a balanced budget at full-employment levels.

Proponents of an activist fiscal policy failed, however, to persuade Congress to accept standby presidential authority to lower taxes when recession threatened or to approve a broad range of countercyclical spending measures. Congress also was unwilling to embrace the "new economics" of full-employment budgets and full-scale stimulus. The budget deficit therefore remained the focal point for debates in Congress over fiscal policy, and the combined budgetary pressures of the VIETNAM WAR and GREAT SOCIETY spending programs exacerbated that debate.

Lyndon Baines Johnson first tried to finance the war and his domestic agenda without a tax increase, but this led to growing deficits and rising inflation. Johnson finally proposed a tax increase in 1967, but Congress stalled its passage until the middle of the following year. The budget was brought into balance in fiscal year 1969, but inflation and economic growth problems were to persist over the next decade.

Under Richard M. Nixon, fiscal policy shifts were rapid and economic successes temporary. Nixon entered office committed to inflation control and balanced budgets. Rising unemployment and rising inflation, however, led him to adopt fiscal stimulus to combat the former and wage and price controls to arrest the latter. The economy had improved sufficiently in 1972 to assist in Nixon's reelection, but inflation rates soon started to climb and, after the 1973 oil embargo, reached double-digit levels.

In 1974, Congress decided that it would formulate alternative budgets and fiscal policy. One of Nixon's last acts in office was signing the 1974 CONGRESSIONAL BUDGET AND IMPOUNDMENT CONTROL ACT, which established a new congressional budgetary process and added confusion over political institutional leadership responsibilities to the growing discord over fiscal policy management.

The short-lived presidency of Gerald Ford began with proposals for tax increases and spending controls to reduce inflation. As the economy moved into recession, Ford abandoned his anti-inflation program, proposing tax cuts and investment tax credits to spur growth. Congressional Democrats responded with proposals for spending stimulus and higher deficits. As a result, fiscal policy management was debated within an increasingly short-term framework. Ford was able to block some Democratic spending initiatives but was unable to persuade Congress to accept structural tax reforms or to consider seriously long-term fiscal policy objectives.

The focus on short-term solutions became even more pronounced under President Jimmy Carter, resulting in a series of abrupt policy reversals. The emphasis was on economic stimulus during Carter's first two years, but then inflation started to climb, accelerated by an oil-price shock in 1979. When the Federal Reserve tightened monetary policy, interest rates soared. Carter now moved to balance the budget and bring inflation under control, but the economy was moving into recession with double-digit inflation. There was confusion about how to deal with "stagflation," and the Carter administration and Congress decided that the best political response was to balance the budget. The full-employment budget concept was ignored, leaving Democrats with no credible arguments to defend demand-stimulus policies.

**Supply-Side and Deficits.** Prior to becoming President, Ronald Reagan had insisted on the primacy of deficit reduction over tax cuts. As President, Reagan reversed ground, adopting supply-side economic prescriptions of tax cuts to promote growth. With congressional Democrats in disarray, Reagan was able to gain passage of an enormous tax cut in 1981, coupled with a considerably smaller package of spending cuts.

Supply-side economics differed from Keynesian theory in its exclusive commitment to tax-cut stimulus and in its focus on increasing incentives through marginal tax rate reductions. Supply-side proponents argued that tax cuts would spur productivity and output, expanding national income and ultimately offsetting tax revenue losses. During 1981 and 1982, however, the recession deepened, and budget deficits rose to unprecedented peacetime levels.

The economy began to improve late in Reagan's first term, and the Federal Reserve's disinflation policies were also having the desired effect. What proved insoluble thereafter was the political impasse over budget deficits. Despite the prolonged and vigorous economic recovery, the budget deficit remained high. When George Bush took office in 1989, deficits were running at $150 billion, and it was hoped that continued economic growth, along with modest policy adjustments, could reduce these levels. Instead, the economy moved into recession, and deficits more than doubled.

The emergence of huge structural BUDGET POLICY deficits made aggressive fiscal policy management extremely difficult. As a result, the President and Congress relied to a considerable extent on automatic stabilizers to provide economic stimulus. In addition, dependence on the Federal Reserve increased, with monetary policy playing an increasing role in economic management. For Presidents, the imbalance between economic leadership responsibilities and institutional resources became more and more pronounced, thus constraining presidential leadership in fiscal policy management.

[See also TAX POLICY.]

### BIBLIOGRAPHY

Heller, Walter W. *New Dimensions of Political Economy.* 1967.
Kimmel, Lewis. *Federal Budget and Fiscal Policy, 1789–1958.* 1959.
Savage, James D. *Balanced Budgets and American Politics.* 1988.
Stein, Herbert. *Presidential Economics: The Making of Economic Policy from Roosevelt to Reagan and Beyond.* 1984.
White, Joseph, and Aaron Wildavsky. *The Deficit and the Public Interest.* 1989.

DENNIS S. IPPOLITO

**FISH, HAMILTON** (1808–1893), governor of New York, Senator, Secretary of State. Born in New York City, Hamilton Fish moved from law into politics as a Whig member of Congress in 1842. He served as governor of New York from 1849 to 1850 and as U.S. Senator from 1851 to 1857. Fish is best known as President Ulysses S. Grant's Secretary of State from 1869 to 1877. Although neither brilliant nor innovative, he conducted the country's foreign relations with a sure hand through a wide range of complex issues. At the outset he confronted the prospect of war between France and Prussia. That war came in July 1870. Following the Prussian victory at Sedan in September, Fish offered the good offices of the United States in arranging a fair and lasting peace. When Prussia declined the offer and proceeded to acquire Alsace, much of Lorraine, and a huge indemnity, Fish predicted that the peace would be short-lived.

Britain's concern over the German threat to the European balance of power offered Russia an occasion to defy the British-dictated Black Sea clauses of the Treaty of Paris (1856). The resulting Anglo-Russian crisis presented Fish an opportune moment to demand a settlement of the *Alabama* claims, based on the destruction of northern commerce by English-built Confederate cruisers during the CIVIL WAR. Determined to avoid a clash with the United States, the British, in the TREATY OF WASHINGTON (1871), agreed to a settlement of the *Alabama* claims through arbitration. In August 1872 the Geneva Tribunal rendered a judgment of $15.5 million in favor of the United States.

In April 1869 Cuban nationalists declared a republic and demanded independence from Spain. Fish urged the Madrid government to institute reforms in the interest of peace but resisted pressure for direct U.S. involvement. Spain offered reforms but contingent on a cessation of the revolt. Meanwhile the struggle for CUBA raged on at enormous cost. By late 1876 both sides concluded that neither could win. Finally in February 1878 the Pact of Zanjon brought peace to Cuba. Fish's policy of exerting pressure on Spain while avoiding intervention in Cuba held to the end. On Fish's recommendation the American minister in Hawaii negotiated a reciprocity treaty with that country in January 1875. On every international front Fish conducted a successful, fundamentally conservative, diplomacy.

### BIBLIOGRAPHY

Campbell, Charles S. *The Transformation of American Foreign Relations, 1865–1890.* 1976.
Fuller, Joseph. "Hamilton Fish." In vol. 7 of *American Secretaries of State and Their Diplomacy.* Edited by Samuel F. Bemis. 1958.
Nevins, Allan. *Hamilton Fish: The Inner History of the Grant Administration.* 1957.

NORMAN A. GRAEBNER

**FLAG, PRESIDENTIAL.** The first regulation authoritatively prescribing a flag signifying the presence of the President of the United States was issued by Secretary of the Navy Gideon Welles on 18 April 1865. It authorized display of the American flag at a ship's main masthead while the President was on deck.

In 1866 the "Union Flag," or "Jack," a blue, rectangular flag, studded with a constellation of white stars, equal in number to the States, was designated to be hoisted in honor of the Commander in Chief. Four years later, the navy returned to using the American flag on such occasions. A far more dramatic change took place in 1882, when the navy approved the first distinctive presidential flag with a blue background and the U.S. coat of arms in the center.

After waiting thirty-three years, the WAR DEPARTMENT followed the navy's lead in 1898. Its design consisted of a large blue star centered on a scarlet background and encircled by a white star for each state, and a white star in each of the four corners. The U.S. coat of arms was placed upon the center star.

Three years later, President Theodore Roosevelt found it confusing to have two presidential flags with different designs and directed that only the navy's should be retained. The presidential flag used by the army and navy for the next several years were identical, except that the color field of the army's was scarlet and the navy's blue. In 1912, President William Howard Taft issued an executive order officially designating the color field as blue.

Finally in 1916, President Woodrow Wilson adopted an official design for the presidential flag consisting of a blue field with four white stars, one in each corner, and the presidential coat of arms in the center. The flag remained unchanged until 1945, when President Franklin D. Roosevelt decided it was inappropriate for the flag of the Commander in Chief to have only four stars when fleet admirals and generals of the army had five stars in their flags.

Roosevelt's initiative ultimately led to the adoption of a new design by his successor, Harry S. Truman, in October 1945. President Truman's executive order called for a dark blue rectangular flag bearing the presidential coat of arms in proper colors, surrounded by forty-eight white stars. President Dwight Eisenhower, in 1959 and 1960 EXECUTIVE ORDERS, added two additional stars to reflect the admission of Alaska and Hawaii as states.

[*See also* SEAL, PRESIDENTIAL.]

### BIBLIOGRAPHY

DuBois, Arthur E., comp. "History of the Seal, Flags, and Colors of the President of the United States of America." Typed manuscript. U.S. Army Institute of Heraldry.

Patterson, Richard S., and Richardson Dougall. *The Eagle and the Shield*. 1976.

STEPHEN W. STATHIS

**FLAG DESECRATION.** American Presidents and presidential candidates have long identified themselves with the national flag. Portraits of Presidents since the days of George Washington have included flags waving in the background. As early as the famous "Log Cabin" presidential campaign of 1840, William Henry Harrison was commonly portrayed as the occupant of a humble log cabin, which had an American flag flying from its roof. Other campaigns before the CIVIL WAR featured advertisements that included flags in which the stars had been removed and replaced with the likeness of candidates, or with the names of both presidential and vice presidential candidates written on the white stripes. Much of the rhetoric that immediately preceded the outbreak of the Civil War involved the protection of the flag at Fort Sumter. Shortly after the North's victory at Charleston in 1865, President Lincoln decreed that the same flag that had been removed when Union forces were evacuated four years earlier be returned to the fort and flown after a ceremony that included singing the "Star Spangled Banner."

By the mid-nineteenth century, the national flag had become a potent symbol, often identified with the person of the President. Yet flag etiquette was far from being observed by the public, and even by Presidents and other public figures. Lincoln, for example, was photographed during the Civil War dining at a table covered with a flag. Nor was flag desecration a national concern until several decades later, when many states passed flag-protection legislation aimed primarily at preventing the commercial exploitation of the flag on labels and in advertisements. Symbolic political dissent, such as the burning of the flag in protest, was also outlawed, but prosecutions were rare. The first United States Supreme Court case dealing with flag desecration involved prosecution of the manufacturer of "Stars and Stripes" beer, whose label included a flag. In *Halter v. Nebraska* (1907), the Court upheld Nebraska's flag protection statute, stating that "love [of the country] will diminish in proportion as respect for the flag is weakened."

*Halter* was decided some two decades before the Supreme Court held that the protections of the First Amendment apply to states as well as to the federal government, and federal laws prohibiting flag desecration were not enacted until the VIETNAM WAR era. In the meantime, WORLD WAR I and the red scare during 1919 effectively changed the focus of flag enthusiasts from commercial exploitation to political dissent. By 1939 and the outbreak of WORLD WAR II in Europe, hostility toward those who refused to salute the flag or spoke disparagingly of it was widespread, often violent. In 1940 fifteen hundred Jehovah's Witnesses, whose beliefs include a literal interpretation of the biblical injunction against the worship of graven images, were victims of mob violence. It was in this atmosphere that the Supreme Court upheld the expulsion of children from public school for refusing to salute the flag in *Minersville School District v. Gobitis*. The Court reversed itself three years later in the landmark decision *West Virginia Board of Education v. Barnette* (1943), which held that states could not compel veneration of the flag. Although *Barnette* did not directly involve desecration, its principles were fundamental to later decisions invalidating state and federal flag protection legislation. A mandatory salute or pledge of allegiance, the Court ruled, was contrary to the very freedoms the flag symbolized.

President Dwight Eisenhower's decision in 1954 to include the words "under God" in the Pledge of Allegiance added to a growing sense of the flag's sanctity. But protest against American involvement in Vietnam during the late 1960s drew national media attention, especially after a flag burning in New York City in 1967. Within months, the House of Representatives had passed the first federal bill against flag desecration, but the Senate did not act until mid 1968. The statute made it a federal crime to cast contempt knowingly upon the flag through mutilation, burning, or defacement. At about this time, President Richard M. Nixon and other Americans took to wearing flag lapel pins as a sign of patriotism.

In 1984, as the Republican national convention in Dallas renominated President Ronald Reagan and Vice President George Bush, a group of protestors demonstrating in Dallas burned a flag in protest against United States policies at home and abroad. Texas convicted them under its Venerated Objects Law. When the *Texas v. Johnson* case was reviewed by the Supreme Court in 1989, George Bush was President. His campaign had featured attacks against Democratic candidate Michael Dukakis for vetoing a Massachusetts law that mandated the Pledge of Allegiance in public schools. Dukakis explained that he had relied on the *Barnette* case, but Bush's tactics were an effective means of questioning his opponent's patriotism. In *Texas v. Johnson* the Court declared the Texas law unconstitutional by a vote of 5 to 4. President Bush spoke out against the decision, saying that he reacted "viscerally" to contempt for the flag, and declaring that he would "uphold our precious right to dissent, but burning the flag goes too far." Congress acted swiftly, the only real debate occurring between those who supported a constitutional amendment outlawing flag desecration, and those who proposed strengthening the federal statute passed in the Vietnam era. At least partially because enacting legislation was easier,

Congress passed the Flag Protection Act of 1989, which included a fine and jail sentence for intentionally mutilating the flag, by burning or otherwise. The statute became law without the President's signature, evidently because President Bush favored a constitutional amendment.

The law was immediately tested by protestors who burned flags in Seattle and Washington, D.C. The two federal prosecutions that resulted were both declared unconstitutional by federal trial courts early in 1990, and the Supreme Court heard arguments in May. Less than a month later, the Supreme Court once again issued a 5 to 4 decision, holding in *United States v. Eichman* (1990) that the government could not justify infringement of first amendment rights simply to protect the flag's status as a symbol. In reaction, President Bush and members of Congress repeated their calls for a constitutional amendment. But public opinion had cooled over the intervening year, and many Americans reacted against what they perceived as partisan maneuvering and grandstanding that accompanied flag-protection rhetoric. By the end of June 1990, the move to amend the Constitution had failed in both the Senate and the House.

Although the battle over flag desecration appeared to have subsided, changes in Court personnel, namely the resignations of Justice William Brennan, who wrote both the *Texas* and *Eichman* majority opinions, and Justice Thurgood Marshall, who joined the two opinions, may reopen the possibility that punishment for flag desecration will someday be held constitutional.

### BIBLIOGRAPHY

Furlong, William Rea, and Byron McCandless. *So Proudly We Hail: The History of the United States Flag.* 1981.

Goldstein, Robert Justin. "The Great 1989–1990 Flag Flap: An Historical, Political, and Legal Analysis." *University of Miami Law Review* 45 (1990): 18–106.

Guenter, Scot M. *The American Flag, 1777–1924: Cultural Shifts from Creation to Codification.* 1990.

Manwaring, David Roger. *Render Unto Caesar: The Flag-Salute Controversy.* 1962.

Michelman, Frank. "Saving Old Glory: On Constitutional Iconography." *Stanford Law Review* 42 (1990): 1337–1364.

NORMAN DORSEN

**FORCE ACT** (1870). Spearheaded by Representative Benjamin Butler of Massachusetts and several other RADICAL REPUBLICAN leaders, the Force Act (also known as the Enforcement Act of 1870 and as the KU KLUX KLAN ACT of 1870) represented the federal government's first serious attempt to enforce the Fifteenth Amendment. Designed to curb anti-Republican and vigilante violence in the RECONSTRUCTION South, the Force Act made the bribery or intimidation of voters in congressional elections a federal criminal offense. Under section 6, two or more persons conspiring to deprive a citizen of any right of citizenship or disguising their identities for the purpose of preventing a citizen from exercising his or her constitutional rights were guilty of a felony. If the process of intimidation led to other crimes, the conspirators could be tried in federal court and subjected to penalties equivalent to those assessed under state law. The Force Act also empowered the President to use federal troops to enforce the law's provisions. Predictably, the leaders of the DEMOCRATIC PARTY condemned the granting of such sweeping powers, excoriating the Force Act as the entering wedge of executive and military despotism. As an ex-general, President Ulysses S. Grant was especially vulnerable to such charges, but the Democrats' fears proved to be unfounded. Grant played only a minor role in the drafting and passage of the Force Act, and once it became law he made little effort to enforce it. During the fall 1870 elections, intimidation of freedmen and other southern Republicans was rampant, but only a few arrests were made. Although he acknowledged the Klan's violations of the Fifteenth Amendment, Grant was unwilling to support the few federal officials in the South who were determined to enforce the new law. The Grant administration eventually used section 6 of the 1870 Force Act as a basis for federal indictments of Ku Klux Klan members, but only after a lengthy congressional investigation of the Klan's activities and after the passage of two additional enforcement acts in February and April 1871.

BIBLIOGRAPHY

Foner, Eric. *Reconstruction: America's Unfinished Revolution, 1863–1877.* 1988.
McFeely, William S. *Grant, A Biography.* 1981.
Swinney, Everette. "Enforcing the Fifteenth Amendment, 1870–1877." *Journal of Southern History* 28 (May 1962): 202–218.
Trelease, Allen W. *White Terror: The Ku Klux Klan Conspiracy and Southern Reconstruction.* 1971.

RAYMOND ARSENAULT

**FORCE BILL.** The TARIFF ACT OF 1832 provoked the legislature of South Carolina into summoning a convention which subsequently passed an Ordinance of NULLIFICATION on 24 November 1832 declaring the tariff laws of 1828 and 1832 unconstitutional and "null, void, and no law, nor binding" upon South Carolina. After 1 February 1833, collection of tariff duties within the state would be unlawful. Any attempt to coerce the state into compliance would result in SECESSION from the Union.

In a proclamation to the people of South Carolina dated 10 December 1832, President Andrew Jackson rejected the notion that a state had the power to annul federal law. Disunion by armed force, he warned, was treason. He then asked Congress on 16 January 1833 for a Force Bill authorizing him to summon the military to put down possible rebellion. The notion that the people of one state could absolve themselves from the Union without the consent of the other states, he said, was "utterly repugnant" to the principles and ideals upon which the American government had been founded. As CHIEF EXECUTIVE, he declared, he must enforce the laws; revenue owed the government would be collected.

Jackson further requested authorization to close any port of entry he deemed necessary and locate it somewhere else. By moving the customs he would force the nullifiers to go to considerable lengths to carry out their threat. His request, he insisted, required no new legislation, simply the enforcement of existing laws.

This War Bill, or Bloody Bill, as some Southerners called it, passed the Senate 20 February 1833. To a man, the nullifiers in the chamber walked out. John Tyler of Virginia cast the single vote against the bill. The vote was thirty-two to one. The House passed it on 1 March by the vote of 149 to 48. The following day Jackson signed the measure.

At the same time, Congress passed the Compromise Tariff of 1833. South Carolina then repealed its Ordinance of Nullification but defiantly nullified the Force Bill.

BIBLIOGRAPHY

Ellis, Richard E. *The Union at Risk: Jacksonian Democracy, States' Rights, and the Nullification Crisis.* 1987.

ROBERT V. REMINI

**FORD, BETTY** (b. 1918) First Lady, wife of Gerald Ford. Although she moved into the White House without going through a national campaign, Elizabeth Bloomer Warren Ford had been a congressman's wife since 1949 and was well acquainted with political life. Within weeks of becoming FIRST LADY, she held her own press conference where she spoke openly of her plan to work for the EQUAL RIGHTS AMENDMENT and of her support for the Supreme Court's *Roe v. Wade* (1973) decision on abortion. Very shortly she broke another tradition when she permitted press releases on her surgery and treatment for breast cancer. Betty Ford lobbied state legislators to support the Equal Rights Amendment and spoke candidly on national television about various family matters.

Her personal popularity is generally acknowledged as her primary asset to her husband's presidency, although he admitted that he considered her opinion when deciding to pardon Richard Nixon. She was less successful in her bid to have her husband name a woman to the Supreme Court or as his running mate in 1976.

### BIBLIOGRAPHY

Ford, Betty (with Chris Chase). *The Times of My Life*. 1978.
Tobin, Leesa E. "Betty Ford as First Lady: A Woman for Women." *Presidential Studies Quarterly* 20 (1990): 761–768.
Weidenfeld, Sheila Rabb. *First Lady's Lady*. 1979.

BETTY BOYD CAROLI

**FORD, GERALD R.** (b. 1913), thirty-eighth President of the United States (1974–1977). Gerald Rudolph Ford—popularly known as "Jerry"—was the first President to reach the White House through the procedure established by the TWENTY-FIFTH AMENDMENT, promulgated in 1967. He fell narrowly short of election to a full term in 1976. Ford's tenure was briefer than that of any but four Presidents, and the shortest among the nine Vice Presidents who have filled out the term of a President. His administration produced no landmark legislative enactments or era-making foreign policy triumphs. Yet he restored the legitimacy of the presidency after the scandal-torn Nixon administration, contributed to gradual reduction of international tensions, and dealt effectively with surging inflation and the worst economic recession since the Great Depression of the 1930s. Probably his greatest achievement, as the title of his memoir, *A Time to Heal*, suggests, was to begin the process of closing wounds to national confidence and cohesion left by more than a decade of domestic political turmoil and draining military involvement in Southeast Asia.

**Youth and Prepresidential Career.** Ford was born in Omaha, Nebraska, on 14 July 1913, son of Leslie King, a wool trader, and Dorothy Gardner King, and was christened Leslie King, Jr. Two years later the marriage broke up and the young mother took her son to live with her parents in Grand Rapids, Michigan. She soon met and married Gerald R. Ford, proprietor of a small paint manufacturing business. Her son's name was changed to Gerald R. Ford, Jr., though the

senior Ford did not legally adopt him until several years later.

Ford retained no conscious memory of his mother's first marriage, which he later learned had been stormy, and was not told that he was adopted until he was "twelve or thirteen." His only encounter with his biological father came when he was seventeen and Leslie King, passing through Grand Rapids on a car trip, stopped at a diner where Ford was employed as a part-time short-order cook and introduced himself—a meeting that Ford later described as deeply traumatic.

Ford seems otherwise to have enjoyed a secure childhood and early youth in a typical middle-class, midwestern, small-city environment. The Fords were Episcopalians, which set them a bit apart from the prevailing Dutch Calvinism of Grand Rapids in the 1920s. The senior Ford met financial difficulties during the depression, but young Jerry won a full scholarship to the University of Michigan. At Michigan, from which he graduated in 1935, he played center on the varsity football team, being named to a national all-star team in his senior year. He considered becoming an economist but doubted that he could make a good living at it and decided to study law instead. He was admitted to Yale Law School and graduated in 1941 in the top quarter of his law school class.

Ford began practicing law in Grand Rapids, where he soon became active in the locally dominant REPUBLICAN PARTY. In the years preceding America's entry into WORLD WAR II, Ford had shared the isolationism then popular in the Midwest and warmly championed by Grand Rapids' most celebrated citizen, Senator Arthur Vandenberg. After the Japanese attack on PEARL HARBOR, Ford joined the navy as an ensign. Wartime service in the Pacific convinced him that "the United States . . . could no longer stick its head in the sand as an ostrich." He returned to Grand Rapids in 1946 an "ardent internationalist."

With quiet encouragement from Vandenberg, who had also been converted during the war to internationalism, Ford entered the 1948 Republican primary for the U.S. House of Representatives and easily defeated the incumbent. He went on to victory in the general election. While running for Congress, Ford courted and married Betty Warren [*see* FORD, BETTY], a local beauty.

In the House, Ford was named to the powerful Appropriations Committee; he specialized in military matters and acquired a thorough knowledge of the federal budget. In 1959, Ford participated in the coup by which Charles Halleck of Indiana ousted Joseph Martin of Massachusetts as House minority leader.

Ford and his associates, however, soon became dissatisfied with Halleck's alliance with conservative southern Democrats, which they believed was blocking development of the Republican Party in the South and undercutting traditional Republican support for progressive civil rights legislation. After the 1964 election, in which Republicans suffered heavy losses in the House accompanying BARRY GOLDWATER's landslide defeat by Lyndon B. Johnson for the presidency, Ford challenged Halleck for the minority leadership. Ford won by a vote of 73 to 67.

As minority leader, Ford pursued courses of fiscal conservatism, moderate progressivism on domestic issues such as civil rights and education, and foreign policy internationalism. After Richard M. Nixon's election as President in 1968, Ford regarded himself as floor leader for the administration as well as leader of the House minority. On a number of domestic issues, such as welfare reform, he loyally supported the administration's relatively progressive proposals rather than following his own more conservative instincts. By forming shifting coalitions with conservative, moderate, and even liberal Democrats he was able to achieve passage of parts of Nixon's domestic program (which sometimes were later blocked in the Senate.)

As internal opposition to American military involvement in Vietnam became increasingly intense during the early 1970s, Ford led a coalition of hawks in the House that repeatedly blocked efforts by the dovish majority in the Senate to establish a fixed date for final American withdrawal from Southeast Asia. In June 1973, however, as support for continuation of the VIETNAM WAR dwindled even among House Republicans, Ford joined the Senate minority leader, Hugh Scott, in pressuring Nixon into agreeing to terminate American combat activities in Southeast Asia by the middle of August.

Ford's highest political ambition had been to become Speaker of the House. When the Republicans failed to make significant gains in the House in 1972 despite Nixon's landslide reelection, he concluded that his party was unlikely to win control of the House in "the foreseeable future." He decided he would run once more for reelection and then retire from the House at the end of 1976.

**Succession to the Presidency.** In October 1973, Vice President SPIRO T. AGNEW, as part of a plea bargain to escape prosecution for bribery charges, resigned. Meanwhile, investigations of the WATERGATE AFFAIR had begun.

Nixon nominated Ford to succeed to the vice presidency—apparently largely because he believed Ford would be easily confirmed. He was right. On 6 December 1973, Ford was sworn in as Vice President.

Ford entered the vice presidency convinced that efforts to impeach Nixon would fade, and that he would carry out his planned retirement from public life at the end of 1976. Events proved otherwise. On 9 August 1974, Nixon, on the verge of impeachment, resigned, and Ford succeeded to the presidency.

The most controversial act of Ford's presidency—which may have cost him election to a full term—occurred only four weeks after his administration began. On Sunday, 8 September, after attending church services, he announced that he had granted a "full, free, and absolute pardon unto Richard Nixon for all offenses" committed while President.

Skeptical commentators and many ordinary citizens have speculated, without evidence, that Ford must have made some kind of deal with Nixon, or with Nixon's chief of staff Alexander Haig, to issue the pardon in return for smooth succession to the presidency. Ford's own explanation in his memoir was that he was convinced that a trial of Nixon would last at least two years, dividing the nation and sapping vital governmental energies, including his own. Along with these practical considerations, an important factor was probably the one he mentioned when the pardon was granted: he believed that Nixon "and his loved ones have suffered enough."

**The Ford Team.** During his first months in the White House, Ford, following advice of a kitchen cabinet of former House colleagues and business lobbyists, moved to replace the tight hierarchical structure through which Nixon had managed the presidency with a looser staff structure, under which several top assistants would have easy access to the President. Donald Rumsfeld, who had been serving as ambassador to NATO, took Haig's place as WHITE HOUSE CHIEF OF STAFF, but many Nixon appointees stayed on in secondary positions on the WHITE HOUSE STAFF—largely because competent replacements could not readily be found. Robert Hartmann, a former journalist who had been Ford's principal assistant in the House, became chief speechwriter and political counselor—not answerable to Rumsfeld.

For the vacant vice presidency Ford nominated NELSON A. ROCKEFELLER, recently retired after three-and-a-half terms as governor of New York, and leader of the Republican Party's progressive wing. Rockefeller, who had three times sought the presidency himself, accepted Ford's nomination on condition that he be given a large role in formulating and directing domestic policy. Both congressional liberal Democrats and conservative Republicans, who had never forgiven Rockefeller for leading the opposition to Goldwater at the 1964 Republican convention, took advantage of the vice presidential confirmation hearings to subject the nominee to prolonged interrogation and to probe details of the Rockefeller family fortune. Rockefeller was not confirmed until near the end of December 1974.

The new Vice President brought with him an extensive staff of governmental specialists, most of whom had formerly served him in New York. But Rumsfeld, who believed Rockefeller had been promised too much authority, had by then solidified his position in the White House, and the Vice President never was able to play the major role in domestic policy he had expected.

Throughout Ford's presidency acrimonious feuds tore the White House staff, delaying decisions and disrupting administrative efficiency. This was partly because of the necessarily quick and fairly haphazard way in which the staff was assembled after Nixon's resignation. But it also reflected Ford's administrative style, formed in Congress, where consensus takes precedence over efficiency. Hartmann, who knew Ford as well as anybody, later said that the President used squabbles among his staff to prevent action on matters on which he had not yet focused his attention.

Most members of Nixon's Cabinet at first remained in place. Some of the stronger individuals among these, such as Secretary of the Treasury William Simon and Secretary of Defense James Schlesinger, had grown used to operating almost autonomously during the final chaotic months of Nixon's presidency. Secretary of State HENRY A. KISSINGER, who also functioned as director of the NATIONAL SECURITY COUNCIL within the White House, was a celebrated international figure. Ford initially allowed many policy decisions by Cabinet secretaries that, in other administrations, would have required White House clearance.

By fall 1975, however, Ford had determined that the time had come to draw more authority back into the White House, and to change the executive branch lineup in a way that would put more of his personal stamp on policy. On 2 November, Ford announced that Rumsfeld would replace Schlesinger, whose public arrogance and clumsy relations with Congress had increasingly nettled the President, as Secretary of Defense, and that George Bush, whom Ford had made American representative in Beijing, would replace William Colby, a Schlesinger ally, as director of the CENTRAL INTELLIGENCE AGENCY. Richard Cheney [see CHENEY, DICK], Rumsfeld's young assistant, became White House chief of staff. Elliot Richardson, who had resigned as Attorney General in 1973 rather than carry out Nixon's order to fire the Watergate special prosecutor, was named Secretary of Commerce. Kiss-

inger, while remaining Secretary of State, was required to yield his role as director of the National Security Council to his assistant, Brent Scowcroft. Finally, and most painfully, Ford informed Rockefeller that conservative opposition dictated that he choose a different running mate for the Republican ticket in 1976.

The Cabinet with which Ford entered the election year was probably stronger than any of Nixon's, and somewhat more weighted toward the moderate-to-progressive side of the Republican Party. Edward Levi, president of the University of Chicago, had become Attorney General to repair the damage suffered by the Department of Justice during the Watergate affair. Simon provided a strong conservative voice at the Treasury. The major service departments were led by vigorous constituency advocates, notably Richardson at Commerce, Carla Hills at Housing and Urban Development, and William Coleman at Transportation.

**Relations with Congress.** The 1974 midterm congressional elections, held under the shadow of Watergate, had produced large Democratic gains. The Democratic majority in the House rose to just over the two-thirds needed to pass bills over the President's veto. The Democratic majority in the Senate, though not quite so overwhelming, was more than enough to dominate legislative business.

Ford's long experience in Congress and his friendly personal relationships with Democratic leaders in both houses gave him tactical advantages that Nixon had lacked. The bitter antagonism that had developed between Nixon and the Democratic majorities in Congress never took hold under Ford. But fundamental differences over economic policy produced a series of pitched legislative battles.

Ford vetoed more bills relative to time in office, an average of 26.4 a year, than all but three Presidents: Grover Cleveland, Franklin D. Roosevelt, and Harry S. Truman. Most of the vetoes by Cleveland, Roosevelt, and Truman, however, had been of private bills, passed at requests by members of Congress to deal with particular problems of individual constituents. All but five of Ford's sixty-six vetoes were of bills dealing with substantive policy issues.

Many of Ford's vetoes were delivered against major appropriations bills, passed by the Democratic Congress to counter the deep recession of 1974–1976. Such budget-breaking expenditures, the President argued, would set off a new round of inflation. Other vetoes were used to protect the EXECUTIVE POWERS of the President, under attack after Watergate, and to uphold the administration's positions in foreign policy and energy policy. Despite the huge Democratic majorities in Congress, Ford, by maintaining relative unity among the Republican minority and shrewd bargaining with approachable Democrats, was able to block attempted overrides of all but twelve of his vetoes.

**Domestic Policy.** The Ford administration's domestic policy agenda, though including a number of positive initiatives, was devoted mainly to combating the economic scourges of inflation and recession and to dealing with the energy crisis that had begun with the Arab oil embargo of 1973.

When Ford entered the presidency, consumer prices were rising at an annual rate of more than 12 percent—the first time since the 1940s the national economy had reached the frightening level of double-digit inflation. Nixon's experiment with wage and price controls had not only failed but also had helped build inflationary pressures that were now exploding in the economy. On 8 October 1974, Ford proposed in a speech before Congress that to reduce inflation there be a one-year 5 percent surcharge on corporate and personal income taxes and a deep cut in federal spending. (The message was best remembered for the President's much derided suggestion that citizens join the fight against inflation by wearing WIN—Whip Inflation Now—buttons.)

Before Congress could give serious consideration to Ford's program it had become clear that the more pressing threat to the economy was the recession that had begun early in 1974 and suddenly accelerated in the fall. Gross national product fell 7.5 percent in constant dollars during the fourth quarter and by December unemployment had risen to 7.2 percent.

In his 1975 state of the union message Ford reported to Congress: "The state of the union is not good." To overcome the growing recession the President proposed, in place of the tax surcharge he had called for a few months earlier, a $16 billion tax cut. To offset the inflationary effects of the tax cut, Ford recommended a moratorium on new federal programs and a ceiling on domestic spending.

The Democratic majority in Congress responded, as unemployment rose to a peak of 8.9 percent in May, by pushing through appropriations far in excess of those called for in the administration's budget and passing a tax cut almost 50 percent greater than that proposed by Ford. Using the veto weapon, Ford turned back many of the spending increases and held out for a tax bill closer to his own recommendation.

Ford coordinated the administration's approach to economic matters through an Economic Policy Board he set up in the White House under the direction of William Seidman, an old friend from Grand Rapids whom he had brought to Washington while he was Vice President. The Economic Policy Board was chaired by Treasury Secretary Simon, and included the chairman of the Council of Economic Advisers, Alan Greenspan, the director of the OFFICE OF MANAGEMENT AND BUDGET, James Lynn, and the heads of several other relevant departments and agencies. Simon emphatically reenforced Ford's conservative instincts on economic policy. Lynn and his deputy, Paul O'Neill, carried on much of the day-to-day trench warfare against growth in federal spending. Greenspan provided intellectual analysis and rationalization that played a major role in guiding administration policy.

The growth of federal ENTITLEMENT programs, giving individuals and states and localities legal rights to income, Greenspan argued, was driving up federal expenditures with dire consequences for the nation's economic future. Fighting recession through the familiar means of massively increasing federal spending, he maintained, would worsen this potentially disastrous trend. Greenspan rejected the conventional wisdom that there was a trade-off between inflation and recession. Inflationary government spending, he claimed, while it might bring short-term relief, would plant the seeds for an even worse bout of recession within a few years.

In December 1975, as Congress prepared to adjourn for the year, Ford and the Democratic leadership agreed to a compromise through which the President accepted the Democrats' proposed tax cut in return for a promise to restrain federal spending. When Congress returned in 1976, with the economy little improved, the barrage of budget-breaking appropriations was resumed with little regard for the December agreement. But Ford at least had increased moral force with which to support his vetoes.

The recession that began in 1974 was made even more onerous for consumers by the huge increase in gas and oil prices that had followed the 1973 Arab oil embargo (imposed as retaliation for American support of Israel during the Yom Kippur War.) Though the embargo had been lifted in March 1974, the international price of oil, set by the Organization of Petroleum Exporting Countries (OPEC), remained ten times what it had been only five years before.

The power of OPEC, almost everyone agreed, made it essential that the United States become "energy independent," or at least greatly reduce its dependence on foreign oil. Ford in his 1975 state of the union message proposed to approach this goal by decontrolling the price of domestically produced oil and increasing fees on imported petroleum, coupled with a windfall profits tax on oil companies. The result, Ford conceded, would be even higher gas and oil prices, but domestic production would be stimulated.

The Democratic leadership in Congress rejected Ford's plan, arguing that it would hurt consumers while further enriching big oil companies, and proposed in its place a package of import quotas and tax incentives for production of more fuel efficient automobiles. Arguing between the two sides continued through 1975, with Democratic members of Congress from the oil-producing states generally supporting the administration.

Vice President Rockefeller entered the fray with a plan, prepared by his staff of economists and lawyers, to create a $100 billion government corporation, which he called the Energy Independence Authority (EIA), to provide loans and guarantees to private companies developing new domestic energy sources. EIA was hotly opposed within the administration by Simon, Greenspan, and Lynn, and more quietly by Rumsfeld, on grounds that it would be enormously costly and violated principles of free-market economics. Ford nevertheless submitted the plan to Congress—but did almost nothing to promote its enactment.

In December 1975, Ford agreed to sign legislation passed by the Democratic majority in Congress that temporarily rolled back prices of domestically produced oil. In return Congress gave the President authority to carry out gradual decontrol of prices of all petroleum products over a forty-month period. Simon, privately, and many conservatives outside the administration, publicly, were harshly critical of Ford, claiming he had given in because he feared the political effects of rising fuel oil prices in New Hampshire at the time of the PRESIDENTIAL PRIMARY in February 1976. By the end of 1976, however, Ford had about half-completed the process of decontrolling petroleum prices. On the day before he left office in January 1977, he ordered elimination of most remaining controls—an action quickly rescinded by the incoming Carter administration.

Beside abolishing many controls on petroleum prices, Ford proposed economic DEREGULATION of the railroad, aviation, and trucking industries, and created a regulatory reform task force to identify other areas in which deregulation would be economically and socially desirable. Only railroad deregulation had been achieved by the time Ford left office, but the groundwork had been laid for other regulatory reforms later carried out under Carter.

Ford proposed a number of domestic service initiatives, including catastrophic health insurance for persons over sixty-five, federal support for economic renewal of depressed zones in inner cities, and consolidation of so-called categorical grants to states and localities into a few broad, largely unrestricted "revenue sharing" grants for services such as health care and education. Democrats in Congress, expecting election of a Democratic President in 1976, gave most of these scant attention.

Ford's approach to domestic policy issues was basically conservative, in the sense of emphasizing freedom of the private economy and assigning primary responsibility for performance of most domestic government services to the states and localities. But he saw an important role for the federal government in responding to public needs that were not being fully met by the private sector or the states and localities. At the start of the 1976 general election campaign he announced that in a full term he would devote more attention to improving federal participation in dealing with "quality of life" concerns such as housing, education, health care, protection against crime, and recreation.

**Foreign Policy.** During the early months of his presidency, Ford gave almost free rein to Secretary of State Kissinger in directing foreign policy. Perceptions among both the American public and foreign leaders of Kissinger's mastery in conducting international relations, and Ford's awareness of his own limited experience in the field, made it prudent for the President to appear for a time to defer to his Secretary of State.

To the end of Ford's term Kissinger's role in formulating and carrying out foreign policy remained central. But as the President's confidence grew he began asserting himself more on international affairs. On his numerous trips abroad he developed warm relationships with leaders of allied powers, particularly James Callaghan in Britain, Helmut Schmidt in West Germany, and Valéry Giscard d'Estaing in France, and achieved footings of wary mutual respect with the communist rulers of the Soviet Union and the People's Republic of China. After the Cabinet shakeup in the fall of 1975, Rumsfeld as Secretary of Defense played an important part in shaping foreign policy. Scowcroft as director of the National Security Council proved not to be Kissinger's pawn, as many had expected, and exerted considerable behind-the-scenes influence. Simon at the Treasury was influential in forming international economic policy.

During the winter of 1975, communist armies swept over South Vietnam and Cambodia, taking advantage of the withdrawal of most American support forces after 1973. Ford asked for a fresh infusion of American aid but the Democratic majority in Congress refused. On 29 April 1975, Ford ordered evacuation of the last American troops from Saigon and the South Vietnamese government capitulated to the communists. "This action," the President said, "closes a chapter in the American experience."

Ford continued Nixon's policies of maintaining close ties within the Western alliance and moving toward more harmonious relations with the Soviet Union and the People's Republic of China. He set out, however, to reverse the decline in military spending that had taken place under Nixon. As a result of cuts in American defense expenditures, he observed, the international military balance was shifting toward the Soviet Union.

During 1975 and early 1976 Kissinger negotiated with the Soviets for a more comprehensive treaty limiting production and deployment of NUCLEAR WEAPONS, SALT (STRATEGIC ARMS LIMITATION TALKS) II. Rumsfeld, speaking for the Pentagon military establishment, insisted on better terms for the United States than Kissinger believed were obtainable. Ford, largely because of concern that conservative criticism of the administration's alleged softness toward the Soviet Union was building support for the rival presidential candidacy of Ronald Reagan, ultimately sided with Rumsfeld and the Pentagon. SALT II was put off to another day.

In November 1974, Ford met in Vladivostok with Soviet leaders, and in December 1975, traveled to China where he took the measure of the communist leadership succeeding the aged Mao Tse-tung. In August 1975, Ford joined Soviet Communist Party boss, General Secretary Leonid Brezhnev, and leaders of other European nations in signing the Helsinki accords, ratifying the boundaries of European countries established at the end of WORLD WAR II and vaguely committing signators to facilitate the free international movement of people and ideas—a charter much criticized by conservatives, who claimed that Ford and Kissinger had in effect accepted Soviet domination of Eastern Europe.

The administration, largely at the instigation of Kissinger, gave increased attention to developing nations. In April 1976, Kissinger, who formerly had assumed the indefinite continuation of white-minority rule in southern Africa, announced in Zambia that the United States would work to install black-majority governments in Rhodesia (later Zimbabwe) and by implication South Africa. The following month the Secretary of State at a United Nations conference in Kenya called for creation of a world resources bank. In September 1976, Rhodesian Prime Minister Ian Smith accepted Kissinger's proposal for transition to a black-majority government.

Within the UNITED NATIONS the United States fought, unsuccessfully, in November 1975, against a resolution sponsored by developing and communist-bloc countries equating Zionism with racism. In the Middle East the United States in 1975 served as midwife to an interim agreement between Israel and Egypt, and in 1976 sought, with little success, to end the civil war in Lebanon.

**The 1976 Election.** Soon after he became President, Ford decided that he would be a candidate for election to a full term in 1976. He expected to have little trouble securing the Republican nomination and was therefore startled by Ronald Reagan's success in gathering support among conservative Republicans in 1975 for an insurgent candidacy. From December 1975, when a national poll showed Reagan leading Ford among Republican voters, until the Republican national convention in August 1976, administration policy was deeply affected by eagerness to appease the Republican right. Drawing on support from party regulars and moderates and from some conservatives like BARRY GOLDWATER who resisted rejecting an incumbent President, Ford eked out a narrow victory over Reagan at the convention. He chose as his vice presidential candidate Senator Robert Dole of Kansas, who had backing among conservatives and was strong in the midwestern farm belt where Ford feared defections like those that helped defeat THOMAS E. DEWEY in 1948 (the year of Ford's first election to the House).

Association of the Watergate scandal with the Republican Party and the continued weakness of the economy in early 1976 seemed to give the Democrats a clear advantage at winning the presidency. Former Governor Jimmy Carter of Georgia capitalized on the desire among many voters to find a leader in no way connected with the scandals, assassinations, and debates over the Vietnam War that had plagued national politics during the prior ten years. Carter won the nomination at the Democratic national convention in July. At the end of the convention a national poll found Carter leading Ford by 33 percentage points.

Ford's general election campaign began with his presiding over the bicentennial celebration on 4 July 1976. Ford and his campaign manager, JAMES A. BAKER III, thereafter ran a skillful campaign designed to associate the President with national pride and reviving public confidence in the nation's future. Unemployment began to fall. Ford's insistence on treating inflation as the number one enemy seemed to be working.

During the early fall Ford steadily gained on Carter. The economic recovery stalled in September but growing doubts among the electorate over Carter's qualifications to be President continued to shift support to Ford. In the first televised debate between the candidates in Philadelphia on 23 September, Ford came out clearly ahead in public perceptions. But in the second debate in San Francisco on 6 October on foreign policy, which was thought to be Carter's area of greatest vulnerability, Ford stumbled into asserting that there was "no Soviet domination of eastern Europe" (partly through confused language but probably also because of lingering resentment over the charge that he had sold out Eastern Europe at Helsinki). This blunder, richly highlighted by the media, revived concern among many voters that Ford might not quite be up to the presidency. The third debate in Williamsburg on 22 October ended inconclusively.

On election day, 2 November, Carter won 50.1 percent of the popular vote to 48 percent for Ford, producing a margin for Carter in the ELECTORAL COLLEGE of 297 to 240 (one elector voted for Reagan). A shift of 9,000 votes in Ohio and Hawaii would have kept Ford in the White House (though still well behind in the popular vote.) Though disappointed at the result, Ford took satisfaction that he had almost closed the gap in what had seemed an impossible race, while refusing to increase government spending for an economic quick fix in the election year. By the time he left office in January 1977, the economic recovery was back on track and annual inflation had fallen below five percent.

After leaving the presidency Ford busied himself in a number of political, educational, and sporting activities. In 1980 he briefly considered joining the Republican ticket as Reagan's running mate before negotiations on this improbable match collapsed on the night of Reagan's nomination.

Ford's administration helped lay the foundation for the swing to more conservative governmental policies carried out under Ronald Reagan and George Bush in the 1980s. His most important contribution to political life, however, was his association of honor and decency with the presidency at a time when public confidence in all national institutions was severely strained.

### BIBLIOGRAPHY

Ford, Gerald R. *A Time to Heal: The Autobiography of Gerald R. Ford.* 1979.

Hartmann, Robert T. *Palace Politics: An Insider's Account of the Ford Years.* 1980.

Hyland, William. *Mortal Rivals: Superpower Relations from Nixon to Reagan.* 1987.

Nessen, Ron. *It Sure Looks Different from the Inside.* 1978.

Osborne, John. *White House Watch: The Ford Years.* 1978.

Porter, Roger B. *Presidential Decision Making: The Economic Policy Board.* 1980.

*Public Papers of the Presidents of the United States: Gerald R. Ford.* 6 vols. 1974–1977.

Reichley, A. James. *Conservatives in an Age of Change: The Nixon and Ford Administrations.* 1981.

Simon, William E. *A Time for Truth.* 1978.

Thompson, Kenneth W., ed. *The Ford Presidency: Twenty-Two Intimate Perspectives of Gerald R. Ford.* 1988.

A. JAMES REICHLEY

**FORDNEY-McCUMBER TARIFF ACT** (1922). One of the principal actions of the Harding administration, the Fordney-McCumber Tariff Act of 1922 proved a jumble of schedules, higher than the Wilson administration's UNDERWOOD TARIFF ACT of 1913, with an average level of 38.5 percent, but lower than the WILSON-GORMAN TARIFF ACT of 1894 at 41 percent, the DINGLEY TARIFF ACT of 1897 at 46 percent, and the PAYNE-ALDRICH TARIFF ACT of 1909 at 40.7 percent. Its principal difference lay in protection of agricultural products and in President Warren G. Harding's insistence upon Section 315, empowering the President to raise or lower rates up to 50 percent within the limits of equalizing foreign and domestic costs of production.

From the beginning the Harding administration desired protection. Wilson on the day before he left office, 3 March 1921, vetoed an emergency tariff bill. Harding revived it; after repassage he signed it in May 1921. Next came the more permanent enactment, distinguished during its passage by name-calling and near fisticuffs. Named after Rep. Joseph W. Fordney (R-Mich.), and Sen. Porter J. McCumber (R-N. Dak.), the bill passed the House, 210 to 90, the Senate 43 to 28, and Harding signed it 21 September 1922.

The new tariff brought little rejoicing. Farmers had championed it because they attributed the drastic drop in prices in 1920 to foreign competition. They gradually realized it was because of collapse of an inflationary spiral after WORLD WAR I, together with overproduction when Europe's farmers returned to production. Failure of European nations to pay their so-called war debts during the 1920s could be attributed to the higher tariff. The return to protectionism displayed the failure of the Harding administration and its successors to understand the country's new creditor status. Nor did the flexibility provision bring flexibility, for Harding told the Federal Tariff Commission "not to throw a monkey-wrench into the machinery," that is, essentially to let congressional schedules alone. His successor, Coolidge, agreed, lowering rates on three items and raising them on seven.

BIBLIOGRAPHY

Murray, Robert K. *The Harding Era: Warren G. Harding and His Administration.* 1969.

ROBERT H. FERRELL

## FOREIGN AFFAIRS: AN OVERVIEW.

The term *foreign affairs* is not in the United States Constitution. The Constitution does not assign authority to "conduct foreign relations" or to "make foreign policy," and the powers allocated to the different branches of government do not coincide neatly with such categories of responsibility. To understand the constitutional dispositions for what we call foreign affairs it is necessary to examine the Constitution—its blueprint, design, and history.

**The President's Foreign Affairs Powers.** "The transaction of business with foreign nations is Executive altogether," Thomas Jefferson wrote. ALEXANDER HAMILTON read the constitutional provision that "the executive Power shall be vested in a President" as a general grant of all executive power, understood to include the control of foreign relations (subject only to conditions and limitations expressed or implied). The Supreme Court of the United States, building on a statement by JOHN MARSHALL, referred in UNITED STATES V. CURTISS-WRIGHT EXPORT CORP. (1936) to "the very delicate, plenary and exclusive power of the President as the sole organ of the federal government in the field of international relations."

Presidents have cited those and other statements to support a "plenary and exclusive" power over U.S. foreign affairs. If those assertions were an accurate description of the President's constitutional authority, this essay could be a brief sentence. Authoritative pronouncements, however—and even presidential claims—are not as extravagant as those terms may suggest. John Marshall (then still a member of Congress) spoke of the President as the "sole organ of the Nation in its external relations, and its sole representative with foreign nations"—an exclusive organ of communication and representation, not a sole repository of power to determine the foreign policy of the United States. For Hamilton, the Constitution gave the President authority that today might be described as power to conduct foreign relations and execute foreign policy; even for Hamilton the Constitution did not vest in the President exclusive authority to determine foreign policy. The Supreme Court's later dictum confirmed only what Marshall had said, that the

President was "sole organ"; it did not suggest that the President had "plenary and exclusive power" to make all the decisions and to take all the actions that add up to the foreign policy of the United States.

Presidential claims, too—even at their most extravagant—have respected limitations on presidential power expressed in the Constitution (for example, the need for the Senate to consent to treaties and appointments); some limitations implicit in grants of authority to other branches (such as the power to declare war [*see* WAR, DECLARATION OF] given to Congress); other limitations that may be implied in the structure of the Constitution and of the system of government it created.

After two hundred years, however, the President dominates American foreign affairs—far beyond what the Constitution expresses or plausibly implies, far beyond what the Framers contemplated or might have foreseen. Two hundred years of national history have given the presidency a virtually exclusive role in the conduct of foreign relations and a paramount role in the making of foreign policy. Congress honors the President's primacy; the courts defer to it. But the President's part can be understood only in relation to that of Congress, which retains "the power of the purse," its essential legislative role in foreign as in domestic affairs, and other designated responsibilities in foreign affairs, notably the power to decide for war or peace.

**The Presidency in Constitutional Text.** In constitutional principle, the exercise of political power has to be justified in the constitutional text or by implication. The President's express powers in foreign affairs are few and appear to be meager. According to Article II, Section 2, he has power to make treaties, but only with the ADVICE AND CONSENT of the Senate, and provided two-thirds of the Senators present concur. He can appoint ambassadors, but only with the advice and consent of the Senate. He receives foreign ambassadors, but that seems to be a constitutional "assignment" rather than an important source of power.

In time, Presidents began to make much of the clause declaring that "the President shall be COMMANDER IN CHIEF of the Army and Navy of the United States." As written, and as originally conceived, that clause appears to be a designation of function rather than an independent grant of important power. Learning the lessons of the American Revolution, the Framers sought to create a single command (to avoid command by Congress or by congressional committee) and they sought to assure civilian control; but they did not consider the office of Commander in Chief to be a repository of any independent political authority. If

Congress maintained an army and navy, the President would be their commander; if Congress declared war, or if the United States were attacked, the President would command the forces provided by Congress to prosecute the war or defend the United States. Nothing in the text or in the history of its promulgation suggests that the Commander in Chief was to have authority to deploy the armed forces for political purposes determined by him.

On the face of the Constitution, that is the sum of presidential power. Alexander Hamilton's argument that the clause providing "the Executive Power shall be vested" in the President was an explicit grant of power to conduct and control foreign relations, is less than obvious, was sharply rejected by James Madison, and has not been authoritatively accepted. (Justice Robert H. Jackson in YOUNGSTOWN SHEET & TUBE CO. V. SAWYER [1952] failed to see in that clause "a grant in bulk" of all executive power, but only "an allocation to the Presidential office of the generic powers" specified later in that article of the Constitution.)

Traditional modes of constitutional interpretation might find in the spare allocations of the text more than appears. The power to appoint ambassadors and authority to receive ambassadors [see AMBASSADORS, RECEIVING AND APPOINTING] can plausibly be read to imply authority to recognize (or not to recognize) governments, to maintain (or not to maintain) relations with a particular country. But constitutional interpretation is not an exact science. Some authority that might be claimed by the President as implied in one of his powers might be claimed by Congress by implication from one of its enumerated powers. For example, the power to terminate a treaty may be implied in the President's power to make treaties, but Congress may claim it as within its authority to regulate commerce with foreign nations, or to decide for war or peace. And much of what has been claimed for the President seems to be beyond the reach of plausible constitutional interpretation.

In *Curtiss-Wright,* Justice George Sutherland offered a bold essay with a bold thesis: in foreign affairs the powers of the United States derive not from the Constitution but from this country's international sovereignty, and the U.S. government therefore has many powers not enumerated in the Constitution. The Court did not proceed to indicate how that extra-constitutional authority of the United States is distributed between Congress and President.

**Intent and Grand Design.** Beyond text and its implications, Presidents have sometimes resorted to larger principles of constitutional construction. A favored source of constitutional meaning is the intent of

the Framers [*see* FOREIGN AFFAIRS: ORIGINAL INTENT]. As regards presidential power in foreign affairs, however, there has been little resort to what the Framers intended, perhaps because what they intended is not easy to determine, perhaps because what they intended is not the large presidential power that proponents of presidential power have favored.

It is far from clear where authority in foreign affairs lies in the grand design of the Constitution. The overall constitutional division between recommending legislation and enacting it, between passing laws and executing them, between appropriating money and spending it, was designed to apply in foreign as in domestic affairs. In foreign affairs, however, the Constitution expressly allocates important powers that do not conform neatly to those divisions. For a major and blatant example, Congress was given the power to decide for war or peace, not a legislative act as commonly understood, in 1787 or now. On the other hand, the President was given the power to make treaties, which frequently have a legislative dimension and are, according to Article VI, the law of the land. Moreover, neither the specific grants of the Constitution nor its grand design clearly allocate authority of continuing importance and controversy (e.g., the power to introduce the armed forces into hostilities that are not war, or to engage in covert intelligence activities [*see* COVERT OPERATIONS].

The debate between Pacificus (Hamilton) and Helvidius (Madison) was essentially a sharp disagreement as to the grand design of the Constitution which both had helped shape (and for the ratification of which both had labored in THE FEDERALIST). Hamilton saw the clause vesting the EXECUTIVE POWER in the President as an explicit grant to him of the control of foreign relations except in so far as the Constitution imposed conditions on this power (such as the requirement of Senate consent to treaties or to the appointment of ambassadors), or insofar as the Constitution expressly allocated authority to Congress, as in the power to regulate foreign commerce or to declare war. For Madison, on the other hand, Congress had the principal authority, legislative as well as other policy-making authority, in foreign as in domestic affairs. The President had only the authority expressly bestowed upon him, notably the power to make treaties and to appoint ambassadors, both subject to the advice and consent of the Senate. [*See* HELVIDIUS-PACIFICUS DEBATES.]

Which of these was the grand design of the Framers can be deduced only from the text they produced and the record of their deliberations and other writings, but the Framers were not wholly explicit (or candid), were not always in agreement, and were at times uncertain of their own intentions. They were committed to SEPARATION OF POWERS as a principle of good government and to CHECKS AND BALANCES to prevent the concentration of power, but the political thought in which the Framers were educated provided no conclusive guidance as to the appropriate roles of executive and legislature in foreign affairs; nor did the Framers have a firm idea as to the distribution they desired in the new kind of government they were creating. They began with a legislature, growing out of the Continental Congress, and apparently saw Congress as primary: there is no indication they intended to deny to Congress any legislative or other policy-making authority, other than the TREATY-MAKING POWER. The presidency was a new office, and the Framers were divided and uncertain about it. They recognized the need for an executive and wanted one capable of initiative and planning. But they also feared autarchy and tyranny.

By the text they wrote, surely, the authors of the Constitution evinced no intent to create a powerful presidency. They did not make the President a republican, nonhereditary facsimile of the king of England. Above all, the President was not to have the king's power to go to war. The President was entrusted with the royal power to make treaties, but only subject to the advice and consent of the Senate, indeed of an extraordinary majority—two-thirds—of the Senators present.

What emerged from the CONSTITUTIONAL CONVENTION was in some respects compromise, in some perhaps purposeful ambiguity. In substantial measure, the Framers seemed content to allow the office to be shaped by events, and by George Washington, the man it was generally assumed would be the first incumbent.

**The Growth of Presidential Power.** On balance, the language of the Constitution, the history of its framing, and the intent of the Framers, appear to support Madison's conception of its grand design, but the experience of the nation has tilted toward Hamilton's vision. From the beginning, the nature of the presidential office and the character of foreign relations and of diplomacy contributed to the growth of presidential authority. Unlike Congress, the President is always in session. Unlike Congress, he can act informally, expeditiously, secretly. Early on it was established that the President represented the United States and was the "sole organ" for official communication between the United States and other countries. The President appointed ambassadors and they were his ambassadors, his organs for diplomatic representation and communication, instructed by him and reporting to him. His power to appoint and his authority to receive ambassadors soon translated into power to recognize (or not to recognize) governments, to main-

tain (or not to maintain) diplomatic relations with them. Congress, for its part, early accepted the President's role as sole organ, recognizing his diplomatic expertise as well as his need for secrecy, which nurtured a sense of congressional inadequacy. Presidents did not attempt to exercise legislative power expressly committed to Congress, or to spend money not authorized and appropriated by Congress, but they readily asserted authority not expressly conferred upon them by the Constitution, and Congress acquiesced. From the beginning of the Republic, Congress began to delegate to the President much of its own undoubted authority. What earlier Presidents did with congressional acquiescence, or even by congressional delegation, later Presidents claimed to be within their own constitutional power.

Encouraged by the growth of Presidential power in foreign affairs generally, Presidents began to place the forces Congress had put under their command at the service of their foreign policy: in several hundred instances Presidents deployed U.S. forces for their own foreign policy purposes, short of war. And Congress generally acquiesced. Later, a growing practice of informal consultations between the President and congressional leaders discouraged congressional objections and served to confirm presidential authority to act without formal congressional participation. On occasion, Congress quickly ratified what the President had already done, as in 1950 when Truman sent U.S. forces to fight in the KOREAN WAR and Congress promptly adopted supportive resolutions and appropriations to finance the war. Sometimes Congress delegated its own war powers to the President in terms so broad that he could later claim to have acted under Congress's authority as well as his own, as in the GULF OF TONKIN RESOLUTION of 1964 that gave constitutional legitimacy to the VIETNAM WAR.

Presidential authority in foreign affairs has grown steadily during more than two hundred years. Understandably, perhaps, the President's role grew with the power of the United States. Early in the nineteenth century the international relations of the United States were modest and Presidents were still cautious politically as well as constitutionally. Thomas Jefferson doubted his own authority to do more than deploy the navy for defensive measures to safeguard U.S. shipping against predations by the Barbary Pirates [see BARBARY WAR]. President James Monroe pronounced his famous MONROE DOCTRINE in 1823 but did not press its implications. James Polk, it was later charged, manipulated relations with Mexico and maneuvered Congress to declare war, but he did not fight the MEXICAN WAR until after Congress had declared it.

Opportunities for asserting extraordinary presidential authority became more frequent later in the nineteenth century and early in the twentieth century. With manifest destiny, President Theodore Roosevelt claimed power as "surrogate" of the people to do whatever was not explicitly forbidden to him by the Constitution or by the laws: he dispatched troops, annexed territory, and made international agreements on his own authority [see STEWARDSHIP THEORY]. President Woodrow Wilson armed merchant vessels against German submarine warfare, even in the face of congressional neutrality laws; later he made an armnistice agreement effectively terminating WORLD WAR I. President Franklin D. Roosevelt, without seeking Senate consent, concluded an agreement with Maksim Litvinov, the foreign minister of the Soviet Union, to settle claims of U.S. nationals (as a condition of recognizing the government of the U.S.S.R.) [see UNITED STATES V. BELMONT; UNITED STATES V. PINK]. Later Roosevelt led efforts to help Great Britain resist Adolph Hitler's aggression, by an executive agreement to exchange U.S. DESTROYERS FOR BASES on British territory. During WORLD WAR II, Roosevelt, and later President Harry S. Truman, charted the postwar peace. Truman approved the Nuremberg Charter, planned the UNITED NATIONS, and promoted the MARSHALL PLAN; he fought the Korean War and pursued a Korean armistice, which President Dwight D. Eisenhower later concluded. President John F. Kennedy blockaded Cuba in the CUBAN MISSILE CRISIS, President Lyndon B. Johnson sent marines to the DOMINICAN REPUBLIC. He and President Richard M. Nixon prosecuted the Vietnam War despite growing opposition in Congress. President Jimmy Carter sent marines to Iran in an attempt to extricate American hostages during the IRANIAN HOSTAGE CRISIS [see DESERT ONE]. President Ronald Reagan concluded an agreement to resolve the crisis, sent Marines to Lebanon, invaded GRENADA, mined Nicaraguan waters, and bombed targets in Libya. President George Bush invaded PANAMA and claimed powers to pursue the GULF WAR against Iraq without congressional authorization, although before initiating military force against Iraq, he sought and obtained congressional authorization.

**Treaties and Executive Agreements.** The Constitution expressly confers upon the President the power to make treaties. The President's treaty power is subject to general constitutional restraints, such as the Bill of Rights, but the scope and content of treaties are not otherwise subject to important limitations. He can make treaties "by and with the Advice and Consent of the Senate . . . provided two thirds of the Senators present concur." Originally the Senate's "advice" func-

tion atrophied, and since then formal advice has not been asked and has been rarely given; though the executive branch sometimes consults individual Senators, advice and consent has been essentially reduced to consent. The Senate can refuse consent, or consent on conditions, commonly on conditions of change in or reservations to the treaty. Even after Senate consent, the President may decide not to make the treaty, for example, if he finds conditions imposed by the Senate unacceptable. If the President makes the treaty he is bound by its provisions as the Senate understood them and by any conditions the Senate imposed. A treaty is law of the land and the President "shall take care" that is be faithfully executed. But he can terminate a treaty in accordance with its terms, or denounce a treaty even if by doing so he puts the United States in violation of its international obligations [see TREATY TERMINATION].

Practice has developed an alternative method of concluding international agreements by "Congressional executive agreement," made by the President with the approval of both houses of Congress. Congressional executive agreements have no explicit constitutional underpinnings but they are not controversial and their use in some areas (notably international trade) is established.

From the beginning, Presidents have claimed also power to make some sole EXECUTIVE AGREEMENTS, international agreements on their own authority. The Supreme Court has confirmed the President's authority to make agreements incidental to recognition of a foreign government (as in the agreement between President Roosevelt and Soviet Foreign Minister Maksim Litvinov), and agreements settling international claims (such as that by President Reagan resolving the Iran hostage crisis). In general, however, there is no agreed principle to distinguish agreements that the President can make on his own authority from those requiring the consent of the Senate (or the approval of Congress).

Periodically, the Senate has sought to curtail the President's authority to make sole executive agreements. In 1969, the Senate adopted the nonbinding NATIONAL COMMITMENTS RESOLUTION declaring that the President had no authority to make a national commitment involving "the use of the armed forces of the United States on foreign territory, or a promise to assist a foreign country . . . by the use of the armed forces or financial resources of the United States" without the consent of the Senate to a treaty or the approval of Congress. Periodically, Congress has threatened to limit executive agreements by statute and even by constitutional amendment. In the end, however, Congress enacted only the CASE ACT (1972) requiring the executive branch to transmit to Congress copies of every executive agreement concluded, where necessary under injunction of secrecy. It is difficult to determine whether the obligation to report to Congress has discouraged Presidents from making executive agreements, which the Senate might insist require its consent.

Presidents have not admitted limitations on their power to make executive agreements but they are not unaware that agreements that purport to make law in the United States are subject to challenge in the courts. An agreement that requires implementation by act of Congress or by appropriation of funds depends on the willingness of Congress to accept the authority of the President to conclude that agreement. A President would be rash to conclude an agreement obligating the United States if Congress might decide that it was beyond his authority to make such a promise; but a bold President might make the commitment hoping to force Congress's hand.

**President and Congress.** The President's role in foreign affairs cannot be understood in isolation from that of Congress. In some respects their roles are mutually exclusive, in some they may overlap, in several respects each depends on the other. Principles of separation of powers, and checks and balances pertain in foreign as well as in domestic affairs.

*Exclusive powers.* In principle, the powers vested by the Constitution in the Congress and the President respectively were to be exclusive of each other: Congress alone had legislative power, the President alone had executive power. Congress alone exercises the powers conferred upon it, principally in Article I of the Constitution, the President alone exercises the powers vested in him in Article II. In foreign as in domestic affairs the President cannot make law or take action of legislative character. For example, in 1952 the Supreme Court ruled in *Youngstown Co. v. Sawyer* that President Truman could not direct the U.S. Army to seize private steel mills in order to settle a labor dispute, though the President insisted that steel production was essential to the prosecution of the Korean War. On another occasion, a lower court declared the President lacked authority to impose a tariff on imports without congressional authorization, because the power to regulate commerce with foreign nations is vested in Congress exclusively. The President cannot coin money, raise an army, or maintain a navy. He cannot appropriate funds or expend money even for foreign affairs purposes except pursuant to authorization and appropriation by act of Congress (Article I, Section 9.). In turn, the President alone speaks for and

represents the United States, appoints and receives ambassadors, recognizes governments, conducts diplomatic relations, negotiates with foreign governments, makes, receives, and resolves claims, makes treaties, and commands the armed forces. [*See* DIPLOMAT IN CHIEF.]

In the 1980s and 1990s, there was some confusion as to the authority of the President to take the United States to war. The constitutional allocation to Congress of the power to declare war has been understood to give Congress the power to decide whether the United States shall go to war or remain at peace. Like other express powers of Congress, the authority to decide for war or peace lies with Congress alone. The Framers recognized that if the country were attacked the United States would be at war without any decision by Congress and the President should have authority to defend the United States; if congressional authorization were deemed necessary it could be assumed.

No President has claimed authority to go to war on his own authority. Arguments that the WAR POWER of Congress was not exclusive, that the President had a concurrent, independent power to go to war have not been pressed and have not been taken seriously. In 1950, when President Truman sent armed forces to defend the Republic of Korea, he claimed authority pursuant to the United Nations Charter, which was signed and ratified by the President with the advice and consent of the Senate as a treaty of the United States. In 1991, President Bush claimed that resolutions of the U.N. Security Council authorizing the United States to go to war to liberate Kuwait gave the President constitutional authority to do so without congressional authorization, because he had authority to carry out U.S. treaty obligations under the U.N. Charter. The prevailing view is, however, that Truman and Bush did not have authority to go to war, that the U.N. Charter, though a treaty of the United States, did not confer such authority, and that a Security Council Resolution that was permissive only and did not create a legal obligation upon the United States to go to war could not provide Constitutional authority [*see* UNITED NATIONS PARTICIPATION ACT].

The exclusive power of Congress to declare and make war, and the authority Presidents have claimed to deploy armed forces for foreign-policy purposes short of war, require difficult distinctions and have raised sharp issues as to the power of Congress to regulate Presidential deployments.

*Concurrent authority of President and Congress.* In general, the respective powers of President and Congress are exclusive, but Justice Robert H. Jackson in 1952 had suggested that "there is a zone of twilight in which [the President] and Congress may have concurrent authority—or in which its distribution is uncertain." Foreign affairs is the principal occupant of that twilight zone.

At the end of the twentieth century constitutional jurisprudence accepts the President's power to make foreign-policy decisions and take foreign-policy actions other than those of legislative character or that are otherwise within powers expressly vested in Congress. But the powers of Congress have also grown large, and some matters as to which Presidents have exercised authority may also be within the powers of Congress—under its commerce power, its power to define offences against the law of nations, its war power, under other enumerated powers including its power to make laws to carry out its powers or those of the other branches, or under an unenumerated foreign-affairs power deriving from the international sovereignty of the United States.

Concurrent authority for the President and Congress inevitably brings the possibility of competition for initiative or for conflicting actions. For a long time that danger remained academic as Congress remained inactive giving the President free rein, but in the wake of the WATERGATE AFFAIR and evidence of other executive abuse of authority such as the IRAN-CONTRA AFFAIR, Congress became "activist." Beginning in the 1970s, Congress adopted the WAR POWERS RESOLUTION, enacted legislation to regulate covert intelligence activities (dirty tricks, as distinguished from intelligence gathering), and tightened restrictions on executive discretion—in the sale of arms or in granting financial assistance to governments thought to be involved in terrorism or drug smuggling, or guilty of consistent patterns of gross violations of internationally recognized HUMAN RIGHTS.

With the rise of congressional activism in the 1970s, the President sought to move the focus of constitutional debate: Presidents no longer thought it necessary to argue that they had the unenumerated powers they had been exercising; they insisted that such powers were exclusive, and that Congress did not have power to monitor and regulate them. The issue was no longer the President's power, but the power of Congress. Presidents charged Congress with being "imperial," implying that congressional regulation was improper, usurping, unconstitutional.

Such Presidential claims and arguments are generally difficult to sustain. History has given the President large powers in foreign affairs as executive and as Commander in Chief beyond the few expressly provided; it has not recognized those powers as exclusive. History has not limited congressional authority. It has not recognized the President's authority to flout acts of Congress or to refuse to take care that the laws be faithfully executed. Authority to disregard acts of Congress has no support in the classic sources claimed for broad presidential authority. Hamilton argued for presidential authority to act (in one instance, to proclaim NEUTRALITY in foreign wars) when Congress is silent; he did not suggest that the President could act contrary to congressional legislation, or even that the powers of Congress should be narrowly construed so as to allow for greater executive power. Neither John Marshall nor the Supreme Court in *Curtiss-Wright* said or implied anything that would warrant the President to flout congressional legislation unless it sought to invade his authority as "sole organ" for representation and communication. In *Youngstown Co. v. Sawyer,* Justice Jackson wrote "When the President takes measures incompatible with the expressed or implied will of Congress, his power is at its lowest ebb, for then he can rely only upon his own constitutional powers minus any constitutional powers of Congress over the matter."

In the War Powers Resolution, Congress declared its view that the President has no independent constitutional authority to introduce U.S. armed forces "into hostilities, or into situations where imminent involvement in hostilities is clearly indicated by the circumstances," except in response to an attack on the United States or its armed forces. In the absence of a declaration of war or authorization by statute, the resolution requires the President to consult Congress before introducing U.S. armed forces into hostilities, to report to Congress whenever he had done so, and to terminate the involvement after sixty days (or after ninety days in emergency and unavoidable military necessity), unless Congress authorized the involvement to continue. President Nixon vetoed the resolution claiming it was unconstitutional, but Congress passed it over his veto. Presidents have continued to challenge the constitutionality of the resolution and have sometimes flouted its provisions.

The War Powers Resolution has been criticized for poor drafting and deep ambiguity, but except for its "legislative veto" provision it is difficult to fault it on constitutional grounds. In his veto message Nixon challenged the resolution's validity because it "would attempt to take away . . . authorities which the President has properly exercised under the Constitution for almost 200 years." But whether they were in fact exercised "properly" has not yet been authoritatively determined. In any event, Presidents exercised those powers when Congress was silent; there was no precedent for the introduction of U.S. forces into hostilities by the President in the face of congressional prohibitions or limitations, or for any other unilateral executive actions contrary to congressional legislation.

If the President presses his resistance to congressional regulation of his concurrent authority, Congress will usually prevail, in constitutional principle and in political practice, if only because it holds the purse strings. Under the Constitution the President cannot spend a dollar unless Congress has authorized and appropriated the money. Where the President has independent, exclusive authority to act, Congress is constitutionally bound to implement his actions, notably by appropriating the necessary funds. For example, Congress may not properly refuse to appropriate funds for the salary of the Secretary of State or for the costs of an embassy in a foreign country. But when the President seeks funds for purposes that Congress is persuaded are beyond his constitutional authority, it can properly frustrate the presidential purpose by withholding appropriations. (It can also resist such presidential action by threat of IMPEACHMENT.)

***Usurpation, interference, and failure of cooperation.*** Issues that have bedeviled the separation of powers in domestic matters have application in foreign affairs. In general, Congress cannot retain for itself a legislative veto to withdraw authority delegated to the President or to interfere with the President's execution of the laws; it can do so only by statute, by an act of Congress adopted by both houses subject to presidential veto. The power of Congress to investigate is subject to the uncertain limitation of the President's EXECUTIVE PRIVILEGE, though that privilege is probably not as immune from congressional probing as he would like it to be. For his part, the President cannot refuse to execute the laws, and he must spend and may not impound or defer the expenditure of funds that Congress directed the President to spend. (Congress has adopted anti-IMPOUNDMENT legislation, and Presidents have acquiesced.)

**Constitutionalism and Democracy.** Much has changed since governmental authority in foreign affairs was allocated in 1787. The President has become "the presidency," with a large executive bureaucracy. The Congress of the Framers' generation has grown and has been transformed into a complex of numerous committees and subcommittees and a huge staff. Over the centuries, each branch of the federal government has aggrandized its constitutional powers and has developed large extraconstitutional powers, the consequence of political parties and patronage, of size and complexities, of the growth of the United States and of a changing world.

Constitutional ideology and national interest require improved processes and procedures that will assure that major decisions are based on the full political authority of the United States, on the powers of Congress and the President. The principle of checks and balances suggests that war and peace and other powers of major national import should not be in the hands of the executive alone. Since the Constitution was adopted, the United States has become a more authentic democracy, its government more authentically representative. Principles of constitutionalism, democracy, and representative government require that important decisions have the consent of both branches, each differently democratic, each differently representative.

BIBLIOGRAPHY

Corwin, Edward S. *The President, Office and Powers, 1787–1984: History and Analysis of Practice and Opinion.* 1984.
Glennon, Michael J. *Constitutional Diplomacy.* 1990.
Fisher, Louis. *Constitutional Conflicts between Congress and the President.* 3d ed. 1991.
Henkin, Louis. *Constitutionalism, Democracy, and Foreign Affairs.* 1990.
Henkin, Louis. *Foreign Affairs and the Constitution.* 1972.
Koh, Harold Hongju. *The National Security Constitution: Sharing Power after the Iran-Contra Affair.* 1990.
Pyle, Christopher H., and Richard M. Pious. *The President, Congress, and the Constitution: Power and Legitimacy in American Politics.* 1984.
Sofaer, Abraham D. *War, Foreign Affairs, and Constitutional Power: The Origins.* 1976.

LOUIS HENKIN

**FOREIGN AFFAIRS: ORIGINAL INTENT.** The Framers intended that the President should be a joint participant in the field of foreign affairs, but a subordinate one. They meant the Senate to be the principal architect of foreign policy, while Congress devised policy concerning matters of war. The President was to be Congress's agent: as DIPLOMAT IN CHIEF he would control the ceremonial functions of representing the United States in its foreign relations, personally or through diplomats, and as COMMANDER IN CHIEF he would conduct wars authorized by Congress.

**In the Constitution.** No executive branch existed under the Articles of Confederation; Congress possessed all powers that in England belonged to the EXECUTIVE PREROGATIVE. When at the CONSTITUTIONAL CONVENTION the Virginia Plan proposed an executive department without mentioning executive powers, delegates expressed opposition to the executive possessing any powers regarding war and peace. The New Jersey Plan authorized the executive to enforce federal acts, appoint lesser officers, and direct military operations. Every delegate who spoke about the executive, including James Madison, the probable author of the Virginia Plan, declared that by definition EXECUTIVE POWER did not extend to foreign policy. JAMES WILSON observed that the executive was the legislature's agent and enforced its policies. Delegates as unlike as Wilson and Roger Sherman agreed that the executive should carry out national laws and make appointments not otherwise vested in Congress. Even ALEXANDER HAMILTON, who later espoused a powerful executive, urged that the Senate should have "the sole power of declaring war, the power of advising and approving all Treaties," and the power to make all appointments except department heads.

In early August 1787, when the Committee of Detail reported a draft Constitution to the convention, it did nothing to alter the existing consensus that the executive power was primarily ministerial in nature, nearly devoid of discretion and leadership. The Committee of Detail understood that power to mean an authority to execute faithfully the laws of the United States, to be Commander in Chief of the armed forces, and to receive ambassadors. The legislature would retain the power to make war, raise armies, build fleets, and even to "call forth the aid of the militia, in order to execute the laws of the Union, enforce treaties, suppress insurrections, and repel invasions." The Senate would possess the sole power to make treaties and appoint ambassadors.

When the convention considered the recommendations of the Committee of Detail, it substituted the word "declare" for "make," thus proposing that Congress should have the power to declare war. The change was made to allow the President "to repel sudden attacks," a power of the Commander in Chief requiring no legislative deliberation. The change in wording took nothing from Congress and added nothing to the executive. The Commander in Chief would possess no authority over the decision to make war.

When the convention reviewed the TREATY-MAKING POWER, Madison noted that the President should be the Senate's "agent," or deputy. GOUVERNEUR MORRIS believed that treaties should be ratified as laws, that is, that they should be approved by both houses of the legislature. Large-state delegates, including Madison and Morris, revealed unease about the Senate alone controlling the treaty power. Because they had lost their battle for proportional representation in both houses, large-state delegates looked for ways to contain the power of the Senate, where the states had equal representation. Still indecisive about the respective roles of the Senate and the President after three months of deliberation, the convention agreed

to the creation of another committee to consider recommendations on undecided matters. In early September, the Committee on Postponed Parts urged that the President should be joined with the Senate in making treaties and appointing ambassadors. The same committee urged that Congress should have the power to issue letters of MARQUE AND REPRISAL. The fact that the convention unanimously accepted that recommendation shows that even though it finally agreed that the President should share diplomatic powers, it believed that he should have no role in the decision to make war.

Although making the President a party to treaties constituted a striking change from all that had gone before, it did not indicate a new decision that the President should formulate foreign policy. Moreover, the requirement of a two-thirds majority vote of the Senate for confirmation of treaties checked any independent authority of the President in foreign affairs. He would need ADVICE AND CONSENT for diplomatic appointments as well as treaties, and he could not initiate wars. In English history, *advice and consent* was a way of designating legislative authority. No bill could be enacted or made into law by the king without the advice and consent of both houses of Parliament. The use of that formula by the convention retained the connotation that the legislature would be responsible for the conduct of foreign affairs. Hamilton, in *Federalist* 75, expressed that understanding when he said that although the power of making treaties was a shared one, the treaty power "will be found to partake more of the legislative than of the executive character." Advice and consent referred, too, to the President's APPOINTMENT POWER. The convention authorized him to take the initiative in making appointments but not in making treaties. The President makes treaties by and with the advice and consent of the Senate, but he "shall nominate, and by and with the Advice and Consent of the Senate, shall appoint. . . ." The word *advice* was used to involve the Senate in foreign policy decisions and negotiations before as well as after the fact. The word *consent* applied to ratification. Together, "advice and consent" meant a deliberative involvement on the Senate's part.

Although the convention belatedly adopted its committee's recommendations to involve the President in diplomacy, nothing said during the debate suggested that the convention had made any significant change or had substantially augmented executive powers. Speaker after speaker emphasized the powers of the Senate in the area of foreign affairs. No one hinted that the President would have an important independent role in treaty making.

When the Committee of Style put the Constitution in final shape, it placed the paragraph on the power of the President to make treaties and appointments with the advice and consent of the Senate in Article II, which deals with the executive power. Two days before the convention adjourned, it considered Article II without noting the fact that the treaty-power provision had been shifted from the article on the legislative to the article on the executive. Nobody thought that the new placement of the treaty power indicated an enhancement of presidential authority. The expectation remained that the Senate would dominate the making of foreign policy as much as Congress controlled the decision to make war.

**The Ratification Debate.** The authors of THE FEDERALIST reflected what supporters of the Constitution meant in the matter of Senate versus presidential control of foreign policy. JOHN JAY, one of the authors, was the nation's most experienced diplomat and knew better than anyone the weaknesses of American foreign policy under the Articles of Confederation. When he wrote *Federalist* 64 he was Secretary of Foreign Affairs for the Continental Congress. Endorsing the joint responsibility vested by the Constitution in the President and Senate, Jay expected the Senate to make foreign policy and the President to carry it out. Anyone under the misimpression that the Framers intended an IMPERIAL PRESIDENCY or a doctrine of INHERENT POWERS should read Hamilton's *Federalist* 69, contrasting the powers of the President with the royal prerogative. In *Federalist* 75, Hamilton, like Jay, conveys the impression that the President would execute the Senate's foreign policy.

Proponents of ratification widely shared the opinions of Hamilton and Jay, although a few preferred a greater role for the President in exercising the diplomatic authority of the nation. Significantly, no one believed that the President should have a more important role than the Senate in foreign affairs. Opponents of ratification tended to oppose presidential powers. They preferred the Articles of Confederation, which had no executive branch and vested all diplomatic and war powers in the Congress. Yet they showed very little dissatisfaction with clauses bearing on foreign affairs or the war powers. Of all the recommendations state conventions made for amending the Constitution, only one dealt with the power of Congress to declare or make war. New York wanted to require a two-thirds vote. Similarly, Virginia wanted a larger majority for confirming treaties. If Anti-Federalists had expected the President to dominate foreign policy, they would have vehemently denounced the Constitution for that reason.

The consensus of 1787–1789 disintegrated briefly in 1793, when Hamilton utterly reversed his opinion by advocating a presidential power to declare NEUTRALITY without senatorial advice and consent. He favored the President's having an inherent executive authority to do whatever he wished as long as it was not expressly prohibited by the Constitution. Hamilton's position was not accepted before Abraham Lincoln's aggressive exercise of powers to save the Union during the CIVIL WAR, and it was not until the twentieth century that the doctrine of inherent executive powers received widespread endorsement.

That doctrine usually seeks mistaken support from historical precedents, such as a remark—yanked out of context—made by Thomas Jefferson when he was Secretary of State; Jefferson's strong endorsement of executive powers referred only to RECEIVING AND APPOINTING AMBASSADORS, not to the making of foreign policy. Similarly, JOHN MARSHALL's 1800 declaration about the President as "sole organ of the nation in its external relations, and its sole representative with foreign nations" meant nothing more than that only the President communicates with foreign nations. In *Talbot v. Seeman* (1801), Chief Justice Marshall declared, "The whole powers of war being by the Constitution . . . vested in Congress, the acts of that body can alone be resorted to as our guide in the enquiry." President Jefferson, lacking congressional authorization, refused to take aggressive action against the Barbary pirates who had proclaimed enmity to the United States, but he dispatched the navy as a show of force—no more. If the original intent of the Framers with respect to foreign affairs had prevailed, we should now be discussing an "imperial Senate" rather than an imperial presidency.

### BIBLIOGRAPHY

Bestor, Arthur. "Separation of Powers in the Domain of Foreign Affairs: The Intent of the Constitution Historically Examined." *Seton Hall Law Review* 5 (1974): 527–666.
Levy, Leonard W. *Original Intent and the Framers' Constitution.* 1988.
Thach, Charles C. *The Creation of the Presidency, 1775–1789.* 1922.

LEONARD W. LEVY

**FOREIGN AID.** Since WORLD WAR II each American President has sponsored the dispensation of varying mixtures of billions of dollars' worth of loans, monetary grants, weaponry, foodstuffs, and technical expertise to other countries. Most foreign aid has originated from the political motive of countering a foreign threat to U.S. interests. During World War II the administration of Franklin D. Roosevelt provided military assistance to nations fighting against the Axis powers even before the United States entered the conflict at the end of 1941. After the war the focus of foreign aid shifted from defeating the Axis to countering the influence of the Soviet Union and other communist countries and movements. While geopolitics most often justified American foreign assistance, humanitarian concerns also played a significant role in encouraging Presidents to request and Congress to authorize hundreds of billions of dollars in foreign aid.

**World War II and After.** The modern history of foreign aid began in 1940, when the Roosevelt administration looked for ways to support the nations fighting Germany and Japan. Hamstrung by laws preventing American arms sales to nations at war while the United States remained neutral, Roosevelt in the summer of 1940 authorized transferring fifty overage destroyers to Britain in exchange for U.S. leases on British naval bases in the Caribbean. The needs of Britain and China (the two powers actively fighting Germany and Japan in late 1940) could not be met by a such a simple, one-time solution. In early 1941 Roosevelt pressed Congress to pass the LEND-LEASE ACT, granting the President power to provide war material to nations whose defense he deemed in the interest of the United States. Attempting to quiet objections that the plan would revive the discredited arms transfers of WORLD WAR I, Roosevelt explained that the goods would be returned after the war. In fact, they were used in the fighting. Lend-lease provided the tools for the Allies both before and after the United States entered the war. From March 1941 to June 1945 the United States provided approximately $31 billion in lend-lease aid to Great Britain, the U.S.S.R., and other allies in Europe, as well as to China, India, and several African and Middle Eastern countries.

In 1943, by which time an eventual Allied victory seemed certain, the Roosevelt administration began planning American reconstruction aid for areas ravaged by the war. In the process, the United States went beyond the unilateral donations of lend-lease toward creation of multilateral foreign-aid agencies, helping, for example, to set up the United Nations Relief and Reconstruction Agency. At the Bretton Woods conference of July 1944 Roosevelt stressed that prosperity and a resurrection of international trade would minimize the kinds of rivalries that had led to World War II. Accordingly, in the BRETTON WOODS AGREEMENT he agreed that the United States would take a leading role in the International Bank for Reconstruction and Development (World Bank) and the International Monetary Fund—the former providing funds for war-torn economies and the latter helping governments create the stable and convertible currencies necessary for international trade to thrive.

The administration of Harry S. Truman created the framework for most subsequent U.S. foreign-assistance programs. As tensions rose between the United States and the Soviet Union in the years following World War II, policymakers believed that more unilateral U.S. aid efforts were necessary in the emerging COLD WAR. In March 1947 Truman asked Congress for $120 million in military aid to Greece and Turkey to counter the influence of the Soviet Union in the eastern Mediterranean. In words that later came to be known as the TRUMAN DOCTRINE, the President pledged U.S. support for "free peoples everywhere who are resisting subjugation by armed minorities or outside pressures." In June 1947 Secretary of State GEORGE C. MARSHALL promised economic assistance to Europe. Over the next year American and European officials worked out details concerning how aid would be used. From 1948 until 1953 the European Recovery Program, or MARSHALL PLAN, provided $18 billion in economic assistance to the nations of Western Europe. The Marshall Plan became the most successful foreign-aid program in history, enabling Western European economies to commence an extraordinary expansion and providing social and political stability.

Truman extended foreign aid beyond Europe and into the military as well as the economic sphere. In eighteen months from the end of 1947 to the beginning of 1949 the Truman administration promised economic assistance to defeated Japan and military and economic assistance to the Nationalist government of China and to South Korea. (This assistance promoted rapid economic expansion in Japan, Taiwan, and South Korea after the end of the KOREAN WAR in 1953.) In his 1949 inaugural address, Truman announced the POINT FOUR PROGRAM of technical and financial assistance to Asia, Africa, and Latin America. The Korean War intensified the Truman administration's desire to counter a Soviet or communist military threat. In 1951 Congress passed the Mutual Security Act (MSA) to coordinate military and economic aid to nations assisting the United States in opposing the Soviet Union or other communist governments or movements. Three-quarters of the $8 billion in foreign assistance appropriated under the MSA went for military grants or loans to friendly governments.

The administration of Dwight D. Eisenhower was less enthusiastic about direct governmental foreign assistance than the Truman administration had been. Eisenhower continued the program of military assistance, primarily to Korea, South Vietnam, Nationalist China, and the European allies, but the administration reduced direct economic assistance. Both the administration and Congress preferred to encourage private American firms to invest directly or to lend money overseas. One exception to the general shift away from economic assistance in the 1950s came in the form of food assistance. Trying to reduce huge domestic crop surpluses, the Eisenhower administration encouraged passage of the Agricultural Trade Development and Assistance Act of 1954 (Public Law 480). Under this law the U.S. government bought surplus crops from American farmers, sold them in poor countries for local currency, and used the nonconvertible receipts to pay for development projects.

**Kennedy's Overhaul of Foreign-Aid Policy.** The Eisenhower administration's skepticism about the benefits of government-sponsored, civilian foreign-aid projects provoked opposition from some academic economists who studied economic growth. One prominent economist, MIT professor Walt W. Rostow, argued that providing capital and technical assistance to poor nations would give them the necessary boost to modernize their economies. President John F. Kennedy adopted many of Rostow's ideas when he advocated a complete overhaul of American foreign-aid policy. Kennedy urged expansion on all fronts—more economic assistance, more military aid, and more technical advice. Congress responded with the Foreign Assistance Act of 1961. The new foreign-aid program expanded nonmilitary assistance and created the Agency for International Development to manage foreign assistance.

Kennedy hoped to duplicate the success of the Marshall Plan in the Western Hemisphere with the creation in 1961 of the ALLIANCE FOR PROGRESS. Designed as an ambitious partnership between Washington and the governments of South and Central America and the Caribbean, the Alliance for Progress was supposed to provide education, to reform land ownership, to reduce mortality, and to build a foundation for economic expansion. It did not realize its lofty goals. Advocates promised more than could realistically be achieved, and it proved more difficult to eradicate the historical poverty of the Western Hemisphere than it had to reconstruct the economies of a previously prosperous Europe. Moreover, the administration of Lyndon B. Johnson cut back on the Alliance for Progress as the VIETNAM WAR absorbed the bulk of foreign-assistance funds.

In 1961 Kennedy and Congress created the PEACE CORPS, one of the most popular and enduring foreign-aid programs. The program was conceived as a crusade against communism, with Kennedy promising that "our young men and women, dedicated to freedom, are fully capable of overcoming the efforts of Mr. Khrushchev's missionaries who are dedicated to undermining that freedom." Over the next thirty years more than eighty thousand mostly young volunteers served in nearly one hundred countries around the globe. In the early years, most Peace Corps volunteers worked in education. From the administration of Richard M. Nixon onward, however, Washington shifted its focus away from enticing volunteers fresh from college toward recruiting older, more experienced people who could offer specific kinds of technical assistance.

**Modifications and Criticisms.** From the mid 1960s to the early 1990s the United States maintained the structure of foreign aid created in the initial period of the cold war, but each administration after Kennedy modified the assistance programs. Changes in economic theory and political challenges to the United States combined to force adjustments in foreign-aid policy. Economists began to doubt that the development promised in the 1950s would occur as quickly as had been expected. Economic assistance therefore shifted from development toward meeting basic human needs. More important changes involved the redirection of foreign aid to military assistance. Military aid to South Vietnam became the major component of foreign assistance in the Johnson and early Nixon administrations. The NIXON DOCTRINE's promise to supply weaponry to anticommunist nations led to more than $13 billion in arms sales to Asia and the Middle East. The administration of Jimmy Carter attempted to curtail arms sales and channel humanitarian assistance through multilateral aid agencies. Yet these changes were more rhetorical than real, and Carter, like his immediate predecessors, authorized enormous military-assistance packages to a few American allies in the Middle East and Southeast Asia. Ronald Reagan's administration further militarized foreign aid, helping friendly governments in Central America, the Middle East, and Asia. The end of the cold war brought another reevaluation of foreign-aid policies. The administration of George Bush refrained from initiating a massive new Marshall Plan, which would have been funded mostly by the United States, to help the economies of Eastern Europe and the former Soviet republics convert to the free-market system. The Bush administration did, however, cooperate with Eastern European nations and Japan in providing technical expertise to reform the economies of the former Soviet empire.

Foreign aid provoked continual political debate in

the United States throughout the fifty-year period from the beginning of World War II to the end of the cold war, with Presidents customarily favoring foreign aid while members of Congress and the general public viewed it with suspicion. Some critics of assistance derided it as a wasteful extravagance, which neither purchased friends abroad nor contributed to foreign countries' economic welfare. Other opponents of foreign aid charged that too much assistance had gone toward countering a perceived communist threat and too little toward improving the lives of people in countries that received the aid.

Foreign aid left a mixed record of successes and failures. The military aid provided during World War II was a major factor enabling the defeat of Germany, Italy, and Japan. The United States helped feed Europe in the immediate aftermath of the war. The Marshall Plan was the most successful U.S. foreign-assistance program, helping restore prosperity to Western Europe and enabling its nations to resist domestic social upheavals. The United States also helped Japan's economic reconstruction after World War II.

Encouraged by successes in Europe and Japan, advocates of foreign aid after 1953 often called for new "Marshall Plans" to address such diverse problems as poverty in Latin America or Southeast Asia or the conversion of the economies of the states of Eastern Europe and the defunct Soviet Union from communism to free markets. Yet only the Peace Corps ever gained the widespread approval in the United States and abroad that the Marshall Plan had engendered. Even there, achievements were more symbolic than real, since the Peace Corps often accomplished more in terms of the personal fulfillment of volunteers than actual economic advance in the countries where it operated. Critics offered various reasons for the relative lack of success of foreign aid. Some argued that the ideas underlying foreign aid rested on flawed economic theories. Most observers of foreign-aid policy believed that the uneven economic and social progress it engendered derived from preoccupation with meeting foreign military threats and inadequate attention to the economic and social needs of poor countries.

## BIBLIOGRAPHY

Hogan, Michael J. *The Marshall Plan.* 1987.
Kimball, Warren. *The "Most Unsordid Act," Lend-Lease, 1939–1941.* 1969.
Packenham, Robert A. *Liberal America and the Third World.* 1983.
Rostow, Walt W. *Eisenhower, Kennedy, and Foreign Aid.* 1985.
Wilhelm, John, and Gerry Feinstein, eds. *Foreign Assistance: Investment or Folly?* 1984.
Wood, Robert E. *From Marshall Plan to Debt Crisis.* 1986.

ROBERT D. SCHULZINGER

**FOREIGN INTELLIGENCE SURVEILLANCE ACT** (1978). Enacted in October 1978, the Foreign Intelligence Surveillance Act (FISA; 50 U.S.C. 1801–1811) became effective in May 1979. For almost forty years, the executive branch had claimed the authority to approve warrantless ELECTRONIC SURVEILLANCE of domestic communications based on inherent, constitutionally based EXECUTIVE POWER to protect the NATIONAL SECURITY and conduct FOREIGN AFFAIRS. Reacting against this practice, Congress intended that FISA would provide the exclusive basis for authorizing a broad range of electronic surveillance and monitoring activities engaged in by the federal government within the borders of the United States for national security purposes.

These activities include the use of wiretapping, concealed microphones, closed-circuit television, transponders (or "beepers"), telephone tracing devices, and interception of certain types of radio communications. The statute identifies the permissible targets of these surveillance activates as a variety of "foreign powers"—foreign governments, terrorist or political groups, and organizations controlled by such governments or groups—and individuals who can be identified as an "agents of a foreign power."

In most circumstances, the authority to conduct such activities must be obtained from a federal district court judge who has been designated by the Chief Justice of the United States as a member of the Foreign Intelligence Surveillance Court. There are seven such judges. They serve rotating seven-year terms and are collectively referred to as the "FISA court." FISA judges may be appointed from any district in the country. They visit Washington, D.C., on a regular basis to review government applications for national security–related electronic surveillance.

The ATTORNEY GENERAL must review and approve each application prior to its submission to the FISA court. Alternately, where the surveillance activity is directed against communications solely among or between foreign powers or at property under foreign government's open and exclusive control, and where there is little likelihood that any communications being made by any United States person will be acquired, the Attorney General may authorize the surveillance without reference to the FISA Court.

Surveillance under FISA may be authorized when its purpose is the acquisition of *foreign intelligence.* The statute defines that term to include information that relates to, or, where the information involves a United States person, is necessary to, United States national defense or foreign affairs, protection against grave hostile acts, terrorism, sabotage, or clandestine intelligence activities by or on behalf of a foreign power.

The term *United States person* defines the class of individuals and groups who are afforded greatest protection under the statute. This class includes U.S. citizens, permanent resident aliens, groups composed largely of such citizens or aliens, and business entities incorporated in the United States. Persons and groups within this class may be targets of surveillance only when the government is able to show that their activities are not only of foreign intelligence interest but also may violate a criminal law.

In reviewing an application to use surveillance, a FISA court judge is required to determine that the location that will be subject to the surveillance will be used by the targeted foreign power or agent and that the government will conduct the surveillance under appropriate procedures to minimize the acquisition, retention, and dissemination of information concerning unconsenting United States persons. Applications to the FISA court must include certifications from senior government officials attesting to the foreign intelligence purposes of the activity. If approved, the surveillance may be conducted for up to ninety days for an individual or a full year for an establishment. These surveillances may be renewed for similar time periods if relevant standards are satisfied.

The Chief Justice is also empowered to designate three federal appellate judges to the FISA appeals court. The sole function of this body is to hear appeals by the government in any instance where a FISA court judge has denied the government's application for a surveillance order. This appeals court has never met, however, since the FISA court had issued more than six thousand FISA surveillance orders through the end of 1991 without a single denial.

### BIBLIOGRAPHY

Cinquegrana, Americo R. "The Wall (and Wires) Have Ears: The Background and First Ten Years of the Foreign Intelligence Surveillance Act of 1978." *University of Pennsylvania Law Review* 137 (1989): 793.

Meason, James E. "The Foreign Intelligence Surveillance Act: Time for Reappraisal." *International Lawyer* 24 (Winter 1990): 1043.

Shapiro, Ira S. "The Foreign Intelligence Surveillance Act: Legislative Balancing of National Security and the Fourth Amendment." *Harvard Journal of Legislation* 15 (1978): 119.

AMERICO R. CINQUEGRANA

**FOREIGN SERVICE.** The American Foreign Service is the corps of professional diplomats responsible to the President for the implementation of foreign policy. The service had its origins during the Revolution. Congress sent Benjamin Franklin, John Adams, and JOHN JAY to European capitals to encourage support for the colonies during the War of Independence, and in 1783 Franklin crowned his diplomatic career with the signing of the Treaty of Paris, in which Britain formally recognized the colonies as independent.

Thomas Jefferson, after serving as minister to France from 1784 to 1789, became the first Secretary of State, presiding over a Department of Foreign Affairs, with a staff of four clerks and two messengers. Acting under authority of Article II of the Constitution, George Washington sent his first two diplomatic representatives to France and Spain and appointed seventeen consuls and vice consuls, principally to cities where American traders were active. Separate diplomatic and consular services evolved, with political PATRONAGE largely determining their membership until the early years of the twentieth century.

The Rogers Act of 1924 combined the Diplomatic and Consular Services into a unified service and made all Foreign Service Officers (FSOs) "subject to promotion by merit." The Foreign Service Act of 1946 provided for the first comprehensive personnel system for the service and for training facilities in a Foreign Service Institute. Under President Carter's strong leadership, the merit system was further strengthened in later governing legislation, the Foreign Service Act of 1980, a companion piece to the CIVIL SERVICE REFORM ACT of 1978.

By 1992 the Foreign Service Officer corps had grown to include approximately four thousand FSOs (of whom about 20 percent were women), their number and their responsibilities reflecting America's enormously expanded role on the world stage. Entry into the officer corps is highly competitive.

Officers enter the service with a basic orientation course at the Foreign Service Institute of the DEPARTMENT OF STATE, and many can expect to return there during their careers for language training or for midcareer and senior-level study in subjects such as management and economics. A small number can expect to advance further into the Senior Foreign Service (SFS)—roughly equivalent to counterparts in the SENIOR EXECUTIVE SERVICE (SES) of the CIVIL SERVICE— with ascending ranks of counselor, minister counselor, career minister and, in rare instances, career ambassador (the top rank of service). Traditionally, approximately 70 percent of American embassies are headed by ambassadors nominated from the career service;

the balance are political appointees. Promotions within the service are based on merit, reviewed annually by selection boards. Mandatory retirement is at age sixty-five.

The Foreign Service staffs some 260 embassies and consular posts in those countries with which the United States maintains diplomatic relations, plus representation in UNITED NATIONS headquarters, specialized multilateral organizations such as the World Health Organization, and regional groupings such as NATO and the European Community. FSOs also serve in offices of the Department of State in partnership with civil service personnel, their positions ranging from that of Deputy Secretary of State to assistant and deputy assistant secretaries, to country desk officers. Some do excursion tours in other government departments, including the NATIONAL SECURITY COUNCIL, the DEPARTMENT OF DEFENSE, and congressional offices. Overseas, the officer corps of the service is supplemented by some five thousand foreign service specialists.

The Foreign Service also includes about nine hundred Foreign Service Information Officers (FSIOs) of the United States Information Agency (USIA), who plan and conduct information and cultural programs abroad; nearly two thousand career professionals in the Agency for International Development (AID), who help develop and administer economic and technical assistance programs overseas; some two hundred officers of the Foreign Commercial Service (FCS) of the DEPARTMENT OF COMMERCE, serving as commercial attachés in embassies abroad; and about 125 with the Foreign Agricultural Service (FAS) of the DEPARTMENT OF AGRICULTURE. Numerous other departments and agencies are also represented in the Foreign Service abroad, including the Department of Defense, the CENTRAL INTELLIGENCE AGENCY, the Drug Enforcement Agency, and the Environmental Protection Agency. Finally, Peace Corps Volunteers serve in many countries, acting in effect as grass-roots diplomats in the overall diplomatic service of the United States.

The modern Foreign Service is thus vastly larger and more diverse than ever. Yet its basic function remains what it has always been: the implementation of American foreign policy under the direction of the nation's DIPLOMAT IN CHIEF, the President, and his principal foreign affairs adviser, the Secretary of State. That implementation process involves essentially four basic tasks. The first is reporting: keeping policymakers in Washington informed of the course of events in a given country and how they impact American interests. Even with the speed and pervasiveness of today's information age, carefully nuanced analysis by diplomats abroad still provides essential information for policymakers in Washington.

The second of these basic tasks is negotiating: the Foreign Service discussing with host governments the content of agreements—bilateral and multilateral, large and small, ranging from arms-reduction treaties to consular conventions and, increasingly, major understandings on transnational issues such as the environment. A third task is protection: acting to ensure that American interests in a given country and American citizens who travel or do business there have equal access to the laws and judicial processes of that country. A fourth and fundamental assignment is representation: articulating American values and policies to peoples and governments abroad.

## BIBLIOGRAPHY

Macomber, William B. *The Angels' Game: A Handbook of Modern Diplomacy*. 1979.

Mayer, Martin. *The Diplomats: The Real People Behind the Events in an Unreal World*. 1983.

Miller, Robert H. *Inside an Embassy: the Political Role of Diplomats Abroad*. 1992.

Newsom, David D. *Diplomacy and the American Democracy*. 1988.

Plischke, Ed. *Modern Diplomacy: The Art and the Artisans*. 1979.

Steigman, Andrew L. *The Foreign Service of the United States: First Line of Defense*. 1985.

L. BRUCE LAINGEN

**FORRESTAL, JAMES V.** (1892–1947), Secretary of the Navy, Secretary of Defense. President Franklin Roosevelt recruited James Forrestal in 1940 to help with the increasingly urgent task of military preparedness, seventeen months before the Japanese attack on PEARL HARBOR. As Navy Under Secretary (1940–1944), in full charge of procurement, Forrestal directed the building of the largest, most powerful fleet in history. The forging of this military instrument was a precondition of victory in the Battle of the Atlantic against German submarines, in the cross-channel landings at Normandy that led to the final defeat of Nazi Germany, and in the vast reaches of the Pacific against the air, naval, and ground forces of Imperial Japan.

As Navy Secretary (1944–1947), Forrestal helped persuade President Harry S. Truman to modify the doctrine of unconditional surrender so as to permit the emperor of Japan to remain as nominal sovereign. By means of this cosmetic accommodation, the United States was able to avoid the terrible trauma of large-scale invasion and to establish conditions for a remarkably peaceful occupation of Japan. Forrestal persuaded Truman to assure absolute U.S. postwar control over the Pacific islands wrested from Japan at such high cost in American lives and also to establish a permanent U.S. naval presence in the Mediterranean. This latter move had the strategic effect of ending Soviet pressures against Greece and Turkey and of assuring a non-Communist victory in the crucial 1948 Italian elections.

Forrestal was the principal architect of the NATIONAL SECURITY COUNCIL, the mechanism designed to assure formal coordination of foreign and defense policy, intelligence, and mobilization planning, and which was at the center of COLD WAR policy-making under every President from Truman to George Bush.

As Navy Secretary, Forrestal defended the navy's determination to avoid change in the organization of the military services, and argued against President Truman's proposal to "unify" the army, navy, and air force under a single Secretary of Defense. His vigorous advocacy before Congress succeeded in weakening the authority granted to the new CABINET position in the NATIONAL SECURITY ACT OF 1947 that created the National Military Establishment (later renamed the Department of Defense in 1949). Then ironically, Forrestal accepted appointment as the nation's first Secretary of Defense, and discovered he had seriously underestimated the bitter intractability of the problem. Inherent interservice rivalries were intensified by the new prominence of air power, by the ongoing revolution in weapons (not only nuclear weapons, but also the prospect of ballistic and guided missiles), and by the impact of suddenly tight postwar budgets on services grown accustomed to no limits on spending. Forrestal's inability to resolve the hard questions of how the military services should divide available moneys and should control specific missions and weapons gradually cost him the confidence of President Truman. Exhausted from his endless efforts to achieve interservice agreement on strategies and budgets, hounded by savage and distorted press attacks, especially by Drew Pearson and Walter Winchell, that depicted him as "the most dangerous man in America," Forrestal suffered a profound sense of personal failure and fell into a state of clinical depression from which he never recovered. Two months after his resignation from office in March 1949, he took his own life by jumping from a window on the sixteenth floor of the Bethesda Naval Hospital.

## BIBLIOGRAPHY

*The Forrestal Diaries.* Edited by Walter Millis and E. S. Duffield. 1951.
Hoopes, Townsend, and Douglas Brinkley. *Driven Patriot—The Life and Times of James Forrestal.* 1992.
Rogow, Arnold A. *James Forrestal, A Study of Personality, Politics, and Policy.* 1963.

TOWNSEND HOOPES

**FORTAS, ABE** (1910–1982), presidential adviser, Supreme Court Justice. A brilliant New Dealer, who cashed in on his governmental expertise to become a highly paid Washington lawyer after WORLD WAR II, Fortas successfully defended Lyndon B. Johnson in his disputed 1948 Senate election. In 1965, then President Johnson engineered Justice Arthur Goldberg's resignation so he could offer Fortas, who had remained a valued adviser, a position on the Court.

As a member of the Warren Court majority, Fortas sought to expand civil rights and to expand CIVIL LIBERTIES for juveniles and adults. He insisted on students' rights to engage in nondisruptive protest against the VIETNAM WAR in his opinion for the Court in *Tinker v. Des Moines Independent Community School District* (1969). But Fortas was committed to maintaining a strong national government and presidency, and his devotion to those causes sometimes limited his judicial commitment to civil liberties.

As one White House staffer said, Johnson "refused to be denied access to his best attorney just because he had given him to the Supreme Court." Ever loyal, Fortas responded to the President's calls. The Justice strongly supported the war in Vietnam and advised Johnson to send troops to riot-torn Detroit. Johnson sometimes asked Fortas to predict the Supreme Court's response should cases involving exercises of presidential power come before it. Fortas also spoke with Johnson about at least two cases pending before the Court.

When Chief Justice Earl Warren resigned in 1968, Johnson nominated Fortas to be Chief Justice. Few Senators realized the extent of Fortas's involvement in White House affairs, and none was aware that Justice Fortas discussed confidential issues involving the Court with the President. Nevertheless, Senators hostile to Fortas's liberal judicial activism knew enough about the Fortas-Johnson relationship to make it an issue at his confirmation hearings. Though Fortas misleadingly downplayed his relationship with Johnson and pointed out that Justices had long advised Presidents, opponents charged that the Justice had violated the principle of SEPARATION OF POWERS. Johnson, who had announced he would not seek reelection, could do little for Fortas. The nomination was already doomed when the Senate learned that Fortas, who was dissatisfied with his judicial salary, had engaged in questionable financial practices. Republicans and conservative southern Democrats launched a filibuster, and Johnson sadly withdrew the nomination at Fortas's request.

A year later, an investigative reporter's revelations brought the Justice's financial dealings under renewed scrutiny. Hoping to unseat Fortas and replace him with a more conservative Justice, the Nixon administration worked secretly to force Fortas's retirement. Fortas resigned from the Court in disgrace in 1969.

### BIBLIOGRAPHY

Kalman, Laura. *Abe Fortas: A Biography*. 1990.
Murphy, Bruce. *Fortas: The Rise and Ruin of a Supreme Court Justice*. 1988.

LAURA KALMAN

**FOUR FREEDOMS.** President Franklin D. Roosevelt's Four Freedoms made up his effort to create a body of humane wartime objectives to counter the anticipated criticism of his Lend-Lease program of January 1941 [*see* LEND-LEASE ACT]. Prime Minister Winston Churchill informed Roosevelt on 2 December 1940 that Great Britain could no longer carry the financial burden of its arms purchases in the United States. Clearly such financing would require a special congressional appropriation. The President found the answer in Lend-Lease. As he explained to Treasury Secretary HENRY MORGENTHAU, JR. the United States would make its increased arms production available to Britain as a loan to be repaid after the war.

Roosevelt outlined his program in his annual message of 6 January 1941. The country, he declared, would meet its foreign dangers by augmenting its national defense, giving support to the resolute peoples resisting aggression, and keeping war away from the Western Hemisphere. Above all, he argued, it was essential that the United States not force those fighting Germany to surrender merely because of their inability to pay cash for the weapons they required. Having identified U.S. interests with those of Britain, Roosevelt universalized his peace aims in the form of four essential human freedoms:

The first is freedom of speech and expression—everywhere in the world.

The second is freedom of every person to worship God in his own way—everywhere in the world.

The third is freedom from want—which, translated into world terms, means economic understandings which will secure to every nation a healthy peacetime life for its inhabitants—everywhere in the world.

The fourth is freedom from fear—which, translated into world terms, means a world-wide reduction of armaments to such

a point and in such a thorough fashion that no nation will be in a position to commit an act of physical aggression against any neighbor—anywhere in the world.

Denying that his vision was utopian, Roosevelt proclaimed it attainable in "our own time and generation." It comprised one more chapter, he said, in the country's quest for a world order in which free countries would work together in creating a friendly, civilized society.

### BIBLIOGRAPHY

Kimball, Warren F. *The Most Unsordid Act: Lend-Lease, 1939–1941*. 1969.
Langer, William L., and S. Everett Gleason. *The Undeclared War, 1940–1941*. 1953.
Sherwood, Robert. *Roosevelt and Hopkins*. 1950.

NORMAN A. GRAEBNER

**FOURTEEN POINTS.** On 8 January 1918, President Woodrow Wilson delivered his famous Fourteen Points address to a joint session of Congress. In response to the Bolshevik revolution in Russia and the refusal of the Allies to endorse U.S. aims in WORLD WAR I at the Inter-Allied Conference in Paris, he decided to make this unilateral statement.

Speaking to the whole world through Congress, the President outlined his peace program. He proclaimed ideals of U.S. political culture, including democracy and capitalism, as the foundation for international peace. He called for a new diplomacy with "open covenants of peace, openly arrived at" to replace the old diplomacy of secret treaties and alliances. He advocated freedom of the seas, equality of trade among nations, and elimination of armaments except for domestic safety.

Breaking from the diplomatic tradition of isolating the United States from the Old World, Wilson offered guidelines for settling territorial disputes in Europe and the Middle East. Never before had the United States gone to such lengths to involve itself in the political and territorial questions of the Old World. In his final point, Wilson reaffirmed his commitment to a postwar LEAGUE OF NATIONS to guarantee the political independence and territorial integrity of all states.

Wilson's address found a generally favorable reception among the Allies, but the Central Powers initially rejected it as an inadequate basis for peace. Facing military defeat in October 1918, however, they requested an armistice and appealed for a peace settlement in accordance with the Fourteen Points. Seizing the opportunity, the President sent his close adviser

Colonel EDWARD M. HOUSE to Europe to commit the Allies as well as the Central Powers to his peace program.

Wilson thought that "the essentially American terms" were the first three and the last, the points calling for abolition of secret treaties, freedom of the seas, equality of commercial opportunities, and a League of Nations. The other points, dealing with the political and territorial settlement in the Old World, were less important. The Allies endorsed the Fourteen Points only after expressing their reservations concerning freedom of the seas and reparations. Secretary of State Robert Lansing informed Imperial Germany on 5 November that the Allied and Associated Powers were prepared to establish peace on the basis of the Fourteen Points. Following Kaiser Wilhelm II's abdication, the new republican government in Germany signed the armistice of 11 November 1918, with this promise.

The TREATY OF VERSAILLES, which Wilson and the Allied statesmen negotiated at the Paris Peace Conference in 1919, failed to fulfill Germany's expectations for a peace based on the Fourteen Points. After receiving the treaty at Versailles on 7 May, the Germans denounced it as a flagrant violation of Wilson's principles. They demanded immediate membership in the League of Nations and wanted the Allies to join Germany in disarmament. They resented the loss of their colonies and some of their country to other states, and refused to pay exorbitant reparations. Expecting Wilson to support them, they declined to sign the treaty unless he forced the Allies to revise it. The Germans thus interpreted the Fourteen Points as a guarantee against the consequences of their military defeat.

Wilson's interpretation of his Fourteen Points differed substantially from Germany's. He believed that the treaty generally conformed to his principles. Its conditions, with minor changes, seemed appropriate to him. He anticipated Germany's membership in the League, but only after a period of probation. He saw no reason to appease the Germans, which left them feeling betrayed.

Nevertheless, the American and Allied interpretation of the Fourteen Points prevailed in the peace treaty. The German cabinet, after some of its members were changed, finally decided that it had no alternative but to acquiesce. A new German delegation arrived in Versailles to sign the treaty on 28 June 1919, even though the conflict over the correct interpretation of Wilson's Fourteen Points had not been resolved. Discussion continued into the postwar years as the victorious powers and the defeated enemy struggled over the alternatives of enforcing or revising the Treaty of Versailles.

### BIBLIOGRAPHY

Gardner, Lloyd C. *Safe for Democracy: The Anglo-American Response to Revolution, 1913–1923.* 1984.

Gelfand, Lawrence E. *The Inquiry: American Preparations for Peace, 1917–1919.* 1963.

Link, Arthur S., ed. *Woodrow Wilson and a Revolutionary World, 1913–1921.* 1982.

Nordholt, Jan Willem Schulte. *Woodrow Wilson: A Life for World Peace.* 1991.

Unterberger, Betty Miller. *The United States, Revolutionary Russia, and the Rise of Czechoslovakia.* 1989.

LLOYD E. AMBROSIUS

**FRANKFURTER, FELIX** (1882–1965), Associate Justice of the Supreme Court. A passionate scholar, devoted teacher, and enigmatic Justice, Frankfurter revered the legal process and the Supreme Court's role in American politics. Born on 15 November 1882, in Vienna, Austria, he immigrated with his family to the United States when he was twelve. After growing up in the Lower East Side of New York and graduating from the City College of New York in 1902, he went to Harvard Law School, graduating in 1906.

Frankfurter's career in public service spanned almost sixty years. It began when President Theodore Roosevelt's Attorney General, HENRY STIMSON, persuaded him to become an assistant U.S. attorney for the Southern District of New York. Stimson, Frankfurter's mentor, took him briefly into private legal practice at the end of the Roosevelt administration. In 1910 Stimson became Secretary of War under President William Howard Taft, and Frankfurter accompanied him to Washington, D.C., as an attorney in the Bureau of Insular Affairs. Four years later, Frankfurter accepted a teaching position at Harvard Law School. But he again returned to Washington in 1917–1918, serving as secretary and counselor to President Woodrow Wilson's Mediation Commission, assistant to the Secretary of Labor, and chair of the War Labor Policies Board. In 1919 Frankfurter married Marion A. Denman and returned to Harvard, where he taught until 1939, when Democratic President Franklin D. Roosevelt named him to fill the seat of Justice Benjamin Cardozo. While teaching at Harvard, Frankfurter had maintained close ties and engaged in extensive correspondence with Justices Oliver Wendell Holmes and Louis D. Brandeis, with many other prominent judges and politicians, and with Franklin Roosevelt himself.

At Harvard, Frankfurter had also earned a reputation as a brilliant and charismatic teacher. He taught federal jurisdiction and administrative law but became one of the country's leading authorities on the Supreme Court. Frankfurter used his connections in the capital to place his students as clerks at the Supreme Court and in positions in the Roosevelt administration. He was a prolific writer, regularly contributing articles to the *Harvard Law Review* and other publications. Among his numerous books are *The Business of the Supreme Court* with James M. Landis (1927), *The Labor Injunction* with Nathan Greene (1930), *The Public and Its Government* (1930), *The Commerce Clause under Marshall, Taney, and Waite* (1937), and *Mr. Justice Holmes and The Supreme Court* (1938).

Prior to his appointment to the Court, Frankfurter had established himself as a leading progressive and liberal legal reformer. He publicly defended Nicola Sacco and Bartolomeo Vanzetti, two Italian anarchists convicted of murder on the basis of insubstantial evidence and executed. Their case was a cause célèbre for liberals convinced that Sacco and Vanzetti were prosecuted for their radical political views. Frankfurter's criticisms of that miscarriage of justice in articles and a book, *The Case of Sacco and Vanzetti* (1927), put him in the vanguard of the emerging civil rights movement. He also helped found the American Civil Liberties Union (ACLU) and the *New Republic*, along with promoting the Zionist movement and offering legal advice to the National Association for the Advancement of Colored People (NAACP).

On the Court, Frankfurter produced a steady stream of opinions, while continuing privately to offer advice to Roosevelt on appointments to the executive and judicial branches and other matters. During his twenty-three years on the bench, Frankfurter wrote 263 opinions announcing the Court's decision, another 144 concurring opinions, 282 dissenting opinions, and 73 separate opinions in which he in part concurred and in part dissented. He also published separate statements of his views in 68 other cases. Among his most notable and impassioned opinions was his concurrence in the Little Rock, Arkansas, school desegregation case, COOPER V. AARON (1958), in which he lectured southern lawyers—many of whom had been his students at Harvard—on the correctness and importance of complying with the watershed rulings in *Brown v. Board of Education* I (1954) and II (1955). Another notable opinion was his famous dissent in *West Virginia State Board of Education v. Barnette* (1943), in which the Court reversed its position three years earlier in *Minersville School District v. Gobitis*

(1940), and forbade compulsory saluting of the U.S. flag in public schools.

Frankfurter remained an economic liberal on the Court, supporting Congress's expansive use of its power under the commerce clause to regulate economic relations. He disappointed liberals, however, in breaking with other NEW DEAL Justices over the Court's role in expanding protection for civil rights and liberties. While he conceded that the First Amendment's guarantee of free speech had "preferred position" in constitutional law, he nonetheless concurred with the majority in *Dennis v. United States* (1951), voting to uphold the criminal prosecution of leaders of the Communist Party for their mere advocacy of communism and socialism. His defense of FEDERALISM also led him to oppose others on the Warren Court (1953–1969) who pushed for applying the guarantees of the Bill of Rights for the criminally accused to state as well as federal courts.

On the Court, Frankfurter championed judicial self-restraint and stressed the importance of collective deliberation. He eschewed absolutist interpretations of the Constitution in favor of history, precedent, and pragmatic reasoning. Never ceasing to be an academic, he lobbied and tirelessly engaged other Justices in intellectual combat. At the same time, he was often overbearing, condescending, and manipulative. Ironically, Frankfurter, one of the greatest advocates of an impartial and apolitical Supreme Court, was one of the most political in his judicial and extrajudicial activities. After suffering a debilitating stroke, Frankfurter retired on 28 August 1962. He died on 22 February 1965 at the age of 82.

### BIBLIOGRAPHY

Freedman, Max, ed. *Roosevelt and Frankfurter: Their Correspondence, 1928–1945*. 1967.

Hirsch, H. N. *The Enigma of Felix Frankfurter*. 1981.

Kurland, Philip B., ed. *Felix Frankfurter on the Supreme Court: Extrajudicial Essays on the Court and the Constitution*. 1970.

Kurland, Philip B., ed. *Of Law and Life and Other Things That Matter: Papers and Addresses of Felix Frankfurter, 1956–1963*. 1967.

Murphy, Bruce. *The Brandeis/Frankfurter Connection*. 1982.

DAVID M. O'BRIEN

**FREEDMEN'S BUREAU.** The Bureau of Refugees, Freedmen, and Abandoned Lands was created by the Congress in 1865 to deal with the massive social and economic problems of the South at the end of the CIVIL WAR. Initially suggested by the War Department's American Freedmen's Inquiry Commission to address the needs of the more than 4 million African

Americans emerging from SLAVERY, its responsibilities included the welfare of southern white refugees as well. Congress initially created the bureau for only one year. Under the leadership of General Oliver Otis Howard the bureau founded schools and hospitals, dispensed food, shelter, and other welfare and relief services, provided legal counseling and labor arbitration and settled thousands of freedmen on abandoned and confiscated property.

The establishment of the Freedmen's Bureau marked a major departure for the federal government, which had never before intervened so directly in the individual lives of Americans. Occasioned by the dislocation created by the war, the bureau came to symbolize the growing presence of the federal government. Southern whites, especially the prewar elite, resolved to fight the efforts of the bureau to aid and protect the freedmen. They turned to Tennessean President Andrew Johnson for assistance. Johnson was a determined STATES' RIGHTS advocate, committed to the principle of white supremacy.

Johnson sought to thwart the bureau, disallowing its efforts to provide freedmen with confiscated land—returning it instead to pardoned former Confederates. He reversed army rulings that prevented Confederate veterans from forming militia units, thus endangering bureau programs and freedmen's rights. He disbanded African American military units stationed in the South, thereby increasing the vulnerability of the freedmen. Hearings held by the congressional Joint Committee on RECONSTRUCTION confirmed that the President's actions threatened to return freedmen to virtual slave status as witness after witness told stories of growing southern terrorism. But the President was obdurate. When, in February of 1866, a bill came before him that would have extended the life of the Freedmen's Bureau, Johnson vetoed it, complaining about the dangers of centralized power. His steadfast refusal to compromise with even the moderates in Congress and his support for the rise of conservative white Southern authority eventually led to his isolation and weakened his presidency. By the summer of 1866 moderate Congressmen had joined with radicals to form a veto-proof Congress. In July, Johnson's veto of the freedmen's bureau bill was overridden and the bureau continued its work until 1870 when the last of its educational programs, its most successful venture, came to an end.

The Freedmen's Bureau lasted only a few years but many of its programs reappeared during the twentieth century in the programs of the NEW DEAL and the GREAT SOCIETY. Moreover, its ambivalence about the propriety of government intervention into the lives of poor people and its fears that welfare assistance might create dependency, remain central to the American debate over the wisdom and the effectiveness of federal assistance programs.

### BIBLIOGRAPHY

Benedict, Michael Les. *The Impeachment and Trial of Andrew Johnson.* 1973.

Foner, Eric. *Reconstruction: American's Unfinished Revolution, 1863–1877.* 1988.

Sefton, James E. *Andrew Johnson and the Uses of Constitutional Power.* 1980.

JAMES OLIVER HORTON

**FREEDOM OF INFORMATION ACT** (1966). The Freedom of Information Act (FOIA) establishes a presumptive right of access for any person—individual or corporate, regardless of nationality—to identifiable, unpublished, existing records of the federal departments and agencies. Requesters are not obligated to explain why they are seeking information or to demonstrate a need for it. The statute assumes that the requested records will be forthcoming; any withholding of such materials, in whole or in part, must be justified by the government.

The FOIA specifies nine categories of information that may be protected from mandatory disclosure. These exemptions do not require the withholding of records but merely permit restriction of access in instances where protection is warranted: first, information properly classified as secret for national defense or foreign-policy purposes under criteria established by an EXECUTIVE ORDER; second, information relating solely to internal personnel rules and practices in an agency; third, data specifically excepted from disclosure by another statute that either requires that matters be withheld in a nondiscretionary manner or that establishes particular criteria for withholding or refers to particular types of matters to be withheld; fourth, trade secrets and commercial or financial information obtained from a person and privileged or confidential; fifth, inter- or intra-agency memoranda or letters that would not be available by law except to an agency in litigation; sixth, personnel, medical, and similar files the disclosure of which would constitute an unwarranted invasion of personal privacy; seventh, certain kinds of investigatory records compiled for law-enforcement purposes; eighth, certain information relating to the regulation of financial institutions; and, ninth, geological and geophysical information and data, including maps, concerning wells. Disputes over the availability of information may be appealed to the head of an agency for resolution and ultimately settled in federal court.

Agencies may charge fees for document search, duplication, and review when providing records in response to an FOIA request. Fee options in this regard are specified in the statute and depend on the type of requester involved—a commercial user, an educational or noncommercial scientific institution whose purpose is scholarly or scientific research, a news media representative, or the general public. Allowance is also made for records to be furnished without any charge or at a reduced cost, according to the FOIA, "if disclosure of the information is in the public interest because it is likely to contribute significantly to public understanding of the operations or activities of the government, and is not primarily in the commercial interest of the requester." Aspects of FOIA policy and administration within the executive branch are coordinated by the OFFICE OF MANAGEMENT AND BUDGET and the DEPARTMENT OF JUSTICE.

Congress amended the statute in 1974, 1976, and 1986 to clarify its provisions and otherwise improve its functioning. Diligent and continuous congressional oversight of the administration of the FOIA by agencies not always sympathetic to or supportive of the information-access law has contributed significantly to its effective functioning.

### BIBLIOGRAPHY

Relyea, Harold C. "Access to Government Information: Rights and Restrictions." In *United States Government Information Policies: Views and Perspectives.* Edited by Charles R. McClure, Peter Hernon, and Harold C. Relyea. 1989.

Relyea, Harold C. "Public Access through the Freedom of Information and Privacy Acts." In *Federal Information Policies in the 1980s: Conflicts and Issues.* Edited by Peter Hernon and Charles R. McClure. 1987.

U.S. House. Committee on Government Operations. *A Citizen's Guide on Using the Freedom of Information Act and the Privacy Act of 1974 to Request Government Records.* 102d Cong., 1st sess., 1991. H. Rept. 101–193.

HAROLD C. RELYEA

**FREEMAN, ORVILLE L.** (b. 1918), governor of Minnesota, Secretary of Agriculture. Freeman, who was of Scandinavian descent, was born in Minneapolis, Minnesota, on 9 May 1918. He received a B.A. from the University of Minnesota in 1940 and a law degree from the same school in 1946. Freeman served in the Marine Corps during WORLD WAR II, earning the rank of major. Overcoming a speech impediment from a war wound, Freeman entered politics as an assistant to Minneapolis mayor HUBERT H. HUMPHREY. He ran for state attorney general in 1950 and governor in 1952,

losing both races. In 1954 he succeeded in winning the governorship and was reelected in 1956 and 1958.

During the 1960 presidential campaign Freeman left the Humphrey camp to support John F. Kennedy for the Democratic nomination. Kennedy chose Freeman to make the nominating speech at the Democratic convention in Los Angeles, and Freeman was among the men Kennedy considered for the vice presidency before picking Lyndon B. Johnson. Freeman lost his bid for another term as governor while helping Kennedy win Minnesota. Following the election, Kennedy considered Freeman for several positions. He finally chose him for Secretary of Agriculture in the belief that Freeman's independence from agricultural interests would enable him better to represent administration AGRICULTURAL POLICY. Freeman was not at first interested in the Agriculture Department job but, after a trip to Latin America, he became convinced that the United States' perennial agricultural surplus problem could be well used to relieve hunger and encourage democracy overseas. While governor, he had been advised on agricultural matters by economist Willard W. Cochrane, who had also advised candidate Kennedy. Freeman brought Cochrane to Washington to help fashion the administration's agricultural policies.

As secretary, Freeman helped to reshape agricultural policy. Kennedy, who had only limited interest in agriculture, gave him considerable leeway. With Kennedy's encouragement, the Department of Agriculture expanded its food programs to reach more people with food stamps and through the distribution of surplus commodities. Freeman proposed a strict plan to cut surpluses through mandatory supply management, but neither Congress nor most farmers supported it. He expanded a program of rural development designed to reverse the deterioration of rural communities because of the decline in the number of farms. Foreign assistance also received new emphasis.

Freeman remained secretary after Kennedy's assassination, serving until Johnson left office. He worked with President Johnson to expand food programs as part of the War on Poverty. He also enlisted the department in LADY BIRD JOHNSON's beautification drive. In the mid-1960s, the department, long an advocate of chemical fertilizers and pesticides, began to study the effects of chemicals on the environment and look for alternative ways to eliminate pests. Freeman's ambitious plans for expanding the department's rural-development and poverty work were ultimately scaled back because of the VIETNAM WAR.

After leaving government, Freeman became president of EDP Technology International, Inc., and from 1970 to 1981 he was president of Business International Corporation and then a partner in the law firm of Popham, Haik, Schnobrich, Kaufman, and Doty. He remained active in agricultural matters, especially overseas development, and wrote a number of books and articles in the field.

BIBLIOGRAPHY

Freeman, Orville L. *World without Hunger.* 1968.
Schlesinger, Arthur M., Jr. *A Thousand Days: John F. Kennedy in the White House.* 1965.

DOUGLAS E. BOWERS

**FREE-SOIL PARTY.** Prior to the MEXICAN WAR, Congress avoided the politically explosive problem of SLAVERY in newly acquired territories through compromise. Only the LIBERTY PARTY supported limitations on the institution, but the party's bond with abolitionists sharply limited its voter appeal in 1840 and 1844. In August 1846, however, Representative David Wilmot of Pennsylvania introduced an amendment to an administration-sponsored appropriation bill demanding that slavery be prohibited in any territories that might be gained from Mexico. The insistence on "free soil" in the WILMOT PROVISO posed a direct challenge to the South's access to new territories. Although the proviso failed, it raised troubling constitutional questions about the power of Congress to legislate on such matters.

Theory became reality as American acquisition of California and the Southwest seemed likely by the fall of 1847. Both the WHIG PARTY and DEMOCRATIC PARTY scrambled to deal with the free-soil issue. The Southern Democrat JOHN C. CALHOUN insisted that slaveowners be guaranteed the right to take their property into the territories. Other Democrats chose an alternative, "popular sovereignty," which allowed the people of the territory to decide the status of slavery for themselves.

Free-Soil Democrats, led by Preston King and the Barnburner faction in New York, and like-minded Conscience Whigs rejected such alternatives. They threatened SECESSION and a possible THIRD PARTY movement if their conventions did not select acceptable presidential candidates in 1848. In May, the Democrats chose LEWIS CASS, a Michigan Senator and champion of popular sovereignty while the following month the Whigs proposed a Louisiana slaveowner, General Zachary Taylor. The Barnburners promptly met in Utica and named Democrat Martin Van Buren. Governor SALMON P. CHASE of Ohio urged a national conclave of all free soilers—even though his own Liberty Party had already nominated Senator John P. Hale of New Hampshire as its candidate.

This coalition of Conscience Whigs, free-soil Democrats, and Liberty men from nineteen states met in Buffalo on 9 August and nominated Van Buren over Hale with the Massachusetts Whig Charles Francis Adams as his running mate. Uniting under the banner "Free Soil, Free Speech, Free Labor, and Free Men," the new party also urged federally funded INTERNAL IMPROVEMENTS, free grants of public lands, and a revenue tariff. Although Van Buren did not win any electoral votes in November, the Free-Soil Party garnered over 10 percent of the popular vote (292,000), perhaps influencing the electoral outcomes in New York and Ohio.

The Free Soilers gained in strength throughout the Northeast and Midwest, electing scores of candidates to state and federal offices. The issue itself remained especially prominent until the COMPROMISE of 1850 resolved the status of slavery in the Mexican Cession. Rejecting the compromise, committed Free Soilers nominated John P. Hale in 1852. He foundered, receiving only 5 percent (156,000) of the total, in a race that saw the procompromise Democrat Franklin Pierce triumph over the Whig WINFIELD SCOTT. The passage of the controversial KANSAS-NEBRASKA ACT (1854), however, rejuvenated the cause of free soil.

The Free-Soil Party lasted less than eight years, before its absorption into a broader REPUBLICAN PARTY coalition by 1856. During its brief existence, the Free-Soil Party provided the philosophical underpinnings of human values, rights, and liberties as well as many of the articulate and experienced leaders that helped elect Abraham Lincoln in 1860.

BIBLIOGRAPHY

Blue, Frederick. *Free Soilers: Third Party Politics, 1848–1854.* 1973.
Gienapp, William. *The Origins of the Republican Party, 1852–1856.* 1987.
Rayback, Joseph. *Free Soil: The Election of 1848.* 1970.

JOHN M. BELOHLAVEK

**FRÉMONT, JOHN C.** (1813–1890), explorer, Senator, Republican presidential nominee in 1856, army officer. John Charles Frémont was born in Savannah, Georgia, and reared in Charleston, South Carolina, by his widowed mother after his father, a French émigré, died in 1819. After a brilliant academic career at the College of Charleston, marred by irregular attendance, he served from 1833 to 1836, as a mathematics teacher aboard the naval sloop *Natchez* on a South American cruise. In 1838 he became an army second lieutenant of topographical engineers and for three years assisted Jean Nicholas Nicollet in mapping the area between the upper Mississippi and Missouri rivers. In 1841 he led an expedition to survey the Des Moines River. Earlier he had met seventeen-year-old Jessie Benton, daughter of Senator Thomas Hart Benton, who was active in promoting western explorations. In October 1841 they defied her father's wishes and eloped. The angry father soon forgave them, however, and provided much support for Frémont's career. The ambitious Jessie often pushed Frémont into opportunities for spectacular achievement that made him equally vulnerable to harsh judgments if he failed, and his Benton connections helped him cultivate arrogant attitudes toward superior authority. Frémont's daring, physical toughness, and skill in coping with the wilderness won the respect of Kit Carson and other westerners, but his political judgments were often unwise.

Frémont spent the next few years mapping much of the area between the Mississippi and the Pacific Ocean, but his most successful expedition, in 1843, violated army orders, which his teen-aged bride had conveniently destroyed. This expedition, with Carson as guide, took him to Oregon and California and with Jessie's help he published a detailed report that gave him a national reputation.

In spring 1845 he led sixty-two men on a "scientific" expedition back to California, where he helped promote the "bear flag" revolt of some dissident Americans and joined Commodore Robert Stockton's naval force in conquering that area from Mexico. Appointed governor by Stockton, Frémont refused to step aside for General Stephen W. Kearney, who arrived with official orders to establish a government. For this he was court-martialed and dismissed from the army for insubordination. Benton served as his attorney and argued that Frémont's major sin was not being a West Point graduate. President James K. Polk approved the verdict but remanded the sentence. The angry Frémont resigned and spent the next few years in California, where he struck gold and became a multimillionaire but after a long and expensive litigation lost his property because of a faulty title. Meanwhile, in 1849 he was elected U.S. Senator but had to stand for reelection in 1851 and was defeated by the proslavery party even though the state constitution barred SLAVERY.

In 1853–1854 he led a well-publicized expedition into central Utah and was available when the new free-soil REPUBLICAN PARTY was looking for a popular presidential candidate. He was defeated for President in 1856 in an exciting campaign, but he and Jessie did much to expand the popularity of the new party and help pave the way for Abraham Lincoln in 1860.

When the CIVIL WAR began, Lincoln, on the advice of Postmaster General Montgomery Blair and the Blair family made Frémont a major general in command of the western department in Saint Louis. Organizing and effectively commanding a large, untrained, and ill-equipped army was beyond Frémont's experience and ability. The Blairs and others blamed him for inaction and for the Union defeat at the Battle of Wilson's Creek, in which General Matthew Lyon and Cary Gratz, a Blair cousin, were killed. Frémont answered the criticisms by ordering the emancipation of the slaves and the confiscation of the property of all rebels in Missouri. Still trying to keep the border states from seceding, Lincoln asked Frémont to revoke the order, but Frémont refused. Jessie went to Washington to plead her husband's case, and threatened Lincoln with a military rebellion. In an angry exchange with FRANCIS P. BLAIR, she compared herself to Napoleon's first wife, the Empress Josephine. With no alternative, Lincoln relieved Frémont of the command, but to assuage the anger of congressional radicals he gave Frémont command of another army centered in Virginia. Facing Stonewall Jackson, Frémont performed poorly, and, when his long-time enemy John Pope became his superior commander, Frémont again resigned.

Frémont was nominated for President again in 1864 by a group of RADICAL REPUBLICANS, but rather than endanger Lincoln's reelection he withdrew on condition that Lincoln would discharge Montgomery Blair. For the next several years, he was involved, without financial success, in various western railroad projects. He served without controversy as governor of Arizona Territory from 1878 to 1883 and died in New York City in 1890. The conclusion is inescapable that with his wife's encouragement, Frémont created most of his own problems. His greatest contribution was the mapping and describing of much of the vast American West, which made immigration and settlement faster and easier.

## BIBLIOGRAPHY

Devoto, Bernard. *The Year of Decision.* 1943.
Frémont, Jessie Benton. *Souvenirs of My Time.* 1887.
Frémont, John Charles. *Memories of My Life.* 1887.
Nevins, Allan. *Frémont: Pathmarker of the West.* 1955.

ELBERT B. SMITH

**FRIES REBELLION.** A direct tax to pay for defense provoked a minor revolt in 1799 called Fries Rebellion. In the summer of 1798 Congress in response to insults from France increased military and naval armament as an accompaniment to the ALIEN AND SEDITION ACTS. The cost of these defense measures in the undeclared QUASI-WAR WITH FRANCE, exorbitant by the day's standards, was to be borne in large part by a direct tax on houses (depending on the number of windows), slaves, and land. In March 1799 revolt broke out in three northeastern Pennsylvania counties against this so-called Window Tax. Led by a popular auctioneer, John Fries, local villagers and townspeople harassed tax assessors and refused payment. When on 6 March federal marshals jailed eighteen tax rebels, Fries at the head of more than one hundred followers surrounded the jail at Bethlehem and forced release of the prisoners. Although no shots were fired, many Federalists, including President John Adams, saw the revolt as a dangerous repetition of the 1794 WHISKEY REBELLION and again suggested it was another example of French intrigue.

Adams proclaimed the counties in rebellion on 12 March and ordered Governor Thomas Mifflin of Pennsylvania to call out the state militia while at the same time he dispatched five hundred federal troops. Fries and two of his confederates were captured, brought before the federal district court, found guilty of treason, and sentenced to death. In their instruction to the jury, Supreme Court Justice James Iredell and District Court Justice Richard Peters declared that removing prisoners from federal custody was tantamount to a DECLARATION OF WAR and therefore, treason. Defense counsel, in protest, withdrew. President Adams viewed the actions of the rebels as serious defiance of national authority but remained troubled by procedures and by the harsh punishment. He suggested review with pardon as a possibility, but his Cabinet unanimously advised him against it.

On appeal a second trial was held in April 1800 but again Fries and his cohorts were found guilty of treason. The day before the scheduled hanging, 20 May, Adams pardoned the three tax protesters and declared a general amnesty.

### BIBLIOGRAPHY

Davis, W. W. H. *The Fries Rebellion. 1899.*

Wharton, Francis. *State Trials of the United States during the Administrations of Washington and Adams.* 1849.

STEPHEN G. KURTZ

**FUGITIVE SLAVERY.** Article IV, Section 2, clause 3, of the Constitution provided that "No Person held to Service or Labour in one State, under the Laws thereof, shall, in Consequence of any Law or Regulation therein, be discharged from such Service or Labour, but shall be delivered up on Claim of the Party to whom such Service or Labour may be due." The Framers presumably expected enforcement of this clause by state and local governments, or private citizens. But, in the Fugitive Slave Act of 1793 Congress spelled out procedures for returning runaway slaves.

This law emerged from a controversy over three Virginians who, in 1788, seized a black named John Davis in Pennsylvania and brought him to Virginia as a fugitive slave. Pennsylvania authorities believed Davis was a free black and indicted the Virginians for kidnapping. When the governor of Virginia refused to extradite the kidnappers, Governor Thomas Mifflin of Pennsylvania asked President George Washington to intervene and to seek "the interposition of the Federal Legislature" so as to "obviate all doubt and embarrassment upon a constitutional question so delicate and important." United States Attorney General EDMUND RANDOLPH concluded both governors were wrong and urged them to settle the problem without federal intervention. Randolph advised Washington to stay out of the matter to avoid "establish[ing] a precedent" for federal intervention "in every embryo dispute between States." Nevertheless, Washington eventually turned the matter over to Congress, which adopted the 1793 law regulating both the extradition of fugitives from justice and the return of fugitive slaves.

Under this law, claimants (slaveowners or their agents) who had seized runaways and brought them to any federal, state, or local judge or magistrate had to present "proof to the satisfaction" of the judge that the person seized was the claimant's fugitive slave. A claimant could establish this proof orally or through a certified "affidavit taken before . . . a magistrate" of the claimant's home state. After establishing proof of ownership the judge issued a certificate of removal to the claimant. Anyone interfering with a rendition was subject to a $500 penalty plus the value of any slaves lost and any costs a master incurred in trying to reclaim the slave.

This law never worked well. All responsibility for capturing slaves rested with owners, who were not guaranteed any aid from police officials. Northern judges sometimes declined to participate in fugitive-slave cases and northern legislatures passed "personal liberty laws" to protect free blacks from kidnapping or mistaken seizure. These laws also provided state procedures to facilitate the return of bona fide fugitives, but these laws often added procedural and evidentiary requirements to the federal law. Northern states balanced protecting free blacks from kidnapping with their constitutional obligation to return fugitive slaves.

Before the 1840s Presidents were rarely involved in fugitive-slave cases. President Andrew Jackson sometimes asked potential federal judges about their views on fugitive-slave renditions, but by and large Presidents kept their distance from the problem. This changed after the Supreme Court's decision in *Prigg v. Pennsylvania* (1842).

In *Prigg*, Justice Joseph Story found that the 1793 law was constitutional and that state personal-liberty laws interfering with rendition were unconstitutional. Story characterized the fugitive-slave clause as "a fundamental article" of the Constitution necessary for its adoption, even though Madison's *Notes* from the federal convention, published in 1840, show this was not true. Story urged state officials to continue to enforce the 1793 law but stated they could not be required to do so. A number of states soon passed new personal-liberty laws, prohibiting their officials from acting under the federal law.

Congress amended the 1793 law as part of the COMPROMISE OF 1850. This law placed responsibility for enforcement in the hands of the executive branch, and thus made fugitive-slave rendition an aspect of presidential politics. President Millard Fillmore, who signed the 1850 law, went to great lengths to enforce it, although his efforts often backfired. In 1851 Fillmore participated in the decision to bring treason charges against thirty-eight blacks and five whites in Christiana, Pennsylvania, after a fugitive slave killed a Maryland slaveowner trying to recapture his runaways. The U.S. Attorney was forced to drop all prosecutions after Supreme Court Justice Robert Grier, while riding circuit, ruled in *United States v. Hanway* (1851), that opposition to the fugitive-slave law did not constitute treason. Similarly, the Fillmore administration arranged for the arrest of a slave named Jerry in Syracuse, New York, to prove the law could be enforced in abolitionist centers like upstate New York. This plan miscarried when a mob rescued Jerry and subsequent prosecutions of the rescuers went nowhere. Fillmore hoped his support for the law would gain him an electoral victory in 1852.

In 1854 the Pierce administration used the army, the Marines, the Coast Guard, and numerous federal deputies to remove the fugitive-slave Anthony Burns from Boston. Estimates of the cost of this removal ran as high as $100,000. While proving he could have the law enforced, even in Boston, Pierce also proved that it was in the end counterproductive and enormously expensive to do so.

Rescues in Wisconsin and Ohio led to confrontations between federal and state authorities. In *Ableman v. Booth* (1859) the Supreme Court affirmed the con-

stitutionality of the 1850 law and the supremacy of the federal courts. But Wisconsin authorities continued to challenge federal power. Similarly, after the Oberlin-Wellington rescue in Ohio, state and local officials challenged federal power.

Peaceful enforcement of the 1850 law was more common than violent opposition. Claimants recovered over nine hundred fugitives under the 1850 act. However, southerners estimated that as many as ten thousand slaves escaped during the 1850s.

By 1860 fugitive-slave rendition was a key aspect of the emerging sectional conflict. President Abraham Lincoln believed he had a constitutional obligation to enforce the federal law, but in his inaugural he tiptoed around the question, asking rhetorically, "Shall fugitives from labor be surrendered by national or by State authority? The Constitution does not expressly say." He used the issue to try to persuade the South not to secede by noting that if the Union collapsed "fugitive slaves, now only partially surrendered, would not be surrendered at all."

Ultimately the fugitive-slave laws did little to protect southern property, but did much to antagonize sectional feelings. Southerners saw the North as unwilling to fulfill its constitutional obligation. Northerners believed the South was trying to force them to become slave catchers, and in the process undermining civil liberties in the nation. In 1864 Congress repealed both the 1793 and 1850 laws.

### BIBLIOGRAPHY

Finkelman, Paul. *An Imperfect Union: Slavery, Federalism, and Comity.* 1981.

Finkelman, Paul. "The Kidnapping of John Davis and the Adoption of the Fugitive Slave Law of 1793." *Journal of Southern History* 56 (1990): 397–422.

Finkelman, Paul, ed. *Articles on American Slavery.* Vol. 6: *Fugitive Slaves.* 1989.

Morris, Thomas D. *Free Men All: The Personal Liberty Laws of the North, 1780–1861.* 1974.

Wiecek, William M. *The Sources of Antislavery Constitutionalism in America, 1760–1848.* 1977.

PAUL FINKELMAN

**FULBRIGHT RESOLUTION.** The ATLANTIC CHARTER, agreed to by President Franklin D. Roosevelt and Prime Minister Winston S. Churchill on 14 August 1941, contained a commitment to "create a wider and permanent system of general security" following WORLD WAR II. For four years the White House and Department of State labored to implement this objective. To avoid the pitfalls of the American experience following WORLD WAR I of rejecting membership in both the LEAGUE OF NATIONS and World Court, and seeking to gain advance nonpartisan and international support, they worked closely with the World War II allies and congressional leaders.

Several resolutions were introduced in Congress to advance this process. Following a conference of Republican leaders at Mackinac Island, which endorsed United States participation in an "international cooperative organization," the House of Representatives—by a vote of 360 to 29—passed the Fulbright Resolution on 21 September 1943. It provided congressional authorization for "the creation of appropriate international machinery with power adequate to establish and maintain a just and lasting peace" and support for "participation by the United States therein through its constitutional processes." On 5 November the Senate passed the companion Connally Resolution by a vote of 85 to 5.

Together these resolutions empowered the President and State Department to proceed with devising and negotiating the UNITED NATIONS Charter, signed at the San Francisco Conference on 26 June 1945, and to facilitate American affiliation with the United Nations. These resolutions and actions reversed the traditional American policies of noninvolvement and isolationism, enabling the United States to play a leading role in the establishment and functioning of the United Nations system.

### BIBLIOGRAPHY

Hull, Cordell. *The Memoirs of Cordell Hull. Vol. 2.* 1948. Pp. 1258–1263, 1314.

Sweetser, A. "League of Nations and Associated Agencies: United States Reverses Thinking and Policy on Organized International Cooperation." *International Conciliation* 397 (1944): 140–149, esp. 142–144.

ELMER PLISCHKE

**FULL EMPLOYMENT.** The principle of full employment is that every person willing to work is guaranteed a job as a result of sufficient compensatory government spending to eliminate unemployment. Presidents can do little on their own to guarantee full employment. All of them since Herbert Hoover have been endowed with economic responsibilities but wanting in actual economic powers. Only twice in the late twentieth century were efforts made to enact full employment legislation, both times by liberal Democrats in Congress. Both efforts failed, in part because President Harry S. Truman in 1946 and President Jimmy Carter in 1978 gave little more than pro forma support to initial broad proposals that ended as weak legislation.

The Full Employment Bill of 1946 owed little to the White House. The bill's congressional sponsors believed that the federal government should guarantee full employment. Washington officials would forecast the yearly performance of the national economy and suggest fiscal and monetary strategies useful for achieving full employment. Levels of federal investment, taxation, and expenditure would be arranged in a way consonant with this economic objective. In effect the federal government would manage the economy and keep it prosperous with enough jobs for everyone who wanted to work. Businessmen opposed this principle, and some cooperated with conservative Congressmen to replace the proposed bill with one of their own. The Full Employment Bill passed the Senate but was stalled in a House committee. Truman acquiesced in a new and weaker version to get it out of committee. Federal responsibilities for full employment were reduced to a call for "maximum" employment for those wanting to work "in a manner calculated to foster and promote free enterprise." The only major effect of the bill was the creation of the President's COUNCIL OF ECONOMIC ADVISERS to analyze and report on the state of the economy. But the EMPLOYMENT ACT of 1946 established no machinery for translating governmental proposals into action.

The Full Employment and Balanced Growth Act of 1978, though impelled by stagflation and recession, was also amended to death. It also enunciated grandly vague principles without specifying precise means or ends; it also was eviscerated by conservatives fearful of socialism and by bipartisan fears of runaway spending and inflation. Presidential caution was also crucial.

### BIBLIOGRAPHY

Bailey, Stephen. *Congress Makes a Law: The Story behind the Employment Act of 1946.* 1950.

Mucciaroni, Gary. *The Political Failure of Employment Policy, 1945–1982.* 1990.

Weir, Margaret. *Politics and Jobs: The Boundaries of Employment Policy in the United States.* 1992.

KIM MCQUAID

# G

**GADSDEN PURCHASE.** The Gadsden Purchase was a strip of territory acquired from Mexico in a treaty negotiated by James Gadsden of South Carolina, United States Minister to Mexico, and Gen. Antonio Lopez de Santa Anna, president of Mexico, on 30 December 1853. Franklin Pierce, elected U.S. President on a platform of vigorous expansionism in 1852, was determined to secure from Mexico transit rights across the isthmus of Tehuantepec, which Americans had sought since the early 1840s, and to acquire a part of Sonora and Baja California. These issues as well as border disputes and INDIAN problems had severely strained Mexican–United States relations after the MEXICAN WAR.

Pierce appointed Gadsden to Mexico specifically to negotiate a treaty resolving all these questions. Gadsden, a southern nationalist and railroad promoter most interested in acquiring territory that would facilitate construction of a southern rail line to the Pacific Coast, was joined in Mexico by Christopher L. Ward, a special messenger and secret agent for southern railroad interests who had invested heavily in a Tehuantepec railroad scheme. Ward claimed to have secret instructions from Pierce to promote those schemes.

When Santa Anna agreed to sell only a small strip of wasteland along the border for $15 million dollars, Pierce was so disappointed that he refused to submit the draft treaty to the Senate. But since Santa Anna had also granted generous transit rights to Americans in Tehuantepec and had agreed to American demands relating to border and Indian questions in exchange for American assumption of all American claims against Mexico, a majority in Pierce's Cabinet supported the treaty. On 10 February 1854, after several months of Cabinet debate, Pierce finally agreed to send the draft treaty to the Senate, however, with the recommendation that a clause favoring a specific southern railroad interest be removed.

The Senate was divided on the treaty along sectional lines, and opponents charged Pierce both with promoting private interests and engaging in corruption and fraud. Pierce was exonerated, but the Senate rejected the treaty by a vote of 17 to 18. The Senate, coming under pressure from lobbyists representing two southern railroad groups that held concessions from Mexico, ultimately agreed to reconsider the draft treaty. On 25 April 1854, the Senate voted 33 to 12 to approve the treaty, but only after reducing the payment to Mexico to $10 million and inserting a clause by which the United States extended protection to both railroad interests.

Pierce disliked the revised treaty more than the original. The United States had acquired a mere 39 million acres of land suitable only as a railroad route, and the new territory provided the United States with neither a natural boundary nor access to the Gulf of California. Pierce realized, however, that due to sectional and partisan divisions the revised treaty was the best that could be achieved, and he was concerned that without such a treaty continued border and Indian disputes with Mexico and the aggressiveness of American railroad interests could lead to war between the two nations. Despite intense opposition from northern railroad interests, the House of Representatives passed the appropriations bill by a vote of 103 to 50. The United States and Mexico exchanged ratifications of the revised treaty on 30 June 1854. The agreement marked the last acquisition of contiguous territory by the United States.

### BIBLIOGRAPHY

Gara, Larry. *The Presidency of Franklin Pierce.* 1991.
Garber, Paul Neff. *The Gadsden Treaty.* 1923.
Nichols, Roy Franklin. *Franklin Pierce, Young Hickory of the Granite Hills.* 2d rev. ed. 1958.

KINLEY BRAUER

**GAG ORDERS.** On various occasions Presidents have attempted to block the flow of information from executive employees to Congress. In 1902 President Theodore Roosevelt issued a "gag order" that prohibited employees of the executive departments from seeking to influence legislation "individually or through associations" except through the heads of departments; failure to abide by this presidential order could result in dismissal from government service. In 1909, President William Howard Taft issued another gag order, this one forbidding any bureau chief or subordinate in government to apply to either house of Congress, to any committee of Congress, or to any member of Congress, for legislation, appropriations, or congressional action of any kind. Such communications could occur only with the consent and knowledge of their department heads. Moreover, Taft's order prohibited executive employees from responding to "any request for information from either House of Congress, or any committee of either House of Congress, or any Member of Congress, except through, or as authorized by, the head of his department."

Congress regarded these presidential orders as direct threats to the ability of the legislative branch to receive whatever information was necessary to legislate and to supervise the executive branch. By adding language to an appropriations bill in 1912, Congress nullified the gag orders issued by Roosevelt and Taft. The debate on the appropriations rider underscored the concern of Congress that the gag orders would put congressional committees in the position of hearing "only one side of a case"—that is, the views of Cabinet officials rather than the rank-and-file members of a department. Members of Congress wanted agency employees to be able to express complaints about the conduct of their supervisors. The purpose of the legislation was to ensure that government employees could exercise their constitutional rights to free speech, to peaceable assembly, and to petition the government for redress of grievances. Congressman James T. Lloyd (D-Mo.) warned that if agency employees could speak only through the heads of the departments, there would be "no possible way of obtaining information excepting through the Cabinet officers, and if these officials desire to withhold information and suppress the truth or to conceal their official acts it is within their power to do so."

Language to nullify gag orders was added as Section 6 to the Postal Services Appropriations Act of 1912. Section 6, known as the LLOYD–LA FOLLETTE ACT, provides a number of procedural safeguards to protect agency officials from arbitrary dismissals. The final sentence of section 6 reads, "The right of persons employed in the civil service of the United States, either individually or collectively, to petition Congress, or any Member thereof, or to furnish information to either House of Congress, or to any committee or member thereof, shall not be denied or interfered with." This sentence was later carried forward in the CIVIL SERVICE REFORM ACT of 1978 and is codified as permanent law (5 U.S.C. 7211).

### BIBLIOGRAPHY

Fisher, Louis. "Congressional-Executive Struggles over Information: Secrecy Pledges." *Administrative Law Review* 42 (1990): 89–107.

LOUIS FISHER

**GALLATIN, ALBERT** (1761–1849), Secretary of the Treasury. Gallatin carried on a Republican financial policy aimed at reducing taxes, government expenditure, and the public debt. Albert Abraham Alfonse Gallatin was born in Geneva, Switzerland, where he received a classical education at the Geneva Academy. At nineteen he emigrated to America and settled in western Pennsylvania. He served in the U.S. House of Representatives from 1795 to 1801 and soon became the Republican leader in the House. His particular area of expertise was public finance, and from the beginning he sought to bring the Treasury Department under congressional oversight. He had served in the House only ten days when he proposed the creation of a watchdog committee to superintend public expenditures. The Ways and Means Committee, as it came to be known, became the principal House organ for controlling the government's financial operations. Gallatin served on the committee until he became President Thomas Jefferson's Secretary of the Treasury in 1801.

Gallatin and Secretary of State James Madison joined with Jefferson to form a virtual triumvirate dedicated to implementing Republicanism. Clearly Gallatin was the one man capable of dismantling the Hamiltonian fiscal system—a foremost objective of the

Republicans. Furthermore he could serve Jefferson effectively as the unofficial liaison with Congress. He was on friendly terms with Republican congressmen, having served for a time as their floor leader, and could work informally with them to push legislation without appearing to violate the SEPARATION OF POWERS by executive encroachment. Acting unobtrusively he enabled Jefferson to have an effective legislative voice without taking on overtones of a monarchical or ministerial system.

Gallatin was in complete agreement with Jefferson's goal of reducing the public debt and ultimately abolishing it. Indeed, he wrote to Jefferson that "reduction of the debt was the principal object of bringing me into office." He also embraced the Republican view of taxation, which encouraged a reliance on import duties as the source of federal revenue and the repeal of all internal taxes. After 1802, when Jefferson signed the bill repealing the internal tax system, 90 percent of federal revenues came from customs and tonnage duties. Like other Republicans, Gallatin was convinced that government expenditures were excessive, and he instituted vigorous programs designed to eliminate wasteful spending. He found little waste on the civilian side and made most cuts by reducing the military. Gallatin and Jefferson believed that reliance on the state militias and a "mosquito fleet" of gunboats would be adequate for the nation's defense.

Under Gallatin's management, the federal government was able, during Jefferson's presidency, to reduce its debts from $80 million to $57 million and to accumulate a treasury surplus of $14 million, despite the unanticipated expense of $15 million for the LOUISIANA PURCHASE.

When the administration adopted the EMBARGO ACTS (1807–1809), Gallatin disapproved. He warned the President that "government prohibitions do always more mischief than had been calculated; and it is not without much hesitation that a statesman should hazard to regulate the concerns of individuals as if he could do it better than themselves." But once the embargo was put in place, he devoted his usual care and skill to enforcing it, even though it necessitated a return to internal taxes and the adoption of oppressive enforcement procedures.

In 1809 when Jefferson left office, Gallatin wanted to resign, but Jefferson and his successor, James Madison, persuaded him to remain. As Secretary of the Treasury under Madison, Gallatin was able to continue Jeffersonian policies and provide continuity in a time of transition. By 1811 the federal debt was reduced to $45 million, and revenues (following the repeal of the embargo) had increased to $14.4 million.

There had been no new borrowing since 1801, and the savings on interest payments amounted to $2 million a year. But the WAR OF 1812 shattered Gallatin's hopes for extinguishing the debt and maintaining the government at a minimal level.

In 1813 he took a leave of absence from the Treasury Department to go to Europe to seek an early peace through negotiations with Russia. In 1814 he was a member of the Peace Commission in Ghent. He continued his service to the nation as a diplomat: he was minister to France (1816–1823) and London (1826–1827). Long after his return to private life, President John Tyler offered him the position of Secretary of the Treasury, but Gallatin said that to accept at age eighty-four "would be an act of insanity." When he died, one newspaper eulogized him as "the last patriarch of the Republican party."

## BIBLIOGRAPHY

Balinky, Alexander. *Albert Gallatin: Fiscal Theories and Policies.* 1958.

Walters, Raymond, Jr. *Albert Gallatin: Jeffersonian Financier and Diplomat.* 1957.

White, Leonard D. *The Jeffersonians: A Study in Administrative History 1801–1829.* 1951.

FORREST MCDONALD

**GARFIELD, JAMES A.** (1831–1881), twentieth President of the United States (1881). As the U.S. President with the second-shortest tenure of office (only two hundred days, eighty of which were spent as a helpless invalid), James Abram Garfield is understandably given short shrift by presidential historians. His significance, however, lies not so much in what he did during his brief term of office but in what his career reveals about the role of the presidency during the latter part of the nineteenth century.

Those years, between RECONSTRUCTION and the SPANISH-AMERICAN WAR, sometimes called the Gilded Age, are often regarded as a low point in presidential power vis-à-vis the Congress. Ohio Senator JOHN SHERMAN summed up the prevalent opinion by declaring, "The executive department of a republic like ours should be subordinated to the legislative department." The British historian James Bryce reinforced this assumption of executive mediocrity by devoting a chapter of his classic 1893 study, *The American Commonwealth*, to explain, as he put it, "Why Great Men Are Not Chosen Presidents."

Garfield both typified and transcended this stereotype of mediocrity. In some respects he blends indistinguishably into that gray procession of (mostly bearded) Presidents from Rutherford B. Hayes to

William McKinley that schoolchildren have such difficulty differentiating. Yet in his life Garfield managed to embody many of his country's most cherished values, and in his public career he demonstrated that not all that glittered in the Gilded Age was gilt.

**Prepresidential Career.** Garfield's nomination as a dark-horse candidate (see DARK HORSES) by the Republican national convention on 8 June 1880 took even some delegates by surprise, but on reflection it can be seen as a supremely logical choice. In many respects Garfield's entire life had been a preparation for the presidency. Born in a log cabin in Orange, Ohio, on 19 November 1831, he was the last President able to claim that politically potent symbol of humble origins. His teenage stint as a canal boy added an image of useful toil, reminiscent of Abraham Lincoln's service as a rail-splitter. Left fatherless as an infant, Garfield was reared by his strong-willed mother, who steered him onto the paths of religion and education. Baptized into the brotherhood of the Disciples of Christ (now the Christian Church) he also attended a Disciples of Christ college in Hiram, Ohio. After broadening his education at Williams College in Massachusetts, he returned to Hiram as a professor of ancient languages, became an ordained minister, and was named President of the college before he was thirty. Elected to the Ohio Senate in 1859, he resigned his seat early in the CIVIL WAR to recruit the Forty-second Ohio Volunteer Infantry and was commissioned the regiment's colonel. After two years of military service in the Army of the Cumberland, culminating with the battle of Chickamauga (for which he won promotion to major general), he assumed a seat in the U.S. House of Representatives, representing Ohio's staunchly Republican Nineteenth District. He held the seat for seventeen years until his 1880 nomination for President.

Thus, in one career, Garfield managed to evoke the cherished symbols of Home, Mother, Church, and Flag. Above all, to a nation that treasured the inspirational tales of Horatio Alger, Garfield was, as Rutherford B. Hayes observed, the ideal candidate because he was "the ideal self-made man."

Garfield had other assets. One was his intimate knowledge of the inner workings of the government acquired as chairman of the House Appropriations Committee. Others included his eloquence, honed in the pulpit, and his professional capacity for sustained intellectual effort, which made him something of a scholar in politics. Physically large, affable, and conciliatory, he was one of the few men in public life with scarcely any enemies. These traits carried him to a position of leadership in the REPUBLI-CAN PARTY and marked him out as a likely presidential possibility.

**Election of 1880.** That his opportunity came sooner, rather than later, was due to the deep divisions within the Republican Party—divisions that threatened to paralyze the Republican national convention of 1880. The front-runner was former President Ulysses S. Grant, hoping for a return to power after a four-year hiatus. His supporters, the self-styled Stalwarts, consisted largely of rotten-borough delegates from the South and the high-handed senatorial triumvirate of Roscoe Conkling, John Logan, and Donald Cameron, who controlled their home states of New York, Illinois, and Pennsylvania.

They were opposed by a loose coalition of midwestern and New England Republicans who felt that it was time for the party to put aside the old issues of Civil War and Reconstruction and move on to fresh faces and new issues. Their leading candidates were JAMES G. BLAINE of Maine and Sherman of Ohio, though scattered support was also expressed for George Edmunds of Vermont and Elihu Washburne of Illinois.

Garfield came to the Chicago convention as a spokesman for Sherman, but his decisive leadership in defeating the unit rule (which would have compelled some state delegations to vote as a bloc, thus insuring Grant's victory) gave the spokesman more prominence than his candidate. Similarly, Garfield's eloquent but curiously lukewarm nominating speech for Sherman boosted his own stock more than the nominee's.

The first ballot revealed the deep split within Republican ranks. Grant led the field with 304 delegates, only 75 short of a majority. Next came Blaine with 284 votes; Sherman trailed with 93. Scattered votes were cast for Edmunds, Washburne, and Minnesota's favorite son, William Windom.

This pattern persisted, ballot after ballot. As the tension mounted, more than one delegate urged Garfield to step forward as a compromise choice to break the deadlock. He steadfastly rejected their pleas, insisting that he must remain loyal to Sherman. His friends had no such inhibitions. Indeed, on the second ballot one had cast an unauthorized vote for the unwilling candidate. On the thirty-fourth ballot Wisconsin unexpectedly switched sixteen votes to Garfield and the astonished convention hall erupted in chaos. Garfield attempted to withdraw his name but was gaveled into silence as state after state impulsively joined the Garfield bandwagon. The Grant forces stood firm, with 306 unshakable delegates, but they were overwhelmed on the thirty-sixth ballot. They were somewhat appeased by being allowed then to choose one of their number, Chester A. Arthur of New

York, to be Garfield's running mate, though some anti-Stalwarts registered their disapproval by voting instead for Mississippi Senator Blanche K. Bruce, the first African American to be so recognized by a major political party.

With a divided Republican Party facing a resurgent Democratic opposition, Garfield's prospects for victory in November seemed bleak. Four years earlier Republican candidate Rutherford B. Hayes had barely eked out a one-vote majority in the ELECTORAL COLLEGE under circumstances that were unlikely to be repeated. With the abandonment of Reconstruction and the subsequent disenfranchisement of Southern black Republicans, the Democrats could count on the 137 electoral votes of the so-called Solid South. If to these they could add fifty votes from northern states still suffering from the economic depression begun in 1873, victory would be theirs.

Faced with these numbers, Garfield's strategy was to mobilize a virtually solid North to counter the Democratic South. The first priority was to heal Republican wounds so that no disgruntled faction would sit on its hands and allow victory to slip away by default.

This was precisely what Roscoe Conkling was threatening to do. He was mollified by the shelving of CIVIL-SERVICE REFORM, an issue that spoilsmen like Conkling despised, and by vague promises that New York Stalwart leaders would be consulted in making appointments. These promises would return to haunt Garfield after his election, but for the moment they were sufficient to tap Stalwart enthusiasm and fundraising ability for Garfield's campaign.

He needed all the help he could get. Departing from their usual pattern of choosing a New York governor as their presidential candidate, the Democrats had nominated General WINFIELD HANCOCK, a Union hero of the battle of Gettysburg, who threatened to cut into the usually dependable Republican bloc of Union veterans.

In such a closely divided electorate, even minor parties could be significant. The PROHIBITION PARTY nominated another Union general, Neal Dow, whose cause was likely to drain more votes from Republicans than from the traditionally hard-drinking Democrats. The GREENBACK PARTY, led by yet another Union general, JAMES WEAVER, threatened to combine with the Democrats rather than allow the notoriously hard-money Garfield to become President.

The local elections in Maine in September showed that this was no idle threat. There, a fusion of Greenbacks and Democrats swept the elections in this normally Republican stronghold, which seemed an ominous harbinger of the general election in November.

This setback galvanized the Republicans into fresh activity. Rather than replaying the stale themes of Civil War and Reconstruction, Blaine called for a fresh emphasis on economic issues. Urging him to "fold up the bloody shirt and lay it away," Blaine persuaded Garfied to shift the main issue to tariff protection. In effect, Blaine and Garfield envisioned a transformation of the Republican Party from the party of the Union to the party of prosperity, a redefinition that would, by the time of McKinley, make it the majority party.

The Democrats failed to meet this challenge. Even though their platform advocated a "tariff for revenue only," they avoided an issue-oriented campaign, concentrating instead on personal assaults on Garfield's character. Ancient scandals and accusations were dredged up to prove Garfield's unfitness—especially his involvement in the CREDIT MOBILIER SCANDAL, in which he had allegedly taken a $329 bribe. Democrats scrawled that number on barns, sidewalks, and gutters as a cryptic reminder.

Garfield refused to respond to these attacks. For one thing, he had a deep-seated personal aversion to parading his own virtue. For another, it was not yet considered proper for presidential candidates to campaign on their own behalf. He did not, however, sit idle. Though he stayed put in his Mentor, Ohio, home of Lawnfield, he gave carefully crafted little speeches to the delegations that daily came to call. By inventing what would come to be known as the front porch campaign, he cleverly managed to circumvent the convention against overt campaigning.

He was also active in shaping campaign strategy. It was Garfield's decision to concentrate Republican resources on the October elections in Indiana. The state was accordingly flooded with speakers, documents, and money. A smashing Republican victory forecast Garfield's success in November. Not even the last-minute appearance of the forged Morey Letter, which suggested that Garfield favored unrestricted Chinese immigration, could prevent Garfield's victory.

Garfield's victory in the November general election was close. In the popular-vote totals, he beat Hancock by fewer than 10,000 votes. But his victory in the Electoral College was decisive: 214 to Hancock's 155. The Greenback Party polled more than 300,000 votes and the Prohibitionists attracted 10,000, leaving Garfield with 48.3 percent of the tally. The congressional elections were also close: the incoming House would be narrowly Republican but the Senate would be evenly divided. Though Hancock captured every one of the old slaveholding states, the Republicans countered by carrying every other state except New

Jersey, Nevada, and California, demonstrating that the country was still politically polarized by the Civil War and its aftermath.

**Garfield's Administration.** His narrow margin of victory imposed on Garfield the obligation to maintain party unity. In forming his CABINET each faction would have to be represented in order to attach its loyalty to the new administration. John Logan was appeased by the selection of Robert Todd Lincoln (son of Abraham Lincoln) as Secretary of War. Southern Republicans were encouraged by the appointment of Louisiana's William H. Hunt to head the Navy Department. Wayne McVeagh's appointment as Attorney General gratified both the reform element, whose views he shared, and Pennsylvania's party boss, Donald Cameron, who was McVeagh's brother-in-law. The post of Secretary of State fell almost inevitably to Garfield's old friend James G. Blaine, the Republican Party's most magnetic leader.

Blaine's appointment created problems. New York's haughty boss, Roscoe Conkling, who was not even on speaking terms with Blaine, demanded that his state and faction be rewarded with an equally prominent place in the new administration. Only the Treasury Department would satisfy him. When Stalwart followers of his were offered what he considered the inferior departments of Justice and the Navy, they declined rather than face Conkling's wrath. That wrath even turned on Garfield, as Conkling harangued the President-elect for over an hour in Conkling's hotel bedroom.

Garfield, at Blaine's prodding, counterattacked by undermining Conkling's grip on New York. Garfield and Blaine intervened in the state's senatorial election in favor of Thomas Platt, who, in return, promised to support all the administration's New York appointments, and they induced Thomas L. James to accept the Postmaster Generalship despite Conkling's objections. This opened the way for Minnesota's William Windom to take the Treasury Department and Iowa's Samuel J. Kirkwood to become Secretary of the Interior. With that, Garfield's long ordeal of Cabinet making was over, just in time for his inauguration on 4 March 1881.

After an uninspired inaugural address, the new President turned to the most immediately pressing task facing his administration—filling the multitude of government jobs. More than 100,000 civilians were employed by the federal government, and, in the absence of a regularized CIVIL SERVICE, all owed their appointments, to one degree or another, to political influence. Other politicians might have enjoyed dispensing all this patronage, but Garfield did not. "I love

to deal with doctrines and events," he declared. "The conflicts of men about men I greatly dislike." Now he found his energy consumed with decisions on "whether A or B shall be appointed to this or that office." Dismayed by the time and effort wasted on such activity, he began to favor some sort of civil service reform, if only to spare future Presidents this ordeal. With Garfield's encouragement, Postmaster General James began to experiment with competitive examinations and other ways to remove political considerations from Post Office appointments.

Other departments also began reform measures. Secretary of the Navy Hunt assembled a board of review whose recommendations would later lead to the creation of a revitalized navy. Attorney General McVeagh began the prosecution (later bungled by his successor) of the Star Route swindlers, who had robbed the Post Office Department of millions of dollars. Treasury Secretary Windom successfully engineered a massive refunding of government bonds.

The most striking activity, as might be expected, came from the State Department, where the dynamic Blaine had too much energy and ambition to be constrained by the customary leisurely pace of American diplomacy. Rather than merely reacting to events, Blaine envisioned a comprehensive reorientation of U.S. foreign policy away from its traditional preoccupation with European relations and toward a greater involvement in Western Hemisphere affairs. In theory, this shift would create a pan-American system in which the United States would guarantee the peace and territorial integrity of Latin America, though in practice Blaine's interventions often resulted only in clumsy meddling.

Since the House of Representatives was not in session during the brief Garfield administration, no legislation was passed. Yet even had more time been granted him, it is unlikely that Garfield would have promoted many significant measures. His view of the presidency, shaped by his congressional experience, was a highly limited one. The President, he argued, had no right to "use the power of his great office to force upon Congress his own peculiar views of legislation." On the other hand, when it came to appointments, he strongly believed that the President must have the right to select officials of his choosing without interference from that "corrupt and vicious practice" known as senatorial courtesy. This conviction led to the most dramatic struggle of the Garfield presidency.

The conflict arose from the still-unresolved schism within the Republican Party. Despite Conkling's obstructionism, Garfield still hoped to appease the lordly New York chief by awarding Conkling's friends high office. These concessions upset Blaine, who demanded that equal recognition be given to Blaine's own New York followers, especially William H. Robertson. Caught in a tug-of-war, Garfield tried to mediate by finding a place for Robertson as collector of the Port of New York.

This was no ordinary government job but a highly lucrative post supervising more than fifteen hundred workers. Four years earlier, when President Hayes had attempted to appoint another Conkling foe to the post, Conkling had successfully appealed to senatorial courtesy to defeat the nomination. Now, though he raged in fury, tied the Senate in knots, and for a time, paralyzed the government, his cause was hopeless in the face of Garfield's resolute determination to maintain the prerogatives of his office. Fearful of losing presidential favors, Conkling's fellow Senators abandoned him and the principle of senatorial courtesy, particularly after it became apparent that the public, hungry for leadership, was rallying behind the President. Rather than acquiesce in Robertson's confirmation, Conkling heeded the suggestion of his junior colleague Platt (who was torn between his promise to Blaine and his loyalty to Conkling) that they both resign from the Senate in protest.

Garfield's victory was complete. After fifteen years of presidential weakness, he had demonstrated the power inherent in the office to dominate his party and overawe the Senate. The issue of Robertson may have been petty, but the result was to begin shaping the presidency into its twentieth-century form.

**Death and Subsequent Influence.** After a shaky start, the Garfield administration had pulled itself together. The President could turn to his next challenge, the intractable Southern Question. Breaking with his passive view of the presidency, he planned to propose a program of federally sponsored education that he hoped would do for southern blacks what education had done for him—place them on the path to middle-class respectability.

Garfield was discussing these plans with Blaine as they strolled through Washington's Baltimore & Potomac train station on 2 July when a shabby, bearded religious fanatic and political hanger-on named CHARLES GUITEAU, who was convinced he carried a commission from God, pumped two bullets into the President's back.

For eighty days the wounded President slid slowly toward death while a morbidly fascinated nation hung on every bulletin from the sickroom. As an invalid, Garfield became what he had not been in health: a genuinely popular hero. In so doing, he prefigured another modern aspect of his office: the President as

celebrity, rising above politics to become a symbol of national unity. The massive outpouring of grief that followed his death on 19 September 1881 at Elberon, New Jersey, was more extravagant that that which had accompanied Lincoln's death and was further proof of the hold the presidency had begun to assume on the nation's imagination. Judged by the standards of legislation passed and crises resolved, the brief Garfield administration may seem a nullity. But in the evolution of the presidency, it marks a milestone.

### BIBLIOGRAPHY

Brown, Harry James, and Frederick D. Williams, eds. *The Diary of James A. Garfield.* Vol. 4, 1878–1881. 1981.

Clancy, Herbert J. *The Presidential Election of 1880.* 1958.

Doenecke, Justus D. *The Presidencies of James A. Garfield and Chester A. Arthur.* 1981.

Hoogenboom, Ari. *Outlawing the Spoils: A History of the Civil Service Reform Movement, 1865–1883.* 1961.

Morgan, H. Wayne. *From Hayes to McKinley: National Party Politics, 1877–1896.* 1961.

Peskin, Allan. *Garfield.* 1978.

ALLAN PESKIN

**GARNER, JOHN NANCE** (1868–1967), thirty-second Vice President of the United States (1933–1941). By personal orientation and experience, John Nance Garner was a creature of Congress who spent three decades progressing to the office he coveted—Speaker of the House. Yet his main contribution to American history came in the distinctive, and diverse, roles he played in relation to the presidency of Franklin D. Roosevelt. Garner was indispensable in securing Roosevelt's nomination and helped enact NEW DEAL legislation. Ultimately, he broke with Roosevelt and as Vice President contested Roosevelt's effort to win a third term.

Born on 22 November 1868 near Detroit, Texas, Garner was first elected to the United State House of Representatives in 1902. During his three decades in Congress, he introduced little legislation and delivered few speeches, preferring to wield influence quietly. Due to his close relationship with President Woodrow Wilson, he served as a liaison between the Wilson White House and Congress. After serving in leadership positions, including as House minority leader from 1928, Garner was elected the thirty-ninth Speaker of the House of Representatives on 7 December 1931 by only three votes in the closest election for that position in modern times.

The following month, William Randolph Hearst began an effort to draft Garner for the Democratic presidential nomination. In a nationally broadcast radio speech on 2 January 1932, Hearst praised Garner as someone who would place "America First"; front-page editorials endorsed him in Hearst newspapers. Although a somewhat reluctant candidate, Garner entered the convention as the third leading candidate behind Roosevelt and ALFRED E. SMITH, the party's 1928 standard bearer. Garner's chances depended on Smith and favorite sons obtaining enough support to deny Roosevelt the necessary two-thirds vote. He was not disposed to deadlock the convention, however, and when, after three ballots Roosevelt was close to, but below, the vote needed for nomination, Garner released his delegates to Roosevelt. In return, he received by prior arrangement the vice-presidential nomination. It was the last time the second spot on the ticket was apparently traded for delegate support to nominate a presidential candidate. The Roosevelt-Garner ticket helped unify the party and illustrated a classic instance of ticket-balancing—a northeastern governor and a southern congressman.

During Roosevelt's first term, Garner was a relatively active and influential Vice President. He regularly attended Cabinet meetings and advised Roosevelt on a range of matters. He occasionally differed with Roosevelt on important issues—Garner, for instance, opposed normalizing relations with Russia—but these disagreements did not undermine the essential relationship. With his extensive legislative experience and contacts, he provided a needed resource in the early Roosevelt administration. As such, he also helped steer NEW DEAL legislation through Congress. In an era before Presidents developed professional legislative liaison offices, Garner often lobbied Senators on administration programs and advised Roosevelt on legislative tactics. Even during the "Second New Deal," during the summer of 1935, Garner worked loyally for Roosevelt's programs despite some misgivings. In 1935 he traveled to the PHILIPPINES, Japan, and China on behalf of the United States, the first foreign travel of an American Vice President in an official capacity; the following year he represented the United States in Mexico. Garner's foreign travels raised his prestige and that of his office.

Garner was reelected Vice President in 1936, only the sixth man to win a second term in that office. Relations with Roosevelt soon soured. They disagreed on numerous policy and political issues—the propriety of sit-down strikes, the COURT-PACKING PLAN, the budget, the administration's involvement in the race for Senate majority leader between Alben W. Barkley and Byron (Pat) Harrison, and the 1938 purge of Democrats Roosevelt did not believe were sufficiently loyal. Gar-

ner worked against some Roosevelt legislative measures and helped frustrate some of the President's aims. Reports of their rift circulated.

Public opinion polls found Garner the clear front-runner for the 1940 Democratic presidential nomination if Roosevelt did not run. Strongly opposed to a third term for Roosevelt, Garner sought the Democratic presidential nomination and entered primaries. The worsening international situation prompted calls for a third term. Roosevelt, although not an announced candidate, defeated Garner handily in Wisconsin, Illinois, California, and other important states.

Roosevelt easily won renomination over Garner, the last time a Vice President has opposed an incumbent President for the nomination. Not surprisingly, Garner was not invited to run again for Vice President. Instead, Roosevelt forced the convention to accept HENRY A. WALLACE, establishing the practice of a presidential candidate dictating the choice of a running mate.

In 1940, after thirty-eight years in Congress and as Vice President, Garner returned to Uvalde, Texas, where he accumulated a fortune from his assorted investments. Until his death on 7 November, 1967 prominent politicians often journeyed to confer with him.

Owing to his stature and skill, and the legislative experience he was able to add to the Roosevelt administration, Garner enhanced the credibility of the vice presidency. He contributed as a presidential adviser and legislative liaison and his occasional foreign travels inaugurated a new role for Vice Presidents. Nonetheless, his second term illustrated inherent limitations in the office. Indeed, he was quoted as describing the vice presidency as not "worth a pitcher of warm spit," a statement some suggest was actually more graphic until censors sanitized it.

## BIBLIOGRAPHY

Cruz, Martha O. *John Nance Garner and the Politics of Opposition: A Study in American Political Realities, 1932–1940.* M.A. thesis, 1971.

Patenaude, Lionel V. "The Garner Vote Switch to Roosevelt: 1932 Democratic Convention." *Southwestern Historical Quarterly* 79 (1975): 189–204.

Patenaude, Lionel V. "Vice President John Nance Garner: A Study in the Use of Influence During the New Deal." *Texana* 11 (1973): 124–144.

Romano, Michael John. *The Emergence of John Nance Garner as a Figure in American National Politics, 1924–1941.* Ph.D. diss. 1974.

Timmons, Bascom N. *Garner of Texas.* 1948

Young, Donald. *American Roulette: The History and Dilemma of the Vice Presidency.* Rev. ed. 1972. Pp. 163–173.

JOEL K. GOLDSTEIN

**GATT (GENERAL AGREEMENT ON TAR-IFFS AND TRADE).** GATT is a remnant of the Charter for an International Trade Organization (ITO) (Havana Charter), envisaged as a specialized agency of the UNITED NATIONS to provide organizational and functional framework and rules for conducting international trade and trade-related operations, not unlike the institutions set up by the BRETTON WOODS AGREEMENTS in other areas of international economic cooperation. For practical reasons, ITO's trade and tariff rules, now known as the GATT, were adopted provisionally in 1947 and entered into force in 1948, whereas the ITO charter itself, agreed to in 1948, became effectively dead in 1950 for lack of sufficient ratification.

For the United States, the GATT is an EXECUTIVE AGREEMENT concluded under the authority of the reciprocal trade agreements legislation and implemented by presidential proclamation rather than a treaty entered into with the ADVICE AND CONSENT of the Senate. At the end of 1992, GATT membership consisted of 105 contracting parties (signatories of the agreement) and 29 countries to which the agreement applies de facto (former dependencies of contracting parties).

A multilateral instrument, GATT operates in three ways: as a framework of rules governing international trade relations; as a forum for trade negotiations aimed at liberalization and greater predictability of the trade environment; and by providing a mechanism for resolving disputes among its members.

GATT rules are based on the following fundamental principles: nondiscrimination—member countries must treat all other members equally with respect to import and export duties and charges (most-favored-nation [MFN] treatment), and imported goods must not be treated less favorably than domestic goods (national treatment); protection through tariffs rather than through nontariff measures; "binding," hence stability, of negotiated tariff concessions; fair competition—rules for dealing with dumping and subsidization of exported goods; general prohibition of quantitative restrictions on imports; in special circumstances, waivers of GATT obligations and trade-restricting safeguard measures; exemptions from the MFN obligation for countries in regional integration groups; more favorable conditions for developing countries (since 1965), including, since 1979, the "enabling clause" for the extension of the generalized system of preferences to developing countries, and special trade treatment for least developed countries; and an exception from normal GATT disciplines for trade in textiles and clothing. The latter is covered by the Multi-Fiber Arrangement (MFA), not part of the GATT but

concluded within its framework in 1974 and extended through 1992.

Seven rounds of multilateral trade negotiations have taken place within the GATT framework: in 1947 (which included the adoption of the GATT itself), 1949, 1951, 1956, 1960–1961 (Dillon Round), 1964–1967 (Kennedy Round), and 1973–1979 (Tokyo Round). While all have dealt with reducing tariff barriers, the Tokyo Round focused particularly on nontariff trade matters and resulted in a number of specialized nontariff agreements ("codes"). These codes apply only among those GATT members that have acceded to them. The eighth (Uruguay) round, begun in 1986, while continuing to deal with tariff and nontariff trade matters, sought to broaden the scope of the GATT by establishing rules also for trade-related services, investment, and intellectual property rights, and creating a Multilateral Trade Organization (MTO).

BIBLIOGRAPHY

Hudec, Robert E. *The GATT Legal System and World Trade Diplomacy.* 2d ed. 1990.

Jackson, John Howard. *The World Trading System: Law and Policy of International Economic Relations.* 1989.

VLADIMIR N. PREGELJ

**GENERAL ACCOUNTING OFFICE (GAO).** Created by the BUDGET AND ACCOUNTING ACT of 1921 to give Congress an independent capacity to audit the executive branch, the General Accounting Office is under the control and direction of the COMPTROLLER GENERAL of the United States. Over time, Congress has increased the powers and responsibilities of the GAO. Presidents and their Attorneys General have frequently raised constitutional objections to the activities of the GAO, especially when it appears that the Comptroller General is carrying out executive duties without being subject to the direct control of the President.

The history of the GAO has important antecedents in the years before the drafting of the Constitution. In 1781, the Continental Congress created a number of executive officers to handle administrative matters. The positions of Secretary for Foreign Affairs and Secretary at War were accepted by Congress as essentially executive in nature. The question of finance proved much more divisive. Robert Morris accepted the new post of Superintendent of Finance, but his request for total control over his subordinates met with legislative opposition. Congress decided to restrict his power to remove subordinates to cases where he had good cause ("incapacity, negligence, dishonesty or other misbehavior"). Moreover, Congress itself appointed the Comptroller rather than allow the Superintendent to make that selection. The Comptroller was a quasi-judicial officer because he superintended the settlement of public accounts and his decision was "conclusive" on all appeals related to the auditing of accounts. Because of these institutional qualities, the Comptroller of 1781 is clearly a forerunner of the Comptroller General.

When Congress created the DEPARTMENT OF THE TREASURY in 1789, it continued the office of Comptroller. Although James Madison argued strongly in favor of giving the President the power to remove the secretaries of Foreign Affairs, War, and Treasury, he insisted that the Comptroller needed a measure of independence from presidential control. The properties of the Comptroller were not "purely of an Executive nature" and seemed to "partake of a Judiciary quality as well as Executive." Because of the mixed nature of this office, Madison said that there might be "strong reasons why an officer of this kind should not hold his office at the pleasure of the Executive branch of the Government." Only by understanding the history of the Comptroller during the Continental Congress could Madison have offered such remarks.

Legislation in 1795 made the Comptroller's decision on certain claims "final and conclusive." In 1817, Congress abolished the offices of accountant in the War and Navy departments and placed the authority to settle all accounts and all claims and demands by or against the United States within the Treasury Department. To discharge these new duties, the statute created four new auditors and an Assistant Comptroller. Other duties were assigned to the Comptroller over the years, but the major organizational change came in 1921, when Congress created the General Accounting Office. In effect, Congress lifted the Comptroller, Assistant Comptroller, and six auditors out of the Treasury Department—literally transferring people, files, furniture, office equipment, and other property to the newly created GAO. The establishment of the GAO was intended to give Congress an institutional capacity to compete with the President's Bureau of the Budget, also created by the 1921 statute.

The Budget and Accounting Act of 1921 describes the GAO as "independent of the executive departments and under the control and direction of the Comptroller General of the United States." The Comptroller General and Assistant Comptroller General are both appointed by the President with the ADVICE AND CONSENT of the Senate and both hold office for fifteen years and may be removed only by a joint resolution of Congress or by IMPEACHMENT.

The GAO audits the executive branch to ensure that funds are spent efficiently and that expenditures are consistent with statutory authority. The 1921 law directed the Comptroller General to report to Congress "every expenditure or contract made by any department or establishment in any year in violation of law." Moreover, the Comptroller General investigates "all matters relating to the receipt, disbursement, and application of public funds." Balances certified by the Comptroller General "shall be final and conclusive upon the executive branch of the Government." Claims and demands by the government or against it are settled and adjusted by the GAO.

The statutory responsibilities assigned to the GAO by the 1921 law have been greatly enlarged over the years. The GAO was strengthened significantly by the Budget and Accounting Procedures Act of 1950 and the Legislative Reorganization Act of 1970. As a result of these statutes and internal reforms, GAO now directs more of its resources to broad program evaluation instead of narrow auditing of agency vouchers. The CENTRAL INTELLIGENCE AGENCY (CIA) is exempt from GAO audits.

GAO's exercise of statutory powers frequently results in collisions with the executive branch, especially the DEPARTMENT OF JUSTICE. Comptrollers General have insisted that their opinions regarding the legality of government expenditures are binding on the executive departments, but ever since 1921 Comptrollers General and Attorneys General have disagreed on statutory interpretations, jurisdiction, and the application of public funds. The ATTORNEY GENERAL has regularly placed limits on the binding nature of GAO decisions. Orders given by the GAO to the executive departments affecting the performance of executive functions have been submitted to the Attorney General for his independent opinion. In some cases the executive departments have refused to comply with GAO decisions.

Occasionally a President has intervened to challenge a GAO decision. In 1944 the Comptroller General ruled that the Committee of Fair Employment Practice, created by EXECUTIVE ORDER and lacking any statutory support, did not have the powers it claimed. This ruling was overridden by a letter written by President Franklin D. Roosevelt. Congress, however, passed legislation to prohibit the use of any appropriation to pay the expenses of any agency established by executive order unless Congress specifically authorized funds for the agency. Disputes between GAO and the executive branch have also been litigated and resolved in federal court.

BIBLIOGRAPHY

Mosher, Frederick C. *The GAO: The Quest for Accountability in American Government.* 1979.

Smith, Darrell. *The General Accounting Office: Its History, Activities, and Organization.* 1927.

Walker, Wallace Earl. *Changing Organizational Culture: Strategy, Structure, and Professionalism in the U.S. General Accounting Office.* 1986.

LOUIS FISHER

**GERRY, ELBRIDGE** (1744–1814), governor of Massachusetts, fifth Vice President of the United States (1813–1814). Despite being a signer of the Declaration of Independence, a governor of Massachusetts, and Vice President of the United States, Gerry is better known as a nonsigner of the Constitution, for his controversial role in the XYZ affair, and for the label "gerrymander" associated with his name. Born in Marblehead, Massachusetts, on 17 July 1744, he was the son of a British immigrant who became one of the richest fishing merchants in Essex County. Gerry graduated from Harvard in 1762, returning in 1765—the year of the Stamp Act—to submit his M.A. thesis, in which he justified the right of faithful subjects to evade arbitrary laws of commerce imposed on them by a government that disregarded sacred property rights.

In 1772 Marblehead elected him to the general court where he encountered his political mentor, Samuel Adams, and helped Adams form the committee of correspondence system, which soon united Massachusetts towns and then all the colonies in a massive anti-British movement.

Gerry's drive toward rebellion received a setback in 1774 in Marblehead's "Smallpox War." During an epidemic Gerry and others started an inoculation program. A mob, fearful that the program might spread rather than check the disease, threatened Gerry's life, burned down his hospital, and ran amok through the streets. He promptly resigned from public office, retired to his home, and sulked. When the British Coercive Acts shut down Boston harbor, creating mass unemployment, Gerry returned to public life and distributed charitable donations that poured in from other colonies.

He was elected to the extralegal Massachusetts Provincial Congress in 1774, serving on the committees of supply and safety. He gathered military supplies for the minuteman forces then forming. Because of these activities he was a marked man and was mentioned in British military dispatches and once barely escaped capture by a British search party.

In 1776 Gerry's political career moved to the national level with his election to the Continental Congress, where he became an early advocate of independence. He signed the Declaration of Independence because it reflected the principles in which he believed: natural rights, strict SEPARATION OF POWERS, honesty and frugality in government, and equal rights. He practiced these principles during his terms in the congress from 1776 to 1781 and from 1783 to 1785. He was one of the most active members of that body, especially in matters dealing with supply and finance.

In 1787, concerned over the breakdown in public order represented by Shays' Rebellion in western Massachusetts, Gerry chose to attend the CONSTITUTIONAL CONVENTION in Philadelphia. At the convention Gerry proved to be a middle-of-the-road nationalist. He hoped to strengthen the central government, yet was also concerned to prevent the government from possessing too much power. His worry about excessive democracy led him to oppose the popular election of both houses of Congress and the President, but he also demanded democratic measures such as the annual election of Congressmen, enumerated powers of government, and a national bill of rights. He remained a "true federalist," advocating a balanced partnership between the central and state governments. Twice he helped rescue the convention from possible disaster; chairing the committee that broke the large state versus small state deadlock with the Connecticut Compromise and casting his vote to approve the compromise by a wafer-thin margin of one state.

In the end, however, Gerry refused to sign the Constitution. He listed three main objections: personal liberties would not be secure without a bill of rights, republican government would not work unless sovereignty was more evenly divided between the central government and the states, and the federal government should not have been given so much military power. Gerry warned that the Constitution would not be ratified without a bill of rights. He was right. State after state approved ratification with the strong recommendation that a bill of rights be added. Gerry staunchly supported the new government, helped to frame the Bill of Rights, and served as Congressman from 1789 to 1793.

In 1797 President John Adams appointed Gerry, John Marshall, and CHARLES COTESWORTH PINCKNEY to go to France to settle several disputes. The French minister of foreign affairs, Talleyrand, and his secret agents (called "X," "Y," and "Z") demanded bribes, causing Gerry's companions to depart in disgust. Gerry, fearing his departure might result in war, disregarded his official instructions and remained in France. His stubborn independence in the so-called XYZ affair proved the right course. Adams subsequently acknowledged that Gerry brought home the assurances that made peace with France possible. [*See* QUASI-WAR WITH FRANCE.]

Gerry served as governor of Massachusetts from 1810 to 1812. His second term was stormy. Despite his long-held belief that political parties were bad, he was reluctantly drawn into partisan politics. Convinced that the Federalists were now monarchists and that some yearned to reunite with Britain, he struck back. He helped to enact an electoral law that came to be called the *gerrymander*. The state was subdivided into senatorial districts so as to consolidate the Federalist vote in a few areas and to give Gerry's Democratic-Republicans an undue advantage. The shape of one electoral district looked like a salamander on the map, and one wit promptly dubbed it a gerrymander. The label stuck, and Gerry's name continues to be associated with the political practice of redistricting electoral areas to concentrate the strength of one party.

In 1812 Gerry, who favored war against Britain, was elected Vice President on the ticket with James Madison. Throughout his years in office, he struggled to maintain his stand against partisan politics. As Vice President he presided over the Senate with decorum, dedication, and a degree of impartiality. But in 1813 he refused to give up the chair—as was the custom at the close of the session—lest William B. Giles, a Virginia Senator who was a peace advocate become president pro tem [*see* WAR OF 1812]. With President Madison ill and Gerry himself in poor health, he feared the presidency might fall into bad hands and that the war might be brought to a close. Fortunately Madison recovered to continue the fighting.

Gerry's relations with two Presidents were symptomatic of his change to more partisan politics. In the XYZ affair, he helped Federalist President Adams prevent a war with France by taking a more moderate political stand as American emissary. During the War of 1812, however, he stood firmly with Jeffersonian President Madison against peace advocates and antiwar Federalists.

Gerry died on 23 November 1814; he was buried in the congressional cemetery.

### BIBLIOGRAPHY

Austin, James T. *Life of Elbridge Gerry*. 2 vols. 1827–1828.

Billias, George Athan. *Elbridge Gerry: Founding Father and Republican Statesman*. 1976.

Gardiner, C. Harvey. *A Study in Dissent: The Warren-Gerry Correspondence, 1776–1792*. 1968.

Morison, Samuel Eliot. "Elbridge Gerry, Gentleman-Democrat." *New England Quarterly* 2 (1929): 3–33.

Shipton, Clifford K. "Elbridge Gerry." In vol. 15 of *Sibley's Harvard Graduates*. Edited by Clifford K. Shipton. 17 vols. 1975.

GEORGE ATHAN BILLIAS

**GETTYSBURG ADDRESS.** The occasion for Abraham Lincoln's most famous speech, one of the few he made as President, was the dedication of a cemetery for the Union soldiers killed in the Battle of Gettysburg (1–3 July 1863). A local citizen named David Wills, who had persuaded Pennsylvania to purchase the land for the cemetery, invited the orator Edward Everett to give the main address, and, weeks later on 2 November, also invited the President.

Time for preparation was short, but, contrary to myth, Lincoln did not dash off the address on the back of an envelope during the train ride to Pennsylvania. He had been thinking for some time about the ideas expressed in the speech. In impromptu remarks to a group of serenaders at the White House on 7 July, for example, Lincoln asked, "How long ago is it?—eighty odd years—since on the Fourth of July for the first time in the history of the world a nation by its representatives, assembled and declared as a self-evident truth that 'all men are created equal.' " Those words foreshadowed the opening of the Gettysburg Address: "Four score and seven years ago our fathers brought forth, upon this continent, a new nation, conceived in liberty, and dedicated to the proposition that 'all men are created equal.' "

At Gettysburg on 19 November 1863, some fifteen thousand people gathered to hear Everett's lengthy address. Lincoln's short speech ended quickly, but Everett himself admitted afterward, "I should be glad, if I could flatter myself that I came as near the central idea of the occasion, in two hours, as you did in two minutes."

Lincoln came to think that his second inaugural address would be the most enduring of his speeches, but many men of letters, including the poet Henry Wadsworth Longfellow, had praised the Gettysburg Address immediately. By 1865 Ralph Waldo Emerson could say that it would "not easily be surpassed by words on any recorded occasion." Broad popular fame came later, encouraged by the practice of reciting the address at Memorial Day ceremonies.

The address beautifully adumbrated Lincoln's late political thought and his rationale for the war. He dated the country's founding from 1776 (1863 minus four score and seven), thus making the Declaration of Independence the crucial document in its history. He maintained that the Union soldiers at Gettysburg had sacrificed their lives to prove that a nation founded on the proposition that all men are created equal might endure. And he called for the living to "resolve that these dead shall not have died in vain, that the nation, under God, shall have a new birth of freedom, and that government of the people, by the people, for the people, shall not perish from the earth."

## BIBLIOGRAPHY

Warren, Louis A. *Lincoln's Gettysburg Declaration: "A New Birth of Freedom."* 1964.

MARK E. NEELY, JR.


**GHENT, TREATY OF.** See TREATY OF GHENT.


**GIFTS TO PRESIDENTS.** Personal gifts given to any federal official may at times raise a suspicion of attempts to curry favor with the official by the donor of the gift, and might give an appearance that the public official is using his or her office for personal gain or private privilege. As explained by the noted ethicist, Sen. Paul Douglas (D-Ill.), the acceptance of gifts and favors by public officials may create a subtle sense of "personal obligation," gratitude or loyalty toward one's "benefactors and patrons." Restrictions thus generally exist on the permissible acceptance of private gifts by federal officials, including the President.

Any restrictions on and regulations concerning the receipt of gifts, favors, and entertainment by federal officials, however, must be balanced with a recognition of innocent expressions of generosity from the public and of normal and permissible personal friendships and relationships. In the case of the President of the United States, any such restrictions on gifts must also must be balanced with the need for the President to perform ceremonial and public functions on behalf of the nation.

The President is restricted in receiving gifts from foreign governments, but has been exempted from specific limitations on the source or value of gifts from the general public. Like all other federal officials, the President may not accept a bribe or an illegal gratuity in return for official acts and may not attempt to coerce a gift from anyone. Annual financial disclosure reports, which the President is required to file publicly, must list all gifts over a specific amount received by the President and the President's spouse and dependent children.

The receipt of gifts by federal officials from foreign governments or from agencies or institutions that represent foreign governments or foreign political entities is restricted by the provisions of the United States Constitution. Article I, Section 9, clause 8 expressly provides that: "No Title of Nobility shall be granted by the United States: And no Person holding any Office of Profit or Trust under them shall, without the Consent of Congress accept of any present, Emolument, Office, or Title, of any kind whatever, from any King, Prince, or foreign State." The purpose of the constitutional restriction on gifts from foreign governments, as noted by Justice Joseph Story, "is founded in a just jealousy of foreign influence of every sort."

Congress has consented to the acceptance of foreign gifts of "minimal value" that are offered as a courtesy or souvenir under the Foreign Gifts and Decorations Act. Minimal value is an amount which is adjusted by the Consumer Price Index every three years; in 1993 it was $200. Additionally, any gift tendered to the President or other federal official from a foreign government may be accepted if it would cause offense or embarrassment to the foreign country or would adversely affect U.S. foreign relations if the gift were refused. In such a case, the President accepts the gift on behalf of the United States and then turns it over to the Government for storage and disposition.

The ethical restraints and regulations in the executive branch of government concerning gifts and favors, promulgated by executive order and regulation, had not traditionally applied to the President of the United States. In 1989, however, in the Ethics Reform Act of 1989, the statutory codification of many of these ethical restraints made such restrictions specifically applicable to all officers and employees of the government, including elected officeholders such as the President. These provisions of law prohibit the receipt of any gifts from prohibited sources, which include those doing business with, seeking action from, or those regulated or affected by a government official or his or her agency or department.

Under regulations that have been promulgated under the statute by the Office of Government Ethics, the President is exempt from such broad ethical restrictions on gifts and may still accept such gifts from the public as long as the gift is not coerced nor in return for an official act. The Office of Government Ethics in promulgating its rules and exceptions noted that: "The ceremonial and other public duties of the President and Vice President make it impractical to subject them to standards that require an analysis of every gift offered."

The President is subject to the federal criminal law barring bribes, the receipt of something of value in return for being influenced in the performance of an official act, and prohibiting illegal gratuities, the receipt of something of value "for or because of" an official act performed or to be performed.

The President, like other high-level federal officials, must publicly file personal financial disclosure statements every 15 May. Any gifts received by the President which aggregate $250 or more in value in a year from any one source, other than from a relative, must be disclosed. Only gifts that are more than $100 in value need to be aggregated for disclosure purposes. Gifts to the spouse and dependent children of the President must also be disclosed unless the gifts are clearly received "totally independent" of the relationship to the President.

### BIBLIOGRAPHY

Douglas, Paul. *Ethics in Government.* 1952.

U.S. Office of Government Ethics. "Standards of Ethical Conduct for Employees of the Executive Branch." Proposed rule. 56 *Federal Register* (23 July 1991): 33778–33815.

U.S. Senate. Committee on Foreign Relations. "Foreign Gifts and Decorations Act." 89th Cong., 2d sess., 1966, S. Rpt. No. 1160.

JACK H. MASKELL

**GOLDWATER, BARRY** (b.1909), Senator, Republican presidential nominee in 1964. Barry Goldwater's nomination as Republican presidential candidate in 1964 was contemporary with the birth of a new REPUBLICAN PARTY and a new set of issues which would give the presidency to the Republicans in five of the following seven presidential elections.

Born on 1 January 1909 in Phoenix, Arizona, Goldwater attended Staunton Military Academy and the University of Arizona, but left college to join the family business. After serving as a pilot in WORLD WAR II, Goldwater entered Arizona politics. He defeated Senate Majority Leader Ernest McFarland in 1952. During his first term in the Senate, Goldwater staked out a position to the right of President Eisenhower by opposing the growth of the administrative state and advocating a strategy of liberation rather than CONTAINMENT toward communism. The core of Goldwater's conviction was a love of personal liberty, property rights, and local self-government. In a year of Republican losses, Goldwater was reelected easily in 1958.

Goldwater's rise to prominence was assisted by a renaissance in American conservatism which began in the period 1955–1964. Through his speeches and books, he became the political symbol of expanding conservative influence in the party.

In 1964, Goldwater was more the candidate of a political movement than a political party. In the pro-

cess of nominating him, the movement took over the Republican Party. The nomination was planned and executed by conservative activists who first met in October 1961 without the knowledge or approval of Senator Goldwater.

Goldwater won a first-ballot victory in San Francisco at a convention characterized by manifest ill-will between the liberal and conservative elements of the party. There were two memorable events, and each played a key role in the campaign. The first was the vigorous booing of Gov. NELSON A. ROCKEFELLER, who responded from the podium by shaking his fist, liberal Republicans sat out the election or voted for President Johnson. The second was Goldwater's paraphrase of a key passage from Aristotle's *Ethics*—"extremism in the defense of liberty is no vice, [and] moderation in pursuit of justice is no virtue"—which was interpreted by the media as evidence of dangerous right-wing extremism.

The relation between Goldwater and the conservatives who nominated him was always an uneasy one, and following the convention, he excluded them from leadership positions in his campaign. In fact, Goldwater was always a conventional Republican whose first loyalty was to party.

A key development of the 1964 general election was the transformation of the southern white presidential electorate from Democratic to Republican, which eventually made the South the most Republican region of the country in presidential elections. The election was contested in the immediate aftermath of the passage of the CIVIL RIGHTS ACT OF 1964, which President Johnson supported and Goldwater opposed (on libertarian, not segregationist, grounds).

Johnson's landslide victory over Goldwater led to the greatest legislative victories of liberalism, but concealed emergent conservative strength. In speaking of a link between personal morality and political happiness, the Goldwater campaign anticipated the culture wars that helped determine the outcome of presidential elections since 1964. And in its warnings of the consequences of liberal principles, it even anticipated the transformation of liberalism in the late 1960s, which drove many former liberals into conservative ranks.

Goldwater served again in the Senate from 1968 to 1986. In later years, he turned further away from the cultural positions of the neoconservatives and the Christian right. His last years in the Senate were marked by an iconoclastic frontier libertarianism (for example, support for *Roe v. Wade*), which increasingly won him more accolades from the left than from the right.

## BIBLIOGRAPHY

Black, Earl, and Merle Black. *The Vital South*. 1992.

Kessel, John H. *The Goldwater Coalition*. 1968.

Nash, George. *The Conservative Intellectual Movement in America since 1945*. 1976.

Rusher, William. *The Rise of the Right*. 1984.

White, F. Clifton, with William J. Gill. *Suite 3505*. 1967.

White, Theodore H. *The Making of the President, 1964*. 1965.

ROBERT C. JEFFREY

**GOLDWATER v. CARTER** 444 U.S. 996 (1979). President Jimmy Carter's unilateral termination of the 1954 Mutual Defense Treaty with Taiwan resurrected the long-standing and largely unresolved, controversy over the locus of the constitutional power of treaty termination. The resulting lawsuit, *Goldwater v. Carter*, presented the first direct challenge to the claim of a presidential power to terminate treaties. The Supreme Court, however, did not reach the merits of the issue. Instead, it dismissed the case as nonjusticiable and thus bypassed an opportunity to chart the constitutional landscape of TREATY TERMINATION.

As a prerequisite to the normalization of relations with Beijing, President Carter announced on 22 December 1978 that he would notify Taiwan of his decision to terminate the Mutual Defense Treaty in accordance with its terms. The treaty provided that either party could terminate the pact one year after notification to the other party. President Carter thus claimed the constitutional capacity to act as the party for the United States government. He defended his decision by invoking the COMMANDER IN CHIEF clause and the President's status as the sole organ of American foreign policy.

Carter's decision to terminate the treaty, which formed the foundation of United States relations with long-time ally, Taiwan, as a necessary condition to the normalization of relations with Beijing, provoked a political firestorm. Senator BARRY GOLDWATER of Arizona and several members of the House and Senate brought a lawsuit in which they challenged Carter's claim that the President possesses unilateral authority to terminate treaties. Goldwater argued that treaties may not be terminated without either the advice and consent of the Senate or approval by Congress. Accordingly, the term *party* in the Mutual Defense Treaty could not be read as a synonym for the President.

*Goldwater v. Carter* invited the Court, on appeal, to draw order from the chaos that characterized the law of treaty termination, a status derived from variety in practice and doctrinal confusion on the proper procedure for the termination of treaties. But the Court, without hearing oral argument, vacated on quasi-jurisdictional grounds the circuit court's judgment for the President and remanded the case with instructions to dismiss the complaint. Justice William Rehnquist wrote an opinion, joined by Chief Justice Warren Burger and Justices Potter Stewart and John Paul Stevens, that held that the case represented a nonjusticiable political question. For this foursome, the case posed a political question simply because it involved the scope of the constitutional power allocated to the President and Congress to conduct American foreign policy. Justice Lewis Powell rejected the invocation of the political question doctrine but concurred in the dismissal of the suit as nonjusticiable for the reason that it was not ripe for judicial review. Justice Thurgood Marshall also joined the dismissal but filed no statement. There were two dissenting opinions. Justices Harry Blackmun and Byron White argued that the Court should have heard oral argument and given the case the plenary consideration it deserved. In another dissent, Justice William Brennan would have upheld the termination for the reason that it flowed from the President's RECOGNITION POWER.

The issue of the locus of the constitutional power to terminate treaties does not, as Justice Brennan wrote in dissent, "conform to any of the analytical threads that make up the political question doctrine." Rehnquist's reliance on the doctrine, moreover, was inconsistent with the Court's two leading cases on the subject, *Baker v. Carr* (1962) and *Powell v. McCormack* (1969). There was, for example, no textual commitment of the issue to any department of government, a test that scholars widely regard as the governing principle of the political question doctrine. Moreover, there were available to the Court, from the realms of historical practice, judicial dicta, and policy considerations, a number of judicially discoverable and manageable standards. In point of fact, the wisdom of terminating a treaty is a political question, but whether the department that terminated a treaty has the constitutional authority to do so is justiciable. At bottom, the Court shirked its duty, as charged by *Marbury v. Madison* to "say what the law is." Throughout its history, the Court has settled a variety of separation-of-powers disputes, including those that involve foreign policy questions. Justice Rehnquist's opinion ignored Justice Brennan's sagacious observation in *Baker v. Carr* that "it is error to suppose that every case or controversy which touches foreign relations lies beyond judicial cognizance."

As a practical matter, the Court's action, or rather its inaction, left the termination of the Mutual Defense Treaty intact. But the fundamental question was left unresolved, and it is not likely to fade away. While the plurality opinion in *Goldwater* does not establish a legal precedent, it is likely to provide agreeable footing for future unilateral presidential treaty terminations.

### BIBLIOGRAPHY

Adler, David Gray. *The Constitution and the Termination of Treaties.* 1986.

Berger, Raoul. "The President's Unilateral Termination of the Taiwan Treaty." *Northwestern University Law Review* 75 (1980): 577–634.

Glennon, Michael J. *Constitutional Diplomacy.* 1990.

Henkin, Louis. "Litigating the President's Power to Terminate Treaties." *American Journal of International Law* 73 (1979): 647–654.

DAVID GRAY ADLER

**GOOD NEIGHBOR POLICY.** United States policy toward Latin America during the presidency of Franklin D. Roosevelt (1933–1945) stressed improved economic and strategic relations with nations of the Western Hemisphere through political cooperation and consultation rather than military INTERVENTIONISM. Driven by a mixture of self-interest, changing perceptions, and idealism, the Good Neighbor Policy mitigated a long tradition of presidential intrusions and annexations in the Caribbean Basin and Latin America and diminished, at least for a time, resentment and mistrust of the old "Colossus of the North" dating back to the nineteenth century.

In his inaugural address of 4 March 1933, Franklin D. Roosevelt dramatically dedicated the United States to "the policy of the good neighbor—the neighbor who resolutely respects himself and because he does so, respects the rights of others." Latin Americans remained highly skeptical on the eve of the Seventh International Conference of American States, in Montevideo, Uruguay, late in 1933. But Roosevelt's Secretary of State, CORDELL HULL, delighted the delegates by supporting a pact that declared "no state has the right to intervene in the internal or external affairs of another." President Roosevelt vigorously supported the new policy of nonintervention, releasing CUBA from the servile terms of the Platt Amendment and ending the twenty-year U.S. Marine occupation of Haiti in 1934. For the first time since 1915, no American troops trod Latin American soil and none returned until President Lyndon B. Johnson's 1965 intervention in the DOMINICAN REPUBLIC.

The Good Neighbor Policy proved its success when the nations of Latin America rallied to the Allied cause at the time of WORLD WAR II. Conferences at Buenos Aires in 1936, Lima in 1938, and Panama in 1939 demonstrated a willingness to take common action to bolster hemispheric defense and to prevent outside intervention in the Western Hemisphere.

Beneath the Roosevelt administration's new posture of military nonintervention, older patterns of U.S. economic and political penetration held firm. When a revolutionary government under Ramón Grau San Martin arose in Cuba in 1933, Roosevelt's administration undermined it by nonrecognition, then supported the corrupt and repressive military regime of Fulgencio Batista, who remained in power until ousted by Fidel Castro in 1959. Still, President Roosevelt's Good Neighbor Policy marked a sharp change from the habitual and heavy-handed intrusions of most of his twentieth-century predecessors and, by respecting the autonomy of most Latin republics, improved America's relations with its southern neighbors at a time of growing danger to world peace and hemispheric security.

### BIBLIOGRAPHY

Dallek, Robert. *Franklin D. Roosevelt and American Foreign Policy, 1932–1945.* 1979.

Dozer, Donald M. *Are We Good Neighbors?: Three Decades of Inter-American Relations, 1930–1960.* 1961.

Gellman, Irwin F. *Good Neighbor Policy: United States Policies in Latin America, 1933–1945.* 1979.

LaFeber, Walter. *Inevitable Revolutions: The United States and Central America.* 1984.

BRIAN VANDEMARK

**GORE, AL** (b. 1948), forty-fifth Vice President of the United States (1993–). Albert Gore, Jr., elected Vice President of the United States in 1992, grew up in politics, as the son of a U.S. Senator from Tennessee. Gore—who took the political name of Al—had served eight years in the House of Representatives and eight in the Senate and became an unexpected hero, even a national heartthrob, in the course of the 1992 campaign. Gore, a handsome man who tends to resemble the cartoon figure Clark Kent, had run a mediocre campaign for the Democratic presidential nomination in 1988. In his attacks on his opponents, he often came across as heavy; he frequently seemed wooden. But Gore, a very smart man and a learner from his own mistakes, was a far better candidate four years later. Some of Gore's friends said that he had mellowed as a result of the near-loss of his young son, Albert, in a freak collision with a car as they left a baseball game and of the long rehabilitation his son, and the rest of the family, went through. Gore and his wife, Tipper, also have three daughters.

Al Gore had a privileged background. He attended one of Washington's most prestigious private schools, St. Alban's, and lived with his parents in a suite in a fine hotel. In summers, the family returned to its farm in Carthage, Tennessee. The younger Gore has always been a complex combination of urbane sophistication and down-home rural folksiness. His father, an early southern progressive who opposed the VIETNAM WAR and lost his Senate seat in 1970, had always been a big influence on his son. But the son, perhaps not wishing to have his political career end the way his father's had, took more centrist positions. Gore, Jr., supported the GULF WAR and was often in the middle on debates over the development of NUCLEAR WEAPONS. He was also a strong environmentalist and early in 1992 published a best-selling book called *Earth in the Balance*. In it, Gore took several strong environmental positions that came under attack by the Republicans during the presidential campaign.

Bill Clinton's choice of Gore as a running mate was an unconventional, and even inspired, decision. The evident good chemistry between Clinton and Gore, former rivals—they came from the same generation of southern Democratic would-be Presidents—and both of them men with confidence in their own brain power, impressed people favorably. Gore had been considered one of the possible, even probable, first tier candidates for the presidency in 1992, but, in the summer of 1991, he decided not to run. Though Gore gave his son's continuing rehabilitation as a reason, George Bush's then high standing in the polls was undoubtedly also a factor.

Clinton, as he campaigned and prepared to govern, gave unprecedented access and influence to his vice presidential selection. Finally, the two families—the Clintons and the Gores—had a strong positive impact when they appeared together in the campaign, as they frequently did. Tipper Gore, a spirited and lovely woman, added a softening note to the group.

After the election, Gore played a major role in helping Clinton assemble his Cabinet and fill other top positions. He was in the meetings Clinton held on whom to select. Carol Browner, the Florida environmental official who was named to head the Environmental Protection Agency, had served on Gore's staff. Gore also played a part in blocking some appointments. It was clear from various public statements on Clinton's part that the President-elect regularly consulted his Vice President-elect on all manner of issues. The public became accustomed to seeing Gore standing beside Clinton as he made announcements or held press conferences. And Gore was expected to play an unprecedentedly strong role as Vice President.

BIBLIOGRAPHY

Clinton, Bill, and Al Gore. *Putting People First: How We Can All Change America.* 1992.
Gore, Al. *Earth in the Balance: Ecology and the Human Spirit.* 1992.

ELIZABETH DREW

**GOVERNMENT CORPORATIONS.** Historically, the federal government has been involved in few commercial-type enterprises. While there were early instances of the federal government participating in corporate enterprises, notably the First and Second BANKS OF THE UNITED STATES, the first time the federal government acquired a corporation outright was in 1903, when the Panama Railroad Company was purchased from the French Panama Canal Company. Since that time a number of corporate bodies have been established; the growth of such enterprises tends to come in spurts and generally in response to emergencies.

The first large-scale use of the corporate option accompanied the mobilization for WORLD WAR I. Later, the Great Depression of the 1930s fostered numerous corporations (e.g., the RECONSTRUCTION FINANCE CORPORATION), and, shortly thereafter, WORLD WAR II prompted the creation of additional corporations. Many of these corporations were abolished after the emergencies or were absorbed into the permanent executive-branch agencies. In later years, the corporate option has been popular not so much because it facilitates the management of commercial-type activities but because it is believed by some to be a legitimate means of circumventing the statutes and regulations (e.g., personnel and salary ceilings) generally applicable to agencies of the executive branch.

**Attempts at Definition.** In 1945, partly in response to the proliferation of corporate bodies created for the war effort, Congress passed the Government Corporation Control Act (31 U.S.C. 9101–9111), which standardized budget, auditing, debt management, and depository practices for those agencies the act enumerated as "government corporations." Government corporations are "agencies" of the United States (*Cherry Cotton Mills v. United States* [1945]) subject to all laws governing agencies except where exempted from coverage by provisions of general laws or by provisions in the enabling act of the corporation. The Control Act does not define what constitutes a corporation; rather, the definition is simply an enumeration of agencies considered corporations. The enumerated corporations are listed as either "wholly-owned" or of "mixed-ownership."

In passing legislation to create a corporation, Congress typically assigns the corporation a separate legal status so that it can sue or be sued, enter into contracts, and own property in its own name. Of greatest importance, Congress generally provides that corporations can "determine the character and necessity of their expenditures and the manner in which incurred, allowed, and paid." This provision exempts corporations from most regulatory and prohibitory statutes applicable to the expenditure of public funds and permits them to function in a commercial manner.

Since there is no uniform definition of what constitutes a corporation, some corporate bodies are not included under the provisions of the Control Act. This being the case, it is not surprising that studies of government corporations differ considerably regarding their number, with totals ranging from thirty-one to forty-seven. The corporations cover the spectrum from large, well-known corporations such as the Tennessee Valley Authority, the UNITED STATES POSTAL SERVICE, and the Federal Deposit Insurance Corporation to small, low-visibility corporate bodies such as the Federal Financing Bank and the Pennsylvania Avenue Development Corporation.

In an effort to provide criteria for determining when the corporate option is appropriate, President Harry S. Truman in his 1948 budget message stated, "Experience indicates that the corporate form of organization is peculiarly adapted to the administration of government programs which are predominately of a commercial character—those which are revenue producing, are at least potentially self-sustaining and involve a large number of business-type transactions with the public." In recent years, Congress, often at the President's behest, has created agencies that are called corporations but that do not meet these criteria. The Corporation for Public Broadcasting and the Legal Services Corporation are examples of "corporations" that do not perform commercial functions but rather are deliberately intended to be insulated from most elements of central management supervision and political accountability.

Regular agencies of the United States receive most of their financial support from funds appropriated by Congress. Government corporations, on the other hand, generally receive most if not all their funds from users of their services. The business character of this relationship, in which the corporate body is obligated to provide services as long as the buyers are willing to pay, means that revenues, expenditures, and even personnel will fluctuate according to consumer demand.

The Control Act requires that enumerated corporations submit to the President business-type budgets that are more or less equivalent to operating plans and assumptions for business in the coming year. The President, and later Congress, may alter these plans, but this rarely happens. Usually, the COMPTROLLER GENERAL is required to apply a commercial-type audit to the corporation balance sheets once every three years. Under ordinary circumstances the Comptroller General cannot disallow corporate expenditures as he can regular agency expenditures. Corporations can generally borrow funds through the Treasury or the Federal Financing Bank. Employees of Government corporations, properly defined, are considered employees of the United States although they may be exempted from CIVIL SERVICE laws and regulations.

**Location, Structure, Governance.** The location, structure, and governance of government corporations vary greatly. Corporate status does not limit where in the executive structure a corporation may be located. Corporations may be located in executive departments (e.g., the St. Lawrence Seaway Development Corporation in the DEPARTMENT OF TRANSPORTATION) or be assigned independent status (e.g., the Export-Import Bank). A government corporation may be structured so that it is merely a financial entity whose employees are actually employees of the parent agency (e.g., the Federal Financing Bank in the DEPARTMENT OF THE TREASURY, the Commodity Credit Corporation in the DEPARTMENT OF AGRICULTURE).

State incorporation laws require boards of directors for private corporations to ensure representation where diversity of ownership is present. In government corporations, however, there is no diversity of ownership and thus there is no need for a board of directors. Boards of directors have come in for criticism for much the same reasons as all forms of plural executive have been criticized since the Federalist period. Single-administrator-headed corporations (e.g., the Government National Mortgage Association, or "Ginnie Mae") are generally viewed by public administrators as being more likely to furnish consistent, professional and accountable leadership.

Arguments favoring the single-administrator-managed corporation notwithstanding, most government corporations do have boards of directors although they differ significantly as to qualifications, powers, and duties. Some corporations have boards composed of CABINET officers and other federal officials serving ex-officio (e.g., the Pension Benefit Guaranty Corporation). Other corporations have mixed boards of federal officials and private citizens (e.g., the Overseas Private Investment Corporation). Some boards have full-time duties (e.g., the Tennessee Valley Authority), while others are large and essentially advisory in character (e.g., the Pennsylvania Avenue Development Corporation). The Board of Governors of the Postal Service chooses and evaluates the performance of the POSTMASTER GENERAL. In most instances where boards include high officers of the executive branch (e.g., the Secretary of the Treasury) as ex-officio members, these members (known as principals) are represented by subordinates. This situation generally results in boards composed at least in part of persons whose primary responsibility is to protect the interests of the parent agency rather than those of the corporation in question.

In recent decades, successive Presidents and the OFFICE OF MANAGEMENT AND BUDGET (OMB) have lost interest in government corporations as a category of organization and have ceased formally to oversee their activities and policies from a presidential perspective. As the managerial capacity of the OMB has declined, Congress has moved in to fill the void, finding variations on the government corporation theme to be an attractive approach for organizing and reorganizing activities of the executive branch. Thus, the government corporation option is under consideration for such agencies as the National Technical Information Service, the Federal Aviation Administration, and the Uranium Enrichment Program.

Government corporations, properly defined and structured, are a useful managerial device for accomplishing public purposes as determined in law. This said, the question remains as to whom these corporations ought to be accountable. What management and oversight responsibilities are appropriate for the President, the OMB, Congress, and the GENERAL ACCOUNTING OFFICE? Given the growing number and importance of government corporations, this question will undoubtedly occupy an increasingly prominent place on the national political agenda.

### BIBLIOGRAPHY

Goldberg, Sidney D., and Harold Seidman. *The Government Corporation: Elements of a Model Charter.* 1953.

Leazes, Francis J. *Accountability and the Business State: The Structure of Federal Corporations.* 1987.

Moe, Ronald C. *Administering Public Functions at the Margins of Government: The Case of Federal Corporations.* 1983.

Musolf, Lloyd. *Uncle Sam's Private Profit-Seeking Corporations.* 1983.

National Academy of Public Administration. *Report on Government Corporations.* 2 vols. 1981.

Seidman, Harold, and Robert S. Gilmour. *Politics, Position, and Power: From the Positive to the Regulatory State.* 4th rev. ed. 1986.

U.S. Comptroller General. *Profiles of Existing Government Corporations.* 1989.

RONALD C. MOE

## GOVERNMENT-SPONSORED ENTERPRISES (GSEs).

The term *government-sponsored enterprise* is not defined in law and therefore is variously defined and interpreted. Some apply the term broadly to include a number of entities enjoying exemptions from most, but not all, laws applicable to federal agencies. Others, including the OFFICE OF MANAGEMENT AND BUDGET (OMB), interpret the term more narrowly. The most widely accepted definition of a GSE is as follows: A GSE is a privately owned, federally chartered financial institution with nationwide scope and specialized lending powers. GSEs are not agencies of the United States but serve as instrumentalities to accomplish a public purpose defined by Congress. The federal government implicitly guarantees the value of GSE obligations and mortgage-backed securities.

Given this definition, six entities in 1991 appeared to qualify for the designation of government-sponsored enterprise: the Federal National Mortgage Association ("Fannie Mae"), the Federal Home Loan Mortgage Corporation ("Freddie Mac"), the Student Loan Marketing Association ("Sallie Mae"), the Federal Home Loan Bank System institutions, the Federal Agricultural Mortgage Association, and the Farm Credit System institutions. Several additional entities—the College Construction Loan Insurance Corporation, the Financing Corporation, and the Resolution Trust Corporation—fit some of the criteria for a GSE but not others.

GSEs have been established by Congress to perform specific credit functions. They primarily act as financial intermediaries to assist borrowers in housing, education, and agriculture. Although GSEs are privately owned, they benefit from government sponsorship. Their securities can collateralize public deposits (e.g., Social Security Administration deposits) and can be held in unlimited amounts by most banks and savings and loans institutions. They are not subject to Securities and Exchange Commission registration requirements, and their corporate earnings are exempt from state and local income taxation. They may borrow from the Treasury, at the Treasury's discretion. Most importantly, the credit market perceives that federal sponsorship of GSEs implies federal guarantee of their corporate debt and obligations. All these factors combine to ensure that GSEs can borrow monies at a lower interest rate than might otherwise be the case.

There is nothing modest about the size and scope of GSEs. The implicit guarantees of GSE obligations by the federal government in 1992 totaled more than $900 billion and was growing rapidly. Although in

1992 the GSEs were considered by the TREASURY DEPARTMENT and the GENERAL ACCOUNTING OFFICE to be in sound financial condition, their creditworthiness was not always so sure. In 1988, the federal government was forced to authorize $4 billion of financial assistance for one insolvent GSE, the Farm Credit System. Also, Fannie Mae was in trouble in the early 1980s, when its capitalization dropped until the corporation had a market worth of negative $11 billion. These instances, plus the sheer size and growth of the unfunded liability upon the Treasury, has prompted concern about the efficacy of the regulation of GSEs.

Insofar as GSEs are regulated, their regulation is the responsibility of those agencies charged with programmatic responsibilities (e.g., DEPARTMENT OF HOUSING AND URBAN DEVELOPMENT) for the GSEs' chartered areas of activity. This form of regulation has been criticized as ineffectual, leaving the federal Treasury, and thus taxpayers, at considerable risk. The President and the executive branch have relatively little legal authority or institutional capacity to affect the operations of GSEs, nor have they exhibited much interest in developing comprehensive regulation of GSEs. The GSEs, among the strongest and wealthiest lobbying groups in Washington, generally oppose efforts to bring GSEs under stronger, centralized regulation.

As previously noted, GSEs are instrumentalities, not agencies, of the federal government. As instrumentalities, they are not subject to the management laws applicable to agencies. At present, there is no generic law defining the authorities, responsibilities, and accountability of GSEs. Each GSE is subject only to the provisions of its enabling statute. This segmented regulation is cited by critics as a source for the uneven oversight of GSEs, and in 1992 Congress was considering legislation to establish a single regulatory agency for the financial and management affairs of GSEs defined as a distinct category of organization.

GSEs are controversial. Supporters of the GSE concept are vigorous in their arguments that GSEs are performing crucial financial intermediary functions that would not otherwise be performed, or would be performed poorly, by the private sector. Supporters point out that the GSEs supply much-needed national refinancing of locally initiated mortgages at low cost to borrowers and at minimal risk to the taxpayers. It is true, they admit, that the profits of these firms have been extremely high and the rewards to officers great (In 1991, Robert Maxwell, the president of Fannie Mae, retired and received a $27 million retirement package), but supporters claim that such rewards are commensurate with the success of the operations. The fact that GSEs are taking over an increasing percentage of their respective markets, supporters say, is proof of their efficiency and not a consequence of the market advantages provided by the implicit federal subsidy of their activities.

Critics argue that GSEs, no matter how financially sound they may appear to be, are an essentially flawed instrument for the achievement of policy objectives agreed to by the President and Congress. Critics predict that GSEs, combining as they do elements of both the governmental and private sectors, will inevitably produce severe distortion in the capital marketplace, encourage monopolistic behavior on the part of the GSEs, and dominate the political actors charged with protecting the public interest, as opposed to the private interest, of GSEs. They contend that GSEs "privatize profits and socialize risks." To critics, GSEs are part of the problem of financial institutions in the United States, not part of the solution. Friends and foes of GSEs agree on at least one point: GSEs are a major element in the growing "quasi government" that challenges the capacity of the President to maintain effective leadership over the administration of the U.S. government.

### BIBLIOGRAPHY

Moe, Ronald C., and Thomas H. Stanton. "Government-Sponsored Enterprises as Federal Instrumentalities: Reconciling Private Management with Public Accountability." *Public Administration Review* 49 (1989): 321–329.

Stanton, Thomas H. *A State of Risk: Will Government-Sponsored Enterprises Be the Next Financial Crisis?* 1991.

U.S. Congressional Budget Office. *Controlling the Risks of Government-Sponsored Enterprises.* 1991.

RONALD C. MOE

**GRAMM-RUDMAN-HOLLINGS ACTS** (1985, 1987). These acts, the first passed in 1985 (GRH I) and the second in 1987 (GRH II), established multiyear deficit-reduction timetables for bringing the federal budget into balance. Both measures set declining maximum deficit amounts intended to balance the budget over a six-year period. Both also provided for automatic enforcement, through SEQUESTRATION or spending cuts to reduce excess deficit amounts if deficit ceilings were breached. While selected features of the GRH bills remain in effect, their basic approach has been abandoned.

The Omnibus Budget Reconciliation Act and BUDGET ENFORCEMENT ACT of 1990 ostensibly refined and extended GRH II. In fact, complicated spending and revenue controls were substituted for deficit ceilings.

The verdict of most BUDGET POLICY analysts was that the GRH experiment was largely a failure, since it did not resolve, and perhaps exacerbated, the policy impasse that caused structural deficit problems. As a consequence, the GRH deficit-reduction goals were missed by huge margins.

The GRH bills formally amended the 1974 CONGRESSIONAL BUDGET AND IMPOUNDMENT CONTROL ACT. Their common premise was that the threat of massive spending cuts required to bring the budget into balance would force the President and Congress to negotiate timely and prudent agreements to reduce deficits. Instead, generous deficit ceilings early in the GRH timetable, along with questionable budget accounting practices, postponed the GRH showdown until 1990, by which time compliance had become impossible.

**GRH I.** The Balanced Budget and Emergency Deficit Control Act of 1985 was signed into law by President Ronald Reagan less than three months after having been introduced by Republican Senators Philip Gramm and Warren B. Rudman and Democratic Senator Ernest F. Hollings. GRH I was a major revision of the federal budgetary process, and its rush to passage was unusually swift for a measure of such significance. GRH I attracted strong bipartisan support, at least publicly, because of a widespread perception that the federal deficit problem was becoming intractable. For fiscal years 1983 through 1985, deficits had averaged over $200 billion, and negotiations between the Reagan administration and Congress on a deficit-reduction agreement for fiscal year 1986 had collapsed. As a result, deficit projections for the remainder of the decade were enormous.

GRH I attempted to break the political deadlock through declining deficit ceilings that would bring the budget into balance in fiscal year 1991. If the President and Congress failed to comply with each annual deficit ceiling, any excess deficit for that year would be eliminated through automatic spending cuts or sequestration. Under GRH I, taxes were excluded from the automatic deficit-reduction procedure. GRH I also exempted certain programs, such as SOCIAL SECURITY, from any automatic cuts, and it limited the allowable maximum reductions in several others, such as Medicare. For defense programs and nonexempt domestic programs, however, automatic cuts were to be divided equally. The GENERAL ACCOUNTING OFFICE (GAO) was granted authority to write sequestration reports, after which final sequestration orders were to be issued by the President.

The GAO's role in the sequestration process was immediately and successfully challenged in court as an impermissible congressional intrusion into the executive process, but not before a fiscal year 1986 sequester order was implemented on 1 March 1986. The sequester order was invalidated by the Supreme Court as part of its decision in BOWSHER V. SYNAR (1986), forcing enactment of legislation to restore the spending cuts. The first year under GRH achieved some modest successes, with GRH procedures helping to block discretionary spending increases and to facilitate passage of the Tax Reform Act of 1986.

**GRH II.** In 1987, a modified GRH measure (the Balanced Budget and Emergency Deficit Control Reaffirmation Act) was enacted that granted the OFFICE OF MANAGEMENT AND BUDGET (OMB) authority to implement the sequestration process, while according the President limited discretion in apportioning any defense sequesters that might occur. The major change in GRH II, however, was extension of the timetable for balancing the budget for an additional two years (to fiscal year 1993), with limits on the maximum permissible cuts for fiscal years 1988 and 1989, regardless of the deficit. As a result, only short-term actions were taken under GRH II, and these did little to reduce structural deficits.

GRH II was invoked by President Reagan in 1987, and a $23 billion sequestration order was issued for fiscal year 1988. This was then repealed under a two-year budget agreement reached between the Reagan administration and Congress in response to the October 1987 stock market crash. This budget agreement included tax increases and spending cuts that were supposed to ensure compliance with the GRH maximum deficit, but the actual fiscal year 1988 and fiscal year 1989 deficits were well above the GRH II limits.

The lack of significant deficit-reduction progress continued under the administration of George Bush. In 1989, another budget agreement was reached that purportedly complied with the $100 billion maximum deficit for fiscal year 1990. In fact, the actual deficit for fiscal year 1990 was more than double the GRH maximum.

The final unraveling of GRH II occurred the following year. President Bush's fiscal year 1991 budget recommended no major policy changes, while showing compliance with the $64 billion GRH maximum deficit. By early spring, new administration estimates revealed a widening deficit gap, with the prospect of perhaps a $100 billion sequestration necessary to comply with GRH II. Since a sequestration of this magnitude was simply not feasible for the defense and nondefense discretionary programs to which it would have been applied, the Bush administration and Congress proceeded to formulate an alternative budget-control agreement for fiscal years 1991 through 1995. The GRH II timetable was abandoned. Instead, the 1990 agreement set annual limits on discretionary spending and established controls to maintain baseline revenue and entitlement levels.

In signing legislation implementing the 1990 budget agreement, President Bush called it the "toughest enforcement system ever," saying, "The Gramm-Rudman-Hollings sequester process is extended and strengthened." In fact, the 1990 budget agreement acknowledged what GRH I and II had shown. The President and Congress could agree to control deficits, but they could not agree on the policy changes needed for effective control.

### BIBLIOGRAPHY

Calmes, Jackie. "Gramm-Rudman-Hollings: Has Its Time Passed?" *Congressional Quarterly Weekly Report* 47 (1989): 2684–2688.
Penner, Rudolph G., and Alan J. Abramson. *Broken Purse Strings: Congressional Budgeting 1974 to 1988*.1988.
Schick, Allen. *Reconciliation and the Congressional Budget Process*. 1981.

DENNIS S. IPPOLITO

**GRANT, ULYSSES S.** (1822–1885), eighteenth President of the United States (1869–1877). On 5 December 1876 Congress met in joint session to hear a clerk read Ulysses Grant's eighth and last annual message. The President began in a fashion unprecedented in the audience's collective memory: "It was my fortune, or misfortune, to be called to the office of Chief Executive without any previous political training. From the age of 17 I had never even witnessed the excitement attending a Presidential campaign but twice antecedent to my own candidacy, and at but one of them was I eligible as a voter. Under such circumstances," he declared, "it is but reasonable to suppose that errors of judgment must have occurred."

Grant considered "differences of opinion" between himself and "writers and debaters" to be expected, but not to be "evidence of blunder" on his part. "Mistakes have been made, as all can see and I admit," he continued. His hollow defense cited the "assistants" around him, "in nearly every case selected without a personal acquaintance with the appointee," but upon congressional recommendations. "Failures," he asserted, "have been errors of judgment, not of intent."

Thus did the man who had attained the highest military rank since George Washington, defeated the enemies of the Union in the CIVIL WAR, and entered the White House as the most popular man in the country, conclude an eight-year presidency. Behind this remarkable and at points disingenuous apology lay memories of a life throughout which the shadows of failure had dogged the footsteps of glory.

Born the son of a tanner in rural Ohio in 1822, Grant grudgingly accepted an appointment to West Point in 1839. He graduated slightly below mid class in 1843. As a young infantry officer in the MEXICAN WAR, he earned citations for gallantry and learned about leadership and resoluteness from General Zachary Taylor. Rather than be court-martialed, he quit the army in 1854, drifted ignominiously from farmer to real estate agent to customs clerk, and wound up in his brothers' leather store in Galena, Illinois. In the spring of 1861, the cannon's roar at Fort Sumter called the nation to arms, and the erstwhile obscure captain soon became colonel of an Illinois volunteer infantry regiment. Early command embarrassments almost ruined his career, and the debacle at Shiloh in April 1862 produced heavy criticism. Lincoln supported Grant, the list of victories in the western theater grew, and in the spring of 1864 Grant became Commanding General of the Army. He thus exercised overall military command for the final year of the war.

Grant's military career ended in unparalleled success; his political career ended in a complex of bittersweet emotions. Grant left office in 1877 not in the least doubtful of his own worth and integrity, and left with pride in certain accomplishments. He also saw himself as the target of unfair attacks and undeserved criticism. He thought himself the victim of partisan scheming, the loser-but-still-statesman when petty politicians successfully blocked his favorite proposals. So much did he want vindication that, following a trip around the world, he entered the race for the 1880 nomination, losing to James A. Garfield on the thirty-sixth ballot.

**Preparation for the White House.** Grant's name as a presidential possibility began to appear in the press in the autumn of 1863, as Union armies stood in Tennessee, poised on the threshold of the Confederate heartland. This man of silent ambition, the son of poverty, failure, and disrespect, might well be excused for thinking of the presidency as the ultimate vindication. There would be times when he would believe, and nearly say, that the country owed him the presidency for his wartime services. But while the war lasted, there were more important goals, and Grant could turn aside hints, rumors, and speculations with the simple, honest, and patriotic response that his current duty was to win the war as soon as possible. In this fashion he could also avoid the kind of melodramatic pronouncements employed in later years by his friend William T. Sherman.

Grant could also thereby avoid any friction with Abraham Lincoln. He understood very clearly the relationship of politics and military command in wartime. He knew that total war required total victory, and that total victory required a cooperative effort between military and civil authorities. Lincoln and Grant, who before the war would have been thought improbable experts in their fields, had formed a winning team in which each needed the other to achieve complete success. And within the equality there was also an inherent superiority that Grant also understood. As a soldier of democracy, Grant accepted the doctrine of civilian control of military power. Lincoln need not fear that the Galena tanner would become the man on horseback.

Had Grant gone to Ford's Theater with Lincoln that April night in 1865, as the plan at one point had been, there would have been two bullets fired, one ending a presidency, the other preventing one. But his wife, Julia Dent Grant, could not abide the thought of smiling her way through a mediocre comedy in the company of MARY TODD LINCOLN. So the Grants did not go, JOHN WILKES BOOTH fired only once, and Grant's relationship to the presidency changed forever. The old comfortable rapport between two mutually respecting men would change and with it, perhaps, some aspects of the military-civilian equilibrium. For all his courage in the secession winter of 1861 and his mortal risks during the war, the new President, Andrew Johnson, was no Lincoln in the hearts of his countrymen. They offered him good will on his accession, but they honored Grant more. Now it was indeed possible for general to eclipse President, and a dangerous thing too, for Johnson was no Lincoln when it came to tolerance and forbearance in politics.

Johnson, as a lifelong Democrat and a border-state Unionist, was an obvious war-coalition vice presidential partner for Lincoln in 1864. But now he was President, with minimal ties to the REPUBLICAN PARTY and a limited personal following. Like Grant, Johnson was a son of poverty and failure. His long road back to respectability, however, had started before Grant's, and Johnson was already a veteran Congressman while Grant was still a nondescript subaltern in a lonely infantry garrison on a desolate Pacific coast. Johnson's ambition, easily as large as Grant's, was also much less discreet, and if, as seemed likely, he coveted a presidential election in his own right in 1868, a face-off with Grant was a distinct possibility.

For the remainder of 1865, President Johnson determined RECONSTRUCTION policy toward the South while the Army, on occupation duty, oversaw it. Grant, as Commanding General, endeavored to cooperate

with Johnson, yet it soon became apparent that the President's policy would result in a return to power by the secessionist aristocracy while affording little protection of Unionists or blacks. The assembling of Congress in December 1865 opened a new phase of the controversy. There ensued an institutional struggle—"wranglings," in Grant's later phrase—for control of Reconstruction. By March 1867 Congress had clearly prevailed, with passage over presidential vetoes of the First Reconstruction Act and the TENURE OF OFFICE ACT.

Having just led the armies that preserved the Union, Grant had no intention of seeing the fruits of victory lost in the politics of Reconstruction. In the spirit of Appomattox, Grant did not want a punitive peace. He wanted an honorable restoration, but on terms that would make secession forever impossible and would protect Southern Unionists and blacks. His loyalty to the Army also led to concern that soldiers in the South, fulfilling the most politically delicate duties in Army history, would be caught in the partisan crossfire.

Grant therefore moved closer to the congressional position on Reconstruction, though not, at least initially, to a presidential bid. Politics held no attraction for him. During the war he had had his fill of politically motivated generals. In his scheme of things, politicians were venal, self-seeking manipulators who were clearly outranked by statesmen, who had the best interests of the whole people in mind. Yet if Grant did not pursue the parties, they certainly pursued him during the early years of Reconstruction. Some Democrats hoped that with Grant they could wash away the memories of General GEORGE B. McCLELLAN's defeat in 1864. Grant, however, was an improbable Democrat. He had voted for James Buchanan in 1856 only because the other choice was General JOHN C. FREMONT, and after four years of war, Grant shared the common view that Democrats were the party of disunion. Indeed, the fear of a Democratic victory in 1868 was one thing that brought Grant into the Republican fold.

The Republicans, however, were not of a single mind. Many moderates early accepted Grant as a winning choice. He was safe on Reconstruction and silent—and therefore presumably nondivisive rather than uninformed—on vexing economic issues such as currency, banks, and the tariff. For many leading RADICAL REPUBLICANS, however, like Thaddeus Stevens, Benjamin Wade, Wendell Phillips, and SALMON P. CHASE, Grant was too silent—and therefore potentially unsafe, or at least not radical enough—on Reconstruction. Privately, Grant had come to accept the necessity for black suffrage, but publicly he remained a mask of circumspection, which kept his relations with the President manageable and also pleased those in the Radical Republican camp, like Wade and Chase, who went to bed each night dreaming of the mansion on the Avenue.

The later half of 1867 proved critical in Grant's path toward the presidency. Johnson, still determined to control Reconstruction (and Grant himself if possible), suspended Secretary of War EDWIN M. STANTON in August and appointed Grant Acting Secretary. Grant found his new position somewhat anomalous and awkward, but he accepted it to avoid a politically worse situation. Meanwhile, Northern voters in November repudiated a number of Radical Republican candidates as well as black suffrage, thus emboldening Democrats to think of victory in 1868 and convincing more Republicans that Grant was indispensible. The Senate reconvened in December and shortly voted to disallow (under the Tenure of Office Act) Johnson's suspension of Stanton. Johnson hoped Grant would join him in defying the Senate. Grant refused, and a difference of opinion over what Grant had promised the President led to an unseemly newspaper quarrel in which Johnson impugned Grant's honor and integrity.

This dire mistake was sufficient to drive Grant into an open break with the President, which in turn finally made him more acceptable to the radicals. The President presently removed Stanton outright, which triggered the 24 February 1868 IMPEACHMENT OF ANDREW JOHNSON for HIGH CRIMES AND MISDEMEANORS. Grant had never reflected on the constitutional niceties of IMPEACHMENT, or indeed on the constitutional independence of the executive branch. He did support the impeachment, and although he did not make a public spectacle of his views he was not above buttonholing moderate Senators on public conveyances and encouraging them to vote for conviction. Near the end of the trial, the Republican national convention met and overwhelmingly chose Grant as the nominee, along with SCHUYLER COLFAX for Vice President. The Democrats chose HORATIO SEYMOUR and Francis P. Blair.

The campaign, during which Grant stayed home and let supporters speak for him, emphasized Reconstruction issues above all else, and when it was over Grant had won by a margin of 300,000 votes out of more than 5.7 million cast. His winning margin was less than the total number of blacks who voted Republican, but he also outpolled other Republican candidates (in Congressional elections, etc.) by more than 100,000 votes. Americans seemed to trust the man, regardless of his lack of policy statements and the party's list of platitudes. Never one to show much emotion, Grant listened disinterestedly to the returns at Congressman Elihu Washburne's house in Galena,

sauntered home at a late hour, found Mrs. Grant still up, and said, "I am afraid I am elected."

**The Character of Grant's Presidency.** It has often been observed that military men do not make good Presidents and that Ulysses Grant is a classic example of this failure. The adage is simplistic with regard to the presidency generally and to Grant in particular. One might better say that the American people have expectations of their military heroes that are too high for the man and the people to meet. Late-twentieth-century Americans very much want their Presidents to be great men but make it extremely difficult for them to be so. Lyndon B. Johnson, for instance, in his televised memoirs from the hill country of central Texas, told journalist Walter Cronkite, "You know, the hardest thing was not to do what was right, but to know what was right." So might Ulysses Grant have said from the front porch in Galena in 1877, though he would not have thought so in 1868.

Grant entered the presidency committed to racial justice, a peaceful sectional reconciliation, and a rather generalized sense of economic and material progress for all Americans, particularly those whose struggles had been similar to his own. These things he took to be basic principles that all should support. Yet he had no conception of what he as President needed to do to bring them to fruition. Racial justice in the North was often denied by the same people who demanded it for the South—a contradiction that the Republican platform, speaking of black suffrage, had almost authorized. Racial justice in the South, not having been established in 1865 (if indeed it could have been), could not be secured after 1869 without massive federal effort. And the economic resources that would make possible Grant's vision of progress also contributed to the greatest period of venality and corruption in American politics to that time.

From nomination through inauguration Grant had been saying that he "would have no policy to enforce against the will of the people." To his audiences this meant relief at not encountering another Andrew Johnson, but to Grant it meant that he could be "a purely administrative officer" without responsibility for developing policy. In his desire to be President of all the people, Grant would have happily employed Theodore Roosevelt's phrase "steward of the people" without understanding its potential. For Roosevelt it facilitated an expansive interpretation of the first sentence of Article II of the Constitution: "The executive power shall be vested in a President of the United States." That wonderful, passive-voice vagueness enabled Roosevelt to claim that he could do anything executive in nature and not otherwise forbidden that the national interest required, from stealing PANAMA to threatening to abolish college football. Grant, on the other hand, as a practitioner of constitutional power relationships within the federal government, was a congressional supremacist .

Being an activist President was not only outside Grant's cast of mind, it was also outside the boundaries of political prudence. He was, after all, following by only one year a narrowly failed presidential impeachment. And that event, in addition to its various other dimensions, was clearly a legislative challenge to executive policy-making, and ultimately to executive independence. Only infrequently did Grant persist in the face of congressional opposition, and when he did, he personalized the issues in rather the same way Johnson had.

To his credit, during the war Grant had understood the relationship of military and political factors. And he had been the military half of a well-functioning team. Now, in peacetime, the issues were mostly political rather than military, and there was no team. Lincoln was dead. Grant had no teacher. Following their quarrel, Grant and Johnson honored public decorum if not historical tradition by keeping out of each other's way on Inauguration Day. Millard Fillmore and Franklin Pierce would have done well to keep quiet, even if asked for advice on being President. Grant entered the White House a lonely man in the middle of a large adulatory crowd. He left it still lonely, in a crowd of decidedly mixed sentiments.

**Grant's Cabinet.** Grant's closest friend and confidant was General John A. Rawlins, who had started out with him as a lieutenant and aide-de-camp in 1861, remained with Grant to become his military chief of staff and then Secretary of War for five months at the start of Grant's first term. Rawlins had high ethical standards, political shrewdness, and a loyalty to Grant that never interfered with forthrightness. General Sherman was also important, but he was too mercurial and hated politics too much to rise beyond Commanding General of the Army, where he served throughout Grant's presidency. After Rawlins's death from tuberculosis in the summer of 1869, there was no one to replace him.

Since Grant was comfortable in the company of officers, it was hardly surprising that many of his presidential staff aides had been wartime subordinates, and since he distrusted politicians it was hardly surprising that his initial Cabinet had no party heavyweights. Grant kept the country in suspense for weeks after his election, consulted with almost no one, including even nominees (a continuing habit that led to embarrassing declinations) and constructed a Cabinet of miscellaneous friends, affable lightweights, and successful businessmen.

Elihu Washburne, Grant's Congressman and early defender, bumbled around the State Department for a week before being shunted off to France as minister. A. T. Stewart, first in line for the Treasury Department, was a wealthy importer and therefore not eligible under a 1789 statute. Grant's simple solution was to ask the Senate to waive the law. This unavailing, Stewart offered an arrangement that looked like a purchase, and finally withdrew. As a courtesy to the able General John Schofield, Grant carried him over briefly in the War Department before giving it to the abler Rawlins, but the Navy Department went to Adolph Borie. This wealthy and sophisticated friend of Grant's, non-Navy to the core and non-interested to the eyebrows, often said, "The Department is managed by Admiral [David Dixon] Porter; I am only a figurehead." Fragile in health and even more fragile in political substance, he did not last through Grant's first summer.

Three of the original Cabinet members were reformers who favored merit rather than party résumés in making appointments, but two of them soon departed. Jacob D. Cox, former governor of Ohio and wearer of wartime stars, brought the concept of CIVIL SERVICE REFORM to the Interior Department, but his relations with Grant deteriorated and he resigned in bitterness in 1870. Ebenezer Rockwood Hoar, Grant's first Attorney General, was an erudite if stiff-necked New England judge who was quite willing to gainsay Senators on judicial appointments and who found himself rudely sacrificed by Grant in the interest of political expediency. Only John Creswell, the Postmaster General, father of the penny postcard, reducer of postal rates, and reformer of contract practices, survived until 1874.

There was, indeed, a rather narrow profile for success in Grant's Cabinet. A nonpolitician (or a politician without enemies) had an advantage; a good war record also helped, as did moderate wealth manifested with gentility, and a home state that afforded geographical balance. Learning, culture, and sophistication could not be such as to make the supersensitive President uncomfortable; ambition and self-confidence could not be prevailing traits; and one simply could not raise questions about the integrity of Grant's appointee-friends without making the fatal mistake of questioning the President's own integrity.

Small wonder, then, that the seven chairs at Grant's Cabinet table often had new occupants and that on each new vacancy Grant passed over able men because of defects that were quite insignificant. Including temporary appointments, the seven positions were held by twenty-five men over the course of eight years. Lincoln and Johnson together had only had nineteen.

Out of all the Cabinet members, only HAMILTON FISH, who succeeded Washburne as Secretary of State, seemed to have all the requirements, and he stayed throughout Grant's presidency. A New York lawyer and prewar politician, he had been a strong Unionist but not an officeholder during the conflict. Grant got him into the Cabinet only with difficulty and kept him there despite his frequent offers to resign. After the death of Rawlins, Fish's counsel became even more important, for despite Fish's cultured, upper-class background and courtly manner, Grant genuinely liked him. The accomplishments of Grant's administration in foreign policy were the work of Fish; Grant's defeats, on the other hand, were principally of his own doing. Fish was a spokesman for caution and stability, yet his influence in two areas was not without controversy, since he was a conservative, hard-money man, and he had limited interest in federal solutions to racial questions. Both of these problems would continually plague Grant's presidency.

Early in the first term came Black Friday (24 September 1869), an event that combined controversy over fiscal policy with scandal in high places. Jay Gould and James Fisk, two financiers, were speculating in gold. They hoped to buy as much as possible at a low price of about $130 per ounce, hold it, force the price as high as possible, and make huge profits by selling at $160 or higher. Under the law, the Treasury could influence the price by selling gold or not, as the Secretary of the Treasury might decide. The schemers hoped to keep the Treasury from selling gold, thereby creating an artificial scarcity that would drive the price higher. Gould and Fisk worked on Grant, who had no understanding of monetary theory and its applications, to convince him to keep Treasury Secretary George Boutwell from selling gold. The schemers wanted to be seen in Grant's company as often as possible, to convince investors that they could influence government policy. For a while it worked: the price of gold reached $162, but by that time Grant realized he had been used. Boutwell put $4 million in gold on the market, the price fell steadily by the hour, and many investors were ruined. A chief gold broker was A. R. Corbin, a relative of Julia Grant, and critics charged that not only she but several of Grant's aides had profited as well. Even though some of the evidence remains obscure, it was clear that greed and corruption could stalk as near the presidency as was necessary for unscrupulous men's success.

Another first-term fiscal issue led to charges that Grant had packed the Supreme Court. Paper currency issued to help finance the war had been declared to be legal tender by an act of Congress, and the constitutionality of that statute had been before the Supreme Court since December 1867. In February 1870 the Court, by a vote of 4 to 3, partially voided the statute, but two seats on the nine-member body were vacant at the time. Grant had attempted to fill these vacancies in December 1869 by nominating Stanton and Hoar. The Senate happily confirmed Stanton (who died within days) and in a fit of petty vengeance tabled the nomination of the better-qualified Hoar. On the same day that the Court announced the legal tender decision, Grant nominated William Strong and Joseph Bradley to the two vacancies. Both were confirmed, though not without partisan grumbling, and in a second case both joined the previously dissenting minority to create a 5 to 4 vote upholding the statute. This outcome, together with the coincidence of timing, led to charges that Grant had packed the Court to achieve a desired result. In truth, Grant had no advance knowledge of the Court's vote and had been considering both men for weeks without any commitments regarding their views, which in fact coincided with those of most state courts and prominent Republican lawyers. Moreover, Grant's choices bucked the announced preferences of importuning Senators for a radical rather than the conservative Republican Strong and for a Southerner instead of Bradley.

Grant made two other appointments to the Supreme Court. In 1872 Justice Samuel Nelson of Pennsylvania resigned. Once again Grant denied Southern aspirations by rejecting both the distinguished Thomas J. Durant of Louisiana, a Lincoln Unionist of 1860, whom he had also rejected in 1869, and federal judge Thomas Duval of Texas. He sidestepped the brilliant but pricklishly ambitious Benjamin Bristow, recently Solicitor General, and Bristow's own candidate, Kentuckian John Marshall Harlan, whose eventual appointment by Rutherford B. Hayes led to a long and distinguished Supreme Court career. Grant satisfied his own pettiness by rejecting the able William M. Evarts, who had skillfully defended Johnson in the Senate, and finally, after weeks of rumors, nominated the man he had already chosen, Ward Hunt. Grant's last vacancy to fill was the chief justiceship in 1873. After a six-month comic opera involving rumors, leaks, nominations, withdrawals, pestering wives, septuagenarian Democratic fossils, and scheming partisan Senators, Grant settled on Morrison R. Waite. The Senate snatched him up by a vote of 63 to 6, because "he is an honest man and a fair lawyer and that is as much as we can reasonably expect from the President."

The Senate must consent not only to judicial nominees but also to the ratification of treaties. Grant's efforts early in his first term to annex the Caribbean nation of Santo Domingo (now the DOMINICAN REPUBLIC) showed just how difficult this process might be. An independent country, Santo Domingo was habitually insolvent and wracked by rebellion. Its dictator-president, Buenaventura Báez, would happily have sold his island country to the United States for as much as he could get (for himself), and Grant happily concluded that the idea was excellent. He had visions of a major naval base, extensive American investment, and, most importantly, a homeland for American blacks, who he hoped would migrate there in large numbers and establish a black state for admission to Congress, thereby solving the race problem. Grant was truly sincere, but his first effort to exercise the President's legitimate constitutional function as director of American FOREIGN AFFAIRS proved disastrous.

Acting largely independently of Fish, who had no interest in such schemes, Grant entrusted negotiations to former wartime aide Orville Babcock, an opportunist with a presence either real or shadowy in almost all the swirling controversies of Grant's presidency. Babcock arranged a treaty, but Grant had also ignored the views of Charles Sumner, the powerful chairman of the Senate Foreign Relations Committee. Sumner, a leading radical on issues of race and Reconstruction, favored assistance and protection for blacks at home rather than moving them elsewhere. He killed the treaty and in the process attacked Babcock's integrity, thus earning Grant's undying enmity.

Grant's notion that annexing Santo Domingo would solve the racial question, in addition to being naive, was also not part of a comprehensive plan. This kind of piecemeal approach was a frequent defect of Grant's perception of the presidency. On important issues he often proceeded with a frustrating combination of impulsiveness and lassitude. Reconstruction, viewed over the course of Grant's eight years, was an example. Grant was committed to racial justice but also to sectional reconciliation, a difficult combination. White Southerners insisted on home rule—that is, that the federal government should keep hands off racial matters and local politics—and many Northerners took greater interest in national economic expansion than in continued reconstruction. Grant preferred to administer congressional enactments rather than to provide executive leadership. On occasion he could act vigorously, as in 1871, when after a year of caution he ordered concerted use of military and judicial power to enforce laws aimed at stopping violence and intimidation by the KU KLUX KLAN. Thousands of arrests and

prosecutions resulted, especially in South Carolina, Mississippi, and North Carolina, and for a time peace and order prevailed at Southern polls.

Critics charged Grant with military despotism, however, and by 1873, when rival state governments fought for control of Louisiana in an atmosphere of violence and electoral fraud, Grant's response was more restrained than it had been in 1871. As one state after another faced Democratic efforts to get rid of Republican regimes and as harried Republican officials wired Washington pleading for federal troops, Grant and his Attorney General responded that "the whole public is tired of these annual autumnal outbreaks in the South," saying that state militias should handle the problems. Grant did authorize the use of federal troops in some locations, but when the state elections of 1876 again produced two rival governments in Louisiana, each clamoring for federal recognition, Grant took no action until his last week in office and then refused to recognize either, thus leaving the problem to his successor.

**Reelection and Second Term.** Reconstruction and civil service reform were two of the most volatile political issues for Grant. Together they formed the major basis of opposition to his reelection in 1872. A coalition of dissident elements within the Republican Party organized under the Liberal Republican banner. Some believed Grant and the party were too radical on the Southern question; others complained that Grant had reneged on his early concern for merit over partisanship in appointments; others thought the tariff too protectionist or the money policy too conservative. This scatteration of viewpoints made the Liberal Republican platform a mess, as did the breakaway faction's decision to unite with the Democrats and prevail on them to accept as a joint candidate HORACE GREELEY, a quixotic editor whom the Democrats had spent decades gleefully trashing. The only unifying theme was opposition to Grant, whose war record still carried great popularity in spite of first-term misadventures. Still, a more plausible opponent, such as the very able (and very available) Charles Francis Adams, would likely have produced quite a different result, since many Grant voters could not picture the fantastic Greeley in the White House. Grant won with 56 percent of the popular vote, higher than anyone else between Andrew Jackson and Theodore Roosevelt but only slightly better than his 1868 count.

This winning spirit, however, did not shape Grant's second term into a successful presidency. The panic of 1873 ushered in a depression that lasted well past Grant's departure from the White House. Southern whites held out, aggressively, until the North tired of efforts to prevent them from having their way. Scandals continued, and they got worse. The WHISKEY RING frauds, in which distillers and revenue agents conspired to defraud the government of taxes on millions of gallons of liquor annually, spelled the doom of many of Grant's appointees, including his private secretary, Orville Babcock. He resigned following his trial, in which the President's remarkable deposition attesting to Babcock's character offset a mass of evidence of guilt and led to Babcock's acquittal. And since Grant could not tolerate anyone who impugned his friends, the estrangement with Treasury Secretary Bristow, who ferreted out the frauds, led to Bristow's resignation from the Cabinet.

War Secretary William Belknap found himself under investigation in the spring of 1876 for bribery and corruption in the awarding of Indian Agency contracts and was saved from conviction only by Grant's agreement to his breathless, weeping plea for an instantly accepted resignation, since at that very moment, down Pennsylvania Avenue, the House was voting Belknap's impeachment. Twenty-three Senators reluctantly voted for acquittal on the ground that the resignation deprived the Senate of jurisdiction, and outrage against Grant mounted. Within months Navy Secretary William Robeson faced investigation over grain contracts and came near impeachment, but remained in the Cabinet in consequence of Grant's inaction. Indeed, over the course of eight years, all of the executive departments had been under congressional investigation at one time or another for irregularities large or small.

Ulysses S. Grant left the presidency in 1877 with mixed emotions. Following the apology with which his last annual message began, he went on to describe the material and commercial condition of the country in favorable terms, to detail excellent relations with foreign countries, and to remind the country at substantial length that if partisan opposition had not defeated his idea of annexing Santo Domingo, "the country would be in a more prosperous condition to-day, both politically and financially."

There had indeed been accomplishments during Grant's eight years. The country was in better economic condition than it had been at the end of the Civil War, with a stable currency, confidence in the national credit, and an industrial revolution in continuing progress. An important and dangerous foreign controversy, involving reparations from Britain for wartime damages caused by the *Alabama* and other British-built Confederate commerce raiders, had been settled fairly without war. Two lingering problems over the Canadian boundary were put to rest by a new survey of the forty-ninth parallel and by arbitration to determine ownership of the San Juan Islands. Yet all of these were really accomplishments of the administration rather than the man. In none of them was the presence of Grant the vital fulcrum between success and failure. He may indeed have been a better practitioner of the art of politics when he left office than when he assumed it. That learning process, however, contributed nothing favorable to the moral and ethical climate of politics, nor did it contribute anything to the strength and effectiveness of the presidency as an institution.

## BIBLIOGRAPHY

Catton, Bruce. *U. S. Grant and the American Military Tradition.* 1954.
Cunliffe, Marcus. *The Presidency.* 3rd ed. 1987.
Dawson, Joseph G., III. *Army Generals and Reconstruction: Louisiana, 1862–1877.* 1982.
Grant, Ulysses S. *Personal Memoirs.* 2 vols. 1885–1886.
Hesseltine, William B. *Ulysses S. Grant, Politician.* 1935.
Keller, Morton. *Affairs of State.* 1977.
McFeely, William S. *Grant: A Biography.* 1981.
Sefton, James E. *Andrew Johnson and the Uses of Constitutional Power.* 1980.
Sefton, James E. *The United States Army and Reconstruction, 1865–1877.* 1967.
Simpson, Brooks D. *Let Us Have Peace: Ulysses S. Grant and the Politics of War and Reconstruction, 1861–1868.* 1991.
Woodward, C. Vann, ed. *Responses of the Presidents to Charges of Misconduct.* 1974.

JAMES E. SEFTON

**GREAT DEBATE OF 1951.** The great debate, in January to April 1951, centered on the issue of how the United States should implement its military obligation to the North Atlantic Treaty Organization (NATO): whether the number of troop divisions to be deployed in Europe should be determined by the President or by Congress. As the debate began, the KOREAN WAR was going badly. China had entered the war and rapidly captured Seoul and Inchon. When President Harry S. Truman announced his decision to send American ground forces to strengthen NATO, Senators who favored a regional defense of the United States objected, and the press quickly labeled the ensuing discussions the great debate over foreign policy. Truman feared a hostile Soviet move in Europe while the United States was distracted in Korea.

The leading opposer of President Truman's policy was Robert A. Taft of Ohio, Senate Republican Leader. Taft had voted against American military commitments to Europe in 1940–1941 and against the NATO treaty in 1949. In a ten-thousand-word speech on 5 January 1951, the longest of the great debate, Taft contended that the President had no power to send forces abroad, without consulting Congress and without Congress's approval. Taft endorsed the resolutions to that effect introduced by Senator Kenneth S. Wherry (R-Neb.) and Frederic R. Coudert, Jr. (R-N.Y.) [see Coudert Resolution]. United States forces had been sent to Korea without notice or discussion with Congress. Neither NATO nor the United Nations Charter, Taft said, empowered the President to deploy troops abroad without Congress's approval and specification of their number.

The superior size of Soviet Union forces and the Soviet's possession of the atomic bomb, Taft argued, rendered futile any defensive effort by American forces on the European mainland. A better strategy was for United States sea and air forces to fight the Soviets from island bases. Taft urged a scaling back of commitments abroad, except for those to Israel and Formosa and NATO countries. He feared that sending troops now would commit the United States to a mainland strategy and preclude an island-base strategy.

President Truman's Senate supporters declared that Taft offered Europe the prospect of being bombed again by United States planes and cited the inadequacy of sea-air forces in aiding South Korea. Taft was reminded that his father, President William Howard Taft, in his book, *Our Chief Magistrate and His Powers,* stated that the President has authority "to order the army and navy where he will." But Senator Taft contended that under the NATO Treaty, Congress retained the power to decide when and how many troops should be sent to Europe.

As it continued, the debate centered on the military budget and the Wherry resolution. In a press conference of 12 January, Truman said that while the President has the untrammeled right to send troops anywhere in the world, he would consult with the Senate Foreign Relations and Armed Services Committees before dispatching more troops to the NATO forces. In a nationally televised address, Herbert Hoover called for a diminution of American commitments abroad.

The prestigious supreme commander of NATO forces, Dwight D. Eisenhower, after a tour of NATO capitals, reported to an informal joint session of the House and Senate on 1 February that American troops in Europe should be increased, but that no rigid formula be established, especially since the foremost need was equipment. Senator Paul Douglas (D-Ill.) said that although the President had authority to send troops abroad, he should not do so without congres-

sional approval, since the step involved too much responsibility for the President to act alone. Douglas felt Congress's role was limited to debate, and the President was the ultimate decider of troop deployment.

Ultimately, the Wherry resolution and other resolutions that barred the dispatch of additional troops to Europe without congressional approval were defeated. A consensus emerged that Europe's defense was essential to American security. Nonetheless, the Truman administration suffered a defeat when a sense of the Senate resolution was adopted on 2 April, which had no binding effect on the President, declaring that no additional ground troops should be sent to Europe without congressional approval. President Truman ignored the limitation and hailed the resolution for its support of the North Atlantic Treaty.

### BIBLIOGRAPHY

Acheson, Dean. *Present at the Creation.* 1969.
Donovan, Robert J. *Tumultuous Years: The Presidency of Harry S. Truman, 1949–1953.* 1982.
Patterson, James T. *Mr. Republican.* 1972.
Truman, Harry S. *Memoirs.* 2 vols. 1955–1956.

LOUIS W. KOENIG

**GREAT DEPRESSION.** See New Deal.

**GREAT SOCIETY.** The successor to the New Deal of Franklin D. Roosevelt and the Fair Deal of Harry S. Truman, the Great Society of Lyndon B. Johnson was the theme of his presidential campaign in 1964, and shortly became the domestic theme of his administration. Johnson set forth the outlines of the Great Society in a commencement address at the University of Michigan at Ann Arbor on 22 May 1964. The phrase is generally credited to Richard Goodwin, a speechwriter and White House assistant, although it had been used as the title of a book published in 1914 by Graham Wallas, a prominent Fabian socialist, which Goodwin said he had not heard of. The speech itself was the work of Goodwin and Jack Valenti, a principal aide to the President. The concept reflected Johnson's fondest hope for America.

Johnson's guiding star was Franklin Roosevelt, with whom he seems to have felt himself in historical competition. An old photograph of the young Johnson in conversation with his hero hung in the family quarters of the White House. The caption, Johnson's own, read, "I listen." Shortly after becoming President, Johnson said, "In both pride and humility, I readily admit that my own course in life has been influenced by none so much as this great man."

About to take office in his own right, Johnson was determined to out-Roosevelt Roosevelt. His would be an outsize program for the renewal of America. "The Great Society," he declared, "rests on abundance for all. It demands an end to poverty and racial injustice, to which we are totally committed in our time." He proceeded to enumerate the elements of the larger vision he was eager to realize: a society in which every child would have the opportunity "to enrich his mind and to enlarge his talents," in which leisure time would be a joyous rather than a boring experience, in which cities would be enabled to meet "not only the needs of the body and the demands of commerce but the desire for beauty and the hunger for community," and in which the means would be at hand to help people "renew contact with nature" and restore America's beauty. To further his goals, Johnson announced his intention to hold a series of White House conferences on the principal challenges he had enumerated; he hoped that from these meetings the practical plans for addressing his goals would emerge. Finally, he asserted that the achievement of his wide-ranging goals would require "new concepts of cooperation [and] a creative federalism, between the National Capital and the leaders of local communities."

Even before the landmark speech in Michigan, as early as his state of the union message to Congress in January 1964, Johnson had added a new crusade to his quest for civil rights legislation, which he had undertaken as a memorial to the slain President John F. Kennedy. This new theme, which would be central to the Great Society, was, as Johnson put it, an "unconditional war on poverty in America." The details, shortly to be revealed, were the product of a task force already at work when Johnson took office. In the early 1960s, affluent Americans had rediscovered the "other America"—that is, the impoverished America—through an influential book of that name by the social critic Michael Harrington and through television documentaries that brought the theretofore undiscussed subject into millions of homes. In March 1964 the White House sent Congress its Economic Opportunity bill, which provided a potpourri of proposals soon enacted into law. It created the Job Corps, which offered employment to inner-city young people between the ages of sixteen and twenty-one; the Head Start program for disadvantaged preschool children; work-study jobs for college students; grants to farmers and small businesses in rural areas; loans to businesses willing to give work to the so-called hard-core unemployed; Volunteers in Service to America (VISTA), a

domestic version of the Peace Corps designed to provide aid to deprived communities; and the Community Action Program, whose purpose was to enable the impoverished to participate in the management of the programs that were designed to help them.

In mid-1965, Joseph A. Califano, a thirty-four-year-old, Brooklyn-born lawyer, came to the White House from the Pentagon and was soon named the President's Special Assistant for Domestic Affairs. Before Johnson left office, Califano had in fact become a "deputy President" for domestic affairs. Under Califano, a myriad of task forces on a multitude of issues were organized, producing a spate of bills sent to Capitol Hill for passage. When the Eighty-ninth Congress—which the President delighted in calling "the Great Eighty-ninth Congress"—finally adjourned on 22 October 1966, it had passed 97 of the 113 major measures that Johnson had called for. In succeeding years Congress, dominated by Democrats, continued to pile act upon act.

In addition to legislation supporting the war on poverty, laws were placed on the books providing health care for the elderly; immigration reform; education for underprivileged children; facilities for research on cancer, stroke, and heart disease; aid for the arts; protection of air and water quality; the creation of "model cities" programs; payment of rent supplements; and funds for urban mass-transit improvements. The list goes on: rehabilitation programs for drug addicts, a teacher corps, vocational retraining for the unemployed, consumer protection, truth-in-packaging laws, protection for children from unsafe toys and hazardous products, highway and tire safety, bail and judicial reform, public-health reorganization, fish and wildlife preservation, parcel-post reform, freedom of information, a new GI bill, the Asian Development Bank, clean rivers legislation, mine safety laws, and narcotics rehabilitation programs. Johnson, keeping in mind the fact that Roosevelt had passed only five major bills in his famous first Hundred Days, boasted, "There never has been an era in American history when so much was done for so many in such a short time."

The monetary cost of all of this would be high, but Johnson was determined to stick with his tax cut of 1964, fearing a slowdown in the economy. Meanwhile, the VIETNAM WAR was heating up and making huge demands for funds. The President divined that the United States was rich enough to have "both guns and butter," but the long-term effect was to generate larger and larger federal budget deficits, a major expansion of the money supply, and steep inflation. The administration seemed inattentive to the growing competition that the United States was beginning to face from Germany, Japan, and emerging industrial nations, which in the long run would render quixotic the country's traditional profligacy with its resources.

Worse, the Great Society never captured the public's imagination. It was dazzled and dizzied by the array of laws passed on so many subjects that it was either unfamiliar with or not interested in. Even in the White House, there was sometimes a feeling that the frenzy of proposing bills bordered on being a caricature of the New Deal. Moreover, Johnson's unflagging energy and uncommon ability to force Congress to his will seemed at odds with the general public's feeling that, after a long generation of governmental activism, it was time to rest for a while. And in an era of rising democracy throughout the world, it struck many people as anachronistic that the U.S. government was exponentially increasing its management of individual lives, businesses, and organizations.

For all its vaunted goals and rhetoric, the Great Society aroused expectations that could not be realized, and it overemphasized the power of the federal government efficiently to manage the variety of undertakings the new laws provided for. Few would argue that the problems that Johnson was attempting to address did not require attack. But the 1960s were not the 1930s. At a time of general well-being, most white working people—the nucleus of the old New Deal and Fair Deal political coalition—did not any longer feel dependent on largess from Washington and were indifferent, if not hostile, to sharing their prosperity with the less fortunate. Others were offended by feckless improvisation by a White House sometimes seemingly bent on innovation for its own sake. Still others saw in the uneven performance of the multitude of programs and agencies fresh evidence of governmental mismanagement and waste.

Despite Johnson's frustration at not being able, despite valiant efforts, to gain the public affection he craved, the Great Society lives on—in health care for the elderly and indigent, in government environmental regulation, in Head Start, in the achievements of the National Institutes of Health, in the food-stamp program, in auto safety regulation, and in the continuing focus of attention on racial injustice. Most profoundly, one finds the spirit of the Great Society in the revived notion that the federal government has ignored for too long the intimate needs of the people. In his memoirs, Johnson wrote that if he had been given a second chance, "I would not have abandoned a single major program that we instituted. I would not have postponed a single law that we recommended and passed." Still, in private he once confessed that his

administration had attempted "to do too much too quickly." Califano, writing many years later, concluded that Johnson had "left plenty of achievements to build on and plenty of mistakes to learn from" but that history would have to record that "Johnson cared and that he tried."

## BIBLIOGRAPHY

Bornet, Vaughn Davis. *The Presidency of Lyndon B. Johnson.* 1983.
Califano, Joseph A., Jr. *The Triumph and Tragedy of Lyndon Johnson.* 1991.
Johnson, Lyndon B. *My Hope for America.* 1964.
Johnson, Lyndon B. *The Vantage Point: Perspectives of the Presidency 1963–69.* 1991.
Kearns, Doris. *Lyndon Johnson and the American Dream.* 1976.
Rulon, Philip Reed. *The Compassionate Samaritan: The Life of Lyndon Baines Johnson.* 1981.
Valenti, Jack. *A Very Human President.* 1975.

HENRY F. GRAFF

**GREELEY, HORACE** (1811–1872), newspaper editor, Whig and Republican activist, Liberal Republican presidential nominee in 1872. Horace Greeley built the *New York Tribune* into one of the most important and largest newspapers in America. Known for his widely publicized antislavery, temperance, and communitarian sympathies, Greeley also had the reputation for overbearing political ambitions, ambitions that went largely unfulfilled.

Born in rural poverty in Amherst, N.H., and possessing very little formal education, Greeley became a printer's apprentice at the age of fourteen. By twenty, Greeley was on his own in New York, working in the city's expanding newspaper industry.

By the end of the 1830s, Greeley had firmly established himself in New York Whig politics. With Thurow Weed and WILLIAM SEWARD's help (both of whom would later be Greeley's political rivals), Greeley began editing two WHIG PARTY organs: The *Jeffersonian* and the *Daily Whig.* During the presidential campaign of 1840, Greeley edited the *Log Cabin,* the first mass-circulation Whig newspaper. Copying the popular electioneering style pioneered by the Democrats, Greeley's *Log Cabin* did much to publicize the supposedly egalitarian roots of William Henry Harrison.

In 1841, Greeley launched the *New York Tribune.* Under his editorship, the *Tribune* became the most important newspaper in New York, partly because Greeley managed to place Charles A. Dana, James S. Pike, Richard Hildreth, and Margaret Fuller on his staff. The *Tribune,* however, was very much Greeley's paper. In his highly popular if erratic editorials (to which he signed his name) his own reform ideas emerged. He identified with New York working men and became involved with the utopianism of Charles Fourier. He was also a political reformer and moralist, advocating temperance, high tariffs, land cooperatives, women's rights, and became the first president of the New York Printers' Union.

In the 1840s, Greeley emerged as a strong voice in the antislavery movement. He opposed the Mexican War and supported the Wilmot Proviso, hoping to eliminate slavery but also protect the Union. He endorsed Zachary Taylor in the election of 1848 and warned of the dangers of the Democrat Lewis Cass. Rejecting the Compromise of 1850, Greeley's antislavery commitment further radicalized him in the 1850s. Arguing against any federal protection of slavery, he became deeply embroiled in the Kansas-Nebraska crisis. He blamed much of bleeding Kansas on President James Buchanan, who supported the pro-Southern Lecompton constitution of Kansas. Greeley called on Northerners to arm free soilers in the territories.

Greeley helped form the Republican Party, and the *Tribune* became one of the first newspapers to endorse the party. As a Republican, he intrigued against his New York rival William Seward, helping to deny Seward the presidential nomination in 1856 and 1860. At the 1856 Republican convention, Greeley worked for John C. Fremont's nomination. In 1860, as a delegate from Oregon, he supported Edward M. Bates of Missouri but willingly supported Abraham Lincoln's eventual nomination. Greeley himself failed to win Seward's Senate seat in 1861 and later lost congressional elections in 1868 and 1870.

Greeley's position on the Civil War was complex. Initially disavowing any attempt to compromise with the breakaway South, he emerged as a partisan of the Radical Republicans, siding with Salmon P. Chase in his struggles against Seward inside Lincoln's Cabinet. Greeley pushed Lincoln for early emancipation and, as did other Radicals in the party, became impatient with the President's handling of the war. By 1863, however, Greeley was an advocate of peace negotiations. In July 1864, he went (with Lincoln's shrewd blessing) on a peace mission to Canada to negotiate with what he thought were empowered emissaries of the Confederacy. Nothing came of the meeting in Niagara Falls, and Greeley returned politically embarrassed.

After the war, he sided with Radicals against Andrew Johnson during Reconstruction. The *Tribune* later turned against Ulysses S. Grant. Disgruntled with Grant, Grant's support of Roscoe Conkling in New York politics, and the Grant administration's indiffer-

ence to Civil-Service Reform, Greeley was driven from the Republican mainstream. In Cincinnati on 1 May 1872 the Liberal Republican movement met to find an appropriate anti-Grant candidate. The Cincinnati convention comprised several disparate elements: Republicans dissatisfied with the Grant administration's corruption, notably Carl Schurz, some former antislavery Republicans, southern Democrats, and spoilsmen. Before the convention, Charles Francis Adams, David Davis, and Schurz were clear leaders of the movement. Adams's refusal to politick eliminated him from the ticket; Schurz was born in Germany and therefore could not compete for the presidency; and reformers blocked the opportunist Davis's rise. To the surprise of many, the convention chose Greeley for the presidential ticket; his running mate was B. Gratz Brown, governor of Missouri and a rival of Schurz's in that state.

The presidential campaign was a monumental disaster for Greeley. Expecting defeat or antagonized by the ticket, several leaders of the movement simply did not campaign. The Liberal Republicans adopted a low-tariff platform; Greeley was an avid protectionist. He further antagonized potential supporters with his prohibitionist beliefs. Discredited by his wartime performance and accused correctly of an inconsistency of policy and temperament, Greeley lost resoundingly to Grant, despite his reluctant endorsement by the Democrats. He carried only six states (southern and border states) and received 2.8 million votes to Grant's 3.6 million. Humiliated in defeat, Greeley died on 30 October 1872.

### BIBLIOGRAPHY

Iseley, Jeter A. *Horace Greeley and the Republican Party*. 1947.
Van Deusen, Glyndon G. *Horace Greeley: Nineteenth-Century Crusader*. 1953.
Wilentz, Sean. *Chants Democratic*. 1984.

JOHN F. WALSH

**GREENBACK PARTY.** This minor party was an inflationist movement in the post–Civil War era. Because of inadequate specie reserves the federal government had issued paper currency, called greenbacks, to help finance the Civil War. The government proposed to limit the quantity of such notes and to redeem them in gold sometime after the war. The expanded wartime currency supply appeared to help sustain economic growth, although the new currency was often discontinued in favor of gold and silver.

Once the conflict was over, diverse interests—some debtor elements in the Midwest, agrarians, labor spokesmen, and a few businessmen interested in rapid growth—hoped to retain the greenbacks, both to sustain economic expansion and to limit the alleged power of gold-standard interests. Greenback supporters were willing to risk inflation for an expanded money supply. Some people also proposed to exchange some federal bonds for greenbacks, thus reducing government interest charges and removing perceived favoritism to holders of tax-exempt redeemable bonds. Fully as diverse a constituency favored retiring the greenbacks and returning to specie payments, chiefly to avoid inflation and to have "honest money" based on gold and silver. This group included some eastern bankers and businessmen as well as laissez-faire theorists. The issue combined the perceived economic advantages of several groups, sectionalism, and philosophical differences.

A number of small parties supporting Greenback ideas appeared. The most prominent was the Greenback, or Independent National, Party, which nominated the New York businessman and philanthropist Peter Cooper for President in 1876. He received eighty thousand votes, and supporters may have helped defeat the gold-standard Democrat SAMUEL J. TILDEN in that disputed election. Hard times following the panic of 1873 made Greenback ideas appealing to more debtors and unemployed, and partisans captured about fifteen seats in the congressional elections of 1878. In 1880 an expanded coalition party broadened its platform to include a graduated income tax, women's suffrage, and railroad regulation. Its candidate, JAMES B. WEAVER of Iowa, received about 300,000 votes, but only ten Greenback candidates won congressional seats. The party's fortunes then steadily declined. Gold payments were resumed in 1879, a more broadly based free-silver movement developed, and public attention turned to other issues. In 1884 the Greenbackers supported Benjamin F. Butler, who fared badly. The Greenback movement's educational and propaganda efforts had to some extent succeeded, however, and many supporters were folded into the Populist revolt of the 1890s [see POPULISM].

### BIBLIOGRAPHY

Friedman, Milton, and Anna Jacobsen Schwartz. *A Monetary History of the United States, 1867–1960.* 1969.
Haynes, Frederick E. *Third Party Movements since the Civil War.* 1916.
Unger, Irwin. *The Greenback Era.* 1964.

H. WAYNE MORGAN

**GREENE v. McELROY** 360 U.S. 474 (1959). This case decided whether a CABINET-level department un-

der presidential authority could deny employment in defense-related private industry by using a security system that accepted "faceless accusers." For William L. Greene, the highly successful vice president and general manager of a California company called ERCO (Engineering and Research Corporation), this issue was crucial. Did the U.S. Department of Defense have the constitutional authority to remove individuals from employment in private industries by means of procedures that denied them the traditional procedural safeguards of confrontation and cross-examination of witnesses provided by the Sixth Amendment? Not only was Greene unable to confront and cross-examine his accusers, but the members of the governmental clearance boards did not see the accusers or know their identities.

A divided Supreme Court upheld Greene's contention that by having his security clearance removed, he was severely limited in his work opportunities and that the hearing he had been given denied traditional requirements for fair procedures. The Court did not determine whether these procedures comported with Sixth Amendment requirements. Nor did it directly address questions about the interaction of presidential and congressional powers. Instead, Chief Justice Earl Warren, writing for the majority, simply decided that "in the absence of explicit authorization from either the President or Congress the clearance board members were not empowered to deprive Greene of his job in a proceeding in which he was not afforded the safeguards of confrontation and cross-examination."

Justice Tom C. Clark wrote a long and bitter dissenting opinion in which he claimed that the majority had improperly addressed the constitutional issues, thus weakening presidential authority to protect NATIONAL SECURITY. Clark accused the majority of establishing Greene's "right to have access to military secrets." Clark's dissent provoked a strong rejoinder from Justice John M. Harlan, who, with Justice FELIX FRANKFURTER, wrote a concurring opinion. Harlan accused Clark of yielding to the temptation of "colorful characterization." Like PETERS v. HOBBY (1955), *Greene* provides an illustration of the fact that the Supreme Court of the United States is generally reluctant to decide on the merits a direct constitutional challenge to the authority of the President. As in previous decisions involving the faceless accuser issue, the Court's majority was characteristically cautious in delineating the reasons for denying broad-constructionist Presidential dismissal authority. But it is important to note that in the 1950s and 1960s such authority was indeed interpreted narrowly. Thus it is not surprising that such decisions aroused congressional opposition.

BIBLIOGRAPHY

Bontecou, Eleanor. *The Federal Loyalty-Security Program.* 1953.

Fisher, Louis. *Constitutional Conflicts between Congress and the President.* 3d ed. 1991.

Pritchett, C. Herman. *Congress versus the Supreme Court.* 1961,

JOHN R. SCHMIDHAUSER

**GRENADA INVASION.** In 1979, the Marxist New Jewel Movement, led by Maurice Bishop, seized power in the tiny Caribbean island nation of Grenada. When Ronald Reagan became President in 1981, he suspended further U.S. economic assistance to Grenada in protest over Bishop's close ties to CUBA's Fidel Castro and his support of the Sandinista revolution in Nicaragua. A few Americans continued to visit the island, although tourism was hampered by the lack of a modern international airport. The closest ties between the United States and Grenada resulted from the presence on the island of nearly one thousand American students at the St. George's University College of Medicine.

On 12 October 1983, a militant faction of the New Jewel Movement, led by General Hudson Austin, overthrew Bishop's government. The rebels imposed martial law and murdered Bishop, who had recently moved away from his alliance with Cuba. Although the dean of the medical college announced that his students were not threatened by the strict curfew imposed by the new regime, officials in Washington expressed concern. Their fears intensified on Sunday, 23 October, when a terrorist attack on a barrack in Beirut killed 241 marines. Frustrated at the inability to retaliate for the humiliation in Lebanon, Reagan recalled that the new government of Grenada had promised to use a Cuban labor brigade to complete construction of a new airport runway long enough to accommodate military aircraft. On 25 October, after quickly consulting with the members of the little known Organization of Eastern Caribbean States, Reagan ordered nineteen hundred U.S. troops plus three hundred personnel from nearby islands to Grenada to liberate the island from what Reagan called "a brutal gang of thugs." The invaders encountered little resistance from the Grenadan armed forces and some tougher fighting from the armed Cuban construction battalion. The invasion succeeded within a week at a cost of 18 U.S. dead and 106 wounded. American soldiers rescued the medical students, who probably had not been in much danger before the arrival of the U.S. forces.

The operation proved highly popular in the Caribbean and the North American mainland. The inhabitants of Grenada welcomed the American soldiers as saviors and expected them to create democracy and prosperity on the island. American forces were removed by mid-December and free elections were held in 1984. Yet the economic assistance promised by the United States never materialized. The invasion also won applause in the United States. The media carried pictures of hundreds of medical students falling to their knees and kissing American soil at Air Force bases upon their return from Grenada. The invasion became an issue during the 1984 presidential election campaign, as Reagan and his supporters pointed to popularity as proof of the success of an assertive foreign policy. Reference to Grenada in 1984 was especially damaging to the candidacy of WALTER MONDALE, the Democratic Party's nominee. Like many Democrats in Congress and specialists on international affairs, Mondale had initially opposed the use of military force in Grenada. They charged that the operation revived the bad memories of high-handed U.S intervention in the Caribbean and Central America. Soon most of the domestic critics either changed their minds or held their tongues after realizing how popular the invasion was with the Grenadians and most U.S. citizens. Initially many South American members of the ORGANIZATION OF AMERICAN STATES and NATO allies had also disapproved of the use of force. They too reversed their objections or suppressed them after realizing how popular Washington's actions had been with the Grenadians and the governments of neighboring Caribbean states.

BIBLIOGRAPHY

Gilmore, William C. *The Grenada Intervention: Analysis and Documentation.* 1984.

Lewis, Gordon. *Grenada: The Jewel Despoiled.* 1987.

O'Shaughnessy, Hugh. *Grenada Revolution: Intervention and Aftermath.* 1984.

ROBERT D. SCHULZINGER

**GROUPTHINK.** A phenomenon identified by Irving Janis, *groupthink* refers to a deterioration of mental efficiency, reality testing, and moral judgment in policy-making groups when members become more concerned with maintaining the group's cohesiveness and agreement than with critically and realistically evaluating information about policy options. Groupthink is associated with highly cohesive in-groups in which a tendency to seek concurrence dominates the group's deliberations about important policy decisions.

Janis developed the concept from case analyses of presidential and policy-making groups involved in foreign policy fiascoes. The classic prototype of groupthink is President John F. Kennedy's advisers' support of the ill-fated decision to launch the BAY OF PIGS INVASION of CUBA in 1961. Janis's reading of Arthur M. Schlesinger, Jr.'s account of the Bay of Pigs decision in his book *A Thousand Days* led him to infer that a concurrence-seeking process was subtly at work in Kennedy's highly cohesive team that prevented members from debating the real issues and risks of the CIA's invasion plan.

The causes of groupthink are a cohesive in-group of policymakers and advisers whose members are insulated from outside information, lack of methodical procedures for generating and evaluating alternatives, and a directive leader who promotes a favored viewpoint.

Eight symptoms of groupthink have been identified: an illusion of invulnerability; collective efforts to rationalize the group's decision; an unquestioned belief in the group's inherent morality; a stereotyped view of rivals and enemies as weak, evil, or stupid; direct pressure on dissenting group members to conform; self-censorship of doubts and counterarguments; an illusion of unanimity; and the emergence of self-appointed "mindguards."

Janis argues that Kennedy's highly cohesive group of advisers exhibited many symptoms of groupthink. Group members displayed an illusion of invulnerability as they basked in the optimism and confidence of the NEW FRONTIER. They held negative stereotypes about Cuban leader Fidel Castro, who was regarded as a weak, "hysteric" leader whose army was ready to defect. Although members seemed unanimous about the invasion plan, it was subsequently revealed that DEAN RUSK and Arthur Schlesinger had private doubts and that therefore there was only an illusion of unanimity. Some members, such as Rusk and Schlesinger, suppressed their personal doubts; and ROBERT F. KENNEDY, who took the role of "mindguard", urged potential dissenters to close ranks with the President.

Janis offers two examples of well-thought-out decisions—the making of the MARSHALL PLAN and the CUBAN MISSILE CRISIS—to demonstrate that groupthink is due to faulty processes, not incompetent decision-makers. The Cuban missile crisis involved the same key people responsible for the Bay of Pigs fiasco. In this case, however, John Kennedy deliberately missed some earlier meetings of his advisers, encouraged open questioning and discussion, introduced outside opinions, and appointed Robert Kennedy as a devil's advocate to challenge every proposal.

Janis also postulates that groupthink played a major role in Harry S. Truman's advisers' support of the decision to escalate the KOREAN WAR, in the support given by Lyndon B. Johnson's "Tuesday luncheon group" to the escalation of the VIETNAM WAR, and in the cover-up of the WATERGATE AFFAIR by some of Richard M. Nixon's advisers. Other cases analyzed for groupthink include Admiral Husband Kimmel's in-group of naval commanders at PEARL HARBOR and Neville Chamberlain's inner circle, whose members supported appeasement of Hitler. The groupthink framework has also been applied to the failed attempt to rescue American hostages in Tehran during the Jimmy Carter administration [*see* DESERT ONE; IRANIAN HOSTAGE CRISIS] and to the *Challenger* space shuttle disaster (Esser and Lindoerfer, 1989). In all these cases, group members ignored or downplayed repeated warnings and information that the favored policy would lead to disaster.

A review of the historical examples cited by Janis indicates that a President's directive style of leadership (in which a favored policy alternative is promoted) together with group insulation are the most reliable predictors of groupthink (McCauley, 1989). Several critics, however, have questioned the role of groupthink in Truman's decision to cross the thirty-eighth parallel (Alsop, 1973), Kennedy's Bay of Pigs decision (Etheredge, 1985) and Johnson's decision to escalate the Vietnam War (Barrett, 1988).

While the concept of groupthink remains an important, although partial, explanation for the occurrence of these historic fiascoes, the term groupthink has entered the vocabulary of the social sciences because of its intuitive appeal and because it serves as a reminder of the hazards of high-pressure group decision making.

## BIBLIOGRAPHY

Alsop, Stewart. Review of *Victims of Groupthink*. *New York Times*, 26 January 1973.

Barrett, D. M. "Political and Personal Intimates as Advisers: The Mythology of Lyndon Johnson and the 1965 Decision to Enter the Vietnam War." Paper presented at Midwest Political Science Association Meetings. April 1988.

Esser, James, and Joanne Lindoerfer. "Groupthink and the Space Shuttle Challenger Accident." *Journal of Behavioral Decision Making* 2 (1989): 167–177.

Etheredge, L. S. *Can Governments Learn? American Foreign Policy and Central American Revolutions*. 1988.

Janis, Irving L. *Groupthink: Psychological Studies of Policy Decisions and Fiascoes*. 1982.

Janis, Irving L. *Victims of Groupthink*. 1971.

Janis, Irving, and Leon Mann. *Decision Making: A Psychological Analysis of Conflict, Choice and Commitment*. 1977.

McCauley, Clark. "The Nature of Social Influence in Groupthink." *Journal of Personality and Social Psychology* 57 (1989): 250–260.

Schlesinger, Arthur M., Jr. *A Thousand Days.* 1965.
Smith, S. "Groupthink and the Hostage Rescue Mission." *British Journal of Political Science* 15 (1984): 117–126.

LEON MANN

## GUADALUPE HIDALGO, TREATY OF. See Treaty of Guadalupe Hidalgo.

## GUITEAU, CHARLES (1841–1882), assassin of President James A. Garfield. A one-time disciple of John Humphrey Noyes's radical Perfectionism, an unsuccessful lawyer, itinerant evangelist, deadbeat, wife beater, and mentally unhinged egoist of grandiose pretensions, Charles Julius Guiteau was a far more complex case than the usual label of "disappointed office seeker" would indicate. Although he did hound the recently elected President, James A. Garfield, for an appointment to the diplomatic service, his real reason for "removing" the President, he insisted, was divine inspiration, not thwarted ambition.

Convinced that his act would unite the Republican Party and make his name immortal, Guiteau stalked the President for six weeks, finally catching him on 2 July 1881 in the waiting room of the Baltimore & Potomac train station in Washington, D.C., just as Garfield was leaving the city for a summer vacation. Guiteau pumped two .44 caliber bullets into the President's back and surrendered himself to the police.

Garfield died on 19 September 1881 and Guiteau was tried the next year: he was convicted and on 30 June 1882 summarily hanged while reciting a childish poem of his own composition.

### BIBLIOGRAPHY

Peskin, Allan. *Garfield.* 1978.
Rosenberg, Charles E. *The Trial of the Assassin Guiteau: Psychiatry and Law in the Gilded Age.* 1968.

ALLAN PESKIN

## GULF OF TONKIN RESOLUTION. The Gulf of Tonkin Resolution, passed by Congress in August 1964, provided President Lyndon B. Johnson with broad legal authority to wage combat against North Vietnamese aggression. The Johnson administration later claimed that the resolution, in combination with U.S. membership in the Southeast Asia Treaty Organization (SEATO), provided a "functional equivalent" to a Declaration of War.

Acting upon the recommendation of Secretary of Defense Robert S. McNamara, President Johnson had instructed the Joint Chiefs of Staff to prepare a program of graduated military pressure against North Vietnam. The President soon approved covert operations along the North Vietnamese coast. Operation Plan 34A was part of the progressively escalating pressure against North Vietnamese coastal installations. The U.S. Navy also began by sending destroyers up the Gulf of Tonkin for intelligence-gathering purposes.

On 2 August 1964, the U.S. destroyer *Maddox* was returning from one of these electronic espionage missions when North Vietnamese torpedo boats fired on her. The attack was repulsed. Rather than withdrawing U.S. ships from this danger zone, the President ordered another destroyer, the *C. Turner Joy*, to join the *Maddox* in the Gulf of Tonkin. On 4 August, both the *Maddox* and the *C. Turner Joy* reportedly came under attack by torpedo boats. Considerable doubt exists as to whether this second attack ever took place. While there is little doubt that North Vietnamese gunboats were operating in the area, weather conditions were so bad and tensions aboard ship so high that Johnson later quipped, "For all I know, our Navy was shooting at whales out there." But circumstantial evidence was all Johnson needed for ordering reprisals against the North.

The President later met with congressional leaders and sought assurance that his action would be supported. On 10 August 1964, Congress passed (by a vote of 88 to 2 in the Senate and 416 to 0 in the House) the Southeast Asia Resolution (often called the Gulf of Tonkin Resolution), which provided Johnson with a broad grant of power that Johnson used as legal justification for prosecuting the Vietnam War. The key part of the resolution read: "The Congress approves and supports the determination of the President, as Commander in Chief, to take all necessary measures to repeal any armed attack against the forces of the United States and to prevent further aggression. The United States regards as vital to its national interest and to world peace the maintenance of international peace and security in Southeast Asia . . . to take all necessary steps, including the use of armed force, to assist any member of protocol states of the Southeast Asia Collective Defense Treaty requesting assistance in defense of its freedom."

Johnson's firm but restrained response won broad popular support; his ratings in the Louis Harris poll, for example, skyrocketed from 42 to 72 percent overnight. Yet, members of Congress had acted in order to create a traditional unified front for presidential action in foreign policy. They had also acted on the basis of false information. The Johnson administration had permitted electronic surveillance in areas likely to provoke Vietnamese response and the attack was not completely unprovoked. In 1966 Sen. Wayne Morse (one of two Senators originally opposed to the resolution) introduced an amendment to repeal the resolution. The amendment was defeated 92 to 5. The Gulf of Tonkin Resolution was terminated by Congress in May 1970.

### BIBLIOGRAPHY

Gelb, Leslie H., with Richard K. Betts. *The Irony of Vietnam: The System Worked*. 1979.

Karnow, Stanley. *Vietnam: A History*. 1983.

Stockdale, Jim, and Sybil Stockdale. *In Love and War*. 1984.

U.S. Senate. Committee on Foreign Relations. *Termination of Middle East and Southeast Asia Resolutions: Report to Accompany Senate Concurrent Resolution 64, May 15, 1970*. 91st Cong., 2d sess., 1970.

Windchy, Eugene C. *Tonkin Gulf*. 1971.

LARRY BERMAN

**GULF WAR.** During the Iran-Iraq war of the 1980s the United States opened diplomatic relations with Iraq, which it had accused of supporting international terrorism. It also supplied Iraq with sensitive satellite intelligence data because it wanted to ensure that Islamic fundamentalist Iran would not come to dominate the Middle East. Although the United States did not approve of the brutal actions of Iraq's leader, Saddam Hussein, after the war it saw him as potentially pragmatic and hoped to normalize relations with Iraq more fully. The United States extended credit for the purchase of U.S. grain and allowed the transfer of dual use (civilian and military) technology from U.S. firms.

The end of the war with Iran left Iraq depleted by many casualties and deeply in debt. This large debt burden, some of which was owed to Kuwait, increased Saddam Hussein's resentment of Kuwait's alleged "stealing" of oil from the Rumaila oil field that extended under both countries. Saddam also wanted greater access to the Arabian Gulf and claimed two islands, Warba and Bubiyan, that were controlled by Kuwait. He also accused Kuwait of waging economic war on Iraq by producing more oil than OPEC quotas allowed.

In spring and summer 1990 Saddam had been making increasingly belligerent speeches about Kuwait and Israel, but the United States continued to want to normalize relations and felt that Saddam could best be dealt with by working diplomatically to moderate his behavior. U.S. diplomacy was thus conciliatory. Even in July 1990 U.S. Ambassador April Glaspie told Saddam that the United States would not interfere with differences among Arab nations.

Despite Saddam's bellicose words the United States did not think that a full-scale attack was imminent, and neither did Iraq's immediate neighbors in the region. When Saddam began to deploy about 100,000 troops along the border with Kuwait, the United States interpreted it as more of his usual saber rattling. But intelligence estimates turned out to be wrong when Iraqi forces invaded and occupied Kuwait with overwhelming force and began to deploy troops along the border with Saudi Arabia. After the invasion, Iraq controlled 20 percent of the world's oil reserves; if it invaded Saudi Arabia it would control 40 percent.

The U.S. reaction to the invasion was initially cautious, but after consulting with his advisers and Prime Minister Thatcher of Great Britain, President Bush declared the invasion of Kuwait "would not stand." Over the next several weeks the United States began the deployment of 200,000 troops to protect Saudi Arabia, and President Bush knitted together a broad-based, international coalition against Saddam's aggression. On 25 August the UNITED NATIONS Security Council passed Resolution 665, which authorized U.N. members to enforce the economic embargo on Iraq.

As fall 1990 wore on, the embargo became effective in cutting off imports and exports; but by late October President Bush became convinced that economic sanctions were not going to be effective in persuading Saddam to leave Kuwait. After the congressional elections in early November the President announced an increase of U.S. troop strength in the region from 200,000 to more than 400,000.

Congressional reaction to the initial deployment of troops to defend Saudi Arabia in August 1990 was favorable. Members of Congress felt that the deployment was defensive in nature and constitutionally within the discretion of the President. Early in the fall both houses of Congress passed resolutions supporting the President's actions. But when the President announced the doubling of troop strength in November, serious concerns were raised by Democrats in Congress. President Bush had not consulted with Congress or forewarned its leadership, and the implication of the doubling of U.S. forces was probable war.

While the United States could resupply the 200,000 troops already in Saudi Arabia for a year or two if necessary, the logistical volume necessary to supply 500,000 troops could not be sustained indefinitely. In addition, the difficulty of maintaining such a large fighting force throughout a hot 1991 summer increased pressure for an early offensive against Iraq. It was becoming evident that the President was leaning toward an offensive to drive Saddam out of Kuwait; and members of Congress, particularly Democrats, felt that the constitutional provision that only Congress could declare war was being ignored. [*See* WAR, DECLARATION OF.]

As the United States moved closer to war, Congress became increasingly nervous about its constitutional prerogatives. The Bush Administration, however, was arguing that it did not need congressional approval to begin offensive action against Iraq but that it could begin hostilities under the authority of the President's power as COMMANDER IN CHIEF.

In December 1990, fifty-six members of Congress sued the administration in federal court (*Dellums v. Bush*) to forbid the president to attack Iraq without a declaration of war from Congress. The court refused to hear the case fully because only 56 of 535 members of Congress were party to the suit. But in dicta the court declared that "the plain language of the Constitution" makes it "clear that congressional approval is required if Congress desires to become involved."

The issue, however, became moot when the administration decided to ask Congress to vote on a resolution of support for the administration's military actions. After several days of somber debate both Houses on 12 January 1991 approved a resolution authorizing the President to use military force against Iraq. Even though the action was not a formal declaration of war, Speaker of the House Thomas Foley said that the votes in Congress amounted to "the moral and constitutional equivalent of a declaration of war."

In the early morning (Baghdad time) of 17 January 1991 the United States began the air war with intensive bombing of Iraq that disabled its air defenses and, over the next four weeks, systematically destroyed much of Iraq's military and economic infrastructure. On 23 February U.S. and allied ground forces swept into Iraq. In a battle that lasted only one hundred hours, Iraq's ability to mount military resistance was overcome and President Bush called a halt to the hostilities.

In the peace agreements after the war Iraq agreed to abide by the U.N. resolutions. Saddam Hussein, however, remained in power, and when President Bush left office in 1993, Saddam was continuing to resist U.N. efforts to assure that his nuclear weapons programs were abandoned.

### BIBLIOGRAPHY

Ridgeway, James. *The March to War.* 1991.
Whicker, Marcia, James P. Pfiffner, and Raymond Moore, eds. *The Presidency and the Gulf War.* 1933.
Woodward, Bob. *The Commanders.* 1991.

JAMES P. PFIFFNER

**GUNBOAT DIPLOMACY.** In the broadest sense, gunboat diplomacy is the use of force or the threat of force by one government to intimidate another. In U.S. history, the term generally refers to the policing role of the U.S. Navy in the Caribbean and Central America from the mid-nineteenth century until the early 1930s, though later exercises of U.S. power in the region (for example, President Lyndon B. Johnson's dispatch of troops to the DOMINICAN REPUBLIC in April 1965 and President George Bush's decision to invade PANAMA in December 1989) resurrected charges of gunboat diplomacy. Most of these interventions were of short duration and occurred when local governments, threatened by disorder, proved unable to provide guarantees for the security of foreign lives and property. Between 1900 and 1934, when U.S. strategic concerns (identified with the defense of the PANAMA CANAL) and business interests greatly expanded in the Caribbean region, gunboat diplomacy became synonymous with the blatant exercise of U.S. power.

No U.S. President of this era exploited gunboat diplomacy more effectively than Theodore Roosevelt, who relied on the navy to back up his forceful policies in the Caribbean. The pattern was firmly established in 1902, when CUBA acquired independence only after relinquishing to the United States the right of intervention and, in the same year, when U.S. naval officers mediated a civil conflict between conservatives and liberals in Panama, then a province of Colombia. In 1903, Roosevelt again used naval power in Panama to protect Panamanians who were amenable to giving the United States major concessions in a new canal treaty.

Roosevelt also intruded in a Venezuelan crisis of 1902 and 1903, brought on by a British and German blockade of the Venezuelan coast. The experience alerted Roosevelt to growing public concern over the European (especially German) presence in the region and strengthened arguments that the United States should play the role of policeman in Latin America.

Roosevelt's announcement in late 1904 that the United States must play the role of policeman in Latin America—a policy known as the Roosevelt Corollary to the MONROE DOCTRINE—gave gunboat diplomacy the imprimatur of official U.S. policy. Presumably, such a policy would obviate the sending of large numbers of troops to fight a guerrilla war (as had occurred in the PHILIPPINES after 1898) or the creation of a U.S. military government on foreign soil. As things turned out, the use of gunboat diplomacy to further broad political goals proved increasingly inadequate. The policy failed to resolve the Cuban political crisis of 1905 and 1906 and Roosevelt sent an army of pacification to the island, where it remained for more than two years.

Gunboat diplomacy also failed to bring lasting peace among the warring states of Central America.

President William Howard Taft, alert to the pitfalls of gunboat diplomacy, replaced it with DOLLAR DIPLOMACY, whereby U.S. financial and economic power ("dollars instead of bullets") would be able to achieve compliance with U.S. policies. Dollar diplomacy proved inadequate in Nicaragua, where the United Fruit Company subsidized a rebellion against the national government. Once installed, the new government was kept in power only by the landing of three thousand U.S. Marines and seamen in 1912. In the aftermath, Nicaragua and Honduras became de facto protectorates of the United States.

In the 1912 presidential campaign, Woodrow Wilson condemned both gunboat and dollar diplomacy as unwarranted exercises of U.S. power. Nonetheless, President Wilson practiced his own version of gunboat diplomacy in Mexico, Haiti, the Dominican Republic, and Central America. When diplomatic pressures foundered, he authorized military interventions in Veracruz (1914), Haiti (1915), and the Dominican Republic (1916).

In 1920, the U.S. Navy created the Special Service Squadron to patrol the Pacific coast of Central America, but here, as in the Caribbean, the use of gunboat diplomacy seemed less necessary than it had earlier. There was no longer a German threat, the Panama Canal appeared secure, and compliant governments ruled in the region. Under President Warren G. Harding, the United States began to dismantle the protectorate system, but U.S. leaders did not abandon gunboat diplomacy. Troops landed in Honduras during the civil war of 1923 and 1924 and, most seriously, in Nicaragua in late 1926. The latter display of gunboat diplomacy resulted in a major intervention of five thousand American soldiers to prop up a friendly government, hold an election, and pursue the guerrilla leader Augusto C. Sandino. Clearly, gunboat diplomacy had failed in its purpose. The landing of troops to safeguard property and foreign lives was counterproductive. In 1930, the State Department concluded that the United States did not require the Roosevelt Corollary to exercise the right of intervention; the following year, Secretary of State HENRY L. STIMSON announced that U.S. property holders in Nicaragua must look to Managua, not Washington, for protection.

The Nicaraguan experience dictated that the United States required a more practical approach to policing the Caribbean—to wit, governments in power that were not only pro-American but capable of defending themselves and, of course, U.S. interests. This decision, which appeared sensible to a generation weary of the taint and the cost of gunboat diplomacy, bequeathed another legacy—an informal alliance between the United States and governments more responsive to foreign than to their own national interests.

## BIBLIOGRAPHY

Challener, Richard. *Admirals, Generals, and American Foreign Policy, 1898–1914.* 1973.

Healy, David. *Drive to Hegemony: The United States in the Caribbean, 1898–1917.* 1988.

Langley, Lester D. *The Banana Wars: United States Intervention in the Caribbean, 1898–1934.* 2d ed. 1988.

Munro, Dana Gardner. *Intervention and Dollar Diplomacy in the Caribbean, 1900–1921.* 1964.

Munro, Dana Gardner. *The United States and the Caribbean Republics, 1921–1933.* 1974.

LESTER D. LANGLEY

# H

**HABEAS CORPUS, SUSPENSION OF.** The Constitution provides in Article I, Section 9, that "The Privilege of the Writ of Habeas Corpus shall not be suspended, unless when in Cases of Rebellion or Invasion the public Safety may require it." Most authorities assumed that only Congress enjoyed this power. Neither the WHISKEY REBELLION nor the WAR OF 1812 provoked suspension, though General Andrew Jackson imposed martial law on New Orleans and defied a writ of habeas corpus in 1815.

Thus the only precedent for President Abraham Lincoln's action during the CIVIL WAR had been set by Jackson, the first Democratic President. In an 1844 congressional debate Whigs had expressed disapproval of Jackson's action. Later, many Republicans valued writs of habeas corpus as devices for freeing fugitive slaves.

But history made little difference to Lincoln, who, though a Whig turned Republican, was also the only President to face a large rebellion. Within two weeks of the firing on Fort Sumter, while Congress was not in session, Lincoln suspended the writ of habeas corpus around Washington, D.C. On 24 September 1862, he suspended it, and imposed martial law in certain cases, throughout the nation. Tens of thousands of civilians were arrested by military authority during the war, and over four thousand were tried by military commissions. On 3 March 1863, Congress passed a Habeas Corpus Act legalizing suspension but, with deliberate ambiguity, left unclear whether it deemed the President's previous suspensions legal. The U.S. Supreme Court did not consider the question during the war (*see* MERRYMAN, Ex PARTE).

After the war the Supreme Court (in Ex PARTE MILLIGAN) condemned the use of military trials where ordinary civil courts were open. The decision was remarkably nonpartisan (Lincoln, a Republican, had appointed five of the Court's members).

No President since Lincoln's day has faced rebellion or foreign invasion, and the Civil War was so vast and so threatening to the life of the Union that it provides no analog to any other event in American history. JEFFERSON DAVIS provides the only relevant comparison. The president of the Confederacy, laboring under the same constitutional restrictions, asked his Congress for authority to suspend the writ; he did not act unilaterally, as Lincoln did. Suspension was permitted only for limited periods. The Confederate army, after a brief experiment in Texas in 1862, did not employ military commissions. Yet, proportionate to population, about the same number of civilians suffered incarceration in Confederate military prisons.

BIBLIOGRAPHY

Neely, Mark E., Jr. *The Fate of Liberty: Abraham Lincoln and Civil Liberties*. 1991.

MARK E. NEELY, JR.

**HAGERTY, JAMES** (1909–1981), presidential press secretary. James C. Hagerty was widely regarded as an outstanding WHITE HOUSE PRESS SECRETARY (in the opinion of the CBS journalist and anchorman Dan Rather, *the* best in the second half of the twentieth century). He became a newspaper reporter in 1934, when he worked for the *New York Times* as campus correspondent for Columbia University during his student days. He stayed with the *Times* until 1943, when he became New York governor THOMAS E. DEWEY's press secretary. He stayed with Dewey through

Dewey's 1944 and 1948 presidential campaigns. In 1952 Dewey "loaned" Hagerty to Republican presidential candidate Dwight D. Eisenhower.

Following his election, Eisenhower appointed Hagerty to the post of White House press secretary. He was immensely popular with the WHITE HOUSE PRESS CORPS because of his simple recipe for working with the reporters: "Make it as easy as possible for them to get what they want—and don't lie." He was responsible for many innovations, the most important of which was to allow live television and radio coverage of presidential news conferences.

Hagerty was unusual among press secretaries in that he participated regularly in staff conferences to discuss policy. Eisenhower trusted his judgment, especially but not exclusively on dealing with the press. Perhaps his most critical moment came in 1955, when Eisenhower suffered a heart attack. As the President recuperated, Hagerty was his source for news and information. He explicitly followed Eisenhower's order, "Tell the truth, the whole truth; don't try to conceal anything." Hagerty did just that, setting a precedent for revealing information about the President's health (Woodrow Wilson's condition had been hidden from the American people following his 1919 stroke). Hagerty played a key role in persuading Eisenhower to run for a second term. He stayed at his post through the full two terms of the Eisenhower administration.

## BIBLIOGRAPHY

Ambrose, Stephen E. *Eisenhower: The President.* 1984.
Hagerty, James C. Diary. Eisenhower Library, Abilene, Kans.

STEPHEN E. AMBROSE

**HAIG v. AGEE** 453 U.S. 280 (1981). The *Haig* case upheld Secretary of State Alexander Haig's revocation of the passport of ex-CIA agent Philip Agee. The decision illustrates the Supreme Court's shift in perspective concerning presidential power in cases involving government claims of NATIONAL SECURITY. The Court discussed the respective rights of Congress and the President to regulate foreign travel by Americans and the process of weighing presidential claims of national security harm against individual CIVIL LIBERTIES.

The Secretary of State had revoked Agee's passport on the grounds that his activities were causing serious damage to the national security and foreign policy of the United States. Agee had worked for the CENTRAL INTELLIGENCE AGENCY from 1957 to 1968 in the clandestine operations division, serving as an undercover

agent. In 1974, in the midst of revelations of illegal CIA activities, Agee announced a campaign to abolish the CIA and in 1975 wrote a book criticizing the CIA, *Inside the Company: CIA Diary.* As part of this campaign, Agee publicly revealed the identity of undercover CIA agents, employees, and sources around the world. The government charged that these revelations prejudiced the ability of the United States to obtain intelligence and were followed by episodes of violence against the persons identified. For purposes of the litigation, Agee conceded that his activities had caused damage to the national security. Although Agee's disclosures violated his employment agreement with the CIA, which prohibited him from disclosing classified information, the CIA could not effectively enforce the agreement because Agee mostly lived overseas during this time.

The revocation of Agee's passport was based on State Department regulations under the Passport Act of 1926. That act provides that the Secretary of State shall issue passports "under such rules as the President shall designate" [*see* TRAVEL, RIGHT TO]. Agee challenged the revocation on the grounds that the applicable regulation had not been authorized by Congress and was thus invalid. The appeals court agreed that Congress had not authorized the regulation either by expressly delegating such power to the executive branch or by approving any long-standing executive practice of denying passports on national security grounds.

The Supreme Court reversed the appeals court decision. The Court stated that the issuance of passports is an aspect of foreign relations and that, while there is plenary presidential power in that field, there is only a limited judicial role. Although the Court did not explicitly decide whether, in the absence of a congressional statute authorizing such passport regulations, the President would have inherent authority to impose such restrictions, it described the Passport Act as a congressional recognition of presidential authority. This was in marked contrast to the earlier decisions in *Kent v. Dulles* (1958) and *Aptheker v. Secretary of State* (1964), in which the Court, believing that revocation of passports was a legislative matter entrusted to Congress and related to its foreign commerce power, had been scrupulous in requiring explicit congressional delegation of authority before the President could limit international travel through revocation of passports. Although the Court in *Haig* rested its decision on a finding that Congress had approved the State Department regulations, in analyzing the question the Court deferred to the executive on all important issues. The dissenting opinion by Justices Brennan and Marshall specifically objected that delegations of power to the executive branch that curtail aspects of liberty, such as the right to travel, must be construed narrowly, that is, to limit rather than expand presidential power.

The Supreme Court also rejected Agee's constitutional challenge to the revocation of his passport. The Court announced a distinction between the freedom to travel outside the United States and the right to travel within the United States and held that the freedom to travel abroad is "subordinate to national security and foreign policy considerations" and therefore may be subject to reasonable government regulation. Again, the Court abandoned the analysis, used in earlier cases, that traveling abroad is part of an individual's constitutionally protected liberty, which may only be curtailed in narrow circumstances. The Court also spoke about the importance of national security even when there is no war. Some scholars argue that in this decision, the Court lost sight of the traditional function of the judiciary as the arbiter and protector of individual liberty against overbroad government claims of power and necessity.

BIBLIOGRAPHY

Dorsen, Norman, Paul Bender, Burt Neuborne, and Joel Gora. *Political and Civil Rights in the United States.* Supplement. 1982. Chap. 11.
Koh, Harold Hongju. *The National Security Constitution.* 1990.

KATE MARTIN

**HAITI.** Born of a slave rebellion against France, the Caribbean republic of Haiti has preoccupied U.S. Presidents from George Washington, whose administration wrangled with the strategic and political issues in the Haitian revolution, to Bill Clinton, who inherited from George Bush the threat of massive Haitian emigration to the United States. Fearful of the impact of Haitians' triumph over slavery on U.S. slaves, the American government refused to recognize Haiti until 1862. In 1915, largely out of apprehension over German influence there, Woodrow Wilson sent Marines to occupy Haiti, and the United States ruled the country through client governments until 1934.

For strategic and economic reasons, Presidents since Dwight D. Eisenhower have quietly acknowledged that although palpably undemocratic rule in Haiti may be unpleasant to contemplate, it reinforces U.S. Caribbean policy and, just as important, provides a labor force for offshore multinationals. The Haitian dictator Jean-Claude ("Baby Doc") Duvalier had the preposterous notion that he would turn Haiti into a

Caribbean "Taiwan." The plan collapsed, and Duvalier's regime merely continued the persecution of political enemies, especially on the democratic left, and the impoverishment of the Haitian people that had characterized the rule of his father, François ("Papa Doc") Duvalier. When escaping Haitians began perilous sea voyages to the United States, the official U.S. position was that most were fleeing poverty and thus not entitled to asylum. Post-Duvalier Haiti, however, is far more complex—a society in which ordinary people and popular organizations believe in democracy and challenge the pretensions of elites who desire maintenance of the status quo: an orderly Haiti where an impoverished majority defers to the elites' rule.

After pressure from the ORGANIZATION OF AMERICAN STATES and the Bush administration, which came under increasing criticism for its policies toward undocumented Haitian immigrants, Haitian voters in December 1990 elected Jean-Baptiste Aristide, a former priest with a long record of working with the poor, as president. He was overthrown in September 1991 in a military coup. The United States joined a trade embargo against Haiti. Those who suffered, however, were poor Haitians. Thousands tried to flee. They were intercepted by the U.S. Coast Guard and turned back or brought to Guantánamo Naval Base on CUBA for detention. A small percentage obtained asylum in the United States, but most were sent back. In the U.S. Congress, old cries about a racist immigration policy were revived.

BIBLIOGRAPHY

Plummer, Brenda Gayle. *Haiti and the United States: The Psychological Moment.* 1992.
Wilentz, Amy. *The Rainy Season: Haiti Since Duvalier.* 1989.

LESTER D. LANGLEY

**HAMILTON, ALEXANDER** (1755/7–1804), first Secretary of the Treasury. A major figure in the establishment of the national government under the Constitution, a capitalist economy, and national political parties, Hamilton is linked with the first four Presidents of the United States. Reared in the British West Indies, he based his political conceptions on British progress after the Glorious Revolution of 1689, its unity under parliamentary rule, and its military and economic power. George Washington, Thomas Jefferson, John Adams, and James Madison depended on this tradition as well, but they also absorbed the principles of freedom and equality that were generated by the seventeenth-century civil war in Britain and transported to America as the colonies were founded.

Hamilton came to New York in 1773, rising to eminence as Washington's military aide and by marriage into the landed aristocracy. He joined the Nationalist movement led by Congress's Superintendent of Finance, Robert Morris, and with Washington and Madison he assisted Nationalist efforts to strengthen the central government and revitalize the economy. He later combined with them to sponsor the CONSTITUTIONAL CONVENTION. Hamilton, Madison, and JOHN JAY wrote THE FEDERALIST, with Hamilton actually drafting most of the articles.

Washington appreciated Hamilton's qualities, saying of him in 1781 that few men of his age and position had "a more general knowledge than he possesses . . . or . . . exceed him in probity and virtue." When Washington died in 1799, Hamilton said "He was an Aegis very essential to me." Washington's patronage was indeed vital to Hamilton's career. During Washington's presidency, Hamilton was virtually a prime minister, and his influence persisted through much of John Adams's term.

As head of the Treasury, Hamilton put the Nationalist program into high gear. Following his directives, Congress saddled the federal government with nearly all public debts, foreign and domestic, federal and state. Federal debts took the form of public securities; funding them created capital for private investment. Functions of the central government expanded, those of the states declined, and within the decade federal taxes extended to levies on land and slaves.

In conformity with the dictum that "public and private credit are closely allied, if not inseparable," Hamilton constructed the BANK OF THE UNITED STATES, new public securities comprising four-fifths of the initial capital. In 1791 he launched the incorporation of large-scale manufactures with machine technology, enterprises of a half-million dollars or more, competitive with foreign industry, supervised by skilled immigrants, and worked by countryside labor. Manufactures, he observed, were everywhere the harbinger of social progress, taking hold in the more advanced nations of the world.

From Madison's standpoint, Hamilton was trying "to *administration* the Government into a thing totally different from that which he and I both knew perfectly well had been understood and intended by the Convention who framed it and by the People adopting it." Previously allied in pursuit of national unity, Madison and Hamilton had parted ways. Madison in 1790 headed opposition to Hamiltonian funding in the House of Representatives. Acceding finally to federal assumption of state debts, Madison and Jefferson secured location of the national capital in western Virginia.

Hamilton prevailed with respect to the Bank of the United States. Opposition, again led by Madison in the House, boiled down to the question of constitutionality. Washington asked his Cabinet for written opinions. He was quickly persuaded by Hamilton, who concocted a manifesto of IMPLIED POWERS: "Every power vested in a government is in its nature sovereign, and includes by force of the term, a right to employ all the means requisite." Jefferson, who resigned from the Cabinet in December 1793, concluded that "monocrats" planned to introduce an "English constitution . . . forming like them a monied interest, by means of a funding system . . . and to make it an engine in the hands of the executive branch of the government which might enable it to assume by degrees a kingly authority."

By 1792 most of Hamilton's economics were institutionalized, and political parties began to form as people took sides with Federalists versus Democratic-Republicans. An intrusive factor that affected the whole decade, however, was the ideology of the French Revolution and the imperialism it spawned. Enthusiasm for the French version of democracy declined as Americans witnessed the effects of the guillotine and military conquests. Hamilton, as always, had a low opinion of "the multitude," and in 1800 he wrote that the revolution in France "after her early beginnings has been always to me an object of horror."

Confronted by war between Britain and France in 1793, Jefferson and Hamilton differed over the French alliance that had helped Americans win their revolution. Jefferson wanted to affirm the treaty of alliance with France, Hamilton to deny its current existence. Washington simply issued a PROCLAMATION OF NEUTRALITY. The main threat to American neutrality, however, lay not in obligation to France but in quarrels with Britain left over from the Revolution, as well as British seizure of "neutral" American vessels in the French West Indies. Hamilton, whose domestic system was menaced by British estrangement, worked hard for reconciliation. The resulting JAY'S TREATY dispelled many hostilities.

As relations with the British became friendlier, relations with the French cooled. American and French vessels clashed on the high seas in the undeclared QUASI-WAR WITH FRANCE. Congress in 1798 authorized President Adams to raise a "Provisional Army" of ten thousand men in case of foreign war. General Washington was to head it, but since he was aged, it was understood that active leadership would fall to the second-in-command. Although Hamilton had commanded the regular army from 1796 on, and in 1798 was busy appointing Federalist officers for additional forces, members of the Cabinet, with Hamilton's collaboration, induced Washington to demand Hamilton's appointment as second-in-command of the Provisional Army, whenever it was raised. Adams's will as President had been overridden by Hamilton's influence, and he had to comply, but Adams never lost the resentment he felt at being deprived of his rightful stature.

Hamilton had a taste for military force. In 1783 he had tried to manipulate the Newburgh Conspiracy, a plot to incite rebellion or the semblance of it by American officers. Washington simply refused to countenance this and put an end to the conspiracy. A decade later Hamilton personally led the military suppression of the WHISKEY REBELLION. In foreign affairs, Hamilton's aim in 1800 was mainly territorial conquest. "We ought certainly," he wrote, "look to the possession of the Floridas and Louisiana, and we ought to squint at South America"—aided by the British fleet.

The military buildup and the exploitation of Washington's prestige made Adams realize how much his Cabinet was dominated by the "hypocrite" Hamilton. Consulting nobody, he dispatched a commission to negotiate with France and obtain a treaty. He dismissed the Secretary of State and the Secretary of War. He let the legislation behind military expansion and the Provisional Army expire unexecuted. He later wrote, "I desire no other inscription over my gravestone than 'Here lies John Adams, who took upon himself the responsibility of peace with France in the year 1800.'"

Hamilton published a long indictment of Adams and his policies, but it discredited only Hamilton himself. In the election of 1800 he supported Jefferson to prevent his hated New York rival, AARON BURR, from occupying the presidency and to heap on Democratic-Republicans the responsibility for the national disasters he foresaw. Actually, Hamilton's unrepented attack on Adams and his conduct during the election broke up the FEDERALIST PARTY and ended his political career. Burr killed him in a duel in 1804.

### BIBLIOGRAPHY

Cooke, Jacob E. *Alexander Hamilton.* 1982.

Cooke, Jacob E., ed. *Alexander Hamilton: A Profile.* 1967.

Ferguson, E. James, et al., eds. *The Papers of Robert Morris, 1781–1784.* 1973–.

McDonald, Forrest, *Alexander Hamilton: A Biography.* 1979.

Miller, John C. *Alexander Hamilton: A Portrait in Paradox.* 1959.

Mitchell, Broadus. *Alexander Hamilton: The National Adventure, 1788–1804.* 1962.

Syrett, Harold C., et al., eds. *The Papers of Alexander Hamilton.* 1961–1987.

E. JAMES FERGUSON

**HAMLIN, HANNIBAL** (1809–1891), fifteenth Vice President of the United States (1861–1865). Han-

nibal Hamlin was born in Paris Hill, Maine, on 27 August 1809. He received his education in local schools, including a year at Hebron Academy. In 1830, he briefly edited the *Oxford Jeffersonian,* a Jacksonian Democratic newspaper, while tilling his late father's acres and studying law on his own. A brief apprenticeship in a Portland law firm was followed by admission to the Maine bar in 1833 and a move to Hampden with his bride Sarah Jane Emery Hamlin. In 1835, he won a seat in Maine's House of Representatives, serving six terms, three of them as speaker. A Jacksonian Democrat, he took antislavery ground that he would never abandon until the CIVIL WAR—opposition to expansion of SLAVERY on moral grounds while rejecting the radical abolitionist approach.

In 1843, Hamlin went to Washington as a member of the U.S. House of Representatives. He supported former President John Quincy Adams's assault on the "gag rule" and loyally defended Maine's economic interests. He opposed Texas annexation on antislavery grounds and coauthored the WILMOT PROVISO to bar slavery from any territory gained by the United States in the MEXICAN WAR.

Hamlin ran unsuccessfully for the U.S. Senate in 1846 but won a seat in 1848 to fill the unexpired term of deceased Senator John Fairfield. In 1850, he opposed those elements of the COMPROMISE OF 1850, especially the Fugitive Slave Act, perceived as advancing slavery's fortunes. In fact, this Democrat supported Whig President Zachary Taylor in his opposition to the comprehensive Compromise. That same year he won a full Senate term by a paper-thin margin, in the face of bitter proslavery Democratic opposition in the Maine legislature.

Senator Hamlin vigorously opposed the KANSAS-NEBRASKA ACT of 1854, defying President Franklin Pierce and finally breaking with the DEMOCRATIC PARTY in 1856 and joining the Republicans. Elected governor of Maine that same year, he resigned the office early in 1857 to return to the Senate.

Hamlin had some hope of being a favorite son candidate for President at the 1860 Republican national convention, but he quietly supported Lincoln and found himself as the running mate of the man from Illinois. Hamlin saw the vice presidency as political oblivion but worked hard behind the scenes for Republican victory. He found this "second office of the land" every bit as frustrating and boring as he had feared, especially during the Civil War when he itched for action and influence. His first biographer, grandson Charles Eugene Hamlin, claimed that disgruntled RADICAL REPUBLICANS offered to support Vice President Hamlin as Lincoln's replacement in 1864 but this tale has little historical probability. True, Hamlin was more radical on slavery issues than his wartime chief, urging emancipation and arming of freedmen earlier than Lincoln felt appropriate, but he loyally supported the President throughout the war.

His stunning defeat for renomination by Andrew Johnson of Tennessee at the National Union Party convention in 1864 was thus all the more painful. Hamlin took solace in the belief that he was Lincoln's personal choice, until he learned twenty-five years later that the President had personally engineered his replacement by Johnson. And Hamlin, a shrewd and pragmatic Republican leader with sterling antislavery credentials would surely have been a more successful President than the stubborn, hapless Democrat Andrew Johnson.

Appointed collector of the Port of Boston by President Johnson, Hamlin resigned in 1866 over RECONSTRUCTION policy and vowed that he would have voted for the President's conviction had he been a Senator in 1868.

The following year, Hamlin returned to the Senate and served until 1881. He supported President Ulysses S. Grant but was no friend of President Rutherford B. Hayes. He worked hard for the presidential nomination of his friend and fellow-Mainer JAMES G. BLAINE in 1876 and 1880, who, as Secretary of State, engineered Hamlin's appointment as minister to Spain in 1881. He died on 4 July 1891.

### BIBLIOGRAPHY

Hamlin, Charles Eugene. *The Life and Times of Hannibal Hamlin.* 1899.
Hatch, Lewis Clinton. *Maine: A History.* 3 vols. 1919.
Hatch, Louis C. *A History of the Vice-Presidency of the United States.* Revised and edited by Earl L. Shoup. 1934.
Hunt, H. Draper. *Hannibal Hamlin of Maine: Lincoln's First Vice-President.* 1969.

H. DRAPER HUNT

**HAMPTON & CO. v. UNITED STATES** 276 U.S. 394 (1928). *J. W. Hampton, Jr., & Co. v. United States* is an important case in the evolution of constitutional doctrine of the DELEGATION OF LEGISLATIVE POWER. The Tariff Act of 1922 (42 Stat. 858) empowered the President to increase or decrease duties imposed by the act to ensure that domestic goods could compete with imports. The act provided some criteria to guide the President in changing the duties. Whenever the President, upon investigation of the differences in costs of production of articles, determined that the duties fixed in the statute did not equalize the differences in costs of production, he was authorized to proclaim the changes in classifications or increases or decreases in any rate of duty provided in the statute.

J. W. Hampton, Jr., & Company, an importer, challenged the constitutionality of the Tariff Act after it was assessed by the collector of customs, acting under a presidential order, a duty of six cents per pound, two cents per pound more than the statutorily established level. The Supreme Court upheld the law as constitutional, finding that Congress adopted in statute the method by which a member of the executive branch would carry out legislative policy and make whatever adjustments were necessary to conform the duties to the standard underlying congressional policy.

The Court continued:

Congress may feel itself unable conveniently to determine exactly when its exercise of the legislative power should become effective, because dependent on future conditions, and it may leave the determination of such time to the decision of an Executive. The true distinction, therefore, is, between the delegation of power to make the law, which necessarily involves a discretion as to what it shall be, and conferring an authority or discretion as to its execution, to be exercised under and in pursuance of the law. The first cannot be done; to the latter no valid objection can be made.

The fact that the delegation dealt with taxes and customs duties posed no problem for the Court: "If Congress shall lay down by legislative act an intelligible principle to which the person or body authorized to fix such rates is directed to conform, such legislative action is not a forbidden delegation of legislative power." Although the President cannot be delegated the authority to levy taxes to regulate commerce or to raise revenue, the statute did not attempt an unlawful delegation of legislative authority. It delegates to the President the power to find facts, not the power to make law."

### BIBLIOGRAPHY

Corwin, Edward S. *The President: Office and Powers, 1787–1984.* 1984.

GARY C. BRYNER

**HANCOCK, WINFIELD** (1824–1886), soldier, Democratic presidential nominee in 1880. By nominating Winfield Scott Hancock as its presidential candidate in 1880, the DEMOCRATIC PARTY adopted the strategy usually employed by the Republicans during the Gilded Age: the selection of a Union general as the party's standard-bearer.

Born in Norristown, Pennsylvania, Hancock graduated from West Point in 1844 in time to serve in the

MEXICAN WAR. During the CIVIL WAR he earned the nickname Hancock the Superb, particularly for his conduct at the Battle of Gettysburg. During RECONSTRUCTION he was briefly military commander of the Department of Louisiana and Texas, where his evident sympathy for white southerners and alleged fulminations against "nigger domination" gained the approval of Democrats but the condemnation of congressional Republicans, who forced his removal from that post.

That controversy brought Hancock political attention and made him a strong contender for the Democratic presidential nomination in 1868. After losing that bid to HORATIO SEYMOUR, Hancock remained in the army, but his political ambitions persisted. In 1880 he launched a better-organized effort that took advantage of the leadership vacuum left in the Democratic Party in the aftermath of the disputed PRESIDENTIAL ELECTION OF 1876. On 24 June 1880, at the Democratic national convention in Cincinnati, Ohio, Hancock was nominated on the second ballot. His running mate was William H. English, of Indiana.

The nomination took even seasoned political observers by surprise, but they conceded it was a strong one. "For the first time in twenty years the Democracy did not blunder," said an alarmed Republican. He had reason for alarm. With the abandonment of Reconstruction and the subsequent disenfranchisement of southern black Republicans, any Democratic nominee was assured the electoral votes of the so-called Solid South. If a few large northern states, such as New York and Indiana, were added, an electoral majority could easily be assembled. Hancock's Pennsylvania birth, his New York residence and, above all, his war record—which could cut into the usually dependable Republican vote of Union veterans—were formidable assets.

His chief liability was his lack of civil experience. Nor was his personality suited for the rough-and-tumble of politics. Smug and phlegmatic, he was dismissed by a Republican newspaper as "a good man, weighing two hundred and fifty pounds."

Since nineteenth-century presidential candidates, unlike aspirants for lesser offices, were not expected to campaign on their own behalf, these drawbacks were not immediately apparent. Initial gambling odds gave the edge to Hancock over his Republican rival, James A. Garfield, a Civil War general with seventeen years congressional experience. This early confidence seemed justified by the 13 September gubernatorial election in Maine, usually a dependable Republican stronghold, which was swept by a candidate supported by a fusion of the GREENBACK PARTY and the Democratic Party.

This unexpected setback shocked Republicans into activity. Seizing upon a phrase in the Democratic platform advocating "a tariff for revenue only," they changed the thrust of their campaign from the dependable invocation of the Civil War (the so-called bloody shirt) to a new emphasis on the protective tariff. Hancock played into their hands by dismissing the tariff as purely "a local question." The cartoonist Thomas Nast portrayed a befuddled General Hancock plaintively asking, "Who is Tariff, and why is he for Revenue Only?"

While the galvanized Republicans raised fresh issues and large contributions, the complacent Democrats, led by their tightfisted and unimaginative chairman, William H. Barnum, waged a mean-spirited, negative campaign, content with dredging up scandals from Garfield's past, such as the $329 he allegedly received from involvement in the CREDIT MOBILIER SCANDAL. The smashing Republican victory in the October election in Indiana revealed the bankruptcy of these tactics and foreshadowed Hancock's defeat in November—a defeat that not even Barnum's desperate exploitation of the forged Morey Letter (which imputed pro–Chinese-immigration sentiments to Garfield) could avert.

Hancock's margin of defeat was narrow in the popular vote (fewer than ten thousand votes) but decisive in the ELECTORAL COLLEGE, which Garfield carried 214 to 155. Although the Democrats took all the old slaveholding states, they won no electoral votes in the rest of the nation other than New Jersey, Nevada, and California. A solid Democratic South was now confronted by a nearly solid Republican North.

For Hancock personally, this result was probably fortunate. Given his political naïveté, his lack of civilian experience, and his commitment to white supremacy, it is unlikely that the presidency would have enhanced his reputation.

### BIBLIOGRAPHY

Clancy, Herbert J. *The Presidential Election of 1880*. 1958.
Hancock, Almira R. *Reminiscences of Winfield Scott Hancock*. 1887.
Jordan, David M. *Winfield Scott Hancock: A Soldier's Life*. 1988.
Peskin, Allan. *Garfield*. 1978.

ALLAN PESKIN

**HARDING, WARREN G.** (1865–1923), twenty-ninth President of the United States (1921–1923). Elected President in 1920, Warren Gamaliel Harding was the first Chief Executive to move directly from the Senate to the White House. He was the first to be elected in a presidential race in which women could vote. He amassed over 16 million votes, nearly twice as many as any previous candidate. The 1920 election was also the first in which election returns were announced on the radio.

**Early Career.** Born on 2 November 1865, in Blooming Grove, Ohio, Harding was the first of eight children of George and Phoebe Harding. He developed an interest in publishing when his father became part owner of the *Argus*, a newspaper in Caledonia, Ohio. Harding worked for the newspaper, setting type and running the press, until he entered Ohio Central College at the age of fourteen. He was graduated in 1882 and took a job teaching in a rural school.

Soon Harding returned to his first love—publishing. In 1884, with the help of two partners, John Sickel and Jack Warwick, he purchased, for three hundred dollars, the bankrupt Marion *Star*. Shortly, his two partners allowed him to buy out their interests and assume full ownership of the newspaper. By the mid 1890s the *Star* was prospering.

In 1891 Harding married Florence Kling DeWolfe. In many ways it was an unusual match. She was five years older than he, divorced, and pregnant. Disowned by her family, she was supporting herself by giving piano lessons. Harding nicknamed her "Duchess." The wife of the handsome Harding was plain, ungraceful, and stubborn, but she was also forceful, ambitious, and competent. The *Star* began to prosper when she took over the bookkeeping and management.

Harding entered politics in 1892 when he ran for county auditor; he was soundly beaten. Seven years later, he won a seat in the Ohio senate. He earned a solid reputation among voters, and especially with the REPUBLICAN PARTY. Being a good party man ensured his steady rise in Ohio politics; he won reelection to the state senate and in 1903 was elected lieutenant governor. In 1909 he ran for the governorship, but the Republicans were split and he lost his base of support and the election as well.

At first Harding was reluctant to reenter politics. His chief persuaders were his wife and HARRY M. DAUGHERTY, a lawyer who had managed Harding's gubernatorial campaign and would continue to figure prominently in his political career. In 1914, Harding ran for the United States Senate and won handily.

His term in the Senate was not particularly distinguished in producing legislation. Nevertheless, the personable and friendly Harding made few enemies and was popular among his colleagues for voting consistently along party lines. During his tenure in the Senate there were many controversial votes to cast: the nation's entry into WORLD WAR I, participation in the LEAGUE OF NATIONS, and the constitutional measures of PROHIBITION and women's suffrage. On these issues Harding's voting record reflected the Republican Party platform. His strong party loyalty combined with his winning personality, fine speaking voice, and warm presence were positive features as he entered the presidential race of 1920.

**The Election of 1920.** The 1920 Republican primaries rendered no clear winner, and, at the start of the national convention in June 1920 in Chicago, Harding's nomination seemed unlikely. The delegates were deadlocked between Frank O. Lowden and Leonard Wood. But by the seventh ballot Harding, who had been in fourth place, was beginning to gain strength. His steady surge continued through the eighth and ninth ballots; on the tenth he won the nomination.

Stories immediately began to circulate that a coterie consisting of few powerful Senators, governors, and party bosses had engineered Harding's nomination. There were allegations that party bosses had met in a smoke-filled hotel room the night before the vote and settled on Harding as the presidential candidate for the party. While one or more such meetings undoubtedly took place, this account ignores Harding's preparation for the convention. Harding and his advisers, who had foreseen a possible impasse between Wood and Lowden, campaigned with a stymied convention in mind. A lack of structure, rather than boss control, made Harding's nomination possible at the convention. Nearly half the delegates were uninstructed. Frustrated by multiple ballots, many remembered friendly Senator Harding from the important state of Ohio. He seemed to be on the right side of the issues and on the wrong side of no one.

Having achieved the nomination (Calvin Coolidge was the vice presidential nominee), Harding did not stump the country. He stayed in Ohio and ran his campaign from the porch of his home, greeting thousands of well-wishers and speaking informally with them, careful to avoid sensitive subjects. His Democratic opponent, JAMES M. COX, whose running mate was Franklin D. Roosevelt, meanwhile campaigned furiously across the country. After the turmoil of the war, widespread labor strikes, and the red scare, Harding offered calm. In one of his most frequently quoted passages, which would later come to symbolize his campaign, he said, "America's present need, is not heroics, but healing; not nostrums, but normalcy; not revolution, but restoration; not agitation, but adjustment; not surgery, but serenity; not the dramatic, but the dispassionate; not experiment, but equipoise; not submergence in internationality, but sustainment in triumphant nationality."

Voters apparently agreed with Harding's assessment of the country's needs. He was elected by the largest popular majority in American history up to that time—60.2 percent. He had been the candidate who best represented a change from the Wilson administration, which had lost its focus. As President, Harding would have to face up to a postwar recession with widespread unemployment and low farm prices.

**Harding's Administration.** Harding tended to his first presidential duty before his inauguration. In choosing his CABINET he revealed how seriously he could approach the presidency and remain very much the Ohio politician.

For most of his appointments, Harding named men of experience and intelligence. As Secretary of State he chose CHARLES EVANS HUGHES, former New York governor and Republican presidential candidate in 1916. Henry C. Wallace of Iowa, editor of the widely known farm journal *Wallace's Farmer* became Secretary of Agriculture; Herbert Hoover, director of postwar relief efforts and of the United States Food Administration would be a distinguished Secretary of Commerce; and ANDREW W. MELLON, a multimillionaire who had amassed his fortune running a bank in Pittsburgh, became Secretary of the Treasury.

But Harding assumed from the first that at least two Cabinet posts should go to old friends and political supporters. As a result, two positions fell to Harding cronies: Albert Fall, a Senator from New Mexico, was named Secretary of the Interior; and Harry Daugherty, Harding's campaign manager, became ATTORNEY GENERAL. These appointments led to some criticism of his administration and gave credence to the rumors that during the convention Harding had promised political favors in return for the nomination. Both men were later to be implicated in the official corruption and scandal that destroyed the reputation of the entire administration. Meantime, however, Harding's presidency made a number of contributions to the country.

In 1921, the President participated in the Washington Naval Conference, which was an international meeting for limitation of armaments. The conference arranged for limits on the number of warships among the signatories and for a few other guarantees of peace. Harding wanted to move the country away from the circumstances that had brought it into World War I; the Senate ratified some treaties designed by the conference [*see* TREATY OF WASHINGTON (1921–1922)], though not until after Harding's death.

Another significant contribution of the Harding administration was the creation, in 1921, of the Budget Bureau. CHARLES G. DAWES was named its first director. His primary job was to create a national budget. By the second fiscal year of Harding's term,

his procedures reduced federal spending by nearly one-third. These changes contributed to the recovery of business from its postwar recession and to the prosperity of the later twenties.

Yet scandal and corruption plagued the administration. While the evidence does not suggest that Harding himself took part in illegal activities, much of what occurred was due to his personal limitations. As the CHIEF EXECUTIVE it was Harding's responsibility to exercise discipline over subordinates and to evaluate their behavior. But friendship and loyalty were to him paramount virtues.

With the 1924 reelection campaign looming, Harding felt uneasy about the political environment. In the 1922 elections, the Republican majority had been reduced in both houses of Congress. Harding worried that this indicated a loss of support for his administration. To remedy the situation, he schedule a speaking tour of the country in June 1923, which included a stop in Alaska. The trip's original purpose was to clear up minor policy questions involving chiefly fishing rights and to give the President, who had a chronic heart ailment and had had a bad case of the flu, a much-needed rest.

As the presidential train traveled across the country in the summer heat, Harding's spirits began to improve. His speeches were well received as he approached Alaska. It was not until the party was returning south that the President began to seem deeply troubled. He had apparently begun to confront mounting evidence that some of his administration was corrupt. On 26 July he spoke at the University of Washington. That evening on the train to San Francisco, he suffered nausea and pain, which Surgeon General Charles E. Sawyer diagnosed, perhaps for the benefit of the press, as a recurrence of indigestion caused by tainted crab meat. Other doctors feared heart difficulties and arranged for specialists, including Dr. Ray Lyman Wilbur, president of Stanford University, to meet the train at San Francisco. It became obvious that the President had also developed pneumonia.

Over the next three days Harding's health seemed to improve. Then, on 2 August 1923, he died suddenly after an apparent brain hemorrhage. Doctors, including Wilbur, agreed that this was the probable cause of death, but Mrs. Harding's refusal to allow an autopsy later contributed to rumors that the President might have been poisoned.

The news of Harding's death shocked and grieved America. He had been a consistently popular President. Services were held in Washington, D.C., and Harding was laid to rest in Marion, Ohio.

**The Harding Scandals.** Three major scandals have permanently labeled the Harding administration as one of the most corrupt in American history. Although there were rumors of scandal in the spring of 1923 while Harding was on his trip to Alaska, these scandals were not exposed until after his death. Their exposure lent some validity to stories of an Ohio gang, operating out of the "little green house on K Street," selling its influence. Many historians believe that the scandals themselves were greatly exaggerated and that there was no sinister Ohio gang. Yet, these rumors rapidly tarnished the posthumous image of the President and obscured his achievements.

*Charles Forbes.* One scandal centered on the director of the Veterans Bureau, Charles Forbes. A recent and shallow friendship with Harding had bought his appointment. In late 1922 evidence accumulated about Forbe's illegal activities. Under his direction the Veteran's Bureau was selling medical supplies for a fraction of their value, while he was receiving kickbacks. Forbes had also maneuvered shady deals involving hospital sites and construction contracts. Upon learning of Forbes's activities, Harding simply let Forbes resign. When the public became aware of his misdeeds, the Senate held its own investigation. Forbes was indicted and was later convicted for conspiracy to defraud the government.

*Jesse Smith.* Another scandal involved Jesse Smith, who committed suicide a few weeks after the resignation of Forbes in early 1923; the news stunned Washington.

Smith had been a general aide and longtime associate of Harry Daugherty but had held no official position in the government; nonetheless, he occupied a desk in the Justice Department. He and others were selling their somewhat limited influence to those dealing in illicit liquor, or wishing to buy government property illegally, or engaged in various other minor swindles. Rumors about Smith's activities circulated freely just before Harding's death in the spring of 1923.

Not wishing a repeat of the Forbes incident, Harding asked Daugherty to send Smith back to Ohio. Smith became mentally unbalanced and on 30 May 1923, burned all his papers and shot himself. Harding and Daugherty publicly claimed that Smith had killed himself due to depression caused by his diabetic condition. Nevertheless, it placed Harry Daugherty under a cloud of suspicion that he could never fully clear away, although a congressional inquiry after Harding's death could not prove any direct involvement of Daugherty in the scandal.

*Teapot Dome.* The most famous scandal of the Harding years—and one of the best known in American history—involved the leasing of oil rights. It was disclosed in April 1922 that private drilling rights had been granted without competitive bidding to Edward L. Doheny for Elk Hills, California, and to Harry F. Sinclair for Teapot Dome, Wyoming, both naval oil reserve areas. The Interior Department explained that secrecy surrounded the leases because they involved NATIONAL SECURITY issues. But Senator ROBERT M. LA FOLLETTE of Wisconsin demanded a full investigation of the incident and placed Senator Thomas Walsh of Montana in charge.

The Walsh investigation stretched out for more than a year. Senate hearings finally began on 24 October 1923, almost simultaneously with those on the Veteran's Bureau. Secretary of the Interior Albert Fall at first seemed to be free of guilt, but information revealing that he had made many improvements on his New Mexico ranch began to change that estimate. Doheny admitted that he had paid Fall $100,000 for his influence and it was also later revealed that Sinclair had made a similar payment. In litigation that lasted until 1930, Fall was convicted of bribery and sentenced to prison. Doheny and Sinclair were both acquitted of conspiracy or bribery.

Though the TEAPOT DOME SCANDAL involved only one federal official and was very limited in scope, it did irreparable harm to the legacy of Harding and his administration, although the President himself was never implicated.

*Nan Britton.* Other charges were made public after Harding's death, more personal in nature, that contributed to the erosion of his reputation. In 1927 Nan Britton published *The President's Daughter.* Her book alleged that she had engaged in a long affair with President Harding, which had resulted in the birth of a daughter. Although firm proof of Nan Britton's story remains unavailable, the appearance in 1964 of love letters between Harding and a hometown department store owner's wife added some credibility to her claims.

**An Assessment.** Harding had tried to be a progressive and creative Chief Executive. He proposed a Department of Public Welfare and encouraged cooperation between the federal and state government on health and sanitation. Realizing the growing significance of the automobile, he supported a program of extensive highway construction. In the expanding radio and aviation industries, the President and his Secretary of Commerce used broad powers previously given them by Congress to protect public safety and ensure fairness to regulate these fledgling concerns.

Perhaps Harding's greatest service to the nation came in overseeing its readjustment after World War

I. He personally exercised an important soothing effect on the entire country. By the time of his death the country was calm, and the basis for a decade of prosperity had been laid.

## BIBLIOGRAPHY

Adams, Samuel Hopkins. *Incredible Era: The Life and Times of Warren Gamaliel Harding.* 1964.

Mee, Charles L. *The Ohio Gang: The World of Warren G. Harding.* 1981.

Murray, Robert K. *The Harding Era: Warren G. Harding and His Administration.* 1969.

Murray, Robert K. *The Politics of Normalcy: Governmental Theory and Practice in the Harding-Coolidge Era.* 1973.

Russell, Francis. *The Shadow of Blooming Grove: Warren G. Harding in His Times.* 1968.

Sinclair, Andrew. *The Available Man: The Life behind the Mask of Warren Gamaliel Harding.* 1965.

Trani, Eugene P. *The Presidency of Warren G. Harding.* 1977.

DONNA GIORDANO and DAVID BURNER

**HARRISON, BENJAMIN** (1833–1901), twenty-third President of the United States (1889–1893). The only grandson of a President (William Henry Harrison, ninth President) to serve as President, Harrison, the son of John Scott Harrison and Elizabeth Irwin, was born on his grandfather's estate in North Bend, Ohio, on 20 August 1833. Another Benjamin Harrison, his great-grandfather, signed the Declaration of Independence. The Harrisons have been described as "America's foremost political dynasty" of the mid to late nineteenth century. Combined with three additional factors, this background placed Harrison among the most available candidates for a Republican presidential nomination in the late nineteenth century. First, Harrison's record had demonstrated unshakable devotion to the party. Second, he had added to his reputation with distinguished service in the CIVIL WAR. Third, Harrison represented Indiana, one of only four swing states in the late nineteenth century (along with New York, New Jersey, and Connecticut), which could have gone to either party in a presidential election.

**Early Career.** Harrison graduated from Miami University in Oxford, Ohio, in 1852, soon married Caroline Scott, and, after studying law for two years, moved to Indianapolis in 1854 to begin his law practice. Harrison actively supported the new REPUBLICAN PARTY in the presidential election of 1856, establishing his credentials as one of the young men who served as "founding fathers" of the party, and soon launched his own political career. He was elected city attorney in 1857, became secretary to the Republican state com-

mittee in 1858, and won the lucrative position of reporter for the Indiana supreme court in 1860. Leaving his wife and two young children behind, Harrison went off to serve in the Civil War, organizing the seventieth Indiana Regiment in July 1862. Under the command of General William Tecumseh Sherman, Harrison displayed conspicuous gallantry during the campaign in Georgia in 1864 and became brevet brigadier general in February 1865.

Harrison returned to Indiana a legitimate war hero. Only thirty-two-years old, he concentrated over the next decade on building his reputation in the legal community. While others talked of nominating him for a seat in Congress or for governor, Harrison slowly and steadily moved up the ladder in the Indiana Republican establishment. In August 1876, when the party's candidate for governor was forced to withdraw in a scandal, Harrison agreed to run. He lost the contest by five thousand votes, but his strong campaign and service to the party only added to his stature. With the death of Senator Oliver P. Morton in 1877, Harrison emerged as the leader of the party in Indiana and was in a perfect position to begin to establish a reputation outside of his home state. President Rutherford B. Hayes considered Harrison for a Cabinet position, then appointed him to the Mississippi River Commission in 1879, giving Harrison visibility on the national level for the first time. Not even Harrison would have imagined, however, that he would be in the White House within a decade.

Harrison served as chairman of the Indiana delegation to the Republican national convention of 1880, where he supported the charismatic and controversial Senator JAMES G. BLAINE, who was making his second attempt to win the presidential nomination. Blaine had been the leading candidate in 1876, but he had lost the nomination to Hayes. When President Hayes chose not to seek a second term, Blaine found himself locked in a classic confrontation with the legendary Ulysses S. Grant, who was bidding for a nomination that could have led to a third term as President. Only on the thirty-fifth ballot did Harrison join the compromise move in favor of James A. Garfield. Harrison had done nothing to alienate Blaine, who would be in a position to make or break the political fortunes of potential Republican presidential candidates throughout the 1880s. As the most prominent Republican in Indiana, Harrison had a choice of rewards after the victory in the presidential election of 1880. President Garfield wanted Harrison in his Cabinet. Instead, the Indiana legislature sent Harrison to the Senate in 1881, giving him the opportunity to build his reputation over the next six years.

At the Republican national convention of 1884, President Chester A. Arthur, who had taken office after the assassination of President Garfield in 1881, faced significant opposition in his bid for the nomination. Members of the Indiana delegation wished to nominate Harrison for the top spot on the ticket. They met resistance from Walter Q. Gresham, a maverick Indiana Republican who had presidential ambitions of his own. Gresham, who had built a reputation by condemning political corruption and calling for tariff reform, had lost a battle with Harrison for control of the Republican Party in Indiana. Gresham had enough influence with the delegation, however, to prevent Harrison's nomination. As it turned out, Gresham had done more for Harrison's political future than he could have imagined. He had spared Harrison from being in the position of challenging Blaine, who finally won the presidential nomination in 1884.

Though Blaine lost to Grover Cleveland, the Democratic candidate, by a very narrow margin in the presidential election of 1884, he remained the leading candidate for another presidential nomination in 1888. In the interim, a dedicated group of supporters, led by Louis T. Michener, Harrison's closest political ally in Indiana, and Wharton Barker, a Philadelphia banker, went to work to make sure that Gresham would not be in a position to block the nomination of Harrison in 1888. Harrison would be made available in case Blaine decided not to run. At the same time, Harrison's availability became obvious to an increasing number of Republicans outside Indiana, even though, in the constantly changing political situation that was typical of Indiana, the legislature denied Harrison a second term in the Senate in 1887.

**The Election of 1888.** Neither Harrison nor any other Republican could have been nominated at the Republican national convention of 1888 if Blaine had wanted the prize. Blaine, however, steadfastly refused to run again, and he provided a dramatic boost for Harrison's chances when, on 1 March 1888, he ruled out every potential candidate except Harrison and emphasized, "The one man remaining who in my judgment can make the best run is Benjamin Harrison." The results of the first ballot at the convention had Harrison in fifth place, behind Senator JOHN SHERMAN of Ohio, Gresham, now a judge of the Seventh United States Circuit Court, Chauncey M. Depew of New York, a railroad magnate, and Governor Russell A. Alger of Michigan. Actually, Harrison was in perfect position as "everybody's second choice." When Depew dropped out before the fourth ballot, most of New York's huge bloc of seventy-two votes

went to Harrison, and the bandwagon effect led to Harrison's nomination on the eighth ballot. The delegates then chose LEVI P. MORTON, a New York banker, who had served two terms in Congress and four years as minister to France, as Harrison's running mate.

When President Grover Cleveland decided to wage the campaign of 1888 on the issue of tariff reform, Harrison responded with an eloquent defense of the tariff in more than ninety speeches from the front porch of his home in Indianapolis. The Harrison-Morton ticket carried the most important swing states, New York and Indiana, and won a total of 233 electoral votes to 168 for President Cleveland. The popular vote detracted somewhat from Harrison's legitimacy, however, when the Solid South provided enough support for Democrat Cleveland to give him close to 100,000 votes more than Harrison in the nationwide total. Still, the Republican Party had control of the White House and working majorities in both Houses of Congress (a margin of twelve votes in the House and ten votes in the Senate) for the first time in fifteen years. The euphoria might have led Republican leaders, including Harrison, to overlook the fact that the voters had not provided an overwhelming mandate.

Harrison has been described by historians, without exception, as aloof, cold, reserved, and self-contained, with a "formal dignity" and "glacial demeanor," which seemed to some as indifference on the part of the President. David Muzzey said of Harrison, a devout Presbyterian with a "minister's conscience," that he was not adept at the political arts: he could not exaggerate, flatter, or misrepresent. As President-elect, Harrison immediately demonstrated the accuracy of this assertion by George Mayer: "No President was more effective as a campaigner and less effective as a party leader." While Harrison really had no choice but to appoint Blaine as Secretary of State for the second time (Blaine had held the position in the Garfield administration in 1881), he then filled the rest of the places in his Cabinet with decent, honest, solid but "obscure" Republicans from the Midwest and Northeast. Not one of Blaine's Cabinet colleagues had a significant political following that could have added in any way to the President's clout within his own party.

In the most eloquent description of Harrison as the nation's CHIEF EXECUTIVE, H. Wayne Morgan insists, "Harrison was a strange political figure on the American scene. He understood national goals for both his party and country, but could not stoop even slightly to make others see." In the process of selecting his Cabinet, Harrison had alienated some of the most powerful figures in the Republican Party. The boss in New

York, Thomas C. Platt, had expected a Cabinet position, as had James S. Clarkson of Iowa, national vice chairman of the party. The boss in Pennsylvania, Senator Matthew Quay, national chairman of the party, could not believe that Harrison had ignored every one of his recommendations. Harrison, who spent four to six hours a day during the first eighteen months in office filling patronage positions because he found it difficult to delegate authority, accepted fully responsibility for his decisions in regard to the Cabinet. From the beginning, however, the command structure of the party felt that Harrison had forgotten who had produced the victory in the presidential election of 1888.

**Domestic Policy.** Historians have insisted over the past hundred years that Harrison's record in the area of domestic policy reveals one of the least successful Presidents in the history of the nation. He will, for instance, always be identified with two of his more colorful and controversial appointments. Corporal James R. Tanner, commissioner of pensions, during just six months in office did his best to grant pensions or increase pensions for as many veterans of the Civil War as possible. Clarkson, who reluctantly accepted a consolation prize, agreeing to serve as first assistant Postmaster General, in just eighteen months in office rewarded thousands of loyal Republicans all across the country with fourth-class postmaster positions. Typically for Harrison, the antics of Tanner and Clarkson have tended to overshadow another important decision: Harrison also launched the career of Theodore Roosevelt on the national level, appointing him a Civil Service commissioner.

In much the same manner, Harrison has been identified with the record of a Congress that seemed out of control, the "Billion Dollar" Congress of 1890. Actually, Republicans were in control of both the executive and legislative branches of the federal government and produced the most active Congress of the half century between the administrations of President Abraham Lincoln and President Woodrow Wilson. Voters of the time may not have been ready for such a level of activity. In particular, contemporaries believed that two major pieces of legislation, the McKINLEY TARIFF and the Sherman Silver Purchase Act, had a disastrous impact on the nation's economy. Many opposed the controversial Lodge elections bill, dubbed the "Force Bill," which was an attempt led by Representative Henry Cabot Lodge, to protect the right of former slaves to vote in the South and had passed the House of Representatives. There was a tendency at the time, one which historians have upheld, to criticize Harrison for "allowing" the Congress

to have its way. Once again, the silver and tariff legislation and the Lodge bill have obscured the fact that the same Congress, working with the same President, also produced the landmark SHERMAN ANTI-TRUST ACT.

Both the House of Representatives and the Senate had experienced revolutions of sorts in 1890. Speaker of the House Thomas B. Reed had suddenly and dramatically forced the minority Democrats in the House to confront the modern era. He had ruled that the opposition could not delay pending legislation with the traditional tactic of the "silent" or "disappearing" quorum, calling for a quorum and refusing to answer to their names. Reed insisted that the Democrats were "present," which they could not deny, and ensured that the legislative program of the Republicans, no matter how controversial, could pass the House on a party-line vote. Such "abuse of power" would return to haunt the Republicans and, yet again, contemporaries associated the President, the leader of the party, with the machinations of the Speaker who became known as Czar Reed.

At the same time, six new states (North Dakota, South Dakota, Montana, Washington, Idaho, and Wyoming) admitted to the Union in 1889–1890 produced twelve Republican members of the Senate who arrived with their own agenda. They would not provide the necessary votes for any pending legislation, holding hostage the McKinley tariff, which would benefit the industrial states, without a guarantee of reciprocal support for passage of the Sherman Silver Purchase Act, demanded by the agricultural and mining states. This silver bloc included at least four more Senators, from the mining states of Colorado and Nevada, and received regular support from the four Senators representing the agricultural states of Kansas and Nebraska. Thus, Republicans in the Northeast and Midwest were forced to work out a deal with their colleagues in the West. Both wings of the party may have been satisfied, but the silver and tariff legislation contributed to the disaster awaiting the Republicans in both the congressional election of 1890 and the presidential election of 1892. In other words, the Republican leaders in Congress would drag Harrison down to defeat with them.

Republicans at the national level had chosen to ignore voter discontent in the Midwest, which had become obvious in 1889, even before the party ever enacted its legislative program in Congress. The Republican Party had been active at the state level as well, and these Republicans joined their colleagues in Congress in casting a shadow over the President's political future. Representing the native born, Protestant, middle and upper classes, Republicans had alienated many in the working class, particularly German and Irish Catholics, over a variety of social issues. In state after state, Republicans led the fight to ban the Sunday sale of alcoholic beverages. Some called for a total PROHIBITION on the sale of alcoholic beverages. Finally, in a reflection of the growing nativist sentiment in the Midwest and across the nation, Republicans demanded the compulsory use of English as the language of instruction in all schools. On this issue alone, the large number of Germans who tried to preserve their culture and language in private schools had no choice but to turn to the DEMOCRATIC PARTY.

Both Iowa and Ohio elected Democratic governors in 1889, only a preview of the series of setbacks facing the Republicans. After passage of the silver and tariff legislation, with the Lodge bill pending, indeed, as Richard Jensen has said, "Never in its history did the GOP [Grand Old Party] labor under such burdens as the 1890 campaign imposed." Harrison tried to save the day with a campaign tour of almost three thousand miles across the Midwest. He had put his reputation on the line, and the magnitude of the defeat further tarnished his image. In an election complicated by the emergence of the Populist Party, a response to growing discontent in the agricultural areas of the Great Plains, Republicans were reduced to a small minority in the House of Representatives, losing about eighty seats. In the aftermath of the landslide, observers, including many in the Republican Party, had no reason to believe that Harrison was the one to lead a Republican comeback in 1892. In many respects, he had become a LAME DUCK.

**Foreign Affairs.** Even Harrison's own activism, displaying what has been called a "spirit of chauvinism" in the conduct of the nation's foreign policy, would not be enough to win a second term in the White House. Nevertheless, a series of historians who have revised the interpretation of American expansion overseas in the late nineteenth century have acknowledged Harrison's role as a creator of the "new empire." Harrison vigorously championed a "large" policy, which linked construction of a modern navy with the need to complete a Central American canal and to acquire naval bases in the Caribbean and in the Pacific. He has been described by John Grenville and George Berkeley Young as, "the first President since the Civil War who fully recognized the need to coordinate the strategic, diplomatic, and the economic factors of policy."

Harrison and Secretary of the Navy Benjamin F. Tracy secured congressional approval to build the first three American battleships in 1890 (part of the unprecedented appropriations package passed by the "Billion Dollar" Congress). The *Indiana*, the *Massachu-setts*, and the *Oregon* were designated "coastline" battleships to emphasize their defensive purpose. Just two years later, however, Congress approved construction of the *Iowa* in 1892, the first "seagoing" battleship, an indication that the United States might be prepared to do more than merely defend its interests. In the Pacific, for instance, in 1889 Harrison approved participation with Great Britain and Germany in a three-power protectorate, a first for the United States, over the Samoan Islands. Closer to home, Harrison hosted the first modern Pan-American Conference in 1889–1890, a serious attempt to build bridges and develop trade with the nations of the hemisphere.

Harrison most clearly demonstrated what has been described, without qualification, as an aggressive, belligerent, firm, and militant foreign policy when he brought the nation to the brink of war with Chile in 1891–1892. A deteriorating relationship with the government that had taken power in a Chilean civil war led to an unfortunate incident in October 1891, the murder by a mob of two American sailors on shore leave in Valparaiso. When Chile refused to act quickly in response to demands for an apology and for reparations, Harrison mobilized the fleet and delivered an ultimatum in January 1892. Chile, a nation of only 2 ½ million, had no choice but to yield. Rear Adm. Bancroft Gherardi described the result: "Our demonstration brought home to Chile [the] fact that [the] United States as a government is no longer to be trifled with."

Finally, Harrison tried to launch the new empire five years before the SPANISH-AMERICAN WAR of 1898. The leaders of a coup in the Hawaiian Islands overthrew the monarchy and proclaimed creation of a republic on 17 January 1893. They then sought annexation by the United States [see HAWAII, ANNEXATION OF]. Harrison responded favorably, leading the new republican government and the United States to sign a treaty of annexation within a month, on 14 February. In reality, however, there was no chance that the Senate would ratify the treaty given the political situation in 1893. Even if unanimous in their support of the treaty, the forty-seven Republicans in the outgoing Senate could not have hoped to produce the fifty-nine of eighty-eight votes required for ratification. The treaty had been doomed by the outcome of the presidential election of 1892, which brought Democrat Grover Cleveland back to the White House and gave the Democrats a majority in the incoming Senate as well. Cleveland, who had no interest in Hawaii or any other elements of the new empire, simply withdrew the treaty from the Senate on 9 March and, in a partisan move, ordered an investigation into events surrounding the coup and the treaty negotiations.

**The Election of 1892.** At the Republican national convention in June 1892, the delegates, despite significant opposition, nominated Harrison on the first ballot. Clarkson, Platt, Quay, and their allies supported Blaine, who had resigned as Secretary of State on the eve of the convention, in a desperate bid to stop Harrison. The President received 535 votes, but 182 votes went to Blaine and another 182 delegates supported Governor William McKinley of Ohio, whose turn would come just four years later. For the first time in the history of the nation, both candidates of the major parties had been President, and they offered the voters a dignified but unspectacular campaign. Only the upstart Populist Party brought some excitement to the contest. The Republican Party seemed adrift, badly divided and led by a President whose heart was not in the campaign. Mrs. Harrison, suffering from tuberculosis, died on 25 October. Harrison seemed anxious to get through the formalities of the election process and to return to private life. The outcome was predictable. Cleveland carried 277 electoral votes to only 145 for Harrison and 22 for the Populists.

Harrison accepted defeat graciously and returned to Indianapolis to resume his law practice. As President he had visited California during the course of a nine-thousand-mile trip across the nation in April and May 1891, and he returned to the West Coast to deliver a series of lectures at Stanford University in 1894. The last years of his life were not completely happy for Harrison. His older children never accepted Harrison's decision in 1896 to marry the much younger Mary Lord Dimmick, the widowed niece of his first wife. The estrangement became permanent with the birth of a daughter in February 1897. Harrison then accepted a very large fee and agreed to serve as chief counsel for Venezuela in its decades-old boundary dispute with British Guiana. In May 1899, Harrison went to Europe for the first time to participate in the arbitration of the case. After his return to the United States, Harrison toured the Northwest early in 1900 and vacationed that summer in upstate New York. Harrison died on 13 March 1901.

### BIBLIOGRAPHY

Grenville, John A. S., and George Berkeley Young. *Politics, Strategy, and American Diplomacy: Studies in Foreign Policy, 1873–1917.* 1966.

Jensen, Richard. *The Winning of the Midwest: Social and Political Conflict, 1888–1896.* 1971.

Knoles, George Harmon. *The Presidential Campaign and Election of 1892.* 1942.

LaFeber, Walter. *The New Empire: An Interpretation of American Expansion, 1860–1898.* 1963.

Marcus, Robert D. *Grand Old Party: Political Structure in the Gilded Age, 1880–1896.* 1971.

Mayer, George H. *The Republican Party, 1854–1964.* 1964.

Morgan, H. Wayne. *From Hayes to McKinley: National Party Politics, 1877–1896.* 1969.

Muzzey, David S. *James G. Blaine: A Political Idol of Other Days.* 1934.

Sievers, Harry J., S.J. *Benjamin Harrison.* 3 vols. 1952–1968.

Socolofsky, Homer E., and Allan B. Spetter. *The Presidency of Benjamin Harrison.* 1987.

Williams, R. Hal. *Years of Decision: American Politics in the 1890s.* 1978.

ALLAN B. SPETTER

**HARRISON, WILLIAM HENRY** (1773–1841), ninth President of the United States (1841). Harrison was the first President elected by the WHIG PARTY. Born in Virginia, he was the first President elected from the Old Northwest—a region that would produce nearly half of all Presidents in the century starting with Harrison's election. His INAUGURAL ADDRESS was the longest in history, and, entering the office just after his sixty-eighth birthday, he was the oldest man to become President until the 1981 inauguration of sixty-nine-year-old Ronald Reagan. Harrison was also the first President to die in office. His death, only a month after his inauguration, meant as well that his tenure in office was the shortest in American history.

**Military Career.** Harrison came from a distinguished Virginia family. His father, Benjamin Harrison, served in the Virginia House of Delegates and was his state's governor. As a delegate to the Continental Congress, Benjamin Harrison was a signer of the Declaration of Independence. In 1787 William Henry entered Hampton-Sidney College, but in 1790 he entered medical studies, first in Richmond, and later in Philadelphia, where he studied with Dr. Benjamin Rush. When his father died in 1791, Harrison left his studies and entered the army as a commissioned officer. Harrison remained in the army until 1798, serving for a time as the aide-de-camp to General Anthony Wayne. In 1798 he became the secretary of the Northwest Territory. In 1799 Harrison became the Territory's delegate to Congress. There he helped move Ohio toward statehood. With the division of the Northwest in 1800, Harrison became the first governor of the new Indiana Territory. There he endorsed petitions to Congress to repeal or modify the prohibition of SLAVERY in the Northwest Ordinance. When the petitions failed, Harrison undermined the Ordinance by adopting a slave code for the territory based on Virginia laws. As a slaveholding Virginian, he sympathized with the many masters already in the territory who wanted to open Indiana to slavery.

In 1811 Harrison gained his nickname, Tippecanoe, by leading an army of a thousand militiamen and regular soldiers against a Shawnee settlement along the Tippecanoe Creek, in present-day Indiana. Harrison's surprise morning assault on the Shawnee was successful, but at the cost of nearly 20 percent of his soldiers. Moreover, within months the Shawnee had returned to this area under the leadership of Tecumseh, who was absent from his settlement at the time of Harrison's attack. During the WAR OF 1812 Harrison led various armies, acting simultaneously as the commander of the Indiana militia (because he was the territorial governor) and under a commission from the Governor of Kentucky. Later in 1812 President James Madison gave him a regular appointment in the United States Army as commander of all forces in the Northwest, and in that capacity he rose to the rank of major general. He eventually defeated the British and their Indian allies in a series of battles which culminated at the Battle of the Thames, in present-day Ontario. Among those who died in the battle was the Shawnee leader Tecumseh, who had previously resisted Harrison's policy of encroachment on INDIAN land. After the war, Harrison compelled most of the native peoples in the Northwest to accept treaties dictated on his terms. In 1814 Harrison left the army a war hero, although somewhat damaged by questions surrounding the financing of his commissaries and some complaints about his leadership by other officers.

**In Congress.** In 1814–1815 Harrison negotiated various Indian treaties at the behest of President Madison; and from 1816 to 1819 he served as Congressman from Ohio. Despite the views of his constituents, Harrison opposed restrictions of slavery in the western territories, consistent with his background as a Virginia slaveowner (he inherited slaves from his father) and his support of allowing slavery in the Northwest Territory. Thus, during the Missouri debates Harrison always voted with the southern members of Congress.

In 1817 Harrison had become a director of the Cincinnati branch of the Second BANK OF THE UNITED STATES, no doubt leading to his support for the bank in the 1830s. However, in 1819 he ran for the Ohio senate as an opponent of the bank. In the senate he continued to oppose the Bank, but also argued against the constitutionality of Ohio's law taxing the bank. On this point he accepted the holding of Chief Justice JOHN MARSHALL in *McCulloch v. Maryland* (1819). While Harrison gained popularity for his opposition to the bank, he lost it by still opposing resolutions advocating restrictions on slavery. This partly explains his defeat for the governorship in 1820 and then the refusal of the Ohio legislature to send him to the U.S. Senate later that year. When his state senate term expired in February 1821, Harrison was reduced to seeking private employment for the first time since he had entered in the Army in 1791. In 1822 Harrison again tried, and failed, to win election to the U.S. Senate. Later that year he also lost a campaign for the U.S. House of Representatives. After fruitless attempts to gain a diplomatic appointment, Harrison finally won Ohio's Senate seat in 1825, largely through his association with HENRY CLAY's 1824 presidential campaign. Clay carried Ohio in 1824, and enough supporters of Clay entered the legislature to give Harrison his Senate victory.

Harrison served in the Senate for three years, largely devoting himself to military issues. In 1828 Harrison became the American minister to Colombia. Again, Harrison's close ties to Clay led to his new appointment. The election of Andrew Jackson ended Harrison's diplomatic career, and in fall 1829 he returned to his farm in Ohio. In 1831 he tried to return to the Senate, but lost. In 1832 he was a member of the board of visitors of West Point, but neither this nor his appointment in 1834 as a county recorder constituted a political comeback.

**A Candidate of the Whigs.** While out of office, Harrison was not out of the public eye. In 1835 opponents of Andrew Jackson began touting Harrison as a potential presidential candidate. In 1836 the Whig Party was barely more than a loosely formed coalition of politicians unified only by their opposition to Andrew Jackson and his heir apparent, Martin Van Buren. The party held no convention for the 1836 campaign, and refused to field a single candidate. Instead, four Whigs—Harrison from Ohio, DANIEL WEBSTER from Massachusetts, Hugh White from Tennessee, and Willie P. Mangum from North Carolina—campaigned against Van Buren.

Thus, in 1836 Harrison was not encumbered by a PARTY PLATFORM. He indicated his support for distributing surplus revenue to the states—an antebellum version of revenue sharing—and also declared he would do the same with revenue gained from future land sales. He indicated mild support for INTERNAL IMPROVEMENTS and completely hedged his bets on rechartering the Bank of the United States. Disingenuously asserting that he had never had anything to do with banks (forgetting he was once a director of the Cincinnati branch of the Bank of the United States) and that he personally opposed a national bank, but also said he would sign a bank bill if Congress passed one. In this campaign Harrison also declared his opposition to any interference with slavery in the southern states or the District of Columbia. Appealing to the South while trying at the same time not to alienate the North, he endorsed colonization as the only legitimate way to deal with slavery. Oddly enough, some southerners, including John C. Calhoun, believed that Harrison was some sort of abolitionist because he supported colonization. Ironically, at that time all northern anti-slavery advocates had followed William Lloyd Garrison and David Walker in their denunciation of colonization as a proslavery scheme to remove free blacks from the nation.

The Whig strategy was to deny Van Buren a majority of electoral votes by having different candidates beat him in different sections of the country, thus throwing the election into the House of Representatives. Harrison was the most successful of the anti-Van Buren candidates, winning 73 electoral votes and 36 percent (549,567) of the popular vote. Moreover, in the North and upper South he ran nearly as well as (or better in some states than) Van Buren. The other Whig candidates won 51 electoral votes, while Van Buren carried 170 electoral votes. The popular vote was much closer, with Van Buren carrying a scant 50.8 percent (761,549) of the vote while the four Whig candidates won 736,250 votes.

**The Election of 1840.** Harrison's strong showing in 1836 made him an obvious candidate for 1840. Indeed, even before the 1836 election was decided, William H. Seward of New York urged Whigs to rally behind Harrison in 1840 as the "candidate of continuation," and as early as 1837 Harrison began working toward the nomination. In 1838, in rejecting overtures from the Anti-Masonic Party to run on its ticket, Harrison made clear his intent on running as Whig—and as the only Whig—in the 1840 campaign. That summer he gave speeches in the Midwest to bolster his candidacy. In March 1839 Daniel Webster announced his support for Harrison. Webster had hoped for the nomination himself, but seeing no chance, he backed Harrison, in part to stop his rival, Henry Clay. In December 1839 the Whig convention met in Harrisburg, Pennsylvania. Thurlow Weed, the leader of the New York Whigs, arrived at the convention determined to stop Clay. Weed, Seward, and others maneuvered the convention into adopting something akin to the modern unit rule for state delegations, and in this way Harrison won the nomination. Weed ostensibly supported General Winfield Scott, but he was equally willing to back Harrison. On the first ballot of the convention the combined Harrison-Scott vote was 151 to Clay's 103. Clay left the convention disappointed and angry; Seward and Webster returned home elated. As in 1836, the Whigs failed to create a platform.

Harrison's 1840 campaign was remarkable for its use of symbolism. Early in the campaign the Demo-

cratic editor of the *Baltimore Republican* sarcastically said of Harrison: "Give him a barrel of hard cider and pension of two thousand a year, and, our word for it, he will sit the remainder of his days in a log cabin by the side of a 'see coal' fire and study moral philosophy." Although Harrison came from a wealthy and educated background, his supporters jumped on this editorial to portray Harrison as a candidate of the common people. He became the "log cabin candidate." A campaign picture portrayed him in front of a log cabin with a spade in his hand, as if the patrician general-politician was a common farmer. The *Harrison Almanac* portrayed the candidate pushing a plow behind two horses, while the *Hard Cider and Long Cabin Almanac* showed Harrison standing in front of a log cabin filling cups of cider and saying "I'll supply you all with true Hospitality." In New York Horace Greely published a campaign newspaper, the *Log Cabin*. Harrison's supporters produced pins, buttons, letterheads, fans, handkerchiefs, and other campaign items with a log cabin on them. With the slogan and "Tippecanoe and Tyler too," Harrison's supporters remade their candidate into a national war hero. Harrison's might be characterized as the first singing campaign of American history. Everywhere his supporters sang Harrison's praises to the tunes of popular songs. Greely published the *Log Cabin Songbook* for personal and political profit, while E. G. Booz, of Philadelphia, begin selling whiskey in bottles shaped like log cabins. With only slight exaggeration, it might be said that Americans sang, drank, and paraded Harrison into the White House.

Harrison's campaign took advantage of the suffrage expansion stimulated by Jacksonian democracy. The patrician Whig outdid the Democrats at their own game—appealing to the middle class and common farmers of the age. Thus a party made up generally of businessmen, planters, and professionals was able to make substantial inroads into traditional Democratic constituencies. The campaign successfully portrayed the incumbent Martin Van Buren as the representative of privilege. As one song noted:

> Let Van from his coolers of silver drink wine
> And lounge on his cushioned settee
> Our man on a buckeye bench can recline
> Content with hard cider is he.

Following in the footsteps of both previous northern Presidents, Martin Van Buren failed to win reelection.

Harrison's success was not entirely a result of campaign hoopla. Although the Panic of 1837 was waning, much of the nation blamed Van Buren for the economic crisis. Throughout the crisis Van Buren had stuck with his hard money policy and his staunch opposition to the Bank of the United States. Moreover, Van Buren lacked the charisma and stature of his predecessor, Andrew Jackson. Finally, having held the White House for three terms, by 1840 the Jacksonians were out of ideas and energy. The nation was ripe for a change, and Harrison's log cabin campaign was ideal for the mood of electorate.

Over 80 percent of the nation's eligible voters cast ballots in this heated contest. The Harrison-Tyler ticket won 52.9 percent of the popular vote and an overwhelming 234 out of 294 electoral votes. While not a landslide popular victory, the results were a substantial turn-around for a new party. Harrison carried all but seven states, including every large state except Virginia, his running mate's home. Harrison's long coattails turned a 28 to 22 Democratic majority in the Senate into a 28 to 22 Whig majority. The Whigs also took over the House, with a 133 to 102 majority.

**A Brief Presidency.** Harrison offered a CABINET position to Henry Clay, but the Kentuckian, still nursing his wounds from failing to get the nomination, declined. This left the best Cabinet position for Daniel Webster; and when offered any spot in the administration, he chose Secretary of State. Webster expected to dominate the aging and politically inexperienced President. Webster also edited Harrison's inaugural address.

The long speech may have cost Harrison his life. For over an hour and a half he read the text on a cold March day, coatless and hatless. Here Harrison set out a coherent theory of Whig politics—that the President should be the servant of the people and particularly of the Congress. He asserted that the greatest danger to liberty in America was the growth of executive power. Unlike Jackson, Harrison did not plan to expand the power of the President and thwart Congress through the excessive use of vetoes. Harrison declared the veto was "a conservative power, to be used" for only three purposes: "to protect the Constitution from violation," to protect "the people from the effects of hasty legislation," and "to prevent the effects of combinations violative of the rights of minorities." In a direct slap at Jackson's bank veto, Harrison declared that the courts were the final arbiter of the constitutionality of laws. Harrison did not endorse a recharter of the Bank of the United States, but he did quote President James Madison's arguments in favor of the bank's legitimacy on the basis of "repeated recognitions" of its constitutionality. Moreover, Harrison was on record as opposing the INDEPENDENT TREASURY program of Van Buren and the Democrats. In his inaugural Harrison also reiterated his opposition to relying solely on specie,

implying that his banking policy would include currency.

Once sworn in, Harrison then turned to filling offices. Once again, he angered Clay by distributing most of his PATRONAGE to the Seward-Webster-Weed wing of the party. Harrison further angered Clay by refusing to call for an immediate special session of Congress. Clay was eager for such a session, and was counting on exercising power in the new Whig regime from the floor of the Senate. Secretary of State Webster, however, supported waiting, and Harrison announced a special session of Congress for the end of May to face the nation's difficult financial condition.

Although busy appointing people to office, Harrison did not share the Jacksonian belief that "to the victors go the spoils." Thus, while numerous Democrats lost their government jobs, Harrison did not order the wholesale and immediate removal of Democrats. Harrison had campaigned for CIVIL SERVICE REFORM, and actually hoped to bring it about. Another Whig reform was to create something akin to cabinet government, with the President first among equals. This would have been an ideal system for a someone of Harrison's limited political background and age.

Harrison apparently caught a cold during his inauguration, and this developed into pneumonia two weeks later. On 27 March Harrison was confined to his bed; and on Sunday, 4 April, a month after his inauguration, he died.

Harrison's presidency was too short to allow any kind of serious analysis. It seems likely he would have eventually balked at following the lead of Congress. Similarly, he might have chaffed as the first among equals within his Cabinet. It is also not clear how long he could have resisted the pressures of Whigs around the country who wanted him to fire and replace all Democratic officeholders with Whigs. But such speculations are just that.

Harrison's death devastated the Whigs. After twelve years of the Democratic rule, the descendants of the national Republicans who had created the Whig party were finally in power. They had the chance to recreate the Bank of the United States, perhaps pass a new tariff, and in other ways regulate the economy to help the commercial interests that dominated the party. But all these possibilities were buried with Harrison. John Tyler, the Vice President, was a STATES' RIGHTS Democrat who had joined the Whigs as much out of his personality difference with the Jacksonians as over political issues. In the Senate Tyler had supported Jackson on the bank veto, his opposition to internal improvements, and his opposition to high tariffs. Tyler was a default candidate for the vice presidency. He was popular with some who hated Jackson and Van Buren, but had never been a true Whig. Harrison's death ironically put a non-Whig into the White House only a month after the Whigs thought they had entered the executive mansion for four years.

BIBLIOGRAPHY

Logan Esarey, ed., *The Messages and Letters of William Henry Harrison.* 2 vols. 1922.
Finkelman, Paul. "Evading the Ordinance: The Persistence of Bondage in Indiana and Illinois." *Journal of the Early Republic* 9 (Spring 1989): 21–52.
Goebel, Dorothy Burne. *William Henry Harrison: A Political Biography.* 1926.
Peterson, Norma Lois. *The Presidencies of William Henry Harrison and John Tyler.* 1989.

PAUL FINKELMAN

**HATCH ACT** (1939). The Hatch Act (53 Stat. 1147) is officially titled an "Act to Prevent Pernicious Political Activities." Its purpose is to prevent partisanship and partisan coercion within the federal CIVIL SERVICE and to restrict the partisan political activities of federal employees. It seeks to create a politically neutral civil service that will serve the public interest rather than being the tool of one party or another. Among its general prohibitions are these: using official authority to manipulate individuals, who are seeking or receiving governmental funds, for partisan purposes; taking an active part in political management or in political campaigns; and belonging to a political party or organization that advocates overthrow of the constitutional government.

The act has been controversial for several reasons. It makes what are acts of virtuous citizenship for private individuals, such as taking part in a partisan campaign, crimes for federal employees. Constitutionally, many—including a three-judge federal district court—have thought the act is poorly drafted in the sense that it fails to specify with reasonable precision what it prohibits. Politically, the act prevents unions representing federal employees from mobilizing their members for partisan activities. This is probably more costly to the Democrats.

The Hatch Act is also called the First Hatch Act to distinguish it from a second that was enacted in 1940 to place similar restrictions on state and local employees whose positions are at least partly funded by the federal government. The act was enforced by the U.S. Civil Service Commission until it was replaced by the MERIT SYSTEMS PROTECTION BOARD in 1979. Neither the commission nor the board has ever been able to provide an all-inclusive list of exactly what the act prohibits.

The act's constitutionality has been upheld by narrow margins in two Supreme Court decisions. In *United Public Workers v. Mitchell* (1947) the Court upheld the statute by a 4 to 3 margin. In *United States Civil Service Commission v. National Association of Letter Carriers* (1973), it split 6 to 3 on the same issues. In the former case, the Court found that despite the potential infringement of federal employees' First Amendment rights, Congress did have the power to regulate their partisan activities in the interests of governmental efficiency. In the latter case, the Court reiterated the importance of efficiency and found that the act was neither unconstitutionally vague nor overbroad.

Ever since the mid 1970s, there have been concerted efforts by Democrats in Congress to modify the Hatch Act. These have been unsuccessful, however, in overcoming presidential vetoes or threats thereof. Hatch Act reform and "un-Hatching" federal employees are almost always on the present-day policy agenda regarding the federal service.

BIBLIOGRAPHY

Benda, Peter, and David H. Rosenbloom. "The Hatch Act and the Contemporary Public Service." In *Agenda for Excellence.* edited by Patricia Ingraham and Donald Kettl. 1992.
Rose, Henry. "A Critical Look at the Hatch Act." *Harvard Law Review* 70 (1962): 510–516.
Rosenbloom, David H. *Federal Service and the Constitution.* 1971.

DAVID H. ROSENBLOOM

**HAWAII, ANNEXATION OF.** The Hawaiian Islands, because of their strategic location, favorable climate, and amiable people, were a welcome port-of-call for American merchants, sealers, and whalers throughout the nineteenth century. The fertile lands of these islands also attracted American sugar and rice planters. By mid-century, American merchants, businessmen, and planters dominated the Hawaiian economy and had acquired political authority, while American missionaries extended and solidified American influence. Although Americans in the United States were lukewarm toward the acquisition of Hawaii, American residents in Hawaii, with the support of Hawaiian King Kamehameha III, promoted annexation. In 1854 they offered a treaty of annexation to President Franklin Pierce, who had been elected in 1852 on an expansionist platform. Their attempt failed when Pierce objected to a clause in the draft treaty forbidding the extension of slavery to the islands. Thereafter, Hawaiian monarchs lost interest in annexation and began an effort to reduce American involvement in the government.

A renewed movement for annexation began in 1892 after the American MCKINLEY TARIFF ACT of 1890, which provided bounties for domestic sugar producers, caused losses of $12 million to American planters in Hawaii. An agent from a small, secret group of annexationists lobbied American officials in Washington, including Benjamin Harrison's Secretaries of State, JAMES G. BLAINE and John W. Foster. While American officials in Washington were more interested in making Hawaii a protectorate than a colony, the American minister in Hawaii, John L. Stevens, became an ardent annexationist. When in January 1893 Americans in Hawaii staged a revolution to depose Hawaiian Queen Liliuokalani, Stevens quickly committed American naval forces, without which the revolution would have failed. The revolutionary government immediately sent agents to the United States to negotiate a treaty of annexation.

President Harrison supported annexation and rushed a hastily negotiated treaty to the Senate on 15 February 1893. But he had only two weeks left in office, and Democratic opposition prevented the Senate from acting before the inauguration of his successor, Grover Cleveland.

On taking office, Cleveland repudiated American involvement in the Hawaiian revolution, withdrew the treaty from the Senate, and removed Stevens from office. He was unwilling, however, to involve American forces in the restoration of the Hawaiian government, and the revolutionary provisional government refused to give up power. It established the Republic of Hawaii on 4 July 1894, which Cleveland regretfully but promptly recognized.

Cleveland's actions sparked a debate in the United States between annexationists and antiannexationists that lasted well into the succeeding administration of William McKinley. The Republicans adopted an annexationist plank in their platform in 1896, which McKinley fully supported. Pressure from Japan for protection for its nationals in Hawaii and Hawaiians' fears of Japanese aggression following their refusal to admit twelve hundred Japanese immigrants led the Hawaiian government to make another appeal to the United States for annexation. To counter Japanese interest in Hawaii, McKinley negotiated a new treaty of annexation in Washington, which was sent to the Senate on 16 June 1897. Following a Japanese protest, McKinley and the annexationists emphasized the Japanese menace, but Democratic and Republican anti-imperialists blocked approval.

When the SPANISH-AMERICAN WAR broke out, McKinley threatened to annex the Hawaiian Islands by decree as a war measure. Congress responded with a joint resolution of annexation [see ANNEXATION BY JOINT RESOLUTION]. On 15 June, the House voted 209 to 91 in favor of annexation; the Senate agreed by a vote of 42 to 21 on 6 July 1898. McKinley approved the resolution on the following day, and on 12 August 1898, Hawaii became a formal possession of the United States.

The annexation of Hawaii was the first American acquisition of a heavily populated noncontiguous territory that, it was thought, was not destined to become a state. Thus, the United States seemingly abandoned its long-standing and uncompromising anti-imperialist policy and became a colonial empire.

### BIBLIOGRAPHY

Dobson, John. *Reticent Expansionism: The Foreign Policy of William McKinley.* 1988.
Pratt, Julius William. *Expansionists of 1898: The Acquisition of Hawaii and the Spanish Islands.* 1936.
Russ, William Adam. *The Hawaiian Republic, 1894–98, and Its Struggle to Win Annexation.* 1961.
Stevens, Sylvester Kirby. *American Expansion in Hawaii, 1842–1898.* 1945.
Tate, Merze. *The United States and the Hawaiian Kingdom: A Political History.* 1965.

KINLEY BRAUER

**HAWLEY-SMOOT TARIFF ACT.** See SMOOT-HAWLEY TARIFF ACT.

**HAY, JOHN** (1838–1905), private secretary to Abraham Lincoln, presidential biographer, Secretary of State. Born in Indiana, John Milton Hay grew to maturity in Illinois. He graduated in 1858 from Brown University. After Lincoln's election, John G. Nicolay, a journalist working as Lincoln's secretary, hired the Brown graduate, and together they formed the most famous presidential staff of the nineteenth century. Nicolay and Hay, along with one assistant, screened visitors, sorted incoming mail, drafted routine correspondence and, in short, performed the office chores of Lincoln's White House. In 1865 Hay gained appointment as Secretary of Legation in Paris, leaving for Europe after Lincoln's assassination.

After service in Vienna and Madrid, Hay returned in 1870 to the United States and started a career in journalism. Marriage in 1874 to the daughter of a wealthy Cleveland family gave him financial security. In due time he turned to writing poetry; wrote an antilabor novel, *The Bread-Winners;* and, with Nicolay, published *Abraham Lincoln: A History*, in ten volumes in 1890.

Disenchanted with the Republican Party in the Grant years, Hay came back to his political home by 1876 and stayed there. He became Assistant Secretary of State in 1878, vowed to leave politics in 1881, but never did. In 1897 McKinley appointed him ambassador to Great Britain and in 1898 made him Secretary of State, an office he held until his death.

Hay became an imperialist, not as shrill as Theodore Roosevelt, but deeply involved in retaining the PHILIPPINES after the SPANISH-AMERICAN WAR of 1898 and in other policies meant to advance Anglo-Saxonism. His OPEN DOOR policy to maintain China's independence and avert China's making territorial and trade concessions to greater powers did not succeed. The HAY-PAUNCEFOTE TREATY of 1901, however, effectively removed Great Britain from Central America and helped make possible the construction of an American canal between the oceans. He played a larger role in foreign policy under McKinley than under Roosevelt.

BIBLIOGRAPHY

Clymer, Kenton J. *John Hay: The Gentleman as Diplomat.* 1975.
Dennet, Tyler, ed. *Lincoln and the Civil War in the Diaries and Letters of John Hay.* 1939.

MARK E. NEELY, JR.

**HAYES, RUTHERFORD B.** (1822–1893), nineteenth President of the United States (1877–1881). Born 4 October 1822 in Delaware, Ohio, Hayes was proud of his New England ancestry but even prouder to be a Buckeye. His father, Rutherford Hayes, died before Hayes was born, and his mother, Sophia Birchard Hayes, with some financial help from her youngest brother Sardis Birchard, raised Hayes and his older sister Fanny.

**Early Career.** After attending preparatory schools in Norwalk, Ohio, and Middletown, Connecticut, Hayes in 1838 entered Kenyon College at Gambier, Ohio, and in 1842 graduated at the head of his class. After reading law for a year at Columbus, Ohio, under the tutelage of a local lawyer, Hayes entered the Harvard Law School and received his Bachelor of Laws degree in 1845. While at Harvard, he studied under Supreme Court Justice Joseph Story, an experience that confirmed Hayes's sympathy for the WHIG PARTY.

From 1845 to 1849, Hayes practiced law in Lower Sandusky (later Fremont), Ohio, but in 1850 he struck out on his own and settled in Cincinnati. There he achieved prominence, and, on 30 December 1852, married Lucy Ware Webb, a recent graduate of Wesleyan Female College in Cincinnati, a devout Methodist, and a reformer with strong temperance and abolitionist beliefs. In contrast, Hayes, a lifelong worshiper of Ralph Waldo Emerson, neither experienced conversion nor joined a church. Regularly attending church services with Lucy, Hayes explained, "Where the habit does not Christianize, it generally civilizes."

Before his marriage Hayes showed little interest in reform. He was a man of reason, not emotion, a conservative who adhered to traditional values. His commitment to reason and justice enabled Lucy to make Hayes a moderate reformer. Beginning in 1853 he defended runaway slaves, and later, to prevent the spread of SLAVERY into western territories, he joined the REPUBLICAN PARTY. Entering politics, Hayes from 1858 to 1861 held his first office as Cincinnati's city solicitor.

When the lower southern states seceded (1860–1861), Hayes was willing to let them go, but he was infuriated when on 12 April 1861 their new Confederacy attacked Fort Sumter at Charleston, South Carolina. Encouraged by Lucy, he went off to war, preferring to "be killed in the course of it than to live through and after it" without having taken part in it. In June he was commissioned a major in the Twenty-third Ohio Volunteer Infantry. Hayes served with conspicuous gallantry throughout the CIVIL WAR, was wounded five times (once seriously), and emerged from the war a major general and a member of Congress.

In Congress from 1865 to 1867, Hayes consistently supported Radical RECONSTRUCTION measures and as chair of the Joint Committee on the Library worked hard to develop the Library of Congress into a great institution. He did not enjoy being a Representative and was happy to resign to run for governor of Ohio. Elected and reelected, Hayes served from 1868 to 1872 and thought his greatest achievements were the ratification of the Fifteenth Amendment and the establishment of the Ohio State University.

Despite his friendship with Liberal Republicans and his awareness of Ulysses S. Grant's shortcomings as President, Hayes loyally supported Grant's reelection in 1872, and even ran for Congress (unsuccessfully) to help the Republican ticket in Cincinnati. Although observers thought Hayes would secure a Cabinet post, Grant merely offered to make him the assistant U.S. treasurer at Cincinnati. Hayes refused this inferior appointment, quit politics and Cincinnati, and in May 1873 returned to Fremont.

After Hayes retired the Republican Party fell into disarray. Ohio Democrats captured the governorship in 1873, and a severe financial panic that year, followed by a deepening economic depression, enabled the Democrats in 1874 to win control of the next national House of Representatives. Enormous pressure developed in Ohio and in the nation to increase the amount of inflated greenbacks in circulation. The depression also threatened Hayes's private fortune—which was tied up in real estate investments—but, although he was "one of the noble army of debtors," Hayes abhorred inflation. From his perspective outside politics, he began to emphasize reconciliation with the South, rather than radicalism, and to affirm his bent for CIVIL-SERVICE REFORM. Desperate to reverse their decline, Ohio Republicans in 1875 turned to their best vote-getter and nominated Hayes for a third term as governor. When Hayes won by a narrow margin, his supporters advocated his nomination for President in 1876 [see ELECTION, PRESIDENTIAL, 1876].

**A Disputed Election.** Recognizing that his "availability" was his strength, Hayes did little to secure the nomination. When his more powerful rivals failed—because they were perceived as too corrupt, or too reform-minded, or too identified with the Grant administration, or too radical—availability did the work, and Hayes received the nomination. The reputation of the Democratic nominee, Gov. SAMUEL J. TILDEN of New York, as a reformer and the continuing economic depression made the campaign difficult for Republicans. In addition Democrats used violence and the threat of violence to keep black and white Republicans in the South from voting. On the basis of votes cast Tilden appeared victorious, but Republicans successfully contested Democratic claims to have carried Florida, Louisiana, and South Carolina. Republicans controlled the administrations and the official election returning boards in those states and disqualified enough Democratic ballots (where intimidation occurred) to produce Republican majorities. Claiming they were defrauded, the Democrats sent conflicting sets of elector's votes to Washington, D.C., for the official count that would elect the next President.

The electoral votes were to be counted at a joint session of Congress (where the Democrats had a majority) by the president of the Senate (who was a Republican). Since the Democrats would not let the president of the Senate decide which votes to count and the Republicans would not allow the joint session to decide, Congress in 1877 created the ELECTORAL COMMISSION of five Senators, five Representatives, and five Supreme Court Justices that would balance seven Republicans with seven Democrats and rely on Associate Justice David Davis, a political independent, to make a nonpartisan decision. After the Democrats

helped elect Davis to the Senate, he disqualified himself. He was replaced on the commission by a Republican Associate Justice who voted with his party, giving the disputed votes to Hayes by an 8 to 7 vote.

With the presidency lost, the Democrats used delay and chaos to extract concessions from Republicans. Their objective was the removal of federal troops supporting Republican regimes in Louisiana and South Carolina—the Democrats had already captured the Florida state government—and to a lesser extent federal support for southern railroad construction. Democrats also hinted that, if sufficiently rewarded with federal offices, a significant number of them—especially those with Whig or unionist backgrounds—would join the Republicans in organizing the next House of Representatives. Although Hayes made no concessions beyond what he had said at the start of the campaign, Grant and Ohio politicians close to Hayes assured Democrats from Louisiana and South Carolina that the troops supporting Republican governments would be withdrawn as long as the civil rights of blacks were respected. With these assurances, enough Democrats ceased to obstruct the count, and on 2 March 1877 Hayes was declared President.

**Haye's Administration.** While some Chief Executives have confronted great crises upon entering office, no other President began his term with a vast segment of the population believing he had been elected by fraud. In addition to that severe handicap, Hayes had to govern with the opposing DEMOCRATIC PARTY in control of the House of Representatives and after the midterm election of 1878 in control of both houses of Congress.

Hampered by a hostile Congress, Hayes faced serious problems. During the Grant administration, particularly after the panic of 1873, Northern support for Radical Reconstruction had eroded, while Southern opposition to it had grown violent. By the time Hayes took office, Radical Reconstruction had virtually disappeared. The only remaining Southern Republican governments were in Louisiana and South Carolina, where—because they were challenged by rival white-supremacy Democratic governments—their existence depended on support by federal troops. The claim of these Republican governments to legitimacy was logically as compelling as Hayes's title to the presidency; the same Republican-controlled election boards had declared both the state and national tickets victorious. Hayes had to determine quickly whether he could or should support these Republican governments.

In addition, many Americans demanded civil-service reform to eliminate the corruption that seemed to permeate the government under Grant. Wishing to divorce the CIVIL SERVICE from politics and to develop a professionalized bureaucracy, they argued that appointments should be made on the basis of merit—determined by competitive examinations open to all—and that civil servants should not be assessed to pay for political campaigns. But most Republican politicians, convinced that reform would destroy party organization, were hostile to reformers, whom they thought were impractical, and to their program, which they thought was visionary.

Further problems were engendered by the severe depression that enveloped Americans from coast to coast. For those suffering from the depression, Reconstruction and corruption were issues of little importance. Besides hurting the Republican Party, which was in power when it struck, the depression led to the Great Strike of 1877, to increased agitation against Chinese laborers in California, and to strident demands for expansion of the currency.

Hayes dealt with these problems himself. His small staff merely handled visitors and correspondence. Twice-weekly Cabinet meetings provided counsel, but Hayes did not slavishly follow the opinion of his Cabinet. Secretary of the Treasury JOHN SHERMAN, Secretary of State William Maxwell Evarts, and Secretary of the Interior Carl Schurz proved to be his most helpful advisers. Even though Hayes had been a Whig before the Civil War and was trying to revive and realign southern Whigs, he moved away from the Whig ideal of a weak President who would be subservient to Congress, be deferential to his Cabinet, and allow virtual autonomy to heads of departments.

**Domestic Affairs.** In deciding issues, Hayes was principled yet practical, cautious yet courageous, open to advice yet not easily influenced, and definitely not manipulated. Decisive, diligent, conscientious, and consistent, he did not panic under stress, endured criticism and hostility with few complaints, was slow to anger, and bore few grudges. He was a patient reformer, confident that ultimately his modest goals would be achieved. With these attitudes Hayes was as successful in handling his problems as the circumstances of his presidency allowed.

Hayes's decision to withdraw federal support in April 1877 from the Republican governments in Louisiana and South Carolina was a response to harsh political realities, rather than a response to any deal made during the count. No matter how legitimate they were, these governments could only be maintained by a military force. Hayes knew that the Democratic House of Representatives would not appropriate money for such a force and that northern public opinion would not sustain such a policy. The question

was not whether the troops should be withdrawn, but when the troops would have to be withdrawn. From this weak bargaining position, Hayes extracted promises from the rival Democratic governments of Louisiana and South Carolina to guarantee the voting and civil rights of all black and white citizens. Hayes was naive in accepting these soon-to-be-broken promises at face value, but he had no other viable option.

Although Hayes had to abandon the Republican governments in Louisiana and South Carolina, he never abandoned his commitment to civil rights and to equal educational and economic opportunities. He was conscientious, humane, fair, and just with everyone, but the disadvantaged particularly attracted his attention. He was an advocate of prison reform and was generous and fearless in using his pardoning power. Hayes also tried to deal justly with the Native Americans [see INDIANS] and during his administration ceased the policy of uprooting peoples and removing them to Indian Territory. He tried to eliminate fraud by reforming the Indian Bureau, and to reduce violence his administration introduced Native American police to keep order on reservations and made strenuous efforts to keep white settlers out of Indian Territory. Hayes worked to integrate Native Americans into the dominant society by promoting education, individual land ownership, and citizenship.

Hayes embraced civil-service reform to a greater degree than any of his predecessors. His pushing reform alienated many Republican politicians but especially Sen. Roscoe Conkling of New York. In June 1877, Hayes ordered federal civil servants not to "take part in the management of political organizations, caucuses, conventions, or election campaigns," and he prohibited political assessments on federal officeholders. In September 1877 he began a battle with Conkling for control of the New York customhouse. By defeating Conkling, Hayes also defeated the idea of senatorial courtesy, the notion that Senators could control civil-service appointments in their states. On Hayes's insistence the merit system was applied in the New York customhouse, and the results achieved there caused the public to perceive civil-service reform, not as the hobby of impractical visionaries, but as a necessity demanded by the growing complexity of the nation's bureaucracy. The CIVIL SERVICE ACT (1883) passed not only because reformers exploited the circumstances of James A. Garfield's assassination but also because the Hayes administration had demonstrated the value of the merit system.

Against great odds Hayes defended the prerogatives of his office and enhanced its power and prestige. By the end of his administration Congressmen, Senators, and others could suggest appointments to Hayes, but no one could dictate them. After a spectacular battle in 1879, he also defeated congressional attempts to force him to approve legislation against his will. The Democratic Congress attached riders to appropriation bills that would destroy laws enforcing voting rights under the Fourteenth and Fifteenth amendments. Sensing correctly that northern public opinion would rally to support the federal supervision of congressional and presidential elections, Hayes vetoed appropriation bills with riders; and ultimately Congress—under the lash of public opinion—passed money bills without the obnoxious riders.

Hayes also vetoed popular legislation that would have expanded the currency and excluded Chinese laborers from the migrants who were allowed into the United States. Hayes's successful veto of the Chinese Immigration bill (1879), which Secretary of State Evarts prepared, was the only veto that Hayes did not write himself. After this veto, Hayes moved to placate Californians by appointing a commission to negotiate a treaty with China permitting limits on immigration (ratified in 1881).

Hayes's anti-inflation policy was successful. Although he could not kill the Bland-Allison silver-coinage bill (1878), which Congress immediately passed over his veto, he reduced its inflationary effect by coining the minimum number of silver dollars required. Near the end of his administration, Hayes claimed that his currency policies—his hard-money stance and especially the resumption of specie payments, which in January 1879 placed the United States back on the gold standard—had restored the confidence of investors in particular and the business community in general. With abundant capital and low interest rates, industries were thriving, railroads were expanding, and foreign trade was increasing. The business cycle was primarily responsible for the economic boom, but it had not been hampered by Hayes's policies. Even though his inflationist opponents were closer to the twentieth-century concept of a managed currency than was Hayes—with his stubborn faith in the gold standard—the fact remains that his currency notions prevailed during a stunning business revival.

Hayes was a man of moderation as well as of principle. His sympathy with labor, but not labor unions, in part accounts for his restrained, legalistic response to the Great Strike in July 1877, which saved both lives and property. The strike was unprecedented in its scope and violence, but Hayes remained calm and responded with federal troops only to proper requests by local and state authorities who had exhausted local means to keep the peace. Although railroad and business leaders demanded that he call up volunteers to suppress the strike, Hayes did not take this action, which probably would have provoked further violence. By using wisely the available small regular army detachments and by neither operating the railroads nor using the mails as a pretext for intervention, Hayes avoided a confrontation between strikers and federal forces. He neither broke the Great Strike nor did the bidding of the railroads, but he did cooperate with local and state authorities to end rioting, looting, and burning.

Hayes was able and lucky. Although he ignored and offended many party leaders, he was a shrewd judge of what the rank-and-file Republicans thought, and his policies attracted the voters. He took office in the middle of a terrible depression, but during his term prosperity returned to the nation. The Republican Party, with its tarnished image newly polished by Hayes, triumphed in 1880 with a Hayes lieutenant, James A. Garfield, at its head. Credit for this success and for a unified Republican Party belong largely to Hayes. If a politician is to be judged by his victories at the polls, Hayes was phenomenally successful.

The political genius of Hayes lay in his moderation, in combining old virtues with new ideas, in mixing sensible proportions of principle and pragmatism. In his wide travels and frequent speeches, Hayes exploited issues and appealed to a broad range of public opinion. Rather than rely on state and local political organizations led by Senators and Congressmen, Hayes embraced the politics of reform and took a modest step on the path that would be followed by the great presidential leaders of the twentieth century. Yet his honesty, simplicity, and decency echoed the pristine values of the early American Republic.

**Retirement.** In retirement at Fremont, Hayes vowed to promote the welfare of his family, town, state, and country. He read widely, monitored public events, and commented on them in his voluminous correspondence and diary. Out of power and without responsibility, Hayes often expressed his views more pointedly than he had expressed them while in office. But his denunciation of giant monopolistic corporations and his support of federal railroad regulation in 1887, when Congress passed the INTERSTATE COMMERCE ACT, reflected a change, not in his principles, but in the nation's economy that was being reshaped by combinations; not in his beliefs, but in the intensity with which they were felt.

Hayes believed that education would ultimately cure most of the problems in American society and consequently made education his "hobby." Even when President, he was a conscientious trustee of the Peabody Fund, which helped to educate both blacks and whites in the South, and as the first president of the board of trustees of the Slater Fund he worked diligently from its creation in 1882 to educate blacks. Not only did Hayes attend all meetings of these organizations, he also wrote numerous letters in support of them, made inspection tours, and urged that the federal government subsidize the education of poor children. Hayes also served on the boards of trustees of Ohio State, Ohio Wesleyan, and Western Reserve universities and faithfully performed the prosaic tasks assigned to him. On all of these boards, he argued that from primary school through college traditional disciplines should be supplemented with practical courses in manual training and the mechanical arts.

In keeping with his faith that education and training could cure social ills, Hayes in 1883 accepted the presidency of the National Prison Association. When governor in 1870, he had presided over the first National Prison Congress, which was held in Cincinnati. He had long corresponded with prison reformers, and his interest in that cause had been heightened by his experience, both as a criminal lawyer and as an executive armed with the pardoning power. For the remainder of his life, Hayes headed that association and worked for a penal system that would be just, rational, and humane. He was desirous of reforming all criminals, including those guilty of capital crimes, believing that their lives could be reclaimed and that the death penalty should be abolished.

Lucy Hayes, who supported her husband in his reform and philanthropic activities, suffered a stroke and died in June 1889. Her death was a severe blow to Hayes. He continued to attend trustee meetings and to work for the causes that these organizations represented, but he was ready to follow Lucy. A few months after his seventieth birthday an attack of angina pectoris felled him in Cleveland, where he was on Ohio State University business. The pain was as intense as his most severe Civil War wound, but, after some brandy, he insisted on returning home, saying he would rather die there than live anywhere else. Three days later, on 17 January, his life ended.

### BIBLIOGRAPHY

Barnard, Harry. *Rutherford B. Hayes and His America*. 1954.

Davison, Kenneth E. *The Presidency of Rutherford B. Hayes*. 1972.

Hayes, Rutherford B. *Hayes: The Diary of a President, 1875–1881, Covering the Disputed Election, the End of Reconstruction, and the Beginning of Civil Service*. Edited by T. Harry Williams. 1964.

Hoogenboom, Ari. *The Presidency of Rutherford B. Hayes*. 1988.

Hoogenboom, Ari. *Outlawing the Spoils: A History of the Civil Service Reform Movement, 1865–1883*. 1961.

Polakoff, Keith Ian. *The Politics of Inertia: The Election of 1876 and the End of Reconstruction*. 1973.

Williams, Charles Richard. *The Life of Rutherford Birchard Hayes: Nineteenth President of the United States*. 2 vols. 1914.

ARI HOOGENBOOM

**HAY-PAUNCEFOTE TREATY.** For the United States the Isthmus of PANAMA gained special strategic significance with its acquisition of California in 1848. In the CLAYTON-BULWER TREATY of 1850 the United States and Great Britain agreed that any future canal through Central America would be subject to joint control, would remain unfortified, and would be neutralized for use by all nations. The issue of a canal remained dormant until the long ninety-eight-day voyage of the battleship *Oregon* from the Pacific coast to CUBA in 1898. Clearly the requirements of U.S. commerce and naval defense following the SPANISH-AMERICAN WAR emphasized the need of an American-controlled interoceanic waterway. In March 1899 Congress authorized the examination of all possible routes for such a canal. Still the country could scarcely contemplate the building of an interoceanic canal without some modification of the Clayton-Bulwer Treaty.

Secretary of State JOHN HAY succeeded in negotiating the Hay-Pauncefote Treaty with Great Britain in 1900. The treaty satisfied Hay but not the U.S. Senate. Hay had failed to secure the American right to fortify as well as build a canal. The Senate amended the treaty so drastically that the British government refused to ratify it. Hay responded by condemning the Senate for its allegedly anti-British prejudices. He complained to one correspondent that he had underestimated the Senate's ignorance, spite, and cowardice. He threatened to resign in protest. Still Hay could not deny the validity of the Senate's criticism and proceeded to reopen negotiations. The second Hay-Pauncefote Treaty, signed on 18 November 1901, granted the United States everything that the Senate had demanded, especially the right to fortify any canal the United States might construct. The British willingly surrendered their canal rights, preferring the extension of U.S. influence in the Caribbean to any compromise with world opinion in their struggle for South Africa.

### BIBLIOGRAPHY

Campbell, Charles S., Jr. *Anglo-American Understanding, 1898–1903*. 1957.

Dennett, Tyler. *John Hay: From Poetry to Politics*. 1934.

Gelber, Lionel M. *The Rise of Anglo-American Friendship: A Study in World Politics, 1898–1906*. 1938.

NORMAN A. GRAEBNER

**HEALTH, PRESIDENTIAL.** Because of the primitive state of medical science during the late eighteenth and most of the nineteenth century, Presidents of that era often received appallingly poor treatment for their ills, sometimes resulting in their deaths. Retired from the presidency, George Washington in 1799 came down with an inflammation of the throat and died after one day's treatment with emetics and cathartics. In 1841, William Henry Harrison delivered his inaugural address (longer than any of his predecessors') standing in the cold without wearing an overcoat. An old man, he fell ill with pneumonia, which was complicated by a chronic intestinal inflammation. His doctors did their worst, prescribing an eight-day regimen that included suction cups, stinging ointments, and cathartics of calomel and castor oil followed by more calomel, rhubarb, and ipecac, then opium, camphor, and brandy, topped off with a Seneca Indian recipe of crude petroleum and Virginia snakeweed. Harrison died a month after his inauguration. Just a few years later, President Zachary Taylor stood in the broiling summer sun listening to the dedicatory speeches for the Washington Monument; perhaps out of boredom, he partook of a large bowl of cherries cooled by ice that had been made from contaminated water. He fell ill with typhoid fever, which doctors treated with brandy and opium, and in a few days died of "severe bilious intermittent fever with congestion."

Three other Presidents of the nineteenth century, including William McKinley at the century's turn in 1901, suffered from inadequate medical care. Chester A. Arthur suffered from Bright's disease, an affliction of the kidneys. He had frequent attacks of illness during his presidency and died a year after leaving office. The shootings of James A. Garfield and of McKinley were followed by medical attention as the patients "lingered," to use the nineteenth-century term; in the case of Garfield, who lingered for two and a half months, it is clear that there was gross medical negligence. His doctors probed for the bullet when they should have let it alone, infecting the patient with unsterilized instruments and even inserting their fingers in the wound. They converted the bullet's entry cavity from a finger-length three and a half inches to a pus-oozing canal twenty inches long. Despite this maltreatment, Garfield's death was the work of his assassin: his splenic artery, torn by the bullet, at last ruptured, and he died. In McKinley's case, the wounded President was operated on in a small emergency hospital, a dimly lit place on the grounds of the Pan-American Exposition in Buffalo, New York, and was thereafter taken to a private house—surprising, because an excellent general hospital was nearby.

For the hundred years from the beginning of Grover Cleveland's second presidency in 1893 through the end of George Bush's presidency in 1993, the health of American Presidents was, in general, remarkably poor. Of the eighteen Presidents who served from 1893 to 1993, five (Wilson, Harding, Franklin Roosevelt, Eisenhower, and Kennedy) suffered serious illnesses, and two (Harding and Roosevelt) died of natural causes while in office.

President Cleveland underwent a hurried operation for cancer of the jaw on 1 July 1893, while aboard a friend's yacht in New York harbor. The hurry was unnecessary, since Cleveland's malady, verrucous carcinoma, does not metastasize, but his doctors did not know that. Although Cleveland's death in 1908 was probably due to stomach cancer, this later illness was unrelated to his cancer of the jaw.

The worst instance of presidential ill health was that of Woodrow Wilson, who long before running for the presidency had a history of cardiovascular disease, leading to probable strokes in 1896, 1904, 1906, and 1909. He suffered a massive cerebral thrombosis on 2 October 1919, which left his left arm and leg nearly paralyzed and his mind greatly impaired. He should have resigned immediately, in favor of Vice President THOMAS R. MARSHALL, but he clung to the presidency, during the very time the TREATY OF VERSAILLES, containing the Covenant of the LEAGUE OF NATIONS, lay before the Senate. Wilson would even have accepted another term if he could have obtained it, and shortly before the 1920 Democratic national convention in San Francisco, which rejected him in favor of Governor JAMES M. COX of Ohio, he went so far as to compose his acceptance speech.

At the time of his inauguration in 1921, Warren Harding had a systolic blood pressure of 180—uncontrollable, for this was long before the invention of effective medication for hypertension. (The normal range is between 100 and 140). During a trip to Alaska in the summer of 1923 Harding was in heart failure, and his condition was misdiagnosed as food poisoning by his personal physician, Brigadier General Charles E. Sawyer. Arriving back in San Francisco, Harding walked from the train to an automobile that took him to the Palace Hotel, where four other physicians joined Sawyer in treating the President. They administered digitalis, but Harding died of a heart attack five days later, on 2 August. Cardiology was then in its infancy, and Harding's doctors certified the cause of death as apoplexy (i.e., stroke).

Presidents Franklin Roosevelt and Dwight Eisenhower, like Wilson, suffered from severe cardiovascular disease. In 1941, Roosevelt's systolic blood pressure reached 188, and by 1944 it had risen to even more alarming heights—on one occasion to 240. In March 1944, he came under the care of a skilled cardiologist, Lieutenant Commander Howard G. Bruenn, who virtually replaced Roosevelt's personal physician, Vice Admiral Ross T. McIntire (McIntire had diagnosed the President's illness as bronchitis). Bruenn gave Roosevelt digitalis, which probably prevented Roosevelt from dying in the summer of 1944. His survival enabled his renomination and election to a fourth term, which lasted only until 12 April 1945, when a massive cerebral hemorrhage caused his death. Eisenhower, who took office in January 1953, suffered a major heart attack in 1955 (he may have had two prior heart attacks, in 1949 and in April 1953). He recovered from the attack of 1955, but at that time he probably suffered a left ventricular aneurysm, a highly dangerous condition in that era (contemporary statistics indicated that 89 percent of heart attack victims with aneurysms died within five years). The President's cardiovascular condition complicated his operation for Crohn's disease (ileitis, or closing of the small bowel) in 1956, and the slight stroke Eisenhower suffered the next year was probably the result of an embolus from the aneurysm.

President John F. Kennedy's Addison's disease, a malady in which the adrenal glands atrophy, was controllable with medication, but it made him a poor candidate for any operation, such as that that had been performed on his back in 1954, which nearly cost him his life. The operation probably kept him out of a wheelchair, but his congenitally weak back plagued him throughout his short presidency.

Other Presidents who suffered, at least temporarily, from illness while in office include Lyndon B. Johnson, who underwent a gall bladder operation in 1965 (Johnson had had a major heart attack in 1955), Ronald Reagan, who had an operation for colon cancer in 1985 and a prostatectomy two years later, and George Bush, whose Graves' disease (an overactive thyroid) was diagnosed when he developed an arrhythmia of the heart.

Presidential illness is an extremely serious matter, obviously bearing on how well the President can execute the duties of office. The record of Presidents' willingness to disclose their medical conditions is discouraging: seven of the eighteen Presidents who served from 1893 to 1993 hid information concerning their illnesses, and in five of these cases the illnesses were so serious that they ought to have prevented the men from running for office in the first place or from running for reelection (as with Franklin Roosevelt's third and fourth terms). Although the TWENTY-FIFTH AMENDMENT to the Constitution, adopted in 1967, provides a procedure for removing an ill President from office, it provides no guarantee that he will be removed, nor can it fully protect against a President's

ability to put himself back in office through a simple assertion of full recovery.

BIBLIOGRAPHY

Abrams, Herbert L. "The President Has Been Shot": Confusion, Disability, and the 25th Amendment in the Aftermath of the Attempted Assassination of Ronald Reagan. 1992.

Crispell, Kenneth R., and Carlos F. Gomez. Hidden Illness in the White House. 1988.

Ferrell, Robert H. Ill-Advised: Presidential Health and Public Trust. 1992.

MacMahon, Edward B., and Leonard Curry. Medical Cover-ups in the White House. 1987.

Park, Bert Edward. The Impact of Illness on World Leaders. 1986.

Post, Jerrold M., and Robert S. Robins. When Illness Strikes the Leader: The Dilemma of the Captive King. 1993.

ROBERT H. FERRELL

**HEALTH AND HUMAN SERVICES, DEPARTMENT OF.** The Department of Health and Human Services (HHS) is responsible for providing health care and social services to millions of Americans. HHS runs 250 separate programs. Its fiscal 1993 budget of $585 billion is the largest of all federal departments and accounts for almost 40 percent of all that the federal government spends. Indeed, the HHS budget exceeds the combined budgets of all fifty states (excluding federal funds they receive) and is larger than the budgets of all countries in the world, except the United States, Germany, and Japan. Each time the consumer price index rises 1 percent, the HHS budget rises almost $4 billion. HHS directly employs about 120,000 people and indirectly pays the salaries of another one million people, in state and local government and on private payrolls, who operate its programs.

**History.** The department was established as the Department of Health, Education, and Welfare (HEW) by President Dwight D. Eisenhower in 1953. President Lyndon B. Johnson turned HEW into the government's largest department when he placed most of his GREAT SOCIETY social programs and the heavy social artillery of his War on Poverty there. During Johnson's presidency (1963–1969), HEW was given responsibility to execute the following programs and laws: Head Start for preschool children; the Elementary and Secondary Education Act, which provides billions of dollars of aid to help schools with high concentrations of poor children; a series of higher education measures that provides grants and loans to help college students defray the cost of their education; Medicare, which provides health care for Americans over sixty-five years of age and those who are permanently disabled; Medicaid, which provides health care for millions of "medically indigent" Americans, largely single-parent mothers and their children who receive benefits under the Aid For Dependent Children (AFDC) program and poor senior citizens in nursing homes; laws to establish community health centers and regional medical centers for heart, cancer, and stroke; funds that substantially increased the federal government's investment in biomedical research; laws that prohibit discrimination on the basis of race, creed, sex, or ethnic origin in federally funded health and education programs.

In 1979, at President Jimmy Carter's recommendation, the Congress took the "E" out of HEW and created a separate Cabinet-level DEPARTMENT OF EDUCATION. The Department of Health and Human Services, as it exists in the early 1990s, was established at that time.

**Sections of HHS.** HHS is formally divided into four sections: the Social Security Administration, which administers social security and welfare programs; the Public Health Service, which includes the National Institutes of Health and Food and Drug Administration; the Health Care Financing Administration, which administers Medicare and Medicaid; and the Administration for Children and Families, which administers service programs for older Americans, children and families.

The Public Health Service (PHS) studies infectious diseases, control of epidemics, and care of American INDIANS on their reservations. The members of PHS are doctors, nurses, and a variety of paramedicals and other professionals, headed by the Surgeon General of the United States.

The Food and Drug Administration, established in 1906, is responsible for assuring that the nation's food supply is safe and properly labeled and that pharmaceutical and medical devices like prostheses are safe and effective before they are marketed. FDA's regulations and actions affect products that account for 25 cents of each dollar American consumers spend.

The National Institutes of Health (NIH) started with a budget of less than $50,000 in 1930. The NIH comprises the world's largest and greatest medical research complex. The first institute dedicated to a specific disease was the National Cancer Institute created in 1937. Since then a number of mission-oriented institutes have been established, including: the National Heart, Lung, and Blood Institute, the National Eye Institute, and the National Institutes of Dental Research; Mental Health; Neurological and Communicative Disorders and Stroke; Arthritis, Diabetes,

*Secretaries of Health, Education, and Welfare*

| President | Secretary of Health, Education, and Welfare |
| --- | --- |
| 34 Eisenhower | Oveta Culp Hobby, 1953–1955 Marion B. Fulson, 1955–1958 Arthur S. Flemming, 1958–1961 |
| 35 Kennedy | Abraham A. Ribicoff, 1961–1962 Anthony J. Celebrezze, 1962–1963 |
| 36 L. B. Johnson | Anthony J. Celebrezze, 1963–1965 John W. Gardner, 1965–1968 Wilbur J. Cohen, 1968–1969 |
| 37 Nixon | Robert H. Finch, 1969–1970 Elliot L. Richardson, 1970–1973 Caspar W. Weinburger, 1973–1974 |
| 38 Ford | Caspar W. Weinburger, 1974–1975 F. David Mathews, 1975–1977 |
| 39 Carter | Joseph A. Califano, Jr., 1977–1979 Patricia Roberts Harris, 1979–1981 |

*Secretaries of Health and Human Services*

| President | Secretary of Health and Human Services |
| --- | --- |
| 40 Reagan | Richard S. Schweiker, 1981–1983 Margaret M. Heckler, 1983–1985 Otis R. Bowen, 1985–1989 |
| 41 Bush | Louis W. Sullivan, 1989–1993 |
| 42 Clinton | Donna E. Shalala, 1993– |

[a] The Department of Health and Human Services succeeded the Department of Health, Education, and Welfare in 1981, two years after the creation of the Department of Education; Secretaries of Health, Education, and Welfare are included in this table. For a list of Secretaries of Education, see EDUCATION, DEPARTMENT OF.

Digestive, and Kidney Diseases; Allergy and Infectious Diseases; Child Health and Human Development; Environmental Health Services; Alcohol Abuse and Alcoholism; and Drug Abuse. Since the late 1970s, the national government, almost entirely through these institutes, has been funding 90 percent of the basic biomedical research performed in America.

HHS also houses the Center for Disease Control, which is headquartered in Atlanta, Georgia. CDC is the nation's nerve center to keep track of infectious diseases and collect many health statistics. It monitors all infectious diseases, from children's ailments like measles, to sexually transmitted diseases like AIDS, gonorrhea, and syphilis, and provides data essential to protect the public health and to assist biomedical research efforts.

HHS programs directly serve one in every five Americans and they touch virtually every citizen at one time or another during his or her life. The department provides cash payments to the elderly, poor, blind, and disabled; kidney dialysis to any who need it; runaway youth shelters; assistance for blind vendors; rescue for abused children; treatment for heroin and cocaine addicts; immunization against childhood diseases like measles, mumps, and whooping cough; rehabilitation for the disabled.

Through its Older Americans program, HHS annually serves more than 150 million meals to almost four million senior citizens at more than 10,000 senior centers it supports across the country, and in the homes of shut-ins. Medicare, the HHS program to provide health services to Americans over 65 and the permanently disabled, pays 25 million bills each month; Medicaid, the program for poor people, pays another 70 million, including many for drug prescriptions. Each day HHS's Social Security Administration receives 25,000 claims; each night the system's computers make millions of entries on individual wage files so workers will receive their proper benefit upon retirement.

**Programs and Controversies.** Because HHS touches so many Americans personally, its actions have provoked wide-ranging and intense controversies that often embroil the President. Just before Thanksgiving in 1959, the HEW Secretary, Arthur Fleming, stopped the sale of canned cranberries and cranberry products in the United States because of concern about adulteration. To execute the law banning any food additive that caused cancer when ingested by animals, Secretary Robert Finch, in 1970, removed the artificial sweetener cyclamates from the market and almost destroyed the soft drink industry in the United States. In 1976, Secretary David Matthews pressed President Gerald Ford to mount the program to protect the nation against the killer swine flu, an unprecedented and ill-starred attempt to inoculate the entire American population. In the 1960s and 1970s, HEW's Civil Rights division placed the presidency at the center of bitter racial controversies as it sought to carry out its congressional mandate to integrate the nation's school systems. In 1978, Secretary Joseph A. Califano, Jr., mounted a major antismoking campaign, which marked the start of the steady decline in smoking among American adults, but which also embroiled the President in political controversy with tobacco-producing states and the cigarette industry. In 1979, the department issued the first Surgeon General's Report on Health Promotion and Disease Prevention, setting goals for a healthier America. The antismoking campaign continued under Surgeon General C. Everett Koop during the 1980s, and HHS set new goals for a healthy America in 1990, thus making health promotion and disease prevention one of the department's central responsibilities.

The department's funding of health programs has put it at the center of controversies such as ABORTION, whether to fund heart transplants, whether to fund expensive neonatal health centers for premature babies, whether to reimburse hospitals for use of expensive life-extending equipment on terminally ill patients, and how to conduct fetal research. Many of these controversies, notably abortion, have engaged Presidents and presidential candidates.

HHS administers the Aid For Dependent Children program, the welfare payments to poor single parents and children that has been a center of controversy since the 1950s. The political and legislative battles have focused on the need to put welfare parents to work and to get absent fathers to pay support for their children. The program's Child Support Enforcement Administration, which was begun in the 1970s, now leads a nationwide effort to locate fathers who are not making support payments and get them to fulfill their responsibility to support their children.

**Accomplishments of HHS.** HHS programs are directed in good measure at America's most vulnerable citizens—the poor, the sick, the old, the disabled, the minorities.

During its history, HHS provided the funds to start the television program "Sesame Street"; financed research that led to cures for some children stricken with leukemia; helped minority students become doctors, lawyers, and professors; spearheaded the World Health Organization's successful effort to eradicate smallpox; furnished social, health, and educational services to Southeast Asian refugees in the wake of the VIETNAM WAR and to Jews escaping from the Soviet Union; and funded the expansion of American medical schools.

BIBLIOGRAPHY

Davis, Karen, and Cathy Schoen. *Health and the War on Poverty.* 1978.
Marmor, Theodore. *The Politics of Medicare.* 1977.

JOSEPH A. CALIFANO, JR.

**HEALTH, EDUCATION, AND WELFARE, DEPARTMENT OF.** For a general overview of the Department of Health, Education, and Welfare, see HEALTH AND HUMAN SERVICES, DEPARTMENT OF. For discussion of the education functions of the department, see EDUCATION, DEPARTMENT OF.

**HEALTH POLICY.** By the 1990s health policy had become one of the President's most significant responsibilities. Health is one of America's top three industries, alongside agriculture and construction. Health spending is nearly $1 trillion a year, about 15 percent of the nation's gross domestic product, and the federal government is the nation's largest purchaser of health care. Federal health care programs, like Medicare, Medicaid, the Veterans Administration hospital system, and health insurance plans that the national government provides for its millions of employees, set the standards of care and reimbursement policies that most other large purchasers follow. As a result, the President is deeply involved in American health policy.

In the earliest days of the Republic, the national government's involvement in matters of health policy was largely through the Public Health Service. The Public Health Service was established in 1789, as the Marine Hospital Service. Its function was to serve merchant seamen and navy personnel. In the late nineteenth and early twentieth centuries, Congress expanded the mission of the Public Health Service to include the study of infectious diseases and the control of epidemics.

During his first term in office President Franklin D. Roosevelt considered shoehorning health-care benefits into the proposal he submitted to Congress in 1935 to establish the SOCIAL SECURITY system, but he dropped the idea for fear of being unable to pass the basic retirement income package.

**The Effect of World War II.** It was WORLD WAR II that began to inject the national government—and hence the President—more deeply into health policy. As part of the national mobilization essential to the war effort, the federal government was required to make substantial investments in health care training and medical research. Desperate for doctors and nurses, the armed forces drafted as many medical professionals as possible and trained even more. The military conducted research on everything from frostbite to malaria, from venereal disease to surgical and burn procedures.

Much of that effort continued after the war, and biomedical research became the first medical arena the federal government entered on a major scale. In 1944, Congress gave the Surgeon General of the United States sweeping powers to support research in the diseases and disabilities of human beings. The National Institutes of Health (NIH), created in 1930, started with a budget of $50,000. At the end of World War II, the multi-million dollar military research effort was transferred to NIH. By 1947, NIH had become the nation's preeminent center for medical research, with a budget of $8 million. By the 1990s, its budget topped $8 billion and the federal government

was funding 90 percent of the nation's basic biomedical research. The President appoints the director of the National Institutes of Health, subject to Senate confirmation. As a result, the President has become engaged in the inevitable controversies that attend the responsibility to set the biomedical research agenda for the nation. Presidents have found themselves entangled, for example, in controversies over the appropriate boundaries of fetal research and the appropriate funding level for AIDS research.

World War II also helped spawn America's pharmaceutical industry. As this industry discovered miracle drugs and medical devices, such as antibiotics, hypertension medication, heart valves and artificial limbs, the Food and Drug Administration (FDA), which had been created in 1906 during President Theodore Roosevelt's administration, became a major player in health policy. By the second half of the twentieth century, the FDA became another source of presidential responsibility and power. The FDA is responsible to see that pharmaceuticals and medical devices are safe and effective, and that certain foods and cosmetics are safe and properly labeled, before they can be marketed. This responsibility has put Presidents into the center of policies and controversies touching millions of Americans.

**Growing Federal Involvement.** In 1945, President Harry S. Truman proposed a sweeping national health insurance program to cover all Americans, even those, like agricultural workers, not then protected by Social Security. Truman also urged massive new government investments to build hospitals across the United States, expand the Public Health Service, and support medical research. Largely because of the opposition of the American Medical Association, Truman was unable to persuade Congress to enact his health insurance plan. But Congress did pass legislation to build hospital beds and, as health care became of greater concern to the American people, began to fund certain health services for old and poor Americans.

President Lyndon B. Johnson made the federal government and the presidency a major component of America's health care system. He persuaded Congress to pass the Medicare program to provide health care for the elderly and Medicaid to provide care for most of the poor. He turned the National Institutes of Health into the dominating force in basic biomedical research in America and established the federal role in building community health centers, immunizing children, and training doctors and nurses.

The nationalization of health-policy issues has placed an enormous political burden on the President. The Supreme Court, in *Roe v. Wade* (1973), gave a woman, under certain circumstances, a constitutional right to an ABORTION as an element of her right to privacy. With Medicaid funding health care for poor women, it soon became the major funder of abortions in the United States and placed the national government and inevitably the President in the middle of the controversy as to whether federal funds should be used to fund abortions.

As the federal government became the largest purchaser of health care, it placed the President into a position to set much of the nation's health policy: setting the basic research agenda, affecting the cost of health care and its availability to millions of Americans, and establishing levels of reimbursement for health care providers like doctors and hospitals. This made the President the most formidable policymaker in terms of America's health care system. In addition the Surgeon General of the United States became more aggressive in promoting healthy habits. Thus, the national government mounted antismoking campaigns and undertook efforts to educate Americans about the dangers of alcohol abuse and the importance of healthy diets. This inevitably embroiled the President in controversies with the tobacco, alcohol, and food industries.

As biomedical science continues to push the envelope of ethics and public policy, the President will continue to find himself in the center of controversies and the debate of ethical questions such as: the appropriate limits of fetal research, the extent to which the federal government should fund use of life-extending equipment for terminally ill patients, the extent to which tax funds should be used to keep severely disabled neonatal babies alive, and whether rationing of health care should be encouraged by the national government.

One of the most formidable challenges for American health policy is to seek ways to provide quality care for all Americans at a reasonable cost. This issue is incredibly complicated, as it involves the training of doctors and paramedicals, the regulation of research, the role of hospitals, the financing mechanisms of insurers and health maintenance organizations, the pricing of pharmaceuticals and medical devices—all in the context of the human reality that "No care is too expensive for my parents, spouse, siblings, or children when they are in pain."

### BIBLIOGRAPHY

Aaron, Henry J., and William B. Schwartz. *The Painful Prescription.* 1984.

Starr, Paul. *The Social Transformation of American Medicine.* 1984.

JOSEPH A. CALIFANO, JR.

**HELVIDIUS-PACIFICUS DEBATE.** The outbreak of war between Britain and the revolutionary republic of France in 1793 provoked the first serious debate about the allocation of authority to make and conduct foreign policy under the Constitution. The principals in this debate were Secretary of the Treasury ALEXANDER HAMILTON, writing as Pacificus, and Congressman James Madison, writing as Helvidius. The two men had collaborated in drafting and ratifying the Constitution as well as writing the authoritative commentary of THE FEDERALIST; now their disputes over financial and foreign policy were a driving force behind the organization of the nation's first POLITICAL PARTIES.

In mid April 1793, President Washington asked his Cabinet to consider what course of policy the United States should pursue. Three circumstances framed the basic context of discussion. The first was that Congress was in recess until December; the second was that the United States was still tied to France by the treaty of alliance of 1778; the third was that Edmond Genet, the newly arrived envoy from France, was already barnstorming northward from Charleston, South Carolina, seeking to rally public support for his country while issuing commissions for American privateers to raid British shipping. Within the administration, Hamilton argued that the terms of the treaty did not oblige the United States to support France or even to honor its financial obligations to that country until it could be determined that a stable government existed there. On the other side, Secretary of State Thomas Jefferson favored recognition of the new government, formal reception of Genet, and in general, a policy that would be sympathetic toward France without running the risk of war. The President sided with Hamilton, issuing a proclamation that, without invoking NEUTRALITY by name, nevertheless sought to pursue an impartial policy toward the belligerents.

Although this disagreement was primarily a dispute over policy, it had constitutional implications as well. Could the executive branch of government unilaterally commit the nation to neutrality, when that decision depended on the interpretation of a treaty, and the Constitution divided authority over treatymaking between the President and Senate? Or should the administration not have to consult both houses of Congress, if it was in effect deciding a matter of war and peace, and the Constitution entrusted the power to declare war to Congress?

The President's neutrality proclamation did not quiet public debate over the wisdom of its policy, however. In an effort to sway public opinion to support the proclamation, Hamilton, in late June 1793, began publishing his Pacificus letters. Beyond defending the wisdom of neutrality, Hamilton made a bold case for the plenary power of the executive branch of the government in the overall framing and conduct of foreign policy. In contrast to Article I of the Constitution, which granted Congress only enumerated powers, Hamilton observed that Article II declared that "The executive Power shall be vested in a President of the United States," and that this grant was modified only by such particular exceptions as were found elsewhere in the text of the Constitution. Under this interpretation, the only legitimate foreign policy powers of the Senate were to be found in the ADVICE AND CONSENT clause for treatymaking and ambassadorial appointments, while those of Congress extended only to DECLARATION OF WAR. All other aspects of foreign relations, Hamilton concluded, fell under the rubric of executive power, including interpreting the obligation of treaties or deciding questions of neutrality.

Alarmed over the tenor and substance of this argument, which he knew to be Hamilton's, Secretary of State Jefferson pressed a reluctant Madison to expose its errors. In his Helvidius essays, which began appearing in late August 1793, Madison argued that Pacificus was attempting to import into the new Constitution ideas and principles that were more properly associated with the practices of monarchical regimes in Europe. By claiming that the executive alone was empowered to judge whether or not a cause for war existed, Madison noted, Pacificus was in effect seeking to negate the right of Congress to decide matters of war and peace. To demonstrate that the views of Pacificus clashed with the original understanding of the allocation of powers under the Constitution, Madison periodically quoted passages from *The Federalist* in which his coauthor Hamilton had taken pains to explain just how prudently the Constitution had divided power over foreign relations between the President and Congress.

Concerned as both sets of essays were with particular conditions of neutrality and the obligations of treaties, their authors nevertheless opened a field of controversy that remains unresolved today.

### BIBLIOGRAPHY

Rutland, Robert A., et al., eds. *The Papers of James Madison.* 17 vols. (1962–1991). Vol. 15. 1985.
Syrett, Harold C., and Jacob E. Cooke, eds. *The Papers of Alexander Hamilton.* 26 vols. (1961–1979). Vol. 15. 1969.

JACK N. RAKOVE

**HENDRICKS, THOMAS A.** (1819–1885), twenty-first Vice President of the United States (1885). Tho-

mas A. Hendricks was something of an anomaly among nineteenth-century Vice Presidents. Unlike most of the twenty-four men who occupied the office during that century, Hendricks had been a serious presidential contender prior to taking the second spot. Moreover, in two instances Hendricks was involved in events that focused attention on gaps in America's provisions for filling the presidency.

Hendricks served in the House of Representatives, United States Senate, and as governor of Indiana during a political career that spanned nearly forty years. He was most noteworthy, however, as a perennial candidate for the Democratic presidential nomination, seeking the nomination on all but one occasion between 1868 to 1884.

Hendricks emerged as one of the leading Democratic candidates in 1868. Though a westerner, he appealed to many in the East who shared his belief that federal obligations should be repaid in gold, but HORATIO SEYMOUR won the nomination.

Hendricks did not figure in presidential nominating politics in 1872, ironically, the only year that he received electoral votes for President. When HORACE GREELEY died between the popular vote and meeting of the electors, Hendricks received forty-two of his sixty-two votes.

In 1876, Hendricks again emerged as a leading candidate for the Democratic nomination. Having run as a "hard money" candidate in 1868, Hendricks emerged as the "greenback" or "soft money" candidate in 1876 and ran a distant second in the balloting to the eventual nominee, SAMUEL J. TILDEN. He received the vice presidential nomination without opposition. The ticket of Tilden and Hendricks represented a classic instance of ticket-balancing—a New York governor and an Indiana Senator, a hard-money man and a greenbacker. Although they won the popular vote, they lost by a single electoral vote when the Republican-dominated ELECTORAL COMMISSION awarded disputed electoral votes to Rutherford B. Hayes.

After another unsuccessful quest for the Democratic presidential nomination in 1880, Hendricks tried to advance his own candidacy again four years later. His efforts failed again to produce the presidential nomination he coveted; again he settled for the second spot on the ticket, this time with Grover Cleveland, governor of New York. Hendricks' selection unified the party, provided geographic balance, and helped the ticket in a competitive state.

Cleveland and Hendricks were elected in 1884. Shortly into their term, rumors began to circulate of a rift between Cleveland and Hendricks, fueled in part by the suggestion that the party's old guard favored

Hendricks for the presidential nomination in 1888. Hendricks's health was already failing before his nomination; he died on 25 November 1885 less than nine months into the term.

Hendricks's death focused attention on a defect in America's law relating to presidential succession. The Presidential Succession Act of 1792 placed the president pro tem of the Senate and Speaker of the House of Representatives behind the VICE PRESIDENT in the line of PRESIDENTIAL SUCCESSION. At Hendricks's death, there was not a president pro tem of the Senate or Speaker of the House and neither house was in session. When they reconvened shortly after Hendricks's death, the Republican Senate elected the Republican Senator JOHN SHERMAN of Ohio as president pro tem, raising the specter that Cleveland's death would change partisan control of the White House. Accordingly, in 1886, Congress changed the succession provision to place CABINET members, not congressional leaders, behind the Vice President.

### BIBLIOGRAPHY

Cook, Theodore P. *The Life and Public Services of Hon. Samuel J. Tilden, Democratic Nominee for President of the United States: To Which Is Added a Sketch of the Life of Hon. Thomas A. Hendricks.* 1876.

Eaton, Herbert. *Presidential Timber: A History of Nominating Conventions, 1868–1960.* 1964

Feerick, John D. *From Failing Hands.* 1965. Pp. 140–146.

Holcombe, John W., and Hubert M. Skinner. *Life and Public Services of Thomas A. Hendricks with Selected Speeches and Writings.* 1886.

JOEL K. GOLDSTEIN

**HICKENLOOPER AMENDMENTS** (1963, 1964). Senator Bourke B. Hickenlooper of Iowa gave his name to two amendments to the foreign assistance laws of the United States, both designed to protect investments of U.S. nationals against expropriation by foreign governments. The first Hickenlooper Amendment, enacted in 1963 in response to Cuban nationalization of private interests, provided that foreign assistance shall not be given to any state that has nationalized property of U.S. nationals without prompt, adequate, and effective compensation. That amendment was not applied frequently and its deterrent influence is difficult to assess. It appears to have had the desired effect in at least one instance in which the government of Sri Lanka decided to compensate U.S. nationals so as not to be denied foreign assistance.

The second Hickenlooper Amendment was adopted by Congress in 1964 to overrule BANCO NACIONAL DE CUBA v. SABBATINO, in which the Supreme Court applied the ACT OF STATE DOCTRINE to give effect to an expropriation by CUBA of property of U.S. nationals without just compensation. The amendment provides that courts should not apply the act of state doctrine in a case in which a claim of title to property is based upon "a confiscation . . . in violation of the principles of international law." The amendment authorizes application of the act of state doctrine in a particular case if the President determines that the national interest requires it.

By mandating the exception, the second Hickenlooper Amendment may be seen as providing legislative support for the judge-made act of state doctrine generally where the amendment does not apply.

Following the second Hickenlooper Amendment courts refused to give effect to the expropriation at issue in *Sabbatino* and in other cases. There appears to have been no case in which the President certified that national interest required that the Hickenlooper Amendment not be given effect and the act of state doctrine be applied.

The Hickenlooper Amendments remain part of U.S. law but their significance has diminished as foreign investments of U.S. nationals have become subject to different arrangements with the host government (such as joint ventures) that do not invite expropriation, and are protected by networks of investment agreements and by agreements for arbitration.

### BIBLIOGRAPHY

Vandevelde, Kenneth J. "Reassessing the Hickenlooper Amendment." *Virginia Journal of International Law* 29 (1988): 115–167.

LOUIS HENKIN

**HIDDEN-HAND PRESIDENT.** The concept of a hidden-hand presidency was introduced to describe the distinctive leadership style of President Dwight D. Eisenhower, which was not evident to Eisenhower's contemporaries, especially those outside his inner circle. The concept, which has application beyond Eisenhower, takes account of the persistent, but more or less deliberately concealed leadership that the declassified records of his presidency show Eisenhower to have exhibited.

Eisenhower seemed at the time of his presidency to be the very model of a nonleader, delegating authority to such strong-minded and visible aides as his Secretary of State, JOHN FOSTER DULLES and his WHITE HOUSE CHIEF OF STAFF, SHERMAN ADAMS. Years later, when the archives were opened, it became evident that he was very much the central figure in his administration's policy making, but that he relied to an unusual degree on aides to announce and execute policies, especially controversial policies. As more aspects of Eisenhower's political style were revealed, it became evident that this impression of political passivity was engendered by a feature of his style that had broader implications for presidential leadership. He resolved the built-in conflict between the American President's ecumenical role as head of state and his intrinsically divisive responsibilities as principal national political leader by hiding his hand in many of his administration's more controversial actions while playing up his status as the symbolic leader of all the nation.

In essence, Eisenhower placed far more emphasis on getting results and, in particular, on anticipating and avoiding negative political eventualities, than on bargaining and conflict management. He also placed no premium on advertising his own political skill. His strategies included working through intermediaries; studious adaptation of his language to circumstances, including skilled use of ambiguity; and self-conscious use of subordinates in ways that played to their strengths and served administration purposes.

In a larger sense, the hidden-hand model of presidential leadership includes all the low-profile and indirect ways in which Eisenhower sought to have an impact. By doing so, it stands in direct contrast to the model of presidential leadership enunciated by Richard Neustadt in his classic study *Presidential Power*, which predicates a President who seeks to affect events by deliberately signaling to other members of the political community that he is a skilled, determined leader. Eisenhower's consistently popular leadership acquired particular interest as a result of the failures of many of his successors to maintain the requisite public support to govern effectively. But the extent to which Eisenhower's results were produced by his style and his successors' difficulties by their failure to act as he did remains to be systematically explored.

### BIBLIOGRAPHY

Ambrose, Stephen E. *Eisenhower: The President.* 1984.
Greenstein, Fred I. *The Hidden-Hand Presidency: Eisenhower as Leader.* 1982.
Neustadt, Richard E. *Presidential Power and the Modern Presidents: The Politics of Leadership from Roosevelt to Reagan.* 1st ed. 1960. 3d ed. 1990.

FRED I. GREENSTEIN

**HIGH CRIMES AND MISDEMEANORS.** The constitutional grounds for IMPEACHMENT are generally termed high crimes and misdemeanors. Article II, Section 4 of the Constitution provides that the Presi-

dent, as well as the VICE PRESIDENT and all civil officers, "shall be removed from Office on Impeachment for, and Conviction of, Treason, Bribery, or other high Crimes and Misdemeanors." "Treason" is defined in Article III, Section 3; "bribery" has an established meaning both at common law and under federal criminal statutes. "High crimes and misdemeanors" is a less familiar term, whose origin is traceable to the British parliamentary common law of crimes.

According to James Madison's notes on the CONSTITUTIONAL CONVENTION, the term was added to the impeachment provision at the suggestion of George Mason of Virginia. As reported by the committee of eleven, the draft constitution limited the grounds for impeachment to treason and bribery. Mason objected that the provision was too limited: "Treason as defined in the Constitution will not reach many great and dangerous offenses," including "attempts to subvert the Constitution." Mason proposed adding "maladministration," then included as a basis for impeachment and removal in a number of state constitutions. Madison responded that "so vague a term will be equivalent to a tenure during pleasure of the Senate," and Mason substituted "other high crimes & misdemeanors . . . agst. the State." To avoid ambiguity, the last phrase was later amended to "against the United States," and then finally deleted by the Committee on Style and Arrangement.

While British impeachments provided "the model from which the idea of this institution has been borrowed," as ALEXANDER HAMILTON wrote in FEDERALIST 65, impeachment in Britain played a different role. Impeachment convictions could lead to criminal penalties, and impeachments could be directed at ordinary citizens—for "high crimes" against the system of government—as well as public officials. Impeachment was a substitute for trial in the criminal courts for high officers of the government and could reach ordinary, as well as high crimes.

In the American system, impeachment is a mechanism for removing officers of the government, including the President; it cannot be used to impose criminal sanctions on officers or citizens. There is no congressional common law of crimes, and since 1812 no federal common law of crimes at all.

The subjects of impeachment, Hamilton wrote, "are those offences which proceed from the misconduct of public men, . . . from the abuse of public trust"—offenses that are "of a nature which may with peculiar propriety be denominated POLITICAL, as they relate chiefly to injuries done immediately to the society itself." Impeachment proceedings "can never be tied down by such strict rules, either in the delineation of the offence by the prosecutors, or in the construction of it by the judges, as in common cases serve to limit the discretion of the courts in favor or personal security."

Nonetheless, at least since the impeachment trial of Supreme Court Justice Samuel Chase in 1804, it has been argued that "high crimes and misdemeanors" means indictable criminal offenses, specific violations of known law. Lawyers for Presidents Andrew Johnson and Richard M. Nixon made this argument in their defense.

The more widely held view, consistent with past American impeachment cases and with constitutional history, is that impeachment is not restricted to cases of criminal wrongdoing. The crucial consideration, at least in presidential impeachment proceedings, is not whether conduct would be criminal if engaged in by a private citizen but the effect of the conduct on the functioning of government. A President is subject to impeachment, under this view, for conduct that is seriously incompatible with either the constitutional form and principles of government or the proper performance of the constitutional duties of the presidential office.

### BIBLIOGRAPHY

Farrand, Max, ed. *The Records of the Federal Convention of 1787*. 1937. Pp. 64–69, 550.

Labovitz, John R. *Presidential Impeachment*. 1978. Pp. 1–131.

Story, Joseph. *Commentaries on the Constitution of the United States*. 1833. sections 749, 763.

U.S. House of Representatives. Committee on the Judiciary. *Constitutional Grounds for Presidential Impeachment: Report by the Staff of the Impeachment Inquiry*. 93d Cong., 2d sess., 1974.

JOHN R. LABOVITZ

**HOBART, GARRET A.** (1844–1899), twenty-fourth Vice President of the United States (1897–1899). With the possible exception of Chester A. Arthur, no man ever entered the office of VICE PRESIDENT with a more modest public résumé than Garret A. Hobart. Yet, like Arthur, Hobart demonstrated that conventional credentials do not always provide the best indicator of the aptitude of the President or Vice President.

Hobart was born on 3 June 1844. He served as speaker of the New Jersey State Assembly and as president of the New Jersey State Senate and was active in some important Republican campaigns there but never held any of the offices—governor, Senator, congressman, Cabinet member—that typically provided Vice Presidents.

Hobart did, however, command strong support in his party in his home state and became the Republican vice presidential candidate in 1896. He was nominated on the first ballot (by a 2 to 1 vote) on the ticket with William McKinley. As a native son of New Jersey, he was expected to help carry that pivotal state. Hobart helped manage the national campaign and his presence on the ticket probably helped produce a ninety thousand-vote margin in New Jersey. His strong support of the gold standard helped influence that party's position on it.

Hobart approached the vice presidency with misgivings, telling his wife that "when I realize all that it means in work, worry, and loss of home and bliss, I am overcome, so overcome I am simply miserable." In view of his success as Vice President, Hobart's trepidation was unfounded.

Although Hobart lacked experience in prominent political positions, he had advantages that many Vice Presidents of his era lacked. Most nineteenth-century Vice Presidents and Presidents came from different wings of their party. They were placed on the ticket to provide a balance often without participation of the Chief Executive. Separated from the President by ideology and bound to them by no personal allegiance, Vice Presidents had little or no loyalty to the administration. Hobart's circumstances were unique. He was ideologically compatible with the President. In addition, Hobart developed a warm personal relationship with McKinley, and his wife often visited the First Lady, who had long been an invalid. The Hobart's rented a house near the White House; the physical proximity encouraged frequent social meetings. The two families vacationed together and shared some holidays. McKinley routinely solicited his Vice President's views on matters of state. The two met regularly and McKinley went out of his way to promote Hobart. Due in part to McKinley's conspicuous efforts, Hobart was often referred to as "Assistant President."

Perhaps due to his experience chairing New Jersey's legislative bodies, Hobart was skilled at presiding over the Senate. He took that duty seriously and regularly discharged it. He prepared assiduously, followed the debates carefully, and personally ruled on parliamentary questions promptly rather than deferring to the parliamentarian. He became immensely popular with Senators, virtually none of whom had known him previously, and was able to help the McKinley administration improve its standing with Congress.

Hobart increased the stature of the vice presidency. As Senator Henry Cabot Lodge observed: "He restored the vice presidency to its proper position and lifted it up before the people to the dignity and importance which it merits."

Hobart collapsed in the spring of 1899 and never

recovered. He died on 21 November 1899. His death marked the sixth time a Vice President died in office and the eleventh time the office was vacant.

Had Hobart lived he no doubt would have won nomination to seek a second term with McKinley. Inasmuch as no Vice President since DANIEL D. TOMPKINS (1817–1825) had been selected to a second term with the same President, that in itself would have been a singular accomplishment. Instead, Hobart's death provided the opening that resulted in Theodore Roosevelt's nomination as Vice President and, upon McKinley's death, his succession to the presidency.

### BIBLIOGRAPHY

Feerick, John P. *From Falling Hands.* 1965.
Hobart, Jennie Tuttle (Mrs. Garret A.). *Memories.* 1930.
Magie, David. *Life of Garret Augustus Hobart—Twenty-Fourth Vice President of the United States.* 1910.
*Memorial Addresses on the Life and Character of Garret A. Hobart Delivered in the Senate and House of Representatives.* 1900.

JOEL K. GOLDSTEIN

**HOMES, PRESIDENTIAL.** There is perhaps no more revealing or erratic group of historic houses than the homes of the American Presidents. They vary from the log cabin Lincoln knew as a boy to the sprawling estate of Franklin Delano Roosevelt. The various houses occupied by a President of the United States are always objects of curiosity as soon as the individual moves to the WHITE HOUSE. The homes of the Presidents are of several types, including birthplaces, the earliest being John Quincy Adams's simple New England farmhouse in Quincy (at the time of his birth, Braintree), Massachusetts; longtime family homes, as Washington's at MOUNT VERNON and Franklin D. Roosevelt's neo-Georgian mansion at HYDE PARK; houses occupied before the presidency but not after, as John F. Kennedy's row house in the Georgetown section of Washington, D.C.; and houses built for or acquired for retirement, such as Martin Van Buren's Italianate Lindenwald on the Hudson, near Kinderhook, New York.

All the Presidents except John Tyler, Zachary Taylor, Richard M. Nixon, Jimmy Carter, Gerald R. Ford, and George Bush have house sites open to the public in the United States; houses survive for these seven, but they are still privately owned. John Tyler's rambling wooden plantation house, Sherwood Forest, in Virginia, alone remains in the hands of the descendants of the President who, in retirement, gave his house this peculiar name because he considered himself a Robin Hood in politics. Zachary Taylor's brick farmhouse in Louisville, Kentucky, stands in a subdivision, while his sugar plantation in Louisiana is now part of the town of Baton Rouge. Richard M. Nixon's birthplace, a bungalow in Yorba Linda, California, is in private ownership, as is his later tile-roofed, stucco villa at San Clemente, California, on the Pacific Ocean. Gerald Ford's modest suburban house in Alexandria, Virginia, is still owned by him, as is his more extensive current residence at Rancho Mirage in California. The site of his birthplace in Omaha, Nebraska, is marked with a historical monument. Jimmy Carter's childhood home in Archery, Georgia, a bungalow with a long front porch, is a private residence, as is his own house in Plains. Ronald Reagan's boyhood home in Dixon, Illinois, can be seen, but other homes he used, as his residence in Pacific Palisades, California, and his current residences in Bel Air and Rancho del Cielo are not open to the public. The shingle-style summer house of George Bush at Kennebunkport, Maine, a rambling seaside house, was owned by his father and is the home of longest duration in Bush's life. His residence in Houston, Texas, is an apartment. Bill Clinton's residence at the time of his election to the presidency in 1992 was the white-columned, plantation style Governor's Mansion of Arkansas, at Little Rock.

**Antebellum Period.** The premier presidential site is Mount Vernon, on the Potomac River below Washington, D.C. Few houses in American history more clearly represent their builders than this wooden mansion of many additions, brought at last to architectural unity just after the American Revolution by the heroic riverfront porch of square piers or box columns that Washington planned himself and called a "pilastrade." Mount Vernon was already a busy site for tourists during Washington's presidency in the 1790s. After his death in 1799 visitors increased so that by the early 1820s regular steamers carried boatloads there to view the tomb and mansion of the "Father of His Country." At last, the heirs of Washington had to move out, for peace of mind. The house in disrepair was purchased in 1858 by the Mount Vernon Ladies' Association of the Union. Today it remains in their hands, both shrine and exemplary historic house museum.

The five Presidents who followed Washington, up to Jackson, are represented in historic houses that they occupied before the presidency or built or finished during their time in the White House. Both the Adamses, father and son, lived in the find old Adams house in Quincy, its low-ceiling rooms filled with their memorabilia, from spectacles to Louis XV furniture acquired by John Adams while serving as American minister to France. Jefferson's MONTICELLO, his extraordinary attempt to adapt aristocratic French taste from *ancien régime* to American architecture for upper-class living, is a subtle mirror of a man enthralled with invention and experimentation, as well as expressions of social status. The MONTPELIER that James Madison made from his father's simple brick house extolls with its homely neoclassicism that brilliant President's commitment to republicanism for America. Highlands, built near Monticello by James Monroe, is a compelling wooden farmhouse he built in his younger days; Oak Hill, near Leesburg, Virginia, Monroe built while he was President, using the White House architect James Hoban and building materials paid for by the government, for which he later had to answer. Of these houses only Oak Hill is still a private home. The rest are museum houses, like most presidential home sites, and open to the public with guided tours.

It was after Jackson came to the White House that presidential residences began to take on a public interest. Mount Vernon's influence on the Presidents themselves was very great. Andrew Jackson, the first military hero to serve as President since Washington, saw a comparison between himself and Washington and consequently took a great interest in the estate. He journeyed there numerous times on navy steamers to admire it. The Washington descendants presented him with the general's leather-covered swivel desk chair; when the Mount Vernon orange house burned in 1833, Jackson ordered one built at the White House to house a sago palm rooted by Washington and saved from the fire. When Jackson's own residence, the Hermitage in Nashville, Tennessee, burned to its brick walls in 1833, he ordered its rebuilding and added not only a heroic colonnade, reminiscent of Mount Vernon, but a driveway similar to the one at Mount Vernon, forming a shape somewhat like that of a guitar. The house was in public hands in the 1850s, about the time Mount Vernon was purchased by the Mount Vernon Ladies' Association of the Union, but it was not to be a museum until the 1880s.

Andrew Jackson's conscious reflection of Washington's residence in his own was picked up by his successor, Martin Van Buren. Both he and Jackson conferred on wallpapers and other details for Lindenwald, but the house with its tall central tower bore no architectural likeness to Mount Vernon. James K. Polk, who also liked to visit Mount Vernon, sensed his importance as the man who had expanded the nation to the Pacific and purchased a retirement house in Nashville, Tennessee, which he and his wife hoped would prevail as their Mount Vernon. He carefully filled Polk Place with artifacts of his presidency and his era before his sudden death in 1849 three months after his retirement. The former President was buried there, and his wife, Sarah, inherited the house for life; upon her death it went to the city of Nashville as a museum. The city tore it down in the 1890s. Polk's memorabilia is displayed in his parents' house in Columbia, Tennessee, thirty miles away.

William Henry Harrison's Grouseland in Vincennes, Indiana, is a fine house of red brick built about 1815. Harrison's birthplace at Berkeley Plantation in Virginia is near Tyler's Sherwood Forest and open to the public. The Gothic-style mansion Millard Fillmore built in Buffalo, New York, in the late 1830s is gone, but the cabin where he was born in Moravia, New York, has been reconstructed, and the first house he built, a late Federal-style cottage, still stands in East Aurora, New York, though it is private and not available to be seen inside.

Two handsome white New England clapboard houses commemorate the early life of Franklin Pierce, the first at Hillsboro, New Hampshire, and the second in Concord, while the house in which he died in 1869 is privately owned. James Buchanan's log cabin birthplace stood in Stoney Batter, Pennsylvania, but was moved to the grounds of Mercersburg Academy in Mercersburg, Pennsylvania, where it is open to visitors. Better known is his beautiful country mansion Wheatland, in Lancaster, Pennsylvania, which is filled with personal memorabilia of his twenty bachelor years there and his four years in the White House.

**Lincoln to the Present.** President Abraham Lincoln never planned to return to live in Springfield, Illinois, after he left his two-story frame house, which he occupied from 1844 until 1861; his Springfield home remains the site museums associated with his life. Lincoln's birthplace, a log cabin on Sinking Spring near Hodgenville, Kentucky, is probably conjectural. A photograph of the authentic cabin was taken while Lincoln was still alive, but after the CIVIL WAR the cabin was taken down and moved many times, being put up again in various configurations. It was reerected at last in 1911 inside a pillared Beaux-Arts shrine, using the early photograph as a guide. Lincoln's early boyhood home on Knob Creek, also near Hodgenville, is reconstructed, and the foundations of the cabin near Lincoln City, Indiana, where he lived into young manhood are preserved in a park setting. Andrew Johnson left a handsome brick residence in Greenville, Tennessee, now a museum. His childhood home, a small, Dutch-roofed building, stands reconstructed in Raleigh, North Carolina.

President Ulysses S. Grant's birthplace, a small clapboard cottage, is restored near Point Pleasant, Ohio, and the broad-eaved, brick house the citizens of Galena, Illinois, presented to him after the Civil War that he owned until he moved to New York City in 1880, has been restored. The mountain cottage where he died in 1885 remains as he left it, some ten miles outside Saratoga Springs, New York. Rutherford B. Hayes's birthplace, a typical Midwest two-story brick house in Delaware, Ohio, was demolished, but he himself saw to the perpetuation of his tranquil residence Spiegel Grove at Fremont, to which is attached the first presidential library, built and funded largely by the estate of the history-conscious Hayes, his wife Lucy, and their eldest son, Webb. In retirement President Hayes employed agents to attend sales of White House furnishings and retrieve at any price items from his presidency. Hayes's efforts were the first conscious return to the Mount Vernon idea since Polk forty years before.

James A. Garfield's quaint stick-style house, Lawnfield, was built only five years before his assassination at the age of 49. His log cabin birthplace is a replica, but the fine bungalow built in Pasadena, California, for his widow by the architects Greene & Greene stands in prime condition, a private residence. Chester A. Arthur's birthplace stands in reproduction at Fairfield, Vermont, but no other site commemorates him, for his brownstone on Lexington Avenue long ago surrendered to the urban expansion of New York City. Grover Cleveland's birthplace, the Presbyterian Manse in Caldwell, New Jersey, has been kept as a house museum. Westland, the ample neocolonial mansion that was his retirement home in Princeton, New Jersey, still stands as a private home.

Benjamin Harrison's birthplace in North Bend, Ohio, a fine Greek Revival residence of brick, was torn down in 1959. The tall, comfortable house to which he added deep porches and occupied from 1874 to 1901 in Indianapolis, Indiana, contains his personal memorabilia and is a museum open to the public. William McKinley's birthplace and his home in Canton, Ohio, from which he conducted the famous Front Porch Campaign of 1896 have been demolished. Theodore Roosevelt's birthplace, a Manhattan brownstone, was reconstructed after its demolition and has been a museum for over a half-century. Sagamore Hill, his rambling farmhouse near Oyster Bay, Long Island, New York, was built for his first wife Alice Lee and occupied by him and his second wife Edith. On her death in 1948, 29 years after his, it became a museum, with very few of the original furnishings removed. Of special interest is the large trophy room and library added while he was President and in the new Beaux-Arts style he introduced to the White House, not the quaint Queen Anne style of the original Sagamore Hill built in 1883.

William Howard Taft's boyhood home dating from 1850s in Cincinnati, Ohio, was restored and is maintained by the National Park Service. Others of the numerous houses that figured in his life are not accessible to the public but are still in use at private residences. Woodrow Wilson's birthplace and home for nine months was the old Presbyterian manse in Staunton, Virginia, a house museum and open to the public, as is his boyhood home, the only home his parents ever owned, at Columbia, South Carolina. His other houses are private residences, except for his last one, a tall Adamesque mansion in the embassy district of Washington, D.C., willed by his last wife EDITH WILSON to the National Trust for Historic Preservation in 1961. It is rich with lore of Wilson's presidency, including his clothing, books, and personal possessions, as well as those of Mrs. Wilson.

Warren G. Harding's widow, Florence, willed their residence in Marion, Ohio, to the nonprofit Harding Memorial Association and it is operated as a museum, fully restored with most of the belongings she left. The birthplace of Calvin Coolidge at Plymouth, Vermont, is restored to the appropriate year 1872, while his father's later house, a white-frame farmhouse in the same town, was dedicated unchanged by President Coolidge's son John as a museum to his parents. Here by the light of a kerosene lamp Coolidge took his oath of office from his father in 1923, on the news that President Harding had died in San Francisco.

Herbert Hoover was born in a small frame house in West Branch, Iowa. The house and much of the village today is part of the Hoover Library complex. His boyhood was spent in the home of an uncle in Newberg, Oregon, and Hoover lived to attend its dedication as a museum. Franklin D. Roosevelt presented his estate on the Hudson River at Hyde Park, New York, to the American people while he was still President. The house, which he helped remodel into its present neo-Georgian form, was his father's Queen Anne mansion, Springwood, and was the house in which Roosevelt was born. On the grounds are the presidential library and gravesite, and nearby is Eleanor Roosevelt's Val-Kill, a small retreat designed for her and built in the mid 1920s. A feature of the Springwood experience is listening to a tour made on tape by Mrs. Roosevelt of her memories of each room in the house. Another important Roosevelt site is the Little White House at the poliomelytis encampment at Warm Springs, Georgia, where he died in 1945.

President Harry S. Truman's birthplace is a tiny frame house in Lamar, Missouri, where he lived until the age of about ten. It is restored, but the house in Independence, Missouri, where he spent most of his boyhood is private and much remodeled from its original appearance. The house most associated with President Truman was the home of his Wallace in-laws, an ample frame house of two stories, frosted with gingerbread in the Queen Anne style and painted white. BESS TRUMAN's grandfather built the house, which became her parents' home around 1900, and home to the Trumans, with the in-laws, beginning in 1919. It is open to the public, left as it was when Mrs. Truman died in 1982. Dwight D. Eisenhower's birthplace in Denison, Texas, a wide frame house with three abrupt gables, is a museum, as is the somewhat similar, though smaller family home in Abilene, Kansas, which has been a house museum since 1947. President Eisenhower's 500-acre farm in Pennsylvania, near the battlefield of Gettysburg, is a homey, brick farmhouse and is open to the public.

John F. Kennedy's birthplace and home for four years, a three-story house in Brookline, Massachusetts, set close in line with other, similar wooden houses, is a museum house, but the other houses associated with his life remain private. On the other hand, many houses commemorate the life of Lyndon B. Johnson, not the least the unpretentious, boxy, much-extended ranch house near Stonewall, Texas, which is available for tours. Nearby is Johnson's birthplace, the school he attended, his boyhood home, and his burial site, all open to the public and in more or less close proximity to the Pedernales River.

**Memorials and Museums.** While the historic house museum did not come into its own in the United States until the 1920s, the restoration of presidential sites started earlier. In Lancaster, Pennsylvania, James Buchanan's niece Harriet Lane Johnson established his home, Wheatland, as a museum in the late nineteenth century. Lincoln's Springfield house was given to the state of Illinois by his son in 1887. Agitation for the restoration of Monticello began late, not long before WORLD WAR I, and the site was acquired for memorial purposes only in 1923; not long after, the Adams houses in Quincy, Massachusetts, became museum properties.

Today about half the presidential house sites open to the public are owned by the federal government or by state governments. Most of the others are owned by private, nonprofit organizations of one kind or another. The trend over recent years has been for private groups to turn the sites over to the National Park Service, as in 1962 with Theodore Roosevelt's Sagamore Hill, which was by then owned by the nonprofit Theodore Roosevelt Association. Still other sites, such as the Hermitage and Mount Vernon, have flourished in the hands of private organizations for over a century.

The interest of the Presidents in providing memorials to themselves made its first manifestation in houses with Jackson. Whether Jefferson, a true house-lover, was ever concerned with this is not known; his circumstances were so desperate at the end of his life that he attempted to put Monticello up for a lottery. Obviously he would have wished things to be otherwise, but he never referred in writing to the perpetuation of his country home. Washington employed two lawyers to catalog his vast papers and housed them at Mount Vernon with the papers, but he never mentioned restoration of his house. Polk was the first to specify his private funds as a means to a memorial to his presidency and Hayes was the only other.

But the idea of one's house as a memorial, dramatized in the great success of George Washington's house as a public attraction, was clearly evident with all the Presidents since Jackson. None took bold steps to assure this until more than a century later when Franklin D. Roosevelt placed his home at Hyde Park under ownership of the federal government in 1939 as a historic site, with the proviso that his family had life tenancy. While still President he saw to the construction by a private foundation of an archive building with an office for his use. This has been followed by subsequent Presidents in one sense, the establishment of presidential libraries, commenced with private donations and eventually maintained by the government under the National Archives.

The preservation of historic houses has naturally followed. President Roosevelt's family elected not to remain at Hyde Park and the mansion became a museum. Following President Harry S. Truman's death and that of his wife, their house in Independence, not far from the Truman Library, was open to the public by the National Park Service. Eisenhower's presidential retreat and retirement home near Gettysburg, Pennsylvania, went to the National Park Service on Mrs. Eisenhower's death in 1979, although the Eisenhower Library is far distant in Kansas. There is as yet no Kennedy house site. Lyndon Johnson bequeathed his LBJ Ranch, near Austin, Texas, to the National Park Service, with a life right to use by Mrs. Johnson. John F. Kennedy's birthplace in Brookline, Massachusetts, became a National Park Service site in 1967. Jimmy Carter has given title to his ranch-style residence in Plains, George, to the National Park Service, with the right to remain there for his and Mrs. Carter's lifetimes.

The presidential houses show the homelife of the occupants and hold a never-ending fascination as domestic settings in which human beings reached for greatness. In America's historic preservation movement the homes of the Presidents, with their enormous public appeal, call for a certain accuracy of restoration and interpretation. It is generally true of all the sites that they are valuable tools in the teaching of history in a popular mode.

## BIBLIOGRAPHY

Jones, Cranston. *Homes of the American Presidents.* 1962.
Kochmann, Rachel M. *Presidents: Birthplaces, Homes, and Burial Sites.* 1976.

WILLIAM SEALE

**HOMESTEAD ACT** (1862). The Homestead Act opened up unoccupied federal land under Union control and offered 160 acres to any American citizen over age twenty-one and the head of a family. In return, the homesteader had to pay a registration fee ranging from $26 to $34, farm the land and maintain continuous residence on it for five years. Alternatively, the five-year residence requirement could be reduced to six months if the homesteader chose to pay $1.25 per acre. Homesteaders had to swear future loyalty to the Union. Specifically excluded from its benefits, however, was anyone who had raised arms against the United States. Between June 1863 and June 1864 farmers acquired more than 1.2 million acres under the act.

With the country in the midst of the CIVIL WAR, the act in part stimulated needed economic activity and bolstered public confidence, making it an effective wartime measure. Moreover, the Republican platform in the election of 1860 had included a homestead plank, one that lured many voters to that party's camp. By signing the bill, President Abraham Lincoln fulfilled a major pledge of the REPUBLICAN PARTY. In a February 1861 speech to Germans in Cincinnati, Lincoln stated: "In regard to the Homestead Law, I have to say that . . . I am in favor of cutting up the wild lands into parcels, so that every poor man may have a home."

Earlier homestead legislation, long part of the Free-Soil movement and Northern expansion plans, repeatedly met with defeat, primarily at the hands of Southerners. The slaveholding South helped defeat earlier bills, and an act passed in 1860 met with President James Buchanan's veto. Now, with secessionist Southerners out of Congress, the Republican Congress passed the new act with overwhelming majorities. The Homestead Act's grant of free land to northern farmers ended nearly fifteen years of agitation. Lincoln enthusiastically signed the law on 20 May 1862.

The Homestead Act reflected Lincoln's and the Republican Party's ideology of free soil and free labor.

Moreover, the act's proponents hoped to end the dominance of large landholders and speculators in the westward expansion, as well as ensure continued Republican political success. Arguably, the Homestead Act represented one of the moral high points of Republican ideals. During RECONSTRUCTION the act was supplemented by the Southern Homestead Act of 1866, which opened up federal lands in Southern states to both blacks and whites.

## BIBLIOGRAPHY

Lanza, Michael L. *Agrarianism and Reconstruction Politics: The Southern Homestead Act.* 1990.
Nevins, Allan. *The Emergence of Lincoln.* 2 vols. 1950.

NICHOLAS AHARON BOGGIONI

**HONEYMOON PERIOD.** The presidential honeymoon is the interval between the election of a new President and the point at which disenchantment is voiced by substantial segments of the public, the press, and Congress. When President Gerald R. Ford declared to a joint session of Congress that, "I do not want a honeymoon with you. I want a good marriage," he was seeking to extend this auspicious period.

With a newly elected President, there is excitement, and the initial evaluation of PUBLIC OPINION is positive. The press typically treats a new CHIEF EXECUTIVE favorably. The news is primarily about appointments and general plans for the future, and the opposition is relatively silent so as not to appear to be sore losers. Thus, the cues on which the public may base its evaluations of the President are supportive of the White House.

Other factors buttress this favorable start to a presidency. Americans tend to have approving opinions of people. They have a general disposition to prefer, to learn, and to expect positive relationships more than negative relationships and to perceive stimuli as positive rather than negative. This orientation provides the foundation for the predisposing factor called the positivity bias.

The causes of the positivity bias are not well known, but it seems to have the greatest potential for influence in ambiguous situations, such as the beginning of a President's term. New occupants of the White House are unknown to the public as chief executives and therefore may receive the benefit of the doubt in the public's evaluation of them.

Some authors have found evidence of a bandwagon effect in which, after an election, people, especially those who had voted for the loser, tend to view the winner more favorably than they did before the election. This depolarization of politics and the positivity bias itself probably help to give most Presidents a boost in the polls early in their terms.

As a President performs his duties, the public may begin to perceive more implications of presidential policies for their own lives. If people view these policies unfavorably, they may be more receptive to negative information about the President. The conventional wisdom is that the honeymoon period is a short one, with the rest of the term characterized by a decline in the polls.

Presidential honeymoons with the public are not always short-lived, however. Declines do take place, but they are neither inevitable nor swift. President Dwight D. Eisenhower maintained his standing in the public very well for two complete terms. President John F. Kennedy held his public support for two years, as did Ford, once he suffered his sharp initial decline following his pardon of Richard Nixon after only a month in office. Both Presidents Ronald Reagan and George Bush experienced considerable volatility in their relations with the public, but their records certainly do not indicate that the loss of public support is inexorable or that it cannot be revived and maintained. Richard M. Nixon's approval levels were also quite resilient for his entire first term. Lyndon B. Johnson's and Jimmy Carter's approval losses were more rapid, although Johnson's initial ratings were inflated due to the unique emotional climate at the time he assumed office following the assassination of Kennedy. The same was true, of course, for Ford, who assumed office after Nixon resigned.

Thus, honeymoons are not necessarily fleeting phenomena in which new occupants of the White House receive a short breathing period from the public. Instead, the President's constituents seem to be willing to give a new chief executive the benefit of the doubt for some time. It is up to each President to exploit the goodwill provided by the public's predisposition and use it as a foundation on which to build solid support for his administration.

Perhaps the most important consequence of a honeymoon period is for the President's ability to lead Congress. First-year proposals have a considerably better chance of passing Congress than do those sent to the Hill later in an administration. Thus, Presidents are frequently advised to be ready to send legislation to the Hill early in the first year of their terms to exploit the honeymoon atmosphere that typically characterizes this period. President Lyndon B. Johnson explained, "You've got to give it all you can in that first year. . . . You've got just one year when they treat you right and before they start worrying about them-

selves." Kennedy, Johnson, Reagan, and to some extent President Jimmy Carter took advantage of this opportunity, whereas Eisenhower, Nixon, and Bush did not.

Although the prospects of passage are enhanced if legislation moves quickly, there are good reasons why many Presidents are not able to ensure that it does. For example, Carter's proposals for energy, welfare reform, and the containment of hospital costs were complex and controversial policies that took a long time to draft and to clear relevant offices in the White House. He could not turn to a well-established party program as Kennedy and Johnson could.

There is of course an alternative to the methodical, time-consuming drafting of legislation. The President might choose simply to propose a policy without thorough analysis to exploit the favorable political climate of his honeymoon. This appears to have been the strategy of Reagan's White House regarding the budget cuts passed by Congress in 1981. The departments (including Cabinet members) and their expertise were kept at a distance during decision making. According to the Budget Director, David Stockman, "None of us really understands what's going on with all these numbers." Lyndon Johnson's legislation to establish the War on Poverty in 1964 is often faulted for having been understood by virtually no one.

Although the strategy of "move it or lose it" may increase the probability of a bill's passage and not affront the sensibilities of someone with Ronald Reagan's lack of concern for details, it is not difficult to understand why someone with the temperament of Jimmy Carter may eschew such a process.

Presidential honeymoons, then, can play an important role in a presidency. But neither their duration nor their significance should be exaggerated.

### BIBLIOGRAPHY

Brody, Richard A. *Assessing the President.* 1991.
Edwards, George C., III. *Presidential Approval.* 1990.
Light, Paul C. *The President's Agenda.* Rev. ed. 1991.
Mueller, John E. *War, Presidents, and Public Opinion.* 1970.

GEORGE C. EDWARDS III

**HOOVER, HERBERT** (1874–1964), thirty-first President of the United States (1929–1933). Herbert Clark Hoover was born in the Quaker village of West Branch, Iowa, orphaned at an early age, and sent to Oregon to live with relatives. He entered Stanford University as a member of its "pioneer" class in 1891. Graduating four years later with a degree in geology, he subsequently entered the employ of San Francisco mining engineer Louis Janin and in 1897 was hired by a British company, Bewick, Moreing, initially serving as an evaluator and manager of mining properties in Western Australia and later as the company's representative in the Chinese Engineering and Mining Company. In 1901 he became a partner in Bewick, Moreing and over the next seven years helped to build its reputation for business progressiveness and financial probity. In 1908 he left the firm to pursue business interests of his own, and in the years that followed he became a specialist in mining finance and the reorganization of failing enterprises. As a "doctor of sick mines," Hoover became both wealthy and internationally recognized, and by 1914 he had become increasingly interested in questions of institutional reform, social betterment, and professionalization. Having made his fortune, he was eager for public service and actively explored the possibilities in publishing and in philanthropic and governmental administration.

**Early Political Career.** Following the outbreak of WORLD WAR I in 1914, Hoover became involved in relief work, initially as director of efforts to rescue Americans who were stranded in Europe and then as organizer and director of the Commission for Relief in Belgium. When the United States entered the war in 1917, he seemed the logical choice for wartime Food Administrator, and in this position he became one of Woodrow Wilson's best known and most widely acclaimed war-effort managers. Seeking to preserve as much "voluntarism" as possible, he laid great stress on public-private cooperation, community pressure, educational publicity, and the use of the government's purchasing power as the best ways to secure the desired economic behavior. In the immediate postwar period, as director of American relief efforts in Europe, as vice chairman of President Wilson's Second Industrial Conference, as the organizer and first president of the Federated American Engineering Societies, and as an unsuccessful contender for the Republican presidential nomination, Hoover continued to preach a "progressivism" that emphasized the need for economic management and social reintegration but insisted that these were best provided through government-encouraged private and community action rather than through a managerial or welfare state. His book *American Individualism* (1922) was a philosophical statement of how such principles could meet modern needs while avoiding what he saw as the evils of statism and collectivism.

In 1921 Hoover entered Warren G. Harding's Cabinet as Secretary of Commerce, and over the next seven years he used this position to mount concerted attacks on a variety of national economic and social problems. The nation suffered, he argued, from organizational and informational gaps that could be filled through appropriate forms of scientific inquiry, professional leadership, and association-building. From the whirl of conferences, committees, and commissions that he set in motion came new structures and networks intended to level out the business cycle, reduce industrial waste, enhance social harmony, promote new and larger markets, and implement a variety of other social-betterment projects. Contemporaries were convinced that no Cabinet officer had ever been engaged in so wide a diversity of activities, and to some observers it appeared that Hoover had made himself not only Secretary of Commerce but undersecretary of everything else. Not only did he expand the conventional duties of the COMMERCE DEPARTMENT; he was also instrumental in shaping the period's diplomacy; working out its labor settlements; devising schemes for agricultural reconstruction and relief; organizing resource development programs; promoting child welfare, home economics, and employment management; and writing such laws as the Federal Radio Act, the Air Commerce Act, and the Railway Labor Act. In each of these areas, Hoover left a legacy that would influence future policy developments.

By 1928 Hoover had acquired a reputation as the nation's troubleshooter ad hence a man capable of dealing with almost any problem that might arise. To his many admirers, he was the scientific engineer, the successful businessman, the great humanitarian, the disinterested expert, and the public-spirited nonpolitician all rolled into one. In the eyes of many, his deficiencies as a political leader—particularly his protective reserve, overly sober demeanor, and lack of skill in the oratorical and political arts—counted more as virtues than as defects. When Calvin Coolidge announced that he would not seek reelection, Hoover became the leading contender for the Republican presidential nomination, which he secured with ease at the party's convention in 1928. In the election that followed, he handily defeated his Democratic opponent, ALFRED E. SMITH of New York, whose urban origins, Roman Catholicism, and opposition to PROHIBITION all counted against him in the southern and western states and led many Democrats there to announce their support for Hoover. When the votes were counted, Hoover had carried forty states (including seven states in the previously Solid South), polled 58 percent of the popular vote, and won the ELECTORAL COLLEGE by a count of 444 to 87.

**The New Day.** During the 1928 campaign, Hoover had talked about a "New Day" in America—a time when poverty would disappear and abundance would make possible ever rising standards of living and individual and social well-being. This New Day was to be ushered in by the kind of organizational and fact-finding projects that he had undertaken as Secretary of Commerce, and in the early months of his administration a number of such projects were launched. Such agencies as the President's Research Committee on Social Trends, the Commission on the Conservation and Administration of the Public Domain, and the National Commission on Law Observance and Enforcement were brought into existence. Administrative reorganizations to improve the performance of the Indian, Veterans, Prisons, and Prohibition bureaus were undertaken as well. And under Ray Lyman Wilbur, Hoover's Secretary of the Interior, plans were laid for transforming the INTERIOR DEPARTMENT into a department of public works and public welfare and using it to fill organizational and informational gaps in such areas as child protection, housing, education, and recreation. In staffing the government, the President found places for numerous "Hoover men" eager to participate in new "Hooverization" projects. But at the Cabinet level, he did make a number of concessions to political and partisan needs: the continuation of AN-DREW W. MELLON as Secretary of the Treasury and the appointments of Walter Brown as Postmaster General, James W. Good as Secretary of War, Arthur M. Hyde as Secretary of Agriculture, and HENRY L. STIMSON as Secretary of State.

In his efforts to usher in the New Day, Hoover also tried to bring better organization to the agriculture sector, which had never fully recovered from the recession of 1920–1921. What the farmers needed, Hoover had argued through much of the 1920s, was a properly developed set of agricultural marketing associations that would enable them to become more businesslike. In 1929 this continued to be his solution for the farm problem, and, in a special session of Congress convened shortly after his inauguration, he was successful in blocking other farm-relief schemes and securing the passage of the Agricultural Marketing Act, which was based on his prescriptions. It established the Federal Farm Board, whose purpose was to represent the various interests in agriculture. Initially provided with a fund of $500 million, the board had as its job to build an appropriate set of marketing associations, to provide such groups with technical and financial aid, to lend them money to facilitate orderly marketing, and to form emergency stabilization corporations to help them cope with demoralized markets. Although the Farm Board failed to achieve its goals, it did leave a legacy of new associations and much resentment on the part of private grain merchants and other middlemen.

Aside from this agricultural legislation, however, the special session produced relatively little. Tariff revision, originally intended to facilitate agricultural adjustment, bogged down and had to be postponed to the regular session, and efforts to modify the immigration quotas established in the 1920s were unsuccessful. Nor did several other initiatives produce much except a foretaste of future political difficulties. A national oil conference, intended to reduce waste and promote oil conservation, produced little but criticism. Measures to strengthen prohibition enforcement led to heightened criticism from urban politicians and civil libertarians. And a Southern policy, intended to consolidate Republican political gains among southern whites, was successful chiefly in alienating northern liberals and African Americans. In areas where problem-solving called more for political artistry than for expert commissions and businesslike organizations, the new administration was already acquiring a reputation for ineptitude and insensitivity.

**The Great Depression.** The great test of Hoover's ideology and prescriptions, however, came with the stock market crash of October 1929. As the great bull market of the late 1920s collapsed in an orgy of panic selling, the President insisted that the basic economy was "fundamentally sound" and promptly took actions intended to short-circuit the business cycle and organize a quick recovery from the effects of speculative excesses. In essence, these actions amounted to the creation of three organizations believed capable of curbing deflationary forces and getting expansion started again. In late 1929 he persuaded the U.S. Chamber of Commerce to create the National Business Survey Conference, which was to work through some 170 trade associations to dispel gloom and obtain compliance with business pledges of wage maintenance and new investment. Shortly thereafter came the similarly organized National Building Survey Conference, the aim of which was to implement pledges of new or expanded construction. And in early 1930 a new Division of Public Construction began working to accelerate federal building projects and to secure the pledges of states and cities to increase their expenditures on public works. In addition, Hoover was successful in securing a temporary tax cut, monetary expansion measures from the Federal Reserve Board, and a pledge of labor peace from the American Federation of Labor and other unions—all measures that were supposed to facilitate the work of the recovery organizations.

Initially, both the President and leading economic experts were optimistic about the workability of the recovery program. Such economists as Irving Fisher and John Maurice Clark believed that the program could bridge the recession, calling it "a great experiment in constructive industrial statesmanship." In

May 1930 Hoover told the nation that this "great economic experiment" had succeeded to "a remarkable degree." By the fall of 1930, however, the economy was again reeling under the impact of new layoffs, worsening farm distress, mounting bank failures, and declining business expectations. Making matters worse was an intensifying international trade war aggravated by the passage in June 1930 of the protectionist SMOOT-HAWLEY TARIFF ACT. Over a thousand economists petitioned Hoover, urging him to veto the tariff bill, but the President was anxious to get the tariff debate over and he signed the measure into law.

Refusing to concede that Hoover's recovery prescriptions had been tried and found wanting, the administration responded to the developments of late 1930 with new Hoover-style organizations and continued resistance to calls for governmental controls and federal relief. In August, the President organized the National Drought Committee to mobilize community-relief machinery in areas hit by the twin scourges of depression and drought. During the same period, the Federal Farm Board established machinery through which it made emergency purchases and conducted acreage-reduction drives for wheat and cotton. In October came the President's Emergency Committee for Employment, intended to serve as a mobilizer, coordinator, and informational clearing house for community-centered or business programs of relief, job creation, and work sharing. Modeled on the organization that Hoover had helped to create following the President's Conference on Unemployment in 1921, the new agency was supposed to relieve distress while preserving local initiative and saving the unemployed from the character-destroying effects of a federal dole. Headed by Arthur Woods, the same man who had headed the 1921 organization, it generated much publicity but was soon under attack for providing press releases rather than jobs and social benefits.

In early 1931, Hoover again declared that this "mobilized voluntary action" was proving its strength, but again he spoke too soon. In the spring of 1931 a financial panic in Europe made the depression a worldwide phenomenon and triggered a further contraction in the United States. Again Hoover's efforts to halt and reverse the contraction were ineffective and seemed only to discredit further his ideas and policies. In July 1931 he secured a one-year suspension of international debt and reparations payments, an arrangement known as the Hoover Moratorium. Yet recovery abroad did not follow, and in the face of continuing contraction at home the administration abandoned further efforts to maintain wage rates and farm prices, took new steps intended to forestall a

federal dole, and focused most of its attention on trying to save the American monetary and banking system. In October the nation's leading financiers were called into conference and persuaded to establish the National Credit Association, intended as a vehicle through which the stronger banks would cooperate to save the weaker ones. But in operation the arrangement proved ineffective, and in December 1931 Hoover urged the creation of a governmental finance corporation modeled on the one that had been established during World War I and empowered to make emergency loans to needy financial institutions.

Hoover's call for emergency federal financing signified a new willingness to support recovery measures involving a larger role for the national government, and in 1932 this became even more apparent. In January he approved legislation creating the RECONSTRUCTION FINANCE CORPORATION, initially authorized to make loans to needy banks and railroads and subsequently to local relief and public works agencies. Also passed in 1932 were laws expanding the lending powers of the Farm Loan and Federal Reserve systems, creating a new system of home loan banks, and authorizing the diversion of Farm Board surpluses to relief purposes. A new network of federal recovery and relief agencies was created to administer such measures. Yet even as the federal government's role expanded, Hoover continued to stress the emergency and supportive nature of this expansion and to place the major reliance for recovery on "mobilized voluntary action" in the private sector. His new economy and budget-balancing measures were intended to encourage such private initiatives, and in August 1932 he took the lead in creating another network of banking and industrial committees as the means of promoting credit expansion and new investment outlays. Recovery, he kept saying, would come through a revival of credit and confidence in the business world, not through raids on the public treasury or the substitution of public for private enterprise.

Yet recovery did not come. A brief upturn in August and September of 1932 was followed by a worsening economic crisis during Hoover's last six months in office, and the great majority of Americans did not agree with Hoover's claim that recovery was being delayed by business fears of the political future and Democratic flirtations with unsound monetary and fiscal proposals. On the contrary, most had come to see Hoover as an obstacle to recovery—clinging stubbornly to a failed political philosophy while doing his best to block more promising forms of action. In his struggle against the Great Depression, Hoover had shown himself to be anything but a do-nothing President, and in his moves toward greater government involvement he had taken actions foreshadowing portions of Franklin D. Roosevelt's NEW DEAL. But his search for recovery had been a failure both economically and politically. The depression had worsened, and in the end he was unable to prevent the forms of governmental intervention that he still regarded as incompatible with a progressive national future.

Meanwhile, the persistence and deepening of the Great Depression had also worked to undermine and discredit Hoover's efforts to make his presidency an instrument of institutional and social reform. He had hoped to use it to continue the task of filling organization and informational gaps that were allegedly responsible for persisting national ills and problems. After the crash, however, such projects were forced to take a back seat to recovery considerations, and increasingly they were seen by critics as inadequate, unrealistic, and intended primarily to block the measures that the nation really needed.

This pattern was particularly characteristic of Hoover's efforts to improve the nation's social welfare and resource conservation systems. In the welfare field, the President's research committee became an industrious amasser of social data, and national conferences were convened on child protection and home ownership. But the followup machinery produced by the conferences accomplished relatively little; most of the grand scheme for a new federal agency to build a better-organized and better-informed system of welfare institutions had to be abandoned; and demands kept growing for expanding the public sector in ways that Hoover continued to oppose. The story was much the same in the conservation field. There the administration was able to get the Hoover Dam project under way, to expand the national park system, and to conduct valuable experiments in improved forestry and oil-reserve management, but its more ambitious designs, particularly those for a national waterway plan, better utilization of the public lands, and new river development projects, were never fulfilled. A treaty with Canada for Saint Lawrence River development was never ratified, and the stalemate that Hoover had inherited on Tennessee River development persisted. He vetoed Senator George Morris's bill for a Tennessee Valley Authority empowered to take over federal facilities at Muscle Shoals and build and operate other multipurpose dams, and he could not persuade Congress to adopt his own plan for a developmental agency composed of private-sector and local government representatives.

Hoover's other reform projects included schemes for reorganizing the executive branch, professionaliz-

ing the federal law enforcement apparatus, and improving the lot of racial minorities. But again, efforts to implement the schemes proved generally unsuccessful, and in reform circles they tended to be regarded as too little, too late. The reorganization plans were all rejected by Congress in 1932. The attack on the problem of crime led only to limited changes in prison practice, administrative procedure, and the judicial appointment process. And the limited efforts to improve INDIAN services, black education, and black business opportunities quickly incurred the enmity and criticism of such militant groups as the Indian Defense Association and the National Association for the Advancement of Colored People (NAACP). They criticized the administration not only for its stinginess but also for its assimilationist attitudes toward Indian cultures, its discrimination against African American soldiers and their families, its decision to embrace "lily-whiteism" in its southern policy, and its lack of concern for lynching atrocities in the South. In 1930 the NAACP strongly opposed the president's appointment of Judge John J. Parker of North Carolina to a vacancy on the Supreme Court, and it subsequently took credit for helping to block senatorial confirmation. The incident was a significant milestone along the route that would eventually take most African Americans out of the REPUBLICAN PARTY.

**Foreign Affairs.** In its conduct of foreign policy, the Hoover administration also found its hopes frustrated, yet it could claim two major diplomatic achievements. One was the London Naval Treaty of 1930, which extended the naval limitations agreed to in Washington, D.C., in 1921 and added a new set of limitations in the previously unrestricted categories of cruisers, destroyers, and submarines. The other was substantial progress in developing a new Latin American policy that foreshadowed the GOOD NEIGHBOR POLICY associated with the presidency of Franklin Roosevelt. Prior to his inauguration, Hoover had toured Latin America, and early in his administration actions were undertaken to upgrade the U.S. diplomatic service in the region, encourage greater inter-American cooperation, and pave the way for military withdrawal from HAITI. The administration also made it clear that the MONROE DOCTRINE would no longer be used to justify police actions in the area, and despite pressures from American investors Hoover rejected proposals for collecting debts by force and allowed the debt defaults and political upheavals caused by economic contraction to run their course without American military intervention. By 1932 the unstable and distressed conditions in Latin America could be cited as evidence of a failed diplomacy, but that diplomacy had also improved relations in ways that contributed to the success of the Good Neighbor initiatives of Hoover's successor.

One of the period's greatest diplomatic challenges was that posed by the impact of the depression on world trade and investment and on the structure of war debts and reparations negotiated after World War I. The real need, so various analysts have argued, was for an international recovery program featuring debt cancellation, emergency credits, tariff revision, joint monetary action, and the United States' acceptance of its responsibility to act as a lender of last resort. But the Hoover administration's willingness to act was limited to the Hoover Moratorium of 1931, a supplementary standstill agreement on repayment of private loans to Germany, and subsequently unsuccessful efforts to negotiate a reduction of land armaments. At times, the administration spoke the language of recovery through international cooperation, but in operation its defense of high protective tariffs, its suspicion of European snares and entanglements, and its insistence on treating debts and reparations as issues unconnected with each other contributed to the economic nationalism that plagued the world throughout the 1930s. Nor was the Hoover administration receptive to schemes for granting diplomatic recognition to the Soviet Union and seeking to develop new markets there. This had the support of sizable segments of the American business community, but Hoover remained opposed on both practical and moral grounds.

Like its immediate predecessors, moreover, the Hoover administration rejected the idea of preserving peace through a system of collective security. It instead placed its faith in such instruments as the World Court, the KELLOGG-BRIAND PACT outlawing aggressive war, and the complex of treaties negotiated at the Washington Conference [see TREATY OF WASHINGTON (1921–1922)], none of which had the enforcement machinery to deal with aggressors. The court, even had it had the American adherence that Hoover was unable to secure, had little prospect of becoming an effective guarantor of international rights and agreements. Invocations of the Kellogg-Briand Pact were of little value in either the Russo-Chinese dispute of 1929 or in the Manchurian crisis of 1931 and 1932. Efforts to invoke the Washington treaty system did nothing to halt Japanese aggression and conquest in Manchuria. The only sanctions applied to Japan were of the moral variety embodied in the Stimson Doctrine of nonrecognition of "immoral" and "illegal" Japanese conquests. Following its enunciation in early 1932, Secretary Stimson wanted to threaten the addition of economic sanctions, but Hoover feared that this would only strengthen the Japanese militarists and decided instead to offer assurances that no such sanctions would be used.

Judged by their larger goals—especially the visions of a world redeemed through American-style business and governmental organization—the Hoover administration's foreign policies were failures. The hopes for a more rational, prosperous, and progressive world were not realized, and nothing effective was done to curb or control the economic and political forces eventually responsible for WORLD WAR II. Recent studies of the period's diplomacy, however, have shown it to be less isolationist, more sophisticated, and more skilled than once thought. And some of its defenders have argued that in its perceptions of the limits of American power and its skepticism about entangling commitments and military solutions it showed more wisdom than the diplomacy that followed.

**Defeat in 1932.** As Hoover's diplomatic, reform, and recovery projects failed, he was also faring badly as a political leader, failing to hold together and govern through the coalition that had elected him. One aspect of the changing political situation was a growing reservoir of anti-Hooverism that produced an increasingly negative presidential image. Another was the rise of antiadministration forces in Congress, reflected in Democratic capture of the House of Representatives in 1930 and in increasingly frequent congressional rebellions against administrative leadership. Still another was eroding Republican Party strength, manifested particularly in the collapse of efforts to make Republicanism respectable in the South, the growth of protest politics in the rural Midwest, and the strong tendency for newly politicized ethnic and labor groups to vote Democratic. Nor were Hoover's political fortunes helped by his actions in July 1932 against the BONUS ARMY of World War I veterans that gathered in Washington to lobby for immediate maturity-value redemption of their bonus insurance certificates. Although historians would subsequently discover that General Douglas MacArthur had violated presidential orders in driving the demonstrators out of their encampment at Anacostia Flats, this was not disclosed at the time. Instead, Hoover tried to defend the action as necessary for dealing with a group increasingly controlled by communists and criminals, and in doing so he opened himself to further charges of hard-heartedness, insensitivity, and paranoia.

At the Republican convention in 1932, Hoover faced a great deal of pessimism but no serious challenges to his renomination. He also believed that in nominating Franklin Roosevelt of New York, the Democrats had provided him with the weakest of several possible opponents. During the campaign that followed, Hoover tried his best to educate citizens concerning his administration's achievements, his critics' political irresponsibility, and the potential "chaos and degeneration" inherent in the proposals and prescriptions of his opponent. His hope for reelection, however, rested mostly on misperceptions concerning Roosevelt's personal qualities and political appeal. In reality, Roosevelt proved to be a highly effective campaigner who succeeded in keeping Hoover on the defensive and taking advantage of the popular desire for change, with the result that the President lost by a larger margin than he had won by four years earlier. On election day he carried only six states, for an electoral count of 59 to Roosevelt's 472. In the popular column the count was 27,821,857 for Roosevelt to only 15,761,841 for Hoover.

The period between Hoover's defeat and Roosevelt's inaugural, a period generally known as the interregnum, became the nadir of the Great Depression. Unemployment climbed to approximately 25 percent of the workforce, and a new banking crisis paralyzed the nation's financial machinery and forced many states to declare bank holidays shutting down their banks or severely restricting their operations. To Hoover the answer lay in a restoration of confidence, and to achieve this he tried, through a series of exchanges with Roosevelt, to commit the incoming administration to a program of budget balancing, sound money, and war-debt renegotiation. Roosevelt, however, refused to make any such commitments, and the change of administrations, on 4 March 1933, came at a time of continuing economic crisis. Hoover's administration, in part because of the burst of activity and change of mood that followed, would enter public memory as a time of despair and defeatism and would continue to be portrayed as such in historical accounts. Largely forgotten were the hopes with which it began, the optimistic innovativeness with which it attempted to short-circuit the business cycle, the reform projects that remained a part of its social agenda, and the interventionist political philosophy that shaped its attitudes concerning proper and improper forms of governmental action.

**The Former President.** As an ex-President, Hoover remained active in Republican Party politics and public policy debates and after 1933 became an outspoken critic of the New Deal, particularly in his *Challenge to Liberty* (1934) and his subsequent "addresses upon the American road." He also took a strong interest in Stanford University, especially in its Food Research Institute and in the Hoover Institution on War, Revolution, and Peace. During the World War II period, he initially supported noninterventionism, tried unsuccessfully to establish food relief programs for popula-

tions in German-occupied countries, and sought but was denied a role in the war government. After the war, he became associated with groups advocating minimal punishment and an early peace treaty for Japan, economic reconstruction for Germany, and a "fortress America" as the best defense against the communist threat. As attitudes toward him mellowed, Hoover became a venerable elder statesman who served successively as coordinator of the European Food Program in 1947, chairman of the Commission for Reorganization of the Executive Branch from 1947 to 1949, and chairman of a second Commission on Reorganization from 1953 to 1955 [*see* HOOVER COMMISSIONS]. In addition, he published his memoirs, wrote histories of the Wilson administration and America's post–World War I relief operations, and worked on but failed to publish a history of communist influences on the West. He died on 24 October 1964 and is buried on a hillside in West Branch, Iowa, near his birthplace and the presidential library that houses his papers.

Among historians the nature of Hoover's presidency and its place in American history have remained controversial matters. Since the 1960s, however, the lines of controversy have tended to shift from negative-versus-positive portrayals of Hoover as an anti-Roosevelt to disputes about the efficacy and wisdom of Hoover's progressivism as opposed to the New Deal variety. The major accomplishment of revisionist scholarship has been to recover and document the managerial, organizational, and reformist dimensions of the Hoover administration, thus undercutting the premises of "rugged individualism" that underlay both the older liberal and the older conservative positions. There has been continuing disagreement, however, about the wisdom and workability of the Hooverian alternative to the New Deal state. Some revisionists, particularly those most critical of New Deal reform, have been impressed by Hoover's designs for containing the bureaucratic state through changes in private-sector and community institutions. But most studies of the Hoover system in action have concluded that the mechanisms envisioned or created were inadequate to deal with the problems they sought to solve. While supporting the view of the Hoover presidency as progressive and interventionist, such studies still see it as a failed presidency, economically, politically, diplomatically, and ideologically.

## BIBLIOGRAPHY

Barber, William J. *From New Era to New Deal: Herbert Hoover, the Economists, and American Economic Policy, 1921–1933.* 1985.
Burner, David. *Herbert Hoover: A Public Life.* 1979.
DeConde, Alexander. *Herbert Hoover's Latin American Policy.* 1951.

Dodge, Mark M., ed. *Herbert Hoover and the Historians*. 1989.

Fausold, Martin L. *The Presidency of Herbert C. Hoover*. 1985.

Ferrell, Robert H. *American Diplomacy in the Great Depression: Hoover-Stimson Foreign Policy, 1929–1933*. 1957.

Hamilton, David E. *From New Day to New Deal: American Farm Policy from Hoover to Roosevelt, 1928–1933*. 1991.

Hoff-Wilson, Joan. *Herbert Hoover: Forgotten Progressive*. 1975.

Nash, George H. *The Life of Herbert Hoover*. 2 vols. 1983, 1988.

Romasco, Albert U. *The Poverty of Abundance: Hoover, the Nation, the Depression*. 1965.

Schwarz, Jordan A. *The Interregnum of Despair: Hoover, Congress, and the Depression*. 1970.

ELLIS W. HAWLEY

**HOOVER, J. EDGAR** (1895–1972), Director of the Federal Bureau of Investigation. Appointed Director of the Bureau of Investigation in 1924, John Edgar Hoover inherited a scandal-ridden agency (renamed the FEDERAL BUREAU OF INVESTIGATION in 1935) enmeshed in controversy precipitated by findings of 1920–1924 of abusive investigative activities. Therefore, the new director was to be subject to the direct supervision of the Attorney General, and the agency's role was to be limited to investigating violations of federal statutes. Hoover moved quickly to lift the cloud of scandal by upgrading qualifications for bureau personnel and instituting administrative procedures to ensure accountability. With time the FBI's influence expanded and Hoover came to be feared or revered as an all-powerful official (although he was theoretically subordinate to the Attorney General). This increased influence was largely the result of Hoover's relation with successive Presidents, a relationship based not on personal friendship but on a shared interest in expanding FBI investigative authority.

On the one hand, executive directives triggered the FBI's expanded role beyond seeking information of federal statutory violations. In a secret meeting with Hoover in August 1936, President Franklin Roosevelt requested a report on "fascist and communistic" activities; following up on a June 1939 directive, in September 1939 Roosevelt directed the FBI to take charge of investigations involving espionage, sabotage, and violations of neutrality laws and, more important, to receive information from local police agencies (and, after 1943, from patriotic citizens) pertaining to "subversive activities." Hoover interpreted these presidential directives as authorizing the FBI to collect noncriminal information about dissident and radical activists. The FBI's monitoring of subversive activities acquired further legitimacy from executive orders issued by President Harry S. Truman in 1947 and by

President Dwight D. Eisenhower in 1953, requiring security clearances for incumbent and applicant federal employees. Under Hoover's direction, the resulting FBI security investigations extended to compiling massive internal security files on any individual or organization suspected of "potential disloyalty," given that current and future security dismissals were to be based on ascertainment of such evidence.

Concurrently, President Roosevelt by a secret directive of May 1940 authorized FBI "national defense" wiretapping, despite the 1934 Federal Communication Act's ban. President Truman unknowingly expanded this wiretapping authorization in July 1946, by signing a letter drafted by Hoover but sent by Attorney General Tom Clark, ostensibly seeking his reaffirmation of Roosevelt's 1940 directive. In May 1954, President Eisenhower's Attorney General, HERBERT BROWNELL, authorized Hoover to approve microphone installations (bugging), put in place by means of trespass, during NATIONAL SECURITY investigations. In both areas of wiretapping and bugging, the secret method of authorization, and the insistence of Attorneys General that this practice not become known provided leeway quickly exploited by Hoover to expand FBI ELECTRONIC SURVEILLANCE, sometimes without the Attorney General's prior authorization; installed taps and bugs, moreover, were never reauthorized. This practice continued until Attorney General NICHOLAS deB. KATZENBACH instituted new rules in 1965 requiring the Attorney General's prior authorization and reauthorization of all taps and bugs. Congress's legalization of wiretapping and bugging in 1968, however, and the broad claim of "inherent" presidential national security powers made by the administration of Richard M. Nixon subverted Katzenbach's restrictions. The Nixon administration also pressured Hoover to expand FBI investigative activities, even if they were "clearly illegal" as under the aborted Huston Plan of July 1970.

Under Hoover's careful supervision, however, including institution of separate record-keeping procedures for politically sensitive reports, the FBI assumed the character of an intelligence arm of the White House. Whether responding to presidential requests for reports on critics of presidential policies or for investigations of the source of leaks or volunteering similar information to the White House, Hoover provided intelligence that serviced presidential political and policy interests. Because this reporting bypassed the Attorney General, Hoover's independence was enhanced. The sensitivity of some requests also limited the ability of Presidents to oversee Hoover's agency—these included Roosevelt's 1940 request for information about former Republican President Herbert

Hoover, Truman's 1945 request for investigations about the "disloyalty" of Roosevelt holdovers in the executive branch, Lyndon Baines Johnson's 1964 request leading to the dispatch of a thirty-man FBI squad to the Democratic National Convention, and Nixon's 1970 request for a list of homosexuals "and other stuff" on members of the Washington press corps. Presidential tolerance of the FBI's surveillance of noncriminal activities invited Hoover to compile information about suspect political and immoral activities of even Presidents and their families (including John F. Kennedy, Dwight D. Eisenhower, ELEANOR ROOSEVELT), members of Congress, and influential public leaders and reporters (such as ADLAI E. STEVENSON and Joseph Alsop).

This presidential support continued even in the wake of the disclosures of the mid 1970s of the scope of Hoover's abuses. Responding to demands to preclude future abuses, the only restrictions instituted after 1975 were by executive order—whether the restrictive guidelines issued by Attorney General Edward Levi in March 1976 or the permissive March 1983 guidelines of Attorney General William French Smith.

### BIBLIOGRAPHY

Gentry, Curt. *J. Edgar Hoover: The Man and the Secrets.* 1991.
Powers, Richard. *Secrecy and Power: The Life of J. Edgar Hoover.* 1987.
Theoharis, Athan, and John Stuart Cox. *The Boss: J. Edgar Hoover and the Great American Inquisition.* 1988.

ATHAN G. THEOHARIS

**HOOVER COMMISSIONS.** In the immediate aftermath of WORLD WAR II, there was a fairly broad consensus favoring governmental "retrenchment." Such sentiment had its origins both in earlier Progressive doctrine stressing economy and efficiency in government and in the obvious need to reevaluate the administration of numerous agencies and programs in the wake of the depression, the war, and demobilization. Congress responded to this situation by establishing two commissions to study the organization and management of the executive branch. The first (1947–1949) and second (1953–1955) Hoover Commissions were so named because they were both chaired by former President Herbert Hoover.

**The First Commission.** In 1946, Republicans took control of both the House and Senate while the White House remained occupied by a Democrat, Harry S. Truman. In the new Congress, legislation (61 Stat. 246) was passed unanimously to establish a commission to make recommendations on how best to reorganize the executive branch. The commission, formally titled the Commission on Organization of the Executive Branch of the Government, was to be a "mixed commission" composed of appointees named by both the President and Congress, with an even number of Republicans and Democrats.

Much of the commission's first year was spent debating its mandate. Were the recommendations to be confined to management and structural changes to improve the performance of government, or should the commission become involved in policy questions such as recommending the elimination of agencies and programs? For all practical purposes this debate was settled by the 1948 presidential election, when Truman unexpectedly won reelection. From that point on, Hoover and the commission shifted their emphasis from retrenchment to the enhancement of the managerial authority of the President and his departmental secretaries. Truman, although protective of the residuals of the NEW DEAL, was also sympathetic to the scientific management ideals of Progressivism. Therefore, his and Hoover's philosophies were not far apart.

Early on, the commission divided its job among task forces, each with its own staff. This decision was crucial because it influenced, if it did not actually predetermine, the thrust of the analyses and recommendations the committee would consider. Each task force submitted its report with recommendations to the commission. No single commission report was written and forwarded to the President and Congress; rather, nineteen separate reports were submitted over three months, the final report in May 1949. These reports were later compiled into a single document and published by a private firm.

The doctrine underlying most of the recommendations was that responsibility for making policy and setting standards ought to be centralized in the President, central managerial agencies, and department secretaries rather than being devolved to the agency level. The commission criticized the tendency toward dispersing functions to independent agencies and called for a renewed, hierarchical structure. The commission was generally pleased with the development of the EXECUTIVE OFFICE OF THE PRESIDENT (EOP) and recommended that the EOP's units be strengthened.

The record of acceptance of commission recommendations was impressive. A number of major laws were passed based on commission recommendations, for example, the Federal Property and Administrative Services Act (63 Stat. 377), which created the General Services Administration. Concentrating on the reorganization of departments, agencies, and certain functions, however, tends to obscure what was to many the principal accomplishment of the first Hoover Commission, namely the enhancement of the presidential office as manager of the executive branch.

**The Second Commission.** Critics of government growth were somewhat disappointed with the results of the first Hoover Commission, however, and eagerly sought a second Hoover Commission when the Republicans took over the White House and both Houses of Congress in 1953. This time the commission was to go after the "roots of big government" and eliminate programs and agencies if necessary. President Dwight D. Eisenhower unenthusiastically signed the bill (67 Stat. 184) passed unanimously by Congress to create a second Hoover Commission patterned largely after the earlier commission. As was his political style, Eisenhower created an alternate commission, the President's Advisory Committee on Government Organization (PACGO), chaired by NELSON A. ROCKEFELLER, to give him a counterbalancing stream of assistance and recommendations.

The very nature of the second commission's philosophy ensured that its results would not receive as favorable a reception as had those of the first commission. Its terms of reference were broad and ill-defined, and the timing of its report was miscalculated. Indeed, the mood of the country had shifted away from retrenchment and toward greater governmental involvement in the economic and social spheres.

The second commission was never able to write a single, comprehensive report; rather, it submitted a number of edited task-force reports to the President and Congress. The premises underlying the reports and the recommendations of the task forces were not all in agreement, so there were doctrinal inconsistencies and disputes. Supporters of the commission, however, kept track of the fate of its 314 specific recommendations and were pleased with the statistical results if not the policy consequences.

In the opinion of many observers, the fundamental deficiency of the second commission was that, unlike the earlier BROWNLOW COMMITTEE (1937) and the first Hoover Commission, it lacked an "administrative model" for evaluating recommendations. Goals and means were conceptually confused in the task force reports. The standard terms of discourse associated with the Progressive era—"economy and efficiency," "streamlining," and so on—were of decreasing utility in improving executive organization and management at midcentury.

In retrospect, the executive branch appears to have been reasonably well managed during the 1940s and 1950s. The managerial agencies (e.g., the Bureau of the Budget) were at the zenith of their strength. While a number of factors may be cited as contributing to this felicitous situation, it would be unfair to ignore the contributions of the two Hoover Commissions. The first commission, especially, argued from first principles stressing the need for political and managerial accountability and clear lines of responsibility. All proposals for change, in the first commission's view, should be measured by whether or not they enhance those values. The influence of the two Hoover Commissions and their administrative philosophy lasted for about two decades.

BIBLIOGRAPHY

Arnold, Peri. *Making the Managerial Presidency: Comprehensive Reorganization Planning 1905–1980.* 1986.

Moe, Ronald C. *The Hoover Commissions Revisited.* 1982.

Pemberton, William E. *Bureaucratic Politics: Executive Reorganization during the Truman Administration.* 1979.

Seidman, Harold. *Politics, Position, and Power: From the Positive to the Regulatory State.* 4th ed. 1986.

U.S. Commission on Organization of the Executive Branch of the Government. *Hoover Commission Report.* 1949.

RONALD C. MOE

**HOPKINS, HARRY** (1890–1946), relief administrator, presidential adviser. One of the premier presidential aides of his century, Harry Lloyd Hopkins possessed the human sympathy, objectivity, and ability to dissect issues necessary to understand President Franklin D. Roosevelt's methods and goals and achieve them with unsurpassed originality and skill.

Roosevelt chose Hopkins to head the Federal Emergency Relief Administration, which allocated funds to the states for unemployment relief in the Great Depression. During the winter of 1933–1934, Hopkins organized a massive program of federal work relief, which in the form of the WORKS PROGRESS ADMINISTRATION (WPA) became the administration's principal weapon against the depression. Hopkins supported Roosevelt by allocating projects and leaders to local officials who supported the NEW DEAL. He also supported organized labor, another key element in the New Deal coalition, and was an eloquent spokesman for all Americans' right to rewarding employment.

When WORLD WAR II erupted, Roosevelt appointed Hopkins special assistant to organize lend-lease aid. Skilled at winning others' confidence, Hopkins created "the Hopkins Shop," a complex web of interests and relationships that coordinated allocations with military strategy and strengthened U.S. relations with Great Britain and the Soviet Union.

At the major summit conferences of World War II, Hopkins emerged as an important figure in U.S.

diplomacy. In 1944 he extended his influence directly into the conduct of foreign policy by moving members of his lend-lease team into key State Department positions. At the YALTA CONFERENCE in February 1945 Hopkins and his diplomatic team helped Roosevelt pursue an overall U.S. strategy of becoming the broker between Great Britain and the Soviet Union.

After Roosevelt's death, President Harry S. Truman sent Hopkins to Moscow to resolve issues that had deadlocked the UNITED NATIONS conference in San Francisco. Hopkins won Soviet concessions on the vital issues, and the conference was successfully carried on.

BIBLIOGRAPHY

McJimsey, George. *Harry Hopkins: Ally of the Poor and Defender of Democracy.* 1987.
Sherwood, Robert E. *Roosevelt and Hopkins.* 1953.

GEORGE MCJIMSEY

**HOT-LINE AGREEMENT.** The hot line is a special teletype circuit linking Washington and Moscow, which speeds communication between Russian—originally Soviet—leaders and American Presidents. Installed on 30 August 1963, the hot line reduces the danger of delay and misunderstanding.

The American terminus of the hot line is located in the offices of the JOINT CHIEFS OF STAFF, and the other terminus is in the Kremlin. The 7,100-mile-long circuit stemmed from a Memorandum of Understanding between American and Soviet representatives on 20 June 1963. The system's primary circuit, a duplex cable, permits simultaneous transmission in both directions between Washington and Moscow.

The need for the hot line became evident during the 1962 CUBAN MISSILE CRISIS when four hours were required to transmit messages, including time for translation, coding, decoding, and customary diplomatic presentation, between President John F. Kennedy and President Nikita Khruschev. The hot line was activated in the 1967 Middle East Six Day War, when President Lyndon B. Johnson moved to head off the Soviet's possible intrusion. President Richard M. Nixon used the hot line in the India-Pakistan crisis of 1971 and the 1973 Middle East War.

President Lyndon B. Johnson valued the hot line as a means of immediately engaging the Soviet head of government and his top advisers, but the rapidity of communication necessitated extra care in weighing words and phrases. Since the 1970s, with the improved communications facilities of the embassies, the hot line has worked more slowly and is little used or needed.

BIBLIOGRAPHY

Johnson, Lyndon Baines. *The Vantage Point.* 1971.
Kissinger, Henry. *White House Years.* 1979.
Sorensen, Theodore C. *Kennedy.* 1965.

LOUIS W. KOENIG

**HOUSE, EDWARD M.** (1858–1938), presidential adviser, diplomatic representative. House was Woodrow Wilson's chief adviser and negotiator in ending WORLD WAR I and formulating the peace treaty.

A man of inherited wealth, Edward Mandell House, known as Colonel House (an honorary title from Texas), had acquired a taste for politics while serving as an unpaid campaign manager and political adviser to four governors of his native state of Texas between 1892 and 1902. Although House first met Woodrow Wilson on 24 November 1911, he played only a minor role in Wilson's presidential nomination and election campaign of 1912. However, their personal friendship developed rapidly after the November election and House soon became Wilson's most trusted political adviser. They worked closely together in the selection of Wilson's Cabinet, and House was active in the passage of Wilson's legislative program in 1913–1914. House always preferred to work behind the scenes; he never desired an official government position.

House's interest began to shift toward foreign policy as early as 1913, and after the outbreak of World War I, he became Wilson's most important adviser on foreign affairs. Wilson sent him on informal diplomatic missions to Europe as early as 1914; after the war began, he was sent to implement Wilson's repeated efforts to mediate the conflict and bring about a negotiated peace. Following the entrance of the United States into the war in 1917, House was heavily involved in negotiations with the western European nations allied against Germany. In September and October 1917, at Wilson's request House set up an organization of experts, known as The Inquiry, to study problems that would arise in a future peace settlement. House's greatest diplomatic moment occurred in November 1918 when he persuaded British and French leaders to accept an armistice with Germany based on Wilson's FOURTEEN POINTS address to Congress 8 January 1918.

Wilson gave House the only official position of his career when he appointed him one of the five American commissioners to negotiate peace. Wilson himself headed the mission and House worked closely with him on such projects as the LEAGUE OF NATIONS covenant during the first weeks in Paris. When Wilson returned to the United States in February 1919, he left

House in charge of the negotiations. When the President returned to Paris in March, he was horrified to discover that House had conceded many demands of the British and French, most notably in agreeing to separate the League covenant from the peace treaty with Germany. Wilson had great difficulty in recovering the lost ground and his friendship with House, and hence House's political influence, deteriorated rapidly. The two men never saw each other again after Wilson sailed for the United States in June 1919.

### BIBLIOGRAPHY

Floto, Inga. *Colonel House in Paris: A Study of American Policy at the Paris Peace Conference 1919.* 1973. Reprint ed. 1980.

George, Alexander L., and Juliette L. George. *Woodrow Wilson and Colonel House: A Personality Study.* 1956. Reprint ed. 1964.

Neu, Charles E. "Woodrow Wilson and Colonel House: The Early Years, 1911–1915." In *The Wilson Era: Essays in Honor of Arthur S. Link.* Edited by John Milton Cooper, Jr., and Charles E. Neu. 1991.

JOHN E. LITTLE

**HOUSING AND URBAN DEVELOPMENT, DEPARTMENT OF.** The first presidential policy initiatives in the field of housing and urban development were relatively straightforward and modest both in program and organizational arrangements. They were about housing per se—not urban development—and they were advanced in pursuit of the grander objectives of peace and prosperity. Programs were lodged in agencies, not departments, and Presidents gave them only sporadic attention.

**Federal Housing Programs.** Publicly supported federal housing first appeared during WORLD WAR I under the auspices of the U.S. Housing Corporation, whose mandate was first to build and then to liquidate housing for war workers (the corporation endured until 1942). Later, in the NEW DEAL years, the Federal Housing Administration (FHA) was created (1934) to direct federal mortgage insurance programs (the Farmers Home Administration and the Veterans Administration would subsequently carry out similar programs). In 1937 the U.S. Housing Authority was established to provide grants and loans to local public housing authorities. In 1942 Franklin D. Roosevelt created the National Housing Agency in a partly successful effort to unify these scattered efforts, and a few years later Harry S. Truman undertook a similar reorganization, establishing the Housing and Home Finance Agency (HHFA). Throughout these years, however, housing remained the principal mission assigned to these agencies, and federal involvement in housing was justified principally on the grounds of war needs or economic recovery.

*Secretaries of Housing and Urban Development*

| President | Secretary of Housing and Urban Development |
|---|---|
| 36 L. B. Johnson | Robert C. Weaver, 1966–1968<br>Robert C. Wood, 1969 |
| 37 Nixon | George W. Romney, 1969–1973<br>James T. Lynn, 1973–1974 |
| 38 Ford | James T. Lynn, 1974–1975<br>Carla Anderson Hills, 1975–1977 |
| 39 Carter | Patricia Roberts Harris, 1977–1979<br>Moon Landrieu, 1979–1981 |
| 40 Reagan | Samuel R. Pierce, Jr., 1981–1989 |
| 41 Bush | Jack F. Kemp, 1989–1993 |
| 42 Clinton | Henry G. Cisneros, 1993– |

The impetus for the establishment of the Cabinet-level Department of Housing and Urban Development (HUD) was different. The 1950s witnessed a growing concern for cities, their fiscal stability, and the health of urban communities. Creating decent housing remained a central part of HUD's program, but a broader set of urban concerns was now surfacing. Strong and vigorous leadership by the mayors of major American cities, for the first time in league with downtown business executives, was stimulated to action by the 1954 Housing Act, which authorized the federal urban renewal program. The mayors' and business leaders' calls for federal attention were supported by the analyses of social scientists, who in the 1950s "discovered" cities and, using new empirical methods of research, forecast that the quality of urban life was at risk. These two forces—the new breed of politically powerful and policy-oriented big city mayors and business leaders and the new breed of articulate, policy-oriented academics—combined forces to lobby for the cities' having a place at the Cabinet table. During the 1960 campaign, they persuaded John F. Kennedy to commit himself to a new urban program and a new department to carry it out.

At the recommendation of his pre-inauguration task force, President Kennedy tried to keep his commitment. He overrode objections from the professional staff in the EXECUTIVE OFFICE OF THE PRESIDENT and proposed the new department to Congress. But Kennedy had appointed Robert Weaver, an African American, as the administrator of HHFA (Weaver was at that time the highest-ranking black in the executive branch). Chiefly because of this, southern members of Congress, anticipating that Weaver would be named thus the first black Cabinet member, killed the Kennedy proposal. It remained for Lyndon B. Johnson to persuade Congress to agree to the establishment of HUD, which he did in 1965—in the euphoric early period of the GREAT SOCIETY.

**A Confusion of Purposes.** HUD's establishment, however, did not make clear its central purpose. Rather, it confused it. Senator Abraham Ribicoff, the leader of the Senate fight to establish the department, under pressure from mortgage bankers and home builders insisted that housing programs maintain a separate identity. They were to be "coordinated" with other urban programs. Mayors and community and academic leaders pressed for the primacy of general urban interests, going so far as to propose the elimination of the word *housing* from the department's title. (They dropped this proposal when a White House task force pointed out the acronym would then be DUD.)

HUD's departmental structure reflected its conflict of purposes and the ambivalence over its goals. HUD absorbed the same constituent units of HHFA, with the FHA accorded quasi-autonomous status, plus two new programs of rent supplements as well as the Model Cities program. Rather than HUD's being a coordinating office, as the legislation had mandated, a presidential EXECUTIVE ORDER authorized the department to be a "convenor" of other departments with urban interests. HUD did not absorb the fledgling antipoverty program (the Office of Economic Opportunity), then an Executive Office agency. Neither were urban environmental programs nor the farm and veteran home loan guarantee programs transferred to the new department.

With an incomplete portfolio, insufficient to convey the image of an organization equally concerned with social as well as physical urban issues, HUD remained bifurcated. Its early years were marked by continuing presidential interest and concern, by major legislative victories, especially in the 1966 and 1968 Housing and Urban Development Acts, and by vigorous program execution (although this was hamstrung by dwindling appropriations as the VIETNAM WAR escalated). But in the tumultuous events of the late 1960s HUD had neither a honeymoon cruise nor a shakedown.

The administrations that followed Johnson's were ideologically and rhetorically hostile to the Kennedy-Johnson emphasis on cities. Yet, somewhat ironically, HUD fared well. Richard M. Nixon's first HUD Secretary, George Romney, embraced and energetically executed the main provisions of the 1968 act, although some of the private housing construction authorized proved ill advised. Romney's successors maintained relatively low profiles, but a substantial pipeline of projects kept the major programs active, albeit with new names, until well into the Carter administration. Even as the department dropped from public view, congressional appropriations continued to increase. What constrained HUD in the Carter years was not ideology but inflation, the oil crisis, and the IRANIAN HOSTAGE CRISIS, all of which diverted attention from domestic programs.

The Reagan administration, which had neither ideological nor program sympathy for HUD, savaged the department. Ideologically, the New Federalism, which mandated the devolution of formerly federal responsibilities to the states, left little room for a national role in urban affairs. Programmatically, HUD's operating budget fell 57 percent, the largest cut suffered by any federal department during the Reagan years. Program cuts in federally assisted housing, community block grants, and urban development action grants were similarly reduced. Even worse for the department's reputation, a series of scandals lost an estimated $2 billion dollars to fraud and mismanagement. The department's record of passivity in legislative initiatives and low visibility throughout the tenure of Secretary Samuel Pierce compounded the pattern of failure.

**HUD's Cabinet Status.** During the Bush administration Secretary Jack Kemp brought vigorous leadership to the department, and the 1990 Housing and Urban Development Act represented the first comprehensive strategy in a generation to provide affordable housing, encourage home ownership, and undertake to empower the poor. The central issue, as throughout the 1980s, was whether appropriations sufficient to respond to the needs of cities would be forthcoming. In 1992, even after the Chicago flood and the Los Angeles riots, that issue remained unresolved.

With more than twenty years of departmental experience to review and the tenures of nine secretaries to appraise, what reckoning can be made of the tenth Cabinet department? As far as HUD's organizational status is concerned, the department never received sustained presidential attention except during the Johnson administration. Not only was its secretary never a member of the "inner" CABINET (i.e., the counselors to the President), but, in terms of political power, Washington observers rank HUD close to the bottom of the "outer" Cabinet, where secretaries are often reduced to being advocates of particularistic interests—pleaders not counselors—and are frequently written off as mere captives of their clienteles.

Judged internally, HUD was still beset by internal controversy: housing programs still vied with more general urban development programs for the attention of the secretary and to secure a priority position in budget and staffing. Unlike the staffs of the State, Defense, and Health and Human Services departments, HUD's senior professional staffs could claim no particular expertise nor superior knowledge of problems or prescriptions for their solution. The FOR-

EIGN SERVICE, the military, and government health professionals all enjoy such status, but HUD's knowledge of housing and urban affairs, mostly resting in the disciplines of economics and sociology, is challenged by its clients in the housing industry and local governments and by experts in think tanks and universities. Neither the statistics HUD produces nor the reports it issues enjoy a special stamp of superiority.

Moreover, HUD's jurisdiction is limited, as other housing and community facility programs are assigned to the departments of Agriculture, Interior, Labor, Health and Human Resources, and Transportation. The loss of the mass transportation programs, which HUD originally administered, to the DEPARTMENT OF TRANSPORTATION sharply restricted HUD's capacity for strategic urban planning. Moreover, the Treasury Department, in setting interest rates, has a critical impact on the prosperity of the housing industry but is often indifferent to it. When the Treasury assumed responsibility for President Nixon's revenue-sharing program, HUD's prestige again suffered severely.

HUD's clienteles do not compensate for the department's low status. The building industry, comprising homebuilders, realtors, mortgage financiers, unions, and building goods manufacturers, is the most potent, but even these interests lose out when the well-being of the national economy is at stake. Further, they tend to tilt HUD toward housing policy and away from urban development. The mayors, community development leaders, housing consumers, and representatives of the urban poor are much less influential, inside or outside Washington.

In the early 1990s, HUD remained a department that had not succeeded in establishing clear and mutually reinforcing goals. It aided housing chiefly by subsidizing interest rates, not by addressing the problems of spiraling land costs or the potential of new technology to transform the building industry. It had lost ground in jurisdictional turf battles within the executive branch, just as the cities had lost ground to the states in the receipt and management of federal grants. Without a President willing to back a new urban initiative and reorganization plan to pull the fragmented urban programs together, HUD faced the prospect of a continuing long, cold slide toward mediocrity in the quality of its leadership and administrative skill and the relevance of its programs to the urban ills it was created to alleviate.

[*See also* HOUSING POLICY.]

### BIBLIOGRAPHY

Hanson, Royce. *The Evolution of National Urban Policy, 1970–80: Lessons From the Past.* 1982.

Kaplan, Marshall, and Franklin James. *Federal Housing Agencies and National Housing Policies.* 1988.

Orlebeke, Charles J. "Chasing Urban Policy: A Critical Retrospect." In *The Future of National Urban Policy.* Edited by Marshall Kaplan and James Franklin. 1990.

Peterson, George E., and Carol W. Lewis, eds. *Reagan and the Cities.* 1986.

Redford, Emmette S., and Marlan Blisset. *Organizing the Executive Branch: The Johnson Presidency.* 1981.

Weaver, Robert C. "The First Twenty Years of HUD." *American Planning Association Journal* 51 (1985): 463–474.

ROBERT WOOD

**HOUSING POLICY.** From the vantage of the American presidency, housing policy is a Johnny-come-lately to the national agenda of executive branch concerns, appearing only in the 1940s. More precisely, when housing has occasionally squirmed its way onto the agenda, it has frequently come covertly, under the wraps of a larger national purpose—as part of a national recovery program, for example, or of a grateful country's partial reward to its veterans. Further, during the 1960s a convergence of tumultous political events blurred distinctions between CIVIL RIGHTS POLICY, urban policy, and housing policy and blended all three into the legislative programs of the GREAT SOCIETY. Finally, in a housing industry that, superficially, is a textbook model of laissez-faire economics but that nonetheless requires substantial subsidies, a long-standing policy debate has divided supply-side policy advocates from demand-side proponents. The recognition of these four attributes of housing policy—its comparative newness, its frequent disguise as "higher" policy, its conflation with other national endeavors, and the theoretical economic controversy that has plagued it—is the beginning of wisdom in understanding how America houses, or does not house, its people.

**Toward National Policy.** Until sporadic national initiatives appeared, housing was (and still largely remains) the province of the private sector. In post–CIVIL WAR industrializing America, business built cities. Jobs were created and households located as a result of thousands upon thousands of individual economic decisions—decisions about land use and prices, industrial and service investments, market calculations and exploitation. The marketplace reigned supreme, and the provision of public facilities and services followed its decision.

In the late nineteenth century the housing industry seemed the epitome of classical capitalist economics. A large number of home-builders appeared: originally members of the respective crafts, carpenters, masons, then plumbers and electricians, graduated to the ranks of general contractors and increasingly worked in league with architects as townhouses and apartment houses replaced cottages. A large number of home buyers appeared as well, as the American commitment to home ownership became embedded in the culture with an ideological life of its own, so that by the turn of the century a majority of families were in fact home owners.

The public sector first intervened at the local level in 1916, with the pioneering New York City zoning law. The Herbert Hoover administration made a tentative effort to nationalize zoning and building code standards, but the Great Depression and WORLD WAR II were the real catalysts for federal involvement in housing. The National Housing Act (1934) provided federal housing insurance for home mortgages; the Wagner-Steagall Act (1937) provided federal low-interest loans to aid local public housing authorities; and the Lanham Act (1940) mandated the construction of houses for wartime workers. These laws were enacted not to declare a public interest in housing per se but rather as financial supports to insolvent bank systems, as public works to speed economic recovery, and as part of the "arsenal of democracy" that would defeat the Axis powers.

Even the "mother of all housing laws," the Housing Act of 1949, which for the first time contained an explicit commitment that all Americans should have "a decent home in a suitable environment," was justified by its key sponsors, Senators Paul Douglas and Robert Taft, in grander terms. As the legislative record shows, their objectives were to help veterans find homes in suburbia and to restore city public housing and slum neighborhoods neglected during the war.

In the 1950s federal interest in housing continued to be indirect. Presidential attention was forthcoming, yet, ironically, federal initiatives in downtown renewal and highways during these years actually decreased the stock of urban housing. At the same time, mortgage insurance continued to underwrite the suburban explosion and made possible the privately developed mass-produced tract home construction that Levittown, Long Island, came to symbolize as well as the now-obsolete shopping centers that pockmark the former outskirts of metropolitan regions.

To his credit, President Dwight D. Eisenhower opposed building interstate expressways through the core cities and supported urban renewal primarily as an effort to restore downtown retail areas. Nonetheless, the net effect of "urban renewal" was a sharp reduction in affordable housing for low- and moderate-income families in the cities. In the 1960s, this process of loss was stepped up: as the highway and renewal programs moved into full swing, the overall

housing inventory reduction was 6.4 million units, or 10.7 percent.

**Expansion of Housing Programs.** With the housing industry clearly in trouble and central-city populations dropping precipitously in the 1960s, Presidents and their administrations acknowledged for the first time a national public interest in housing per se. John F. Kennedy's preinaugural task force on housing, followed by Lyndon B. Johnson's two task forces on urban and metropolitan problems, initiated a series of new programs that year after year expanded the federal role in housing.

Under Kennedy the relocation of families displaced by renewal projects was subsidized and for the first time the private sector was encouraged by subsidies to build housing for low- and moderate-income families. Johnson first extended aid in the rent-supplement program, then in the 1966 Demonstration Cities and Metropolitan Development Act (better known as Model Cities), and, finally, capped the decade's effort with the massive quantitative commitment of the 1968 Housing and Urban Development Act. This law authorized the construction of twenty-six million housing units over the following ten years, six million of them earmarked for poor families. In the same year, the Fair Housing Act introduced a desegregation component to all programs under the aegis of the DEPARTMENT OF HOUSING AND URBAN DEVELOPMENT, the establishment of which had first been proposed by Kennedy and which had finally been effected under Johnson in 1965. The 1966 and 1968 acts were breakthrough presidential commitments, designed to fulfill, twenty years later, the 1949 Housing Act's declaration that every American family was entitled "to a decent home in a suitable environment."

To date (1992) the 1968 act has proven to be the high-water mark of housing policy. Under Richard M. Nixon's HUD Secretary, George Romney, the department moved expeditiously to meet the annual schedules necessary to complete the ten-year goal of twenty-six million units, and for a time succeeded. Nixon, however, declared the urban crisis solved, and although the NEW FRONTIER and the Great Society programs continued under different names well into the Jimmy Carter administration, presidential attention to domestic matters shifted to ENVIRONMENTAL POLICY.

Throughout the 1970s housing policy remained entangled with civil rights and urban policy. The Fair Housing Act of 1968 was explicit in its efforts to open suburban communities to minority families. As community development and block grants came into play alongside housing programs in the 1974 Housing and Urban Development Act, HUD's focus was still perceived as big-city oriented. Although President Carter continued most of the housing initiatives of the 1960s, the oil crisis and the spiraling inflation of the late 1970s sharply limited housing starts, especially city-subsidized ones. Moreover, in the 1970s the first explicit confrontation among supply-side and demand-side experts broke out with the enactment of "voucher" programs advocated by the supply siders, especially those made available to poor urban families who rented their homes.

So the confusion worsened. Was HUD's major mission to provide housing assistance for the majority of homeowners as well as for the poor? Was its focus to be urban development, with special attention to urban neighborhood rehabilitation? Were HUD's programs a critical component in civil rights strategy—ensuring free access by minorities to all housing markets and so lightening the burden of court-mandated school desegregation? So far as presidential policy was concerned, the 1970s—Nixon, Gerald Ford, and Carter—gave mixed signals.

**Under Reagan and Bush.** In the 1980s the Ronald Reagan administration showed no hesitation in clarifying housing policy. First, the private market would prevail; in Reagan's first six years, authorizations for federal housing subsidies fell from $30 billion to $7.9 billion. Second, insofar as housing subsidies were to exist, they should come in the form of vouchers, regardless of what vacancy rates for affordable housing might be. Third, the largest building subsidies, effected by the tax breaks of the 1981 Tax Act and the banking deregulation laws of 1983, went to commercial, not residential, building—a ninefold increase of off-budget tax incentives from $2 billion to $19 billion. A massive boom in nonresidential construction and high-income condominiums resulted, while the 1986 Tax Reform Act effectively shut the door on tax credits for subsidized housing. Another result was the collapse of the savings and loan industry, which had naively ventured into the commercial real estate market and been corrupted by it [see SAVINGS AND LOAN DEBACLE].

The George Bush administration's principal housing policy was contained in the 1990 Housing and Urban Development Act. This act held the promise of restoring attention to public housing by providing the first substantial subsidy authorization for affordable housing in twenty years. It also evoked themes of neighborhood empowerment and home ownership that had been absent since the 1960s. Whether appropriations sufficient to the policy commitment would be forthcoming remained unclear, and whether the divergent strands of housing, urban, and civil rights policies could be brought together in a coherent strat-

egy was also an open question. More fundamentally, whether the supply- or demand-side strategies for subsidies would prevail remained unlikely to be settled without empirical economic analysis to replace ideological debate.

So, in the early 1990s, housing policy remained a Johnny-come-lately, a "sometime thing" for presidential concern. Except for campaign strolls through the slums, it typically bores the incumbent in the White House.

### BIBLIOGRAPHY

Browning, Rufus P., Dale Marshall, and David Tabb. *Protest Is Not Enough.* 1984.

Frieden, Bernard, and Lynne Sagalyn. *Downtown, Inc.: How America Rebuilds Cities.* 1989.

Hanson, Royce, ed. *Rethinking Urban Policy.* 1983.

Kaplan, Marshall, and Franklin James, eds. *The Future of National Urban Policy.* 1990.

Kaplan, Marshall, and Peggy Cuiciti, eds. *The Great Society and Its Legacy.* 1986.

Schwartz, David C., Richard C. Ferlauto, and Daniel N. Hoffman. *A New Housing Policy for America.* 1988.

Wood, Robert. *The Necessary Majority: Middle America and the Urban Crisis.* 1972.

ROBERT WOOD

**HOWE, LOUIS MCHENRY** (1871–1936), journalist, political adviser. Howe had become attached to Franklin D. Roosevelt when the latter was a state senator in 1911. The two remained close until Howe's death. Devoting himself entirely to Roosevelt's political fortunes, Howe became his most effective and influential organizer and strategist. Roosevelt appointed Howe secretary to the President, a position Howe used to limit access to the President and to keep his position as principal adviser. But amid the complexities of the evolving NEW DEAL, Howe's influence with Roosevelt diffused into that of troubleshooter who smooth talked, flattered, and occasionally supported disappointed Cabinet members, Congressmen, and other potential troublemakers. Working with Postmaster General and political patronage boss JAMES A. FARLEY, Howe played an important role in balancing politics and expertise in staffing the fledgling New Deal agencies.

Howe was especially close to ELEANOR ROOSEVELT and promoted her public image to show the administration's sympathy for the downtrodden. His pet interests were the CIVILIAN CONSERVATION CORPS and Subsistence Homesteads. Howe effectively sheltered the CCC from scandal and administrative conflict, but when he involved himself directly in administrative detail his desire for fast results and his lack of ability seriously embarrassed the subsistence projects. He also championed legislation to strengthen federal police powers in the face of the so-called crime wave of 1933–1934.

Howe was essentially a phrasemaker and political maneuverer who saw politics as a means to gain office but not to change society. He was uncomfortable with the dynamic administrative drive of a HARRY HOPKINS and the theoretical prescriptions of a REXFORD G. TUG-WELL and always feared their methods would embarrass Roosevelt. He sympathized, however, with the sufferings of the "little man," whom the depression so cruelly treated, and distrusted Wall Street. He was loyal to Roosevelt but in a protective and narrowly political way that limited Howe's role in the administration of one of the century's master political executives.

### BIBLIOGRAPHY

Rollins, Alfred B., Jr. *Roosevelt and Howe*. 1962.

GEORGE MCJIMSEY

**HUGHES, CHARLES EVANS** (1862–1948), governor of New York, Associate Justice of the Supreme Court, Republican presidential candidate in 1916, Secretary of State, Chief Justice of the United States.

The Republican Party drafted him for the presidential nomination in 1916 as the candidate most likely to mend the split between party conservatives and progressives that had made possible the election of the Democrat, Woodrow Wilson, in 1912. Though Hughes had previously maintained that a Supreme Court Justice should not bring the integrity of the judicial system into question by consenting to run for high office, he convinced himself in 1916 that the future of his party and the nation made it his duty to accept the nomination. Though a man of high intelligence, he proved to be an inept political strategist and a campaigner who conspicuously lacked the common touch. More important, Wilson and the Democratic Party largely succeeded in preempting the great issues of progressivism and peace. Wilson and Congress had in 1916 enacted most of the social reform legislation advocated by the PROGRESSIVE [BULL MOOSE] PARTY in 1912. Both Wilson and the other leaders of the Democratic Party were able to capitalize on the strong desire of most of the American people to stay out of WORLD WAR I: "He kept us out of war" became the Democratic rallying cry. Hughes, with his demands for stronger defense of American rights both in Europe and Mexico, was unfairly portrayed as the candidate who would bring war to the nation. Wilson was re-

elected by only a narrow margin of 9,129,606 popular and 277 electoral votes to 8,538,221 popular and 254 electoral votes for Hughes. Hughes came close to sweeping the East and Middle West, but Wilson won all of the South and most of the western states.

In December 1920 President Warren G. Harding seems to have chosen Hughes for Secretary of State simply because he was the best qualified Republican available for the position. In contrast to Wilson, who kept control of foreign affairs firmly in his own hands and wrote, or at least revised, most important diplomatic documents himself, Harding both by inclination and as a deliberate policy left both the formulation and implementation of foreign policy to Hughes. Hughes in turn made a point of keeping Harding fully informed through daily visits or telephone conversations. He customarily accompanied his statements of facts with definite proposals for action, which Harding almost invariably approved. Hughes was careful not to clash with Harding's own general inclinations in regard to American foreign policy, and he above all avoided embroiling the President with the Senate and its Foreign Relations Committee. Hughes was keenly sensitive to the limits of what was politically possible. Thus, in the face of Senate intransigence, he soon abandoned his own desire to have the United States enter the LEAGUE OF NATIONS and settled instead for a separate peace treaty with Germany that ended the still-existing state of war and reserved to the United States all rights granted to it in the TREATY OF VERSAILLES. Hughes dealt similarly with all other problems of foreign affairs arising from World War I. After Harding's death on 2 August 1923, President Calvin Coolidge also allowed Hughes the dominant role in American foreign relations.

Hughes was appointed Chief Justice by Herbert Hoover in 1930. During his tenure (1930–1941) the Supreme Court ruled that several important acts passed by Congress as part of President Franklin D. Roosevelt's NEW DEAL program were unconstitutional. Two of these acts involved improper delegations of legislative power to the executive, and in another case the Court limited the President's REMOVAL POWER. Roosevelt responded in 1937 with his so-called COURT-PACKING PLAN to increase the number of Justices on the ground that the Court was not abreast of its work. The plan aroused a storm of opposition in Congress and in the nation at large and was rejected by the Senate Judiciary Committee several months later. Meanwhile, Hughes had written a letter to the committee, on 21 March 1937, in which he convincingly repudiated Roosevelt's claim. More important, the Court soon thereafter handed down several decisions that upheld important acts of Roosevelt's legislative program. Hughes always denied that he and his judicial colleagues had undergone a sudden change of heart because of the Court-packing plan. Many scholars, however, believe that Hughes did seek to defend the Court by leading it in a new direction more in line with the thought of the New Deal era.

### BIBLIOGRAPHY

Glad, Betty. *Charles Evans Hughes and the Illusions of Innocence: A Study in American Diplomacy.* 1966.

Hughes, Charles Evans. *The Autobiographical Notes of Charles Evans Hughes.* Edited by David J. Danelski and Joseph S. Tulchin. 1973.

Link, Arthur S., and William M. Leary, Jr. "Election of 1916." In vol. 3 of *History of American Presidential Elections, 1789–1968.* Edited by Arthur M. Schlesinger, Jr., Fred L. Israel, and William P. Hansen. 4 vols. 1971.

Perkins, Dexter. *Charles Evans Hughes and American Democratic Statesmanship.* 1956.

Pusey, Merlo J. *Charles Evans Hughes.* 2 vols. 1951.

JOHN E. LITTLE

**HUGHES-RYAN AMENDMENT** (1974). The Hughes-Ryan Amendment to the Foreign Assistance Act of 1961 established a basic framework for congressional oversight of executive-initiated covert operations. It was enacted in 1974, a period in which Congress was reasserting its constitutional role vis-à-vis the President over U.S. foreign policy decision making.

The amendment provided that:

> No funds . . . may be expended by or on behalf of the Central Intelligence Agency for operations in foreign countries other than activities intended solely for obtaining necessary intelligence, unless and until the President finds that each such operation is important to the national security of the United States and reports, in a timely fashion, a description and scope of such operations to the appropriate committees of Congress.

The public disclosure of a series of dubious CENTRAL INTELLIGENCE AGENCY covert operations conducted during the 1960s and early 1970s such as assassination plots against foreign leaders and aiding the overthrow of democratically elected governments, led to calls for more congressional control over heretofore unilateral presidential initiatives. In August and September 1974 various Senators and Representatives proposed either limiting or banning CIA covert operations intervening in the affairs of other countries. Some members of Congress argued that there is no justification in our democratic system for covert operations that result in assassinations or political disruptions of another country's internal affairs.

These proposals were defeated, in part due to arguments that Congress did not have enough information about CIA covert operations. Instead, Sen. Harold Hughes and Rep. David Ryan introduced separate legislation designed to require the President to provide notification to the relevant congressional committee of covert operations abroad.

The purpose of the amendment allowed Congress to acquire information about covert operations so as to be able to make decisions about the legitimacy of such activities. Congress mandated that the President provide notification of covert operations but not seek congressional approval before initiating such activities.

The Hughes-Ryan Amendment was the first congressional attempt to provide legislative oversight of presidentially initiated covert operations. Ironically, the amendment also was read to provide the first explicit congressional authorization for executive covert operations. Executive covert operations had not been explicitly recognized as a part of the CIA's functions when Congress enacted the NATIONAL SECURITY ACT of 1947, which established the CIA. After 1974, Congress could no longer evade its responsibility for CIA covert actions.

Senator Hughes believed that his amendment provided a temporary arrangement, until more permanent regulations on the President's power to initiate covert actions could be developed. However, this temporary arrangement has remained in effect, although Congress has made improvements in the oversight scheme with the Intelligence Oversight Act of 1980 and again in 1991.

### BIBLIOGRAPHY

Cinquegrana, Americo R. "Dancing in the Dark: Accepting the Invitation to Struggle in the Context of 'Covert Action': The Iran-Contra Affair and the Intelligence Oversight Process." *Houston Journal of International Law* 11 (1988):177, 182–187.

JULES LOBEL

**HULL, CORDELL** (1871–1955), Representative, Senator, Secretary of State. The longest-serving Secretary of State in American history—eleven and a half years—Hull held the top post in Franklin D. Roosevelt's CABINET throughout the NEW DEAL and most of WORLD WAR II. He tirelessly championed free trade, markedly improved U.S. relations with Latin America, and successfully advocated postwar collective security. For this last work, President Roosevelt praised Hull as the "father of the UNITED NATIONS" and he received the Nobel Peace Prize in 1945.

Although Roosevelt and Hull liked and respected each other and shared many political experiences and principles, Roosevelt frequently preferred to act as his own Secretary of State. He often sought diplomatic advice from Under Secretary of State Sumner Welles and Treasury Secretary HENRY MORGENTHAU, JR. Differences of personality accentuated the distance between the President and his Secretary of State. Roosevelt was daring and flexible; Hull was deliberate and sometimes rigid. Roosevelt once confided to W. Averell Harriman that he found his Secretary of State "forceful, stubborn, [and] difficult to handle."

As a result, Hull's influence on the President, his impact on the formulation and execution of U.S. foreign policy, and even his personal control of the State Department remained tightly circumscribed. Roosevelt did not invite Hull to his first meeting with Churchill nor any of his subsequent Big Three summit conferences. Hull privately criticized "the White House attitude and treatment of the Department and encroachment in foreign affairs" on many occasions, but he always publicly deferred to Roosevelt's personal style of diplomacy with equanimity and grace.

Before PEARL HARBOR, Hull concentrated his energies on reciprocal trade, the GOOD NEIGHBOR POLICY, and Far Eastern issues. His wartime efforts focused largely on Congress and postwar affairs. Like the President he served, Hull's memory of Wilson's tragic failure to secure Senate approval of the TREATY OF VERSAILLES and the LEAGUE OF NATIONS heavily colored his approach to the creation of a new collective security organization during World War II. He used his high political standing in Congress to build crucial bipartisan support for the idea of a United Nations, convinced this offered the best hope for its future.

### BIBLIOGRAPHY

Hull, Cordell. *The Memoirs of Cordell Hull.* 2 vols. 1948.
Pratt, Julius W. *Cordell Hull.* 2 vols. 1964.

BRIAN VANDEMARK

**HUMAN RIGHTS.** The emphasis on human rights in American foreign policy is popularly associated with the presidency of Jimmy Carter and is encapsulated in Carter's inaugural address statement: "Our commitment to human rights must be absolute. . . . Because we are free we can never be indifferent to the fate of freedom elsewhere. Our moral sense dictates a clearcut preference for those societies which share with us an abiding respect for individual human rights." As President, Carter spoke of human rights in evangelical tones and did much to give the issue prominence in the national and international arenas. Yet the attribution of the human-rights campaign to Carter has been both overstated and misunderstood.

The concept of inalienable rights is embedded in the founding documents of the United States, including the Declaration of Independence and the Bill of Rights; it is an integral part of the American ethos. Carter's crusade for human rights continued a moralistic U.S. foreign-policy tradition, with roots traceable to the beginning of the Republic. Even the term *human rights* was used by Thomas Jefferson who, in 1809, wrote that America was "the solitary republic of the world, the only monument of human rights . . . the sole depository of the sacred fire of freedom and self-government, from hence it is to be lighted up in other regions of the earth, if other regions of the earth shall ever become susceptible to its benign influence."

In the twentieth century, several Presidents enunciated an expanded version of the American mission: beyond furnishing a "monument of human rights" and serving mankind by the power of its example, the United States should actively strive to universalize American values. President Woodrow Wilson's FOURTEEN POINTS and President Franklin D. Roosevelt's FOUR FREEDOMS were the primary archetypes of this broadened version of the American mission. In the same tradition were President Harry S. Truman's promise "to assist free peoples to work out their own destinies" and President John F. Kennedy's pledge that the United States would "pay any price, bear any burden . . . to assure the survival and the success of liberty." Carter's campaign was essentially a new variant on old themes.

Among the distinguishing features of the new policy was the attempt to institutionalize human rights concerns and ensure that they were regularly factored into the processes of U.S. bilateral and multilateral diplomacy, foreign aid, and trade. Military intervention was ruled out as an instrument of enforcement. The impulses that generated the policy and the first critical steps to implement it emanated from Congress in the early 1970s and predated the Carter presidency.

By the time of Carter's inauguration, Congress had conducted important hearings on human rights; adopted the 1974 Jackson-Vanik Amendment conditioning the grant of most-favored-nation status to Soviet-bloc countries on liberalized emigration practices; passed resolutions expressing the sense of Congress that aid should be withheld from gross human rights violators; and in 1975–1976, enacted mandatory legislation requiring the STATE DEPARTMENT to submit reports regarding the observance of human rights by recipients of U.S. foreign aid and denying

U.S. security and economic assistance to governments that engaged "in a consistent pattern of gross violations of internationally recognized human rights." Congressional policy was not totally rigid. Thus, Jackson-Vanik allowed the President extensive waiver authority; security assistance might be extended to offending states on the basis of the U.S. national interest and economic assistance granted if it "directly" benefited the "needy people" of the country concerned.

Congressional initiatives on human rights were an integral part of a general post-VIETNAM WAR (and later, post-WATERGATE AFFAIR) backlash against both the IMPERIAL PRESIDENCY and the *Realpolitik* of the Nixon-Ford-Kissinger era. While conceding congressional authority to legislate on human rights, President Gerald R. Ford and Secretary of State HENRY KISSINGER doubted the wisdom of such legislation, preferring that human-rights abuses be addressed by flexible presidential responses and quiet diplomacy. Nevertheless, both Ford and Kissinger began increasingly to employ human rights rhetoric; and in 1975 an Office of Human Rights and Humanitarian Affairs was established in the State Department.

Carter incorporated the human-rights theme into his electoral campaign at a late stage and hesitatingly, apparently after pressure from Senator Henry Jackson. Earlier Carter had criticized the Helsinki Accords and had deemed the Jackson Amendment "ill advised." In writing on foreign policy in his 1975 book *Why Not the Best?*, although he called for a more moral foreign policy, Carter did not use the term "human rights." During the drafting of the Democratic platform, his delegates were passive on human rights; and even after the GEORGE MCGOVERN and Henry Jackson wings of the DEMOCRATIC PARTY agreed on a strong human-rights plank (the former for use against right-wing dictatorships, the latter for flaying Soviet abuses), Carter at first deemphasized the issue. Later, however, he effectively utilized the theme, primarily in an anti-Soviet context, in his debate with President Ford; and it was, as noted, a major motif in his inaugural address.

In office, Carter continued to give the matter of human rights great prominence (especially during the first two and a half years of his tenure), and overall his relationship with Congress in this sphere was cooperative rather than confrontational. One indication of the new policy focus was the growth of the human-rights bureaucracy. At Carter's request Congress upgraded the Office of Human Rights to a bureau headed by an Assistant Secretary of State. Beyond that, human-rights officers operated in all American embassies abroad and within the various regional bureaus of the State Department. In the NATIONAL SECURITY COUNCIL, Carter created an Interagency Group on Human Rights and Foreign Assistance.

Other Carter initiatives entailed drawing closer to the international community on human-rights matters. Carter persuaded Congress to repeal the Byrd Amendment, which had permitted the United States to violate a UNITED NATIONS Security Council ban on the importation of chrome from Rhodesia. He signed and sent to the Senate three U.N. treaties on human rights (the Convention against Racial Discrimination and the covenants on Civil and Political Rights and on Economic and Social Rights) and the American Convention on Human Rights. Though to all of these he attached far-reaching reservations designed to please the Senate more than the human-rights lobby, the Senate failed to ratify them.

Besides these and other symbolic acts, the Carter administration terminated or restricted aid to a long list of countries, many of them in Latin America (including Argentina, Bolivia, Chile, El Salvador, Guatemala, HAITI, Nicaragua, Paraguay, and Uruguay). But the primary mode of implementing human-rights policy remained under Carter, as under his predecessors, quiet diplomacy. The administration's claims of success in getting thousands of political prisoners freed were contested by others and could not be readily verified.

As Carter's human-rights policy unfolded, its conceptual and practical difficulties became ever more apparent. Which rights, for example, should be most emphasized? Secretary of State Cyrus Vance spoke of three categories of rights: "the right to be free of governmental violation of the integrity of the person, including torture, cruel, inhuman or degrading treatment or punishment, and arbitrary arrest or imprisonment"; economic and social rights; and civil and political liberties. Formally, no preference was expressed for any category, but Vance intimated that the first might be emphasized as most amenable to rapid improvement. Congressional legislation had also highlighted this category.

Was the purpose of the human-rights policy merely to dissociate the United States from unsavory regimes (as the human-rights statutes implied), thereby improving America's image in the world and allowing Americans to feel better? Or was it to improve the human-rights records of offenders? If the latter, was it realistic to abjure active intervention in all instances? Might not the cut-off of aid injure the local inhabitants more than it punished the offending regimes? How was the policy to be reconciled with American strategic interests? Was the United States to target only weak states over which it had aid leverage and ignore worse (even genocidal) offenders on the left and right?

Before long, disillusionment set in among both liberal and conservative elements of the coalition formerly supporting the policy. All agreed that the policy lacked coherence and involved "selective indignation." Liberals contended that the abuses of many rightist governments were ignored; conservatives objected that the policy was too anti-ally and insufficiently anti-Soviet. Decisions seemed often to be the haphazard result of bureaucratic wrangling among the State Department bureaus and between State and other Cabinet departments (such as Defense, Treasury, Agriculture, and Commerce). Fissures also emerged in the executive-legislative coalition on the issue, and the Carter administration, like its predecessor, pleaded for authority to handle the aid-rights conundrum on a flexible case-by-case basis.

Toward the end of Carter's tenure, a sense of unease with his human-rights policy was fairly widespread. The 1979 replacement of Anastasio Somoza by the Sandinistas in Nicaragua and of the Shah by the Khomeini fundamentalists (and hostage-takers) in Iran constituted a major watershed. Conservatives charged that by hounding friendly authoritarian governments without examining the credentials of the likely alternatives, Carter had paved the way for regimes that were far worse than their predecessors, both for U.S. interests and the human rights of the local population. Some liberals, on the other hand, reproached the administration for not dissociating itself earlier and more unequivocally from the fallen regimes.

Against this background, the Reagan administration resolved to modify the previous policy; but congressional pressures, events abroad, and the institutionalization of the earlier human-rights campaign induced far greater continuity of policy than many predicted.

Initially, the Reagan administration promised a human-rights policy that would be more antitotalitarian than antiauthoritarian; more anti-adversary than anti-ally; more sensitive to terrorism as the greatest threat; more aware of the alternatives to the existing regimes; and more prone to use the effective methods of quiet diplomacy than public denunciation and denial of aid. Elliott Abrams (who was appointed Assistant Secretary of State for Human Rights after the failed nomination of Ernest Lefever, an outspoken critic of Carter's human-rights policy) was instrumental in enunciating a new focus for Reagan's human-rights policy. Instead of treating only the symptoms of human-rights abuse, the administration would treat the disease, the lack of free elections and a democratic infrastructure. Some criticized this as a smokescreen, the substitution of a "manipulable political science standard" for "widely accepted concern for the security of the person."

The Reagan administration record on human rights was notable in several respects. Senate approval was obtained for the Genocide Convention, which had languished in the Senate for almost four decades, a casualty of the BRICKER AMENDMENT controversy of the early 1950s. The human-rights bureaucracy was increased. Above all, the administration encouraged (though somewhat reluctantly) the democratization of Chile, Haiti, and the Philippines. The principal executive-congressional clash concerned South Africa. Reagan opposed economic sanctions on the grounds that they would greatly harm the nonwhite majority, but he was overruled by Congress.

Ironically, the Bush administration, which witnessed an unprecedented worldwide spread of democracy, gave less prominence to the issue of human rights than did its two predecessors, made less effort to enunciate a coherent doctrine, and responded to the dramatic developments and challenges of its incumbency with notable confusion and lack of inspiration. The administration also clashed frequently with Congress on human-rights-linked issues such as the grant of most-favored-nation status to China after the Tiananmen Square massacre; the arming of terrorist states (including Iraq before the Persian GULF WAR); legislation regarding the victims of torture; economic aid to El Salvador and Peru; and policy toward the Kurds and the components of Yugoslavia. Support for Kuwait was necessarily posited by Bush as a matter of legitimacy rather than democracy.

Bush administration initiatives on human rights included support for ratification of the International Covenant on Civil and Political Rights; a proposal, adopted by the U.N. General Assembly, to establish a U.N. electoral commission to help states guarantee free and fair electoral processes; the listing of human rights (but not democracy) as one of four key elements of the new world order; and the inclusion of both human rights and democracy among the five requirements that Secretary of State James Baker notified former Soviet republics they would have to meet to qualify for U.S. recognition and aid.

Human-rights concerns will likely remain part of U.S. foreign policy for some time to come. With the end of the COLD WAR, as certain strategic worries recede, human-rights considerations may become more prominent because more affordable. On the other hand, U.S. human-rights policy will still have to take into account U.S. geopolitical interests, the local alternatives to unsatisfactory situations, and as Cyrus Vance admonished, "the limits of our power and our wisdom." Simplistic presidential pronouncements notwithstanding, the issue of human rights, by its nature, raises more questions than it answers.

## BIBLIOGRAPHY

Brown, Peter G., and Douglas MacLean, eds. *Human Rights and U.S. Foreign Policy: Principles and Application.* 1979.

Forsythe, David P. *Human Rights and U.S. Foreign Policy: Congress Reconsidered.* 1988.

Frankel, Charles. *Human Rights and Foreign Policy.* 1978.

Kommers, Donald P., and Gilburt D. Loescher, eds. *Human Rights and American Foreign Policy.* 1979.

Muravchik, Joshua. *The Uncertain Crusade: Jimmy Carter and the Dilemmas of Human Rights Policy.* 1986.

Rubin, Barry M., and Elizabeth P. Spiro, eds. *Human Rights and U.S. Foreign Policy.* 1979.

Schlesinger, Arthur M., Jr. "Human Rights and the American Tradition." *Foreign Affairs* 57 (1978): 503–526.

Vogelgesang, Sandy. *American Dream, Global Nightmare: The Dilemma of U.S. Human Rights Policy.* 1980.

MICHLA POMERANCE

**HUMPHREY, HUBERT H.** (1911–1978), thirty-eighth Vice President of the United States (1965–1969), Senator, Democratic presidential nominee in 1968. Hubert Horatio Humphrey was born in the prairie town of Wallace, South Dakota. His father, a druggist, later moved the family to Doland, South Dakota, where Humphrey spent his childhood and early adult years. After graduating from the University of Minnesota and acquiring a master's degree in political science at Louisiana State University, Humphrey began work as a college instructor in Minneapolis. His public career began in 1940 when he was appointed director of a local program of the Works Progress Administration (WPA). Humphrey became more active in Minnesota politics and in 1943 ran unsuccessfully for mayor of Minneapolis, losing narrowly to the incumbent. Running again in 1945, at the age of thirty-four, he was overwhelmingly elected mayor.

**Senator and Vice President.** In 1948, Humphrey campaigned for a seat in the United States Senate. At the Democratic Party's national convention that summer, he earned his first notice in national politics, delivering a fiery speech in favor of the administration's civil rights plank in the party platform. "The time has arrived," he said, "for the Democratic Party to get out of the shadow of states' rights and walk forthrightly into the bright sunshine of human rights."

Elected in 1948 and reelected in 1956, Humphrey soon became a prominent voice of liberalism in the Senate and the country. In 1960 he announced his candidacy for President. Badly financed from the start and lacking a genuine national constituency, he was beaten by John F. Kennedy in Humphrey's neighboring state of Wisconsin. A few weeks later in the West Virginia primary, another defeat by Kennedy brought his ill-fated campaign to a close.

Humphrey returned to the Senate, and early in 1961 he became the majority whip. For the next few years, he worked closely with Presidents Kennedy and Lyndon B. Johnson on a rushing river of new legislation: the Peace Corps, nuclear disarmament, youth employment, wilderness protection, economic opportunity, and on and on into every nook and cranny of American life. In 1964 he was chosen to be the floor leader for the most important bill of its time, the Civil Rights Act of 1964. For months he worked to solidify support in his own party and to attract the Republican support needed to prevent the bill's death by filibuster. Especially important was the politicking he did with Republican leader Everett M. Dirksen, whose eventual support turned the tide in favor of enactment. The passage of the civil rights bill was Humphrey's greatest legislative achievement.

Lyndon Johnson was watching. In 1964 Johnson was preparing to run for a new presidential term and needed a running mate. He was widely viewed as an odds-on favorite for election in the fall, so there was much interest among leading Democrats in joining what promised to be a successful ticket. Humphrey's name was at the top of nearly everyone's list of vice presidential candidates. But Johnson enjoyed suspense, and he was especially concerned that there be some drama at the Democratic convention in Atlantic City, since there was no mystery about his own nomination. He dragged out the selection of a running mate until the last minute, constantly floating new names as possibilities and puncturing the conventional wisdom. Only hours before the convention's vote, after subjecting a humiliated Humphrey to his suspense game, did Johnson announce his selection of the Minnesota Senator as his running mate.

Johnson and Humphrey swept to a landslide victory over the Republicans Barry Goldwater and William E. Miller in the fall with a margin of almost 16 million popular votes. What followed was not a period of triumph for Humphrey but years of forced obscurity, disdain, and belittlement by Johnson, and political abandonment by many of his old allies in national politics. Johnson rarely sought Humphrey's advice on matters of importance and often excluded him from White House discussions. Humphrey had to defend administration policies he had played no role in helping to formulate. He soldiered on, an administration loyalist.

After 1965, the United States commitment of forces in the VIETNAM WAR came to dominate the concerns of the President and the country. As the war declined in popularity, Humphrey became a target of vilification for antiwar activists. In many ways, these were Humphrey's natural allies. Had he not been Vice President, he might well have been a leader among those questioning the war. Instead, he became a leading spokesman for the administration's policies in Vietnam, his speeches sounding increasingly shrill and defensive as opposition to the war mounted.

**Presidential Candidate.** Humphrey's life took a dramatic and unexpected turn on 31 March 1968, when Johnson announced that he would not seek reelection. Two Democrats—Senators EUGENE McCARTHY of Minnesota and ROBERT F. KENNEDY of New York—had already entered the primaries to challenge Johnson. It was late in the process to mount a campaign from scratch, but on 27 April 1968, Humphrey announced his candidacy for the Democratic nomination for President.

With the support of many labor leaders and important local Democratic officials, Humphrey decided not to compete in the remaining primaries. His strategy assumed that McCarthy and Kennedy would wound each other so badly in the primaries that Humphrey could secure the nomination by building delegate strength in those states where primaries had little or no impact on delegate selection. When Robert Kennedy was assassinated on the night of the California primary, the hand of tragedy cleared the largest obstacle from Humphrey's path to the nomination.

Humphrey was nominated by the Democrats at their convention in Chicago, but the price of that victory was very high. Conflict over the war and over its nominating rules tore the Democratic Party apart. The streets of Chicago were full of angry antiwar protesters who were viciously set upon by the Chicago police. Television carried the wrenching images of a hemorrhaging Democratic Party and a country at war with itself. From these smoldering ashes rose the deeply wounded presidential candidacy of Hubert Humphrey.

Humphrey had to contend not only with a REPUBLICAN PARTY unified behind Richard M. Nixon and the insurgent independent candidacy of Alabama Governor GEORGE WALLACE but also with the fissure lines in his own party. Democratic support for Humphrey was far from certain. As the fall campaign wore on, Humphrey was increasingly haunted by his association with the war policies of the Johnson administration. Still Vice President and a man who valued political loyalty, Humphrey nevertheless understood that he needed to chart his own course on Vietnam or his candidacy was doomed.

In a critical speech in Salt Lake City on 30 September 1968, he promised that "as president, I would stop the bombing of [North Vietnam] as an acceptable risk for peace because I believe it could lead to success in the negotiations and a shorter war." This statement was, in fact, only a minor variation from the administration's policy, but it helped convince reluctant Democrats that, if elected, Humphrey would be his own man on Vietnam. The heckling of his speeches dropped off, local officials began to appear at his campaign stops, and his standing in the opinion polls rose.

By the last weekend of the campaign, the final national polls called it a dead heat. And it was. Of 72 million votes cast, Nixon beat Humphrey by only 510,000—one of the closest outcomes in American history. It was a miraculous political rally for Humphrey; to his dying day he was certain that he could have won if only the campaign had lasted a week longer.

**Return to the Senate.** Humphrey returned to private life after the election but not for long. He was elected to the Senate from Minnesota two years later, and in 1972 he was again a candidate for President. This time he battled his way through the primaries but failed to secure enough delegates to wrest the nomination from Sen. GEORGE McGOVERN of South Dakota.

Humphrey returned to the Senate, where his legislative skills and the respect he commanded on both sides of the aisle allowed him to become a senior statesman in that body. In 1976 he again contemplated a campaign for the Democratic nomination for President, but his opportunity evaporated as Jimmy Carter began to build delegate strength through the primaries.

Humphrey did run for reelection to the Senate in 1976, winning by more than 800,000 votes. But just before the election, he underwent an operation for cancer. The progress of the disease could not be completely deterred, and it ended his life on 13 January 1978.

Humphrey's death brought an outpouring of tribute and love. He was praised for his contributions to national progress and particularly his legislative accomplishments on behalf of children, the poor, and minorities. Many called him the greatest legislator of the twentieth century. But he was praised as well for his joyous and robust optimism, for a spirit that eschewed meanness and placed great faith in the goodness of the American people. At his funeral in Washington, his protégé and friend, Vice President WALTER

MONDALE, said, "He taught us all how to hope and how to live, how to win and how to lose. He taught us how to live and, finally, he taught us how to die."

### BIBLIOGRAPHY

Berman, Edgar. *Hubert: The Triumph and Tragedy of the Humphrey I Knew.* 1979.

Cohen, Dan. *Undefeated: The Life of Hubert H. Humphrey.* 1978.

Humphrey, Hubert H. *The Education of a Public Man: My Life and Politics.* 1976.

Sherrill, Robert, and Harry W. Ernst. *The Drugstore Liberal.* 1968.

Solberg, Carl. *Hubert H. Humphrey: A Political Biography.* 1984.

White, Theodore H. *The Making of the President 1968.* 1969.

G. CALVIN MACKENZIE

**HUMPHREY'S EXECUTOR v. UNITED STATES** 295 U.S. 602 (1935). *Humphrey's Executor,* which established the limits of a President's REMOVAL POWER, arose out of a 1933 conflict between a Federal Trade Commissioner, William Ewart Humphrey, and President Franklin D. Roosevelt.

In 1925, President Calvin Coolidge, seeking to create a conservative majority on the Federal Trade Commission (FTC), had appointed Humphrey, who as a Representative from Washington state and subsequently as a lobbyist for lumber interests had earned a reputation as an ardent Republican partisan and supporter of big business. Progressives denounced him as a "Jesse James," and Senator George Norris (R-Neb.), called him "the greatest reactionary of the country." So effective was Humphrey in turning the commission in a rightward direction that when Herbert Hoover reappointed him in 1931, twenty-eight Senators voted not to confirm. By the time Roosevelt took office in 1933, Humphrey had become the most prominent symbol of an entrenched conservative bureaucracy.

Roosevelt resolved to get rid of Humphrey, especially because Congress in 1933 had given the FTC additional powers under two newly enacted laws, the NATIONAL INDUSTRIAL RECOVERY ACT, and, more particularly, the Securities Act of 1933. Since Humphrey's six-year term would not expire until 1937, the President sought to persuade him to leave voluntarily. He later claimed he had evidence that Humphrey had taken bribes, but instead of citing any substantive reason for demanding the resignation, Roosevelt on 31 August 1933 wrote Humphrey a maladroitly worded letter that said, "I do not feel that your mind and my mind go along together."

When Humphrey refused to step down, Roosevelt removed him from the FTC on 7 October and appointed a replacement. Humphrey countered on 28 December by filing suit in the U.S. Court of Claims contesting his removal and demanding back salary. On 14 February 1934, Humphrey died, but the executor of his estate, Samuel Rathbun, maintained the suit. The U.S. Court of Claims, in turn, certified two questions to the U.S. Supreme Court: Was the President's power to discharge commissioners restricted by the 1914 FTC statute to specific causes such as malfeasance in office? And, if so, was such a limitation on his removal authority constitutional?

Roosevelt was confident of victory in this case because his legal advisers had assured him he had ample authority. The Supreme Court had never questioned the DECISION OF 1789, when Congress had acknowledged, somewhat ambiguously, the right of the President to dismiss the Secretary of Foreign Affairs without its consent, and as recently as 1926, in MYERS v. UNITED STATES, the Court, in a 6 to 3 decision, had sustained President Woodrow Wilson's dismissal of a postmaster without the consent of the Senate. In a sweeping opinion, Chief Justice William Howard Taft had upheld an extremely broad removal power for the President.

On 27 May 1935, the Supreme Court, in an opinion by Justice George Sutherland, ruled 9 to 0 that the President had exceeded his authority in discharging Humphrey. The doctrine of illimitable power of removal, Sutherland said, violated the principle of SEPARATION OF POWERS. Sutherland, who had joined in Taft's opinion in *Myers,* acknowledged that in that opinion "expressions occur which tend to sustain the government's contention" in *Humphrey's Executor,* but he dismissed them as dicta with no force. Unlike Myers, who was a "purely executive" functionary, Humphrey, as a Federal Trade Commissioner, occupied "no place in the executive department," for the FTC was "an agency of the legislative or judicial departments" that exercised "quasi-legislative or quasi-judicial powers." In creating such an agency, Congress had undoubted authority to set terms of tenure of commissioners "and to forbid their removal except for cause in the meantime."

Sutherland's opinion elicited a mixed response. Commentators scoffed at the assertion that a regulatory commission was in no way situated in the executive branch, and the President was angered at the refusal of the Court to concede that, in firing Humphrey, he was acting on the authority of an opinion written by the Chief Justice of the United States less than a decade earlier. On the other hand, those who believed that commissioners should be free of the fear of political reprisal hailed the ruling as a charter of liberation for regulatory tribunals. Furthermore, unlike other decisions of the pre-1937 Court, *Humphrey's Executor* was never reversed, and in WIENER V. UNITED STATES (1958) and MORRISON V. OLSON (1988) the principle was even expanded.

### BIBLIOGRAPHY

Cushman, Robert E. *The Independent Regulatory Commissions.* 1941.

Leuchtenburg, William E. "The Case of the Contentious Commissioner: *Humphrey's Executor v. U.S.*" In *Freedom and Reform: Essays in Honor of Henry Steele Commager.* Edited by Harold M. Hyman and Leonard W. Levy. 1967.

WILLIAM E. LEUCHTENBURG

**HYDE PARK.** During Franklin Delano Roosevelt's twelve years (1933–1945) as President, Hyde Park, New York, was, in the words of author Geoffrey C. War, "one of the world's most familiar datelines." At his summer White House, Roosevelt met privately with a broad array of national and world leaders. Several of his famous radio FIRESIDE CHATS originated from the living room–library of the Big House, as his family liked to call it.

Springwood, the Roosevelt family estate situated on a bluff overlooking the Hudson River, mirrors the personality of Roosevelt and his parents. FDR, the only child of James and Sara Roosevelt, was born there on 30 January 1882. He grew to manhood, brought his wife Eleanor to live in 1905, and raised their children among the estate's tranquil woods. In 1911, from the front porch of Springwood, Roosevelt launched his political career as a New York State senator. Later, the home provided a respite from the rigors of being Assistant Secretary of the Navy (1913–1920), governor of New York (1928–1932), and President (1933–1945). When Franklin Roosevelt contracted polio in 1921, it was to Springwood that he retreated to begin his rehabilitation.

When it was decided in 1915 that a larger home was needed to accommodate Franklin's growing family and increasing political importance, the house was more than doubled in size and transformed from a country place into an imposing mansion. Although many of FDR's ideas were incorporated in the renovation, his mother made sure that the interior retained much of its original charm and grace.

Life at Springwood, however, was difficult for ELEANOR ROOSEVELT. Her mother-in-law was always the woman of the house and in charge of all of its affairs. Ultimately, Eleanor found solace at Val-Kill, a beautiful, serene spot on the eastern side of the estate where FDR constructed a stone cottage of Dutch colonial design for her and her friends in 1925. A decade later, she converted a building a short distance away into a home for herself where she worked and entertained guests for the remainder of her life.

President Roosevelt and his mother bequeathed Springwood to the American people in 1938 and it was dedicated as a National Historic Site by President Harry S. Truman on 12 April 1946, the first anniversary of Roosevelt's death. The site, which is administered by the National Park Service, also includes a coach house and stables, gardener's cottage, greenhouse, rose garden, large ice house, and the grave sites of Franklin and Eleanor. The Franklin D. Roosevelt Library, containing manuscripts, books, and other historical materials dealing with his life, is adjacent to the site.

### BIBLIOGRAPHY

Gurney, Gene, and Clare Gurney. *FDR and Hyde Park.* 1970.

Hyde Park Historical Association. *Springwood: Birth Place of Franklin Delano Roosevelt.* 1993.

Ward Geoffrey C. "The House at Hyde Park." *American Heritage* 38 (April 1986): 41–46, 48–50.

STEPHEN W. STATHIS

# I

**ICKES, HAROLD** (1874–1952), Secretary of the Interior and head of the Public Works Administration (PWA). A progressive journalist and lawyer, Harold Le Claire Ickes went to Washington in 1933 and quickly became a key player in Franklin D. Roosevelt's CABINET and a member of his intimate circle of advisers; his detailed *Secret Diary* remains a critical (though hardly objective) source of insights into NEW DEAL politics. Long committed to conservation and opposed to powerful utilities companies, Ickes turned his twin appointments as Secretary of the Interior and head of the PUBLIC WORKS ADMINISTRATION (PWA) into a major power base. The PWA built hundreds of hospitals, sewer systems, highways, and power systems, including such landmarks as the San Francisco–Oakland Bay Bridge and the Lincoln Tunnel between New York and New Jersey. Also under Ickes's general direction was the construction of massive power projects such as Boulder Dam (later renamed Hoover Dam). Such projects served Ickes's interest in conservation as well as the New Deal's interest in public relief, though the PWA's projects were later eclipsed by the job-creation programs of HARRY HOPKINS's WORKS PROGRESS ADMINISTRATION (WPA). During WORLD WAR II Ickes served as administrator for petroleum and solid fuels.

As an adviser to the President and especially through his close friendship with ELEANOR ROOSEVELT, Ickes wielded considerable influence within the administration on behalf of a variety of progressive concerns. He was perhaps the leading New Deal supporter of the interests of African Americans. He spoke out against the Nazi persecution of Jews and against the wartime internment of JAPANESE AMERICANS. He opposed the antics of the House Un-American Activities Committee under the chairmanship of Representative Martin Dies (D-Tex.), though he allowed Roosevelt to convince him not to make his opposition public.

Ickes's power, tenacious personality, and passionate commitment to progressive causes made him a force to be reckoned with. These same factors also guaranteed that Ickes would run up against other powerful figures. He fought with Hopkins about public works, with Secretary of Agriculture HENRY A. WALLACE for control of the Forest Service, and with congressional conservatives on a host of issues (Ickes, with Hopkins, THOMAS CORCORAN, and others, was behind the unsuccessful congressional "purge" of 1938, in which Roosevelt tried to rid Congress of Conservative Democrats who opposed the New Deal). After Roosevelt's death, Ickes clashed with President Harry S. Truman, and in 1946 resigned all his government posts.

### BIBLIOGRAPHY

Ickes, Harold L. *The Secret Diary of Harold L. Ickes.* 3 vols. 1953–1954.

Watkins, T. H. *Righteous Pilgrim: The Life and Times of Harold L. Ickes, 1874–1952.* 1990.

WILLIAM LASSER

**IMMIGRATION ACT** (1924). The 1924 Immigration Act was the culmination of a process begun in 1882 that steadily narrowed entry into the United States. The criteria that it established set the basic limits of American IMMIGRATION POLICY until 1965. President Wilson had pocket vetoed the first version of the 1921 act, but Harding approved it and its extension in 1922. President Coolidge gladly signed the 1924 act

785

into law. Herbert Hoover specifically approved of the act and Franklin Roosevelt was uncharacteristically silent about it. Harry Truman and John F. Kennedy denounced its principles as prejudiced and unworthy of a democracy, and Lyndon Johnson put a quietus to its principle of ethnic discrimination in signing the immigration act of 1965.

The 1924 act was intended both to reduce significantly the number of immigrants and to favor those from northwestern Europe—British, Germans, and Scandinavians—as opposed to those from eastern and southern Europe—Italians, Poles, Eastern European Jews, Southern Slavs, and Greeks. It excluded immigrants from Asia as "aliens ineligible to citizenship" but left immigration from the New World relatively unchecked. The law also incorporated previous restrictions which had barred criminals, persons who failed to meet certain moral standards, persons with various diseases, paupers, certain radicals, and illiterates.

The chief method used was a quota system, a device first introduced in the Emergency Quota Act of 1921. Under the 1924 act quotas were first calculated at 2 percent of the number of persons of each eligible nationality recorded in the 1890 census, which pro-restrictionists called the Anglo-Saxon census as it antedated the great surge of so-called new immigrants. After 1929 there was a National Origins Quota System, and under both systems there were some 150,000 quota spaces. In addition there were non-quota immigrants: spouses or unmarried minor children of American citizens, returning previously admitted immigrants, ministers of religion, professors and certain members of their families, and students.

The law provided that national origin was to be determined by calculating "the number of inhabitants in [the] continental United States in 1920 whose origin by birth or ancestry" was attributable to each nation. But the definition of "inhabitants in [the] . . . United States in 1920" excluded any immigrants from the New World and their descendants; any Asians and their descendants; the descendants of "slave immigrants"; and the descendants of "American aborigines." Using these twisted criteria a committee of scholars under the auspices of the American Council of Learned Societies created the numbers to help the government calculate the quotas.

The "scientific" quotas, first promulgated by President Hoover in 1929, awarded more than half the quota spaces—83,304—to Great Britain and Ireland, almost a quarter—36,149—to Germanic Europe and Scandinavia, and left just over a fifth—33,135—to the rest of the eligible Old World.

As an additional method of restriction, all immi-

grants were required to obtain a visa from an American consulate, which gave the American consular service a potential stranglehold on immigration which was to cost many would-be refugees from Europe their lives in the Nazi era.

In terms of advocates' goals, the 1924 act was a relative success. Immigration, which had run at about a million annually before WORLD WAR I was reduced considerably. After 1930 the Great Depression was even more successful: in four consecutive years, 1932 through 1935, more persons emigrated from the United States than immigrated to it.

Although the 1924 act remained on the books, after 1943 its provisions were gradually eroded by statutory and administrative relaxation. Under the Displaced Persons Act of 1948, for example, quotas could be "mortgaged." Within four years enough Latvians had been admitted to mortgage the tiny Latvian annual quota of 286 persons to A.D. 2274. Nevertheless congressional nativists kept the quota system in the 1952 McCARRAN-WALTER ACT, passed over Truman's veto, and maintained it until Johnson's reforms were enacted in 1965. Those reforms substituted hemispheric caps for national quotas and created a system under which family reunification became the guiding principle.

### BIBLIOGRAPHY

Daniels, Roger. *Coming to America: A History of Immigration and Ethnicity in American Life.* 1990.
Higham, John. *Strangers in the Lane.* 2d ed. 1955. Repr. 1988.
Hutchinson, E. P. *Legislative History of American Immigration Policy.* 1981.

ROGER DANIELS

**IMMIGRATION AND NATURALIZATION SERVICE v. CHADHA.** See INS v. CHADHA.

**IMMIGRATION POLICY.** American immigration policy can conveniently be divided into five phases.

**Unrestricted Immigration, to 1882.** In the early decades of its existence, the United States provided a generalized welcome to all comers but had no immigration policy. Apart from the abolition of the slave trade in 1809, there was no immigration legislation at all, although in 1798 and 1819 Congress did require that all arrivals be enumerated. President Tyler put it nicely in an 1841 message to Congress:

We hold out to the people of other countries an invitation to come and settle among us as members of our rapidly growing family, and for the blessings which we offer them we require of them to look upon our country as their country and unite with us in the great task of preserving our institutions and thereby perpetuating our liberties.

But the arrival of large numbers of poor Catholic immigrants, mostly from Ireland, helped cause an anti-immigrant reaction and some eastern states passed legislation taxing arriving immigrants. In the *Passenger Cases* (1849) the Supreme Court disallowed these taxes, holding that immigration was subject only to federal regulation, even though no federal laws existed. Despite much anti-immigrant agitation in the antebellum years, no legislation resulted and the CIVIL WAR, in which many immigrants fought for the Union, created a nationalism that embraced immigrants. As the REPUBLICAN PARTY platform in 1864 put it, "foreign immigration . . . should be fostered and encouraged."

Beginning with Ulysses Grant, Presidents began to call for some kinds of immigration restriction and Congress began to act. In 1875 the first restrictive immigration statute was enacted, making it a crime for Americans to participate in the Asian "cooly-trade" and barring the entry of persons under sentence for nonpolitical felonies, of persons whose sentences had been remitted on condition of emigration, and of women "imported for the purposes of prostitution." No enforcement bureaucracy was created and it is not clear that even one immigrant was kept out by the act.

Controversy about Chinese immigrants created the first friction between the legislative and executive branches over immigration policy. Congress, sensitive to demands from the Far West and from trade unions, debated the exclusion of Chinese as early as 1870. In 1879 President Hayes vetoed an exclusion bill, arguing that, since immigration from China was covered by the 1869 Burlingame treaty, Congress was usurping presidential authority and that the matter could be better settled by negotiation.

In 1880 both major parties had anti-Chinese planks in their platforms. Early in 1882, after a new treaty with China recognized the right of the United States to suspend immigration, Congress passed a bill barring Chinese immigration for twenty years. President Arthur vetoed it saying that twenty years was too long. Congress responded by passing the CHINESE EXCLUSION ACT, which forbade the immigration of Chinese laborers for ten years and reaffirmed the bar against the naturalization of Chinese, but did allow the entry of Chinese "merchants."

**Increasing Restrictions, 1882–1921.** The first general restriction of immigration was enacted later in 1882. Although the law may not have kept out a single immigrant, it applied a fifty-cent head tax on incoming passengers and authorized the exclusion of "any convict, lunatic, idiot, or any person unable to take care of himself or herself without becoming a public charge." By the end of WORLD WAR I seven major classes of immigrants had been barred: Asians (save for Japanese and Filipinos), criminals, persons who failed to meet certain moral standards, certain poor persons who failed to meet certain moral standards, certain poor persons, certain sick persons, certain radicals, and illiterates.

Only the restriction on illiterates created major controversy. Three Presidents—Cleveland, Taft, and Wilson—vetoed literacy-test bills, largely on the grounds that illiteracy was the fault of the societies from which the immigrants came. Finally enacted over Wilson's second veto in 1917, the much debated measure had little effect as educational standards in most of Europe had risen by then.

But listing all the restrictions should not obscure the fact that immigration policy was still relatively permissive. Between 1892 and 1921, 308,835 aliens were excluded from the United States, more than half of them on the grounds that they were "likely to become a public charge." Since nearly 21 million persons successfully immigrated during those years, the rejection rate at American ports of entry was about 1.5 percent. (Uncounted others were rejected by physical examinations at ports of embarkation.)

**Greatest Restriction, 1921–1943.** Law enacted in 1921 and 1924—and supported by Presidents Harding and Coolidge, most politicians and the general public—made rejection a majority phenomenon. The Emergency Quota Act of 1921 and the IMMIGRATION ACT of 1924 placed severe limits on the number to be admitted, deliberately discriminated against southern and eastern Europeans, and required all immigrants to obtain a visa, placing great power in the hands of the consular service. More positively, the law created a "non-quota" category for close relatives of Americans, making family reunification an element of policy. In addition, as the Great Depression began, President Hoover, by administrative fiat changed the "likely to become a public charge" provision from a measure that kept out those who were held to be incompetent into one that kept out the poor.

The Great Depression proved to be an even more effective barrier than legislation: in several years of the 1930s more persons emigrated than immigrated. Franklin Roosevelt, who changed so much of American life, never once spoke of reforming general immigration policy. Since the United States had no refugee policy, the laws and regulations enacted to inhibit immigration also operated to keep out refugees.

**Relaxing Restriction, 1943–1965.** In 1943, Franklin Roosevelt persuaded Congress to repeal Chinese exclusion, award Chinese a tiny quota, and allow them to be naturalized. This seemingly minor act was the hinge on which the golden door began to swing open wider, largely because, in the half century that followed, foreign policy was more important than immigration policy. It was difficult to claim leadership of the "free world" when American policy barred most of the peoples of the world. Piecemeal liberalization quickly followed: Filipinos and "natives of India" were granted immigration and naturalization rights in 1946. After difficult fights led by President Truman in 1948 and 1950, relatively large numbers of displaced persons were admitted outside the quotas and in 1952 the otherwise reactionary McCARRAN-WALTER ACT extended the right of immigration and naturalization to all groups while retaining the discriminatory quota system. Truman, who favored a greater liberalization, had his veto overridden.

He then appointed a commission that proposed a liberal policy in its report, *Whom We Shall Welcome*. This policy was largely espoused by John Kennedy and put into effect by the immigration act of 1965 pushed through by Lyndon Johnson. In the meantime, a whole host of ad hoc COLD WAR refugee programs was installed by presidential directives and later approved by Congress. The misbegotten VIETNAM WAR produced the most massive refugee program of all. In 1980, at the urging of President Carter, who saw it as part of his HUMAN RIGHTS policy, Congress enacted, for the first time, a general refugee act whose major assumption was that refugees and asylum seekers of all kinds would be a continuing factor in American immigration.

**Renewed Heavy Immigration, Since 1965.** The changed world situation and the 1965 act and its successors have produced a major shift in patterns of American immigration, a shift not envisaged by the legislation's drafters. Where once European immigration dominated, after 1965 immigration from Asia and Latin America has. Those regions have accounted for more than 80 percent of all legal immigration, and more than 90 percent if illegal or "undocumented" entrants could be counted.

By 1992 two contrary attitudes toward immigration policy had become prevalent. On the one hand, most Americans seemed to have positive attitudes toward past and much present immigration, as the great popularity of the magnificent immigration museum on Ellis Island showed. On the other hand, some of the most numerous immigrant groups, particularly those from Latin America, were seen as economic and social threats in a time of lowered economic expectations. Although the political platforms of both political parties had positive things to say about immigration, many analysts wondered whether American immigration policy was about to undergo another major change of direction.

BIBLIOGRAPHY

Daniels, Roger. *Coming to America: A History of Immigration and Ethnicity in American Life*. 1990.

Fuchs, Lawrence H. *The American Kaleidoscope: Race, Ethnicity, and the Civic Culture*. 1990.

Hutchinson, E. P. *Legislative History of American Immigration Policy, 1798–1965*. 1981.

ROGER DANIELS

**IMMUNITY, PRESIDENTIAL.** The Constitution does not specify whether the President possesses any immunity from the judicial process. It does accord members of Congress explicit privileges from arrest and from suits for their legislative conduct. The absence of a parallel set of textual immunities for the President may imply that he possesses none. Yet concern was expressed at the CONSTITUTIONAL CONVENTION that subjecting the President even to IMPEACHMENT could impair his capacity to perform the duties of the office. Hence it is unlikely that the Framers thought that the President could be treated like an ordinary individual by the courts. Congress has not legislated on the subject. A statute purporting to regulate the President's exposure to compulsory process, civil damages, or criminal sanctions might be invalidated on SEPARATION OF POWERS grounds. Consequently, delineation of presidential immunities has been left to the courts.

The question of a President's immunity is sensitive for several reasons. First, his office is owed the respect due to the head of a coequal branch of government. Second, if the President must respond in any way to judicial process, and especially if he is amenable to trial, there is potential for interference with his constitutional duties. And third, fear of civil or criminal liability could deter a President from vigorously pursuing the public interest. Yet powerful competing considerations exist as well. If ours is truly to be a government "of laws, and not of men," no one should be above the law. Presidents have power to do great harm as well as good—it would be unfortunate if either affected individuals or the general public were unable to obtain redress for presidential wrongdoing. The courts have tried to balance these values.

**Immunity in History.** For most of the history of the United States it was unclear that the President could be directly subjected to any kind of compulsory court process. In the treason trial of AARON BURR in 1807, Chief Justice John Marshall, sitting as a circuit judge, directed a subpoena for evidence to President Thomas Jefferson. Jefferson complied "voluntarily," protesting any obligation to do so, and there the matter rested for many years. In MISSISSIPPI v. JOHNSON (1867), the Court refused to forbid President Andrew Johnson to enforce Reconstruction legislation. The decision rested, though, on the discretionary nature of the President's statutory duties and the consequent inappropriateness of enjoining his exercise of those duties in advance, rather than on his amenability to suit. Effective legal control of presidential actions was routinely maintained by reviewing the actions of subordinates. For example, in YOUNGSTOWN SHEET & TUBE CO. v. SAWYER (1952), the Court enjoined the Secretary of Commerce from carrying out the President's order to seize the steel mills to prevent a wartime strike. *Youngstown* confirmed the principle first established in MARBURY v. MADISON (1803), that the courts can compel high executive officers to comply with statutory limitations on their power.

Finally, in UNITED STATES v. NIXON (1974), the Supreme Court enforced a subpoena directly against the President for evidence in a criminal trial of several of his closest aides. The Court recognized a qualified EXECUTIVE PRIVILEGE to refuse to reveal presidential discussions and records. This privilege, based on general separation-of-powers concepts, stemmed from the functional need of the President for candid advice in policy formulation. Nevertheless, the Court held that the needs of the courts overrode the privilege in this specific case. It emphasized the narrowness of the subpoena and the power of the trial court to prevent unnecessary intrusion into presidential confidentiality by reviewing pertinent records in camera. In other situations involving military and foreign affairs secrets, the privilege has been treated as absolute, as in *United States v. Reynolds* (1953).

Article I, Section 3, of the Constitution does provide that impeached officers may be prosecuted. As applied to the President, this may mean that impeachment must precede any prosecution. (Some other officers have been prosecuted first and impeached afterwards, however.) It is also unclear whether a sitting President may be indicted and prosecuted for crime. None has ever been indicted, although President Nixon was named as an unindicted coconspirator by the grand jury investigating the WATERGATE AFFAIR.

Before the 1970s, civil damages actions against Presidents were extremely rare, and none ever proceeded to trial. *Livingston v. Jefferson* (C.C. Va. 1811) was the best-known early attempt to sue a President for damages. Chief Justice Marshall, sitting as a circuit judge, dismissed on a technicality a damages suit against Thomas Jefferson for an action taken pursuant to his presidential duties. The Supreme Court eventually erected a general barrier to successful civil actions against executive officers by holding that these officers possessed complete immunity from common law tort claims for actions taken in their official capacity. In *Spalding v. Vilas* (1896), the Court, granting immunity to the Postmaster General, emphasized that the public interest required the immunity in order to assure that officials would fearlessly execute their duties. The Court reaffirmed *Spalding* in *Barr v. Matteo* (1959) by holding a federal officer immune for acts taken within the "outer perimeter" of the line of duty. In *Westfall v. Erwin* (1988), however, the Court required that an official must have been exercising government discretion when taking action for which immunity was claimed. Congress subsequently amended the Federal Tort Claims Act (28 U.S.C. 2680) to substitute the United States as defendant and to waive sovereign immunity for the new liability created by *Westfall*.

The potential for civil actions against Presidents became real when the Supreme Court held in *Bivens v. Six Unknown Named Agents of Federal Bureau of Narcotics* (1971), that the Constitution directly authorizes civil actions against federal officers who violate constitutional rights of individuals. After *Bivens*, citizens possessed a claim to assert against Presidents who had injured them, but the question remained whether defendants in *Bivens* suits could assert any immunity from damages. In *Butz v. Economou* (1978), the Court granted a Secretary of Agriculture a qualified immunity from damages, if the action taken was neither malicious nor clearly illegal.

In NIXON v. FITZGERALD (1982), involving President Richard M. Nixon's removal of a civilian from the air force, the Court decided that the President possesses an absolute immunity from civil damages when he acts within the "outer perimeter" of his official duties. In justifying the extension of complete immunity to the President, the Court emphasized the likelihood that the prominence of the presidency would draw lawsuits, the existence of other checks on presidential behavior (such as congressional and press scrutiny of his actions), and the possibility of other relief for injured individuals. The breadth of the decision appears to make the President immune in any civil case. A companion case, *Harlow v. Fitzgerald* (1982), involved the extension of presidential immunity to his immediate aides. The Court decided that these aides are entitled only to the qualified immunity that is available to other executive officers. It modified that immunity, however, to eliminate the element of subjective malice. The Court thought that too many baseless claims could proceed to trial where allegations of malice were made, because an officer could not readily negate them. The net effect of the two cases is to permit some checking of a President through his aides.

### BIBLIOGRAPHY

Carter, Stephen. "The Political Aspects of Judicial Power: Some Notes on the Presidential Immunity Decision." *University of Pennsylvania Law Review* 131 (1983): 1341–1399.

Fisher, Louis. *Constitutional Conflicts between Congress and the President.* 3d ed. 1991.

Ray, Laura K. "From Prerogative to Accountability: The Amenability of the President to Suit." *Kentucky Law Journal* 80 (1991–1992): 739–790.

Shane, Peter M., and Harold H. Bruff. *The Law of Presidential Power.* 1988.

Tribe, Laurence H. *American Constitutional Law.* 2d ed. 1988.

HAROLD H. BRUFF

**IMPEACHMENT.** The constitutional procedure for removing a President from office is called impeachment. Article II, Section 4 of the Constitution provides that the President (as well as the Vice President and all civil officers) "shall be removed from office on Impeachment for, and conviction of, Treason, Bribery, or other HIGH CRIMES AND MISDEMEANORS." The House of Representatives initiates the procedure by voting an accusation—an impeachment—that it then prosecutes in the Senate. Just as the House has "the sole Power of Impeachment" (Article I, Section 2), the Senate has "the sole Power to try all Impeachments" (Article I, Section 3). When sitting for the purpose of an impeachment trial, members of the Senate "shall be on Oath or Affirmation"; when the President is tried, the Chief Justice presides. Conviction requires a two-thirds vote of the members of the Senate who are present. "Judgment in Cases of Impeachment shall not extend further than to removal from Office, and disqualification to hold and enjoy any Office of honor, Trust or Profit under the United States; but the Party convicted shall nevertheless be liable and subject to Indictment, Trial, Judgment and Punishment, according to Law" (Article I, Section 3).

**The Framers' Debates.** The Framers of the Constitution tailored the impeachment provisions with a view to the removal of the President. They followed the procedural model of English impeachments, which had been adopted in most of the states. The power of originating the inquiry—preferring an impeachment—was placed in the hands of a legislative body because, ALEXANDER HAMILTON wrote, impeachment is a legislative remedy, "an essential check in the hands of that body upon the encroachments of the executive." It was lodged in the House, "those who represent the great body of the people," James Iredell told the North Carolina ratifying convention, "because the occasion for its exercise will arise from acts of great injury to the community, and the objects of it may be such as cannot be easily reached by an ordinary tribunal."

The Framers had difficulty deciding how impeachments should be tried. They rejected trial by the Supreme Court because it might try the President on a criminal charge after the impeachment trial and because the Court, as GOUVERNEUR MORRIS said, "were too few in number and might be warped or corrupted." The Senate was considered to be the only body that would be unbiased by an accusation brought by the House. Any other tribunal, Iredell said, might "be too much awed by so powerful an accuser." But there was concern that the Senate would be too lenient. For example, James Monroe complained to the Virginia ratifying convention: "To whom is he responsible? To the Senate, his own council. If he makes a treaty, bartering the interests of the country, by whom is he to be tried? By the very persons who advised him to perpetrate the act. Is this any security?"

The impeachment procedure was criticized because the President was not suspended from office during the trial. "[W]hen he is arraigned for treason," George Mason warned the Virginia convention, "he has the command of the army and navy, and may surround the Senate with thirty thousand troops." Impeachments will come too late, Fisher Ames of Massachusetts told the House in 1789: "[W]hile we are preparing the process, the mischief will be perpetrated, and the offender will escape." Impeachment was a "dilatory and inefficient process," John Vining of Delaware said. "[W]hat delays and uncertainty with the forms of trial, details of evidence, arguments of counsel, and deliberate decision!" Theodore Sedgwick of Massachusetts concurred: impeachment was a "tardy, tedious, desultory road."

**Impeachments of Other Officials.** These representatives were endorsing the President's power to remove executive officers. Just one subordinate executive officer has ever been impeached, Secretary of War William W. Belknap in 1876 for bribery. He resigned hours before the House voted unanimously to impeach him; the Senate acquitted him, with twenty-two of the twenty-five senators who voted not guilty expressing the view that the Senate lacked jurisdiction as a result of his resignation. Senator William Blount was impeached in 1797 for sedition and conspiracy. The Senate, which had already expelled Blount, dismissed the impeachment.

Impeachment has been used principally against federal judges. Thirteen have been impeached, and a number of others were subject to impeachment resolutions and investigations in the House that did not lead to impeachment. Of the thirteen, seven were convicted, four were acquitted, and two resigned. In the three most recent cases—all convictions—a committee of the Senate heard the evidence, and only closing arguments were made to the full Senate.

The most significant of the judicial impeachments involved Supreme Court Justice Samuel Chase. A partisan Federalist, Chase was impeached in 1804 by a Republican House. He was charged, in the words of one of the House managers prosecuting the impeachment at his Senate trial in 1805, with "perverting the high judicial functions of his office for the purposes of individual oppression, and of staining the pure ermine of justice by political party spirit." Eight articles of impeachment charged judicial misconduct while sitting as a circuit justice in 1800 and 1803. During the trial, Chase's defense counsel emphasized that the articles alleged no indictable crime or known wrong and that the impeachment was itself a partisan use of judicial process. The Senate acquitted him on each article, although a majority voted guilty on three of them. The outcome led Thomas Jefferson to reflect, some years later, that "impeachment is an impracticable thing, a mere scare-crow."

**Andrew Johnson.** Only two Presidents, a century apart, have been the subject of impeachment proceedings—Andrew Johnson in 1868 [*see* IMPEACHMENT OF ANDREW JOHNSON] and Richard M. Nixon in 1974.

In December 1867, after a ten-month investigation, the House Judiciary Committee reported a resolution of impeachment against President Johnson. Five Radical Republicans on the committee voted for the resolution; two moderate Republicans and two Democrats voted against. For the committee majority, George S. Boutwell acknowledged to the House that "no specific, heinous, novel offense" was charged against President Johnson but rather "a series of acts, . . . a succession of events" all pointing to the charge that "he used as he had the opportunity, and misused as necessity and circumstances dictated, the great powers of the nation with which he was intrusted, for the purpose of reconstructing this Government in the interest of the rebellion." For the Republican minority of the committee, Chairman James F. Wilson contended that the House

"must be guided by some rule in this grave proceeding." Johnson was "the worst of the Presidents," but he should not be impeached for "a bundle of generalities" such as those reported by the committee. The House rejected the impeachment resolution by a vote of 57 to 108.

Two and one-half months later, in February 1868, President Johnson ordered the removal from office of Secretary of War EDWIN M. STANTON and authorized Maj. Gen. Lorenzo Thomas to act as interim secretary. The TENURE OF OFFICE ACT, which Congress passed in 1867 over Johnson's veto, provided that officers appointed with the ADVICE AND CONSENT of the Senate would hold office until their successors were similarly appointed. CABINET officers were subject to removal with the advice and consent of the Senate. When the Senate was in recess, the President could suspend an officer and appoint a temporary replacement until the Senate met again and decided whether the officer could be removed. In August 1867, President Johnson had suspended Stanton; in January 1868, the Senate refused to concur in the suspension. The Tenure of Office Act carried a criminal penalty for violations, which it declared to be "high misdemeanors."

The same day President Johnson ordered Stanton's removal, the Senate passed a resolution stating that "under the Constitution and laws . . . the President has no power to remove the Secretary of War and to designate any other officer to perform the duties of that office *ad interim*." The following day, the House Committee on Reconstruction reported a resolution of impeachment. Two days later, the House impeached Johnson by a vote of 126 to 47. "The logic of the former case is made plain, not to say perfect, by the sequence in the present one," James F. Wilson told the House. President Johnson "has presented to us . . . a high misdemeanor known to the law and defined by statute."

The House appointed a select committee to draft articles of impeachment against Johnson. It reported back charges based entirely upon the events surrounding the orders for the removal of Stanton and the designation of Thomas as interim secretary. The House adopted nine articles, each pleading a legal variant of a "high crime" or a "high misdemeanor" from these events.

After the House elected managers to prosecute the impeachment in the Senate, they proposed two broader charges, which the House added to the articles. Article 10 alleged that Johnson had made "intemperate, inflammatory, and scandalous harangues" against Congress and laws enacted by it, by which he brought the office of President "into contempt, ridicule, and disgrace, to the great scandal of all good citizens." Article 11 charged that President Johnson had declared that the Thirty-ninth Congress was not authorized to execute legislative power, but was a Congress of only part of the states, and that, in pursuance of this declaration, he had attempted to prevent the execution of the Tenure of Office Act by preventing Stanton from resuming the functions of Secretary of War after the Senate refused to concur in his suspension, to prevent the execution of the Army Appropriations Act, and to prevent the execution of the Reconstruction Act. (The Thirty-ninth Congress had passed all three laws in 1867.)

The trial focused on the removal of Stanton and the interim appointment of Thomas. Johnson's defense counsel made a number of arguments, not all of them consistent: He had not violated the Tenure of Office Act because there was only an attempt to remove, not a removal. The Tenure of Office Act did not apply to Stanton or the temporary designation of Thomas. The act was unconstitutional. If the act did apply and was constitutional, Johnson should not be removed for a mistaken interpretation of law, made in good faith and with the advice of his Cabinet. Furthermore, Johnson intended to test the constitutionality of the law, which he had a right—even a duty—to do. If he had no such right, he should not be removed for a good faith mistake in construing his constitutional duties and powers. Finally, there was no public injury; it was at best a technical-crime, insufficient cause to remove the President from office.

The House managers, having found their "perfect" case in what they thought was an easily proved statutory "high misdemeanor," were constrained by the pretextual charge they chose to prosecute. The Tenure of Office Act simply would not bear the intense scrutiny to which it was put during the trial. The defense, not the managers, was able to invoke the responsibilities, powers, and duties of the presidential office. Having pleaded specific crimes, the managers were hampered in arguing that President Johnson had committed great constitutional wrongs.

The Senate ultimately voted on only three articles—Article 11 and two articles concerning the Thomas appointment. Each failed by a single vote, with thirty-five Republicans voting guilty and twelve Democrats and seven Republicans voting not guilty. The defense arguments clearly bore fruit with the Republicans voting for acquittal. In written opinions, six of these Senators explained their votes on the basis of statutory construction, Johnson's intent, the supposed justification for his conduct, and the lack of gravity of the offense. Senator Charles Sumner, who declared

Johnson guilty of all the articles "and infinitely more," wrote that one of these opinions, by Senator P. G. Van Winkle of West Virginia, treated the impeachment "as if it were a prosecution for sheep-stealing in the police court of Wheeling."

The Johnson impeachment, wrote Clinton L. Rossiter in the 1950s, was "vengefully political in motivation and purpose"; his acquittal "made clear for all time that impeachment is not . . . a political process for turning out a President whom a majority of the House and two-thirds of the Senate simply cannot abide." Presidential impeachment was considered to be a constitutional dead letter.

**Richard M. Nixon.** The revelation of the WATERGATE AFFAIR and President Nixon's order to fire Special Prosecutor Archibald Cox, who was investigating it, changed this perception. The House Judiciary Committee began an inquiry in November 1973 to determine whether grounds existed to impeach President Nixon. The investigation lasted some eight months. It focused on evidence of wrongdoing by Nixon, including information provided by the federal grand jury investigating the Watergate cover-up, which ultimately named President Nixon an unindicted co-conspirator in an obstruction of justice.

In July 1974, the Judiciary Committee voted to report three articles of impeachment to the House. Each of the articles charged that President Nixon had violated his constitutional oath faithfully to execute the office of President and to preserve, protect, and defend the Constitution and his constitutional duty to take care that the laws by faithfully executed.

Article 1 focused on the Watergate cover-up. It charged that President Nixon had prevented, obstructed, and impeded the administration of justice by engaging personally and through his subordinates and agents in a plan or course of conduct to obstruct investigation of the Watergate break-in; to cover up, conceal, and protect those responsible; and to conceal the existence and scope of other unlawful covert activities. It specified nine means used to implement the course of conduct or plan. The Committee voted 27 to 11 to adopt this article.

Article 2 alleged abuse of presidential power. It charged that President Nixon had repeatedly engaged in conduct violating the constitutional rights of citizens, impairing the due and proper administration of justice and the conduct of lawful inquiries, or contravening the laws governing executive agencies and the purposes of these agencies. Included in specifications were misuse of the Internal Revenue Service; improper electronic surveillance by the FEDERAL BUREAU OF INVESTIGATION and SECRET SERVICE; creation of a secret investigative unit (the "plumbers") within the EXECUTIVE OFFICE OF THE PRESIDENT; failure to act when he knew that close subordinates were impeding investigations; and interference with the FBI, the Justice Department, the Special Prosecutor, and the CENTRAL INTELLIGENCE AGENCY. The Committee adopted this article by a vote of 28 to 10.

Article 3 dealt with President Nixon's refusal to produce tape recordings of his private conversations and other materials subpoenaed by the committee for its impeachment investigation. It alleged that he had "interposed the powers of the Presidency against the lawful subpoenas of the House of Representatives, thereby assuming to himself functions and judgments necessary to the exercise of the sole power of impeachment vested by the Constitution in the House of Representatives." The committee voted 21 to 17 to report this article.

The committee rejected two other proposed articles by votes of 26 to 12. One alleged that President Nixon authorized, ordered, and ratified the concealment of information from Congress and supplied Congress with false and misleading statements about American bombing operations in Cambodia during the VIETNAM WAR. The other charged that President Nixon fraudulently failed to report income and claimed unauthorized deductions on his federal tax returns and that he received unconstitutional emoluments in the form of government expenditures on his privately owned homes.

During the deliberations of the committee, both proponents and opponents of President Nixon's impeachment agreed that grounds for impeachment would exist if he had engaged in serious violations of his constitutional duties, as defined by the constitutionally prescribed oath and the constitutional provision that the President "shall take Care that the Laws be faithfully executed." Even those who voted against the impeachment articles acknowledged that "high crimes and misdemeanors" need not be violations of criminal law, although some contended that proof of criminal or wrongful intent was required. The minority of the committee that opposed impeachment asserted that the evidence was inadequate to support the charges and that the allegations were insufficiently grave to warrant the extreme step of impeachment and removal from office.

The committee conducted its inquiry more like an adjudication than the preparation of an accusation for prosecution before the Senate. It permitted counsel for President Nixon to argue his case and to examine witnesses. It required clear and convincing evidence of the allegations included in articles of impeachment.

Six days after the Judiciary Committee finished its deliberations on articles of impeachment, President Nixon released transcripts of three recorded conversations that were among those he had withheld from the committee. The Supreme Court had ordered production of these and other recordings for use in Watergate cover-up prosecutions, rejecting Nixon's claim of EXECUTIVE PRIVILEGE in a unanimous opinion. Even those who had voted against the impeachment articles considered one of the newly released recordings to be a "smoking gun," proving Nixon's early involvement in the cover-up. Nixon's remaining support evaporated, and he conceded that the new evidence made his impeachment by the House "virtually a foregone conclusion." Three days later, he resigned from office.

**An Assessment.** In the aftermath of the Nixon resignation, there was consensus that the constitutional system had worked. Like the Johnson trial, the Nixon impeachment seemed to demonstrate that the outcome of a presidential removal proceeding depends much more upon establishing guilt of serious wrongdoing than on partisanship. The constitutional requirement of a two-thirds vote by the Senate necessitates, as a practical matter, that members of the President's own political party support impeachment and removal. "The security to innocence" from this requirement is, as Alexander Hamilton wrote, "as complete as itself can desire."

But the Nixon proceeding again demonstrated that the procedure for removing a President is cumbersome and time-consuming. The first impeachment investigation of Andrew Johnson took ten months. When it voted to impeach Johnson, the House acted quickly—his orders to remove Stanton and install Thomas were issued on a Friday afternoon, the House impeached the following Monday. Even in that case, however, the Senate trial was not completed for nearly three months. In Nixon's case, it took eight months before the Judiciary Committee was able to recommend articles of impeachment; had the impeachment gone forward, it would have taken several months more for trial.

Nor, because impeachment is such a rare event, have the procedures been modernized or tailored to the constitutional purpose of the undertaking. Articles of impeachment, each considered and voted upon separately, are anachronistic and may obscure the crucial issue in an impeachment proceeding—whether the wrongful conduct of the President, taken as a whole, is sufficiently serious to warrant removal from office. Other elements of the process similarly reflect formalities of the eighteenth century, long obsolete elsewhere in the law, and tend to impart an inappropriate aura of a criminal prosecution to the proceeding.

Presidential impeachment is an uncomfortable enterprise for legislators and citizens alike. It poses fundamental questions about the nature of American government, which it forces Congress to address in the midst of a governmental crisis, without much guidance from precedent. It requires clear-cut choices—to accuse or not, to adjudge guilty or not—by the branch of government most prone to compromise or defer controversial decisions.

The Framers of the Constitution viewed the President's eligibility for reelection every four years as the principal mechanism for ensuring responsibility in the office. James Madison described it as "an impeachment before the community, who will have the power of punishment by refusing to re-elect him." This accountability has been attenuated by the two-term limitation of the TWENTY-SECOND AMENDMENT. The President's amenability to criminal prosecution and civil suit has likewise been reduced. Although the Framers envisioned that the President, even while in office, would be subject to legal process, the Supreme Court held in 1982 that a President or former President is absolutely immune from civil suit for conduct while in office. And the Watergate criminal case, in which President Nixon was not indicted but merely named as a conspirator, suggests that prosecution of an incumbent President, although constitutionally permissible, is unlikely to be pursued.

Impeachment itself has proved to be an unwieldy weapon. Its presence in the constitutional arsenal, however, undoubtedly serves as a deterrent to presidential malfeasance. No President would want to face the obloquy of being the first to be convicted upon an impeachment, of having "his very name . . . become a word to frighten children with throughout the land," as one of Andrew Johnson's defense counsel put it. From this perspective, the most important precedent concerning presidential impeachment may prove to be an extraconstitutional one: President Nixon's resignation to avoid impeachment, trial, and probable removal from office.

### BIBLIOGRAPHY

Benedict, Michael Les. *The Impeachment and Trial of Andrew Johnson.* 1973.
Bushnell, Eleanore. *Crimes, Follies, and Misfortunes: The Federal Impeachment Trials.* 1992.
Hoffer, Peter Charles, and N. E. H. Hull. *Impeachment in America, 1635–1805.* 1984.
Labovitz, John R. *Presidential Impeachment.* 1978.
Rehnquist, William H. *Grand Inquests: The Historic Impeachment of Justice Samuel Chase and President Andrew Johnson.* 1992.
Smith, Samuel H., and Thomas Lloyd, eds. *Trial of Samuel Chase, An Associate Justice of the Supreme Court of the United States, Impeached by the House of Representatives for High Crimes and Misdemeanors before the Senate of the United States,* 2 vols. 1970. Reprint of 1805 ed.
U.S. House of Representatives. *Impeachment of Richard M. Nixon, President of the United States: Report of the Committee on the Judiciary.* 93d Cong., 2d Sess., H. Rept. No. 93-1305. 20 August 1974.
U.S. Senate. *Trial of Andrew Johnson, President of the United States, Before the Senate of the United States, on Impeachment by the House of Representatives for High Crimes and Misdemeanors.* 40th Cong., 2d Sess. 2 vols. 1970. Reprint of 3 vol. 1868 ed.

JOHN R. LABOVITZ

## IMPEACHMENT OF ANDREW JOHNSON.

President Andrew Johnson is the only President to have been impeached by the House of Representatives. The House voted to impeach Johnson on 24 February 1868. On 29 February it filed particular articles (formal charges) and added two others on 3 March. The trial began with presentation of the articles to the Senate on 4 March and concluded on 26 May 1868, with the Senate failing to convict the President by a margin of one vote.

The Constitution authorizes the House of Representatives, on a majority vote, to bring an IMPEACHMENT to the Senate for trial. Conviction requires a two-thirds vote of the Senate, and the punishment is removal from office. The definition of the Constitution's grounds for impeachment—"High Crimes and Misdemeanors"—has been a matter of dispute. During the controversy over Johnson's impeachment, many Republicans insisted that the terms referred not only to indictable crimes but also to abuse of power. Democrats, who supported Johnson's RECONSTRUCTION policies, as well as some of the more conservative Republicans argued that impeachment required indictable crimes.

**The Dispute with Congress.** The roots of the Johnson impeachment lay in the dispute between the President and Congress concerning Reconstruction of the Union after the CIVIL WAR and who had the authority to make Reconstruction policy. President Johnson favored a lenient policy that permitted former Confederates to retain political power in the South and left southern states with nearly untrammeled authority to define and limit the rights of the newly freed slaves. Most Republicans wanted to displace the old Southern political leadership and insisted that the freedmen be guaranteed at least basic civil rights. Johnson insisted that as COMMANDER IN CHIEF of the armed forces it was his obligation to reestablish civil government in the South and that Congress had little authority on this question. Republicans insisted that restoration to the Union required the agreement of both Congress and the President through formal legislation.

The dispute led to a crisis in American government. Over Johnson's veto, Congress passed legislation that defined black Americans as citizens and forbade violation of their basic civil rights. It proposed a constitutional amendment to accomplish the same ends and to disqualify Confederate leaders from holding political office. When southern whites, encouraged by Johnson, continued to resist, Republicans passed the Reconstruction Act, which placed the southern states under military authority once again and required the organization of new state governments under constitutions guaranteeing equal civil rights and enfranchising black men.

Johnson bitterly resisted this program. He used his presidential powers to obstruct its operation, hoping frustrated northern voters would eventually turn against its authors. His Attorney General took no steps to enforce the civil rights legislation. The Cabinet appointed government officers who were not required to take loyalty oaths. Johnson forced the return of property the government had seized from Confederates and designated for the use of former slaves. He replaced military officers who vigorously enforced the Reconstruction Act with others who sympathized with southern whites. Most ominously, he denied the constitutionality of the state governments created under the Reconstruction Act, laying the foundation for a confrontation over which southern votes, if any, would count in the presidential and congressional elections of 1868.

In the course of this struggle, Johnson used his authority over the CIVIL SERVICE to remove Republican officeholders and replace them with men loyal to him. Republicans responded with the TENURE OF OFFICE ACT, which limited the President's power to remove government officials without Senate approval [see also REMOVAL POWER]. Opponents denied the measure's constitutionality, and even supporters disliked the provision that prevented the President from making changes in his Cabinet without approval by the Senate. A compromise purposely left unclear whether the law protected the Cabinet.

**Impeachment.** RADICAL REPUBLICANS began demanding that the House impeach Johnson as early as January 1867. More conservative Republicans, however, feared to take such an extreme step and referred the matter to the House Judiciary Committee, which was known to be opposed to impeachment. As Johnson continued to obstruct Republican policy, pressure for impeachment grew. It reached a peak when Johnson, apparently to gain complete control of the army, suspended Secretary of War EDWIN M. STANTON in accordance with the Tenure of Office Act in August 1867, naming General Ulysses S. Grant as a temporary replacement. However, Democratic successes in the state elections of 1867 tempered the anti-Johnson feeling of some Republicans. Although the House Judiciary Committee narrowly recommended in November 1867, that Johnson be impeached, the House defeated the resolution the following month, with at least some Republicans saying that only a clear violation of law could constitute an impeachable offense.

In January 1868, the Senate formally refused to accede in Stanton's removal. According to the Tenure of Office Act, that decision reinstated Stanton as Secretary of War. But Johnson was determined to remove Stanton. On 21 February he appointed a new temporary Secretary of War and once again notified Stanton of his removal. Fearing that such outright defiance meant Johnson was prepared to go to any length to frustrate their Reconstruction policy, House Republicans on 24 February almost unanimously passed a new impeachment resolution. Having earlier defeated the resolution to impeach Johnson for abuse of power, the House passed nine narrow, legalistic impeachment articles, all either charging a violation of the Tenure of Office Act or that the President had appointed a new Secretary of War without Senate confirmation, as required by the Constitution. Only at the last moment did the House add tenth and eleventh articles that alleged a general conspiracy to undermine Congress and defeat the operation of the Reconstruction laws.

**Trial.** Although House Republicans and Radical Republican Senators urged a quick trial, conviction, and removal, most Republican Senators joined Democrats to give Johnson a fair hearing. Johnson's legal counsel relied on three basic arguments in response to the charge that the President had violated the Tenure of Office Act. First, they argued that the President had the right to refuse to enforce a law he thought was unconstitutional, especially if the law was aimed at him and the only way to test its constitutionality before the courts was to disobey it. Second, they claimed that the President did not have criminal intent because his only purpose in violating the law was to test it before the courts. Third, they argued that Secretary of War Stanton was not covered by the law and that therefore the President had not violated it by ordering his removal. In response to the charge Johnson had violated the Constitution by appointing Stanton's replacement without Senate confirmation, Johnson's lawyers cited a large number of instances where Presidents had made temporary appointments without Senate confirmation.

The managers of the House's case for impeachment responded that the President had no right to violate a law once it was duly passed over his veto; that even if his intent were to test the law's constitutionality, that intent did not vitiate his culpability; and that the law did cover Stanton. But most of all, they insisted that the President must be held to a higher standard of obedience to law than are ordinary citizens. Over the objections of Johnson's counsel, they insisted that the President had acted in a political context and for political reasons and, citing the eleventh impeachment article, stressed that the Senate must not close its eyes to the context in which the trial was proceeding and the dangerous consequences of an acquittal.

On 16 May the Senate voted on the eleventh article. The vote to convict—35 to 19—fell one vote short of the margin necessary. Having received assurances that Johnson would not continue to undermine the Republican Reconstruction program, seven Republican Senators joined all the Democrats in voting not guilty, primarily on the grounds that Stanton was not covered by the law. In an effort to exert political pressure on their recalcitrant colleagues, the Republicans adjourned the trial for ten days. They then voted on the first and second articles, with the same result. With that, Republicans voted to adjourn the trial *sine die* (indefinitely).

### BIBLIOGRAPHY

Benedict, Michael Les. *The Impeachment and Trial of Andrew Johnson.* 1973.

DeWitt, David Miller. *The Impeachment and Trial of Andrew Johnson, Seventeenth President of the United States: A History.* 1903.

Dunning, William A. "The Impeachment and Trial of President Johnson." In *Essays on the Civil War and Reconstruction, and Related Topics.* 1898.

Trefousse, Hans L. *Impeachment of a President: Andrew Johnson, the Blacks, and Reconstruction.* 1975.

MICHAEL LES BENEDICT

**IMPERIALISM.** America's venture into imperialism—the extension of political authority through force—focused on the Pacific region and Caribbean in the late nineteenth and early twentieth century. The United States, unlike other imperial powers, did not create its empire by dispatching military forces specifically to establish control over generally defenseless areas. Instead it exploited opportunities created by war or the internal instabilities and weaknesses of

regions regarded strategically important. This accounts for the ease and almost total disregard of means by which the United States established its colonial empire. Europe's successful African and Asian ventures in the 1880s failed to enlist the United States in the competition for empire. Still events in the Pacific and the Caribbean were slowly, almost imperceptibly, transforming the country's global outlook. What attracted Americans to the immense world of the Pacific was not only the opportunities for trade and investment but also the knowledge that the civilizations of the Pacific could not resist the power, technology, and organizational skills of the Western world. After 1890 the application of American will in the Orient appeared so effortless that it ultimately led to expanded objectives, illusions of omnipotence, and wars exorbitantly expensive.

Under the prodding of Anson Burlingame, the first U.S. minister to China in 1861, the United States developed a paternalism toward that amorphous empire that eventually made its defense the keystone of American policy in the Pacific. At the same time the United States contributed much to Japan's modernization. Meanwhile the United States in 1867 claimed the Midway Islands in the north central Pacific. In subsequent years it demonstrated a growing interest in Hawaii, Korea, and Samoa, where it faced powerful German and Japanese competition. Despite potential dangers two forces accelerated the country's Pacific encroachments. One was the missionary zeal to bring order and progress to the world's backward regions. To the expansionist Josiah Strong Christianity and civil liberty, as keys to Western civilization, had contributed most to the elevation of the human race. "It follows, then," he wrote in 1885, "that the Anglo-Saxon, as the great representative of these two ideas . . . , is divinely commissioned to be, in a peculiar sense, his brother's keeper. Add to this the fact of his rapidly increasing strength in modern times, and we have well nigh a demonstration of his destiny." The more tangible incentive to American activity in the Pacific lay in the quest for world markets that accompanied the impressive growth of American industrial and agricultural production after the CIVIL WAR. Alfred Thayer Mahan's influential book, *The Influence of Sea Power upon History* (1890), advocated the acquisition of island outposts to protect the country's shipping.

Benjamin Harrison's presidency (1889–1893) established the foundations of an American empire in the Pacific. In August 1891 Secretary of State JAMES G. BLAINE suggested to Harrison that "there are only three places that are of value enough to be taken, that are not continental. One is Hawaii and the others are Cuba and Porto Rico. . . . Hawaii may come up for decision at any unexpected hour." In February 1893 the Harrison administration negotiated an annexation treaty with Hawaiian commissioners; the incoming President Grover Cleveland rejected it. Cleveland was equally critical of the previous administration's involvement in Samoa. Anti-imperialists warned the nation against assuming commitments outside the Western Hemisphere. Colonial acquisitions, declared William Graham Sumner, a sociologist at Yale University, would be burdens, not gains. The anti-imperialists demonstrated their power when they defeated another Hawaii annexation treaty in 1897.

Within a year the SPANISH-AMERICAN WAR had broken the power of anti-imperialism and pushed the United States onto the world stage. On 1 May 1898, within days after the outbreak of the war, a war ostensibly to free CUBA, Commodore George Dewey's American squadron destroyed Spain's Pacific fleet in Manila Bay. This sudden display of U.S. naval power and the possibilities it opened for empire-building were not lost on a group of well-placed expansionists in Washington. During June, Congress annexed Hawaii by joint resolution. Meanwhile President William McKinley moved to establish American control of the PHILIP-PINES, already freed except for the capital city of Manila by Emilio Aguinaldo's Filipino insurgents. On 13 August the Spaniards, by previous arrangement, surrendered Manila to American forces.

As Spanish territory the Philippines, unlike Hawaii and Samoa, had been off limits to American imperial ambitions. But the decision to destroy Spanish power in Manila closed all easy avenues of retreat. Having liberated the islands, the United States had either to restore them to Spain—which was impossible—free them, transfer them to another power, or retain them. During the summer of 1898 politicians, editors, intellectuals, missionary societies, and commercial groups clamored for retention. On September 16 President McKinley instructed his peace commission that American arms, with no thought of acquisition, had brought the country duties and obligations to humanity that it could not ignore. During December the Peace Commission in Paris negotiated a treaty that conveyed the Philippines, Guam, and PUERTO RICO to the United States in exchange for $20 million. After a long, bitter, and sometimes brilliant debate the Senate approved the treaty in February 1899 by a vote of 57 to 27, one more than necessary to gain the required two-thirds. That decision incited the costly and divisive Filipino war for possession of the Philippines that lasted until Aguinaldo's capture in 1902.

Secretary of State JOHN HAY'S OPEN DOOR notes of 1899 and 1900 appeared to save China from dismemberment by Russia, Great Britain, France, Germany, Italy, and Japan. In the process they created a powerful, if informal, U.S. commitment to China's political, economic, and administrative integrity. Thereafter the United States faced Russia and Japan, two dominant powers in the Far East with interests in China far greater than those of the United States, as potential enemies in the western Pacific. Yet editors, politicians, and businessmen, seeing only a succession of apparently triumphant national involvements in the Pacific, looked confidently to the Far East as the new stage of American activity and lightly assigned to Washington the major responsibility for the region's peaceful evolution.

American intervention in the Caribbean began with the destruction of Spanish power in Cuba during the Spanish American War. Except for the annexation of Puerto Rico in 1899, the United States, as in China, sought, not territory, but peace, stability, and economic opportunity. Through the Platt Amendment of 1901 the United States gained control over Cuba's external policies even as it attempted to stabilize the Cuban government and economy through a continuing military occupation. In 1903 the United States engineered the Panamanian revolution, acquired the desired Panama Canal Zone, and soon established a protectorate over the new Republic of Panama. Theodore Roosevelt's interventionism in the Caribbean reached its ultimate form in his corollary of the MON-ROE DOCTRINE, proclaimed in 1904. Roosevelt saw clearly that European creditors would interfere in the internal affairs of the Latin American states unless the United States assumed responsibility for the financial policies of the Caribbean republics. Roosevelt established control of the customs administration of Santa Domingo. In 1912 the Taft administration placed marines in Nicaragua to support a pro-U.S. regime. Political disturbances in HAITI prompted Woodrow Wilson to order marines into that country in July 1915 and establish a protectorate to control that country's finances. Within a year Wilson sent marines to Santa Domingo to establish peace and the possibilities of economic development. Wilson placed troops in Mexico, purchased the Virgin Islands, and negotiated the Bryan-Chamorro Treaty to obtain a water route through Nicaragua as well as important leaseholds at each end of the proposed canal.

Republicans condemned Wilson's Caribbean interventions. In 1924 the Coolidge administration signed a treaty with Santo Domingo that removed the marines; a year later Coolidge ended the thirteen-year military occupation of Nicaragua. The decision was premature. In 1926 marines reentered Nicaragua to defend the conservative government against a liberal assault. An election in 1927 satisfied both sides, but the continued resistance of rebel leader Augusto Sandino prompted Coolidge to continue the marine occupation of Nicaragua. The rising Latin American indignation toward Washington's unequal treatment of the Caribbean states burst forth in the Pan-American Conference at Havana in January 1928. Responding to domestic as well as foreign pressures, J. Reuben Clark, Under Secretary of State, repudiated American interventionism under the Roosevelt Corollary in his *Memorandum on the Monroe Doctrine*. In adopting the views of the *Memorandum*, President Herbert Hoover and his Secretary of State, HENRY L. STIMSON, abandoned the policies of the past. During 1931 Stimson ordered the marines out of Nicaragua. President Franklin D. Roosevelt completed the withdrawal of the marines from Nicaragua in 1933 and from Haiti a year later. With the formal U.S. endorsement of the Latin American resolution against foreign intervention at the Seventh International Conference of American States at Montevideo in December 1933, the era of American interventionism in the Caribbean came to an end.

### BIBLIOGRAPHY

Anderson, David L. *Imperialism and Idealism: American Diplomats in China, 1861–1898.* 1985.

May, Ernest R. *Imperial Democracy: The Emergence of America as a Great Power.* 1961.

Morgan, H. Wayne. *America's Road to Empire: The War with Spain and Overseas Expansion.* 1865.

Rystad, Goran. *Ambiguous Imperialism: American Foreign Policy and Domestic Politics at the Turn of the Century.* 1975.

Welch, Richard E. *Imperialists and Anti-Imperialists: The Debate Over Expansionism in the 1890's.* 1972.

NORMAN A. GRAEBNER

**IMPERIAL PRESIDENCY.** The American Constitution envisages a strong presidency within an equally strong system of accountability. The term *imperial presidency* arose in the latter days of the administration of Richard M. Nixon to describe the result when the constitutional balance between EXECUTIVE POWER and PRESIDENTIAL ACCOUNTABILITY is upset in favor of executive power.

The imperial presidency thesis argues that the perennial threat to the constitutional balance comes from foreign affairs. Confronted by presidential initiatives in domestic policy, the countervailing branches of the national government—the legislative and the judiciary—have ample confidence in their own information and judgment. In this area they do not hesitate to challenge what they deem executive aggrandizement, nor do they lightly surrender power to the presidency. The media and PUBLIC OPINION, those extraconstitutional checks on the abuse of executive power, are similarly assured in dealing with domestic policy.

But confronted by presidential initiatives in foreign affairs, Congress and the courts, along with the press and the citizenry too, often lack confidence in their own information and judgment and are therefore more easily intimidated by executive authority. The inclination in foreign policy is to let the President have the responsibility and the power—a renunciation that results from congressional pusillanimity as well as from presidential rapacity. The more acute the crisis, the more power flows to the President.

"It is chiefly in its foreign relations," as Alexis de Tocqueville noted early on, "that the executive power of a nation finds occasion to exert its skill and its strength. If the existence of the American Union were perpetually threatened, if its chief interests were in daily connection with those of other powerful nations, the executive would assume an increased importance." But the young republic Tocqueville visited in the 1830s had lived, at least since the WAR OF 1812, in happy isolation from world power struggles. So "the President of the United States," Tocqueville observed, "possesses almost royal prerogatives which he has no opportunity of exercising."

By the twentieth century the United States itself had become a world power, its interests in daily connection with those of other powers; and the half century from Pearl Harbor to the breakup of the Soviet Union was experienced as a time of perpetual threat to the existence of the American Union. The chronic international crisis known as the COLD WAR at last gave Presidents the opportunity for sustained exercise of those almost royal prerogatives. What began as EMERGENCY POWERS temporarily confided to Presidents soon hardened into prerogatives claimed by Presidents as constitutionally inherent in the presidential office: thus the imperial presidency.

**The Early Republic.** The rise of the imperial presidency ran against the original intent of the Framers. With the war-making propensities of absolute monarchs in mind, the Framers of the Constitution took care to assign the vital foreign policy powers exclusively to Congress. Article I gave Congress not only the appropriations power—itself a potent instrument of control—but also the power to regulate commerce, to declare war, to raise and support armies, to provide and maintain a navy, to make rules for the government and regulation of armed services, and to grant letters of MARQUE AND REPRISAL. This last provision represented the eighteenth-century equivalent of retaliatory strikes and empowered Congress to authorize limited as well as general war.

Even ALEXANDER HAMILTON, the constitutional convention's foremost proponent of executive energy, endorsed this allocation of powers. "The history of human conduct," he wrote in FEDERALIST 75, "does not warrant that exalted opinion of human virtue which would make it wise to commit interests of so delicate and momentous a kind, as those which concern its intercourse with the rest of the world, to the sole disposal of . . . a President of the United States." What seemed at stake was not only the wisdom of the policy but the freedom of the people. "Perhaps it is a universal truth," said James Madison, "that the loss of liberty at home is to be charged to provisions against danger, real or pretended, from abroad."

The specific grants of authority to the executive in foreign policy were trivial compared with the authority specifically granted to Congress. The presidency was given the power of RECEIVING AND APPOINTING AMBASSADORS and, by implication, of serving as the channel of communications to foreign states. The President as COMMANDER IN CHIEF was given the power to direct the armed forces once war was authorized or begun and, by implication, the power to repel sudden attacks when Congress was not in session. However, Article II vested general executive power in the presidency. And, as *Federalist* 64 and 75 emphasized, the structural advantages of the presidency—unity, decision, secrecy, despatch, stability of purpose, special sources of information—made the executive the prime agent in dealings with foreign states.

Those structural advantages worked against the Framers' original intent. The pattern of presidential aggrandizement under the spur of international crisis was visible from the start. In opposition Thomas Jefferson had been the apostle of strict construction and the foe of executive initiative. But viewing problems from the White House, he sent a naval squadron to the Mediterranean under secret orders to fight pirates in the BARBARY WAR, applied for congressional sanction six months later, then misled Congress as to the nature of his orders. He unilaterally authorized the seizure of armed vessels in waters extending to the Gulf Stream, engaged in rearmament without congressional appropriations, withheld information from Congress and invoked John Locke's doctrine of emergency prerogative—the law of self-preservation—to justify action beyond congressional authorization.

Early Presidents did not hesitate to engage in what later generations called COVERT OPERATIONS against foreign states and to do so without congressional knowledge. James Madison sent Joel K. Poinsett as a secret agent (see PRIVATE ENVOYS) to Latin America and winked at his clandestine revolutionary adventures in Argentina and Chile; the Secretary at State removed Poinsett's despatches from State Department files lest Congress request them. Both Madison and James Monroe used covert action to facilitate the annexation of Florida.

Presidential adventurism in the early republic differed in salient respects, however, from the Imperial presidency. As Abraham D. Sofaer shows in his magistral work, *War, Foreign Affairs, and Constitutional Power: The Origins,* early Presidents deliberately selected venturesome agents, deliberately kept their missions secret, deliberately gave them vague instructions, deliberately failed either to approve or to disapprove their constitutionally questionable plans, and deliberately denied Congress the information to determine whether aggressive acts were authorized—all precisely because the Presidents wanted their men in the field to do things they knew lay beyond their constitutional right to command. "At no time," Sofaer writes of the early period, "did the executive claim 'inherent' power to initiate military action."

**Lincoln and Franklin D. Roosevelt.** The early Presidents thus usurped power, and usurpation creates no constitutional precedents. It is the assertion of INHERENT POWERS that defines the imperial presidency and creates precedents for the future. The contrast in constitutional claims between the emergency policies of Abraham Lincoln and Franklin D. Roosevelt and those of post-WORLD WAR II Presidents illustrates the distinction.

Both Lincoln and Roosevelt were well aware what the Constitution said about the war-making power. In 1848 Lincoln called the MEXICAN WAR illegal and unconstitutional because it was unilaterally provoked, so he believed, by President James K. Polk. The Founding Fathers at Philadelphia, Lincoln said, had "resolved to so frame the Constitution that no one man should hold power of bringing this oppression [war] upon us." Similarly Roosevelt in 1940, promising supplies to a French government under Nazi assault, carefully added: "These statements carry with them no implication of military commitments. Only Congress can make such commitments."

Yet after the attack on Fort Sumter in 1861, Lincoln, on his own, without congressional authorization, assembled the militia, enlarged the army and navy beyond their authorized strength, called out volunteers for three years' service, spent unappropriated public funds, suspended habeas corpus, arrested persons "represented" as involved in "disloyal" practices, and instituted a naval blockade of the rebel states. Similarly in 1941, when German submarine warfare threatened to sever the lifeline of supplies to Britain, Roosevelt, on his own, without congressional authorization, dispatched troops to Iceland, instituted a convoy system, issued a "shoot-on-sight" order to the navy, and launched an undeclared war in the North Atlantic.

But neither President based his action on claims of inherent power. His emergency measures, Lincoln told Congress when he finally convoked a special session, "whether strictly legal or not, were ventured upon under what appeared to be a popular demand and a public necessity; trusting then as now that Congress would readily ratify them." Roosevelt, like Lincoln, relied on his sense of popular demand and public necessity. The passage of the LEND LEASE ACT (1941) after uninhibited public and congressional debate had aligned the United States with Great Britain in the European war. If Congress voted arms to Britain as national policy, then, inferentially, national policy was to make sure the arms got to Britain. Roosevelt added a murky proclamation of "unlimited national emergency." But, like Lincoln, he made no claims of inherent power to do what he believed necessary to save the nation.

Both Lincoln and Roosevelt undertook acts they knew to be beyond the Constitution. Both did so in times of transcendent crisis when the life of the nation seemed truly at stake. Both acted, knowingly or not, on Locke's doctrine of emergency prerogative, trusting that Congress would eventually approve their actions. Both men understood and affirmed that emergency prerogative must expire with the emergency. "The Executive power itself," said Lincoln, "would be greatly diminished by the cessation of actual war." "When the war is won," said Roosevelt, "the powers under which I act automatically revert to the people—to whom they belong." Neither Lincoln nor Roosevelt claimed an inherent and routine presidential right to do what they did. That claim, the essence of the imperial presidency, was a product of the second half of the twentieth century.

**Resistance to Presidential Power.** The sporadic appearance of international crisis before World War II also delayed the emergency of the imperial presidency. For, while war increased presidential power, peace brought a reaction against executive excess.

The CIVIL WAR, Henry Adams wrote, "for the time obliterated the Constitution." It produced what Benjamin R. Curtis, one of the two dissenting justices in DRED SCOTT V. SANDFORD (1857), charged was "a military despotism." But once the crisis ended, the other two branches of government lost no time in reasserting their constitutional powers. A year after Appomattox the Supreme Court held EX PARTE MILLIGAN (1866) that Lincoln's prosecution of a proslavery conspirator under martial law behind the lines violated the Constitution. In another two years Lincoln's successor in the White House found himself at the bar of impeachment. The republic entered the era characterized by Woodrow Wilson as one of "congressional government."

Wilson himself, writing a new preface to *Congressional Government* after the SPANISH-AMERICAN WAR, remarked on "the greatly increased power . . . given the President by the plunge into international politics." When foreign policy became the nation's dominant concern, Wilson said, the executive "must of necessity be its guide: must utter every initial judgment, take every first step of action, supply the information upon which it is to act, suggest and in large measure control its conduct." As President during WORLD WAR I, Wilson acted on his own model.

But once again the return of peace shrank presidential power, as the Senate quickly showed by rejecting the TREATY OF VERSAILLES. In the next decade Roosevelt, a mighty domestic President, could not prevent Congress from imposing rigid NEUTRALITY legislation that put American foreign policy in a straitjacket while Germany and Japan ran amok in Europe and Asia.

The end of WORLD WAR II brought the usual diminution of presidential power. A year after Roosevelt's death his successor was so unpopular that voters said "To err is Truman" and elected a Republican Congress. The next year Congress gained posthumous revenge against the powerful wartime President by proposing what became the TWENTY-SECOND AMENDMENT, thereby limiting all future Presidents to two terms.

**Rise of the Imperial Presidency.** But this time the diminution was brief. The cold war, by generating a climate of sustained and indefinite crisis, aborted the customary reversion of power to the coordinate branches. The most visible sign of growing executive imperialism was the transfer of the power to go to war from Congress to the presidency. Ten years after Roosevelt told France that only Congress could make military commitments, President Harry S. Truman, confronted by the North Korean invasion of South Korea, sent American forces to war on his own.

Senator Robert A. Taft, finding "no legal authority" for Truman's decision, offered to support a joint resolution sanctioning military intervention. Without such a resolution, Taft said, "We would have finally terminated for all time the right of Congress to declare war, which is granted to Congress alone by the Constitution." But Truman was persuaded by DEAN ACHESON, his Secretary of State and an eminent lawyer, that the presidency had an inherent power to commit the country to war.

In support of this claim, the State Department produced a litany of nineteenth-century military interventions taken on unilateral presidential initiative. Were these in fact precedents for war against North Korea? The nineteenth-century actions were not directed against sovereign states. Nearly all were undertaken to protect lives and property of American citizens against stateless and lawless bands—revolutionaries, angry mobs, savage tribes, brigands, pirates. Such interventions differ fundamentally from wars against organized governments both in the juridical status of the combatants and in the limited nature of the conflict. Presidents had decided that "police actions," not mounted against sovereign states and not requiring special appropriations, did not rise to the dignity of formal congressional concern.

A secondary argument rested on the resolution of the United Nations Security Council authorizing member states to oppose North Korean aggression. But a UN resolution does not nullify the constitutional requirement of congressional action.

Defenders of inherent presidential war-making power invoked the Supreme Court's decision in UNITED STATES. V. CURTISS-WRIGHT EXPORT CORP. (1936). This decision did not, however, sanction unilateral presidential power to go to war. The case did not even involve the war-making power. And, far from affirming inherent executive authority, the Court affirmed the power of Congress to impose arms embargoes and further affirmed the right of Congress to delegate to the President power to institute a particular embargo. The decision, in the words of Justice Robert H. Jackson in a later case (YOUNGSTOWN SHEET & TUBE CO. V. SAWYER [1952]) "involved, not the question of the President's right to act without congressional authority, but the question of his right to act under and in accord with an Act of Congress."

In writing the *Curtiss-Wright* decision, Justice George Sutherland faced potential embarrassment. The year before a unanimous court had struck down the NATIONAL INDUSTRIAL RECOVERY ACT as an unconstitutional delegation of congressional power to the President. It was therefore necessary in *Curtiss-Wright* to distinguish delegation in domestic policy from delegation in foreign policy. Drawing this distinction led Sutherland into dubious historical excursions and expansive language about the "plenary and exclusive power" of the President in foreign affairs. But these were obiter dicta. *Curtiss-Wright* gave the imperial presidency rhetorical encouragement, not constitutional vindication.

Historically, Congress had preserved the rough balance of the Constitution because it retained three vital powers: the war-making power; the power of the purse; and the power of oversight and investigation. In 1950 it relinquished the war-making power. Truman fought in Korea, Lyndon B. Johnson in Vietnam, and Richard M. Nixon in Cambodia without believing that their despatch of troops into combat required explicit congressional authorization (Congress provided ambiguous authorization in the case of Vietnam through the 1964 GULF OF TONKIN RESOLUTION). In 1969–1974, the Nixon administration tried systematically and, until the WATERGATE AFFAIR, successfully to restrict the other two powers: countering the power of the purse by the doctrine of the unlimited impoundment of appropriated funds and countering the power of oversight and investigation by the doctrine of unreviewable EXECUTIVE PRIVILEGE (a novel term, first used officially in 1958) and the extension of the executive secrecy system. Had Nixon succeeded in imposing these doctrines on top of his amplified claims for the presidential war-making power, he would have gravely weakened Congress as a serious partner in the constitutional order.

Nixon carried the imperial presidency still further by using against his political opponents at home— "enemies," he called them—powers that the presidency had accumulated to save the republic from foreign foes. Invoking NATIONAL SECURITY as an all-purpose justification, he set up a secret White House posse to burgle offices, forge historical documents, and wiretap officials, embassies, newspapermen, and "enemies." "When the President does it," Nixon claimed in 1977, "that means that it is not illegal." Congress eventually roused itself. Articles of impeachment charged Nixon with acting "in a manner contrary to his trust as President and subversive of constitutional government," and Nixon resigned rather than be impeached and face a trial.

The imperial presidency reached its climax with Nixon. The post-Watergate reaction cut back on some presidential excesses. None of Nixon's successors, for example, used emergency powers against political opponents. The presidency of Jimmy Carter even led to concerns about the impotence of the office. "We have not an imperial presidency," former President Gerald Ford said in 1980, "but an imperiled presidency." But such lamentations were soon refuted when Ronald Reagan showed that a President with only a vague understanding of issues could still dominate the government and lead the country.

Nor did the reaction constrain executive assumption of the war-making power. Reagan in the case of GRENADA and George Bush in the cases of PANAMA and Iraq insisted on what Bush called "the President's constitutional authority to use the armed forces to defend vital U.S. interests." In the Iraq case Congress rescued Bush from a constitutional conflict by voting to authorize the PERSIAN GULF WAR. However, the end of the cold war materially weakened the national security argument for the imperial presidency.

Critics of the imperial presidency thesis argued that it exaggerated presidential strength, pointing to the chronic inability of Presidents to get many things they desire. Even when the imperial presidency culminated in Nixon, the President lived in a state of chronic and profane frustration, unable to command Congress, the judiciary, the press, the universities, unable even to get the FEDERAL BUREAU OF INVESTIGATION, the CENTRAL INTELLIGENCE AGENCY, and the Internal Revenue Service to do his bidding.

Administrative frustrations are real and exasperating; but they do not cancel the constitutional and institutional powers of the office or the President's capacity to decide policies and set goals. Functional necessities guarantee the indestructibility of the presidential office. A system based on the separation of powers among three nominally equal branches has an inherent tendency toward stalemate. One of the branches must take the initiative if the system is to move. The executive branch alone is structurally capable of taking that initiative.

A strong presidency therefore remains the key to the American system. When the constitutional balance between power and accountability is maintained, a President—as many have shown—can be effective without becoming imperial. The system indeed requires strong Presidents—but strong within the Constitution.

### BIBLIOGRAPHY

Corwin, E. S. *The President: Office and Powers, 1787–1984.* 5th rev. ed. Edited by R. W. Bland, T. T. Hindson and J. W. Peltason. 1984.

Cox, H. B. *War, Foreign Affairs, and Constitutional Power, 1829–1901.* 1984.

Ford, Henry Jones. *The Rise and Growth of American Politics.* 1898.

Glennon, Michael J. *Constitutional Diplomacy.* 1991.

Goldsmith, William J. *The Growth of Presidential Power.* 3 vols. 1974.

Henkin, Louis J. *Foreign Affairs and the Constitution.* 1972.

Koh, Harold H. *The National Security Constitution.* 1990.

Neustadt, Richard E. *Presidential Power and the Modern Presidents.* 1990.

Pious, Richard M. *The American Presidency.* 1979.

Schlesinger, Arthur M., Jr. *The Imperial Presidency.* 1973. Rev. ed. with epilogue, "After the Imperial Presidency." 1989.

Sofaer, Abraham D. *War, Foreign Affairs, and Constitutional Power: The Origins.* 1976.

Wormuth, F. D., and E. B. Firmage. *To Chain the Dog of War.* 2d rev. ed. 1989.

ARTHUR M. SCHLESINGER, JR.

**IMPLIED POWERS.** Because the Constitution does not purport to be an exhaustive catalog of powers, the problem of discovering implied powers in its interstices is frequently encountered. It is met, as are other problems of constitutional construction, by the examination of experience in the light of constitutional principle. In this article the term *implied powers* will be used in a comprehensive sense, to include all powers not enumerated in the constitutional text.

Many judges and other writers on constitutional problems find the source of such powers in one or another of the ENUMERATED POWERS, or in a combination of several. In other cases, implied powers are derived from the nature and sovereignty of the nation, the grand design of its polity, or similar axioms of political theory deemed to be embodied in the Constitution.

Some argue that implied powers are less legitimate than those mentioned in the constitutional text. They would confine the authority of government strictly to the enumerated powers, especially in the case of the President, whom they view with suspicion as a potential tyrant. This position is clearly untenable. IN RE NEAGLE (1890) declares that "any obligation fairly and properly inferrible" from the Constitution and the statutes is a law within the meaning of the word "law" as if it were absolutely expressed therein.

Three factors make the task of attributing implied powers to the President particularly complex: the importance of the presidency in the political strategy of the Constitution; the fact that the President is endowed with extensive and rather vaguely defined authority in the sphere of international relations; and the fact that the President is often said to possess INHERENT POWERS, or the residual powers, of sovereignty, sometimes identified with the prerogative powers of the British crown.

In his important study of the presidency, Charles C. Thach, Jr., concludes that Article II "admits an interpretation of executive power much wider than that outlined by the enumerated powers." This result, he concludes, was intended by the Framers because the CONSTITUTIONAL CONVENTION was dominated by a fear of unbridled legislative power and by the conviction that a strong and accountable national executive was needed "to counterbalance legislative predominance. The state legislatures' excesses and the incompetency of Congress as an administrative body produced the Presidency." Thach's view encourages the implication of Presidential powers rather freely in order to keep the self-aggrandizing propensities of Congress within tolerable limits.

The bills that established the first four departments of the executive branch required Congress to confront the question whether the Constitution gave the President the implied power to remove officials of the government as well as to appoint them. After extensive debate, Congress left the matter largely to practice and the Courts. James Madison argued forcefully that the President could not be expected faithfully to execute the laws unless he could dismiss subordinates. Madison's view was sustained in MYERS v. UNITED STATES (1926), which gave a broad reading of the President's REMOVAL POWER.

In general, history has accepted Madison's view that the President has an implied power to remove at least his CABINET officers and other high-ranking officials with policy-making responsibilities. They serve at the President's pleasure. On the other hand, Congress has established CIVIL SERVICE systems of various kinds; they all involve limitations on the President's power to dismiss. Congress has authorized appointments for fixed terms as well. And the President's removal power does not extend to members of INDEPENDENT COMMISSIONS, as the Supreme Court held in HUMPHREY'S EXECUTOR v. UNITED STATES (1935).

Article II, Section 3, prescribes that the President shall receive ambassadors and other public ministers, a provision sometimes understood as a routine ceremonial duty as head of state. The duty of receiving ambassadors and other public ministers, has, however, been read to imply the President's sole power of diplomatic recognition, for example; the sole power to conduct foreign relations; the sole power to negotiate treaties which are mentioned in the Constitution, and EXECUTIVE AGREEMENTS, which are not mentioned [see RECOGNITION POWER].

Executive agreements are frequently used in the conduct of international relations. Some, such as trade agreements, are authorized by statutes, but other executive agreements are entered into solely on the President's constitutional authority. In UNITED STATES v. PINK (1942), the Supreme Court declared that an assignment of property claims incidental to agreement on the terms of recognition was part of the "supreme law of the land," as if an executive agreement were a treaty. And GOLDWATER v. CARTER (1979) did not reject President Jimmy Carter's power to abrogate a defense treaty with Taiwan as incident to his decision to establish diplomatic relations with the People's Republic of China.

Other executive agreements are made by the President alone in the course of diplomatic negotiations. In 1957, for example, the United States acted as a secret mediator in helping to persuade Israel to evacuate the Sinai Desert after the Suez Crisis of 1956. To achieve agreement between Egypt and Israel, President Dwight D. Eisenhower guaranteed that the United States would, if necessary, use force to keep the Straits of Tiran open to Israeli shipping. That promise was treated as binding by President Lyndon B. Johnson in the Six-Day War of 1967.

The importance of the President's special responsibility for the conduct of FOREIGN AFFAIRS is again illustrated by an episode during President Ulysses S. Grant's administration. It involved granting permission to land international submarine cables on American soil. In the absence of legislation, President Grant authorized a French company to connect by cable a town in Massachusetts to the French city of Brest. The President was reluctant to act without a statute but finally yielded to an Attorney General's opinion and granted the license. The Attorney General explained that the President's implied power to issue the license was based on the fundamental rights that "grow out of the jurisdiction of the nation over its own territory and its international rights and obligations as a distinct sovereignty." For these reasons, the Attorney General concluded, "the President is not limited to the enforcement of specific acts of Congress" (22 *Ops. Att'y Gen.* 13).

No President has claimed that the President's powers over cable connections or international electronic transmission facilities are exclusive. Clearly, the regulation of such activities comes well within any definition of Congress's power to legislate on matters of interstate and foreign commerce. But both constitutional usage and judicial opinions recognize presidential power to act and even to take military action without prior statutory authority in the conduct of foreign relations, so long as he does not trespass on Congress's exclusive authority to declare war or violate any other principle of constitutional law. For example, the President cannot "dispose of the liberty" of a fugitive from justice by extraditing him to another country in the absence of a statute or treaty conferring the power (*Valentine v. United States* [1936]).

The President's constitutional authority to respond to national emergencies and threats to public order raises similar issues. Cases such as IN RE DEBS (1895) and *In re Neagle* (1890) can be explained only if one accepts as a major premise the doctrine that the President's executive power conferred by Article II is not a mere designation of status but a grant of authority, including EMERGENCY POWERS that may go well beyond the enumerated powers, depending on circumstance. The same principle, on a much larger scale, is required to justify the constitutional propriety of what President Abraham Lincoln did between the time of the attack on Fort Sumter and Congress's meeting to ratify his actions [see CIVIL WAR], and some of the initiatives of Presidents Woodrow Wilson and Franklin D. Roosevelt before the United States formally entered WORLD WAR I and WORLD WAR II.

## BIBLIOGRAPHY

Corwin, Edward S. *The President: Office and Powers, 1787–1984.* 1940. 5th rev. ed. by Randall W. Bland, Theodore T. Hindon, and Jack W. Pelstson, 1984.

Schwartz, Bernard. *A Commentary on the Constitution of the United States, The Powers of Government.* Vol. 2: *The Powers of the President.* 1962.

Thach, Charles C., Jr. *The Creation of the Presidency, 1775–1789.* 1922.

Van Alstyne, William W. "The Role of Congress in Determining Incidental Powers of the President and of the Federal Courts: The Horizontal Effect of the Sweeping Clause. *Law and Contemporary Problems* (1976): 102–134.

EUGENE V. ROSTOW

**IMPOUNDMENT.** Presidents and other executive-branch officials impound funds when they do not spend the full amount appropriated by Congress. In most cases, the executive's withholding of funds does not present a problem. It is widely recognized that impoundments for purely routine managerial functions do not represent a threat to legislative prerogatives. Some impoundments, however, encroach upon the ability of Congress to make policy and decide budget priorities. As House Appropriations Committee chairman George Mahon remarked in 1949, "Economy is one thing, and the abandonment of a policy and program of the Congress another thing." Because of abuses during the Richard M. Nixon administration, Congress passed the IMPOUNDMENT CONTROL ACT of 1974 to control presidential impoundments.

It has long been the practice of the executive branch to regard appropriations as permissive rather than mandatory, unless Congress specifies in law that all funds must be spent. From the days of George Washington, then, impoundment has occurred whenever spending has fallen short of appropriations. Routine withholdings occur to effect savings, to respond to changing events, and for other basic managerial reasons.

Attorney General Judson Harmon declared in 1896 that an appropriation was not mandatory "to the extent that you are bound to expend the full amount if the work can be done for less." To guard against wasteful spending, Congress passed legislation in 1905 to require that appropriations be apportioned by monthly or other allotments, so "as to prevent undue expenditures on one portion of the year that may require deficiency or additional appropriations to complete the service of the fiscal year." That language was refined the following year to limit the freedom of departmental heads to waive or modify the apportion-ment requirement. When part of appropriated funds is apportioned to an agency for spending, some of the funds are placed in budgetary reserve.

In 1942, President Franklin D. Roosevelt defended budgetary reserves as sound fiscal practice. To mandate the full expenditure of funds, he said, "would take from the Chief Executive every incentive for good management and the practice of commonsense economy." In 1950 the House Appropriations Committee emphasized that economy "neither begins nor ends in the Halls of Congress." An appropriation of a given amount for a particular activity constituted "only a ceiling upon the amount which should be expended for that activity." Administration officials were expected to render all necessary service "with the smallest amount possible" within the limit established by Congress.

Impoundment to effect savings could be distorted by ambitious executive officials to frustrate congressional policy. That potential for abuse was recognized by both branches. President Roosevelt, in his remarks in 1942, said that budgetary reserves to prevent deficiencies or to effect savings were not "a substitute for item or blanket veto power, and should not be used to set aside or nullify the expressed will of Congress." The 1950 statement by the House Appropriations Committee warned that while it was "perfectly justifiable and proper for all possible economies to be effected and savings to be made," there was no justification to use impoundment "to thwart a major policy of Congress." Congress appropriates monies months—and sometimes years—in advance of the time when agencies actually obligate and spend funds, so, in addition to using impoundment to effect savings, Presidents have sometimes withheld funds because of changing events. An early example of this practice occurred in 1803, when President Thomas Jefferson withheld $50,000 that Congress had appropriated for the purchase of gunboats. Jefferson did not impound the funds to frustrate congressional policy, however: as he explained, as a result of the LOUISIANA PURCHASE the funds appropriated for gunboats would remain unexpended because the "favorable and peaceable turn of affairs on the Mississippi rendered an immediate execution of that law unnecessary." A year later, having taken the time to study the most recent models of gunboats, he informed Congress that he was proceeding with the program.

Execution requires managerial judgments, and an administrator may have a number of other valid reasons for suspending a program or payment. In *Decatur v. Paulding* (1840), the Supreme Court supported an impoundment decision by the Secretary of the Navy, who had withheld payment from a widow although her claim was based on a resolution passed by Congress. The Court found that if the Secretary had mechanically followed the direction of Congress, without exercising judgment or discretion, the widow would have received two pensions (one from the specific resolution adopted on her behalf and a second from a general pension bill) and that the Secretary had properly concluded that Congress could not have intended double benefits.

In addition to these explicit or implied authorities, executive officials may have other legitimate reasons for withholding funds. A number of statutes have established spending ceilings, requiring the President to impound appropriated funds. The CIVIL RIGHTS ACT OF 1964 empowers the President to withhold funds from federally financed programs in which there is discrimination by race, color, or national origin. And states that have failed to enact billboard-control legislation, as required by federal law, have been threatened with the loss of federal aid to highway improvement.

The major problem in executive-legislative relations over impoundment power came during the Nixon administration, when executive officials claimed that they had unilateral constitutional powers to withhold funds. During a news conference on 31 January 1973, President Nixon asserted that the constitutional right of a President to impound funds for the purpose of combating inflation or avoiding a tax increase was "absolutely clear." Other officials in his administration maintained that impoundment was consistent with the President's constitutional duty to "take care that the laws be faithfully executed" and "was authorized by the constitutional provisions that vest the executive power with the President."

These announcements broke new ground. Although officials in the Nixon administration invoked the Jefferson incident as an acceptable precedent, Jefferson's action was temporary and provoked by changing events. The Nixon administration claimed the right to terminate programs, thereby directly challenging the right of Congress to make policies and decide priorities.

The Nixon impoundments were unprecedented in their scope and severity. Never before had congressional priorities and prerogatives been so altered and jeopardized. During December 1972 and January 1973, the administration announced major cancellations and cutbacks. Frequently the actions were defended on the superficial grounds that Congress had failed to enact mandatory language for the programs. In other words, the mere existence of discretionary authority, which Congress had granted to enable executive officials to administer the programs more effectively, was used as an excuse to cancel the programs in their entirety.

The programs affected by the Nixon impoundments included the Rural Environmental Assistance Program, the Water Bank Program, the emergency loan program of the Farmers Home Administration, the Rural Electrification Administration, rural water and sewer grants, housing projects, and other federal programs. The largest amount was withheld from the clean water program: exactly half of the $18 billion that Congress had provided for three years was impounded by the administration.

Federal courts handed down approximately eighty decisions that ruled on the impoundment theories of the Nixon administration. With the exception of three cases in the lower courts, the administration lost every one. Only one case, *Train v. City of New York* (1975), reached the Supreme Court, and the administration lost that one as well.

As part of the Budget Act of 1974, Congress passed the Impoundment Control Act to restrict presidential withholding of appropriated funds. Under the terms of this legislation, the President must submit reports to Congress on two types of impoundment: *rescissions*, which are proposals to terminate funds, and *deferrals*, which are proposals to delay the expenditure of funds. For a rescission, the President needs the support of both houses of Congress through a regular bill or joint resolution. He must obtain that approval within forty-five days of continuous session (which excludes legislative adjournments for more than three days). Under the 1974 act, either house of Congress could pass a resolution to disapprove deferrals, but that type of LEGISLATIVE VETO was declared unconstitutional by the Supreme Court in INS v. CHADHA (1983). As a result of *Chadha* and a court decision in 1987 concerning deferrals by the Reagan administration, deferral authority has been limited to routine, managerial actions. Presidents may no longer defer funds simply because they do not support the policies enacted into law by Congress.

Used with restraint and circumspection, impoundment had been used by Presidents without precipitating major crises. But during the Nixon years restraint was replaced by abandon, precedents were stretched past their breaking point, and statutory authority was pushed beyond legislative intent. For all its trappings of conservatism and "strict constructionism," the Nixon administration never demonstrated an understanding of the concepts that lie at the heart of the political system: a respect for procedure, a sense of comity and trust between the branches, and an appreciation of limits and boundaries. Without good faith and integrity on the part of executive officials, the delicate system of nonstatutory controls, informal understandings, and discretionary authority could not last. At a time when public programs could have benefited from flexibility and executive judgment, Congress was forced to pass legislation with mandatory language and greater rigidities. That part of the Nixon legacy cast a shadow over future administrations.

### BIBLIOGRAPHY

Fisher, Louis. *Presidential Spending Power.* 1975.
Pfiffner, James P. *The President, the Budget, and Congress: Impoundment and the 1974 Budget Act.* 1979.
Schick, Allen. *Congress and Money.* 1980.

LOUIS FISHER

**IMPOUNDMENT CONTROL ACT** (1974). Enacted in 1974 in response to President Richard M. Nixon's refusal to spend funds appropriated by Congress the Impoundment Control Act specifies procedures for two types of IMPOUNDMENT: *rescissions,* or terminations of funds, and *deferrals,* or delays in the spending of funds. In general, the burden is on the President to rescind funds, while Congress is required to disapprove deferrals. Because of court rulings during the Ronald Reagan administration, the President's ability to defer funds has been substantially curtailed.

If a President decides to rescind funds, he must submit a special message to Congress specifying the funds proposed for rescission; the account, department, or establishment involved; the reasons the funds should be rescinded; the estimated fiscal, economic, and budgetary effect of the proposed rescission; and all facts, circumstances, and considerations related to the rescission. Unless Congress completes action on a rescission bill within forty-five days of continuous session (which does not count legislative adjournments of more than three days), the President must release the funds and make them available for obligation by the agency.

In the case of deferrals, the President must again submit a special message to Congress identifying the funds proposed to be deferred; the account, department, or establishment involved; the period of time proposed for deferring the funds; the reasons for the proposed deferral, including any legal authority invoked to justify the deferral; the estimated fiscal, economic, and budgetary effect of the proposed deferral; and all facts, circumstances, and considerations

related to the deferral. A deferral may not be proposed for any period of time extending beyond the end of the fiscal year in which the special message is transmitted to Congress.

Under the Impoundment Control Act, either house of Congress could disapprove a deferral and force the release of funds for obligation by an agency. The Supreme Court, however, declared this type of LEGISLATIVE VETO unconstitutional in INS v. CHADHA (1983). This meant that the President now had deferral authority without the legislative check of a one-house veto. For a few years the Reagan administration and Congress reached a compromise to avoid this type of presidential abuse, but with passage of the GRAMM-RUDMAN-HOLLINGS ACT in 1985 the administration proceeded to defer large amounts to restrict spending.

In *City of New Haven v. United States* (1987) a federal appellate court held that the legislative veto in the Impoundment Control Act was not severable from the deferral authority. The statute's language and its legislative history convinced the court that Congress would not have delegated deferral authority to the President without the one-house veto. The court thus ruled that if the legislative veto was unconstitutional the deferral authority fell with it. Congress promptly enacted that policy into law (101 Stat. 785, sec. 206). The effect was to restrict future deferrals to routine, administrative actions. Presidents may not propose deferrals simply because they disagree with the policy and programmatic choices made by Congress.

### BIBLIOGRAPHY

Fisher, Louis. *Presidential Spending Power.* 1975.
Pfiffner, James P. *The President, the Budget, and Congress: Impoundment and the 1974 Budget Act.* 1979.
Schick, Allen. *Congress and Money: Budgeting, Spending, and Taxing.* 1980.

LOUIS FISHER

**INAUGURAL ADDRESSES.** An inaugural address is the first public expression that a President makes after taking the simple thirty-five-word PRESIDENTIAL OATH OF OFFICE. It is a unique moment in the American experience when political differences are momentarily put aside as the nation listens intently to the philosophy, aspirations, themes, and goals that will shape the next four years.

Although not constitutionally required, every ceremony since George Washington's 30 April 1789 inauguration has included an address. Washington's initial speech as President was delivered in the Senate Chamber of Federal Hall in New York City. Between 1793 and 1813, inaugural addresses were delivered either in the House or Senate chamber. Outdoor public inaugurations began with James Monroe in 1817. Only on four occasions since has the inaugural address been given in the warm confines of the Capitol.

Inaugural addresses were initially carried by horseback or stage to an awaiting nation, and then later by train and telegraph. Not until Calvin Coolidge's 1925 inauguration was an address broadcast by radio. Live television coverage began in 1949 with Harry S. Truman.

The shortest inaugural speech, George Washington's second, was only 135 words and contained but four sentences. William Henry Harrison's 8,445 word address was the longest, taking nearly two hours to deliver. A month later, Harrison died of pneumonia that started with the cold he caught during the snowy ceremony.

On the average, inaugural addresses have run about 2,400 words. Only a few have been universally acclaimed as being truly memorable, but all afford a picture window on history. Their story lines have covered the faith of Presidents, the special destiny of the American Republic, the nation's growth and expansion, the development of foreign policy, the treatment of ethnic minorities, economic fluctuations, and the evolution of the presidency, as well as numerous other issues. It is after all, as George Bush aptly observed in 1989, "democracy's big day."

**Economic Fluctuations.** One of the most closely observed aspects of American life noted in inaugural addresses has been the state of the economy. At his second inauguration, Thomas Jefferson announced that the elimination "of unnecessary offices, of useless establishments and expenses," had enabled his administration to discontinue "internal taxes." Although the nation was deep in debt by James Monroe's 1817 inauguration, he maintained that the "great amount of our revenue and the flourishing state of the Treasury are full proof of the competency of the national resources for any emergency."

Martin Van Buren's glowing description of "an aggregate of human prosperity" found no where else in the world proved to be misplaced optimism as the entire nation, within months, faced a financial panic. Ulysses S. Grant promised that the "great debt" incurred in preserving the Union would be paid off as quickly as possible.

Amidst prosperity "without parallel in our history," James A. Garfield took office in 1881. "Ample employment," however, soon gave way to the Panic of 1884. Five years later, Benjamin Harrison promised, and then worked to deliver, an administration in which expenditures were "made with economy and only upon public necessity."

For William McKinley, the "best way for Government to maintain its credit is to pay as it goes—not by resorting to loans, but by keeping out of debt—through an adequate income secured by a system of taxation, external or internal, or both." William Howard Taft also felt government had a responsibility "to be as economical as possible, and to make the burden of taxation as light as possible."

As the Great Depression deepened in early 1933, Franklin D. Roosevelt's first inaugural address offered hope to the disillusioned nation. Within the first paragraph was the line destined to be among his most famous: "the only thing we have to fear is fear itself," he said. "This great nation," he counseled the American people, "will endure as it has endured, will revive and will prosper."

In 1937, Roosevelt still saw "one third of a nation ill-housed, ill-clad, ill-nourished." These bleak conditions were not, however, in his mind a picture of despair. He had painted this picture "in hope—because the Nation, seeing and understanding the injustice in it, proposes to paint it out."

**Ethnic Minorities.** A prominent concern of newly inaugurated Presidents during the nineteenth century was the acculturation of ethnic minorities. Prior to the CIVIL WAR, the plight of American INDIANS and the question of SLAVERY were of particular interest. Jefferson acknowledged that the Indians had been overwhelmed by an "overflowing population from other regions" and "reduced within limits too narrow for the hunter's state." James Monroe called on Congress to develop a plan to care appropriately for them, while Andrew Jackson promised "humane and considerate attention to their rights." Yet, nearly half a century later, Ulysses S. Grant admitted little had changed. Grover Cleveland challenged the American people to treat the Indians "honestly" and "with forbearance," but then the Indians were forgotten.

The question of slavery was even more challenging. Martin Van Buren, James K. Polk, Franklin Pierce, and James Buchanan gave support to the institution of slavery in their inaugural remarks. South Carolina had already seceded when Abraham Lincoln renounced any "purpose, directly or indirectly, to interfere with the institution of slavery in the States where it exists." The Civil War freed the slave to become a citizen, but Ulysses S. Grant did not feel social equality was a "subject to be legislated upon." He was unwilling to do anything "to advance the social status of the colored man, except to give him a fair chance to develop what there is good in him."

Government, Rutherford B. Hayes stressed, had a moral obligation "to employ its constitutional powers and influence to establish the rights of the people it emancipated." The "advance of 4,000,000 people from a condition of servitude to that of citizenship," however, "could not occur without presenting problems." Four years later, James A. Garfield called emancipation the "most important political change since the adoption of the Constitution." Yet in 1909, William Howard Taft concluded it was "not the disposition or within the province of the Federal Government to interfere with regulation by Southern States of their domestic affairs."

Following the Civil War, inaugural addresses also began to contain expressions of concern about the growing number of foreign immigrants. We need rigidly enforced laws, Grover Cleveland argued, prohibiting Chinese immigrants from competing with American labor when they had no intention of acquiring citizenship and insisted on retaining repugnant habits as well as customs. Benjamin Harrison sought the exclusion of all races, "even the best, whose coming is necessarily a burden upon our public revenues or a threat to social order. These should be identified and excluded." President Taft focused on minimizing the "evils likely to arise from" the admission of Asian immigrants.

"Justice," Lyndon B. Johnson told his fellow countrymen in 1965, "requires us to remember that when any citizen denies his fellow, saying: 'His color is not mine,' or 'his beliefs are strange and different,' in that moment he betrays America, though his forebears created this nation." Jimmy Carter hoped his presidency would be remembered as one that "had torn down the barriers that separated those of different race and region and religion, and where there had been mistrust, built unity, with a respect for diversity."

**Foreign Affairs.** Presidents talked of foreign relations, which had held their attention since the beginning. While Thomas Jefferson sought "honest friendship with all nations, entangling alliances with none" in his first inaugural speech, James Madison was not so generous in 1813. His second inaugural provided justification for war against Great Britain.

Although Ulysses S. Grant vowed to "respect the rights of all nations," he made it clear in 1869, that if "others departed from this rule in their dealings with us, we may be compelled to follow their precedent." Similarly, William McKinley spoke in 1897 of pursuing "a firm and dignified foreign policy." In 1905, Theodore Roosevelt confidently declared that the United States had "become a great nation, forced by the fact of its greatness into relations with the other nations of the earth, and we must behave as beseems a people with such responsibility." Americans had also become, as Woodrow Wilson observed, "a composite and cosmopolitan people." America stood "firm in armed neutrality," but, Wilson warned, it could still be drawn into WORLD WAR I because our "fortunes as a nation are involved whether we would have it so or not." While Warren G. Harding wanted "no part in directing the destinies of the Old World" following the war, Calvin Coolidge conceded, "we cannot live to ourselves alone."

Franklin Roosevelt's fourth address, a mere 573 words, delivered near the end of WORLD WAR II, emphasized that Americans had "learned to be citizens of the world, members of the human race. We have learned the simple truth, as Emerson said, that 'The only way to have a friend is to be one.' "

A combative Harry S. Truman accused the communists of trying to prevent "world recovery and lasting peace." His speech outlined four points of action: continued use of the MARSHALL PLAN, creation of an Atlantic defense pact, technical and scientific assistance to underdeveloped nations, and grants or loans to those countries.

Dwight D. Eisenhower stressed that he was willing to use force to deter aggression, saying: "In the final choice a soldier's pack is not so heavy a burden as a prisoner's chains." John F. Kennedy was also willing to "pay any price, bear any burden, meet any hardship, support any friend, oppose any foe, in order to assure the survival and the success of liberty."

As the communist world began to crumble in 1989, George Bush enthusiastically announced that "great nations of the world are moving toward democracy through the door of freedom."

**Calls for Reform.** A democracy, on occasion, is in need of reform. It was the earnest desire of Ulysses S. Grant in 1873, to correct CIVIL SERVICE abuses. Four years later, Rutherford B. Hayes appealed for both CIVIL SERVICE REFORM and "a change in the system of appointment itself." Using even stronger language, James A. Garfield called for the regulation of the civil service by law. Grover Cleveland saw civil service reform as a way of protecting the American people from incompetency, while William McKinley felt reform was necessary to "retaining faithful and devoted public servants in office."

Benjamin Harrison used his 1885 address to challenge the nation's great corporations to "more scrupulously observe their legal limitations and duties," and suggested that Congress should enact more adequate pension laws. A myriad of reform proposals were espoused by William Howard Taft, including calls for relieving the railroads from certain antitrust restrictions, reorganization of the DEPARTMENT OF JUSTICE, the Department of Commerce and Labor, and the Interstate Commerce Commission, as well as revision of the antitrust and interstate commerce laws "which shall secure the conservation of our resources."

After four years as President, Woodrow Wilson confidently declared at the outset of his second term that "no equal period in our history has been so fruitful of important reforms in our economic and industrial life or so full of significant changes in the spirit and purpose of our political action." Under his leadership, there had been tariff reductions, banking reforms, stronger antimonopoly legislation, assistance to agriculture, and conservation legislation. Herbert Hoover's 1929 address focused on the need for dealing with crime and the abuses under the Eighteenth Amendment (PROHIBITION) because of the failure of many state and local officials to enforce the law zealously.

**Faith in Greater Power.** Virtually every President in inauguration remarks has professed a belief in, and reliance on, a Supreme Being. Washington emphasized that every step by which the American people "have advanced to the character of an independent nation seems to have been distinguished by some token of providential agency." Thomas Jefferson sought the "favor of that Being in whose hands we are, who led our fathers, as Israel of old, from their native land and planted them in a country flowing with all the necessaries and comforts of life."

Humbly invoking God for "wisdom and firmness," James Buchanan hoped to avoid civil war and restore harmony and friendship among the several States. Looking upon the blood and ruin of the Civil War, Abraham Lincoln read perhaps the single most moving paragraph of all inaugurations: "With malice toward none, with charity for all, with firmness in the right as God gives us to see right, let us strive on to finish the work we are in, to bind up the nation's wounds."

As World War II entered its final stages, Franklin D. Roosevelt prevailed on "Almighty God . . . for the way to see our vision clearly—to see the way that leads to a better life for ourselves and for all our fellow men— to the achievement of His will, to peace on earth." By remaining steadfast "in our faith in the Almighty," Harry S. Truman declared four years later, "we will advance toward a world where man's freedom is secure."

If we failed as a nation, Lyndon B. Johnson said, "then we have forgotten in abundance what we learned in hardship: that democracy rests on faith, that freedom asks more than it gives, and that the judgment of God is harshest on those who are most favored." "Ours was," Jimmy Carter reminded us, "the first society openly to define itself in terms of both spirituality and human liberty."

**Growth and Expansion.** When "George Washington, placed his hand upon the Bible" in 1789, Ronald Reagan recalled on the occasion of the fiftieth inaugural, he "stood less than a single day's journey by horseback from raw, untamed wilderness. There were four million Americans in a union of thirteen colonies. Today, we are sixty times as many in a union of fifty States." The excitement, as well as the apprehension that accompanied that expansion, is a well-recorded inaugural theme.

The LOUISIANA PURCHASE, Jefferson explained in his second inaugural, had "been disapproved by some from a candid apprehension that the enlargement of our territory would endanger its union." He reasoned, however, that it was "better that the opposite side of the Mississippi should be settled by our own brethren and children than by strangers of another family." In 1821, James Monroe boasted of the acquisition of Florida that opened "to several States a free passage to the ocean" and secured the United States "against all future annoyance from powerful Indian tribes."

After James K. Polk took his oath in 1845, he excitedly announced that the number of states had grown from thirteen to twenty-eight, two having joined the Union within the past week. Polk was somewhat premature in granting Texas statehood, as that did not actually occur for another ten months. In his mind, however, annexation of the territory had settled the issue. He also felt it a "duty to assert and maintain" the Oregon Territory by constitutional means.

Franklin Pierce, like Polk, argued that concern about the ability of the American system to survive territorial expansion and an augmented population had proven unfounded. Instead, the country, he felt, had experienced "an additional guaranty of strength and integrity of both" at both the state and federal level.

Lincoln's anxiety, understandably was quite different, as he spoke directly to Southerners in 1861. "We can not remove our respective sections from each other," he reminded them, "nor build an impassable wall between them."

**Greatness of America.** "Preservation of the sacred fire of liberty and the destiny of the republican model of government," Washington proclaimed at his first inauguration, has been "entrusted to the hands of the American people." His successors have carried that message forward with great regularity on inauguration day.

The "existence of such a government as ours for any length of time," John Adams reasoned, "is a full proof of a general dissemination of knowledge and virtue throughout the whole body of the people." James Monroe was convinced the American system had "shunned all the defects which unceasingly prey on the vitals and destroyed the ancient Republics."

"Our Government," Martin Van Buren proudly declared, "quietly but efficiently performs the sole legitimate end of political institutions—in doing the greatest good to the greatest number—we present an aggregate of human prosperity surely not elsewhere to be found." For James K. Polk, the American system of "well-regulated self-government" as the "most admirable and wisest . . . ever devised by human minds."

On the eve of the twentieth century, James A. Garfield found it inspiring "to remember that no great emergency . . . has ever arisen that has not been met with wisdom and courage by the American people." Theodore Roosevelt stressed that "no people on earth have more cause to be thankful" than Americans. "Much has been given us, and much will rightfully be expected from us."

"Nowhere else in the world," Woodrow Wilson said in 1913, "have noble men and women exhibited in more striking forms the beauty and energy of sympathy and helpfulness and counsel in their efforts to rectify wrong, alleviate suffering, and set the weak in the way of strength and hope." "Because of what America is and what America has done," Calvin Coolidge reminded his countrymen, "a higher hope inspires the heart of all humanity."

Americans, Franklin Roosevelt cautioned in 1941, must never let the "sacred fire of liberty," as our first President proclaimed, "be smothered with doubt and fear." If we do, "then we shall reject the destiny which Washington strove so valiantly and so triumphantly to establish."

America's role as a defender of freedom, John F. Kennedy believed, was a responsibility the citizenry should not shirk from. "My fellow Americans," he told us, "ask not what your country can do for you: Ask what you can do for your country. My fellow citizens of the world: Ask not what America will do for you, but what together we can do for the freedom of man."

Few inaugural addresses have better explained the relationship of the presidency to the American people in preserving freedom than James K. Polk's eloquent remarks of 4 March 1845:

> Although in our country the Chief Magistrate must almost of necessity be chosen by a party and stand pledged to its principles and measures, yet in his official action he should not be the first President of a part alone, but of the whole United States. While he executes the laws with an impartial hand, shrinks from no proper responsibility, and faithfully carries out in the executive department of the government the principles and policy of those who have chosen him, he should not be unmindful that our fellow-citizens who have differed with him in opinion are entitled to the full and free exercise of their opinions and judgments and that the right of all are entitled to respect and regard.

### BIBLIOGRAPHY

Campbell, Karlyn Kohrs, and Kathleen Hall Jamieson. "Inaugurating the Presidency." *Presidential Studies Quarterly* 15 (Spring 1985): 394–411.

Lott, Davis Newton, ed. *The Presidents Speak: The Inaugural Addresses of the American Presidents from Washington to Nixon.* 1969.

Schlesinger, Arthur M., Jr. and Fred L. Israel. *The Chief Executive: Inaugural Addresses of the Presidents of the United States from George Washington to Lyndon B. Johnson.* 1965.

STEPHEN W. STATHIS

**INAUGURATION.** "I do solemnly swear [or affirm] that I will faithfully execute the office of President of the United States, and will to the best of my ability, preserve, protect, and defend the Constitution of the United States." With these words, prescribed by the Constitution, each American President since George Washington has assumed the mantle of CHIEF EXECUTIVE. The quadrennial thirty-five-word swearing-in ceremony takes only two minutes. All other activities associated with inaugurals—the receptions, concerts, spectacular parades, lofty addresses, and grand balls—are products of custom and tradition rather than law.

When VICE PRESIDENTS succeed to the presidency on the death or resignation of an incumbent, all ceremonial formalities are dispensed with except the presidential oath. On four of the six occasions when inauguration day has fallen on a Sunday, Presidents chose to be sworn in twice—first, without fanfare, at the White House and then, on the following Monday at a public ceremony at the Capitol.

On the morning of the first inauguration—30 April 1789—cannons thundered in salute, church bells rang for nearly half an hour, and many people began their day in their places of worship praying for the new government and new President. The first inauguration was eight weeks late because the House of Representatives did not have a quorum to count the electoral votes until 6 April. It then took another week for a messenger to carry the news of Washington's election from New York to Mount Vernon. The ceremony took place on the portico of New York City's Federal Hall.

Washington's second inauguration was held in the Senate Chamber of Independence Hall in Philadelphia. John Adams's 1797 installation as President took place in the House Chamber. Thomas Jefferson, the first President to be inaugurated in Washington, took his oath of office in the Senate Chamber in 1801 and 1805. The scene shifted to the House for James Madison's 1809 and 1813 ceremonies.

Speaker of the House HENRY CLAY's stubbornness made inaugurals an outdoor affair. In 1817, Clay refused to allow the Senators to bring their forty "fine red chairs" into the House Chamber for James Monroe's first oath-taking, and the ceremony simply moved outside. Although rain and snow forced Monroe's second inaugural back to the House chamber in 1821, the outdoor swearing-in at his first inaugural set a precedent that with few exceptions, has been followed ever since. Beginning in 1981, the ceremony was shifted from the East to the West Front of the Capitol, where it would be visible to a larger number of spectators.

Since the third inauguration, the oath has been administered by the Chief Justice of the United States, except for the half-dozen men who succeeded by death and chose the nearest judge for their emergency ceremonies. JOHN MARSHALL holds the record of nine inaugural ceremonies (1801–1833), followed by ROGER B. TANEY with seven (1837–1861), and Melville Fuller with six (1889–1909).

Franklin D. Roosevelt's second inaugural, in 1937, was the first to be held on 20 January, following adoption of the TWENTIETH AMENDMENT in 1933. The official date for the inaugural was changed from 4 March (originally set by the Continental Congress and confirmed by the Second Congress), because it was felt that too much time lapsed between the election and inauguration, especially in the case of LAME-DUCK PRESIDENTS. Also, prior to 1937, the new Vice President had taken his oath of office in the Senate Chamber and not with the President. On 20 January 1945, Roosevelt was sworn-in for his fourth term in a simple ceremony on the south portico of the White House, the only inaugural to be held there. Roosevelt's departure from the traditional pomp and pageantry was prompted by a behind the scenes disagreement with the congressional inaugural committee over what amount of money was to be appropriated for the ceremony. Ultimately, Roosevelt decided to hold the ceremony at the White House. The result was one of the most austere ceremonies in history.

Although INAUGURAL ADDRESSES often have been characterized as less than inspiring, they have on occasion accurately captured the unique demands of an era and have moved the nation: Abraham Lincoln's masterful second inaugural address ("With malice toward none, with charity for all, with firmness in the right . . . "),

Franklin D. Roosevelt's assurance that "the only thing we have to fear is fear itself," and John F. Kennedy's "ask not what your country can do for you"—each holds an honored place in history and not for eloquence alone.

George Washington, who started the precedent of delivering an inaugural address, also gave the shortest—135 words—in 1793. In addition, he began the tradition of professing a belief in, and reliance on, a Supreme Being in his address, and taking the oath of office with his hand on a Bible.

The first official inaugural ball, according to most historians, was hosted by James and DOLLEY MADISON in 1809 at Long's Hotel on Capitol Hill. Four hundred people made the select guest list. At Madison's second inauguration in 1813, eight thousand clamored to get into the ball at the Davis Hotel on Pennsylvania Avenue.

Between 1913 and 1929, and during WORLD WAR II, there were no official balls. President Woodrow Wilson asked that there be no inaugural balls for both his first (1913) and second (1917) oath taking. President Warren G. Harding (1921) planned initially to revive the custom but subsequently changed his mind and a charity ball was held instead. Charity balls were also given to launch the Coolidge (1925) and Hoover (1929) administrations. In 1937, an Inaugural Concert served as a substitute for a ball. Inaugural balls made a comeback following the war. In 1969, there were six, and in 1981, for the first time, a ball was held overseas, honoring Ronald Reagan in Paris, and satellite balls were held across the country. For the 1985 and 1989 inaugurations, there were nine balls.

Inaugural parades down Pennsylvania Avenue following the swearing in ceremony began in 1889. Earlier parades had started at the White House and escorted the President to the Capitol. The parades have included everything from a float with a weaving mill (1841), a hot air balloon (1857), ten thousand lantern-bearing marchers singing campaign songs (1877), and Buffalo Bill (1889), to a calliope playing "I'm Just Wild About Harry" (1949), and a reproduction of the LBJ Ranch (1965). Dwight D. Eisenhower was even lassoed by a cowboy at his 1953 parade.

Although Theodore Roosevelt did not follow his daughter Alice's suggestion in 1905 to have the Democratic losers march down Pennsylvania Avenue in chains, there were coal miners with lights on their helmets, American Indians in headdress, the black troops of the famous 9th Cavalry that had ridden with him at Santiago, and his beloved Rough Riders. President John F. Kennedy's PT-109 boat and the eight surviving members of the crew he commanded in World War II, together with thirty thousand other participants passed by the White House reviewing stand in 1961.

Instead of riding at the head of the inaugural parade to the White House, a jubilant Jimmy and ROSALYNN CARTER, with their daughter Amy, startled parade officials and delighted the crowds in 1977 when they walked the entire sixteen blocks to the White House. The coldest day in inaugural history, 20 January 1985, forced cancellation of the parade for the first time in history, and Ronald Reagan began his second term in the Capitol Rotunda. Although it was not quite as cold in 1873, it was frigid enough for the champagne to freeze at the reception for Ulysses S. Grant. When John F. Kennedy became President, an estimated one million people braved a chilling twenty-two-degree temperature, a nineteen-mile-per-hour wind, and eight inches of snow to see the 1961 inaugural parade.

It was not snowing on 4 March 1841, but it was chilly and overcast when William Henry Harrison, at age sixty-eight, wearing neither overcoat nor hat, rode a white charger in a two-hour procession from the White House to the Capitol. After delivering the longest inaugural address (8,445 words), Harrison returned in another slow-moving parade, shook hands with thousands of well-wishers, and then attended three balls. What started as a cold shortly after the inauguration quickly became pneumonia and Harrison died one month later.

Though the trappings have changed and the ceremony now is witnessed by thousands of spectators and watched on television by millions around the world, inaugurations continue to symbolize the permanence of the nation and the peaceful transfer of power in the world's greatest democracy. Inaugurations play a legitimating role in the American democratic process and offer the best affirmation available of Lincoln's view that "when an election is past, it is altogether fitting a people that until the next election they should be one people." An inauguration represents a healthy middle ground between a coronation and a coup d'état.

BIBLIOGRAPHY

Durbin, Louise. *Inaugural Cavalcade.* 1971.
Hughes, Patrick. "Inaugural Day Weather." *NOAA* (National Oceanic and Atmospheric Administration) 15 (Winter 1985): 4–8.
*The Inaugural Story 1789–1969.* 1969.

STEPHEN W. STATHIS

**INCOMPATIBILITY CLAUSE.** The Constitution prohibits members of either house of Congress from "holding any Office under the United States." This provision, found in Article I, Section 6, clause 2, is called the incompatibility clause. It is one of several provisions intended to keep the branches of government separate. Because of the incompatibility clause, the American system of SEPARATION OF POWERS is constitutionally distinct from the British parliamentary system, in which members of the legislative branch can serve as ministers in the executive branch.

The incompatibility clause has existed for two centuries without any definition or application by federal courts. When a question regarding the clause reached a federal district court in 1971, in a case involving the right of members of Congress to hold commissions in the armed forces reserves, the judge remarked that the "meaning and effect of this constitutional provision have never before been determined by a court," and three years later the Supreme Court held in *Schlesinger v. Reservists to Stop the War* (1974) that the reservists lacked standing to bring the case. In response to the objection that if the courts fail to resolve the issue of the incompatibility clause then as a practical matter no one can, the Court replied, "Our system of government leaves many crucial decisions to the political branches." In 1977, when the Justice Department examined the issue of whether members of Congress may hold commissions as officers in the armed forces reserves, it concluded that the "exclusive responsibility for interpreting and enforcing the Incompatibility Clause rests with Congress."

BIBLIOGRAPHY

Fisher, Louis. "Separation of Powers: Interpretation outside the Courts." *Pepperdine Law Review* 18 (1990): 57–93.

LOUIS FISHER

**INDEPENDENT CANDIDATES.** See THIRD-PARTY CANDIDATES.

**INDEPENDENT COMMISSIONS.** Independent commissions are multimembered bodies that perform regulatory and adjudicatory functions outside the executive branch and not under the direct control of the President. Their virtues are that, ideally, they can carry out their responsibilities in an unbiased manner and can implement regulatory legislation through the application of expert knowledge and group deliberation by a body relatively stable in its membership because of staggered terms. Their clearest drawback is their insulation from political accountability and from the political protection that the President can provide.

At first, the constitutional validity of the commissions was attacked on the ground that they united the powers of lawmaker, prosecutor, and judge in the same entity. Frequently, this attack was leveled by those subject to regulation, but not all the criticism was self-serving, and for a long time it cast a shadow over the commissions' legitimacy. This conjunction of powers, however, is not unique to the commissions; it characterizes regulatory agencies within the executive branch as well. The need for general administrative reform was an important aspect of antiregulatory arguments in the 1930s, and, following the report of the Attorney General's Committee on Administrative Procedure in 1941, Congress, after WORLD WAR II, passed the ADMINISTRATIVE PROCEDURE ACT to segregate regulatory and adjudicatory functions without requiring the division of agencies into separate bodies. The constitutionality of this arrangement is now generally accepted.

A distinct separation-of-powers attack on the commissions is that their independence impermissibly creates a fourth branch of government and undercuts the President's constitutional powers. Because Article II, without qualification, vests the executive power in the President, it is argued that no executive power may validly be exercised except by those who are under his direct control, for only in this way will he be able to discharge the constitutional responsibility to "take care that the laws be faithfully executed."

The independence of the first regulatory commission—the Interstate Commerce Commission (ICC), created in 1887 to regulate railroads—did not result from a conscious congressional desire to insulate it from the authority of the President. What Congress wished to guarantee was independence from partisan bias, and it did so through a requirement that not more than a bare majority of the commissioners could belong to the same political party (a stipulation applied to several subsequent commissions). Independence from the President, as such, was not an apparent subject of legislative concern. In fact, Congress initially placed the ICC within the Department of the Interior, but the Secretary requested termination of this arrangement, which was ended in 1889, perhaps to prevent domination of the commission by the incoming President, Benjamin Harrison, previously a railroad lawyer. The commission form was chosen after the model commonly employed for railroad regulation by the states, which alone had been engaged in regulation until the Supreme Court, in *Wabash, St. Louis and Pacific Railway v. Illinois* (1886), suddenly forced this responsibility on the federal government by ruling that the states were constitutionally forbidden to regulate interstate rail-road rates. The President was given authority to remove members of the ICC for inefficiency, neglect of duty, or malfeasance in office, but this measure was intended as a means by which incompetent commissioners could be removed prior to the completion of their statutorily specified terms rather than as a deliberate curtailment of an unlimited presidential removal power.

But Presidents soon began to look upon commissions as diminishing their authority. In 1908 Theodore Roosevelt sent a message to Congress insisting that executive functions should only be carried out by entities answerable to the President. Congress showed little inclination to accede to such a request. The first chairman of the ICC was the renowned constitutional scholar Thomas M. Cooley, who made sure that the commission operated under sound procedures and brought it substantial prestige. As the need for regulation of other types of business activity became apparent early in the twentieth century, Congress chose to make further use of the commission form. Four new commissions were established during the administration of Woodrow Wilson, who supported them but made clear that he believed he had the authority to direct their efforts and sought ex officio membership on them for executive-branch officials. Presidents Warren G. Harding, Calvin Coolidge, and Herbert Hoover also anticipated being able to influence the work of the commissions, either by personal contacts with commissioners or by forcing their resignations. Commissions were required to submit their budgets to Congress through the executive branch.

Although the regulatory commission was an important instrument in the vast expansion of federal authority during the NEW DEAL, Franklin D. Roosevelt was unprepared to tolerate policy formulation and implementation by agencies outside his control. His power to appoint the entire membership of the commissions created during his presidency served to insure that their actions would conform to his desires, but he had no such ability to control the older commissions. In 1933 he summarily removed William Humphrey from the Federal Trade Commission, citing no reason except policy disagreement, even though the FEDERAL TRADE COMMISSION ACT only authorized removal for inefficiency, neglect of duty, or malfeasance in office. Roosevelt's action was challenged in the Supreme Court, which, in HUMPHREY'S EXECUTOR v. UNITED STATES (1935), unanimously held that restriction of the President's removal power was constitutionally permissible. The Court distinguished MYERS v. UNITED STATES (1926), in which it had been held that Congress could not constitutionally require that the Senate concur in the President's dismissal of a postmaster because such a restriction was an improper interference with the constitutional power and responsibilities of the President. It declared that *Myers* only applied to limitations on the President's authority to remove officials exercising purely executive power, and, since independent commissions were bodies whose duties were "quasi-legislative" and "quasi-judicial," the power to remove commissioners was validly subject to congressional restriction.

The reasoning of *Humphrey's Executor* was highly dubious. The duties of a Federal Trade Commissioner are surely executive in large part and are in no way different from those of many executive-branch officers who, under *Myers,* are removable by the President at will. But the controversy over Humphrey's removal underscored the plain fact that the actual independence of the commissions turns not on whether they are located inside or outside the executive branch, or on what their duties are, but on whether the President can remove commissioners without cause. If a President can do so, the commissions are not independent.

Certainly, for Roosevelt and his supporters, the notion that the effectuation of New Deal programs could be obstructed by commissioners who were holdovers from the past was unacceptable, and the commissions, like the courts, became targets of the administration. Following his landslide reelection in 1936, Roosevelt appointed a committee of distinguished students of government and administration under the chairmanship of Louis Brownlow to prepare a report for submission to Congress advocating centralized presidential control over all administrative activities of the federal government. The BROWNLOW COMMITTEE, formally designated the President's Committee on Administrative Management, took dead aim at the independent commissions. It declared that it would be more accurate to describe them as the "irresponsible" commissions, and condemned them as "a headless 'fourth branch' of the Government, a haphazard deposit of irresponsible agencies and uncoordinated powers," which "enjoy power without responsibility" and "leave the President with responsibility without power."

But the Brownlow report, like the COURT-PACKING PLAN, was rejected by Congress, which not even in the heyday of the New Deal was prepared to accept the dramatic shift in the balance of political power that would result from granting the President absolute authority over the execution of all federal laws and policies. However, keeping the commissions free from presidential control leaves them, as many commentators have noted, with little protection against congressional influence through the appropriations process, oversight by committees, and personal contacts by members of Congress and their staffs. Political accountability through the President may be replaced by accountability to a small number of strategically situated members of Congress. And because regulated groups can concentrate their efforts at lobbying and persuasion on a single locus of regulation, there has been evidence of "capture" of commissions by those who are supposedly subject to their regulatory authority. Nevertheless, despite their shortcomings, independent commissions offer a promise of fairness and consistency in the administration of regulatory legislation that cannot be quickly dismissed by those who are uneasy about the complete concentration of administrative authority in the executive branch. Thus, the first HOOVER COMMISSION, making recommendations in 1949 to Harry S. Truman on executive organization, and James Landis, reporting to John F. Kennedy in 1960 on administrative agencies, declared that their retention was appropriate and desirable.

But such a spirit of accommodation has not been shared by all administrations, even though it is obvious that the duties of some regulatory entities, such as the FEDERAL ELECTION COMMISSION, necessitate that they be entirely free from political influence. Richard Nixon's Advisory Council on Executive Organization, chaired by Roy Ash (the ASH COUNCIL), recommended in 1971 that the majority of existing commissions be replaced by agencies headed by a single individual removable at the will of the President. Although Congress remained unwilling to accede to such recommendations, the administration of Ronald Reagan saw an apparent opportunity to end the independence of the commissions through judicial action when, for a time in the 1980s, the Supreme Court seemed willing to place strict limits on Congress's power to interfere with the exercise of executive authority. The Reagan administration was no less anxious than the Roosevelt administration had been to bend all government agencies to its will, although for altogether different purposes, and thus sought to take advantage of this emerging judicial attitude. In 1985 Attorney General EDWIN MEESE III announced that "we should abandon the idea that there are such things as 'quasi-legislative' or 'quasi-judicial' functions that can be properly delegated to independent agencies or bodies." The Solicitor General, while disavowing any intent to call into question the constitutionality of the independent commissions, argued before the Supreme Court in BOWSHER V. SYNAR (1986) that the President possesses illimitable constitutional authority to remove at will any federal officer appointed by him who is responsible for the administration of the law except where the officer's administrative responsibilities are ancillary to the performance of adjudicatory functions; he also questioned the continued vitality of *Humphrey's Executor* as a precedent.

Although the original draft of Chief Justice Warren Burger's majority opinion in *Bowsher* seemed to endorse these contentions, the Court carefully noted in its final opinion that its holding disallowing the assignment of executive duties to the COMPTROLLER GENERAL did not implicate the validity of the independent commissions because it turned on the fact that the Comptroller General was removable by Congress, not that he was not removable by the President. And the Court categorically rejected the administration's position on the commissions in MORRISON v. OLSON (1988), where it sustained the constitutionality of an independent counsel over the lone dissent of Justice Antonin Scalia, who argued for absolute presidential REMOVAL POWER. Speaking for the majority, Chief Justice William H. Rehnquist confined the holding in *Myers* to the proposition that Congress could not give itself a role (except through the IMPEACHMENT process) in the removal of executive officials, and he reaffirmed the result, but not the reasoning, of *Humphrey's Executor.* The Court agreed with the holding that Congress can limit the President's power to remove a commissioner, not because the commission does not exercise executive power, as *Humphrey's Executor* reasoned, but because the Constitution does not require that the President have uncontrolled removal power over every officer with administrative responsibilities.

The *Morrison* decision would appear to settle beyond doubt the constitutional validity and viability of independent commissions. It establishes that the President's ability to remove commissioners is subject to reasonable restrictions not involving actual congressional participation in the removal decision, and that the commissions' independence may be protected by statute. As Justice Byron R. White has observed, "the Court has been virtually compelled to recognize that Congress may reasonably deem it 'necessary and proper' to vest some among the broad new array of governmental functions in officers who are free from the partisanship that may be expected of agents wholly dependent upon the President."

### BIBLIOGRAPHY

Bernstein, Marver H. *Regulating Business by Independent Commission.* 1955.

Cushman, Robert E. *The Independent Regulatory Commissions.* 1941.

Miller, Geoffrey P. "Independent Agencies." *Supreme Court Review* (1986): 41–97.

Steele, Charles N., and Jeffrey H. Bowman. "The Constitutionality of Independent Regulatory Agencies under the Necessary and Proper Clause: The Case of the Federal Election Commission." *Yale Journal on Regulation* 4 (1987): 363–392.

Strauss, Peter L. "The Place of Agencies in Government: Separation of Powers and the Fourth Branch." *Columbia Law Review* 84 (1984): 573–669.

U.S. Senate. Committee on Governmental Affairs. *Study on Federal Regulation,* Vol. 5: *Regulatory Organization.* 95th Cong., 2d Sess., 1977. S. Doc. No. 95–91.

U.S. Senate. Committee on the Judiciary. *Separation of Powers and the Independent Agencies: Cases and Selected Readings.* 91st Cong., 1st Sess., 1969. S. Doc. No. 91–49.

Verkuil, Paul R. "The Purposes and Limits of Independent Agencies." *Duke Law Journal* (1988): 257–279.

Verkuil, Paul R. "The Status of Independent Agencies after *Bowsher v. Synar.*" *Duke Law Journal* (1986): 779–805.

DEAN ALFANGE, JR.

**INDEPENDENT COUNSEL.** Originally called a special prosecutor, an independent counsel is an official appointed under the Ethics in Government Act of 1978 (28 U.S.C. secs. 591 et seq.) to investigate allegations of serious wrongdoing by the President, Cabinet officials, and certain other high-level executive-branch and presidential campaign personnel. In the wake of the WATERGATE AFFAIR, Congress created the independent-counsel process to prevent the under-prosecution of executive-branch malfeasance that could occur because of the conflict of interest inherent in leaving the policing of the executive to the Justice Department alone.

**Appointment, Powers, and Removal.** Under the act, the ATTORNEY GENERAL has ninety days to investigate, once specific information is presented suggesting that an official covered by the statute has committed a serious federal offense. If the Attorney General determines within that time that no further investigation is warranted, then no action occurs. If, however, the Attorney General refuses or is unable to make that determination, the matter is referred to a special panel of the U.S. Court of Appeals for the District of Columbia Circuit, which appoints an independent counsel. The order of appointment specifies the scope of the counsel's investigation, which may be amended on petition of the counsel or at the initiative of the Attorney General.

It is customary for the court to seek prestigious members of the bar, often from the same political party as the person being investigated, to act as independent counsel. Prominent independent counsels in the late 1980s included Laurence Walsh, a retired federal judge and former head of the American Bar

Association, appointed to investigate the IRAN-CONTRA AFFAIR, and another distinguished retired judge, Arlin Adams, appointed to investigate a financial scandal in the DEPARTMENT OF HOUSING AND URBAN DEVELOPMENT (HUD). Once appointed, an independent counsel has powers comparable to those of a U.S. attorney or other Justice Department prosecutor charged with a similar investigation. These include the ability to conduct a grand jury investigation, to pursue all necessary evidence and witnesses, and ultimately to decide whether matters assigned to the counsel warrant prosecution.

The relative independence of the independent counsel is secured not only by his or her judicial appointment but also by statutory protection against discharge. Independent counsels ordinarily have job tenure until they determine that all matters within their jurisdiction are adequately resolved. They may be removed only by personal action of the Attorney General, and then only for "good cause, physical disability, mental incapacity, or . . . other condition that substantially impairs" the independent counsel's job performance. As a consequence, the Attorney General—and, thus, the President—is without power to threaten an independent counsel with removal because of disagreements about the conduct of an investigation or prosecution. Decisions regarding the sufficiency of evidence for an indictment, the appropriateness of alternative investigative techniques, witness selection, and so on, are entirely within the independent counsel's discretion.

**Special Prosecutors and Independent Counsels.** Strictly speaking, it was not necessary for Congress to enact the Ethics in Government Act to provide at least some prosecutors with greater-than-usual decisional independence. The Justice Department is authorized to appoint special attorneys for important matters; it had used that authority, for example, to appoint Archibald Cox as special prosecutor for the Watergate investigation. The Justice Department promised Cox he would not be discharged except for malfeasance or incapacity. When the department broke its commitment, however, and fired Cox for pursuing a subpoena of certain tapes of telephone conversations of Richard M. Nixon (tapes later successfully obtained by Cox's successor, Leon Jaworski), the episode persuaded Congress that executive forbearance was not reliable as the sole source of prosecutorial independence in highly sensitive matters.

The Justice Department has not altogether abandoned its special-prosecutor procedure, however. When a scandal broke in 1991 concerning the alleged theft and resale by Justice Department officials of a computer program for tracking litigation, Attorney General William Barr appointed as his special prosecutor retired federal judge Nicholas Bua, under regulations assuring his independent decision making. The highly sensational accusations had been given credibility by the fact that counsel for the victim of the alleged crime, a computer-software company called Inslaw, Inc., was Elliot Richardson, the former Attorney General whose refusal to fire Watergate special prosecutor Cox was a critical event in the unfolding demise of the Richard M. Nixon administration. Similarly, Barr appointed retired judge Malcolm Wilkey as special prosecutor to investigate the 1992 House of Representatives bank scandal, after it was revealed that the bank had permitted hundreds of members of Congress to cash overdrawn checks.

Numerous independent counsels were appointed between 1976 and 1991, some to investigate particular individuals for discrete alleged violations, others to investigate all wrongdoing in connection with substantial scandals. Five individual investigations that were referred to independent counsel concluded without indictment. These targeted Hamilton Jordan and Tim Kraft, both aides to Jimmy Carter; Ronald Reagan's first Secretary of Labor, Ray Donovan; Reagan administration Attorney General EDWIN MEESE III; and Theodore Olson, Assistant Attorney General under Reagan. Two other investigations, targeting Reagan aides Michael Deaver and Lyn Nofziger, produced indictments and convictions, although Nofziger's conviction was overturned on appeal based on the trial court's misinterpretation of the relevant criminal statute.

Two broader independent-counsel investigations focused on the Iran-contra scandal and on allegations of fraud and embezzlement in the administration of HUD loan programs under Reagan's HUD Secretary, Samuel Pierce. The Iran-contra investigation produced a number of indictments and convictions, although two principal convictions—of former NATIONAL SECURITY ADVISER John Poindexter and of his aide, Col. Oliver North, were overturned on appeal because insufficient steps were taken to prevent the inculpatory use at trial of immunized congressional testimony. The HUD investigation elicited its first indictment and guilty plea in early 1992. Although this record suggests a system that is successful overall, it bears noting that a defendant such as Theodore Olson, who ultimately was not prosecuted, still had to endure a twenty-eight-month investigation and $1.3 million in legal fees before being cleared.

**Constitutionality and Institutional Impact.** When a statutory special-prosecutor process was first proposed in Congress, the Gerald Ford administration opposed it as an unconstitutional incursion into executive authority, a position later taken by the Reagan administration as well. In a sweeping 7-to-1 opinion, however, the Supreme Court in MORRISON V. OLSON (1988) upheld the constitutionality of independent counsel and rejected the claim that the President had inherent constitutional power to control the policy-making discretion of all federal prosecutors.

The lack of direct executive control, however, does not eliminate all Justice Department influence regarding the conduct of prosecutions against targets of independent counsel. For example, the independent counsel's investigation of the Iran-contra affair repeatedly raised issues of access to classified documents, access that the Justice Department sometimes opposed. Should an independent counsel seek presidential evidence, whether documents or testimony, the Justice Department would likewise be available to defend a presidential assertion of EXECUTIVE PRIVILEGE.

The established constitutionality of the independent-counsel process does not eliminate all concern for its fair operation. For example, because the statute requires the Attorney General to initiate an investigation whenever significant information is presented regarding possible serious wrongdoing by any person within the act's purview, it is relatively easy for members of Congress to trigger the independent-counsel process against politically vulnerable officials. It is also true that the individual targets of independent-counsel investigations are subject, unlike other criminal defendants, to the prosecutorial judgments of officials who, unlike ordinary Justice Department attorneys, are not disciplined by any competing demands for their highest priority law enforcement efforts.

It is thus unsurprising that Congress has fine-tuned the independent-counsel process from time to time. In 1982, reacting to claims of undue stringency, Congress amended the original statute to make it easier for the Attorney General to decline to pursue an investigation under the act. In 1987, however, Congress determined that it had inadvertently created too great a loophole for evading the independent-counsel process, and it again tightened up the process. For example, Attorneys General had claimed authority under the 1982 amendments to forgo prosecution based on their determination that the potential defendants lacked the state of mind necessary to violate the criminal law involved. The 1987 amendments removed that discretion.

Presumably to temper any potential for unfairness, Congress has always designed the independent-counsel process as a compromise between prosecutorial accountability to the President and complete independence. Thus, the act applies only to a limited number of officials with regard to whom the executive branch's conflicts of interest in self-regulation would be most dramatic. Further, although the statute directs certain acts by the Attorney General, there is no court review of the Attorney General's decisions under the statute. Thus, if the Attorney General decides either that given information is insufficient to trigger a preliminary investigation or that the appointment of independent counsel is unwarranted after such an investigation, no one may use the judicial process to compel the investigation to proceed.

The system also offers a political advantage to the executive. As exemplified by the investigation of Attorney General Meese, who had been the focus of substantial adverse publicity because of his financial dealings and alleged intervention in legal proceedings on behalf of friends, a decision by independent counsel not to prosecute is likely to have a much greater effect in resuscitating the reputation of the accused official than would a similar judgment by the Justice Department. For this reason, although the statutory authority to appoint independent counsels lapsed in December 1992, it would be surprising if the process were not ultimately reauthorized.

### BIBLIOGRAPHY

Bruff, Harold. "Independent Counsel and the Constitution." *Willamette Law Journal* 24 (1988): 539–563.

Carter, Stephen. "The Independent Counsel Mess." *Harvard Law Review* 102 (1988): 105–141.

Eastland, Terry. *Ethics, Politics, and the Independent Counsel: Executive Power, Executive Vice, 1789–1989.* 1989.

Harriger, Katy Jean. *Independent Justice: The Federal Special Prosecutor in American Politics.* 1992.

Shane, Peter M. "Independent Policymaking and Presidential Power: A Constitutional Analysis." *George Washington Law Review* 57 (1989): 596–626.

PETER M. SHANE

**INDEPENDENT TREASURY.** The Independent Treasury, or the Subtreasury, was a system that enabled the national government to conduct its own financial affairs, collecting taxes and disbursing its own funds in specie without the use of a national bank or any state banks. In 1832, after President Andrew Jackson vetoed the recharter of the Second BANK OF THE UNITED STATES, he removed federal deposits from the bank and placed them in state banks. By 1838 President Martin Van Buren endeavored to separate the national government from the state banks by creating the Independent Treasury as a repository for all federal funds. Congress accepted the Independent

Treasury in June 1840, after Van Buren had made the system a key element of his presidency. In 1841 Presidents William Henry Harrison and John Tyler, following the WHIG PARTY platform, began dismantling the Independent Treasury.

Democratic President James K. Polk was determined to separate the federal government from the banks. In 1846 Congress reestablished the Independent Treasury and through various modifications this system remained until the last subtreasury closed in 1921.

Through the Independent Treasury Polk hoped to divorce the national government from both a powerful central bank and state banks. The system was designed to protect public money and to furnish safe currency while continuing to collect and disburse only specie. Federal revenues went into subtreasuries, essentially collecting stations in major cities around the nation. The system successfully placed limitations on the expansion of credit and made the use of specie, public and private, more widespread. But the Independent Treasury never accomplished its goals. In times of prosperity the Treasury accumulated surplus revenues, which took hard money out of circulation. This had a deflationary effect, restricting credit and limiting the expansion of trade and production. During an economic crisis, however, the requirement that taxes be paid in specie led individuals to hoard hard money, retarding the economy by limiting credit and slowing growth.

President James Buchanan in 1857, hailing the Independent Treasury, claimed that it had no negative effect on business, that the expense to run the system was minimal, and that it secured a sound currency. But the intensity and size of the CIVIL WAR overwhelmed the Independent Treasury. On 6 January 1862 the Independent Treasury ceased payment in specie and issued greenbacks, thus withdrawing from the spirit and goals of the 1846 law by failing to do business in hard money. Additionally the exigencies of the Civil War led the government to rely on banks to market war bonds.

The various crises and panics between the Civil War and WORLD WAR I demonstrated the inadequacies of the Independent Treasury. In 1846 the Treasury had little influence on big business, but by the 1870s its credit limitation proved too restrictive. Credit had become the blood of modern society, and without it industry and business would have been ruined. The change from an agrarian society to an industrial society, with an increase in the use of banks and credit, ran counter to the goals and purposes of the Independent Treasury. The system set up by Polk and Van Buren was ultimately inadequate for a modern industrial society based on credit, and was subsequently replaced by the modern FEDERAL RESERVE SYSTEM.

### BIBLIOGRAPHY

Hurd, John R. *A National Bank, or No National Bank; An Appeal to the Common Sense of the People of the United States, Especially of the Laboring Classes.* 1842.

Kinley, David. *The History, Organization, and Influence of the Independent Treasury of the United States.* 2d ed. 1968.

Kinley, David. *The Independent Treasury of the United States and Its Relations to the Banks of the Country.* 1910.

Peterson, Norma Lois. *The Presidencies of William Henry Harrison and John Tyler.* 1989.

Studenski, Paul, and Herman E. Krooss. *Financial History of the United States: Fiscal, Monetary, Banking, and Tariff, Including Financial Administration and State and Local Finance.* 2d ed. 1952.

RONALD FISCHER and PAUL FINKELMAN

**INDIANS.** U.S. Presidents' influence on Indian policy has been great. For Presidents, Indians have represented a bother—a "problem"—and resolution of the "Indian problem" has never been achieved, since it is defined by the Indians' persistent and unique legal and cultural presence in the United States. The government exchanged gifts and promises for Indian lands, hoping that the Indian population would eventually disappear through decline or assimilation. Instead, diverse Indian peoples and their cultures and tribal governments have managed to survive, continuing to remind the United States of its legal and moral responsibilities.

Presidents have occasionally mentioned Indians in their INAUGURAL ADDRESSES, but the nation has rarely been so concerned with Indians to warrant a President's full attention. Although the Constitution gives the executive branch of the federal government authority over Indian affairs, Presidents have always had the opportunity to distance themselves from policymaking. Cahuilla Indian Rupert Costo, an Indian-rights advocate, author, and editor, stated that Presidents have had a "role in determining policy, initiating actions, signing or vetoing legislative acts, and in fact deciding the fate of the Indian Tribes"; however, individual Presidents have inherited Indian policies that they have then adjusted to fit current circumstances or they have applied existing ideas, popular outside of government, to alter the direction of the U.S. government's Indian policy. Presidential policy has not so much resulted from sensitivity to Indians as from interest groups' pressure to resolve issues involving Native Americans.

**The Policy of Removal.** Two years before George Washington became President, Secretary of War Henry Knox had recommended to the Congress, that it would be too expensive in lives and money to abandon the colonial practice of recognizing Indians' "right of soil" and negotiating purchases of land through formal treaties. As Washington's Secretary of War, Knox established the new country's Indian policy. Washington and his immediate successors wanted to obtain Indian land cheaply and morally and hoped to avoid confrontations between pioneers and Indians through central government control. They assumed that Indians would decline in numbers, cede their land, and eventually become "civilized," melting into the non-Indian population.

The collapse of this assumption forced a shift in Indian policy. Vast little-known lands to the west stimulated Thomas Jefferson's conceptualization of the alternative policy, removal. Indians obstructing civilization's expansion would be pushed westward. In 1803 Jefferson sent Meriwether Lewis and William Clark on a surveying expedition beyond the distant limits of the Louisiana Territory, a journey that took them through many Indian homelands. In the early nineteenth century, Presidents realized that non-Indians would continue to push westward beyond the government's control, that Indians were unwilling to cede their lands peacefully, and that Indians were failing to recognize the "superiority" of non-Native Americans' development. Lewis and Clark's reports confirmed the feasibility of a removal policy.

James Monroe opposed the removal of the Cherokees as "revolting to humanity and utterly unjustifiable," yet a few years later, Andrew Jackson, the renowned Indian-fighter, eagerly enforced the Indian Removal Act of 1830, oblivious to Supreme Court opinions. Jackson refused to enforce the Court's decision against the state of Georgia in the case of *Worcester v. Georgia* (1832), in which the court said that the national government had exclusive jurisdiction in the Cherokee Nations' territory. During Jackson's administration thousands of eastern Indians were forcibly removed to the west: thousands died on the way, while others suffered at the hands of swindlers, land speculators, and government contractors. Martin Van Buren continued Jackson's policy of forced removal.

The expansionist President James K. Polk was second only to Jefferson in annexing Indians' territory to the United States. Adding the Oregon Territory and the Mexican Cession, Polk encouraged immigration into Indian land while ignoring promises to protect the Indian and Mexican residents.

**Reservations or Assimilation.** During the 1850s, the government began developing a reservation policy as a solution to Indian-white confrontations in the west. Presidents continued to hope that the size of the reservations would gradually shrink as the residents abandoned hunting for farming and raising livestock. Millard Fillmore's representatives negotiated the reduction of many California Indians' landholdings, putting Indians onto reservations, but when the treaties failed to pass the Senate, he did not renegotiate them or even inform the Indians that the treaties were void.

Abraham Lincoln's administration was embroiled not only in the CIVIL WAR but in many Indian wars as well. The HOMESTEAD ACT (1862) was a directly aggressive act against Indians, opening their land in Kansas and Nebraska to white homesteaders. Secretary of State WILLIAM H. SEWARD purchased Alaska, adding Inuit and Aleut populations to the United States. As non-Indians continued their invasion westward in the post–Civil War years, the Indian wars persisted. Commissioners were sent to inform Plains Indians that they had to move to reservations far from emigrants and railroads.

Ulysses S. Grant saw the Indian service as a good place to retire unneeded army officers, but Congress banned that policy early in 1870. In response to Congress and to a rising sentiment demanding Christian justice for Indians, Grant turned control of Indian agencies over to different Christian denominations. Distributing responsibilities in this way spurred interdenominational conflicts, and the rivalry persisted, eventually leading to the withdrawal of government subsidies to all contract schools on the reservations. Grant's Peace Policy, with its emphasis on treating Indians with kindness and justice, did not change the general objectives of U.S. Indian policy.

As the nineteenth century neared its close, the government policy was to separate Indians from their tribes and free the government from its expensive treaty obligations. Aiming to make Native Americans into farmers and ranchers, Congress attempted to shrink the size and number of reservations, finally passing the General Allotment Act (also known as the Dawes Severalty Act, 1887), which provided 160-acre allotments to Indian heads of families.

Schools were a primary means for the government to train Indian children in vocational skills to enable them to support themselves. Off-reservation boarding schools were too expensive for the money-conscious Congress of the mid 1800s, and they gave way to on-reservation day schools. Reformers such as Commissioner of Indian Affairs Thomas Morgan believed, as Morgan put it, that "education should seek the disintegration of the tribes"—that is, that schools should assist Indians in assimilating into the larger culture.

Benjamin Harrison and Grover Cleveland reformed the administration of the Indian Service by extending the federal CIVIL SERVICE to include school superintendents and teachers, physicians, agency clerks, and storekeepers. Theodore Roosevelt continued to reform Indian Service bureaucrats while seizing Indians' "surplus" land. Such reforms did withdraw Indian Service appointments from the realm of presidential PATRONAGE, but competent administrators were not necessarily sensitive to Indians' interests. Also during Roosevelt's administration, the Secretary of the Interior made the first oil and gas leases on Indian lands, the Blue Lake region in New Mexico—sacred to Taos Pueblo Indians—was made part of the Blue Lake Wilderness Area, and two and a half million acres of Indian reservation lands became national forests.

Twentieth-century Presidents' Indian policies reflected the advances of two contending factions: the assimilationists and the cultural pluralists. Finally, Indian participation also came to influence Indian policy. While Woodrow Wilson was preoccupied with WORLD WAR I (in which many Indians volunteered to fight), his Indian Commissioner, Cato Sells, eagerly issued fee patents, which enabled Indians to dispose of their land freely, to "competent" Indians, those who were less than one-half Indian or had graduated from a government school, because he thought it a crime to leave so much land and natural resources unused. The government liberated Indians by giving them unrestricted ownership of their land. Wilson's administration aimed to free Indians from wardship status and federal supervision.

**Termination.** From Wilson's to Warren G. Harding's administration, the federal government continued to free itself of responsibility to Indians. Albert Fall, Harding's Secretary of the Interior, tried repeatedly to apply the Dawes Act to the Indians of the Southwest.

In the 1920s, those who would reform Indian policy, led by the educator and social worker John Collier, campaigned for Indian civil liberties, conservation of reservations, preservation of Indian cultures, and extension of federal assistance. Indian opposition to federal government policy compelled the Bureau of Indian Affairs (BIA) under Calvin Coolidge to ask the Brookings Institution to review federal policy and recommend improvements. The result was *The Problem of Indian Administration* (also known as the Meriam Report), submitted in 1928. Critical of federal policy, the Meriam Report condemned the Dawes Act for failing to benefit Indians and encouraged abandoning assimilationist policy for a policy of cultural pluralism. The report also urged increasing funds for Indian health and education programs. Herbert Hoover's administration took steps to implement the Meriam Report recommendations to improve health care and education and to decentralize the BIA, but it failed to end the allotment policy or increase tribal decision-making powers.

Franklin D. Roosevelt appointed John Collier to be his Commissioner of Indian Affairs. Collier immediately set out to change the government's Indian policy, first by achieving the repeal of the Dawes Act and by stopping sales of allotted lands. He proposed the Indian Reorganization Act (also known as the Wheeler-Howard Act of 1934) and used Roosevelt's NEW DEAL programs to promote Indian arts and crafts, to reclaim and improve Indian lands, and to gain jobs for Indians. White opposition to Collier's programs arose because of their expense and their expansion of bureaucracy; among Indians, opposition arose over the programs' imposition of the Secretary of the Interior as a final authority over tribal affairs.

In 1946 Congress created the Indian Claims Commission to decide disputes between the federal government and Indians. Although Indians won many cases and received monetary awards, the commission generally strengthened the case for terminating federal supervision of Indians. Harry S. Truman's acting Commissioner of Indian Affairs, William Zimmerman, sanctioned the termination movement when he agreed that certain tribes were wealthy and acculturated enough to survive on their own without federal protection. Dwight D. Eisenhower signed into law the termination of federal controls over western Indians. Termination bills continued to be introduced into Congress during the 1950s, but in 1958 Secretary of the Interior Fred Seaton announced that no more tribes would be terminated without Indian consent.

While Congress proceeded to terminate federal responsibility for Indians, Commissioner of Indian Affairs Dillon Myer tried to solve unemployment problems on reservations by encouraging young Indians to relocate in industrialized urban areas. The policy of relocating Indians away from reservations declined after 1958 because nearly half the Indians involved ultimately returned to the reservations. From the late 1950s, federal subsidies for Indian vocational training and on-the-job training helped reduce Indian unemployment. Congress appropriated large budgets for Indian education during the 1960s.

During the Kennedy and Johnson administrations, antipoverty programs targeted Indians as well as non-Indians. Beginning in 1961, Indian activist organizations pressured the Kennedy administration to reduce the influence of the BIA and increase the level of Indian participation in policy-making, program design, and budgeting. Appropriations for health services had begun to rise dramatically during Eisenhower's administration, and increases continued through the Kennedy and Johnson years. Improved health—and the employment and training of Indians in the health-care field—followed the shift in responsibility for Indian health care from the BIA to the Public Health Service.

In 1970, President Richard M. Nixon asked Congress to increase funds for Indian health and economic development, to repudiate termination, to empower tribes to operate federally funded programs, to return Blue Lake to the Taos Indians, to increase education funds for Indians in public schools (and channel them through tribal governments), and to allow Indians to enter into long-term leases of their lands to non-Indians.

In the late 1970s, Indian victories in the courts over land, water, and fishing rights contributed to an anti-Indian backlash in public opinion. Jimmy Carter tried to treat Indians as if they were not politically separate. Although Ronald Reagan promised to deal with tribes on a government-to-government basis, he reversed trends in Indian policy dating back to the Eisenhower administration. He reduced funds for Indian social programs, and his Commission on Indian Reservation Economies recommended a policy shift toward encouraging private ownership and the individual profit motive and against tribal identity and autonomy.

The images of many popular Presidents may seem to tarnish when one takes account of their perspective on American Indians and their participation in forming federal Indian policy. One needs to consider that popular Presidents' popularity has been the result of their expressing and representing the interests of the non-Indian populace. Presidents are political creatures who respond to political forces, and through most of U.S. history Presidents have felt little pressure from Indians and a great deal from non–Native Americans.

### BIBLIOGRAPHY

Costo, Rupert. "Presidents of the United States in American Indian History." *The Indian Historian* 1 (1968): 4–13.

Fixico, Donald. *Termination and Relocation: Federal Indian Policy, 1945–1960.* 1986.

Horsman, Reginald. *Expansion and American Indian Policy, 1783–1812.* 1967.

Prucha, Francis Paul. *American Indian Policy in the Formative Years: The Indian Trade and Intercourse Acts, 1790–1834.* 1962.

Prucha, Francis Paul. *The Great Father: The United States Government and the American Indians.* 2 vols. 1984.

U.S. Commissioner of Indian Affairs. *Annual Reports to the Secretary of the Interior.* 1849–present.

Washburn, Wilcomb E., ed. *Handbook of North American Indians.* Vol. 4: *History of Indian-White Relations.* 1988.

SEAN O'NEILL

**INELIGIBILITY CLAUSE.** Article I, Section 6, clause 2 of the Constitution prohibits any member of Congress from being appointed to any federal position "which shall have been created, or the Emoluments whereof shall have been encreased" during the member's term of office. The Framers designed this ineligibility clause to prevent the executive from using the APPOINTMENT POWER to corrupt legislators. They knew that the English crown had used appointments to undermine the independence of Parliament.

Interpretations of the ineligibility clause by Congress and the executive branch have far outweighed contributions from the courts. In two instances, the executive branch showed a willingness to reach a settlement with Congress in order to nominate a member of Congress who was ineligible under a literal reading of the Constitution. In the first case, President William Howard Taft wanted Senator PHILANDER KNOX to serve as Secretary of State, even though the salary for that office had been increased during Knox's term. As a way of removing part of the constitutional problem, Congress passed legislation to reduce the compensation of the Secretary of State to the previous level. That did not satisfy the literal meaning of the ineligibility clause, but it took away the appearance of gain and corruption.

A similar situation occurred in 1973, when President Richard M. Nixon wanted to nominate Senator William Saxbe to be Attorney General. The salary for that office had been increased during Saxbe's term as Senator. The Justice Department concluded that Saxbe would be eligible if Congress passed legislation setting his salary as Attorney General at the level established before the increase. "Neither the public, the Executive branch, nor the Legislative branch is well-served by a prohibition so broad that it overcorrects and needlessly deprives members of Congress of opportunities for public service in appointive civil offices." The legislation passed, and Saxbe become Attorney General.

The courts have done little to clarify the boundaries of the ineligibility clause. Senator Hugo Black was nominated to the Supreme Court in 1937 even though a retirement system for the judiciary had been enacted that year, while Black served in the Senate, but the Supreme Court avoided the constitutional issue by holding in *Ex parte Levitt* (1937) that the plaintiff lacked standing to bring the suit. More recently, the nomination of Congressman Abner Mikva to the District of Columbia circuit was challenged because the salaries of federal judges had been increased during Mikva's term in Congress. Once again, in *McClure v. Carter* (1981), a federal court tossed out the suit because of lack of standing. The Justice Department had reasoned that Mikva's appointment to the federal bench was not barred by the ineligibility clause because the scheduled salary increase had not taken effect at the time of Mikva's nomination and that if it had he could be given the same statutory relief that Senators Knox and Saxbe had enjoyed.

BIBLIOGRAPHY

Fisher, Louis. "Separation of Powers: Interpretation outside the Courts." *Pepperdine Law Review* 18 (1990): 57–93.

LOUIS FISHER

**INF (INTERMEDIATE-RANGE NUCLEAR FORCES) TREATY.** Most of the attention that was paid to United States–Soviet Union nuclear ARMS CONTROL efforts focused on strategic weapons— the most powerful systems, capable of reaching all the way from one superpower's home territory into the other. But other types of NUCLEAR WEAPONS also pose enormous threats and might in some circumstances be even more likely to be used. The Intermediate-range Nuclear Forces (INF) Treaty was crafted to deal with these types of weaponry—missile systems capable of ranges between roughly three hundred and three thousand miles.

The United States and the Soviet Union had long deployed various types of INF weapons on the territory of their European allies. The United States, moreover, had studiously refrained from issuing any sort of "no first use" pledge, seeking to reserve the possibility that American nuclear weapons in Europe might be employed if a Soviet or Warsaw Pact westward attack otherwise threatened to overwhelm numerically outmanned NATO forces. [See FIRST USE OF NUCLEAR WEAPONS].

In the late 1970s, the Soviet Union began to deploy a new generation of INF missile, the SS-20, which was larger, more powerful, and capable of reaching greater distances than its predecessors. In response, NATO, at the prodding of President Jimmy Carter, adopted a two-track policy of, first, preparing to deploy its own new version of INF weaponry (consisting of 464 ground-based cruise missiles and 108 Pershing II ballistic missiles) in configurations comparable to the Soviets', and, second, offering to negotiate toward a treaty that would fairly regulate both sides' missiles on the European continent.

Moscow initially resisted this tactic, protesting against the projected deployments, attempting to rally Western European political opinion, and boycotting the negotiations. Eventually, however, the talks resumed, and President Ronald Reagan adopted the "zero option" objective, attempting to ban, not simply restrict, INF missiles and to abolish them on a worldwide basis, not simply in Europe. A variety of interim compromises was evaluated, and eventually the American position embraced a "double zero" approach— that is, desiring to outlaw not only the relatively longer-range INF forces that had been the original subject of negotiations but the relatively shorter-range devices as well. At length, the Soviets agreed.

On 8 December 1987, President Reagan and Soviet General Secretary Mikhail Gorbachev signed the INF treaty, and, after a stormy ratification process, the agreement entered into force. The treaty provided for the supervised dismantling and destruction of an entire category of deployed nuclear weaponry, the first disarmament accord to do so. It also mandated an elaborate exchange of weapons-related data, enforcing a degree of openness previously adamantly resisted by the U.S.S.R., and called for a thirteen-year period of intrusive on-site inspections inside the military establishments of the United States and the Soviet Union, thereby setting a precedent for even more invasive verification arrangements necessary for the subsequent START (STRATEGIC ARMS REDUCTION TALKS) agreement. The INF treaty restored a large measure of the DETENTE relationship that had deteriorated during the early 1980s and capped a remarkable evolution in President Reagan's attitude toward the Soviet Union.

BIBLIOGRAPHY

Risse-Kappen, Thomas. *The Zero Option: INF, West Germany, and Arms Control.* 1988.

Talbott, Strobe. *Deadly Gambits: The Reagan Administration and the Stalemate in Nuclear Arms Control.* 1984.

U.S. Arms Control and Disarmament Agency. *Arms Control and Disarmament Agreements: Texts and Histories of the Negotiations.* 1990.

DAVID A. KOPLOW

**INFORMATION SECURITY OVERSIGHT OFFICE (ISOO).** The Information Security Oversight Office is responsible for monitoring, reviewing, making recommendations, and issuing rules and regulations for classifying and declassifying NATIONAL SECURITY information in the executive branch. Its jurisdiction covers approximately eighty agencies—including the DEPARTMENT OF DEFENSE and the CENTRAL INTELLI-

GENCE AGENCY (CIA)—which generate approximately seven million classification actions annually. The office, which reports annually to the President, is located in the General Services Administration (GSA) but takes its policy and program direction from the NATIONAL SECURITY COUNCIL (NSC), a part of the EXECUTIVE OFFICE OF THE PRESIDENT.

ISOO is a relatively small organization, with a staff of fifteen and a budget of $1.24 million in fiscal year 1992. It requested an increase for an additional five positions and $600,000 in fiscal year 1993, to oversee the National Industrial Security Program, which covers private contractors who handle CLASSIFIED INFORMATION.

There have been proposals in Congress that have focused on strengthening ISOO's independence, authority, and resources, in order to increase further its oversight capabilities and, in turn, improve controls over the classified information system.

The office's heritage dates to President Richard M. Nixon's 1972 EXECUTIVE ORDER on classified information (E.O. 11652), which first created an oversight body in this field, the now-defunct Interagency Classification Review Committee. The committee, composed of representatives of the major classifying agencies, was originally housed in the Executive Office of the President and later in the National Archives and Records Service (then a part of GSA) when the Archivist headed it. These two predecessor locations help to explain ISOO's current dual position (still located in GSA but receiving policy direction from the NSC). The Information Security Oversight Office itself was officially established by President Jimmy Carter in 1978 (E.O. 12065)—as a separate office within GSA—in order to increase oversight over the classification system.

ISOO currently operates under President Ronald Reagan's executive order (E.O. 12356) on National Security Information, which replaced Carter's in 1982. ISOO issued the directive that implemented Reagan's order later in the same year. The Director, charged with monitoring agency compliance with the President's order, can also review agency declassification guidelines and regulations and require them, subject to appeal to the NSC, to be changed if not consistent with Executive Order 12356 or ISOO's directive. The Director also has authority to conduct on-site reviews of the information security program of each agency. He can be denied access by the head of the agency to certain categories of information, however, if such access would pose an exceptional national security risk; in that event, the Director may appeal the denial to the NSC.

The Director, moreover, prescribes standard personnel forms to implement the information security program. In 1987, one of the secrecy agreements—because it included the vague term "classifiable information"—generated a substantial amount of controversy, court challenges by federal employees, and congressional restrictions on its implementation. Later, the term was dropped and new language inserted.

ISOO's Director convenes and chairs interagency meetings to study and make recommendations to improve the security classification system. The Director also oversees an ongoing effort to develop a new executive order on the classification system.

## BIBLIOGRAPHY

Fisher, Louis. "Congressional-Executive Struggles over Information: Secrecy Pledges." *Administrative Law Review* 42 (1990): 89–107.

Garfinkel, Steven. "Executive Coordination and Oversight of Security Classification Administration." *Government Information Quarterly* 1 (1984): 157–164.

Kaiser, Frederick M. "The Amount of Classified Information: Causes, Consequences, and Correctives of a Growing Concern." *Government Information Quarterly* 6 (1989): 247–266.

U.S. Information Oversight Office. *Annual Reports* (1978).

FREDERICK M. KAISER

**INHERENT POWERS.** In the contest over the control of American government, predicted in THE FEDERALIST, Presidents have claimed several forms of power. Least controversial are those powers expressly granted in Article II, such as the power to receive ambassadors. More controversial, but well established, are the powers implied from specific grants, especially those broad responsibilities expressly conferred, such as the function of COMMANDER IN CHIEF, or executing the laws.

To have separate meaning, arguments based on "inherent power" should be understood as those claims to authority that have no express basis from which such powers can be fairly implied. Claims to implied powers may be so tenuous that they, too, should be equated with claims that certain authority is "inherent" in certain presidential functions—or overall combinations of functions.

Claims of inherent powers have arisen most often in connection with the conduct of foreign policy and NATIONAL SECURITY affairs. The most frequent bases for claiming inherent powers are Article II, Section 1, providing "the executive Power shall be vested in a President of the United States of America," and Section 3, directing the President to "take Care that the

Laws be faithfully executed." According to the argument based on this theory, by vesting the EXECUTIVE POWER in a President, Article II grants the officeholder all the powers that are naturally vested in a sovereign nation. The office possesses a "residuum" of power, independent of the specific powers and duties assigned to it by the Constitution and federal statutes.

In 1936, the Supreme Court in UNITED STATES V. CURTISS-WRIGHT EXPORT CORP. identified sovereignty as the basis of the President's inherent power to conduct foreign affairs, tracing the power not to the Constitution, but to the British Crown. "Sovereignty is never held in suspense. When, therefore, the external sovereignty of Great Britain in respect to the colonies ceased, it immediately passed to the union." The foreign policy power, according to the Court, is a "very delicate, plenary and exclusive power of the President as the sole organ of the federal government in the field of international relations—a power which does not require as a basis for its exercise an Act of Congress." The need for a single voice, expertise, and secrecy properly make foreign affairs the domain of the executive.

Adherents of the "delegated" or "formal" powers theory dispute the existence of powers beyond those identified in the Constitution. William Howard Taft wrote, "the President can exercise no power which cannot be fairly and reasonably traced to some specific grant of power or justly implied and included within such grant as proper and necessary." Under this view, Article II, Section 1, only creates the office of the President, while the rest of Article II delineates its functions. Any other reading, according to this theory, makes superfluous the enumerated powers in Sections 3 and 4.

The *Curtiss-Wright* opinion has been vigorously criticized as vague, unnecessary, and lacking proper judicial restraint. Subsequent decisions, such as YOUNGSTOWN SHEET & TUBE CO. V. SAWYER (1952), have signaled less sympathy toward claims of inherent powers in the domestic arena, even during wartime. *New York Times Co. v. United States* (1971) disallowed prior restraint of publication and UNITED STATES V. UNITED STATES DISTRICT COURT (1972) disallowed warrantless national-security searches. Particularly vulnerable to attack are claims that the President is authorized to rely on "inherent" power to act contrary to a legislative determination based on clearly expressed or implied legislative authority. As Justice Robert Jackson wrote in his famous concurring opinion in *Youngstown*, "When the President takes measures incompatible with the expressed or implied will of Congress, his power is at its lowest ebb, for then he can rely only upon his own constitutional powers minus any consti-

tutional powers of Congress over the matter." ALEXANDER HAMILTON, in his famous argument as Pacificus, wrote that the President could cause war by refusing to accept an ambassador, but not where Congress has required otherwise. If an express grant of power to the President may in some circumstances be overridden by Congress, so too could a power claimed to "inhere" in the executive function [see HELVIDIUS-PACIFICUS DEBATES].

While the Constitution does not explicitly incorporate residual powers for the CHIEF EXECUTIVE, Presidents have occasionally claimed an inherent EMERGENCY POWER to act in the nation's essential interests, at their own risk. Examples of such claims are Thomas Jefferson's explanation for purchasing naval supplies without legislative authority to defend against an expected British attack on the *Chesapeake*, James Madison's explanation of Andrew Jackson's declaration of emergency after the Battle of New Orleans, and Abraham Lincoln's explanation for curtailing civil liberties upon the outbreak of the CIVIL WAR [see also HABEAS CORPUS, SUSPENSION OF]. As Arthur M. Schlesinger, Jr., a critic of the inherent powers theory, has observed, even if the "idea of prerogative was not part of presidential power as defined in the Constitution . . . there is reason to believe that the doctrine that crisis might require the executive to act outside the Constitution in order to save the Constitution remained in the back of [the Framers'] minds." John Locke in his *Second Treatise on Government* argued for an executive power, particularly during emergencies, to act "according to discretion for the public good, without the prescription of law and sometimes even against it." While Taft advocated a system based on enumerated powers, for example, he said that executive power should be limited "so far as it is possible . . . consistent with that discretion and promptness of action that are essential to preserve the interests of the public in times of emergency, or legislative neglect or inaction."

The claim to an inherent power to exceed the Constitution in emergencies differs significantly, however, from the claim that such actions are in fact authorized by the Constitution. Each exercise of the emergency power, as understood by Locke, Jefferson, Lincoln and others, by definition exceeded authority conferred by the Constitution, and therefore subjected the President's conduct to legislative, judicial, and public review, including possible IMPEACHMENT.

## BIBLIOGRAPHY

Corwin, Edward S. *The President: Office and Powers 1787–1957.*

Fisher, Louis. *Constitutional Conflicts between Congress and the President.* 3d ed. 1991.

Pious, Richard M. *The American Presidency.* 1979.

Schlesinger, Arthur M., Jr. *The Imperial Presidency.* 1973.

Sofaer, Abraham D. "Emergency Power and the Hero of New Orleans." *Cardozo Law Review* 2 (1981): 233.

Sofaer, Abraham D. *War, Foreign Affairs, and Constitutional Power: The Origins.* 1976.

ABRAHAM D. SOFAER

**IN RE DEBS.** See DEBS, IN RE.

**INSPECTORS GENERAL.** Offices of inspector general (IG) consolidate authority over auditing and investigations within a federal department or agency. The contemporary effort to create such units by public law—as permanent, nonpartisan, independent offices—began in 1976 with a single office. The concept and constructs have since been extended to 61 current federal organizations, including all CABINET departments and the largest agencies as well as a wide variety of commissions, government corporations, boards, and foundations. The IGs in the departments and largest agencies are nominated by the President and confirmed by the Senate; they can be removed only by the President and not the agency head. The APPOINTMENT POWER and REMOVAL POWER over IGs in the smaller entities, by comparison, are held by the agency head.

**Establishment of the Offices.** Significant legislative initiatives to establish these offices occurred in 1976, when the first IG was created; in 1978, when the Inspector General Act was passed; and in 1988, when major amendments to the act were approved. These efforts reflected substantial bipartisan support in both chambers of Congress, usually in the face of opposition from the affected departments and agencies. Conflicts between the executive and legislative branches have also arisen over IG reporting requirements to Congress and removal of the IGs by the President.

All but one of the sixty-one IGs fall directly or indirectly under the Inspector General Act of 1978, as amended (5 U.S.C. Appendix 3). Fifty-nine are expressly under the act; and the Inspector General in the Government Printing Office, a legislative branch organization, follows its basic provisions (44 U.S.C. 3901). The only exception is the Inspector General in the Central Intelligence Agency (CIA). Although modeled after the IGs under the 1978 Act, the CIA Inspector General has less authority and autonomy than its counterparts (P.L. 100-193).

The President's Council on Integrity and Efficiency (PCIE), established by Ronald Reagan in 1981 (Executive Order 12301), and the Executive Council on Integrity and Efficiency (ECIE) by George Bush in 1992 (Executive Order 12805), serve as coordinating mechanisms for the IGs and other officials. Both headed by the deputy director of the OFFICE OF MANAGEMENT AND BUDGET, the two Councils issue annual reports on IG activities and sponsor a number of committees that deal with matters affecting the IG community.

The effort to establish statutory OIGs was designed to replace a system that was deficient in detecting and preventing waste, fraud, and abuse in federal programs and operations. The preexisting system relied on administratively created units that had proved defective because of inherent limitations on their stability, independence, resources, and authority. These units, moreover, had no direct or immediate reporting mandates to the agency head let alone to Congress or to the ATTORNEY GENERAL (if they uncovered suspected illegalities).

The IG effort arose in the aftermath of the WATERGATE AFFAIR and other abuses in the executive that eroded trust and confidence in it. Along with this, major financial scandals affected the agencies in question and thus served as catalysts for several important legislative developments. The first of the contemporary IGs, created in 1976 in the Department of Health, Education, and Welfare (now HEALTH AND HUMAN SERVICES), for instance, followed revelations of widespread fraud in medicare and medicaid programs, which had become a campaign issue in the presidential election that year. Two years later, the Inspector General Act of 1978 was approved during the exposure of pervasive, long-standing violations of procurement laws and policies in the General Services Administration (GSA), one of twelve departments or agencies covered by the new act. The best efforts of the Carter administration, including the creation of an administrative OIG in GSA, had proven inadequate. A more powerful, permanent office was seen as necessary to correct the underlying defects in detecting and preventing such abuses.

Two major enactments—the Inspector General Act of 1978 and its 1988 amendments—established the majority of the offices and standardized the powers, duties, and responsibilities of the IGs. The 1978 IG Act (P.L. 95-452) set up offices in twelve departments and agencies and provided for the basic purposes, authorities, duties, and responsibilities of the IGs. A decade later, the 1988 amendments to the Inspector General Act (P.L. 100-504) extended the offices to the few remaining Cabinet departments and major agencies without them, standardized their powers and authorities, and added specific items to the semiannual reports from the IGs (and companion reports from the head of the agency). The amendments also created a new set of IGs in the mostly smaller federal entities.

**Duties and Powers.** The inspectors general have been granted broad authority "to promote economy, efficiency, and effectiveness in the administration of, and to prevent and detect fraud and abuse in the [agency's] programs and operations." These include the power to: conduct audits and investigations throughout their respective establishments; have direct access to all information, documents, records, reports, audits, and reviews throughout the establishment; issue subpoenas under their own authority for information and documents; receive complaints from employees, whose confidentiality is to be protected; administer oaths for taking testimony; have direct and prompt access to the head of the agency; hire and control their own personnel and resources; and request assistance directly from any federal, state, or local government agency.

The statutory inspectors general have also been given a substantial amount of independence from political pressures and agency officials, who might be subject to an IG investigation or audit. Protection of the IGs' independence—as well as the integrity of their audits and investigations—is built into the requirements for their appointment and removal; restrictions on agency supervision; prohibitions on IGs assuming program operating responsibilities; protections surrounding their resources and appropriations; and obligations to report to the Attorney General, agency head, and Congress.

**Independence.** The IGs are to be selected without regard to partisan affiliation and on the basis of integrity and demonstrated ability in accounting, auditing, financial analysis, law, management analysis, public administration, or investigation. Making the IGs presidential nominees confirmed by the Senate (in the Cabinet departments and larger federal agencies), moreover, gives them the same status as the head and other top agency officials who hold confirmed positions.

If the President (or agency head, where appropriate) removes an IG, the President (or head) must communicate the reasons to Congress. The severest challenge to the IGs' independence in this regard occurred in 1981, less than three years after passage of the 1978 act. On the day Ronald Reagan became President, he summarily dismissed all the confirmed statutory IGs (fourteen at the time) and one confirmed deputy IG. This action was criticized—by both Republicans and Democrats in Congress—for undercutting the independence and nonpartisan nature of the inspectors general, thereby politicizing the offices. Even-

tually, about half of the fired officers were reinstated to IG posts.

Under the IG act, the inspectors general serve only under the "general supervision" of the head of the agency. No agency official can "prevent or prohibit the Inspector General from initiating, carrying out, or completing any audit or investigation, or from issuing any subpoena during the course of any audit or investigation." Exceptions to this exist only for the Departments of DEFENSE, JUSTICE, and TREASURY. In these cases, the department head may interfere only for certain specified reasons, dealing mostly with national security or ongoing criminal investigation. And Congress must be notified of the action.

The IGs are precluded from assuming "program operating responsibilities" and from putting their own recommendations for corrective action into effect. This prohibition prevents them from being placed under the direction of other agency officials. It also prevents a conflict of interest from arising as it would if an inspector general investigated or audited a program or activity which his or her own office was carrying out.

All the statutory IGs are granted control over their resources, including authority to hire their own staff and to request assistance directly from other federal agencies. The offices of inspector general in the larger federal establishments (where the IGs are presidential appointees) also have a separate appropriations account.

The IGs' reporting requirements—to the Attorney General, the agency head, and Congress—not only support their autonomy and the integrity of their operations but also contribute to the ability of other government organizations to oversee and investigate executive activities. The IGs, for instance, are directed to "report expeditiously to the Attorney General whenever the Inspector General has reasonable grounds to believe there has been a violation of Federal criminal law."

Inspectors general are also required to keep the head of the establishment and Congress fully and currently informed by specific reports—semiannual and immediate reports—and such other means as testimony at congressional hearings. The IG reports to the agency head (who transmits them to Congress) are not to be cleared or censored by the head, though the head may append comments. This protection is fundamental to the independence and integrity of the IG, who may discover wrongdoing by the head or other agency officials. In addition to semiannual reports, the IGs can issue immediate reports concerning particularly serious or flagrant problems. These reports also go to the agency head who must transmit them, along with any comments, to Congress within seven days. IGs, however, have rarely issued these immediate reports. They are sometimes characterized as "silver bullets," because, if shot, they could terminate the IG's relationship with agency management.

## BIBLIOGRAPHY

Adair, John J., and Rex Simmons. "From Voucher Auditing to Junkyard Dogs: The Evolution of Federal Inspectors General." *Public Budgeting and Finance* 8 (1988): 91–100.

Dempsey, Charles L. "The Inspector General Concept: Where It's Been, Where It's Going." *Public Budgeting and Finance* 5 (1985): 39–51.

Gates, Margaret J., and Marjorie Fine Knowles. "The Inspector General Act in the Federal Government: A New Approach to Accountability." *Alabama Law Review* 36 (1985): 473–513.

Kaiser, Frederick M. "The Watchers' Watchdog: The CIA Inspector General." *International Journal of Intelligence and Counterintelligence* 3 (1989): 55–75.

Moore, Mark H., and Margaret Jane Gates. *Inspectors-General: Junkyard Dogs or Man's Best Friend.* 1986.

U.S. Department of the Treasury. Office of Inspector General. *Agents for Preventing and Detecting Fraud and Waste: A Report on the Tenth Anniversary of the Inspector General Act of 1978.* 1988.

U.S. House of Representatives. Committee on Government Operations. *The Inspector General Act of 1978: A Ten-Year Review.* 100th Cong., 2d Sess., 1988.

FREDERICK M. KAISER

**INSTITUTIONAL PRESIDENCY.** Scholars and commentators use the concept of the institutional presidency to describe the complex organizational and procedural structure that has developed to support the modern presidency. The institutional presidency originated with the creation of the EXECUTIVE OFFICE OF THE PRESIDENT (EOP) in 1939. The formation of the EOP followed a recommendation by the President's Committee on Administrative Management, better known as the BROWNLOW COMMITTEE, that the President needed staff support to manage the ever-increasing executive and administrative responsibilities of the office. Since 1939, the EOP has grown and diversified, becoming a primary resource for advice to and operational support for the President.

Each President inherits executive roles from his predecessor, then modifies and personalizes them, thereby increasing the need for specialized, yet adaptable, institutional support. The institutional presidency, with its flexible constellation of offices and functions, has developed to fill this need and has become a key element of the post–WORLD WAR II presidency. The core components of the institutional presidency include the WHITE HOUSE STAFF, the NATIONAL SECURITY COUNCIL, the COUNCIL OF ECONOMIC ADVISERS, the OFFICE OF SCIENCE AND TECHNOLOGY POLICY, the offices of the VICE PRESIDENT and FIRST LADY, the OFFICE OF MANAGEMENT AND BUDGET, the COUNCIL ON ENVIRONMENTAL QUALITY, the OFFICE OF THE U.S. TRADE REPRESENTATIVE, the OFFICE OF POLICY DEVELOPMENT, and the OFFICE OF ADMINISTRATION. Many other offices, councils, and boards have temporarily served the institutional presidency, including the Office of War Mobilization and Reconversion (1943–1946), the Office of Economic Opportunity (1964–1975), the Council on Wage and Price Stability (1974–1981), and the Office of National Drug Control Policy (1989–). Such bodies have often emerged as responses to particular presidential needs; if the needs persist, the offices are likely to become institutionalized, or permanent.

The institutional presidency responds not only to changing policy priorities from one administration to the next but also to the personality and management styles of successive Presidents. Because of this flexibility, the institutional presidency is characterized by both continuity and discontinuity. The institutional presidency is therefore viewed as a process of growth, diversification, and adaptation rather than as a discrete organizational entity.

## BIBLIOGRAPHY

Burke, John P. *The Institutional Presidency*, 1992.

Gilmour, Robert S. "The Institutionalized Presidency: A Conceptual Clarification." In *The Presidency in Contemporary Context.* Edited by Norman Thomas. 1975.

Wyszomirski, Margaret Jane. "The Discontinuous Institutional Presidency." In *Executive Leadership in Anglo-Saxon Systems.* Edited by Colin Campbell, S.J., and Margaret Jane Wyszomirski. 1991.

MARGARET JANE WYSZOMIRSKI

**INS v. CHADHA** 462 U.S. 919 (1983). In this landmark case, the Supreme Court struck down as unconstitutional a one-house LEGISLATIVE VETO in an immigration statute. The broadness of the ruling invalidated all other existing legislative vetoes. After 1983, however, Congress and the executive branch created a new set of legislative vetoes, both statutory and informal, and no legal challenges were filed in court to contest them.

The case involved Jagdish Rai Chadha, an East Indian born in Kenya and bearing a British passport. He had outstayed his student visa and was threatened with deportation from the United States. Following statutory procedures, he presented his case to an administrative hearing at the Immigration and Naturalization Service and argued that deportation would result in "extreme hardship." He received a favorable decision from an immigration judge. His name was among those of 340 persons that the Attorney General sent to Congress, recommending suspension of deportation. Pursuant to statutory authority, the House of Representatives disapproved six names from the list, Chadha's among them.

In *INS v. Chadha*, the Court held that the one-house veto in the immigration statute violated the Constitution's principle of bicameralism, which requires action by both houses of Congress, and the PRESENTATION CLAUSE, which requires that all bills must be presented to the President for his signature or veto. Chief Justice Warren Burger wrote the opinion for the Court, announcing that whenever congressional action had the "purpose and effect of altering the legal rights, duties and relations of persons" outside the legislative branch, Congress must act through both houses in a bill that is presented to the President. He was joined in the opinion by five Justices. Justice Lewis Powell, Jr., concurred in the judgment but stated his preference for a more narrowly drawn holding that would be confined to cases (like Chadha's) where Congress tried to override adjudicatory decisions.

Justice Byron White issued a lengthy dissent, condemning the majority for adopting a rigid, formalistic model of SEPARATION OF POWERS. In a separate dissent, Justice William Rehnquist objected that the one-house veto could not be severed from the discretionary authority given to the Attorney General to suspend deportations. If the legislative veto was invalid, the discretionary authority should fall with it, Rehnquist argued. The legislative history of the statute convinced Rehnquist that Congress had delegated the authority only on the condition that it would retain a legislative veto to control the administration.

The Court's decision contains many deficiencies. First, the decision to sever the legislative veto while retaining the balance of the statute meant that the Attorney General now had unchecked authority to suspend deportations.

Second, the Court stated that it was insufficient for Congress to argue that the legislative veto was "efficient, convenient, and useful in facilitating functions of government." According to the Court, that defense of the legislative veto, standing alone, would "not save it if it [was] contrary to the Constitution. Convenience and efficiency are not the primary objectives—or the hallmarks—of democratic government." The majority opinion claimed that it was "crystal clear from the records of the Convention, contemporaneous writings and debates, that the Framers ranked other values

higher than efficiency." This is bad history. The record from 1776 to 1787 provides abundant evidence that the Framers were very much concerned with making government more efficient and effective. The Articles of Confederation was replaced precisely because they failed to provide an efficient, effective framework for government, and the new Constitution was intended to redress many of the administrative deficiencies of the Continental Congress.

Third, the Court misunderstood the relationship between the legislative veto and the presentation clause. The President exercises a veto to check legislation that is ill-considered or that might encroach on the President's office. The Court implied that the legislative veto frustrated these constitutional purposes by evading the President's veto. That theoretical concern has little application to the legislative veto. Consider a specific type of legislative veto: if, for example, the President presented a reorganization plan to Congress and either house disapproved, presidential powers would not be affected; the structure of the executive branch would remain as before, and in this case the President would not need the veto power to protect executive prerogatives.

Fourth, it was not clear that the House of Representatives altered Chadha's legal rights. The Attorney General's suspension of Chadha's deportation was conditioned on the availability of a one-house veto. The House acted pursuant to a statute. Far from altering Chadha's legal rights, the House was fulfilling the procedures established by statute.

Finally, the Court declared that no constitutional provision allowed Congress "to repeal or amend laws by other than legislative means pursuant to Art. I." When the House adopted a one-house veto to disapprove Chadha's suspension, it was not repealing or amending a law. It was following the procedure already enacted into law. It was the Court, in *Chadha*, that effectively repealed or amended the immigration law by striking the legislative veto and allowing the balance of the statute to remain in force.

The Court's misreading of history, congressional procedures, and executive-legislative relations proved costly to its own prestige. Its theory of government was very much at odds with the practices developed over the years by the political branches. Neither agency heads nor members of Congress wanted the static model advanced by the Court. Executive officials still sought substantial discretion in administering delegated authority; legislators still wanted to control that authority without having to pass more laws.

The inevitable result of this decision was a record of noncompliance, subtle evasion, and a system of lawmaking more convoluted, cumbersome, and covert than before. In many cases the Court's decision simply drove underground a set of legislative and committee vetoes that once operated in plain sight. Congress continued to put legislative vetoes (of the committee veto variety) in bills, and both Presidents Reagan and Bush signed such bills into law.

From the date that *Chadha* was decided in 1983 to the end of 1992, Congress created more than two hundred new legislative vetoes. By 1992, none of those had been litigated, nor were they likely to be, since they appeared in appropriations bills that expired after a year and it was doubtful that anyone would have standing to bring a suit. If someone did, the case would probably become moot before a ruling could be issued. In addition to legislative vetoes that appear in statutes, Congress perfected a range of informal, nonstatutory procedures that permit congressional committees to review and approve certain agency actions.

### BIBLIOGRAPHY

Craig, Barbara Hinkson. *Chadha: The Story of an Epic Constitutional Struggle.* 1988.
Elliott, E. Donald. "INS v. Chadha: The Administrative Constitution, the Constitution, and the Legislative Veto." *Supreme Court Review* 1983: 125–176.
Fisher, Louis. *Constitutional Conflicts between Congress and the President.* 3d ed. 1991.

LOUIS FISHER

**INTEGRATION OF THE MILITARY.** For discussion of Harry S. Truman's order desegregating the military, see EXECUTIVE ORDER 9981.

**INTELLIGENCE COMMUNITY.** Within the U.S. federal government more than forty agencies, known collectively as the intelligence community, have responsibilities for intelligence operations at home and abroad. Together these agencies employ more than 150,000 people and spend some $30 billion each year. They represent the largest information-producing apparatus in the history of the world.

The primary mission of the intelligence community is to provide intelligence (information) for the National Command Authority—the President, the CABINET, and the JOINT CHIEFS OF STAFF—and for the Congress. The various data-collection and espionage activities and operations dedicated to this objective are known collectively as the National Foreign Intelligence Program (NFIP).

Beneath the President and the NATIONAL SECURITY COUNCIL (NSC) in the intelligence chain of command stands the Director of Central Intelligence (DCI), who is in charge of the entire intelligence community. This official also heads America's premier intelligence organization, the CENTRAL INTELLIGENCE AGENCY (CIA). In this capacity, he is known as the DCIA (Director of the CIA).

The expression intelligence *community* is something of a misnomer, belying the competition for influence among the intelligence agencies. Relationships among them have often been discordant and the DCI's control over them quite loose. The National Security Agency (NSA) and the Defense Intelligence Agency (DIA), for instance, are part of the Department of Defense, so they have another boss as well—the Secretary of Defense, who unlike the DCI enjoys cabinet rank. Historically, the rivalry between the CIA and the military intelligence agencies has often been bitter.

Of the many agencies comprising the intelligence community, a few are preeminent in terms of budgets, personnel, technology, and influence: the CIA, the NSA, the DIA, the intelligence units within the military services, the State Department's Bureau of Intelligence and Research (INR), the National Reconnaisance Office (NRO), and the intelligence units within the FEDERAL BUREAU OF INVESTIGATION (FBI), the Department of the Treasury, and the Department of Energy.

Overseas, the main emphasis of the CIA is on the recruitment of spies from America's major adversaries. The CIA's case officers in the field attempt to observe, gain access to, recruit, and, finally, manage espionage agents inside these "hard target" countries. The CIA also conducts COVERT OPERATIONS around the globe in an attempt to shape world events to conform with U.S. aspirations. Further, the CIA engages in counterintelligence, that is, the thwarting of foreign intelligence services bent on infiltrating U.S. intelligence services. At home, the CIA's emphasis is on analysis—interpreting data collected through open sources, technical espionage (satellites and reconnaisance airplanes, for example), and classic spying (human intelligence). Analysts at CIA headquarters in Langley, Virginia, prepare reports to keep policymakers informed about world events.

The National Security Agency, which is within the organizational domain of the Department of Defense, is the chief technological intelligence arm of the U.S. government. The NSA staffs some two thousand fixed listening posts around the world to intercept and decipher coded messages sent by foreign governments and military units. Large circular antennae in various locations overseas scan the airwaves for coded messages; so do flying and seaborne interceptors. This interception of various signals and communications by the NSA falls under the rubric of signals intelligence. A torrent of data pours from the skies into NSA headquarters at Fort Meade, Maryland, where it is translated, organized, and disseminated to other intelligence agencies. The NSA is also the nation's cryptological, or codebreaking, center.

The Department of Defense created the Defense Intelligence Agency in 1961 to improve the coordination and analysis of intelligence collected by the military services. Located at Bolling Air Force Base near Washington, D.C., the DIA enjoys the backing of the Secretary of Defense in intergovernment councils, but it has had only limited success in overcoming the preference of the military services to keep intelligence policy decentralized within their own organizations.

Housed in the Department of State, the Bureau of Intelligence and Research—though small—has earned a reputation for careful intelligence analysis. The INR's primary objective is to introduce into intelligence reports a sensitivity to diplomatic implications of world developments. The National Reconnaisance Office, the most secretive agency in the community, directs the U.S. satellite and air reconnaissance spy programs. The FBI's intelligence units consist of an Internal Security Branch, which gathers information on "extremists" who might pose a threat to U.S. security, and a Counterintelligence Branch, which guards against foreign spies and terrorists within the United States. The Treasury Department is home to the SECRET SERVICE, the Internal Revenue Service (IRS), and the Customs Bureau, which gather intelligence on individuals who pose a threat to U.S. officials, fail to pay their taxes, or import contraband goods. The Energy Department has an International Security Affairs division that monitors nuclear testing and the international transfer of nuclear materials. The degree to which DCIs have succeeded in coordinating these main elements in America's intelligence colossus has been limited.

### BIBLIOGRAPHY

Bamford, James. *The Puzzle Palace.* 1984.
Johnson, Loch K. *A Season of Inquiry: Congress and Intelligence.* 1988.
Ransom, Harry Howe. *The Intelligence Establishment.* 1970.
Richelson, Jeffrey. *The U.S. Intelligence Community.* 1985.
Turner, Stansfield. *Secrecy and Democracy: The CIA in Transition.* 1985.

LOCH K. JOHNSON

**INTELLIGENCE OVERSIGHT ACT** (1980). This act was the culmination of Congress's desire to reassert a significant role over presidential foreign policy decision making in the aftermath of the VIETNAM WAR and the WATERGATE AFFAIR. When the nation and a reawakened Congress discovered that the CENTRAL INTELLIGENCE AGENCY (CIA) had been engaged in a number of unsavory projects during the 1960s and early 1970s, such as assassination plots against foreign leaders, and aiding the overthrow of democratically elected governments, the drive for legislative oversight of presidentially initiated COVERT OPERATIONS gained momentum. In December 1974, Congress enacted the HUGHES-RYAN AMENDMENT requiring the President to notify various congressional committees of CIA covert operations in a timely fashion. The next month, the Senate voted to establish a special committee to investigate intelligence activities, and the House of Representatives took similar action shortly thereafter.

The Senate Select Committee to Study Governmental Operations with Respect to Intelligence Activities, popularly known as the CHURCH COMMITTEE after its chairman, Sen. Frank Church, recommended the adoption of a legislative charter and the establishment of a permanent Senate Committee on Intelligence to oversee CIA activities. In 1976 and 1977, the Senate and House acted to establish permanent intelligence oversight committees.

The Senate Committee on Intelligence spent almost three years drafting a broad charter for the INTELLIGENCE COMMUNITY. The charter (S. 2284) contained comprehensive restrictions on intelligence activities and procedures for CONGRESSIONAL OVERSIGHT. While that new charter was based on President Jimmy Carter's own Executive Order 12036, administration officials eventually opposed its adoption because they did not want to give those restraints the force of law. Many other critics opposed the bill because it was too permissive, and the broad charter was never enacted. One small part of the charter—the legislative oversight provisions—was, however, enacted as the Intelligence Oversight Act of 1980.

The Intelligence Oversight Act maintained and improved on the basic notion of congressional oversight established by the Hughes-Ryan Amendment. As with the amendment, the oversight act's basic framework required the President to find that a covert operation was important to U.S. NATIONAL SECURITY and to notify the relevant congressional committees. That act did not require that those committees approve covert operations as a condition precedent to their initiation.

The new act broadened the intelligence activities that had to be reported to include activities conducted by any agency of the United States, not just the CIA. It also mandated that prior notification of covert activities be provided to the relevant committees. The act also required executive branch officials to furnish information or materials requested by the intelligence committees and report in a timely fashion any illegal intelligence activity or significant intelligence failures.

The Carter administration fought for and won several provisions in the act. First, the number of committees that the executive had to report to was reduced from eight to the two (House and Senate) permanent intelligence committees. Second, in response to the administration's concerns that the prior notification requirement would reduce the President's flexibility to deal with extraordinary circumstances requiring speed or secrecy, two exceptions were made to the oversight act's prior notice requirement.

The first exception allowed the President to limit prior notice in order to meet extraordinary circumstances affecting vital interests of the United States to eight designated congressional leaders instead of the full intelligence committees. The second exception was designed to overcome executive complaints that prior notice might intrude on the President's constitutional powers. It allowed the President to dispense with prior notice altogether when the President believed the Constitution allowed unilateral action but instead to inform the intelligence committees of covert operations afterwards "in a timely fashion."

The IRAN-CONTRA AFFAIR involved the second exception to the prior notification requirement of the 1980 act. The Reagan administration had not provided notice to Congress of the sale of arms to Iran or of the NATIONAL SECURITY COUNCIL's support for the contras in Nicaragua. The majority report of the congressional committees investigating the Iran-contra affair criticized this failure on two grounds. First, the President alone is required to make a determination to delay notice of a covert operation in order to ensure that the President takes personal responsibility for such a weighty decision. President Ronald Reagan did not make a personal determination to withhold the information on the contra support activity. Second, the President withheld notification of the arms sale to Iran for over one year; Congress only learned about the covert operation through newspaper reports. The Iran-contra report criticized this failure to notify as not being the "timely" notice required by the exception to the prior notice requirement.

In the aftermath of the Iran-contra affair, congressional efforts focused on tightening the oversight process. Congress sought to confine the "timely notice" provision of the 1980 act to within forty-eight hours after the covert operation is initiated. Ultimately, the Intelligence Oversight Act of 1991 was adopted, which made only minor changes in the oversight framework.

The 1991 act required that the President personally authorize any covert action, and that the action be "necessary to support identifiable foreign policy objectives of the United States." The President must make this determination in a written finding usually made contemporaneously, but not more than forty-eight hours after the decision is made. The act also clarified the definition of covert action but made no major changes in the notification provisions to Congress. President George Bush nonetheless killed the 1991 act by POCKET VETO because he claimed that it "purports to regulate diplomacy by the President" by mandating oversight of any request by the United States to a foreign government or a private citizen to conduct covert actions. President Bush also objected to the Congressional explanation accompanying the bill, which interpreted the act as requiring that prior notice could only be withheld in "exigent circumstances," and then only for "a few days." He claimed that such an interpretation would "unconstitutionally infringe on the authority of the President." The offensive provision and interpretation were removed and the President signed the Intelligence Authorization Act for fiscal year 1991.

Questions remain as to whether the present statutory framework still provides the President with too much unilateral authority over covert operations, particularly paramilitary operations. Some scholars and officials have suggested that at least with respect to covert war explicit congressional approval and not mere notification is constitutionally required.

### BIBLIOGRAPHY

Highsmith, Newell L. "Policing Executive Adventurism: Congressional Oversight of Military and Paramilitary Operations." *Harvard Journal on Legislation* 19 (1982): 327, 354–368.

Paterson, Thomas G. "Oversight or Afterview? Congress, the CIA, and Covert Action since 1947." In *Congress and the United States Foreign Policy: Controlling the Use of Force in the Nuclear Age.* Edited by Michael A. Barnhart. 1987.

JULES LOBEL

**INTELLIGENCE OVERSIGHT BOARD.** See PRESIDENT'S INTELLIGENCE OVERSIGHT BOARD.

**INTEREST GROUPS, PRESIDENTS AND.** Presidents feel the constant presence and pressure of interest groups, as both positive and negative forces. Interest groups are as important for a President as he is for them because they represent a resource for the President in governing and when seeking reelection.

In 1983, President Ronald Reagan complained about the efforts of banking-community interest groups to repeal a 10-percent withholding tax on savings account funds: "One of the most important pieces of legislation to be considered by the Congress this year is being held hostage by a small but highly funded and organized special interest group." Reagan was forced to sign the legislation, which provided for a rollback in the withholding, even though he did not believe in that portion of the measure. President Reagan's frustration is evidence of the importance that interest groups have gained in the policy-making process. They are no longer merely forces that one can choose to deal with or not; a President needs their support to govern.

In 1974 President Gerald Ford established the OFFICE OF PUBLIC LIAISON (OPL) to deal with interest groups. In so doing, he formalized what had become a crucial relationship for all modern Presidents. The institutionalization of interest groups into the White House structure is both a sign of the strength that such groups have in the national political system and a source of added strength for them. The OPL gives groups an open channel to the White House to plead their case for their policy interests.

Interest groups have long been recognized as an important element in American politics. Early commentators on our system noted their significance. Even prior to the ratification of the Constitution, James Madison was worrying about the strength of factions. In 1832 Alexis de Tocqueville noted the tendency of Americans to form associations to accomplish political ends. While there has long been a recognition that groups have an impact on policy at the national level, for most of U.S. history the focus of interest-group action was the Congress, not the President. Groups directed their electoral efforts toward the President's national party, not the President himself. Prior to the creation of the OPL, there were people on the WHITE HOUSE STAFF whose job it was to deal with interest groups, but their efforts were aimed primarily at groups' roles in elections and were often channeled through the national committee of the President's party.

**The Policy Environment.** A confluence of elements brought interest groups into the presidential foreground. Three of the most important of these elements are the public's demand for a broad range of new domestic social and economic programs, the increase in the number of groups directing their efforts toward influencing policy in a single policy area, and the inability of congressional and political party leadership to deliver their members' support for a President's policy programs.

*Making policy.* Domestic policy in the 1990s was different from what it was in the 1960s because of the increased policy responsibilities that the national government had assumed in the interim. Some of the new policy areas developed during that time include HEALTH POLICY (e.g., Medicare and aid to lower-income people, women, and infant children), CIVIL RIGHTS POLICY (e.g., equal employment, voting, and housing rights for African Americans and other racial and ethnic minorities, women, and the disabled), EDUCATION POLICY (e.g., aid to colleges for construction, student loan programs, Head Start), consumer interests (automobile safety, consumer products safety), ENERGY POLICY (e.g., alternative fuels, fuel conservation, fuel supplements for the poor), ENVIRONMENTAL POLICY (e.g., clean air, wild rivers, toxic waste disposal, forest preservation), HOUSING POLICY (e.g., construction, equal access, rent supplements), urban policy (e.g., development grants, mass transportation), and workplace policy (e.g., occupational safety, with regulations for safety in both big and small businesses). This is but a small selection from the large number of programs that were begun and expanded. And each policy area has its own constellation of interest groups surrounding it and demanding a role in shaping programs and their implementation.

All the new areas of federal policy-making have put additional demands on the President and the Congress that interest groups have sought to direct. Interest groups both created and were created by the expanded policy agenda. Jack Walker, a political scientist who conducted a major study of 564 interest groups at the national level, found that half the groups he studied were created in the period following WORLD WAR II. He also found that many had located their headquarters in Washington, D.C., only since 1960: 66 percent of groups in his study had had Washington headquarters in 1960, while twenty years later 90 percent had headquarters in the nation's capital. Growth in the number of lobbyists working in Washington was very rapid. *Congressional Quarterly*, in its *Guide to Congress*, estimates that the number of people lobbying for interest groups in Washington rose from four thousand in 1977 to somewhere between ten and twenty thousand in 1982.

*Divided government.* The President, aside from the Vice President, is the only nationally elected official and, consequently, the only one who can claim to represent the national perspective necessary in developing national policy programs. But Presidents' constitutional resources have often proved thin as they have tried to persuade Congress—particularly when Congress is controlled by the opposing party—to do what they think necessary. Policy demands increased at about the same time that the institutions of Congress and the political parties were least able to offer the leadership to deliver on them. The phenomenon of DIVIDED GOVERNMENT, in which the presidency and either or both houses of Congress are controlled by different political parties, has created significant problems in the President's ability to lead Congress—as have the institutional changes that have decentralized the congressional power structure. Between 1952 and 1992, different parties controlled the presidency and at least one house of Congress for twenty-six of those forty years.

Dwight D. Eisenhower was the last President who was able to deal effectively with the opposing party's majority in Congress because the opposing party's congressional leaders were still in a position to speak for the members of their party's congressional delegation and had strong bases for persuading them to follow their leadership. He was victorious on votes in the Congress an average of 72.2 percent of the time during his eight years. After Eisenhower left the White House, Speaker of the House Sam Rayburn died and Senate majority leader Lyndon B. Johnson left the Senate for the vice presidency; party differences soon began to translate into policy-making problems. Presidents Richard M. Nixon, Gerald Ford, Ronald Reagan and George Bush were far less successful in their dealings with Congress than Eisenhower had been. Their victory percentages on votes in the Congress were, respectively: 67.2 percent (Nixon), 57.6 percent (Ford), 61.9 percent (Reagan), and 54.7 percent (Bush, first two years). Clearly, Presidents have needed every resource possible in their efforts to convince a reluctant Congress to adopt their programs. Interest groups have proven to be such a resource.

**Interactions.** The President and the White House staff have three basic interactions with interest groups: electoral support; the use of interest groups and their resources to win policy battles; and demands by interest groups for White House services, intervention, and presidential policy support. The expense of presidential campaigns has escalated at the same time that political parties have lost some of their organizational viability, particularly to provide a large part of the resources needed by a presidential candidate to win election. When organizing their campaigns, presidential candidates have turned to interest groups to help provide some of the resources that parties once contributed.

***Elections.*** General election campaign costs have risen dramatically since Eisenhower's day. In 1952, when he ran for the first time, he and his Democratic opponent, ADLAI E. STEVENSON, spent a combined total of $11.64 million. Twenty years later, when President Nixon ran for reelection in 1972, the total had risen to $91.4 million. With the enactment of a federal matching program for presidential campaign funds, limits have been placed on presidential campaign spending. Still, in 1988, the two major-party candidates spent $92.2 million in the general election. [*See also* CAMPAIGN FINANCES.]

Candidates have been able to meet growing demands for funds through establishing new funding sources, especially PACS (POLITICAL ACTION COMMITTEES). PACs, the campaign funding operations run by individual interest groups, are an outgrowth of the campaign financing reform legislation of 1974, which sought to reduce the influence of individuals who could give large sums of money. PACs have become critically important sources of funding for congressional and, to a lesser extent, presidential campaigns. PACs are allowed to give $5,000 per election contest while individuals can give only $1,000 for each primary and each general election campaign. At the end of 1974 there were 608 PACs, but that number had grown to 4,172 by 1990.

As the number of PACs grew, so did their total contributions to campaigns for national offices. In 1978, the contributions of PACs to congressional campaigns totaled $34.1 million. In 1990, the figure had grown to $149.9 million. In 1990 the percentage of congressional campaign funds coming from PACs grew to 41 percent for House candidates and 21 percent for Senate candidates. These developments in campaign funding resulted in interest groups insinuating themselves into the political process in a new way. The President is not as dependent on groups for money as are persons running for Congress because of public financing of presidential elections and limits placed on the amounts that can be spent. But he is affected by the funding practices of the Congress. He must try to convince members to support him when they may feel they owe loyalty to those who funded them. The President therefore vies with interest groups for the attention of members of Congress.

***Domestic agenda.*** The domestic arena is where a President most needs interest groups and the support they represent. In a policy battle, such as that faced by President Reagan on his tax increase provisions in 1982, a group can offer a President at least two things: manpower and information, which, when combined produce a way for the President to reach out to constituents directly. While he does so regularly through the news media, he can reach individuals around the country much more directly by way of interest groups and, at the same time, have them pick up the bill.

Tax increases are generally a hard sell, and the tax increase of 1982 was no different. The natural difficulty of the issue made it particularly important to create a support group early in the fight. Since the tax was going to be felt by businesses, it was crucial to the legislation's passage to gain the support of the business community. Through the OPL, a coalition of supporters was established that provided the White House with political information on both supporters and opponents in the business community. A steering committee was put together, with representatives from major business organizations such as the National Association of Realtors, the National Association of Manufacturers, the National Council of Life Insurance, and the American Business Conference.

The support and attention of these groups helped neutralize the impact of the opposition the legislation faced from the Chamber of Commerce and the American Farm Bureau Federation. In addition to political information, the groups on the steering committee provided resources that the White House did not have. "The Realtors can send out half a million Mailgrams within 24 hours," said Wayne Valis, who worked in the OPL in the Reagan administration and handled the passage of the tax legislation. "If they have a hundred target congressmen, they can get out 100,000 Mailgrams targeted by district," Valis added. The White House staff had neither the resources nor the flexibility to get into action the way the interest groups did.

As government has taken a more active role in creating domestic policy programs, interest groups have increased their demands for White House services, intervention, and support. Their relations are now organized mainly through the OPL. The office is the entry point for most groups needing White House help or support and operates as an administrative broker for groups, directing them toward the other federal offices where their issues are being dealt with or toward people within the White House who are involved in programs related to their interests.

*Administrative broker.* Many of the tasks performed by the OPL can be categorized as casework: "If the National Maritime Union has a particular problem with something the Department of Commerce is doing, you track it down and set up a session where everybody can talk," commented Robert Bonitati, who worked in the OPL during the early Reagan years and was responsible for dealing with labor issues. Getting the White House involved on its behalf is a significant plus for an interest group: "It has a great impact when you call from here," said Morton Blackwell, who handled religious issues and groups for the office during President Reagan's first term.

The broker role played by the White House usually involves the OPL, the staff in the political operation, or the domestic policy staff. The OPL directs interest groups to the places where action on their issues is being taken. The Political Affairs Office handles interest-group participation in electoral coalitions. The domestic policy staff responds to interest-group demands when legislation is developing. Sometimes, when legislation is particularly important, all these units become involved.

The White House serves as a legislative broker in instances of policy paralysis, when groups cannot work out their differences. An excellent example of such a situation occurred in the Jimmy Carter administration, when business and Jewish groups reached a stalemate over how to fashion legislation that would outlaw the participation of American companies in an Arab-led boycott of companies doing business with Israel. Business groups were worried about losing the business of Arab countries. The Jewish groups wanted to prevent U.S. companies from going along with the Arab boycott. The White House mediated between the members of a task force that included representatives from both business, as represented by the Business Roundtable, and Jewish groups, as represented by the Anti-Defamation League of B'nai B'rith. "Both sides were in touch with [Stuart] Eizenstat [White House domestic policy chief], and he played the honest broker role," commented Irving Shapiro, a past president of the Business Roundtable and of the DuPont Company, who was involved with both groups. "He was looking for solutions, not rhetoric or theory," Shapiro said. When the representatives of the two groups came up with a compromise proposal, President Carter sent it to Congress.

In a political environment that makes leadership and consensus building difficult, the President needs support to make policy on those issues on which the public demands action. Interest groups can be important partners in that effort.

## BIBLIOGRAPHY

Alexander, Herbert. *Financing Politics: Money, Elections, and Political Reform.* 4th ed. 1992.

Cigler, Allan J., and Burdett A. Loomis, eds. *Interest Group Politics.* 1983.

Edwards, George. *At the Margins: Presidential Leadership of Congress.* 1989.

Kumar, Martha Joynt, and Michael Baruch Grossman. "The Presidency and Interest Groups." In *The Presidency and the Political System.* Edited by Michael Nelson. 1984.

Polsby, Nelson W. "Interest Groups and the Presidency: Trends in Political Intermediation in America." In *American Politics and*

*Public Policy.* Edited by Walter Dean Burnham and Martha Wagner Weinberg. 1978.

Rockman, Bert A. *The Leadership Question: The Presidency and the American System.* 1984.

Schlozman, Kay Lehman, and John T. Tierney. *Organized Interests and American Democracy.* 1986.

Walker, Jack L. "The Origin and Maintenance of Interest Groups in America." *American Political Science Review* 77 (1983): 390–406.

MARTHA KUMAR

## INTERIOR, DEPARTMENT OF THE.

On 3 March 1849, the last day of James Knox Polk's administration, Congress enacted legislation to create a fifth CABINET agency, to be called the Home Department, or the Department of the Interior. The idea for such an agency was almost as old as the nation. A department for domestic affairs was considered in 1789, but, instead, both domestic and foreign concerns were lodged in the DEPARTMENT OF STATE. Proposals for a Home Department continued to be discussed for more than half a century.

The vast land acquisitions resulting from the Mexican War enormously enlarged the domestic responsibilities of the federal government and gave the idea new impetus, and Polk's Secretary of the Treasury, Robert J. Walker, championed it. The General Land Office, which oversaw and disposed of lands in the public domain, had been placed in the Department of the Treasury because of the revenues generated from land sales. In his 1848 annual report, Walker pointed out that the duties of the Land Office had little to do with his department's other functions. The functions of the Patent Office in the State Department, the Indian Affairs office in the WAR DEPARTMENT, and the pension offices in the War and Navy departments were equally remote from the primary responsibilities of those departments, he added. All, he declared, should be brought together in a new Department of the Interior. These ideas were incorporated in the 1849 bill creating the department.

For the first Secretary of the Interior, President Zachary Taylor turned to Thomas Ewing, a colorful son of rural Ohio. A frontier lawyer, a U.S. Senator, and Secretary of the Treasury under Presidents William Henry Harrison and John Tyler, Ewing had long been a force in Ohio's Whig councils. One of Ewing's tasks was to locate satisfactory office space to house his department. Completion of the east wing of the Patent Office building in 1852 finally provided the Secretary with suitable quarters, and the two remaining wings, finished in 1856 and 1867, provided additional space. Although some personnel worked elsewhere in the city, the Patent Office building remained the headquarters of the Department of the Interior until 1917.

Interior commanded a huge PATRONAGE reservoir and Secretary Ewing launched such a wholesale replacement of officeholders in the bureaus he inherited that opposition newspapers branded him "Butcher Ewing." Heated controversies with congressional Democrats over his use of the spoils system prevented him from devoting much attention to organizing his department, and the task of setting an administrative course for the fledgling Cabinet agency fell to subsequent secretaries.

Interior lacked the clear role definition other departments enjoyed, but it nevertheless played a role in national affairs larger than the sum of its parts. In one way or another, all the responsibilities entrusted to it had to do with the internal development of the nation or the welfare of the American people. It was this fundamental responsibility that united the large, permanent bureaus with smaller transitory offices. The former gave the department strength and continuity, while the latter dramatized its versatility as a force in government. By offering a repository for functions that did not fit elsewhere, Interior enabled Congress more easily to accept and to discharge responsibilities for the internal needs of a rapidly growing nation. Some bureaus, charged with missions of growing importance to the nation, matured and later split off to become independent Cabinet departments and agencies. Among these were the agricultural division of the Patent Office, which became the DEPARTMENT OF AGRICULTURE in 1862; the Bureau of Labor, established in Interior in 1884, which became the Department of Commerce and Labor in 1903; and the DEPARTMENT OF ENERGY, formed in 1977.

A sampling of tasks assigned the Interior Department suggests the scope of its cares in the last half of the nineteenth century. Responsibilities ranged from the conduct of the decennial census to the colonization of freed slaves in Haiti, from the exploration of western wilderness to oversight of the District of Columbia jail, from the regulation of territorial governments to the construction of the national capital's water system, from management of hospitals and universities to maintenance of public parks. Such functions, together with basic responsibilities for Indians, public lands, patents, and pensions, gave Interior officials an extraordinary array of concerns.

Because western issues stimulated the department's birth, the West has always been the scene of many of its activities. Two of its major bureaus, Indian Affairs and the General Land Office, operated chiefly in the West and performed duties vital to western interests. Be-

*Secretaries of the Interior*

| President | Secretary of the Interior | President | Secretary of the Interior |
|---|---|---|---|
| 12 Taylor | Thomas Ewing, 1849–1850 | 28 Wilson | Franklin K. Lane, 1913–1920 |
| 13 Fillmore | T. M. T. McKennan, 1850 | | John B. Payne, 1920–1921 |
| | Alex H. H. Stuart, 1850–1853 | 29 Harding | Albert B. Fall, 1921–1923 |
| 14 Pierce | Robert McClelland, 1853–1857 | | Hubert Work, 1923 |
| 15 Buchanan | Jacob Thompson, 1857–1861 | 30 Coolidge | Hubert Work, 1923–1928 |
| 16 Lincoln | Caleb B. Smith, 1861–1863 | | Roy O. West, 1928–1929 |
| | John P. Usher, 1863–1865 | 31 Hoover | Ray Lyman Wilbur, 1929–1933 |
| 17 A. Johnson | John P. Usher, 1865 | 32 F. D. Roosevelt | Harold L. Ickes, 1933–1945 |
| | James Harlan, 1865–1866 | 33 Truman | Harold L. Ickes, 1945–1946 |
| | Orville H. Browning, 1866–1869 | | Julius A. Krug, 1946–1949 |
| 18 Grant | Jacob D. Cox, 1869–1870 | | Oscar L. Chapman, 1949–1953 |
| | Columbus Delano, 1870–1875 | 34 Eisenhower | Douglas McKay, 1953–1956 |
| | Zachariah Chandler, 1875–1877 | | Frederick A. Seaton, 1956–1961 |
| 19 Hayes | Carl Schurz, 1877–1881 | 35 Kennedy | Stewart L. Udall, 1961–1963 |
| 20 Garfield | Samuel J. Kirkwood, 1881 | 36 L. B. Johnson | Stewart L. Udall, 1963–1969 |
| 21 Arthur | Samuel J. Kirkwood, 1881–1882 | 37 Nixon | Walter J. Hickel, 1969–1970 |
| | Henry M. Teller, 1882–1885 | | Rogers C. B. Morton, 1971–1974 |
| 22 Cleveland | Lucius Q. C. Lamar, 1885–1888 | 38 Ford | Rogers C. B. Morton, 1974–1975 |
| | William F. Vilas, 1888–1889 | | Stanley K. Hathaway, 1975 |
| 23 B. Harrison | John W. Noble, 1889–1893 | | Thomas S. Kleppe, 1975–1977 |
| 24 Cleveland | Hoke Smith, 1893–1896 | 39 Carter | Cecil D. Andrus, 1977–1981 |
| | David R. Francis, 1896–1897 | 40 Reagan | James G. Watt, 1981–1983 |
| 25 McKinley | Cornelius N. Bliss, 1897–1899 | | William P. Clark, 1983–1985 |
| | Ethan A. Hitchcock, 1899–1901 | | Donald P. Hodel, 1985–1989 |
| 26 T. Roosevelt | Ethan A. Hitchcock, 1901–1907 | 41 Bush | Manuel Lujan, Jr., 1989–1993 |
| | James R. Garfield, 1907–1909 | 42 Clinton | Bruce Babbitt, 1993– |
| 27 Taft | Richard A. Ballinger, 1909–1911 | | |
| | Walter L. Fisher, 1911–1913 | | |

tween 1850 and 1857, in cooperation with the U.S. Army, Interior's Mexican Boundary Commission surveyed the new international boundary agreed upon in the treaties ending the MEXICAN WAR and formalizing the 1853 GADSDEN PURCHASE. In 1858–1860, Interior commissioners fixed and marked the disputed boundary between Texas and New Mexico.

Rivalries between Interior and the War Department over exploring and mapping the West in the post–CIVIL WAR years raised concerns in the scientific community, as well as in official Washington. As a result, in 1879, all the western surveys were consolidated within the Interior Department in the newly formed United States Geological Survey. The Department assumed special responsibility for the West's scenic treasures as well. In 1872 Congress established the world's first national park—Yellowstone—under Interior jurisdiction. Others, including Sequoia, Yosemite, and Mount Rainier, were created during the 1890s.

Despite its western emphasis, Interior from its outset conducted major programs of nationwide applica-

tion. One such program, which assumed enormous magnitude and consequences in the 1880s, was the pensioning of the Union army and navy veterans. (In 1885 there were 1.5 million such veterans.) By 1890 Interior's Pension Bureau employed more than six thousand agents, medical examiners, and clerks.

Interior's fourth major bureau from its inception until 1925 was the Patent Office. Reflecting the burgeoning technology of the industrial revolution, the protection of inventions by government patents assumed growing importance in the latter half of the nineteenth century. By 1890 patent officials received more than 41,000 applications and issued more than 26,000 patents annually.

From its first days Interior bore a special relationship to the District of Columbia. At one time or another, the Secretary's federal city responsibilities have covered public buildings, parks, police, the jail, a street railway linking Washington and Georgetown, a railroad bridge across the Potomac, and the city's water supply. The Secretary also supervised various institutions serving the capital's health, education, and welfare needs.

As the twentieth century opened, the Department of the Interior became increasingly concerned with efforts to reorient the nation's traditional practices of handling natural resources—land, timber, water, minerals, and wildlife. Most nineteenth-century Americans assumed these resources to be inexhaustible and believed government regulation of their exploitation to be alien to democratic principles. In the prevailing view, Interior's mission was to dispose of government resources to private enterprise, both individual and corporate. A few people of vision, however, dissented from this philosophy. One was Secretary Carl Schurz, who fought to halt the devastation of forests in the public domain. The Forest Reserve Act of 1891, promoted by President Benjamin Harrison's Interior Secretary, John W. Noble, and the creation of the first national parks marked a modest shift in the traditional philosophy. But not until Theodore Roosevelt's administration (1901–1909) did the doctrine of Schurz and his sympathizers become a national crusade. The crusaders gave it a label that has endured: conservation.

Among the results of this movement was legislation providing for construction of dams and aqueducts to water arid and semiarid lands in the West, to be carried out by the Reclamation Service of the Geological Survey. Later Bureau of Reclamation projects, including such world-famous works as the Hoover and Grand Coulee dams, the All-American Canal in California, and the Alva Adams Tunnel beneath the Continental Divide in Colorado, brought water and flood control, electric power, and recreational resources to vast areas formerly incapable of sustaining major settlement, crop production, and industrial development.

The conservation crusade of the early twentieth century and the formation of other departments to address other concerns resulted in a sharper focus in Interior on natural resources and a drift away from the grab-bag "home department" concept. Interior is no longer the "Department of Miscellany," but primarily a land-managing agency, controlling one third of all U.S. land. As of 1992, it had under it ten bureaus: the National Park Service, the Office of Surface Mining Reclamation and Enforcement, the Minerals Management Service, Land Management, the Fish and Wildlife Service, the Bureau of Indian Affairs, Territorial and International Affairs, Mines, Reclamation, and the U.S. Geological Survey.

For most of its life, Interior has been relatively anonymous among Cabinet departments. Its very name, conveying only the vaguest impression of its functions, has contributed to its indistinct image. Occasionally during the twentieth century, however, forceful or colorful Interior secretaries—including Franklin K. Lane, Albert B. Fall, HAROLD L. ICKES, STEWART L. UDALL, and JAMES WATT—and controversies have brought unaccustomed publicity and prominence to the department.

### BIBLIOGRAPHY

Forness, Norman O. "The Origins and Early History of the United States Department of the Interior." Ph.D. dissertation, Pennsylvania State University, 1964.

Learned, Henry B. "The Establishment of the Secretaryship of the Interior." *American Historical Review* 16 (1911).

Trani, Eugene. "The Secretaries and Under Secretaries of the Department of the Interior." Typescript, Department of the Interior Library, 1966.

*United States Government Manual* 1991/92. 1992.

Utley, Robert M., and Barry Mackintosh. *The Department of Everything Else.* 1989.

E. C. BEARSS

**INTERMEDIATE-RANGE NUCLEAR FORCES TREATY.** See INF (INTERMEDIATE-RANGE NUCLEAR FORCES) TREATY.

**INTERNAL IMPROVEMENTS.** The power of the federal government to construct, operate, and maintain internal improvements projects—especially roads, harbors, and bridges—has divided the Republic since the administration of George Washington. The transportation legacy of the colonial era left American port cities loosely linked to the countryside and each other by rivers, the Atlantic Ocean, and often impassible dirt roads. State and local governments of the era, sometimes in partnership with private enterprise, moved quickly to fill the need. By 1820 they had produced a "turnpike revolution" of almost four thousand miles of road.

National appropriations for harbor improvements commenced in 1789 and reflected the pro-improvements philosophy of the ruling FEDERALIST PARTY. When the more conservative Democratic-Republicans attained power in 1801, they agreed that federal monies could be provided for certain interstate improvements. The national government could not, however, engage in local projects or in repair and maintenance, or launch a systematic program without a constitutional amendment.

In 1806, Thomas Jefferson, utilizing the rationale of promoting national defense and the postal service, approved the initial survey for the National (Cumberland) Road. Anticipating excess revenues in the Treasury, the President argued for spending on "roads, rivers and canals." He urged Congress to pass an amendment, however, to legitimatize such expenditures. Although none was forthcoming, construction of the road—built with the proceeds of the sale of public lands—began in Maryland in 1811 and extended to Vandalia, Illinois by 1838.

The WAR OF 1812 revealed the inadequacies of transporting soldiers and supplies as well as the need to bring American goods closer to favorable markets. The Speaker of the House of Representatives, HENRY CLAY of Kentucky, capitalized on the patriotism of the postwar era to push his AMERICAN SYSTEM, including internal improvements, through the Democratic-Republican Congress in 1816–1817. Clay received support from President James Madison, who also endorsed such measures but who, reflecting the views of Jefferson, recommended the passage of an appropriate amendment to the Constitution. When Congress ignored his request and proceeded to adopt legislation that would funnel profits from the newly chartered BANK OF THE UNITED STATES to construct roads and canals, Madison vetoed this Bonus Bill on 3 March 1817.

The third member of the Virginia dynasty, James Monroe, continued the tradition of urging internal improvements conditioned on a constitutional amendment. Congress failed to recommend such a measure. Thus, when a bill to allow Congress to collect tolls for the repairs and maintenance of the Cumberland Road appeared on the President's desk in 1822, he summarily vetoed it. Monroe did, however, endorse the General Survey Bill of 1824, which authorized a study of roads and canals needed for military purposes.

While the federal government remained relatively passive, state governments during the ERA OF GOOD FEELINGS invested millions of dollars in internal improvements. The election of Andrew Jackson in 1828 as standard-bearer of the fledgling DEMOCRATIC PARTY brought a new style of government to the capital but not a repudiation of Jeffersonian philosophy on internal improvements. During his tenure in the White House, Old Hickory approved millions of dollars for a variety of internal improvement projects deemed constitutionally correct. He rebelled, however, at a bill for the construction of a Kentucky highway linking Lexington—the hometown of his archrival Henry Clay—with Maysville. The President vetoed the measure of 1830 as an intrastate venture. Except for an occasional post road, Congress removed itself from highway construction for almost a century.

Funding for other improvements rapidly became a partisan political issue. Whigs supported an active role for the federal government, while Democrats would share national funds but wanted minimal government involvement. A Whig-dominated Congress passed the Land Act of 1841, a proposal to distribute a portion of the proceeds from public land sales to the states for internal improvements. Unfortunately, the measure became intertwined with the tariff issue and encountered the resistance of southern Democrats. President John Tyler, a Virginian and longtime opponent of federally financed improvements, vetoed the bill in the summer of 1842.

Democratic Chief Executives held the line on all types of projects. James K. Polk reiterated the Jefferson-Jackson position when he twice vetoed rivers and harbors bills. He urged that the states, with the approval of Congress, levy tonnage duties and utilize the proceeds for improvements projects.

Democrat Franklin Pierce represented a transitional attitude on the issue. He repeatedly vetoed internal improvements bills. Falling back on Jefferson's argument of military necessity, however, Pierce did endorse several coastal projects in the South. The concept of a Pacific railway had also won the approval of prominent Democrats, including Secretary of War JEFFERSON DAVIS, and the President approved land grants for railway construction in 1853. Sectional animosity and fraud, however, destroyed all hopes for success.

The election of Abraham Lincoln and the REPUBLICAN PARTY in 1860 set the trend for the remainder of the century. As the heirs to the WHIG PARTY's economic views, the Republicans boosted improvements, especially railroads. The Pacific Railway Act of 1862 commenced a massive land grant giveaway that totaled more than 130 million acres and millions of dollars in loans. This largesse, increasingly bipartisan after the CIVIL WAR, enabled the railway corporations to crisscross the nation with 200,000 miles of track by 1900.

Late nineteenth-century Presidents based their opposition to improvements on economics, not constitutionality. Chief Executives of both parties endorsed expensive internal improvements in the freewheeling Gilded Age. Only when they encountered a particularly outrageous bill, such as the multimillion-dollar pork-barrel rivers and harbors bill of August 1882, might a President (in this case Chester A. Arthur) veto the measure. Highway expansion, however, continued to languish until state governments, under pressure from automotive enthusiasts, began a good roads movement by the time of WORLD WAR I. The ensuing regeneration of American roads climaxed in 1956, when Congress through the Interstate Highway Act voted $26 billion to help finance 42,000 miles of construction.

### BIBLIOGRAPHY

Goodrich, Carter. *Government Promotion of American Canals and Railroads, 1800–1900.* 1960.
Jordan, Philip D. *The National Road.* 1948.
Taylor, George R. *The Transportation Revolution, 1815–1861.* 1951.

JOHN M. BELOHLAVEK

## INTERNATIONAL EMERGENCY ECONOMIC POWERS ACT (1977).

Enacted in 1977, the International Emergency Economic Powers Act (IEEPA) authorizes the President to take certain specified actions "to deal with any unusual and extraordinary threat, which has its source in whole or substantial part outside the United States, to the national security, foreign policy, or economy of the United States, if the President declares a national emergency with respect to such threat." A presidential declaration of national emergency, made pursuant to the NATIONAL EMERGENCIES ACT of 1976, is effective until its anniversay date or unless terminated sooner by the President or by a duly enacted joint resolution of disapproval. A national emergency may be extended if the President, within the ninety-day period prior to the anniversary date, gives notice to Congress and in the *Federal Register* that the declaration is to continue in effect.

To exercise the authority provided by the IEEPA, the President must specify that he is activating the statute when making his national-emergency declaration. He may, through regulations, instructions, or licenses, investigate, regulate, or prohibit any transactions in foreign exchange; transfers of credit or payments between, by, through, or to any banking institution, to the extent that such transfers or payments involve any interest of any foreign country or a national thereof; and the importing or exporting of currency or securities by any person—individual or corporate—subject to the jurisdiction of the United States. Furthermore, he may also "investigate, regulate, direct and compel, nullify, void, prevent or prohibit, any acquisition, holding, withholding, use, transfer, withdrawal, transportation, importation or exportation of, or dealing in, or exercising any right, power, or privilege with respect to, or transactions involving, any property in which any foreign country or a national thereof has any interest." The statute specifies that the President, "in every possible instance, shall consult with the Congress before exercising any of the authorities granted by" it and "shall consult

regularly with the Congress so long as such authorities are exercised."

The statute grew out of congressional assessments in the early 1970s of the scope and exercise of national-emergency powers. The National Emergencies Act of 1976 established a national-emergency declaration procedure; modified, repealed, and continued certain emergency-law provisions; and directed pertinent congressional committees to examine the continued provisions with a view to revision and reform. One of those provisions, section 5(b) of the Trading with the Enemy Act of 1917, had been interpreted to give the President vast domestic and international economic regulatory authority during war or "any other period of national emergency declared by the President." With the subsequent enactment of the IEEPA, section 5(b) was limited to a "time of war," and the IEEPA provided the framework for exercising specified international economic-emergency powers. In the past several years, the IEEPA has been invoked to hold or control the United States-held assets of Iran, Nicaragua, Libya, PANAMA, Iraq, and HAITI.

### BIBLIOGRAPHY

Bowman, Mary Margaret Coughlin. "Presidential Emergency Powers Related to International Economic Transactions: Congressional Recognition of Customary Authority." *Vanderbilt Journal of Transnational Law* 11 (1978): 515–534.
Mannheimer, Rita. "Amendments to the Trading with the Enemy Act Limit Presidential Power to Regulate International Economic Transactions." *International Trade Law Journal* 3 (1978): 413–420.
U.S. House. Committee on International Relations. *Trading with the Enemy: Legislative and Executive Documents Concerning Regulation of International Transactions in Time of Declared National Emergency.* 94th Cong., 2nd sess., 1976. Committee Print.

HAROLD C. RELYEA

## INTERNATIONAL LAW, PRESIDENT AND.

Presidents are subject to the limits of international law when those limits are specifically recognized through the TREATY-MAKING POWER. Under the Constitution, self-executing treaties are the law of the land and must be faithfully executed by the President. Since the earliest days of the Republic, customary norms of international law that have not been incorporated in a treaty or statute have also been viewed as a part of federal law. The President's constitutional obligation to comply with customary international law is, however, unclear. The Supreme Court has not definitively decided that question, and ATTORNEY GENERAL opinions and lower court decisions have reached conflicting positions.

**Views of the Framers.** Substantial evidence indicates that the Framers viewed customary international law as constitutionally limiting the President' discretion in conducting foreign policy. The America that drafted and ratified the Constitution and took its place as an independent nation was a weak nation. It sought to ensure that its leaders did not take precipitous action that could lead to its destruction.

In their famous HELVIDIUS-PACIFICUS DEBATES in 1793, both James Madison and ALEXANDER HAMILTON recognized that the President had a constitutional duty to enforce international law. Hamilton utilized the President's duty to execute the law of nations to support George Washington's authority to issue the PROCLAMATION OF NEUTRALITY:

> The Executive is charged with the execution of all laws, the law of Nations as well as the Municipal law, which recognizes and adopts those laws. It is consequently bound, by faithfully executing the laws of neutrality, when that is the state of the Nation, to avoid giving a cause of war to foreign Powers.

Madison sought a narrower view for presidential authority that would not, in his opinion, impinge on congressional WAR POWERS:

> That the executive is bound faithfully to execute the laws of neutrality, whilst those laws continue unaltered by the competent authority, is true; but not for the reason here given, to wit, to avoid giving cause of war to foreign powers. It is bound to the faithful execution of these as of all other laws, internal and external, by the nature of its trust and the sanction of its oath.

While Hamilton and Madison may have used the law of nations for different purposes, they agreed that the President was obligated to faithfully execute the laws of nations.

Madison returned to this theme five years later in his dispute with the John Adams administration's conduct of the QUASI-WAR WITH FRANCE. Adams had prohibited the arming of ships in United States ports as a violation of NEUTRALITY, but as tensions mounted between France and the United States, the President revoked the prohibition, thereby granting "an indirect license to arm." Congress had not yet acted. Madison complained that the President had no power to grant such an indirect license, writing, "The first instructions were no otherwise legal than as they were in pursuance of the law of nations, and consequently in execution of the law of the land. The revocation of the instructions is a virtual change of the law, and consequently a usurpation by the executive of a legislative power." During the ensuing debate over relations with France, various congressmen noted, without contradiction, that the President could use the nation's armed forces only in a "manner authorized by the law of nations."

The Framers' view that the President was constitutionally required to comply with and enforce customary international law flowed from their general SEPARATION OF POWERS perspective—to wit, that certain foreign policy decisions were, in Hamilton's words, "so delicate and momentous" that entrusting them "to the sole disposal" of the President is inappropriate. These separation-of-powers concerns apply to decisions to violate international law. As Michael Glennon pointed out in a 1986 article, violations of international law may lead to serious costs: diplomatic isolation, loss of prestige, countermeasures, economic sanctions, and damages. The international outcry provoked by the Supreme Court's decision in *United States v. Alvarez-Machain* (1992), permitting the President to kidnap Mexican citizens and bring them to trial in the United States, illustrates why actions in violation of international norms ought to be subject to the restraint of collective decision making.

**Court Cases.** The Supreme Court's opinion in *Brown v. United States* (1814) further supports international law limits on the President's powers as COMMANDER IN CHIEF and other FOREIGN AFFAIRS powers. The question before the Court was whether the President could confiscate enemy property in the United States after war had been declared, even though Congress had not authorized such confiscation. The executive branch argued that the DECLARATION OF WAR itself gave the President the right to seize and condemn enemy property. Chief Justice John Marshall canvassed international law and held that the scope of the President's constitutional war powers should be construed consistently with the law of nations to require congressional authorization prior to executive seizure of alien property. For Marshall, " in expounding that constitution [of the United States], a construction ought not lightly to be admitted which would give to a declaration of war an effect in this country it does not possess elsewhere."

The government, in arguing for greater war powers, recognized that congressional action was probably necessary for the executive to take actions that violated international law. The executive argued that the President could seize all property that, according to the modern law of nations, is subject to confiscation, "although it might require an act of the legislature to justify the condemnation of that property which, according to modern usage, ought not to be confiscated."

Marshall responded to this argument by noting that this modern usage "is a guide which the sovereign follows or abandons at will" and that "although it cannot be disregarded by him without obloquy, yet it may be disregarded." Marshall's statement has sometimes been taken to mean that customary international law could be abandoned at will by the President, but the context of his remarks make clear that Marshall meant no such thing. He viewed the international norm involved as a permissive rule that allowed sovereigns to take enemy property upon a war's commencement, although as a policy matter this was generally discouraged. Application of this permissive rule was, to Marshall, "a question rather of policy than of law." Like other questions of policy, Marshall thought that the question of whether to confiscate enemy property was a legislative determination. Marshall's point was not that customary international law could be abandoned at will but rather that this was a discretionary rule that the legislative and not executive branch could decide to disregard.

Justice Joseph Story dissented. He agreed that the international law rule was permissive, but to him that meant that the President had the constitutional authority to seize enemy property. The President's constitutional war power to carry on war could only be limited by statute or the law of nations, and Congress had not yet limited the President.

Attorney General WILLIAM WIRT agreed with Justice Story in an 1822 opinion, concluding that the obligation of the President, as executive officer, to enforce the laws of the country extended to the "general laws of nations." Attorney General James Speed also agreed in 1865, stating that the laws of war,

> like the other laws of nations, . . . are of binding force upon the departments and citizens of the Government, though not defined by any law of Congress . . . . Under the Constitution of the United States no license can be given by any department of the Government to take human life in war, except according to the law and usages of war. (11 *Op. Att'y Gen.* 297, 299–301)

**Twentieth-Century Developments.** The twentieth century brought a change in U.S. government attitudes toward limiting the President's discretion based on international law. In *The Paquete Habana* (1900), the Supreme Court struck down actions by naval officers as violations of international law. While Justice Horace Gray's opinion noted that international law was a part of our law, it qualified that statement by stating that international law was binding "where there is no treaty, and no controlling executive or legislative act or judicial decision."

Many examples can be cited of twentieth-century Presidents dispatching U.S. troops to intervene in the internal affairs of other sovereign nations. The United States has often been unwilling to accept the law of nations when it has limited its own foreign policy options. With the onset of the COLD WAR, that attitude was reinforced. In 1954, the first of the HOOVER COMMISSIONS warned, "We are facing an implacable enemy whose avowed objective is world domination by whatever means and at whatever cost. There are no rules in such a game. Hitherto acceptable norms of human conduct do not apply." In that ideological context it was unlikely that the executive would accept, or Congress and the judiciary impose, the limitations of international law on the President's use of force abroad.

The end of the cold war and President George Bush's purported search for a "new world order" raised new possibilities for rediscovering the original interrelationship between constitutional and international law restraints. The rationales utilized over the previous half-century for removing restraints on the President's conduct of foreign policy no longer applied with the same force. While the United States still faced many enemies in the world and dangerous dictators, terrorists, and drug traffickers continued to abound, the "implacable enemy" seeking "world domination" had disintegrated.

Of course, international law rules have different degrees of clarity and strength. The vaguer the rule, the more discretion the President will have in deciding whether a particular act violates international law. There are, however, many rules of international law that are clear: a nation cannot use force to kidnap another nation's citizen within the other country's territory; a nation cannot intentionally bomb civilian targets; a nation cannot mine another country's harbors without notice, nor can it attempt to assassinate another country's leader in peacetime.

Despite these generally accepted limits, the JUSTICE DEPARTMENT claims the inherent constitutional authority to use force to kidnap foreign citizens and bring them to trial in the United States. While not explicitly ruling on the constitutionality of such actions, the Supreme Court in *Alvarez-Machain* held that such kidnappings, even if violative of customary international law, could not be remedied in domestic courts. The Court's opinion implicitly upheld the President's power to take such action in violation of customary international law.

The recent trend has clearly been to uphold the President's constitutional power to use force and take other actions that violate customary international law. Important separation-of-powers concerns, the early constitutional history of our nation, and the contemporary situation in the world do, however, suggest the necessity for a reconsideration of these recent rulings.

**The Role of Congress.** Article I, Section 8, clause 10 of the Constitution explicitly grants Congress the power to define and punish violations of the law of nations. Thus, Congress can constitutionally define a number of actions as violations of the law of nations and make them crimes under U.S. law. Congress could constitutionally prohibit such acts as mining another nation's harbors, launching a first-strike tactical nuclear attack during a war, using chemical weapons to repulse an enemy attack, shooting prisoners of war, assassinating civilians, or covertly intervening in another nation's affairs by assassinating its leader. Since the President could not legally violate any of these statutes, he would have no plenary or sole power to conduct warfare in violation of international law as incorporated in congressional statutes.

Even if the President's role as Commander in Chief generally gives him the sole power to choose which tactics and weapons to utilize in warfare, that power is limited by Congress's power to define offenses against international law. If Congress leaves that power unexercised, it must still be presumed that the President will follow international law, even if no criminal sanctions apply. The rule firmly entrenched in our jurisprudence from *Murray v. The Schooner Charming Betsey* (1804) is that "an act of Congress ought never to be construed to violate the law of nations, if any other construction remains." That doctrine reflects a presumption that Congress intends to maintain the rules of international law absent express, intentional derogation. It follows that congressional silence should mean that Congress wants the President to follow international law.

In sum, the values of world order and justice reflected in international law are related to the concern for CHECKS AND BALANCES on arbitrary governmental conduct that underlie separation of powers. This relationship dictates that, where United States policy violates existing treaties or customary norms of international society, such action requires the greater scrutiny provided by joint decision making of Congress and the President through the regular statutory process.

### BIBLIOGRAPHY

Glennon, Michael J. "Can the President Do No Wrong?" *American Journal of International Law* 80 (1986): 923–930.

Charney, Jonathan. "The Power of the Executive Branch of the United States Government to Violate Customary International Law." *American Journal of International Law* 80 (1986): 913–922.

Lobel, Jules. "The Limits of Constitutional Power: Conflicts between Foreign Policy and International Law." *Virginia Law Review* 71 (1985): 1071–1180.

Jay, Stewart. "The Status of the Law of Nations in Early American Law." *Vanderbilt Law Review* 42 (1989): 819–849.

Henkin, Louis. "The President and International Law." *American Journal of International Law* 80 (1986): 930–938.

Leigh, Monroe. "Is the President above Customary International Law?" *American Journal of International Law* 86 (1986): 757–763.

JULES LOBEL

## INTERSTATE COMMERCE ACT

**INTERSTATE COMMERCE ACT** (1887). Railroad discrimination against shippers had aroused their ire in the years following the CIVIL WAR. Farmers, merchants, and manufacturers at places where railroads had no competition paid higher rates than those who shipped goods farther distances between competing points. In addition large shippers where competition existed often received illegal rebates (discounts) giving them an advantage over smaller and less fortuitously located competitors. Responding to the outrage of disadvantaged shippers, states passed "Granger Laws" regulating rates. When in 1886 the Supreme Court in *Wabash v. Illinois* declared those laws unconstitutional, the pressure on Congress for unprecedented federal regulation of railroads proved irresistible.

Shippers—whether they were merchants, farmers, or industrialists—and those railroad managers who recognized the inevitability of regulation shaped the Interstate Commerce Act, but its hardcore support in Congress came from the Midwest and the South. A House of Representatives bill, reflecting the interests of shippers, prohibited rebates, the long-and-short-haul abuse, and railroad pools and relied on the courts for enforcement, while a less stringent Senate bill, more palatable to railroads, permitted pools and relied on a commission for enforcement. The Interstate Commerce Act compromised their differences. It called for "reasonable and just" rates, outlawed discrimination, prohibited pools, created an Interstate Commerce Commission (ICC)—without specific power to set rates—and left a loophole in the long-and-short-haul clause.

President Grover Cleveland, who had no effect on the passage of the act, appointed a strong ICC—headed by Thomas M. Cooley—which proceeded to set rates. The ICC was reasonably effective for a decade, but in 1897 the Supreme Court in the *Maximum Freight Rates* decision denied that the ICC could set rates and in *Alabama Midland* it destroyed the ICC's control over the long-and-short-haul abuse, reducing the ICC to a collector of statistics.

### BIBLIOGRAPHY

Hoogenboom, Ari, and Olive Hoogenboom. *A History of the ICC: From Panacea to Palliative.* 1976.

Martin, Albro. "The Troubled Subject of Railroad Regulation in the Gilded Age—a Reappraisal." *Journal of American History* 61 (1974): 339–371.

Purcell, Edward A. "Ideas and Interests: Businessmen and the Interstate Commerce Act." *Journal of American History* 54 (1967): 561–578.

ARI HOOGENBOOM and OLIVE HOOGENBOOM

**INTERVENTIONISM.** Interventionism is the term given to diverse currents of opinion that favored some form of U.S. involvement in the burgeoning world crisis of the late 1930s and early 1940s. In almost every way, the term defies precise description. Similarly elusive is the relationship between the various interventionist forces and the administration of President Franklin D. Roosevelt.

The immense problems created by the depression distracted America's attention from world affairs. Roosevelt ignored NATIONAL SECURITY issues in the 1932 campaign and promised not to seek membership in the LEAGUE OF NATIONS.

Opinion about American foreign policy during the depression decade was shaped by an aversion to war, given focus by memories of WORLD WAR I, together with an antipathy to the militant expansionism of Japan, Italy, and Germany. The Manchurian crisis of 1931–1932 prompted no significant calls for any action stronger than nonrecognition of Japanese territorial gains. Nazism began to be taken seriously with the party purge of mid 1934 in Germany, but even so Hitler represented an evil rather than a threat to 1930s America.

The initial stages of Italian and German expansionism tended to intensify Americans' desire to preserve peace by insulating the United States from events across the Atlantic. Mussolini's invasion of Ethiopia in 1935 attracted wide attention and prompted public demonstrations by both supporters and critics. The official response debated in the United States was negative in character—embargoes on arms and raw materials.

The balance between antiwar feeling and a desire to oppose fascism and Japanese militarism gradually shifted during the late 1930s in favor of the latter. Roosevelt's 1937 quarantine speech and his state of the union addresses of 1938 and 1939 established his leadership in the interventionist movement.

Events themselves exercised much the greatest influence on American opinion as FOREIGN AFFAIRS enlarged their claim on public attention. Almost without exception, events broadened and intensified American hostility toward the future Axis partners. Until 1940 this opposition seldom led to calls for intervention overseas. Even Japan's bombing of the U.S. gunboat *Panay* produced no such outcry. Instead,

it bolstered support for passage of the Ludlow Amendment, which would have required a popular referendum before a DECLARATION OF WAR could take effect. Every opinion poll showed that overwhelming majorities wanted to stay out of war. Public calls for the use of American influence continued to emphasize the curtailment of U.S. trade as the preferred foreign policy weapon. It is indicative of the public mood that the first major group formed as a result of the Sino-Japanese war was called the Committee for Non-Participation in Japanese Aggression and that it was criticized for being too confrontational.

War in Europe at first resulted in surprisingly modest changes in American policy. Germany received harsh criticism in the press, as Japan had for its conduct in China. At home the issue as the proposed repeal of the embargo on arms sales to belligerent nations. Roosevelt formulated the case for repeal, emphasizing that the embargo represented an abandonment of traditional neutral rights and in effect favored Germany. Britain and France were the obvious beneficiaries of repeal, but advocates scrupulously avoided defending change on those grounds. The name of an ad hoc group formed to marshal public support for repeal, the Non-Partisan Committee for Peace through Revision of the Neutrality Act, described with tortuous accuracy the public stance of the administration. The choice of name was no accident, for Roosevelt advised its leadership just as he also encouraged prominent Catholics and labor leaders to voice support for his policy. Repeal passed because it could convincingly be represented as a peace measure.

The German defeat of France in the summer of 1940 forced Americans to address the potential conflict between their desire to stay at peace and their wish to see Hitler stopped. In beginning to face this dilemma, Americans discovered bitter divisions within the body politic.

In one sense, the magnitude of Nazi achievements, especially when combined with Japan's continued expansion in Asia, circumscribed the forces of intervention. Despite substantial increases in military spending since 1937, the U.S. Army was far too weak to be a decisive force in Europe. In any case, the proportion of Americans favoring immediate entry into the European war was only 14 percent of all those polled in the summer of 1940. Support drifted upward over the next eighteen months but never comprised more than a quarter of the population. Roosevelt insisted upon a substantial consensus in favor of any initiative, and he steadfastly refused to advocate war. He ran as a peace candidate in the 1940 presidential campaign.

So intervention would have to stop short of outright

war. Aid to Britain thus became the central issue, overshadowing concern over the situation in the Pacific. Most interventionists stressed the benefits to the United States of continued British resistance. The British might yet defeat Hitler outright; at worst they delayed the Nazi onslaught and bought vital time for America to rearm. The largest and best-known interventionist group, the Committee to Defend America by Aiding the Allies, consistently justified aid on those grounds. Its first leader, William Allen White, carefully positioned the committee to lead public opinion as Roosevelt wished. A powerful faction of the committee, labeled the Century Group, insisted on a more aggressive stance and ousted White early in 1941. They quickly found that many within the committee still hung back, and consequently they formed a new group, Fight for Freedom, to advocate an outright declaration of war.

Many interventionists increasingly resorted to personal attacks upon the patriotism of their isolationist opponents. Led by Roosevelt, the administration and its allies in the media employed similar tactics. Isolationists responded in kind. Groups like the Council for Democracy adopted a more constructive tone on behalf of interventionism, with scant success. The controversies of 1941 were ferocious and left scars that the war itself did not begin to heal. No consensus was achieved.

Interventionism was validated by WORLD WAR II in the eyes of most Americans. The Truman administration later invoked memories of the 1930s to build support for a policy of global activism on a scale unimaginable only fifteen years earlier.

### BIBLIOGRAPHY

Cole, Wayne S. *Roosevelt and the Interventionists, 1932–1945*. 1983.

Dallek, Robert. *Franklin D. Roosevelt and American Foreign Policy, 1932–1945*. 1979.

Doenecke, Justus D., and John E. Wilz. *From Isolation to War, 1931–1941*. 2d ed. 1991.

Heinrichs, Waldo. *Threshold of War: Franklin D. Roosevelt and American Entry into World War II*. 1988.

Schneider, James C. *Should America Go to War?: The Debate over Foreign Policy in Chicago, 1939–1941*. 1989.

JAMES C. SCHNEIDER

**INVESTIGATIONS, CONGRESSIONAL.** Congressional investigations have left an indelible mark on the course of American history. Phrases such as "Teapot Dome," "Watergate," and "Iran-contra" have become part of the popular vernacular as a result of congressional investigations. And a number of well-known figures in American political history—CHARLES EVANS HUGHES, Hugo Black, Harry S. Truman, Joseph McCarthy, and Sam Ervin, to name a few—first obtained national prominence through their involvement in such investigations. Indeed, it is not exaggeration to say that the political rise ("Mr. Hiss, are you now or have you ever been a member of the Communist Party?") and fall ("What did the President know and when did he know it?") of one American President, Richard M. Nixon, were directly linked to congressional investigations.

Congress's power to investigate, recognized as an implicit element of its authority to legislate under Article I, Section 1, of the Constitution, draws its historical foundation from early British parliamentary practice. The first congressional investigation dates back to 1792, when a special committee of the House of Representatives was formed to investigate the military defeat of Major General Arthur St. Clair and his troops by Indians in the Ohio frontier.

High-profile congressional investigations, like those during the WATERGATE AFFAIR and the IRAN-CONTRA AFFAIR, often undertaken by select investigative committees, generate the most public attention. Far more common, however, are the scores of investigations conducted each year by standing committees of Congress in furtherance of their continuing legislative and oversight responsibilities.

**Oversight Investigations.** Congressional committees carry on these investigations for a variety of reasons, none more important than CONGRESSIONAL OVERSIGHT of the administration of the laws by the executive branch. Implicit in our tripartite system of government is the need for some mechanism through which Congress can assess the adequacy of existing laws and the efficacy of their administration. Congress's investigatory powers supply this mechanism. William Pitt the elder stated in 1742, "[W]e are called the Grant Inquest of the Nation, and as such it is our duty to inquire into every step of public management, either abroad or at home, in order to see that nothing has been done amiss." Although Pitt's words were directed at the parliamentary system, a similar view was expressed by Senator Sam Ervin about the American system of government based on the separation of powers, "Of considerable importance is Congress's power to investigate the executive branch. We do not live in a monarchy but in a democracy where governmental functions are shared by three equal branches. The White House is the people's house, not an imperial palace. The executive branch is not above the law."

In the latter part of the twentieth century, two examples of these types of oversight investigations were Watergate and Iran-contra. Watergate involved an investigation into the 17 June 1972 break-in of the offices of the Democratic National Committee by five individuals with ties to the Republican National Committee. Suspicions that prominent members of the Nixon administration either knew of or participated in the crime prompted the Senate to establish the Select Committee on Presidential Campaign Activities, chaired by Senator Ervin, to investigate the break-in and any subsequent cover-up. The investigation and hearings resulted in the conviction of high-ranking members of the administration and IMPEACHMENT proceedings by the House Judiciary Committee, prompting Richard Nixon to become the first President in the history of the United States to resign.

The Iran-contra affair involved the investigation of joint House and Senate committees into a covert operation conducted by the administration of President Ronald Reagan. The operation involved a series of arms sales to the government of the Ayatollah Khomeini in Iran in an effort to secure the release of American hostages, and the transfer of the proceeds of those sales to the contras—the armed resistance movement opposing the communist government in Nicaragua—at a time when Congress had voted to deny them military aid. The investigation revealed that retired military officers, senior members of the National Security Council, and the CENTRAL INTELLIGENCE AGENCY Director, William Casey, were all implicated in the operation and subsequent cover-up effort.

History will probably view the Iran-contra investigation less favorably than it has Watergate. To a remarkable degree, the Iran-contra hearings were dominated by some of the witnesses, in particular the "can do" lieutenant colonel, Oliver North. Additionally, the two most important criminal convictions arising from the scandal, those of North and the NATIONAL SECURITY ADVISER, John Poindexter, were ultimately thrown out as a direct result of Congress's decision to grant them limited immunity for their congressional testimony.

**Powers of Inquiry.** Congress has a number of tools at its disposal to carry out its investigations, including the power to require by subpoena the attendance of witnesses and the production of documents, the power to punish for CONTEMPT OF CONGRESS the refusal to comply with a subpoena, the threat of criminal prosecution for giving "perjured" or false testimony, and the power to compel a witness who has asserted his Fifth Amendment privilege against self-incrimination to testify under a grant of limited immunity. These tools play a prominent role in the investigatory process.

Although broad, Congress's powers of inquiry are not unfettered. There must be a valid legislative pur-

pose for conducting an investigation. Congress cannot probe into purely private affairs or expose private activity solely for the sake of doing so. Nor can it usurp the functions of the executive and judicial branches by prosecuting, trying, and convicting individuals for criminal offenses. Furthermore, the fundamental freedoms guaranteed by the Constitution cannot be infringed. The Fifth Amendment privilege against self-incrimination, the Fourth Amendment protection against unreasonable search and seizure, and the First Amendment freedom from forced revelations of thoughts and beliefs or unwarranted intrusions into past associations all apply in the context of congressional investigations. Finally, the procedural rules of each house and its committees and subcommittees that affect the rights of witnesses—for example, open versus closed hearings, protection of confidential materials, broadcasting of hearings, questioning of witnesses, and the role of counsel—are judicially cognizable and also must be observed.

**Executive Branch Resistance.** Congressional investigations of the executive branch have not infrequently given rise to a "clash of absolutes" between the two political branches; the executive can assert a right to withhold from disclosure information Congress deems necessary to execute its oversight responsibilities. The executive branch has advanced a number of grounds, often grouped together under the rubric EXECUTIVE PRIVILEGE, to justify its refusal to provide the requested information. These grounds include NATIONAL SECURITY, confidentiality of presidential communications, protection of predecisional intragovernmental opinions, and the secrecy of law enforcement investigatory files.

Since the Watergate affair of the 1970s, courts have become involved, albeit in a limited fashion, in attempting to referee these interbranch skirmishes. The 1974 decision of the United States Supreme Court in UNITED STATES v. NIXON recognized for the first time a constitutional basis for executive privilege. The *Nixon* case, however, involved the special prosecutor's subpoena of the tape recordings of President Richard M. Nixon's conversations, for use in a criminal trial, and not the assertion of the privilege in response to a congressional demand for information. The scattered judicial precedents that have addressed this latter question have set forth no clear rules of law, and thus the scope of the privilege is largely undefined.

As a result, the resolution of executive privilege disputes with Congress has largely been the product of the politics of the moment. Typically, both sides stake out intractable positions, a test of political will ensues, and after some period of time, a political compromise is fashioned. These compromises are often extremely complex, as illustrated by the 1982 inquiry of a Senate select committee into Abscam and other law enforcement activities of the FEDERAL BUREAU OF INVESTIGATION, a scandal that in the period 1978–1980 had resulted in the criminal conviction of one Senator and six Representatives. Under the terms of the elaborate access agreement negotiated between the committee and the Department of Justice, the committee was provided access to more than twenty thousand pages of FBI documents generated during the covert stage of the Abscam operation. However, the Department of Justice, under which the FBI operates, was permitted to withhold grand jury materials and certain prosecutorial memoranda (although oral briefings on the factual material contained in the memoranda were provided). The department was also permitted to withhold documents that might compromise ongoing investigations or reveal confidential sources of investigative techniques (although it was required to describe each document and the basis of the refusal to disclose, in addition to providing the committee an opportunity to propose conditions under which such documents might be disclosed). For its part, the committee retained its right to subpoena and seek access judicially to all restricted categories of documents. And the committee agreed to a "pledge of confidentiality" whereby it could use and publicly disclose in its hearings and final report information derived from the Department of Justice documents but could not publicly identify the specific documents from which the information was obtained.

The rise in instances of conflict between the two political branches, as well as the increasing size of the legislative bureaucracy, suggest that congressional investigations will continue to play a prominent role in the future. In the right hands, congressional investigations can be an effective instrument for exposing government corruption and maladministration, and for providing the electorate with a better education about the American system of government than any civics textbook. If abused, witnesses' reputations can be irreparably damaged, public confidence undermined, and the credibility of Congress itself diminished.

## BIBLIOGRAPHY

Dash, Sam. *Chief Counsel: Inside the Ervin Committee—The Untold Story.* 1976.

Grabow, John C. *Congressional Investigations, Law and Practice.* 1988.

Hamilton, James. *The Power to Probe: A Study of Congressional Investigations.* 1976.

Schlesinger, Arthur M., Jr., and Roger Burns. *Congress Investigates: A Documented History 1792–1974.* 1975.

Taylor, Tolford. *Grand Inquest: The Story of Congressional Investigations.* 1955.

JOHN C. GRABOW and COURT E. GOLUMBIC

**IRAN-CONTRA AFFAIR.** The Iran-contra affair was one of the principal constitutional crises of the American republic. The affair had two interconnected parts: the sale of arms to Iran, which was widely understood to be in exchange for the freeing of American hostages; and, in defiance of the expressed will of Congress, the financial and other support given by the Reagan administration to the contras—the armed opposition to the Sandinista government of Nicaragua. Taken together, the events spanned a period of five years, from the first effort by the Congress in 1982 to restrict aid to the contras, to the appointment in 1986 of congressional committees and a special counsel to investigate the sales to Iran and the diversion of profits from that sale to the contras.

**Outlines of the Affair.** The events of each part of the affair are exceedingly complex. They had, moreover, no substantive connection to one another, becoming joined only through the activities of Colonel Oliver North, who was on the staff of the NATIONAL SECURITY ADVISER to President Ronald Reagan, and of the network of people that he assembled.

*The Nicaraguan contras.* In July 1979 the long-lasting Somoza dictatorship in Nicaragua came to an end, overthrown by a broad revolutionary coalition known as the Sandinista National Liberation Front. The Carter administration's response to the new government was one of goodwill, tempered by a desire to prop up the moderates in the coalition and prevent the extremists from seizing control.

President Reagan, upon assuming office, reversed the Carter administration policy and suspended aid to the Nicaragua government. By 1982, the United States was the principal sponsor of a covert military operation in support of the Nicaraguan contras' effort to overthrow the Sandinista regime. This covert operation was contrary to the expressed United States policy that the American government was engaged only in interdicting the flow of Nicaraguan arms to those in El Salvador friendly to the Sandinistas. Information that this was not the prime object of American aid led to the first BOLAND AMENDMENT of December 1982, which said, in part, that the CENTRAL INTELLIGENCE AGENCY and the DEPARTMENT OF DEFENSE were prohibited from using any funds "for the purpose of overthrowing the Government of Nicaragua." The Boland Amendment was attached to a defense appropriations bill for fiscal year 1983 and signed to go into effect from 21 December 1983 until 8 December 1984. With these events the "contra" part of the affair began.

The Reagan administration made continuous efforts to circumvent this ban by drawing in other countries to support the contras. It also simply ignored the ban, having the CIA mine three Nicaraguan ports. The result was a second Boland Amendment, also attached to a Defense Department appropriations bill, that was signed by the President on 12 October 1984. This amendment was even more restrictive and direct than the first. It prohibited any direct or indirect military or paramilitary support for the contras from 3 December 1984 to 19 December 1985 whether by the CIA, the Defense Department or "any other agency or entity of the United States involved in intelligence activities".

Even after the Boland amendments, President Reagan commented that he was still committed to holding the contras together "body and soul." As a result, Colonel North, who had become the principal point of contact between the United States government and the contras, found himself in an expanded role.

Those who wrote the second Boland Amendment were clear that it was meant to cover all agencies of the United States involved in intelligence activities including the NATIONAL SECURITY COUNCIL and its staff headed by the national security adviser to the President. Their statements on the floor of the Congress affirmed this. But because the NSC was not specifically named, and because it was ostensibly not engaged in gathering intelligence, a loophole was thought to exist by some and Colonel North was used to exploit it. The staff of the national security adviser picked up the work previously carried on by the CIA in support of the contras.

*Iranian arms sales.* Particularly important for Colonel North and those who relied on him was the question of how to secure funds for the contras now that the Congress had denied them aid. They hit upon the stratagem of soliciting funds from foreign countries who, because they wished to retain the goodwill of the United States, could be prevailed upon to support the contras. They also successfully approached private American citizens who could be convinced that the Sandinistas were part of a worldwide communist threat. To coordinate this fund-raising and to transport its fruits to the contras, North assembled a network of people in and out of government that included most importantly a retired general, Richard Secord.

North remained in charge of the support of the contras until the effort collapsed into scandal in late 1986. By then the operation had become intertwined with efforts of the Reagan administration to sell arms to Iran. The connection to the contra operation occurred when a portion of the funds received from the arms sales was diverted to contra support. In effect,

Colonel North and those for whom he worked had found yet another source of funds for the contras outside the regular appropriation of funds by the Congress. (By mid 1986, Congress in fact resumed funding for the contras, but by this time the whole affair was showing signs of coming apart.)

The background to the sale of arms to the Iranians begins with the overthrow of the Shah of Iran in 1979 and the creation of a Muslim state hostile to the United States. The new regime had been causing difficulties for American foreign policy, not the least of which was the taking of American hostages who were kept captive in Iran for some fourteen months [*see* IRANIAN HOSTAGE CRISIS]. In the spring of 1983, the Reagan administration had become so determined to punish the new regime that it embarked upon an effort to convince all nations not to sell arms to Iran, accusing the Iranian government of supporting international terrorism. The administration said repeatedly that it would not deal with terrorists, and specifically that it would not bargain for the release of hostages, which by then included seven Americans held in Lebanon by pro-Iranian groups. The fate of these hostages, however, weighed heavily on the administration, particularly on President Reagan, but there was no easy way to secure their release, especially if bargaining with Iran was ruled out.

Despite the administration's pronouncements, American intelligence had been regularly approached with suggestions that if the United States would provide arms to Iran, the Iranian government would provide various favors in return. In mid 1985, the United States accepted one such approach. Those organizing the approach, an assorted set of international deal-makers, contended that a moderate faction could be bolstered in Iran through the sale of arms to that country. American officials concluded that there were at least two potential benefits to the scheme: it might lead to the freeing of the hostages, and it would increase the probability of an Iranian regime more sympathetic to the United States.

Through a complex series of steps, the Israeli government was drawn into the proposed sale of arms. In August 1985, the American administration authorized the Israelis to go ahead with the sale of American-made missiles in what turned out to be, even if not intended by all involved, an arms-for-hostage deal. As a consequence of the Israeli sale, one American hostage was released.

By late 1985, Colonel North had become the key person from the American side in the undertaking to sell arms to the Iranians. After the first sale in August-September of 1985, a second sale by the Israelis was authorized by Reagan administration officials in November. With this sale, American involvement grew deeper, as complications arose that only the United States could disentangle. In the end, the problems could not be overcome and the sale was aborted.

***The Iran-contra connection.*** The deepening American involvement raised the question of a PRESIDENTIAL FINDING. This is a document that must by law be prepared when the President decides that a covert operation is needed for national security reasons. Any such finding must be followed by a report of such operations to the Congress. No such finding was prepared before the first sale. After the fact, however, one was prepared that also made clear that the administration understood it was engaged in an arms-for-hostage deal.

The complications of the second arms sale led American officials to decide that the whole operation should be under their direct control, rather than being effectively directed by the international deal-makers who had first approached the U.S. government. This required two more findings and a complex arrangement, engineered by Colonel North, that was designed to hide the fact that the United States, in contradiction of its often-stated policy, was now selling arms directly to the Iranians to secure the return of its hostages. The administration was in fact divided over this course of action, but with President Reagan's acquiescence it went ahead. Arms were delivered to the Iranians in several installments from February to October 1986 via a set of intermediaries. As a result, a second hostage was released.

The use of intermediaries for the arms sale set up the possibility that a substantial amount of money could be diverted to the contras since the funds from the sale were deposited in an account controlled by one of these intermediaries, Richard Secord, who was also one of the principals in the network that North had recruited to support the contras. The diversion was made and the selling of arms to Iran was joined to the support of the contras.

In late 1986, details of the Iran-contra affair started to leak out. The publicity led to various speeches and press conferences by the Reagan administration in October and November that were designed to explain the deals with Iran and the diversion of funds from the arms sales to the contras. The revelations also led to the appointment by President Reagan of former Senator John Tower to investigate the whole affair [*see* TOWER COMMISSION], the appointment of independent counsel Lawrence Walsh, and the announcement by the House and Senate of their intention to hold hearings on both the arms sales and the secret military assistance to the contras. The Congress duly held the hearings and the report was issued in November 1987. Judge Lawrence Walsh obtained a number of guilty pleas and convictions from his investigation. Two of the principal convictions (Oliver North and John Poindexter) were overturned on appeal because of the limited immunity granted by Congress for their testimony. The appeals court held that testimony from witnesses at their trials had been tainted by information given to Congress under the immunity grant.

**Constitutional Issues.** The Iran-contra affair was not only a case of good plans gone awry or bad ones being pursued with clumsy zeal. More importantly, it showed an executive branch willing and able to violate the constitutional prerogatives of the Congress. Even more ominously, the affair indicated not just a violation of the Constitution but its *unworkability* in foreign affairs. The Iran-contra affair is suggestive of a serious weakness in the whole constitutional design.

To understand the nature of this constitutional violation and constitutional weakness is to understand how the SEPARATION OF POWERS system must function. In order for this system to work there must be comity between the branches: they need to cooperate in a system of shared powers. Cooperation between the President and Congress is the principal source of the energetic government that the Founders of the American republic sought to create. The foundation of this comity is the constitutionally ordained powers of each branch that can be used to compel the cooperation of the others. The aim of the Founders was that each branch would have the means and motive to play its constitutional role when the government acted.

But in foreign affairs, if the President or those who act for him, do not think that congressional views must be taken into account as a matter of constitutional right, they will not only attempt to circumvent the Congress, by and large they will succeed. There is little to stop them, as Madison, the principal architect of the Constitution, understood. In a letter to Thomas Jefferson, Madison wrote, that the "management of foreign affairs appears to be the most susceptible of abuse of all trusts committed to a Government." This, he continued, was because foreign affairs could "be concealed or discussed, or disclosed in such parts and at such times as will suit particular views." Woodrow Wilson made the connection to PRESIDENTIAL-CONGRESSIONAL RELATIONS when he said "hostile or designing officials can always hold [Congress] at arms length by dexterous evasions and concealments."

The Constitution may be, as one of its great students, Edward Corwin, said, "an invitation to struggle" between the President and Congress in foreign affairs, but for the struggle to be a productive one, each branch must be in a position to force the other's cooperation. And that is the difficulty. Congress's ability to do so is weak—and the executive's ability to engage in dexterous evasions and concealments is great. In the end, Congress's ability to force cooperation rests on its power of IMPEACHMENT. But that is so weighty a step that the Congress is unlikely to see it as a ready remedy for its weakness. As a result, comity principally rests on the belief of each branch that the other has a rightful and useful role to play.

Comity in foreign affairs depends, therefore, on the relatively weak reed of mutual respect between the branches. It rests on Congress's view that the Constitution gives the President wide discretion in foreign affairs. With some notable exceptions, recent constitutional history has shown few difficulties here, and the Iran-contra affair was no different in this respect. More precariously, comity also rests on the executive's conviction that the best understanding of the Constitution requires it to take account of the legislature's views.

For much of American history, this weakness in constitutional design did not cause great problems. The pressures on the Constitution were limited because the United States had not yet assumed great and continuing burdens in foreign affairs. The Iran-contra affair, however, revealed just how weak the reed of mutual respect has become with the ascent of the United States to the status of a world power. In particular, it showed executive branch officials disregarding Congress's legitimate role in foreign affairs, one based primarily on its power to appropriate money and secondarily on its power to oversee the activities of the executive branch.

The Iran-contra affair demonstrated that the executive branch was in fact unwilling to show the necessary respect for Congress's constitutional prerogatives in foreign affairs. In particular, and of the gravest importance, was the executive's attempt to evade congressional control of appropriations.

American views of congressional powers in fiscal matters stem largely from English experience. Historically, English kings and queens could run their foreign policies as long as they had the resources to do so. An important impetus to constitutional government was the monarch's need to raise money. If Parliament was to levy taxes, it could require both that monarchical discretion be curbed and that parliamentary views of how the money was to be spent should carry weight. In short, Parliament must have the power of appropriation.

The American system inherited and developed this tradition. Thus the Constitution says "No Money shall be drawn from the Treasury, but in Consequence of Appropriation by Law." If such congressional power—to specify the purposes for which money raised through taxation shall be spent—were absent, the principle of popular consent to taxation would be nugatory. Money lawfully raised through taxation could be spent in whatever fashion the executive chose.

The American constitutional tradition is thus plain. Allowing the President to spend funds not lawfully appropriated would mean that the President is the government of the United States. This is not what the Constitution says. If Congress does not appropriate money, money cannot be spent. Any attempt by a President or executive branch officials to raise and spend money outside the appropriations process is unconstitutional. Yet, there is every reason to believe that the executive's disregard of Congress's powers will continue to happen. The Iran-contra affair indicates that the separation of powers in foreign affairs is in grave trouble. If it in fact collapses, then the Founders' constitutional design for foreign affairs will have proved to be too weak to stand up to the role the United States has chosen for itself in world affairs.

### BIBLIOGRAPHY

Draper, Theodore. *A Very Thin Line: The Iran-Contra Affairs.* 1991.

Glennon, Michael J. *Constitutional Diplomacy.* 1990.

Henkin, Louis. *Foreign Affairs and the Constitution.* 1972.

Koh, Harold Hongju. *The National Security Constitution.* 1990.

National Security Archive. *The Chronology: The Documented Day-by-Day Account of the Secret Military Assistance to Iran and the Contras.* 1987.

Schlesinger, Arthur M., Jr. *The Imperial Presidency.* 1973.

U.S. House of Representatives. Select Committee to Investigate Covert Arms Transactions with Iran. Select Committee on Secret Military Assistance to Iran and the Nicaraguan Opposition. *Report of the Congressional Committees Investigating the Iran-Contra Affair.* H. Rept. 100-13; S. Rept. 100-216. 100th Cong., 1st sess., 1987.

Wormuth, Francis, and Edwin Frimage. *To Chain the Dogs of War.* 2d ed. 1989.

STEPHEN L. ELKIN

**IRANIAN HOSTAGE CRISIS.** From 1953 until the mid 1970s, the United States maintained close relations with the government of Shah Mohammed Reza Pahlavi of Iran. In 1978, however, relations between the two countries grew strained as political opposition to the Shah's regime led to intense civil strife. In January 1979, after weeks of angry demonstrations, an ailing Shah fled Iran and sought refuge in several countries, ending up in the United States.

Within weeks, the Ayatollah Ruhollah Khomeini, a fundamentalist Islamic leader living in exile in France, returned to Iran and became its de facto ruler.

On 4 November 1979, Iranian militants overran the United States embassy compound in Tehran. The militants, who claimed loyalty to Khomeini's government, kept fifty-two American citizens hostage and held them for the next 444 days. In response, President Jimmy Carter conducted one of the most dramatic exercises of a President's peacetime foreign-affairs power in United States history.

Almost immediately, Carter declared a national emergency and imposed a trade embargo and an extraterritorial freeze upon Iranian assets under the INTERNATIONAL EMERGENCY ECONOMIC POWERS ACT of 1977. Carter ordered discontinuation of all oil purchases from Iran for delivery to the United States, unsuccessfully sought multilateral economic sanctions against Iran through the United Nations, and ultimately cut off nearly all lines of communication and travel to Iran.

At about the same time, Carter took action against Iranian nationals in the United States. After breaking diplomatic relations with Iran, he ordered the Iranian embassy and consulates closed and expelled Iranian diplomats after declaring them *persona non grata*. He further instructed that Iranian citizens be denied visas for future entry and directed the Attorney General to issue regulations requiring Iranian students to report to local immigration offices for visa checks. In November 1979, the United States also brought a contentious lawsuit against Iran in the International Court of Justice. The suit ultimately succeeded, resulting in the World Court's declaration that Iran's capture and detention of the American hostages violated its international legal obligations to the United States under the Vienna Conventions on Diplomatic and Consular Relations.

None of these nonmilitary attempts succeeded in securing the hostages' release from captivity. On 24–25 April 1980, a frustrated Carter attempted an unsuccessful military raid into Iranian territory aimed at rescuing the hostages. Carter sent eight American helicopters to a remote staging area in the middle of Iran, known as DESERT ONE, where they met cargo planes carrying commandoes for a military incursion into Tehran. Desert One proved a disastrous failure. Three of the helicopters broke down, forcing Carter to abort the mission. Upon evacuating the site, two aircraft collided, killing eight Americans, and Secretary of State Cyrus Vance resigned in opposition to the secret operation.

The Shah's death in July 1980 eliminated a key point in controversy between the United States and Iran: whether the U.S. should assist Khomeini in securing the Shah's return to Iran. Perhaps more important, in September 1980, war broke out between Iran and Iraq, which dramatically enhanced Iran's willingness to settle the crisis. In September 1980, secret settlement negotiations began in earnest between the two governments, through the intermediation of the government of Algeria. Iran's American bank creditors also began secret negotiations with Iranian officials regarding the unfreezing of the frozen assets. Khomeini's government finally outlined four conditions as the prerequisite to the release of the hostages: the return of the Shah's wealth to Iran; the cancellation of both private and public claims against Iran; the unfreezing of all Iranian assets; and a commitment from the United States not to interfere in Iran's internal affairs.

In November, Carter was defeated for reelection by Ronald Reagan, in good measure because of Carter's failure to resolve the hostage crisis. Thereafter, negotiations through Algerian intermediaries intensified, with the United States being represented by Deputy Secretary of State Warren Christopher. On 19 January 1981, the two nations agreed that Iran would release the American hostages in exchange for a U.S. pledge of nonintervention into Iranian internal affairs and the delivery to an escrow account of all frozen Iranian assets in the United States and abroad subject to the jurisdiction of the United States. The delivery of some $8 billion would constitute the largest financial transaction in history to date. The parties proceeded to enter four EXECUTIVE AGREEMENTS in all—later known as the Algiers Accords—which went on to rescind virtually every economic or political sanctions measure taken by the United States against Iran during the preceding 14 months. The accords suspended all private claims by American commercial entities and transferred them to arbitration before the Iran-U.S. Claims Tribunal, a newly established international tribunal in the Hague that distributed awards from an account containing more than $1 billion in unfrozen Iranian assets.

On 20 January 1981, the day that President Carter left office, the two countries finally concluded the agreement, and the hostages were released thirty minutes after Ronald Reagan was inaugurated President. Soon after the release, some commentators suggested that the Algiers Accords were void under INTERNATIONAL LAW because they had been negotiated under duress. Nevertheless, in February, the Reagan administration ratified the Algiers Accords, triggering intensive domestic litigation in which private parties claimed that the agreement constituted an unlawful taking of American citizens' property. In July 1981, a near-unanimous Supreme Court upheld the President's constitutional and statutory authority to conclude the Algiers Accords in DAMES & MOORE V. REGAN.

Nearly a decade later, former Carter administration officials alleged that the Reagan presidential campaign had in fact conspired with the Iranian government deliberately to delay the release of the fifty-two hostages until after the presidential election. These officials claimed that the Reagan-Bush campaign had made clandestine overtures to Iran and arranged illegal arms shipments through Israel to forestall an October surprise, whereby the Carter administration would win the hostages' release just before the presidential election, and thereby win reelection. In August 1992, Congress conducted an inquiry into these charges but they remained unsubstantiated.

### BIBLIOGRAPHY

Carter, Jimmy. *Keeping Faith: Memoirs of a President.* 1982.
Sick, Gary. *October Surprise: America's Hostages in Iran and the Election of Ronald Reagan.* 1991.
Smith, Gaddis. *Morality, Reason and Power: American Diplomacy in the Carter Years.* 1986.

HAROLD HONGJU KOH

**IRON TRIANGLES.** Government policies and programs create communities of common interest among the individuals and groups that create, nurture, implement, or benefit from these policies. Scholars and journalists have identified in particular the three-way policy-making alliances of congressional committees, executive agencies, and clientele interest groups. Iron triangles is one label for these arrangements; related terms include *cozy triangles, policy whirlpools,* ISSUE NETWORKS, or *triple alliances.* Scholars prefer the term *subgovernments.*

These networks control policy making in numerous policy fields such as milk pricing, sugar quotas, oil production, and weapons-system contracting. In veterans affairs, for example, the key players are the House and Senate veterans committees, the DEPARTMENT OF VETERANS AFFAIRS, and key veterans groups such as the American Legion, Veterans of Foreign Wars, and Vietnam Veterans. If groups within such networks agree on their objectives, they can control the policy outcomes. This power is not really the result of a conspiracy; it merely shows that those most directly affected by a policy tend to control the outcome as long as the general public is not alerted.

Executive agencies, legislative committees, and associated lobby groups have long worked in tandem to pursue their common interests. Arthur Maass's 1951 study of the links between the Army Corps of Engineers and the House and Senate Public Works committees was a pioneering description of this type of mutually beneficial alliance. From his 1965 study of INDIAN affairs policies, J. Leiper Freeman generalized the relationship into a model of policy making throughout the entire political system. Executive agencies responsible for running particular programs, he noted, commonly forged close ties with both the legislative committees responsible for enacting the statutes on which their authority rested and the clientele groups served by these programs and policies. Although Presidents have "considerable leeway" in influencing subsystem participants (especially the bureaucrats), the participants' narrow agendas limit Presidents' incentives for involvement.

In this scheme, each segment of a triangle (or subgovernment) is expected to serve its own interests by supporting the goals of the other two participants in the policy-making system. Such an alliance is more or less a closed system of decision making. Members of Congress who do not serve on the committee included within the triangle, and segments of the population that are not part of the agency's clientele, are excluded from effective participation in the policy-making decisions of these subgovernments. Presidents intrude upon these established networks with caution, or not at all.

These relationships are far from static, however. External developments exert constant pressure for change. A scandal over a drug with disastrous side effects for pregnant women and their babies pressured legislators in the 1960s to set stricter drug-testing standards. A 1966 pre-Christmas mail breakdown in Chicago "triggered public concern over postal issues that eventually shattered the monolithic, clientele-dominated environment of the [Post Office] Committee." Postal-reform advocates seized upon the event, and a March 1970 postal strike aiming to wrest policy from the clientele-committee alliance eventually resulted in the 1970 postal reorganization [*see* UNITED STATES POSTAL SERVICE]. But the public's attention span is short. After such upheavals, the subgovernments may slip back into a stable pattern. At best, a new balance of power is imposed by the brief crisis and public outcry.

The complexity and fluidity of the links between interest groups and government have threatened the hegemony of the iron triangles. It is increasingly difficult, for example, to prevent outsiders from invading a subgovernment's policy-making enclave. First, overlapping committee jurisdictions and the proliferation of subcommittees and informal groups on Capitol Hill offer additional points of entry through which legislators—even those outside the traditional networks—can gain a voice in the subgovernment's policy questions. Special-interest caucuses provide alternative channels of influence for lawmakers not on the relevant committee. More than a hundred of these caucuses seek policies favorable to their constituencies. Executive agency jurisdictions, like those of congressional panels, also overlap. The external effects of one agency's decisions reverberate in other policy settings.

The subgovernments' ability to dominate given policy arenas shifts with historical changes in institutions, processes, and the larger political environment. In 1978, Hugh Heclo asserted that the old triangles had been replaced by issue networks—knowledgeable people and groups that flow in and out of several policy areas. Participants in issue networks are united in their policy expertise but they lack full control over the policies themselves. Several factors have contributed to the decline of iron triangles' control over policy-making: the rise of large numbers of new citizens' groups and advocacy organizations, new patterns of investigative reporting and the enlarged role of the media in national politics, the greater policy-making role of the federal courts, and the increasing aggressiveness of Presidents intent on controlling the bureaucracy.

Yet iron triangles are by no means extinct in American political life. Cooperation is still a leading characteristic of the linkage between executive agencies and legislative committees. Agencies cannot survive or prosper without support from Capitol Hill committees, and members of Congress dare not ignore the services or regulations produced by these agencies, much less their effect on constituents. Lobby groups devote much of their influence to nurturing these policies and bending them to their members' benefit. But because their direct and visible effects are narrow, these policies only sporadically arouse the interest of Presidents, the mass media, or the electorate.

### BIBLIOGRAPHY

Davidson, Roger H. "Breaking Up Those 'Cozy Triangles': An Impossible Dream?" In *Legislative Reform and Public Policy.* Edited by Susan Welch and John G. Peters. 1977.
Fenno, Richard F., Jr. *Congressmen in Committees.* 1973.
Freeman, J. Leiper. *The Political Process: Executive Bureau–Legislative Committee Relations.* 1965.
Heclo, Hugh. "Issue Networks and the Executive Establishments." In *The New American Political System.* Edited by Anthony King. 1978.
Maass, Arthur A. *Muddy Waters.* 1951.

ROGER H. DAVIDSON

**ISOLATIONISM.** No American President since George Washington has ever tried to isolate the United States from the rest of the world. The United States always had economic and cultural relations with other countries. It established diplomatic relations with European governments more than a decade before Washington became President. The term "isolationism" never was applied to American foreign policies by any of its Presidents in the eighteenth and nineteenth centuries.

The term *isolationism* was invented and applied by people who wanted the United States to turn away from its traditional foreign policies toward policies they thought would be more realistic in the twentieth century. To accomplish that radical change it was believed necessary to make the older policies appear worse than they actually were. The term "isolationism" has performed that denigrating role.

The traditional foreign policies pursued by the United States during its first 125 years under the Constitution were not literally isolationist. Traditionally, the United States under its first twenty-seven Presidents opposed involvement in internal political and military affairs of Europe and opposed entering permanent alliances with foreign states. The United States guarded its sovereignty and freedom of action in FOREIGN AFFAIRS. That did not mean that Americans had no interest in Europe or were unaffected by developments there.

Those traditional policies were a natural product of American experiences. Most citizens of the United States (or their parents or ancestors) had fled from things in England or Europe they had not liked: war, poverty, and oppression. They wanted none of that in America. The wide Atlantic magnified the moral and political differences between the Old World and the New.

No United States military forces fought on the European continent from the time America proclaimed its independence in 1776 until after Congress declared war on Germany in 1917. The United States fought its War for Independence, the War of 1812, the MEXICAN WAR, the CIVIL WAR, and the SPANISH-AMERICAN WAR all without sending troops to fight in Europe. It ended its alliance with France after it had served its purpose in helping win independence from England. After that alliance ended in 1800 the United States did not enter another alliance with European states until it joined the North Atlantic Treaty Organization nearly a century and a half later.

Those traditional policies did not rule out American activity and expansion in other parts of the world. The United States established its initial boundaries, bought the Louisiana Territory [see LOUISIANA PURCHASE] acquired Florida from Spain, annexed the independent country of Texas [see TEXAS, ANNEXATION OF], divided the Oregon Territory with England [see OREGON TREATY], annexed California and the southwest, purchased the Gadsden Territory [see GADSDEN PURCHASE], bought Alaska from Russia [see ALASKA PURCHASE TREATY], acquired part of Samoa, annexed the independent country of Hawaii [see HAWAII, ANNEXATION OF] acquired PUERTO RICO, Guam, and the PHILIPPINES by war from Spain, obtained control of the PANAMA CANAL Zone, and expanded its trade and investments all over the world—all without sending troops to fight in Europe and or entering alliances with foreign governments. All that was accomplished without departing from policies that, in the twentieth century, have been called "isolationist."

Twentieth-century departures from those traditional policies have been associated particularly with strong Presidents such as Woodrow Wilson and Franklin D. Roosevelt. But in the eighteenth and nineteenth centuries some of America's greatest Presidents helped formulate policies that in the twentieth century have been called "isolationist." President Washington proclaimed American NEUTRALITY in the wars in Europe. In his FAREWELL ADDRESS he advised: "The great rule of conduct for us, in regard to foreign nations, is, in extending our commercial relations, to have with them as little *political* connection as possible" [emphasis in original]. He contended that it was America's "true policy to steer clear of permanent alliances with any portion of the foreign world," and that America could depend on "temporary alliances" to cope with "extraordinary emergencies." Those views were consistent with the preferences of most Americans then and for more than a century to come.

John Adams listened approvingly when a European diplomat told him that America should "have sense enough to see us in Europe cut each other's throats with a philosophical tranquility." As America's second President, Adams resisted involvement in war with France and engineered the agreement that ended America's alliance with that European power.

Thomas Jefferson, the third President and one of its greatest, advised against "entangling alliances," accomplished the Louisiana Purchase expanding America's territory to the Pacific, and struggled to prevent involvement in the Napoleonic Wars.

John Quincy Adams was more experienced in foreign affairs than any other President, but neither as James Monroe's Secretary of State nor as President did he depart from those traditional policies. As Secretary of State he told an audience, in 1821, that America was "the well-wisher to the freedom and independence of all. She is the champion and vindicator only of her own." He helped formulate the MONROE DOCTRINE that was consistent with America's traditional policies. James K. Polk provoked war with Mexico in 1846 partly to acquire California and the Southwest for the United States. But he entered no alliances and did not send troops to fight in Europe. Under President Franklin Pierce the United States did not become involved in the Crimean War.

Abraham Lincoln and his Secretary of State WILLIAM H. SEWARD preserved the Union partly by successfully preventing European intervention in the Civil War. And when Seward (under President Andrew Johnson) negotiated the purchase of Alaska, he was wholly within the confines of America's traditional policies.

As a consequence of the Spanish-American War of 1898, the United States under President William McKinley greatly expanded its overseas empire without intervening in Europe and without entering alliances.

In the twentieth century under the leadership of Woodrow Wilson and Franklin D. Roosevelt the United States gradually departed from those traditional policies toward a policy of multilateral collective security in world affairs. The Japanese attack on PEARL HARBOR was the turning point.

In more fundamental terms, however, Wilson and Roosevelt were leading America in new directions in foreign affairs that changing circumstances at home and abroad mandated. After WORLD WAR II the alarming power of the Soviet Union and the People's Republic of China could only be turned back by the power of the United States.

And within the United States the growth of productive industries and financial resources projected America's economy all over the world. Those economic developments encouraged the urbanization of American society, as did stepped-up immigration. The result was an erosion of rural bases for "isolationism." Steamships, telegraph, cable, telephone, radio, automobiles, and airplanes spectacularly speeded communication and travel. Improved education, travel, news coverage, and television helped make Americans more aware of what was happening abroad. Intercontinental bombers, missiles, and nuclear warheads made any thought of return to America's traditional policies of the eighteenth and nineteenth centuries impossible.

Americans and their political leaders differ among themselves on when, where, and how the United States should involve itself abroad, but they will not return to the policies of noninvolvement in Europe and no entangling alliances. Neither conditions abroad nor those within the United States permit such a return to the past. President George Bush's leadership of multinational forces in the GULF WAR to turn back Iraq's conquest of Kuwait was based on similar reasoning and language that Wilson and Franklin Roosevelt had used against more formidable challenges earlier in the twentieth century. Because of changed circumstances at home and abroad, the United States will not revert back to the traditional policies of nonentanglement and noninvolvement in Europe that characterized American foreign affairs during the first 140 years of its independent history—policies that in the twentieth century have been called "isolationist."

### BIBLIOGRAPHY

Cole, Wayne S. *Roosevelt and the Isolationists, 1932–45*. 1983.

Cooper, John Milton, Jr. *The Vanity of Power: American Isolationism and the First World War, 1914–1917*. 1969.

Doenecke, Justus D. *Not to the Swift: The Old Isolationists in the Cold War Era*. 1979.

Dowty, Alan. *The Limits of American Isolation: The United States and the Crimean War*. 1971.

Rippy, J. Fred, and Angie Debo. "The Historical Background of the American Policy of Isolation." *Smith College Studies in History* 9 (1924): 71–165.

Savelle, Max. "Colonial Origins of American Diplomatic Principles." *Pacific Historical Review* 3 (1934): 334–350.

Weinberg, Albert K. "The Historical Meaning of the American Doctrine of Isolation." *American Political Science Review* 34 (1940): 539–547.

WAYNE S. COLE

**ISRAEL.** When World War II ended in 1945 the immediate issue for Jews was what to do with several hundred thousand survivors of the murder of six million Jews. Most of these refugees could not go home again, and the majority insisted on starting a new life in Jewish Palestine. President Harry Truman took up their cause and kept urging the British government to admit at least a hundred thousand immediately. The British resisted this demand; they would not admit more Jews while dealing, ever less successfully, with armed rebellion by Arabs and counterfire—and illegal immigration–by Jews. American Jews mounted ever more intense pressure on Truman, and he became ever testier. The State Department, headed by George C. Marshall, was opposed to pushing the British on the issue of refugees, and it was vehemently against the creation of a Jewish state in part of Palestine. Truman was pro-Jewish. He also knew that he would need the votes of Jews in the 1948 election, and he was deeply influenced by Eddie Jacobson, a former business partner and one of his closest friends. On his own testimony and that of his family and of his closest personal circle, he decided to overrule Marshall (whom Truman revered) because of Truman's sympathy for the refugees and his conviction, nourished by his religious faith, that the Jews had a right to their own land. When Great Britain decided in 1947 to lay down the mandate for Palestine, Truman instructed his delegates to the United Nations to vote and to lobby for partition of the country into a Jewish and an Arab state. Despite some hesitation and confusion in the weeks immediately before the state of Israel was declared on 14 May 1948, Truman again overruled the State Department and recognized the new state, de facto, eleven minutes after it formally came into being. Without his personal support from 1945 to 1948, Israel would not have been voted into being by the United Nations, and Palestine would have remained, indefinitely, a theater for guerilla warfare.

President Dwight D. Eisenhower became deeply involved in Israel when, in October 1956, a coalition of Great Britain, France, and Israel attacked Egypt to seize the Suez Canal. The Israeli army occupied all the Sinai Peninsula in a four-day campaign. Eisenhower was furious at all three allies because he held that the Suez Canal was an international waterway. Great Britain and France withdrew almost immediately but Israel, which had joined the war in order to stop terrorist raids from Eygptian-controlled Gaza, would not budge. After months of wrangling and threats of U.N. sanctions proposed by Eisenhower, Israel withdrew and agreed that the United Nations would police its border with Gaza and that the American government would increase its financial aid to the new state.

The next major American involvement with Israel came when Lyndon Johnson worked to prevent the outbreak of the Six-Day War in June 1967. After Israel's victory, he supported Israel's refusal to evacuate the territories that it had occupied unless the Arabs agreed to make peace and to establish secure frontiers. In 1968 Johnson agreed to supply Israel with military aircraft, thus creating the precedent that has turned the United States into Israel's major source for weapons that it does not produce itself.

Richard Nixon helped increase both civilian and military aid to Israel during his time in office. He was especially involved in the effort to help Russian Jews emigrate and worked hard to persuade the Soviet Union to let more Jews out. In October 1973, when Egypt attacked Israel on Yom Kippur, Nixon decided to fulfill, immediately and generously, Israel's request to be resupplied. In the diplomatic efforts to end the war, Nixon and Secretary of State Henry Kissinger presided over an even-handed solution that did not completely humiliate the Eygptians but left Israel in control of the Sinai.

When Gerald Ford succeeded Nixon, he kept Kissinger in office; together they continued the effort to make peace between Israel and the Arabs. Kissinger effected two partial withdrawals by Israel in the Sinai peninsula but no breakthrough. Jimmy Carter attempted to continue the pressure on Israel to yield territory for peace, but his early attempts failed. Carter's great moment came in 1979, the year after the Egyptian president, Anwar Sadat, made his historic trip to Jerusalem. When negotiations had stalled, Carter invited Sadat and Menachem Begin, the prime minister of Israel, to CAMP DAVID. In almost two weeks of uninterrupted negotiation, Carter brokered an agreement for peace and full diplomatic relations between Egypt and Israel. The governing conditions were Israel's assent to return all the Sinai to Egypt and to bargain with the Palestinians in the territories about interim autonomy and, three years later, about their ultimate status. The documents were signed on the lawn of the White House by Begin and Sadat, with Carter as witness. [See CAMP DAVID ACCORDS].

Ronald Reagan was the most emotionally and unconditionally pro-Israel of all his predecessors. His main preoccupation for most of his presidency was the fight against the Soviet Union, the "evil empire." Israel was a staunch and dependable ally which needed to be supported with aid and supplied with planes. To be sure, Reagan did not neglect friendly Arab states, especially Saudi Arabia, to which he sold advanced planes in 1983 over the objections of the pro-Israel lobby. On the other hand, Reagan did not object to the policy of the Likud government, under Begin and Shamir, that increased Jewish settlement on the West Bank. When Israel invaded Lebanon in June 1982, Reagan helped extricate the Palestine Liberation Organization (PLO) fighters and leaders headed by Yasir Arafat, but he did not force Israel to withdraw or lessen his support for its government.

George Bush was more critical of Israel than was Reagan, and he and Secretary of State JAMES A. BAKER III worked in vain to stop the Israeli government's aggressive policy of settlement. Bush wanted to reduce aid to Israel by the amount it was spending on the settlements, but he did not succeed. Bush and Baker did manage to convoke peace negotiations between Israel and the Palestinians in the territories (with the PLO in the wings) and all the bordering Arab states, which began in October 1991 in Madrid. Bush's obvious displeasure with the policies of the Likud and his desire for a more flexible government in Jerusalem was a factor in the defeat of the Likud-led coalition by the Labor Party and its allies in the Israeli elections of June 1992. It is not certain that negotiations, suspended after a 1992 meeting in Washington, D.C., will produce a peace treaty unless Bill Clinton invests as much of himself in the process as Carter did at Camp David.

## BIBLIOGRAPHY

Grose, Peter. *Israel in the Mind of America.* 1983.
Hertzberg, Arthur. *The Jews in America: Four Centuries of an Uneasy Encounter.* 1989.
McCullough, David. *Truman.* 1992.
Shapiro, Edward. *The Jewish People in America.* Vol. 5: *A Time for Healing: American Jewry since World War II.* 1992.

ARTHUR HERTZBERG

**ISSUE NETWORKS.** Observers have used a variety of terms to describe policy-making structures within America's separated and fragmented political institutions. Terms such as *subgovernments, policy subsystems,* and *policy communities* have been coined, usually to characterize the ongoing relationships that can develop among interest groups, legislative committees, and executive agencies dealing with a common subject matter. When these relationships take the form of tripartite alliances that are self-governing and virtually immune from outside political influences, they are typically referred to as IRON TRIANGLES. By contrast, the term *issue network* denotes roughly the opposite type of policy subsystem. Here, interactions are multipolar rather than three-cornered, more open than insulated, and more fluid than stable over time. Some have also argued that the issues around which issue networks arrange themselves are often more explicitly and heavily invested with value conflicts (environmental risks or abortion rights, for example) than are the issues that more conventional subgovernments struggle over—involving, for example, the distribution of material economic benefits.

In the policy-making process, issue networks can be thought of as a political configuration somewhere between a shared-attention group and a shared-action group. An issue network is like a shared discussion group without a designated discussion leader. A network is composed of individuals who not only pay attention to what they consider a particularly important aspect of public policy but who also regard one another as knowledgeable about the meaning of those issues and the options available for solving problems. These common attributes do not imply, however, that participants in the network will unite into a coalition or conventional interest organization capable of taking joint action. Standard views of subgovernments tend to define policy as arising out of conflict among a set of power brokers as to who gets what and when and how they get it. The issue-network perspective also sees policy-making as a conversation in which problems are puzzled over, identified, and refined and in which meanings are sought in the public forum. For the modern presidency, issue networks pose a series of difficulties and opportunities. These are inherent in the defining features of such networks.

An issue network's multipolarity means that on many policy matters, Presidents cannot expect the relevant actors to fit into a given triangle of congressional committee, executive agency, and major interest group(s). This reflects not only a growing fragmentation and overlap of authority within established institutions but also highlights the fact that, since the NEW DEAL and the social reforms of the 1960s and 1970s, government activism has been associated with an increased mobilization of competing policy activists in think tanks, public interest or consumer groups, academic centers, the media, consulting firms, nonprofit corporations, and other organizations.

Even without this proliferation of voices, greater openness in policy-making processes has reduced the possibility of behind-the-scenes bargaining and compromise among political leaders. Public access to records and deliberations in government decision making has increased markedly since the 1950s. So, too, have access to the courts and judges' willingness to intervene in making and remaking public policies. Lines of public access have also widened via the work of investigative reporters, policy newsletters, and new technologies for direct mail and telecommunications targeted at specialized audiences.

The combination of greater openness and more participants demanding government to solve more value-laden problems can obviously spell trouble for PRESIDENTIAL LEADERSHIP. There are fewer reliable blocks of support enabling Presidents to build enduring electoral and governing coalitions. Institutional or partisan loyalties become more contingent and dependent on the issue in question. Alliances are likely to be transitory. Any given position is likely to be challenged by a mobilization of countervailing experts. Thus the policy environment becomes more unpredictable and less receptive to any bargains struck by a given set of organizational leaders, whether in the White House, Congress, or elsewhere. Strategies of persuasion are further complicated as politicians use the advanced marketing techniques of pollsters, political consultants, and media advisers to help position themselves on issues when addressing a segmented public. Projecting an image of having a "correct" stance on an issue can easily get in the way of the hard work of actually constructing public policy.

Issue networks, however, also present opportunities for presidential leadership. In the first place, the general public is likely to find the incessant debates among policy activists arcane and confusing. This situation tends to leave the President as the one comprehensible figure to whom the public might look to make sense of what is going on—"the vision thing" as George Bush put it. This expectation can be a burden, but it can also create an opportunity for someone who believes in, and can communicate, his or her larger message.

Likewise, if a President has strong preferences in given policy areas, the networks of policy activists can provide a valuable pool of personnel for filling appointive positions in the executive branch. By picking and choosing among such activists, Presidents can staff important government positions with people who are likely to be more knowledgeable and committed to the cut and thrust of policy debate than are conventional party or interest-group representatives.

Additionally, if the White House is really interested in learning about the complexities of an issue, the information and argumentation that flow through issue networks can be helpful in reality-testing and in avoiding half-baked presidential initiatives. Of course, if inaction is a President's preferred policy, the complex and often self-canceling nature of network debates can also be a useful device.

Finally, Presidents can try to adapt to the more fluid environment of alliance building and persuasion. Given the instability of traditional electoral and governing coalitions, issue networks can be an important resource for constructing the ad hoc majorities that have to be put together from one policy matter to the next. To do so, White House liaison activities must go beyond providing access or consulting with this or that group. Such outreach activities must try to mobilize the networks of policy activists that cut across organizational hierarchies and institutional boundaries.

## BIBLIOGRAPHY

Berry, Jeffrey M. "Subgovernments, Issue Networks, and Political Conflict." In *Remaking American Politics*. Edited by Richard Harris and Sidney Milkis. 1989.

Bosso, Christopher J. *Pesticides and Politics: The Life Cycle of a Public Issue*. 1987.

Heclo, Hugh. "Issue Networks and the Executive Establishment." In *The New American Political System*. Edited by Anthony King. 1978.

Knoke, David. *Political Networks*. 1990.

Peterson, Mark A. "Interest Mobilization and the Presidency." In *The Politics of Interests*. Edited by Marc P. Petracca. 1992.

HUGH HECLO

**ITEM VETO.** See VETO, ITEM.